The Environment Through the Lens of International Courts and Tribunals

Edgardo Sobenes · Sarah Mead · Benjamin Samson
Editors

The Environment Through the Lens of International Courts and Tribunals

ASSER PRESS

Springer

Editors
Edgardo Sobenes
ESILA
The Hague, The Netherlands

Sarah Mead
Amsterdam, The Netherlands

Benjamin Samson
Université Paris Nanterre
Angers, France

ISBN 978-94-6265-506-5 ISBN 978-94-6265-507-2 (eBook)
https://doi.org/10.1007/978-94-6265-507-2

Published by T.M.C. ASSER PRESS, The Hague, The Netherlands www.asserpress.nl
Produced and distributed for T.M.C. ASSER PRESS by Springer-Verlag Berlin Heidelberg

This T.M.C. ASSER PRESS imprint is published by the registered company Springer-Verlag GmbH, DE part of Springer Nature.
The registered company address is: Heidelberger Platz 3, 14197 Berlin, Germany

Foreword

'[T]he environment is under daily threat'. This statement was made by the International Court of Justice (ICJ) in its advisory opinion rendered in 1996 in the case concerning the *Legality of the Threat or Use of Nuclear Weapons.*[1]

Such an assessment is still valid today. In light of current environmental challenges—*inter alia*, climate changes and global warming, illegal, unreported and unregulated fishing activities and overexploitation of fishery resources, deforestation, plastic debris, air, water and land pollution—the status of the environment is even more alarming in 2021 than it was 25 years ago. This is so, in spite of the proliferation of international treaties, recommendations and guidelines that aim to preserve and protect the environment.

The dire situation of the fauna and flora of our planet may be a matter of surprise given the abundance of existing international environmental norms. But the adoption of treaties and other rules of international law does not in itself guarantee that the environment is properly protected in practice. An effective regime of protection requires that, in addition to the existence of legal norms, tools and mechanisms be put into place to ensure compliance therewith, to monitor their implementation and to provide legal recourses should they be breached.

It is against this background that the contribution of international courts and tribunals in promoting compliance with environmental rules needs to be assessed. International courts and tribunals may play a useful role when cases involving alleged violations of obligations under environmental law are brought before them. They may settle environmental disputes and avoid their aggravation, clarify the interpretation and scope of the rules concerned, and order reparation.

For the past 30 years, international courts and tribunals have not remained inactive in the environmental field. On the contrary, they have been seized of a growing number of environmental cases, and their decisions (judgments or advisory opinions) have contributed to the development of a broad corpus of environmental rules and

[1] ICJ, *Legality of the Threat or Use of Nuclear Weapons*, Advisory Opinion, 8 July 1996, ICJ Reports 1996, p. 241, para 29.

principles. Mention may be made, for example, of the 'concept of sustainable development', to which the ICJ referred to as early as 1997 in its Judgment in the case concerning the *Gabčíkovo- Nagymaros Project (Hungary/Slovakia)*,[2] or the obligation to 'undertake an environmental impact assessment where there is a risk that the proposed industrial activity may have a significant adverse impact in a transboundary context',[3] whose binding character under international customary law was affirmed in 2010 by the ICJ in its *Pulp Mills* judgment, and also by the International Tribunal for the Law of the Sea (ITLOS) in its Advisory Opinion of 2011.[4]

In this context, it is worth noting that the book *The Environment through the Lens of International Courts and Tribunals*, co-edited by Edgardo Sobenes, Sarah Mead and Benjamin Samson comes at the right time. Of course, the fact that this is a timely publication is not the only reason for which the co-editors and the different contributors are to be commended. The added value of the book is to offer in one volume a comprehensive and systematic overview of the different legal issues relating to the handling of environmental cases by international courts and tribunals.

In Part I, readers are given a detailed presentation of the various international courts and tribunals which may have jurisdiction on environmental issues. Besides the ICJ, ITLOS, WTO dispute settlement mechanism and the International Criminal Court, the book also covers more recent developments before regional courts—mainly in the context of human rights—and commercial and investment arbitration tribunals.

A legal battle may be lost or won on procedural grounds. Therefore, it is useful for litigants to be fully aware of procedural and jurisdictional challenges which may be faced during international proceedings. Part II responds to such a need by reviewing in a systematic manner a number of key notions such as jurisdiction, access to courts and tribunals and evidence. Access to international justice is probably the most crucial element to keep in mind in an international legal order without a court possessing general compulsory jurisdiction. This explains why existing compulsory regimes for the settlement of environmental disputes, such as Part XV of the United Nations Convention on the Law of the Sea, are particularly attractive for States willing to engage in international litigation. Part II also includes a chapter on provisional measures before international courts and tribunal. The emphasis put on provisional measures is fully justified. Provisional proceedings may constitute an efficient tool whenever it is necessary to prevent serious harm to the environment pending a decision on the merits.

The co-editors have rightly allocated part of the publication (Part III) to the consideration of issues relating to the future of environmental litigation. The part addresses new trends and ideas, such as the role of international litigation in a context marked

---

[2] *Gabčíkovo-Nagymaros Project (Hungary v Slovakia)*, Judgement, 25 September 1997, ICJ Reports 1997, p. 78, para 140.

[3] ICJ, *Case Concerning Pulp Mills on the River Uruguay (Argentina v Uruguay)*, Judgment, 20 April 2010, ICJ Reports 2010, p. 83, para 205.

[4] ITLOS, *Responsibilities and obligations of States with respect to activities in the Area*, Advisory Opinion, 1 February 2011, ITLOS Reports 2011, p. 50, para 145.

by an increased recourse to municipal courts in environmental litigation, and the potential role of the United Nations Security Council in dealing with environmental emergencies.

At a time when confidence in the multilateral legal order and the peaceful settlement of international disputes remains fragile, it is a source of comfort to see that more than twenty international practitioners and academics (with a composition which reflects gender balance and includes representatives of the new generation) have united their efforts to provide to the public what may be characterized as a guide to international environmental litigation. Legal norms to protect the environment do exist. It remains to be hoped that this new publication will contribute to a greater use of international courts and tribunals in order to protect our common environment.

Louvain-la-Neuve, France
September 2021

H. E. Mr. Philippe Gautier
Registrar, International Court of Justice

Preface

As litigators and scholars specialised in international law with a deep concern for the environmental crises upon us, this book aims to put the spotlight on how international courts and tribunals are addressing issues relating to the environment. It is our view that, only with a clear sense of the state of play, can we determine whether the system of international dispute resolution is up to the task of protecting our most precious asset: the natural world.

The book covers the full range of international, regional and transnational courts and tribunals, with a focus on their treatment of the environment. Presented in three parts, the book addresses how individual courts and tribunals engage with environmental matters (Part I); compares the manners in which these courts and tribunals are resolving key issues common to environmental litigation (Part II); and delves into future opportunities and developments in the field (Part III). The book therefore serves as both an essential aid to scholars and students engaged in research in this ever-developing field, and practitioners involved in environmental litigation.

The breadth of international courts and tribunals covered in this book can only be achieved through an edited volume: each contributor has brought their specialist knowledge and experience to the task of preparing their respective chapters. We, the editors, are deeply grateful for their commitment to the project—despite the delays and difficulties caused by the COVID-19 pandemic. We also extend our sincere gratitude to our assistant editor, Joseph Reeves, who has been instrumental in bringing the final manuscript together.

For better or worse, the sovereign state remains at the heart of the international legal system. Yet it is evident that the system has failed to pay adequate attention to the interconnected nature of the natural world. Our flourishing as a global community therefore depends on the ability for our systems to change—and the system of international dispute resolution is no different. It is our hope that, by showing how international courts and tribunals have fared to date, this book lays the foundation for further research aimed at identifying ways to strengthen the system of international disputes resolution towards the better protection of our global environment for future generations.

The Hague, The Netherlands — Edgardo Sobenes
Amsterdam, The Netherlands — Sarah Mead
Angers, France — Benjamin Samson

Contents

About the Editors

Edgardo Sobenes is an international lawyer with extensive experience in international litigation before the International Court of Justice and a unique practice in coordinating and managing international legal teams. His consultancy practice focuses on issues concerning public international law, international disputes, and procedural support. Currently he is the President of the Nicaraguan Branch of the International Law Association, and the creator and host of the first Podcast about international law in Spanish (Hablemos de Derecho Internacional—HDI). He guest lectures globally on topics related to international law and international litigation, and has written extensively in the field of public international law. He holds an Advanced LL.M. in Public International Law and International Dispute Settlement from Leiden University and an International Master's in Law from the University of Barcelona and ISDE.

Sarah Mead is a New Zealand-trained lawyer specialising in international environmental law and international human rights law. She presently works as a Senior Legal Associate at the Climate Litigation Network, an international project of the Urgenda Foundation which brought the ground-breaking climate change litigation against the Dutch State. Sarah also co-leads the IUCN World Commission on Environmental Law project: *Judicial Handbook on Climate Litigation.* She has published widely on topics relating to international environmental law, international climate change law and policy, and small island-states. She holds an Advanced LL.M. in Public International Law from Leiden University.

Benjamin Samson holds a Ph.D. in law from Université Paris Nanterre. He specialises in public international law, international investment law and law of the sea. He has extensive experience acting as counsel for governments in proceedings before the International Court of Justice, the International Tribunal for the Law of the Sea and the Permanent Court of Arbitration. He was a Visiting Scholar at the George Washington University School of Law (Washington D.C.) (2017), and has taught international law and international dispute settlement at various universities in France. He has published a book and several articles on various international law issues.

Joseph Reeves is a Ph.D. candidate at the University of Angers, from which he holds a degree in international law. His doctoral research focuses on animal law. As a research assistant, he has taught international and European law at different French universities and has written in the fields of environmental law, European law, investment law, and human rights law. He has also advised various non-profit organisations on questions relating to animal law, European law and French administrative law.

Chapter 1
Emergence of International Environmental Law: A Brief History from the Stockholm Conference to Agenda 2030

Sumudu Atapattu

Content

Abstract This chapter provides an overview of the emergence of international environmental law from the Stockholm Conference in 1972 to the adoption of the Sustainable Development Goals in 2015. It discusses the major milestones as well as principles that have emerged and their impact on international environmental law

S. Atapattu (✉)
Research Centers and International Programs, University of Wisconsin Law School, Madison, Wisconsin, United States
e-mail: sumudu.atapattu@wisc.edu

Human Rights Program, UW-Madison, Madison, Wisconsin, United States

Raoul Wallenberg Institute for Human Rights, Lund, Sweden

Center for International Sustainable Development Law, Montreal, Canada

E. Sobenes et al. (eds.), *The Environment Through the Lens of International Courts and Tribunals*, https://doi.org/10.1007/978-94-6265-507-2_1

(IEL), especially the report of the World Commission on Environment and Development (1987) and sustainable development. The chapter surveys the evolution of IEL under three subheadings: (a) during the pre-sustainable development era—from the Stockholm Conference in 1972 to the World Commission on Environment and Development in 1987; (b) the post-sustainable development advancements from the Rio Declaration of 1992 to Rio+20 in 2012 with particular emphasis on the impact of sustainable development on IEL; and (c) globalization, the Anthropocene and the Sustainable Development Goals. The chapter also discusses some of its unique features such as the extensive use of soft law instruments, the framework/protocol approach, linkages with other disciplines and the North-South divide. It briefly surveys the regulation of the global commons as well as the activities of non-state actors. It concludes by summarizing the achievements, challenges and the future trajectory of IEL. It argues that IEL needs to devise novel legal tools and principles to confront the challenges posed by global environmental challenges, especially climate change, and urgently rethink the capitalist model of development that has given rise to extensive environmental destruction.

Keywords International Environmental Law · Climate change · Sustainable development · World Commission on Environment and Development · Sustainable Development Goals · Soft law · Anthropocene · Stockholm Declaration on the Human Environment · Rio Declaration on Environment and Development

1.1 Introduction

Modern international environment law dates back to the UN Conference on the Human Environment held in 1972,[1] even though several conservation treaties were in existence at the turn of the 20th century.[2] No textbook on international law carried a chapter on the topic and there were certainly no textbooks on it. Despite this late start, international environmental law (IEL) has flourished with many of its topics,[3] and even sub-topics,[4] attracting textbooks. Its evolution within a span of five decades is remarkable.

---

[1] UN Conference on the Human Environment held in Stockholm. United Nations 1972; Handl 2012.

[2] Examples include: Convention for the Protection of Birds Useful to Agriculture (1902); Treaty for the Preservation and Protection of Fur Seals (1911); General Convention Relating to the Development of Hydraulic Power Affecting More than One State (1923); Convention on Certain Questions Relating to the Law on Watercourses (1929). See Hunter et al. 2015, p. 137; and the table of treaties in Sands et al. 2018.

[3] For example, climate change, sustainable development and the link between human rights and environment have attracted a large number of publications. Other topics include biodiversity, ozone depletion, water pollution, air pollution, hazardous waste, and trade and environment.

[4] Sub-topics include trade and environment, carbon trading, REDD, climate refugees, climate litigation, the Paris Agreement, indigenous peoples and traditional knowledge, and gender and environmental protection.

IEL did not evolve in a systematic manner. It simply responded to various environmental challenges as they arose. Its evolution has revolved around four major international conferences and its principles are scattered across a plethora of multilateral, regional and bilateral treaties, thousands of soft law instruments and a handful of judicial decisions. No Universal Declaration of Environmental Principles similar to the Universal Declaration of Human Rights exists.[5] Yet, despite its rather ad hoc development, it is possible to find an overarching framework, a coherent body of legal principles, and compliance mechanisms.

This chapter provides an overview of the emergence of IEL from the Stockholm Conference in 1972 to the adoption of the Sustainable Development Goals in 2015.[6] It will discuss the major milestones as well as principles that have emerged and their impact on IEL, especially the report of the World Commission on Environment and Development (WCED) and sustainable development. It proceeds in seven sections. Section 1.2 provides an overview of the evolution of IEL from the pre-sustainable development era to the Anthropocene. Section 1.3 is devoted to a discussion of selected principles of IEL—the principle of harm prevention and the obligation not to cause damage to the environment of other states and to the global commons; the common but differentiated responsibility principle; inter and intra-generational equity principle; the precautionary principle; and environmental impact assessment and public participation. Section 1.4 highlights some of the unique features of IEL—the extensive use of soft law; the framework/protocol approach in designing legal obligations; and linkages with other areas such as economic activities; trade and investment; human rights, justice and good governance; and the North-South divide in shaping IEL. Section 1.5 surveys the regulation of the global commons including the common heritage of mankind principle, while Sect. 1.6 briefly discusses the attempts made to and the norms that have emerged to regulate activities of non-state actors. Section 1.7 concludes with some final thoughts on achievements, challenges and the future trajectory. It argues that IEL needs to devise novel legal tools and principles to confront the challenges posed by global environmental challenges, especially climate change, and urgently rethink the capitalist model of development that has given rise to much environmental destruction.

---

[5] See Hunter et al. 2015, p. 433. This, by itself, is not a problem and the Stockholm Declaration has, to some extent, played this role. The Universal Declaration of Human Rights was adopted in 1948 and forms the foundation of modern human rights law. See De Schutter 2010.

[6] United Nations General Assembly 2015, Transforming Our World: Agenda 2030 for Sustainable Development (Agenda 2030), UN Doc. A/RES/70/1.

1.2 Evolution of International Environmental Law[7]

The evolution of IEL will be discussed under three subheadings: the pre-sustainable development era—from the Stockholm Conference in 1972 to the WCED in 1987; the post-sustainable development era advancements from Rio Declaration of 1992 to Rio+20 in 2012 with particular emphasis on the impact of sustainable development on IEL; and globalization, the Anthropocene and the Sustainable Development Goals.

1.2.1 Pre-sustainable Development Era

By the late 1960s several European states were beginning to feel the negative consequences of 'acid rain',[8] a by-product of industrial activities. Because the consequences were felt far away from the source and these sources were outside their territories, an international response was required. Sweden suggested an international conference in 1968 to address these emerging environmental challenges and offered to host it in 1972.

North–South divisions plagued the conference from the start. Developing countries, many of whom were newly independent and not feeling the negative impacts of industrialization, wanted to ensure that their sovereign right to develop was preserved. Having finally achieved the majority in the UN General Assembly, G-77 and China sponsored a series of resolutions 'affirming their right to development, their sovereignty over natural resources and the need to handle environmental policies at the national level'.[9] A resolution on development and environment was adopted shortly before the Stockholm Conference,[10] recognizing that 'no environmental policy should adversely affect the present and future development possibilities of developing countries'[11] and affirming the sovereign right of each country to plan its own economy, define its own priorities, and determine its own environmental standards and criteria. The resolution also expressed the view that most environmental problems in developing countries are caused by a lack of economic resources and

[7] See Yang and Percival 2009, p. 616, who define 'global environmental law' as 'the set of legal principles developed by national, international, and transnational environmental regulatory systems to protect the environment and manage natural resources.' This must be distinguished from 'international environmental law' which is the body of law governing the global environment. While there are national legal principles that have become part of IEL (see discussion below), there is a distinct body of laws governing environmental issues that affect two or more states or the global environment. According to Sands et al. 2018, p. 14, 'international environmental law comprises those substantive, procedural and institutional rules of international law that have as their primary objective the protection of the environment.'

[8] See Hunter et al. 2015, Chapter 10.

[9] Ibid., p. 138.

[10] United Nations General Assembly 1972, Resolution on Development and Environment, UN Doc. A/RES/2849 (XXVI) (Stockholm Declaration).

[11] Ibid., para 3.

that the quality of human life depends on resolving environmental problems which have their origins in underdevelopment itself. The United States of America and the United Kingdom voted against the resolution while almost all the other industrialized countries abstained.[12] This was the mindset of countries going into the Stockholm conference.

Considered as one of the most successful conferences held up to that point, 113 countries participated in the conference although only two heads of state—from Sweden and India—attended. Despite being a soft law instrument,[13] the Stockholm Declaration on the Human Environment adopted at the Conference laid the foundation for modern international environmental law.[14] It also laid the foundation for the subsequent acceptance of sustainable development, although the term itself did not appear in the Declaration. It emphasized the importance of integrating environment with development and 'internationalized' environmental protection despite the insistence by developing countries that environmental protection should be subject to national law and policies. Its near-endorsement of a human right to a healthy environment is noteworthy:

> Man has the fundamental right to freedom, equality and adequate conditions of life, in an environment of a quality that permits a life of dignity and well-being, and he bears a solemn responsibility to protect and improve the environment for present and future generations [….][15]

Later documents unfortunately failed to develop and adopt a distinct right to a healthy environment which remains a gap in contemporary international human rights law.[16] Regional human rights treaties, on the other hand, have been much more forthcoming,[17] as have regional human rights institutions and national judiciaries.[18]

Another influential provision in the Declaration that is now considered as having crystallized into a customary law principle governing the environment is Principle 21:

> States have, in accordance with the Charter of the United Nations and the principles of international law, the sovereign right to exploit their own resources pursuant to their own environmental policies, and the responsibility to ensure that activities within their jurisdiction

[12] This resolution emphasized developing countries' strong belief that environmental protection should not interfere with their development agenda and that environmental protection should be left to individual countries. See Hunter et al. 2015, p. 140.

[13] See discussion in Sect. 1.4.1.

[14] Stockholm Declaration, above n 10.

[15] Ibid. Principle 1.

[16] See Atapattu and Schapper 2019, p. 3.

[17] These are: American Declaration of Rights and Duties of Man, adopted at the Ninth International Conference of American States, Bogota, Colombia, 2 May 1948; African Charter on Human and Peoples' Rights, opened for signature 27 June 1981, 1520 UNTS 217, entered into force 21 October 1986; Convention on Access to Information, Public Participation in Decision Making and Access to justice in Environmental Matters (Aarhus Convention), opened for signature 25 June 1998, 2161 UNTS 447, entered into force 30 October 2001.

[18] See Pedersen 2018, p. 86; Atapattu and Schapper 2019, chapters 4 and 8.

> or control do not cause damage to the environment of other States or of areas beyond the limits of national jurisdiction.[19]

The Stockholm Conference legitimized international action in relation to the environment, spurred action at the national level and recognized the link between economic development and environmental protection. Subsequent to the Conference, the United Nations Environment Program (UNEP) was established which, to date, continues as the international organization and focal point relating to the global environment. Around this time, many national laws and institutions were also adopted along with a proliferation of environmental treaties.[20]

Despite these noteworthy developments, the North-South tensions influenced the Stockholm Conference and 'have continued to play a central role at the major international gatherings on environmental protection held since.'[21] These tensions prompted the UN General Assembly to appoint a commission in 1983 to look into ways to reconcile economic development with environmental protection. Thus, the World Commission on Environment and Development headed by the then Prime Minister of Norway, Gro Harlem Brundtland, was born.

1.2.2 Post-sustainable Development Era

The mandate given to the WCED was to formulate 'a global agenda for change' and to, inter alia, propose long-term environmental strategies for achieving sustainable development by 2000 and beyond.[22] The central message of the report—sustainable development—had a huge impact on the development of international environmental law. Defined as 'development that meets the needs of the present without compromising the ability of future generations to meet their own needs',[23] sustainable development has become one of the most influential concepts of international law. The WCED sent an urgent message to states to change their destructive practices: 'we are unanimous in our conviction that the security, well-being and very survival of the planet depend on such changes, now.'[24] The WCED report had a direct bearing

---

[19] United Nations General Assembly 1972, Principle 21. See also Hunter et al. 2015, p. 142; Sands et al. 2018, p. 202.

[20] An often forgotten, yet important instrument is the World Charter for Nature adopted by the UN General Assembly to celebrate the 10th anniversary of the Stockholm conference. It was the first instrument to adopt a set of principles to protect nature. It recognized that nature should be protected irrespective of its worth to human beings and laid the first seeds of the precautionary principle, EIA and sustainable development. UN General Assembly, World Charter for Nature 1982, UN Doc. A/RES/37/7.

[21] See Michelson 2015, p. 109. See also Ntambirweki 1991.

[22] See WCED 1987, p. ix.

[23] Ibid., p. 43.

[24] Ibid., p. 23.

on the UN Conference on Environment and Development (Rio Conference) held in 1992.[25]

Instead of trying to improve the definition of sustainable development, the Rio Declaration sought to give it content. Thus, the Rio Declaration embodies substantive components, procedural components, linkages and tools to achieve sustainable development. In this sense, the Rio Declaration can be considered one of the most influential instruments on sustainable development to have been adopted by the international community.

The substantive components include the principle of equity (both inter- and intra-generational); sustainable utilization of natural resources; the principle of integration; and the right to development.[26] The procedural components include, as embodied in Principle 10, access to information, participation in decision-making and access to remedies which form part of international human rights law.[27] Many of these components have normative effect and states must fulfil these requirements in relation to development activities within their territories.

The most significant contribution of the Rio Declaration was the recognition of sustainable development as the overarching framework for environmental governance and the adoption of principles and tools to achieve it: environmental impact assessment (Principle 17), the polluter pays principle (Principle 16), the precautionary principle (Principle 15), and the common but differentiated responsibility principle (Principle 7). It identified women, youth, and indigenous peoples as groups requiring special protection (Principles 20, 21 and 22 respectively) and linkages with areas such as warfare (Principle 24) and peace (Principle 25).

The journey of sustainable development, which began with the adoption of the WCED report, got a considerable boost with the adoption of the Rio Declaration which essentially 'put meat on the bones'. Its binary nature consisting of two pillars changed to encompass a third pillar with the adoption of the Copenhagen Declaration on Social Development,[28] which was later affirmed in the Johannesburg Declaration on Sustainable Development:[29]

> Accordingly, we assume a collective responsibility to advance and strengthen the interdependent and mutually reinforcing pillars of sustainable development—economic development, social development and environmental protection—at the local, national, regional and global levels.[30]

---

[25] See Report of the UN Conference on Environment and Development, Rio de Janeiro, 3–14 June 1992, UN Doc. A/CONF.151/26/Rev.l (Vol l). See in particular the Rio Declaration on Environment and Development, Annex 1, p. 3 (Rio Declaration). See also Sand 1992, p. 209.

[26] See Birnie et al. 2009. See also Sands et al. 2018, p. 219.

[27] See Rio Declaration, above n 25.

[28] United Nations (1995) Report of the World Summit for Social Development, Copenhagen, 6–12 March, UN Doc. A/CONF.166/9 (Copenhagen Declaration).

[29] United Nations, Johannesburg Declaration on Sustainable Development 2002, UN Doc. A/CONF.199/20.

[30] Ibid., para 5. See Jacob 1999, who argues that sustainable development is a 'contestable concept' which has two levels of meaning—the first level is unitary but vague and the concept is defined by reference to core ideas (similar to democracy and liberty). The second level of meaning is how the

In many respects, the Rio+20 conference held to celebrate the 20th anniversary of the Rio Conference, was a disappointment. Its unambitious agenda consisted of just two broad themes—promoting a green economy as the vehicle to achieve sustainable development and strengthening the institutional framework to achieve that.[31] While the final document titled *The Future We Want* endorsed the international community's commitment to sustainable development, the Rio+20 conference failed to capture the excitement and promise of its predecessor, the Earth Summit.

However, sustainable development has survived the ebbs and flows in enthusiasm. It provides the overarching framework for the myriad of environmental principles that developed in a rather ad hoc manner and lacked an organizing principle.[32] If only from this perspective, sustainable development plays an important role. Sustainable development also internationalized the development process, thereby bringing the economic development process of states subject to international scrutiny: 'The most potentially far-reaching aspect of sustainable development is that for the first time it makes a state's management of its own domestic environment a matter of international concern in a systematic way.'[33] Thus, sustainable development is now entrenched in IEL and some scholars believe that a separate branch of international law called international sustainable development law has now emerged.[34]

1.2.3 Globalization, Anthropocene and Sustainable Development Goals (SDGs)

The promising start to sustainable development made with the adoption of the Rio Declaration met its match with the rise of globalization, another 'whirlwind force'[35] to sweep the world:

> The emergence of globalization as the predominant economic trend in the 1990s set up an inevitable potential conflict with the goals of sustainable development proclaimed at Rio. Many of the same policy makers that embraced sustainable development also embraced globalization, as the engine that would deliver the promises of Rio.[36]

Many believed that the policies of globalization with its emphasis on market forces, technological changes and undermining environmental and social safeguards

---

concept should be interpreted in practice. He identifies six core ideas of sustainable development: environment-economy integration; futurity; environmental protection; equity; quality of life; and participation. See also Boyle and Freestone 1999. For a critique, see Dawe and Ryan 2003.

[31] See Hunter et al. 2015, p. 182.

[32] See Hunter et al. 2015, p. 169; Atapattu 2019.

[33] See Birnie et al. 2009, p. 124.

[34] See Cordonier Segger and Khalfan 2004, and Principle 27 of the Rio Declaration, above n 25, which calls upon states to cooperate in good faith to develop 'international law in the field of sustainable development.'

[35] See Hunter et al. 2015, p. 175.

[36] Ibid.

was antithetical to the objectives of sustainable development.[37] It is no secret that the trade agenda was promoted at the expense of the environmental agenda with the World Trade Organization and the World Bank playing a major role. Structural adjustment policies and deregulation of multinational corporations that benefited the Global North were promoted while pro-poor, environmentally friendly policies were rejected which negatively impacted small scale farmers and other vulnerable communities in the Global South.[38] These negative impacts led Nobel laureate Joseph Stiglitz to note that globalization is not working for the environment or for the world's poor.[39] The negative impact of globalization was recognized in the Johannesburg Declaration on Sustainable Development which noted:

> Globalization has added a new dimension to these challenges. The rapid integration of markets, mobility of capital and significant increases in investment flows around the world have opened new challenges and opportunities for the pursuit of sustainable development. But the benefits and costs of globalization are unevenly distributed, with developing countries facing special difficulties in meeting this challenge.[40]

Forces of globalization continue to date and has diverted attention from sustainable development. As noted, the agenda of the Rio+20 conference held in Brazil in 2012 was 'strikingly unambitious'.[41] This lackluster situation was reinvigorated somewhat with the adoption of the Sustainable Development Goals (SDGs) in 2015.[42] For the first time, the global community adopted a common global agenda on *all* three dimensions of sustainable development, articulating that SDGs are integrated and indivisible and are based on human rights.[43] Comprising 17 goals and 169 targets, SDGs are an ambitious global agenda that seek to address, inter alia, poverty as well as climate change. However, SDGs continue to promote economic growth as the vehicle for poverty alleviation when the negative consequences of limitless growth are apparent in the form of the externalities that it has created:

> Goal 8, for example, seeks to increase GDP growth in the least developed countries along with higher levels of economic productivity in all countries. By failing to acknowledge the need to reduce economic growth in affluent countries in order to improve living standards in poor countries without exceeding ecological limits, the SDGs 'fail to reconcile the contradiction between growth and sustainability at the core of sustainable development.'[44]

The latest 'catch phrase' to enter the global scene is the Anthropocene. Scientists believe that we have entered a new geologic epoch called the 'Anthropocene' in which

---

[37] See Yang and Percival 2009, pp. 641–42 who point out that while globalization in the form of trade liberalization and the growth of MNCs has facilitated externalization of pollution and environmental degradation, it has also led to more positive outcomes via environmental self-regulation.

[38] See Gonzalez 2017, p. 218.

[39] See Stiglitz 2001, referred to in Hunter et al. 2015, p. 177.

[40] Johannesburg Declaration on Sustainable Development, above n 29, para 14.

[41] See Hunter et al. 2015, p. 181.

[42] See UN General Assembly 2015.

[43] Ibid., para 18. Agenda 2030, above n 6, affirms the importance of the UDHR and human rights treaties and the responsibility of states to respect human rights and fundamental freedoms for all, without distinction of any kind (para 19) and gender equality (para 20). Cf. Knox 2015.

[44] See Atapattu et al. 2020, quoting Adelman 2018, p. 34.

human beings are the primary driver of environmental destruction.[45] This epoch 'is characterized by human domination and disruption of Earth system processes essential to the planet's self-regulating capacity'.[46] This generalized statement blurs the fact that more affluent segments of society are responsible for this destruction and that environmental crises are intrinsically connected to global economic policies that have colonial and post-colonial origins.[47] International law has enabled the entrenchment of these policies and practices.[48] Climate change, massive loss of biological diversity, and generation of toxic chemicals are just the tip of the iceberg. Many impoverished and minority communities continue to suffer the negative impacts of these environmental crises disproportionately, leading to justice concerns.[49]

1.3 Selected Principles of International Environmental Law

In addition to sustainable development, other principles of IEL have now emerged.[50] These principles play an important role, from providing guidance to states to design obligations in a particular area, to courts and tribunals to resolve disputes when they arise. They also provide guidance to states when negotiating treaties and other instruments.[51] While some principles have been borrowed from general international law,[52] others are unique to IEL.[53] These principles are substantive or procedural in nature although a clear distinction is hard to draw.[54] We now turn to a brief survey of some of these principles here.

---

[45] See Crutzen 2002, referred to in Gonzalez 2017.

[46] See Gonzalez 2017, p. 219.

[47] Ibid., p. 220.

[48] Ibid., p. 222.

[49] There is considerable literature on environmental justice. See, generally, Agyeman et al. 2003; Foster 1998; Bullard 2005; Boyd 2019. See also Principle 14 of the Framework Principles on Human Rights and the Environment 2018, UN Doc. A/HRC/37/59 proposed by John Knox, former UN Special Rapporteur on Human Rights and Environment.

[50] See, generally, Sands et al. 2018; Birnie et al. 2009; Hunter et al. 2015; Dupuy and Vinuales 2015; Atapattu 2006; Rosencranz 2003, p. 309; Brown Weiss 2011, p. 37; and Bodansky 2009.

[51] See Hunter et al. 2015, pp. 438–439.

[52] Principles of sovereignty and state responsibility are examples.

[53] The common but differentiated responsibility principle is a good example.

[54] See Brunnée 2018.

1.3.1 Obligation not to Cause Environmental Harm and the Principle of Prevention

The corollary of the cardinal principle of state sovereignty is the duty not to cause environmental harm beyond states' borders. Enshrined in Principle 21 of the Stockholm Declaration, and reaffirmed in the Rio Declaration[55] and treaties,[56] the obligation of harm prevention has now become a customary international law principle governing the environment.[57] This principle has its roots in the common law principle of *sic utere tuo ut alienum non laedus* ('do not use your property to harm another') and has been affirmed in several cases. In the *Corfu Channel Case*, the ICJ referred to 'every state's obligation not to allow knowingly its territory to be used for acts contrary to the rights of other States.'[58] This principle was affirmed in the environmental context in the ICJ advisory opinion on the *Legality of the Threat or Use of Nuclear Weapons*:

> The existence of the general obligation of States to ensure that activities within their jurisdiction and control respect the environment of other States or of areas beyond national control is now a part of the corpus of international law relating to the environment.[59]

While the Principle 21 formulation is considered a well-established customary international law principle, several questions remain: (a) what is the level of harm that would trigger this obligation; (b) what is the standard of care that states are required to abide by;[60] (c) what activities are under the jurisdiction or control of states; and (d) what remedies should be available to states that suffer damage? The answers depend on the context of each case and whether there are other obligations

---

[55] Rio Declaration, above n 25.

[56] See for example Convention on Long-range Transboundary Air Pollution, opened for signature 13 November 1979, 1302 UNTS 217, entered into force 16 March 1983; Vienna Convention for the Protection of the Ozone Layer, opened for signature 22 March 1985, 1513 UNTS 293, entered into force 22 September 1988; Stockholm Convention on Persistent Organic Pollutants, opened for signature 22 May 2001, 2256 UNTS 119, 17 May 2004; United Nations Framework Convention on Climate Change, opened for signature 9 May 1992, 1771 UNTS 107, entered into force 21 March 1994 (embodies Principle 21 verbatim in the Preamble without mentioning Principle 21); and Convention on Biological Diversity, opened for signature 5 June 1992, 1760 UNTS 79, entered into force 29 December 1993 (embodies Principle 21 verbatim in Article 3 titled 'principle' without mentioning Principle 21).

[57] See Hunter et al. 2015, p. 473; Sands et al. 2018.

[58] ICJ, *Corfu Channel (UK v Albania)*, Judgement, 9 April 1949, ICJ Reports 1949, p. 22.

[59] ICJ, *Legality of the Threat of Nuclear Weapons*, Advisory Opinion, 8 July 1996, ICJ Reports 1996, para 29–30. This was affirmed in ICJ, *Case Concerning Pulp Mills on the River Uruguay (Argentina v Uruguay)*, Judgment, 20 April 2010, ICJ Reports 2010, p. 14; and ICJ, *Gabčíkovo-Nagymaros Project (Hungary v Slovakia)*, Judgment, 25 September 1997, ICJ Reports 1997, p. 7.

[60] In the *Pulp Mills* case, the ICJ referred to the obligation to act with due diligence in respect of all activities which take place under the jurisdiction and control of each party. Elaborating on what this obligation entails, the ICJ stated: 'it is an obligation which entrails not only the adoption of appropriate rules and measures, but also a certain level of vigilance in their enforcement and the exercise of administrative control applicable to public and private operators, such as the monitoring of activities undertaken by such operators, to safeguard the rights of the other party', para 197.

in place that establish more precise standards. Although this principle is useful in the context of transboundary environmental issues, it is less useful to seek damages in relation to global issues such as climate change because, due to the multitude of sources, actors and victims, and the time lags involved, it is difficult to establish the causal link between the activity and damage.[61] However, the basic obligation of harm prevention is applicable to all activities of states.

A manifestation of the principle of sovereignty is the permanent sovereignty over natural resources principle. Its adoption was championed by developing countries who wanted to assert their sovereignty over their natural resources, after having gained independence after years of colonialism. General Assembly Resolution 2158 affirmed 'the inalienable right of all countries to exercise permanent sovereignty over their natural resources in the interest of their national development, in conformity with the spirit and principles of the Charter of the United Nations…'.[62] It also called on states to achieve the maximum possible development of natural resources of developing countries in accordance with national laws and regulations. However, with the advent of sustainable development and the principle of prevention, the efficacy of this principle has diluted somewhat as states are required to balance development activities with their environmental and social impact regardless of their impact beyond national borders.

With the advent of sustainable development as a principle, states are now required to prevent environmental harm even *within* their territory—giving rise to the principle of harm prevention. This principle is useful vis-à-vis global problems as states are required to prevent environmental harm irrespective of a transboundary element.[63] Environmental impact assessment, discussed below, is a useful tool to give effect to the principle of prevention as it 'emphasizes the need to anticipate environmental damage and to act proactively and cooperatively to avoid or minimize the risk'.[64] The principle of prevention emphasizes that preventing environmental harm is better and less costly than relying on remedial measures and/or providing compensation for damage. Moreover, some environmental damage may be irremediable.

[61] These legal issues were brought to the forefront in the Inuit petition filed before the Inter-American Commission on Human Rights in 2005 against the United States. The petition is available here: http://climatecasechart.com/climate-change-litigation/non-us-case/petition-to-the-inter-american-commission-on-human-rights-seeking-relief-from-violations-resulting-from-global-warming-caused-by-acts-and-omissions-of-the-united-states/. Accessed 23 March 2022. See also Farber 2007, p. 1615.

[62] See Hunter et al. 2015, p. 443; and Schrijver 1997.

[63] See Duvic-Paoli 2018.

[64] See Hunter et al. 2015, p. 477. See discussion below in Sect. 1.3.5.

1.3.2 Common but Differentiated Responsibility Principle[65]

The principle of common but differentiated responsibility (CBDR) serves as an exception to the sovereign equality principle. It gave rise to intense North-South debate at the time of its adoption,[66] and continues to be a hotly debated principle. It underlies the legal regimes governing ozone depletion[67] and climate change.[68] Reflecting core elements of equity, the CBDR principle acknowledges that the contribution to certain global environmental problems, their impact as well as the ability to address them, differ widely across states. It 'presents a conceptual framework for compromise and cooperation in meeting future environmental challenges, because it allows countries that are in different positions with respect to specific environmental issues to be treated differently'.[69] The Rio Declaration incorporates this principle:

> States shall cooperate in a spirit of global partnership to conserve, protect and restore the health and integrity of the Earth's ecosystem. In view of the different contributions to global environmental degradation, States have common but differentiated responsibilities. The developed countries acknowledge the responsibility that they bear in the international pursuit of sustainable development in view of the pressures their societies place on the global environment and of the technologies and financial resources they command.[70]

The UN Framework Convention on Climate Change (UNFCCC) includes CBDR as one of its guiding principles.[71] Including a specific provision on principles is rather unusual in environmental treaties and the adoption of this provision was contentious.[72] CBDR does not play a major role in relation to mitigation commitments under the Paris Agreement as the parties opted for bottom-up, voluntary commitments ostensibly to get around the CBDR principle. However, the principle continues to play an important role in relation to adaptation, climate finance, and the loss and damage mechanism.[73] The Paris Agreement is to be 'implemented to reflect equity and the principle of common but differentiated responsibilities and respective capabilities, in the light of different national circumstances.'[74] The CBDR principle

---

[65] See, generally, Cullet 2003; Rajamani 2006; French 2000; Stone 2004; Halvorssen 1999.

[66] See Atapattu 2015, p. 93.

[67] See Montreal Protocol on Substances that Deplete the Ozone Layer, opened for signature 16 September 1987, 1522 UNTS 3, entered into force 1 January 1989.

[68] See UNFCCC, above n 56; and the Kyoto Protocol to the United Nations Framework Convention on Climate Change, opened for signature 11 December 1997, 2303 UNTS 162, entered into force 16 February 2005.

[69] See Hunter et al. 2015, pp. 463–64. See also Rajamani 2016, pp. 493–514.

[70] Principle 7, Rio Declaration, above n 25.

[71] See UNFCCC, above n 56.

[72] See Atapattu 2015, p. 93, and Yamin and Depledge 2004, p. 70 who point out that Article 3 'does not refer to historic contribution to climate change as originally proposed by some developed countries but presents a more balanced approach emphasizing Parties' responsibilities as well as their present-day capabilities.'

[73] See Bodansky et al. 2017, p. 219.

[74] Preamble, Paris Agreement, opened for signature 12 December 2015 (2015), UN Doc. FCCC/CP/2015/L.9, Annex, entered into force 4 November 2016.

breaks new ground in international law[75] and its adoption even in its diluted form[76] was a major victory for developing countries.

1.3.3 *Inter- and Intra-generational Equity Principle*

Also grounded in the principle of equity are the principles of inter and the intra-generational equity—which form part of the substantive components of sustainable development. The inter-generational equity principle acknowledges that many of our decisions have an impact on future generations and hence, they should be 'given a seat at the table' when making decisions.[77] The climate crisis has brought the importance of this principle to the forefront. The UNFCCC calls upon parties to protect the climate system for the benefit of present and future generations of humankind.[78]

According to the theory of inter-generational justice which seeks to sustain the welfare and well-being of all generations, 'each generation has an obligation to future generations to pass on the natural and cultural resources of the planet in no worse condition than received and to provide reasonable access to the legacy for the present generation.'[79] This requires each generation to conserve options, quality and access to resources.

The most celebrated decision that discusses the inter-generational equity principle is the *Minors Oposa case* from the Philippines:

> Petitioners minors assert that they represent their generation as well as generations yet unborn. We find no difficulty in ruling that they can, for themselves, for others of their generations and for the succeeding generations, file a class suit. Their personality to sue in behalf of the succeeding generations can only be based on the concept of intergenerational responsibility insofar as the right to a balanced and healthful ecology is concerned...... Needless to say, every generation has a responsibility to the next to preserve that rhythm and harmony for the full enjoyment of a balanced and healthful ecology. Put a little differently, the minors' assertion of their right to a sound environment constitutes, at the same time, the performance of their obligation to ensure the protection of that right for the generations to come.[80]

This decision shows how developments at the international level can influence judicial decisions at the national level. The ICJ referred to the inter-generational

---

[75] See Atapattu 2015, p. 98.

[76] Ibid. p. 96. The original formulation of the CBDR principle referred specifically to the historic responsibility of Northern states but was dropped due to opposition by Northern countries especially, the US which appended an 'interpretative clause' to Principle 7 when signing the Rio Declaration, above n 25.

[77] See Hunter et al. 2015, p. 460. For the seminal work on the Inter-generational equity principle, see Brown Weiss 1996.

[78] UNFCCC, above n 56, Preamble and Article 3.

[79] See Brown Weiss 2011, p. 37.

[80] Supreme Court of the Philippines, *Minors Oposa v. Secretary of the Department of Environment and Natural Resources*, Judgement, 30 July 1993, 33 ILM 173.

equity principle in its advisory opinion on *The Legality of the Threat of Use of Nuclear Weapons*.[81] The ICJ noted that 'the environment is not an abstraction but represents the living space, the quality of life and the very health of human beings, including generations unborn.'[82]

On the other hand, southern countries argue that the emphasis on future generations should not obscure the inequity in the current generation which should be addressed *before* equity among generations is addressed.[83] In other words, the intra-generational equity principle requires that economic, social and environmental injustices that plague the current generation should be addressed, especially, the disproportionate burden of environmental costs placed on certain communities. The environmental justice movement seeks to address the unequal burden of polluting activities on low-income and minority communities.[84]

The Rio Declaration embodies both principles. Principle 3 provides that: 'The right to development must be fulfilled so as to equitably meet developmental and environmental needs of present and future generations,'[85] while Principle 5 emphasizes the need to eradicate poverty 'in order to decrease the disparities in standards of living and better meet the needs of the majority of the people of the world'.[86] Agenda 2030 with its 17 Sustainable Development Goals (SDGs) that range from poverty alleviation[87] to addressing climate change,[88] embodies both inter and intra generational equity aspects. Many environmental treaties also embody these two principles.[89]

1.3.4 Precautionary Principle

Another controversial yet important principle that has given rise to intense debate is the precautionary principle. It recognizes that scientific certainty often comes too late and therefore, scientific uncertainty should not be used as an excuse to postpone cost effective preventive measures. Like the principle of prevention, the precautionary principle entails taking anticipatory action to avoid irreparable environmental harm

---

[81] See ICJ, *Legality of the Threat or Use of Nuclear Weapons*, above n 59, p. 95.

[82] Ibid. para 29.

[83] See Atapattu 2015, p. 92.

[84] See Kuehn 2000, p. 10681; Gonzalez 2012, pp. 77–98; and Foster 1998, p. 52.

[85] See Rio Declaration, above n 25, Principle 3.

[86] Ibid., Principle 5. Principle 6 of the Rio Declaration is another manifestation of the intra-generational equity principle. It requires the special situation and needs of developing countries, particularly the least developed countries to be given special priority.

[87] See Agenda 2030, above n 6, SDG 1.

[88] Ibid., SDG 13.

[89] See for example UNFCCC, above n 56; Paris Agreement, above n 74; and Convention on Biological Diversity, above n 56.

before it occurs: 'Indeed, the precautionary principle can be viewed as the application of the principle of prevention where the scientific understanding of a specific environmental threat is not complete.'[90]

This principle reflects the important relationship that environmental issues have with science.[91] Many of the environmental laws cannot be designed without a sound scientific basis. When there is scientific uncertainty or science is conflicting, designing an effective legal regime becomes problematic. Moreover, states have used scientific uncertainty as an excuse not to take preventive measures.[92] The precautionary principle was born in an effort to address this situation. The IPCC reports which play an important role in relation to climate change is a good example of this relationship.[93]

Principle 15 of the Rio Declaration embodies the precautionary principle. It provides that:

> In order to protect the environment. The precautionary approach shall be widely applied by States according to their capabilities. Where there are threats of serious or irreversible damage, lack of full scientific certainty shall not be used as a reason for postponing cost-effective measures to prevent environmental degradation.[94]

The precautionary principle has been included in many treaties, including the Montreal Protocol,[95] the UNFCCC,[96] and the Biosafety Protocol.[97] The UNFCCC includes it as a principle under Article 3:

> The Parties should take precautionary measures to anticipate, prevent or minimize the causes of climate change and mitigate its adverse effects. Where there are threats of serious or irreversible damage, lack of full scientific certainty should not be used as a reason for postponing such measures, taking into account that policies and measures to deal with climate change should be cost-effective so as to ensure global benefits at the lowest possible cost [...][98]

---

[90] See Hunter et al. 2015, p. 478.

[91] See Sands et al. 2018, p. 6.

[92] The United States referred to scientific uncertainty as one of the reasons for withdrawing from the Kyoto Protocol in 2001. See Phillipson 2001, pp. 288–304.

[93] The Intergovernmental Panel on Climate Change (IPCC) was established by the UN to synthesize science relating to climate change. Its reports have influenced climate negotiations and are widely regarded as reflecting the status of climate science. See www.ipcc.ch/.

[94] Principle 15, Rio Declaration, above n 25.

[95] The Preamble refers to the need to take precautionary measures to control the substances that deplete the ozone layer, with the ultimate objective of eliminating them on the basis of scientific knowledge, taking into consideration technical and economic considerations.

[96] Principle 3, UNFCCC, above n 56.

[97] Article 1 of the Cartagena Protocol on Biosafety to the Convention on Biological Diversity, opened for signature 29 January 2000, 2226 UNTS 208, entered into force 11 September 2003, refers specifically to Principle 15 of the Rio Declaration, above n 25.

[98] Article 3(3), UNFCCC, above n 56. Draft Article 3 gave rise to intense debate during negotiations. See Bodansky 1993; Atapattu 2017, p. 247.

The most extensive application of the precautionary principle can be found in the Straddling Fish Stocks Agreement adopted in 1995.[99] In addition to not referring to taking cost-effective measures, it also provides that the absence of adequate scientific information (as opposed to certainty) *shall not* be used as a reason for postponing conservation measures.

The precautionary principle has been applied in international and domestic judicial decisions.[100] In the *Gabcikovo Nagymaros* case, the ICJ referred the need to take newly developed norms of environmental law into account when implementing the treaty between the parties and to take precautionary measures:

> The Court is mindful that, in the field of environmental protection, vigilance and prevention are required on account of the often irreversible character of damage to the environment and of the limitations inherent in the very mechanism of reparation of this type of damage.[101]

Other institutions and dispute settlement mechanisms that have addressed the precautionary principle include the WTO,[102] the International Tribunal for the Law of the Sea (ITLOS),[103] and the European Union,[104] although their approach to its application has differed somewhat.

---

[99] Agreement on the Conservation and Management of Straddling Fish Stocks and Highly Migratory Fish Stocks, opened for signature 8 September 1995, UN Doc. A/CONF.164/37, entered into force 11 December 2011.

[100] See for e.g. Supreme Court of India, *Vellore Citizens Welfare Forum v Union of India and Others*, Judgment, 28 August 1996; Supreme Court of India, *Narmada Bachao Andolan v Union of India and Others*, Judgment, 18 October 2000.

[101] *Gabcikovo Nagymaros,* above n 59, paras 140 and 113.

[102] *In the Beef Hormone case* the EU invoked the precautionary principle as a justification for its decision to regulate GMOs in food. US argued that EU's actions were not scientifically based and, therefore, contrary to WTO rules. The WTO dispute settlement body sided with the US. See WTO, *European Communities—Measures Concerning Meat and Meat Products (Hormones),* Appellate Body Report, 16 January 1998, WT/DS26/AB/R WT/DS48/AB/R.

[103] In the *Southern Bluefin Tuna Cases,* petitioners (New Zealand and Australia) argued that parties must act consistently with the precautionary principle. Japan not surprisingly denied its application. The Tribunal noted: 'The parties should in the circumstances act with prudence and caution to ensure that effective conservation measures are taken to prevent serious harm to the stock of southern bluefin tuna' and also referred to scientific uncertainty regarding measures to be taken to conserve Bluefin tuna stocks. The separate opinions of Judges Laing and Treves specifically referred to the precautionary principle. The latter judge noted that a precautionary approach is inherent in the notion of provisional measures. See ITLOS, *Southern Bluefin Tuna Cases (New Zealand and Australia v Japan),* Provisional Measures, 27 August 1999, ITLOS Reports 1999, p. 268. See Marr 2000. In the *MOX Plant case,* also before the ITOLS, Ireland argued that the precautionary principle places the burden on the UK to demonstrate that no harm would arise from the operation of the MOX plant. While the Tribunal called upon the parties to cooperate with one another and enter into consultations, it did not refer to the precautionary principle. See ITLOS, *The MOX Plant Case (Ireland v United Kingdom),* Provisional Measures, 13 November 2001, ITLOS Reports 2001, p. 89.

[104] EU adopts the following test to determine the legality of measures based on the precautionary principle—whether they are proportional to the chosen level of protection; non-discriminatory in their application; consistent with similar measures taken; based on an examination of potential benefits and costs of action or inaction; subject to review in light of new scientific data; and capable of assigning responsibility for producing scientific evidence. See Communication from the Commission on the Precautionary Principle, COM (2000) 1, Summary (2 February 2000).

Despite the controversy surrounding the principle, the precautionary principle plays an important role in the decision-making process and 'provides a framework for governments to set preventative policies where existing science is incomplete or where no consensus exists regarding a particular threat.'[105] On the one end of the spectrum, it is no more than the preventive approach. On the other extreme, it reverses the burden of proof.[106] While there doesn't seem to be a uniform understanding of its meaning among states, the precautionary principle likely requires that activities and substances which may be harmful be regulated or even prohibited even in the absence of conclusive evidence about their harmful impact.[107]

1.3.5 Environmental Impact Assessment and Public Participation

Environmental Impact Assessment (EIA) is a tool that originated from the national level[108] and became part of international law.[109] Principle 17 of the Rio Declaration embodies this but gives deference to national law.[110] It seeks to implement the principle of prevention, discussed above.[111] As a public document that is subject to public participation in most countries, EIA paved the way for the convergence between human rights and environmental issues. Principle 10 of the Rio Declaration embodies participatory rights which are also established principles of human rights law:

> Environmental issues are best handled with the participation of all concerned citizens, at the relevant level. At the national level, each individual shall have appropriate access to information concerning the environment that is held by public authorities, including information on hazardous materials and activities in their communities, and the opportunity to participate in decision-making processes. States shall facilitate and encourage public awareness

---

[105] See Hunter et al. 2015, p. 479.

[106] See Atapattu 2006, Chapter 3.

[107] See Sands 1994.

[108] The US was the first country to adopt environmental impact statements for major federal projects. See Craik 2008 for a discussion of the evolution of EIA under domestic law and international law.

[109] See Sand 2006, p. 519, who, when referring to the dynamic relationship between domestic and international law, distinguishes between 'horizontal diffusion' (when environmental policies and laws spread among countries) and 'vertical transplants' (when MEAs draw on domestic environmental laws and policies). See also Wiener 2001, pp. 1295–1371, for a slightly different view based on comparative law, and Yang and Percival 2009, p. 626.

[110] See Principle 17, Rio Declaration, above n 25: 'Environmental impact assessment, as a national instrument, shall be undertaken for proposed activities that are likely to have a significant adverse impact on the environment and are subject to a decision of a competent national authority.' See also Framework Principle 8.

[111] See Brunnée 2018.

> and participation by making information widely available. Effective access to judicial and administrative proceedings, including redress and remedy, shall be provided.[112]

Together, these three rights—access to information, participation in the decision-making process and access to remedies—are considered access rights[113] or democracy rights relating to the environment.[114] Principle 10 was the impetus for the adoption of the Aarhus Convention[115] which was the first environmental treaty, albeit regional, to incorporate these participatory rights. Latin America adopted a similar treaty in 2018.[116] In the *Pulp Mills* case between Uruguay and Argentina, the ICJ held that conducting EIAs 'has gained so much acceptance among States that it may now be considered a requirement under general international law .... where there is a risk that the proposed industrial activity may have a significant adverse impact in a transboundary context, in particular on a shared resource.'[117] The Court further noted that due diligence and the duty of vigilance and prevention that EIA implies would not have been fulfilled if a party undertaking such an activity did not conduct an EIA which, the Court held, applied even in the absence of a transboundary impact.[118]

1.4 Unique Features of IEL

While general international law forms the foundation of IEL and many of the early principles were borrowed from international law, IEL has adopted its own principles and procedures. Moreover, it has developed several unique features that will be summarized in this section.

1.4.1 Use of Soft Law Instruments

Although not unique to this field, the extensive use of soft law instruments is an important feature of IEL. In fact, the very first document that formed the foundation of this field—the Stockholm Declaration—is a soft law instrument. Since then,

---

[112] Principle 10, Rio Declaration, above n 25. See Sands et al. 2018, Chapter 14; Kravchenko 2009; and Framework Principles 9 and 10, above n 49.

[113] See the Access Initiative at WRI, www.wri.org/our-work/project/access-initiative-tai.

[114] See Cordonier Segger and Khalfan 2004.

[115] See Aarhus Convention, above n 17.

[116] Regional Agreement on Access to Information, Participation and Justice in Environmental Matters in Latin America and Caribbean, opened for signature 4 March 2018, LC/L.4059/Rev.8, entered into force 22 April 2021.

[117] *Pulp Mills on the River Uruguay (Argentina v Uruguay)*, above n 59.

[118] Ibid., para 120. Some countries, such as Canada and Sri Lanka, have gone even further and require the preparation of sustainable development assessments. See Impact Assessment Act, SC 2019, c 28, s 1 (Canada); Federal Sustainable Development Act, SC 2008, c 33 (Canada); and Sustainable Development Act, No 19 of 2017 (Sri Lanka).

hundreds of soft law instruments have been adopted on various topics. Some soft law instruments paved the way for the adoption of treaties later.[119] Others provided guidance to states.

While an in-depth discussion of soft law instruments is not possible here, suffice it to say that soft law plays an important role in developing the law particularly in newly emerging areas, shaping national law, and consolidating existing laws.[120] However, not all soft law instruments play a role in shaping law. There are many kinds of soft law instruments and there is a hierarchy among them. Declarations of high-level conferences which are adopted by states enjoy higher status than codes of conduct adopted by non-state actors such as development banks or industry. Similarly, UN General Assembly resolutions adopted by consensus will enjoy a higher status than a resolution adopted by an academic body such as the International Law Association.

Thus, the significance of soft law instruments should be evaluated on a case by case basis. Because they are flexible, easy to adopt, and do not need to be ratified, states often opt for soft law instruments—at least at the beginning. The same is true when science is uncertain but action is warranted. In that sense, there are similarities between soft law instruments and framework treaties, discussed next. Even more radically, some international institutions have been established by soft law instruments—UNEP, the premier international institution on the environment, was established by a UN General Assembly resolution.[121] Similarly, the Arctic Council was established by a non-binding instrument.[122] With the proliferation of soft law instruments, states have begun paying closer attention to the language included in them with some even going to the extent of inserting 'interpretative statements' to them,[123] akin to reservations to treaties. Despite the significance of these soft law

[119] Examples include: Bonn Guidelines on Access to Genetic Resources and Fair and Equitable Sharing of Benefits Arising from their Utilization (2002), https://www.cbd.int/doc/publications/cbd-bonn-gdls-en.pdf accessed 20 June 2020; and the Nagoya Protocol on Access to Genetic Resources and the Fair and Equitable Sharing of Benefits arising from their Utilization to the Convention on Biological Diversity, opened for signature 29 October 2010, 3008 UNTS, entered into force 12 October 2014; Cairo Guidelines and Principles for the Environmentally Sound Management of Hazardous Waste and the Basel Convention on the Control of Transboundary Movements of Hazardous Wastes and their Disposal, opened for signature 22 March 1989, 1673 UNTS 57, entered into force 5 May 1992.

[120] See Hunter et al. 2015, p. 350.

[121] UN General Assembly Resolution 2997 (XXVII) 1972. See Hunter et al. 2015, p. 191, and Sands et al. 2018, p. 63. UNEP was established as a program, rather than a specialized agency which, together with limited financial resources, has constrained its ability to function effectively. See also Brown Weiss 2011, p. 24.

[122] The Arctic Council was established by the Ottawa Declaration on the Establishment of the Arctic Council in 1996. The Declaration is available here: https://oaarchive.arctic-council.org/bitstream/handle/11374/85/EDOCS-1752-v2-ACMMCA00_Ottawa_1996_Founding_Declaration.PDF?sequence=5&isAllowed=y. Accessed 20 June 2020.

[123] Examples include the 'interpretative statements' made by the US to the Rio Declaration (Article 7 on the CBDR) and to the UN Declaration on the Right to Development (1986), adopted by UN General Assembly resolution 41/128, 4 December 1986. See Hunter et al. 2015, p. 450.

instruments, they are not binding (unless they have been incorporated into treaties) and cannot hold states responsible for their failure to fulfil these commitments.[124]

1.4.2 Framework/Protocol Approach

Another technique that states have adopted in the environmental field is the 'framework/protocol' approach in response to scientific uncertainty and/or lack of political will.[125] In situations where there is insufficient political support to adopt a treaty with binding obligations but there is sufficient scientific proof to show that a particular issue needs attention, the framework/protocol approach has proven to be effective. While it is essentially a tactic to 'buy more time', it has been effective at establishing an institutional framework to facilitate exchange of information, research and other activities. When science became more established states have supplemented the framework with more stringent obligations in protocols. This approach has been adopted in relation to regional seas,[126] long-range transboundary air pollution,[127] ozone depletion,[128] climate change,[129] and with a modification in relation to biodiversity.[130]

As noted, framework conventions are similar to soft law instruments in practice as the language employed is rather soft and vague. It is important to remember, however, that framework conventions are still treaties and the provisions of the Vienna Convention on the Law of Treaties[131] apply to them. Despite the vague language used in them, the commitments are binding on states. In fact, when the US withdrew from the Kyoto Protocol, some scholars argued that the US was in violation of the

---

[124] See Dupuy 1991; Palmer 1992, p. 259; and Sand 1992.

[125] See Brown Weiss 2011, p. 7; Hunter et al. 2015, p. 353.

[126] See Barcelona Convention for the Protection of the Mediterranean Sea Against Pollution, opened for signature 16 February 1976, 1102 UNTS 27, entered into force 12 February 1978.

[127] UNECE, Convention on Long-Range Transboundary Air Pollution, opened for signature 17 November 1979, 1302 UNTS 217, entered into force 16 March 1983 and its protocols.

[128] Vienna Convention for the Protection of the Ozone Layer, opened for signature 22 March 1985, 1513 UNTS 293, entered into force 22 September 1988; and the Montreal Protocol, above n 67, and London Amendments.

[129] UNFCCC, above n 56; Kyoto Protocol above n 68; and the Paris Agreement, above n 74. Whether the Paris Agreement is a 'protocol' under the UNFCCC is a hotly debated issue. See Bodansky 2016, p. 142. The Paris Agreement is a unique document because it adopts a hybrid approach to obligations and encapsulates voluntary emission reduction commitments in a binding framework.

[130] Convention on Biological Diversity, above n 56. Biosafety Protocol, above n 97; Nagoya Protocol, above n 119; and Nagoya-Kuala Lumpur Supplementary Protocol on Liability and Redress to the Cartagena Protocol on Biosafety, opened for signature 15 October 2010, UN Doc. UNEP/CBD/BS/COP-MOP/5/17, entered into force 5 March 2018.

[131] Vienna Convention on the Law of Treaties, opened for signature 23 May 1969, 1155 UNTS 331, entered into force 27 January 1980.

UNFCCC.[132] It is usually a pre-requisite that in order to sign a protocol, states must become parties to the framework convention first.[133]

1.4.3 Linkages

Environmental issues do not operate in a vacuum and are closely intertwined with economic activity. More often than not, environmental pollution and degradation are byproducts and externalities of economic development. Until the advent of sustainable development as the overarching framework to govern economic activity, environmental degradation was considered an externality. Now sustainable development requires states to consider environmental protection and social development as integral components of the economic development process. Climate change is an excellent example of our economic activities gone awry and is considered the biggest market failure ever.[134]

Another important relationship is the link with human rights, justice and good governance. Many poor and marginalized communities are disproportionately affected by polluting industries and studies have consistently shown that such industries are predominately located in poor and marginalized communities.[135] The environmental justice movement was born out of this disproportionate impact.[136] Moreover, because the environmental legal regime lacks a sophisticated institutional framework to seek redress, victims of environmental abuse have resorted to the human rights machinery. While international human rights law does not yet recognize a right to a healthy environment as a distinct right, regional human rights instruments do,[137] and many judiciaries have generated a significant body of jurisprudence on environmental rights by interpreting existing rights expansively.[138] Moreover, over 100 constitutions around the world now recognize some form of environment rights[139] and many believe that the time is now ripe to recognize a distinct right to a healthy environment.[140] While this development is yet to take place, procedural environmental rights—right to information, participation in the decision-making process and right to remedies—are established rights and overlap with procedural components

---

132 See Hunter et al. 2015, p. 677.

133 Article 23 of the Kyoto Protocol, above n 68, makes it clear that it is open for signature by states and regional integration organizations that are parties to the Convention (meaning the UNFCCC).

134 See Klein 2014.

135 See Foster 1998, p. 52.

136 See Kuehn 2000.

137 See above n 17 for these regional instruments.

138 See Reports of the Special Rapporteurs on Human Rights and Environment, John Knox and David Boyd, especially the mapping report by Knox (2013): www.ohchr.org/EN/Issues/Environment/SREnvironment/Pages/MappingReport.aspx. Accessed 20 June 2020. See also Atapattu and Schapper 2019, Chapter 8.

139 See Boyd 2012; May and Daly 2015.

140 See Knox and Pejan 2018.

of sustainable development and principles of good governance.[141] Many instruments recognize the relationship between sustainable development and good governance.[142]

The relationship with trade and investment is another important, yet vexing, issue. While international trade has led to considerable economic growth worldwide,[143] trade liberalization has also contributed to much environmental degradation.[144] This relationship is mainly threefold: (a) using trade measures to implement environmental treaties; (b) whether 'production and process methods' (PPMs) are compatible with GATT core principles; and (c) the scope of environmental exceptions to GATT.[145] Several environmental treaties have used trade measure to ensure compliance. Thus, for example, the Ozone regime bans trade in controlled substances with non-parties.[146] The debate on PPMs has been the most controversial in the context of 'like products' in relation to the most favored nations obligation (MFN) and national treatment. Many disputes have arisen in relation to this and whether process and production methods should be taken into consideration when evaluating whether products are 'like products'.[147] GATT panels tended to adopt a restrictive approach based on physical likeness. However, environmentalists argue that how a product is manufactured and disposed of should be taken into consideration (a 'cradle to grave' approach) when deciding whether products are similar. Many believe that harmonization through multilateral environmental agreements is the best approach, so as to avoid differing domestic environmental laws.[148] The third area of contention has been in relation to the exceptions found in Article XX of the GATT in interpreting

---

[141] See Atapattu and Schapper 2019, Chapter 16. Council of Europe (2008): Principles of Good Governance: www.coe.int/en/web/good-governance/12-principles-and-eloge. Accessed 20 June 2020.

[142] See Johannesburg Declaration, above n 29; Agenda 2030, above n 6.

[143] See Hunter et al. 2015, p. 1221; Sands et al. 2018, Chapter 18.

[144] Ibid.

[145] See Hunter et al. 2015, p. 1253–1280.

[146] See Article 4 of the Montreal Protocol, above no 67. Whether this is incompatible with the MFN provisions of GATT is debatable. However, the general consensus is that as long as these measures are part of MEAs and not individual action, such measures are acceptable. See also the Basel Convention, above n 119 and the Basel Ban, opened for signature 22 September 1995, UNEP Decision 11/12, entered into force 5 December 2019; and the Bamako Convention on the Ban of Import into Africa and the Control of Transboundary Movement and Management of Hazardous Wastes from Africa, opened for signature 30 January 1991, 2101 UNTS 177, entered into force 22 April 1998.

[147] These include WTO, *United States—Measures concerning the Importation, Marketing and Sale of Tuna and Tuna Products,* Recourse to Article 21.5 of the DSU by Mexico, Appellate Body Report, WT/DS381/AB/RW; WTO, *United States-Import Prohibition of Certain Shrimp and Shrimp Products,* Recourse to Article 21.5 by Malaysia, Appellate Body Report, WT/DS58/AB/RW; WTO, *EC—Measures Affecting Asbestos and Asbestos-Containing Products*, Appellate Body Report, 12 March 2001, WT/DS135/AB/R. For a discussion of these cases, see Hunter et al. 2015, Chapter 17; Sands et al. 2018, Chapter 18.

[148] See Hunter et al. 2015, p. 1259.

'necessary to protect human, animal or plant life or health' and 'relating to the conservation of exhaustible natural resources…'.[149] These provisions have attracted many disputes, but these challenges have so far not involved measures taken under multilateral environmental agreements.[150] Similarly, conflicts between bilateral investment treaties and environmental issues have also arisen[151] and given the close relationship between trade, investment and the environment, it is likely that these disputes will continue.

1.4.4 North–South Divide

The disparity in the global community between the affluent Global North and their poorer counter-parts in the Global South has given rise to many divisions and at times paralyzed negotiations at the global level.[152] One of the most contentious areas has been climate change although these North-South tensions date back to the decolonization era. As Atapattu and Gonzalez note:

> North-South conflicts originating in the economic realm have profoundly shaped the evolution of international environmental law and policy. The global North industrialized and developed by exploiting the planet's natural resources without regard for the environmental consequences. Northern consumption patterns, which are increasingly emulated by Southern elites, have brought the planet's ecosystems to the brink of collapse and will constrain the development options of present and future generations, particularly in the global South.[153]

The environmental agenda and global negotiations are dominated by the North and many Southern nations view Northern demands for environmental protection as hypocritical, given their enormous ecological footprint and believe that the North owes an ecological debt to the South.[154] These tensions continue to date by diluting obligations and affecting negotiations, but they have also resulted in the adoption of novel legal principles such as the CBDR. Most environmental treaties reflect compromises along North-South lines.[155]

---

149 Article XX, General Agreement on Tariffs and Trade, opened for signature 30 October 1947, 55 UNTS 187, entered into force 1 January 1948. However, it was incorporated into the WTO Agreement, which entered into force on 1 January 1995: www.wto.org/english/docs_e/legal_e/gatt47.pdf. Accessed 20 June 2020.

150 See Hunter et al. 2015, p. 1278.

151 Ibid.

152 For an in-depth discussion of the North-South divide in relation to environmental issues, see Alam et al. 2015.

153 See Atapattu and Gonzalez 2015, pp. 9–10.

154 Climate change negotiations reflect these tensions. See Patz et al. 2007, p. 397.

155 See Alam et al. 2015 for a discussion of how North-South divisions have influenced the development of IEL.

1.5 Regulation of the Global Commons

Principle 21 of the Stockholm Declaration was one of the first instruments to recognize the need to protect the global commons from environmental pollution which referred to the responsibility of states to protect the areas beyond the limits of national jurisdiction. Called the global commons, these areas comprise the high seas (beyond the 200 mile exclusive economic zone), the sea bed, outer space and Antarctica.[156] The main principle underlying these areas is *res communes*—that the resources belong to everybody—and no state can subject these areas to its sovereignty.[157] Article 87 of the UN Convention on the Law of the Sea (1982) provides: 'The high seas are open to all States, whether coastal or land-locked. Freedom of the high seas is exercised under the conditions laid down by this Convention and by other rules of international law [...]'.[158] At the beginning, there were no rules to govern the commons' resources and the high seas fisheries were subject to the right of capture.[159] However, this penalized those who did not have the technology or resources, especially developing countries and land-locked countries. Therefore, the need was felt to adopt a new conceptual framework to govern the resources of the global commons. Thus, the common heritage of mankind principle was born. While it provides an important framework, it has also attracted criticism mainly due to its benefit sharing requirement.[160]

Some treaties embody this principle. For example, the Moon Treaty provides that the moon shall be used exclusively for peaceful purposes[161] while the moon and its natural resources are the common heritage of mankind.[162] It further provides that 'the moon is not subject to national appropriation by any claim of sovereignty, by mean of use or occupation or by any other means.'[163] State parties have the right of exploration on the basis of equality and non-discrimination. They are required to establish an international regime for: the orderly and safe development of natural resources of the moon; rational management of those resources; expansion of opportunities of those resources and equitable sharing by all states in the benefits derived from those resources with the interests of developing countries and those countries that contributed to the exploration of those resources being given special consideration.[164]

---

156 See Hunter et al. 2015, p. 451; Sands et al. 2018, p. 12 and Chapters 11 and 13.

157 Thus, Article 89 of the UN Law of the Sea Convention (UNCLOS), opened for signature 10 December 1982, 1833 UNTS 3. entered into force 16 November 1994, provides: 'No state may validly purport to subject any part of the high seas to its sovereignty.'

158 Ibid., Article 87.

159 See Hunter et al. 2015, p. 451.

160 See Baslar 1998; and Noyes 2011.

161 Article 3, Agreement Governing the Activities of States on the Moon and Other Celestial Bodies (Moon Treaty), opened for signature 5 December 1979, 1363 UNTS 3, entered into force 11 July 1984.

162 Ibid., Article 11(1).

163 Ibid., Article 11(2).

164 Ibid., Article 11(7).

As can be expected, this provision became quite controversial and many space-faring nations did not ratify the treaty. The same provisions were included in the Law of the Sea Convention which similarly became controversial. The relevant provisions of the Law of the Sea Convention provide as follows:

> The Area and its resources are the common heritage of mankind... No state shall claim or exercise sovereignty or sovereign rights over any part of the Area or its resources... All rights in the resources of the Area are vested in mankind as a whole... [T]he Authority shall provide for the equitable sharing of financial and other economic benefits derived from activities in the Area [...][165]

This benefit sharing aspect led several developed countries, especially the United States and United Kingdom, to refuse to ratify the Convention. Fearing that the entire treaty regime would collapse, Part XI was amended after the Convention was opened for signature.[166]

While its application is rather limited, the common heritage principle has four characteristics: non-appropriation (no state can appropriate these areas); international management (an international organization or body to be in charge of managing these areas); shared benefits (resources of the global commons should be shared among all countries); and use for peaceful purposes (these areas cannot be used for military purposes).[167] More recently, states have opted to apply the more neutral principle of common concern of mankind to issues like biodiversity[168] and climate change.[169]

1.6 Regulation of Activities of Non-state Actors

One of the most challenging issues for international law has been the regulation of activities of non-state actors, especially multinational corporations which have, over the years, been guilty of causing massive environmental damage as well as human rights abuse in developing countries.[170] Under traditional international law, only states have rights and responsibilities. This traditional view has slowly eroded as more and more non-state actors have begun playing a greater role in shaping international law and monitoring activities of states. While states remain full subjects of

---

[165] UNCLOS, above n 157, Part XI which defines both the 'Area' and 'Authority'.

[166] See Agreement Relating to the Implementation of Part XI of the United Nations Convention on the Law of the Sea of 10 December 1982, UN Doc. A/RES/48/263, 17 August 1994. Although the US has signed the Convention, it has so far not ratified it.

[167] While it is highly likely that the 'Star Wars' program of the US was contrary to this principle, the US reaffirmed its commitment to the demilitarization of space after the Cold War. See Hunter et al. 2015, p. 455.

[168] See Convention on Biological Diversity, above n 89, Preamble.

[169] See UNFCCC, above n 56, Preamble and Article 3.

[170] See Atapattu 2018, pp. 431–454.

international law, other actors such as NGOs, business community, industry, multinational corporations, subnational governments, academics (epistemic communities) and even individuals have begun playing an important role at the international level.[171] Their involvement is particularly significant in the environment field.[172]

States are under a general obligation to ensure that their activities do not cause damage to the environment of other states and become responsible under international law for their failure to control the activities of private persons; whether this obligation extends to multinational companies for activities in other states is debatable. In June 2014 at the initiative of Ecuador, the UN Human Rights Council adopted a resolution,[173] which created an intergovernmental working group 'whose mandate shall be to elaborate an internationally legally binding instrument to regulate, in international human rights law, the activities of transnational corporations and other business enterprises.'[174] Negotiations are continuing on a draft prepared by the working group and it remains to be seen where this attempt will lead.[175] On the positive side, the draft adopts an expansive definition of 'human rights violation or abuse' which includes violations of environmental rights.[176] Attempts at adopting a treaty to regulate activities of business enterprises have thus far failed, with the North supporting a minimalist approach to preserve its economic prosperity and the South intent on achieving prosperity, advocating a binding code.[177]

The Guiding Principles on Business and Human Rights[178] is another attempt to bring business enterprises within the human rights framework which, as discussed, include instances of environmental degradation.[179] Proposed by John Ruggie, these Guiding Principles are based on three pillars: (a) the state's duty to *protect* against human rights abuses by third parties, including business; (b) the corporate responsibility to *respect* human rights; and (c) greater access by victims to an effective *remedy*,

[171] See Brunnée 2018 who notes that IEL must address the challenge posed by non-state actors who are responsible for most instances of environmental damage and that states act only as intermediaries when they take on community interests and their task is often to influence the activities of non-state actors.

[172] See Hunter et al. 2015, p. 254; Brown Weiss 2011, pp. 18–22; Sands et al. 2018, pp. 89–96.

[173] UN Human Rights Council, UN Doc. A/HRC/RES/26/9, 14 July 2014.

[174] Ibid., para 1.

[175] Legally Binding Instrument to Regulate, in International Human Rights Law, the Activities of Transnational Corporations and other Business Enterprises, OEIGWG Chairmanship Revised Draft 16 July 2019: https://www.ohchr.org/Documents/HRBodies/HRCouncil/WGTransCorp/OEIGWG_RevisedDraft_LBI.pdf. Accessed 20 June 2020.

[176] According to draft Article 1(2), '"Human rights violation or abuse" shall mean any harm committed by a State or a business enterprise, through acts or omissions in the context of business activities, against any person or group of persons, individually or collectively, including physical or mental injury, emotional suffering, economic loss or substantial impairment of their human rights, *including environmental rights*' (emphasis added).

[177] See Puvimanasinghe 2015, p. 320.

[178] Guiding Principles on Business and Human Rights: Implementing the UN Protect, Respect and Remedy Framework (2011): www.ohchr.org/Documents/Publications/GuidingPrinciplesBusinessHR_EN.pdf. Accessed 20 June 2020.

[179] See Sect. 1.4.3 on linkages.

both judicial and non-judicial.[180] This is a significant, albeit soft law attempt, to bring the business community within the human rights framework. While some businesses have voluntarily adopted this framework, its success will depend on these principles being adopted and implemented by the business community widely. There is no doubt that their active participation is necessary for its success.[181]

1.7 Conclusion: Achievements, Challenges and Future Trajectory

International environmental law has come a long way since the Stockholm Conference of 1972. Not only has it blossomed into a separate branch of international law in a relatively short span of time, some of its topics have become separate areas of law in their own right. Climate change is a good example of this evolution. The achievements of IEL are many: IEL has seen the adoption of many treaties, led to the development of principles and non-compliance procedures,[182] established institutions, and shaped national law and institutions, all within the span of five decades.

Moreover, as this volume demonstrates, international dispute settlement mechanisms and their jurisprudence in this area have proliferated which has contributed to the development of IEL and especially, its principles.[183] From arbitral tribunals to human rights bodies, these institutions have dealt with cases involving environmental degradation. One of the most important decisions of the International Court of Justice is the *Gabcikovo* case where the Court had to balance environmental protection, on the one hand, and economic development, on the other.[184] Although obiter, the separate opinion of Judge Weeramantry in this case discussed sustainable development extensively.[185] The Court's advisory opinion on the *Legality of Nuclear Weapons* consolidated the customary status of Principle 21 of the Stockholm Declaration.[186] Other courts have also contributed to the development of IEL. Among them, the

---

[180] Above n 178. See https://www.business-humanrights.org/en/un-secretary-generals-special-representative-on-business-human-rights/un-protect-respect-and-remedy-framework-and-guiding-principles. Accessed 20 June 2020.

[181] See Puvimanasinghe 2015, p. 322, and Atapattu and Schapper 2019, Chapter 14.

[182] See Sands et al. 2018, p. 172 who note that one of the most significant developments in IEL has been the emergence of non-compliance procedures under various treaties. The first non-compliance procedure was established under the Montreal Protocol on Substances that Deplete the Ozone Layer, including an Implementation Committee. Other non-compliance procedures include those under the Basel Convention, the Biosafety Protocol, above n 97, POPs Convention, Kyoto Protocol and the Aarhus Convention. According to Sands et al. 2018, the non-compliance procedure established under the Kyoto Protocol is 'among the most comprehensive and rigorous established thus far', p. 173.

[183] See Sands et al. 2018, pp. 178–192.

[184] *Gabcikovo Nagymaros,* above n 59.

[185] Ibid., Separate Opinion, Judge Weeramantry.

[186] Other cases include the *Pulp Mills on the River Uruguay, (Argentina v Uruguay),* above n 59; ICJ, *Whaling in the Antarctic (Australia v Japan: New Zealand intervening)*, Judgment, 31 March

Advisory Opinion of the ITLOS in relation to Responsibilities of States in the Area is significant.[187] Other institutions include the WTO Dispute Settlement Body which has dealt with many trade cases involving environmental measures,[188] the European Court of Justice,[189] and human rights courts.[190] Together, these dispute settlement bodies have contributed to the development of IEL and consolidated its principles.

Despite these achievements, IEL faces many challenges. Global environmental problems, a byproduct of economic development, have emerged requiring cooperation by the entire international community. Never before has the international community faced so many environmental challenges, ranging from hazardous wastes to climate change:

> Global statistics are sobering. The world has entered a sixth wave of mass extinction where, according to some estimates, 27,000 species vanish every year and about one million species currently face extinction. Climate change is accelerating more rapidly than scientists predicted…. In 2016, the world generated 242 billion tons of plastic waste. If present trends continue, there will be more plastic in the oceans than fish by 2050. Between 1945 and the present, the worldwide generation of hazardous waste increased from 5 million to 400 million tons *per year*. … Every year, air pollution kills more than 7 million people, while lack of access to fresh water and sanitation has been linked to the death of 5 million people per year.[191]

Climate change with its far-reaching consequences will define the way we live, the way we do business, how we travel, where we live, our consumption patterns (even possibly what we eat) and our very development path. It requires us to devise new legal strategies, principles and institutions to address the unprecedented challenges posed by it. From forced displacement of millions of people to the submergence of sovereign states, climate change will require us to adapt existing legal principles and adopt new ones.

Sustainable development is here to stay. It provides us with an alternative paradigm to develop, an alternative to neo-liberal market-based policies that have caused environmental destruction.[192] If we are to avoid a catastrophic future for our children and

---

2014, ICJ Reports 2014, p. 226; ICJ, *Certain Activities Carried out by Nicaragua in the Border Area (Costa Rica v Nicaragua) and Construction of a Road in Costa Rica along the San Juan River (Nicaragua v Costa Rica)*, Judgment, 16 December 2015, ICJ Reports 2015, p. 665. The Aerial Herbicide Spraying case between Ecuador and Columbia involved extensive environmental and human rights issues including the extraterritorial application of human rights law, but the case was later settled by the parties.

[187] ITLOS, *Responsibilities and Obligations of States Sponsoring Persons and Entities with Respect to Activities in the Area*, Advisory Opinion, 1 February 2011, ITLOS Reports, p. 10.

[188] See Hunter et al. 2015, p. 17; Sands et al. 2018, Chapter 18.

[189] See Sands et al. 2018, p. 187 (and references cited in note 353).

[190] See Anton and Shelton 2011, Chapter 5; Kravchenko and Bonine 2008, Chapter 2.

[191] See Atapattu et al. 2020 (footnotes omitted).

[192] There is an increasing demand for 'degrowth' in affluent countries. See Akbulut et al. 2019; Schneider et al. 2010; and Research and Degrowth 2010. The Declaration was adopted at the Economic Degrowth for Ecological sustainability and Social Equity Conference in Paris in April 2008.

grandchildren we must adjust our consumerist lifestyle now. We must ensure those who are less fortunate than us have a decent standard of living. Notions of justice and equity demand us to do this before it is too late.

Post Scriptum

Since writing this chapter, the UN Human Rights Council adopted a resolution recognizing, for the first time, a human right to a safe, clean, healthy and sustainable environment (October 2021), https://undocs.org/a/hrc/48/l.23/rev.1 (accessed November 2021).

References

Adelman S (2018) The Sustainable Development Goals, Anthropocentrism and Neoliberalism. In: French D, Kotzé L (eds) Global Goals: Law, Theory & Implementation. Edward Elgar, Cheltenham, pp 15-40

Agyeman J, Bullard RD, Evans B (2003) Just Sustainabilities. Development in an Unequal World. Earthscan, London

Akbulut B, Demaria F, Gerber JF, Martinez-Alier J (2019) Who promotes sustainability? Five theses on the relationships between the degrowth and environmental justice movements. Ecological Economics 165:106418

Alam S, Atapattu S, Gonzalez C, Razzaque J (eds) (2015) International Environmental law and the Global South. Cambridge University Press, New York

Anton DK, Shelton DL (2011) Environmental Protection and Human Rights. Cambridge University Press, New York

Atapattu S (2006) Emerging Principles of International Environmental Law. Transnational, New York

Atapattu S (2015) The Significance of International Environmental Law Principles in Reinforcing or Dismantling the North-South Divide. In: Alam S, Atapattu S, Gonzalez C, Razzaque J (eds) International Environmental law and the Global South. Cambridge University Press, New York, p 74

Atapattu S (2017) Climate Change, International Environmental Law Principles, and the North-South Divide. Transnational Law & Contemporary Problems 26:247

Atapattu S (2018) Extractive Industries and Inequality: Intersections of Environmental Law, Human Rights, and Environmental Justice. Arizona State Law Journal, 50:2:431-454

Atapattu S (2019) From 'Our Common Future' to Sustainable Development Goals: Evolution of Sustainable Development under International Law. Wisconsin International Law Journal, 36:2:215

Atapattu S, Gonzalez G, Seck S (2020) Intersections of Environmental Justice and Sustainable Development: Framing the Issues. In: Atapattu S, Gonzalez G, Seck S (eds) Cambridge Handbook on Environmental Justice and Sustainable Development

Atapattu S, Schapper A (2019) Human Rights and the Environment: Key Issues. Routledge, Abingdon, Oxford

Baslar K (1998) The Concept of the Common Heritage of Mankind in International Law. Martinus Nijhoff, The Hague

Birnie P, Boyle A, Redgwell C (2009) International Law and the Environment. Oxford University Press, Oxford

Bodansky D (1993) The United Nations Framework Convention on Climate Change: A Commentary. Yale Journal of International Law 18:451

Bodansky D (2009) Art and Craft of International Environmental Law. Harvard University Press, Cambridge, MA
Bodansky D (2016) The Legal Character of the Paris Agreement. RECEIL 25:2:142
Bodansky D, Brunnée J, Rajamani L (2017) International Climate Change Law. Oxford University Press, Oxford
Boyd D (2012) The Environmental Rights Revolution: A Global Study of Constitutions, Human Rights, and the Environment. UBC Press, Vancouver
Boyd D (2019) A Safe Climate: A Report of the UN Special Rapporteur on Human Rights and Environment: www.srenvironment.org/report/a-safe-climate-human-rights-and-climate-change. Accessed 30 June 2020
Boyle A, Freestone D (1999) International Law and Sustainable Development: Past Achievements and Future Challenges. Oxford University Press, Oxford
Brown Weiss E (1996) In Fairness to Future Generations: International Law, Common Patrimony, and Intergenerational Equity. Transnational, New York
Brown Weiss E (2011) The Evolution of International Environmental law. Japanese Yearbook of International Law 54:1
Brunnée J (2018) International Environmental Law and Community Interests: Procedural Aspects. In: Benvenisti E, Nolte G, Yalin-mor K (eds) Community Interests across International Law. Oxford University Press, Oxford
Bullard RD (ed) (2005) The Quest for Environmental Justice: Human Rights and the Politics of Pollution. Sierra Club Books, San Francisco
Cordonier Segger MC, Khalfan A (2004) Sustainable development law: principles, practices, and prospects. Oxford University Press, Oxford
Craik N (2008): International Law of Environmental Impact Assessment: Process, Substance and Integration. Cambridge University Press, Cambridge
Crutzen PJ (2002) Geology of Mankind-The Anthropocene. Nature 415:23
Cullet P (2003) Differential Treatment in International Environmental Law. Routledge, London
Dawe N, Ryan K (2003) The Faulty Three-Legged Stool Model of Sustainable Development. Conservation Biology, 17:5: www.researchgate.net/publication/228595015_The_Faulty_Three-Legged-Stool_Model_of_Sustainable_Development Accessed 20 June 2020
De Schutter O (2010) International Human Rights Law. Cambridge University Press, Cambridge
Dupuy P-M, Vinuales JE (2015) International Environmental Law. Cambridge University Press, Cambridge
Dupuy P-M (1991) Soft Law and the International law of the Environment. Michigan Journal of International Law 12:420
Duvic-Paoli LA (2018) The Prevention Principle in International Environmental Law. Cambridge University Press, Cambridge
Farber D (2007) Basic Compensation for Victims of Climate Change. University of Pennsylvania Law Review 155:1615
Foster S (1998) Justice from the Ground Up: Distributive Inequities, Grassroots Resistance and the Transformative Politics of the Environmental Justice Movement. California Law Review 86:4:775-841
French D (2000) Developing States and International Environmental Law: The Importance of Differentiated Responsibilities. ICLQ 49:35
Gonzalez C (2012) Environmental Justice and International Environmental Law. In: Alam S, Bhuiyan JH, Chowdhury TMR, Techera E (eds) Routledge Handbook in International Environmental Law. Routledge, London
Gonzalez C (2017) Global Justice in the Anthropocene. In: Kotze LJ (ed) Environmental Law and Governance for the Anthropocene. Hart
Halvorssen A (1999) Equality Among Unequals in International Environmental Law. Routledge, New York

Handl G (2012) Declaration of the United Nations Conference on the Human Environment (Stockholm Declaration), 1972 and The Rio Declaration on Environment and Development, 1992. UN Audiovisual Library of International Law. https://legal.un.org/avl/pdf/ha/dunche/dunche_e.pdf

Hunter D, Salzman J, Zaelke D (2015) International Environmental Law and Policy. Foundation Press, St. Paul, MN

Jacob M (1999) Sustainable Development as a Contested Concept. In: Dobson A (ed) Fairness and Futurity: Essays on Environmental Sustainability and Social Justice. Oxford University Press, Oxford

Klein N (2014) This Changes Everything: Capitalism vs. The Climate. Simon & Schuster, New York

Knox J (2015) Human Rights, Environmental Protection and Sustainable Development Goals. Washington International Law Journal 24:517

Knox JH, Pejan R (eds) (2018) The Human Right to a Healthy Environment. Cambridge University Press, New York

Kravchenko S, Bonine J (2008) Human Rights and the Environment: Cases, Law, and Policy. Carolina Academic Press, Durham, North Carolina

Kravchenko S (2009) Is Access to Environmental Information a Fundamental Human Right? Oregon Review of International Law 11:227

Kuehn R (2000). A Taxonomy of Environmental Justice. Environmental Law Reporter 30:10681

Marr S (2000) The Southern Bluefin Tuna Cases: The Precautionary Approach and Conservation and Management of Fish Resources. European Journal of International Law 11:815-31

May JR, Daly E (2015) Global Environmental Constitutionalism. Cambridge University Press, New York

Michelson K (2015) The Stockholm Conference and the Creation of the South-North Divide in International Environmental Law. In: Alam S, Atapattu S, Gonzalez C, Razzaque J (eds) International Environmental Law and the Global South. Cambridge University Press, New York, p 109

Ntambirweki J (1991) The Developing Countries in the Evolution of an International Environmental Law. Hastings International and Comparative Law Review 14: 905

Noyes J (2011) Common Heritage of Mankind: Past, Present and Future. Denver Journal of International Law and Policy 40:447

Palmer G (1992) New Ways to Make International Environmental Law. AJIL 86:2:259

Patz J et al (2007) Climate Change and Global Health: Quantifying a Growing Ethical Crisis. EcoHealth 4:397

Pedersen OW (2018) The European Court of Human Rights and International Environmental Law. In: Knox JH, Pejan R (eds) The Human Right to a Healthy Environment. Cambridge University Press, New York

Phillipson M (2001) The United States withdrawal from the Kyoto Protocol. Irish Jurist, New Series, 36:288-304

Puvimanasinghe S (2015) From a Divided Heritage to a Common Future? International Investment Law, Human Rights, and Sustainable Development. In: Alam S, Atapattu S, Gonzalez C, Razzaque J (eds) International Environmental Law and the Global South. Cambridge University Press, New York, p 317

Rajamani L (2006) Differential Treatment in International Law. Oxford University Press, Oxford

Rajamani L (2016) Ambition and Differentiation in the 2015 Paris Agreement: Interpretative Possibilities and Underlying Politics. ICLQ 65:493

Research and Degrowth (2010) Degrowth Declaration of the Paris 2008 Conference. Journal of Cleaner Production 18:523

Rosencranz A (2003) The Origins and Emergence of International Environmental Norms. Hastings International and Comparative Law Review 26:309

Sand P H (1992) UNCED and the Development of International Environmental Law. Journal of Natural Resources and Environmental Law 8:209

Sand P H (2006) Global Environmental Change and the Nation State: Sovereignty Bounded. In: Winter G (ed) Multilevel Governance of Global Environmental Change: Perspectives from Science, Sociology and the Law. Cambridge University Press, New York
Sands Ph (1994) The "Greening" of International Law: Emerging Principles and Rules. Indiana Journal of Global Legal Studies 1:293
Sands Ph, Peel J, Fabra A, MacKenzie R (2018) Principles of International Environmental Law. Cambridge University Press, Cambridge
Schneider F, Kallis G, Martinez-Alier J (2010) Crisis or opportunity? Economic degrowth for social equity and ecological sustainability. J Cleaner Prod 18:511
Schrijver N (1997) Sovereignty over Natural Resources: Balancing Rights and Duties. Cambridge University Press, Cambridge
Stiglitz J (2001) Globalization and its Discontents. WW Norton & Company, New York
Stone C (2004) Common but Differentiated Responsibilities in International Law. American Journal of International Law 98:276
United Nations (1972) Report of the United Nations Conference on Human Environment, UN Doc. A/CONF.48/14/REV.1
United Nations (1995) Report of the World Summit for Social Development UN Doc. A/CONF.166/9 (Copenhagen Declaration)
United Nations Conference on Environment and Development (1992) Report of the UN Conference on Environment and Development, UN Doc. A/CONF.151/26/Rev.l (Vol l)
United Nations General Assembly (1972) Resolution on Development and Environment, UN Doc. A/RES/2849 (XXVI) (Stockholm Declaration)
United Nations General Assembly (2015) Transforming Our World: Agenda 2030 for Sustainable Development, UN Doc. A/RES/70/1
WCED (1987) Our Common Future. Report of the World Commission for Environment and Development. Oxford University Press, Oxford
Wiener JB (2001) Something Borrowed for Something Blue: Legal Transplants and the Evolution of Global Environmental Law. Ecology Law Quarterly 27:4:1295-1371
Yamin F, Depledge J (2004) The International Climate Change Regime: A Guide to Rules, Institutions and Procedures. Cambridge University Press, Cambridge
Yang T, Percival RV (2009) The Emergence of Global Environmental Law. Ecology Law Quarterly 36:615

Sumudu Atapattu Director, Research Centers and International Programs, University of Wisconsin Law School, Executive Director, Human Rights Program, UW-Madison; Affiliated faculty, Raoul Wallenberg Institute for Human Rights, Sweden and Lead Counsel for Human Rights, Center for International Sustainable Development Law, Canada.

Part I
A Fragmented Jurisdictional Landscape

Chapter 2
The International Court of Justice and the Protection of the Environment

Anne Coulon

Contents

Abstract This chapter focuses on the role of the International Court of Justice (ICJ) with respect to the protection of the environment. It examines the tools that are at the Court's disposal to tackle the specific challenges raised by environmental cases. Three main themes are considered. First, the mechanisms available for assembling and examining evidence relevant to the determination of environmental issues are explored. Second, the chapter examines the scope of the Court's power to indicate provisional measures protecting the environment against irreparable harm while proceedings are pending in a case before it. Third, it highlights the ICJ's contribution

A. Coulon (✉)
Temple Garden Chambers, Lange Voorhout 82, 2514 EJ The Hague, The Netherlands
e-mail: annecoulon@tgchambers.com

E. Sobenes et al. (eds.), *The Environment Through the Lens of International Courts and Tribunals*, https://doi.org/10.1007/978-94-6265-507-2_2

to the development and clarification of international law relevant to the protection of the environment. These topics are examined in light of the Court's treatment of the key relevant cases that have been submitted to it since environmental concerns emerged at the international level. The Court's contribution through the exercise of its advisory function is also addressed. This overall analysis of the ICJ's role demonstrates that the Court has had, and will continue to have, a decisive and positive impact both on the clarification of the relevant rules of international law to provide clear guidance in the field and on the resolution of environmental disputes.

Keywords International Court of Justice · Environment · Environmental Law · Transboundary Harm · Environmental claims · Scientific evidence · Burden of proof · Provisional Measures and Interim Relief · Due diligence · Precautionary principle · Environmental Impact Assessment · Rules of Environmental Law · Environmental damage · Compensation

2.1 Introduction

The International Court of Justice (the Court or the ICJ) has a natural role to play in the field of environmental protection. Not only does its status as the principal judicial organ of the United Nations[1] give it a legitimacy to decide novel legal issues that no other court or tribunal can claim, but the fact that it is the only international court with general subject-matter jurisdiction makes it an obvious forum to bring environmental disputes, especially in the absence of a specialised jurisdiction established to deal with such claims.

This certainly explains why States have entrusted the Court with situations involving environmental issues very early on. They have done so directly by submitting contentious cases to the Court, requesting the latter to judicially settle their disputes. They have also turned to the Court indirectly, through voting within the appropriate bodies in favour of resolutions seeking advisory opinions. An analysis of the Statute and the Rules of Court, along with an examination of the Court's response when it has been seised of such matters, is necessary to evaluate the ICJ's capacity to tackle the particular challenges raised by these types of issues.

Those challenges are, essentially, threefold. First, environmental cases often involve complex factual issues. It is therefore critical for any court seised of such cases to be able to obtain the necessary evidence and to satisfactorily analyse it. Secondly, because of the potentially irreversible character of damage caused to the environment, it is crucial to have the power to intervene in an escalating situation in order to prevent irreparable harm being incurred while judicial proceedings are going on in a contentious case. Finally, because of the rise of environmental issues on the international stage and the rapid evolution of the corresponding rules of international law in the field, States have needed guidance in identifying their rights and obligations with respect to environmental protection. Undoubtedly, the main strength of the ICJ

[1] UN Charter, Article 92.

lies in its demonstrated capacity to rigorously identify and clarify said rules, thereby consolidating a coherent jurisprudence on the basis of which to settle present and future disputes. This is where the Court has made its most significant contribution with respect to the protection of the environment.

This chapter will deal with these points in turn. Before doing so, however, it is necessary to briefly recall the basic principles governing the functioning of the Court, in particular those applicable to the determination of its jurisdiction. In addition, an initial overview of the key cases submitted to the Court in which environmental issues have arisen will be provided to introduce the main developments in this field.

2.2 The Principles Governing ICJ Action

The International Court of Justice has a contentious and an advisory function, both of which may be relevant when it comes to the protection of the environment.

2.2.1 The ICJ's Contentious Function

According to Article 38, para 1 of its Statute, the function of the Court is to decide in accordance with international law such disputes as are submitted to it; as is well known, only States may be parties to cases before the Court.[2]

It follows, from the outset, that there are three fundamental limitations to the Court's potential action regarding environmental protection: first, the limitation of the Court's jurisdiction to cases brought by States against other States means that only cases where at least one Government considers that its interests are at stake will reach the Court. As a result, a number of legal questions are less likely to be decided by the ICJ.[3] In particular, since individuals have the main interest in having States' human rights obligations that relate to environmental concerns clarified and complied with, regional courts and tribunals that allow for direct access by individuals to the judges have a greater chance to be seised of such issues. Moreover, since the existence of a dispute between the Parties[4] is a condition of the Court's jurisdiction,[5] the Court will only pronounce judgment 'in connection with concrete cases', where

[2] See Statute of the International Court of Justice, 26 June 1945, entry into force 24 October 1945, Article 36(1).

[3] As one author notes, 'States generally have little inclination to engage in proceedings against one another to address global environmental problems, as such proceedings would involve diplomatic costs not justified by the achievement of any specific national interest.' See Mayer 2018, p. 240.

[4] While Article 38, para 1 only refers to 'disputes', Article 36, para 2 specifies that the Court has jurisdiction in all 'legal disputes' that may arise between States parties to the Statute having made a declaration in accordance with that provision.

[5] See, most recently: *Obligations concerning Negotiations relating to Cessation of the Nuclear Arms Race and to Nuclear Disarmament (Marshall Islands v India)*, Jurisdiction and Admissibility,

there exists 'an actual controversy involving a conflict of legal interests between the parties'.[6] When exercising its contentious jurisdiction, the Court cannot and will not determine the applicable law with regard to a hypothetical situation, and the fact that some States may manifest a common interest in having the World Court clarify the applicable rules in the field of environmental protection will not suffice to seise the latter.[7] Finally, the consensual nature of the Court's jurisdiction, which implies that a State can only be made a party to a dispute before the Court insofar as it has accepted the Court's jurisdiction over such dispute, necessarily limits the scope of intervention of the ICJ.[8]

Within the limits of its jurisdiction so defined, the ICJ unquestionably has a role to play in the settlement of disputes involving environmental issues. It is worth pointing out that, in 1993, the Court created a Chamber for Environmental Matters,[9] pursuant to Article 26, para 1, of its Statute. As States did not show an interest in using the Chamber, it was never used and as a result the Court decided not to hold internal elections for the renewal of its composition in 2006. However, as noted by a former President of the Court, 'its very creation, which was never called into question, bears witness to the Court's willingness to use all the tools at its disposal to take careful account of the specific nature of cases involving issues relating to the environment'.[10]

Needless to say, a claim will only be heard by the Court if it is admissible. A party may raise an objection to admissibility if it considers that 'there exists a legal reason, even when there is jurisdiction, why the Court should decline to hear the case, or more usually, a specific claim therein'.[11] In the field of the protection of

Judgment, 5 October 2016, ICJ Reports 2016, p. 269, para 33 ff; *Obligations concerning Negotiations relating to Cessation of the Nuclear Arms Race and to Nuclear Disarmament (Marshall Islands v Pakistan)*, Jurisdiction and Admissibility, Judgment, 5 October 2016, ICJ Reports 2016, p. 566, para 33 ff; *Obligations concerning Negotiations relating to Cessation of the Nuclear Arms Race and to Nuclear Disarmament (Marshall Islands v United Kingdom)*, Preliminary Objections, Judgment, 5 October 2016, ICJ Reports 2016, p. 849, para 36 ff.

[6] *Question of the Delimitation of the Continental Shelf between Nicaragua and Colombia beyond 200 Nautical Miles from the Nicaraguan Coast (Nicaragua v Colombia)*, Preliminary Objections, Judgment, 7 March 2016, ICJ Reports 2016, p. 138, para 123 (*Continental Shelf between Nicaragua and Colombia* (Preliminary Objections)).

[7] This consideration does not apply to the exercise by the Court of its advisory jurisdiction. See Sect. 2.2.1 below.

[8] This chapter won't elaborate on the various ways in which a State can consent to the Court's jurisdiction. On this point, the Handbook published by the International Court of Justice is rather well documented. https://www.icj-cij.org/public/files/publications/handbook-of-the-court-en.pdf. Accessed 21 January 2022.

[9] See https://www.icj-cij.org/en/chambers-and-committees. Accessed 21 January 2022.

[10] Speech of H.E. Mr. Ronny Abraham, President of the International Court of Justice, to the Sixth Committee of the General Assembly (28 October 2016) (President Abraham's 2016 speech to the Sixth Committee). https://www.icj-cij.org/public/files/press-releases/0/19280.pdf. Accessed 21 January 2022.

[11] *Application of the Convention on the Prevention and Punishment of the Crime of Genocide (Croatia v Serbia)*, Preliminary Objections, Judgment, 18 November 2008, ICJ Reports 2008, p. 456, para 120.

the environment, issues of standing[12] are likely to become particularly relevant in determining the admissibility of future cases, especially if issues pertaining to State responsibility in relation to climate change are raised.[13]

2.2.2 *The ICJ's Advisory Function*

As already mentioned, the ICJ also has an advisory function: under Article 65, para 1 of its Statute, the Court is competent to give advisory opinions on legal questions referred to it by authorised United Nations organs and specialised agencies. When the Court is seised of a request for an advisory opinion, it must first consider whether it has jurisdiction to give the opinion requested. This requires that the question asked be a 'legal question'.[14] Moreover, the Court will only have jurisdiction if the entity which requested the opinion was entitled to do so. Pursuant to Article 96, paras 1 and 2 of the UN Charter, while the General Assembly and the Security Council of the United Nations may request an advisory opinion on 'any legal question', other organs and specialized agencies may only do so under two conditions: the organ or agency must be duly authorised by the General Assembly to make such a request, and the question on which the opinion is requested must be one 'arising within the scope of [the] activities' of the requesting entity.[15]

---

[12] A claim will only be admissible if the State making it has standing to do so, meaning that it is entitled to invoke the responsibility of the other State party to the case for an alleged breach of the international obligation concerned. For a recent example of a case where the issue of standing was considered as part of the examination of the admissibility of the Applicant's claims, see *Questions Concerning the Obligation to Prosecute or Extradite (Belgium v Senegal)*, Judgment, 20 July 2012, ICJ Reports 2012, pp. 448–450, paras 64–70.

[13] The International Law Commission (ILC) touched upon the question of standing to invoke the violation of international obligations relating to the protection of the environment in its commentaries on draft articles 42 and 48 of its 2001 *Draft Articles on Responsibility of States for Internationally Wrongful Acts*, which deal, respectively, with the invocation of State responsibility by an injured State and by a State other than an injured State acting in the collective interest (see *Yearbook of the International Law Commission, 2001,* vol. II, Part Two). In relation to Article 42(b)(i), the ILC indicated that, '[f]or example a case of pollution of the high seas in breach of article 194 of the United Nations Convention on the Law of the Sea may particularly impact on one or several States whose beaches may be polluted by toxic residues or whose coastal fisheries may be closed. In that case, independently of any general interest of the States parties to the Convention in the preservation of the marine environment, those coastal States parties should be considered as injured by the breach' (see Commentary to Article 42, para 12). In its commentary of Article 48, the Commission used the hypothesis of 'an obligation aimed at protection of the marine environment in the collective interest' as an example of obligation that would be owed to the international community as a whole (see Commentary to Article 42, para 10).

[14] This was last recalled in *Legal Consequences of the Separation of the Chagos Archipelago from Mauritius in 1965*, Advisory Opinion, 25 February 2019, ICJ Reports 2019, p. 95 (*Chagos Advisory Opinion*).

[15] For an application of these criteria, see for example: *Legality of the Use by a State of Nuclear Weapons in Armed Conflict*, Advisory Opinion, 8 July 1996, ICJ Reports 1996, p. 66; *Difference*

The ICJ has in the past pronounced itself on issues relevant to the protection of the environment in the context of advisory proceedings.[16] It is worth recalling that it is in an advisory opinion issued upon the request of the United Nations General Assembly (UNGA or General Assembly) that the Court first recognised the existence of an obligation incumbent upon States to respect the environment.[17] Yet, environmental concerns were not the focus of the proceedings, which concerned the question of the legality of the threat or use of nuclear weapons.[18]

In September 2011, during an address to the 66th regular session of the UNGA, the President of the Republic of Palau raised the need for the General Assembly to seek an advisory opinion from the ICJ 'on the responsibilities of States under international law to ensure that activities carried out under their jurisdiction or control that emit greenhouse gases do not damage other States'.[19] More recently, the Republic of Vanuatu announced its intention to convene 'a historic meeting with delegations from all regions' to discuss the possibility of seeking an advisory opinion from the ICJ 'to promote climate justice'.[20] To this date, such initiatives have not led to the institution of advisory proceedings. However, given the growing concern of States for environmental issues and the very active role played by various organs of the United Nations in this respect, it is not unlikely that the Court be asked to give an advisory opinion on legal issues directly pertaining to the protection of the environment in the future.[21]

Relating to Immunity from Legal Process of a Special Rapporteur of the Commission on Human Rights, Advisory Opinion, 29 April 1999, ICJ Reports 1999, p. 62.

[16] See Sects. 2.6.1 and 2.6.2.

[17] *Legality of the Threat or Use of Nuclear Weapons*, Advisory Opinion, 8 July 1996, ICJ Reports 1996, p. 226 (*Nuclear Weapons Advisory Opinion*).

[18] See Sects. 2.6.1 and 2.6.2.

[19] 'Palau seeks UN World Court opinion on damage caused by greenhouse gases', *UN News*, 22 September 2011. https://news.un.org/en/story/2011/09/388202. Accessed 21 January 2022.

[20] 'Vanuatu to convene historic meeting in The Hague on climate justice and international law', *Daily Post*, 18 March 2020. https://dailypost.vu/news/vanuatu-to-convene-historic-meeting-in-the-hague-on-climate-justice-and-international-law/article_8ab75110-6899-11ea-b546-9f5258ee5e79.html. Accessed 21 January 2022. Vanuatu thereafter confirmed its intention to seek a General Assembly's request for an advisory opinion from the Court. See 'Vanuatu to push international court for climate change opinion', *Reuters*, 25 September 2021. https://www.reuters.com/world/asia-pacific/vanuatu-push-international-court-climate-change-opinion-2021-09-25/. Accessed 21 January 2022. See also 'Vanuatu launches campaign to take climate change to the International Court of Justice', *Radio New Zealand*, 25 September 2021. https://www.rnz.co.nz/international/pacific-news/452264/vanuatu-launches-campaign-to-take-climate-change-to-the-international-court-for-justice. Accessed 21 January 2022.

[21] Let us not forget, however, that the fact that the ICJ has jurisdiction to give an advisory opinion does not guarantee that it will exercise it. Indeed, the Court has emphasised on numerous occasions that is has a discretionary power whether to respond or not to a request for an advisory opinion. That being said, the Court considers that such a request should, in principle, not be refused; accordingly, 'only "compelling reasons" may lead the Court to refuse its opinion in response to a request falling within its jurisdiction'. This was last recalled in the *Chagos Advisory Opinion*, above n 14, paras 63–65.

2.3 An Overview of the Leading Cases

Over the years, States have entrusted the Court with a number of cases involving environmental issues. In particular, the beginning of the twenty-first century was marked by a wave of environmental cases reaching the Court: between 2006 and 2011, the ICJ was seized of no less than five cases involving issues of environmental protection.[22]

Some of the cases submitted to the Court since its creation have been settled by the States concerned before reaching the merits stage. Those cases should not be disregarded when evaluating the role played by the ICJ in resolving disputes involving environmental matters since the Court was chosen by the Parties as the forum to raise their environmental claims. Other cases have been litigated and adjudicated by the Court. The latter, together with the Court's advisory opinion on the legality of the threat or use of nuclear weapons, have generated a considerable body of jurisprudence in which relevant rules of international law applicable to environmental protection have been addressed and defined.

2.3.1 Environmental Cases Settled Out of Court[23]

The first cases directly relevant to the protection of the environment that were brought to the Court were the *Nuclear Tests* cases, introduced against France on 9 May 1973 by Australia and New Zealand, respectively. In those cases, the Applicants contested the conduct by France of nuclear tests in the Pacific, asserting that they were causing damage to human and animal life as well as to the environment.[24] New Zealand maintained, in particular, that undertaking nuclear tests 'violat[ed] the rights of all members of the international community, including New Zealand, to the preservation from unjustified artificial radioactive contamination of the terrestrial, maritime and aerial environment and, in particular, of the environment of the region in which

[22] Those cases were, by ascending chronological order of being filed, the case concerning *Pulp Mills on the River Uruguay (Argentina v Uruguay)*, filed in May 2006, the case concerning *Aerial Herbicide Spraying (Ecuador v Colombia)*, filed in March 2008, the case concerning *Whaling in the Antarctic (Australia v Japan; New Zealand intervening)*, filed in May 2010, the case concerning *Certain Activities Carried Out by Nicaragua in the Border Area (Costa Rica v Nicaragua)*, filed in November 2010, and the case concerning the *Construction of a Road in Costa Rica along the San Juan River (Nicaragua v Costa Rica)*, filed in December 2011.

[23] Note that the case concerning *Certain Phosphate Lands in Nauru (Nauru v Australia)*, which is often referred to as another environmental case settled under the auspices of the ICJ, was voluntarily omitted. Indeed, it is the alleged breach of Australia's obligations under the Trusteeship Agreement for Nauru as well as Australia's alleged failure to respect the right to self-determination of the people of Nauru that were at the core of the dispute, and Nauru insisted on the financial loss it incurred, not the environmental damage caused.

[24] Application instituting proceedings filed by Australia in the Registry of the Court, paras 24–26, 40, 42; Application instituted proceedings filed by New Zealand in the Registry of the Court, paras 13, 22, 25 (New Zealand's Application).

the tests are conducted and in which New Zealand, the Cook Islands, Niue and the Tokelau Islands are situated'.[25] This raised the question of the existence and scope of an international law obligation incumbent upon France not to cause unjustified damage to the environment and of the identity of the obligee or obligees of any such obligation.

Strictly speaking, the dispute was not settled by agreement between the Parties. The Court, however, observed in two separate judgments on the questions of jurisdiction and admissibility that, after the introduction of the case, France had, through various public statements, undertaken not to conduct further tests in the Pacific and that such undertaking was binding upon it. On that basis, it found 'that the claim[s] of [Australia and New Zealand] no longer ha[d] any object and that [it was] therefore not called upon to give a decision thereon'.[26] It is unclear what motivated France to make such statements and whether the ongoing ICJ proceedings played a role at all; in fact the attitude of the French Government towards the Court in this case would seem to indicate that the proceedings were ignored by the Respondent altogether.[27] But the very fact that Australia and New Zealand both decided to seise the Court of the matter illustrates the trust placed in the ICJ as a forum to settle disputes with an environmental component at a time when environmental concerns had only recently emerged. Immediate action was asked from the Court in the form of two requests for provisional measures, to which it responded within six weeks.[28]

Another case with an important environment-related subject-matter that was settled out of Court is the case concerning *Aerial Herbicide Spraying (Ecuador v Colombia).* On 31 March 2008, Ecuador filed an Application instituting proceedings against Colombia, referring to Article XXXI of the Pact of Bogota as the basis for jurisdiction. In its Application, Ecuador alleged that, by spraying toxic herbicides at locations near, at and across its border with Ecuador, Colombia had violated Ecuador's rights under customary and conventional international law.[29] However, on 12 September 2013, Ecuador informed the Court that the Parties had come to an agreement, as a result of which it wished to discontinue the proceedings in the case. After Colombia indicated that it had no objection to the discontinuance of the proceedings, the Court issued an order placing the discontinuance on record and

[25] New Zealand's Application, above n 24, para 28.

[26] *Nuclear Tests (Australia v France)* , Judgment, 20 December 1974, ICJ Reports 1974, p. 272, para 62; *Nuclear Tests (New Zealand v France)*, Judgment, 20 December 1974, ICJ Reports 1974, p. 478, para 65.

[27] France considered that the Court was manifestly not competent in the case, refused to participate in the proceedings, and withdrew its declaration of acceptance of the jurisdiction of the Court under Article 36, para 2 of the Statute.

[28] *Nuclear Tests (Australia v France)*, Interim Protection, Order, 22 June 1973, ICJ Reports 1973, p. 99 (*Nuclear Tests* (Provisional measures Australia)); *Nuclear Tests (New Zealand v France)*, Interim Protection, Order, 22 June 1973, ICJ Reports 1973, p. 135 (*Nuclear Tests* (Provisional Measures New Zealand)). See Sect. 2.4.

[29] The written pleadings filed by the Parties in the case are available on the Court's website. https://www.icj-cij.org/en/case/138/written-proceedings. Accessed 21 January 2022.

directed that the case be removed from the List.[30] As recorded in the Court's Order, the Parties' agreement established, *inter alia*, an exclusion zone, in which Colombia was not to conduct aerial spraying operations. It also set out operational parameters for Colombia's spraying programme and provided for the creation of a Joint Commission to ensure that spraying operations outside the exclusion zone have not caused herbicides to drift into Ecuador.

While the fact that the Parties reached an agreement three weeks before the scheduled start of the oral hearings in the case[31] might be a coincidence, it seems to suggest that the ongoing ICJ proceedings may have prompted said Parties to put an end to their dispute through diplomatic channels. Indeed, it has been argued that the involvement of the ICJ in a case can alter dispute behaviour outside the Court[32] and in the case of *Ecuador v Colombia*, it cannot be excluded that the case facilitated an out-of-court settlement.[33] In any event, cases like the *Aerial Herbicide Spraying* case highlight the potentially broad scope of issues that may come before the ICJ in relation to the protection of the environment.

2.3.2 Environmental Cases Decided by the Court

The first cases decided by the ICJ that had an impact on the protection of the environment were not environmental cases *per se*. Environmental issues were, indeed, only treated incidentally, in relation to the implementation of rules from what could be referred to as traditional fields of international law. Notably, in the case concerning the *Gabčíkovo-Nagymaros Project*, introduced in July 1997 by the Republic of Hungary and the Slovak Republic, the Court addressed the relevance of environmental protection with regard to the law of State responsibility.

A second wave of relevant cases then reached the Court, in which the protection of the environment and the conservation of species was at the heart of the dispute, but the obligations invoked were exclusively treaty obligations. While the settlement of those cases by the ICJ had a direct impact on the protection of the environment, the relevance of the judgments issued is primarily limited to those cases, or to potential

---

[30] *Aerial Herbicide Spraying (Ecuador v Colombia)*, Order, 13 September 2013, ICJ Reports 2013, p. 278.

[31] As reported in the Court's Order, the Parties' agreement was concluded on 9 September 2013. The hearings in the case were scheduled to start on 30 September (see Tomka 2013a, p. 6).

[32] See, for instance: McLaughlin Mitchell and Owsiak 2018 p. 459. As explained by an authoritative commentator, '[t]here clearly exists no objection in principle, given the general political function served by the judicial settlement of international disputes, to States instituting proceedings as a step in the evolution of the diplomatic handling of the affair and as a legitimate means of political pressure, hoping in that way to settle the case out of Court': see Shaw 2016, p. 1238.

[33] This hypothesis was embraced by Judge and former President of the Court Peter Tomka, who, referring to the case of *Ecuador v Colombia*, emphasised the role that the engagement of the Court's amicable judicial process could play in the conduct of peaceful negotiations. See Tomka 2013b, pp. 12–13.

future disputes relating to the interpretation or application of the same treaties. This is true of the case concerning *Whaling in the Antarctic* (*Whaling* case), introduced in May 2010, in which Australia was invoking the violation by Japan of its obligations under the International Convention for the Regulation of Whaling (ICRW) as well as other international conventions concerning the protection of the environment.[34] It also applies, though to a lesser extent, to the case concerning *Pulp Mills on the River Uruguay* (*Pulp Mills* case), filed on 4 May 2006, in which Argentina was alleging a violation of Uruguay's obligations under a bilateral treaty. The relevance of the judgment issued by the Court in this case does go beyond the applicable treaty, insofar as the Court referred to obligations incumbent upon States under general international law as part of its interpretation of the relevant treaty provisions.[35]

More recently, two cases were brought to the Court where the existence and compliance with States' obligations under customary international law relating to the environment was a main issue.

In the case concerning *Certain Activities Carried Out by Nicaragua in the Border Area (Costa Rica v Nicaragua)* (the *Certain Activities* case), introduced in November 2010, Costa Rica made two categories of claims against Nicaragua. According to the Applicant, the Respondent had, firstly, violated its sovereignty over a territory which was in dispute between the Parties but which it alleged was Costa Rican. Costa Rica contested, among other things, the excavation by Nicaragua of several *caños* in that territory, which it argued had caused material damage to its territory and environment. Moreover, Costa Rica also contested the conduct by Nicaragua in Nicaraguan territory of dredging activities that had—allegedly—caused transboundary harm to Costa Rica. According to the Applicant, such conduct was constitutive of a breach of Nicaragua's 'substantive environmental obligation not to cause harm to Costa Rica's territory'.[36] Costa Rica also maintained that Nicaragua had breached its procedural obligations imposed on it by customary international law in the field.

In the case concerning the *Construction of a Road along the San Juan River (Nicaragua v Costa Rica)* (*Road* case), filed in December 2011, Nicaragua alleged the violation by Costa Rica of both procedural and substantive obligations under customary international law relating to the environment in connection with the construction of a road on the Costa Rican side of the border between the two countries. Nicaragua maintained, *inter alia,* that the works undertaken by Costa Rica had

[34] In its Application, Australia had invoked the violation by Japan of its obligations under the Convention on International Trade in Endangered Species of Wild Fauna and Flora (CITES) as well as under the Convention on Biological Diversity. It did, however, progressively abandoned these claims in its pleadings and made no mention of these instruments in its final submissions.

[35] While the Court's jurisdiction in *Pulp Mills* only extended to alleged violations of the Statute of the River Uruguay, the Court explained that, in application of the relevant rules of treaty interpretation, the interpretation of that treaty had to take into account, together with the context, 'any relevant rules of international law applicable in the relations between the parties', which included rules of general international law.

[36] *Certain Activities Carried Out by Nicaragua in the Border Area (Costa Rica v Nicaragua) and Construction of a Road in Costa Rica along the San Juan River (Nicaragua v Costa Rica)*, Merits, Judgment, ICJ Reports 2015, p. 705, para 100 (*Certain Activities; Construction of a Road* (Merits)).

caused significant transboundary harm to the San Juan River, situated in Nicaragua's territory.

Both cases were joined by an Order of 17 April 2013.[37] The Court's judgment in the joined cases, dated 16 December 2015,[38] built on pronouncements already made in the *Pulp Mills* case and embodies the current state of the ICJ's jurisprudence on customary international law concerning transboundary harm.[39]

Having set the scene for the Court's work with regard to environmental protection, an assessment now follows of the Court's strengths and weaknesses in taking up the challenges of environmental cases as identified above, namely the handling of the relevant evidence, the risk that irreparable harm occurs before the case is settled and the necessity to clarify the applicable rules in the field.

2.4 Scientific Evidence in Environmental Cases before the International Court of Justice

Environmental cases often entail a substantial amount of highly technical evidence. It has been argued that, while the ICJ is in a particularly good position to refine the rules of international law relevant to the protection of the environment, it is not, however, equipped to examine and analyse complex scientific evidence.[40] On that basis, its ability to establish relevant facts and therefore to satisfactorily settle environmental disputes has been questioned. Yet, an overview of the rules applicable to the production of evidence and of past cases in which the Court has been confronted with technical evidentiary material shows that it has all the necessary tools at its disposal to deal with intricate environmental cases.

2.4.1 Assembling the Necessary Evidence to Decide Environmental Cases

Just like in other cases, there is no restriction as to the form of the evidence the parties to an environmental case may produce in support of their factual allegations. Written documents, videos, photographs and maps are all examples of evidentiary

[37] *Certain Activities Carried Out by Nicaragua in the Border Area (Costa Rica v Nicaragua)*, Joinder of Proceedings, Order, 17 April 2013, ICJ Reports 2013, p. 166.

[38] *Certain Activities; Construction of a Road* (Merits), above n 36.

[39] The Parties were also alleging the violation of certain treaty obligations: see their final submissions at paras 49 and 52 of the judgment. This chapter will only address the Court's findings regarding customary international law.

[40] See, for instance, *Pulp Mills on the River Uruguay (Argentina v Uruguay)*, Judgment, 20 April 2010, ICJ Reports 2010, Joint dissenting opinion Judges Al-Khasawneh and Simma, para 4.

material used in cases involving environmental issues.[41] Moreover, the Statute and the Rules of Court indicate that the parties can produce expert opinions, provided both in writing, in the form of reports, and orally, in the form of testimonies.[42]

The Statute and the Rules of Court allow the Court to take action if the evidence produced by the parties is not deemed satisfactory. In particular, under Article 62 of the Rules, '[t]he Court may at any time call upon the parties to produce such evidence or to give such explanations as the Court may consider to be necessary for the elucidation of any aspect of the matters in issue, or may itself seek other information for this purpose'.[43] The ICJ can therefore be proactive in the gathering of evidence. Particularly relevant in this context is also the possibility for the Court to arrange for an expert opinion, envisaged by Article 50 of the Statute[44] and Article 67 of the Rules.[45] The Court has made use of these provisions in three cases so far, none of which focused on environmental issues.[46] It is, however, an avenue that may prove very useful in future environmental cases.

In addition to resorting to experts, the Court may decide to conduct a visit to the place or locality to which a case relates. It can do so at any time, either *proprio*

---

[41] For an example of a case where all those were used, see *Certain Activities; Construction of a Road* (Merits), above n 36.

[42] The relevant provisions are to be found in Articles 43 and 44 of the Statute and Articles 50, 57, 58, 63, 64 and 65 of the Rules of Court.

[43] The Court did so recently in relation to the question of reparations in the case concerning *Armed Activities on the Territory of the Congo (Democratic Republic of the Congo v Uganda).* In this case, it requested further evidence from the Parties after they had submitted their written pleadings on the matter; it also asked them methodological questions as well as questions regarding reparation mechanisms and processes. See the Questions put by the Court under Article 62, para 1, of its Rules, available at https://www.icj-cij.org/public/files/case-related/116/116-20180611-OTH-01-00-EN.pdf. Accessed 21 January 2022.

[44] Article 50 of the Court's Statute provides that '[t]he Court may, at any time, entrust any individual, body, bureau, commission or other organization that it may select, with the task of carrying out an enquiry or giving an expert opinion'.

[45] Pursuant to Article 67, para 1, of the Rules of Court, '[i]f the Court considers it necessary to arrange for an enquiry or an expert opinion, it shall, after hearing the parties, issue an order to this effect, defining the subject of the enquiry or expert opinion, stating the number and mode of appointment of the persons to hold the enquiry or of the experts, and laying down the procedure to be followed'. Para 2 indicates that '[e]very report or record of an enquiry and every expert opinion shall be communicated to the parties, which shall be given the opportunity of commenting upon it'.

[46] *Corfu Channel (Great Britain v Albania),* Order, 17 December 1948, ICJ Reports 1948, p. 124; *Maritime Delimitation in the Caribbean Sea and the Pacific Ocean (Costa Rica v Nicaragua),* Order, 31 May 2016, ICJ Reports 2016, p. 235; *Armed Activities on the Territory of the Congo (Democratic Republic of the Congo v Uganda),* Order, 8 September 2020. Note that in the case of the *Democratic Republic of the Congo v Uganda,* in which experts were appointed in the reparations phase, the terms of reference of the experts included, *inter alia,* questions about the loss of natural resources suffered by the Democratic Republic of the Congo (the DRC) in the case. The experts report focuses on the quantity and monetary value, based on average market prices, of gold, diamond, coltan, timber, tin, tungsten and coffee plundered and unlawfully exploited in the DRC (in particular, in the occupied district of Ituri) during the relevant period. As specified in the report, the questions—raised by the DRC in its pleadings—of the existence and valuation of a damage to wildlife or of damage resulting from deforestation (beyond the commercial timber trade) were not covered by the report.

motu or at the request of a party.[47] In the case concerning the *Gabčikovo-Nagymaros Project*, the Parties jointly proposed that a visit *in situ* be arranged; in an Order dated 5 February 1997 the Court decided to 'exercise its functions with regard to the obtaining of evidence by visiting a place or locality to which the case relates', having considered that 'this may facilitate its task in the instant case'.[48]

In view of the foregoing, there is no doubt that the ICJ has the means to obtain all the necessary evidence to decide cases involving multifaceted environmental issues. It appears, however, that it has only rarely had recourse to the possibilities offered to it to gather evidence itself. Some may regard this as a weakness;[49] however, it seems reasonable for the Court only to have resort to such tools when necessary, leaving the parties with the prime responsibility for evidence gathering.[50]

2.4.2 Establishment of the Facts in Environmental Cases

Quite distinct from the question of the means to obtain the necessary evidence to decide environmental cases is the question of the treatment by the Court of such evidence. That subject, in turn, raises two issues: first, that of the assessment, by the Court, of the evidence provided, and second, that of the burden of proof.

With regard to the first issue, as highlighted by Judge and former President of the Court Ronny Abraham, since the ICJ is a judicial organ and not a scientific body, it may often benefit from the analytical skills of experts when presented with complex technical and scientific data in environmental cases.[51] This, however, does not change the fact that it is the Court, and the Court alone, that has exclusive responsibility to assess the evidence before it, and that this responsibility may not be delegated to experts.[52] The Court reasserted this principle in its judgment in the joined *Certain Activities* and *Road* cases. It affirmed that it is its duty, 'after having given careful consideration to all the evidence in the record, to assess its probative value, to determine which facts must be considered relevant, and to draw conclusions

---

[47] Article 66 of the Rules provides in relevant part that '[t]he Court may at any time decide, either *proprio motu* or at the request of a party, to exercise its functions with regard to the obtaining of evidence at a place or locality to which the case relates, subject to such conditions as the Court may decide upon after ascertaining the views of the parties'.

[48] *Gabčíkovo-Nagymaros Project (Hungary v Slovakia)*, Order, 5 February 1997, ICJ Reports 1997, pp. 4–5.

[49] In their joint dissenting opinion in the *Pulp Mills* case (above n 40), Judges Al-Khasawneh and Simma criticised the Court for what they considered to be 'a deficient method of scientific fact-finding' and argued that the Court should have arranged for an expert opinion.

[50] This seems all the more reasonable as the parties have, in practice, the best access to all relevant factual and evidentiary material. This assessment could change in cases where one of the parties does not appear before the Court or fails to defend its case: under Article 53, para 2 of the Statute, the Court must, before deciding such cases, 'satisfy itself … that the claim is well founded in fact and law'.

[51] President Abraham's 2016 speech to the Sixth Committee, above n 10, p. 10.

[52] Ibid., p. 8.

from them as appropriate'. The Court, in other words, 'make[s] its own determination of the facts, on the basis of the totality of the evidence presented to it, and … then appl[ies] the relevant rules of international law to those facts which it has found to be established'.[53] And indeed, it did so in these joined cases, just like it had in earlier cases involving scientific data.[54]

With regard to the second issue, namely the burden of proof, it is well established that, '[a]s a general rule, it is for the party which alleges a fact in support of its claims to prove the existence of that fact'. Nevertheless, the Court has clarified that this rule is not 'an absolute one' and that '[t]he determination of the burden of proof is in reality dependent on the subject-matter and the nature of each dispute brought before the Court; it varies according to the type of facts which it is necessary to establish for the purposes of the decision of the case'. In particular, the procedural nature of the obligation whose violation is invoked and the negative nature of the facts alleged may have an impact on the bearer of the burden of proof. The Court has made clear that in some occurrences, 'neither party is alone in bearing the burden of proof'.[55]

A first reading of the judgment issued on 31 March 2014 in the *Whaling* case[56] may cast doubt on the validity of these principles in the case and, by extension, in cases where similar issues would be raised. It will be recalled that Australia was alleging a breach by Japan of its obligations under the ICRW on the basis that the latter was granting special permits authorizing the killing of whales under a whaling programme (JARPA II) which, according to the Applicant, was not 'for the purposes of scientific research'.[57] The Court considered that the question whether a programme is for purposes of scientific research within the meaning of the Convention is an objective one and proceeded to answer it on that basis.[58] It considered that the evidence introduced by Japan showed that there were 'weaknesses in Japan's explanation' and

---

[53] *Certain Activities; Construction of a Road* (Merits), above n 36, p. 726, para 176. The Court had already affirmed this principle in *Pulp Mills on the River Uruguay (Argentina v Uruguay)* , Judgment, 20 April 2010, ICJ Reports 2010, p. 72, para 168 (*Pulp Mills* (Judgment)).

[54] See, for instance: *Whaling in the Antarctic (Australia v Japan: New Zealand intervening)*, Judgment, 31 March 2014, ICJ Reports 2014, p. 226 (*Whaling in the Antarctic* (Judgment)). The Court's treatment of expert evidence in the case, in particular the adoption of a procedure of examination, cross-examination and re-examination of party-appointed experts, followed by questions of the judges, has been favourably received (see, for instance, Mbengue 2016, p. 539; see also Sands 2016, p. 30). This procedure was later followed in the *Certain Activities* and *Road* cases (note that in these proceedings, the experts were simply asked to confirm orally their written statement in lieu of examination-in-chief).

[55] *Ahmadou Sadio Diallo (Republic of Guinea v Democratic Republic of the Congo),* Merits, Judgment, 30 November 2010, ICJ Reports 2010, pp. 661–662, paras 54–56. On evidence and the burden of proof, see also Chap. 17.

[56] *Whaling in the Antarctic* (Judgment), above n 54.

[57] Australia invoked the violation by Japan of various provisions of the Schedule to the ICRW, which set forth restrictions on the killing, taking and treating of whales. Japan, for its part, argued that its whaling programme was not subject to these restrictions, on the basis that it fell within the scope of Article VIII of the ICRW, according to which the killing, taking, and treating of whales 'for purposes of scientific research' shall be exempt from the operation of the Convention.

[58] *Whaling in the Antarctic* (Judgment), above n 54, p. 254, para 67.

that it raised a series of 'doubts' relating to Japan's alleged scientific purpose.[59] It concluded that 'the evidence [had] not establish[ed] that the programme's design and implementation [were] reasonable in relation to achieving its stated objectives' and concluded that the JARPA II programme was not a programme 'for the purposes of scientific research'.

As pointed out by several dissenting judges[60] and acknowledged by one concurring judge,[61] the burden seemed to be on the Respondent to prove that its whaling programme was indeed for the purposes of scientific research, and not on the Applicant to substantiate its claim that it was not. One could speculate as to the reasons behind the Court's approach: was it because, given the fact that conservation of species was at stake, 'the principle of prevention and the precautionary principle … [were] to inform and conform any programmes under special permits within the limited scope of Article VIII of the ICRW', as one judge would have hoped to see recognized?[62] Probably not, as evidenced by that very judge's separate opinion.[63] Was it a consequence of the Court's interpretation of the relevant provisions of the Convention, in particular Article VIII?[64] Or was it because Australia was alleging a negative fact, namely, the absence of scientific purpose behind Japan's JARPA II programme, that the Court considered Japan had to establish the existence of such purpose? In any event, the Court's reasoning neither suggests that the Court intended to modify the principles applicable to the burden of proof, nor that any such modification would be the result of the environmental nature of the dispute. In the more recent judgment issued in the joined cases between Costa Rica and Nicaragua, concerning protection against transboundary harm, each party was treated as bearing the burden of proving the facts which it alleged.[65]

It follows that the aforementioned principles concerning the burden of proof, which were formulated by the Court in general terms and have been elaborated in the context of cases involving issues of a diverse nature,[66] must be considered to apply

---

[59] Ibid., p. 274, para 153, pp. 279-280, paras 178–179, p. 284, para 194, p. 289, para 209, pp. 289–290, para 212 and p. 293, para 226.

[60] *Whaling in the Antarctic* (Judgment), above n 54, Dissenting Opinion of Judge Owada, p. 318, para 43; Dissenting Opinion of Judge Abraham, pp. 328–329, para 31; Dissenting Opinion of Judge Bennouna, pp. 341 and 345.

[61] Judge Xue, commenting on the question of the sample sizes, indicates, *inter alia*: 'In my view, Japan fails to explain to the satisfaction of the Court how the sample sizes are calculated and determined with the aim of achieving the objectives of the programme. Technical complexity of the matter does not release it of the burden of proof, as the issue lies at the core of the dispute' (*Whaling in the Antarctic* (Judgment), above n 54, Dissenting Opinion of Judge Xue, p. 427, para 25).

[62] *Whaling in the Antarctic* (Judgment), above n 54, Dissenting Opinion of Judge Cançado Trindade, p. 374, para 70.

[63] Ibid., p. 375, para 71.

[64] See *supra* note 56. As pointed out by the Court, issues concerning the interpretation of Article VIII were central to the case (*Whaling in the Antarctic* (Judgment), above n 54, p. 249, para 50).

[65] See in particular paras 119–120, 192–196, 203–207, 211–213, 216 of the 2015 Judgment in the joined cases.

[66] Among said cases, we find the *Pulp Mills* case, which raised issues relating to the protection of the environment.

in the field of environmental protection. Such rules have the advantage of offering both consistency and a degree of flexibility which may be welcome in environmental cases, where facts can prove particularly difficult to establish.

2.5 The Role of the Court in Preventing Irreparable Damage to the Environment

As pointed out at the beginning of this chapter, one of the challenges posed by environmental cases is the risk that irreparable damage will be caused before the Court issues a decision on the merits.

Pursuant to Article 43 of the Court's Statute, the procedure in contentious cases consists of a written and an oral part. The written proceedings consist of the communication to the Court and to the parties of memorials, counter-memorials and, if necessary, replies. An overview of the Court's orders fixing time-limits shows that the time period given to the parties to prepare their first piece of written pleadings is only exceptionally fixed under six months and that it often goes up to a year. On top of that, it is not unusual for a second round of written pleadings to be ordered before the case proceeds to the hearing phase.[67] This explains why there is an average period of a little over three and a half years between the institution of proceedings and the delivery of a final Judgment by the Court in contentious cases.[68] To avoid a future decision on the merits being prejudiced by irreparable harm caused during this time to the rights recognized to a Party, the Court can indicate provisional measures of protection.

Article 41, para 1, of the Court's Statute provides that '[t]he Court shall have the power to indicate, if it considers that circumstances so require, any provisional measures which ought to be taken to preserve the respective rights of either party'. Such measures may be indicated at the request of the Applicant or the Respondent. While the Statute does not specify the conditions under which provisional measures will be indicated, those have been clearly identified by the Court in its jurisprudence.[69]

First, the Court will only be able to indicate provisional measures in a case if it has *prima facie* jurisdiction to decide that case on the merits.[70] Secondly, the rights whose

[67] On the length of written and oral pleadings, see the 2018 Interim Report submitted by the Committee on the Procedure of International Courts and Tribunals of the International Law Association (ILA) to the 78th Biennial Conference of the ILA, available on the ILA's website.

[68] Abraham 2016, p. 300. The cases completed since 2016 did not substantially affect the then calculated average period.

[69] Those conditions have been consistently applied by the Court. They were last recalled in the Court's Orders of 7 December 2021, indicating provisional measures in two cases concerning the *Application of the International Convention on the Elimination of All Forms of Racial Discrimination (Armenia v. Azerbaijan and Azerbaijan v. Armenia).*

[70] This means that the Court must be satisfied that the provisions relied upon by the Applicant appear to afford a basis on which its jurisdiction could be founded, with such a finding being

protection is sought by the party requesting the measures must be at least plausible.[71] Thirdly, a link must exist between the rights which form the subject of the proceedings before the Court on the merits of the case and the provisional measures being sought. Finally, and very importantly, the power of the Court to indicate provisional measures will be exercised only if there is a real and imminent risk that irreparable prejudice will be caused to the rights in dispute or that the disregard of a party's plausible rights lead to irreparable consequences before the Court gives its final decision in the case. The Court, in other words, will only indicate provisional measures if there is urgency.[72]

The Court made clear that, when provisional measures are indicated in a case, these measures are binding on the parties[73] and indeed, a failure to respect such measures will be considered a breach of the State's international obligations and may give rise to a finding of the Court to this effect.[74] Provisional measures are, therefore, a powerful tool to protect the rights of the parties to a case before the Court pending a decision on the merits. They can, as a consequence, be a powerful tool to protect the environment against a risk of irreparable prejudice. This is all the more important as, as pointed out by the Court, damage to the environment often is of an irreversible character and there are inherent limitations in the mechanism of reparation of this type of damage.[75]

The Court has been requested to order provisional measures in the majority of environmental cases that have come before it. The decisions it made in respect of those requests show that, in cases where the protection of the environment is sought by a party, the criteria governing the indication of provisional measures remain unchanged. In particular, the Court does not consider that *any* pollution or other kind of damage to the environment amounts to irreparable damage. The environmental nature of the damage feared does not discharge the party requesting protective

---

without prejudice to the Court's final decision on the question of the jurisdiction to deal with the merits of the case.

[71] As recalled by the Court, the *raison d'être* of provisional measures is to preserve the rights which may subsequently be adjudged to belong to either party (see *Certain Activities Carried Out by Nicaragua in the Border Area (Costa Rica v Nicaragua)*, Provisional Measures, Order, 8 March 2011, ICJ Reports 2011, p. 18, para 53 (*Certain Activities* (Provisional Measures 2011)). Therefore, the Court cannot and will not impose measures on a sovereign State if there is no reason to believe that the prescribed action corresponds to an obligation the Court could recognise to respect another State's right. As with the finding on *prima facie* jurisdiction, a finding of the Court on the plausibility of a party's rights at the provisional measures stage will not prejudice the Court's finding on the alleged rights on the merits.

[72] The Court's jurisprudence makes clear that there is urgency when the acts susceptible of causing irreparable prejudice can occur at any moment before the Court makes a final decision on the case.

[73] *LaGrand (Germany v United States of America)*, Judgment, 27 June 2001, ICJ Reports 2001, p. 506, para 109.

[74] Ibid., para 128(5); *Certain Activities; Construction of a Road* (Merits), above n 36, p. 740, para 229(3).

[75] *Gabčíkovo-Nagymaros Project (Hungary v Slovakia)*, Judgment, 25 September 1997, ICJ Reports 1997, p. 78, para 140 (*Gabčíkovo-Nagymaros* (Judgment)).

measures conclusively to establish that such damage would be irreparable, nor that the risk is real that such damage occur imminently.

This was particularly apparent in the treatment made by the Court of Argentina's request for provisional measures in the *Pulp Mills* case[76] and of Nicaragua's request for provisional measures in the *Road* case.[77] In both cases, the Applicant maintained that local species and the ecosystem of, respectively, the river Uruguay and the San Juan river, were at serious risk of irreparable harm.[78] In support of its Request, Argentina referred to various studies indicating that the activities undertaken by Uruguay could have a negative impact on the environment and argued that the resulting prejudice would be, by definition, irreparable, since 'the restoration of the *status quo ante* could not be envisaged, satisfaction would be inappropriate, and compensation would be precluded' for damage of this kind.[79] Argentina implied that a precautionary approach was adequate when assessing the reality of the existence of a risk to the environment and it referred to decisions on provisional measures adopted by the International Tribunal for the Law of the Sea[80] to support its position, arguing that the latter 'showed that it was aware of its responsibilities in respect of environmental protection'.[81] In the *Road* case, Nicaragua adopted the same approach, arguing that the construction of a road by Costa Rica would cause severe environmental damage to the environment and that such damage would be irreparable since, in particular, there would be 'no way to recover the prior environmental values and intact ecosystem'.[82]

In both cases, the Court disregarded the notion that any damage to the environment would be irreparable and implicitly rejected the idea that the degree of risk required to indicate provisional measures in environmental cases could be any lower than in other cases. It considered that the evidence provided by the Applicants was not sufficient to establish the irreparable character of the damage they argued would occur in the absence of provisional measures, and concluded that the circumstances were not such as to require the exercise of its power to indicate provisional measures.

[76] *Pulp Mills on the River Uruguay (Argentina v Uruguay)*, Provisional Measures, Order, 13 July 2006, ICJ Reports 2006, p. 113 (*Pulp Mills* (Provisional Measures 2006)).

[77] *Construction of a Road in Costa Rica along the San Juan River (Nicaragua v Costa Rica); Certain Activities Carried Out by Nicaragua in the Border Area (Costa Rica v Nicaragua)*, Provisional Measures, Order of 13 December 2013, ICJ Reports 2013, p. 398 (*Construction of a Road; Certain Activities* (Provisional Measures 2013)).

[78] *Pulp Mills* (Provisional Measures 2006), above n 76, p. 121, para 35; *Construction of a Road; Certain Activities* (Provisional Measures 2013), above n 77, paras 26–28.

[79] Verbatim Record 2006/46, p. 65–66 (Pellet).

[80] ITLOS, *Southern Bluefin Tuna (New Zealand and Australia v Japan)*, Provisional Measures, Order, 27 August 1999, ITLOS Reports 1999, p. 280; *Land Reclamation in and around the Straits of Johor (Malaysia v Singapore)*, Provisional Measures, Order, 8 October 2003, ITLOS Reports 2003, p. 10.

[81] Verbatim Record 2006/48, pp. 45–46 (Pellet). Note that the concept of 'precautionary approach' was not referred to as such.

[82] Verbatim Record 2013/28, pp. 31–33 (McCaffrey). Nicaragua relied principally on an expert report it had commissioned with a view to demonstrating the existence of a risk of irreparable damage to the environment.

It appears from the foregoing that the ICJ is rather strict in its appreciation of whether a particular situation calls for the indication of provisional measures of protection of the environment. The above mentioned *Nuclear Tests* cases could seem to have set a different trend. In those cases, Australia and New Zealand had filed requests for provisional measures in which they invoked, *inter alia,* the need to preserve the environment from radioactive contamination. Australia, in particular, maintained that the prejudice caused by further nuclear tests on the environment would be 'irremediable by any payment of damages'.[83] The Court considered that, since 'the information submitted to [it] … *d[id] not exclude the possibility* that damage to [New Zealand and Australia] might be shown to be caused by the deposit on [their respective] territory of radio-active fall-out resulting from [nuclear] tests and to be irreparable',[84] it should indicate interim measures of protection.[85] Two observations must be made in this regard: first, the risk of damage to the environment was not the only risk invoked by the Applicants and indeed, the danger to human life and health was particularly emphasised and surely played a significant role in the Court's reasoning; secondly, almost fifty years have passed since the Court ordered provisional measures in these cases, during which the conditions for the indication of provisional measures have been refined and, arguably, become more stringent.

This does not mean that the ICJ cannot or will not protect the environment through the indication of provisional measures. And indeed, the Court indicated provisional measures to protect, *inter alia,* Costa Rica's plausible rights of sovereignty as well as environmental rights connected thereto in the *Certain Activities* case, having found that the course of the San Juan river was at a real and imminent risk of being diverted and that this would cause irreparable prejudice to said rights.[86]

However, provisional measures cannot be requested to protect the environment against *any* harm; only a protection from irreparable harm can be obtained through these means. Establishing that the risk that such irreparable harm will occur is not only real but imminent can be a major challenge for a State requesting interim measures of protection. That being said, the jurisprudence of the ICJ in relation to provisional measures has the advantage of being well-defined, which, in turn, ensures a high degree of predictability of its decisions on the matter.

[83] *Nuclear Tests* (Provisional measures Australia), above n 28, p. 104, para 27.

[84] Ibid., p. 105, para 29; *Nuclear Tests* (Provisional Measures New Zealand), above n 28, p. 141, para 30.

[85] *Nuclear Tests (Australia v France)*, above n 28, p. 105, para 29; *Nuclear Tests (New Zealand v France)*, above n 28, p. 141, para 30 (emphasis added).

[86] *Construction of a Road; Certain Activities* (Provisional Measures 2013), above n 77, p. 354. See in particular paras 49–50.

2.6 The ICJ's Contribution to the Clarification of the Rules of International Law Relating to the Protection of the Environment

As indicated at the beginning of this chapter, the ICJ, in the exercise of its contentious as well as its advisory function, has contributed considerably to the development and clarification of international law relating to the protection of the environment. Starting with the recognition of a general obligation to respect the environment, the Court has then shown how environmental protection can be relevant in the application of the rules of various fields of international law. More recently, the Court has had the occasion to significantly clarify the rules of customary international law relating to the prevention of transboundary harm and the principles applicable to compensation of environmental damage.

2.6.1 Recognition of an Obligation in Relation to Environmental Protection

In December 1994, the United Nations General Assembly requested the Court to render an advisory opinion on the following question: 'is the threat or use of nuclear weapons in any circumstance permitted under international law?'. The question asked did not directly address the subject of environmental protection. Yet, during the proceedings before the Court, the question of the legality of the use of nuclear weapons with regard to international environmental law was raised. While some States argued that 'any use of nuclear weapons would be unlawful by reference to existing norms relating to the safeguarding and protection of the environment, in view of their essential importance', others took the view that any such norms could only ever be binding in times of peace and were therefore irrelevant when it came to the use of nuclear weapons in hostilities.[87]

In its advisory opinion, the Court 'recognize[d] that the environment is under daily threat and that the use of nuclear weapons could constitute a catastrophe for the environment. [It] also recognize[d] that the environment is not an abstraction but represents the living space, the quality of life and the very health of human beings, including generations unborn.'[88] Most importantly, it indicated that '[t]he existence of the general obligation of States to ensure that activities within their jurisdiction and control respect the environment of other States or of areas beyond national control is now part of the corpus of international law relating to the environment'.[89]

---

[87] *Nuclear Weapons Advisory Opinion*, above n 17, p. 241, paras 27–28.

[88] Ibid., pp. 241–242, para 29.

[89] Ibid.

The Court did not elaborate further on the scope or content of this 'general obligation', but its statement, which was regularly referred to in subsequent decisions,[90] undoubtedly opened the door to the development of international environmental law.

2.6.2 *The Relevance of Environmental Protection in Various Fields of International Law*

The relevance of the *Nuclear Weapons* advisory opinion goes beyond the recognition of the 'general obligation' mentioned above. The Opinion contains interesting elements regarding the protection of the environment in the law of armed conflict. A little more than a year after this Opinion, the Court had the opportunity to clarify how the protection of the environment could be invoked in the context of another field of international law, namely the law of State responsibility. More recently, in its 2009 judgment settling a dispute regarding navigational and related rights between Costa Rica and Nicaragua, the Court showed how the recognition of the legitimacy of environmental concerns could play a role in the application of the law of treaties. These contributions will be examined in turn.

2.6.2.1 The Protection of the Environment and the Law of Armed Conflict

In the *Nuclear Weapons* advisory opinion, the Court stated, in apparent reference to both general international law and relevant treaties, that 'existing international law relating to the protection and safeguarding of the environment … indicates important environmental factors that are properly to be taken into account in the context of the implementation of the principles and rules of the law applicable in armed conflict'.[91]

The need to consider environmental issues in the implementation of some of these 'principles and rules', namely those relevant to the exercise of the right to self-defence, was emphasized. In the words of the Court, 'States must take environmental considerations into account when assessing what is necessary and proportionate in the pursuit of legitimate military objectives. Respect for the environment is one of the elements that go to assessing whether an action is in conformity with the principles of necessity and proportionality.'[92]

The Court did not identify the precise environmental factors to be considered nor the manner in which those must be taken into consideration. Those questions remain open for determination in the future.

---

[90] See, for instance, *Gabčíkovo-Nagymaros* (Judgment), above n 75, p. 41, para 53; *Pulp Mills* (Judgment), above n 53, pp. 55–56, para 101; *Certain Activities; Construction of a Road* (Merits), above n 36, pp. 711–712, para 118.

[91] *Nuclear Weapons Advisory Opinion*, above n 17, p. 243, para 33.

[92] Ibid., p. 242, para 30.

2.6.2.2 The Protection of the Environment and the Law of State Responsibility

The question whether a State's will to protect the environment could be relevant when applying the principles and rules of State responsibility was raised before the Court in the case concerning the *Gabčíkovo-Nagymaros Project*. The case was not about the protection of the environment *per se*; the dispute rather focused on the status and alleged breaches of a bilateral treaty governing the construction and functioning of a barrage system on the Danube. Yet, given the subject-matter and the very terms of the treaty, as well as the facts surrounding the case, the protection of the environment was at the heart of the Parties' arguments. It is worth mentioning that the Court's judgment referred to the concept of sustainable development and that the Court indicated that the 'new norms and standards' developed with respect to environmental protection 'have to be taken into consideration, not only when States contemplate new activities but also when continuing with activities begun in the past'.[93]

Of particular interest for the purposes of the implementation of the law of State responsibility in environmental cases was the fact that Hungary relied, *inter alia,* on a 'state of ecological necessity' to justify the fact that it suspended and abandoned works that it was committed to perform in accordance with the relevant treaty and related instruments. Hungary maintained in that regard that it could not accept the ecological risks arising from the barrage project with respect to water quality, fauna and flora.[94] This state of necessity, said Hungary, precluded the wrongfulness of its conduct. Without accepting the validity of any doctrine of ecological necessity, Slovakia maintained that in any event the facts of the case would not amount to such ecological necessity.[95]

On the one hand, the Court made clear that the need to protect the environment could justify non-compliance with an international obligation on the part of a State on the grounds of necessity. This is so because a State's concern for its natural environment may be considered as relating to an 'essential interest' of that State, within the meaning of the customary rule of State Responsibility relating to necessity.[96]

On the other hand, it stressed that the need for environmental protection could only serve as a basis to invoke a state of necessity in case of a real and imminent peril for the environment. Mere uncertainties as to the consequences for the environment of complying with an international obligation, however serious, 'could not, alone, establish the objective existence of a "peril" in the sense of a component element of a state of necessity'.[97] On that basis, the Court concluded that there was an absence of a state of necessity in the case.

This might seem at odds with the Court's assertion, at a later stage in the same judgment, of its mindfulness that, 'in the field of environmental protection, vigilance

---

[93] *Gabčíkovo-Nagymaros* (Judgment), above n 75, pp. 77–78, para 140.

[94] Ibid., pp. 35–36, para 40.

[95] Ibid., p. 37, para 44.

[96] Ibid., pp. 40–41, paras 52–53.

[97] Ibid., pp. 41–42, para 54.

and prevention are required on account of the often irreversible character of damage to the environment and of the limitations inherent in the very mechanism of reparation of this type of damage'.[98] The Court's reasoning, however, clarified that the rules governing necessity as a ground for precluding wrongfulness will not be altered by the environmental aim behind a State action. In particular, a precautionary approach will not alter the exceptional character of necessity.

2.6.2.3 The Protection of the Environment and the Law of Treaties

It was not until twenty years later that the Court was called upon to examine the legal relevance of the will to protect the environment in another case, this time in relation to the implementation of the law of treaties. In the case concerning *Navigational and Related Rights* between Costa Rica and Nicaragua, the Court was asked to decide whether Nicaragua had violated its obligations under a bilateral treaty which, on the one hand, established Nicaragua's exclusive *dominium* and *imperium* over the waters of the San Juan river and, on the other hand, guaranteed Costa Rica a right of free navigation on the said waters.[99] The Court first confirmed the existence and scope of Costa Rica's right under the treaty, before moving to the question of the extent to which the exercise of said right was subject to Nicaragua's power of regulation under the same instrument.

In its judgment, the Court observed that 'where the parties have used generic terms in a treaty, the parties necessarily having been aware that the meaning of the terms was likely to evolve over time, and where the treaty has been entered into for a very long period or is "of continuing duration", the parties must be presumed, as a general rule, to have intended those terms to have an evolving meaning.'[100] This statement was made in connection with the interpretation of the term 'comercio' as used in the treaty provision affirming Costa Rica's navigational rights 'con objectos de comercio'.[101]

The Parties agreed and the Court confirmed that, under the régime established by the 1858 Treaty, Nicaragua had the power to regulate the exercise by Costa Rica of its

---

[98] Ibid., pp. 77–78, para 140.

[99] The relevant provision was Article VI of the Jerez-Cañas Treaty, a Treaty of Limits concluded between the Parties on 15 April 1858. In its Spanish version, which is the only authoritative one, Article VI reads in relevant part as follows: 'La República de Nicaragua tendrá exclusivamente el dominio y sumo imperio sobre las aguas del río de San Juan desde su salida del Lago, hasta su desembocadura en el Atlántico; pero la República de Costa Rica tendrá en dichas aguas los derechos perpetuos de libre navegación, desde la expresada desembocadura hasta tres millas inglesas antes de llegar al Castillo Viejo, con objetos de comercio, ya sea con Nicaragua ó al interior de Costa Rica por los ríos de San Carlos ó Sarapiquí, ó cualquiera otra vía procedente de la parte que en la ribera del San Juan se establece corresponder á esta República'.

[100] *Dispute regarding Navigational and Related Rights (Costa Rica v Nicaragua)*, Judgment, 23 July 2009, ICJ Reports 2009, p. 243, para 66 (*Navigational and Related Rights* (Judgment)).

[101] The Parties disagreed as to the meaning and proper translation of the words 'con objectos de comercio', which the Court established means 'for the purposes of commerce'. See ibid., p. 240, paras 56–57.

right to freedom of navigation, provided in particular that the regulations adopted by Nicaragua pursued a legitimate purpose.[102] Because the legitimate purpose requirement was not expressly mentioned in the relevant treaty provision the Court did not apply as such the above mentioned principle of interpretation to the determination of what would fall under the legitimate purpose qualification. It did, however, follow a similar approach, stating that 'over the course of the century and a half since the … Treaty was concluded, the interests which are to be protected through regulation in the public interest may well have changed in ways that could never have been anticipated by the Parties at the time: protecting the environment is a notable example'.[103] It then proceeded to demonstrate that, in adopting certain measures which have been challenged, Nicaragua was 'pursuing the legitimate purpose of protecting the environment'.[104]

It appears from the Court's reasoning that it considered that the Parties must be presumed to have intended the scope of Nicaragua's regulatory powers to evolve with the concerns States would be facing over time, to include the now legitimate aim to protect the environment. While the Court's decision was limited to the applicable treaty, it may very well be relevant when interpreting other treaty provisions in the future.[105]

2.6.3 Clarification of the Rules of International Environmental Law Relating to Transboundary Harm

As already mentioned, the 2015 judgment issued in the *Certain Activities* and the *Road* cases significantly clarified the state of customary international law relating to transboundary harm. In particular, the judgment confirmed that general international law imposes two sets of obligations on States carrying out, in their territory, activities that may be harmful to the environment in another State: first, obligations of a

[102] *Navigational and Related Rights* (Judgment), above n 100, pp. 249–250, para 87.

[103] Ibid., p. 250, para 89.

[104] Ibid., p. 250, para 89, p. 254, para 104, p. 256, para 109, p. 258, para 118, pp. 261–262, para 127 and pp. 26–266, para 141.

[105] Note that the Court was called upon applying treaties directly relevant to the protection of the environment in several cases. In addition to bilateral treaties, it dealt with the interpretation and application of, *inter alia,* the following multilateral conventions: the International Convention for the Regulation of Whaling (see *Whaling in the Antarctic* (Judgment), above n 54), the Convention on Wetlands of International Importance especially as Waterfowl Habitat, known as the Ramsar Convention (see *Certain Activities; Construction of a Road* (Merits), above n 36, pp. 707–708, paras 106–107, pp. 708–709, 109–110, p. 724, para 165, p. 725, para 172 and pp. 737–738, paras 218–220) and the 1992 Convention on Biological Diversity (see *Certain Activities; Construction of a Road* (Merits), above n 36, pp. 707–708, paras 106–107, pp. 709–710, para 111, p. 723, para, 163–164 and pp. 737–738, paras 218–220). The relevant developments have not been included in this chapter, which aims at dealing with issues of general relevance and therefore does not cover the interpretation by the Court of specific treaty provisions when the relevance of the Court's reasoning is limited to those provisions.

substantive nature, and second, obligations of a procedural nature. More importantly, the judgment clarified the content and scope of such obligations.

2.6.3.1 States' Substantive Obligations under Customary International Law Concerning Transboundary Harm

With regard to substantive obligations, the Court confirmed that, under general international law, '[a] State is ... obliged to use all the means at its disposal in order to avoid activities which take place in its territory, or in any area under its jurisdiction, causing significant damage to the environment of another State'.[106]

Emphasis must be placed on the use of the word significant, and indeed the Court's analysis shows that only activities causing significant transboundary harm could amount to a breach of substantive obligations under customary international law. The Court did not insist on that requirement in the *Certain Activities* case, since it considered that the dredging activities led by Nicaragua in its own territory had not caused *any* transboundary harm to Costa Rica, from which it naturally followed that Nicaragua had not breached its substantive obligations under international environmental law.[107] In the *Road* case, however, there was evidence that the construction works undertaken by Costa Rica had had some impact on the San Juan River, situated in Nicaragua's territory. The Court considered that Nicaragua had not proved that those works had caused significant transboundary harm and that, '[t]herefore, Nicaragua's claim that Costa Rica breached its substantive obligations under customary international law concerning transboundary harm must be dismissed'.[108]

Proving such significant harm will often imply producing highly technical evidence, and it has been argued that 'the findings of the Court underscore the difficulty for States of making out a case of transboundary environmental harm when the cause of the harm is incremental rather than sudden'.[109] However, where there is sufficient evidence of significant harm, there is scope for the Court to find that violations have occurred.

---

[106] *Certain Activities; Construction of a Road* (Merits), above n 36, pp. 711–712, para 118. The Court referred back to its statement to this effect in its judgment in the *Pulp Mills* case (above n 53, pp. 55–56, para 101).

[107] *Certain Activities; Construction of a Road* (Merits), above n 36, p. 710, para 113 and p. 712, paras 119—120.

[108] See in particular para 217 of the Judgment.

[109] McCaffrey 2018, p. 366

2.6.3.2 States' Procedural Obligations under Customary International Law Concerning Transboundary Harm

The ICJ clarified that, under customary international law, two kinds of procedural obligations may become relevant when a State considers engaging in an activity potentially harmful to the environment of another State: first, an obligation to assess the transboundary impact of such activity and second, an obligation to notify, and consult with, the concerned neighbouring State.

The first obligation 'could be described as a two-step procedural obligation',[110] which applies not only to industrial activities, but 'generally to proposed activities which may have a significant adverse impact in a transboundary context', in particular, on a shared resource.[111] It derives from the State's obligation to exercise due diligence in preventing significant transboundary harm[112] and must be fulfilled before embarking on any such activity.[113]

First, the State must ascertain whether the activity entails a risk of significant transboundary harm, on the basis of an objective evaluation of all the relevant circumstances.[114] This can be done, for instance, by way of a preliminary assessment of the risk posed by the activity.[115] The second step of the obligation is only triggered if a risk of significant transboundary harm is indeed found to exist: in that case, the State must then carry out an environmental impact assessment—or EIA—to confirm whether the risk is real and, if so, to evaluate its nature and scope.[116] That obligation, held the Court, 'is a continuous one, and … monitoring of the project's effects on the environment shall be undertaken, where necessary, throughout the life of the project'.[117]

The Court clarified the interplay between domestic law and international law in this respect. In particular, it made clear that the domestic law of the State contemplating the activity plays no role in the determination of the existence of the obligation to carry out an EIA. In particular, the existence of an emergency exemption from the obligation to carry out an EIA under domestic law is irrelevant when it comes to determining whether a State is under an obligation to carry out such assessment

---

[110] President Abraham's 2016 speech to the Sixth Committee, above n 10, p. 7.

[111] *Certain Activities; Construction of a Road* (Merits), above n 36, pp. 706–707, para 104.

[112] Ibid.

[113] For the requirement to fulfil this obligation before even starting the contemplated activity, see in particular p. 723, para 161.

[114] *Certain Activities; Construction of a Road* (Merits), above n 36, pp. 706–707, para 104 and p. 720, para 153.

[115] Ibid., p. 720, para 154.

[116] Ibid., pp. 706–707, para 104 and p. 720, para 153.

[117] Ibid., pp. 722–723, para 161; *Pulp Mills* (Judgment), above n 53, pp. 83–84, para 205. On that point, it is worth noting that, in its judgment in the case concerning the *Gabčíkovo-Nagymaros Project,* the Court had already referred to the growing 'awareness of the vulnerability of the environment and the recognition that environmental risks have to be assessed on a continuous basis'. See *Gabčíkovo-Nagymaros* (Judgment), above n 75, p. 67, para 112.

under international law.[118] However, the judgment left open the question whether there is, under international law, an emergency exemption from the obligation to carry out an EIA.[119]

In cases where the State is indeed under an obligation to carry out an EIA, it is for that State 'to determine in its domestic legislation or in the authorization process for the project, the specific content of the environmental impact assessment required in each case, having regard to the nature and magnitude of the proposed development and its likely adverse impact on the environment as well as to the need to exercise due diligence in conducting such an assessment'.[120]

As mentioned above, customary international law recognizes the existence of another type of procedural obligation in this context, namely an obligation to notify and consult. This obligation only arises if the EIA confirms that there is a risk of significant transboundary harm and if the State nevertheless plans to go ahead with the activity. In this case, the State will be required 'to notify, and consult in good faith with the potentially affected State, where that is necessary to determine the appropriate measures to prevent or mitigate that risk.'[121]

The 2015 Judgment underscores that, when a State has violated its procedural obligations as defined above, a Court's declaration to this effect may constitute an appropriate measure of satisfaction.[122]

2.6.3.3 Remaining Uncertainties as to the Scope of States' Obligations under Customary International Law Concerning Transboundary Harm

So far, the ICJ has only been seized of cases were the activities said to be dangerous for the environment were carried out by the States themselves. In the *Pulp Mills* case, Argentina was referring to the negative environmental effects of the authorization, construction and future commissioning of two pulp mills by the Uruguayan State. In the *Certain Activities* case, Costa Rica reproached Nicaragua with conducting works—notably dredging of the San Juan River—in violation of its international obligations, and at the heart of the case concerning the *Construction of a Road along the San Juan River* were construction works carried out by Costa Rica along the border separating the territories of the two countries.

While the Court's jurisprudence leaves no doubt about the fact that both the substantive and the procedural obligations identified above apply in cases where the

---

118 *Certain Activities; Construction of a Road* (Merits), above n 36, pp. 721–722, para 157.

119 As the Court considered that such emergency was not constituted in the case, it did not need to address that question. See para 159 of the Judgment.

120 *Certain Activities; Construction of a Road* (Merits), above n 36, pp. 706–707, paras 104 and pp. 721–722, para 157; *Pulp Mills* (Judgment), above n 53, pp. 83-84, para 205.

121 *Certain Activities; Construction of a Road* (Merits), above n 36, pp. 706–707, paras 104 and p. 724, para 168.

122 Ibid., pp. 738–739, para 224.

State embarks on public works, the question whether the same obligations exist with respect to activities carried out by private entities was never raised before the Court which, therefore, did not address it.

On this point, it must be noted that, on its face, the scope of the substantive obligation, as defined by the Court, seems broad enough to apply to such activities. Indeed, in the Court's words,'[a] State is ... obliged to use all the means at its disposal in order to avoid *activities which take place in its territory, or in any area under its jurisdiction*, causing significant damage to the environment of another State'.[123]

However, the wording used by the Court when it comes to the procedural obligations appears more restrictive. In the words of the Court, '*a State must, before embarking on an activity* having the potential adversely to affect the environment of another State, ascertain if there is a risk of significant transboundary harm, which would trigger the requirement to carry out an EIA'.[124] Moreover, the Court explained that '[t]he obligation in question rests on the State pursuing the activity'.[125] Similarly, the Court referred to an obligation to notify and consult incumbent on 'a State planning an activity' that carries a risk.[126]

The question whether a State would be under any procedural obligation with respect to activities carried out by private entities on its territory was not at issue in the *Certain Activities* and the *Road* cases[127] and the answer to that question seems to remain open. Interestingly, the Inter-American Court of Human Rights, referring to the ICJ's judgment in the joined cases, indicated that the obligation to carry out an environmental impact assessment when there is a risk of significant harm 'rests with the State that plans to implement the activity or under whose jurisdiction it will be implemented'.[128] According to the Inter-American Court, this obligation 'is independent of whether a project is being implemented directly by the State or by private individuals'.[129]

2.6.4 Clarification of the Principles Applicable to Compensation for Environmental Damage

In its Judgment in the *Certain Activities* and the *Road* cases, the Court found that Nicaragua had the obligation to compensate Costa Rica for material damages caused

[123] Ibid., pp. 711–712, para 118 (emphasis added).

[124] Ibid., pp. 706–707, para 104 (emphasis added)

[125] Ibid., p. 720, para 153.

[126] Ibid., p. 724, para 168.

[127] Note that this question was never raised before the Court.

[128] Inter-American Court of Human Rights, Advisory Opinion, 15 November 2017, oc-23/17: 'The environment and human rights', para 158.

[129] Ibid., para 160.

by its unlawful activities on Costa Rican territory.[130] Since the unlawful activities were carried out by Nicaragua in Costa Rican territory, in violation of the latter's territorial sovereignty, the harm caused to Costa Rica was not a transboundary harm and as a result, the question whether Nicaragua's activities had caused *significant* damage to Costa Rica was not at stake; any material damage caused gave rise to compensation. The Court settled the question of compensation in a judgment issued on 2 February 2018.[131]

In these proceedings, Costa Rica claimed, on the one hand, compensation for costs and expenses allegedly incurred as a result of Nicaragua's activities on Costa Rican territory. On the other hand, it also claimed compensation for environmental damage resulting from such activities.[132] It is the first time that the ICJ was called upon to adjudicate a claim for compensation for this kind of damage and the judgment significantly clarified the applicable legal principles.[133]

In the judgment, the Court recalled the obligation to make full reparation for the damage caused by a wrongful act[134] and reaffirmed that compensation may be an appropriate form of reparation, 'particularly in those cases where restitution is materially impossible or unduly burdensome'.[135] It warned, however, that compensation 'should not have a punitive or exemplary character'.[136]

The 2018 judgment confirms that awarding compensation requires the Court to ascertain, firstly, whether a damage exists, secondly, what the extent of such damage

---

[130] *Certain Activities; Construction of a Road* (Merits), above n 36, p. 740, para 229(5)(a). In para 229(5)(b), the Court decided that, 'failing agreement between the Parties on [the] matter within 12 months from the date of this Judgment, the question of compensation due to Costa Rica will, at the request of one of the Parties, be settled by the Court'.

[131] *Certain Activities Carried Out by Nicaragua in the Border Area (Costa Rica v Nicaragua)*, Compensation, Judgment, ICJ Reports 2018, p. 15 (*Certain Activities* (Compensation)).

[132] Ibid., p. 27, para 36.

[133] During the oral hearings in the reparations phase of the case concerning *Armed Activities on the Territory of the Congo*, held in April 2021, the Parties referred to the findings of the Court in the *Certain Activities* case when discussing the DRC's claim for compensation in respect of the prejudice caused to its natural resources by Uganda. In this case, the DRC referred to the climate impact of deforestation as well as to the resulting damage to biodiversity and to the habitat of animal species as part of its claim concerning the prejudice to its natural resources. The Applicant also referred to the damage caused to its fauna, in particular through the killing of animals and the harming of their habitat in Congolese national parks. In its Memorial, filed in September 2016, the DRC had assessed the damage to its fauna by reference to the commercial value of the animal species concerned; the Applicant had clarified, however, that it was 'not … claiming a commercial value *as such*, but … using that value in order to assess the ecological and economic injury suffered by the DRC' (see para 5.153-5.154 of the Memorial of the DRC on the question of reparations (emphasis in the original)). Note that Uganda challenges the fact that the DRC's claims concerning deforestation and damage to fauna fall within the scope of the Court's judgment on the merits and maintains that, in any event, these claims are unfounded and must be rejected. The case is currently under deliberation.

[134] *Certain Activities* (Compensation), above n 131, p. 26, para 30.

[135] Ibid., para 31.

[136] Ibid.

is—if it does indeed exist—and thirdly, whether there is a direct and certain causal nexus between the wrongful act and the injury suffered.[137] Finally, it requires the Court to assign a monetary value to the damage caused.[138] These requirements, which were identified by reference to the Court's jurisprudence in compensation cases involving damages unrelated to the environment, were found equally applicable to claims for compensation for environmental damage. The ICJ therefore clarified that the environmental nature of a damage does not alter the legal principles applicable to compensation. The Court, however, gave specifics related to environmental damage when it comes to applying those principles.[139]

2.6.4.1 The Recognition of Different Types of Damage

The 2018 judgment shows that, in case of environmental damage, compensation is not only due for expenses incurred by the injured State as a consequence of a damage caused to the environment; it is also due for damage caused to the environment, in and of itself.[140] The Court thereby clarified that the impairment or loss of the ability of the environment to provide goods and services can be compensated under international law.[141]

In that regard, it is apparent from the Court's reasoning that, in cases where damage was caused to the environment, two types of situations may arise: in some cases, natural recovery is sufficient to return an environment to the state in which it was before the damage occurred, and in others, natural recovery is not sufficient, and active restoration measures are instead required. The Court specified that compensation for environmental damage may therefore include, on the one hand, indemnification for the impairment or loss of environmental goods and services in the period prior to recovery, and, on the other hand, payment for the restoration of the damaged environment.[142]

2.6.4.2 The Evaluation of Environmental Damage

With regard to the extent of the environmental damage, the Court specified that 'the absence of adequate evidence as to the extent of material damage will not, in all situations, preclude an award of compensation for that damage.'[143] In this regard, it cited an arbitral decision in which the tribunal, referring to situations in which 'the tort itself is of such nature as to preclude the ascertainment of the amount of

[137] Ibid., p. 26, para 32.

[138] Ibid.

[139] See also Chap. 18.

[140] *Certain Activities* (Compensation), above n 131, p. 28, para 41.

[141] Ibid., para 42.

[142] Ibid., pp. 28–29, paras 42–43.

[143] Ibid., pp. 26–27, para 35.

damages with certainty', indicated that 'while the damages may not be determined by mere speculation or guess, it will be enough if the evidence show the extent of the damages as a matter of just and reasonable inference'.[144]

2.6.4.3 The Establishment of Causation in Case of Environmental Damage

With respect to causation, the Court observed that particular issues may arise in cases of alleged environmental damage. It referred, as examples, to the possibility of a damage due to several concurrent causes, or to cases in which the state of science regarding the causal link between the wrongful act and the damage may be uncertain. The Court stated that such difficulties must be addressed 'as and when they arise in light of the facts of the case at hand and the evidence presented to the Court'.[145] It made clear that 'ultimately, it is for the Court to decide whether there is a sufficient causal nexus between the wrongful act and the injury suffered'.[146]

2.6.4.4 The Valuation of Environmental Damage

Finally, in order to determine the amount of compensation appropriate in a given case, the damage caused to the injured party must be valuated.[147] In other words, a monetary value must be assigned to it. This logically and necessarily applies in cases of environmental damage; yet, for obvious reasons, assigning a monetary value to this kind of damage may prove difficult. In that regard, the Court noted that 'international law does not prescribe any specific method of valuation for the purposes of compensation for environmental damage'.[148] It added that such a valuation must be made 'tak[ing] into account the specific circumstances and characteristics of each case'. What matters, said the Court, is to have recourse to elements that 'offer a reasonable basis for valuation'.[149]

The relevance of the findings of the Court with respect to the payment required for compensation for restoration measures was limited to the case at hand. The Court, however, made interesting findings with respect to the compensation due for the impairment or loss of the environmental goods and services of the impacted area in the period prior to recovery; those will certainly serve as a frame of reference in future cases involving issues of compensation for environmental damage.

The judgment demonstrates in particular that, in some instances, it may be appropriate to approach the valuation of environmental damage 'from the perspective of

---

[144] Ibid., referring to *Trail Smelter Arbitration*, Award, 11 March 1941, 3 RIAA 1905, p. 1920.

[145] *Certain Activities* (Compensation), above n 131, p. 26, para 34.

[146] Ibid.

[147] See also Chap. 17.

[148] *Certain Activities* (Compensation), above n 131, p. 31, para 52.

[149] Ibid.

the ecosystem as a whole, by adopting an overall assessment of the impairment or loss of environmental goods and services prior to recovery, rather than attributing values to specific categories of environmental goods and services and estimating recovery periods for each of them'.[150] And indeed, an overall approach was deemed appropriate in the context of the *Certain Activities* case for several reasons. While those were specific to the case under consideration, they could prove relevant in other cases too.

First, a damage to one particular type of environmental good or service in one area may cause damage to many other goods and services in that same area; an overall valuation allows account to be taken of the correlation between the harms caused.[151] Secondly, in some areas the environmental goods and services provided are not only extremely important, they are also 'closely interlinked'; this was the case in respect of the protected wetland affected in the *Certain Activities* case, in the words of the Court one of 'the most diverse and productive ecosystems in the world'.[152] Implicit in the Court's reasoning is the idea that a more global consequential damage to the environment may result from the impairment of one or more categories of environmental goods and services in such an area; an overall valuation can account for that reality. Thirdly, in the view of the Court, an overall valuation allows 'to take into account the capacity of the damaged area for natural regeneration', without having to establish a single recovery period for all the affected environmental goods and services—an exercise which it said cannot be achieved in situations where various environmental goods and services require a different amount of time to return to their pre-damage condition.[153]

Of course, valuating environmental harm will only become necessary if it is established that such harm has indeed occurred. The presence of the above mentioned elements does not therefore relieve the Applicant from the obligation to establish that environmental damage has occurred. The 2018 Judgment shows that, even when an overall valuation of the damage is appropriate, the different categories of environmental goods and services for which an impairment has been established will all be taken into account in the process.[154]

2.7 Conclusion

This chapter has focused on the capacity of the ICJ to deal with cases relating to the protection of the environment and on the contribution of the jurisprudence developed by the Court in the field. It has shown, in particular, that the ICJ has played a pivotal role in clarifying the relevant rules of general international law,

---

[150] Ibid., p. 37, para 78.

[151] Ibid., paras 79 and p. 38, para 82.

[152] Ibid., p. 37, para 80.

[153] Ibid., p. 38, paras 81–82.

[154] Ibid., pp. 38–38, paras 84–86.

which will certainly guide States in their action and facilitate the peaceful settlement of future environmental disputes.

The Court's role with respect to the protection of the environment is destined to become even more important as States' environmental concerns keep growing. A dispute involving key issues concerning the law of international watercourse and the protection of the environment has already been submitted to the Court, which awaits a pronouncement.[155] Moreover, many questions that have not yet reached the Court might do so in the future. For instance, the question of the emergence of obligations *erga omnes* in the field of environmental protection has caused a flurry of academic writing.[156] Specific issues might also arise in relation to the reparation for damage resulting from a breach of a State's obligation not to cause significant transboundary harm, since in such a case only one part of environmental damage, beyond a certain threshold, would result from an internationally wrongful act. The ICJ will address these issues if and as they are submitted to it; in doing so, the Court will be able to draw on its long and proven track record to tackle and resolve those challenges.

References

Abraham R (2016) Presentation of the International Court of Justice over the Last Ten Years. Journal of International Dispute Settlement 7:297-307

Dupuy P-M, Viñuales JE (2018) International Environmental Law. Cambridge University Press, Cambridge

Fitzmaurice M (2013) The International Court of Justice and International Environmental Law. In: Tams CJ, Sloan J (eds) The Development of International Law by the International Court of Justice. Oxford University Press, Oxford, pp 353-374

International Court of Justice (2019) Handbook. https://www.icj-cij.org/public/files/publications/handbook-of-the-court-en.pdf. Accessed 21 January 2022

Mayer B (2018) The International Law on Climate Change. Cambridge University Press, Cambridge

Mbengue MM (2016) Scientific Fact-finding at the International Court of Justice: An Appraisal in the Aftermath of the Whaling Case. Leiden Journal of International Law 29:529-550

---

[155] The case concerning the *Status and Use of the Waters of the Silala*, introduced by Chile against Bolivia on 6 June 2016, is now ready for hearing. In its Application, Chile requests the Court, *inter alia,* to adjudge and declare that 'Bolivia has an obligation to take all appropriate measures to prevent and control pollution and other forms of harm to Chile resulting from its activities in the vicinity of the Silala River' as well as 'to cooperate and to provide Chile with timely notification of planned measures which may have an adverse effect on shared water resources, to exchange data and information and to conduct where appropriate an environmental impact assessment, in order to enable Chile to evaluate the possible effects of such planned measures'. Bolivia formulated counter-claims, the admissibility of which Chile did not object to (see the Court's Order of 18 June 2019 fixing time-limits for the submission by Chile of an additional pleading related solely to the counter-claims).

[156] See, for example, Dupuy and Viñuales 2018, pp. 52–53; Fitzmaurice 2013, pp. 357–358; Peel and Sands 2018, pp. 158-159. See also Wojcikiewicz Almeida 2019, pp. 163–188, which discusses the link between community interests, *erga omnes* obligations and third-party intervention before the ICJ.

McCaffrey SC (2018) Environmental Law and Freshwater Ecosystems. In: Sobenes E, Samson B (eds) Nicaragua before the International Court of Justice. Impacts on International Law. Springer, Cham, pp 347-367

McLaughhlin Mitchell S, Owsiak AP (2018) The International Court of Justice. In: Howard RM, Randazzo KA (eds) Routledge handbook of judicial behavior. Routledge, New York, pp 445–467

Peel J, Sands Ph (2018) Principles of International Environmental Law. Cambridge University Press, Cambridge

Sands Ph (2016) Climate Change and the Rule of Law: Adjudicating the Future in International Law. Journal of Environmental Law 28:19-35

Shaw MN (2016) Rosenne's Law and Practice of the International Court: 1920-2015. Brill Nijhoff, Leiden and Boston

Tomka P (2013a) Speech to the Sixty-Eighth Session of the General Assembly of the United Nations, 31 October 2013. https://www.icj-cij.org/public/files/press-releases/2/17672.pdf. Accessed 21 January 2022

Tomka P (2013b) Inaugural Hilding Eek Memorial Lecture at the Stockholm Centre For International Law And Justice: 'The Rule of Law and the Role of the International Court of Justice in World Affairs'. https://www.icj-cij.org/public/files/press-releases/8/17848.pdf. Accessed 21 January 2022

Wojcikiewicz Almeida P (2019) International Procedural Regulation in the Common Interest: The Role of Third-Party Intervention and *Amicus Curiae* before the ICJ. The Law & Practice of International Court and Tribunals 18:163-188

Anne Coulon Public international lawyer, Associate Member at Temple Garden Chambers.

Chapter 3
International Tribunal for the Law of the Sea

Lan Ngoc Nguyen

Contents

Abstract While the United Nations Convention on the Law of the Sea (UNCLOS) places significant emphasis on the protection of the marine environment, the interpretation of the relevant rules under UNCLOS and the application of general environmental principles to the marine environment are not always straightforward. The role of judicial bodies in clarifying these rules to protect and preserve the marine environment is therefore especially important. This chapter aims to examine the contribution of the International Tribunal for the Law of the Sea ('ITLOS' or 'the Tribunal') to the protection of the marine environment. To that end, the chapter first examines the procedural rules that are relevant to disputes relating to the marine environment. It then analyses how ITLOS has interpreted and applied important principles of environmental law in the context of the marine environment in its jurisprudence. Based on these findings, the chapter assesses the strengths and weaknesses of ITLOS in contributing to the protection of the marine environment. The chapter concludes that

L. N. Nguyen (✉)
Faculty of Law, Economics and Governance, Utrecht University School of Law, Netherlands
Institute for the Law of the Sea, Utrecht, The Netherlands
e-mail: l.n.nguyen@uu.nl

Centre for Water, Oceans and Sustainability Law, Utrecht University, Newtonlaan 201, 3584 BH Utrecht, The Netherlands

E. Sobenes et al. (eds.), *The Environment Through the Lens of International Courts and Tribunals*, https://doi.org/10.1007/978-94-6265-507-2_3

the Tribunal's examination of important environmental principles lends an authoritative voice to endorsing their importance in the context of the marine environment and helps to enrich the case law that deals with them, thus providing guidance for States in the implementation of the principles. At the same time, one should be reasonable in what can be expected of ITLOS in terms of its contributions to the protection of the marine environment due to the inherent jurisdictional limitations upon dispute settlement bodies.

Keywords International Tribunal for the Law of the Sea (ITLOS) · marine environment · arovisional measures · advisory proceedings · precautionary principle · duty to cooperate · duty to conduct environmental impact assessment

3.1 Introduction

The protection of the marine environment assumes a special place under the United Nations Convention on the Law of the Sea ('UNCLOS' or 'the Convention'). Not only does the Convention prescribe States' rights and obligations regarding the conservation of marine resources in the maritime zones falling under their jurisdiction, it also devotes an entire Part XII to the 'Protection and Preservation of the Marine Environment'. However, while innovative, Part XII provides a general framework for the protection of the marine environment, and focuses primarily on prevention of marine pollution. Due to the zonal approach to maritime regulation that UNCLOS adopts, other aspects of the protection of the marine environment are not contained in Part XII but found in other parts of the Convention, for example, the conservation of marine resources in Part V on Exclusive Economic Zone (EEZ) or protection of the marine environment in the seabed in areas beyond national jurisdiction in Part XI on the Area. As a result, while UNCLOS gives considerable attention to the protection of the marine environment, the application of the relevant rules is not always straightforward. Against that background, the role of judicial bodies in clarifying these rules in order to ensure and promote the goal of UNCLOS to protect and preserve the marine environment is especially important. As stated by the President of the Third Conference on the Law of the Sea, '[e]ffective dispute settlement would also be the guarantee that the substance and intention within the legislative and language of the convention will be interpreted both consistently and equitably.'[1]

This chapter aims to examine the contribution of the International Tribunal for the Law of the Sea ('ITLOS' or 'the Tribunal') to the protection of the marine environment. The chapter is structured as follows. Section 3.2 provides a brief overview of the position of ITLOS within the dispute settlement system of UNCLOS and of the relevant procedural rules that may have a bearing on the ability of ITLOS to hear and decide on disputes relating to the marine environment. Section 3.3 then analyses the cases decided by ITLOS that relate to different aspects of marine environmental

---

[1] Nordquist 1985, p. 10.

protection—focusing particularly on how ITLOS has interpreted and applied important principles of environmental law in the context of the marine environment, then offers some observations regarding the Tribunal's interpretation and application of these principles. Section 3.4 takes stock of the ITLOS' jurisprudence and assesses its strengths and weaknesses in dealing with environmental disputes. Section 3.5 concludes.

3.2 The Relevant Procedural Rules of ITLOS

Article 287 of UNCLOS provides for the competence of four dispute settlement bodies, namely the International Court of Justice (ICJ), ITLOS and two ad hoc tribunals, one constituted under Annex VII and one under Annex VIII. ITLOS is thus only one of the choice of procedures available for dispute settlement under UNCLOS. Similar to the tribunals mentioned, under Article 288(1), ITLOS has the jurisdiction to settle disputes that 'concern the interpretation and application of the Convention'. This article thus sets the parameters, in terms of the subject-matter (jurisdiction *rationae materiae)*, within which UNCLOS tribunals are to operate. However, ITLOS's compulsory jurisdiction comes only in Section 2 of Part XV, following Section 1 which allows States to adopt other means of dispute settlement of their choice. It is also subjected to the limitations and exclusions included in Section 3. Space does not allow for a detailed elaboration of all the conditions contained in these two sections. Section 3.2.1 will therefore only highlight those provisions that may impact ITLOS' ability to deal with issues relating to the protection of the marine environment. Furthermore, although ITLOS is only one of the options which State parties can select under UNCLOS, it still has a special place in the Convention for several reasons. In the context of marine environmental protection, ITLOS' residual jurisdiction for provisional measures and its power to give advisory opinions are of particular relevance. The rules regarding ITLOS' jurisdiction in these two types of proceedings will thus be examined in Sect. 3.2.2. Finally, Sect. 3.2.3 provides some remarks relating to applicable law.

3.2.1 Jurisdiction in Contentious Proceedings

As mentioned, the compulsory jurisdiction of ITLOS is restricted by the conditions contained in Section 1 and Section 3 of Part XV of UNCLOS. The most relevant articles for the purposes of this chapter are Article 281 under Section 1 and Article 297(3) under Section 3. It should be noted that ITLOS has not had the opportunity to examine these articles in great detail in its case law. Instead, it is Annex VII arbitral tribunals that have shed light on their interpretation and application. Similarly, as will become clear below, ITLOS has not specifically dealt with the protection of the marine environment in any contentious proceedings. Thus, the impact of the procedural rules analysed below on the way ITLOS deals with marine environmental protection cannot be verified in practice. However, because the tribunals under Article 287 all operate under the same jurisdictional framework of Part XV, an exposition of the relevant procedural rules is still pertinent as the interpretation of this article may have important implications for ITLOS.

Article 281 essentially provides that, when the parties have agreed to another means of dispute settlement, UNCLOS tribunals can only exercise jurisdiction if the parties have not been able to settle the dispute between them using the means agreed *and* the parties have not agreed to exclude further procedures, including recourse to the UNCLOS dispute settlement procedures. This second requirement of Article 281 was at issue in the *Southern Bluefin Tuna* arbitration.[2] Japan in this case argued that the jurisdiction of the Annex VII tribunal could not be triggered because the parties had already agreed to use the dispute settlement procedures under Article 16 of the Convention on the Conservation of Southern Bluefin Tuna (CCSBT) which excluded recourse to UNCLOS dispute settlement procedures.[3] The majority in *Southern Bluefin Tuna* agreed with Japan, holding that although Article 16 of the CCSBT did not expressly exclude the applicability of the procedures of Section 2 Part XV of UNCLOS, 'the absence of an express exclusion of any procedures in Article 16 is not decisive'.[4] What was important in the tribunal's view was the existence of an express obligation to continue to seek resolution of the dispute in paragraph 2 of Article 16 by the means listed in para 1.[5] This meant that the existence of any list of dispute settlement methods and a commitment to resolving the dispute by peaceful means would suffice as an agreement to exclude resort to UNCLOS procedures under Article 281.[6]

In 2016, the majority's interpretation of Article 281 in *Southern Bluefin Tuna* was explicitly rejected by the *South China Sea* arbitral tribunal when deciding whether Article 281 applied to exclude the tribunal's jurisdiction to hear the dispute brought by the Philippines against China concerning the South China Sea, given that there were several instruments containing the parties' agreement to settle their disputes by a variety of peaceful means.[7] The tribunal concluded that 'Article 281 requires some clear statement of exclusion of further procedures'.[8] The *South China Sea* tribunal's decision meant that the bar for the invocation of Article 281 to exclude the jurisdiction of UNCLOS tribunals has now been set relatively high—an explicit exclusion of resort to UNCLOS procedures would be needed.

---

[2] *Southern Bluefin Tuna Case (Australia and New Zealand v Japan)*, Award on Jurisdiction and Admissibility, 4 August 2000, 39 ILM 1359.

[3] Ibid., para 34.

[4] Ibid., para 57.

[5] Ibid.

[6] Churchill 2006, p. 403.

[7] *South China Sea Arbitration (Philippines v China)*, Award on Jurisdiction and Admissibility, 27 August 2013, PCA Case No 2013–19.

[8] Ibid., para 223.

It is clear that in the aftermath of the two arbitrations, there exists a divergence in the interpretation of Article 281. This divergence results in a lack of clarity regarding the effect of Article 281 on the jurisdiction of UNCLOS tribunals, including ITLOS, to deal with issues relating to marine environmental protection which are also regulated in other conventions or treaties that contain their own dispute settlement provisions. Given the existence of various international treaties besides UNCLOS which meet these two requirements, it is open to question the extent to which Article 281 will limit the competence of ITLOS to deal with disputes concerning the protection of the marine environment that may also arise under other international treaties.

Turning to Article 297(3) which excludes disputes concerning coastal States' sovereign rights over living resources in the EEZ from the compulsory jurisdiction of UNCLOS tribunals, the complicated design of UNCLOS regarding fisheries competences means that the scope of application of Article 297(3) is not always clear. The decisions of Annex VII arbitral tribunals have clarified several aspects of this provision, two of which are worth mentioning. First, according to the arbitral tribunal in *Chagos MPA*, Article 297(3) excludes disputes relating to procedural obligations, including the obligations to consult and coordinate pursuant to Articles 63, 64 and 194 of UNCLOS and Article 7 of the 1995 UN Fish Stocks Agreement.[9] Second, the tribunal in *Chagos MPA* confirmed that the limitations contained in Article 297(3) still applied to the straddling fish stocks that were found in the EEZ of the coastal State.[10] While the tribunal acknowledged the shortcomings of a jurisdictional separation of disputes relating to fisheries in the EEZ and those in the high seas, this was the approach adopted by the State Parties, to which the tribunal stayed faithful. This firm statement on the applicability of Article 297(3) to straddling stocks may have important implications for disputes arising from the UN Fish Stocks Agreement, for example from Article 7 on the compatibility between conservation and management measures for areas under national jurisdiction and beyond.

The interpretation of Article 297(3) in case law shows that it has the potential to restrict the ability of ITLOS to deal with issues relating to the protection of marine living resources found in the EEZ. In particular, ITLOS will not have the competence to examine whether procedural obligations relating to the conservation of marine living resources insofar as they are found in the EEZ. ITLOS will also not be able to deal with disputes relating to straddling stocks.

3.2.2 Provisional Measures and Advisory Proceedings

With regards to the jurisdiction of ITLOS in provisional measures proceedings, the requirements for prescribing provisional measures stipulated under Article 290 do not in general differ to a great extent from those of the ICJ or other courts, with two noteworthy exceptions. First, under Article 290(1), ITLOS may prescribe provisional

---

[9] *Chagos Marine Protected Area Arbitration (Mauritius v United Kingdom)*, Award, 18 March 2015, PCA Case No 2011-03, 21 RIAA 359, para 534.

[10] Ibid., para 301.

measures not only to preserve the rights of the parties as normally seen in other courts, but also to 'prevent serious harm to the marine environment'. This second basis for ITLOS to prescribe provisional measures is quite unique, and offers the Tribunal the opportunity to contribute to the protection of the environment already from an earlier phase of the proceedings. Second, whereas for most other courts, a request for provisional measures would normally be brought before the body which will eventually hear the merits of the case, under Article 290(5), ITLOS has the competence to prescribe provisional measures for cases for which the parties have chosen an Annex VII Arbitral Tribunal to hear the case, pending the latter's constitution. This residual jurisdiction again allows ITLOS to play a greater role in provisional measures proceedings, particularly those concerned with 'preventing serious harm to the marine environment' as mentioned above.

Turning to its advisory jurisdiction, ITLOS as the permanent court established under UNCLOS has the jurisdiction to give advisory opinions. However, unlike the ICJ, the advisory function is not explicitly conferred upon ITLOS as a whole but only on the Seabed Dispute Chamber ('SDC' or 'the Chamber'). According to Article 191 of UNCLOS, the SDC is mandated to 'give advisory opinions at the request of the Assembly or the Council on legal questions arising within the scope of their activities'. The SDC has indeed exercised this advisory jurisdiction in one instance in the *Advisory Opinion on Activities in the Area*.[11]

More controversial has been the question regarding whether ITLOS as a full tribunal also has jurisdiction to give advisory opinions. This had been a topic of much debate in the scholarly community as UNCLOS does not explicitly provide for such jurisdiction as in the case of the SDC.[12] ITLOS finally resolved this issue in 2015 in the *Advisory Opinion on IUU Fishing*.[13] The request for the Advisory Opinion was brought by the Sub-Regional Fisheries Commission (SRFC) on the basis of the Convention on the Determination of the Minimal Conditions for Access and Exploitation of Marine Resources within the Maritime Areas under Jurisdiction of the Member States of the SRFC (MCA Convention). ITLOS founded its advisory jurisdiction on the basis of a combined reading of Article 288(1) of UNCLOS, Article 21 of ITLOS Statute and Article 138 of the Rules of Procedure of ITLOS. More specifically, ITLOS held that Article 21 of the ITLOS Statute, existing independently of Article 288 of the Convention,[14] allows the tribunals to exercise jurisdiction over not only 'disputes' and 'applications' but also 'all matters provided for in any other agreement which confers jurisdiction on the Tribunal'.[15] The words 'all matters' in ITLOS's view, 'must mean something more than only "disputes"' and

---

[11] ITLOS, *Responsibilities and obligations of States with respect to Activities in the Area*, Advisory Opinion, 1 February 2011, ITLOS Reports 2011, p. 10.

[12] See for example Kim 2010, p. 1; Jesus 2006, p. 39; Rosenne 1998, p. 487; You 2008, p. 360; Ndiaye 2010, p. 565.

[13] ITLOS, *Request for Advisory Opinion submitted by the Sub-Regional Fisheries Commission*, Advisory Opinion, 2 April 2015, ITLOS Reports 2015, p. 4.

[14] Ibid., para 52.

[15] Ibid., para 4.

'that something more must include advisory opinions if specifically provided for in any other agreement'.[16] ITLOS also found that 'the prerequisites that need to be satisfied before the Tribunal can exercise its advisory jurisdiction' under Article 138 of the Rules were further met in that instance.[17]

ITLOS' decision to establish advisory jurisdiction despite the lack of express authorisation under UNCLOS has faced much opposition from States—as evident in the proceedings of the Advisory Opinion on IUU Fishing, and scholarly criticism.[18] However, establishment of the full ITLOS tribunal's advisory jurisdiction has certainly opened a wider door for ITLOS to play a more active role in developing the law of the sea, including issues relating to the protection of the marine environment. It is worth noting that as ITLOS' power to render advisory opinions is dependent on the authorisation of 'any other agreement', it is possible that ITLOS may be requested to address questions that go beyond the scope of UNCLOS. In fact, on 31 October 2021, Antigua and Barbuda and Tuvalu signed an agreement which establishes a Commission of Small Island Developing States on Climate Change and International Law. This Commission is authorised to request an advisory opinion from ITLOS on the legal responsibility of States for carbon emissions, marine pollution, and rising sea levels. It is yet unclear how the specific questions will be formulated, but the first issue, for example, may well touch upon legal questions that are beyond the scope of UNCLOS. It remains to be seen whether and to what extent ITLOS will deal with them.

3.2.3 Applicable Law

While ITLOS' jurisdiction is limited to disputes that arise under the Convention, it must be acknowledged that there are tools available under UNCLOS that allow ITLOS to resort to other rules of international environmental law in interpreting UNCLOS provisions. Two provisions are worth highlighting.

The first is Article 293 on Applicable Law which allows the Tribunal to apply 'other rules of international law not incompatible with this Convention' in deciding cases before it. Article 293 has been used by ITLOS, for example in *M/V Saiga (No 2),* to expand its jurisdictional scope by bringing issues which were not provided for under UNCLOS into its jurisdictional ambit.[19] However, the arbitral tribunal in *MOX Plant* adopted an opposite understanding of the relationship between Articles 288(1) and 293. It held that 'there is a cardinal distinction between the scope of its jurisdiction under Article 288, para 1 of the Convention, on the one hand, and the law to be applied

---

[16] Ibid., para 56.

[17] Ibid., para 59.

[18] See for example Ruys and Soete 2016, p. 155; Lando 2016, p. 441.

[19] *M/V 'SAIGA' (No. 2) (Saint Vincent and the Grenadines v Guinea),* Judgment, 1 July 1999, ITLOS Reports 1999, p. 10, para 155.

by the Tribunal under Article 293 of the Convention on the other hand.'[20] The use of Article 293 is sometimes accompanied by reference to Article 31(3) of the Vienna Convention on the Law of Treaties (VCLT). In the *South China Sea Jurisdiction and Admissibility Award*, for example, the arbitral tribunal stated that although it did not have jurisdiction to decide on violations of the Convention on Biodiversity (CBD), it could consider the relevant provisions of the CBD for the purposes of interpreting the content and standard of Articles 192 and 194 of UNCLOS. The use of standards contained in external treaties for the purposes of interpreting provisions of UNCLOS, according to the tribunal, was made possible thanks to Article 293(1) UNCLOS on Applicable Law and Article 31(3) of the VCLT.[21]

The second provision related specifically to environmental issues is Article 297(1). The arbitral tribunal in *Chagos MPA* interpreted Article 297(1)(c) to allow UNCLOS tribunals to deal with disputes relating to international rules and standards for the protection and preservation of the marine environment that involve 'the contravention of legal instruments beyond the four corners of the Convention itself.'[22] According to the tribunal, this article thus serves as a *renvoi* to the sources of law beyond UNCLOS itself.[23]

The interpretation of the abovementioned articles potentially allows ITLOS to play an important role not only in the protection of the marine environment under UNCLOS, but also in ensuring that UNCLOS provisions relating to the protection of the environment develop in tandem with other rules of international law.

3.3 ITLOS Jurisprudence Concerning Marine Environmental Protection

To date, ITLOS has not had the opportunity to deal with the protection of the marine environment in any contentious proceedings, only in provisional measures and advisory opinion proceedings. Despite the limited number of cases, ITLOS' decisions have contributed to clarifying important principles under international environmental law, namely the precautionary principle, the duty to cooperate, and the obligation to conduct environmental impact assessment. This section will examine the ways in which ITLOS dealt with each of these principles and offer some observations concerning its interpretation and application of the principles.

---

[20] *The MOX Plant case (Ireland v United Kingdom)*, Order No. 3: Suspension of Proceedings on Jurisdiction and Merits, and Request for Further Provisional Measures, 24 June 2003, para 19.

[21] *South China Sea (Philippines v China)*, above n 7, para 176.

[22] *Chagos Marine Protected Area Arbitration (Mauritius v United Kingdom)*, above n 9, para 316.

[23] Ibid.

3.3.1 *The Precautionary Principle*

3.3.1.1 The Relevant Cases

The *Southern Bluefin Tuna* case was the first instance in which the precautionary principle was invoked before ITLOS. In this case, Australia and New Zealand alleged that Japan, by unilaterally designing and undertaking an experimental fishing programme, failed to comply with obligations to conserve and cooperate in the conservation of the Southern Bluefin Tuna (SBT) stock in accordance with, inter alia, the precautionary principle.[24] Pending the constitution of Annex VII arbitral tribunal, the Applicants requested that ITLOS prescribe provisional measures to ensure that 'the parties act consistently with the precautionary principle in fishing for SBT pending a final settlement of the dispute'.[25]

While the Applicants did not base their claims on any provisions of Part XII, ITLOS confirmed in the Order for provisional measures that 'the conservation of the living resources of the sea is an element in the protection and preservation of the marine environment'.[26] This paved the way for ITLOS to take into account environmental principles to deal with the conservation of living resources. The tribunal acknowledged that the SBT 'is severely depleted and is at its historically lowest levels and that this is a cause for serious biological concern'. [27] On this basis, it held that 'the parties should in the circumstances act with prudence and caution to ensure that effective conservation measures are taken to prevent serious harm to the stock of SBT'.[28] Most importantly, ITLOS held in paras 79 and 80, which deserve to be quoted in full, that:

> 79. Considering that there is scientific uncertainty regarding measures to be taken to conserve the stock of southern bluefin tuna and that there is no agreement among the parties as to whether the conservation measures taken so far have led to the improvement in the stock of southern bluefin tuna;
>
> 80. Considering that, although the Tribunal cannot conclusively assess the scientific evidence presented by the parties, it finds that measures should be taken as a matter of urgency to preserve the rights of the parties and to avert further deterioration of the southern bluefin tuna stock.[29]

---

[24] Australia and New Zealand asked ITLOS in their written pleadings to take into account 'the parties' obligations under general international law, in particular the precautionary principle'. See Request for the Prescription of Provisional Measures Submitted by New Zealand, para 1: www.itlos.org/fileadmin/itlos/documents/cases/case_no_3_4/request_new_zealand_eng.pdf Accessed 24 February 2020; Request for the Prescription of Provisional Measures Submitted by Australia, para 1: www.itlos.org/fileadmin/itlos/documents/cases/case_no_3_4/request_australia_eng.pdf Accessed 24 February 2020.

[25] *Southern Bluefin Tuna (New Zealand v Japan; Australia v Japan)*, Provisional Measures, 27 August 1999, ITLOS Reports 1999, p. 280, para 34.

[26] Ibid., para 70.

[27] Ibid., para 71.

[28] Ibid., para 77.

[29] Ibid., paras 79 and 80.

Although ITLOS did not explicitly refer to the precautionary principle, there are elements in these two paragraphs which signalled the application of this principle.[30] ITLOS highlighted the lack of scientific certainty regarding the measures to be taken and their effectiveness in conserving the stock, but nonetheless still decided to prescribe measures in order to prevent further deterioration to the stock. Coupled with the reference to 'caution and prudence', it does not seem difficult to conclude that ITLOS intended to apply the precautionary principle. In fact, the two paragraphs cited above show that the precautionary principle served as the main basis for the prescription of provisional measures in this case.

ITLOS, however, did not confirm the status of the precautionary principle as a rule of customary international law as contended by the Applicants. It is interesting to note that in Judge Treves' Separate Opinion, he argued that such a confirmation was not necessary,[31] as 'a precautionary approach seems to be inherent in the very notion of provisional measures.'[32] Judge Treves' reasoning implied that, in his view, the basis for the application of the precautionary principle was found in the Convention itself, particularly in the requirement of 'urgency' under Article 290(5). This view has received support from another scholar, who argues that the inclusion of the 'serious harm to the marine environment' as a basis for the prescription of provisional measures enhances the precautionary aspect of provisional measures.[33]

The precautionary principle also arose in *MOX Plant* concerning Ireland's challenge to the commission and operation of the MOX Plant by the UK.[34] In its Written Request, Ireland contended that the precautionary principle had attained the status of a customary international rule and, as such, it was binding on both parties.[35] In the context of a provisional measures proceeding before ITLOS, Ireland argued that the precautionary principle should inform the tribunal's assessment of the urgency of the measures that it was required to take in respect of the operation of the MOX plant.[36] The UK, on the other hand, maintained that due to the lack of proof and on the facts of this case, the precautionary principle had no application.[37]

ITLOS in this case adopted a more cautious approach when dealing with the precautionary principle than in *Southern Bluefin Tuna*. Despite both parties' reference to the legal status of the principle and to the insufficiency of scientific data, ITLOS

---

[30] Several judges confirmed in their separate and dissenting opinions that the prescription of the provisional measure was based upon the considerations of the precautionary principle. See *Southern Bluefin Tuna (New Zealand v Japan; Australia v Japan)*, above n 25, Sep. Op. Treves, para 8; Sep. Op. Laing, para 19; Sep. Op. Shearer, para 6.

[31] Ibid., Sep. Op. Judge Treves, para 9.

[32] Ibid.

[33] Foster 2013, p. 268.

[34] ITLOS, *MOX Plant (Ireland v United Kingdom)*, Provisional Measures, 3 December 2001, ITLOS Reports 2001, p. 95.

[35] Request for Provisional Measures and Statement of Case Submitted on Behalf of Ireland, para 97: www.itlos.org/fileadmin/itlos/documents/cases/case_no_10/request_ireland_e.pdf Accessed 24 February 2020.

[36] Ibid.

[37] *MOX Plant (Ireland v United Kingdom)*, above n 34, para 75.

did not address any of these issues in its Order. ITLOS rejected Ireland's request for provisional measures due to the lack of urgency of the situation required for provisional measures under Article 290(5).[38] However, in the Provisional Measures Order, the Tribunal still used the term 'prudence and caution' seen in *Southern Bluefin Tuna* in order to require the parties to cooperate 'in exchanging information concerning risks or effects of the operation of the MOX plant and in devising ways to deal with them'.[39] The use of 'prudence and caution' was not supported by any discussion, particularly on scientific uncertainty or risk of harm, thus it is unclear as to whether ITLOS actually intended to invoke the precautionary principle in this case. In any event, ITLOS' refusal to apply the precautionary principle to grant Ireland the requested provisional measures could be seen as a retreat from the strong endorsement that ITLOS had shown for the principle in *Southern Bluefin Tuna*. As argued by one commentator, the characteristics of the MOX Plant dispute suggested that it was a 'text book' example of a situation that would require the precautionary principle.[40] ITLOS, therefore, would seem to have missed an important opportunity to make a meaningful contribution to clarifying this increasingly important but still rather vague principle of environmental law.

In the *Land Reclamation* case concerning Malaysia's allegations that Singapore had violated UNCLOS by conducting land reclamation activities in the Straits of Johor, Malaysia also invoked the precautionary principle when requesting provisional measures.[41] Singapore, on the other hand, argued that there was no room to apply the precautionary principle in the case in question.[42] Similar to the approach taken in the *MOX Plant* case, ITLOS did not discuss the precautionary principle when considering Malaysia's allegations that Singapore's activities in the Straits of Johor could cause irreparable prejudice to Malaysia's rights or serious harm to the marine environment. Instead, ITLOS only recalled the familiar phrase 'prudence and caution' to require the parties to 'establish mechanisms for exchanging information and assessing the risks or effects of land reclamation works and devising ways to deal with them in the areas concerned'.[43] The use of the phrase 'prudence and caution' bore resemblance to that used in *MOX Plant*.

Finally, the *Advisory Opinion on Responsibilities and Obligations of States with respect to Activities in the Area* presented the occasion in which ITLOS came the closest to endorsing the status of the precautionary principle. The SDC was requested to answer three questions submitted by the International Seabed Authority (ISA) concerning the responsibilities, obligations and liability of UNCLOS States Parties with respect to the sponsorship of activities in the Area. Unlike previous cases in which the precautionary principle was invoked as a matter of customary international

[38] Ibid., para 81.

[39] Ibid., para 84.

[40] Stephens 2009, p. 234; McDorman 2001, p. 531.

[41] ITLOS, *Case Concerning Land Reclamation by Singapore in and around the Straits of Johor (Malaysia v Singapore)*, Provisional Measures, 8 October 2003, ITLOS Reports 2003, p. 10.

[42] Ibid., para 75.

[43] Ibid., para 99.

law, the precautionary principle is clearly stipulated in the Regulations on Prospecting and Exploration for Polymetallic Nodules in the Area (Nodules Regulations), and the Regulations on Prospecting and Exploration for Polymetallic Sulphides in the Area (Sulphides Regulations). These are binding instruments and are applicable to exploration activities in the Area.[44] As a result, the SDC in the *Advisory Opinion on Activities in the Area* found that the implementation of the precautionary approach as defined in these Regulations was a binding obligation on sponsoring States. [45] Although the general obligation to implement the precautionary principle already exists in the Sulphides Regulation, the SDC, in what could be described as an *obiter dictum*, went on to say that:

> [T]he precautionary approach has been incorporated into a growing number of international treaties and other instruments, many of which reflect the formulation of Principle 15 of the Rio Declaration. In the view of the Chamber, this has initiated a trend towards making this approach part of customary international law.[46]

Even though the SDC did not explicitly state that the principle was a customary rule, this statement came closer to accepting the customary nature of the principle than any other tribunals had, and have, to date.

The SDC also took the opportunity to shed some light on the meaning and application of this principle, albeit only in relation to the activities provided for in the Regulations. The Chamber explained that Principle 15 of the Rio Declaration contained two sentences, of which the second specified the scope of application of the precautionary principle. In particular, the second sentence of Principle 15 of the Rio Declaration set the scale of harm to 'serious or irreversible damage' and limited the measures to be taken to only 'cost-effective measures'.[47] Moreover, the Chamber also noted that the Rio Declaration also allowed for certain flexibility in the application of the principle, in light of the phrase 'applied by States according to their capabilities'.[48] The SDC interpreted this to mean that, in the context of the Advisory Opinion, 'the requirements for complying with the obligation to apply the precautionary approach may be stricter for the developed than for the developing sponsoring States'.[49] This statement created a link between the precautionary principle and the principle of 'common but differentiated responsibility' widely recognised under international environmental

---

[44] Regulations on Prospecting and Exploration for Polymetallic Nodules in the Area, ISBA/19/C/17 (amended) (22 July 2013); Regulations on Prospecting and Exploration for Polymetallic Sulphides in the Area, ISBA/16/C/L.5 (6 May 2010). Regulation 31, para 2 of the Nodules Regulations and Regulation 33, para 2 of the Sulphides Regulations require sponsoring States as well as the Authority to 'apply a precautionary approach, as reflected in Principle 15 of the Rio Declaration' in order 'to ensure effective protection for the marine environment from harmful effects which may arise from activities in the Area'. See *Responsibilities and obligations of States with respect to Activities in the Area,* above n 11, para 125.

[45] Ibid., para 127.

[46] Ibid., para 135.

[47] Ibid., para 128.

[48] Ibid., para 129.

[49] Ibid., para 161.

law.[50] In addition, the SDC also stated that 'the precautionary approach is also an integral part of the general obligation of due diligence of sponsoring States'.[51] This was the first time in which an international tribunal analysed the structure and meaning of the precautionary principle as contained in Principle 15 of the Rio Declaration in any detail, providing an important clarification of the meaning and application of this principle.

3.3.1.2 Some Observations Regarding the Precautionary Principle

A perusal of ITLOS' cases shows that ITLOS was the first tribunal to have applied the precautionary principle in *Southern Bluefin Tuna* in 1999, albeit without calling it by name. It should be noted that the precautionary principle is recognised in almost all fisheries instruments post-UNCLOS.[52] Such widespread recognition perhaps gave ITLOS the incentive to be more readily accepting of the precautionary principle in fisheries conservation cases, such as *Southern Bluefin Tuna,* as compared to marine pollution cases, such as *MOX Plant* or *Land Reclamation*. Even though ITLOS did not explicitly state that the precautionary principle had become part of customary international law, the SDC's view that there was now a trend towards making this approach part of customary law was the boldest acknowledgement of the principle by any international tribunal. ITLOS, therefore, can be said to be the forerunner in the adoption of the precautionary principle.

Notwithstanding ITLOS' acknowledgment of the precautionary principle, due to the fact that the principle has been dealt with mostly in provisional measure proceedings, the application of the precautionary principle seems to have been informed by the nature of these types of proceeding. In terms of the threshold for the severity of harm, ITLOS in *Southern Bluefin Tuna* read the gravity of harm contained in Article 290, i.e. 'serious harm', as the triggering point for the application of the precautionary principle. With regards to the burden of proof, the provisional measures cases all seem to indicate that ITLOS did not reverse the burden of proof. The applicants still bore the obligation to prove 'serious harm' to the environment when requesting precautionary measures from the respondents. However, it is arguable that, as Judge Wolfrum acknowledged in *MOX Plant*,[53] the reversal of the burden of proof was not undertaken in the case because ITLOS was only required to establish *prima facie* jurisdiction in provisional measures. Therefore, the refusal to reverse the burden

[50] Cullet 2015, p. 229.

[51] *Advisory Opinion on Activities in the Area,* above n 11, para 131.

[52] This has prompted the argument that even though precaution in fisheries management has yet to reach the status of customary international law, a new norm of marine living resources management is emerging. See Kaye 2001, p. 261.

[53] *MOX Plant (Ireland v United Kingdom)*, above n 34, Separate Opinion of Judge Wolfrum, para 3.

of proof in ITLOS case law was dictated by the exceptional nature of provisional proceedings.[54]

In the context of an advisory proceeding, the *Advisory Opinion on Activities in the Area* was among the first to clarify the link between the precautionary principle and several other environmental obligations. In earlier cases, namely *MOX Plant* and *Land Reclamation*, ITLOS already hinted at the link between the precautionary principle and procedural obligations, using 'prudence and caution' as the basis for prescribing provisional measures which were of a procedural nature, such as the duty to cooperate.[55] The SDC, however, expanded the relationship between the precautionary principle not only to the duty to cooperate, but also to the principle of 'common but differentiated responsibility' and due diligence. As ITLOS was only required to examine the precautionary principle in the abstract in an advisory proceeding, it did not elaborate more on the peculiarities of these links.

In short, ITLOS' decisions have added an authoritative voice to endorsing the status and applicability of the precautionary principle to marine environment protection under UNCLOS. ITLOS has also contributed to clarifying certain elements of the principle's normative content, although the contribution was limited by the nature of the proceedings in which the principle was examined.

3.3.2 Duty to Cooperate

3.3.2.1 The Relevant Cases

ITLOS had the opportunity to discuss the duty to cooperate in protecting the marine environment both in the context of prevention of marine pollution and conservation of marine living resources.

In relation to cooperation to prevent marine pollution, the duty to cooperate took centre stage in the *MOX Plant* and *Land Reclamation* cases. In *MOX Plant*, Ireland alleged that, inter alia, the UK breached its obligations under Articles 123 and 197.[56] Although ITLOS did not find that there was urgency requiring the provisional measure requested by Ireland, it still prescribed provisional measures requiring both parties to cooperate and enter into consultations regarding several issues. In one of the most important paragraphs of the Order, ITLOS stated that:

The duty to cooperate is a fundamental principle in the prevention of pollution of the marine environment under Part XII of the Convention and general international

[54] It should be noted that a refusal to reverse the burden of proof could also be seen in the *Pulp Mills* case by the ICJ in the context of a contentious proceeding. See ICJ, *Pulp Mills on the River Uruguay, (Argentina v Uruguay)*, Judgement, 20 April 2010, ICJ Reports 2010, p. 14, para 164.

[55] Note, however, that ITLOS' prescription of procedural measures not requested by the applicants, was not without criticism, both by the individual judges and some commentators. See Morgan 2001, p. 182.

[56] *MOX Plant (Ireland v United Kingdom)*, above n 34, para 26.

law and that rights arise therefrom which the Tribunal may consider appropriate to preserve under article 290 of the Convention.[57]

In saying so, ITLOS affirmed that the duty to cooperate existed beyond the confines of UNCLOS and had become part of general international law. Furthermore, ITLOS held that 'prudence and caution require that Ireland and the UK cooperate in exchanging information concerning risks or effects of the operation of the MOX plant and in devising ways to deal with them, as appropriate'.[58] As already mentioned, ITLOS used precaution as the basis for the need to cooperate, which in turn, required the exchange of information between the parties. In prescribing its provisional measure, ITLOS held that 'Ireland and the UK shall cooperate and shall, for this purpose, enter into consultations [...]'[59] The duty to cooperate in this case, thus, included the obligation to exchange information and to enter into consultation.

ITLOS' approach in *MOX Plant* was subsequently adopted in *Land Reclamation*. It should be noted, however, that this case was not entirely similar to *MOX Plant*. Firstly, Malaysia when requesting provisional measure did not bring up the issue of cooperation, at least by name. In its Request, Malaysia asked the Tribunal to order Singapore to provide Malaysia with full information concerning the current and projected works, to afford Malaysia a full opportunity to comment upon the works and their potential impacts; and to agree to negotiate with Malaysia concerning any remaining unresolved issues.[60] All of these may be part of the duty to cooperate, as has been held in the *MOX Plant* case, but some of them also exist as independent obligations under UNCLOS. Secondly, in response to several of Malaysia's requests, Singapore gave assurances and undertakings which indicated Singapore's readiness and willingness to enter into negotiations, to give Malaysia a full opportunity to comment on the reclamation works and their potential impacts, and to notify and consult Malaysia before it proceeded to construct any transport links. Singapore also extended an explicit offer to share the information that Malaysia requested, and re-examine its works in the case that Malaysia was not convinced by the evidence supplied.[61] Despite placing Singapore's commitments on records, ITLOS still found the level of cooperation between the parties insufficient. ITLOS recalled the statement made in the *MOX Plant* case that 'the duty to cooperate is a fundamental principle in the prevention of pollution of the marine environment under Part XII of the Convention and general international law'.[62] In almost identical wording to the *MOX Plant* case, ITLOS then held that 'prudence and caution require that Malaysia and Singapore establish mechanisms for exchanging information and assessing the

---

[57] Ibid., para 82.

[58] Ibid., para 84.

[59] Ibid., operative para 1.

[60] Request for Provisional Measure Submitted by Malaysia, para 13: www.itlos.org/fileadmin/itlos/documents/cases/case_no_12/request_malaysia_eng.1.pdf. Accessed 24 February 2020.

[61] *Case Concerning Land Reclamation by Singapore in and around the Straits of Johor (Malaysia v Singapore)*, above n 41, para 76.

[62] Ibid., para 92.

risks or effects of land reclamation works and devising ways to deal with them in the areas concerned'.[63]

The provisional measures eventually prescribed echoed many of Singapore's commitments. ITLOS required Malaysia and Singapore to cooperate, for the purposes of which, to enter into consultations, exchange information, assess risks and most importantly, establish a group of independent experts with a mandate to conduct a study to determine the effects of Singapore's land reclamation, to propose measures to deal with any adverse effects of such land reclamation; and to prepare an interim report on the subject of infilling works in Area D at Pulau Tekong.[64] Although the duty to cooperate was not invoked by Malaysia in its submissions, the whole case in the end revolved around this duty.

Turning to cooperation in conserving marine living resources, ITLOS had the opportunity to deal with this issue most prominently in the *Advisory Opinion on IUU Fishing*. In this instance, in determining coastal States' obligation in ensuring the sustainable management of transboundary stocks, ITLOS held that both the duty to cooperate and the duty to seek to agree under Articles 63(1) and 64(1) were 'due diligence' obligations which required the States concerned to consult with one another in good faith, pursuant to Article 300 of the Convention.[65] These obligations were thus an obligation of conduct and State parties had to consult each other with a view to reaching an agreement on measures to conserve and develop the fish stocks. They were not, however, under an obligation to reach such an agreement. ITLOS only required that consultation be meaningful, in the sense that substantial effort should be made by all States concerned.[66] ITLOS also attempted to specify the conservation and management measures that coastal States should take to fulfil the obligation to cooperate. For example, ITLOS stated that the measures should ensure that the shared stocks would not be endangered by over-exploitation or that they should be designed to maintain and restore stocks at levels which can produce maximum sustainable yield.[67] These requirements, however, were more focused on the objectives that conservation and management measures should achieve, rather than on what the measures should be. They were, moreover, just repeating what was already provided for more generally under the Articles 61 and 62 on conservation and utilisation of marine sources. Lastly, with regard to migratory stocks, particularly tuna in this case—a highly migratory species under Annex I of UNCLOS, ITLOS held that the Member States of the regional fisheries organisation had the obligation under Article 64(1) to seek to agree upon the conservation and management measures in regard to stocks that occur both within the EEZ of other Member States and in an area beyond and adjacent to these zones.[68] ITLOS required the measures to be taken pursuant to the obligation under Article 64(1) to be consistent and compatible with

[63] Ibid., para 99.

[64] Ibid., para 106.

[65] Ibid., para 210.

[66] Ibid.

[67] Ibid., para 208.

[68] *Advisory Opinion on IUU Fishing,* above n 13, para 215.

those taken by the appropriate regional organisation, for example the International Commission for the Conservation of Atlantic Tunas in the case of tuna.

Judge Paik was not impressed with the lack of clarification on the meaning and scope of the duty to cooperate in managing the shared resources laid down in the relevant provisions of the Convention.[69] Having established that it was unclear under UNCLOS how the obligation to cooperate was to be performed, Judge Paik commented that:

> In addressing the problem arising from the lack of cooperation in this case, simply emphasizing the obligation of cooperation or repeating the relevant provisions of the Convention would hardly be sufficient. In a sense, it begs the question what specifically is required to discharge that obligation, a question this Opinion does not answer satisfactorily.[70]

He instead turned to and sought guidance in the 1995 UN Fish Stocks Agreements, Article 7 of which contains several concrete obligations to give effect the duty to cooperate.[71]

The *Advisory Opinion on IUU Fishing* brought about a commendable development in that it confirmed that coastal States' obligations to conserve and manage living resources in the EEZ under Article 61 formed part of the sustainable development of ocean resources, placing UNCLOS firmly within the wider framework of sustainable development. However, the Advisory Opinion was limited on the substance of the two important obligations under Articles 63 and 64. Other than elucidating the nature and objectives of the obligations, it did not expand in any detail on what these obligations entail or what was expected of States to fulfil the obligation to cooperate in conserving and managing trans boundary stocks.[72]

3.3.2.2 Some Observations on the Duty to Cooperate

ITLOS' decisions on the duty to cooperate have made some important contributions to the status and content of the duty. The duty to cooperate is now acknowledged to be part of general international law, as held by ITLOS in *MOX Plant* and confirmed in *Land Reclamation*. The duty to cooperate is found to be applicable to all aspects of the protection of the marine environment, including the conservation of marine resources as affirmed in the *Southern Bluefin Tuna* case and the prevention of trans boundary pollution as in *MOX Plant* and *Land Reclamation*.

The scope of the duty to cooperate has also been clarified to a certain extent. The duty to cooperate, at least in the prevention of marine pollution, comprises more

---

[69] ITLOS, *Request for Advisory Opinion submitted by the Sub-Regional Fisheries Commission*, Separate Opinion of Judge Paik, 2 April 2015, ITLOS Reports 2015, para 31.

[70] Ibid., para 34.

[71] Ibid., para 36.

[72] Note that the ICJ also refused to read anything of substance into the duty to cooperate in *Whaling*. However, some of the separate and dissenting judges argued that the duty should be given a very significant substantive content. See ICJ, *Whaling in the Antarctic (Australia v Japan: New Zealand intervening)*, Judgment, 31 March 2014, ICJ Reports 2014, p. 226, paras 13–17.

concrete obligations, namely, the obligations to exchange information, to consult with other States potentially affected by the planned activities, to jointly study the impacts of the activity on the marine environment, monitor risks or the effects of the operation, and devise measures to prevent pollution of the marine environment. When it comes to the conservation of marine resources, however, ITLOS has been less successful in defining the contours of the obligation to cooperate with regards to shared stocks. This also highlights the issue found in several of ITLOS decisions concerning the duty to cooperate. With the exception of *Land Reclamation* in which ITLOS prescribed at least one concrete measure to be taken by the parties to discharge the duty to cooperate, it was generally much more general or, in the words of Judge *ad hoc* Shearer in the *Southern Bluefin Tuna* case, too 'diplomatic', with regard to the measures to be taken so as to fulfil the duty to cooperate. States retain wide discretion as to the manner in which to fulfil their duty to cooperate.

3.3.3 Duty to Conduct EIA

3.3.3.1 The Relevant Cases

The obligation to carry out an environment impact assessment (EIA) is provided for in Article 206 of UNCLOS.[73] Beyond the Convention, the ICJ in *Pulp Mills* recognised that this obligation also existed under general international law 'where there is a risk that the proposed industrial activity may have a significant adverse impact in a transboundary context, in particular, on a shared resource'.[74] The status of this obligation under international law is, therefore, no longer subject to debate. It is the content of the obligation that is still shrouded in uncertainty.

In *MOX Plant*, one of Ireland's allegations was that UK had refused to carry out a proper assessment of the impacts on the marine environment of the MOX plant and associated activities.[75] Ireland argued that even though the UK in 1993 had carried out an EIA on the basis of which the commission of the MOX Plant was authorised, the 1993 Impact Assessment Statement was not adequate as it did not address the potential harm of the MOX Plant to the marine environment of the Irish Sea.[76] Meanwhile, the UK contended that it had adduced evidence to establish that the risk of pollution from the operation of the MOX plant would be infinitely small and that the commissioning of the MOX plant would not cause serious harm to the

[73] Article 206 UNCLOS provides that: When States have reasonable grounds for believing that planned activities under their jurisdiction or control may cause substantial pollution of or significant and harmful changes to the marine environment, they shall, as far as practicable, assess the potential effects of such activities on the marine environment and shall communicate reports of the results.

[74] *Pulp Mills on the River Uruguay (Argentina v Uruguay),* above n 54, para 83.

[75] *MOX Plant (Ireland v United Kingdom),* above n 34, para 26.

[76] Ibid.

marine environment or irreparable prejudice to the rights of Ireland.[77] ITLOS, for its part, did not address the adequacy or lack thereof of the 1993 Impact Assessment Statement in its Provisional Measure Order.

In *Land Reclamation*, Malaysia also alleged that Singapore had not, prior to commencing its current land reclamation activities, conducted and published an adequate assessment of their potential effects on the environment and on the affected coastal areas.[78] Even though Singapore argued that the land reclamation had not caused any adverse impact on Malaysia, the Tribunal found that an EIA had not been undertaken by Singapore.[79] This fact proved to be crucial in the granting of provisional measures as ITLOS held that in the absence of the EIA, it could not be excluded that the land reclamation works might have adverse effects on the marine environment.[80] Consequently, although ITLOS did not order Singapore to suspend its land reclamation activities as requested by Malaysia, it ordered the establishment of a group of experts whose mandate was to 'study the effects of Singapore's land reclamation and to propose, as appropriate, measures to deal with any adverse effects of such land reclamation'.[81] The task assigned to this group was in effect that of EIA, the results of which would form the basis for any actions as agreed by the two parties. Similar to *MOX Plant*, the lack of EIA did not prompt ITLOS to grant the applicant the provisional measures that the latter had requested. However, EIA formed the crux of the provisional measure that ITLOS eventually prescribed.

In the *Advisory Opinion on Activities in the Area*, ITLOS managed to shed further light on the obligation to conduct EIA. With regard to activities in the Area, the obligation to carry out an EIA, besides finding a basis in Article 206, is also found in the Annex to the 1994 Agreement as well as the Nodules Regulations and the Sulphides Regulations.[82] Notwithstanding this fact, the SDC still added that an obligation to conduct an EIA was a general obligation under customary international law.[83] It recalled the statement made by the ICJ concerning EIA in *Pulp Mills*, but stated that although EIA in that case was discussed in a transboundary context, the obligation to conduct an EIA:

> [M]ay also apply to activities with an impact on the environment in an area beyond the limits of national jurisdiction; and the Court's references to 'shared resources' may also apply to resources that are the common heritage of mankind.[84]

---

[77] Ibid., paras 72–73.

[78] *Case Concerning Land Reclamation by Singapore in and around the Straits of Johor (Malaysia v Singapore),* above n 41, para 22.

[79] Ibid., para 95.

[80] Ibid., para 96.

[81] Ibid., para 106.

[82] The relevant provisions of these Regulations require the sponsoring States not only to individually ensure compliance by the sponsored contractor with this obligation but also to cooperate with the Authority in the establishment and implementation of impact assessments. *Responsibilities and obligations of States with respect to Activities in the Area*, above n 11, para 141.

[83] Ibid., para 145.

[84] Ibid., para 148.

With regard to the content of the obligation to conduct an EIA, the SDC did not leave it open as did the ICJ in *Pulp Mills*. In the specific context of activities in the Area, the SDC pointed out that the content of the obligation to conduct an EIA was specified in the Nodules Regulations, Sulphides Regulations and the Recommendations for the Guidance of the Contractors for the Assessment of the Possible Environmental Impacts Arising from Exploration for Polymetallic Nodules in the Area.[85] Furthermore, the SDC held that 'EIAs should be included in the system of consultations and prior notifications set out in article 142 of the Convention with respect to resource deposits in the Area which lie across limits of national jurisdiction.'[86] There has been uncertainty regarding the relationship between EIA and other procedural obligations, particularly consultation with and notification to the affected population.[87] The SDC's abovementioned statement confirmed that EIA under UNCLOS was part of the obligation to consult and notify, insofar as activities in areas beyond national jurisdiction are concerned. The ICJ in 2015 in fact confirmed this close relationship between the obligation to conduct EIA and the obligation to notify and consult in *Construction of a Road*.[88]

3.3.3.2 Some Remarks on the Obligation to Conduct EIA

Despite requiring the conduct of an EIA, Article 206 of UNCLOS does not elaborate on the content of this obligation. In their written submissions to the Annex VII arbitral tribunal in *MOX Plant*, Ireland was particularly mindful of the fact that Article 206 did not impose any specific obligations on the UK regarding EIA, but argued nonetheless that the arbitral tribunal, in interpreting and applying Article 206, 'should take into account the common standards of EIA in other instruments such as the UNEP EIA Principles or the Espoo Convention'.[89] The UK, for its part, argued that by virtue of the terms 'reasonable grounds' and 'as far as practicable' under Article 206, States retained the discretion as to the manner in which EIA should be carried out.[90] The disagreement between Ireland and the UK raises the question as

[85] Ibid., para 149.

[86] Ibid., para 148. The Recommendations are issued by the Legal and Technical Commission which is mandated by the Regulations to provide recommendations of a technical or administrative nature to contractors to assist them in the implementation of the rules, regulations and procedures of the Authority. Despite having no binding effect, these Recommendations are to be taken into account by States. See: www.isa.org.jm/files/documents/EN/7Sess/LTC/isba_7ltc_1Rev1.pdf. Accessed 24 February 2020.

[87] See for example Dupuy and Viñuales 2015, p. 70; Okanawa 1997, p. 275; Birnie et al. 2009, p. 105.

[88] *Certain Activities Carried out by Nicaragua in the Border Area (Costa Rica v Nicaragua) and Construction of a Road in Costa Rica along the San Juan River (Nicaragua v Costa Rica)* [2015] ICJ Rep 665, para 10.

[89] *The MOX Plant case (Ireland v United Kingdom)*, above n 20, Memorial of Ireland, para 7.16: www.pca-cpa.org/Ireland%20Memorial%20Part%20II2340.pdf?fil_id=223. Accessed 24 February 2020.

[90] Ibid., paras 5.14–5.32.

to whether and to what extent Article 206 can be informed by existing standards of EIA found in other international instruments.[91] It is interesting to note that the SDC in its *Advisory Opinion on Activities in the Area* was willing to interpret the Nodules Regulations in light of the development of the law contained in the subsequent Sulphides Regulations. More specifically, the Nodules Regulations did not mention the precautionary principle and only contained a very general provision on 'best environmental practice'. Nevertheless, the SDC had no hesitation in reading the precautionary principle and the requirement to apply 'best environmental practices' found under the Sulphides Regulations into the Nodules Regulations.[92] This practice may signal the Tribunal's willingness to read existing international environmental standards into other instruments into UNCLOS.

In conclusion, the most significant contribution of UNCLOS tribunals to the development of the duty to conduct an EIA has been the strengthening of its status and importance in cases of transboundary harm. In terms of the normative content of the obligation, there are perhaps merits in the comments of one scholar that ITLOS case law on EIA 'has barely scratched the surface'.[93] ITLOS' decisions concerning EIA threw little new light on what the duty involves or the criteria based on which an EIA would be considered satisfactory. Both the *MOX Plant* and the *Land Reclamation* cases involved submissions requiring the interpretation and application of Article 206. In neither of the cases, however, was the alleged lack of EIA considered for the prescription of provisional measures. The only exception was the *Advisory Opinion on Activities in the Area*, in which the SDC was able to clarify the content of the duty to conduct an EIA thanks to the specific Rules and Regulations concerning the activities in the Area. These Rules and Regulations, however, contain criteria that are applicable in a very limited context with specific actors, and thus may not readily be extended to other instances in which the duty also arises.

3.4 Strengths and Weaknesses of ITLOS in Dealing with Environmental Protection

3.4.1 Strengths

All of the cases before ITLOS that relate to the protection of the marine environment were brought in the context of provisional measures and advisory proceedings. As mentioned, Article 290 requires ITLOS to prescribe provisional measures to either preserve the rights of the parties or prevent serious harm to the marine environment. However, one scholar has argued that it is States that bring the cases, not the

[91] Craik 2008, p. 120.

[92] *Responsibilities and obligations of States with respect to Activities in the Area,* above n 11, paras 136 and 137.

[93] Boyle 2007, p. 378.

marine environment, therefore, there is no guarantee that the marine environment may benefit from the measures prescribed or that the development of principles of marine environment protection may occur during the process of dispute resolution.[94] In fact, another commentator has observed that: 'The Tribunal has [...] never granted such measures solely on that basis.'[95] However, as *Land Reclamation* shows, provisional measures requiring serious and meaningful cooperation played an important role in not only resolving disputes between the parties but also in the protection of the marine environment in the Straits of Johor.[96] It follows that the protection of the parties' interests and the goal of protecting the marine environment are not mutually exclusive. Provisional measures ordering the disputing parties to undertake a joint monitoring or EIA or requiring the parties to cooperate to ensure conservation and optimum utilisation of a fish stock and to devise measures to prevent land-based marine pollution 'can contribute to enforce community interests regarding marine environmental protection,[97] while at the same time, serving to protect the rights of the parties. ITLOS' decisions in provisional measures proceedings, therefore, have shown that, despite their limitations, they can still play an important role in advancing environmental interests. Moreover, in more recent cases such as *Ghana/Cote d'Ivoire*, ITLOS has been more explicit in citing the prevention of the serious harm to the environment as a basis for prescribing provisional measures.[98] This was despite of the fact that the Special Chamber was not convinced that Côte d'Ivoire had 'adduced sufficient evidence to support its allegations that the activities conducted by Ghana in the disputed area are such as to create an imminent risk of serious harm to the marine environment'.[99] The explicit reliance on preventing serious harm in the operative paragraphs buttressed the holding that 'the risk of serious harm to the marine environment is of great concern to the Special Chamber'.[100]

Second, in rendering its provisional orders, ITLOS has not adopted a narrow or fragmented interpretation of marine environment protection, but has instead opted for a more holistic understanding of what marine environmental protection comprises. ITLOS in *Southern Bluefin Tuna* regarded the conservation of marine living resources,[101] despite not explicitly provided for in Part XII, as a component of marine environment protection. As mentioned from the outset, the obligations concerning the conservation of marine resources and prevention of marine pollution are scattered in different parts of UNCLOS, primarily due to the zonal approach that the Convention adopts. By bringing them together, ITLOS confirmed that they

[94] Rashbrooke 2004, p. 515.

[95] Proelss 2017, p. 1873.

[96] Treves 2006.

[97] Tanaka 2014, p. 365.

[98] ITLOS, *Dispute Concerning Delimitation of the Maritime Boundary between Ghana and Côte d'Ivoire in the Atlantic Ocean (Ghana/Côte d'Ivoire)*, Judgment, 23 September 2017, ITLOS Reports 2017, para 108.

[99] Ibid., para 67.

[100] Ibid., para 68.

[101] *Southern Bluefin Tuna Cases (New Zealand and Australia v Japan)*, above n 25, para 70.

are integral components of marine environmental protection. Such an approach has enabled ITLOS to extend obligations found under Part XII concerning primarily the prevention of marine pollution to the conservation of fisheries.[102]

Third, it has been argued that advisory proceedings are more likely to give international courts and tribunals leeway to develop the law. As the legal questions submitted for advisory opinions are usually formulated in a more abstract and general manner, and not confined to the facts of the case, the interpretation and clarification of the law in advisory proceedings have the potential to transcend the particular instance and have wider applicability. The same could arguably be said for ITLOS. As both advisory requests concerned different issues relating to the protection of the marine environment, ITLOS was able to examine in great detail, thereby clarifying several important principles relating to the protection of the marine environment in the two advisory opinions. While the conclusion of ITLOS to establish advisory power for the full tribunal was, as analysed in Sect. 3.2, not without controversy, it opens the door for ITLOS to play a more significant role in clarifying and developing principles to protect the marine environment. This advisory jurisdiction may allow State parties to an institutional body established under the currently-negotiated international legally binding instrument under the United Nations Convention on the Law of the Sea on the conservation and sustainable use of marine biological diversity of areas beyond national jurisdiction (BBNJ ILBI), to request advisory opinions from ITLOS relating to the conservation of marine resources in areas beyond national jurisdiction. Moreover, it is interesting to note that in both advisory proceedings, ITLOS allowed not only States but also international organisations to make written statements, and in the Advisory Opinion on *IUU Fishing*, non-governmental organisations such as World Wild Fund International submitted amicus curiae briefs.[103] The advisory jurisdiction of ITLOS, therefore, also has the potential to allow for more inclusive participation of all actors in the protection of the marine environment.

Finally, the most significant contribution of ITLOS towards the development of the law on marine environment protection is the clarification of the status of several principles of environmental law. In particular, ITLOS confirmed that the duty to cooperate and the obligation to conduct an EIA are now all part of general international law. With regard to the controversial precautionary principle, while not explicitly acknowledging its customary status, ITLOS is the only international tribunal to date which has given a green light to the precautionary principle belonging to the corpus of general international law, as demonstrated in the *Advisory Opinion on Activities in the Area*. ITLOS also shed light on the precautionary principle as provided for under Principle 15 of the Rio Declaration, establishing a connection between the precautionary principle and the principle of common but differentiated responsibility, and the principle of due diligence. All these aspects of the precautionary principle had

---

102 *Request for Advisory Opinion submitted by the Sub-Regional Fisheries Commission*, above n 13, paras 216 and 217.

103 See ITLOS page for the Advisory Opinion on Activities in the Area: https://www.itlos.org/en/main/cases/list-of-cases/case-no-17/. Accessed 24 February 2020. For the Advisory Opinion on IUU Fishing: https://www.itlos.org/en/main/cases/list-of-cases/case-no-21/ Accessed 24 February 2020.

not been discussed to a great extent in international jurisprudence before and thus, mark an important contribution of ITLOS to the development of the principle. The keenness of UNCLOS bodies to accept emerging principles which are either still controversial or vague in their content and bring them into the corpus of UNCLOS shows that the tribunals are open to treating the Convention as having an evolving nature, and that they are willing to interpret UNCLOS in line with new developments in the field. This approach is highly welcome and reasonable, for UNCLOS came into being at a time when international environmental law was not yet fully developed and had only started to gather attention.

3.4.2 Weaknesses

The first weakness lies in the limited number of cases in which ITLOS has had the opportunity to deal with marine environmental protection. Its ability to make wide-ranging contributions is thus constrained. This can be explained by the jurisdictional constraints as specified in Sect. 3.2, placing limitations on what ITLOS can do. As ITLOS only has jurisdiction under the Convention pursuant to Article 288(1), it would be unable to deal with all marine environmental protection issues that arise, unless there is a sufficient link to one or more provision of the Convention. Moreover, as analysed in Sect. 3.2.1, Articles 281 and 297(3) may impose further restrictions on the jurisdictional scope of ITLOS. The interpretation of these articles in case law to date has created significant uncertainty regarding the extent to which ITLOS can have a say at all in certain environmental issues, including those that are regulated under other conventions other than UNCLOS and those that relate to the conservation of marine living resources in the coastal States' EEZ. It is worth mentioning that in the most revised draft text of the BBNJ ILBI, it has been proposed that 'the provisions relating to the settlement of disputes set out in Part XV of the Convention apply mutatis mutandis to any dispute between States Parties to this Agreement concerning the interpretation or application of this Agreement, whether or not they are also Parties to the Convention'.[104] As many of the issues regulated under the new agreement are likely to also be found under other international instruments, the conflicting interpretation of Article 281 casts serious doubt over the extent to which ITLOS may be able to play a role in protecting the marine environment beyond national jurisdictions under this new agreement. While, as mentioned in Sect. 3.3, there are tools that allow ITLOS to deal with issues beyond UNCLOS, the interpretations of articles such as Article 293 and Article 297(1) to expand the jurisdiction of the tribunals under Article 287 UNCLOS has not been without controversy.[105]

[104] Revised draft text of an agreement under the United Nations Convention on the Law of the Sea on the conservation and sustainable use of marine biological diversity of areas beyond national jurisdiction, Article 55: https://undocs.org/en/a/conf.232/2020/3. Accessed 24 February 2020.

[105] For critiques of the interpretation of Article 297(1), see for example Talmon 2016, para 927; Allen 2017, p. 313.

Consequently, caution would need to be exercised in using these articles just to give ITLOS more opportunities to hear environmental cases, so as not to circumvent the jurisdictional constraints that are imposed upon ITLOS under the Convention.

This may not be a weakness in a strict sense that can be blamed on ITLOS itself, as this was the decision of the drafters of the Convention to establish the dispute settlement system in such a way. However, these constraints should be taken into account in order to manage expectation regarding the role of ITLOS. In any case, it is worth remembering that the contribution of ITLOS—as a dispute settlement body—to the development of the law necessarily transpires through the decisions rendered in the course of settling disputes or issuing advisory opinions. The decision to bring cases or advisory requests to international courts and tribunals, in turn, rests entirely with States. It is impossible to predict with any degree of certainty when States are willing to do so, and the proceedings under Part XV of UNCLOS have indeed been rather haphazard in nature.

Second, looking at the cases that ITLOS has had the chance to deal with, there also exist certain weaknesses. The fact that international courts and tribunals acknowledge and confirm the existence of environmental principles may not necessarily mean they have meaningfully shed light on the normative content of these principles. International courts have had the tendency to pay lip-service to environmental principles, partly contributing to what one commentator terms as the 'myth system' of international environmental law—a set of ideas often considered part of customary international law but which do not reflect state practice, and instead are merely 'collective ideals of the international community' which 'have the quality of fictions or half-truth.'[106] Therefore, unless the normative content of the principles is clarified so as to expose clear obligations on States, the customary status or otherwise of the principles is of little meaning in practice.

The precautionary principle was applied in provisional measure proceedings in *Southern Bluefin Tuna.* However, given the nature of the proceedings (provisional), its normative content, such as the threshold to trigger the application of the precautionary principle under UNCLOS, was informed by Article 290. This may restrict the applicability of the conclusions to other cases. In respect of the obligation to cooperate, ITLOS confirmed the link between the duty to cooperate and other duties, such as the duty to conduct consultation, duty to exchange information, duty of prior notification, in the context of preventing marine pollution. In the conservation of marine resources, ITLOS however remains overly coy when it comes to specifying concrete measures for States to fulfil the duty to cooperate, leaving much room to be filled. Similarly, ITLOS did not manage to shed much light on the obligation to conduct an EIA. Except for the link between EIA and the duty to consult and notify relevant stakeholders, the content of the obligation to conduct an EIA under Article 206 of UNCLOS remains unclear, as is the question as to whether there is a common global minimum for the standards of EIA or whether it is at the discretion of States.

---

[106] Bodansky 1995, p. 105.

3.5 Conclusion

This chapter has sought to examine the contribution of ITLOS to the protection of the marine environment. By analysing the cases that ITLOS has dealt with to date, it has shown that ITLOS has had the opportunity to engage with various environmental principles in the context of the marine environment. In doing so, it has contributed to clarifying the legal status and normative content of several principles, such as the precautionary principle, the duty to cooperate and EIA. However, the case law has also shown that ITLOS has missed several opportunities to contribute further to developing these principles. That said, the Tribunal's examination of the principles, even when limited, lends an authoritative voice to endorsing their importance and helps to enrich the case law that deals with them, providing some guidance for States in the implementation of the principles. At the same time, one should be reasonable in what can be expected of ITLOS in terms of its contributions to the protection of the marine environment. There are inherent limitations upon dispute settlement bodies such as ITLOS, particularly in terms of jurisdictional scope, that will constrain them from playing a greater role in developing the law. ITLOS will have to strike a careful balance between seizing the opportunity to contribute to the development of environmental principles and staying within the limits of its jurisdiction in order to maintain its legitimacy and authority.

References

Allen S (2017) Article 297 of the United Nations Convention on the Law of the Sea and the Scope of Mandatory Jurisdiction. Ocean Development & International Law 48:313-330
Birnie P et al (2009) International Law and the Environment. Oxford University Press, Oxford
Bodansky DM (1995) Customary (and Not So Customary) International Environmental Law. Indiana Journal of Global Legal Studies 3:105-119
Boyle A (2007) The Environmental Jurisprudence of the ITLOS. International Journal of Marine and Coastal Law 22:369-381
Churchill R (2006) Some Reflections on the Operation of the Dispute Settlement System of the UN Convention on the Law of the Sea During its First Decade. In: Barnes R et al (eds) The Law of the Sea: Progress and Prospects. Oxford University Press, Oxford
Craik N (2008) The International Law of Environmental Impact Assessment: Process, Substance and Integration. Cambridge University Press, Cambridge
Cullet P (2015) Common but Differentiated Responsibility. In: Viñuales JE (ed) The Rio Declaration on Environment and Development: A Commentary. Oxford University Press, Oxford
Dupuy PM, Viñuales JE (2015) International Environmental Law. Cambridge University Press, Cambridge
Foster C (2013) Science and the Precautionary Principle in International Courts and Tribunals: Expert Evidence, Burden of Proof and Finality. Cambridge University Press, Cambridge
Jesus JL (2006) Commentary on Article 138 of the Rules of the Tribunal. In: Rao PC, Gautier P (eds) The Rules of the International Tribunal for the Law of the Sea: A Commentary. Martinus Nijhoff, Dordrecht
Kaye SM (2001) International Fisheries Management. Kluwer Law International, The Hague

Kim DY (2010) Advisory Proceedings before the International Tribunal for the Law of the Sea as an Alternative Procedure to Supplement the Dispute-Settlement Mechanism under Part XV of the United Nations Convention on the Law of the Sea. Issues in Legal Scholarship doi: https://doi.org/10.2202/1539-8323.1116

Lando M (2016) The Advisory Jurisdiction of the International Tribunal for the Law of the Sea: Comments on the Request for an Advisory Opinion Submitted by the Sub-Regional Fisheries Commission. Leiden Journal of International Law 29:441-461

McDorman T (2001) International Tribunal for the Law of the Sea. YBIEL 21:531

Morgan DL (2001) A practitioner's critique of the Order Granting Provisional Measures in the Southern Bluefin Tuna case. In: Moore JN, Nordquist MH (eds) Current Marine Environmental Issues and the International Tribunal for the Law of the Sea. Martinus Nijhoff, The Hague

Ndiaye TM (2010) The Advisory Function of the International Tribunal for the Law of the Sea. Chinese Journal of International Law 9:565-587

Nordquist MH (1985) United Nations Convention on the Law of the Sea, 1982: A Commentary, Vol V. Martinus Nijhoff, Dordrecht

Okanawa P (1997) Procedural Obligations in International Environmental Agreements. British Yearbook of International Law 67:275-336

Proelss A (2017) United Nations Convention on the Law of the Sea: A Commentary. CH Beck/Hart/Nomos, Munich/Oxford/Baden-Baden

Rashbrooke G (2004) The International Tribunal for the Law of the Sea: A Forum for the Development of Principles of International Environmental Law? International Journal of Marine and Coastal Law 19:515-536

Rosenne S (1998) International Tribunal for the Law of the Sea: 1996–97 Survey, International Journal of Marine and Coastal Law 13:487-514

Ruys T, Soete A (2016) 'Creeping' Advisory Jurisdiction of International Courts and Tribunals? The Case of the International Tribunal for the Law of the Sea. Leiden Journal of International Law 29:155-176

Stephens T (2009) International Courts and Environmental Protection. Cambridge University Press, Cambridge

Talmon S (2016) The Chagos Marine Protected Area Arbitration: Expansion of the Jurisdiction of UNCLOS Part XV Courts and Tribunals. International & Comparative Law Quarterly 65:927-951

Tanaka Y (2014) Provisional Measures Prescribed by ITLOS and Marine Environmental Protection, Proceedings of the Annual Meeting of the American Society of International Law 108:365-367

Treves T (2006) A System for Law of the Sea Dispute Settlement. In: Barnes R et al (eds) The Law of the Sea: Progress and Prospects. Oxford University Press, Oxford

You KJ (2008) Advisory Opinions of the International Tribunal for the Law of the Sea: Article 138 of the Rules of the Tribunal, Revisited. Ocean Development & International Law 39:360-371

Lan Ngoc Nguyen Assistant Professor, Utrecht University School of Law and Senior Associate Researcher, Netherlands Institute for the Law of the Sea, Utrecht Centre for Water, Oceans and Sustainability Law, Faculty of Law, Economics and Governance, Utrecht University, The Netherlands. This chapter was funded by the ERC Research Project 'Accommodating New Interests at Sea: Legal Tools for Sustainable Ocean Governance' (SUSTAINABLEOCEAN).

Chapter 4
The Protection of the Environment Through Inter-State Arbitration

Brian McGarry

Contents

Abstract The present chapter assesses the treatment of procedural issues in inter-State arbitrations relating to environmental protection, and identifies the substantive contributions of this form of dispute settlement to international environmental law and governance. This chapter first identifies the roles that inter-State arbitral tribunals have played in resolving jurisdictional questions and conducting incidental proceedings in disputes relating to environmental protection, including questions arising under *lex specialis* instruments such as the UN Convention on the Law of the Sea. The chapter then overviews the codification and application of standing procedural texts in environmental arbitration, including the Permanent Court of Arbitration's 2001 Optional Rules for Arbitration of Disputes Relating to the Environment and/or Natural Resources. It thereafter surveys classic and contemporary examples of cases relating to environmental protection, illustrating how inter-State arbitral tribunals have throughout history defined the normative content and status of environmental legal instruments through their analyses of applicable law (including their treatment of customary international law and general principles of law). Finally, the author concludes with observations on the notion of jurisdictional fragmentation, as well as the potential future role of inter-State arbitration in environmental protection and regulation.

Keywords Inter-State disputes · environmental law · arbitral jurisdiction · arbitral procedure · UNCLOS · PCA Environmental Rules · customary international law · general principles of law · cross-fertilization

---

B. McGarry (✉)
Grotius Centre for International Legal Studies, Faculty of Law, Leiden University, Leiden, The Netherlands
e-mail: b.k.mcgarry@law.leidenuniv.nl

E. Sobenes et al. (eds.), *The Environment Through the Lens of International Courts and Tribunals*, https://doi.org/10.1007/978-94-6265-507-2_4

4.1 Introduction

Inter-State dispute settlement mechanisms provide a path to legal accountability in transboundary environmental disputes, which often involve traditional governmental competences and sensitive territorial or economic interests.[1] The question then arises as to how different inter-State mechanisms utilize distinct approaches to resolving environmental disputes. International arbitration tribunals, for example, have relied upon a broader range of case law than institutions such as the International Court of Justice (ICJ), which has often been averse to citing decisions from beyond the Great Hall of Justice.[2]

This is partly due to arbitration's longer history, and a general preference for arbitration over judicial settlement in the compromissory clauses of contemporary environmental conventions.[3] Yet the cross-fertilizing tendencies of arbitration also arise from its comparatively unmoored character. Inter-State arbitration encompasses the need to flexibly adapt to legal approaches dictated by parties—in the absence of institutional prerogatives—without betraying the coherence of multilateral legal instruments. For this reason, arbitral tribunals possess a heightened interest in citing prior cases decided by other bodies, in order to improve perceptions of their awards' legal 'correctness', and the prospect of voluntary implementation.

The present chapter assesses the treatment of procedural issues in inter-State arbitrations relating to environmental protection, and identifies the substantive contributions of this form of dispute settlement to international environmental law and governance. Section 4.2 of this chapter identifies the roles that inter-State arbitral tribunals have played in resolving jurisdictional questions and conducting incidental proceedings in disputes relating to environmental protection, including questions arising under *lex specialis* instruments such as the UN Convention on the Law of the Sea (UNCLOS). Section 4.3 overviews the codification and application of standing procedural texts in environmental arbitration, including the Permanent Court of Arbitration's 2001 Optional Rules for Arbitration of Disputes Relating to the Environment and/or Natural Resources (PCA Environmental Rules). Section 4.4 surveys classic and contemporary examples of cases relating to environmental protection,

---

[1] For illustrations of the environmental practice of mixed tribunals, see e.g., on the use of regional human rights courts to apply related obligations, ECHR, Grand Chamber, *Öneryıldız v Turkey*, 30 November 2004, Case No. 48939/99 (concerning protection of the right to life); on the development of counterclaims procedure in investor-State arbitration to obtain compensation for environmental damage caused by foreign nationals, *Burlington Resources Inc. v Republic of Ecuador*, Award, 7 February 2017, ICSID Case No. ARB/08/5. As to the use of domestic courts in transboundary environmental disputes, sovereign immunity is a general obstacle to obtaining and enforcing domestic judgments against a foreign State; however, domestic courts have recently made notable strides in holding their own governments accountable for international environmental obligations. See, e.g., the decision of the Supreme Court of the Netherlands (Hoge Raad) in *Urgenda Foundation v State of the Netherlands*, Judgment, 20 December 2019.

[2] See Alschner and Charlotin 2018, p. 83.

[3] See, e.g., United Nations Convention on the Law of the Sea, 10 December 1982, 1833 UNTS 3, entered into force 16 November 1994 (UNCLOS), Article 287(5).

illustrating how inter-State arbitral tribunals have throughout history defined the normative content and status of environmental legal instruments through their analyses of applicable law (including their treatments of customary international law and general principles of law). Section 4.5 concludes with observations on the notion of jurisdictional fragmentation, as well as the potential future role of inter-State arbitration in environmental protection and regulation.

4.2 Jurisdictional Questions and Incidental Proceedings

Jurisdictional instruments in contemporary inter-State arbitrations illustrate the above said connection between environmental protection and questions of territorial sovereignty and regulatory control. Of particular note is UNCLOS, which served as the jurisdictional basis for 14 inter-State arbitrations between 1998 and 2019.[4] The Convention establishes arbitration as the default means of binding dispute settlement, and permits any party to an interpretation or application dispute unresolved through amicable means to institute these proceedings unilaterally.[5]

As opposed to proceedings before the ICJ or the International Tribunal for the Law of the Sea (ITLOS)—in which institutional rules automatically bifurcate cases to address preliminary objections on a *prima facie* basis—UNCLOS leaves it to the discretion of individual tribunals whether to take this approach.[6] In so doing, tribunals have formulated ad hoc rules of procedure which borrow verbatim from the threshold in the ICJ Rules of Court as to whether the objection 'possess[es] an exclusively preliminary character'.[7] Thus whereas the *South China Sea* arbitration was bifurcated to first address jurisdictional questions in the absence of China's formal participation in the case,[8] the *Chagos Marine Protected Area* tribunal decided to address the UK's objections to jurisdiction following a hearing on the merits.[9]

---

[4] This figure includes the first UNCLOS arbitration, *Southern Bluefin Tuna*, and 13 subsequent cases administered by the PCA. It does not include cases unilaterally instituted as arbitrations, which were thereafter removed by agreement to the International Tribunal for the Law of the Sea. See further PCA, 'United Nations Convention on the Law of the Sea', https://pca-cpa.org/en/services/arbitration-services/unclos/ Accessed 1 July 2020.

[5] UNCLOS, above n 3, Articles 286–287.

[6] See ibid., Annex VII, Article 5.

[7] *Cf.* ICJ Rules of Court, Article 79*ter*(4) (as amended 21 October 2019); *South China Sea Arbitration (Philippines v China)*, Rules of Procedure, 27 August 2013, PCA Case No. 2013-19, Article 20(3).

[8] See *South China Sea Arbitration (Philippines v China)*, Procedural Order No. 4, 21 April 2015, PCA Case No. 2013-19.

[9] See *Chagos Marine Protected Area Arbitration (Mauritius v UK)*, Procedural Order No. 2 (Application to Bifurcate Proceedings), 15 January 2013, PCA Case No. 2011-03. For another example of unitary proceedings despite jurisdictional objections to UNCLOS arbitrations with environmental consequences, see also discussion of *Barbados v Trinidad and Tobago* in Kwiatkowska 2007, pp. 917 and 928.

Indeed, one of the clearest overlaps between territoriality and environmental governance in recent inter-State arbitral practice is the *Chagos* arbitration, in which the UK objected that Mauritius had clothed a land sovereignty dispute as a dispute about area-based management tools in the marine environment. The tribunal upheld this objection in its 2015 award, finding that it lacked jurisdiction under UNCLOS to determine whether the UK's disputed sovereignty over a neighbouring archipelago gave it 'coastal State' status for marine protection purposes (a matter later addressed by the ICJ).[10] Seven months after the *Chagos* award, the *South China Sea* arbitral tribunal—including one of the *Chagos* arbitrators who dissented on this jurisdictional finding—would instead conclude that UNCLOS empowered it to identify the marine entitlements of insular features subject to sovereignty disputes, so long as they 'cannot sustain human habitation or economic life of their own'.[11] The 2020 *Black Sea, Sea of Azov, and Kerch Strait* arbitral award affirmed the *Chagos* approach by finding that it lacked jurisdiction under UNCLOS to identify a rightful 'coastal State' for marine environmental protection purposes.[12] While ITLOS appears likely to draw from such awards when addressing related questions in a currently pending dispute,[13] the somewhat discordant approaches of these tribunals to the jurisdictional consequences of disputed sovereignty makes ITLOS's path difficult to foresee.

UNCLOS practice also highlights how the regime-crossing nature of disputes concerning environmental protection may give rise to questions of comity and admissibility issues such as *lis pendens*. For example, fisheries regimes reflect links between environmental disputes and international economic law, including trade rules subject to dispute settlement before the World Trade Organization (WTO) or regional trade bodies. As such, they have resulted in parallel proceedings between such bodies and UNCLOS dispute settlement mechanisms—a phenomenon which has historically led to amicable settlement (most recently in the 2014 termination of the *Atlanto-Scandian Herring* arbitration).[14] As noted by the *Southern Bluefin Tuna* arbitral tribunal, UNCLOS may be unable to establish a 'truly comprehensive regime' in

---

[10] See *Chagos Marine Protected Area Arbitration (Mauritius v UK)*, Award, 18 March 2015, PCA Case No. 2011-03, paras 163, 222 and 547; ICJ, *Legal Consequences of the Separation of the Chagos Archipelago from Mauritius in 1965,* Advisory Opinion, 25 February 2019, ICJ Reports 2019, p. 95, paras 79–82 and 183.

[11] See the tribunal's subsequent summary of these findings in *South China Sea Arbitration (Philippines v China)*, Award, 12 July 2016, PCA Case No. 2013-19, para 691; *cf.* UNCLOS, above n 3, Article 121(3). See further *Chagos Marine Protected Area Arbitration (Mauritius v UK)*, Dissenting and Concurring Opinion of Judges Kateka and Wolfrum, 18 March 2015, PCA Case No. 2011-03.

[12] See further *Coastal State Rights in the Black Sea, Sea of Azov, and Kerch Strait (Ukraine v Russia)*, Award on Preliminary Objections, 21 February 2020, PCA Case No. 2017-06; Schatz 2020.

[13] See ITLOS, 'Dispute Concerning Delimitation of the Maritime Boundary between Mauritius and Maldives in the Indian Ocean (Mauritius/Maldives): Preliminary objections submitted by the Republic of Maldives', Press Release No. 299, 19 December 2019, https://www.itlos.org/fileadmin/itlos/documents/press_releases_english/PR_299_en.pdf.

[14] See *Atlanto-Scandian Herring Arbitration (Denmark in respect of the Faroe Islands v EU)*, Termination Order, 23 September 2014, PCA Case No. 2013-30. See also ITLOS, *Conservation and Sustainable Exploitation of Swordfish Stocks—Chile v EU)*, Order, 16 December 2009, ITLOS Reports 2008–2020, p. 13.

the jurisdictional sense.[15] Indeed, ITLOS in the *MOX Plant* provisional measures proceedings confirmed the exclusivity of UNCLOS dispute settlement mechanisms only to those disputes 'concern[ing] the interpretation and application of the Convention and no other agreement'.[16] In this case, which concerned information-sharing obligations under UNCLOS, a subsequently constituted arbitral tribunal would ultimately defer to the European Court of Justice's (ECJ) proceedings concerning the exclusivity of its competence in the matter.[17] These cases also overlapped in parties and subject-matter with the *OSPAR* arbitration, concerning related obligations under a regional environmental treaty.[18]

Turning from questions of jurisdiction and admissibility, we may query the use of judicial procedural mechanisms in the inter-State arbitration of environmental disputes. In this light, it may be recalled that the principal difference between procedure before international institutional courts and ad hoc arbitral tribunals is the parties' freedom to establish their own rules in the latter setting. This is of course not unique to environmental disputes, but *lex specialis* jurisdictional instruments may nevertheless confer certain relevant powers upon tribunals, such as concern what the ICJ and ITLOS characterize as incidental proceedings.[19] Beyond the aforementioned preliminary objections to jurisdiction and admissibility, the most relevant examples of incidental proceedings in contemporary inter-State arbitration are requests for provisional measures, intervention, and counterclaims.

One aspect of provisional measures in contemporary inter-State arbitrations that is specific to environmental disputes is true as well for proceedings before ITLOS. The dispute settlement provisions of UNCLOS enable a tribunal to prescribe provisional measures to prevent serious harm to the marine environment, irrespective of the requested measures or respective rights of the parties.[20] Requests for provisional

[15] ITLOS, *Southern Bluefin Tuna—Australia and New Zealand v Japan*, Award on Jurisdiction and Admissibility, 4 August 2000, 23 RIAA 1, para 62. Whereas all subsequent UNCLOS arbitrations have been administered by the PCA, the arbitral proceedings in *Southern Bluefin Tuna* were administered by the International Centre for Settlement of Investment Disputes.

[16] *MOX Plant (Ireland v UK)*, Provisional Measures, 3 December 2001, ITLOS Reports 2001, p. 95, para 52.

[17] See *MOX Plant (Ireland v UK)*, Procedural Order No. 3, 24 June 2003, PCA Case No. 2002-01; *MOX Plant (Ireland v UK)*, Procedural Order No. 6, 6 June 2008, PCA Case No. 2002-01.

[18] See *OSPAR Arbitration (Ireland v UK)*, Final Award, 2 July 2003, PCA Case No. 2001-03. The tribunal in this case would fill its mandate without the comity offered by the *MOX Plant* tribunal to the ECJ. Its treatment of the merits of that dispute remains notable in the context of the present chapter for its characterization of customary international law and general principles as, for practical purposes, subsidiary sources of law in disputes alleging the breach of conventional rules. See ibid., para 84.

[19] See ICJ Rules of Court, Articles 73–89; ITLOS Rules of the Tribunal, Articles 88–106 (as amended 25 September 2018).

[20] See UNCLOS, above n 3, Article 290(1).

measures under UNCLOS are moreover notable because ITLOS retains authority to prescribe such measures prior to the constitution of an arbitral tribunal.[21]

The bilateral tradition of inter-State arbitration contrasts sharply with the plethora of multilateral interests in environmental disputes, such as concern marine resources. This highlights the absence of provisions enabling third-State intervention in the rules of procedure of inter-State arbitration tribunals. The *South China Sea* arbitration featured requests to participate as observers to the oral hearings in The Hague, but no request to intervene in a sense granting rights of active participation in the proceedings.[22] The *Bangladesh v. India* UNCLOS arbitration proceedings, which concerned control of resources in the parties' exclusive economic zones and continental shelves, were instead coordinated with parallel proceedings before ITLOS in *Bangladesh/Myanmar*.[23] Judge Anderson (formerly of ITLOS) has suggested that India might have better served the regional unity of these disputes through intervention before ITLOS, rather than through separate proceedings.[24] Notably however, this institutional fragmentation in multilateral disputes has not given rise to normative fragmentation. Indeed, the arbitral tribunal in *Bangladesh v. India* (in which three arbitrators served concurrently at ITLOS) adapted reasoning from the ITLOS Judgment in *Bangladesh/Myanmar*, which was itself a reflection of earlier jurisprudence from both the ICJ and the *Barbados v. Trinidad and Tobago* arbitration.[25]

The ability of respondents in inter-State environmental arbitrations to present counterclaims will also rely upon the specific provisions of ad hoc procedural rules and the discretion of the tribunal. While questions of counterclaim procedure were alluded to in *Barbados v. Trinidad and Tobago* arbitration,[26] the *Guyana v. Suriname* arbitration is more notable in this context. While the arbitral tribunal's rules of procedure were silent on counterclaims procedure, it considered that it had jurisdiction over threat-of-force and State responsibility claims arising under the UN Charter and general international law because they were sufficiently connected to (and moreover 'not incompatible with')[27] the main maritime claims arising under UNCLOS in this case.[28]

---

[21] See ibid., Article 290(5). For an example of an inter-State arbitration based on a bilateral environmental treaty (and thus without a standing body of judges ready to issue provisional measures).

[22] See further McGarry 2018, p. 101.

[23] Both of these proceedings were instituted by Bangladesh as UNCLOS arbitrations on 8 October 2009. While *Bangladesh/Myanmar* was removed to ITLOS by agreement of the parties, resulting in a Judgment on 14 March 2012, the arbitration tribunal in *Bangladesh v India* would not issue Procedural Order No. 1 in that case until 28 August 2013.

[24] See further Anderson 2012, pp. 823–824.

[25] See *Delimitation of the Maritime Boundary in the Bay of Bengal (Bangladesh/Myanmar),* Judgment, ITLOS Reports 2012, p. 4, para 184 (citing *Barbados v Trinidad and Tobago*, Award, 11 April 2006, PCA Case No. 2004-02, para 223). See also *Bangladesh/Myanmar*, ibid., paras 185, 233, 264 and 326 (citing *Maritime Delimitation in the Black Sea (Romania v Ukraine),* Judgment, 3 February 2009, ICJ. Reports 2009, p. 61, paras 77, 116, 120, 122, 137 and 201).

[26] See *Barbados v. Trinidad and Tobago* Award, above n 25, paras 213–214.

[27] See the applicable law provisions in UNCLOS, above n 3, Article 293(1).

[28] *Guyana v. Suriname*, Award, 17 September 2007, PCA Case No. 2004-04, paras 403–406, 410 and 423. See further Antonopoulos 2014, pp. 18–19. Some UNCLOS provisions limit sources of

While the institution of incidental proceedings can reflect elements of party strategy in dispute settlement, it is worth recalling that respondents occasionally make a strategic choice not to appear in inter-State arbitrations. In disputes concerning environmental resources or sovereignty, the State may be more likely to adopt a position of non-participation from the inception of the proceedings, as seen in the *South China Sea* arbitration.[29] As such, the tribunal is well-prepared to establish rules preserving the rights of the non-appearing State—a presumption already enshrined in *lex specialis* instruments such as UNCLOS.[30] In another instance of cross-fertilization, such tribunals have generally borrowed a flexible approach from the ICJ's case law by finding that diplomatic communications (rather than formal submissions in the proceedings) can be understood to constitute a 'plea concerning jurisdiction'.[31]

4.3 Codification and Application of Procedural Instruments

More than a decade after the adoption of the 2001 PCA Environmental Rules, the International Bar Association characterized them as 'the first and [still] only procedural arbitral rules drafted specifically with environmental disputes in mind'.[32] Certain differences between these Rules and the organization's current rules of general application, the 2012 PCA Arbitration Rules (PCA 2012 Rules), mirror revisions that the PCA made when consolidating its earlier institutional rules.[33] Indeed, the Introduction to the Environmental Rules states that they reflect adaptations based on the most recent UN Commission on International Trade Law Arbitration Rules then in force (1976 UNCITRAL Rules), whereas the PCA 2012 Rules

applicable law in broader terms, such as through express reference to Article 38 of the ICJ Statute. See, e.g., UNCLOS, above n 3, Article 83(1).

29 See, e.g., *South China Sea*, Award, above n 11, paras 28–29.

30 *Cf*. UNCLOS, above n 3, Annex VII, Article 9; ITLOS Statute, Article 28; ICJ Statute, Article 53.

31 Cf. *South China Sea*, Procedural Order No. 4, above n 8, p. 6; ICJ, *Fisheries Jurisdiction (UK v Iceland)*, Order, 18 August 1972, Joint Dissenting Opinion of Judges Bengzon and Jiménez de Aréchaga, ICJ Reports 1972, p. 184.

32 International Bar Association 2014, p. 140.

33 For examples of these earlier procedural rules, see e.g. *Croatia/Slovenia*, Final Award, 29 June 2017, PCA Case No. 2012-04 (applying PCA rules specifically designed for arbitrations between two States); *Delimitation of the Abyei Area between the Government of Sudan and the Sudan People's Liberation Movement/Army*, Award, 22 July 2009, 30 RIAA 145 (applying PCA rules specifically designed for mixed arbitrations). On the jurisdictional difficulties of raising the *Croatia/Slovenia* award's non-implementation before regional courts, see further General Court, *Slovenia v Croatia*, Judgment, 31 January 2020, Case No. C-457/18.

in some respects parallel changes that had been incorporated into the 2011 UNCITRAL Rules.[34] Other aspects of the Environmental Rules reflect procedural interests specific to environmental disputes.[35] While these rules may be applied in disputes of either a public or private nature, this section of the present chapter considers their suitability to the unique interests of inter-State proceedings. This question is given further weight by the as-yet unused ITLOS Chamber for Marine Environment Disputes, as well as the discontinuance of the ICJ's Chamber for Environmental Matters.[36]

Parties may consent to such rules on an ad hoc basis, through instruments that incorporate them by reference, or through contracts such as those based on the Model Emissions Reduction Purchase Agreements (ERPA) developed by the International Emissions Trading Association.[37] As of 2019, parties had utilized these rules in four PCA-administered (investor-State) arbitrations arising under ERPA dispute settlement provisions, concerning the sale and purchase of Certain Emissions Reductions Units and related Clean Development Mechanism projects under the 1997 Kyoto Protocol.[38] Future applications of the PCA Environmental Rules may arise under the compromissory clause of the 2003 Protocol on Civil Liability and Compensation for Damage Caused by the Transboundary Effects of Industrial Accidents on Transboundary Waters (which incorporates them by reference, but which has thus far attracted only one party).[39]

One of the clearest distinctions between ad hoc arbitration and institutional adjudication is the power of arbitrating parties to affect the composition of the tribunal. In this light, the Introduction to the PCA Environmental Rules further indicates that one innovation which 'reflect[s] the particular characteristics of disputes having a natural resources, conservation, or environmental protection component' is the 'establishment of a specialized list of arbitrators [...] and a list of scientific and technical experts' through these Rules.[40] Article 8(3) distinguishes this list of arbitrators as an expertise-based alternative to persons already nominated by States to

---

34 See generally Meshel 2016.

35 See further Ratliff 2001, p. 887.

36 See further ITLOS 2020, 'Chambers' https://www.itlos.org/the-tribunal/chambers/; ICJ 2020, 'Chambers and Committees' https://www.icj-cij.org/en/chambers-and-committees ('[I]n 1993 the Court created a Chamber for Environmental Matters, which was periodically reconstituted until 2006. However, in the Chamber's 13 years of existence no State ever requested that a case be dealt with by it. The Court consequently decided in 2006 not to hold elections for a Bench for the said Chamber').

37 See further IETA 2006.

38 The Protocol concerns the 1992 UN Framework Convention on Climate Change. See further Levine and Peart 2019, pp. 209, 238.

39 The Protocol on Civil Liability and Compensation for Damage Caused by the Transboundary Effects of Industrial Accidents on Transboundary Waters (Kiev, 21 May 2003) is a treaty protocol to the 1992 Convention on the Protection and Use of Transboundary Watercourses and International Lakes (Helsinki, 17 March 1992) and to the 1992 Convention on the Transboundary Effects of Industrial Accidents (Helsinki, 17 March 1992). Hungary acceded to the Protocol in 2004.

40 See PCA Environmental Rules, Introduction, paras (i) and (v).

the PCA's general-purpose roster of Members of the Court.[41] Similarly, the most notable distinction between the Environmental Rules and the general-purpose PCA 2012 Rules in regards to the appointment of experts is the inclusion in the former's Article 27(5) of a list of experts (maintained by the PCA Secretary-General) who are 'considered to have expertise in the scientific or technical matters in respect of which these Rules might be relied upon'.[42] In keeping with principles of party autonomy in arbitration, however, both lists of arbitrators and experts are illustrative, and do not prevent parties from appointing other individuals.[43] Indeed, the possibility of appointing arbitrators who do not specialize in environmental disputes is to an extent envisaged in Article 24(4) of the Environmental Rules, which provides that the tribunal may request parties 'to provide a nontechnical document summarizing and explaining the background to any scientific, technical or other specialized information which the arbitral tribunal considers to be necessary to understand fully the matters in dispute'.[44]

In terms of the incidental proceedings discussed in the preceding section of this chapter, one notable consideration which distinguishes the PCA Environmental Rules from the PCA 2012 Rules is the stipulation of subject-matter requirements regarding counterclaims. Article 19(3) of the Environmental Rules includes more inclusive language concerning the counterclaim's connection 'arising out of, or in connection with' the main claim,[45] but expressly limits sources of applicable law which may support a counterclaim to those stipulated in the requirements for the notice of arbitration.[46] Regarding provisional measures, as with arbitrations under UNCLOS, those under the Environmental Rules empower the tribunal through Article 26(1) to 'take any interim measures [...] it deems necessary to preserve the rights of any party or to prevent serious harm to the environment'.[47] The clearest distinctions in this respect are the power to 'take' (rather than ITLOS's power to 'prescribe', and

[41] PCA Environmental Rules, Article 8(3): 'In appointing arbitrators pursuant to these Rules, the parties and the appointing authority are free to designate persons who are not Members of the Permanent Court of Arbitration at The Hague. For the purpose of assisting the parties and the appointing authority the Secretary-General will make available a list of persons considered to have expertise in the subject-matters of the dispute at hand for which these Rules have been designed'.

[42] *Cf*. PCA 2012 Rules, Article 29.

[43] In at least one case under the PCA Environmental Rules, an appointment was made using this list of arbitrators. See P. Sands, 'Climate Change and the Rule of Law: Adjudicating the Future in International Law' (UK Supreme Court, 17 September 2015).

[44] *Cf*. PCA 2012 Rules, Article 27(4).

[45] *Cf*. PCA 2012 Rules, Article 21(3).

[46] For these notice requirements, see PCA Environmental Rules, Article 3(3)(c) (requiring 'reference to any rule, decision, agreement, contract, convention, treaty, constituent instrument of an organization or agency, or relationship out of, or in relation to which, the dispute arises').

[47] *Cf*. PCA 2012 Rules, Article 26(1).

the ICJ's functionally equivalent power to 'indicate'),[48] as well as the absence of express authority to take such measures on the tribunal's own initiative.[49]

This recalls other fundamental procedural distinctions between arbitration and adjudication, which are equally relevant to arbitration under the PCA Environmental Rules and arbitration rules of general application. For example, there is no prospect of third-party intervention envisaged in the Environmental Rules, in keeping with principles of party autonomy in arbitration.[50] Nor do these principles make any concession to the heightened public interest that may accommodate environmental disputes, as reflected in the Environmental Rules' stipulation that '[t]he award may be made public only with the consent of all the parties'.[51] Somewhat more surprisingly, whereas the PCA 2012 Rules include a provision specifically devoted to site visits—reflecting then-recent development of this procedure in the PCA-administered *Guyana v. Suriname* and *Kishenganga* arbitrations—the PCA Environmental Rules include no express reference to this practice.[52] These distinctions from practice before institutional bodies such as the ICJ and ITLOS can have consequences for litigation strategies, which parties may wish to consider when determining the most appropriate forum to resolve an environmental dispute between States.

As rules of procedure used primarily in mixed arbitrations, the prospect of applying the PCA Environmental Rules in inter-State proceedings recalls the limited role that procedural instruments of general application have played in inter-State arbitrations concerning sensitive environmental and territorial matters. These include soft law instruments such as the International Bar Association Guidelines on Conflicts of Interest in International Arbitration (IBA Guidelines), which endorses an 'appearance of bias' standard for challenges to arbitrators.[53] In the PCA-administered *Chagos* arbitration (concerning the UK's establishment of a marine protected area in disputed territory), Mauritius cited such instruments in support of its challenge to the independence and impartiality of a member of the tribunal (and then-Member of the ICJ).[54] Yet the tribunal '[did] not consider the many [...] texts invoked by Mauritius, in

[48] *Cf*. ITLOS Statute, Article 25(1); ICJ Statute, Article 41(1). See further ITLOS, *M/V 'Saiga' (No. 2) (Saint Vincent and the Grenadines v Guinea),* Provisional Measures, 11 March 1998, ITLOS Reports 1998, p. 24, para 48 (referring to 'the binding force of the measures prescribed'); ICJ, *LaGrand (Germany v US),* Judgment, 27 June 2001, ICJ Reports 2001, p. 466, para 109 ('reach[ing] the conclusion that orders on provisional measures under Article 41 have binding effect').

[49] See PCA Environmental Rules, Article 26(1). See similarly UNCLOS, above n 3, Article 290(3). See contra ICJ Rules of Court, Article 75(1) (acknowledging the Court's *proprio motu* power to indicate provisional measures without any request from the parties).

[50] See *contra* ICJ Statute, Articles 62–63; ITLOS Statute, Articles 31–32.

[51] PCA Environmental Rules, Article 32(6).

[52] See *Guyana v. Suriname*, Award, above n 28, paras 108–126; *Indus Waters Kishenganga Arbitration (Pakistan v India),* Partial Award, 18 February 2013, PCA Case No. 2011-01, paras 33–40, and 77–88.

[53] See IBA 2014.

[54] See *Chagos Marine Protected Area (Mauritius v UK),* Reasoned Decision on Challenge, 30 November 2011. PCA Case No. 2011-03.

particular the IBA Guidelines, to be relevant for the purposes of its analysis in the present proceedings',[55] and found that a party must demonstrate a higher standard of 'actual bias' to successfully challenge an arbitrator in inter-State proceedings.[56]

4.4 Substantive Contributions to Environmental Protection

The present section of this chapter illustrates how inter-State arbitral tribunals contribute to the development of international environmental law and environmental governance. While environmental protection in the 21st century requires multilateral rules, the sensitivity of sovereign territorial and economic interests makes it uniquely difficult to negotiate well-defined terms in environmental conventions. This difficulty is evident in the work of consensus-based fora such as the Conferences of Parties to the UN Framework Convention on Climate Change and the Convention on Biological Diversity, which have in recent years relied upon their environmentalist mandates to justify the adoption of legal instruments over Members' objections.[57]

Because rules and principles codified in this manner tend to utilize vague terms, international courts and tribunals have throughout the history of environmental law applied legal texts through a still-emergent 'common law' approach to adjudication.[58] In this manner, the coherence of international environmental governance has been fortified through the participation of tribunals, which must apply environmental law as codified by its stakeholders in taciturn or impracticably broad terms.[59] Moreover, in environmental treaty regimes providing for compulsory and binding (or even quasi-judicial)[60] dispute settlement, the mere prospect of a developmental interpretation

[55] Ibid., para 165.

[56] Ibid., paras 167 ('the system of inter-State dispute settlement is based upon the consent of the Parties, and more specifically upon the rules of public international law [...] Mauritius has not demonstrated that the rules adopted by non-governmental institutions such as the IBA have been expressly adopted by States [...] nor fall within any other of the sources of international law'); 169 ('the Tribunal is not convinced that the Appearance of Bias Standard as presented by Mauritius and derived from private law sources is of direct application in the present case').

[57] See Schermers and Blokker 2018, p. 570, Sect. 779B (framing these 2002 and 2010 conferences as demonstrating that 'the strong collective political will to achieve results may prevail over the wish not to take decisions without consensus').

[58] See generally Brown 2007.

[59] For a theoretical perspective, see further Bianchi 2018, p. 28.

[60] On the recent use of quasi-judicial fora such as the UN Human Rights Committee to seek State responsibility for climate change, see (2019) Torres Strait Islanders take climate change complaint to the United Nations https://www.theguardian.com/australia-news/2019/may/13/torres-strait-islanders-take-climate-change-complaint-to-the-united-nations Accessed 1 July 2020. On the use of compulsory UNCLOS conciliation to establish State regulatory jurisdiction and a cooperative framework regarding natural resources in the continental shelf, see *Timor Sea Conciliation (Timor-Leste v Australia)*, Report and Recommendations of the Compulsory Conciliation Commission, 9 May 2018, PCA Case No. 2016-10, paras 45–47 (regarding the suspended *Timor Sea Treaty Arbitration* and the *Article 8(b) Arbitration* proceedings), Annex 28. Such delimitations may be drawn

of legal sources arguably encourages States to amicably resolve, on bilateral terms, questions that could not be addressed with sufficient precision in a multilateral forum.

The impact of inter-State arbitration as a means of settling environmental disputes may be viewed in terms of influence beyond the *res inter alios acta* character of these awards.[61] These impacts are seen in arbitrations giving rise to subsequent litigation by parties, such as the related ICJ advisory proceedings and pending ITLOS contentious proceedings instituted by Mauritius following the *Chagos* arbitration.[62] They may be seen as well in the incorporation of arbitral findings when codifying treaties, such as the adoption in the 1958 Geneva Convention on the High Seas of a rule pronounced in the 1905 *Muscat Dhows* award recognizing the exclusive sovereign authority of States to prescribe their own rules for flagging vessels (which can give rise to 'flags of convenience', and laxed regulation of vessel-source pollution).[63] As further discussed below, such impacts are also seen in the gradual cross-fertilization of arbitral jurisprudence. Indeed, while the ICJ in 1960 avoided taking a position on the specific character of the above stated rule, by 1999 ITLOS would clarify the rule in terms aligning with that earlier award's expansive construction of flag-State prerogatives under customary international law.[64]

Several inter-State arbitrations have left a normative legacy of precipitating and developing international environmental law. Perhaps the earliest example of the arbitral development of general principles in international environmental law is the nineteenth century *Behring Fur Seal* case.[65] By approaching the dispute as a matter concerned with the scope of coastal States' rights over the neighbouring high seas—and thus favouring the long-established principle of *mare liberum*—the tribunal

---

as between States or as between a State and the international community. In the latter instance, these cases establish lines between the regulatory jurisdiction of a coastal State and the institutional jurisdiction of the International Seabed Authority (which implements the principle of the common heritage of mankind). See further UNCLOS, above n 3, Articles 136, 157 and 187–189.

[61] While this traditional rule, as codified in Article 59 of the ICJ Statute, limits the de jure force of ICJ legal conclusions to the parties to the case, the legacy of ICJ case law makes clear that case-specific findings in Judgments have influenced the practice of non-party States, such as the non-party implementation of customary rules identified in the ICJ's 1951 *Fisheries* Judgment. Through the cross-fertilization of judicial dialogue, the findings of other inter-State bodies (including arbitral tribunals) may similarly challenge rigid notions of *res inter alios acta* in international dispute settlement. See further Fitzmaurice 1958, p. 170; McGarry 2017, p. 339.

[62] See *Chagos* Advisory Opinion, above n 10; *Mauritius/Maldives*, Press Release, above n 13.

[63] See *Muscat Dhows (France/UK)*, Award, 8 August 1905, 9 RIAA 83; Convention on the High Seas (Geneva, 29 April 1958). On historical and comparative links between vessel-source pollution and flags of convenience, see further Dempsey and Helling 1980.

[64] *Cf. Constitution of the Maritime Safety Committee of the International Maritime Consultative Organization*, Advisory Opinion, 8 June 1960, ICJ Reports 1960, p. 171; ITLOS, *M/V 'Saiga' (No. 2) (Saint Vincent and the Grenadines v Guinea)*, Judgment, 1 July 1999, ITLOS Reports 1999, paras 80–81 and 83 (finding that the absence of a 'genuine link' between flag State and vessel does not entitle other States to refuse to recognize a vessel's nationality).

[65] See *Award between the United States and the United Kingdom relating to the rights of jurisdiction of United States in the Bering's sea and the preservation of fur seals*, Award, 15 August 1893, 28 RIAA 263.

determined that the US possessed no right to unilaterally regulate high seas fisheries.[66] This arbitration remains notable as well for the tribunal's incorporation of the general principle of good faith in finding a legal prohibition against exercising rights for the sole purpose of injuring another State.[67] The seminal *Lac Lanoux* arbitration (concerning the use of lake waters by France and Spain) would later enrich this principle with the tribunal's observation that, as a general proposition, bad faith cannot be presumed.[68] These pronouncements of the doctrine of abuse of rights are closely linked to the principle of *sic utere tuo ut alienum non laedas*, which would later be reflected in Principle 21 of the Stockholm Declaration and Principle 2 of the Rio Declaration.[69]

The arbitration of transboundary resource disputes has provided particularly fruitful ground for identifying customary rules and general principles in international environmental law. Without referring to State practice, the 1938 *Trail Smelter* award found a customary legal duty to prevent activities within Canada's territory from causing injury in or to US territory.[70] This significantly predated the 'environmentalisation' of the same rule of transboundary harm in Principle 21 of the 1972 Stockholm Declaration, which the *Iron Rhine* tribunal later framed as central to the codification and development of international environmental law.[71] While the 1957 *Lac Lanoux* award had referred to 'international practice' to support its decision that, with respect to their shared river, Spain did not possess a veto right capable of paralyzing France's regulation of resources in French territory, it cited little authority beyond a general liberalism toward case-based normative development in the 1925 *Tacna-Arica* award.[72] Despite the absence of prior State practice supporting the *Trail Smelter* and *Lac Lanoux* decisions, both have been accepted and indeed heralded as milestones in international environmental law.[73]

These two landmark arbitrations demonstrate the significance of consensus among tribunals as to the existence and character of a customary rule. For example, while the tribunal in the *Lac Lanoux* arbitration found that France had not breached its obligation to take into account Spain's interests in the course of negotiations, it stated that 'the rule that states may utilize the hydraulic power of international watercourses cannot be established as a custom, even less as a general principle of law'.[74] Yet

---

[66] See further Lowe 2007, pp. 236 and 238.

[67] See Mbengue and McGarry 2019, pp. 408 and 424.

[68] See *Lac Lanoux (France/Spain)*, Award, 16 November 1957, 12 RIAA 281, 308. See further Epiney 2006.

[69] See Sands 1995, p. 123.

[70] See *Trail Smelter Arbitration*, Award, 11 March 1941, 3 RIAA 1905.

[71] See further *Arbitration Regarding the Iron Rhine Railway (Belgium/Netherlands)*, Award, 24 May 2005, PCA Case No. 2003-02, para 59 ('Since the Stockholm Conference on the Environment in 1972 there has been a marked development of international law relating to the protection of the environment').

[72] See *Lac Lanoux* Award, above n 68, pp. 306–307 (citing *Tacna-Arica Question (Chile/Peru)*, Award, 4 March 1925, 2 RIAA 921). See further Birnie and Boyle 1992, pp. 128 and 130.

[73] See Sands 1995, p. 191; Birnie and Boyle 1992, pp. 89–90 and 102–3.

[74] *Lac Lanoux* Award, above n 68, p. 130. See further McIntyre 2006, pp. 157–210.

when the case is viewed alongside *Trail Smelter*, a more basic rule emerges de facto, whereby States should not damage the environment of other States.[75] Following *Lac Lanoux*, there has been greater certainty that a properly seized tribunal would identify and apply that customary rule by reference to these two cases. In this manner, cross-fertilization and legitimization between these two tribunals has likely reduced the number of foreseeable instances of transboundary environmental harm in the year since.

Many principles of wide-ranging application have nevertheless possessed particular salience for the development of international environmental law through inter-State arbitration. In this respect, the *Trail Smelter* award is notable for its application of the principle of equity,[76] which had been developed in a fisheries regulation context in the 1910 *North Atlantic Fisheries* award,[77] and which was also characterized in contemporaneous cases at the PCIJ as regards treaties providing for the arbitration of riparian disputes.[78] The principle of due diligence is a prime example of how general principles that surface in international environmental law may be construed so broadly as to be too imprecise for courts and tribunals to apply confidently. Indeed, the *Trail Smelter* award's dictum that States have an obligation of best efforts to avoid damaging other territories was seen in the Stockholm era to require further development and normative anchoring in order to produce concrete legal obligations.[79]

The precautionary principle plays a significant role in contemporary environmental relations and international dispute settlement. This has been due in part to the practice of UNCLOS. Environmental protection cases have been instituted with concurrent requests for arbitration and ITLOS provisional measures since the 1999 Order in *Southern Bluefin Tuna*, establishing an early progressive stance in the development of the precautionary principle.[80] Yet the 2016 *South China Sea* award, which concluded that case without any provisional findings from ITLOS, notably omitted any reference to the precautionary principle in its treatment of allegations of environmental degradation.[81]

---

[75] See Atapattu 2006, p. 2.

[76] See *Trail Smelter*, Award, above n 70.

[77] See *North Atlantic Fisheries Case (UK/US)*, Award, 7 September 1910, 11 RIIA 167.

[78] See PCIJ, *Diversion of Water from the Meuse*, Judgment, 28 June 1937, PCIJ Ser. A/B, no. 70, p. 77; PCIJ, *Diversion of Water from the Meuse*, Individual Opinion of Judge Hudson, 28 June 1937, PCIJ Ser. A/B, no. 70, pp. 76–77. See further Sands et al. 2012, p. 119.

[79] See Lang 1999, pp. 157–58.

[80] In light of scientific uncertainty concerning the appropriate fisheries conservation measures to be taken, ITLOS ruled that the parties should 'act with prudence and caution to ensure that effective conservation measures are taken to prevent serious harm to the stock of southern bluefin tuna'. *Southern Bluefin Tuna (New Zealand and Australia v. Japan)*, Provisional Measures, 27 August 1999, ITLOS Reports 1999, p. 280. See also *Southern Bluefin Tuna*, Award, above n 15, para 77. See further de Sadeleer 2002, p. 23.

[81] See generally *South China Sea* Award, above n 11.

The *South China Sea* arbitration nonetheless provides insight into other general principles relevant to environmental disputes (and, of course, the law of the sea).[82] Stressing that it was 'particularly troubled' by concerns that China had harmed the marine environment through its construction activities and fishing practices, the tribunal applied the principle of due diligence in especially strict terms.[83] It interpreted the rules found in Part XII of UNCLOS in light of the broader 'corpus of international law relating to the environment', imputing to Article 192 'a due diligence obligation to prevent the harvesting of species that are recognized internationally as being at risk of extinction and requiring international protection'.[84]

Inter-State environmental arbitrations have more broadly contributed to the development of relevant areas of general international law, such as through clarification of the sources of international law. For example, the 1999 *Eritrea/Yemen* and 2007 *Guyana v. Suriname* awards (concerning, inter alia, harmful alterations of the marine environment) contributed to a chorus of courts and tribunals characterizing the 1958 Geneva Convention on the Continental Shelf as a codification of customary international law.[85] The *Iron Rhine* arbitration award—which gave rise to three subsequent requests for interpretation[86]—is particularly emblematic of the difficulty of systematizing the sources of law classified in Article 38(1) of the ICJ Statute and assigning them a coherent nomenclature. This dispute concerned Belgium's right of transit under the parties' 1839 Treaty of Separation and the Netherlands' efforts in the 1990s to designate nature reserves laying across the route of a partially unused

---

[82] On future reference to the 2016 *South China Sea* Award's interpretation of UNCLOS Article 121 (defining the status and entitlements of insular features) in disputes involving non-parties to UNCLOS, see Collins 2019 (examining this in the hypothetical context of Scottish statehood). The groundwork for such reference may be traced to the 1992 *Saint-Pierre-et-Miquelon* award, which has been viewed as implicitly endorsing UNCLOS Article 121 (defining the status and entitlements of insular features) as a codification of customary law several years before UNCLOS entered into force. See e.g. de la Fayette 1993, pp. 85–86. This is a more taciturn approach than the tribunal's treatment of other provisions of UNCLOS. See *Delimitation of the Maritime Areas between Canada and France (Canada/France)*, Award, 10 June 1992, 21 RIAA 265, paras 42 (Article 76), 51, 88 (Article 58), n 45 (Article 6).

[83] *South China Sea*, Award, above n 11, para 957. See further Mbengue 2016, pp. 285–287.

[84] *South China Sea*, Award, above n 11, para 956.

[85] See *Agreement to Arbitrate Dated 3 October 1996 between Eritrea and Yemen*, Award of the Arbitral Tribunal in the Second Stage (Maritime Delimitation), 17 December 1999, PCA Case No. 1996-04, paras 131–132; ibid., Annex III, Article 1(a) (concerning the parties' negotiated prohibition of explosives-based fishing or marine pollution); *Guyana v Suriname*, Award, above n 28, paras 296, 335, 338, 342 and 392; ibid., paras 467 and 470 (distinguishing the legality of acts based on whether they cause 'physical change to the marine environment'). See further *Delimitation of the Continental Shelf between the UK and France (France/UK)*, Decision, 30 June 1977, 18 RIAA 3; *Maritime Delimitation in the Area between Greenland and Jan Mayen (Denmark v Norway)*, Judgment, 14 June 1993, ICJ Reports 1993, p. 38, paras 9, 43, 46, 51 and 56.

[86] See *Arbitration Regarding the Iron Rhine Railway (Belgium/Netherlands)*, Interpretation of the Award of the Arbitral Tribunal, 20 September 2005, PCA Case No. 2003-02, paras 1–2. For illustration of the limited scope of post-award requests which may be made in arbitrations concluded by special agreement (and relevant for environmental protection purposes), see *Eritrea-Ethiopia Boundary Commission*, Decision Regarding the Request for Interpretation, Correction and Consultation Submitted by Ethiopia on 13 May 2002, 24 June 2002, PCA Case No. 2001-01.

railway.[87] After considering the treaty rules applicable to the parties' dispute, the tribunal observed:

> [I]nternational environmental law has relevance to the relations between the Parties. There is considerable debate as to what, within the field of environmental law, constitutes "rules" or "principles"; what is "soft law"; and which environmental treaty law or principles have contributed to the development of customary international law. Without entering further into those controversies, the Tribunal notes that in all of these categories "environment" is broadly referred to as including air, water, land, flora and fauna, natural ecosystems and sites, human health and safety, and climate. The emerging principles, whatever their current status, make reference to conservation, management, notions of prevention and of sustainable development, and protection for future generations.[88]

The prospect of interpreting antique treaties in the context of modern environmental disputes recalls the role that inter-State tribunals have played in the development of doctrines of treaty interpretation. For example, the *Iron Rhine* tribunal framed both ICJ case law and Article 31(3)(c) of the 1969 Vienna Convention on the Law of Treaties as supporting the proposition that 'an evolutive interpretation, which would ensure any application of the treaty that would be effective in terms of its object and purpose, will be preferred to a strict application of the intertemporal rule'.[89] The Court of Arbitration in the *Kishenganga* case, which was instituted under the 1960 Indus Waters Treaty in a dispute between India and Pakistan regarding a hydroelectric project, would adopt similar reasoning in 2013:

> It is established that principles of international environmental law must be taken into account even when (unlike the present case) interpreting treaties concluded before the development of that body of law. *The* Iron Rhine *Tribunal applied concepts of customary international environmental law to treaties dating back to the mid-nineteenth century, when principles of environmental protection were rarely if ever considered in international agreements and did not form any part of customary international law.* Similarly, the International Court of Justice in *Gabčíkovo–Nagymaros* ruled that, whenever necessary for the application of a treaty, "new norms have to be taken into consideration, and [...] new standards given proper weight". It is therefore incumbent upon this Court to interpret and apply this 1960 Treaty in light of the customary international principles for the protection of the environment in force today.[90]

The approach of these tribunals is consistent with the aforementioned gap-filling function of general legal principles, as a treaty cannot through silence preclude the potential application of subsequently emergent principles relating to the environment.[91] In this regard, a direct line may be traced between these contemporary inter-State tribunals and earlier landmark inter-State arbitrations. These include the Franco-Mexican Commission's dictum in the 1928 *Georges Pinson* award that 'every

---

[87] See *Iron Rhine*, Award, above n 71.

[88] Ibid., para 58 [*emphasis added*].

[89] Ibid., para 80.

[90] *Kishenganga,* Partial Award, above 52, para 452 [*emphasis added*].

[91] See Boyle 1997, pp. 13 and 15. One could similarly characterize principles concerning good neighbourliness and abuse of rights. See further Teclaff 1974, p. 229; Ballenegger 1975, pp. 67 et seq.

international convention must be deemed tacitly to refer to general principles of international law for all questions which it does not itself resolve in express terms and in a different way'.[92]

Beyond influencing the development of international environmental (and general international) law, inter-State arbitrations have clarified links between environmental law and the rules of other specialized legal regimes, such as international human rights. Indeed, such tribunals have arguably framed the subsequent definition of such rules by the ICJ. For example, the Eritrea-Ethiopia Boundary Commission laid normative foundations for the ICJ's later finding that the practices of local populations may serve as a basis for recognizing customary rights to shared natural resources.[93] More recently, the 2015 *Arctic Sunrise* and 2016 *Duzgit Integrity* awards—which concerned environmental protests on an oil platform and allegations of illegal oil transfer at sea, respectively—addressed the question of a tribunal's power to apply human rights instruments in UNCLOS arbitrations. The latter tribunal framed normative influence between these regimes in fairly permissive terms, observing that while it '[did] not have jurisdiction to determine breaches of obligations not having their source in [UNCLOS] (including human rights obligations) as such, [it] may have regard to the extent necessary to rules of customary international law (including human rights standards) not incompatible with the Convention'.[94] As such, while compulsory arbitration under UNCLOS places *ratione materiae* limits on which treaties tribunals may directly apply, such tribunals have nevertheless applied functionally equivalent customary rules and general principles.

Inter-State arbitral tribunals have in this manner applied classical sources of international law not only to fill lacunae in treaty instruments, but also to affirm the mutual supportiveness of environmental norms and rules and principles derived from other regimes. Indeed, the doctrine of mutual supportiveness in contemporary disputes requires harmonization if possible in a given instance,[95] as the UN International Law Commission acknowledged in its 2006 report on fragmentation in international law.[96] Moreover, by applying principles of a cross-regime nature (such as sustainable

---

[92] *Georges Pinson*, Award, 19 October 1928, 5 RIAA 327, para 50.

[93] *Cf. Eritrea-Ethiopia Boundary Commission (Eritrea/Ethiopia)*, Decision Regarding Delimitation of the Border between Eritrea and Ethiopia, 13 April 2002, PCA Case No. 2001-01, para 7.3; *Dispute regarding Navigational and Related Rights (Costa Rica v Nicaragua)*, Judgment, 13 July 2009, ICJ Reports 2009, p. 213, para 141.

[94] *Duzgit Integrity Arbitration (Malta v. São Tomé and Príncipe)*, Award, 5 September 2016, PCA Case No. 2014-07, para 207. *Cf. Arctic Sunrise* Arbitration (Netherlands v. Russia), Award on the Merits, 14 August 2015, PCA Case No. 2014-02, paras 197–198.

[95] See generally Boisson de Chazournes and Mbengue 2011, pp. 1615–1638; Pavoni 2010, p. 649.

[96] Report of the Study Group of the International Law Commission finalized by M. Koskenniemi, 'Fragmentation of international law: difficulties arising from the diversification and expansion of international law', UN Doc. A/CN.4/L.682, 13 April 2006, para 43 ('[A]lthough the two norms seemed to point in diverging directions, after some adjustment, it is still possible to apply or understand them in such way that no overlap or conflict will remain. This may [...] take place through *an attempt to reach a resolution that integrates the conflicting obligations in some optimal way in the general context of international law*') [*emphasis added*]. See further International Law Commission, 'Identification of customary international law: The role of decisions of national courts in the

development) in disputes relating to environmental protection, tribunals have further stymied compulsions toward fragmentation in international law.[97]

4.5 Conclusion

As the present chapter and its immediate neighbours have been included in this edited volume to illustrate a 'fragmented jurisdictional landscape', it is worth recalling that jurisdictional fragmentation in the current patchwork of environment-related instruments does not necessarily imply normative fragmentation in the resulting case law. Indeed, the foregoing illustrates how inter-State arbitral tribunals have played a foundational and ongoing creative role in the development of international environmental law, and how in so doing they have relied upon jurisprudential cross-fertilization. This practice improves not only the coherence of the field, but also the likelihood that the parties and observers will view an award as authoritative. In this sense, the vantage from which society views the work of justice affects the legitimacy it attributes to legal process, as well as the normative legacy of resulting decisions.[98]

Jurisdictional fragmentation is to an extent ameliorated in the environmental field through jurisdictional links between international courts and ad hoc commissions established to resolve natural resource disputes.[99] The 'shadow' of these links is also evident in natural resource arbitrations in which the parties transferred the case to an institutional body early in the proceedings,[100] as well as in ICJ cases where the parties' *compromis* foresaw the possibility of removing the case to arbitration.[101]

case law of international courts and tribunals of a universal character for the purpose of the determination of customary international law. Memorandum by the Secretariat', UN Doc. A/CN.4/691, 9 February 2016, para 4 ('A domestic judicial decision might also be relevant for the purpose of the identification of general principles of law').

97 See Abi-Saab 1999, p. 926; Ross 2009, p. 32; Lowe 2016, p. 30; Andenas and Chiussi 2017, p. 50; McGarry 2018, p. 115. On the rush of international initiatives for the trans-sectoral codification of environmental law 'principles' beginning in the 1980s, see further Sand 2008, p. 38.

98 See Lord Hewart's axiom that 'justice should not only be done, but should manifestly and undoubtedly be seen to be done' in *R v. Sussex Justices, ex parte McCarthy* [1924] 1 KB 256. See generally von Bogdandy and Venzke 2014; Cegla Center for Interdisciplinary Research of the Law 2013.

99 See, e.g., PCIJ, *Territorial Jurisdiction of the International Commission of the River Oder*, Judgment 10 September 1929, PCIJ Ser. A, No. 23, p. 27 (resolving a multilateral appeal from States Parties to the arbitration treaty establishing the Commission on the River Oder, in part by relying on principles such as 'the requirements of justice and the considerations of utility'). See also PCIJ, *Jurisdiction of the European Commission of the Danube*, Judgment, 8 December 1927, PCIJ Ser. B, No. 14, p. 6.

100 See, e.g., *M/V 'Virginia G' (Panama/Guinea-Bissau)*, Judgment, 14 April 2014, ITLOS Reports 2014, p. 4; *Delimitation of the Maritime Boundary between Ghana and Côte d'Ivoire in the Atlantic Ocean (Ghana/Côte d'Ivoire)*, Judgment, 23 September 2017, ITLOS Reports 2017, p. 4; *M/T 'San Padre Pio' (No. 2) (Switzerland/Nigeria)*, ITLOS Case No. 29, Order of 7 January 2020.

101 See, e.g., Treaty between the Government of Canada and the Government of the United States of America to Submit to Binding Dispute Settlement the Delimitation of the Maritime Boundary in the Gulf of Maine Area (Washington, 29 March 1979), Article III (enabling either party to unilaterally

Cross-systemic dialogue between international tribunals and domestic or regional bodies may continue to reduce both jurisdictional and normative fragmentation. The compulsory arbitration provisions of UNCLOS have played a significant role in reinforcing this dialogue, as seen in fisheries cases with parallel trade disputes before the WTO,[102] and in ECJ proceedings arising from inter-State arbitrations under UNCLOS and regional environmental treaties.[103]

The semantic flexibility of customary rules and general principles, as codified in environmental treaties and soft law instruments, appears likely to continue to strengthen the progressive development of international environmental law through arbitral interpretation. The multiplication of international courts and tribunals increases opportunities for judges and arbitrators to contribute to the specificity and consolidation of this body of law and practice. Indeed, a direct line may be drawn from the pioneering work of arbitration in this field and recent efforts towards the conventionalization of these normative developments in binding form.[104] While biological threats such as COVID-19 and other emergent global challenges should remind us that bilateral dispute settlement is not a substitute for robust political cooperation in a multilateral policy and regulatory framework,[105] inter-State tribunals nevertheless remain vital to the refinement of rules and principles underlying future environmental protection and human security.

References

Abi-Saab G (1999) Fragmentation or Unification: Some Concluding Remarks. New York University Journal of International Law and Policy 31(4):919–934

Alschner W, Charlotin D (2018) The Growing Complexity of the International Court of Justice's Self-Citation Network. European Journal of International Law 29:1:83–112

Andenas M, Chiussi L (2017) General principles and the coherence of international law – Principes généraux et cohérence du droit international. University of Oslo Faculty of Law Research Paper No. 2017-14 https://papers.ssrn.com/sol3/papers.cfm?abstract_id=2939082 Accessed 1 July 2020

Anderson D H (2012) Delimitation of the Maritime Boundary in the Bay of Bengal (Bangladesh/Myanmar). Case No. 16. American Journal of International Law 106:4:817–824

Antonopoulos C (2014) Counterclaims before the International Court of Justice. T.M.C. Asser Press, The Hague

remove the ICJ's *Gulf of Maine* case to a Court of Arbitration if the ICJ had not constituted a Special Chamber 'in a manner acceptable to the Parties').

[102] See discussion of the *Atlanto-Scandian Herring* and *Swordfish* disputes, above n 14.

[103] See discussion of the *MOX Plant* and *OSPAR* disputes, above n 17–18. On the arbitration of riparian disputes before regional institutions, see generally Meshel 2018, p. 55.

[104] See UN General Assembly, 'Towards a Global Pact for the Environment', A/RES/72/777, 10 May 2018. See further International Group of Experts for the Pact 2017.

[105] Some US legal observers have nevertheless encouraged a rush to the courtroom. See, e.g., Kraska 2020, China is Legally Responsible for COVID-19 Damage and Claims Could Be in the Trillions https://warontherocks.com/2020/03/china-is-legally-responsible-for-covid-19-damage-and-claims-could-be-in-the-trillions/ (Accessed 1 July 2020); Tzeng 2020.

Atapattu S A (2006) Emerging Principles of International Environmental Law. Transnational Publishers, Ardsley

Ballenegger J (1975) La Pollution en Droit International. Droz, Geneva

Bianchi A (2018) International Adjudication, Rhetoric and Storytelling. Journal of International Dispute Settlement 9:1:28–44

Birnie P W, Boyle A E (1992) International Law and the Environment. Oxford University Press, Oxford

Boisson de Chazournes L, Mbengue M (2011) A "Footnote as a Principle'. Mutual Supportiveness in an Era of Fragmentation. In: Hestermeyer H P, König D, Matz-Lück N, Röben V, Seibert-Fohr A, Stoll P-T, Vöneky S (eds) Coexistence, Cooperation and Solidarity – Liber Amicorum Rüdiger Wolfrum, vol. II. Martinus Nijhoff, The Hague, pp 1615–1638

Boyle A (1997) The *Gabčíkovo–Nagymaros* Case: New Law in Old Bottles. Yearbook of International Environmental Law 8:1:13–20

Brown C (2007) A Common Law of International Adjudication. Oxford University Press, Oxford

Cegla Center for Interdisciplinary Research of the Law (ed) (2013) International Courts and the Quest for Legitimacy. Theoretical Inquiries in Law 14(2)

Collins R (2019) Sovereignty has 'Rock-all' to do with it...or has it? What's at stake in the recent diplomatic spat between Scotland and Ireland? EJIL:Talk! https://www.ejiltalk.org/sovereignty-has-rock-all-to-do-with-it-or-has-it-whats-at-stake-in-the-recent-diplomatic-spat-between-scotland-and-ireland/ Accessed 1 July 2020

de la Fayette L (1993) The Award in the Canada-France Maritime Boundary Arbitration. International Journal of Marine and Coastal Law 8:1:77–103

Dempsey P S, Helling L L (1980) Oil Pollution by Ocean Vessels – An Environmental Tragedy: The Legal Regime of Flags of Convenience, Multilateral Conventions, and Coastal States. Denver Journal of International Law and Policy 10:1

de Sadeleer N (2002) The Effect of Uncertainty on the Threshold Levels to Which the Precautionary Principle Appears to be Subject. In: Sheridan M, Lavrysen L (eds) Environmental Law Principles in Practice. Bruylant, Brussels, pp 17–43

Epiney A (2006) Lac Lanoux Arbitration https://opil.ouplaw.com/view/10.1093/law:epil/9780199231690/law-9780199231690-e154 Accessed 1 July 2020

Fitzmaurice G (1958) Some Problems Regarding the Formal Sources of International Law. In: van Asbeck F M (ed) Symbolae Verzijl, présentées au professeur J.H.W. Verzijl à l'occasion de son 70e anniversaire. Martinus Nijhoff, The Hague

International Bar Association (IBA) (2014) IBA Guidelines on Conflicts of Interest in International Arbitration (as amended 10 August 2015) https://www.ibanet.org/Document/Default.aspx?DocumentUid=E2FE5E72-EB14-4BBA-B10D-D33DAFEE8918 Accessed 1 July 2020

International Court of Justice (ICJ) (2020) Chambers and Committees https://www.icj-cij.org/en/chambers-and-committees Accessed 1 July 2020

International Emissions Trading Association (IETA) (2006) Code of CDM Terms. Version 1.0 https://www.ieta.org/resources/Resources/Trading%20Documents/ietacodeofcdmtermsv%201%202.pdf Accessed 1 July 2020

International Group of Experts for the Pact (2017) Draft Global Pact for the Environment https://globalpactenvironment.org/uploads/EN.pdf (Accessed 1 July 2020)

International Tribunal for the Law of the Sea (ITLOS) (2020) Chambers https://www.itlos.org/the-tribunal/chambers/ Accessed 1 July 2020

Kwiatkowska B (2007) The 2006 Barbados/Trinidad and Tobago Maritime Delimitation (Jurisdiction and Merits) Award. The American Journal of International Law, Volume 101, No 1, pp 149–157

Lang W (1999) UN-Principles and International Environmental Law. Max Planck Yearbook of United Nations Law 3:157–172

Levine J, Peart N (2019) Procedural issues and innovations in environment-related investor-State disputes. In: Miles K (ed) Research Handbook on Environment and Investment Law. Edward Elgar, Northampton, pp 209–243

Lowe V (2007) International Law. Oxford University Press, Oxford
Lowe V (2016) The Limits of the Law. In: Recueil des cours [Collected Courses], Volume 379. Martinus Nijhoff Publishers, Leiden, pp 9–34
Mbengue M (2016) The South China Sea Arbitration: Innovations in Marine Environmental Fact-Finding and Due Diligence Obligations. AJIL Unbound: Symposium on the South China Sea Arbitration 110:285–289
Mbengue M, McGarry B (2019) General Principles of International Environmental Law in the Case Law of International Courts and Tribunals. In: Andenas M, Fitzmaurice M, Tanzi A, Wouters J (eds) General Principles and the Coherence of International Law. Brill, Leiden, pp 408–441
McGarry B (2017) The Development of Custom in Territorial Dispute Settlement. Journal of International Dispute Settlement 8(2):339–365
McGarry B (2018) Third Parties and Insular Features after the South China Sea Arbitration. Chinese (Taiwan) Yearbook of International Law and Affairs 35:99–135
McIntyre O (2006) The Role of Customary Rules and Principles of International Environmental Law in the Protection of Shared International Freshwater Resources. Natural Resources Journal 46:157-210
Meshel T (2016) Optional Rules for Arbitration of Disputes Relating to Natural Resources and /or the Environment: Permanent Court of Arbitration (PCA) https://www.mpi.lu/fileadmin/mpi/medien/research/MPEiPro/Optional_Rules_for_Arbitration_law-mpeipro-e2810.pdf Accessed 1 July 2020
Meshel T (2018) Inter-State Fresh Water Dispute Resolution: Some Reflections on River Basin Organizations as Arbitral Institutions. Yearbook of International Environmental Law 29:55–76
Pavoni R (2010) Mutual Supportiveness as a Principle of Interpretation and Law-Making: A Watershed for the 'WTO-and-Competing-Regimes' Debate? European Journal of International Law 21:3:649–679
Ratliff D (2001) The PCA Optional Rules for Arbitration of Disputes Relating to Natural Resources and/or the Environment. Leiden Journal of International Law 14:4:887–896
Ross A (2009) Modern Interpretations of Sustainable Development. Journal of Law and Society 36:1:32–54
Sand P H (2008) The Evolution of International Environmental Law. In: Bodansky D, Brunnée J, Hey E (eds) The Oxford Handbook of International Environmental Law. Oxford University Press, Oxford
Sands Ph (1995) Principles of Environmental Law Volume I: Frameworks, standards and implementation. Manchester University Press, Manchester
Sands Ph, Peel J, MacKenzie R (2012) Principles of International Environmental Law. Cambridge University Press, Cambridge
Schatz V (2020) The Award concerning Preliminary Objections in *Ukraine v. Russia*: Observations regarding the Implicated Status of Crimea and the Sea of Azov, EJIL:Talk! https://www.ejiltalk.org/the-award-concerning-preliminary-objections-in-ukraine-v-russia-observations-regarding-the-implicated-status-of-crimea-and-the-sea-of-azov/ Accessed 1 July 2020
Schermers H G, Blokker N M (2018) International Institutional Law. Brill, Leiden
Teclaff L (1974) The Impact of Environmental Concern on the Development of International Law. In: Teclaff L, Utton A (eds) International Environmental Law. Praeger, New York
Tzeng P (2020) Taking China to the International Court of Justice over COVID-19, EJIL:Talk! https://www.ejiltalk.org/taking-china-to-the-international-court-of-justice-over-covid-19/ Accessed 1 July 2020
von Bogdandy A, Venzke I (2014) In Whose Name? A Public Law Theory of International Adjudication. Oxford University Press, Oxford

Brian McGarry Assistant Professor of Public International Law, Grotius Centre for International Legal Studies, Faculty of Law, Leiden University

Chapter 5
The World Trade Organization Dispute Settlement Mechanism

Stephanie Switzer

Contents

Abstract The relationship between trade and environmental protection is one that has provoked much by way of debate. While there is recognition within WTO legal texts that trade liberalisation can have an impact upon environmental protection, much of the more contentious issues pertaining to the relationship between trade and the environment have been left to the WTO dispute settlement system to pronounce on. This chapter assesses the strengths and weaknesses of the WTO dispute settlement system as a forum for resolving disputes involving environmental matters. This chapter argues that while the jurisprudence of the WTO dispute settlement system has been sensitive to the idea that countries should have sufficient policy space to enact measures for environmental purposes, significant question marks remain over a number of questions such as how non-WTO law should be treated within the WTO dispute settlement system. With an increasing range of environmental threats facing the world, not least the spectre of climate change, change is needed within the WTO to better ensure a mutually supportive relationship between trade and environmental protection.

Keywords Trade and environment · exhaustible natural resources · WTO dispute settlement · renewable energy · Appellate Body

S. Switzer (✉)
Centre for Environmental Law and Governance, University of Strathclyde, Glasgow, Scotland
e-mail: Stephanie.switzer@strath.ac.uk

E. Sobenes et al. (eds.), *The Environment Through the Lens of International Courts and Tribunals*, https://doi.org/10.1007/978-94-6265-507-2_5

5.1 Introduction

The origins of the modern trading system, as encompassed in the World Trade Organisation (WTO), lie in the aftermath of the 2nd World War with the formation of the General Agreement on Tariffs and Trade (GATT) in 1947. With 23 original contracting parties, the GATT was to act as a provisional agreement to liberalise tariffs prior to the introduction of a permanent entity for the governance of international trade, the International Trade Organisation (ITO).[1] Due to reluctance on the part of the US Congress to ratify the Havana Charter that would have brought the ITO in effect, the ITO failed to come into being. The result of this was that the 'temporary' GATT developed over time an institutional structure, increased its Membership and oversaw eight rounds of trade negotiations. The last of these rounds was the so-called Uruguay Round. Launched at Punta del Este in 1986, the Uruguay round encompassed negotiations on a wide range of areas relevant to trade, including intellectual property, agriculture and subsidies. Perhaps the most important act of the Uruguay Round, however, was the decision to form a World Trade Organisation, which entered into force as an institution in 1995.[2] The WTO incorporates the original GATT 1947 as part of the GATT 1994,[3] which is one of the so-called 'covered agreements' of the WTO.

The WTO has, as at December 2020, 164 Members and with the accession of Russia in 2012, includes all major trading nations as Members. The foundational source of WTO law is the Marrakesh Agreement Establishing the World Trade Organisation which, while relatively short, notes that all 'agreements and associated legal instruments included in Annex 1, 2 and 3 … are integral parts of this Agreement.'[4]

The central focus of this chapter is the operation of the Dispute Settlement Understanding (DSU), particularly with respect to how the WTO dispute settlement system has dealt with disputes involving environmental matters. The WTO does not have unrestrained free trade as its goal.[5] Indeed, the preamble to the Marrakesh Agreement Establishing the WTO recognises that relations 'in the field of trade and economic endeavour' should allow for 'the optimal use of the world's resources in accordance with the objective of *sustainable development*, seeking both to protect and preserve the environment and to enhance the means for doing so'.[6] The compromise recognised in this preambular provision—that growth, whether it be economic

---

[1] For a background on the formation of the GATT, see Trebilcock and Howse 2005, pp. 23–24.

[2] Marrakesh Agreement Establishing the World Trade Organisation, 15 April 1994, 1867 UNTS 154, entered into force 1 January 1995 (WTO Agreement).

[3] General Agreement on Tariffs and Trade Article XX, Oct. 30, 1947, 61 Stat. A-11, 55 UNTS 194, as amended by Marrakesh Agreement Establishing the World Trade Organization, April 15, 1994, Annex 1A, 1867 UNTS 154, 33 ILM 1125 (hereinafter GATT 1994).

[4] Annex 1A at present contains 13 agreements relevant to trade in goods, including the GATT 1994; Annex 1B contains the General Agreement on Trade in Services while Annex 1C contains the Agreement on Trade Related Aspects of Intellectual Property (TRIPS). Annex 3 contains a Trade Policy Review Mechanism while Annex 2 contains the Dispute Settlement Understanding (DSU).

[5] Hoekman 2016, p. 1087.

[6] WTO Agreement, above n 2, preamble (emphasis added).

growth or a rise in living standards—should not be at the expense of the environment or sustainable development more generally, provides important background to understanding the legal compact of the WTO.[7] The placement of the principle of sustainable development in preambular language means that it operates at the level of general principle and is not binding in the way that other provisions of the WTO agreements are.[8] However, this preambular statement is accompanied by numerous provisions within the WTO covered agreements which attempt to strike a balance between a Member's 'right to regulate' for environmental purposes with the other trade related goals of the WTO.[9] There is, however, no specific legal agreement on the relationship between trade and environmental protection and accordingly, important questions of Members' regulatory space to enact environmental measures have—at least in part—been left to the dispute settlement system to deliberate upon.

As we will see, the relationship between trade and environmental protection is one that has provoked much by way of debate, including question marks over the relationship between WTO law and multilateral environmental agreements (MEAs).[10] The extent to which the WTO dispute settlement system can, and moreover should, apply other provisions of international law so as to 'defragment' the public international law system and ensure the mutual supportiveness of WTO law is a further, related issue, that has arisen in the context of the trade and environment relationship.[11] While there is some reference within the WTO legal texts to the fact that trade liberalisation can impact environmental protection, as noted above, much of the more contentious issues pertaining to the relationship between trade and the environment have largely been left—arguably purposely[12]—to the dispute settlement system to pronounce on.

Given the above context, the general aim of this chapter is to assess the strengths and weaknesses of the WTO dispute settlement system as a forum for resolving disputes involving environmental matters. The next section (Sect. 5.2) provides an overview of the WTO and its dispute settlement system. This is followed (Sect. 5.3) by a discussion on certain of the more significant disputes that the WTO dispute settlement system has heard involving trade and the environment. After this (Sect. 5.4), we will assess strengths and weaknesses of the WTO dispute settlement system as a forum for resolving disputes involving environmental matters. In line with other scholars, it will be argued that the WTO dispute settlement system, and in particular the Appellate Body, have been sensitive to the concerns of certain constituencies that the WTO should provide space for countries to enact measures for environmental purposes with an impact upon trade. However, despite such sensitivity, question

---

[7] Trachtman 2017, pp. 273–274.

[8] Lydgate 2012, p. 624.

[9] Trachtman 2017, p. 274.

[10] Kulovesi 2016, p. 49.

[11] Kulovesi 2016.

[12] Indeed, from the early days of the GATT, certain commentators placed significant prominence on dispute settlement and were 'intrigued' by using it as 'a format for studying environment and trade issues', see discussion in Brown Weiss 2016, p. 367.

marks remain over a number of questions such as to how international law agreements emanating from outside the WTO, such as MEAs, should be treated within the dispute settlement system. With an increasing range of environmental threats facing the world, not least the spectre of climate change, change is needed within the WTO to better ensure a mutually supportive relationship between trade and environmental protection.

5.2 An Overview of the WTO and Its Dispute Settlement System

5.2.1 Operation of the Dispute Settlement System

At the date of writing,[13] Members have lodged almost 600 disputes before the WTO dispute settlement body, with over 350 formal rulings issued.[14] Compared to certain other international adjudicatory systems such as ITLOS and the ICJ, Members have made extensive use of the WTO dispute settlement system.[15] This section will provide an overview of the operation of the dispute settlement system, with consideration given, *inter alia*, to its jurisdiction, evidentiary requirements, the burden of proof and issues of applicable law. Where possible, commentary will be entered into on how these issues interface with the relationship between trade and environmental protection though a more detailed treatment of such issues will be provided in the following Section (Sect. 5.3).

As noted above, the WTO Understanding on Rules and Procedures for the Settlement of Disputes—known as the WTO Dispute Settlement Understanding (DSU)—sets out the governance framework for dispute settlement under the WTO.[16] The mandate of the WTO dispute settlement system is set out in Article 3.2 DSU as being: ‘security and predictability to the multilateral trading system. The Members recognise that it serves to preserve the rights and obligations of Members under the covered agreements, and to clarify the existing provisions of those agreements in accordance with the customary rules of interpretation of public international law.’

However, while the mandate granted to the WTO dispute settlement at first sight appears quite broad, the third sentence of Article 3.2 notes the somewhat ‘circumscribed’[17] nature of this mandate. The third sentence to Article 3.2 directs that, ‘(r)ecommendations and rulings of the Dispute Settlement Body (DSB) cannot add to or diminish the rights and obligations provided in the covered agreements.’ In

[13] February 2021.

[14] WTO Dispute Settlement Body.

[15] Van Den Boscche and Zdouc 2017, p. 165.

[16] WTO, Dispute Settlement Rules: Understanding on Rules and Procedures Governing the Settlement of Disputes, Marrakesh Agreement Establishing the World Trade Organization, Annex 2, 1869 UNTS 401, 33 ILM 1226 (1994) (DSU).

[17] Van Den Boscche and Zdouc 2017, p. 190.

essence, the rulings of the WTO dispute settlement system cannot 'make law.' Accordingly, as noted by Devaney, the mandate of the dispute settlement system is quite constrained when compared with that of the ICJ, with the latter also tasked with the progressive development of international law.[18]

The WTO DSB administers the dispute settlement system. The DSB comprises representatives of all WTO Members. It is essentially the WTO General Council sitting in another guise.[19] The dispute settlement process commences with a request for consultations by the complaining Member. In terms of locus standi, only WTO Members may bring a dispute—and indeed, be the subject of a complaint—before the dispute settlement system. Interested Members with a substantial interest in the dispute[20] may act as 'third parties' to the dispute. The DSU recognises the right to third parties to be heard and to make submissions.[21] Only Members may be third parties.

The rules on standing are significant from an environmental perspective; environmental interest groups and indeed international environmental organisations do not have *locus standi* to bring a dispute to the WTO. They may submit *amicus curiae* briefs—discussed below—but, as will be argued, this process is quite limited. It does not, for example, guarantee a right to be heard or a right of access to the dispute settlement system by non-WTO parties.

5.2.1.1 The Consultations and the Panel Stage

As noted above, all disputes commence with a request for consultations by the complaining Member. The consultations stage has proven quite successful in helping to resolve disputes,[22] though in the event that the parties are unable to resolve the matter through consultations within 60 days of the commencement of consultations,[23] the complaining party may seek formal adjudication before a dispute settlement Panel. The complainant must provide a written 'summary of the legal basis of the complaint sufficient to present the problem clearly.'[24]

The dispute settlement Panel is an *ad hoc*, as opposed to standing body,[25] and usually consists of three panellists though there is provision for a five Member Panel if the parties to the dispute so agree.[26] A single Panel—as opposed to multiple

[18] Devaney 2016, p. 129.

[19] WTO Agreement, above n 2, Article IV.3.

[20] DSU, above n 16, Articles 4.11, 10 17.4.

[21] Ibid., Article 10.

[22] Davey 2014, p. 688.

[23] DSU, above n 16, Article on the procedure for consultations.

[24] Ibid., Article 6.2.

[25] Ibid., Article 8 on the composition of Panels.

[26] Ibid., Article 8(5).

Panels—may be established 'whenever feasible',[27] where two or more Members request the establishment of a Panel in relation to the same matter.

The function of the Panel is set down in Article 11 DSU as being to make an

> objective assessment of the matter before it, including an objective assessment of the facts of the case and the applicability of and conformity with the relevant covered agreements, and make such other findings as will assist the DSB in making the recommendations or in giving the rulings provided for in the covered agreements.

The usual 'terms of reference' of a Panel require it to examine '*in light of the relevant provisions of … the covered agreements* (emphasis added),' the claims set out in request by the complaining Member to establish a Panel.[28] What this means in practical terms is that a complainant cannot make new claims after the establishment of the Panel.[29] While the parties involved may agree to special terms of reference, such agreement is rare.[30] The reference to the 'covered agreements' of the WTO in Article 11 DSU is notable in that it is clear the focus of the WTO dispute settlement system is very much on WTO law, rather than on clarifying the relationship between WTO law and other areas of international law such as the relationship between WTO law and MEAs. While issues of jurisdiction and applicable law are discussed further below, the circumscribed nature of the Panel's remit, as set down in Article 11 DSU, is to be noted at this juncture.

The DSU sets out quite detailed provisions in respect of the timelines to govern dispute settlement proceedings. Panel proceedings are tasked, as a 'general rule', to take no more six months—three in urgent cases such as those involving perishable goods—and should '(i) no case exceed nine months.'[31] While the emphasis in the DSU upon strict timescales can be contrasted with the ICJ and ITLOS,[32] in practice, and in part due to the increased complexity of disputes being brought before the WTO dispute settlement system, these timeframes are oftentimes exceeded.[33] Notably, there is no fast-track procedure for disputes involving environmental concerns though to the extent a dispute involving environmental aspects would be considered as 'urgent', the parties could avail of the more compressed timeframe of three months for Panel proceedings set out in the DSU.[34]

Once the parties have had an opportunity to make submissions and the Panel has deliberated on the issues before it, the Panel will issue its report to the parties involved in the dispute. The report is then circulated to the wider Membership before publication on the WTO website.[35] Panel reports are not binding until formal adoption

---

[27] Ibid., Article 9(1).

[28] Ibid., Article 7.1.

[29] Van Den Boscche and Zdouc 2017, p. 220.

[30] Ibid., p. 221.

[31] DSU, above n 16, Articles 12.8 to 12.9.

[32] Subedi 2010, p. 180.

[33] Davey 2014, p. 691.

[34] See e.g. DSU, above n 16, Article 12.8.

[35] Van Den Boscche and Zdouc 2017, pp. 277–278.

by the DSB. The DSU mandates that adoption occurs within 60 days of the publication unless there is either a consensus against its adoption (the so-called 'negative consensus' or 'reverse consensus' rule) or the complaining party or the defending Member lodges an appeal.[36] In other words, in the absence of an appeal, adoption of Panel reports is quasi-automatic. This is a significant change from the practice of dispute settlement under the precursor to the WTO, the GATT, in respect of which panel reports were only adopted if all parties—including the losing party—agreed to adoption. The now infamous *Tuna—Dolphin* GATT panel reports—discussed below in Sect. 5.3.1.1—which are considered a nadir in the relationship between trade and environmental, were in fact not adopted, a situation which is highly unlikely to arise nowadays given the negative consensus rule. Therefore a ruling which was fundamentally at odds with environmental norms—while very unlikely to arise in practice—would nevertheless almost certainly be adopted due to the reverse consensus rule.

5.2.1.2 The Appellate Body Stage

The WTO Appellate Body hears appeals from the Panel stage. In contrast to the Panel, the Appellate Body is a standing body. As noted by Van Den Bossche and Zdouc, the WTO dispute settlement system is one of only a handful in the international system to make provision for appellate review.[37] While establishment of an Appellate Body within the WTO was something of an afterthought,[38] in its early days, it was praised as the 'jewel in the crown' of the trading system.[39] Around 70% of Panel reports have been appealed.[40]

The DSU directs that the Appellate Body shall have seven Members, each with four-year terms, renewable once.[41] Divisions of three Appellate Body Members hear appeals. Only the parties—not including third parties—to a dispute can appeal a Panel report[42] and appeals can only be lodged on the basis of 'issues of law covered in the Panel report and legal interpretations developed by the Panel.'[43] Members cannot appeal findings of fact and there is no remand authority for the Appellate Body to refer issues back to the Panel for further assessment.[44] In terms of its mandate, the Appellate Body 'may uphold, modify or reverse the legal findings and conclusions of the Panel.'[45]

---

[36] DSU, above n 16, Article 16.4.

[37] Van Den Boscche and Zdouc 2017.

[38] Van den Boscche 2005.

[39] Creamer 2019.

[40] Bacchus and Lester 2020, p. 186.

[41] DSU, above n 16, Article 17.2.

[42] Ibid., Article 17.4.

[43] Ibid., Article 17.6.

[44] See discussion in Pierola 2005, pp. 193–216.

[45] DSU, above n 16, Article 17.13.

All WTO Members are required to agree—or at least not disagree—on the appointment of individuals to the Appellate Body. Since 2016, the US has blocked the appointment of new Members as well as the reappointment of existing Appellate Body Members with the result that since December 2019, the Appellate Body has ceased to have enough Members to function.[46] While the causes of the so-called Appellate Body crisis are outside the scope of this chapter,[47] the lack of a functioning Appellate Body has (at least) two practical consequences for the operation of the WTO. The first consequence relates to the adoption of Panel reports; while WTO Members are still utilising the dispute settlement process,[48] the Dispute Settlement Body cannot adopt if an appeal is lodged.[49] There is nothing to prevent the losing side from appealing 'into the void',[50] thereby effectively blocking the adoption of the Panel report and rendering it devoid of legal force.

Numerous proposals have been made to avoid appeals being lodged into the 'void.' These include that at the outset of a dispute, parties agree not to appeal.[51] Certain Members have also moved forward to develop and alternative arbitration forum as a 'stop-gap'[52] alternative to the Appellate Body through the creation of a multi-party interim appeal arbitration arrangement—the MPIA.[53] Article 25(1) DSU provides the legal authority for the creation of the MPIA. This provision offers the possibility 'for expeditious arbitration within the WTO as an alternative means of dispute settlement which can facilitate the solution of certain disputes that concern issues that are clearly defined by both parties' with the procedures to be followed under arbitration required to be agreed by the parties involved.[54]

As at December 2020, the EU and 22 other Members are participants to the MPIA.[55] The participating parties to the MPIA have agreed 'to resort to arbitration under Article 25 of the DSU as an interim appeal arbitration procedure ... so long as the Appellate Body is not able to hear appeals of Panel reports in disputes among

---

[46] Three Appellate Body members are required to hear appeals; Article 17.1 DSU. By December 2019, the number of Appellate Body members had reduced to one. For discussion, see Hoekman and Mavroidis 2020b.

[47] And indeed, these causes have been well documented elsewhere; see, for example, Hoekman and Mavroidis 2020a.

[48] At the date of writing, the most recent request for consultations was November 2020; see WTO 2020b.

[49] In full, DSU, above n 16, Article 16.4, '(w)ithin 60 days after the date of circulation of a panel report to the Members, the report shall be adopted at a DSB meeting unless a party to the dispute formally notifies the DSB of its decision to appeal or the DSB decides by consensus not to adopt the report'.

[50] As, for example, has already occurred; see WTO, *United States—Countervailing Measures on Softwood Lumber from Canada—Notification of an appeal by the United States under article 16 of the Understanding on Rules and Procedures governing the Settlement of Disputes*, Panel Report, 29 September 2020, WT/DS533/5.

[51] WTO 2020a.

[52] European Commission 2020a.

[53] WTO 2020c.

[54] DSU, above n 16, Article 25(2).

[55] European Commission 2020b.

them due to an insufficient number of Appellate Body Members.'[56] The parties involved have already appointed ten arbitrators under the MPIA,[57] which largely mirrors WTO processes with, for example, three arbitrators appointed to arbitrations. While the creation of the MPIA as a stopgap is outside the scope of this chapter, it is nonetheless important to note its significance to the multilateral trade system. If it ends up hearing 'appeals' on matters pertaining to trade and environment, much critical attention will be paid to the resulting jurisprudence.

5.2.1.3 Jurisdiction

Leaving aside the issue of the Appellate Body crisis for now, and as summarised by Van Den Boscche and Zdouc, the jurisdiction of the WTO dispute settlement system is compulsory, exclusive and contentious.[58] A compulsory aspect of WTO Membership is acceptance of the jurisdiction of the dispute settlement system as part of the 'package deal' of WTO Membership.[59] The lack of exceptions to such compulsory jurisdiction has led Subedi, for example, to remark that the dispute settlement system of the WTO is the 'only truly compulsory system currently extant in the international field.'[60] Jurisdiction is exclusive in the sense that Members *may only* seek redress of violations of WTO obligations or other nullification or impairments of benefits through recourse to the WTO dispute settlement.[61] Finally, the WTO dispute settlement system only operates when there is an actual 'live' dispute between Members; in contrast with the ICJ, it does not enjoy any form of advisory jurisdiction. Accordingly, in the absence of an actual dispute, there is no scope, for example, for a Member to seek an advisory opinion on the WTO legality of a proposed of trade-impacting environmental measure. Arguably, this may have a chilling effect on the willingness of Members to utilise trade measures to pursue environmental goals.

---

[56] WTO 2020d, para 1.

[57] WTO 2020e.

[58] Van Den Boscche and Zdouc 2017, pp. 168–169.

[59] Ibid. This may be compared with the ICJ, which under Article 36 of the ICJ Statute cannot force States to accept jurisdiction; see e.g. ICJ, *and East Timor (Portugal v Australia)*, Judgment, 30 June 1995, ICJ Reports 1995, p. 90.

[60] Subedi 2010, p. 179. Subedi does, of course, recognise that dispute settlement under the 1982 UNCLOS does have compulsory aspects, but argues that 'both in terms of the number of cases referred to the International Tribunal for the Law of the Sea (ITLOS) and other arbitral tribunals and the significant exceptions to compulsory jurisdiction' mean that the WTO is the 'only truly' compulsory system internationally.

[61] Van Den Boscche and Zdouc 2017, p169, drawing on Article 23.1 DSU which notes that 'When Members seek the redress of a violation of obligations or other nullification or impairment of benefits under the covered agreement or an impairment of any objectives of the covered agreements, they *shall* have recourse to, and abide by, the rules and procedures of this Understanding' (emphasis added).

5.2.1.4 Mutually Acceptable Solutions

Formal adjudicatory proceedings *are not* the optimal outcome sought by the DSU. Rather, as noted in Article 3.7 DSU, 'A solution *mutually acceptable* to the parties to a dispute and consistent with the covered agreements is clearly preferred (emphasis added).' Other mechanisms to resolve a dispute are available under the DSU, including good offices, conciliation and mediation.[62] Such processes are voluntary under the DSU,[63] and unlike under the Law of the Sea Convention,[64] and indeed many other treaties, the WTO DSU contains no formalised provisions on conciliation.[65] The only relevant mention(s) of conciliation and mediation are made in Article 5(6); that the Director General of the WTO may offer, in an *ex officio* capacity, good offices, conciliation or mediation and the provision in Article 24(2) that 'Director-General or the Chairman of the DSB shall, upon request by a least-developed country Member offer their good offices, conciliation and mediation with a view to assisting the parties to settle the dispute, before a request for a Panel is made.' Such processes are 'almost never used.'[66] In addition, while in principle, the parties to a dispute may request the establishment of a working party—and this certainly occurred in the early days of the GATT 1947—there is no formal mention made within the DSU of either working parties or processes for their establishment.[67] Recourse to arbitration under Article 25 DSU is also possible though Members have seldom used this provision.[68] The creation of the MPIA will almost certainly change this.

Finally, other mechanisms such as the raising of 'specific trade concerns' under the WTO Technical Barriers to Trade (TBT) and Sanitary and Phytosanitary Measures (SPS) Committees also provide Members with various fora to air and indeed settle disputes informally in these areas of WTO law.[69] More generally, WTO committee work may allow for grievances to be aired and settled before they reach the more formal stage of dispute settlement proceedings governed by the DSU.[70] While the more informal role played by WTO committees will not be considered further in this piece, it is important to underscore the importance of this largely 'hidden'[71] aspect of WTO governance in helping to resolve trade conflicts. In line with the practice of others commentators in the arena of trade and environmental protection,[72] this

---

[62] DSU, above n 16, Article 5(1).

[63] Ibid.

[64] Tanaka 2018, p. 288.

[65] Ibid. Note that certain commentators such as Georges Abi-Saab would argue that the GATT 1947 dispute settlement system was akin to a conciliation system; see Abi-Saab 2005, p. 8.

[66] Busch and Pelc 2014, p. 408.

[67] Merrills 2005, p. 217.

[68] *See* WTO, *United States—Section 110(5) of the US Copyright Act—Recourse to Arbitration under Article 25 of the DSU*, Award of the Arbitrators, 9 November 2001, WT/DS160/ARB25.

[69] WTO 2018; Horn et al 2013.

[70] WTO 2018; Horn et al. 2013.

[71] Lang and Scott 2009.

[72] See Cosbey and Mavroidis 2014b, p. 289.

chapter therefore does not seek to denigrate the utility and moreover effectiveness of specific trade concerns though due to the confines of space, the focus of this chapter is on disputes on trade and environment protection heard before the dispute settlement system. Further attention is given to the role of the Committee on Trade and Environment below (Sect. 5.3.1).

5.2.1.5 Applicable Law

In terms of applicable law, Article 7 DSU sets out the 'terms of reference' for a Panel and instructs it to 'address the relevant provisions in any covered agreement or agreements cited by the parties to the dispute.' At least two competing interpretations exist as to the scope of this provision; that a Panel may *only* apply the WTO covered agreements when arbitrating on a dispute *or* that it lays out a minimum requirement and does not preclude reference to non-WTO rules by a Panel.[73] Pauwelyn, who espouses the latter view, notes that the practice of the Panel and Appellate Body has been such that they have not limited themselves to considering only WTO law in their deliberations.[74] Accordingly, both Panel and Appellate Body reports have at times referred to the general principles of international law,[75] customary international law[76] as well as non-WTO law Treaties.[77] As we shall see, references to such non-WTO sources have included Convention on International Trade of Endangered Species of Wild Flora and Fauna (CITES).[78]

As noted above, Article 3.2 DSU directs that the underpinning purpose of the dispute settlement system is the settlement of disputes 'in accordance with customary rules of interpretation of public international law.'[79] By extension, the Appellate Body has noted that WTO law 'is not to be read in clinical isolation from public international law.'[80] The Appellate Body has recognised that Articles 31 and 32 of the Vienna Convention of the Law of Treaties (VCLT) constitute the customary rules of interpretation of public international law. Despite this recognition, and the inclusion therein of the principle of systemic integration under VCLT Article 31(3)(c) which states that '(t)here shall be taken into account, together with the context: (a)ny relevant rules of international law applicable in the relations between the parties', there is still a lack of certainty as to how non-WTO norms can be taken into account

[73] See discussion in Pauwelyn 2008, p. 7.

[74] See generally Pauwelyn 2008, p. 7.

[75] See discussion in Cameron and Gray 2001, pp. 248–298.

[76] See discussion in Cameron and Gray 2001, pp. 248–298.

[77] See generally Pauwelyn 2008, pp. 7–8.

[78] Convention on International Trade in Endangered Species of Wild Fauna and Flora, 3 March 1973, 993 UNTS 243, entered into force 1 July 1975 (CITES).

[79] See discussion in Pauwelyn 2008, pp. 7–8.

[80] WTO, *United States—Standards for Reformulated and Conventional Gasoline*, Appellate Body Report, 29 April 1996, WT/DS2/AB/R, p. 17 (*US—Gasoline*).

in WTO jurisprudence.[81] While numerous commentators[82] have called for greater recourse under the dispute settlement system to the principle of systemic integration, the Appellate Body has been rather circumspect in its approach to this issue, clarifying that 'a delicate balance must be struck between, on the one hand, taking due account of an individual WTO Member's international obligations and, on the other hand, ensuring a consistent and harmonious approach to the interpretation of WTO law among all WTO Members.'[83] Indeed, as we will see in our discussion of the dispute of *US—Shrimp*, there is a lack of clarity as to when, and more significantly, how, a Panel or Appellate Body will consider and apply relevant provisions of MEAs.[84]

While non-WTO law may be referred to and indeed used as an aid to interpretation within the WTO dispute settlement system, it is unlikely that other sources of international law *will* be held to have modified existing WTO rights and obligations, or that a party to a non-WTO Agreement can invoke its terms as a defence to a violation of WTO rules.[85] Accordingly, in *Peru – Agricultural Products*, the Appellate Body held that other treaties do not modify WTO obligations pursuant to Article 41 of the VCLT. Article 41 provides for *inter se* agreements to modify multilateral treaties between certain of the parties only. The non-application of Article 41 VCLT was because 'the WTO Agreements contain specific provisions addressing amendments, waivers, or exceptions … which prevail over Article 41.'[86] While the dispute concerned a regional trade agreement between Peru and Guatemala that Peru claimed allowed it to maintain non-WTO compliant agricultural duties, it is likely the case that MEAs would not in general be considered capable under the WTO dispute settlement system of modifying the rights and obligations of Members under WTO law.[87]

Finally, the dispute settlement system may hear disputes brought 'pursuant to the consultation and dispute settlement provisions of the agreements listed in Appendix 1 to the [DSU].'[88] In other words, the *jurisdiction* of the Panel and the Appellate Body is such that it may only hear claims related to one or more of the WTO covered agreements but jurisdictional concerns are separate from questions of the *applicable law* that a Panel or the Appellate Body may consider in a particular dispute.[89]

---

[81] Kulovesi 2016, p. 57.

[82] See e.g. Kulovesi 2016.

[83] WTO, *European Communities and Certain Member States—Measures Affecting Trade in Large Civil Aircraft*, Appellate Body Report, 18 May 2011, WT/DS316/AB/R, paras 844–845.

[84] Kulovesi 2016, p. 57.

[85] C.f. Pauwelyn 2003, pp. 473–491.

[86] WTO, *Peru—Additional Duty on Imports of Certain Agricultural Products*, Appellate Body Report, 31 July 2015, WT/DS457/AB/R, para 5.112; cited and discussed in Trachtman 2017, p. 302.

[87] See Trachtman 2017, pp. 302–303.

[88] DSU, above n 16, Article 1.

[89] See generally Pauwelyn 2008, p. 7.

5.2.1.6 Burden of Proof

The DSU is silent on a number of important issues, including the burden of proof applicable under the dispute settlement system.[90] However, in *US—Wool Shirts and Blouses,* the Appellate Body noted that 'various international tribunals, including the International Court of Justice, have generally and consistently accepted and applied the rule that the party who asserts a fact, whether as a claimant or the respondent, is responsible for providing proof thereof.'[91] It is therefore for the complaining party to establish a prima facie case in relation to its claims. Once the complaining party has met the requirement, it is for the defending party to rebut the prima facie case.[92] In respect of the invocation of an exception, the party invoking that particular exception owes the burden of proof. As Grando notes, however, both the Appellate Body and Panel have struggled with defining what is and is not an exception[93] though GATT Article XX, which as we will see is a central provision in the relationship between trade and the environment is firmly recognised as an affirmative exception.[94]

5.2.1.7 The Standard of Review, Fact-finding and Evidence

In terms of the standard of review to be employed, Article 11 DSU requires the Panel to 'make an objective assessment of the matter before it, including an objective assessment of the facts of the case and the applicability of and conformity with the relevant covered agreements'.[95] While there is no provision within the DSU in respect of rules of evidence, the Panel is empowered under Article 13 DSU to 'seek information and technical advice from any individual or body which it deems appropriate ... (and to) seek information from any relevant source and ... consult experts to obtain their opinion on certain aspects of the matter.' While the latter provision may seem to be quite far reaching,[96] and indeed, potentially beneficial in cases involving environmental protection, Panels have not fully utilised their broad

---

[90] Though a small number of provisions exist within individual WTO covered agreements directly allocating the burden of proof, e.g. Article 10.3 of the Agreement on Agriculture; see Grando 2010, p. 152.

[91] WTO, *US-Measures Affecting Imports of Woven Wool Shirts and Blouses from India,* Appellate Body Report, 25 April 1997, WT/DS33/AB/R, 335 (*US—Wool Shirts and Blouses*).

[92] WTO, *United States—Sections 301–310 of the Trade Act of 1974,* Panel Report, 25 January 2000, WT/DS152/R, para 7.14. For an excellent discussion on fact-finding and the burden of proof under WTO law, see Grando 2010.

[93] Grando 2010, pp. 153–154.

[94] WTO, *US—Wool Shirts and Blouses*, above n 91, para 337.

[95] Note that Article 17.6 of the WTO Anti-Dumping Agreement sets out a special standard of review to be applied to anti-dumping investigations; this shall not be considered in this chapter.

[96] An example of a panel consulting experts pursuant to its authority under Article 13 DSU can be found in WTO, *United States—Import Prohibition of Certain Shrimp and Shrimp Products*, Panel Report, 15 May 1998, WT/DS58/R, paras 5.1 et seq. (*US—Shrimp (Panel Report)*).

fact-finding authority and instead have relied largely on evidence submitted to them by the parties.[97]

The Appellate Body has directed that Members are 'under a duty and an obligation to "respond promptly and fully" to requests made by Panels for information under Article 13.1 of the DSU'[98] and Panels may draw inferences from facts, 'including the fact that (a Member) had refused to provide information sought by the Panel.'[99] The Appellate Body's mandate is 'limited to issues of law covered in the Panel report and legal interpretations developed by the Panel', and so it does not have a fact finding role as such, instead relying on evidence submitted to the Panel.[100] As noted above, the Appellate Body does not have remand authority to remand a dispute back to a Panel.

Of particular note is that both the Panel and the Appellate Body have the authority to consider *amicus curiae* briefs. This power is not explicitly set out in the DSU. Instead, this authority derives from, *inter alia*, a broad reading of Article 13 DSU (the right of a Panel to seek information)[101] and Article 17.9 DSU (the right of the Appellate Body to draw up its own procedures for review).[102] While certain commentators have noted the potential of *amicus curiae* briefs to open up 'a green cosmopolitan public sphere that seeks more reflexive modernization and facilitates horizontal forms of regime accountability',[103] in practice both the Panel and the Appellate Body have been relatively circumspect in considering briefs received. As argued by Squatrito, briefs considered primarily are those endorsed by one of the disputing Members as well as those that cohere with the previous findings of the dispute settlement system.[104] Accordingly, there are limits to which *amicus curiae* briefs will be accepted and considered, thereby limiting the potential of environmental groups and organisations to influence disputes involving environmental concerns.

5.2.1.8 Precedent

There is no formal system of precedent within the WTO dispute settlement system and the findings of both the Appellate and the Panel are not binding, 'except with

[97] Devaney 2016, p. 132 and 140–141. Note that there are also special expert bodies established under a number of the covered agreements; see discussion in Devaney 2016, pp. 138 to 139.

[98] WTO, *Canada—Measures Affecting the Export of Civilian Aircraft*, Appellate Body Report 2 August 1999, WT/DS70/AB/R, para 187 (*Canada—Aircraft*).

[99] Ibid., para 203.

[100] Devaney 2016, p. 141.

[101] See WTO, *United States—Import Prohibition of Certain Shrimp and Shrimp Products*, Appellate Body Report, 12 October 1998, WTO/DS58/AB/R, para 108 (*US—Shrimp (Appellate Body Report)*).

[102] WTO, *United States–Imposition of Countervailing Duties on Certain Hot-Rolled Lead and Bismuth Carbon Steel Products Originating in the United Kingdom*, Appellate Body Report, 10 May 2000, WTO/DS138/AB/R, para 39.

[103] Eckersley 2007.

[104] See generally Squatitro 2018.

respect to resolving the particular dispute between the parties to that dispute.'[105] It is also to be remembered that Article 3.2 DSU is explicit in its direction that, '(r)ecommendations and rulings of the DSB cannot add to or diminish the rights and obligations provided in the covered agreements' of the WTO. However, at the same time, the Appellate Body has held that 'absent cogent reasons, an adjudicatory body will resolve the same legal question in the same way in a subsequent case.'[106] By extension, the Appellate Body has directed that in respect of Panel proceedings 'to rely on the Appellate Body's conclusions in earlier disputes is not only appropriate, but is what would be expected from Panels, especially where the issues are the same'.[107]

5.2.1.9 Enforcement

Unlike in certain other systems of international dispute settlement, provisional measures are not available under the WTO DSU.[108] This is particularly relevant for environmental disputes since in other international fora, provisional measures do play an important role in the domain of environmental protection.[109]

Following a dispute, and assuming a Panel or the Appellate Body finds inconsistency with a provision of a covered agreement, 'it shall recommend that the Member concerned bring the measure into conformity with that agreement.'[110] Unless either side lodges an appeal, and as noted above, the DSB automatically adopt reports of the Panel unless there is a consensus among the Parties against adoption.[111] Similarly, in respect of the adoption of reports of the Appellate Body, Article 17.14 DSU sets out that,

> An Appellate Body report shall be adopted by the DSB and unconditionally accepted by the parties to the dispute unless the DSB decides by consensus not to adopt the Appellate Body report within 30 days following its circulation to the Members.

As noted above, however, the Appellate Body is no longer functional, raising concerns that the losing side to a Panel report could lodge an appeal effectively into

[105] WTO, *Japan—Taxes on Alcoholic Beverages*, Appellate Body Report, 1 November 1996, WT/DS8/AB/R, WT/DS10/AB/R, WT/DS11/AB/R 14, p. 97 at 107–108.

[106] WTO, *United States—Final Anti-Dumping Measures on Stainless Steel from Mexico,* Appellate Body Report, 30 April 2008, WT/DS344/AB/R, para 160, (*US—Stainless Steel (Mexico)*).

[107] WTO, *United States—Sunset Reviews of Anti-Dumping Measures on Oil Country Tubular Goods from Argentina—Recourse to Article21.5 of the DSU by Argentina*, Appellate Body Report, 17 December 2004, WT/DS268/AB/RW, para 188.

[108] For a discussion on provisional measures within international legal processes more generally, see Miles 2017.

[109] Miles 2017.

[110] Article 19(1) DSU.

[111] DSU, above n 16, Article 16.4.

the 'void', thereby preventing the report's adoption.[112] Under the MPIA, the DSB is notified of arbitrations but does not formally adopt them.[113]

5.2.1.10 Surveillance, Compensation and Suspension of Concessions

Leaving aside for now the legal and practical issues associated with the current Appellate Body crisis, under the 'normal' functioning of the dispute settlement system, the DSB performs a surveillance function in respect of the implementation of Panel and Appellate Body reports. In the event that immediate compliance is not possible, the Member concerned is given a 'reasonable period of time' to implement the findings of the Panel or Appellate Body and bring itself into compliance. If the parties cannot agree as to what constitutes a 'reasonable period of time', arbitration may be sought with a maximum of fifteen months acting as a starting point for the arbitrator.[114] The parties can see further recourse to dispute settlement, including to the original Panel, in the event of disagreement on whether implementation has in fact occurred.[115]

Should the reasonable period of time expire and the losing side have failed to bring itself into compliance, the complainant may seek compensation on a voluntary basis from the defendant.[116] Compensation is relatively uncommon, in part because it requires agreement from the losing party but also because its application must be consistent with the covered agreements. The practical consequence of this is that compensation needs to be applied, inter alia, on a Most-favoured nation basis.[117]

In the absence of mutual agreement on compensation, the Member concerned may seek authorisation from the DSB to 'suspend' concessions. In real terms, this gives the Member the right to enact trade retaliation. Trade retaliation cannot be instituted unilaterally without the authorisation of the DSB. It is also prospective and cannot therefore take into account prior damage. The general principle governing the suspension of concessions is that it should be in the same sector as any violation or nullification and impairment occurred but if it would not be practical or effective to do so, suspension of concessions in another sector—so-called cross retaliation—may be authorised.[118]

As underscored in Article 21.1 DSU, 'Compensation and the suspension of concessions or other obligations are temporary measures … neither … is preferred to full implementation of a recommendation to bring a measure into conformity with the covered agreements.' While arguably the possibility of the suspension of concessions gives the WTO dispute settlement system 'teeth' that certain other international dispute settlement processes do not have, the system has been used only

[112] Pauwelyn 2019.

[113] MPIA, Annex 1, para 16.

[114] DSU, above n 16, Article 21.3(c).

[115] Ibid., Article 21.5.

[116] Ibid., Article 22.2.

[117] See discussion in Van Den Boscche and Zdouc 2017, p. 204.

[118] Busch and Pelc 2014.

infrequently[119] and has been the subject of extensive criticism.[120] Indeed, the WTO itself has no enforcement powers and instead operates as a decentralised system of self-enforcement.[121] In addition, the system of retaliation is ill suited to provide a remedy for environmental harms, focused as it is on trade, as opposed to other harms.

5.3 Significant Environmental Disputes Within the WTO Dispute Settlement System

Having provided an overview of the operation of the WTO dispute settlement system, our attention now turns to the specific issue of how the WTO dispute settlement system has dealt with issues pertaining to the relationship between trade and environment. This section will commence with a short introduction to the various environmental provisions in the WTO agreements before a discussion is then engaged in on certain WTO key disputes that have dealt with environmental concerns. It is to be noted that the confines of space preclude a discussion of all disputes dealing with issues related to the environment. However, it is intended that the selected disputes will help to draw out certain of the key themes applicable to discussions on the treatment of environmental protection under the dispute settlement system.

5.3.1 Environmental Provisions in the WTO Covered Agreements

There is no freestanding agreement on Trade and Environment within the WTO. At the same time, however, and as underscored by Hoekman, the WTO does not have unrestrained free trade as its goal.[122] Sustainable development as well as preservation and protection of the environment feature prominently in the preamble to the Marrakesh Agreement establishing the WTO. In addition, numerous provisions exist within the WTO 'covered' agreements allowing Members to enact measures for environmentalesque purposes which would otherwise be in breach their WTO obligations. Under the TRIPS Agreement, for example, Members may exclude from patentability inventions, 'the prevention within their territory of the commercial exploitation of which is necessary … to protect human, animal or plant life or health or to avoid serious prejudice to the environment…'[123] A further example can be found under

---

[119] Ibid.

[120] See e.g. Davey 2014.

[121] Busch and Pelc 2014.

[122] Hoekman 2016, p. 1087.

[123] WTO, Agreement on Trade-Related Aspects of Intellectual Property Rights, Apr. 15, 1994, Marrakesh Agreement Establishing the World Trade Organization, Annex 1C, 1869 UNTS 299, 33 ILM 1197 (1994), Article 27.2.

the TBT Agreement in respect of which Members are required to ensure that technical regulations 'are not more trade restrictive than necessary to fulfil a legitimate objective, taking into account the risks non-fulfilment would create.' Such legitimate objectives are noted under the TBT Agreement to include 'protection of human health or safety, animal or plant life or health, or the environment' though it is to be noted that this list is not exhaustive.

Perhaps the most well-known provision of WTO law associated with a Member's right to regulate for environmental purposes is Article XX of the GATT. A wealth of case law related to the relationship between trade and environment exists in respect of the operation of the GATT Article XX defence. It is often used as a justification either for a breach of the so-called national treatment provision outlined in GATT Article III and the most-favoured nation clause in GATT Article I.1, or the prohibition of quantitative restrictions set out in GATT Article XI.

In essence, GATT Article XX grants Members policy space to enact measures that would otherwise be in breach of a Member's obligations under the GATT so long as the measure in question is justifiable under one of the subparagraphs of GATT Article XX as well as the provisions of its chapeau. To expand, the chapeau to GATT Article XX directs that a measure may only pass muster under one of the subparagraphs of GATT Article XX to the extent that it is 'not applied in a manner which would constitute a means of arbitrary or unjustifiable discrimination between countries were the same conditions prevail, or a disguised restriction on international trade.' In this way, the GATT Article XX exception attempts to carefully circumscribe the relationship between a Member's obligations under the GATT and its right to regulate. Should a Member seek to rely on the GATT Article XX defence, the Panel/Appellate Body will firstly assess whether the measure in question falls within one of the subparagraphs of the Article XX and assuming that it does, the examination will then turn to whether the measure fulfils the requirements of the chapeau.[124]

In terms of the subparagraphs of GATT Article XX most relevant to environmental protection, GATT Article XX(b) allows for measures 'necessary to protect human, animal or plant life or health' while Article XX(g) provides legal cover for measures 'relating to the conservation of exhaustible natural resources if such measures are made effective in conjunction with restrictions on domestic production or consumption.' Article XX(a) further provides an exception for measures 'necessary to protect public morals.'[125]

Notably, while, as we will see below, the text of GATT Article XX(a), (b) and (g) can and indeed have been interpreted to allow for otherwise GATT violating measures to be taken for environmental ends, it must also be underlined that there is no explicit reference in the text of GATT Article XX environmental protection more

---

[124] WTO, *US—Gasoline*, above n 80, p. 22.

[125] This defence was relevant in the dispute of WTO, *EC–Seal Products,* Appellate Body Report, 22 May 2014, WT/DS400/AB/R, WT/DS401/AB/R. The protection of animal welfare by the EU was accepted as a matter of public morality and was thereby able to avail of the GATT Article XX(a) defence, albeit the particular measures in question failed to pass muster under the chapeau to GATT Article XX.

generally, nor to more specific environmental concerns such as climate change.[126] With very limited exceptions, the GATT Article XX defence is only available as a defence to a breach of the GATT. It is not therefore available to justify a breach of, for example, the provisions of the WTO Agreement on Subsidies and Countervailing Measures.[127]

In addition to the numerous provisions of the WTO covered agreements which attempt to grant Members policy space to enact environmental measures which would otherwise be in breach of their WTO obligations, the WTO Committee on Trade and Environment also provides an institutional forum for discussions of the relationship between trade and environmental protection.[128] Under the WTO Doha Round launched in 2001, a Special Session of the Committee on Trade and Environment was tasked, inter alia, to negotiate on 'the relationship between existing WTO rules and specific trade obligations set out in multilateral environmental agreements.' A large number of multilateral environmental agreements allow for trade related measures[129] and the Doha Round negotiations were to be conducted 'with a view towards enhancing the mutual supportiveness of trade and environment.'[130] To date, negotiations have not concluded.

5.3.1.1 Discussion and Analysis of Key Disputes Relating to Environmental Concerns

Arguably, the most appropriate starting point to assess the treatment of environmental concerns under the dispute settlement system of the trade regime is *Tuna-Dolphin*. These infamous disputes were conducted under the GATT 1947, and were litigated on before the coming into force of the WTO as an institution. Nevertheless, they are significant in that they set the scene for the later confrontation of trade and environmental issues in the WTO.

Tuna—Dolphin

In the GATT Panel report of *Tuna – Dolphin*[131] (first dispute), the GATT Panel was required to consider the GATT legality of a US import embargo applied to tuna, depending upon where the tuna was caught and the particular method used to catch the tuna. While there was no doubt that aspects of the measure constituted a breach of

---

126 On this note, see Cima 2018, pp. 668–669.

127 See discussion in Feld and Switzer 2012.

128 For a discussion of the operation of the Committee on Trade and Environment, see Sinha 2013 and Teehankee 2020. See also WTO, Decision on Trade and Environment, Ministerial Decision of 14 April 1994, 33 ILM 1267 (1994).

129 WTO 2017.

130 WTO, Ministerial Declaration of 14 November 2001, WTO Doc. WT/MIN(01)/DEC/1, 41 ILM 746 (2002), para 31.

131 GATT *United States – Restrictions on the Imports of Tuna,* Dispute Panel Report, 3 September 1991, unadopted, BISD 39S/155 (*Tuna-Dolphin (1991)*) .

GATT Article XI:1, which prohibits the imposition of quantitative restrictions,[132] the more pertinent question for the Panel was the applicability of the GATT Article XX(b) and (g) defences to the US measure. In a controversial finding, the Panel held that the unilateralism inherent in the US measure was such that it could not find a safe harbour under GATT Article XX(b) with a similar finding made in respect of GATT Article XX(g).[133] In the view of the Panel, the risks of allowing such unilateralism were simply too great to the trading system; doing so could fundamentally undermine the rights of the contracting parties under the GATT.[134] As contended by Howse: '[t]he Panel based its decision on an intuition that trade measures to protect the environment might somehow open the door to "green" protectionism, thereby threatening the market access negotiated in the GATT framework'.[135]

A second *Tuna—Dolphin* Panel[136] dealing with a similar set of facts came to the same conclusion and struck down the measure at issue, albeit the second Panel's interpretation of the freedom of contracting parties to enact measures with potential impact upon other parties was slightly broader than the first Panel.[137] While under the pre-WTO system of dispute settlement the losing party could block the adoption of a Panel report and neither GATT Panel report was adopted, their combined effect was such as to introduce a concern among environmentalists that free trade would always trump other concerns such as environmental protection.[138] As we will see, the *Tuna-Dolphin* reports are now considered something of an 'outlier'[139] in terms of the WTO jurisprudence on trade and environment, with the implication of the first Panel's findings that the GATT was a sort of 'centralized authority, the permission of which was required to pursue the social agenda at home'[140] now firmly rejected.

---

[132] Ibid. paras 5.17–5.19.

[133] The panel was also asked to consider the compliance of dolphin safe labelling requirements but found they were not incompatible with US obligations under the GATT; GATT, *Tuna-Dolphin (1991)*, above n 131, paras 5.41–5.44.

[134] GATT, *Tuna-Dolphin (1991)*, above n 131, para 5.27.

[135] Howse 2002, p. 491.

[136] GATT, *United States—Restrictions on Import of Tuna*, Dispute Panel Report, 16 June 1994, 33 ILM 839 (1994).

[137] As noted by Howse 2002, p. 491 (footnote 9), while the first panel had introduced a jurisdictional limitation on the freedom of action of contracting parties under GATT Article XX, this limitation was dealt with differently by second panel; p. 491. According to Howse, in the 'second Tuna/Dolphin ruling, the panel rejected the territorial limitation that the first Tuna/Dolphin panel had placed on Article XX, instead suggesting that Article XX(b) and (g) could not apply to measures that would only be effective in protecting the environment were other countries to change their policies'.

[138] Howse 2002, p. 491.

[139] Cosbey and Mavroidis 2014b, p. 289.

[140] Cosbey and Mavroidis 2014b, p. 294.

US—Shrimp

With the coming into force of the WTO, the scene was set for a confrontation between the trade community and environmentalists. The WTO dispute of *US—Shrimp* provided the first significant opportunity for the Appellate Body in particular to establish its approach to the relationship between trade and environmental protection.[141]

The dispute of *US—Shrimp* concerned what in essence was an import ban imposed by the United States on shrimp caught using methods liable to produce high levels of mortality in sea turtles. Since 1990, US domestic trawlers had been required to install turtle excluder devices (TEDs) and/or introduce so-called 'tow time restrictions'.[142] In 1989, the US Congress also enacted legislation requiring that only shrimp from countries certified as having a regulatory programme for turtle protection similar to that of the US or a fishing programme with no risk to turtles could be imported, with certification to take effect by 1991 and every year thereafter.[143] A later set of regulations, together with a 1995 court case,[144] led to a general import ban on shrimp from countries whose fleet did not employ TEDs together with a certification programme.[145]

The complainants in the dispute, India, Malaysia, Thailand and Pakistan, alleged numerous breaches of the GATT that they contended were not justifiable either under GATT Article XX(b) or (g). The Panel found a breach of GATT Article XI[146]—the prohibition on quantitative restrictions—and agreed with the complainants that this breach was not justified under GATT Article XX. The Panel rejected the GATT Article XX defence on the basis of a narrow reading of the GATT Article XX chapeau. As summarised by the Appellate Body, the Panel held that:

> [i]f an interpretation of the chapeau of Article XX were followed which would allow a Member to adopt measures conditioning access to its market for a given product upon the adoption by exporting Members of certain policies, including conservation policies, GATT 1994 and the WTO Agreement could no longer serve as a multilateral framework for trade among Members as security and predictability of trade relations under those Agreements would be threatened.[147]

In essence, according to the Panel, the unilateral aspects of the US measure were such that the measure was bound to fail under the scrutiny of the chapeau to GATT Article XX. On appeal, the Appellate Body agreed that the US measures were not justifiable under GATT Article XX. Significantly, however, the Appellate Body diverged from some of the central reasoning of the Panel. It found that:

---

[141] Though earlier disputes had dealt with issues pertaining to trade and environmental protection; e.g. WTO, *US—Gasoline*, above n 80. The confines of space preclude an exhaustive analysis of all disputes dealing with environmental issues.

[142] WTO, *US—Shrimp (Panel Report)*, above n 96, paras 2.6 & 2.17.

[143] Ibid., paras 2.7–2.8.

[144] Ibid., paras 2.8–2.10.

[145] Ibid., paras 2.11–2.16.

[146] Ibid., para 7.13. Indeed, the US did not dispute this aspect of the complainants' argument.

[147] WTO, *US—Shrimp (Appellate Body Report)*, above n 101, para 112.

> conditioning access to a Member's domestic market on whether exporting Members comply with, or adopt, a policy or policies unilaterally prescribed by the importing Member may, to some degree, *be a common aspect of measures falling within the scope of one or another of the exceptions* (under GATT Article XX) [emphasis added].[148]

The Appellate Body continued that:

> it is not necessary to assume that requiring from exporting countries compliance with, or adoption of, certain policies (although covered in principle by one or another of the exceptions) prescribed by the importing country, renders a measure a priori incapable of justification under Article XX. Such an interpretation renders most, if not all, of the specific exceptions of Article XX inutile, a result abhorrent to the principles of interpretation we are bound to apply.[149]

Described by Cosbey and Mavroidis as 'one of the most remarkable U-turns on trade and environment,' the above findings of the Appellate Body underlined that a trade measure enacted for environmental purposes should not be struck down on the narrow grounds that it is unilateral.[150] This marked a significant divergence from the findings of the GATT Panel in *Tuna-Dolphin*, which notably the Appellate Body failed to cite.

While the US lost the dispute (albeit it was successful in later Article 21.5 DSU compliance proceedings), the findings of the Appellate Body in respect of why are instructive for better understanding this foundational jurisprudence on the trade and environment nexus. In addition to its clarification that unilateralism may be a 'common aspect of measures' falling within the scope of GATT Article XX, the dispute is also significant for the Appellate Body's interpretative approach to the meaning of exhaustible natural resources under GATT Article XX(g). Adopting a dynamic and evolutionary interpretation[151] of this phrase, the Appellate Body held that:

> [t]he words of Article XX(g), "exhaustible natural resources", were actually crafted more than 50 years ago. They must be read by a treaty interpreter in the light of contemporary concerns of the community of nations about the protection and conservation of the environment.[152]

Accordingly, and with reference to the principle of sustainable development embodied in the preamble to the WTO Agreement, the Appellate Body held that living natural resources which Members sought to conserve could fall within the legal scope of exhaustible natural resources.[153] This was significant as the complainants had alleged that only mineral and non-living resources such as oil and gas would be considered as 'exhaustible' within the context of GATT Article XX (g).[154] In adopting

[148] Ibid., para 121.

[149] Ibid.

[150] Cosbey and Mavroidis 2014b, p. 289.

[151] WTO, *US—Shrimp (Appellate Body Report)*, above n 101, para 130.

[152] Ibid., para 128.

[153] Ibid., paras 128–131.

[154] See discussion in WTO, *US—Shrimp (Appellate Body Report)*, above n 101, para 127. For a useful overview of more recent jurisprudence in respect of GATT Article XX(g), see Chi 2014.

its evolutionary interpretation of this phrase, the Appellate Body drew inspiration from a range of international instruments, including Article 56 of the United Nations Convention on the Law of the Sea. This refers to natural resources as 'either living on non-living.'

In terms of whether the sea turtles that the US sought to protect are 'exhaustible natural resources', the Appellate Body again turned to other sources of international law as context for its examination. It noted that under Annex 1 of the Convention on International Trade of Endangered Species of Wild Flora and Fauna (CITES), all seven species of sea turtle are noted as being 'species threatened with extinction which are or may be affected by trade.'[155] Given this listing, the Appellate Body held that 'the exhaustibility of sea turtles would in fact have been very difficult to controvert.'[156]

The dispute was also significant for the Appellate Body's examination of the function of the chapeau to Article XX. While the Appellate Body rejected the notion that unilateralism was prohibited *per se* under GATT Article XX, it underlined that the chapeau is the embodiment of a recognition of the requirement to strike a balance between the right of Members to utilise the exceptions under GATT Article XX(a) to (g), and the need to protect the rights of other Members from being impeded upon.[157] The Appellate Body found that the US measure did in fact constitute unjustifiable discrimination – thereby failing to adhere to the fundamental requirements of the chapeau. One aspect of such discrimination was that the US imposed a blanket obligation on countries intending to import into the US as they had to adhere to the same requirements as that imposed on US domestic trawlers.[158] In the view of the Appellate Body:

> [w]e believe that discrimination results not only when countries in which the same conditions prevail are differently treated, but also when the application of the measure at issue does not allow for any enquiry into the appropriateness of the regulatory programme for the conditions prevailing in those exporting countries.[159]

Furthermore, while the US had engaged in negotiations on the measure with respect to western countries, the same was not the case in relation to the complainants, with the Appellate Body questioning whether 'across-the-board negotiations with the objective of concluding bilateral or multilateral agreements'[160] had been engaged in. While there is no 'free standing duty to negotiate outlined in GATT Article XX', according to Howse,

---

155 CITES, above n 78, Article II.1, cited in WTO, *US – Shrimp (Appellate Body Report)*, above n 101, para 132.

156 WTO, *US – Shrimp (Appellate Body Report)*, above n 101, para 132.

157 Ibid. para 156; in full: 'we consider that it embodies the recognition on the part of WTO Members of the need to maintain a balance of rights and obligations between the right of a Member to invoke one or another of the exceptions of Article XX, specified in paragraphs (a) to (j), on the one hand, and the substantive rights of the other Members under the GATT 1994, on the other hand'.

158 Ibid., para 161.

159 Ibid., para 165.

160 Ibid., para 166.

> (1) undertaking serious negotiations with some countries and not with others is, in circumstances such as these, "unjustifiable discrimination," and (2) that a failure to undertake serious negotiations may be closely connected with, and indeed part and parcel of, various discriminatory effects of a scheme, and may reinforce or perhaps even tip the balance towards a finding that those discriminatory effects amount to "unjustifiable discrimination" within the meaning of the chapeau.[161]

There is much to praise in respect of the decision in *US – Shrimp*, not least the Appellate Body's reliance upon the provisions of other sources of international law as relevant context for the interpretation of WTO law. However, Kulovesi notes that while this was indeed a welcome development, the Appellate Body could have done more to clarify the nature of the relationship between WTO law and MEAs and other instruments of international environmental law.[162] Accordingly, the Appellate Body failed to delineate whether it was obligated to rely upon these other sources of law, or whether such a move was a voluntary act on its part.[163] While greater clarity could have been offered by the Appellate Body on this issue,[164] the dispute at least did offer an insight into the sensitivities of the Appellate Body to concerns 'that trade liberalisation and environmental protection agendas are irreconcilable.'[165]

Brazil—Tyres[166]

The pertinent facts of this dispute centre upon the imposition by Brazil of an import ban on retreaded tyres.[167] The ban had been imposed due to both environmental and health concerns relating to the accumulation and disposal of used tyres.[168] In essence, retreaded tyres have a shorter lifespan than new tyres. Retreaded tyres accumulate as waste at a faster level than is the case for new tyres. Waste tyres also form ideal breeding grounds for mosquitos, contributing to outbreaks of serious diseases such as malaria and dengue fever. Burning waste tyres also produces toxic gases. The complainant, the European Communities, argued that the ban contravened GATT Article XI:1. Brazil sought to justify the ban pursuant to GATT Article XX(b) as being 'necessary to protect human, animal or plant life or health.' The ban did not, however, extend to all imported retreaded tyres as following a 2002 ruling by a MERCUSOR Panel, an exception was made for a specific type of retreaded tyres from Mercosur countries. Local retreaders had also successfully used the Brazilian court system to apply for preliminary injunctions against the import ban to import

[161] Howse 2002, p. 505.

[162] Kulovesi 2016, p. 57.

[163] Ibid.

[164] Kulovesi 2016.

[165] See discussion in Stephens 2009, p. 344.

[166] WTO, *Brazil—Measures Affecting Imports of Retreaded Tyres*, Appellate Body Report, 3 December 2007, WT/DS332/AB/R (*Brazil – Tyres (Appellate Body Report)*).

[167] McGrady 2009 provides a useful analysis of this dispute.

[168] WTO, *Brazil—Measures Affecting Imports of Retreaded Tyres*, Panel Report, 12 June 2007, WT/DS332/R, para 7.53 (*Brazil—Tyres (Panel Report)*).

casings.[169] These exceptions would ultimately prove problematic for Brazil's GATT Article XX defence.

At first instance, the Panel held that the import ban did breach GATT Article XI:1 and while it held that the measure could be provisionally justified under GATT Article XX(b), it found that the effect of the preliminary injunctions was such as to undermine the requirements of the GATT Article XX chapeau. The Panel found, however, that the MERCUSOR exception did not breach the conditions of the chapeau, a finding that the European Communities went onto appeal.

In *Brazil—Tyres*, the Appellate Body underscored the 'fundamental principle' that WTO Members have the right to determine their own desired level of protection.[170] In examining the compliance of the Brazil's measures under GATT Article XX(b), the Appellate Body drew on its previous jurisprudence in the dispute of *US – Gambling* so as to elaborate more fully on the meaning of 'necessary' in the text of GATT Article XX(b). In doing so, the Appellate Body quoted *US—Gambling* to note that,

> [the] weighing and balancing process inherent in the necessity analysis "begins with an assessment of the 'relative importance' of the interests or values furthered by the challenged measure" and also involves an assessment of other factors, which will usually include "the contribution of the measure to the realization of the ends pursued by it" and the restrictive impact of the measure on international commerce.[171]

In essence, the requirement of necessity mandates analysis of the 'importance of the interests or values at stake, the extent of the contribution to the achievement of the measure's objective, and its trade restrictiveness.'[172] In terms of the necessity analysis required under Article XX(b), a measure need not be indispensable to be considered 'necessary' but rather must make a 'material contribution to the achievement of the objective' at issue.[173] Such a material contribution need not be assessed quantitatively.[174] Assuming this threshold test is met, a comparison must then be made with other possible alternative measures and the extent to which these might be less trade restrictive while also contributing to achievement of the objective in question.[175] Any such comparison must be carried out in light of the importance of the objective in question.[176]

Notably, the Appellate Body went on to 'rank' particular objectives, agreeing with the Panel that protection of human health is 'both vital and important to the highest

---

[169] Ibid., para 7.140.

[170] *Brazil—Tyres (Appellate Body Report)*, above n 166, para 210.

[171] WTO, *United States—Measures Affecting the Cross-Border Supply of Gambling and Betting Services*, Appellate Body Report, 7 April 2005, WT/DS285/AB/R, para 306, cited in *Brazil—Tyres (Appellate Body Report)*, above n 166, para 143.

[172] *Brazil – Tyres (Appellate Body Report)*, above n 166, para 178.

[173] Ibid., para 150.

[174] Ibid., para 146.

[175] Ibid., para 178.

[176] Ibid.

degree'[177] while protection of the environment is merely noted as being 'important.'[178] While the Appellate Body ultimately agreed with the Panel that the import ban was necessary within the meaning of GATT Article XX(b),[179] the basis for such ranking is unclear,[180] and raises concerns as to the underpinning ideological stance of the Appellate Body in seemingly ranking protection of the environment as less vital than the protection of human health.[181] Indeed, such an anthropocentric approach also fails to grasp the complex interlinkages between human and environmental health and how such concerns cannot be neatly siloed.

Leading on from the above, while the Appellate Body agreed with the findings of the Panel that the measure was necessary, it overturned the Panel's findings that the MERCOSUR exception met the requirements of chapeau. The Appellate Body held in respect of the legal test under the chapeau, discrimination would be arbitrary or unjustifiable if 'the reasons given for this discrimination bear no rational connection to the objective falling within the purview of a paragraph of Article XX.'[182] The MERCUSOR exception, in essence, failed to demonstrate a rational connection to the public health goals that the import ban sought to fulfil. According to the Appellate Body:

> we have difficulty understanding how discrimination might be viewed as complying with the chapeau of Article XX when the alleged rationale for discriminating does not relate to the pursuit of or would go against the objective that was provisionally found to justify a measure under a paragraph of Article XX.[183]

What is notable about this finding is that a full, rather than selective import ban, would undoubtedly have passed muster before the Appellate Body,[184] putting paid to the notion that the jurisprudence of the WTO dispute settlement system will always rule in favour of more, as opposed to less trade.[185]

Canada—Renewable Energy

This dispute, in fact two parallel cases brought by the European Union and Japan, arose from the imposition by Ontario of domestic content requirements for certain generators of renewable energy in order to be eligible for a feed-in tariff programme

---

[177] Ibid., para 179. See discussion in Andersen 2015, p. 397.

[178] Ibid., para 179. See discussion in Andersen 2015, p. 397.

[179] Ibid., para 210.

[180] Andersen 2015, p. 397.

[181] For a general discussion on such issues, see Andersen 2015.

[182] *Brazil—Tyres (Appellate Body Report)*, above n 166, para 227.

[183] Ibid., para 227.

[184] Cosbey and Mavroidis 2014b, p. 299.

[185] Ibid.

(FIT).[186] The programme was designed to increase the levels of renewable electricity within the Ontario energy supply system.[187] Entities participating in the FIT programme were paid a guaranteed price under a 20 or 40-year contract for every kilowatt-hour of eligible electricity generated.[188] An additional requirement under the FIT programme for 'minimum required domestic content levels' was applied to the development and construction of facilities for energy generation from solar photovoltaic (PV) and wind power.[189]

In the dispute, the EU and Japan claimed that the domestic content requirements applicable to solar photovoltaic and wind power generation facilities constituted a prohibited subsidy as defined by Article 3.1(b) and Article 3.2 of the Agreement on Subsidies and Countervailing Measures (SCM). These provisions prohibit 'subsidies contingent, whether solely or as one of several other conditions, *upon the use of domestic over imported goods* (emphasis added).' The complainants also alleged a violation of the national treatment obligation under GATT Article III:4 and Article 2.1 of the Agreement on Trade Related Measures (TRIMS). Both the Panel and the Appellate Body upheld the claim that the local content requirements at issue violated GATT Article III:4 and thus by extension, constituted a violation of TRIMS Article 2.1. Canada had attempted to rely on the Article III:8(a) GATT derogation for government procurement, an argument which was not upheld.[190] In addition, both the Panel and the Appellate Body failed to find a violation of the SCM, albeit in respect of certain aspects of the dispute, they adopted different reasoning. It is the SCM dimension of the dispute that has sparked the most commentary.

Under the WTO SCM, a subsidy exists when 'there is a financial contribution by a government or any public body within the territory of a Member (and ...) a benefit is thereby conferred.'[191] A benefit is conferred when the recipient receives a financial contribution more advantageous than that available on the market.[192] By extension, '(t)hat a financial contribution confers an advantage on its recipient cannot be determined in absolute terms, but requires a comparison with a benchmark,

[186] There has been extensive discussion of this dispute in the literature. See, for example, Espa and Marín Durán 2018; Farah 2015; Farah and Cima 2013; Cosbey and Mavroidis 2014a; Davies 2015; Dawson 2019; Weber and Koch 2015.

[187] WTO, *Canada—Certain Measures Affecting the Renewable Energy Generation Sector*, Appellate Body Report, 24 May 2013, WT/DS412/AB/R (*Canada—Renewable Energy (Appellate Body Report)*); WTO, *Canada–Measures Relating to the Feed-In Tariff Program*, Appellate Body Report, 24 May 2013, WT/DS426/AB/R (*Canada—Feed-In Tariff Program (Appellate Body Report)* para 4.17.

[188] Ibid.

[189] Ibid., paras 4.21–4.23.

[190] The reasoning of the Appellate Body in respect of the legal interpretation of Article III:8(a) was arguably narrower than that employed by the Panel; see discussion in Charnovitz and Fischer 2015.

[191] See WTO, Agreement on Subsidies and Countervailing Measures, Apr. 15, 1994, Marrakesh Agreement Establishing the World Trade Organization, Annex 1A, 1869 UNTS 14, Article 1 for the definition of a subsidy.

[192] WTO, *Canada—Renewable Energy (Appellate Body Report)*); WTO, *Canada—Feed-In Tariff Program (Appellate Body Report)*, above n 187, para 5.163.

which, in the case of subsidies, derives from the market.'[193] In other words, key to the definition of a benefit is the task of defining the benchmark of the relevant market. The Panel was not satisfied that a separate market existed for electricity from wind or solar PV. The Panel instead found that the relevant market was that for all electricity[194] but that no such competitive market for wholesale electricity actually existed or could reasonably be achieved in Ontario due to the levels of intervention required to achieve a satisfactory diversity in sources of supply for electricity.[195] Instead, the Panel observed that one way to assess whether a benefit existed was via, 'the relevant rates of return of the challenged …contracts with the relevant average cost of capital in Canada.'[196] However, in the absence of required information, the Panel was unable to complete its analysis and therefore was unable to uphold the complainants' contentions that a benefit existed.[197]

On appeal, the Appellate Body did not uphold the appellants' claims that a benefit did in fact exist but proceeded along different lines to that of the Panel. The Appellate Body rejected that the relevant benchmark was the wholesale market for electricity as a whole and instead found that the relevant market benchmarks should take account of existence of a separate market for solar PV and wind electricity sector.[198] However, in the view of the Appellate Body, 'where a government creates a market, it cannot be said that the government intervention distorts the market, as there would not be a market if the government had not created it'.[199] Accordingly, for the Appellate Body, it was the market for renewable electricity that should provide the benchmark against which the existence of a benefit should be assessed.[200] In this respect, 'the relevant question is whether wind and solar electricity suppliers would have entered the renewable electricity market given those targets but absent the FIT program, not whether they would have entered the blended electricity wholesale market without the subventions.'[201] However, in the absence of full exploration of relevant evidence by the Panel, the Appellate Body was unable to complete the analysis in respect of

---

[193] Ibid., para 5.164.

[194] WTO, *Canada—Certain Measures Affecting the Renewable Energy Generation Sector*, Panel Report, 19 December 2012, WT/DS412/R, (*Canada—Renewable Energy (Panel Report)*); WTO, *Canada—Measures Relating to the Feed-in Tariff Program*, Panel Report, 19 December 2012, WT/DS426/R (*Canada – Feed-In Tariff Program (Panel Report)*), para 7.318.

[195] Ibid., paras 7.318–7.327.

[196] Ibid., para 7.327.

[197] Ibid., para 7.328.

[198] WTO, *Canada—Renewable Energy (Appellate Body Report)*); WTO, *Canada—Feed-In Tariff Program (Appellate Body Report)*, above n 187, para 5.190. In essence, the 'proper benchmark for wind- and solar PV-generated electricity should take into account the Government of Ontario's definition of the energy supply-mix as including wind- and solar PV-generated electricity, which implies the existence of separate markets for wind- and solar PV-generated electric' para 5.204.

[199] WTO, *Canada—Renewable Energy (Appellate Body Report)*); WTO, *Canada—Feed-In Tariff Program (Appellate Body Report)*, above n 187, para 5.118.

[200] Ibid., para 5.187.

[201] Charnovitz and Fischer 2015, p. 198.

whether a benefit existed and so was unable to assess whether the scheme in question constituted a prohibited subsidy.[202]

The legal test employed by the Appellate Body in this dispute made it virtually 'impossible' for the FIT programme to constitute a subsidy within the meaning of the WTO Agreement on Subsidies and Countervailing Measures (SCM).[203] This was because, the Appellate Body 'in effect, moved the goalpost by redefining the market to be electricity from renewable sources. As a result, the question of whether the prices paid in the FITs are above market prices no longer has an obvious answer'[204] and certainly a much less obvious answer than one if the relevant market had been the wholesale electricity as a whole. Cosbey and Mavroidis have commented on the, 'significant legal acrobatics that the (Appellate Body) had to employ to avoid finding that a FIT—a widespread and effective tool of climate change mitigation policy—was a subsidy.'[205] Of significance within this jurisprudence is that the Appellate Body did not attempt to justify its reasoning by reference to the policy distinction between the two types of electricity production at issue within the dispute; i.e. their respective impacts of renewable energy on the one hand, and electricity powered by fossil fuels on the other, on *climate change emissions*.[206] While attempting to illustrate its environmental *bona fides* by directing that, 'fossil fuel resources are exhaustible, and thus fossil energy needs to be replaced progressively if electricity supply is to be guaranteed in the long term,'[207] the Appellate Body would have been on firmer ground, at least from an environmental law perspective, to have focused on the climate change aspects of the move away from fossil fuels, rather than emphasising the exhaustibility of conventional fuels.[208]

More generally, the dispute leaves open important questions as to the mutual supportiveness of the international trade and climate regimes.[209] Indeed, it has been argued that while the legal acrobatics performed by the Appellate Body here to avoid a finding that the FIT scheme constituted a subsidy was likely the result of a desire to ensure the mutual supportiveness of WTO law with the demands of the environmental community, a finding of a subsidy may well have prompted a more focused and detailed discussion on the need for 'reasonable environmental exceptions in the SCM Agreement'.[210] This would undoubtedly be more beneficial than having to rely on 'judicial creativity' on an ongoing basis.[211]

---

[202] WTO, *Canada—Renewable Energy (Appellate Body Report))*; WTO, *Canada – Feed-In Tariff Program (Appellate Body Report)*, above n 187, paras 5.245–5.246.

[203] See Espa 2019, p. 989.

[204] Charnovitz and Fischer 2015, p. 204.

[205] Cosbey and Mavroidis 2014b, p. 298.

[206] Ibid.

[207] WTO, *Canada—Renewable Energy (Appellate Body Report))*; WTO, *Canada—Feed-In Tariff Program (Appellate Body Report)*, above n 187, para 5.186.

[208] Charnovitz and Fischer 2015, p. 208.

[209] See e.g. Kulovesi 2016. For more a general discussion, see also Amerjee and Nakul Nayak 2014.

[210] Charnovitz and Fischer 2015, pp. 207–209.

[211] Ibid. See also Bigdeli 2014.

US—Tuna II

The *US—Tuna II* dispute centred upon US labelling requirements for use of the terminology of 'dolphin safe' when tuna is sold in the US.[212] In 2008, Mexico brought a dispute to the WTO alleging that the US, in its 'dolphin safe' labelling requirements, had breached numerous provisions of the TBT and the GATT. The US 'dolphin safe' labelling requirements distinguished between tuna depending upon where it was caught and the fishing method used.[213] The essence of these requirements was that tuna caught in the eastern tropical pacific (ETP) using purse seine nets to set on or encircle dolphins would not be eligible for the 'dolphin safe' label. This was the case even if no dolphins were killed or injured in the process. The requirements at issue had a particular impact upon the Mexican tuna fleet.

The Panel in *US—Tuna II* found that the labelling regime constituted a technical regulation and therefore fell within the purview of the TBT Agreement. However, the Panel considered that there had been no breach of the non-discrimination obligation under Article 2.1 TBT.[214] However, the Panel did uphold Mexico's complaint that the US labelling requirement was a violation of Article 2.2 TBT as it was 'more trade restrictive than necessary to fulfil a legitimate objective.'

On appeal, the Appellate Body upheld the Panel's finding that the labelling regime constituted a technical regulation but reversed the Panel's finding that it constituted a breach of Article 2.2 TBT. The Appellate Body found, however, that the US regime *was* in breach of its obligations under Article 2.1 TBT, reversing the Panel's findings on that issue. Article 2.1 TBT requires that any like imported product be granted 'no less favourable treatment' in comparison with a like domestic product. The Appellate Body held that in respect of the obligation contained in Article 2.1 TBT, 'technical regulations may pursue legitimate objectives but must not be applied in a manner that would constitute a means of arbitrary or unjustifiable discrimination.'[215] The Appellate Body found that the difference in labelling regime, depending upon the fishing methods used and where the tuna was caught was not sufficiently justified by the US. In essence, whereas the risk from setting on dolphins in one particular area—the Eastern Tropical Pacific—was fully internalised within the US regime, the same could not be said for tuna caught outside of the ETP using different fishing

[212] There has been extensive discussion of this dispute in the literature. See, for example, Fagundes Cezar 2018; Crowley and Howse 2014; Howse and Levy 2013; Kelly 2014.

[213] WTO, *United States—Measures Concerning the Importation, Marketing and Sale of Tuna and Tuna Products,* Panel Report, 15 September 2011, WT/DS381/R (*US—Tuna II (Panel Report)*) paras 2.9 to 2.26.

[214] Ibid., paras 6.41 to 6.44. The Panel exercised judicial economy in respect of Mexico's claims under GATT Article I:1 and III:4. This was because it considered that 'in addressing all aspects of Mexico's claims under the TBT Agreement, including, but not limited to, its discrimination claims, we have addressed Mexico's claims in a manner sufficient to resolve the dispute'.

[215] WTO, *United States—Measures Concerning the Importation, Marketing and Sale of Tuna and Tuna Products,* Appellate Body Report, 16 May 2012, WT/DS381/AB/R (*US—Tuna II (Appellate Body Report, Appellate Body Report)*) para 213.

methods.[216] Accordingly, the regulation applicable to non-ETP tuna fishing was insufficiently calibrated to the risks involved and hence was too lax.[217] The lack of calibration according to the risk profile involved hence led to the Appellate Body's finding of a breach of the 'no less favourable treatment' obligation set out in Article 2.1 TBT.

In response to the Appellate Body's findings, the US instituted a number of changes to its labelling regime, including the introduction of a requirement that in respect of tuna caught *outside* the ETP using purse seine nets, certification would be required to confirm that no dolphins were killed or seriously injured in the process. Additional tracking and verification requirements were also added for tuna caught *within* the ETP. Compliance proceedings under Article 21.5 DSU were subsequently taken in respect of the new requirements. Breaches of Articles I:1 and III:4 of the GATT were found by both the Panel and the Appellate Body though again, the findings were based on different legal grounds. In relation to whether the measure in question could be justified under GATT Article XX, the Appellate Body found that the conditions of the chapeau were not satisfied. In addition, both the Panel and the Appellate Body again struck down the US regime as being a breach of Article 2.1 TBT, albeit for different reasons. The reasoning here was similar to its first findings in the dispute and concerned the calibration of risk in respect of dolphin injury and mortality.[218] Further changes were made to the US regime with a view to improving the risk calibration of the measure, and in a second set of compliance proceedings, the measure finally passed muster before both the Panel and the Appellate Body.[219]

The facts and indeed legal analysis engaged in in *US—Tuna II* are undoubtedly complex. However, some preliminary points can be made in respect of the analysis engaged in in the dispute and its contribution to the coherence of trade and environment jurisprudence. Of particular note is the Appellate Body's focus on the concept of risk calibration in its non-discrimination analysis under TBT Article 2.1. While it is not to be denied that there was indeed a lack of even-handedness to the US measure,[220] rather than the 'risk-based approach constraining WTO decision-making, it might even reasonably appear that an emphasis on risk unshackled adjudicators from principled constraints.'[221] This is because '(a)s soon as one distinction was addressed, there seemed to be another problematic one to be found.'[222] Furthermore, as articulated by Coglianese and Sapir, the Appellate Body provided little by way of clarification to

---

216 Ibid., para 297; 'The US measure fully addresses the adverse effects on dolphins resulting from setting on dolphins in the ETP, whereas it does "not address mortality (observed or unobserved) arising from fishing methods other than setting on dolphins outside the ETP"'.

217 Ibid.

218 For a useful discussion on the issue of risk calibration, see Coglianese and Sapir 2017.

219 For a useful summary, see https://www.wto.org/english/tratop_e/dispu_e/cases_e/ds381_e.htm Accessed 18 December 2020.

220 Coglianese and Sapir 2017.

221 Ibid., p. 347.

222 Ibid.

guide policy makers[223] on how to manage the process of risk calibration. It is one thing to direct that measures should be calibrated in accordance with the different profiles of risk that may exist, but it is an entirely different task to provide useful guidance on such calibration processes. In the absence of such guidance, profound potential exists for a chilling effect to occur. Furthermore, while the dispute was—eventually—heralded as a 'win' for environmental protection, 'Mexican tuna producers … responded to this dispute by diversifying their export destinations rather than changing their methods to increase their US market share.'[224] Accordingly, while the *legal* results of the dispute were such that US efforts to reduce the practice of 'setting on' dolphins were ultimately upheld, in real terms, the US regulatory efforts also likely brought about trade diversion of Mexican exports to other jurisdictions without such stringent—and costly—requirements.[225]

As explored further below, the jurisprudence of the Panel and of the Appellate Body has many positive aspects in respect of helping to fashion a jurisprudence more responsive to environmental concerns. However, and as demonstrated by *US—Tuna II,* problems do remain, a fact that will be further elucidated in the succeeding section which attempts to assess the strengths and weaknesses of the WTO dispute settlement system as a forum for resolving disputes involving environmental matters.

5.4 Assessment of the Strengths and Weaknesses of the WTO Dispute Settlement System as a Forum for Resolving Disputes Involving Environmental Matters

It is important to underscore that there has been little by way of legal change within the WTO in respect of the relationship between trade and environmental protection.[226] However, as demonstrated above and as argued by Cosbey and Mavroidis, '(t)he case law, by contrast, has showed a significant and welcome evolution… (with) the dominant trend (being) toward deference towards nationally enunciated objectives and the measures chosen to achieve them, even where those measures are trade restrictive.'[227] Such deference marks a considerably *volte face* from the dark days of the GATT era *Tuna-Dolphin* litigation.

Despite the failure of the Doha Round environmental mandate negotiations to conclude, commentators such as Quick would argue against the feasibility and moreover need for further negotiations on the relationship between trade and environmental protection, pointing to the dispute settlement system's ability to 'get the job

223 See generally Coglianese and Sapir 2017.

224 See generally Baroncini and Brunel 2020.

225 See discussion in Baroncini and Brunel 2020.

226 Cosbey and Mavroidis 2014b, p. 300.

227 Ibid.

done.'[228] In a similar vein, Howse has noted the ability of the jurisprudence of the WTO dispute settlement to deftly strike the balance between trade liberalisation on the one hand, and the protection of sensitive interests on the other.[229] In the view of Howse, the Appellate Body has very much crafted its own role, separate from that of the WTO 'insider' community. A central underpinning vision of the Appellate Body was that 'a kind of fundamental balance or equilibrium between an inherent right to regulate and specific disciplines on its use' existed within the WTO Agreements.'[230]

While, however, the Appellate Body has managed to dampen some of the more vehement critiques of how environmental concerns are treated under the WTO dispute settlement, its jurisprudence is not absent of problems. The Appellate Body's 'ranking' of values in *Brazil—Tyres*, for example, evokes an anthropocentric approach which may devalue the position of environmental protection more generally. Furthermore, while the reference to various MEAs in *US—Shrimp* is seemingly positive, more generally, the jurisprudence of the WTO dispute settlement system does not provide 'a solid basis for constructive interaction between the international trade and environmental regimes.'[231] As discussed above, there seems little scope for the WTO dispute settlement system to allow MEAs to be utilised as in a way that modifies the rights and obligations of Members, leading to greater potential for a conflict between WTO law and environmental law.[232]

Leaving it to the dispute settlement system to delineate the appropriate relationship between trade and environmental protection is additionally problematic in that we are reliant upon the 'right' disputes being brought to influence state behaviour. To exemplify, we now have a rich—if still incomplete—jurisprudence on support measures for renewable energy, albeit one that saw the Appellate Body engage in considerable legal acrobatics to avoid a finding of that a subsidy existed. However, we have no case law on support for environmentally destructive fossil fuels.[233]

In a similar vein to Howse, Trachtman praises the 'good instincts' of the Appellate Body and credits it, together with the influence of the wider trade community, for generally making decisions sensitive to the environment.[234] However, he argues that too much emphasis has been placed on such good instincts due to a lack of an internally coherent body of jurisprudence on the relationship between trade and environment. This jurisprudential incoherence poses significant risks of what Trachtman refers to as a 'virtual environmental disaster in Geneva.'[235] Trachtman criticises two particular aspects of this jurisprudence; the tendency of Appellate Body findings to apply in an overly broad manner, such as to invalidate sound environmental regulation, while also at the same time, providing too little of a rationale for allowing

[228] Quick 2013, p. 981.
[229] Howse 2016, p. 9.
[230] Ibid., p. 44.
[231] Kulovesi 2011, pp. 81 to 82.
[232] Trachtman 2017, p. 304.
[233] Asmelash 2015.
[234] Trachtman 2017, p. 274.
[235] Ibid., p. 274.

violations.[236] For example, and as elaborated upon above, while the focus on the calibration of risk which underpinned the *US—Tuna II* case law may at first sight appear 'rational', the lack of clarity over its invocation has the potential to result in incoherence.[237] To the extent that the jurisprudence of the WTO dispute settlement system helps to shape Member's perceptions of the meaning of WTO law,[238] such a lack of clarity over the application of a particular measure could result in a chilling effect. Furthermore, and perhaps more fundamentally, leaving the debate on trade and environment to be developed within and by the dispute settlement system will only get us so far,[239] particularly because the Appellate Body has, particularly recently, been largely comprised of former government officials;' 'trade insiders', as it were.[240] It is difficult to envisage trade insiders pushing a 'strong critique'[241] of current jurisprudence on the relationship between trade and environmental protection. Accordingly, it may be a case of 'too much is never enough' in respect of the dispute settlement system's treatment of trade and environmental protection. In addition, procedural issues, such as the lack of provisional measures, further limit the practical impact of the WTO dispute settlement system as a bulwark against environmental degradation.

5.5 Conclusions

Considerable uncertainty currently exists over the future trajectory of WTO dispute settlement. The Appellate Body system is no longer functioning. To the extent that the task of resolving the relationship between trade and environment has fallen to the WTO dispute settlement system, the system has been able to move beyond the dark days of the GATT Panel reports in *Tuna-Dolphin*. The Appellate Body in particular has been able to craft a jurisprudence that recognises the fundamental right of Members to regulate to protect interests such as environmental protection. However, the jurisprudence of the WTO dispute settlement system in respect of the trade and environmental protection is not without its flaws. Moreover, the current Appellate Body crisis blows into stark relief the risks inherent in the relationship between trade and environment being produced by the dispute settlement system. With an increasing range of environmental threats facing the world, not least the spectre of climate change, it is clear that change is needed within the WTO to better ensure a mutually supportive relationship between trade and environmental protection.

[236] Ibid., pp. 273–275.

[237] Drawing on insights from the excellent piece by Coglianese and Sapir 2017.

[238] Busch and Pelc 2014, p. 412. See also Izaguerri and Lanovoy 2013.

[239] See generally Trujillo 2013.

[240] Pauwelyn 2016.

[241] See generally Offor 2020. See also Boisson de Chazournes 2016.

References

Abi-Saab G (2005) The WTO Dispute Settlement and General International Law. In: Yerxa R, B Wilson (eds) Key Issues in WTO Dispute Settlement: The First Ten Years. Cambridge University Press, Cambridge, pp 7–12

Amerjee A, Nayak N (2014) A 'Heated' Debate: The WTO's Climate Question. Trade, Law and Development 6:1–8

Andersen H (2015) Protection of Non-Trade Values in WTO Appellate Body Jurisprudence: Exceptions, Economic Arguments, and Eluding Questions. Journal of International Economic Law 18:383–405

Anon (2019) United States Continues to Block New Appellate Body Members for the World Trade Organization, Risking the Collapse of the Appellate Process. American Journal of International Law 113:822–831

Asmelash H B (2015) Energy Subsidies and WTO Dispute Settlement: Why Only Renewable Energy Subsidies Are Challenged. Journal of International Economic Law 18:261–285

Bacchus J, Lester S (2020) The Rule of Precedent and the Role of the Appellate Body. Journal of World Trade 54:183–198

Baroncini E, Brunel C (2020) A WTO Safe Harbour for the Dolphins: The Second Compliance Proceedings in the US–Tuna II (Mexico) case. World Trade Review 19:196–215

Bigdeli S Z (2014) Clash of Rationalities: Revisiting the Trade and Environment Debate in Light of WTO Disputes over Green Industrial Policy. Trade, Law and Development 6:177–209

Boisson de Chazournes L (2016) WTO and Non-Trade Issues: Inside/Outside WTO. Journal of International Economic Law 19:379–381

Busch M, Pelc KJ (2014) Dispute Settlement in the WTO. In: Martin L L (ed) The Oxford Handbook of the Political Economy of International Trade. Oxford University Press, Oxford, pp 1–19

Cameron J, Gray K R (2001) Principles of International Law in the WTO Dispute Settlement Body. The International and Comparative Law Quarterly 50:248–298

Cezar R F (2018) The Politics of 'Dolphin-Safe' Tuna in the United States: Policy Change and Reversal, Lock-in and Adjustment to International Constraints (1984-2017). World Trade Review 17:635–663

Charnovitz S, Fischer C (2015) Canada-Renewable Energy: Implications for WTO Law on Green and Not-So-Green Subsidies. World Trade Review 14:177–210

Chi M (2014) 'Exhaustible Natural Resource' in WTO Law: GATT Article XX(g) Disputes and Their Implications. Journal of World Trade 48:939–966

Chisik R, Fang C (2020) Cross-retaliation and International Dispute Settlement. https://ideas.repec.org/p/rye/wpaper/wp078.html Accessed 23 December 2020

Cima E (2018) Promoting Renewable Energy Through FTAs? The Legal Implications of a New Generation of Trade Agreements. Journal of World Trade 52:663–695

Coglianese C, Sapir A (2017) Risk and Regulatory Calibration: WTO Compliance Review of the US Dolphin-Safe Tuna Labeling Regime. World Trade Review 16:327–348

Cosbey A, Mavroidis P C (2014a) A Turquoise Mess: Green Subsidies, Blue Industrial Policy and Renewable Energy: The Case for Redrafting the Subsidies Agreement of the WTO. Journal of International Economic Law 17:11–47

Cosbey A, Mavroidis P C (2014b) Heavy Fuel: Trade and Environment in the GATT/WTO Case Law. Review of European, Comparative & International Environmental Law 23:288–301

Creamer C (2019) From the WTO's Crown Jewel to its Crown of Thorns. AJIL Unbound 113:51–55

Crowley M A, Howse R (2014) *Tuna-Dolphin II*: a legal and economic analysis of the Appellate Body Report. World Trade Review 13:321–355

Davey W J (2014) The WTO and Rules-Based Dispute Settlement: History, Evolution, Operational Success and Future Challenges. Journal of International Economic Law 17:679–700

Davies A (2015) The GATT Article III:8(a) Procurement Derogation and *Canada – Renewable Energy*. Journal of International Economic Law 18:543–554

Dawson A (2019) Safeguarding the Planet? Renewable Energy, Solar Panel Tariffs, and the World Trade Organization's Rules on Safeguards. Trade, Law and Development 11:334–371
Devaney J (2016) Fact Finding Before the International Court of Justice. Cambridge University Press, Cambridge
Eckersley R (2007) A Green Public Sphere in the WTO?: The Amicus Curiae Interventions in the Transatlantic Biotech Dispute. European Journal of International Relations 13(3):329–356
Espa I (2019) New Features of Green Industrial Policy and the Limits of WTO Rules: What Options for the Twenty-first Century? Journal of World Trade 53(6):979–1000
Espa I, Marín Durán G (2018) Renewable Energy Subsidies and WTO Law: Time to Rethink the Case for Reform Beyond Canada – *Renewable Energy/Fit Program.* Journal of International Economic Law 21:621–653
European Commission (2020a) Interim appeal arrangement for WTO disputes becomes effective. https://trade.ec.europa.eu/doclib/press/index.cfm?id=2143 Accessed 23 December 2020
European Commission (2020b) The WTO multi-party interim appeal arrangement gets operational. https://trade.ec.europa.eu/doclib/press/index.cfm?id=2176 Accessed 23 December 2020
Farah P D (2015) WTO and Renewable Energy: Lessons from the Case Law. Journal of World Trade 49:1103–1116
Farah P D, Cima E (2013) Energy Trade and the WTO: Implications for Renewable Energy and the OPEC Cartel. Journal of International Economic Law 16:707–740
Graewert T (2008) Conflicting Laws and Jurisdictions in the Dispute Settlement process of Regional Trade Agreement and the WTO. Contemporary Asia Arbitration Journal 1:287–334
Grando M (2010) Evidence, Proof, and Fact Finding in WTO Dispute Settlement. Oxford University Press, Oxford
Hoekman B M, Mavroidis P C (2020a) Preventing the Bad from Getting Worse: The End of the World (Trade Organization) As We Know It? https://scholarship.law.columbia.edu/faculty_scholarship/2606 Accessed 23 December 2020
Hoekman B (2016) The World Trade Order: Global Governance by Judiciary? European Journal of International Law 27:1083–1093
Hoekman B M, Mavroidis P C (2020b) To AB or Not to AB? Dispute Settlement in WTO Reform. Journal of International Economic Law 23:1–20
Horn H, Mavroidis P C, Wijkstrom, E N (2013) In the Shadow of the DSU: Addressing Specific Trade Concerns in the WTO SPS and TBT Committees. Journal of World Trade 47: 729–759
Howse R (2002) The Appellate Body Rulings in the *Shrimp/Turtle* Case: A New Legal Baseline for the Trade and Environment Debate. Columbia Journal of Environmental Law 27:489–519
Howse R (2016) The World Trade Organization 20 Years On: Global Governance by Judiciary. European Journal of International Law 27:9–77
Howse R, Levy P I (2013) The TBT Panels: *US-Cloves, US-Tuna, US-COOL.* World Trade Review 12:327–375
Izaguerri A, Lanovoy V (2013) The WTO's Influence on Other Dispute Settlement Mechanisms: A Lighthouse in the Storm of Fragmentation. Journal of World Trade 47(3):481–574
Kelly T (2014) Tuna-Dolphin Revisited. Journal of World Trade 48:501–524
Kulovesi K (2011) The WTO Dispute Settlement System: Challenges of the Environment, Legitimacy and Fragmentation. Kluwer, Alphen aan den Rijn
Kulovesi K (2014) International Trade Disputes on Renewable Energy: Testing Ground for the Mutual Supportiveness of WTO Law and Climate Change Law. Review of European, Comparative & International Environmental Law 23:342–353
Kulovesi K (2016) International Trade: Natural Resources and the World Trade Organisation. In: Morgera E, Kulovesi K (eds) Research Handbook on International Law and Natural Resources. Edward Elgar, Cheltenham, pp 46–65
Lang A, Scott J (2009) The Hidden World of WTO Governance. European Journal of International Law 20:575–614
Lydgate E (2012). Sustainable development in the WTO: From mutual supportiveness to balancing. World Trade Review 11:621–639

McGrady B (2009) Necessity Exceptions in WTO Law: Retreaded Tyres, Regulatory Purpose and Cumulative Regulatory Measures. Journal of International Economic Law 12:153–173
Merrills J G (2005) International Dispute Settlement. Cambridge University Press, Cambridge
Miles C A (2017) Provisional Measures before International Courts and Tribunals. Cambridge University Press, Cambridge
Offor I (2020) Animals and the Impact of Trade Law and Policy: A Global Animal Law Question. Transnational Environmental Law 9:1–24
Pauwelyn J (2003) Conflict of Norms in Public International Law: How WTO Law Relates to Other Norms of International Law. Cambridge University Press, Cambridge
Pauwelyn J (2008) How to Win a WTO Dispute Based on Non-WTO Law? Questions of Jurisdiction and Merits. In: Griller S (eds) At the Crossroads: The World Trading System and the Doha Round. Springer, Vienna, pp 1–53
Pauwelyn J (2016) The WTO 20 Years On: 'Global Governance by Judiciary' or, Rather, Member-driven Settlement of (Some) Trade Disputes between (Some) WTO Members? European Journal of International Law 27:1119–1126
Pauwelyn J (2019) WTO Dispute Settlement Post 2019: What to Expect? Journal of International Economic Law 22:297–321
Pierola F (2005) The Question of Remand Authority for the Appellate Body. In: Mitchell D A (ed) Challenges and Prospects for the WTO. Cameron May, London, pp 193–216
Quick R (2013) Do We Need Trade and Environment Negotiations or Has the Appellate Body Done the Job? Journal of World Trade 47:957–983
Sinha M (2013) An Evaluation of the WTO Committee on Trade and Environment. Journal of World Trade 47:1285–1322
Spiegel-Feld D, Switzer S (2012) Whither Article XX? Regulatory autonomy under non-GATT agreements after China—raw materials. Yale Journal of International Law Online 38:16–30
Squatitro T (2018) Amicus Curiae Briefs in the WTO DSM: Good or Bad News for Non-State Actor Involvement? World Trade Review 17:65–89.
Stephens T (2009) International Courts and Environmental Protection. Cambridge University Press, Cambridge
Subedi S P (2010) The WTO Dispute Settlement Mechanism as a New Technique for Settling Disputes in International Law. In: French D et al (eds) International Law and Dispute Settlement: New Problems and Techniques. Hart, Oxford, pp 173–190
Tanaka Y (2018) The WTO Dispute Settlement System. In: Tanaka Y (ed) The Peaceful Settlement of International Disputes. Cambridge University Press, Cambridge, pp 275–310
Teehankee M (2020) Trade and Environment Governance at the World Trade Organization Committee on Trade and Environment. Kluwer Law International/Wolters Kluw
Trachtman J P (2017) WTO Trade and Environment Jurisprudence: Avoiding Environmental Catastrophe. Harvard International Law Journal 58:273–309
Trebilcock M J, Howse M (2005) The Regulation of International Trade. Routledge, Abingdon
Trujillo E (2013) A Dialogical Approach to Trade and Environment. Journal of International Economic Law 16:535–585
Van den Bossche P (2005) From Afterthought to Centrepiece: The WTO Appellate Body and its Rise to Prominence in the World Trading System. https://papers.ssrn.com/sol3/papers.cfm?abstract_id=836284 Accessed 23 December 2020
Van den Bossche P, Zdouc W (2017) The Law and Policy of the World Trade Organization: Text Cases and Materials. Cambridge University Press, Cambridge
Weber R H, Koch R (2015) International Trade Law Challenges by Subsidies for Renewable Energy. Journal of World Trade 49:757–780
Weiss E B (2016) Integrating Environment and Trade. Journal of International Economic Law 19:367–369
WTO (2017) Matrix on Trade-Related Measures Pursuant to Selected Multilateral Environmental Agreements - Note by The Secretariat. https://docs.wto.org/dol2fe/Pages/FE_Search/FE_S_S006.aspx?Query=%28%28%20@Symbol=%20wt/cte/w/160/rev.5%20%29%29&Language=

ENGLISH&Context=FomerScriptedSearch&languageUIChanged=true Accessed 23 December 2020
WTO (2018) Addressing Tensions and Avoiding Disputes: Specific Trade Concerns in the TBT Committee. https://www.wto.org/english/res_e/reser_e/ersd201811_e.pdf Accessed 23 December 2020
WTO (2020a) DDG Wolff urges start of 'serious discussion' on WTO reforms. https://www.wto.org/english/news_e/news20_e/ddgaw_30oct20_e.htm Accessed 23 December 2020
WTO (2020b) Hong Kong, China initiates dispute complaint against US origin marking requirements. https://www.wto.org/english/news_e/news20_e/ds597rfc_03nov20_e.htm Accessed 23 December 2020
WTO (2020c) Multi-Party Interim Appeal Arbitration Arrangement Pursuant to Article 25 of the DSU. https://trade.ec.europa.eu/doclib/docs/2020/march/tradoc_158685.pdf Accessed 23 December 2020
WTO (2020d) Statement on A Mechanism for Developing, Documenting and Sharing Practices and Procedures in The Conduct Of WTO Disputes. https://trade.ec.europa.eu/doclib/docs/2020/april/tradoc_158731.pdf Accessed 23 December 2020
WTO (2020e) Statement on a Mechanism for Developing, Documenting and Sharing Practices and Procedures in the Conduct of WTO Disputes. https://trade.ec.europa.eu/doclib/docs/2020/august/tradoc_158911.12-Suppl.5%20(002).pdf Accessed 23 December 2020
WTO Dispute Settlement. https://www.wto.org/english/tratop_e/dispu_e/dispu_e.htm Accessed 23 December 2020

Stephanie Switzer is a senior lecturer and Co-Director of the University of Strathclyde's Centre for Environmental Law and Governance, Glasgow, Scotland. The author wishes to thank Iyan Offor and Mitchell Lennan for their help, discussions and advice in preparing this chapter. Any errors are the author's own.

Chapter 6
Crimes Against the Environment: What Role for the International Criminal Court?

Steven Freeland

Contents

Abstract Acts perpetrated during the course of warfare have, through the ages, led to significant environmental destruction. These have included situations where the natural environment has intentionally been targeted as a 'victim' or has somehow been manipulated to serve as a 'weapon' of warfare. Until recently, such acts were generally regarded as an unfortunate but unavoidable element of armed conflict, despite their potentially disastrous impacts. The existing international rules have largely been ineffective and inappropriate and have in practical terms done little

S. Freeland (✉)
School of Law, Western Sydney University, Locked Bag 1797, Penrith, NSW 2751, Australia
e-mail: s.freeland@westernsydney.edu.au

Bond University, Robina, Australia

University of Vienna, Vienna, Austria

iCourts Centre of Excellence for International Courts, Copenhagen, Denmark

Université Toulouse, 1 Capitole, Toulouse, France

Hong Kong University, Pok Fu Lam, Hong Kong

Centre for Research in Air and Space Law, McGill University, Montreal, Quebec, Canada

London Institute of Space Policy and Law, London, United Kingdom

Universiti Teknologi MARA (UiTM), Shah Alam, Selangor, Malaysia

E. Sobenes et al. (eds.), *The Environment Through the Lens of International Courts and Tribunals*, https://doi.org/10.1007/978-94-6265-507-2_6

to deter deliberate environmental destruction, particularly when measured against perceived military advantages. However, as the significance of the environment has come to be more widely understood and recognised, this is no longer acceptable, particularly given the ongoing development of weapons capable of widespread and significant damage. This chapter examines the current legal regime under international criminal law relevant to the intentional destruction of the environment during warfare, and argues that such acts should, in appropriate circumstances, be recognised as an international crime and should be subject to more effective rules giving rise to international criminal responsibility within the framework of the Rome Statute of the International Criminal Court.

Keywords international criminal law · international humanitarian law · criminal accountability for deliberate environmental destruction · crimes against the environment

6.1 The Need for International Criminal Justice for the Protection of the Environment

History has borne witness to many deliberate acts aimed at destroying the natural environment during the course of a military conflict. Herodotus described how, in the fifth century BC, the retreating Scythians scorched the earth and poisoned the water wells in an effort to slow the advancing Persian army led by Darius. In 146 BC, Roman troops razed the city of Carthage and poisoned the surrounding soil with salt to prevent its future fertilisation. More recent warfare has seen further examples including:

(a) During the Vietnam War, the United States implemented 'Operation Ranch Hand' to devastating effect to destroy vegetation used by the enemy for cover and sustenance through the use of chemicals such as Agent Orange.[1]
(b) Towards the end of the Gulf War in 1991, retreating Iraqi forces deliberately ignited over 700 burning Kuwaiti oil well heads and emptied millions of barrels of oil into the Gulf waters. These actions gave rise to almost universal condemnation.[2] The then German Chancellor, Helmut Kohl, asserted that this constituted a 'crime against the environment'.[3]
(c) During the course of the 2003 invasion of Iraq, Human Rights Watch estimated that United States and British forces used almost 13,000 cluster bombs and over 1.9 tonnes of depleted uranium,[4] causing very significant environmental

[1] It has been estimated that Operation Ranch Hand destroyed 8% Vietnam's croplands, 14% of its forests, and 50% of its swamp areas: Yuzon 1996, pp. 795–6.

[2] Shortly afterwards, the Parliamentary Assembly of the Council of Europe called for the establishment of a war crimes tribunal to prosecute those responsible for 'this disgraceful attack on the environment': Leibler 1992, p. 68.

[3] Helmut Kohl, Statement by the German Chancellor, Bulletin (Bonn), 9 April 1991, 255.

[4] Haavisto 2005, p. 581.

damage, the extent of which may not be known for a considerable period of time.[5]

(d) The western region of Darfur in Sudan has seen the poisoning of vital water wells and drinking water installations,[6] as part of a deliberate government-supported strategy by the Arab Janjaweed Militia to eliminate or displace the ethnic black Africans living in that region.

As indicated by these examples (there are many more), and notwithstanding (or perhaps because of) its significance to human populations, the targeting of the environment has increasingly become a part of the conduct of armed conflict. Given the diverse ways in which armed conflict might be conducted, particularly in light of the development of weapons technology, there is even greater scope for such destructive actions in future warfare.

In the author's opinion, the most appropriate method to address the issue is not through (civil) environmental protection measures, but rather under international criminal law (although it is hoped that this will have positive consequences for the environment), so that those who intentionally instigate such destruction can be made criminally liable. This chapter therefore examines the existing provisions of the Rome Statute that are, or may be, of relevance to the issue of the protection of the environment, and concludes by offering some comments and suggestions based on this analysis.

6.2 Historical Background

International criminal law has been developing rapidly, particularly over the past two decades. This has principally been through the operation of the United Nations *ad hoc* international criminal tribunals, as well as a number of 'hybrid' or 'internationalised' courts established to deal with international crimes perpetrated during specific conflicts.[7] In addition, the world's first permanent international criminal institution, the International Criminal Court (ICC), was established in 2002. The development

---

[5] Depleted uranium is a by-product of the process of 'uranium enrichment', which involves the separation of the three different uranium isotopes (uranium-238, uranium-235 and uranium-234) as a preliminary step towards the use of nuclear fission as a source of energy (uranium-235 is the most suitable for nuclear fission): Koppe 2006, p. 18.

[6] See United Nations Commission on Human Rights 'Report of the United Nations High Commissioner for Human Rights and Follow-Up to the World Conference on Human Rights: Situation of Human Rights in Darfur Region of the Sudan' (7 May 2004) E/CN.4/2005/3, paras 50 and 73.

[7] The United Nations *ad hoc* Tribunals are the International Criminal Tribunal for the Former Yugoslavia (ICTY)—established by United Nations Security Council Resolution 827, UN Doc. S/RES/827 (1993); and the International Criminal Tribunal for Rwanda—established by United Nations Security Council Resolution 955, UN Doc. S/RES/955 (1994) (ICTR). In December 2010, the Mechanism for International Criminal Tribunals (MICT) was established to continue the 'obligations and essential functions' of the ICTR and the ICTY: United Nations Security Council Resolution 1966, UN Doc. S/RES/1966 (2010). The 'hybrid' or 'internationalised' criminal tribunals include those that operate or have operated in East Timor—established in 2000 by the United

of this system of international criminal justice has been described as 'one of the few bright spots in the recent history of international law'.[8]

The establishment of the ICC dates back to December 1989 when the United Nations General Assembly asked the International Law Commission (ILC) to resume its work on the drafting of a constitutive instrument for an international criminal court,[9] with a jurisdiction that would specifically include drug trafficking.[10] The ILC completed a draft statute and submitted it to the United Nations General Assembly in 1994 (ILC Draft Statute).[11] After further work on the draft by the *Ad Hoc* Committee on the Establishment of an International Criminal Court, and later the Preparatory Committee on the Establishment of an International Criminal Court—a consolidated draft text was ready for submission to a diplomatic conference.

The General Assembly convened the United Nations Diplomatic Conference of Plenipotentiaries on the Establishment of an International Criminal Court (Rome Conference) from 15 June to 17 July 1998, 'with a view to finalizing and adopting a convention on the establishment of an international criminal court'.[12] The Rome Conference was attended by delegations from over 160 States, 30 Intergovernmental Organizations and 230 Non-Governmental Organizations. Right up until the final vote, there remained a number of contentious issues—particularly in relation to the extent of the Court's proposed jurisdiction, as well as its relationship with the United

Nations Transitional Administration in East Timor (UNTAET), pursuant to UNTAET Regulations 2000/11 and 2000/15 (6 March 2000 and 6 June 2000 respectively); Sierra Leone—established by an agreement between the United Nations and the Government of Sierra Leone dated 16 January 2002, pursuant to United Nations Security Council Resolution 1315, UN Doc. S/RES/1315 (2000); and Cambodia—established by an agreement between the United Nations and the Government of Cambodia dated 6 June 2003, pursuant to United Nations General Assembly Resolution 57/228 B, UN Doc. A/RES/72/228(B) (2003). There is also the Special Tribunal for Lebanon, which operates in the Netherlands and was established by United Nations Security Council Resolution 1757, UN Doc. S/RES/1757 (2007).

[8] Jessberger and Geneuss 2013, p. 501.

[9] The ILC had in 1948 already been invited by the United Nations General Assembly to 'study the desirability and possibility of establishing an international judicial organ for the trial of persons charged with genocide and other crimes': United Nations General Assembly Resolution 260 (III) B, UN Doc. A/RES/260(III) (1948). However, the political realities associated with the Cold War meant that, in 1954, the United Nations General Assembly halted work on the drafting of any statute for such a proposed court: see United Nations General Assembly Resolution 897 (IX), UN Doc. A/RES/897(IX) (1954), and United Nations General Assembly Resolution 898 (IX), UN Doc. A/RES/898(IX) (1954). For a description of the evolution of a system of international criminal justice leading up to the establishment of the ICC, see Freeland 2010, pp. 195–210.

[10] United Nations General Assembly Resolution 44/39, UN Doc. A/RES/44/39 (1989), para 1.

[11] Draft Statute for an International Criminal Court, Report of the International Law Commission on Its Forty-sixth session, United Nations General Assembly Official Records 49th Sess., Supp. No. 10, (1994) (ILC Draft Statute).

[12] United Nations General Assembly Resolution 52/160, UN Doc. A/RES/52/160 (1997), para 3.

Nations Security Council. In the end, however, the delegates adopted the final terms of the Rome Statute, albeit not unanimously.[13]

As events at the Rome Conference and subsequently have illustrated, the establishment of the ICC was as political an event as it was significant in the evolution of international criminal justice. The negotiating States, as well as the other stakeholders, represented a multitude of differing views as to how the Court should be structured. The final terms of the Rome Statute were, in many respects, the result of an 'enduring tension inherent in multilateral negotiations between sovereignty and universality',[14] which by necessity required a 'solution' based upon political compromise. This was even the case in relation to the question of what crimes should be included in the Rome Statute,[15] in order that the (draft) instrument could be presented as 'marketable' to the delegates.[16]

The precise scope of those crimes included in the final version of Rome Statute thus represented a *realpolitik* compromise in the circumstances—a careful balance between the important goals of the Court on the one hand,[17] and a politically acceptable series of definitions of proscribed acts to be regarded as international crimes within the jurisdiction of the Court on the other. In such a context, a more expansive approach towards prohibiting intentional environmental damage during armed conflict beyond the scope of what was agreed under Article 8(2)(b)(iv) was not politically feasible. Certainly, also, measures that would specifically protect the environment were not among the principal concerns of the delegates to the Rome Conference.

The ICC has the mandate to play a role when certain international crimes have (allegedly) been committed. As a permanent court, it differs from the *ad hoc* international criminal Tribunals. The International Criminal Tribunal for the Former Yugoslavia (ICTY) and International Criminal Tribunal for Rwanda (ICTR) were set up as 'UN subsidiary organs'[18] *in response to* specific events and were always intended to have a limited life-span, as is indicated by the formulation of the Completion Strategy for those Tribunals.[19] By contrast, the ICC is 'a permanent institution',

---

[13] Of those represented at the Rome Conference, 120 states voted to adopt the Rome Statute. There were 21 abstentions and seven states (China, Iraq, Israel, Libya, Qatar, Yemen and the USA) voted against the resolution.

[14] McCormack and Robertson 1999, p. 636.

[15] For example, several states had argued that the definition of war crimes should include a provision prohibiting the use of nuclear weapons. As the Rome Conference was drawing to a close, these states largely agreed to compromise on this point—with the result that such a provision was not included in the Rome Statute—since they were prepared to 'put the larger goal of achieving an international criminal court first': see Kalivretakis 2001, p. 702.

[16] Williams 2000, p. 546.

[17] See Rome Statute of the International Criminal Court, 17 July 1998, 2187 UNTS 3, entered into force 1 July 2002 (Rome Statute), preamble.

[18] Sarooshi 1999, p. 389.

[19] See *inter alia* United Nations Security Council Resolution 1503 UN Doc. S/RES/1503 (2003); United Nations Security Council Resolution 1534, UN Doc. S/RES/1534 (2004); United Nations Security Council Resolution 1966, UN Doc. S/RES/1966 (2010).

established under a treaty and, as such, is formally independent of the United Nations, although there is clearly an ongoing relationship between the two institutions on several key issues.[20] Unless the Assembly of States Parties to the Rome Statute decides to completely alter the nature or focus of the Court, the ICC will remain in place for the long-term, and will have the potential to play a role in circumstances where 'the most serious crimes of concern to the international community as a whole' have been committed.[21] In this sense, the Court represents an important mechanism of international criminal justice in relation to values and norms that are accepted universally among the international community now and into the future. These values and norms will continue to evolve further in the years and decades to follow in order to address relevant concerns regarding actions taken within the context of armed conflict that may, for example, threaten the future of humanity.

6.3 The Core Crimes Under the Rome Statute

The Rome Statute currently provides that the following crimes fall within the jurisdiction of the ICC:

(a) Genocide—when committed 'with intent to destroy, in whole or in part, a national, ethnical, racial or religious group, as such';[22]
(b) Crimes against humanity—when committed 'as part of a widespread or systematic attack directed against any civilian population, with knowledge of the attack';[23]
(c) War crimes—which usually involves a breach of the 1949 Geneva Conventions,[24] and/or the laws and customs of armed conflict, 'in particular when committed as part of a plan or policy or as part of a large-scale commission of such crimes';[25] and

[20] There is a Negotiated Relationship Agreement between the International Criminal Court and the United Nations (4 October 2004), whose purpose is to 'define [...] the terms on which the United Nations and the Court shall be brought into relationship' (Article 1(1)). In addition, there are a number of provisions in the Rome Statute that formalize various aspects of the specific relationship between the Court and the United Nations Security Council: see, for example, Rome Statute, above n 17, Articles 13(b), 16, 53(2)(c), 53(3)(a), 87(5), 87(7) and 115(b).

[21] Rome Statute, above n 17, preamble, para 4.

[22] See Rome Statute, above n 17, chapeau, Article 6.

[23] Ibid., Article 7(1).

[24] Geneva Convention for the Amelioration of the Condition of the Wounded and Sick in Armed Forces in the Field, 12 August 1949, 75 UNTS 31, entered into force 21 October 1950; Geneva Convention for the Amelioration of the Condition of the Wounded, Sick and Shipwrecked Members of Armed Forces at Sea, 12 August 1949, 75 UNTS 85, entered into force 21 October 1950; Geneva Convention Relative to the Treatment of Prisoners of War, 12 August 1949, 75 UNTS 135, entered into force 21 October 1950; Geneva Convention Relative to the Protection of Civilian Persons in Time of War, 12 August 1949, 75 UNTS 287, entered into force 21 October 1950.

[25] See Rome Statute, above n 17, Article 8(1).

(d) The Crime of Aggression as more recently defined.[26]

These crimes, particularly those of genocide, crimes against humanity and war crimes, are broadly regarded as reflecting universal international criminal norms.[27] Shortly after the conclusion of the Rome Statute, a Trial Chamber of the ICTY described the legal effect of the provisions of the Rome Statute in the following way:

> Depending on the matter at issue, the Rome Statute may be taken to restate, reflect or clarify customary rules or crystallise them, whereas in some areas it creates new law or modifies existing law. At any event, the Rome Statute by and large may be taken as constituting an authoritative expression of the legal views of a great number of States.[28]

Since that time, it has been asserted that the Rome Statute 'purports to contain a comprehensive stocktaking of the current status of customary international law'.[29] This may be over-stating the case, since particular aspects of the definitions of crimes in the Rome Statute, in particular, that of crimes against humanity and war crimes, and the crime of aggression as a whole, most likely also include(d) elements of 'progressive development', rather than already well-established principles of law. Hence, arguments persist as to whether every aspect of the definitions of the crimes in the Rome Statute may (or may not) be identical to current customary international law.[30] Nevertheless, it is generally acknowledged that the general parameters of the core international crimes represent acts that are a gross affront to fundamental norms.

Whilst the Rome Statute does not contain a specific crime of 'crimes against the environment' within the crimes in relation to which the Court has jurisdiction,[31] it does set out the circumstances in which a particular level of damage to the 'natural environment' may constitute a war crime. This represents the first time that the environment has been expressly mentioned in the constitutive documents of any of the international criminal courts/tribunals that have been established.

As a general observation, the inclusion of such a provision within the statute of what is intended to be a *permanent* international criminal court might, potentially, represent an important preliminary step towards individual criminal responsibility for intentional environmental destruction during armed conflict. However, the effectiveness of any provision depends upon its express terms. The reality of the severe

---

[26] See ibid., Article 8 bis.

[27] For the purposes of the discussion that follows in this chapter, these three crimes are referred as the 'core international crimes'.

[28] ICTY Trial Chamber, *Prosecutor v Furundzjia*, Judgment, 10 December 1998, Case No. IT-95-17/1, para 227.

[29] Kalivretakis 2001, p. 684.

[30] See, for example, Cassese 2003, pp. 91–94. See also ICTY Trial Chamber, *Prosecutor v Kupreskic et al*, Judgment, 14 January 2000, Case No. IT-95-16-T, where the Trial Chamber (at para 545) noted that '[b]y requiring that crimes against humanity be committed in either internal or international armed conflict, the [United Nations] Security Council, in establishing the [ICTY], may have defined the crime in Article 5 [of the Statute of the ICTY] more narrowly than is necessary under customary international law'.

[31] This was partly due to the fact that such an idea 'regrettably' failed to gain support in the deliberations leading to the finalization of the Rome Statute: Rest 2004, p. 18.

damage that has been, and inevitably will in the future be inflicted on the environment during the course of armed conflict necessitates an understanding of whether the existing obligations are adequate, or whether, in fact, they may need further development and amendment.

6.4 Jurisdiction of the ICC—A Brief Overview

As noted above, the ICC has jurisdiction in relation to the specific crimes of genocide (Article 6), crimes against humanity (Article 7), war crimes (Article 8), as well as the more recently defined crime of aggression. The specific requirements of the former three crimes, particularly as they might possibly be applied to intentional destruction of the environment during armed conflict, are discussed below.

In general terms, and as is the case with serious crimes under the national law of most countries, these crimes require the presence of both a 'physical' element (*actus reus*) and a 'mental' element (*mens rea*).[32] In terms of the mental element, the Rome Statute sets out a 'default' standard of *mens rea*, which specifies that, for individual criminal responsibility to apply, the material (physical) elements of the crime must be 'committed with intent and knowledge', as those terms are defined in the provision.[33] This standard applies '[u]nless otherwise provided', so that specific crimes may have *mens rea* requirements that differ from the Article 30 standard.

Articles 12 and 13 of the Rome Statute specify the '[p]reconditions to the exercise of jurisdiction' and 'exercise of jurisdiction' by the Court respectively.[34] The Court has jurisdiction over natural persons only—thus excluding the possibility of bringing charges under the Rome Statute against a corporation.[35] In summary, the Court can exercise its jurisdiction in relation to the crimes identified in the Rome Statute in the following circumstances:

(a) where an (alleged) crime has been committed on the territory of a State Party to the Rome Statute;[36]
(b) where a national(s) of a State Party to the Rome Statute is alleged to have committed a crime;[37]
(c) where a situation in which a crime(s) 'appears to have been committed' has been referred to the Prosecutor of the ICC by the United Nations Security Council acting under Chapter VII of the United Nations Charter;[38] or

---

[32] See, for example, Schabas 2000, chapters 4 and 5.

[33] Rome Statute, above n 17, Article 30(1).

[34] There are specific provisions relating to the exercise by the Court of its jurisdiction over the crime of aggression: see ibid, Article 15 bis and 15 ter.

[35] Ibid., Article 25(1).

[36] Ibid., Article 12(2)(a).

[37] Ibid., Article 12(2)(b).

[38] Ibid., Article 13(b).

(d) where a non-State Party to the Rome Statute lodges a declaration with the Registrar of the ICC, accepting the jurisdiction of the Court with respect to the 'crime in question'.[39]

The ICC is also subject to a specific *ratione temporis*. As set out in Article 11 of the Rome Statute, the Court has the power to exercise its jurisdiction with respect to circumstances that may occur *in the future*—that is, at any time after the Rome Statute came into force (1 July 2002).[40]

Finally, the jurisdiction of the Court is subject to the principle of 'complementarity' as established under the Rome Statute. In essence, this means that primary responsibility for the prosecution of these crimes lies with States, and that the ICC therefore operates as a 'court of last resort'. This in itself demonstrates a shift in emphasis from the culture of impunity that had existed before the 1990s, during which time States had been reluctant to try their own nationals for war crimes, 'and even more [so] where crimes against humanity or genocide [were] concerned'.[41]

Article 17 of the Rome Statute applies the complementarity principle in terms of the 'admissibility' of a case. A case is determined by the Court as being inadmissible *inter alia* where:

> (a) The case is being investigated or prosecuted by a State which has jurisdiction over it, unless the State is unwilling or unable genuinely to carry out the investigation or prosecution;
>
> (b) The case has been investigated by a State which has jurisdiction over it and the State has decided not to prosecute the person concerned, unless the decision resulted from the unwillingness or inability of the State genuinely to prosecute;
>
> […]
>
> (c) The case is not of sufficient gravity to justify further action by the Court.[42]

This creates what has been described as a 'presumption in favour of prosecution in domestic courts',[43] given that it accords a priority to national jurisdiction. This

---

[39] Ibid., Article 12(3). For a discussion of the declaration process by non-state parties under Article 12(3) of the Rome Statute, see Freeland 2006; Stahn 2006.

[40] It should be noted, however, that if a state becomes a State Party to the Rome Statute after 1 July 2002, the Court may exercise its jurisdiction only with respect to crimes committed after the entry into force of the Rome Statute for that state, unless that state has made a declaration as a non-state party under Article 12(3) of the Rome Statute: see Rome Statute, above n 17, Article 11(2).

[41] Sands 2003, p. 72.

[42] Rome Statute, above n 17, Article 17(1). The Appeals Chamber of the ICC considered the meaning of the words 'is being investigated' in Article 17(1)(a) of the Rome Statute in Judgment on the appeal of the Republic of Kenya against the decision of Pre-Trial Chamber II of 30 May 2011 entitled 'Decision on the Application by the Government of Kenya Challenging the Admissibility of the Case Pursuant to Article 19(2)(b) of the Statute': Appeals Chamber, *Prosecutor v Ruto, Kosgey and Sang*, 30 August 2011, Case No. ICC-01/09-01/11 OA, and Judgment on the appeal of the Republic of Kenya against the decision of Pre-Trial Chamber II of 30 May 2011 entitled 'Decision on the Application by the Government of Kenya Challenging the Admissibility of the Case Pursuant to Article 19(2)(b) of the Statute': Appeals Chamber, *Prosecutor v Muthaura, Kenyatta and Ali*, 30 August 2011, Case No. ICC-01/09-02/11 OA.

[43] Sarooshi 1999, p. 395.

is to be contrasted with the 'primacy' principle under which the *ad hoc* Tribunals operate.[44]

Article 17(2) specifies those circumstances in which the ICC may determine the 'unwillingness' of a State in a particular case. This may arise in the following situations:

> (a) The proceedings were or are being undertaken or the national decision was made for the purpose of shielding the person concerned from criminal responsibility;
>
> (b) ... an unjustified delay in the proceedings ... inconsistent with an intent to bring the person concerned to justice;
>
> (c) The proceedings were or are not being conducted independently or impartially, and ... are being conducted in a manner ... inconsistent with an intent to bring the person concerned to justice.[45]

In assessing these circumstances, the Court is to have regard to 'the principles of due process recognized by international law'.[46] In determining a State's (in)ability in a particular case, the Court has to consider whether:

> ...due to a total or substantial collapse or unavailability of its national judicial system, the State is unable to obtain the accused or ... evidence or otherwise [is] unable to carry out its proceedings.[47]

6.5 Applicability of the Rome Statute to Environmental Crimes

As mentioned, Article 8(2)(b)(iv) expressly refers to, and 'criminalizes' damage to, the natural environment in certain specific circumstances and will be considered in detail below. Before turning to that specific provision, however, we first consider whether it may be possible that other provisions of the Rome Statute might also be relevant to such acts; specifically, whether the crimes of genocide, crimes against humanity and other war crimes also address the issue to any significant degree. In this way, one can gain a more comprehensive understanding of the applicability of

---

[44] See Articles 9(1) and 9(2) of the Statute of the International Tribunal for the Prosecution of Persons Responsible for Serious Violations of International Humanitarian Law Committed in the Territory of the Former Yugoslavia since 1991, 32 ILM 1159 (ICTY Statute). The Appeals Chamber of the ICTY confirmed the legitimacy of its primacy in Decision on Defence Motion for Interlocutory Appeal on Jurisdiction: ICTY Appeals Chamber, *Prosecutor v Duško Tadić*, 2 October 1995, Case No. IT-94-1, paras 49–64. See also Articles 8(1) and 8(2) of the Statute of the International Criminal Tribunal for the Prosecution of Persons Responsible for Genocide and Other Serious Violations of International Humanitarian Law Committed in the Territory of Rwanda and Rwandan Citizens Responsible for Genocide and Other Such Violations Committed in the Territory of Neighbouring States, between 1 January 1994 and 31 December 1994, 33 ILM 1598 (ICTR Statute), which is in slightly wider terms.

[45] Rome Statute, above n 17, Article 17(2).

[46] Ibid.

[47] Ibid., Article 17(3).

the Rome Statute to acts that might constitute a crime against the environment, as well as the significance of Article 8(2)(b)(iv) itself within the broader schema of crimes within the instrument. In undertaking this exercise, however, it is important to bear in mind that, as provided in the Rome Statute itself:

> The definition of a crime shall be strictly construed and shall not be extended by analogy. In case of ambiguity, the definition shall be interpreted in favour of the person being investigated, prosecuted or convicted.[48]

6.6 Intentional Destruction of the Environment as Genocide?

The word 'genocide' was first coined in 1944 by a Polish-Jewish lawyer, Raphael Lemkin, who lobbied to have the issue of genocide as an international crime discussed at the United Nations General Assembly. The international community ultimately agreed with the assertion that genocide was indeed a crime under international law.[49] There then followed a number of General Assembly Resolutions,[50] culminating in the adoption of the Genocide Convention.[51] This landmark instrument set out an agreed definition of genocide that has since remained largely unchanged.

The Genocide Convention was the first major treaty dealing with human rights issues to be concluded under the auspices of the United Nations. The ICJ has said of the Genocide Convention that:

---

48 Ibid., Article 22(2). In May 2008, the ICC Appeals Chamber endorsed its earlier finding when considering its methodology for the interpretation of the Rome Statute, where it had stated: 'The rule governing the interpretation of a section of the law is its wording read in context and in light of its object and purpose. The context of a given legislative provision is defined by the particular sub-section of the law read as a whole in conjunction with the section of an enactment in its entirety. Its objects may be gathered from the chapter of the law in which the particular section is included and its purposes from the wider aims of the law as may be gathered from its preamble and general tenor of the treaty': Judgment on the appeal of Mr. Germain Katanga against the decision of Pre-Trial Chamber 1 entitled 'Decision on the Defence Request Concerning Languages': Appeals Chamber, *Prosecutor v Germain Katanga*, 27 May 2008, Case No. ICC-01/04-01/07 (OA3), para 39.

49 Some commentators consider that *acts* of genocide had in fact been included within the concept of 'crimes against humanity' as applied in the indictments brought under the Charter of the Nuremberg International Military Tribunal, annexed to the 1945 London Agreement for the Establishment of an International Military Tribunal (8 August 1945) 82 UNTS 279 (Nuremberg Charter): see, for example, Restatement of the Law: Third Restatement of U.S. Foreign Relations Law, Volume 2 (1987), 165, ss 702, Reporters' comments, para 3. However, it is now accepted that, even though they have some common elements, what distinguishes genocide from crimes against humanity is that the crime of genocide is a 'crime of intent' in which a specific 'group' is targeted, and not merely specific individuals within that group; or put another way, 'the ultimate victim of genocide is the group': Judgment on Defence Motions to Acquit: Trial Chamber, *Prosecutor v Sikirica, Dosen and Kolundzjia*, 3 September 2001, Case No. IT-95-8-T, para 89.

50 See, for example, United Nations General Assembly Resolution 96(I), UN Doc. A/RES/96(1) (1946).

51 Convention on the Prevention and Punishment of the Crime of Genocide, 9 December 1948, 78 UNTS 277, entered into force 12 June 1951 (Genocide Convention).

> The origins of the Convention show that it was the intention of the United Nations to condemn and punish genocide as "a crime under international law" involving a denial of the right of existence of entire human groups, a denial which shocks the conscience of mankind and results in great losses to humanity, and which is contrary to moral law and to the spirit and aims of the United Nations.[52]

The crime of genocide as defined in the Rome Statute is drawn from the definition in the 1948 Genocide Convention, which was incorporated as well into the ICTY and ICTR Statutes.[53] The preamble of the Genocide Convention notes that 'at all periods of history genocide has inflicted great losses on humanity'.[54] Genocide has been referred to as the 'crime of crimes'[55] and is often regarded as the most heinous of all violations of human rights.[56] The particular distinguishing characteristic of the crime is, as noted, its focus on 'groups', specifically the intended destruction of entire human groups.[57] It therefore incorporates a very specific *dolus specialis*, being the intent 'to destroy, in whole or in part, a national, ethnical, racial or religious group, as such'.[58]

From the perspective of any prosecution, this specific intent is far more complex in terms of proof than a *general* intent, which might instead be inferred on the basis of a 'reasonable person' test,[59] and/or the default standard of intent set out in Article 30 of the Rome Statute. For this reason, genocide is a very difficult crime to prove in the absence of a clear 'paper trail'—which would not normally exist[60]—although there have since 1998 been several successful prosecutions of genocide before the *ad*

[52] ICJ, *Reservations to the Convention on the Prevention and Punishment of the Crime of Genocide*, Advisory Opinion, 28 May 2951, ICJ Reports 1951, p. 23.

[53] There are, however, some differences between the ICTY and ICTR Statutes on the one hand and the Rome Statute on the other. For example, Article 4(3) of the ICTY Statute, above n 44, and Article 2(3) of the ICTR Statute, above n 44, respectively specify that the following acts are punishable: '(a) Genocide; (b) Conspiracy to commit genocide; (c) Direct and public incitement to commit genocide; (d) Attempt to commit genocide; (e) Complicity in genocide'.

By contrast, these acts are not included in Article 6 of the Rome Statute, above n 17, but are instead incorporated into Article 25(3), which deals with individual criminal responsibility and applies to each of the crimes within the jurisdiction of the Court. The act of 'directly and publicly incit[ing] others to commit genocide' is, however, specifically referred to in Article 25(3)(e) of the Rome Statute.

[54] *Reservations to the Convention on the Prevention and Punishment of the Crime of Genocide*, above n 51, preamble, para 2.

[55] ICTR Trial Chamber, *Prosecutor v Akayesu*, Judgment, 2 September 1998, Case No. ICTR-96-4-T, para 16.

[56] de Vito et al. 2009, p. 37.

[57] Ibid., p. 36.

[58] *Reservations to the Convention on the Prevention and Punishment of the Crime of Genocide*, above n 51, Article II. See also, for example, Rome Statute, chapeau Article 6.

[59] Bassiouni 2000, p. 9.

[60] See, for example, ibid., where Bassiouni suggests that the Genocide Convention, above n 51, was drafted with the Nazi Germany experience in mind, which left behind a very detailed paper trail, but that this is a 'situation [that] never has been repeated'.

hoc Tribunals, and counts of genocide have also been alleged against accused before the ICC.[61]

As for the 'physical' elements, the crime comprises a number of acts of genocide relating to four specific types of group. The concept of genocide based on an intention to destroy a 'political' group was not included in the final definition, despite having been part of both Lemkin's original draft definition, as well as the more general description adopted by the United Nations General Assembly two years prior to the conclusion of the Genocide Convention.[62] Attempts to include political and social groups into the Rome Statute definition were also not accepted at the Rome Conference, as the majority of States present did not want to alter a definition that was clearly recognized under customary international law.[63]

Similarly, the definition of genocide does not appear to include actions intended to destroy (in whole or in part) a group based on their *culture*. Thus, from a legal perspective, there exists no formal concept under international criminal law of 'cultural genocide'.[64]

Acts designed to destroy a group (in whole or in part) could possibly involve the intentional destruction of the environment during armed conflict, as a way of attempting to render impossible the group's ability to continue to exist. The Rome Statute specifies that '[d]eliberately inflicting on the group conditions of life calculated to bring about its physical destruction' would fall within the type of acts that constitute genocide.[65] Under this provision, it is not necessary for the intended 'results'—the *actual* destruction of the group—to occur. A 'result requirement' had been proposed by the United States in the drafting process of the Elements of Crimes under the Rome Statute (Elements of Crimes),[66] but was ultimately not included in the final version.[67]

Although the footnote to Article 6(c) in the Elements of Crimes also envisages a broader range of circumstances,[68] acts such as the poisoning of water wells or destruction of forests upon which local indigenous groups depend could arguably fall

---

[61] See, for example, *Second Warrant of Arrest for Omar Hassan Ahmad Al Bashir*, ICC Pre-Trial Chamber I, *Prosecutor v. Al Bashir ('Omar Al Bashir')*, 12 July 2010, Case No. ICC-02/05-01/09. This accused was also charged with five counts of crimes against humanity and two counts of war crimes.

[62] See United Nations General Assembly Resolution 96(I), UN Doc. A/RES/96(I) (1946), para 4.

[63] See Werle 2005, p. 191.

[64] See, however, ibid. where the author suggests that Article 6(e) of the Rome Statute ('Forcibly transferring children of the group to another group') 'defines a form of cultural genocide'.

[65] Rome Statute, above n 17, Article 6(c).

[66] Article 9(1) of the Rome Statute provides for the adoption of the 'Elements of Crimes' by a two-thirds majority of the Assembly of States Parties to the Rome Statute, and specifies that their function is to 'assist the Court in the interpretation and application of Articles 6, 7 and 8' of the Rome Statute. See also Elements of Crimes (9 September 2002), Article 6(c).

[67] Rückert and Witschel 2001, p. 68.

[68] This footnote provides that: '[t]he 'conditions of life' may include, but is not necessarily restricted to, deliberate deprivation of resources indispensable for survival, such as food or medical services, or systematic expulsion from homes'. See also *Prosecutor v Akayesu*, above n 55, para 506.

within this description, although it is still necessary to demonstrate that the special intention to 'destroy' is directed towards the *physical* destruction (in whole or in part) of the relevant group,[69] rather than, for example, their 'way of life'. As noted, proving the existence of this *dolus specialis* is a difficult exercise, and reliance on this provision to address the intentional destruction of the environment will therefore rarely be applicable.

In addition, it may be that the targeted group that is the subject of the environmental destruction does not constitute one of the established groupings within the definition of genocide. As noted, these groups were 'chosen' very carefully by the international community when originally agreeing the definition of the crime, and various additional groups suggested by Lemkin and others were deliberately not included. That said, the categorization into (one or more of) the four specified groups in the definition of the crime of genocide may not, however, always be quite as clear-cut as might first appear. Schabas has, for example, suggested that the listed groups 'resist efforts at precise definition'.[70]

Nevertheless, it appears highly unlikely that the intentional destruction of the environment during armed conflict would *per se* fall within the (current) definition of genocide. To assert otherwise would, in effect, impose a 'double intent' requirement to what is already a very complex crime. Not only would it be necessary to show the existence of the current *dolus specialis*, but an additional intent—to target the environment as a victim or use it as a weapon—would also be necessary to prove genocide for such acts. This would constitute a redefinition of the crime (at least in relation to circumstances involving the intentional destruction of the environment) and would mean that, for practical purposes, it would be virtually impossible to prove beyond a reasonable doubt the commission of what is a very difficult crime to prove.

In any event, given the 'stigma' associated with this crime of crimes, it would be unlikely that circumstances pointing 'just' to the intentional targeting of the environment alone would be prosecuted as genocide. Consequently, even if acts of this type were such as to (possibly) constitute an act of genocide, it is likely that the Prosecutor would take a conservative approach. To date, prosecution in the international Tribunals for the crime of genocide has generally been 'reserved' for 'high profile' acts that have resulted in, or have been intended to, directly cause very considerable harm to a relevant group.

Moreover, the Elements of Crimes appear to limit any scope for considering intentional environmental destruction as an act of genocide, by stipulating that, for each of the acts that might constitute an act of genocide under the Rome Statute, that act *inter alia* must have taken place 'in the context of a manifest pattern of

---

[69] ICTY Trial Chamber, *Prosecutor v Jelesić*, Judgment, 14 December 1999, Case No. IT-95-10-I, paras 78–83. It has been held by the ICTY Appeals Chamber that the 'in part' requirement refers to a 'substantial part of that group': see ICTY Appeals Chamber, *Prosecutor v Krstić*, Judgment, 19 April 2004, Case No. IT-98-33-A, para 8 and the various references made in paras 8–13.

[70] Schabas 2000, p. 109. See also *Prosecutor v Akayesu*, above n 55.

similar conduct directed against that group or was conduct that could itself effect such destruction'.[71]

This is not to say that the range of acts of genocide may not expand in the future. However, at least in the relatively early stages of the judicial activities of the ICC, there is a need for the Prosecutor, and the Court itself, not to be seen to be 'creating' crimes that are not clearly set out in the Rome Statute, as this flies in the face of the political concerns that lead to the compromised terms of the Rome Statute.

6.7 Intentional Destruction of the Environment as a Crime Against Humanity?

Although 'crimes against humanity' was not formally categorized as a separate crime until after the Second World War, the concept had by that time already been recognized. In May 1915, the Governments of France, Great Britain and Russia made a declaration regarding the massacres of the Armenian population in Turkey, denouncing them as 'crimes against humanity and civilisation for which all the members of the Turkish government will be held responsible together with its agents implicated in the massacres'.[72]

Crimes against humanity were recognized (and codified) in the Nuremberg Charter,[73] and considered in the Judgment of the Nuremberg Military Tribunal, as well as in Law No. 10 of the Control Council for Germany,[74] and the Tokyo Military Tribunal Charter.[75]

Since the Nuremberg and Tokyo Military Tribunal trials, the concept of crimes against humanity has continued to undergo a gradual evolution, firstly in national

---

[71] See Elements of Crimes, Articles 6(a)(4), 6(b)(4), 6(c)(5), 6(d)(5) and 6(e)(7).

[72] See ICTR Trial Chamber, *Prosecutor v Akayesu*, above n 55, para 565 and the corresponding footnote.

[73] See Nuremberg Charter, above n 49, Article 6(c).

[74] See Law No. 10 of the Control Council for Germany, Punishment of Persons Guilty of War Crimes, Crimes Against Peace and Against Humanity (20 December 1945) 36 ILR 31, Article II. This law was enacted to establish a legal basis in Germany for the trial of war criminals who were not prosecuted by the Nuremberg Military Tribunal: Jørgensen 2000, p. 20.

[75] See Charter of the International Military Tribunal for the trial of the major war criminals in the Far East (19 January 1946) TIAS 1589; 4 Bevans 20 (Tokyo Charter), Article 5(c).

cases such as *Eichmann*[76] and *Barbie*,[77] and subsequently as it has been defined in the Statutes of the *ad hoc* international Tribunals[78] and, ultimately, in the Rome Statute itself. The definition of crimes against humanity in the Rome Statute is broader than any previous formulation in several important respects.

Despite this process of evolution and expansion, there is no specific reference to the environment in the definition of crimes against humanity. It is true, however, that certain acts that constitute crimes against humanity might also relate to circumstances where the environment has been intentionally targeted. The Rome Statute defines a crime against humanity as any of a number of specified acts 'committed as part of a widespread or systematic attack directed against any civilian population, with knowledge of the attack'.[79] These include:

> [p]ersecution against any identifiable group or collectivity on political, racial, national, ethnic, cultural, religious, gender ... or other grounds that are universally recognized as impermissible under international law, in connection with any act referred to in this paragraph or any crime within the jurisdiction of the Court.[80]

and '[o]ther inhumane acts of a similar character intentionally causing great suffering, or serious injury to body or to mental or physical health'.[81]

Article 7(1)(h) identifies persecution against 'any identifiable group' or 'collec-tively' on a very broad basis ('any other grounds')—the characterization of the targeted groups for this crime is therefore significantly wider than for the crime of genocide. 'Persecution' is defined for the purposes of Article 7(1) of the Rome

---

[76] District Court of Jerusalem, *Attorney-General of the Government of Israel v Eichmann*, Judgement, 11 December 1961, Criminal Case No 40/61, 36 ILR 5. Eichmann was prosecuted under Israeli law (1951 Nazi and Nazi Collaborators (Punishment) Law) for war crimes, crimes against the Jewish people (the definition of which was modelled on the definition of genocide in the 1948 Genocide Convention) and crimes against humanity. He was convicted by the District Court of Jerusalem and sentenced to death. His appeal to the Supreme Court of Israel was dismissed: Supreme Court of Israel, *Eichmann v Attorney-General of the Government of Israel*, Judgment, 29 May 1962, Criminal Appeal 336/61, 36 ILR 277.

[77] In 1987, Klaus Barbie, who had been the head of the Gestapo in Lyon from November 1942 to August 1943 and was known as the 'Butcher of Lyon', was convicted by the Rhone *Cour d'assises* of 17 counts of crimes against humanity. His appeal was dismissed by the French Court of Cassation: *Féderation National des Déportés et Internés Résistants et Patriotes and Others v. Barbie*, Judgement, 20 December 1985, Case No 85-95166, 100 ILR 330.

[78] Article 3 of the ICTR Statute, above n 44, defines crimes against humanity as any one of a number of enumerated acts '... when committed as part of a widespread or systematic attack against any civilian population on national, political, ethnic, racial or religious grounds'. Article 5 of the ICTY, above n 44, Statute defines crimes against humanity to include the same acts, but '... when committed in armed conflict, whether international or internal in character, and directed against any civilian population'. However, in practice, the ICTY has adopted the criteria mentioned in the chapeau of Article 3 of the ICTR Statute: see, for example, ICTY Appeals Chamber, *Prosecutor v Kupreskic & Ors*, above n 30, para 544; ICTY Appeals Chamber, *Prosecutor v Blaskic*, Judgment, 29 July 2004, Case No. IT-95-14-A, paras 96-126. This practice has been criticised by some commentators: see, for example, Lattanzi 2001, pp. 478–82.

[79] Rome Statute, above n 17, chapeau Article 7(1).

[80] Ibid., Article 7(1)(h).

[81] Ibid., Article 7(1)(k).

Statute as 'the intentional and severe deprivation of fundamental rights contrary to international law by reason of the identity of the group or collectivity'.[82]

The deliberate destruction of a habitat[83] or of access to clean and safe water or food on a significant scale could, in certain circumstances, represent a breach of the fundamental human rights of the individuals within a targeted group, as perhaps might some other acts of environmental destruction. The right to 'adequate food' is, for example, expressly included in Article 11 of the ICESCR,[84] one of the principal human rights instruments that makes up the so-called 'International Bill of Human Rights'.[85] The right to water is, in addition, guaranteed in Articles 11 and 12 of the ICESCR. The duty to provide water is also expressly specified in Article 24 of the Convention on the Rights of the Child,[86] and Article 14 of the Convention of All Forms of Discrimination against Women.[87] In relation to the right to water, the United Nations Committee on Economic, Social and Cultural Rights has stated that:

> Water is a limited natural resource and a public good fundamental for life and health. The human right to water is indispensable for leading a life in human dignity. It is a prerequisite for the realization of other human rights
>
> […]
>
> The right [to water] should also be seen in conjunction with the other rights enshrined in the International Bill of Human Rights, foremost amongst them the right to life and human dignity[88]

Thus, in theory, the terms of Article 7(1)(h) of the Rome Statute might extend to certain acts that intentionally target the environment during armed conflict. One should also note the 'catch all' provision, Article 7(1)(k) of the Rome Statute, referred to above. Once again, one could envisage the possibility of acts that constitute environmental crimes perhaps falling within the terms of that provision.

---

82 Rome Statute, above n 17, Article 7(2)(g).

83 Conservation regimes such as those specified in the European Council Directive 92/43/EEC of 21 May 1992 on the conservation of natural habitats and of wild fauna and flora are not expressly designed, nor appropriate to deal with the intentional destruction of the environment during armed conflict.

84 International Covenant on Economic, Social and Cultural Rights, 16 December 1966, 993 UNTS 3, entered into force 3 January 1976 (ICESCR).

85 The other two instruments that, together with the ICESCR make up the 'International Bill of Human Rights', are the Universal Declaration of Human Rights, adopted by United Nations General Assembly Resolution 217A (III), UN Doc. A/RES/217A (1948), and the International Covenant on Civil and Political Rights, 16 December 1966, 999 UNTS 171, entered into force 23 March 1976.

86 See Convention on the Rights of the Child, 20 November 1989, 1577 UNTS 3, entered into force 2 September 1990, Article 24(2)(c).

87 See Convention on the Elimination of All Forms of Discrimination against Women, 18 December 1979, 19 ILM 33, entered into force 3 September 1981, Article 14(h).

88 United Nations Committee on Economic, Social and Cultural Rights, 'Substantive Issues arising in the Implementation of the International Covenant on Economic, Social and Cultural Rights: General Comment No. 15 (2002)—The right to water (Articles 11 and 12 of the International Covenant on Economic, Social and Cultural Rights)' (November 2002), paras 1 and 3. See also Horn and Freeland 2009, p. 101.

However, it would of course also be necessary to prove the other elements of the crime of crimes against humanity. The chapeau of Article 7 sets out a number of over-arching elements of the crime of crimes against humanity, which must also be present in order to support a conviction. This includes a 'widespread or systematic attack directed against any civilian population'. There has been considerable jurisprudence in relation to the meaning of the concepts of 'widespread' and 'systematic' in this context. The Appeals Chamber of the ICTY has confirmed that '"widespread" refers to the large-scale nature of the attack and the number of targeted persons, while the phrase "systematic" refers to the organized nature of the acts of violence and the improbability of their random occurrence'.[89] In a similar vein, in 2009 a Pre-Trial Chamber of the ICC confirmed that:

> Although the terms "widespread" and "systematic" are not specifically defined in the Statute, the Chamber has previously held that this language excludes random or isolated acts of violence, and that the term "widespread" refers to the large-scale nature of the attack, as well as to the number of victims, while the term "systematic" pertains to the organised nature of the acts of violence and to the improbability of their random occurrence.[90]

The two expressions are set out in the chapeau in the disjunctive ('or') form and are therefore alternate requirements. It is not necessary to demonstrate that the relevant attack meets both criteria—one would be sufficient to support a conviction. Be that as it may, both expressions at least suggest on their face that a crime against humanity will generally only occur in the context of a multiplicity of actions, an observation that is reinforced by Article 7(2)(a) of the Rome Statute, which specifies that an 'attack directed against any civilian population' means:

> ... a course of conduct involving the *multiple commission of acts* referred to in [Article 7(1) of the Rome Statute] against any civilian population, pursuant to or in furtherance of a State or organizational policy to commit such attack;[91]

However, it is still possible for a limited number of acts, or even a single act by an accused, to constitute a crime against humanity, assuming that all other elements of the crime are satisfied, if they are 'a part of [the] attack ... unless those acts may be said to be isolated or random'.[92] Nevertheless, the overall combined effect of these elements, coupled with the fact that there is a need to demonstrate the existence of a 'policy to commit such attack', would seem to make it very difficult to bring acts done with the intent to destroy the environment during armed conflict within the terms of crimes against humanity.

Further, and most significantly for the purposes of this discussion, any possible connection is made even more tenuous due to the requirement that the attack must be

---

[89] *Prosecutor v Blaskic*, above n 78, para 101, referring to ICTY Appeals Chamber, *Prosecutor v Kunarac & Ors*, Judgment, 12 June 2002, Case No. IT-96-23 and IT-96-23/1-A, para 94.

[90] Decision on the Prosecution's Application for a Warrant of Arrest against Omar Hassan Ahmad Al Bashir, *Prosecutor v Al Bashir ('Omar Al Bashir')*, above n 61, para 81.

[91] Rome Statute, Article 7(2)(a) (emphasis added).

[92] *Prosecutor v Blaskic*, above n 78, para 101, referring to ICTY Appeals Chamber, *Prosecutor v Kunarac & Ors*, above n 89, para 96.

directed 'against any civilian population'. In essence, for a crime against humanity to be committed, it is necessary to demonstrate that the civilian population is the 'victim' or 'primary object' of such an attack.[93] Indeed, the 'status of the victim as a civilian' is one of the characterizing features of a crime against humanity.[94] In order to determine whether the attack has been directed against the civilian population in this way, the ICTY has stated that the following factors must be considered:

> …the means and method used in the course of the attack, the status of the victims, their number, the discriminatory nature of the attack, the nature of the crimes committed in its course, the resistance to the assailants at the time and the extent to which the attacking force may be said to have complied or attempted to comply with the precautionary requirements of the laws of war…[95]

Although the intentional destruction of the environment during armed conflict may often be intended as a method of harming specific populations, it is for this reason that the crime of crimes against humanity is not readily applicable in circumstances where it is the *environment* (as opposed to the civilians) that is deliberately targeted as the victim or the primary object of such acts. It is this specific victim perspective that differentiates any notion of a crime *against* the environment from the other core international crimes in the Rome Statute and, as a consequence, such acts will not fall within the requirements of crimes against humanity.

6.8 Intentional Destruction of the Environment as a War Crime?

6.8.1 Article 8(2)(b)(iv)

As noted, the 'natural environment' is expressly referred to in only one provision of the Rome Statute, this being a specific act within the definition of war crimes.[96] Article 8(2)(b)(iv) specifies that, 'in particular when committed as part of a plan or policy or as part of a large-scale commission of such crimes',[97] a war crime within the jurisdiction of the Court includes:

> (b) … serious violations of the laws and customs applicable in international armed conflict, within the established framework of international law, namely, any of the following acts:
>
> […]

[93] *Prosecutor v Kunarac & Ors*, above n 89, para 91.

[94] *Prosecutor v Blaskic*, above n 78, para 107.

[95] *Prosecutor v Kunarac & Ors*, above n 89, para 91; see also *Prosecutor v Blaskic*, above n 78, para 106.

[96] Of course, other 'war crimes' defined in Article 8 of the Rome Statute may also relate to conduct that might indirectly involve damage to the natural environment.

[97] Rome Statute, above n 17, Article 8(1).

> (iv) Intentionally launching an attack in the knowledge that such attack will cause incidental loss of life or injury to civilians or damage to civilian objects or widespread, long-term and severe damage to the natural environment which would be clearly excessive in relation to the concrete and direct overall military advantage anticipated.[98]

As can be seen, the article specifies three 'variants of the offence'[99]—relating to (i) incidental loss of life or injury to civilians; (ii) damage to civilian objects; or (iii) damage to the natural environment. Given the focus of this chapter, it is only the third variant that is the subject of the discussion.

Before assessing the scope of this aspect of the provision, it is necessary to consider its drafting history. Although the notion of the 'criminality' of States for significant environmental damage was, for a period, included in the ILC Draft Articles on State Responsibility,[100] and the concept of individual criminal responsibility for 'widespread, long-term and severe damage to the natural environment' was included in the Draft Code of Crimes against the Peace and Security of Mankind,[101] such actions did not form part of the ILC Draft Statute. Instead, it was suggested that such damage would usually fall within the scope of other crimes already included in the draft text, and that, if that were not the case in a specific situation, it might be that the act does not meet the 'threshold of gravity for an international crime'.[102]

The revised draft version of the Statute, which subsequently formed the basis for the final discussions at the Rome Conference, contained three additional options, other than the version that was ultimately adopted as Article 8(2)(b)(iv), namely:

> (1) 'Intentionally launching an attack in the knowledge that such attack will cause incidental loss of life or injury to civilians or damage to civilian objects or widespread, long-term and severe damage to the natural environment, which is not justified by military necessity';
>
> (2) 'Intentionally launching an attack in the knowledge that such attack will cause incidental loss of life or injury to civilians or damage to civilian objects or widespread, long-term and severe damage to the natural environment';
>
> (3) 'No paragraph'—which would have meant that there would be no prohibition included in the Rome Statute in relation to widespread, long-term and severe damage to the natural environment.[103]

---

[98] Ibid., Article 8(2)(b)(iv).

[99] Werle and Jessberger 2014, p. 493.

[100] See Report of the International Law Commission to the General Assembly on its work of the thirty-second session, [1980] 2 *Yearbook of the International Law Commission* Part II, 32. Draft Article 19 of the 'Draft Articles on State Responsibility for International Wrongful Acts' had provided that an 'international crime' included: '[a]n internationally wrongful act which results from the breach by a State of an international obligation so essential for the protection of fundamental interests of the international community that its breach is recognized as a crime by that community as a whole constitutes an international crime', and included (draft Article 19(3)(d)) 'a serious breach of an international obligation of essential importance for the safeguarding and preservation of the human environment, such as those prohibiting massive pollution of the atmosphere or of the seas'.

[101] [1991] 1 *Yearbook of the International Law Commission* 234. See draft Article 26 of the Draft Code of Crimes Against the Peace and Security of Mankind.

[102] Cassese et al. 2002, pp. 522–523.

[103] See Draft Statute for the International Criminal Court (14 April 1998) Part 2 'War Crimes', ss B(b), as quoted in Drumbl 2000, pp. 622–3.

In the end, a compromise was reached with the final provision requiring a balancing of the damage as against military advantage. In practical terms, this means that environmental issues are 'made secondary' to interests of military importance.[104] In so doing, the provision therefore does not focus on the issues that arise from the intentional targeting of the environment during the course of armed conflict. It fails to recognize the importance of the protection of the environment *as such*, instead falling back on the traditional and outdated approach that environmental harm is to be regarded as an unfortunate 'bi-product' of warfare, even in circumstances where the damage is deliberate and intentional.

Similar language is used in Article 55(1) of Additional Protocol I,[105] and Article I(1) of the ENMOD Convention.[106] Several points bear further elaboration here. First, it is apparent that Article 8(2)(b)(iv) demands a very high threshold of injury to the environment before an act would fall within the scope of the crime. The use of the conjunctive ('and') between the words widespread, long-term and severe, rather than the disjunctive form, has, at least from an environmental protection perspective, effectively meant a 'regression' from the standard that had been specified in the ENMOD Convention (where the disjunctive form is used).[107] Werle and Jessberger explain this variance as follows: 'Since environmental damage can be expected as a collateral consequence in any type of warfare, the requirements were raised in comparison to those in ENMOD'.[108]

Moreover, a comparison of Article 8(2)(b)(iv) with Article 55(1) of Additional Protocol I indicates how the degree of culpable action necessary to amount to a war crime under the Rome Statute appears to have been increased. Acts that would contravene Article 55(1) would not necessarily constitute a war crime under Article 8(2)(b)(iv) of the Rome Statute, since this latter provision includes the need for the damage to be 'clearly excessive'. It is generally agreed that, under customary international law, the parties to an armed conflict are prohibited from causing 'excessive damage to the environment during military operations'.[109] The difficulties relating to the requirement of 'excessive' damage under Article 8(2)(b)(iv) were highlighted in the 2000 Committee Report examining NATO's actions during Operation Allied Force.[110] However, not only must the damage be 'excessive', but it must also be

[104] Drumbl 2000, p. 623.

[105] Protocol I Additional to the Geneva Conventions of 12 August 1949, and relating to the Protection of Victims of International Armed Conflicts, 1125 UNTS 3, 16 ILM 1391 (Additional Protocol I).

[106] Convention on the Prohibition of Military or Any Other Hostile Use of Environmental Modification Techniques, entered into force 10 December 1976, 1108 UNTS 151; 16 ILM 88, entered into force 5 October 1978 (ENMOD Convention).

[107] Drumbl 2000, p. 624.

[108] Werle and Jessberger 2014, p. 493.

[109] See Werle and Jessberger 2014, p. 492 and the references in the corresponding footnote.

[110] Final Report to the Prosecutor of the International Criminal Tribunal for the former Yugoslavia by the Committee Established to Review the NATO Bombing Campaign Against the Federal Republic of Yugoslavia, 13 June 2000, 39 ILM 1257 (Committee Report).

'clearly' so. Irrespective of any uncertainties as to what 'excessive' means, the inclusion of the descriptor 'clearly' suggests an intention to set an even higher level of damage as the requisite threshold, although how this is to be determined is unclear.

There is also no guidance provided as to the meaning of 'widespread', 'long-term' or 'severe' as they appear in Article 8(2)(b)(iv). Under the interpretative guidance provided in relation to their meaning in the ENMOD Convention, these three terms are defined, for the purposes of that Convention, as follows:

> (a) 'widespread': encompassing an area on the scale of several hundred square kilometres;
>
> (b) 'long-lasting': lasting for a period of months, or approximately a season;
>
> (c) 'severe': involving serious or significant disruption or harm to human life, natural and economic resources or other assets.[111]

The breadth of these interpretations, particularly as *all* of the variables must be satisfied ('and'), already sets the bar at a very high point in terms of what level of environmental damage will be necessary before Article 8(2)(b)(iv) might apply.[112] Yet, in relation to the use of these words in Article 55(1) of Additional Protocol I, various commentaries have provided even more restrictive interpretations. In a 1993 report to the United Nations General Assembly, the Secretary-General stated that:

> There are substantial grounds, including from the *travaux préparatoires* of [Additional] Protocol I, for interpreting 'long-term' to refer to *decades rather than months*. On the other hand, it is not easy to know in advance exactly what the scope and duration of some environmentally damaging acts will be.[113]

Naturally, it will be important to develop an understanding as to the scope of these words as they are used in any specific provision of the Rome Statute. The interpretations offered for the purposes of ENMOD 'should not be transferred mechanically' to Article 8(2)(b)(iv).[114] Moreover, the words will not necessarily have the same meaning in different articles of the same instrument—obviously, the context in which a particular word appears is relevant to its precise meaning. For example, the meaning of the word 'widespread' as it appears in the *chapeau* of Article 7(1) (crimes against humanity) will not be the same as its meaning in Article 8(2)(b)(iv). Without a specific definition of such words, it ultimately falls to the Court itself to determine their precise meaning, thus leaving the issue unclear at least until that point.

In the absence of an express definition (or clarification) within the Rome Statute, for the ICC Judges to determine a different (lower) interpretation of these words in the context of environmental damage than the thresholds in the ENMOD Convention

---

[111] 1976 CCD Understanding Relating to Article I of ENMOD, 31 United Nations General Assembly Official Records Supp. No. 27 (A/31/27), Annex I.

[112] Fenrick has suggested, for example, that the threshold would probably not be reached even by 'the sort of damage caused by heavy shelling during World War I battles on the Western Front': Fenrick 1999, p. 197.

[113] United Nations Secretary-General, 'Report of the Secretary-General on the Protection of the Environment in Times of Armed Conflict' (29 July 1993) para 34 (emphasis added).

[114] Werle and Jessberger 2014, p. 493.

and Additional Protocol I, it would be necessary for them to base their conclusions, at least partially, on environmental concerns. This might possibly eventuate, but such an outcome would require the involvement of environmental groups in the proceedings, although it is not entirely clear how this would work in practice.[115] It would also require a 'brave' bench of Judges, given the reality that environmental damage invariably occurs in armed conflict, and the traditional political reluctance to extend the express sanctions against environmental damage beyond what is specifically provided for in the Rome Statute.

In addition, Article 8(2)(b)(iv) requires an assessment of the proportionality of the environmental damage seen in the context of the military contingencies surrounding such actions. The requirement that the anticipated military advantage must be taken into account when looking at the damage to the environment—which was not the case with respect to either of Articles 35(3) or 55(1) of Additional Protocol I—adds to the uncertainty, subjectivity and difficulty of applying the provision. Even if the requisite threshold of widespread, long-term and severe damage is found to have resulted from a particular act, a war crime still would not have been committed if this falls within what was acceptable in the light of the anticipated military advantage.

The Elements of Crimes, when referring to Article 8(2)(b)(iv), emphasize that the military considerations that are to be weighed in determining the proportionality of the act are to be determined on a subjective basis. It provides that:

> The expression 'concrete and direct overall military advantage' refers to a military advantage that is foreseeable by the perpetrator at the relevant time. Such advantage may or may not be temporally or geographically related to the object of the attack … It reflects the proportionality requirement inherent in determining the legality of any military activity undertaken in the context of an armed conflict.[116]

The military 'value' of any particular act(s) is to be determined on the basis of 'the broader purpose' of the particular operation.[117] A determination of whether the relevant act is acceptable will be dependent upon the knowledge of the alleged perpetrator, based on his/her ('foreseeable') perceptions at the time. The Elements of Crimes confirm this as follows:

> … this knowledge element requires that the perpetrator make the *value judgement* as described therein. An evaluation of that value judgement must be based on the *requisite information available to the perpetrator at the time*.[118]

It is highly likely that the terms of Article 8(2)(b)(iv), when read together with the guidance provided by the Elements of Crimes, would 'excuse' many (and possibly all) decisions made by military commanders to intentionally target the environment.[119]

---

[115] One possibility might be for the Judges to require that specific information relating to the relevant environmental concerns be presented, pursuant to Article 64(6)(d) of the Rome Statute, which empowers a Trial Chamber to '[o]rder the production of evidence in addition to that already collected prior to the trial or presented during the trial by the parties'.

[116] Elements of Crimes, Article 8(2)(b)(iv), footnote 36.

[117] Dörmann 2004, p. 173.

[118] Elements of Crimes, Article 8(2)(b)(iv), footnote 37 (emphasis added).

[119] Dörmann 2001, p. 127.

Taking these considerations into account, the terms of Article 8(2)(b)(iv) are therefore, in the words of Okowa, 'heavily tilted in favour of military advantage and against environmental protection'.[120]

In addition, Article 30 of the Rome Statute applies as the default *mens rea* standard for Article 8(2)(b)(iv).[121] The dual requirement of both intention and knowledge further restricts any possible practical application of Article 8(2)(b)(iv). For example, the 2000 Committee Report examining NATO's actions during Operation Allied Force concluded that:

> …the requisite *mens rea* [under Article 8(2)(b)(iv)] on the part of a commander would be *actual or constructive* knowledge as to the grave environmental effects of a military attack; a standard which would be *difficult to establish for the purposes of prosecution* and which may provide an insufficient basis to prosecute military commanders inflicting environmental harm in the (mistaken) belief that such conduct was warranted by military necessity.[122]

It must also be noted that Article 8(2)(b)(iv) is only applicable 'in international armed conflict, within the established framework of international law'. This express limitation restricts its applicability in dealing with the environmental aspects of armed conflict. Earlier drafts of the instrument had included wording similar to Article 8(2)(b)(iv) within Articles 8(2)(c), and 8(2)(e), which both now deal with war crimes committed in an armed conflict 'not of an international character'. This was omitted, however, during the negotiation process and was not included in the final version of the Rome Statute.[123]

Several other provisions in the Rome Statute that originally only applied to international armed conflicts have more recently been extended to the war crimes provisions applying to non-international armed conflicts. However, the scope of Article 8(2)(b)(iv) was never part of that debate. In any event, the definition of a non-international armed conflict in the Rome Statute is itself quite limited.[124]

This is a particularly notable omission given that an increasing number of armed conflicts in the world are of a non-international nature and, in any event, there is no overwhelming logic preventing the applicability of such a provision in relation to internal conflicts. The environmental damage that occurred during the Rwandan and Yugoslav conflicts (the latter being regarded as having the characteristics of both an international and a non-international armed conflict),[125] indicate the extent of environmental destruction that can take place during the course of a 'civil war'. This would be the case, for example, in circumstances where an insurgency group uses a tropical forest as its 'base' and the Government forces, believing that such acts

[120] Okowa 2009, p. 248.

[121] Werle and Jessberger 2014, p. 494.

[122] Committee Report, para 23 (emphasis added).

[123] Drumbl 2000, p. 631.

[124] See Rome Statute, above n 17, Article 8(2)(f). See also Decision on the Prosecution's Application for a Warrant of Arrest against Omar Hassan Ahmad Al Bashir, *Prosecutor v. Omar Hassan Ahmad Al Bashir ('Omar Al Bashir')*, above n 61, para 59.

[125] See, for example, Decision on Defence Motion for Interlocutory Appeal on Jurisdiction, *Prosecutor v Duško Tadić*, above n 44, para 73.

are 'legitimate theaters of operations', deliberately destroy the forest and/or poison water and river systems as part of its attempt to defeat the insurgents.[126]

In sum, therefore, it seems that there is a real risk that, in reality, resort will not be made to the environmental damage variant in Article 8(2)(b)(iv). This provision is but one of a multitude of different war crimes set out in the Rome Statute, and the requirements necessary for it to be applied appear virtually impossible to satisfy in practical terms. Not only are there very significant legal hurdles to overcome in this regard, but this is also a reflection of the resistance towards the issue at the political level, given the general reluctance of states to limit the actions of their own military personnel.

It is true in one respect that express reference to environmental damage as a war crime is to be regarded as a step forward in the development of international criminal law, particularly since there is now a mechanism of international justice—the ICC—through which such acts can be prosecuted. At least the issue has been raised and discussed, and there is an acceptance, in relation to the jurisdiction of the ICC, that completely unfettered environmental destruction is no longer accepted. For example, refer to the fact that the third possible 'no paragraph' option quoted above in the draft version of the Statute was ultimately rejected.

However, as indicated by the discussion above, the issue of intentional environmental destruction during armed conflict still appears at best to be a narrowly defined 'add-on'.[127] The very considerable—perhaps even insurmountable—legal hurdles will, for all practical purposes, serve to curtail any effective prosecution. Indeed, the high damage thresholds and very limited circumstances as to when the provision may be relevant, if anything, serve to reinforce traditional perceptions that environmental concerns will remain very much minor and subsidiary issues when planning and implementing a military action.

6.8.2 Other War Crimes

For the sake of completeness, the remaining acts under Article 8 that might be helpful in addressing the issue of intentional destruction of the environment are addressed. In doing so, it must be noted that the chapeau of Article 8 suggests that the enumerated war crimes within that paragraph are to be regarded as exhaustive, since it has generally been accepted that the use of the words 'namely, any of the following acts'[128] implies exclusivity.[129] As a consequence, it does not appear possible to extend the scope of Article 8 of the Rome Statute beyond the specific war crimes that have

[126] Drumbl 2000, p. 631.

[127] Ibid., 632.

[128] See Rome Statute, above n 17, chapeau of Articles 8(2)(a), 8(2)(b), 8(2)(c) and 8(2)(e) respectively.

[129] Drumbl 2000, p. 633. For a contrary view, see Bruch 2001, p. 719.

been expressly stipulated. This is notwithstanding the fact that Article 21(1)(b) of the Rome Statute provides that the applicable law of the Court shall include:

> In the second place, where appropriate, applicable treaties and the principles and rules of international law, including the established principles of the international law of armed conflict ...[130]

With this caveat in mind, one can list those war crimes provisions that criminalize particular acts, the implementation of which could have destructive effects on the environment. Within the 'grave breaches' provisions, Articles 8(2)(a)(iii) and 8(2)(a)(iv) of the Rome Statute may be relevant. In addition, within the context of an international armed conflict, Articles 8(2)(b)(v), 8(2)(b)(xiii), 8(2)(b)(xvi), 8(2)(b)(xvii) and 8(2)(b)(xviii) also appear to apply to acts that may impact negatively on the environment. The latter two of these provisions relate to the use of weapons that might already be prohibited by some other international agreements.[131] With respect to the prosecution of environmentally destructive acts within the context of a non-international armed conflict, the only possible provisions of relevance are Articles 8(2)(e)(v), 8(2)(e)(xii), and the more recently included Articles 8(2)(e)(xiii) and 8(2)(e)(xiv).

However, each of these provisions, to the extent they may be relevant, do not, either individually or collectively, address adequately all of the fundamental issues associated with the intentional destruction of the environment during warfare.[132] The structure of Article 8 of the Rome Statute thus creates somewhat of a dilemma; in the event that the Prosecutor wishes to proceed against an accused in relation to such damage, they would in all likelihood look at the first instance to Article 8(2)(b)(iv) as the 'standard' for such a war crime. However, as discussed above, there are very significant difficulties associated with proving the requisite threshold requirements of that provision.

On the other hand, a 'fall back' position of resorting to other war crimes, assuming that they may be applicable, and that all of the relevant elements of those crimes have been met, would in most circumstances not cover all of the elements of such damage and, in any event, would not address the specific 'intent' aspect of a crime against the environment—the deliberate targeting of the environment as a victim, and/or its use as a weapon, during armed conflict.

---

[130] Rome Statute, Article 21(1)(b).

[131] See, for example, Geneva Protocol for the Prohibition of the Use in War of Asphyxiating, Poisonous and Other Gases, and of Bacteriological Methods of Warfare, 26 Martens (3rd) 643; Convention on the Prohibition of the Development, Production and Stockpiling of Bacteriological (Biological) and Toxic Weapons and on their Destruction, 10 April 1972, 1015 UNTS 163, entered into force 26 March 1975; Convention on Prohibitions or Restrictions on the Use of Certain Conventional Weapons Which May be Deemed to be Excessively Injurious or to Have Indiscriminate Effects, 10 October 1980, 1342 UNTS 137, entered into force 2 December 1983; Convention on the Prohibition of the Development, Production, Stockpiling and Use of Chemical Weapons and on Their Destruction, 3 September 1992, 32 ILM 800 entered into force 29 April 1997.

[132] See, for example, Ezekiel 2007, pp. 237–9.

6.9 Conclusion

One of the principal goals behind the establishment of the ICC has been the deterrence and punishment of the most serious international crimes, which also 'threaten the peace, security and well-being of the world'.[133] Given the rapid development of technology and the sometimes bewildering shift in geopolitical alliances, such threats are themselves 'fluid' in nature and will almost certainly vary (expand) in the future.

The intentional destruction of the environment during an armed conflict now falls plainly within this description, particularly given the catastrophic environmental damage that may result. However, the limitations of, and uncertainties with the definitions of the existing crimes within the jurisdiction of the Court significantly restrict any attempt to utilize them in such a way so as to comprehensively apply to such acts.

It might be suggested by some that the inclusion of Article 8(2)(b)(iv) of the Rome Statute, which makes express reference to the natural environment, may be sufficient in this regard. Indeed, the fact that there currently exists a specific war crime dealing with the issue might reinforce to most military personnel and others engaged in armed conflict that they cannot act with complete disregard of the environmental impact of their actions. In this regard, it could even be argued that, on a cursory reading, this provision provides some protection to the environment, and that therefore the 'need' to impose an enforcement mechanism has somehow been satisfied.

Yet, this is both simplistic and inaccurate. The intentional destruction of the environment during armed conflict represents a blatant disregard for the environment and for the (potential) consequences of such acts. Article 8(2)(b)(iv) is insufficient and inadequate to address the problem, due to the uncertainties of the provision and the inordinately high threshold level of damage that it requires, and even then only after taking account of the military contingencies.

Moreover, none of the core international crimes within the jurisdiction of the ICC are in terms that would adequately regulate such acts. In relation to these crimes, it will no doubt be important that the Court and the Prosecutor act in such a way as to avoid claims (whether or not justified) that they are perhaps 'overreaching' the boundaries of their respective powers, particularly given the highly political nature of the subject matter of the Court's mandate.

Yet, it is argued that acts done with the intent to cause significant environmental destruction during armed conflict should be prosecuted at the international level in particular circumstances, and certainly in broader terms than appear possible within the existing structure of the Rome Statute.[134] This flows from two important considerations—first, the need to properly formalize the criminalization of such acts through a mechanism (a clearly defined crime) that appropriately addresses their heinous nature; and secondly, that this mechanism should be included within the

---

[133] Rome Statute, above n 17, preamble para 3.

[134] See 'Vulnerable Nations Call for Ecocide to be Recognized as an International Crime' https://www.climateliabilitynews.org/2019/12/06/ecocide-international-criminal-court-vanuatu/. Accessed 10 February 2020.

jurisdiction of the ICC, given the functions of that institution as determined by the broader international community, and the level of seriousness of the actions it addresses. In regards the latter point, the need to ensure the integrity of any such prosecution means that they must be carried out by/through a body that has been created with the general (ideally universal) acceptance of states. As the first and only *permanent* international criminal court, the ICC represents the appropriate judicial 'forum' through which to prosecute such acts.

Hence, we are now at a crossroads—there is, in the author's view, an imperative to address the intentional targeting of the environment during armed conflict, and an appropriate enforcement mechanism exists for that to be done. Yet, Article 8(b)(2)(iv), and indeed the Rome Statute as a whole, is simply not performing the role that it should with respect to such acts and, frankly, is incapable of doing so as presently constituted. This is notwithstanding the Prosecutor's 2016 Policy Paper in which she stated that her Office 'will give particular consideration to prosecuting Rome Statute crimes that are committed by means of, or that result in, inter alia, the destruction of the environment …'.[135] Whilst this policy is laudable and, in theory at least, would give greater scope for victims from affected communities to participate in, and give evidence in cases relating to the impact of deliberate environmental destruction on their lives, in the author's view, it may not be practically feasible under the terms of the Rome Statute as they stand. The current legal framework fails to provide sufficient protection for the environment against such acts and thus fails humanity on this issue.

It is therefore submitted that a new (fifth) crime—'crimes against the environment'—be included within the terms of the Rome Statute so as to create international criminal responsibility in appropriate circumstances for those who deliberately target the environment as a strategy of armed conflict. The author has elsewhere elaborated on this argument and has provided a detailed draft of his proposed definition and structure for this crime.[136]

References

Bassiouni MC (2000) The Normative Framework of International Humanitarian Law: Overlaps, Gaps, and Ambiguities. In: Schmitt M (ed) International Law Studies Volume 75: International Law Across the Spectrum of Conflict. Naval War College, pp 1–55

Bruch CE (2001) All's Not Fair in (Civil) War: Criminal Liability for Environmental Damage in Internal Armed Conflict. Vermont Law Review 25:695

Cassese A (2003) International Criminal Law. Oxford University Press, Oxford

Cassese A, Eser A, Gaja G, Kirsch P, Pellet A, Swart B (eds) (2002) The Rome Statute of the International Criminal Court: A Commentary. Oxford University Press, Oxford

[135] ICC Office of the Prosecutor 2016, p. 14. Policy paper on case selection and prioritisation (15 September 2016).

[136] For a more detailed discussion, including this author's suggestion for the terms of the crime of 'crimes against the environment' to be included into the Rome Statute, see Freeland 2015.

de Vito D, Gill A, Short D (2009) Rape characterized as genocide. SUR International Journal on Human Rights 10:29
Dörmann K (2001) War Crimes in the Elements of Crimes. In: Fischer H, Kress C, Lüder S R (eds) International and National Prosecution of Crimes Under International Law: Current Developments. Verlag Arno Spitz, Berlin, pp 461–488
Dörmann K (2004) Elements of War Crimes under the Rome Statute of the International Criminal Court: Sources and Commentary. Cambridge University Press, Cambridge
Drumbl M (2000) Waging War against the World: The Need to Move from War Crimes to Environmental Crimes. In: Austin J E, Bruch C E (eds) The Environmental Consequences of War: Legal, Economic, and Scientific Perspectives. Cambridge University Press, pp 620–646
Ezekiel A (2007) The Application of International Criminal Law to Resource Exploitation: Ituri, Democratic Republic of the Congo. Natural Resources Journal 47:225
Fenrick W J (1999) Article 8: War Crimes – article 8(2)(b)(iv). In: Triffterer O (ed) Commentary on the Rome Statute of the International Criminal Court: Observers' Notes, Article by Article. Hart Publishing, London
Fischer H, Kress C, Lüder S R (eds) (2001) International and National Prosecution of Crimes Under International Law: Current Developments. Verlag Arno Spitz, Berlin
Freeland S (2006) How Open Should the Door Be? - Declarations by Non-states Parties under Article 12(3) of the Rome Statute of the International Criminal Court. Nordic Journal of International Law 752:211
Freeland S (2010) International Criminal Justice and the Death Penalty. In: Yorke J (ed) The Right to Life and the Value of Life: Orientations in Law, Politics and Ethics. Routledge
Freeland S (2015) Addressing the Intentional Destruction of the Environment during Warfare under the Rome Statute of the International Criminal Court. Intersentia, Cambridge
Haavisto P (2005) The International Responses to the Environmental Impacts of War. Symposium. Georgetown International Environmental Law Review 17:565
Horn L, Freeland S (2009) More than Hot Air: Reflections on the Relationship between Climate Change and Human Rights. University of Western Sydney Law Review 13:101
Jessberger F, Geneuss J (2013) Down the Drain or Down to Earth? International Criminal Justice under Pressure. Journal of International Criminal Justice 11:501
Jørgensen N (2000) The Responsibility of States for International Crimes. Oxford University Press, Oxford
Kalivretakis EI (2001) Are Nuclear Weapons Above the Law? A Look at the International Criminal Court and the Prohibited Weapons Category. Emory International Law Review 15:683
Koppe E (2006) The Use of Nuclear Weapons and the Protection of the Environment During International Armed Conflict. Hart Publishing
Lattanzi F (2001) Crimes Against Humanity in the Jurisprudence of the International Criminal Tribunals for the Former Yugoslavia and Rwanda. In: Fischer H, Kress C, Lüder S R (eds) International and National Prosecution of Crimes Under International Law: Current Developments. Verlag Arno Spitz, Berlin
Leibler A (1992) Deliberate Wartime Environmental Damage: New Challenges for International Law. California Western International Law Journal 23:67
McCormack T, Robertson S (1999) Jurisdictional Aspects of the Rome Statute for the New International Criminal Court. Melbourne University Law Review 23:635
Okowa P (2009) Environmental Justice in Situations of Armed Conflict. In: Ebbesson J, Okawa P (eds) Environmental Law and Justice in Context. Cambridge University Press
Rest A (2004) Enhanced Implementation of International Environmental Treaties by Judiciary – Access to Justice in International Environmental Law for Individuals and NGOs: Efficacious Enforcement by the Permanent Court of Arbitration. Macquarie Journal of International and Comparative Environmental Law 1:1
Rückert W, Witschel G (2001) Genocide and Crimes Against Humanity in the Elements of Crimes. In: Fischer H, Kress C, Lüder SR (eds) International and National Prosecution of Crimes Under International Law: Current Developments 59:68

Restatement of the Law: Third Restatement of U.S. Foreign Relations Law, Volume 2 (1987), 165, ss 702. Reporters' Comments

Sands Ph (2003) After Pinochet: The Role of National Courts. In: Sands Ph (ed) From Nuremberg to The Hague: The Future of International Criminal Justice. Cambridge University Press, pp 68–108

Sarooshi D (1999) The Statute of the International Criminal Court. International and Comparative Law Quarterly 48:387

Schabas W (2000) Genocide in International Law. Cambridge University Press, Cambridge

Stahn C (2006) Why some Doors may be Closed Already: Second Thoughts on a 'Case-by-Case' Treatment of Article 12(3) Declarations. Nordic Journal of International Law 75:243

United Nations Commission on Human Rights (2004) Report of the United Nations High Commissioner for Human Rights and Follow-Up to the World Conference on Human Rights: Situation of Human Rights in Darfur Region of the Sudan. E/CN.4/2005/3 (7 May 2004)

United Nations Secretary General (1993) Report of the Secretary-General on the Protection of the Environment in Times of Armed Conflict. A/48/269 (29 July 1993)

UNTAET Regulations 2000/11 (2000a) (6 March 2000)

UNTAET Regulations 2000/15 (2000b) (6 June 2000)

Werle G (2005) Principles of International Criminal Law. Oxford University Press, Oxford

Werle G, Jessberger F (2014) Principles of International Criminal Law. Oxford University Press, Oxford.

Williams S (2000) The Rome Statute on the International Criminal Court – Universal Jurisdiction or State Consent – To Make or Break the Package Deal. In: Schmitt M (ed) International Law Studies Volume 75: International Law Across the Spectrum of Conflict. Naval War College

Yuzon EF (1996) Deliberate Environmental Modification Through the Use of Chemical and Biological Weapons: "Greening" the Environmental Laws of Armed Conflict to Establish an Environmentally Protective Regime. American University Journal of International Law and Policy 11:793

Steven Freeland Emeritus Professor of International Law, Western Sydney University; Professorial Fellow, Bond University; Visiting Professor, University of Vienna: Permanent Visiting Professor, iCourts Centre of Excellence for International Courts, Denmark; Visiting Professor, Université Toulouse 1 Capitole; Adjunct Professor, Hong Kong University; Associate Member, Centre for Research in Air and Space Law, McGill University; Advisory Board Member, Centre for Research in Air and Space Law, Maharashtra National Law University, Mumbai, Senior Fellow, London Institute of Space Policy and Law; External Examiner, Universiti Teknologi MARA (UiTM), Malaysia. This chapter was completed in April 2020 and builds upon previous research by the author, who can be contacted at s.freeland@westernsydney.edu.au

Chapter 7
The European Court of Human Rights and the Environment

Birgit Peters

Content

Abstract Environmental protection has been a long-standing question before the European Court of Human Rights. The case-law of the ECtHR is vast and extensive. Nevertheless, the protection offered by this regional human rights protection system is still limited. To date, it applies to present generations who claim to be victims of present and immediate threats to those human rights guaranteed by the European

B. Peters (✉)
Faculty of Law, University of Trier, Trier, Germany
e-mail: petersb@uni-trier.de

E. Sobenes et al. (eds.), *The Environment Through the Lens of International Courts and Tribunals*, https://doi.org/10.1007/978-94-6265-507-2_7

Convention on Human Rights (ECHR). Also, the right to a clean and healthy environment is not protected per se under the ECHR. Some might therefore argue that the ECHR is ill-suited to deal with all the threats to the environment with which modern environmental law is faced today, such as the loss of biodiversity and climate change. Others find the ECHR applies also to those scenarios. Taking a middle ground, this contribution looks at the current status of environmental protection offered under the ECHR regime and outlines possible future developments, taking into account some of the recent developments in other international human rights regimes.

Keywords European Court of Human Rights · European Convention on Human Rights · environmental rights · environmental protection · right to a clean and healthy environment

7.1 Introduction: The Environment Before the European Court of Human Rights

The European Court of Human Rights (the Court or ECtHR) is regarded as one of the most successful human rights institutions in the world.[1] The Court has also attained a certain prominence in environmental cases. Since the mid-1990s, the Court has recognised environmental risks and damage with impact on individual human beings as violations of the European Convention on Human Rights (ECHR).[2] Over the years, the Court has applied the ECHR in cases involving threats to all environmental media, whether concerning air, soil or water. It has heard cases being brought by applicants in relation to emissions from gold mines near their homes,[3] the risks of nuclear power plants,[4] passive smoking,[5] the noise from Heathrow airport,[6] or from nearby bars and cafés.[7]

Still, the environmental protection offered by the ECHR is limited. Above all, it is restricted to living, human applicants and to actual or immediate threats to the rights protected by the ECHR. The ECtHR has not yet applied the ECHR in cases concerning future generations, or where only the common interests of nature were

[1] Keller and Stone Sweet 2008, p. 710. The work on this chapter was concluded in March 2020. Legal developments could only be reviewed until that date.

[2] Starting with the case of ECtHR, *López Ostra v Spain*, 9 December 1994, App no 16798/90. (All court cases quoted in the following without a particular denomination of the deciding court are those of the European Court of Human Rights (ECtHR)). Pedersen 2018, p. 86, contends that the ECtHR has put the right to a clean and healthy environment into practice.

[3] ECtHR, *Taşkın v Turkey*, 10 November 2004, App no 46117/99, para 133.

[4] ECtHR, *Balmer-Schafroth and others v Switzerland*, 26 August 1997, App no 22110/93.

[5] ECtHR, *Branduse v Romania*, 27 January 2016, App no 39951/08.

[6] ECtHR, *Hatton v United Kingdom*, 8 July 2003, App no 36002/97, para 120.

[7] ECtHR, *Moreno Gómez v Spain*, 16 November 2004, App no 4143/02, para 61; ECtHR, *Cuenca Zarzozo v Spain*, 16 January 2018, App no 23383/12, para 51.

at stake. Unless the ECtHR interprets the Convention in a different, less anthropocentric, or less 'individualistic'[8] manner, the ECtHR system may therefore be ill-suited for questions of general environmental degradation and some of the major environmental threats of our time, i.e. climate change and the loss of biodiversity. This debate is not entirely new. Already in the 1990s the proper relationship between human rights and the environment was debated.[9] Yet, with the rapid decline of livelihoods and living conditions due to climate change induced weather phenomena and natural disasters, the discussion has gained new momentum.[10] The Court has now received its first climate claims. Some may still conclude[11] that these problems have no direct bearing on humans and thus on individual human rights.[12] Others may argue, now more than ever, that common interests of nature and society have a rightful place in international human rights protection.[13] An intermediate position would maintain that, while there may be conflicts between the human rights and the international environmental regime, both may be united to advance the achievement of their common objectives.[14]

In line with the intermediate approach, this chapter will discuss some of the challenging aspects of environmental protection by the ECtHR. I will focus on those elements of the Court's jurisprudence, which illustrate that the Court has neither denied applications of the ECHR in environmental cases in principle, nor followed a broad approach which attempts to combine the common interests of nature with human rights. Accordingly, this chapter will first address elements pertaining to the forum and standing before the ECtHR. Secondly, I will illustrate the substantive scope of protection that the ECHR offers in environmental cases, including the standard of proof. Thirdly, after debating possible justifications and remedies that may be obtained for human rights violations in cases concerning the environment, I will draw some conclusions as to the strengths and weaknesses of the Court in protecting the environment.

[8] Francioni 2010, p. 50.

[9] Boyle 2009.

[10] Special Rapporteur Environment 2020; Osofsky and Peel 2018, p. 40.

[11] The discussion is not new. See Shelton 1991.

[12] Boyle 2012, p. 613 ff. Most recently the contributions in Voigt 2019, in particular: Petersmann 2019.

[13] IACHR, *The Environment and Human Rights – Requested by the Republic of Colombia*, Advisory Opinion, 15 November 2017, OC 23/17, para 62; most recently: Special Rapporteur Environment 2020; Osofsky and Peel 2018, p. 40; Francioni 2010, p. 41.

[14] Shelton 1991, p. 105ff.

7.2 The ECHR: An Anthropocentric Forum of Environmental Protection?

7.2.1 Introduction

The environmental protection offered by the ECHR is inherently limited by its anthropocentric, or, as Francioni concluded, individualistic,[15] approach. Like many international human rights regimes, the ECHR is focused on the impact of threats on human beings, not on the environment itself.[16] The Convention centres on the protection of the individual: its main aim is safeguarding individual human beings from violations of their rights. Article 1 of the ECHR makes this very clear, noting: 'The High Contracting Parties shall secure to *everyone* within their jurisdiction the rights and freedoms defined in Section I of this Convention.'

Although one could be tempted to conclude that 'everyone' who enjoys the protection of the rights and freedoms defined in the Convention could encompass entities other than humans, such as rivers and natural monuments,[17] articles 34 and 35 of the ECHR dealing with the admissibility of claims before the ECtHR underscore that protection afforded by the ECHR is only rendered to individuals, and for human rights violations within the scope of application of the Convention.[18] Moreover, as the Convention guarantees mostly civil and political rights,[19] it does not leave much room to include common interest or post-individualistic conceptualisations of rights which might include broader conceptualisations of nature protection.[20] I will show this by further illustrating the ECHR's approach discussing the scope of application of the Convention which can be defined as *ratione personae*, *ratione loci*, *ratione temporis* and *ratione materiae*.[21] I will discuss the most relevant elements which point to the anthropocentric character of the forum (*ratione personae* and *materiae*) first before turning to the further elements of forum (*ratione loci* and *temporis*) and to the element of standing, in the section thereafter.

---

[15] Francioni 2010, p. 50.

[16] Bolye 2009, para 4.

[17] For the recognition of rights of rivers in national law compare: Roy 2017.

[18] Articles 34, 35 para 3 lit. a ECHR.

[19] See Section I of the Convention, which is entitled 'rights and liberties'. Only Protocol 1 includes cultural rights, in particular the right to education (Article 2 para 1 of Protocol 1 to the ECHR). The Convention does not guarantee so called collective rights and few social rights, such as the freedom of association. The decision to include only civil and political rights was tactical. See: Harris et al. 2009, p. 3.

[20] Huanacuni 2015, para 2741.

[21] Compare: Schabas 2017, p. 93.

7.2.2 Ratione Personae *Scope of Application of the ECHR*

In most cases concerning the environment, the personal scope of jurisdiction is unproblematic. The ECHR applies to States, from the moment of ratification.[22] Personal jurisdiction may only become an issue, if a State has broken up. Here, it has been the view of the Court that the Convention applies notwithstanding the dissolution or succession, to the people on the territory of the dissolved State.[23]

The matter of jurisdiction is however closely linked to the international responsibility of the State concerned.[24] This will also be discussed in Sect. 7.2.4 below. Especially in climate change cases, environmental damage resulting from climate change may be attributed to more than one State following the principle of shared responsibility.[25] Yet, the matter, that a human rights violation may be attributable to more than one State, does not relieve the States to which the violation is attributable from their responsibility under the Convention.[26]

7.2.3 Ratione Materiae *Scope of Application of the ECHR*

According to Article 1 and Article 35(3)(a) of the ECHR, claims will only be successful before the ECtHR if the applicant can prove a violation *of a right guaranteed by the Convention*. These articles describe the *ratione materiae* jurisdiction of the ECtHR. Hence, also environmental disputes before the ECtHR must concern the rights guaranteed by the ECHR. As the Convention does not guarantee a human right to a clean and healthy environment—the ECtHR has affirmed this time and again in its decisions[27]—claims concerning the environment must revolve around violations of the (mostly civil and political) rights guaranteed by the ECHR,[28] such as the right to life, the prohibition of torture and inhuman and degrading treatment, or the right to a fair trial, etc. The ECHR does not contain many so called social and economic rights, such as the right to health.[29] Nor does it guarantee collective rights, such as the rights of indigenous communities. Accordingly, unless and as far as environmental degradation cannot be recognised as violations of human rights guaranteed by the ECHR, they cannot be subject to a claim before the ECtHR.

---

[22] Schabas 2017, p. 93.

[23] ECtHR, *Bijelić v Montenegro and Serbia*, 28 April 2009, App no 11890/05, para 69.

[24] ECtHR, *Andrejeva v Latvia*, 18 February 2009, App no 55705/00, para 56.

[25] On this see: Liston 2020, p. 250ff.

[26] Ibid.

[27] ECtHR, *López Ostra v Spain*, 9 December 1994, App no 16798/90, para 51; ECtHR, *Hatton v United Kingdom*, above n 6, para 96; ECtHR, *Furlepa v Poland*, 18 March 2008, App no 62101/00, para 2; ECtHR, *Leon and Agniezka Kania v Poland*, 21 October 2009, App no 12605/03, para 98.

[28] Harris et al 2009, p. 3.

[29] The only references to social, cultural and economic or collective rights can be found in Article 11 (freedom of association) and Article 2 of Protocol 1 to the ECHR (right to education).

Other regional human rights conventions allow a broader approach in environmental cases. As is illustrated by Monica Feria-Tinta in Chap. 9 of this volume, the American Convention on Human Rights (ACHR) recognises the right to a clean and healthy environment.[30] The Inter-American Court of Human Rights (IACHR) recently interpreted the right to not only oblige States to protect the life and health of their citizens, but also to oblige States parties to protect the environment for the sake of all organisms that live on this planet.[31] This could go as far as recognising the rights of nature as individual legal personalities with an individual claim to protection.[32] It is not yet clear what the Inter-American-Court intended with this ruling. In the following paragraphs, the IACHR concentrated on extrapolating the integration and recognition of international environmental obligations as part of the positive obligations guaranteed under the ACHR.[33] Hence, the question of whether or not the recognition of the right to a clean and healthy environment required the recognition of the rights of nature, remains unanswered. In any case, the IACHR pointed to the application of international environmental obligations as part of the duty to protect the right to a clean and healthy environment under the Convention. Thus, the IACHR is certainly one of the first human rights courts to ponder the further integration of international environmental protection into the human rights regime.

Despite its innovative character, the decision of the IACHR is not readily transferable to the ECHR regime. The ECHR does not contain any provision like Article 4 of the Protocol to the ACHR, which guarantees the right to a clean and healthy environment. Thus, the interpretation of State's obligations in light of their international environmental obligations is only possible and feasible if a right safeguarded in the ECHR is at stake in a case concerning environmental harm. This will be illustrated further in Sect. 7.4 of this chapter.

7.2.4 **Ratione Loci** *Scope of Application or State Jurisdiction*

The further elements of the forum of application are predetermined by the provision of Article 1 of the ECHR. The reference to 'jurisdiction' links the (territorial) scope of application of the convention to the *authority* of States, not to their territory. Following Article 1 of the ECHR, States are burdened with the obligation to observe and protect the rights guaranteed by the ECHR in the exercise of their jurisdictional authority, be it legislative, executive or judicial.[34] In environmental cases, especially

[30] Article 4 of Additional Protocol on the Protection of Economic, Social and Cultural Rights ACHR (Protocol of San Salvador) 1998 69; African Commission on Human and People's Rights 2015, para 3 (States' responsibilities to protect life 'extend to preventive steps to preserve and protect the natural environment, and humanitarian responses to natural disasters, famines, outbreaks of infectious diseases, or other emergencies.').

[31] IACHR, above n 13.

[32] Ibid.

[33] Ibid., para 63 ff.

[34] Peters and Altwicker 2019, p. 21.

the legislator may be called upon to react to protect the environment. The ECtHR has confirmed in a number of cases that the State was obliged to protect the rights of those affected by relevant legislation.[35] In the *Hatton* case, the Court therefore needed to decide whether the adoption of noise regulation was sufficient to protect the applicants against the noise from Heathrow airport.[36] The administration can also protect the rights of applicants, mostly by granting information and participation rights in administrative decision-making.[37] The judiciary is usually called upon to provide adequate judicial protection according to Article 6 of the ECHR.[38]

In spite of the wording of Article 1 of the ECHR, the Court has emphasised time and again that the principle of territoriality is the primary link for the obligations of the member States flowing from the ECHR.[39] So far, the Court has only accepted cases where the environmental harm occurred in the territory of the State member to the ECHR.[40] This, however, does not exclude that the Convention may apply to cases involving human rights infringements caused by transnational environmental harm. Under certain circumstances—especially since Article 1 of the ECHR refers to jurisdiction and not to territory—States parties to the ECHR are also responsible for actions carried out abroad. This is the personal scope of jurisdiction. In cases not concerning environmental degradation, the ECtHR has accepted personal jurisdiction, where the human rights violation could be attributed to personnel of a member State, who operated on or controlled a third-State's territory. For example, the Court ruled in the renowned *Louizidou* case that States are also responsible for the actions of their personnel in areas where they exercise exclusive jurisdiction, like Turkey in Northern Cyprus.[41] Moreover, in the cases of *Al Skeini* and *Al Jedda*, the ECtHR affirmed that the ECHR can apply in cases where the personnel of member States exercised effective and ultimate authority and control on the ground.[42] The two latter cases concerned the human rights violations by British forces that occurred in Iraqi prisons after the third war in Iraq.[43]

Accordingly, the ECHR may apply extraterritorially, in cases involving environmental harm, as long and as far as the particular harm in question may be attributed

---

[35] See above, Sect. 7.4.2.

[36] See above, Sect. 7.4.2.; ECtHR, *Hatton v United Kingdom*, above n 6, para 98.

[37] See Sect. 7.4.3.

[38] See Sect. 7.4.2.

[39] ECtHR, *Bankovic and others v. Belgium and others*, 12 December 2001, App no 52207/99 para 61 and 67; ECtHR, *Chagos Islanders v the United Kingdom*, 11 December 2012, App no 35622/04, para 70; ECtHR, *Hirsi Jamaa and others v Italy*, 23 February 2012, App no 27765/09, para 71ff.

[40] Council of Europe 2012, 25.

[41] ECtHR, *Loizidou v Turkey*, 18 December 1996, App no 15318/89, para 52.

[42] ECtHR, Al *Skeini and others v United Kingdom*, 7 July 2011, App no 55721/07, para 149 ('authority and control'); ECtHR, Al-*Jedda v United Kingdom*, 7 July 2011, App no 27021/08, para 84 ('ultimate authority and control').

[43] The ECtHR did not rely on the accepted standard of effective control in those cases. On this see: ICJ, *Military and Paramilitary Activities in and against Nicaragua (Nicaragua* v *United States of America),* Merits, Judgment, 27 June 1986, ICJ Reports 1986, para 115; International Law Commission (2001), Article 8; International Law Commission 2011, Article 7.

to the member State following the principle of personal jurisdiction. Yet, as the environmental damage leading to the human rights violation needs to be caused by personnel controlled by the State abroad, few cases concerning transnational environmental damage will actually fall into this category of attribution. It is not very likely that, for instance, a military battalion stationed in a third State contributes to an environmental disaster.

Instead, the majority of cases which tackle the aspect of transnational environmental harm will concern another situation. This can be summarized by the famous *Trail Smelter* arbitration of 1941.[44] The *Trail Smelter* arbitration dealt with the emissions from a smelter in Canada that caused environmental degradation and harm in US territory. In the case, the arbiter established that States are responsible for transnational environmental damage, if the emissions can be attributed to a certain public or private enterprise under the control of the State.[45] Here, 'control' of the State cannot be understood in the sense of personal jurisdiction discussed above. There is no extraterritorial act involved. Rather, the case concerns territorial acts (or omissions) which have extraterritorial effects, either on the nationals of the legislating State or on third State nationals. It deals with the primary responsibility of the legislative –and therefore the original jurisdiction of the State[46]—to prevent transnational environmental damage which results from activities on its very territory. Nonetheless, in *Banković,* the Court found the ECHR did not apply in situations where an act was imputable to a member state of the ECHR, but where the consequences felt fell outside the scope of application of the ECHR.

Therefore, jurisdiction *ratione loci* may only be established, if the Court interprets Article 1 of the ECHR in light of the international environmental principles set in the *Trail Smelter* case. The remaining discussion will then revolve around the nature, scope and reach of state obligations in those cases. In general international law, the general duty to prevent extraterritorial harm crystallized into the customary no-harm/preventive action rule of international law.[47] However, the details of determining the scope and reach of the legislative responsibility to prevent harm are still unclear.[48] Similarly, the ECtHR will have to discuss, whether and how the positive obligations of the States party to the ECHR apply in climate change related

[44] *Trail Smelter Arbitration,* Award, 11 March 1941, 3 RIAA 1905; ICJ, *Legality of the Threat of Nuclear Weapons,* Advisory Opinion, 8 July 1996, ICJ Reports 1996, para 29; ICJ, *Gabčíkovo-Nagymaros Project (Hungary* v *Slovakia),* Judgment, 25 September 1997, ICJ Reports 1997, para 53; ICJ, *Certain Activities Carried out by Nicaragua in the Border Area (Costa Rica v Nicaragua) and Construction of a Road in Costa Rica along the San Juan River (Nicaragua v Costa Rica),* Judgment, 16 December 2015, ICJ Reports 2015, para 162.

[45] *Trail Smelter Arbitration,* above n 44, p. 1965.

[46] Against: Besson 2020.

[47] For its latest affirmation in international environmental law see: ICJ, *Certain Activities Carried out by Nicaragua in the Border Area (Costa Rica v Nicaragua) and Construction of a Road in Costa Rica along the San Juan River (Nicaragua v Costa Rica) (Judgment),* above n 44, para 162; United Nations Secretary General 2018, para 14.

[48] Peters et al. 2020, p. 128.

cases.[49] Also the aspect of causation is disputed and not easy to determine, least of all in human rights cases.[50] As this chapter merely provides an overview of the environmental protection offered by the ECHR regime, I can only point to the general principles of the ECHR regime here. The details must remain for another assessment.

7.2.5 **Ratione Temporis** *Scope of Application of the ECHR*

According to the general rules of international law, States only incur obligations deriving from an international treaty from the moment of ratification.[51] This general rule is only modified, if the obligations that derive from the treaty actually cover a situation that *began before* ratification. Under the ECHR, this exception applies if positive obligations, which may be derived from certain ECHR rights, are at stake.[52] For example, a State can be held liable for breaching Article 2 ECHR, if they did not instigate proceedings in a case concerning a murder, even if that murder happened before the State ratified the Convention. In general, the critical date for the establishment of temporal jurisdiction is the date of the interference with the rights of the Convention.[53] Those general rules also apply in environmental proceedings.

However, in particular in the case of disasters, such as climate change, those principles remain difficult to apply in the individual case at hand. There is an international consensus that obligations of States for emissions contributing to climate change concern the period from 1990 onwards.[54] Current climate science also allows for the attribution of emissions contributing to slow-onset disasters to a particular

[49] On this, see Sect. 7.4, below.

[50] Compare, for example: Maljean-Dubois 2019, para 42; Brunnée 2004. For recent national jurisprudence involving so called climate claims in human rights cases compare: General Court, *Carvalho and Others v Parliament and Council*, Order, 8 May 2019, Case No T-330/18, ECLI:EU:T:2019:324; Netherlands Supreme Court, *State of the Netherlands (Ministry of Economic Affairs and Climate Policy) v Stichting Urgenda*, Judgment, 20 December 2019, ECLI:NL:HR:2019:2007; Human Rights Committee (2020). For decisions before German courts: High Court of Hamm, *Saúl Luciano Lluiya against RWE*, Decision, 30 November 2017; German Constitutional Court, *Friends of the Earth Germany, Association of Solar Supporters, and Others v Germany*, Complaint of 22 November 2018. For a recent decision in the United Kingdom compare: High Court of England and Wales, *R (Friends of the Earth) v Department for Transport & Others*, Judgment, 27 February 2020, Court of Appeal Case Nos: C1/2019/1053, C1/2019/1056 and C1/2019/1145, 2020 EWCA Civ 214.

[51] Vienna Convention on the Law of Treaties, 23 May 1969, 1155 UNTS 331, entered into force 27 January 1980, Articles 14 and 24.

[52] Compare: Schabas 2017, p. 109.

[53] Ovey and White 2006, p. 485; Schabas 2017, p. 108.

[54] United Nations Framework Convention on Climate Change, 1 July 1992, 1771 UNTS 107, entered into force 21 March 1994 (UNFCCC), Article 4 Abs. 2 lit. b; Kyoto Protocol to the United Nations Framework Convention on Climate Change, 12 March 1998, 2303 UNTS 162, entered into force 16 February 2005 (Kyoto Protocol), Article 3 Abs. 1; Paris Agreement, 12 December 2015, UNTS No 54113, entered into force 4 November 2016, Article 2 Abs. 1 lit. a.

State at a particular point in time.[55] The ECtHR can draw upon those insights in climate-change related cases, at least in cases concerning the main emitter States in Europe that have ratified the Convention before 1990.

Still, the human rights obligations of 'younger' ECHR member States needs further consideration.[56] In particular, the ECtHR would need to clarify the exact point in time, when 'younger' ECHR member States incurred a positive obligation to prevent and mitigate the human rights violations resulting from climate change. Several instances may be relevant for this assessment: first, 1990 onwards, when the international consensus settled on global reduction duties. Second, from the date of the individual State's coming into being, if reduction obligations are considered part of the customary no harm principle in international environmental law.[57] Third, from the date of ratification of the respective climate change agreement that gives rise to positive obligations under the ECHR or, fourth, from the date of their ratification of the ECHR.

7.3 Standing

7.3.1 Individuals or their Associations

According to Article 34 of the ECHR, only individuals or their associations may be admitted as applicants before the ECtHR. They must be alive or represented by an applicant who has a legitimate interest in defending their rights.[58] Thus far, the ECHR has not yet admitted unborn, future generations as applicants with a legitimate interest, despite the fact that these generations are the most likely to bear the costs of current environmental degradation.[59] Nor has the Court accepted so-called popular claims (*actio popularis*) that have no nexus to an individual human rights violation,

---

[55] See, for example: World Bank, CO_2 emissions, public data, CC BY-4.0, at: https://data.worldbank.org/indicator/EN.ATM.CO2E.KT?end=2016&start=1990 Accessed 24 February 2021.

[56] Which is true for a number of States members to the ECHR. Compare: Albania (1996), Andorra (1996), Armenia (2002), Azerbeidjan (2001), Bosnia and Herzegovina (2002), Bulgaria (1992), Croatia (1992), Georgia (1999), Hungary (1992), Latvia (1997), Lithuania (1995), Monaco (2005), Montenegro (2006), Moldova (1997), Romania (1994), Russia (1998), Serbia (2004), the Slovak Republic (1993), Slovenia (1994), Ukraine (1997). At: https://www.coe.int/en/web/conventions/full-list/-/conventions/treaty/005/signatures Accessed 24 February 2021.

[57] Voigt 2008, p. 8ff.

[58] Leach 2011, para 4.40 (so-called indirect victims); Meyer-Ladewig et al. 2017, Article 34, para 8.

[59] Compare for a case involving future generations: Supreme Court of the Philippines, *Juan Antonio Oposa et al.,* v *The Honorable Fulgencio S. Factoran, Jr., in his capacity as the Secretary of the Department of Environment and Natural Resources, and the Honorable Eriberto U. Rosario, Presiding Judge of the RTC*, 30 July 1993.

but concern abstract challenges or interests of the public at large.[60] Accordingly, the ECtHR cannot hear cases where only the interests of nature are at stake.

Despite the foregoing, the ECtHR will deal with cases that concern an infringement of the rights of environmental interest organisations, thereby recognising the common interest in the protection of nature defended by those organisations. This jurisprudence developed with the case *Collectif Melox et Mox v France*, where the ECtHR found that Article 6 ECHR—which guarantees the right to a fair trial—could be invoked by an environmental interest organisation where the claim concerned the interests that the organisation defends.[61] In the view of the Court, exercise of the right to participation and information generally contributes to fulfilling an NGO's role in a democratic society.[62] Two further cases also highlight this approach. In *Vides Aizsardzības Klubs v Latvia*,[63] a Latvian environmental interest organisation had published a report on the destruction of certain protected sand dunes in the Gulf of Riga in a local newspaper. The mayor of the community concerned sued the organisation for defamation. The ECtHR, however ruled that Article 10 of the ECHR, which guarantees the right of environmental NGOs to disseminate environmental information, had been violated. The Court also found that Article 10 of the ECHR guaranteed NGOs the right to exercise their role as guardians of environmental law in a democratic society.[64] Another case, *Costel Popa v Romania*, points in a similar direction. In this decision, the ECtHR regarded the failure to register the organisation as an environmental organisation represented an unjustified restriction of Article 11 of the ECHR (which provides for the freedom of assembly and association).[65]

The ECtHR thus has not only confirmed the importance of environmental interest organisations in European society, but also their role as 'watchdog[s] for nature',[66] i.e. their role as representatives of the interests of nature. The decisions therefore illustrate how common environmental concerns may be recognised under the ECHR: they must be defended by environmental interest organisations and the rights of those organisations must be at stake. The ECtHR, is, however, unable to deal with environmental concerns that are not represented by interest organisations and cannot be perceived a violation of their rights. The ECtHR is not a general environmental court: its competence to hear environmental claims is limited to cases that concern violations of the rights of individuals (or their associations).

---

60 Leach 2011, para 4.24; ECtHR, *Ilhan v Turkey*, 27 June 2000, App no 22277/93.

61 ECtHR, *Affaire collectif national d'information et d'opposition à l'usine Melox - Collectif stop Melox et Mox v France*, 12 June 2006, App no 75218/01, para 4ff.

62 ECtHR, *Affaire collectif à l'usine Melox*, App no 75218/01, admissibility decision as quoted in *L'Erablière A.S.B. v Belgium*, para 15.

63 ECtHR, *Vides Aizsardzības klubs v Latvia*, 27 May 2004, App no 57829/00.

64 Ibid., para 42.

65 ECtHR, *Costel Popa v Romania*, 26 July 2016, App no 47558/10.

66 ECtHR, *Vides Aizsardzības klubs v Latvia*, above n 63, para 42.

7.3.2 Victim

For a successful claim before the ECtHR, individuals or their associations must claim that they have been *victims* of human rights violations.[67] In the interpretation of the Court, this entails being 'personally or directly affected'[68] by a violation of the Convention. The Court usually speaks of a 'direct link between the applicant and the harm they consider they have sustained on account of the alleged violation'.[69] The Court also allows claims which concern 'potential victims' of violations of the ECHR, where the violation did not yet occur.[70] In that case, applicants must provide sufficient proof that there is a likelihood that they will be affected by a human rights violation.[71] However, mere speculation is not enough.[72] The cases in which the Court allowed potential victims to address the Court, all concerned instances where the potential infringement of the applicants rights was imminent. For example, in *Soering*, the deportation of the applicant was ordered, but not yet executed.[73] Other cases concerned laws that had already been enacted and were capable of being applied to the applicants' situation.[74]

In line with the primarily anthropocentric character of the forum, the definition of standing therefore concentrates on the immediate effects of (environmental) harm on individual human beings. It will be difficult to establish standing in cases, which are entirely future related. Moreover, it is not always easy to determine when a person (or an association) has been affected in that sense in cases concerning the environment. In fact, persons or associations can be affected by harm to the environment in various ways: the most obvious example is that of individual exposure to environmental contaminants, risk or harm. Yet further criteria may be relevant for determining affectedness: exposure over time may be relevant,[75] as well as the question of whether or not the person lived in the immediate geographical vicinity of the contamination.[76] Eventually and in a broad interpretation of affectedness, persons or associations may also be affected by the beauty of a nearby natural monument,[77] or by the presence of a particular species in their natural habitat.[78]

---

[67] Article 34 ECHR; for the aspects of the victim requirement see: Leach 2011, paras 4.05ff.

[68] Leach 2011, para 4.25.

[69] ECtHR, *Brudnicka and others v Poland*, 3 March 2005, App No 54723/00, para 26.

[70] ECtHR, *Soering v the United Kingdom*, 7 July 1989, App no 14038/88, Series A No 161.

[71] ECtHR, *Segi and others v 15 States of the European Union*, 23 May 2002, App No 6422/02, 9916/02.

[72] Ibid.

[73] ECtHR, *Soering v the United Kingdom*, above n 70.

[74] Compare: ECtHR, *Dudgeon v the United Kingdom*, 22 October 1981, App no 7525/76, Series A No 45, para 39.

[75] ECtHR, *Balmer-Schafroth and others v Switzerland*, above n 4.

[76] ECtHR, *Cordella v Italy*, 24 January 2019, App no 54414/13; 54264/15, paras 100ff.

[77] ECtHR, *Kyrtatos v Greece*, 22 May 2003, App no 41666/98, para 52.

[78] ECtHR, *Lesoochranárske Zoskupenie VLK v Slovakia*, 2 October 2012, App no 53246/08.

As assessment of the exact relation of the individual or association to the environmental harm in question may be the subject of detailed factual assessment, the Court has tended to admit claims as long as the link between the victim and the environmental harm could be established, without further detailed factual assessment. The ECtHR has declined cases where the application concerned an *actio popularis*,[79] or when the facts communicated made it clear that the relation between the victim and the human rights violation was too remote. For example, in the recent *Cordello v Italy* decision, the Court pointed out that some of the applicants had not lived in areas classified by Italy as 'zones of high environmental risk'. The ECtHR therefore concluded that they could not be regarded as victims.[80] For the most part, detailed assessment of the 'link' between the affected person or association and the particular violation of rights is mostly left to the merits stage of the case.

7.4 Substantive Protection in Environmental Proceedings: The Case of Positive Environmental Obligations

7.4.1 Introduction

The ECHR primarily guarantees the obligation of States to *respect* the rights guaranteed in the Convention (Article 1 ECHR), i.e. not to infringe upon the rights of their nationals. Yet, the ECtHR member States are also called upon to *protect* the same rights.[81] The duty to protect is expressed by various positive obligations. Positive obligations calling upon States to use all necessary means to prevent violations of human rights within their jurisdiction[82] have been established under the Convention since the early 1970s. In the first cases that dealt with positive obligations, the Court had to decide on the obligations to protect the right to individual liberty and the justification of the exercise of aggression.[83] In due course, the Court extended its jurisdiction on positive obligations to cases concerning the environment.[84] The following cases illustrate the bandwidth of rights that have been interpreted by the ECtHR to include a duty to protect the individual applicant from environmental threats. The cases also illustrate the range of possible environmental threats which

[79] ECtHR, Di *Sarno and Others v Italy*, 10 January 2012, App no 30765/08, para 80. On the exception from the actio popularis rule, see Sect. 7.2.2, above.

[80] ECtHR, *Cordella v Italy*, above n 76, para 102.

[81] Peters and Altwicker 2019, pp. 20 and 21.

[82] Compare: Harris et al 2009, pp. 6 and 18ff.

[83] For the early case law of the ECtHR on Article 5 ECHR see: ECtHR, *De Wilde, Ooms and Versyp v Belgium*, 18 June 1971, App no 2832/66; 2835/66; 2899/66, para 76; ECtHR, *McCann and others v the UK*, 27 September 1995, App no 18984/92, para 161.

[84] ECtHR, *López Ostra v Spain*, above n 27, para 51; ECtHR, *Hatton v United Kingdom*, above n 6, para 96; ECtHR, *Furlepa v Poland*, above n 27, para 2; ECtHR, *Leon and Agniezka Kania v Poland*, above n 27, para 98.

can lead to a human rights violation. The section thereafter will turn to specific environmental obligations which follow from those human rights guarantees.

7.4.2 Bandwidth of Convention Rights Providing for Positive Obligations to Protect the Environment According to the ECtHR's Jurisprudence

The Court has tackled threats to the right to life, guaranteed by Article 2 of the ECHR, on various occasions. The *Öneryılıdz v Turkey* case[85] concerned the fate of the relatives of the applicant, who were housed on the site of a landfill. A methane explosion destroyed the house of the relatives and nine family members died. The ECtHR decided that the applicant's right under Article 2 of the ECHR had been violated. The government should have taken practical measures to protect the lives of the relatives of the applicant.[86] Although the Court did not confirm a violation of Article 10 of the ECHR, which guarantees the right to information, the Court considered that Article 2 of the ECHR contained a procedural duty to inform the applicant about the risks involved in erecting a house on a former dump site.

In *Branduse v Romania*, the ECtHR affirmed a violation of the prohibition of inhuman and degrading treatment, according to Article 3 of the ECHR.[87] The applicant in that case suffered from hepatitis and hypertension. He was jailed for nine months in a prison cell with 120 other inmates, ninety-nine per-cent of whom smoked. The Court decided that the State should have taken measures to protect the applicant from exposure to smoke exhaled by the other inmates.[88] Its failure to do so amounted to degrading treatment of the applicant.

One of the greatest fields of application in environmental cases is Article 8 of the ECHR, which guarantees the right to private and family life. The Court concluded in the most famous case concerning Article 8 of the ECHR, *Hatton v UK*, which dealt with the noise emissions by Heathrow airport, that the right to enjoy one's personal home included State measures to protect the home from noise emissions.[89] Article 8 has also been considered by the Court in cases such as *Guerra et al v Italy*, where the malfunctioning of a fertilizer plant led to several of the applicants being hospitalized with arsenic poisoning.[90] The Court interpreted the right in Article 8 of the ECHR to contain a right to receive information about the emissions of environmental projects, as the conduct of the local authorities had made it impossible for Ms. Guerra to appraise the risks of living in the vicinity of the plant.[91]

---

[85] ECtHR, *Öneryildiz v Turkey*, 30 November 2004, App no 48939/99.

[86] Ibid., para 90.

[87] ECtHR, *Branduse v Romania*, above n 5.

[88] Ibid., paras 29–30.

[89] ECtHR, *Hatton v United Kingdom*, above n 6, para 96.

[90] ECtHR, *Guerra and Others v Italy*, 19 February 1998, App no 14967/89.

[91] Ibid., para 58, 60.

The right to information guaranteed by Article 10 of the ECHR has only recently been successfully invoked before the ECtHR. Article 10 was considered by the Court, for example, in the case of *Vides Aidzarsibas Klubs*, discussed earlier.[92] The Court emphasised that environmental interest organizations must have access to environmental information and must also have the possibility of disseminating that information. A State should enable environmental interest organizations to fulfil their role as environmental watchdogs in a democratic society.[93]

The Court has also discussed environmental obligations as part of the right to a fair trial guaranteed in Article 6 of the ECHR. The right applies to both civil and criminal proceedings under domestic law,[94] and guarantees a number of particular rights. For civil proceedings it guarantees, amongst others, the right to a reasoned judgment,[95] the right to a fair trial conducted on fair application of the relevant procedure,[96] and the right of access to a court[97] and to enforcement proceedings, which concern the execution of decisions on civil claims.[98] Article 6 of the ECHR may apply if projects or activities with impact on the environment infringe on rights of the applicants guaranteed under domestic law. Those cases can concern violations of emission standards, or omission to guarantee rights to participate in environmental proceedings envisaged at the national level.

Finally, the Court considered violations of the right to property in environmental cases. In the *Öneryıldz* decision quoted above, it established that Article 1 of Protocol No. 1 to the ECHR obliges States to adopt positive measures of protection.[99] States must, in particular, make sure that the right to property is protected by law and that adequate remedies are provided in case violations, loss and/or damage.[100] Last and most importantly, the ECtHR established that the positive obligations developed under Articles 2 and 8 ECHR equally apply to the loss of property, according to Article 1 of Protocol No 1.[101] Articles 2, 8 and 1 of Protocol No 1 of the ECHR therefore establish one standard of protection in cases concerning the environment.

Although the ECtHR has not yet dealt with this matter, the Human Rights Committee which oversees the implementation of the International Covenant on Civil and Political Rights (ICCPR), recently illustrated in a communication against New Zealand that the guarantees of the right to life may also be invoked in climate

---

[92] See above n 63.

[93] Ibid., para 42.

[94] Brems 2005; ECtHR, *Taşkin v Turkey*, above n 3, para 130.

[95] ECtHR, *Hadjianastassiou v Greece*, 16 December 1992, App no 12945/87,

[96] Brems 2005, p. 294.

[97] ECtHR, *Golder v UK*, 21 February 1975, App no 4451/70, para 36; ECtHR, *Philis v Greece*, 27 August 1991, App no 16598/90, para 59; ECtHR, *De Geouffre de la Pradelle v France*, 16 December 1992, App no 12964/87, para 28; ECtHR, *Stanev v Bulgaria*, 17 January 2012, App no 36760/06, para 229.

[98] Grabenwarter 2014, Article 6, para 15.

[99] ECtHR, *Öneryildiz v Turkey*, above n 85, para 134. For a recent decision see: ECtHR, *Kurşun v Turkey*, 20 October 2018, App no 22677/10, para 114.

[100] Ibid., para 114.

[101] Ibid., para 115.

change cases, in particular in *non-refoulement* situations.[102] Those situations bar the sending State from exposing the complainant to life threatening circumstances in their home States, as long as it can be demonstrated that the circumstances existed in general and given the personal circumstances of the applicant.[103] As the violation is determined on the claim made by the applicant in the sending State, it is irrelevant who or which State is ultimately responsible for creating this life-threatening situation in the first place. In climate-change cases and in the actual case before the Human Rights Committee, a claimant who had fled from Kiribati claimed that the situation in his home country had become unbearable due to climate change.[104] The Human Rights Committee established that all States party to the ICCPR have an obligation to protect applicants from threats and life threatening situations—which may include threats created by climate change—that can result in a loss of life.[105] Therefore, they also had a responsibility not to send individuals back into those situations.[106] Following the ECtHR's established jurisprudence, the *non-refoulement* obligation is part of the guarantees of Articles 2 and 3 of the ECHR.[107] Hence, it is probable that the Court may argue similarly in a comparable case.

Further Convention rights have been invoked in national and European climate litigation cases.[108] In addition to Article 2 ECHR, they have raised questions regarding the scope of application of Article 8 of the ECHR.[109] The growing number of national climate cases suggests that the matter will soon come before the ECHR.

To sum up, the ECtHR has affirmed that almost all important civil and political rights of the ECHR may be invoked in cases concerning the environment. It has applied the ECHR to various settings that involve damage to the environment: they are as diverse as passive smoking, health hazards emerging from large industrial projects, or noise emissions. The ECHR might also apply in future climate-change cases involving a violation of the *non-refoulement* prohibition. Considering the bandwidth of cases discussed by the ECtHR, Pedersen concluded that this factually corresponded to the protection of the right to a clean and healthy environment under the ECHR.[110] In any case, the case law of the Court proves that the ECHR is more than fit to address environmental cases.

---

[102] See the reasoning of the HRC, *Ioane Teitiota v New Zealand*, 7 January 2020, CCPR/C/127/D/2728/2016, (*Ioane Teitiota v New Zealand*), para 9.11.

[103] ECtHR, *F.G. v Sweden*, 23 March 2016, App no 43611/11, para 114.

[104] El-Hinnawi 1985, 6. The term is disputed, see: McAdam 2011, 2ff.

[105] *Ioane Teitiota v New Zealand*, above n 102, para 9.4.

[106] Ibid.

[107] See, for example: ECtHR, *F.G. v Sweden*, above n 103, para 110; ECtHR, *Hirsi Jamaa and others v Italy*, above n 39, paras 23 and 134ff.

[108] Compare: *Carvalho and Others v Parliament and Council*, above n 50, *State of the Netherlands (Ministry of Economic Affairs and Climate Policy) v Stichting Urgenda*, above n 50 and High Court of Ireland, *Friends of the Irish Environment* v *Ireland*, Judgment, 19 September 2019.

[109] See both the *Carvalho and Others v Parliament and Council*, above n 50, and *Urgenda Foundation* v *State of the Netherlands*, above n 50, cases.

[110] Pedersen 2018, p. 86.

7.4.3 *Specific Kinds of Positive Obligations Owed to the Protection of the Environment*

7.4.3.1 International Environmental Obligations as Positive Obligations

Having demonstrated that the rights guaranteed under the ECHR may be invoked in a multitude of cases involving environmental damage, I will now spell out in more detail what particular environmental obligations weigh on States in those cases. As positive obligations to protect a particular right are dependent on its scope of application, the specific positive environmental obligations will vary according to the nature and scope of application of the primary right in question. For instance, the positive environmental obligations flowing from the right to a fair trial will be different than those flowing from the right to private life and family. Nonetheless, it is remarkable that the ECtHR has developed a canon of positive environmental obligations, which apply, first and foremost, in cases involving Article 8 of the ECHR, but also in other cases involving violations of Article 2, 6, and Article 1 of Protocol 1 to the ECHR.

First of all, this canon of positive obligations recognizes some of the major principles of international environmental law. For example, in the *Hatton* case, the Court found that although States enjoyed a margin of appreciation when it came to fulfilling the positive obligations under Article 8 ECHR,[111] they had to observe recognized standards of environmental protection. Hence, States have to observe the precautionary principle when it comes to the environmental risks of activities which are still subject to scientific uncertainty. They therefore need to take precautionary measures and protect the rights of the applicants, although it may be uncertain whether or not the threat posed by the environmental project in question is going to materialize.[112] Yet, the precautionary approach is disputed, even in international law.[113] And whereas the Court has referred to the precautionary principle in some cases, more recent decisions cast doubt on whether the Court considers the principles as a recognized standard of international environmental law. In the more recent *Hardy and Maile v the UK* decision, for example, Pedersen argued that the Court left the principle unapplied.[114] The Court nevertheless engaged with the applicant's arguments about the environmental risk posed by the liquefied gas terminals in question

---

[111] ECtHR, *Hatton v United Kingdom*, above n 6, para 98; most recently: ECtHR, *Jugheli and others v Georgia*, 13 July 2017, 38342/05, para 64.

[112] ECtHR, *Tătar v Romania*, 27 January 2009, App no 67021/01, para 88; ECtHR, *Öneryıldız v Turkey*, above n 85, para 90. Compare the precautionary principle as laid down in principle 15 of the Rio Declaration 1992: 'Where there are threats of serious or irreversible damage, lack of full scientific certainty shall not be used as a reason for postponing cost-effective measures to prevent environmental degradation.'

[113] Lee 2018; Wiener 2018.

[114] Pedersen 2018, p. 86, referring to ECtHR, *Hardy Maile v United Kingdom*, 14 February 2012, App no 31965/07.

and thus with the subject matter of the precautionary principle. It also considered the risk assessment carried out by the UK.[115] It merely did not concur with the applicants that their rights under Article 8 of the ECHR could only be protected if the permit to operate the terminals was not granted.[116]

In the *Öneryıldız* case, the Court established that States should prosecute and punish environmental polluters who have caused environmental damage.[117] The case therefore recognized a well-known principle of international environmental law, the polluter pays principle.[118] Another case confirmed two further essential obligations of international environmental law: in *Tătar v Romania*, the ECtHR considered that States must assess the environmental impact of projects that concern the environment (Environmental Impact Assessment),[119] a duty which has been recognized by the International Court of Justice as a duty under customary international law.[120] The case also recognized the precautionary principle,[121] discussed above.

7.4.3.2 Procedural Environmental Obligations

However, most particularly, the Court has interpreted the ECHR to guarantee procedural environmental rights.[122] These are specific environmental obligations concerned with the procedure of environmental decision making which attempt to implement principle 10 of the Rio Declaration, which has been held to embody the principle of environmental democracy.[123] Principle 10 provides:

> Environmental issues are best handled with participation of all concerned citizens, at the relevant level. At the national level, each individual shall have appropriate access to information concerning the environment that is held by public authorities, including information on hazardous materials and activities in their communities, and the opportunity to participate in decision-making processes. States shall facilitate and encourage public awareness and participation by making information widely available. Effective access to judicial and administrative proceedings, including redress and remedy, shall be provided.

---

[115] ECtHR, *Hardy and Maile v United Kingdom*, above n 114, paras 223ff.

[116] Ibid., para 231.

[117] ECtHR, *Öneryıldız v Turkey*, above n 85, para 93.

[118] Sands and Peel 2018, p. 240.

[119] ECtHR, *Tătar v Romania*, above n 112, para 114.

[120] ICJ, *Pulp Mills on the River Uruguay, (Argentina* v *Uruguay),* Judgment, 20 April 2010, ICJ Reports 2010, para 204; ICJ, *Certain Activities Carried out by Nicaragua in the Border Area (Costa Rica v Nicaragua) and Construction of a Road in Costa Rica along the San Juan River (Nicaragua v Costa Rica) (Judgment)*, above n 44.

[121] Sands and Peel 2018, p. 229.

[122] For a detailed assessment of the Court's jurisprudence on this matter see: Peters 2018, pp. 1ff.

[123] United Nations Secretary General 2018, para 14.

Principle 10 sets out three distinctive rights: the right to information, the right to participate in environmental decision-making and the right to access justice in environmental affairs. In wider Europe, they are also guaranteed by the Aarhus Convention, which is one of the most comprehensive treaties providing for procedural environmental rights in environmental decision-making.[124] Nearly all the States party to the ECHR have ratified the Aarhus Convention.[125] Accordingly, the ECtHR has emphasised on many occasions, that it will interpret the rights of the ECHR in light of the Aarhus Convention.[126] Above all, it has held that the right guaranteed in Article 8 of the ECHR must be guaranteed in keeping with the procedural environmental obligations of Principle 10 of the Rio Declaration and the Aarhus Convention. Thus, to safeguard this right, States must inform potential victims of the environmental hazards of the project,[127] provide for their participation in the decision-making processes leading to the permit,[128] and allow for broad access to justice and provide applicants with a possibility to appeal relevant decisions.[129]

But other decisions, too, can be interpreted as realizing procedural environmental rights. Decisions like *Okyay and others v Turkey* and *Taşkin v Turkey*, for example, focused on the right to access to justice as part of the right to a fair trial. In both cases, the Court found the right to a fair trial to be violated, when the applicants had obtained judgments and decisions against the operation of certain environmental projects which impacted on rights of the applicants guaranteed under national law.[130]

Last, the findings of the ECtHR which emphasise the guarantee of the right to information in environmental proceedings, for example the case of *Vides Aidzarsibas Klubs v Latvia*, can be counted as upholding the environmental rights guaranteed by the Aarhus Convention,[131] all the more so since they emphasise the important role of environmental NGOs in democratic societies. This interest-based approach to environmental decision-making is central to the Aarhus Convention.[132]

---

[124] Convention on Access to Information, Public Participation in Decision-Making and Access to Justice in Environmental Matters, 25 June 1998, 2161 UNTS 447, entered into force 30 October 2001 (Aarhus Convention)

[125] Currently, the Aarhus Convention has 39 ratifications and 47 signatory states. For the state of ratifications see https://treaties.un.org/Pages/ViewDetails.aspx?src=IND&mtdsg_no=XXVII-13&chapter=27&clang=_en. Accessed 24 February 2021.

[126] ECtHR, *Taşkin v Turkey*, above n 3, para 99; ECtHR, *Branduse v Romania*, above n 5, para 27; ECtHR, *Grimkovskaya v Ukraine*, 21 July 2011, App no 38182/03, paras 39, 69; ECtHR, *Di Sarno and Others v Italy*, above n 79, para 107; ECtHR, *Tătar v Romania*, above n 112, para 118; ECtHR, *Lesoochranárske Zoskupenie VLK v Slovakia*, above n 78, para 80.

[127] Starting with the case: ECtHR, *Guerra and Others v Italy*, above n 90, paras 58 and 60.

[128] ECtHR, *Grimkovskaya v Ukraine*, above n 126, para 72.

[129] ECtHR, *Taşkin v Turkey*, above n 3, paras 118–119; compare: ECtHR, *Giacomelli v Italy*, 2 November 2006, App no 59909/00, para 83.

[130] ECtHR, *Okyay and others v Turkey*, 12 July 2005, App no 36220/97, paras 72–73; ECtHR, *Taşkin v Turkey*, above n 3, paras 136 and 138.

[131] Similarly: ECtHR, *Sdruženi Jihočeské Matky* v Czech *Republic*, 10 July 2006, App no 19101/03.

[132] Epiney and Sollberger 2002; Ebbesson 2011, p. 248.

7.4.3.3 Preliminary Conclusion for the Kinds of Obligations Owed Under the ECHR in Environmental Cases

The case law of the ECtHR has made it clear that States must observe the positive obligations to protect various civil and political rights enshrined in the ECHR, above all, the right to life, the right to private and family life and the right to a fair trial in environmental contexts. As part of those positive obligations, the Court has recognized some of the most essential standards of international environmental law, like the polluter pays principle, the precautionary principle and the duty to conduct an environmental impact assessment. The Court has also considered that States must adopt adequate standards of protection, which essentially embody the standard of the no-harm rule and punish criminal offenders. Finally, the ECtHR has found that the procedural environmental rights guaranteed in the Aarhus Convention, i.e. the right to information, participation and access to justice in environmental decision-making, constitute positive obligations in cases concerning the environment.

7.4.4 Personal Scope of Application of Positive Environmental Rights and Obligations/Standard of Proof

The ECtHR has established certain minimum standards of proof which applicants must meet to successfully argue that there has been a violation of a positive environmental obligation at the merits stage.[133] On some occasions, those standards were discussed as part of the requirement of standing, or as part of the personal scope of application of the right in question.[134] The case law is not uniform. Moreover, the standards are relative and vary according to the individual right in question. However, some of the case law seems to have consolidated on the standards established for Articles 2, 6, 8 and Article 1 of Protocol 1 to the Convention.

Considering the right to life, the Court established that there must be a real risk that the applicant's life could by harmed by environmental damage.[135] The Court has assumed that a real risk exists, when it is both genuine and imminent.[136] Most importantly, the immediacy of the threat is primarily considered in terms of probability. The Court established that the threat should be understood as a direct threat to the rights of the persons in question.[137]

---

[133] Cf. Pavoni 2015, 89.

[134] Compare the assessment in: Leach 2011, para 4.30; ECtHR, *Grimkovskaya v Ukraine*, above n 126, para 58.

[135] ECtHR, *Öneryıldız v Turkey*, above n 85, para 71.

[136] ECtHR, *Öneryıldız v Turkey*, above n 85, paras 98–101; ECtHR, *Budayeva et al v Russia*, 20 March 2008, App no 15339/02, paras 147–158; ECtHR, *Kolyadenko et al. v Russia*, 28 February 2012, App no 17423/05, paras 165 and 174–180.

[137] See the references at n 136, above.

Regarding the prohibition of torture, the ECtHR found that the ill treatment 'must attain a minimum level of severity'.[138] Again, the Court explained, 'the assessment ...is, in the nature of things, relative; it depends on all the circumstances of the case, such as the nature and context of the treatment, the manner and method of its execution, its duration, its physical or mental effects and, in some instances, the sex, age and state of health of the victim.'[139]

As regards the right to a fair trial according to Article 6 of the ECHR, the ECtHR considered that there must be a direct (i.e. causal) link between the environmental project and the applicant's rights.[140] Like in the case of violations of the right to life, this link can be viewed as established if the project in question poses a 'specific' and 'imminent' danger to the rights of the applicant, according to the ECtHR.[141] Other cases emphasised that the project had to have a direct effect on the applicant's health or well-being.[142] If, however, the case concerns environmental risks with uncertain effects on human health,[143] the Court denies that there has been an effect on the rights of the applicant.

Considering the right to home and family, which is guaranteed by Article 8 of the ECHR, the Court has explained in various cases that those rights are only incurred *ratione personae* to individuals where a certain 'minimum level'[144] has been surpassed: e.g. those for whom environmental projects present a *real risk of damage* to health or family life, or a *significant negative influence or impact* on health and family life.[145] As in the cases of violations of the right to life, the ECHR only grants those rights to persons with a 'sufficiently close' or clear link to the risk in question, such that a certain level of severity is attained.[146] Mere fear of risk is not sufficient.[147] This requires that the risk in question has amounted to actual interference[148] and has attained a certain minimum level;[149] applicants cannot simply complain about a 'negligible detriment in comparison to the environmental hazards

---

[138] ECtHR, *Branduse v Romania*, above n 5, para 26; ECtHR, *Kudła v Poland*, 26 October 2000, App no 30210/96, para 91.

[139] Ibid.

[140] ECtHR, *Balmer-Schafroth and others v Switzerland*, above n 4, para 40; ECtHR, *Athanassoglou and Others v Switzerland*, 6 April 2000, App no 27644/95, para 46–55; ECtHR, *Ivan Atanasov v Bulgaria*, 2 December 2010, App no 12853/03, paras 92, 95.

[141] ECtHR, *Balmer-Schafroth and others v Switzerland*, above n 4; ECtHR, *Athanassoglou and Others v Switzerland*, above n 140.

[142] ECtHR, *Atanasov v Bulgaria*, above n 140, para 93; ECtHR, *Taşkin v Turkey*, above n 3; cf. Morgera 2005, p. 138.

[143] ECtHR, *Balmer-Schafroth and others v Switzerland*, above n 4, para 40.

[144] ECtHR, *Grimkovskaya v Ukraine*, above n 126, para 58.

[145] ECtHR, *Giacomelli v Italy*, above n 129, para 78.

[146] ECtHR, *Taşkin v Turkey*, above n 3, para 113; ECtHR, *Fadeyeva v Russia*, App no 55723/00, 9 June 2005, para 70.

[147] ECtHR, *Hardy and Maile v United Kingdom*, above n 114, para 188.

[148] Ibid.

[149] This may however be reached, if the pollution at issue worsened the general health status of the applicants, see: ECtHR, *Jugheli and others v Georgia*, above n 111, para 71.

inherent to life in every modern city'.[150] Article 8 ECHR cannot apply either if the claims brought before the Court are based on the destruction of nature alone.[151] Neither can applicants claim a violation of Article 8 ECHR merely on the basis that general environmental rules have not been complied with.[152]

Although the standards established by the Court to prove the violation of a Convention right are relative, the ECtHR's case law, especially on Articles 2, 6 and 8 suggests that the Court will only accept claims of applicants who prove that they are faced with a severe, real and imminent risk of a violation of their rights in environmental matters.[153] This entails, amongst other things, that there is a certain probability that the environmental risk or damage will materialize and that there is a sufficient causal relation between the violation of ECHR rights and an environmental damage.

It is likely that the ECtHR will rely on this standard of proof also in climate change cases. In the case against New Zealand, the Human Rights Committee relied on a similar standard of proof. The Human Rights Committee found that the applicant had not established that his right to life would be impaired in such a way that he was bound to suffer an unnatural or early death in his home country.[154] In addition, the Human Rights Committee pointed out that there is also the responsibility of the States affected by climate change: the Human Rights Committee confirmed that the complainant's nation was responsible for the primary protection of the rights of the complainants, in particular in slow-onset disasters, such as sea level rise. It needed to take relevant action in the time that remained to prevent their nationals being exposed to life-threatening and unbearable living conditions.[155] Accordingly, to assume a violation of the right to life by the sending State, the complainant needed to established that these efforts had failed or were fruitless.[156]

The standard of proof is quite demanding and further limits the application of ECHR guarantees in environmental cases. It excludes an invocation of the ECHR against future environmental threats.[157] It also excludes an application of the ECHR in cases that primarily concern the damage to nature. In addition, it prevents an application of the ECHR in cases in which the damage to the rights guaranteed by the ECHR has not yet materialized.

---

[150] ECtHR, *Hardy and Maile v United Kingdom*, above n 114, para 188

[151] ECtHR, *Kyrtatos v Greece*, above n 77, para 54; for a discussion, see Martens 2007, p. 295.

[152] ECtHR, *Atanasov v Bulgaria*, above n 140, paras 75–77.

[153] Compare: Leach 2011, para 4.32.

[154] *Ioane Teitiota v New Zealand*, above n 102, paras 9.7ff.

[155] Ibid., para 9.12.

[156] Ibid.

[157] On this, see Sect. 7.2.2 above.

7.5 Justification for Interferences or the Margin of Appreciation in Cases Concerning Positive Environmental Obligations

Justification for interferences with the rights guaranteed by the ECHR, in particular of those applicable in cases concerning the environment, i.e. Articles 2, 6, 8, 13 and Article 1 of Protocol 1 to the ECHR, are subject to the specific requirements stated in para 2 of each guarantee, with the exception of the prohibition on torture. For example, interferences with the right to a private and family life, home and correspondence guaranteed by Article 8 of the ECHR, can be justified if they are 'necessary in a democratic society in the interests of national security, public safety or the economic well-being of the country'. This section will not discuss the details of possible justifications. Rather, as infringements of the rights guaranteed by the ECHR in environmental cases will mostly occur as a failure to act or by omission on behalf of the State,[158] I want to share some general thoughts on the applicability of justifications in cases involving the failure to meet positive obligations under the ECHR.

Since its engagement with the matter, the Court has held that States usually have a margin of appreciation when it comes to meeting the positive obligations guaranteed under the ECHR in environmental proceedings.[159] The margin varies according to the particular right in question. It will be narrow in cases involving the right to life, and wider in cases involving the right to home and family.[160] States are called upon to fulfil this margin of appreciation in light of their (international) environmental standards and regulations.[161] Nonetheless, they are left with certain discretion as to which particular measure or method is suitable to fulfil the aim of protecting the rights of the ECHR, in light of current (international) environmental law. This includes the weighing of environmental and economic interests and the ultimate decision about the realization of a project that impacts on the environment. Finally, proof of overstepping the margin of appreciation is generally on the applicant.

The *Hatton* case may serve as a good example to illustrate this. In the *Hatton* case, the ECtHR concluded that the United Kingdom had to ensure the protection of the applicants against the noise emanating from Heathrow Airport in order to meet their obligations under Article 8 of the ECHR.[162] The Court found that the UK had fulfilled its obligations by enacting particular noise emission standards in the case at hand.[163] It could not be proven that the government had overstepped its margin of appreciation

---

[158] See Sect. 7.4.2 of this chapter.

[159] See, for example: ECtHR, *Powell and Rayner v United Kingdom*, 21 February 1990, App no 9310/81, para 41; ECtHR, *Hatton v United Kingdom*, above n 6, para 98; most recently: ECtHR, *Jugheli and others v Georgia*, above n 111, para 64.

[160] ECtHR, *Hämalinen v Finland*, 16 July 2014, App no 37359/09, para 67.

[161] See Sect. 7.4.3.1 above.

[162] See Sect. 7.4.2 above. *Hatton v United Kingdom*, above n 6, paras 98 and 100.

[163] ECtHR, *Hatton v United Kingdom*, above n 6, paras 125ff.

in the particular circumstances.[164] In the *Hatton* case, the Court also found that the economic situation in the particular member State determined its possibilities to fulfil the relevant positive obligations.[165] Had the UK, for example, been suffering from a severe economic crisis or generally been in a weak economic situation at the time of the Hatton judgment, less strict noise emission standards could have applied. *Klatt* therefore concluded the Court awarded the UK a margin in end-setting.[166] According to Klatt, the Court left it to the member States to decide whether and on which basis they 'wish to limit the enjoyment of a human right'.[167]

The Court's argument in the *Hatton* judgment is not unproblematic. In the *Hatton* case, the margin of appreciation determined the scope of the positive obligation owed by the UK. In pointing toward the economic interests of the UK, the Court included reasons for the justification of infringements of ECHR rights into the assessment of the margin of appreciation. Combining arguments on the scope of the obligation with possible limitations could circumvent the specific justification provisions of the ECHR. They allow for justifications only under certain conditions (for example, they must be 'necessary in a democratic society'). An expansion of the assessment of the margin of appreciation toward end-setting can therefore only be allowed if the reasons or interests included into the assessment of the margin of appreciation are in line with the justification requirements of the ECHR.[168] In any case, as the margin of end-setting allows for the inclusion of arguments usually concerned with the justification of infringements of ECHR rights, the *Hatton* case aptly demonstrates that there will not be much room for the application of the ECHR's justification provisions. At least reasons for justification will rarely be assessed outside the framework of the margin of appreciation.

7.6 Remedies

Although recent reforms have made it more flexible, for example with the introduction of the pilot judgment procedure,[169] the ECHR-system is not renowned for creative remedies in human rights cases and has only recently expanded its jurisprudence on the matter.[170] Therefore, Leach's conclusion on the remedies awarded by the ECtHR is still valid: 'the Court's primary remedy is a declaration that there has been a violation of the Convention.'[171] That said, applicants may file a claim for just satisfaction, according to Article 41 of the ECHR, which calls upon the Court to

164 Ibid., paras 128–129.

165 Ibid., paras 97 and 116.

166 Klatt 2011, p. 717.

167 Ibid.

168 Ibid.

169 Rules of Court 2020, Article 61.

170 Cornejo Chavez 2017, p. 379.

171 Leach 2011, para 8.01.

award monetary compensation to the applicant. According to the wording of Article 41 of the ECHR, just satisfaction may only be awarded if the Court has affirmed that there was a violation of the Convention and where the national system did not allow for a complete reparation of the human rights violation in question. Further to that, the applicant must establish a clear and causal link between a Convention violation and the damage sustained according to the further rules of the Court.[172] Awards can entail pecuniary damages for actual loss and damages sustained, such as loss of earnings or means for earning a living.[173] The Court may also award non-pecuniary damages, for example for pain, suffering or distress.[174] The final award of just satisfaction lies within the discretion of the Court. The Court has often underlined that decisions will be made on an equitable basis.[175] The Court may conclude that the declaration that the Convention has been violated is sufficient compensation; it may also find that the reparation awarded to the victims is lower than their actual loss.[176] The Court applies general principles to award just satisfaction.[177] Thus, in many cases, it is difficult to discern how the Court arrived at the sum awarded.[178] More recent case-law of the ECtHR evidences that the context of the human rights violation may influence the decision on the award of non-pecuniary damages.[179]

Those general observations also apply to remedies awarded in cases concerning the environment. The Court has awarded just satisfaction in the form of pecuniary and non-pecuniary compensation to be paid to the applicants, in many of its landmark decisions.[180] In the reasons given for the award of damages, the Court mentioned the damage done to the environment merely as a factor which contributed to the adverse living-conditions which the applicants had to tolerate.[181] The ECtHR has not interpreted the provision of Article 41 ECHR to compensate for the loss or damage caused to the environment. Also in the case of remedies, the ECHR system therefore concentrates on the individual and on the damage sustained by individuals.

---

[172] Practice Directions, Rules of Court, paras 7ff.

[173] Leach 2011, para 8.18.

[174] Ibid., para 8.21.

[175] ECtHR, *Scoppola v Italy (No. 2)*, 17 September 2009, App no 10249/03.

[176] Practice Directions, Rules of Court, para 2.

[177] Ibid., paras 10ff.

[178] Leach 2011, para 8.10.

[179] Cornejo Chavez 2017, p. 385.

[180] For a recent example, ECtHR, *Cordella v Italy*, above n 76, para 192. For the classical case-law compare: ECtHR, *Okyay and others v Turkey*, above n 130, para 79; ECtHR, *Öneryıldız v Turkey*, above n 85, para 176; ECtHR, *Hatton v UK*, above n 6, para 155; ECtHR, *López Ostra v Spain*, above n 27, para 71.

[181] ECtHR, *Taşkin v Turkey*, above n 3, para 155.

7.7 Final Conclusions

The environmental protection provided by human rights instruments like the ECHR is mostly anthropocentric. It centres on the protection of humans from infringements of their individual human rights by environmental threats, whether inflicted by the State, or by others. The ECHR is no exception to this rule. Certain gateways nonetheless open the ECHR for broader considerations recognizing common interests of nature. First and foremost, the ECtHR has recognized the role of environmental interest organizations as 'watchdogs for nature'. Therefore, the ECHR may apply if the rights of environmental NGOs have been denied in environmental decision-making. Moreover, the *ratione loci* scope of application of the ECHR is tied to the concept of jurisdiction, mentioned in Article 1 of the ECHR. Therefore, the ECHR may apply in cases concerning transnational environmental harm, as far as the harm may be attributed to a State party to the ECHR according to the principle of personal jurisdiction. This might open the ECHR for claims in so called climate change cases, which usually build on the aspect of transboundary damage. Even though the ECHR can only be invoked if the civil and political rights safeguarded by the Convention have been violated, the ECtHR has applied it in a multitude of cases involving all kinds of environmental threats. The latest jurisprudence of the Human Rights Committee has even pondered their application in the case of climate change. There is no reason why the ECHR could not apply in similar situations.

That said, for the ECtHR to award individual remedies in cases concerning the environment a number of requirements need to be fulfilled: (1) The ECHR guarantees a particular right, which provides for a certain standard of protection. (2) Living persons or their associations invoke a violation of this right a particular case. The ECHR cannot apply with regard to future generations or in contexts concerning the destruction of nature, or natural objects alone. (3) The State fails to provide protection in the individual case. (4) The applicants can prove that they have been affected by the State's inaction. Usually, this entails that the applicants establish that they have been faced with a severe, real and imminent risk of a violation of their rights. (5) The State's failure to protect the applicant's rights is not covered by the margin of appreciation, which States have in fulfilling their positive obligations under the ECHR. (6) The applicant has shown that there was a causal relation between the individual damage sustained and the human rights violation in question.

The ECHR therefore offers an important, but no unconditional possibility of environmental adjudication. Due to the limitations of the ECHR regime, those in favour of general environmental protection may certainly conclude that human rights regimes are ill-suited to protection of the environment. And indeed, the protection provided by human rights regimes like the ECHR does not suffice to combat the actual environmental and climate crises that the world faces today. Yet, no international environmental court is equipped to take measures in the wake of the current crises that exist today. Human rights courts like the ECtHR open a forum, where at least some of the current interests can be heard and discussed. Applicants should not be denied its use.

References

Besson S (2020) Due Diligence and Extraterritorial Human Rights Obligations–Mind the Gap! ESIL Reflection 2020:9

Boyle A E (2009) Environment and Human Rights. Max Planck Encyclopedia of Public International Law, https://opil.ouplaw.com/view/10.1093/law:epil/9780199231690/law-9780199231690-e1948 Accessed 24 February 2021

Boyle A E (2012) Human Rights and the Environment: Where Next? European Journal of International Law 23:613–642

Brems E (2005) Conflicting Human Rights: An Exploration in the Context of the Right to a Fair Trial in the European Convention for the Protection of Human Rights and Fundamental Freedoms. Human Rights Quarterly 27:294–326

Brunnée J (2004) Of Sense and Sensibility: Reflections on International Liability Regimes as Tools for Environmental Protection. The International and Comparative Law Quarterly 53:351–367

Cornejo Chavez L (2017) New Remedial Responses in the Practice of Regional Human Rights Courts: Purposes Beyond Compensation. International Journal of Constitutional Law 15:372–392

Council of Europe (2012) Manual of Human Rights and the Environment. Council of Europe

Crawford J (2018) The Current Political Discourse Concerning International Law. The Modern Law Review 81:1–22

Ebbesson J (2011) A Modest Contribution to Environmental Democracy and Justice in Transboundary Contexts: The Combined Impact of the Espoo Convention and Aarhus Convention. Review of European Community & International Environmental Law 20:248–257

El-Hinnawi E (1985) Environmental Refugees. Unep

Epiney A, Sollberger K (2002) Zugang zu Gerichten und gerichtliche Kontrolle im Umweltrecht. Berichte des Umweltbundesamts. Erich Schmidt Verlag, Berlin

Francioni F (2010) International Human Rights in an Environmental Horizon. European Journal of International Law (2010) 21:41–55

Grabenwarter C (2014) The European Convention on Human Rights: A Commentary. Beck, Munich.

Huanacuni FM (2015) Vivir bien/Buen Vivir, Kindle edn.

Harris D J, O'Boyle M, Bates E, Buckley C (2009) Law of the European Convention on Human Rights. Oxford University Press, Oxford

IPCC (2007) Climate Change 2007: Synthesis Report. Contribution of Working Groups I, II and III to the Fourth Assessment Report of the Intergovernmental Panel on Climate Change [Core Writing Team, Pachauri RK, Reisinger A (eds)]. IPCC, Geneva, Switzerland

Keller H, Stone Sweet A (2008) A Europe of Rights the Impact of the ECHR on National Legal Systems. Oxford University Press, Oxford

Klatt M (2011) Positive Obligations Under the European Convention on Human Rights. Zeitschrift für ausländisches Recht und Völkerrecht 2011:691–718

Leach P (2011) Taking a Case to the European Court of Human Rights. Oxford University Press, Oxford

Lee G S D (2018) Uncertainty, Risk and the (in)Applicability of the Precautionary Principle: Reassessing the Scope of Precaution and Prevention in International Environmental Law. University of Cambridge

Liston G (2020) Enhancing the efficacy of climate change litigation: how to resolve the 'fair share question' in the context of international human rights law. Cambridge International Law Journal 9(2): 241–263

Maljean-Dubois S (2019) Climate Change Litigation. Max Planck Encyclopedia of International Procedural Law. https://opil.ouplaw.com/view/https://doi.org/10.1093/law-mpeipro/e3461.013.3461/law-mpeipro-e3461 Accessed 24 February 2021

Martens M (2007) Constitutional Right to a Healthy Environment in Belgium. Review of European Community & International Environmental Law 16:287–297

Mayer B (2018) Obligations of Conduct in the International law on Climate Change: A Defence. Review of European, Comparative and International Environmental Law 27:130–140

McAdam J (2011) Swimming Against the Tide: Why a Climate Change Displacement Treaty is not the Answer. International Journal of Refugee Law 23:2–27
Meyer-Ladewig J, Nettesheim M, von Raumer S, Kulick A (2017) European Convention on Human Rights (Europäische Menschenrechtskonvention), Commentary. Nomos, Baden-Baden
Morgera E (2005) An Update on the Aarhus Convention and its Continued Global Relevance. Review of European Community & International Environmental Law 14:138–147
Osofsky H M, Peel J (2018) A Rights Turn in Climate Change Litigation? Transnational Environmental Law 7:37–67
Ovey C, White CA (2006) The European Convention on Human Rights, 4th edn. Oxford University Press, Oxford
Pavoni R (2015) Environmental Jurisprudence of the European and Inter-American Courts of Human Rights. In: Boer B (ed) Environmental law dimensions of human rights. Oxford University Press, Oxford, pp 69–106
Pedersen OW (2018) The European Court of Human Rights and International Environmental Law. In: Knox J H, Pejan R (eds) The human right to a healthy environment. Cambridge University Press, Cambridge, pp 86–96
Peters A, Altwicker T (2019) Europäische Menschenrechtskonvention. C.H. Beck, Munich
Peters A, Krieger H, Kreuzer L (2020) Due diligence: the risky risk management tool in international law. Cambridge International Law Journal 9:121–136
Peters B (2018) Unpacking the Diversity of Procedural Environmental Rights: The European Convention on Human Rights and the Aarhus Convention. Journal of Environmental Law 30:1–27
Petersmann M-C (2019) When Environmental Protection and Human Rights Collide: Four Heuristics of Conflict Resolution. In: Voigt C (ed) International Judicial Practice on the Environment: Questions of Legitimacy. Cambridge University Press, Cambridge, pp 239–261
Roy E A (2017) The Guardian, 16.03.2017, at: https://www.theguardian.com/world/2017/mar/16/new-zealand-river-granted-same-legal-rights-as-human-being Accessed 24 February 2021
Sands Ph, Peel J (2018) Principles of International Environmental Law. Cambridge University Press, Cambridge
Schabas W (2017) The European Convention on Human Rights, A Commentary. Oxford University Press, Oxford
Shelton D (1991) Human Rights, Environmental Rights, and the Right to Environment. Stanford Journal of International Law 28:103–138
Voigt C (2008) State Responsibility for Climate Change Damages. Nordic Journal of International Law 77:1–22
Voigt C (ed) (2019) International Judicial Practice on the Environment: Questions of Legitimacy. Studies on International Courts and Tribunals. Cambridge University Press, Cambridge
Wiener J B (2018) Precautionary principle. In: Krämer L, Orlando E (eds) Elgar Encyclopedia of Environmental Law. Edward Elgar Publishing Limited, Cheltenham, pp 174–185

International Documents

Additional Protocol to the American Convention on Human Rights in the Area of Economic, Social and Cultural Rights (Protocol of San Salvador), 14 November 1988, OAS, Treaty Series, no. 69
African Commission on Human and People's Rights (2015), General Comment No. 3 on the African Charter on Human and Peoples' Rights: The Right to Life (article 4), Adopted during the 57th Ordinary Session of the African Commission on Human and Peoples' Rights held from 4 to 18 November 2015 in Banjul, The Gambia
Bankovic and others v. Belgium and others, European Court of Human Rights, Decision, 12 December 2001 (2001)
Duarte Agostinho and others v. Portugal and 32 other member states, ECtHR, Complaint (2020)

Klimaseniorinnen Switzerland and others v. Switzerland, no. 53600/20, ECtHR, Complaint (2020)
Practice Directions, Rules of Court, European Court of Human Rights, https://www.echr.coe.int/Pages/home.aspx?p=basictexts/rules Accessed 24 February 2021
Rio Declaration on the Environment, 31 ILM 874, 1992
Rules of Court (2020), European Court of Human Rights, 1 January 2020
Special Rapporteur of the Human Rights Council on Human Rights and the Environment (2020), David Boyd, Consultations on Human Rights and Biodiversity, 6 April 2020
UN ECE Convention on Access to Information, Public Participation in Decision-making and Access to Justice in Environmental Matters (Aarhus Convention). United Nations Treaty Series 2161:447
United Nations Secretary General (2018), Gaps in International Environmental Law and Environment-Related Instruments: Towards a Global Pact for the Environment, Report, 30 November 2018, UN Doc A 73/419

Birgit Peters Ph.D. LLM, Professor of Public Law, International Law and European Law, University of Trier, Germany.

Chapter 8
European Union Court System and the Protection of the Environment

Olivier Peiffert

Contents

Abstract For almost 30 years, the EU courts have been dealing with many cases relating to environmental protection. This has raised a number of issues relating to access to justice at the EU level. Because of the basic structure of the EU procedural rules, the direct actions brought before the EU Courts, especially actions for annulment, are rather closed to private litigants. The best way to bring a case to the EU courts thus remains the reference by a national court for a preliminary ruling. In this regard, the Court of Justice has focused on enhancing access of litigants to national courts when environmental protection is at stake. This procedural scheme has given rise to certain difficulties regarding EU compliance with the Aarhus Convention.

Keywords EU Courts · access to justice · judicial review of EU legal acts · control of EU Member States · standing to bring proceedings · procedural rights of private litigants · environmental NGOs · Aarhus Convention

---

O. Peiffert (✉)
Sorbonne Nouvelle University—ICEE; General Court of the EU, 13, rue de Santeuil, 75231 Paris Cedex 05 Paris, France
e-mail: olivier.peiffert@sorbonne-nouvelle.fr

E. Sobenes et al. (eds.), *The Environment Through the Lens of International Courts and Tribunals*, https://doi.org/10.1007/978-94-6265-507-2_8

8.1 Introduction

In many legal systems, awareness of the negative impacts of human activities on the environment has led to the adoption in the last 50 years of very developed environmental protection regulations. However, it is the actual observance of environmental law that largely determines its usefulness.[1] The importance of effectiveness in this field explains the growing interest accorded to access to justice in environmental matters. Judicial institutions are increasingly requested to ensure that the environmental law in force is indeed observed by those bound by it, including public authorities. Since natural elements have, in principle, no legal personality, the issue of access to justice in environmental matters lies in the establishment of procedural rights for individuals or NGOs, which allow them to bring legal proceedings when the environment is threatened.[2] In the European Union (EU), access to justice in environmental matters concerns, *inter alia*, the Court of Justice of the European Union (CJEU), that is, the institution composed of both the Court of Justice (the Court) and the General Court (formerly the Court of First Instance).[3]

On the one hand, according to Article 19 of the Treaty on European Union (TEU), the Court of Justice of the EU 'shall ensure that in the interpretation and application of the Treaties the law is observed'. The Court is thus entrusted with interpreting the Treaties and secondary legislation adopted in accordance with those Treaties, and reviewing the legality of this secondary legislation, with the aim of controlling both the institutions and the Member States of the EU. On the other hand, EU institutions have the power to adopt secondary legislation to protect the environment.[4] Since the 1970s, hundreds of legal Acts have been adopted, covering most fields of environmental protection. Nowadays, the protection of *inter alia* animal and plant species, water, soil, air, climate, waste collection and disposal, control of chemicals, GMO or dangerous facilities are all within the ambit of EU law.

The general judicial competence associated with that inflation of EU environmental law explains the now well-established jurisdiction of the EU courts in environmental matters. Numerous cases have reached the Court of Justice of the EU

[1] See e.g. Maljean-Dubois 2017.

[2] See e.g. Bétaille 2016; Truilhé and Hautereau-Boutonnet 2019.

[3] According to Article 19(1) TEU, 'The Court of Justice of the European Union shall include the Court of Justice, the General Court and specialised courts'. Since the removal of the Civil Service Tribunal, there is no longer specialised courts in the EU judicial system. On the jurisdiction of the General Court (formerly the Court of First Instance), see TFEU, Article 256. Concerning the most recent reforms, see Cartier-Bresson and Dero-Bugny 2020.

[4] Originally, the only legal basis for European environmental law was the approximation of national laws affecting the establishment of the common market (current Articles 114 and 115 TFEU). The Single European Act of 1986 enshrined European environmental policy (current Articles 191 to 193 TFEU). At present, most EU legal acts to protect environment are based on Article 114 TFEU (if related to goods or services trade) or on Article 192 TFEU. Concerning the legal basis of the secondary legislation in the field of environmental protection, see e.g., Krämer 2016.

concerning EU environmental protection acts of secondary legislation.[5] Court statistics indeed show that between 2014 and 2018, the Court registered 208 new cases in the field of environmental protection and closed 170 proceedings.[6] During this period, the General Court registered 36 cases and closed 46 in the same field. The growth in environmental litigation before the EU Courts started towards the end of the 1990s,[7] and the figures have remained rather constant in the last decade.

Although the jurisdiction of the Court of Justice of the EU in matters of environmental law is thus well established, access to justice, including for individuals and NGOs, depends on EU procedural law. Indeed, it must be borne in mind that access to the European Courts is carefully regulated, and hence limited, by specific procedural rules, which apply whatever the matter in question. After providing a brief background to the EU judicial system and the Aarhus Convention (Sect. 8.2), this chapter will emphasize that direct actions before the EU Courts are rather closed to individuals (Sect. 8.3), with the result that many cases that reach the Court are by way of references for a preliminary ruling (Sect. 8.4). This could raise certain issues relating to EU compliance with the Aarhus Convention (Sect. 8.5).

8.2 Background

8.2.1 The General Scheme of the Legal Remedies Before the Court of Justice

Without seeking to provide an exhaustive account of the legal remedies before the Courts of the EU, a brief background is provided for context.[8] EU procedural law provides for various categories of legal remedies allowing access to the EU Courts. Formally, one must distinguish direct actions from references for preliminary rulings. First, direct action allows litigants to bring their actions against EU institutions or Member States directly before the EU Courts. The main direct actions are the action for annulment,[9] the action for failure to act,[10] the action for non-contractual liability

[5] Because of the limited length of this chapter, there will be no discussion of the content of secondary legislation, nor of the principles of European environmental law, i.e. principle of prevention, principle of precaution and the polluter-pays principle. Moreover, general international law has a limited influence on EU law, due to the autonomy of the Union's legal order. Therefore, we will not refer to international case law or the rules of general international law.

[6] CJEU, Annual Report 2018 — Judicial Activity, pp. 127, 134, 242 and 245. https://curia.europa.eu/jcms/jcms/Jo2_7000/fr/. Accessed 30 April 2021.

[7] See Krämer 2004.

[8] Concerning the EU Court system, see e.g., Lenaerts et al. 2014; Barents 2020.

[9] TFEU, Article 263.

[10] Ibid., Article 265.

of the EU,[11] and the action for a declaration of failure to fulfil obligations.[12] Such actions shall be brought before the General Court, which gives decisions at first instance, and, more exceptionally, before the Court.[13] In addition, in the context of a direct action, a party might raise a plea of illegality aimed at challenging an act of general application.[14] Second, where the solution of a case before the domestic courts of the Member States is determined by rules of EU law, references for a preliminary ruling enables these courts to refer any question of interpretation of EU law to the Court, as regards both the Treaties and acts of secondary legislation. Reference for a preliminary ruling also allows national courts to raise questions concerning the legality of acts of secondary EU law.[15] It is important to point out that a reference for a preliminary ruling is a procedure for cooperation between a national court and the EU Court: the national court is responsible for referring a question to the EU Court for a preliminary ruling, and defines the terms of that question. The parties to the dispute before the national court only have the status of intervening parties in the proceedings before the Court.

These different legal remedies serve two main purposes. On the one hand, the action for annulment, the action for failure to act, the plea of illegality and the reference for a preliminary ruling on validity seek to ensure that the EU institutions comply with the Treaties, both when acting and failing to act. The action for non-contractual liability of the EU seeks – to a certain extent – to achieve the same purpose, since one of the conditions for granting compensation is that *unlawful* actions of an EU institution causes damage. On the other hand, the action for failure to fulfil obligations and the reference for a preliminary ruling on interpretation ensures that the Member States do not violate binding EU rules.

In the words of the Court, the Treaty thus established 'a complete system of legal remedies and procedures' that makes the EU a Union 'based on the Rule of Law', since 'neither its Member States nor its institutions can avoid a review of the question whether the measures adopted by them are in conformity with the basic constitutional charter, the Treaty'.[16] However, completeness of the EU system of legal remedies is the subject of recurring discussions in jurisprudence,[17] because of its treatment of the actions of private persons. Indeed, in relation to direct actions, access by natural and legal persons to the EU Courts meets specific conditions of *locus standi*, which

[11] Ibid., Articles 268 and 340 (2).

[12] Ibid., Articles 258 and 259.

[13] Articles 50a and 51 of the Statute of the Court of Justice of the EU specifies the division of jurisdiction between the General Court and the Court of Justice. Especially, the actions for a declaration of failure to fulfil obligations are always brought before the Court.

[14] TFEU, Article 277.

[15] Ibid., Article 267.

[16] Court of Justice, *Les Verts v Parliament*, Judgement, 23 April 1986, Case No 294/83, ECLI:EU:C:1986:166, para 23.

[17] See e.g., Arnull 1995, p. 7; Dubout 2007, p. 429; Mastroianni and Pezza 2014, p. 923; Wildemeersch 2019.

relate to the applicants' 'standing to bring proceedings' ('*qualité pour agir*' in the working language of the EU Courts). This chapter will address this issue in detail below.[18]

8.2.2 *The Ratification of the Aarhus Convention by the EU*

Another important factor to understand the debate on access to justice before the EU Courts in environment matters is the ratification by the EU of the Convention on Access to Information, Public Participation in Decision-Making and Access to Justice in Environmental Matters of 25 June 1998 (Aarhus Convention) in 2005.[19] Article 9 of the Aarhus Convention aims at conferring procedural rights to natural or legal persons, especially environmental NGOs, where environmental protection is at stake. In particular, paragraph 3 of that article provides for, *inter alia*, the right to initiate judicial proceedings to challenge acts and omissions by public authorities that contravene provisions of environmental law.[20] It should be made clear that access to this judicial procedure is granted to litigants 'when they meet the criteria, if any', laid down by the domestic law of the parties to the Convention. Thus, Article 9(3) does not establish any real *actio popularis*. Article 9(4) of the Convention states that the remedies must be adequate and effective, fair, equitable, timely and not prohibitively expensive.

Because Article 9(3) of the Convention conditions the right to a judicial remedy on criteria laid down by the parties, the Court held that this provision has no direct effect in EU law.[21] Moreover, the EU Member States do not consider it necessary to reform the EU procedural law laid down in the Treaty on the Functioning of the EU (TFEU) in order to comply with the Convention. The main measure taken in order to adapt the applicants' right to bring an action before the EU Courts is Regulation 1367/2006, known as the 'Aarhus Regulation'.[22] The content of this Regulation will

---

[18] See *infra*, Sect. 8.3.

[19] See Aarhus Convention, opened for signature 25 June 1998 (1998), entered into force 30 October 2001 and Decision 2005/370/EC of the Council on the conclusion, on behalf of the European Community, of the Convention on access to information, public participation in decision-making and access to justice in environmental matters, 17 February 2005, OJEU 2005, L124, p. 1.

[20] Paragraphs 1 and 2 concern legal proceedings to enforce the substantive rights enshrined in the Convention. Paragraph 3 also concerns actions against private individuals, but that aspect is not the central issue in EU litigation.

[21] Court of Justice, *Lesoochranárske zoskupenie*, Judgment 8 March 2011, Case No C-240/09, ECLI:EU:C:2011:125, para 44–45.

[22] Regulation (EC) No 1367/2006 of the European Parliament and of the Council on the application of the provisions of the Aarhus Convention on Access to Information, Public Participation in Decision-Making and Access to Justice in Environmental Matters to Community institutions and vessels, 6 September 2006, OJEU 2006 L264, p. 13.

be set out in more detail later in this chapter.[23] Suffice it to indicate at this stage that it does not create any procedure not grafted onto the existing system.

8.3 Limited Direct Actions for Individuals in Environmental Matters

As pointed out above, some remedies under EU procedural law enable applicants to present their claims directly before the EU Courts.[24] Actions for failure to fulfil obligations make it possible to sanction breaches of EU environmental law by the authorities of the Member States. Actions for annulment, for failure to act and for damages, enable the EU Courts to review measures adopted by EU institutions and bodies. However, these direct actions are rather closed to individuals: infringement proceedings are not available to them (Sect. 8.3.1), and individuals will only rarely have sufficient *locus standi* to bring other forms of direct actions in environmental matters (Sect. 8.3.2).

8.3.1 Infringement Proceedings in Environmental Matters: Effective But Not Available to Individuals

Infringement proceedings are an effective tool for reminding Member States that they have to comply with their obligations under the Treaties or secondary legislation. In practice, it is the Commission, as 'guardian institution of the Treaties', which brings most of those actions.[25] If the Commission considers that a Member State is failing to comply with its obligations, it must first give the Member State an opportunity to submit its observations, before the Commission issues a reasoned opinion. At the end of that pre-litigation stage, the Commission may bring a judicial action if the State in question does not comply with that opinion.[26] The actions are then brought directly before the Court, whose function consists of delivering a declaratory judgment establishing whether a Member State has infringed EU law. If necessary, the Member State will be required to take the measures necessary to conform with the judgment.[27]

In environmental matters, this legal remedy has significant potential. Environmental law is one of the areas of EU law affected by rather serious problems of implementation at the national level, such as failure to communicate information

[23] See *infra*, Sect. 8.3.2.3.

[24] See *supra*, Sect. 8.2.1.

[25] Although Member States may also bring such actions (Article 259 TFEU), State actions remain marginal in practice.

[26] TFEU, Article 258.

[27] Ibid., Article 260.

to the Commission, incorrect transposition of directives or failure to implement secondary legislation. The Commission's Directorate-General for the Environment has developed a strategy to address this issue. According to available statistics, in 2019, the Commission initiated 337 infringement proceedings and brought 51 cases before the Court in the matter.[28] In 2016, the Commission produced a report highlighting that about 244 infringement actions were brought before the Court between 1994 and 2014 against the fifteen Member States which joined the EU before the enlargement of 2004. These actions concerned cases of incorrect application of ten directives on nature protection, waste, water, air and environmental impact studies. For the Commission, these actions enable genuine progress in the effectiveness of national policies for the protection of the environment.[29]

The effectiveness of that legal remedy is reinforced by two important procedural rights granted the Commission. First, where a Member State does not comply with a judgment of the Court on failure to fulfil obligations, the Commission may bring another action before the Court. That procedure may then result in the EU judicature imposing on the Member State in question a penalty payment and/or a lump sum fine. For example, the Court recently ordered Ireland to pay a lump sum of EUR 5 million together with a penalty payment of EUR 15,000 per day in a case involving compliance with the rules on environmental impact assessments.[30]

Second, in the context of an action for failure to fulfil obligations, the Commission may request the Court to adopt interim measures based on Article 279 TFEU. The Commission must then set out the circumstances giving rise to urgency and the pleas of fact and law establishing a *prima facie* case for the interim measures sought. The concerned Member State shall be notified of the application so that it may submit its observations. In cases of extreme urgency, the Court may provisionally grant the application for interim measures, even before the defendant has submitted its observations.[31] Admittedly, interim measures in the context of actions for failure to fulfil obligations within the field of environmental protection are relatively exceptional,[32] so one must not exaggerate their importance. However, the Commission does not hesitate to request such measures where circumstances so require.

---

[28] See https://ec.europa.eu/environment/legal/law/statistics.htm. Accessed 30 April 2021. The difference between those two figures is due to the fact that most of the proceedings are closed at the stage of the pre-litigation procedure.

[29] See European Commission, Study to assist the benefit delivered through the enforcement of EU compliance with legal rules—Purpose report, Publications Office of the European Union, 2016. https://ec.europa.eu/environment/pubs/pdf/Final_report_study_benefits_enforcement.pdf. Accessed 30 April 2021.

[30] Court of Justice, *Commission v Ireland*, Judgment, 12 November 2019, Case No C-261/18, ECLI:EU:C:2019:955.

[31] See Rules of Procedure of the Court of Justice, Article 160(7).

[32] One can only identify a few cases: Court of Justice, *Commission v Italy*, Order, 19 December 2006, Case No C-503/06 R, ECLI:EU:C:2006:800 and in the same case Order, 27 February 2007, ECLI:EU:C:2007:120; Commission *v Poland*, Order, 18 April 2007, Case No C-193/07 R, ECLI:EU:C:2007:218 and *Commission v Malta*, Order, 24 April 2008, Case No C-76/08 R, ECLI:EU:C:2008:252.

In that respect, the *Białowieża Forest* case is a good example. In 2016, the Commission initiated a pre-litigation procedure relating to a timber extraction plan adopted by the Polish authorities in respect of a forest classified as a Natura 2000 site, for infringing certain directives relating to the protection of fauna and flora. On 20 July 2017, the Commission brought an action for failure to fulfil obligations before the Court. In light of information indicating that Poland had already adopted a decision to carry out timber extraction operations, the Commission also made an application for interim measures, and requested the Court to rule on it *inaudita altera parte*. By a first order made on 27 July 2017, the Court ordered Poland to immediately cease the deforestation measures at issue, in view of the risk of serious and irreparable damage to protected countryside, and taking into account the precautionary principle.[33] By a second order of 20 November of that year, after hearing Poland, the Court maintained its interim decision, holding that the Commission's action in the main proceedings could not be considered *prima facie* without reasonable substance, and satisfied the condition of urgency.[34] On 17 April 2018, having acceded to the Commission's request for an expedited procedure,[35] the Court finally held that Poland had infringed the directives at issue.[36]

Although the action for failure to fulfil obligations appears effective, it nevertheless suffers from the length of proceedings. The Commission's obligation to comply with the pre-litigation phase may prove helpful in resolving certain difficulties before the dispute reaches the Court. However, it makes the procedure more cumbersome where the Member States are not cooperative. Moreover, the rules of procedure require the Commission to initiate that procedure twice before the Court can impose financial penalties.[37] In the abovementioned case relating to Ireland's implementation of the Impact Assessment Directive, 18 years elapsed between the Commission's first letter of formal notice and the Court's judgment imposing penalties on that Member State.[38]

---

[33] Court of Justice, *Commission v Poland*, Order, 27 July 2017, Case No C-441/17 R, ECLI:EU:C:2017:622. The precautionary principle had already been invoked by the Court in order to justify the adoption of interim measures: Court of Justice, *Commission v Malta*, Order, 24 April 2008, above n 32, para 37.

[34] Court of Justice, *Commission v Poland*, Order, 20 November 2107, Case No C-441/17 R, ECLI:EU:C:2017:877.

[35] Court of Justice, *Commission v Poland*, Order, 11 October 2017, Case No C-441/17, ECLI:EU:C:2017:794. About the expedited procedure, see Article 134 of the Rules of Procedure of the Court of Justice.

[36] Court of Justice, *Commission v Poland*, Judgment, 17 April 2018, Case No C-441/17, ECLI:EU:C:2018:255.

[37] It is only whether the Commission brings a case on the grounds that a Member State has failed to fulfil its obligation to notify measures transposing a directive that it may demand immediately penalty payment to the Court: see article: see TFEU, Article 260(3).

[38] With regard to the first pre-litigation procedure, see Court of Justice, *Commission v Ireland*, Judgment, 3 July 2008, Case No C-215/06, ECLI:EU:C:2008:380, paras 30–33; on the final stage of the proceedings, see Court of Justice, *Commission v Ireland*, Judgment, 12 November 2019, Case No C-261/18, ECLI:EU:C:2019:955.

Furthermore, it stems from Articles 258 and 259 TFEU that only the Commission and the Member States may bring infringement proceedings before the Court. Therefore, natural persons and environmental NGOs are not entitled to initiate such proceedings. Admittedly, they may lodge a complaint with the Commission if they consider that the authorities of a Member State infringed EU environmental law.[39] However, the Commission has a discretion in assessing whether or not such a complaint should be dealt with, and it is settled case law that a refusal to initiate infringement proceedings is not a challengeable act before the EU Courts.[40] The Aarhus Regulation does not change anything in this respect in the field of environmental protection, since acts of the Commission in the context of infringement proceedings are excluded from its scope.[41] The exclusion of environmental NGOs from direct participation in this process of control of Member States' acts has been subject to criticism in jurisprudence on the ground that the Commission may freely define its priorities for failure to fulfil obligations, having regard to its own political agenda.[42] However, the environmental NGOs could benefit from the Court's case law admitting their intervention in cases relating to environmental protection.[43]

8.3.2 Obstacles to Direct Actions Against EU Institutions in Environmental Disputes

In theory, actions for annulment, for failure to act and to establish non-contractual liability enable any person to bring disputes before the EU Courts on the ground that the EU institutions failed to comply with the environmental protection rules applicable to them.[44] However, admissibility of such remedies is often limited when natural or legal persons bring them.

First, actions for damages are quite rare in environmental protection matters. That rareness can be explained by the substantive conditions of the EU's non-contractual liability:[45] applicants will generally have difficulty in establishing the existence of a

[39] See: https://ec.europa.eu/assets/sg/report-a-breach/complaints_en/index.html. Accessed 30 April 2021.

[40] Court of Justice, *Lütticke v Commission of the EEC*, Judgment, 1 March 1966, Case No 48/65, ECLI:EU:C:1966:8 and *Clarke v Commission*, Order, 1 October 2019, Case No C-284/19 P, ECLI:EU:C:2019:799, para 27.

[41] Regulation (EC) 1367/2006, Article 2(2)(b).

[42] Krämer 2009, p. 13.

[43] Court of Justice, *Bayer CropScience and Bayer v Commission*, Order, 7 February 2019, Case No C-499/18 P, ECLI:EU:C:2019:107, para 6.

[44] Disputes are, in principle, brought before General Court, which gives judgment at first instance by decisions against which an appeal may be brought before the Court. The appeal has no devolutive effect: the Court is limited to reviewing the external validity and internal legality of the decision under appeal. See Naômé 2016.

[45] Following the Court's case law 'the European Union may incur non-contractual liability only if a number of conditions are fulfilled, namely the existence of a sufficiently serious breach of a rule

manifest illegality, direct and certain damage, or a causal link. For example, some applicants recently sought compensation on the ground that the rules on atmospheric emissions from motor vehicles adopted after *Dieselgate* would lead to damage to the air quality they breathe. The General Court rejected that application, holding that these applicants failed to establish the existence of direct and certain damage.[46] The same difficulties arise when companies seek compensation for economic harm supposedly caused by environmental legislation.[47]

Next, actions for failure to act are also rather rare in the field of environmental protection. In any event, they encounter an obstacle of a procedural nature: natural and legal persons must establish they have standing to bring proceedings, which gives rise to significant difficulties.[48] The same difficulties arise in relation to actions for annulment, which are the most common direct actions in environmental matters, and on which we shall focus the analysis here.

8.3.2.1 The Origin of the Obstacles: *Locus Standi* and Subsidiarity of EU Environment Policy

It is apparent from Article 263(2) TFEU that the Member States, the Parliament, the Council of the EU and the Commission may act by right against all acts of the EU institutions producing legal effects. Those litigants are thus 'privileged'. Natural or legal persons, for their part, have the status of 'ordinary' litigants. According to Article 263(4) TFEU, they will establish *locus standi* by right only if they challenge an act of which they are the addressees. On the other hand, where the contested measure addresses another person, or where it consists of a measure of general application, ordinary litigants must establish that they are both directly and individually concerned by it.[49]

---

of law intended to confer rights on individuals, the fact of damage and the existence of a causal link between the breach of the obligation resting on the author of the act and the damage sustained by the injured parties': see e.g., Court of Justice, *Commission v Fresh Marine*, Judgment, 10 July 2003, Case No C-472/00 P, EU:C:2003:399, para 25 and *Artegodan v Commission*, Judgment, 19 April 2012, Case No C-221/10 P, EU:C:2012:216, para 80.

[46] General Court, *Abel and Others v Commission*, Order, 4 May 2018, Case No T-197/17, ECLI:EU:T:2018:258, paras 29–33.

[47] See e.g., General Court, *Enviro Tech (Europe) and Enviro Tech International v Commission*, Judgment, 16 December 2011, Case No T-291/04, ECLI:EU:T:2011:760, paras 140–163; Court of Justice, *Enviro Tech (Europe) v Commission*, Order, 24 January 2013, Case No C-118/12 P, ECLI:EU:C:2013:37 and *Holcim v Commission*, Judgment, 7 April 2016, Case No C-556/14 P, ECLI:EU:C:2016:207.

[48] See General Court, *Federcaccia Toscana and Others v Commission*, Order, 26 October 2017, Case No T-562/15, ECLI:EU:T:2017:765, paras 72–77.

[49] See, in that regard, Lenaerts et al. 2014, paras 7.85.

Direct concern means, in essence, that the contested measure must, in itself, alter the applicant's legal situation.[50] As regards individual concern, it is clear from the *Plaumann* case that:

> persons other than those to whom a decision is addressed may only claim to be individually concerned if that decision affects them by reason of certain attributes which are peculiar to them or by reason of circumstances in which they are differentiated from all other persons and by virtue of these factors distinguishes them individually just as in the case of the person addressed.[51]

It is obvious that this condition will not be easy to meet if the contested act is of general application.

The Lisbon Treaty introduced an amendment in that regard. If the action is brought against a regulatory act not entailing implementing measures, the only condition to be satisfied is that the applicant must be directly concerned.[52] However, first, that amendment does not concern actions against legislative acts.[53] Secondly, it has been interpreted rather restrictively by the Court.[54] The Court judged that this more flexible condition of admissibility does not apply when the contested act produces its legal effects vis-à-vis the applicant only through acts taken by the national authorities as an intermediary.[55]

The logic underlying these procedural rules is that access to EU Courts should not be made available to direct actions beyond cases in which the EU institutions have direct administrative functions, i.e. functions that empower them to take individual measures.[56] In particular, measures of general application should not be open, in principle, to challenge by means of direct action.[57] Thus, where the institutions possess

---

[50] Following the Court's case law, the condition that a natural or legal person must be directly concerned 'requires two cumulative criteria to be met, namely, first, the contested measure must directly affect the legal situation of the individual and, second, it must leave no discretion to its addressees who are entrusted with the task of implementing it, such implementation being purely automatic and resulting from the EU rules alone without the application of other intermediate rules': Court of Justice, *Scuola Elementare Maria Montessori v Commission*, Judgment, 6 November 2018, Cases No C-622/16 P to C-624/16 P, ECLI:EU:C:2018:873, para 42.

[51] Court of Justice, *Plaumann v Commission*, Judgment, 15 July 1963, Case No 25/62, ECLI:EU:C:1963:17, para 223.

[52] TFEU, Article 263(4), final limb.

[53] Legislative acts are the ones adopted by the Council of the EU and, where appropriate, by the European Parliament, in accordance with an ordinary or special legislative procedure: see TFEU, Article 289(3). In short, these first-level measures of general application legally reflect the most important political choices of the EU institutions. Regulatory acts are acts of general application that are not legislative acts. About the concept of regulatory acts, see Court of Justice, *Inuit Tapiriit Kanatami and Others v Parliament and Council*, Judgment, 3 October 2013, Case No C-583/11 P, ECLI:EU:C:2013:625, paras 59–61.

[54] Wildemeersch 2014, p. 155.

[55] Court of Justice, *T & L Sugars and Sidul Açúcares v Commission*, Judgment, 28 April 2015, Case No C-456/13 P, ECLI:EU:C:2015:284, para 40.

[56] For instance, in the field of competition policy, the Commission may adopt individual decisions imposing fines on undertakings or authorising concentrations of undertakings.

[57] Kovar 1999, p. 387.

implementing functions characterized by the adoption of individual measures, those measures may be the subject of an action for annulment by their addressees. A challenge to the legality of acts of general application on the basis of which individual measures are adopted will then be possible by way of a plea of illegality. Where national authorities have to implement EU legislation, it is, in principle, the decisions taken by those authorities that alter the legal assets of natural and legal persons. The addressees of such measures must then bring proceedings – or even 'trigger' a case – before the national courts in order to ensure that the administrative authorities of a Member State do indeed comply with EU law.[58] If there is doubt as to the legality of the EU legislation itself, the national court may refer the matter to the Court for a preliminary ruling. The main justification for this particular organization of the judicial powers is that, in most of the national legal systems, individuals may challenge only administrative measures by way of a direct action, in particular those of direct concern to them. Challenging acts of general application, especially legislative acts, generally arises by way of an exception, in particular through systems of preliminary rulings before constitutional courts.[59]

In the context of EU environmental policy, that logic leads to the restriction of individuals' direct access to the EU Courts. That policy is the result of a balance between the need to combat certain pollution at the supranational level and the need for Member States to adapt their measures in accordance with local considerations, within a Union where national ambitions in relation to the protection of the nature vary widely.[60] EU environmental policy is thus characterized by subsidiarity, particularly favourable to the indirect administration logic. In this field, the bulk of EU legislative production consists of adopting acts of general application, with Directives often being preferred to Regulations. Those acts impose obligations on Member States as much as on individuals, and national administrative authorities will generally be responsible for their implementation. It should be added that the few fields in which the direct administration takes precedence (for example, marketing authorizations for dangerous products or substances, allocation of greenhouse gas quotas, subsidizing activities) concern mostly the regulation of economic activities. Economic operators are thus more likely to be the addressees of individual acts than natural persons or environmental NGOs.

[58] In certain situations, acts of general application of the EU having direct effect alter the legal situation of individuals, without there being any real need for a national implementing decision. As the law stands, direct access to the EU Courts may nonetheless possibly be impossible for challenging those acts. Proceedings before the national courts may, in some way, be 'triggered' in order to be able to benefit from a challengeable decision, and to suggest to the national court to refer for a preliminary ruling. See Coutron 2014, p. 548.

[59] Lenaerts 2009, p. 257.

[60] Blumann 1997, p. 63 and p. 80 ss.; Lenaerts 1993, p. 846; de Sadeleer 2012, p. 73.

8.3.2.2 The Reality of the Procedural Obstacles in the Case Law

A study of the proceedings for annulment case law in environmental matters reveals the reality of the procedural obstacles faced by ordinary litigants. We will address here applications brought by companies, environmental NGOs and natural persons, as well as local authorities of the Member States.

First, economic operators, which are ordinary litigants whether they are legal or natural persons, may consider that a measure of an EU institution seeking to protect the environment prejudices their economic interests. If a company intends to challenge an act of secondary legislation, the specific features of the case in point will determine its *locus standi.*

Thus, a company may in principle challenge legal acts that are of direct and individual concern to it. This remains rare in practice: such a situation can only prevail in the few areas of environmental policy in which EU institutions have direct administrative functions. For instance, under Regulation 517/2014 establishing a system of quotas for marketing fluorinated greenhouse gases, it is for the Commission to adopt implementing decisions setting reference values for each producer or importer of that substance. The latter may then challenge those decisions insofar as it concerns them, without having to justify its standing to bring proceedings.[61]

Beyond these hypotheses, the standing of economic operators to initiate proceedings is more fragile. This is the case where a company challenges a decision addressed to a Member State. Once the national authorities have the responsibility to adopt national measures subsequent to the contested decision, while having a margin of discretion, the claim will be dismissed on the ground that the applicant is not of direct concern, because it is then the national measures which will alter this latter's legal situation.[62] Since the Court considers that a decision addressed to a Member State may be of a general nature vis-a-vis those subject to that State, actions can also be dismissed on the ground that this subject is not of individual concern.[63] The same logic usually justifies the dismissal of proceedings brought by companies against measures of general application. The application will be declared inadmissible on the ground that the applicant is not of individual concern, because the contested

---

[61] See e.g., General Court, *GHC v Commission*, Judgement, 24 June 2015, Case No T-847/14, ECLI:EU:T:2015:428. See also a case in which the locus standi has not been challenged by the General Court: *Mebrom v Commission*, Judgement, 22 May 2007, Case No T-216/05, ECLI:EU:T:2007:148.

[62] On that ground, the General Court has dismissed as inadmissible several actions brought against Commission decisions concerning the national allocation plans for CO^2 quotas adopted in the context of the EU emissions trading system, since the Member States had a margin of discretion to allocate allowances within the limits of the ceiling authorized by the Commission: see e.g., Court of First Instance, *Drax Power and Others v Commission*, Order, 25 June 2007, Case No T-130/06, ECLI:EU:T:2007:188; *Cemex UK Cement v Commission*, Order, 6 November 2007, Case No T-13/07, ECLI:EU:T:2007:331 and *Dykerhoff Polska v Commission*, Order, 23 September 2008, Case No T-196/07, ECLI:EU:T:2008:390.

[63] See, about the national allocation plans for CO^2 quotas mentioned above, Court of Justice, *Saint-Gobain Glass Deutschland v Commission*, Order, 8 April 2008, Case No C-503/07 P, ECLI:EU:C:2008:207.

measure applies to it objectively, in the same way as it applies to all persons falling within its scope, whatever the number of addressees.[64]

It is only when a contested act of general application can be qualified as a regulatory act not entailing implementing measures and directly affecting the applicant that this can get over the *Plaumann* case law obstacle.[65] It must be recalled here that, under the fourth limb of Article 263(4) TFEU, when an action is brought against a regulatory act not entailing implementing measures, the only condition to be satisfied is that the applicant must be directly concerned.[66] It is difficult to evaluate the actual impact of these special conditions of admissibility in environmental disputes, because it is a case-by-case analysis, largely dependent on the general scheme of the regulation concerned and the legal effects its produces. For instance, the General Court found that a decision of the Commission not to include a substance in the Union's list of additives which may be used in plastic materials coming into contact with foodstuffs under Directive 2002/72, was a regulatory act not entailing implementing measures by Member States. Under that Directive, this non-inclusion had the immediate consequence of prohibiting the marketing of the substance, without the Member States needing to adopt any implementing measures.[67] By contrast, the Court considered the fourth limb of Article 263(4) TFEU as inapplicable in a case where the challenged act was a Regulation concerning the placing of plant protection products on the market because this Regulation called for Commission's or Member States' measures of implementation.[68]

Second, natural persons and environmental NGOs regularly bring actions to challenge decisions they consider harmful to the environment. The assessment of their *locus standi* depends on the same factors as those relating to actions initiated by economic operators. However, the likelihood that they will be the addressees of an individual measure is weaker.

---

[64] See, thereto, General Court, *Enviro Tech v Commission*, Judgement, 16 December 2011, above n 47, paras 94–120.

[65] See *supra*, Sect. 8.3.2.1.

[66] A regulatory act not entailing implementing measures under the meaning of Article 263(4) TFEU can be a Directive, a Regulation, a Decision or any other act having legal effects.

[67] General Court, *Microban v Commission*, Judgement, 25 October 2011, Case No T-262/10, ECLI:EU:T:2011:623, paras 26–38. For another example, the General Court annulled a regulation without calling into question the locus standi of the applicant: General Court, *Bilbaina de Alquitranes and Others v Commission*, Judgement, 7 October 2015, Case No T-689/13, ECLI:EU:T:2015:767. In appeal, see Court of Justice, *Commission v Bilbaína de Alquitranes and Others*, Order, 7 July 2016, Case No C-691/15 P, ECLI:EU:C:2016:597. The General Court adopted a perhaps generous approach in some cases delivered before the Court for case law clarification: see General Court, *Romonta v Commission*, Judgement, 26 September 2014, Case No T-614/13, ECLI:EU:T:2014:835, paras 28–38. The analysis of the locus standi has not been challenged in appeal: Court of Justice, *Romonta v Commission*, Order, 13 September 2016, Case No C-565/14 P, ECLI:EU:C:2016:698. About this case law, see de Sadeleer and Poncelet 2013, p. 7.

[68] Court of Justice, *European Union Copper Task Force v Commission*, Judgement, 13 March 2018, Case No C-384/16 P, ECLI:EU:C:2018:176, paras 44–70; for another example, see General Court, *Eurofer v Commission* Order, 4 June 2012, Case No T-381/11, ECLI:EU:T:2012:273, paras 41–63.

That situation arises principally in relation to access to documents. The legal framework for this, Regulation 1049/2001,[69] confers on any person the right to request from an EU institution or agency the disclosure of documents in its possession, subject to certain exceptions. The relevant institution is required to reply within a certain period,[70] by a decision addressed individually to the applicant. This constitutes an act open to challenge.[71] Natural persons and environmental NGOs may therefore rely on that regulation to obtain access to documents on which the institutions have based their decisions in terms of environmental policy, and they have well-established *locus standi* to challenge refusals before the General Court, if necessary.[72]

Beyond that specific field, actions brought by natural persons or environmental NGOs against measures not addressed to them, in particular measures of general application, are generally bound to fail as the law stands. Before the EU ratification of the Aarhus Convention, several associations, including Greenpeace International, and a group of natural persons resident in the Canary Islands, attempted to bring an action for annulment in the interests of the environment. The contested act was a Commission Decision granting Spain financial aid for the construction of two power stations in the Canary Islands. The applicants argued that, since environmental protection was at stake, the Court of First Instance should adopt a liberal interpretation to individual concern, by assessing their *locus standi* in light of the harm they would likely suffer because of a deterioration of the environment. They argued that the Commission's decision could affect their living conditions, quality of life or health, while environmental protection associations invoked their statutory interests.[73] However, the Court of First Instance considered that the nature of the interests in question did not justify derogation from the established principles. It dismissed the action on the ground that the applicants were not individually affected by the contested measure in the sense of the *Plaumann* case law.[74] On appeal, the Court confirmed this reasoning.[75] This 'orthodox' approach to the conditions for admissibility in proceedings relating to environmental protection has been followed

---

[69] Regulation (EC) No 1049/2001 of the European Parliament and of the Council concerning public access to European Parliament, Council and Commission Documents, 30 May 2001, OJEU 2001 L145, p. 43.

[70] Ibid., Articles 7 and 8.

[71] About the act open to challenge under Regulation 1049/2001, see General Court, *Arca Capital Bohemia v Commission*, Judgement, 11 December 2018, Case No T-440/17, ECLI:EU:T:2018:898, paras 16–20.

[72] See e.g., General Court, *Stichting Greenpeace Nederland and PAN Europe v Commission*, Judgement, 21 November 2018, Case No T-545/11 RENV, ECLI:EU:T:2018:817 and *Tweedale v EFSA*, Judgement, 7 March 2019, Case No T-716/14, ECLI:EU:T:2019:141.

[73] Court of First Instance, *Greenpeace and Others v Commission*, Order, 9 August 1995, Case No T-585/93, ECLI:EU:T:1995:147, paras 29–41.

[74] Ibid., paras 48–58.

[75] Court of Justice, *Greenpeace and Others v Commission*, Judgement, 2 April 1998, Case No C-321/95 P, ECLI:EU:C:1998:153.

in subsequent decisions.[76] In certain cases, the acts challenged in vain, for procedural reasons, by 'ordinary' litigants have been annulled as a result of actions brought by 'privileged' litigants, such as Member States, who have a *locus standi* by right.[77]

That jurisprudence has remained constant since the ratification to the Aarhus Convention,[78] even in cases where NGOs have explicitly relied on it, considering it would reinforce their *locus standi*.[79] One of the most recent attempts was an action brought by several natural persons seeking the annulment of certain legislative acts adopted in 2018 to achieve a 40% decrease in greenhouse gas emissions by 2030 compared to 1990 emissions.[80] The applicants claimed to be directly and individually concerned by the contested measures by virtue of their rights under the Charter of Fundamental Rights of the European Union. In the alternative, they took the view that the *Plaumann* case law should be ruled out, in particular in light of the Aarhus Convention. The General Court dismissed their action, and concluded that the allegation of an infringement of fundamental rights could not amount to individual concern to the applicants by the legislative acts in question following the *Plaumann* case law.[81] In other terms, the applicants had confused the conditions of admissibility with those relating to the merits of the action.

Third, and lastly, the local authorities of the Member States are also 'ordinary' litigants within the meaning of Article 263(4) TFEU.[82] It follows that they must therefore also show that they are directly and individually concerned when bringing an

[76] Court of First Instance, *Danielsson and Others v Commission*, Order, 22 December 1995, Case No T-219/95 R, ECLI:EU:T:1995:219 and *Sahlstedt and Others v Commission*, Order, 22 June 2006, Case No T-150/05, ECLI:EU:T:2006:172; Court of Justice, *Sahlstedt and Others v Commission*, Judgement, 23 April 2009, Case No C-362/06 P, ECLI:EU:C:2009:243. In some cases, it is the lack of direct concern which has justify a dismissal: Court of First Instance, *Freiherr von Cramer-Klett and Rechtlerverband Pfronten v Commission*, Order, 22 June 2006, Case No T-136/04, ECLI:EU:T:2006:170.

[77] Court of First Instance, *EEB and Others v Commission*, Order, 28 November 2005, Case No T-94/04, ECLI:EU:T:2005:425 (Order, dismiss) and *Sweden v Commission*, Judgement, 11 July 2007, Case No T-229/04, ECLI:EU:T:2007:217 (annulment).

[78] See e.g., General Court, *Associazione Granosalus v Commission*, Order, 14 February 2019, Case No T-125/18, ECLI:EU:T:2019:92, paras 51–64.

[79] Court of First Instance, *WWF-UK v Council*, Order, 2 June 2008, Case No T-91/07, ECLI:EU:T:2008:170, paras 80–82; Court of Justice, *WWF-UK v Council*, Order, 5 May 2009, Case No C-355/08 P, ECLI:EU:C:2009:286.

[80] The applicants hoped measures to combat climate change more ambitious. This action took place of a wider worldwide strategy, seeking to enhanced climate change policies thanks to legal actions. See Krämer 2019a, p. 213.

[81] General Court, *Carvalho and Others v Parliament and Council*, Order, 8 May 2019, Case No T-330/18, ECLI:EU:T:2019:324, paras 46–55. This judgment was confirmed on appeal: Court of Justice, *Carvalho and Others v Parliament and Council*, Judgment, 25 March 2021, Case No C-565/19 P, ECLI:EU:C:2021:252. In the same vein, see Court of Justice, *Sabo and Others v Parliament and Council*, Order, 14 January 2021, Case No C-297/20 P, ECLI:EU:C:2021:24.

[82] Court of Justice, *Regione Siciliana v Commission*, Judgement, 2 May 2006, Case No C-417/04 P, ECLI:EU:C:2006:282, paras 21–24.

action for annulment in environmental law matters. That demonstration will be difficult[83] where local authorities challenge acts of which they are not the addressees.[84] Thus, for lack of direct concern, the General Court dismissed an action brought by the Brussels Capital Region against the December 2017 Regulation renewing the approval of the active substance glyphosate for five years.[85] This assessment has been confirmed in appeal. The Court judged, inter alia, that the General Regulation concerning the placing of plant protection products on the market leaves a discretion to the Member states when a substance is approved. Any competent national authority (i.e. the Belgian federal government in that case), taking into account the circumstances in its territory, may impose risk mitigation measures, or even forbid the marketing of a product containing that substance.[86]

To conclude, it is worth noting that some authors have criticized the 'orthodox' approach to the conditions for admissibility, especially with regard to the procedural rights of natural persons and NGOs.[87] In particular, some consider that the case law is more flexible in certain spheres of economic law, in particular in disputes concerning State aid control or measures of the common commercial policy where the courts have been able to take into account, inter alia, the existence of procedural law or factual circumstances showing that the applicants are individually concerned.[88]

8.3.2.3 The Limited Scope of the Aarhus Regulation

As pointed out above,[89] in order to apply the Aarhus Convention to the EU institutions, the Parliament and the Council adopted the Aarhus Regulation. That Regulation establishes a system of internal review closely related to proceedings before the EU Court.

---

[83] However, the General Court recently held the Regulation introducing new standards on atmospheric emissions from motor vehicles after *DieselGate* directly affects the cities of Paris, Brussels and Madrid, due to their powers to restrict the circulation of motor vehicles in order to protect air quality. The action was held to be admissible since the contested regulation was, according to the General Court, a regulatory act not entailing implementing measures: General Court, *Ville de Paris v Commission*, Judgement, 13 December 2018, cases T-339/16, T-352/16 and T-391/16, ECLI:EU:T:2018:927, paras 50–84. The question remains whether the Court will confirm this approach: see pending Case No C-178/19 C-179/19.

[84] Court of First Instance, *Região autónoma dos Açores v Council*, Judgement, 1 July 2008, Case No T-37/04, ECLI:EU:T:2008:236; Court of Justice, *Região autónoma dos Açores v Council*, Order, 26 November 2009, Case No C-444/08 P, ECLI:EU:C:2009:733.

[85] General Court, *Région de Bruxelles-Capitale v Commission*, Order, 28 February 2019, Case No T-178/18, ECLI:EU:T:2019:130.

[86] Court of Justice, *Région de Bruxelles-Capitale v Commission*, Judgement, 3 December 2020, Case No C-352/19 P, ECLI:EU:C:2020:978, paras 50–52.

[87] See e.g., regarding to Aarhus Convention, above n 19, Mastroianni and Pezza 2014.

[88] See e.g., Krämer 2017, p. 13.

[89] See *supra*, Sect. 8.2.2.

Under that Regulation, an NGO whose object is environmental protection, is entitled to submit a reasoned request to an institution, agency or body of the EU[90] in order to trigger a review of an act or omission in the field of environmental law. The institution or body concerned must reply to that request within 12 weeks.[91] The Regulation also provides that the applicant NGO 'may institute proceedings before the Court of Justice in accordance with the relevant provisions of the Treaty.'[92] This provision must be read in light of the rules governing direct actions: the applicant is the addressee of the reply to a request for review and therefore, has a well-established standing to bring proceedings – especially an action for annulment – before the EU Courts in case its submission is rejected. If the Court upholds the application, the institution will have to modify the decision, having regard to the reasons for the judge's decision.[93] The case law has specified the practical details of that procedure, in terms which must encourage NGOs to carefully articulate their claims of reassessment. Since the purpose of the review mechanism is to lead the institution concerned to determine whether the act in question is unlawful or unfounded, specific and precise points of fact and law must support the request. In addition, if the party filing the request brings the matter before the EU judicature, it may not make a claim on new grounds or on evidence not appearing in the request for review.[94]

Without addressing the question of the effectiveness of this mechanism,[95] the question that arises here is the extent to which it can extend access to the EU Courts by means of actions brought against decisions refusing reassessment.[96] In this respect, one must take into account the criteria laid down by the Regulation, some of which are restrictive.

First, the mechanism is open only to NGOs whose primary-stated objective is the promotion environmental protection.[97] It does not concern natural persons, economic operators or local authorities of the Member States. Secondly, review is limited to decisions taken 'under environmental law'.[98] This expression may be interpreted strictly, as covering only acts formally deriving from EU environmental policy enshrined in Articles 191 to 193 TFEU, or broadly, as including acts adopted on

---

[90] Beyond the EU institutions, it is necessary to take into account the growing role of EU agencies in environmental matters, as the European Chemicals Agency or the European Food Safety Agency.

[91] See Regulation (EC) 1367/2006, Articles 10 and 11.

[92] Ibid., Article 12(1); the right of action also concerns the infringement by the institution sought of the rules on the review procedure laid down by the regulation: Article 12(2).

[93] TFEU, Article 266. The EU courts shall not have jurisdiction to issue injunctions: General Court, *PAN Europe v Commission*, Order, 12 March 2014, Case No T-192/12, ECLI:EU:T:2014:152, para 15.

[94] Court of Justice, *TestBioTech and Others v Commission*, Judgement, 12 September 2019, Case No C-82/17 P, ECLI:EU:C:2019:719, paras 38, 39, 67 and 68.

[95] In a contribution published in 2018, the authors stated that 35 requests for review had been sent to the Commission. They had all resulted in a decision of inadmissibility or dismissal on the merits: see Brosset and Truilhé-Marengo 2018.

[96] In that regard, see ibid.; de Sadeleer and Poncelet 2013; Pallemaerts 2011, p. 271.

[97] Regulation (EC) 1367/2006, Article 11.

[98] Ibid., Articles 2(1)(g) and 10(1).

other bases as far as they are connected with environmental protection. The General Court opted for the broad interpretation: it annulled a Commission decision rejecting an application for review of genetically modified soybeans marketing authorization on the ground that it related to food safety and health, not to environment protection.[99]

Finally, under the Regulation, the request for review must relate to an 'administrative act' or an 'administrative omission'.[100] In this respect, the Regulation states that 'administrative act' means 'any measure of individual scope ... having legally binding and external effects.'[101] Thus, it is clear that legislative or regulatory acts are excluded from the scope of the Regulation and that a request for review of such acts will be declared inadmissible.

In light of these provisions, the first question raised is whether that limitation of the scope of the internal review mechanism complies with the Aarhus Convention. In the *Vereniging Milieudefensie* and *Stichting Milieu* cases, two actions seeking the annulment of Commission decisions refusing to review measures of general application on the ground that they were not 'administrative acts', were supported by pleas of illegality challenging the provisions of the Aarhus Regulation limiting the scope of review mechanism. At first instance, the General Court, while acknowledging that the measures at issue were indeed of general application, nonetheless granted the requests by declaring the limitation of the review to administrative acts as inapplicable because of its non-conformity with Article 9(3) of the Aarhus Convention.[102] However, the Court set aside these judgments on appeal on the ground that this provision of the Convention does not have direct effect. It also ruled that the Aarhus Regulation was not intended to implement some international obligations within the meaning of the case law about direct effect of WTO law in the EU legal order.[103] Consequently, the Convention cannot lead to a review of legality of secondary legislation.[104]

---

[99] General Court, *TestBioTech v Commission*, Judgement, 14 March 2018, Case No T-33/16, ECLI:EU:T:2018:135.

[100] Regulation (EC) 1367/2006, Article 10(1).

[101] Ibid., Article 2(1)(g). The fact that it does not concern acts not having binding effects is consistent with the traditional case law concerning the act open to challenge. See Mariatte and Ritleng 2011, pp. 45 ss.

[102] General Court, *Stichting Natuur en Milieu and PAN v Commission*, Judgement, 14 June 2012, Case No T-338/08, ECLI:EU:T:2012:300; General Court, *Vereniging Milieudefensie and Stichting Stop Luchtverontreiniging Utrecht v Commission*, Judgement, 14 June 2012, Case No T-396/09, ECLI:EU:T:2012:301.

[103] Where the European Union intends to implement a particular obligation assumed in the context of the agreements concluded in the context of the World Trade Organization or where the EU act at issue refers explicitly to specific provisions of those agreements, the Court should review the legality of the act at issue and the acts adopted for its implementation in the light of the rules of those agreements: Court of Justice, *Fediol v Commission*, Judgement, 22 June 1989, Case No 70/87, ECLI:EU:C:1989:254, paras 19–23; Court of Justice, *Nakajima All Precision v Council*, Judgement, 7 May 1991, Case No C-69/89, ECLI:EU:C:1991:186 paras 29–32.

[104] Court of Justice, *Council and Others v Vereniging Milieudefensie and Stichting Stop Luchtverontreiniging Utrecht*, Judgement, 13 January 2015, Cases No C-401/12 P, C-402/12 P and C-403/12 P, ECLI:EU:C:2015:4 and *Council and Commission v Stichting Natuur en Milieu and Pesticide*

Since this limitation remains in force, the second question concerns the precise meaning of the words 'administrative act'. The concept of 'administrative act' does not correspond to the usual categories of EU legal acts and thus calls for clarification. In particular, it may raise certain difficulties with regard to measures of a hybrid nature. For example, some measures are addressed to Member States, or are requested by economic operators to place a product on the market, but may create, at the same time, rights or obligations for other persons. The case law has provided some clarification on this point. Despite who they are addressed to, or requested by, legal acts are not 'administrative acts' if they are of general application vis-à-vis third parties. This applied to a Commission decision approving a plan for limiting certain industrial emissions notified by a Member State,[105] a Commission decision on the transitional free allocation of CO2 allowances,[106] and the 2016 Regulation provisionally renewing the authorization of the active substance glyphosate.[107]

It follows from the foregoing that the review regime established by the Aarhus Regulation does indeed grant NGOs direct access to the Courts of the EU in order to challenge certain acts not addressed to them, and in respect of which their *locus standi* might have been difficult to establish. However, it has not considerably extended access to the Court for hearing actions for annulment, since it does not allow challenges to measures of general application.

8.4 The Importance of Preliminary Reference in Environmental Litigation

The existence of obstacles for ordinary litigants to bring direct action against acts of Member States or EU institutions does not mean these litigants cannot access EU Courts. According to the general scheme of EU procedural law, it means that the appropriate legal remedy is not a direct action but a preliminary reference.

Where EU institutions do not have direct administrative functions, ordinary litigants should be able to challenge the national measures implementing EU law before

---

Action Network Europe, Judgement, 13 January 2015, Cases No C-404/12 P and C-405/12 P, ECLI:EU:C:2015:5.

[105] General Court, *EEB v Commission*, Order, 17 July 2015, Case No T-685/14, ECLI:EU:T:2015:560, paras 42–49.

[106] General Court, *Frank Bold v Commission*, Order, 29 June 2015, Case No T-19/13, ECLI:EU:T:2015:520, paras 39–45.

[107] General Court, *Mellifera v Commission*, Judgement, 27 September 2018, Case No T-12/17, ECLI:EU:T:2018:616, paras 56–65. This judgment was confirmed on appeal: Court of Justice, *Mellifera v Commission*, Judgement, 3 September 2020, Case No C-784/18 P, ECLI:EU:C:2020:630. However, the Commission considered as admissible applications for review concerning genetically modified soybean marketing authorization, and the authorization of a chemical component, without explaining this admissibility in its decisions. In any cases, the admissibility had make possible a substantive debate before EU Courts: General Court, *TestBioTech and Others v Commission*, Judgement, 15 December 2016, Case No T-177/13, ECLI:EU:T:2016:736 and *ClientEarth v Commission*, Judgement, 4 April 2019, Case No T-108/17, ECLI:EU:T:2019:215.

national courts. If actions brought before the national court concern breaches of EU environmental law by national authorities, the national court may itself draw the appropriate conclusions. The national court would, or should, refer a question to the Court for a preliminary ruling if it encounters difficulties in interpreting the relevant rules.[108] The applicants may also claim that EU acts of secondary legislation themselves contain unlawful provisions. The national court shall refer to the Court for a preliminary ruling if there exists a serious doubt concerning the validity of the act.[109] In any case, one should note that a Member State might be the subject of an action for failure to fulfil obligations if one of its courts infringes EU law, including the obligation to refer a matter for a preliminary ruling.[110]

In environmental litigation, preliminary references are of great importance since direct actions brought by ordinary litigants are generally inadmissible. As a result, the majority of the Court's most relevant and significant judgments in this field have arisen through this remedy.[111] Preliminary reference enables the Court to review by way of exception the legality of acts of the EU institutions relating to environmental protection (Sect. 8.4.1), but also to focus on issues of access to justice, this time before the national courts (Sect. 8.4.2).

8.4.1 The Review by Way of Exception of the Legality of EU Institutions' Acts

An applicant lacking *locus standi* to challenge a measure before the EU Courts will have every interest in triggering a reference for a preliminary ruling on validity. Practice points to a good example: a company wanted to challenge a Directive classifying n-propyl bromide as a dangerous substance. It initially brought an action for annulment before the General Court against that Directive. Next, this company challenged before a Belgian court the measure adopted by the Belgian Government to transpose the same Directive, leading to a referral to the Court for a preliminary ruling on validity. On 15 October 2009, the Court examined the question referred to it for a preliminary ruling, and thus assessed the legality of the Directive at stake.[112] On 16 December 2011, the General Court dismissed the action for annulment on the

---

[108] National courts ruling at last instance shall be obliged in this respect: Court of Justice, *CILFIT v Ministero della Sanità*, Judgement, 6 October 1982, Case No 283/81, ECLI:EU:C:1982:335.

[109] Court of Justice, *Foto-Frost v Hauptzollamt Lübeck-Ost*, Judgement, 22 October 1987, Case No 314/85, ECLI:EU:C:1987:452.

[110] Court of Justice, *Commission v France*, Judgement, 4 October 2018, Case No C-416/17, ECLI:EU:C:2018:811, paras 105–114.

[111] In support of that proposal, one can refer to a book seeking to explain EU environmental law through a case-law study. Most of decisions listed are judgments given on references for a preliminary ruling. See Clément 2016.

[112] Court of Justice, *Enviro Tech (Europe) v Belgium*, Judgement, 15 October 2009, Case No C-425/08, ECLI:EU:C:2009:635.

ground of a lack of individual concern, i.e. without considering the legality of the challenged Directive.[113]

In practice, the Court frequently examines references for preliminary rulings triggered by economic operators.[114] Environmental NGOs or other associations also make use of this remedy. For example, the question whether the general scheme for authorizing GMOs complied with the precautionary principle in case it excludes organisms obtained by mutagenesis was brought under review through a referral for preliminary ruling.[115] The Court also reviewed the legality of the regulation concerning the marketing authorization of plant protection products in light of the precautionary principle. It gave the opportunity to clarify the implications of the principle while considering that regulation was not unlawful.[116]

In the case law, the existence of the preliminary reference on validity explains why the dismissal of an action for annulment for lack of *locus standi* does not breach the right to effective judicial protection, as enshrined in Article 47 of the Charter of Fundamental Rights of the EU.[117] This is perfectly compatible with the traditional understanding of the system of legal remedies before the EU judicature.

8.4.2 Guarantees Concerning Access to National Courts

In view of the division of judicial competences established by the Treaty, the right to bring an action before national courts is crucial. First, as regards ordinary litigants who have no standing to bring an action for failure to fulfil obligations, these courts are responsible for reviewing the Member States' acts in light of EU law. Next, national courts can or must refer certain cases to the Court by way of a preliminary

---

[113] General Court, *Enviro Tech (Europe) and Enviro Tech International v Commission*, Judgement, 16 December 2011, above n 47. The application also contained claim for damages. The General Court rejected it as unfounded, on the ground that the applicant had not succeeded in establishing manifest illegality of the Directive. The General Court's examination was largely linked to the assessment made by the Court in that regard, which took the view that the question referred to it for a preliminary ruling did not support the conclusion that the Directive was unlawful.

[114] See, thereto, Court of Justice, *Gowan Comércio Internacional e Serviços*, Judgement, 22 December 2010, Case No C-77/09, ECLI:EU:C:2010:803 and *Borealis and Others*, Judgement, 8 September 2016, Case No C-180/15, ECLI:EU:C:2016:647.

[115] Court of Justice, *Confédération paysanne and Others*, Judgement, 25 July 2018, Case No C-528/16, ECLI:EU:C:2018:583.

[116] Court of Justice, *Blaise and Others*, Judgement, 1 October 2019, Case No C-616/17, ECLI:EU:C:2019:800. For another example, relating to the Habitats Directive, see: Court of Justice, *Associazione Italia Nostra Onlus*, Judgement, 21 December 2016, Case No C-444/15, ECLI:EU:C:2016:978, paras 40–64.

[117] Court of Justice, *European Union Copper Task Force v Commission*, Judgement, 13 March 2018, above n 68, para 119; Court of First Instance, *Freiherr von Cramer-Klett and Rechtlerverband Pfronten v Commission*, Order, 22 June 2006, above n 76, para 55; General Court, *Carvalho and Others v Parliament and Council*, above n 81, para 52.

ruling. If ordinary litigants do not have access to the national court's jurisdiction, they will also be deprived of indirect access to the Court itself.

In this regard, paragraph 1 of Article 19 TEU stipulates that 'Member States shall provide remedies sufficient to ensure effective legal protection in the fields covered by Union law.' In the field of environmental protection, the implementation of the Aarhus Convention led the EU institutions to adopt specific rules, seeking to enhance access to national courts. However, this is a sensitive area, because there are substantial differences between national legal systems in terms of the conditions governing the admissibility of legal remedies before administrative national courts.[118] Subsidiarity has thus led to a sectoral approach: several Directives relating to environmental protection incorporate procedural provisions. In substance, these provisions provide that members of the public must be able to bring effective legal proceedings, in accordance with the conditions of national law, in order to challenge the legality of national decisions taken within the scope of the Directive in question.[119]

By answering questions referred to it for a preliminary ruling on the interpretation of the above-mentioned provisions, the Court has developed case law concerning different aspects of access to national courts.[120] That case law is, to a great extent, based on an interpretation of secondary legislation in conformity with the Aarhus Convention, which prevails notwithstanding the fact that its provisions do not have direct effect.[121]

First, some questions referred to the Court have concerned various aspects of effectiveness of legal remedies. For instance, the provisions of Directives relating to public participation in environmental decision-making provide that legal proceedings must not be prohibitively expensive. The Court has stated that, within the framework of remedies available under those Directives, applicants should not be prevented from seeking a judicial review because of the burden of the costs.[122] The Court also clarified the right of access to courts provided for by a Directive concerning industrial pollution. It held that the national court hearing an action must have been able to adopt any interim measure capable of ensuring the full effectiveness of the forthcoming decision, such as a provisional suspension of a permit to operate a

---

[118] See Fromont 2006.

[119] For a survey of these directives and a presentation of those provisions, see Brosset and Truilhé-Marengo 2018.

[120] On that case law, see ibid.; Delile 2016, p. 91 and Ryall 2019, p. 116.

[121] About the relationship between direct effect and interpretation in conformity with EU law related to Aarhus Convention, see Schmied 2013, para 1061.

[122] Court of Justice, *Edwards and Pallikaropoulos*, Judgement, 11 April 2013, Case No C-260/11, ECLI:EU:C:2013:221, paras 25–35. Those questions were raised by United Kingdom courts, before which there are considerable risks in terms of costs (almost 100.000 GBP on the case Edwards and Pallikaropoulos). Subsequently, the Court found that the United Kingdom had failed to transpose correctly that obligation: Court of Justice, *Commission v United Kingdom*, Judgement, 13 February 2014, Case No C-530/11, ECLI:EU:C:2014:67, paras 44–63. The Court has clarified its jurisprudence in cases involving other Member States: *North East Pylon Pressure Campaign and Sheehy*, Judgement, 15 March 2018, Case No C-470/16, ECLI:EU:C:2018:185.

polluting installation.[123] The case law extended this last requirement beyond cases where a directive provides for procedural rights.[124]

Next, several principles concern the formal conditions for access to the national courts. The Court, *inter alia*, has consolidated the contentious status of NGOs. As a general rule, national courts have to interpret national procedural law in accordance with Article 9(3) of the Aarhus Convention, in order to enable environmental organizations to challenge any administrative decision that may be contrary to EU environmental law.[125] The procedural rights provided for in certain directives strengthen that requirement. Thus, the Court has held that a national rule subjecting the right to take legal action by environmental organizations to the condition that they comprise more than 2000 members was contrary to the Directives relating to public participation in environmental decision-making.[126] Following the case law, the same Directives also precluded that a review of a decision of a judicial body could be subject to the condition that the appellant association took part in the investigation procedure that gave rise to the contested decision.[127]

The Court went as far as holding that certain fundamental rules of national procedural law shall be set aside insofar as they impede the effectiveness of judicial actions. For example, it has found that the legislative ratification of certain administrative measures could not preclude judicial review of these measures' compliance with a Directive, even though national law does not provide for a right of action against a legislative act.[128] Above all, numerous judgments concern domestic rules on administrative disputes of certain Member States, which subject the admissibility of a request to the infringement of a 'subjective right'. Such rules may treat as inadmissible the claims based on procedural requirements, while certain directives relating to environmental protection are mainly intended to lay down procedural rules, e.g. the Environmental Impact Assessment Directive. They may also limit actions brought by associations in order to defend their statutory objective or the interest of their members.[129]

For instance, under German law implementing the Environmental Impact Assessment Directive, the applicants could challenge a decision approving a plan to construct a work on the ground that no environmental impact assessment was carried

---

[123] Court of Justice, *Solvay and Others*, Judgement, 16 February 2012, Case No C-182/10, ECLI:EU:C:2012:82, paras 105–110.

[124] Court of Justice, *ClientEarth*, Judgement, 19 November 2014, Case No C-404/13, ECLI:EU:C:2014:2382, paras 50–58. However, this is not a genuine innovation, since the obligation to take interim measures to safeguard effectiveness of EU law is well-established: Court of Justice, *Factortame*, Judgement, 19 June 1990, Case No C-213/89, ECLI:EU:C:1990:257, para 21.

[125] Court of Justice, *Lesoochranárske zoskupenie*, Judgement, 8 March 2011, above n 21.

[126] Court of Justice, *Djurgården-Lilla Värtans Miljöskyddsförening*, Judgement, 15 October 2009, Case No C-263/08, ECLI:EU:C:2009:631, paras 40–52.

[127] Ibid., paras 32–39.

[128] Court of Justice, *Boxus and Others*, Judgement, 18 October 2011, Cases No C-128/09 to C-131/09, C-134/09 and C-135/09, ECLI:EU:C:2011:667 and *Solvay and Others*, Judgement, 16 February 2012, above n 123.

[129] Fromont 2006, pp. 178–179.

out. However, the applicants could not plead that such an assessment was carried out but was irregular. Also, the burden of proof that the challenged decision would have been different without the procedural defect was falling on the applicant. The Court held that the Directive interpreted in the light of the objective of giving the public concerned wide access to justice precludes such national procedural rules.[130] Other Judgments confirmed that national rules on administrative disputes could not preclude the examination of claims based on infringements of procedural rules enshrined in the Environmental Impact Assessment Directive.[131]

To take another example, under German law, an environmental protection organization was not entitled to challenge a permit for a coal-fired power station on infringement of the law for the protection of water and nature as those provisions do not confer subjective rights on individuals. The Court considered such national rules incompatible with the Environmental Impact Assessment Directive, especially because the environmental protection organizations should have extensive procedural rights to challenge national decisions on impact assessment.[132]

Some decisions have confirmed these principles, regardless of the existence of procedural rights enshrined in secondary legislation. It follows that natural persons and environmental NGOs may bring an action based on a Directive setting out a clear and unconditional obligation, even if the obligation in question does not give rise to a 'subjective right' within the meaning of national law.[133]

In jurisprudence, that case law has been welcomed in so far as it has consolidated access to national courts in environmental matters despite the rather modest principles laid down in this regard in secondary law. At the same time, it strengthened criticisms of the orthodox approach in relation to the admissibility of direct actions, on the ground that the Court imposes requirements on national courts, which it does not itself observe.[134]

---

[130] Court of Justice, *Gemeinde Altrip and Others*, Judgement, 7 November 2013, Case No C-72/12, ECLI:EU:C:2013:712, paras 42–54.

[131] Court of Justice, *Gruber*, Judgement, 16 April 2015, Case No C-570/13, ECLI:EU:C:2015:231, paras 33 ss. Subsequently, Germany was found to have failed to fulfil its obligations to comply with the Impact Assessment Directive: Court of Justice, *Commission v Germany*, Judgement, 15 October 2015, Case No C-137/14, ECLI:EU:C:2015:683.

[132] Court of Justice, *Bund für Umwelt und Naturschutz Deutschland, Landesverband Nordrhein-Westfalen*, Judgement, 12 May 2011, Case No C-115/09, ECLI:EU:C:2011:289, paras 45–49.

[133] Court of Justice, *Janecek*, Judgement, 25 July 2008, Case No C-237/07, ECLI:EU:C:2008:447, paras 34–39; *Protect Natur-, Arten- und Landschaftschutz Umweltorganisation*, Judgement, 20 December 2017, Case No C-664/15, ECLI:EU:C:2017:987, paras 30–58 and *Wasserleitungsverband Nördliches Burgenland and Others*, Judgement, 3 October 2019, Case No C-197/18, ECLI:EU:C:2019:824, paras 30–46.

[134] See Brosset and Truilhé-Marengo 2018 and Delile 2016

8.5 The Problem of the Compliance with the Aarhus Convention

The foregoing considerations highlight the implications of the general scheme of the EU legal remedies in relation to access to justice in environmental matters. Since the rules on admissibility of direct actions are, in general, rather unfavourable to ordinary litigants, the latter is compelled to turn to the preliminary ruling procedure in order to access the EU Courts.

This scheme gave rise to certain difficulties regarding the Aarhus Convention. In particular, it raised the question as to whether the EU was complying with the obligations laid down in Article 9(3) and (4) of the Convention. According to these provisions, 'members of the public have access to … judicial procedures to challenge acts and omissions by … public authorities which contravene provisions of its national law relating to the environment', and second, these procedures 'shall provide adequate and effective remedies … and be fair, equitable, timely and not prohibitively expensive'.

In 2008, the NGO ClientEarth seized the Aarhus Convention Compliance Committee, established under Article 15 of the Convention. In April 2011, the Committee adopted the first part of its conclusions and recommendations.[135] In essence, in light of Article 2(2)(d) of the Convention, it considered that the impossibility of taking action against legislative acts of the EU could not be criticized.[136] However, after examining the abovementioned case law of the Court of Justice of the EU,[137] it found that inadmissibility of actions for annulment brought by individuals or environmental NGOs against all the acts of general application makes the *Plaumann* case law too strict to comply with Article 9(3) and (4). Furthermore, according to the Compliance Committee, the preliminary ruling mechanism could not compensate for procedural obstacles to actions for annulment, since its effectiveness depends on the legal remedies established by the Member States and on the will of the national courts. However, the Committee reserved its definitive findings, due to pending cases relating to the Aarhus Regulation, in particular the *Stichting Milieu* case, and the Lisbon Treaty's introduction of the fourth limb of Article 263(4) TFEU.

---

[135] Findings and recommendations of the Aarhus Convention Compliance committee with regard to communication ACC/C/2008/32 (Part I) concerning compliance by the European Union, adopted on 14 April 2011.

[136] Following Article 2(2)(d) of the Convention, a regional organization do not act as public authorities when it performs in its legislative capacity, with the effect that these forms of decision-making are not covered by Article 9 of the Convention.

[137] See Sect. 8.3.2.2 above.

The Committee delivered the second part of its conclusions in March 2017,[138] after the Court had set the judgment of the General Court in *Stichting Milieu* aside,[139] leaving the Aarhus Regulation unchanged. Taking into account the *Stichting Milieu* case law, the Committee explained that neither the new conditions of admissibility relating to regulatory acts which do not entail implementing measures,[140] nor the Aarhus Regulation, are enough to affect its provisional conclusions and concluded that the EU is not in compliance with Article 9(3) and (4) of the Aarhus Convention. It recommended either that the competent institutions amend the Aarhus Regulation or adopt appropriate secondary legislation, or that the EU Courts interpret EU legislation in accordance with the Convention.

In view of the sixth session of the meeting of the Parties to the Aarhus Convention in Budva in September 2017,[141] a draft decision restating the conclusions of the Committee was submitted to the parties. In light of those developments, the European Commission has made a proposal on the position to be adopted by the EU. According to the Commission, the Committee did not take into account the specific nature of the EU system of judicial review, especially the central role of national courts as ordinary Courts of EU law and the system of preliminary rulings under Article 267 TFEU. In order to protect these specificities and the autonomy of the EU legal order, the Commission concluded that the EU should reject the Committee's findings.[142] The EU Council has taken a different position. On the ground of the separation of powers within the EU, the EU Council explained that it could not issue instructions or recommendations to the Court of Justice of the EU, and considered that recommendations concerning the EU could not therefore refer to that judicial institution. In addition, it proposed that the meeting of the Parties to the Aarhus Convention 'take[s] note of' the conclusions of the Compliance Committee instead of 'endors[ing]' them.[143] The meeting of the parties has postponed its final decision to the next conference, which will take place in 2021.[144]

---

[138] Findings and recommendations of the Aarhus Convention Compliance committee with regard to communication ACC/C/2008/32 (Part II) concerning compliance by the European Union, adopted on 17 March 2017.

[139] See Sect. 8.3.2.3 above.

[140] See Sects. 8.3.2.1 and 8.3.2.2 above.

[141] Draft decision VI/8f in view of the sixth session of the meeting of the Parties to the Aarhus Convention concerning compliance by the European Union with its obligations under the Convention, 30 June 2017.

[142] Proposal for a Council Decision on the position to be adopted, on behalf of the European Union, at the sixth session of the Meeting of the Parties to the Aarhus Convention regarding compliance case ACCC/C/2008/32, COM(2017) 366 final, 29 June 2017.

[143] Decision (EU) No 2017/1346 of the Council on the position to be adopted, on behalf of the European Union, at the sixth session of the Meeting of the Parties to the Aarhus Convention as regards compliance case ACCC/C/2008/32, 17 July 2017, OJEU 2017 L186, p. 15.

[144] Krämer 2019b, pp. 795 ss.

8.6 Conclusions

At this time, it is difficult to know whether, and to what extent, the conditions regulating access to the EU Courts in environmental matters are likely to evolve.

However, in the author's view, the EU Courts are not necessarily in the best position to modify the EU procedural law concerning admissibility. It is true that specific solutions have been adopted by the Court concerning the admissibility of direct actions in the field of EU economic law, especially regarding the review of State aid decisions or the measures of the common commercial policy.[145] However, this case law is not easily transposable to the environmental field, at least not without risking introducing inconsistencies into the conditions of admissibility of direct actions.[146] The same risk of incoherence exists as regards the reconsideration of the direct effect of the Aarhus Convention: it is rather obvious that Article 9(3) is neither clear nor unconditional.[147] In any event, the abandonment of *Plaumann* case law in environmental matters cannot be done without opening a Pandora's box which may have extensive consequences in all fields of EU litigation. It would modify the repartition of judicial powers between the national courts and the EU courts and could involve a significant increase in the number of cases pending before the latter.

If direct access to the EU Court in environmental matters has to be strengthened in the future, *ad hoc* solutions should perhaps be preferred. In that regard, a revision of the Aarhus Regulation seems to be the least costly solution from the point of view of the consistency of the admissibility rules. It would also entrust the political EU institutions with the responsibility of deciding to what extent the European Courts should contribute to the effectiveness of environmental law.

It has to be noted that the European Commission has recently made a proposal amending the Aarhus Regulation in order to address the concerns expressed by the Aarhus Convention Compliance Committee.[148] The proposal contains notably a new

---

[145] Some consider that the case law is more flexible in certain spheres of economic law that in the field of environmental protection. See e.g., Krämer 2019a.

[146] In disputes concerning State aid control or measures of the common commercial policy, the courts take into account, inter alia, the existence of procedural law or of factual circumstances showing that the applicants are individually concerned. About admissibility of actions concerning the review of State aid decisions or measures to protect trade, see e.g., Mariatte and Ritleng 2011, p. 104 ss. One should bear in mind that procedural rights existing in the field of State aid control or common commercial policy instrument does not have real equivalent in the environmental secondary legislation. In any case, procedural rights are not central when it comes to challenging the merits of a decision concerning State aid and, in the field of the common commercial policy, the case law takes account, inter alia, of the fact that undertakings established in third countries do not always have access to a national court capable of referring questions to the Court for a preliminary ruling (see e.g., Court of Justice, *Allied Corporation e.a. v Commission*, Judgement, 21 February 1984, Cases No 239/82 and 275/82, ECLI:EU:C:1984:68, paras 13 and 15).

[147] It is not obvious that the specific solutions developed about direct effect of WTO law could lead to another solution. One has to take into account that the Court tends to apply those principles in a restrictive way: see Schmied 2013, paras 869 ss.

[148] Proposal for a Regulation of the European Parliament and of the Council on amending Regulation (EC) No 1367/2006 of the European Parliament and of the Council of 6 September 2006

definition of 'administrative acts' including acts of general application and covering 'regulatory acts' under the fourth limb of Article 263(4) TFEU. At the same time, it excludes from the review mechanism the provisions of such 'administrative acts' for which EU law explicitly requires implementing measures at national level. This could make clear that, as regards these provisions, it should be possible to seek remedy before the national courts, with access to the CJEU by way of preliminary ruling.

References

Arnull A (1995) Private Applications and the action for annulment under Article 173 of the EC Treaty. Common Market Law Review 32:7–49

Barents R (2020) Remedies and Procedures Before the EU Courts. Kluwer Law International, Alphen aan den Rijn

Bétaille J (ed) (2016) Le droit à l'accès à la justice en matière d'environnement. Presses de l'Université de Toulouse 1 Capitole, Toulouse

Blumann C (1997) Compétence communautaire et compétence nationale. In: Masclet J-C (ed) La Communauté européenne et l'environnement. La Documentation française, Paris, pp 63–105

Brosset E, Truilhé-Marengo E (2018) L'accès au juge dans le domaine de l'environnement : le hiatus du droit de l'Union européenne. Revue des droits et libertés fondamentaux http://www.revuedlf.com/droit-ue/lacces-au-juge-dans-le-domaine-de-lenvironnement-le-hiatus-du-droit-de-lunion-europeenne/

Cartier-Bresson A, Dero-Bugny D (eds) (2020) Les réformes de la Cour de justice de l'Union européenne. Bruylant, Brussels

Clément M (2016) Droit européen de l'environnement. Larcier, Brussels

Coutron L (2014) L'héritage de l'arrêt UPA. L'Actualité juridique. Droit administratif 548–556

de Sadeleer N (2012) Particularités de la subsidiarité dans le domaine de l'environnement. Droit et société 1:73–90

de Sadeleer N, Poncelet C (2013) Contestation des actes des institutions de l'Union européenne à l'épreuve de la Convention d'Aarhus. Revue Trimestrielle de Droit Européen 1:7–34

Delile J-F (2016) La protection juridictionnelle dans le domaine environnemental en droit de l'Union européenne : la victoire de l'incohérence. In: Bétaille J (ed) Le droit d'accès à la justice en matière d'environnement. Presses de l'Université Toulouse 1 Capitole, pp 91–12

Dubout E (2007) Le 'contentieux de la troisième génération' ou l'incomplétude du système juridictionnel communautaire. Revue Trimestrielle de Droit Européen 3:427–443

Fromont M (2006) Droit administratif des États européens. Presses universitaires de France, Paris

Kovar R (1999) L'identification des actes normatifs en droit communautaire. In: Dony M, De Walsche A (eds) Mélanges en hommage à Michel Waelbroeck. Bruylant, Brussels, pp 387–422

Krämer L (2004) Data on Environmental Judgments by the EC Court of Justice. Journal for European Enviromental & Planning Law 1:127–135

Krämer L (2009) The environmental complaint in EU law. Journal for European Environmental & Planning Law 1:13–35

Krämer L (2016) EU Environmental Law. Sweet & Maxwell, London

Krämer L (2017) Accès à la justice en matière d'environnement - La double mesure de la Cour de justice de l'Union européenne. Revue du droit de l'Union européenne 1:13–39

on the application of the provisions of the Aarhus Convention on Access to Information, Public Participation in Decision-making and Access to Justice in Environmental Matters to Community institutions and bodies, 14 October 2020, COM(2020) 642 final.

Krämer L (2019a) Changement climatique, droits fondamentaux et accès à la justice. Revue du droit de l'Union européenne, 2019 1:213–223

Krämer L (2019b) Protection de l'environnement. In: Blumman C, Picod F (eds) Annuaire de droit de l'Union européenne – 2017. Editions Panthéon-Assas, Paris, p 795

Lenaerts K (1993) The Principle of Subsidiarity and the Environment in the European Union: Keeping the Balance of Federalism. Fordham International Law Journal 17:846–895

Lenaerts K (2009) La systémique des voies de recours dans l'ordre juridique de l'Union européenne. In: De Walsche A, Levi L (eds) Mélanges en hommage à Georges Vandersanden. Bruylant, Brussels, pp 257–282

Lenaerts K, Arts D, Maselis I (2014) EU Procedural Law. Oxford University Press, Oxford

Maljean-Dubois S (ed) (2017) The Effectiveness of Environmental Law. Intersentia, Cambridge

Mariatte F, Ritleng D (2011) Contentieux de l'Union européenne/1. Lamy, Rueil-Malmaison

Mastroianni R, Pezza A (2014) Access of individuals to the European Court of Justice of the European Union under the new text of Article 263, para. 4, TFEU. Rivista Italiana di Diritto Pubblico Comunitario, 5:923–948

Naômé C (2016) Le pourvoi devant la Cour de justice de l'Union européenne. Larcier, Brussels

Pallemaerts M (2011) Access to Environmental Justice at EU Level: has the 'Aarhus Regulation' improved the Situation? In: Pallemaerts M (ed) The Aarhus Convention at Ten: Interactions and Tensions between Conventional International Law and EU Environmental Law. Europa Law Publishing, Groningen, pp 271–312

Ryall A (2019) The Aarhus Convention: Standards for Access to Justice in Environmental Matters. In: Turner S et al. (eds) Environmental Rights: The Development of Standards. Cambridge University Press, Cambridge, pp 116–146

Schmied F (2013) Les effets des accords de l'OMC dans l'ordre juridique de l'Union européenne et de ses Etats membres. LGDJ, Paris

Truilhé È, Hautereau-Boutonnet M (2019) Le procès environnemental - Rapport final de recherche. http://www.gip-recherche-justice.fr/publication/le-proces-environnemental-du-proces-sur-lenvironnement-au-proces-pour-lenvironnement/. Accessed 30 April 2021

Wildemeersch J (2014) L'article 263, alinéa 4, du traité FUE : une modification des conditions de recevabilité du recours en annulation sans (véritables) conséquences. In: Mahieu S (ed) Contentieux de l'Union européenne. Questions choisies. Larcier, Brussels, pp 155–190

Wildemeersch J (2019) Contentieux de la légalité des actes de l'Union européenne : le mythe du droit à un recours effectif. Bruylant, Brussels

Olivier Peiffert Associate Professor (Sorbonne Nouvelle University—ICEE), Legal Secretary at the General Court of the EU. All views expressed herein are personal to the author.

Chapter 9
Inter-American Court of Human Rights

Monica Feria-Tinta

Contents

Abstract In a region rich in natural resources, where mining and exploration and exploitation of oil and gas have featured prominently, the Inter-American System of International Protection of Human Rights has acted as a forum for the settlement of environmental disputes via the gateway of human rights claims. It has in this manner contributed, already for decades, to the justiciability of environmental issues using an evolutive and systemic interpretation of the rights under the American Convention on Human Rights. This chapter examines the doctrines, contributions, and procedural tools at the disposal of the Inter-American System (with a particular focus on the Inter-American Court of Human Rights), as a forum resolving

M. Feria-Tinta (✉)
Twenty Essex Chambers, London, England
e-mail: MFeria-Tinta@twentyessex.com

Lauterpacht Centre for International Law, University of Cambridge, Cambridge, England

E. Sobenes et al. (eds.), *The Environment Through the Lens of International Courts and Tribunals*, https://doi.org/10.1007/978-94-6265-507-2_9

disputes involving environmental matters and providing protection for the environment. The chapter identifies the weaknesses and strengths of the system in dealing with environmental cases and the impact its case law is having on the development of international environmental law. This includes examining the ground-breaking ruling by the Inter-American Court of Human Rights, Advisory Opinion 23 on *Environment and Human Rights*, arguably the most significant ruling on environmental issues of any international court to date. It is posited that the Advisory Opinion not only recognises the right to a healthy environment as fundamental to the existence of humanity, but also that it has the potential to unlock real cross-border remedies for victims of environmental degradation, including influencing climate change litigation across the globe. The chapter closes by looking into the emerging jurisprudence after this crucial development, with the first contentious case acknowledging the right to a healthy environment under the American Convention on Human Rights (the *Lhaka Honhat* case).

Keywords Inter-American Court of Human Rights · Inter-American System of Protection of Human Rights · environmental harm · transboundary harm · diagonal human rights claims · right to life in dignity · right to a healthy environment · positive obligations · procedural obligations in environmental cases · due diligence · provisional measures · friendly settlements · climate change litigation · remedies

9.1 Introduction

In a region rich in resources, where mining (such as gold, silver, iron, copper, coal) and exploration and exploitation of oil and gas have featured prominently, the Inter-American System of International Protection of Human Rights (the Inter-American System) has acted as a forum for the settlement of disputes concerning violations of human rights linked to the environment. These disputes have raised inter alia the rights to health, water, clean environment, property, and cultural rights of indigenous communities living in adversely environmentally affected lands.

As noted elsewhere, traditionally, within public international law, environmental law and human rights law evolved as separate fields of law.[1] Whereas the fundamental tenets of human rights law were adopted as early as 1948,[2] the emergence of international environmental law, a younger field, dates back to about 1972.[3] Despite the apparent separation of these two fields of law, for decades, the Inter-American System's jurisprudence has contributed to the justiciability of environmental issues

[1] Feria-Tinta 2021.

[2] Universal Declaration of Human Rights (1948), Proclaimed by the General Assembly, resolution 217 A (III), A/RES/3/217 A, 10 December 1948.

[3] Fitzmaurice et al. 2010, p. 15.

via an evolutive and systemic interpretation of the rights under the American Convention on Human Rights (the American Convention or the Convention).[4] Unlike the European System, however, this jurisprudence did not develop through the gateway of the right to privacy (as in the case law of the European Convention on Human Rights with the seminal case of *Lopez Ostra v Spain* under Article 8 of the European Convention on Human Rights),[5] but through the gateway of the right to life, in its interrelation with other rights under the American Convention. Indeed, early in its jurisprudence, the Inter-American Court of Human Rights (the Inter-American Court) construed the right to life under the Convention with a focus on positive obligations of the State, ultimately developing the doctrine of the *right to a life in dignity*. This has today influenced the understanding of the notion of right to life, universally, as reflected in the workings of the United Nations Human Rights Committee,[6] and will possibly also cross-fertilise the new generation of environmental degradation and climate change cases before the European Court of Human Rights.

This early important body of law in the Inter-American System recently paved the way for a ground-breaking ruling by the Inter-American Court of Human Rights, the Advisory Opinion on *Environment and Human Rights* (Advisory Opinion 23),[7] arguably the most significant ruling on environmental issues of any international court or tribunal to date. Advisory Opinion 23 not only recognises the right to a healthy environment as fundamental to the existence of humanity, but also has the potential to unlock real cross-border remedies for victims of environmental degradation. This chapter examines the contributions of the Inter-American System, with a particular focus on the Inter-American Court of Human Rights as a forum for resolving disputes involving environmental matters and providing protection for the environment. The chapter also identifies the impact of the system's case law so far on the development of international environmental law. It is divided into three sections.

First, in Sect. 9.2, the salient procedural aspects of the system are introduced and early key jurisprudence on environmental issues arising from the Inter-American System's contentious jurisdiction—both before the Inter-American Commission of Human Rights (the Commission, or the Inter-American Commission) and the Inter-American Court prior to the Advisory Opinion 23—is examined. Within this section, important tools for addressing urgent environmental cases are identified, such as the increasing resort to provisional measures in environmental cases in the Inter-American System, particularly before the Inter-American Commission, as well as *friendly settlements* as a mechanism to resolve disputes which demand action that may not benefit from protracted litigation. This section closes with a review of the

[4] American Convention on Human Rights, 22 November 1969, 1144 UNTS 123, entered into force 18 July 1978.

[5] ECtHR, *López Ostra v Spain*, Judgment, 9 December 1994, App No 16798/90.

[6] Feria-Tinta 2021.

[7] IACHR, *The Environment and Human Rights (State Obligations in Relation to the Environment in the Context of the Protection and Guarantee of the Rights to Life and to Personal Integrity—Interpretation and Scope of Articles 4(1) and 5(1) of the American Convention on Human Rights)*, Advisory Opinion OC-23/18, 15 November 2017, IACtHR Ser. A, No 23 (in Spanish, in the original) (Advisory Opinion 23).

failed opportunity of the Inter-American Commission to deal with the first climate change case which arose in the Inter-American System (the *Inuit* case).[8]

Section 9.3 turns to an analysis of the quantum leap that the Inter-American System made with the Inter-American Court of Human Rights Advisory Opinion 23 (and its significance). Section 9.4 looks into the emerging jurisprudence post-Advisory Opinion 23 with the first contentious case acknowledging the right to a healthy environment under the American Convention on Human Rights (the *Lhaka Honhat* case).[9] The conclusion attempts to identify some of the strengths and weaknesses of the system upon the review of the jurisprudence discussed and sums up the impact that the Inter-American System case law is having on the development of international environmental law.

9.2 The Inter-American System: Contentious Jurisdiction

The critical link between human beings' subsistence and the environment was recognised early in the work of the Inter-American Human Rights Commission.[10] This quasi-judicial organ, which is an autonomous organ of the Organisation of American States (OAS), settles disputes concerning environmental protection cases both under the American Convention on Human Rights,[11] as well as in cases where an OAS member is not a party to the American Convention under the American Declaration of the Rights and Duties of Man (the American Declaration).[12]

The Commission has jurisdiction to deal with individual petitions in accordance with Article 23 of its Rules. There is no victim requirement to act as a petitioner before the Commission. The Rules allow for 'any person or group of persons or non-governmental entity legally recognized in one or more of the Member States of the OAS' to submit petitions to the Commission 'on their own behalf or on behalf of

[8] *Sheila Watt-Cloutier et al v United States,* Petition to the Inter-American Commission on Human Rights, 7 December 2005 (the *Inuit* case).

[9] *Indigenous Communities Members of the Lhaka Honhat Association v Argentina*, Judgment, 6 February 2020, IACtHR Ser. C, No 400 (the *Lhaka Honhat* case).

[10] Inter-American Commission on Human Rights, *Indigenous and Tribal People's Rights over their Ancestral Lands and Natural Resources, Norms and Jurisprudence of the Inter-American Human Rights System*, 30 December 2009. OEA/Ser.I/L/V/II. Doc. 56/09. The Commission is composed of seven members elected in their individual capacity by the General Assembly of the OAS. See Inter-American Commission Rules (Approved by the Commission at its 109th special session held from 4 to 8 December 2000 and amended at its 116th regular period of sessions, held from 7 to 25 October 2002), Article 1.3.

[11] It does so via an integrated approach to rights traditionally considered civil and political in nature (e.g. right to life and freedom from torture) and under the scope of Article 19 (rights of the child), Article 21 (right to property), Article 26 (progressive realisation of economic, social and cultural rights).

[12] American Declaration of Rights and Duties of Man, adopted at the Ninth International Conference of American States, Bogota, Colombia, 2 May 1948. This contains economic, social and cultural rights as well as civil and political rights.

third persons, concerning alleged violations of a human right recognized in, as the case may be, the American Declaration of the Rights and Duties of Man' and other applicable instruments of the Inter-American System.[13]

Article 28 of the Commission Rules establishes the requirements for the consideration of petitions. In order to decide on the admissibility of a matter the Commission shall verify whether the remedies of the domestic legal system have been pursued and exhausted in accordance with the generally recognised principles of international law.[14] There are some exceptions to this rule, which include situations in which the domestic legislation of the State concerned does not afford due process of law for protection of the right or rights that have allegedly been violated; the party alleging violation of his or her rights has been denied access to the remedies under domestic law or has been prevented from exhausting them; or, there has been unwarranted delay in rendering a final judgment under the aforementioned remedies.[15] In cases where the petitioner contends that he/she is unable to prove compliance with the exhaustion of domestic remedies rule, it is up to the State concerned to demonstrate to the Commission that the remedies under domestic law have not been previously exhausted, unless that is clearly evident from the record.[16] In those cases, in which the exceptions to the requirement of prior exhaustion of domestic remedies are applicable, the petition is to be presented within a reasonable period of time.[17] In cases in which the exhaustion of domestic remedies rule applies, petitions must be lodged within a period of six months following the date on which the alleged victim has been notified of the decision that exhausted the domestic remedies.[18] In addition, Article 33 of the Commission's Rules provides that the Commission shall not consider a petition if its subject matter is pending settlement before another international governmental organisation in which the State concerned is a member, or essentially duplicates a petition pending or already examined and settled by the Commission or by another international governmental organization of which the State concerned is a member.[19] Other grounds for the inadmissibility of a petition are if the petition does not state facts that tend to establish a violation of rights or if a petition is 'manifestly groundless'.[20]

The proceedings before the Commission are generally divided into an admissibility stage and a merits stage. As will be discussed below, Article 25 of its Rules also gives the Commission power to issue provisional measures in serious and urgent

---

[13] Inter-American Commission on Human Rights, Res. 1/2013, 18 March 2013, Reform of the Rules of Procedure, Policies and Practices, at 4–17, reprinted in Inter-American Commission on Human Rights, Rules of Procedure of the Inter-American Commission on Human Rights, http://www.oas.org/en/iachr/mandate/Basics/RulesIACHR2013.pdf Accessed 25 June 2015. Rules of the Inter-American Commission, Article 23.

[14] Article 31.1, Rules of the Inter-American Commission, above n 13.

[15] Ibid., Article 31.2 a-c.

[16] Ibid., Article 31.3.

[17] Ibid., Article 32.2.

[18] Ibid., Article 32.1.

[19] Ibid., Article 33.2 a and b.

[20] Ibid., Article 34.

cases, on its own initiative or at the request of a party. Such powers have been used not only in cases brought before the Commission under Article 28 of its Rules, but more generally in serious and urgent cases that are yet not a matter before the Commission, so as to prevent irreparable harm to persons in cases involving OAS member States.

In cases where a petition under Article 28 of the Commission's Rules is lodged in relation to a State member of the OAS which is not party to the American Convention, the Commission's examination of the merits of the case is completed with the issuing of a report under Article 43 of its Rules. The report of the Commission contains recommendations. While the recommendations of the Commission are not strictly speaking legally binding, they are nevertheless authoritative findings with which State members of the OAS should comply in good faith.

In cases in which the petition under Article 28 of the Commission's rules was lodged in relation to a State member of the OAS which is party to the American Convention, individual complaints can potentially be referred to the Inter-American Court if violations are found. In such cases the report issued by the Commission is known as an 'Article 50 report' (issued in accordance with Article 50 of the American Convention on Human Rights). Initially, this is a confidential report (the petitioner does not get a full copy of the report), and the State is given two months to comply with the recommendations of the report. If the State does not comply with the recommendations and it has accepted the jurisdiction of the Inter-American Court in accordance with Article 62 of the American Convention, the Commission 'shall refer' the case to the Inter-American Court 'unless there is a reasoned decision by an absolute majority of the members of the Commission to the contrary'.[21] The Commission gives fundamental consideration to obtaining justice in a given case, based among others, on the nature or seriousness of the violation, the position of the petitioner, the quality of the evidence available, and the need to develop or clarify the case law of the system.[22]

When a case reaches such a stage of the proceedings, it is possible for the victims to participate in the proceedings directly and independently from the Commission (alleged victims have *locus standi* before the Court)—a development that has taken place with recent reforms of the Court's Rules in 2001.[23] Note in that sense that there is a victim-requirement for participation in proceedings before the Inter-American Court. Only alleged victims identified in the case filed by the Commission can appoint a legal representative to participate in the proceedings. Petitioners that are non-victims (e.g. Non- Governmental Organisations) have no procedural standing before the Court unless they are appointed representatives. The notion of 'petitioner' no

---

[21] Ibid., Article 44.1.

[22] Ibid., Article 44.2.

[23] The Court adopted such Rules of Procedure in November 2000 and these came into force on 1 June 2001. See Feria-Tinta 2006, pp. 159–203. Those Rules have been further improved in the current Rules of Procedure of 2009.

longer applies before the Court. The alleged injured party is known as the 'alleged victim'.[24]

The victim has a central position in the law of international protection of human rights.[25] The declaration of victims in the Inter-American System is therefore considered 'fundamental evidence'.[26] The interpretation of the applicable law also follows a victim-centred approach to make rights under the American System have an '*effet utile*'. The Court has held in that sense that the effective protection of human rights constitutes the object and purpose of the American Convention, so when interpreting it the Court shall do so 'in such a way that the system for the protection of human rights has all its appropriate effects' (*effet utile*).[27]

The approach to evidence in the system follows an inquisitorial approach in essence:[28] it is not based solely on the Parties' adversarial role, although parties actively contribute with the evidence in the proceedings. The Court has developed its own Rules for the participation of the parties in the proceedings. Documentary evidence (documents, videos, photographs), witness evidence and expert evidence are admissible and there are strict time limits for the offering of such evidence.[29] Parties also have the opportunity to cross-examine witnesses and to test the evidence.

The system does not have a formalistic approach to evidence but that is not the same as saying it is 'informal'.[30] Evidence that has been produced in *contradictorio* has more weight than documentary evidence the content of which a party may not have had the opportunity to contest. Similarly, witness evidence that has been subject to cross-examination by the other party has more weight than the evidence of declarants that have produced a written statement only. The Inter-American Court evaluates evidence according to the system of *sana crítica* or 'sound judicial discretion' which as aptly noted, 'resembles the way in which common law

[24] Rules of Procedure of the Inter-American Court of Human Rights, 24 November 2009, Article 2(25).

[25] See *Villagrán Morales y Otros vs Guatemala*, Reparations, Judgment, 26 May 2001, IACtHR Ser. C, No 77, Separate Opinion by Judge A. Cançado Trindade, para 15.

[26] *Fernández Ortega and Others v Mexico*, Judgment, 30 August 2010, IACtHR Ser. C, No 215, para 100; Rosendo *Cantú and Others v Mexico*, Judgment, 31 August 2010, IACtHR Ser. C, No 216, para 89.

[27] *The Right to Information on Consular Assistance. In the Framework of the Guarantees of the due Process of Law*, Advisory Opinion OC-16/99, 1 October 1999, IACtHR Ser. A, No 16, para 58.

[28] The organs adjudicating rights under the Inter-American Instruments have the key role to ensure compliance of the State parties with said instruments. Article 58 of the Court's Rules establishes that the Court may at any stage of the proceedings obtain, on its own motion, any evidence it considered helpful and necessary. In particular, it may hear any person whose statement, testimony, or opinion it deems to be relevant including alleged victims, witnesses, and expert witnesses. Therefore, the Court may seek certain pieces of evidence from the parties and it has the power to appoint expert witness not offered by the parties. In *El Amparo v Venezuela*, the Court resorted *propio motu* to an actuarial expert for the calculation of reparations in the case (*El Amparo v Venezuela*, Reparations and Costs, Judgment, 14 September 1996, IACtHR Ser. C, No 28, paras 12 and 28).

[29] On the procedural intricacies of Declarants' evidence see Feria-Tinta forthcoming.

[30] As wrongly noted by Álvaro Paúl 2018, para 4.

judges weigh evidence'.[31] The Court has also developed a system of burden of proof and presumptions through its *jurisprudencia constante.*

An important feature of the Inter-American System is that both the Commission and the Court have consistently held that developments in the corpus of international human rights law relevant to interpreting and applying the American Declaration and the American Convention may be drawn from the provisions of other prevailing international and regional human rights instruments. This includes other Inter-American regional instruments, such as the Additional Protocol to the American Convention on Human Rights in the Area of Economic, Social and Cultural Rights (Protocol of San Salvador).

Increasingly, the justiciability of environmental issues both under the American Declaration and the American Convention is coming under the contentious jurisdiction of the Inter-American organs.[32] A fundamental development in this regard has been, as will be seen below, the acknowledgement of the right to a healthy environment in the Americas. As will be seen in the cases discussed, the Inter-American Commission has been effective in bringing cases of this nature before the Inter-American Court and obtaining reparation for victims, including compensation, measures of satisfaction and guarantees of non-repetition that have made States implement polices to bring their practices into conformity with the American Convention on Human Rights and the American Declaration.

Whilst a contentious climate change case as such has not been brought before the system after the early failed attempt made by the *Inuits* (which is examined below),[33] the Commission has dealt with the topic of climate change as a thematic issue since. It is clear that the jurisprudence of the system has matured to a point where such contentious cases would not only be justiciable but, if framed correctly, successful, adjudicated with the benefit of the jurisprudential developments the system has seen in recent years.

9.2.1 Inter-American Commission on Human Rights

Individual petitions alleging mass violations of economic, social and cultural rights (with related environmental issues at stake) have featured on the docket of the Inter-American Commission for over 20 years. In a region rich in resources, where mining (such as gold), mega energy projects, and exploitation of oil and gas are increasing, the Commission has acted as a forum for the settlement of disputes concerning violations of the right to health, to water, to a clean environment, to property and to cultural rights of indigenous communities living in the affected lands.

The early jurisprudence on environmental issues arising from the Inter-American System's contentious jurisdiction is illuminating for many reasons. The case law

[31] Ibid., para 9.

[32] See Feria-Tinta 2007, pp. 431–459. See also Feria-Tinta 2009, pp. 319–330.

[33] See *Sheila Watt-Cloutier et al v United States*, above n 8.

reviewed in this first section attests to the fact that often it is not that environmental rights are not protected in domestic fora, but rather that States fail to enforce judgments issued by their own domestic courts as *Mapuche Paynemil and Kaxipayiñ Communities v Argentina*[34] instructively shows. International fora act in that sense, as a corrective mechanism to ensure the right to effective judicial protection and access to justice for the realisation of environmental protection in domestic systems. Second, contrary to what is commonly assumed, environmental protection (via the realisation of civil and political rights) is to a great extent often violated by failure to comply with a negative obligation (not to interfere with the enjoyment of a right) rather than by failure to act as a provider of the right. The case of *Maya Indigenous Communities of the Toledo District v Belize*,[35] involving violations threatening the survival of entire communities in Latin America, paradigmatically illustrates this point. Third, the cases reviewed in this section also show that States are increasingly found responsible for failure to ensure the protection of the environment *vis a vis* the action of non-state actors such as corporations causing environmental harm and threatening the lives of indigenous and local communities. Fourth, the cases reviewed herein attest to a common approach taken by different regional organs in relation to the indivisible, interrelated and interdependent nature of rights. As will be seen in this section, such an approach has given rise to a doctrine within the Inter-American system, in relation to the right to life, as entailing, 'the right to a dignified and decent existence' (which encompasses basic economic, social and cultural rights). This is similar to the doctrine of 'implied' rights present in the assessment of cases by the African Commission (e.g. holding that the right to food is implicitly guaranteed in the African Charter in such provisions as the right to life, the right to health and the right to economic, social and cultural development).

9.2.1.1 Early Key Jurisprudence on Environmental Issues

The Case of Community of San Mateo de Huanchor and its Members v Peru

The responsibility of a State for the actions of a non-State actor as a result of toxic waste produced by mining activities affecting an entire community was at the centre of a dispute in the *Community of San Mateo de Huanchor and its Members v Peru* case.[36] The petitioners alleged that the State of Peru had violated the fundamental rights of this community, 'because of the effects being suffered by [its] members […] from the environmental pollution caused by a field of toxic waste sludge in the place called Mayoc, belonging to the Lizandor Proaño S.A. mining company and which

34 Inter-American Commission on Human Rights, Case 12.010, *Mapuche Paynemil and Kaxipayiñ Communities*, 5 February 2013.

35 Inter-American Commission on Human Rights, Report No 40/04 Case 12.053, Merits, *Maya Indigenous Communities of the Toledo District*, Belize, 12 October 2004.

36 Inter-American Commission on Human Rights, Report No 69/04, Petitions 504/03, Admissibility, *Community of San Mateo de Huanchor and its members*, Peru, 15 October 2004.

ha[d] not been removed, although there [was] an administrative order requiring its removal'.[37]

The petitioners further alleged that the mining activities of the said company in an urban area were illegal as they infringed legal provisions for the mining sector.[38] Upon denunciations, the mining activity was brought to a halt by a Ministerial Resolution. Yet nothing had been done about the pollution caused which had allegedly created 'a public crisis in the population of San Mateo de Huanchor'.[39]

The petitioners argued that those most severely affected were the children who showed 'high indices of lead, arsenic, and mercury in their organism, which if not treated will have severe consequences for their integral development because the effects of exposure to the sludge over time are prolonged and heightened when no adequate treatment is given.'[40] It was further argued that the farming activities of the inhabitants had been affected 'by the high content of pollutants, especially lead, cadmium, arsenic and mercury, found in the vegetation of the zone, as a result of the pollution of the land they farm and the water of the Rímac River'.[41] As recorded by the Commission this town had a population of 5,600 people and most of them identified themselves as indigenous.[42] The Commission admitted the case holding that if proven, all these facts could be characterised as 'a violation of the right to personal security, right to property, rights of the child, right to fair trial and judicial protection and the progressive development of economic, social, and cultural rights enshrined in Articles 4, 5, 8, 17, 19, 21, 25, and 26 of the American Convention, related to Articles 1(1) and 2 of the same instrument.'[43] The Commission further provided for a number of precautionary measures for the immediate protection of the affected population whilst the case remained for adjudication on its merits.[44]

Often, it is not that economic, social and cultural rights are not protected in domestic fora but rather, as in the *Community of San Mateo de Huanchor* case, that States do not enforce their own legal provisions for environmental protection domestically or orders issued by domestic courts to that effect.

Indeed, as noticed by the Inter-American Commission itself, in recent years, the case law of the Inter-American System of protection of Human Rights 'has tended

---

[37] Ibid., para 14.

[38] Ibid., para 14.

[39] Ibid., para 26.

[40] Ibid.

[41] Ibid.

[42] Ibid., paras 15 and 16.

[43] Ibid.

[44] According to public sources, the Inter-American Commission is 'still deliberating the merits of the case'. See https://www.ciel.org/project-update/san-mateo-de-huanchor/. Accessed 19 February 2020.

to confirm the enforceability of the right to effective judicial protection in the area of social rights in their individual dimension'.[45]

The Case of Mapuche Paynemil and Kaxipayiñ Communities v Argentina
The case of *Mapuche Paynemil and Kaxipayiñ Communities v Argentina*[46] is another example of a case where there was a failure to enforce a domestic judicial order. Although the right to health, the right to water and the right to a clean environment are central to the claim, the complaint brought against Argentina before the Inter-American System was in fact for failure of the said State to comply with a decision of its own national Courts. The case before the domestic system had been brought under the scope of the rights of the child.

An *Amparo* action (a constitutional course of action) was filed on 24 March 1997 in an Argentine court in order to protect the health of the children and youth of Mapuche communities in Neuquen (Patagonia), exposed to the consumption of water contaminated with lead and mercury. A domestic judicial decision ordering the provincial government to provide an emergency supply of water within two days and a permanent supply of water through any possible means within 45 days was issued on 11 April 1997.[47] The national court also ordered the provincial government to conduct studies to ascertain the level of harm in the population caused by heavy metal contamination and, if harm was found, to provide necessary treatment as well as to take all necessary measures to prevent environmental damage.[48] The contamination of the lands and water resources of the Mapuche population who had traditionally lived in this area, had come about as a result of negligence and bad practices in the hydrocarbon exploitation activities of a transnational company, YPF S.A. and Repsol S.A.. Allegedly, in the mid-1970s, part of the land of the Mapuche indigenous populations had been invaded by oilfield developers, to build an oilfield and a gas-site in Loma de la Lata.[49]

However, the judicial order issued by the domestic Argentine court was not complied with. This gave rise to the filing of a case before the Inter-American Commission, so as to ensure compliance. The case was essentially one of denial of 'access to justice' for the Mapuche indigenous communities.

The right to effective judicial protection is enshrined in Article 25(c) of the American Convention and entails a duty on the part of State parties to 'ensure that the

---

[45] See Inter-American Commission on Human Rights, 'Access to justice as a Guarantee of Economic, Social and Cultural Rights. A review of the Standards Adopted by the Inter-American System of Human Rights' OEA/Ser.L/V/II.129 Doc. 4, 7 September 2007. Original: Spanish.

[46] Inter-American Commission on Human Rights, *Mapuche Paynemil and Kaxipayiñ Communities*, above n 34.

[47] For a copy of the Amparo action, see: http://www.escr-net.org/caselaw/caselaw_show.htm?doc_id=405963. Accessed 19 February 2020.

[48] Falaschi and Nara 2013, p. 2.

[49] Ibid.

competent authority enforces such remedies when granted.'[50] Additional substantive rights that were raised in the claim before the Commission included the right to property and the rights of the child.

In the framework of a hearing before the Inter-American Commission, the State of Argentina undertook to provide medical attention for the young population that had been exposed to the effects of the contamination. The State also agreed that a water treatment plant under construction would be monitored by both Mapuche communities. In the meantime, provision of water in containers (250 litres of water daily to each inhabitant of the community) was to be made available to the population.[51] The acceptance of these communities' right to water by the State concerned was an important precedent in the system regarding the 'right to water'.

The State also agreed to disclose information it held about the Loma de la Lata oilfield. In particular, about the location of abandoned wells, oxidation pools and piping. However, the State mostly failed to implement these undertakings.[52] As noted by a commentator, to date, more than 20 years after the conflict started, the provincial government only provides 120 litres of water to each family per week.[53]

It is uncertain what the situation of the case before the Inter-American Commission is. No report by the Commission has been made public. Proceedings before the Commission are a 'prolonged process'[54] and can easily last over a decade. The Mapuche communities' fight in this case nevertheless may reach the Inter-American Court, thereby creating an important precedent against harmful exploitation practices of transnational entities in the region, giving rise to State responsibility for failure to ensure respect for the fundamental rights of populations affected by these actions.

The Case of the Maya Indigenous Communities of the Toledo District

The Commission examined a claim raising environmental issues against the State of Belize, having as its focus the right to property, under Article XXIII of the American Declaration of the Rights and Duties of Man.[55]

The case of the *Maya Indigenous Communities of the Toledo District*[56] concerned a petition which alleged that Belize had violated the rights of the Maya people by awarding logging and oil concessions on Maya lands without meaningful consultations with them. The concessions had allegedly resulted in substantial environmental harm and irreversible damage to the natural environment upon which the Maya depended.

---

[50] Inter-American Commission on Human Rights, Report No 110/00, case 11.800, *Cesar Cabrejos Bernuy v Peru*, 4 December, 2000, paras 45–47.

[51] Inter-American Commission on Human Rights, *Mapuche Paynemil and Kaxipayiñ Communities*, above n 34.

[52] Ibid.

[53] Maraggi 2017, p. 55.

[54] Shelton 2015, p. 9.

[55] Article XXIII of the American Declaration provides: 'Every person has a right to own such private property as meets the essential needs of decent living and helps to maintain the dignity of the individual and of the home.'

[56] See above n 35.

In its examination of the case, the Commission noted that 'the logging concessions granted by the State cover[ed] areas of land that include[ed] critical parts of the natural environment upon which the Maya people depend[ed] for subsistence, including vulnerable soils, primary forest growth and important watersheds.'[57]

According to the plaintiffs, 'the logging activity undertaken pursuant to the concessions ha[d] affected essential water supplies, disrupted plant and animal life, and, as a consequence, ha[d] affected Maya hunting, fishing, and gathering practices essential to the Maya cultural and physical survival.'[58] In support of these allegations, reports by experts familiar with the environmental status of lands in the Toledo District were provided, as well as affidavits from members of the Maya people themselves concerning the effects of the logging activities on their communities, were submitted.

Citing jurisprudence of the African Commission concerning the impact of resource development activities on an indigenous community in Nigeria,[59] the Inter-American Commission acknowledged the importance of economic development for the prosperity of the populations of the American hemisphere. The Commission, however, emphasised the balance a State needed to strike between the potential benefits brought by multinational corporations in their jurisdictions, and the common good and rights of individuals and local communities. The Commission held:

> [...] development activities must be accompanied by appropriate and effective measures to ensure that they do not proceed at the expense of the fundamental rights of persons who may be particularly and negatively affected, including indigenous communities and the environment upon which they depend for their physical, cultural and spiritual well-being.[60]

The Commission concluded that Belize had violated the right to property in the present case in at least two ways. In the first instance, it had violated such a right 'by failing to take effective measures to recognize the communal property right to the lands that [the Mayas] have traditionally occupied and used and to delimit, demarcate and title or otherwise establish the legal mechanisms necessary to clarify and protect the territory on which their right exists'.[61] Second, Belize had violated that right by granting logging and oil concessions to third parties (the corporation) to utilise the property and resources without effective consultation and the informed consent of the Maya people, with resulting environmental damage.[62]

The Inter-American organs take a broad approach to identifying affected rights, emphasising the interdependence, interrelatedness of rights, and draw on a range of sources to support those rights. In this case, the Commission held that several other rights under international law were also violated by Belize. These included the right to life, the right to religious freedom and worship, the right to a family and

---

[57] Ibid., para 145.

[58] Ibid.

[59] ACHPR, *Social and Economic Rights Action Centre (SERAC) and the Centre for Economic and Social Rights (CESR) v Nigeria*, October 2001, No 155/96.

[60] *Maya Indigenous Communities of the Toledo District*, above n 35, para 150.

[61] Ibid., para 152.

[62] Ibid., para 153.

to protection thereof, and the right to preservation of health and well-being under the American Declaration. Also, the 'right to consultation' implicit in Article 27 of the ICCPR, Article XX of the American Declaration, and the principle of self-determination.[63] Particular importance was given to 'the distinct nature of the right of property as it applies to indigenous people', 'whereby the land traditionally used and occupied by these communities plays a central role in their physical, cultural and spiritual vitality'.[64] It was stressed that for indigenous people, the free exercise of the right to property and the right to equality is essential to the enjoyment and perpetuation of their culture.

The Commission further held that the concept of family and religion within the context of indigenous communities 'is intimately connected with their traditional land, where ancestral burial grounds, places of religious significance and kinship patterns are linked with the occupation and use of their physical territories'.[65]

Finally, the Commission specifically referred to the 'the duty to consult' as a 'fundamental component' of the State's obligations in giving effect to the communal property rights of indigenous peoples in the lands that they have traditionally used and occupied.[66]

The Commission recommended that the State of Belize (a) adopt in its domestic law (and through fully informed consultations with the Maya people) legislative, administrative, and any other measures necessary to delimit, demarcate and title or otherwise clarify and protect the territory in which the Maya people have a communal property right, in accordance with their customary land use practices, and without detriment to other indigenous communities; (b) implement such measures and 'until those measures have been carried out, abstain from any acts that might lead the agents of the State itself, or third parties acting with its acquiescence or its tolerance, to affect the existence, value, use or enjoyment of the property located in the geographic area occupied and used by the Maya people' and (c) repair the environmental damage resulting from the logging concessions granted by the State in respect of the territory traditionally occupied and used by the Maya people.[67]

The Kichwa Peoples of the Sarayaku Community and Its Members v Ecuador

Another claim concerning environmental degradation and indigenous peoples was brought against Ecuador, *The Kichwa Peoples of the Sarayaku Community and its members*,[68] under the American Convention for failing to ensure the protection of indigenous peoples (including children) against the activity of an oil company in their ancestral lands, before the contentious jurisdiction of the Commission.

---

[63] Ibid., para 154.

[64] Ibid., para 155.

[65] Ibid.

[66] Ibid.

[67] Ibid., para 197.

[68] Inter-American Commission on Human Rights, *The Kichwa Peoples of the Sarayaku Community and its members*, Admissibility, Report No 64/04, 13 October 2004, Case 12.465.

The case, filed before the Commission in December 2003, denounced Ecuador for allowing an oil company to carry out activities without the consent of the Sarayaku community, for persecuting community leaders, and for the denial of judicial protection and legal due process to the detriment of the Sarayaku community.[69] As in the case of *San Mateo de Huanchor*, here as well, the Commission granted interim measures of protection.

The case was eventually referred by the Commission to the Inter-American Court. As Ecuador argued in the case before the Court, starting in the 1960s, Ecuador had increased oil exploration activities, focusing its interest in the country's Amazonian region.[70] In 1969, the first reserves of crude oil were discovered in the north-eastern region, and three years later exports began and the region 'became very important from a geopolitical and economic perspective, changing from a 'myth' into a national strategic area.'[71] According to the parties, 'during the 1970s, Ecuador experienced rapid economic growth, a significant surge in exports, and a strong process of modernization of the infrastructure of its main cities'.[72] Yet this 'bonanza' came at a high price for indigenous peoples and their ancestral lands.

The Commission stated that this was a case in which the State had granted a permit to a private oil company to carry out oil exploration and exploitation activities in the territory of the Kichwa Indigenous People of Sarayaku in the 1990s, without previously consulting them and without obtaining their consent. The company had begun the exploration phase, and even introduced high-powered explosives in several places on indigenous territory, thereby creating an alleged situation of risk for the population.[73] For a time, because of that, the Kichwa People had been prevented from seeking means of subsistence and limited their rights to freedom of movement and to cultural expression.

The Court issued a judgment in the case in 2012.[74] The Court found that Ecuador had violated the rights to consultation, to indigenous communal property, and to cultural identity, in the terms of Article 21 of the American Convention, in relation to Articles 1(1) and 2 thereof, to the detriment of the Kichwa Indigenous People of Sarayaku. It also found Ecuador *inter alia* responsible for severely jeopardizing

---

[69] Ibid., para 2. The Petition claimed that Ecuador is consequently responsible for violating the right to property (Article 21), judicial protection (Article 25), due process (Article 8), freedom of movement (Article 22), personal integrity (Article 5), personal liberty and security (Article 7), life (Article 4), freedom of association (Article 16), political participation (Article 23), freedom of expression (Article 13), juridical personality (Article 3), freedom of conscience and religion (Article 12), the rights of the child (Article 19), equality (Article 24), health and culture (Article 26, in accordance with Articles XI and XIII of the American Declaration of the Rights and Duties of Man) under the American Convention on Human Rights, to the detriment of the Sarayaku community. See Organization of American States (OAS), American Convention on Human Rights, 'Pact of San Jose', Costa Rica, 22 November 1969, ('American Convention').

[70] *Kichwa Indigenous People of Sarayaku v Ecuador, Merits and Reparation, Judgment, 27 June 2012,* IACtHR Ser. C, No 245, para 58.

[71] Ibid.

[72] Ibid.

[73] Ibid., para 2.

[74] Ibid.

the rights to life and to personal integrity, recognized in Articles 4(1) and 5(1) of the American Convention, in relation to the obligation to guarantee the right to communal property. Among the measures the Court ordered Ecuador to implement were to 'neutralize, deactivate and, if applicable, remove all pentolite left on the surface and buried in the territory of the Sarayaku People', based on a consultation process with the People, within the time frames and in accordance with the ways and means described in the judgment. It also ordered the State to consult the Sarayaku People in a prior, adequate and effective manner, and in full compliance with the relevant international standards applicable, 'in the event that it seeks to carry out any activity or project for the extraction of natural resources on its territory, or any investment or development plan of any other type that could involve a potential impact on their territory'.[75]

Sheila Watt-Cloutier et al v United States

In contrast to the increasing number of cases addressing environmental issues seized by the Inter-American Commission, the first climate change case ever to reach an international human rights organ, was simply dismissed. This was the case of *Sheila Watt-Cloutier et al v United States*.[76] The petition, filed against the US before the Inter-American Commission in 2005, concerned the effects that global warming was having on the Arctic, which was affecting the way of life and the fundamental rights of the Inuit indigenous peoples. Boldly, it was brought on behalf of all Inuit of the Arctic regions of the US and Canada, a large number of whom had been individualised for the purposes of filing the claim.

The claim provided a full analysis of the alleged violations and described the manner in which global warming and climate change was harming Inuit life and culture. It described that for the Inuit, 'ice is a supporter of life. It brings the sea animals from the north (…) and in the fall it also becomes an extension of Inuit land.'[77]

Highlighting first the extent to which the life and culture of the Inuit was completely dependent on the Arctic environment, the claim argued that 'nowhere on Earth has global warming had a more severe impact than the Arctic.'[78] It was alleged that global warming had already visibly transformed the Arctic, 'altering land conditions',[79] making the weather of the Arctic 'increasingly unpredictable' (with Inuit elders, who have long experience in reading the weather, reporting various changes

---

[75] Ibid., p. 92.

[76] Inter-American Commission on Human Rights, *Sheila Watt-Cloutier et al v United States*, decision, 16 November 2006, Petition 1413/05. See 'Petition Seeking Relief from Violations resulting from Global Warming caused by Acts and Omissions of the United States' . See http://climatecasechart.com/climate-change-litigation/non-us-case/petition-to-the-inter-american-commission-on-human-rights-seeking-relief-from-violations-resulting-from-global-warming-caused-by-acts-and-omissions-of-the-united-states/ Accessed 23 March 2022.

[77] Ibid., p. 39.

[78] Ibid., p. 1.

[79] Ibid., p. 37.

in weather patterns in different areas of the Arctic),[80] 'decreas[ing] water levels in lakes and rivers', and producing 'changes in the location, characteristics and health of plant and animal species'.[81] Moreover, the claim argued that natural drinking water sources had become scarcer and less drinkable, harming Inuit health. This, it was argued, was the result of the combined effect of the decrease in snowfall, permafrost melt, the sudden early melt, erosion, rising temperatures, and changing winds.[82]

The claim further submitted that the 'deteriorating ice conditions have made travel, harvest, and everyday life more dangerous for the Inuit because the location of unsafe ice was harder to predict'.[83] It also argued that '[s]ome previously navigable rivers are now impossible to use for transportation'.[84] Disappearing sea ice, combined with changes in prevailing winds and currents, on the other hand, had wreaked havoc with travel and harvest.[85]

The complaint depicted the Inuit world, the natural world that sustained them as peoples and gave them their cultural identity, being destroyed. The complaint was detailed and supported by scientific data.

It was argued that loss of both permafrost and sea ice had contributed to increasingly devastating coastal erosion which had led to a 'cataclysmic impact on the Inuit',[86] given that most Inuit live, hunt and travel near the coast. The claim argued that Inuit homes and communities were further threatened because of the increased storm surges resulting from the loss of the ice's wave-suppressing effects.[87] Changes in ice and snow had also affected animals on which the Inuit relied, damaging their subsistence, harvest, safety and health. The claim noted that 'ice dependent species such as seals, walrus, polar bears, and sea birds are already suffering population decreases as a result of the disappearing ice.'[88]

The petition also argued that changing species distribution had harmed the nutrition, health and subsistence harvest of the Inuit.[89] In other words, food sovereignty of the Inuit had been adversely affected. For example, the gathering seasons were getting shorter for picking berries, an important component of the Inuit diet. Harvesting of greens had also been affected by climate changes. Important protein sources were also changing location and were of lower quality in some areas.[90] Caribou, moose and various species of waterfowl were likely to undergo shifts in range and abundance.[91] Different species of fish were also moving northward, jeopardizing native

---

[80] Ibid.

[81] Ibid.

[82] Ibid., p. 61.

[83] Ibid., p. 39.

[84] Ibid., p. 65.

[85] Ibid.

[86] Ibid., p. 51.

[87] Ibid.

[88] Ibid., p. 45.

[89] Ibid., p. 54.

[90] Ibid.

[91] Ibid., p. 55.

fish stocks.[92] It was stressed that the Inuit had already noticed a deterioration in their health because of a lack of country food.[93] The shift from traditional diet has created diseases such as diabetes and cardiovascular diseases amongst them.[94]

Lastly, it was argued that the deteriorating ice and snow conditions have also undermined the traditional Inuit way of life.[95] Travelling and harvesting, two critical components of Inuit culture, have been damaged as a result of climate change. The inability to forecast the weather has also diminished the important role of elders in planning hunting, travel and day-to-day preparation for bad weather.[96] Further, because of the deterioration of the snow, the art of building igloos could not easily be passed on to the next generation, resulting in a loss of traditional knowledge about a truly unique feature of Inuit culture.[97] In short, it was argued that the changes described above were 'seriously threatening the Inuit's continued survival as a distinct and unique society.'[98]

The central Inuit argument was that by its acts and omissions the US, which the claim identified as the largest contributor to global warming which had damaging effects on the Inuit, bore State responsibility for the above impacts. The claim argued:

> Among nations, the United States has long been the world's greatest consumer of energy, and hence of fossil fuels [...] throughout the industrial era the United States has had the highest CO_2 emission of any nation.[99]

The claim noted that the US continued to be the world's largest emitter of energy-related CO_2, and that climate change caused by the US government's regulatory actions and inactions (e.g. misleading and ineffective targets, no mandatory controls, no reduction of greenhouse gas emissions, misleading and obscuring climate science, failure to cooperate with efforts to reduce greenhouse gas emissions) were therefore causing Arctic ice to disappear, which was the ancestral land of the Inuit, threatening their survival and violating their rights under the American Declaration. In particular, the right to culture, right to enjoy the lands they have traditionally used and occupied, right to use and enjoy their personal property, right to the preservation of health, right to life, physical integrity and security, right to their own means of subsistence, right to residence and movement, and inviolability of home.

The case was dismissed even before consideration of its admissibility. The Commission decided simply not to process it on the grounds that 'the information it contains does not satisfy the requirements set forth in [the Commission's] Rules'.[100] The letter merely noted that 'the information provided does not enable

---

[92] Ibid., p. 67.
[93] Ibid., p. 55.
[94] Ibid., pp. 62–63.
[95] Ibid., p. 48.
[96] Ibid., p. 58.
[97] Ibid., p. 49.
[98] Ibid., p. 67.
[99] Ibid., p. 68.
[100] Inter-American Commission on Human Rights, Letter dated 16 November 2006. https://graphics8.nytimes.com/packages/pdf/science/16commissionletter.pdf. Accessed 10 March 2020.

us to determine whether the alleged facts would tend to characterize a violation of rights protected by the American Declaration'. This despite the fact that the claim had provided over 150 pages of detailed analysis of the violations under the American Declaration.

The dismissal of the Inuit case was a missed opportunity for the Inter-American System to consider the link between climate change and human rights many years prior to climate change litigation becoming an established strategic legal tool. Nevertheless, the case marked a turning point, namely the recognition of the need to address existential threats such as climate change, as a human rights issue within the Inter-American System, something the Commission started doing by engaging with climate change as a thematic issue in its work.[101] Such engagement has also resulted in attention to the relationship between the private sector and climate change. Early last year, for example, the Commission published a Report on Business and Human Rights which addresses climate change, environmental degradation and the obligations of States to regulate the private sector.[102] The report highlighted the right of access to justice in order to remediate the impact of climate change.[103]

9.2.1.2 Friendly Settlements

On occasion, redress for environmental degradation affecting human rights has come about as a result of negotiations within the framework of friendly settlements under the auspices of the Inter-American Commission. Article 41 of the Rules of the Inter-American Commission provides that 'the Commission shall place itself at the disposal of the parties concerned, at any stage of the examination of a petition or case, with a view to reaching a friendly settlement of the matter [...]'.

Shelton suggests that friendly settlements are 'more effective' than a decision of the Commission on the merits and 'lessen the time required for each case'.[104] She notes that one study found that compliance rates with friendly settlements were almost

---

[101] Hearing on Climate Change before the Inter-American Commission on Human Rights, September 2019.

http://climatecasechart.com/non-us-case/hearing-on-climate-change-before-the-inter-american-commission-on-human-rights/. Accessed 11 March 2020.

[102] Comisión Interamericana de Derechos Humanos, Relatoría Especial sobre Derechos Económicos, Sociales, Culturales y 'Empresas y Derechos Humanos: Estándares Interamericanos' https://www.oas.org/es/cidh/informes/pdfs/EmpresasDDHH.pdf. Accessed 11 March 2020. See in particular paras 233–253.

[103] It stated: 'For the Commission and its REDESCA, it is also a priority that the States guarantee access to justice and reparation for damage in climate matters. This obligation requires States to guarantee the existence of accessible, affordable, timely and effective mechanisms to challenge those actions or omissions that may affect human rights due to climate change and environmental degradation and to obtain reparation for damages arising from the climate risks and the policies adopted in this regard, whether these actions come from the State or through companies.' Ibid., para 251. (Author's translation).

[104] Shelton 2015, p. 9.

double those with Court judgments and five times the rate of compliance with Inter-American Commission decisions.[105] Doubtlessly, friendly settlements constitute a tool to be considered in dispute resolution of environmental issues, even though friendly settlements do not develop law within the system.

In the case of *Mercedes Julia Huenteao Beroiza et al v Chile,*[106] a group of indigenous families settled a dispute following this route. The case was filed on 10 December 2002 for alleged violations of Article 4 (right to life), Article 5 (inhumane treatment), Article 8 (fair trial), Article 12 (freedom of conscience and religion), Article 17 (rights of the family), Article 21 (right to property), and Article 25 (right to judicial protection) of the American Convention on Human Rights. The case revolved around the construction of hydroelectric plants, authorised by the State of Chile, which were to have detrimental consequences on the ancestral land and culture on the Mapuche Pehuenche people of the Upper Bío Bío sector in Chile. The petition alleged that the State of Chile had authorized ENDESA to build a dam that would destroy indigenous land in an irreversible and permanent manner, threatening the Pehuenche culture. The petition requested provisional measures from the Inter-American Commission in order to prevent the State from taking any act that might amplify or exacerbate the dispute and impair the effectiveness of any decision that the Commission might have been likely to adopt in the case. The Commission agreed to grant this request in 2002 and reissued the same in 2003 adding the proviso that the State should 'avoid [...] or suspend [...] any judicial or administrative action that entails eviction of the petitioners from their ancestral lands'.[107] However, by the time the petition was lodged, nearly 70% of the construction of the dam was completed.[108]

The parties eventually agreed to a friendly settlement of the matter. The families agreed to be relocated from their ancestral lands that would be flooded by the dams and accepted in exchange to be granted quality land, technical assistance for agricultural production in their new lands, scholarships for education and a compensation of US$300,000 per family. In the case of the last measure, the State of Chile agreed to act as a guarantor of the obligation that had to be carried out by ENDESA. The State of Chile also undertook to adopt a wide number of measures including, the ratification of ILO Convention No 169,[109] to carry out a constitutional reform to grant constitutional recognition of the indigenous peoples existing in Chile, as well as to refrain from authorising hydroelectric projects in indigenous land in the Upper Bío Bío sector. Although the majority of the families were relocated according to the

[105] See ibid., citing Basch et al 2010.

[106] Inter-American Commission on Human Rights, *Mercedes Julia Huenteao Beroiza and Others*, Report No 30/04, 11 March 2004, Petition 4617/02.

[107] Ibid., para 5 and para 15.

[108] Ibid., para 25.

[109] The ILO Convention No 169 was ratified by the Chilean Senate in March 2008 and became part of Chilean law in 2009. Survival International, 'Key International Law on Tribal Peoples Ratified' 11 March 2008 https://www.survivalinternational.org/news/3122 ; CCTVCOM, 'ILO Convention becomes law in Chile' 16 September 2009 http://english.cctv.com/20090916/101996.shtml. Accessed 19 February 2020.

terms of agreement and compensated, by 2005, the core of the measures that formed part of the friendly settlement were still to be implemented.[110]

The case is instructive to show that whilst friendly settlements can be an important tool to settle disputes without having to go all the way through expensive litigation, it does require careful consideration on the part of the representatives of the victims, before settling the matter out of Court. Bona fides on the part of the State is essential for this mechanism to be effective.

9.2.1.3 Provisional Measures

Provisional measures have increasingly become a tool to avoid irreparable damage in cases of environmental pollution affecting fundamental rights under the American Convention. In accordance with Article 25 of the Rules of Procedure of the Inter-American Commission, 'in serious and urgent cases, and whenever necessary according to the information available, the Commission may, on its own initiative or at the request of a party, request that the State concerned adopt precautionary measures to prevent irreparable harm to persons.' As the text suggests, the Commission 'requests' the State concerned to adopt the measures. It does not issue a legally binding order. However, its request carries the authority of the Commission, which is an organ charged with the 'study and initial processing of petitions lodged' before the Inter-American System of individual petitions.[111] The innovative use of provisional measures in the Inter-American System could well go back to the decade of 2000, in which the Commission ordered a State to provide anti-retroviral medication to 24 persons, carriers of the Human Immunodeficiency Virus/Acquired Immunodeficiency Virus ('HIV/AIDS') in *Jorge Odir Miranda Cortez et al v El Salvador*.[112] Despite being in a state of emergency as a consequence of an earthquake, El Salvador complied with the Commission's provisional measures request.[113]

Provisional measures have also been used to prevent irreversible environmental harm affecting rights under the American Convention. As mentioned before, the Inter-American Commission has also granted precautionary measures in a number of cases concerning environmental damage. In *Community of San Mateo Huanchor*, for example, the Commission adopted precautionary measures to avoid irreparable damage to the victims since the severe environmental pollution caused by the mining sludge field had triggered a public health crisis in the affected community, which entailed a daily risk associated with exposure to the metals in the sludge. In so doing

[110] Inter-American Commission on Human Rights, *Mercedes Julia Huenteao Beroiza and Others*, Breach of the Friendly Settlement Agreement, 19 October 2005.

[111] See Article 41f of the American Convention on Human Rights, above n 4, and Article 26 of the Rules of Procedure of the Commission, above n 13.

[112] Inter-American Commission on Human Rights, *Jorge Odir Miranda Cortez and Others v El Salvador*, Report No 209/01, 20 March 2009, Case No 12.249, para 284.

[113] By 13 January, 2001, information provided by the State indicated that by that date 'anti-retroviral medication had been provided to 11 of the 24 persons included in case 12.249' and the treatment was available for the rest upon appropriate medical evaluation. Ibid., para 23.

the Commission took notice that those who were most severely affected were the children: 'because of their exposure to lead and other mineral waste, the children [were] running the risk of suffering irreparable damage to their neurological abilities and psychological development'.[114] The Commission requested the State of Peru to adopt measures within 15 days which included 'starting up a health assistance and care program for the population of San Mateo de Huanchor, especially its children, in order to identify those persons who might have been affected by the pollution so that they can be given relevant medical care' as well as 'drawing up as quickly as possible an environmental impact assessment study required for removing the sludge containing the toxic waste'.[115]

More recent examples of the use of provisional measures refer to the decision of the Commission on 1 April 2011, granting measures for the members of the indigenous communities of the Xingu River Basin in Pará, Brazil. The request related to the impact of the construction of the Belo Monte hydroelectric power plant, the world's third largest dam, on the right to life and integrity of the communities. The Commission requested that Brazil suspend immediately the licensing process for the Belo Monte Hydroelectric Plant project and stop any construction work from moving forward until the State: (1) conducted free, informed, culturally appropriate consultations, in good faith, and with the aim of reaching an agreement; (2) guaranteed that the indigenous communities have access beforehand to the project's Social and Environmental Impact Study, in an accessible format, including translation into the respective indigenous languages; (3) adopted measures to protect the lives and physical integrity of the members of the indigenous peoples of the Xingu Basin in voluntary isolation, and to prevent the spread of diseases and epidemics in their community, including any diseases derived from the massive influx of people in the region as well as the exacerbation of transmission vectors of water-related diseases such as malaria.[116]

In an example of the Inter-American System being vulnerable to political pressure, in a set-back, four months after granting the precautionary measures, the Commission modified them.[117] Among other things, Shelton notes that as a consequence of receiving the request, Brazil withdrew its OAS ambassador and nominee for the Inter-American Commission and halted its financial contributions.[118] AIDA, the NGO that represented the claimants, complained that four years after the provisional measures were issued, Brazil 'not only breached the precautionary measures, but also

[114] Inter-American Commission on Human Rights, *Community of San Mateo Huanchor*, above n 36, para 11.

[115] Ibid., para 12.

[116] See Inter-American Commission on Human Rights, *Indigenous Communities of the Xingu River Basin, Pará v Brazil,* 1 April 2011, PM 382/10.

[117] AIDA, 'Belo Monte, The Urgency of Effectively Protecting Human Rights', 1 April 2015 https://aida-americas.org/en/blog/belo-monte-urgency-effectively-protecting-human-rights. Accessed 19 February 2020.

[118] Shelton 2015, p. 12.

repeatedly requested that they be lifted'.[119] The government also allowed construction of the Belo Monte Dam to continue, and the project (by 2015) was 70 percent complete.[120]

Despite the experience in the Brazilian case, the use of provisional measures in cases of environmental degradation have continued and the Commission has currently a Special Rapporteur on Economic, Social, Cultural and Environmental Rights. Recently, this office issued a joint statement together with the United Nations Special Rapporteur on Human Rights and the Environment to highlight challenges related to the Covid-19 pandemic and the global environmental crisis. The joint statement inter alia acknowledged that '[t]he current pandemic has revealed the already fragile state of environmental protection in many countries of the Americas. The pandemic has exacerbated existing patterns of inequalities, and it is no coincidence that areas with higher levels of environmental pollution and higher death rates from COVID-19 are the same in which historically discriminated against people live.'[121] It called on States to strengthen their environmental laws, policies, programs and regulations.[122]

9.2.2 The Inter-American Court of Human Rights

Established in 1979, the Inter-American Court of Human Rights is a juridical organ with broad powers to provide reparation (with no parallel in any other region so far). The Court has exercised jurisdiction to that effect, in order to redress violations of economic, social and cultural rights.

The judgments of the Inter-American Court are legally binding and its orders of provisional measures are equally binding. Under its individual petition system, the Court examines claims under the American Convention brought by the Inter-American Commission. Although victims cannot file a case before the Court propio motu, they have locus standi before the Court.

The Inter-American Court has so far made environmental degradation justiciable mainly in cases concerning indigenous peoples' claims. In addition, it has developed important doctrines incorporating economic, social and cultural rights to rights traditionally conceived as 'civil and political' in nature and conceiving reparations so as to redress 'historical wrongs' done to communities and environmental harm.

---

[119] AIDA, 'Belo Monte, The Urgency of Effectively Protecting Human Rights', 1 April 2015 https://aida-americas.org/en/blog/belo-monte-urgency-effectively-protecting-human-rights. Accessed 19 February 2020.

[120] Ibid.

[121] OAS, Press Release 'The Americas: Government should strengthen, not weaken, environmental protection during COVID-19 pandemic' https://www.oas.org/en/iachr/media_center/PReleases/2020/198.asp. Accessed 19 February 2020.

[122] Ibid.

9.2.2.1 The Consolidated Notion of 'the Right to a Life in Dignity' in the Jurisprudence of the Inter-American Court

The Inter-American System went through a period of consolidation through the Inter-American Court's first 25 years of functioning in the interpretation of the substantive law of the system. Through its *jurisprudencia constante* the Court elaborated important doctrines that have given full effect to the American Convention on Human Rights.

One such doctrine is that, in the settlement of contentious cases, the Inter-American Court has developed the right to life so as to encompass the notion of the right to a dignified existence (or the right to a life in dignity) and the right to a decent life. Note that the 'Protocol of San Salvador', contains references to such notions.[123]

The notions of the right to a 'dignified existence' and to a 'decent life' were first referred to by the Inter-American Court in the context of its examination of the rights of the child.[124] In its first contentious case concerning children *Villagrán Morales y Otros v Guatemal*a (Street Children case),[125] the Court established an important principle: that owing to the fundamental nature of the right to life, restrictive approaches were inadmissible and that in essence, 'the fundamental right to life includes not only the right of every human being not to be deprived of his life arbitrarily, but also the right that he will not be prevented from having access to the conditions that guarantee a dignified existence.'[126] In the given case, the Court found that Guatemala had violated Article 4 of the Convention in a twofold way. Not only because their State agents had deprived the victims of their lives but also because it had deprived the victims in the case (children living in the streets), of the minimum conditions for a dignified life.[127]

In its Advisory Opinion *Juridical Condition and Human Rights of the Child,*[128] the Court elaborated on the notion of 'a decent life' (which forms a unity with the notion of 'a dignified existence') as encompassing several aspects with respect to children: conditions of life which ensure dignity, the right to receive the highest priority and the best effort from States, the right to education and the right to health.[129]

This understanding of the right to life has been further consolidated in the context of litigation concerning collectivities, often challenging environmental degradation

---

[123] Reference to the right to living a 'dignified and decent existence' is found for example in Article 6 (Right to Work), Article 7 (Just, Equitable and Satisfactory Conditions of Work), Article 9 (Right to Social Security) and Article 13 (Right to Education) therein.

[124] Article 19 of the American Convention, above n 4.

[125] *Villagran Morales et al case*, Judgment of 19 November, 1999, IACtHR, Series C: No 32.

[126] Ibid., para 144. Emphasis added.

[127] Ibid.

[128] *Juridical Condition and Human Rights of the Child*, Advisory Opinion OC-17/2002, 28 August 2002, IACtHR Ser. A, No 17.

[129] The Court referred to Article 13 (right to education), Article 15 (right to the formation and the protection of families), and Article 16 (rights of children) of the Protocol of San Salvador in its interpretation of Article 19.

and deprivation of their ancestral land, to the detriment of indigenous communities in the Americas. In the indigenous community *Yakye Axa v Paraguay* case,[130] the Court held that Paraguay had violated Article 4 (right to life) of the American Convention because it had failed to ensure this community's 'right to a life in dignity'.[131] The Court concluded that the Yakye Axa community, which belongs to the Enxet Lengua people in Paraguay, had been deprived of its right to property upon its ancestral lands and lived as a consequence in a state of high vulnerability and destitution. The community literally lived alongside the road, in a terrain where it was not possible for them to carry out their traditional agricultural activities, a place lacking sanitation facilities as well as other basic services. The communities did not have access to clean water and their most reliable source was rainwater. It was noted during the proceedings before the Court that members of the community fell sick and children were malnourished through lacking access to clean water, food and other essential necessities. Large tracts of land in the Paraguayan Chaco had been sold through the London stock exchange, to British businessmen and the land was used for cattle ranching.[132] Indeed, Paraguay has one of the highest rates of deforestation in the world, largely due to the rapid expansion of cattle ranching, especially in the western Gran Chaco region.[133]

In the *Yakye Axa* case, the Court ordered that:

> [a]s long as the community remain[ed] without land, given its special conditions of vulnerability and the fact that it is impossible for them to have access to their traditional mechanisms of subsistence, the State will be obliged to supply, in a manner both immediate and regular, sufficient drinking water for the consumption and the personal hygiene of the members of the Community; provide regular medical care and medicines suitable for preserving the health of all persons, especially boys, girls, elderly people and pregnant women, including medicines and treatment suitable for the removal of parasites from all the members of the Community; provide them with food sufficient in quantity, variety and quality to enable the members of the Community *to have the basic conditions required for a life of dignity*; install latrines or any type of suitable sanitary service so that the biological waste of the Community may be managed in an effective and salubrious manner; and endow the school in the current location of the Community with sufficient bilingual materials for the due education of its pupils.[134]

In the case of the *Sawhoyamaxa Indigenous Community v Paraguay*[135] the Court again examined the rights of indigenous peoples deprived of their ancestral lands and living 'in a state of nutritional, medical and health vulnerability, which constantly threatened their survival and integrity'.[136] Here again the Court emphasised the duty

---

[130] *Comunidad Indigena Yakye Axa v Paraguay,* Judgment, 17 June 2005, IACtHR Ser. C, No 125.

[131] Ibid., para 176.

[132] CEJIL, Yayke Axa Community, https://cejil.org/en/yakye-axa-community. Accessed 19 February 2020.

[133] Mongabay (2020) https://news.mongabay.com/2020/04/cattle-put-paraguays-chaco-biome-at-high-risk-but-report-offers-hope/. Accessed 19 February 2020.

[134] *Comunidad Indigena Yakye Axa v Paraguay,* above n 130 (emphasis added).

[135] *Sawhoyamaxa Indigenous Community v Paraguay,* Judgment, 29 March 2006, IACtHR Ser. C, No 146.

[136] Ibid. para 2.

of States to guarantee the creation of conditions that may be necessary in order to prevent violations of the right to life. That is, States are responsible for taking measures to ensure access to conditions that might guarantee a decent life. Judge Sergio García Ramírez reflected in that sense:

> 18. Some remarkable decisions by the Court have shifted the focus towards the other side of the right to life which, seen from yet another perspective, constitutes the other face of State duties: beyond the mere omission curbing arbitrariness or mitigating punishment, action is required to create conditions to guarantee a decent existence. In this view, the right to life is restored to its original status as an opportunity to choose our destiny and develop our potential. It is more than just a right to subsist, but is rather a right to self-development, which requires appropriate conditions [...] for a feasible and full existence, [...].
>
> [...]
>
> 19. The Inter-American Court has forcefully gone a long way in this direction. It has affirmed the duty to provide decent living conditions. It has highlighted the positive duties of the States, and not only their negative obligations. By doing so, it has broadened the horizons of human rights under the aegis of the American Convention. This has been the doctrine firmly upheld by the Court in each and every one of its most recent decisions.[137]

What emerged from such jurisprudence of the Inter-American Court is a consolidated notion of the right to life entailing the concept of the 'right to a life in dignity',[138] which is fundamental to the jurisprudence relating to environmental issues. Notice in that respect that the Spanish *derecho a una vida digna* is broader than the notion behind the term 'right to a decent life' which appears sometimes as its translation. The word 'dignity' refers to something that goes beyond material well-being. It is a concept that has a spiritual dimension. It refers also to the right to have one's identity respected (including the racial, cultural and religious elements of it).[139] *Derecho a una vida digna* therefore entails the duty of the State to ensure that everybody has without discrimination a right to self-development and not just a right to subsist. This requirement to 'provide conditions for a feasible and full existence' is a component of the current understanding of the duties arising from the right to life under the American Convention. The right to life in that sense would encompass material and spiritual aspects inherent to the respect and protection of the dignity of the human person.

---

[137] *Sawhoyamaxa Indigenous Community v Paraguay*, above n 135, paras 18 and 21 (emphasis added).

[138] Ibid. para 153.

[139] Ibid., para 168.

9.3 The Inter-American System Advisory Jurisdiction: The Advisory Opinion of the Inter-American Court of Human Rights on the Environment and Human Rights

A critical development took place before the Inter-American Court of Human Rights not under its contentious jurisdiction but under its advisory functions: the Court's ground-breaking *Advisory Opinion on the Environment and Human Rights*,[140] which in this author's view is the most significant ruling on environmental issues of any international tribunal to date.

In March 2016, Colombia, submitted a Request to the Inter-American Court,[141] asking three main questions, namely (as a précis):

(1) If an individual living in Country A suffers a human rights violation caused by environmental damage emanating from Country B, can that individual bring a claim to hold Country B responsible under the American Convention on Human Rights?

(2) Would Country B breach the American Convention if—by act or omission—it were to cause serious transboundary environmental damage that undermined the rights to life and personal integrity (protected by Articles 4 and 5 of the American Convention) of people living in Country A?

(3) Does the American Convention require Country B to comply with the norms of international environmental law, and does that include, as one necessary mode of compliance, a requirement to carry out an environmental impact assessment of proposed projects with potential transboundary impacts? And if so, what does that obligation generally entail?[142]

Colombia's Request elicited a detailed and carefully reasoned ruling. The Advisory Opinion is the first legal pronouncement ever by an international human rights court with a true focus on environmental law as a systemic whole.[143] It also unequivocally places environmental rights in the sphere of *basic rights* that are justiciable under the American Convention. This matters because, as the UN Special Rapporteur on Human Rights and the Environment, Professor John Knox, observed '[t]he drafters of the seminal human rights instrument, the 1948 Universal Declaration of Human Rights did not include environmental rights'.[144] Yet, as the Inter-American Court noted, without a healthy environment other human rights are often nullified.[145] The

---

[140] Advisory Opinion 23, above n 7.

[141] Request for an Advisory Opinion, presented by the Republic of Colombia, concerning the interpretation of Articles 1(1), 4(1) and 5(1) of the American Convention on Human Rights, 14 March 2016. Available at http://www.corteidh.or.cr/solicitudoc/solicitud_14_03_16_ing.pdf. Accessed 19 February 2020.

[142] Feria-Tinta and Milnes 2018a, p. 3.

[143] Feria-Tinta and Milnes 2018b.

[144] Human Rights Council, Preliminary Report of the Independent Expert on the issue of human rights obligations relating to the enjoyment of a safe, clean, healthy and sustainable environment, John H. Knox, 24 December 2012, UN Doc. A/HRC/22/43, para 7.

[145] Advisory Opinion 23, above n 7, para 59.

lack of an overt mention of environmental rights as basic rights in the Universal Declaration—and indeed the American Convention—is remedied by the Inter-American Court's conclusion.

Colombia's Request represented an intricate intermingling of political and environmental concerns. Its backdrop and impetus were the ongoing disputes with Nicaragua over maritime boundaries,[146] and the threat posed by potentially unbridled infrastructure development in Nicaragua to the vulnerable ecosystems and means of livelihood in Colombia's maritime provinces.[147] In particular, plans by Nicaragua to build, with funding from China, a 170-mile rival to the Panama Canal linking the Caribbean Sea and the Pacific Ocean, dubbed 'the biggest earth-moving operation in history',[148] are considered by scientists to threaten irreversible harm to the marine ecosystem in Caribbean waters. The background to the request was therefore fears that this megaproject would destroy the marine ecosystem in the area (killing reefs, seagrass and fish), followed by chemical pollution and bringing invasive species introduced by shipping lane bottlenecks.[149] A case pending, at admissibility level, before the Inter-American Commission brought by indigenous populations against Nicaragua in relation to the construction of the canal, was likewise in the background.[150] Colombia's Request thus brought under the Court's purview a compelling contemporary issue: the ability (or lack thereof) of international law to regulate unrestrained development of infrastructure megaprojects, not least given the transboundary harms they may cause. As Colombia's Request noted, we are indeed 'living at a time when major infrastructure projects are frequently being built and brought into operation … with effects that may exceed State boundaries'.[151]

Despite this specific context, the Request raised issues that transcended any particular bilateral dispute. Colombia's Request led to a fertile debate before the Inter-American Court, with carefully deliberated interventions by States Parties to

[146] The International Court of Justice had decided a dispute on maritime boundaries between Colombia and Nicaragua adversely to Colombia. *Territorial and Maritime Dispute (Nicaragua v Colombia)* Judgment, ICJ, Reports 2012, p. 624. Following this, Colombia had withdrawn its optional clause declaration under Article 36(2) of the ICJ Statute. As a consequence, Colombia would no longer have a right of recourse to the ICJ against Nicaragua, for example in cases of environmental harm.

[147] This political 'edge' to the Request would doubtless have been apparent to the Inter-American Court, and in any event, the Guatemalan representative at the hearing on Colombia's Request drew attention to the need to ensure that any Advisory Opinion did not undermine the ICJ's settlement of that territorial dispute. Feria-Tinta and Milnes 2018a. The Inter-American Court deftly defused that aspect by concentrating on the issues of principle and avoiding expressing any concrete views on particular instances of pollution sources or their victims.

[148] Gibbs and Elliott 2017.

[149] Feria-Tinta and Milnes 2018c.

[150] Petition 912/14 filed before the Inter-American Commission on Human Rights on 17 June 2014. See Advisory Opinion 23, above n 7, para 25. For further information on the petition, see FIDH report 'Concesión del Canal Interoceánico en Nicaragua: Grave impacto en los Derechos Humanos - Comunidades campesinas movilizadas resisten', September 2016 No 680e. https://www.fidh.org/IMG/pdf/nicaragua680esp2016web-1gg.pdf. Accessed 19 February 2020.

[151] Request at para 9.

the American Convention,[152] intergovernmental organisations,[153] and civil society organisations.[154] A notable feature of the submissions by regional States was the consistent support for recognition of environmental rights, broadly in favour of an affirmative answer to the questions posed in Colombia's Request.[155]

In turn, the Inter-American Court's response to Colombia's three questions was also broadly in the affirmative, in certain respects even more so than the Request had envisaged.[156]

The following sections will focus on four important aspects of the Advisory Opinion: (1) the meaning of jurisdiction in the American Convention covering a State's activities that cause effects outside its territory (i.e. transboundary damage); (2) the Advisory Opinion's emphasis on the inherent relationship between the protection of the environment and the realisation of other human rights (e.g. the right to life);[157] (3) the further affirmation that the notion that the right to life includes a right to live with dignity in the context of environmental degradation; and (4) the notion of due diligence and other procedural obligations as giving effect to the respect of human rights.

9.3.1 The Meaning of Jurisdiction under the American Convention and Potential Diagonal Climate Change Claims

A significant aspect of the Advisory Opinion, for potential transboundary environmental claims, is one that signals the possibility of 'diagonal' human rights claims

---

[152] Argentina, Bolivia, Honduras and Panama made written observations and intervened orally before the Court. Guatemala intervened orally at the hearings. Advisory Opinion 23, above n 7, paras 6 and 9.

[153] The Inter-American Commission on Human Rights, The General Secretariat from the Organisation of American States (OAS) with the International Union for Conservation of Nature's World Commission on Environmental Law, and the International Maritime Organisation.

[154] There were forty-four interventions from civil society.

[155] See Feria-Tinta and Milnes 2018a. One State, Panama, expressed more restrictive views but nonetheless emphasised the importance of States adhering to international environmental norms. Guatemala and Honduras favoured Colombia's position, while Bolivia (which did not submit any written observations) made oral submissions going even further, in line with the Bolivian government's strongly environmentalist and indigenous peoples-oriented stance. Argentina advocated for a more cautious and context-driven approach, but one that was open to 'diagonal' jurisdiction based on concrete facts (similar to the Inter-American Court's eventual ruling).

[156] On the first question, the Inter-American Court adopted a broader approach than Colombia proposed, in that it declined Colombia's invitation to base either substantive State human rights obligations or the scope of '*jurisdiction*' under Article 1(1) of the American Convention on the existence or otherwise of any *other* treaty regime such as the *Convention for the Protection and Development of the Marine Environment of the Wider Caribbean Region*, 24 March 1983, 1506 UNTS 157, entered into force 11 October 1986 ('Cartagena Convention').

[157] Advisory Opinion 23, above n 7, para 47.

(concerning obligations capable of being invoked by individual or groups against States other than their own) in circumstances far broader than those which have been held admissible under the Inter-American system to date. So far, the Inter-American System has taken a cautious approach to extraterritorial obligations. Generally, the relatively few cases found to be admissible in the extraterritorial application of human rights treaties have involved direct exercise of violence by State agents outside a State's borders, and sometimes even that is not enough.[158] The Advisory Opinion makes clear that, in principle, the Inter-American System permits cross-border human rights claims in respect of other types of conduct, such as transboundary pollution and ecological damage.

The Court held that the word 'jurisdiction', for the purposes of the human rights obligations under the American Convention, 'may encompass a State's activities that cause effects outside its territory'.[159] The Court emphasised that States:

> must ensure that activities within their jurisdiction or control do not cause damage to the environment of other States or of areas beyond the limits of their jurisdiction, and that States are obliged to use all available means to avoid activities in their territory, or in any area under their jurisdiction, causing significant damage to the environment of another State.[160]

In this context, one of the most interesting features of the Advisory Opinion is the Court's handling of the concept of 'effective control'. The Court held:

> In cases of transboundary damage, the exercise of jurisdiction by a State of origin is based on the understanding that it is the State in whose territory or *under whose jurisdiction the activities* were carried out that has *the effective control over them* and is in a position to prevent them from causing transboundary harm that impacts upon the enjoyment of human rights of persons outside its territory. The potential victims of the negative consequences of such activities are under the jurisdiction of the State of origin for the purposes of the possible responsibility of that State for failing to comply with its obligation to prevent transboundary damage.[161]

It further concluded:

> When transboundary harm or damage occurs, a person is under the jurisdiction of the State of origin if there is a causal link between the action that occurred within its territory and the negative impact on the human rights of persons outside its territory. The exercise of jurisdiction arises *when the State of origin exercises effective control over the activities that caused the damage and the consequent human rights violation.*[162]

Thus, in the Advisory Opinion, as concerns transboundary environmental harms, '*effective control*' is no longer something which has to be exercised over the territory where the victims were, nor over the victims themselves. Rather, what matters is whether the source state—State X—has effective control over the activities that caused the transboundary harm.

---

[158] See for example the approach taken in the European System: *Banković and Others v Belgium and Others,* Judgment, 12 December 2001, App No 52207/9.

[159] Advisory Opinion 23, above n 7, para 95. (Author's translation).

[160] Ibid., para 97.

[161] Ibid., para 102 (emphasis added).

[162] Ibid., para 104 (h) (emphasis added).

This is significant for potential transboundary cases (and possibly climate change cases) as it opens the door to diagonal claims. The Court's reasoning could be used to support an argument that a State's contribution to the accumulation of greenhouse gases in the atmosphere should result in State responsibility and accountability under the American Convention to victims living in other States.

9.3.2 The Right to Life as a Right to a Healthy Environment

A crucial pronouncement of the Court in the Advisory Opinion is that '[t]he degradation of the environment can cause irreparable damage to human beings, and therefore a healthy environment is a fundamental right for the existence of humanity'.[163]

The Advisory Opinion recognised the right to healthy environment as 'a fundamental right for the existence of humanity', as part of the right to life.[164] The Court further held that 'environmental degradation and the adverse effects of climate change affect the effective enjoyment of human rights' (including, fundamentally, the right to life).[165]

In the Court's view the 'human right to a healthy environment' has collective and individual connotations, being both a 'universal interest [...] owed to present and future generations' and having 'direct or indirect repercussions on people due to its connection with other [individual] rights, such as the right to health, personal integrity or life, among others'.[166]

It was therefore acknowledged that there is an interdependence and indivisibility between human rights and the protection of the environment, giving rise to state obligations.[167] In an interesting passage relevant to future climate change litigation, the Court held that 'climate change has very diverse repercussions for the effective enjoyment of human rights, such as the rights to life, health, food, water, housing and self-determination.'[168] In the same vein, it stressed that 'a critical link between human beings' subsistence and the environment has been recognised in other international treaties and instruments [...] including the International Covenant on Civil and Political Rights.'[169]

---

[163] Ibid., para 59. In the original Spanish: 'La degradación del medio ambiente puede causar daños irreparables en los seres humanos, por lo cual un medio ambiente sano es un derecho fundamental para la existencia de la humanidad.'

[164] Ibid., para 59.

[165] Ibid., para 47.

[166] Ibid., para 59.

[167] Ibid., para 55.

[168] Ibid., para 54.

[169] Inter-American Commission on Human Rights, *Indigenous and Tribal People's Rights over Their Ancestral Lands and Natural Resources, Norms and Jurisprudence of the Inter-American Human Rights System*, OEA/Ser.I/L/V/II. Doc 56/09 (30 December 2009), para 192.

9.3.3 The Positive Obligations Under the Right to Life and the Notion of the Right to Life in Dignity

The Advisory Opinion relied on long-standing jurisprudence of the Court and stated that compliance with the obligations imposed by Article 4 of the American Convention, related to Article 1(1) of this instrument, not only presupposes that no person may be deprived of his or her life arbitrarily (negative obligation) but also, it requires States to take all appropriate measures to protect and preserve the right to life (positive obligations).[170] This is a key consideration concerning the right to life, which has also been embraced more recently by the Human Rights Committee, influenced by jurisprudence of the Inter-American Court.[171]

This approach has enabled the Inter-American Court to examine and establish the violation of Article 4 of the Convention in relation to individuals who did not die as a result of the actions that violated this instrument.[172] It is worth mentioning that this approach to the right to life is also reflected in the jurisprudence of the European Court of Human Rights. In fact, as noted by the Advisory Opinion, the European Court of Human Rights has also found violations of the right to life with regard to individuals who did not die as a result of the acts that violated the European Convention on Human Rights.[173]

Moreover, the Advisory Opinion applies the notion of 'the right to a life in dignity' (reviewed in an earlier section of this chapter) in the context of environmental degradation. The Advisory Opinion is thus authority to assert that a State incurs international responsibility under the American Convention (violating its obligations under Article 4 (right to life)) if it fails to guarantee the right to life, free from environmental degradation, within its jurisdiction.

In the *Yakye Axa case*, (a case quoted by the Advisory Opinion) the Court stated that:

> … one of the obligations that the State must inescapably undertake as a guarantor, to protect and ensure the right to life, is that of generating minimum living conditions that are compatible with the dignity of the human person and of not creating conditions that hinder or impede it. In this regard the State has the duty to take positive, concrete measures geared towards fulfillment of the right to a decent life, especially in the case of persons who are vulnerable and at risk.[174]

---

[170] Advisory Opinion 23, above n 7, para 108.

[171] Article 4 of the American Convention on Human Rights is in similar terms to Article 6(1) of the ICCPR and provides: 'Every person has the right to have his life respected. This right shall be protected by law and, in general, from the moment of conception. No one shall be arbitrarily deprived of this life.'

[172] Advisory Opinion 23, above n 7, para 109.

[173] In this regard, see, ECtHR, *Acar and Others v Turkey*, Judgment, 24 May 2005, App No s 36088/97 and 38417/97, paras 77 and 110, and ECtHR, *Makaratzis v Greece*, Judgment, 20 December 2004, App No 50385/99, paras 51 and 55.

[174] The *Yakye Axa case*, above n 130, para 162. The Court concluded in the case, that Paraguay had violated the right to life because it had failed to ensure the indigenous community's *right to a life in dignity*.

This approach to the right to life, highlighted by the Court in the context of establishing the link between environmental degradation and the right to life in the Advisory Opinion, is crucial to the proper examination of rights under Article 4 of the Convention in a potential climate change case and indeed in any environmental degradation case threatening the quality of life of individuals.

The Court's ruling that States can be accountable for the emission of pollutants from activities in their territory which cause transboundary ecological harm coupled with an approach to the right to life as described above is significant for environmental transboundary claims including climate change claims. If in 2005, the Inter-American Commission decided against accepting a petition by Inuit peoples that climate change was violating their rights, in the light of the Advisory Opinion the arguments of the Inuit (and other vulnerable groups for whom climate change has become an existential threat to their lands, livelihoods and cultures) benefit from enhanced weight of principle and authority.

9.3.4 Procedural Obligations in Environment-related Cases: Due Diligence, the Duty to Prevent Transboundary Harm and Other Procedural Obligations

Finally, in the Advisory Opinion, the Court held that the majority of the environmental obligations rest on a duty of due diligence on the part of the State.[175] Such a duty is understood as an obligation of conduct (i.e. focusing on what States do), and not as an obligation of result (focusing on whether States succeed in achieving a particular result or not).[176]

The Advisory Opinion draws heavily from the 1972 Stockholm Declaration[177] and the 1992 Rio Declaration,[178] treating the principles enunciated in those early non-binding legal instruments—including prevention of environmental harm, the precautionary principle, procedural safeguards, and the obligation of cooperation—as binding legal obligations under the American Convention. It also elaborates on the scope of a number of procedural rights such as access to information, public participation and access to justice.

The Court held in particular that, in order to respect and guarantee rights to life and integrity, States are under a duty to:

(1) Prevent significant environmental damage, both inside and outside their territory;
(2) Regulate, oversee and control the activities under their jurisdiction which may give rise to significant damage to the environment, carry out studies on environmental

[175] Advisory Opinion 23, above n 7, para 124.

[176] Ibid., para 123.

[177] Declaration of the United Nations Conference on the Human Environment, Stockholm, 5-16 June 1972, U.N. Doc. A/Conf.48/14/Rev. 1(1973); 11 ILM 1416 (1972).

[178] Rio Declaration on Environment and Development, Rio de Janeiro, 13 June 1992. UN Doc. A/CONF.151/26 (vol. I); 31 ILM 874 (1992).

impact when there exists a risk of significant damage to the environment, draw up a contingency plan so as to have in place safety measures and procedures for minimising the possibility of major environmental accidents, and mitigating any significant environmental damage that would have ensued, even when this may have occurred in spite of preventive actions on the part of the State;

(3) Act in accordance with the precautionary principle, when faced with possible severe or irreversible damage to the environment, even in the absence of scientific certainty;

(4) Cooperate, in good faith, for the protection against damage to the environment;

(5) Pursuant to that duty of cooperation, notify other States that may be potentially affected when they become aware that a planned activity under their jurisdiction could give rise to a risk of significant cross-border damage, and in cases of environmental emergencies, as well as to consult and negotiate, in good faith, with the States potentially affected by significant cross-border damage;

(6) Guarantee the right of access to information relating to possible negative impact upon the environment, enshrined in Article 13 of the American Convention;

(7) Guarantee the right to public participation of people under their jurisdiction, which is enshrined in Article 23(1) of the American Convention, in the making of decisions and policies that may affect the environment; and

(8) Guarantee access to justice, with regard to State obligations for the protection of the environment.[179]

In short, the implications of the Advisory Opinion 23, are likely to ripple well beyond the Americas. Cross-fertilisation among international judicial bodies is common: the opinion will stand as a marker when the European Court of Human Rights, sooner or later, has to do its own thinking on what 'jurisdiction' means for transboundary environmental damage.

The Opinion's core reasoning could be applied to air pollution, chemicals, and climate change. It may also stimulate new thinking in arguments about international law's (in)ability to regulate the activities of multinational corporations. In any event, the Advisory Opinion is certainly a landmark and a quantum leap in the jurisprudence of the Inter-American system and international human rights law.

A positive observation can be made regarding the power and value of advisory opinions. Cases often take up to ten years to be decided, a major barrier in the Inter-American System of Human Rights. Advisory Opinions, on the other hand, can be applied directly in most jurisdictions within the Inter-American System (as most jurisdictions within are monist systems), making Advisory Opinions a potentially influential legal tool. Seen from this perspective, it is likely that many environmental and climate change cases will be brought before the highest courts in the Americas, in particular Constitutional Courts, applying directly the notions recognised in the Advisory Opinion 23.

---

[179] Advisory Opinion 23, above n 7, para 242.

9.4 Contentious Cases After the Advisory Opinion on Environment and Human Rights: The First Contentious Case on the Right to a Healthy Environment, the Lhaka Honhat Case

The *Lhaka Honhat* case[180] is the first instance in which the Inter-American Court upheld the right to a healthy environment in a contentious case making it justiciable under the American Convention on Human Rights. In this particular case, the claimant raised this right under Article 26 of the Convention (the right to progressive development).[181] The case referred to indigenous communities in the province of Salta, Argentina, alleging that the State had failed to implement measures to stop illegal logging and other harmful activities in their territory, which had altered their indigenous way of life and damaged their cultural identity.

The indigenous peoples argued that 'the environmental degradation of the territory claimed' had been 'a continuous and significant process' that 'started at the beginning of the twentieth century with the introduction of cattle by the criollo settlers.'[182] Further, they posited that 'as a result of over-grazing by the cattle', the 'illegal logging of the forests' and the 'fences put up by the criollo families', the environment had been 'degraded'; moreover, '[t]he cattle have destroyed the herbaceous and arboreal vegetation, and this has ruined the irrigation and regeneration capacity of the land,' which 'has resulted in desertification and fissures.' They added that 'the illegal logging of native forests, using 'mining' methods—indiscriminate and unsustainable extraction—significantly affects the resilience and renewal capacity of tracts of forest.' They also indicated that the loss of flora had an impact on the natural habitat of the wildlife, which also had to compete with the cattle for food and water, adding that the loss of autochthonous flora and fauna was also related to the installation of fencing in the territory, which 'constitutes a natural obstacle' to their development.'[183]

The Court noted that this was the first contentious case in which it had to rule on the rights to a healthy environment, to adequate food, to water and to take part in cultural life based on Article 26 of the Convention. Among other considerations the Court noted that other Inter-American instruments such as Article XIX of the American Declaration on the Rights of Indigenous Peoples refers to the 'the right to protection of a healthy environment,' which includes the right of the indigenous peoples 'to live in harmony with nature and to a healthy, safe, and sustainable environment'; 'to

[180] *Lhaka Honhat*, above n 9.

[181] The provision reads: 'Article 26. Progressive Development: The States Parties undertake to adopt measures, both internally and through international cooperation, especially those of an economic and technical nature, with a view to achieving progressively, by legislation or other appropriate means, the full realization of the rights implicit in the economic, social, educational, scientific, and cultural standards set forth in the Charter of the Organization of American States as amended by the Protocol of Buenos Aires.'

[182] *Lhaka Honhat*, above n 9, para 187.

[183] Ibid.

conserve, restore, and protect the environment and to manage their lands, territories and resources in a sustainable way,' and 'to the conservation and protection of the environment and the productive capacity of their lands or territories and resources.'[184]

In addition to finding a number of violations under the American Convention,[185] the Court concluded that 'the interrelated rights to cultural identity, a healthy environment, adequate food, and water' under Article 26 had been violated in the case. The Court ordered a number of measures be implemented by Argentina, including measures of restitution (i.e. delimit, demarcate and grant a collective title;[186] relocation of the criollo population).[187] The Court also ordered measures of satisfaction and guarantees of non-repetition. A novel aspect of the measures of restitution ordered by the Court were 'measures for restitution of the rights to a healthy environment, food, water and cultural identity'. Namely, that within one year of notification of the judgment, [Argentina] 'shall prepare a report establishing the actions that must be implemented to conserve water and to avoid and rectify its contamination; to guarantee permanent access to drinking water; to avoid the persistence of the loss or decrease in forestry resources and endeavor to recover them, and to facilitate access to nutritional and culturally acceptable food'.[188] Recognising that 'the interrelated rights to cultural identity, a healthy environment, adequate food, and water have been harmed', the Court also ordered that a Community Development Fund for the indigenous culture be set up by Argentina.[189]

Doubtlessly this first contentious case on the right to a healthy environment will be followed by other such decisions under the contentious procedures of the Inter-American Court bolstered by the legal reasoning of the Advisory Opinion 23.

9.5 Conclusion

Despite its challenges (slow procedures and problems of enforcement of decisions issued in the context of contentious cases), the Inter-American System has nevertheless managed to consolidate an important body of law. It has constitutionalised environmental law (including important procedural aspects of environmental law) as part of fundamental human rights for the Americas, with the ground-breaking Advisory Opinion 23. Most countries in the region have monist systems of law in which

---

[184] Ibid., para 248.

[185] Namely the right to property under Article 21, Article 23 (Right to political participation), Right to judicial guarantees under Article 8(1), and Articles 3, 13, 16 and 22(1) (right to recognition of juridical personality or the rights to freedom of thought and expression, freedom of association, and freedom of movement and residence) of the American Convention on Human Rights.

[186] *Lhaka Honhat*, above n 9, para 327.

[187] Ibid., para 329.

[188] Ibid., above n 9, Resolutive point 12.

[189] Ibid., para 338.

the American Convention is directly justiciable, which means that domestic courts will be able to apply the environmental standards held by the Court in domestic cases.

One of the key strengths of the Inter-American System has been its creative jurisprudence. The system has also resorted to innovative uses of provisional measures to address irreversible environmental harm and has used its wide reparation powers (which go well beyond the just satisfaction approach of the European System) to reverse historical wrongs and address environmental degradation in the Americas.

The Inter-American System's substantive approach to the right to life ('right to a life in dignity') which entails a right to live in a healthy environment, has influenced the notion of the right to life adopted by the UN Human Rights Committee, reflected in its recent General Comment 36.[190] From that perspective, environmental degradation and the serious threat of climate change requires States to act to protect the ability of citizens to enjoy a life with dignity.[191] This approach to the right to life has been applied in a recent case before the UN Human Rights Committee raising an environmental issue, in *Portillo,*[192] and is at the basis of the *Torres Strait Islanders* case (the first world-case on climate change).[193] Both of these cases are amongst the most defining cases for the future of humanity, and have crucially benefited from the Inter-American System's understanding of the right to life in contexts of environmental degradation.

As noted in this chapter, the Inter-American Courts' Advisory Opinion will in the same vein, influence the law well beyond the Americas. The opinion is likely to stand as a marker now that the Strasbourg Court has to do its own thinking on what 'jurisdiction' means for transboundary environmental damage in the new generation of environmental/climate change cases already reaching the European Court of Human Rights.[194]

The Inter-American Court's Advisory Opinion core reasoning could be applied to air pollution, chemicals, and climate change. If the Inter-American System had a slow start with the *Inuit* case, the Court's Advisory Opinion 23 is certainly a quantum leap in the jurisprudence addressing environmental harm, including possible climate change claims (diagonal and non-diagonal) under human rights treaties. It may also stimulate new thinking in arguments about international law's (in)ability to regulate the activities of multinational corporations.

---

[190] Human Rights Committee, General Comment No. 36 (2018) on article 6 of the International Covenant on Civil and Political Rights, on the right to life, 30 October 2018. CCPR/C/GC/36 ('General Comment No 36').

[191] Ibid., para 65.

[192] HRC, *Portillo Cáceres and Others v Paraguay*, 20 September 2019, CCPR/C/126/D/2751/2016.

[193] HRC, *Torres Strait Islanders v Australia*, pending, Communication 3624/2019 (petition not publicly available at time of publishing).

[194] See ECtHR, *Duarte Agostinho and Others v Portugal and 32 Other States*, pending, App No 39371/20; *The Guardian,* 'Portuguese Children Sue 33 Countries', 3 September 2020, accessed on 2 February 2021. For a discussion of European cases, see Feria-Tinta 2020.

More immediately, it may first have to be applied to the very problems it was designed to discourage: mega-projects lacking any sincere environmental due diligence, dying reefs, the vulnerable Raizales people, and millions more like them. This ruling brings meaningful redress a major step closer.

In short, the developments in the Inter-American System are shaping environmental law today.

References

AIDA (2015) Belo Monte, The Urgency of Effectively Protecting Human Rights. https://aida-americas.org/en/blog/belo-monte-urgency-effectively-protecting-human-rights. Accessed 25 April 2021.

Basch F et al (2010) The Effectiveness of the Inter-American System of Human Rights Protection: A Quantitative Approach to its Functioning and Compliance with its Decisions. Sur: International Journal on Human Rights 7(2):9–35.

Falaschi C, Nara O (2013) CIDH: La causa No 12.010. Comunidades Mapuche Paynemil y Kaxipayiñ-Neuquen, Argentina.

Feria-Tinta M (2006) La víctima ante la Corte Inter-Americana de Derechos Humanos a 25 años de su funcionamiento. Revista IIDH, 43:159–203.

Feria-Tinta M (2007) Justiciability of Economic, Social, and Cultural Rights in the Inter-American System of Protection of Human Rights: Beyond Traditional Paradigms and Notions. 29 Human Rights Quarterly 29(2):431–459.

Feria-Tinta M (2009) Litigation in Regional Human Rights Systems on Economic, Social and Cultural Rights against Poverty. In: Van Bueren G (ed) Freedom from Poverty as a Human Right. Unesco Publishing, pp 319–344.

Feria-Tinta M (2020) Climate Change Litigation in the European Court of Human Rights: Causation, Imminence and Other Key Underlying Notions. Europe of Rights & Liberties 2021(1):3:52–71 https://www.europedeslibertes.eu/article/climate-change-litigation-in-the-european-court-of-human-rights-causation-imminence-and-other-key-underlying-notions/ Accessed 23 April 2021.

Feria-Tinta M (2021) Climate Change as a Human Rights Issue: Litigating Climate Change in the Inter-American System of Human Rights and the United Nations Human Rights Committee. British Institute of International and Comparative Law, Climate Change Litigation Global Perspectives. Brill, Leiden.

Feria-Tinta M (forthcoming) Declarants: Inter-American Court of Human Rights (ICtHR). Max Planck Encyclopedia of International Procedural Law, OUP.

Feria-Tinta M, Milnes S (2018a) The Rise of Environmental Law in International Dispute Resolution: the Inter-American Court of Human Rights issues a landmark Advisory Opinion on Environment and Human Rights. Yearbook of International Environmental Law 27:1–18.

Feria-Tinta M, Milnes S (2018b) The Rise of Environmental Law in International Dispute Resolution: Inter-American Court of Human Rights issues Landmark Advisory Opinion on Environment and Human Rights, https://www.ejiltalk.org/the-rise-of-environmental-law-in-international-dispute-resolution-inter-american-court-of-human-rights-issues-landmark-advisory-opinion-on-environment-and-human-rights/ Accessed 23 April 2021.

Feria-Tinta M, Milnes S (2018c) How International law could help victims of environmental degradation. The Guardian. https://www.theguardian.com/commentisfree/2018/feb/21/international-law-cross-border-victims-environment-rulings. Accessed 23 April 2021.

Fitzmaurice M, Ong D, Merkouris P (2010) Research Handbook on International Environmental Law. Edward Elgar Publishing, UK.

Gibbs S, Elliott L (2017) China Puts Nicaraguan Canal plan on hold, The Times. https://www.thetimes.co.uk/article/china-puts-nicaraguan-canal-plan-on-hold-vnghd00r8 Accessed 23 April 2021.

Maraggi I (2017) Resistir al avance extractivista: Las Comunidades Mapuche Paynemil, Kaxipayiñ y Campo Maripe frente a los conflictos territoriales en Loma La Lata y Loma Campana, Neuquén (Thesis). https://digital.cic.gba.gob.ar/handle/11746/10069 Accessed 23 April 2021.

Paúl Á (2018) Evidence: Inter-American Court of Human Rights (IACtHR). Max Planck Encyclopedia of International Procedural Law.

Shelton D (2015) The Rules and the Reality of Petition Proceedings in the Inter-American Human Rights System. Notre Dame Journal of International & Comparative Law, 5(2):1–26.

Monica Feria-Tinta is a Barrister at the Bar of England & Wales, a specialist in public international law, practising from Twenty Essex Chambers (London); LL.M; Diploma of the Hague Academy of International Law. She is a Bencher of Middle Temple, a Partner Fellow at the Lauterpacht Centre for International Law, and a Visiting Fellow at Jesus College, University of Cambridge.

Chapter 10
The Protection of the Environment Before African Regional Courts and Tribunals

Makane Moïse Mbengue

Contents

Abstract Despite the scarce jurisprudence, African regional courts and tribunals have contributed significantly to the development of international environmental law by better linking environmental protection and human rights, strengthening the content of the duty of due diligence and shaping proactive environmental remedies. The African Commission and Court of Human and Peoples' Rights, the Court of Justice of the Economic Community of West African States and the Court of Justice of the East African Court of Justice are the most progressive and innovative adjudicatory mechanisms in terms of environmental jurisprudence within the Africa. In contributing to the development of international environmental law, these courts and tribunals engaged in cross-fertilization with other universal or regional courts.

M. M. Mbengue (✉)
Department of Public International Law and International Organization, Faculty of Law, University of Geneva, Geneva, Switzerland
e-mail: makane.mbengue@unige.ch

Sciences Po Paris (School of Law), Paris, France

E. Sobenes et al. (eds.), *The Environment Through the Lens of International Courts and Tribunals*, https://doi.org/10.1007/978-94-6265-507-2_10

Keywords African Commission and Court of Human and Peoples' Rights · Cross-fertilization · Environmental remedies · East African Community · Economic Community of West African States · Regional Economic Communities · right to a healthy environment

10.1 Introduction

In his seminal Separate Opinion in the *Gabcikovo-Nagymaros* case, Judge Weeramantry underlined that '(i)n the context of environmental wisdom generally, there is much to be derived from ancient civilizations and traditional legal systems in Asia, the Middle East, Africa, Europe, the Americas, the Pacific, and Australia—in fact, the whole world. This is a rich source which modern environmental law has left largely untapped.'[1]

Africa's legal wisdom in the field of environmental protection can be traced back to the 13th Century when the Mali Empire, under the reign of Sundiata Keita, adopted in 1236 the Manden Charter (or *Kurukan Fuga*).[2] The Manden Charter which was the Constitution of the Mali Empire contained a specific chapter entitled 'Preservation of Nature' with three provisions dealing with environmental protection. It even appears that one of the most important principles of international environmental law, i.e. the principle of intergenerational equity, was already reflected in the Manden Charter. Indeed, its preamble reads as follows: 'The Children of Sanin and Kroton declare: every human life is a life. It is true that one life comes into existence before another life, But no life is more "senior" or more respectable than any other life, Just as no life is superior to any other life.'[3] The Manden Charter was inscribed in 2009 on the Representative List of the Intangible Cultural Heritage of Humanity kept by UNESCO.

Contemporary African States kept that heritage and have engaged, since their independence, in adopting a comprehensive nexus of legal instruments in relation to environmental protection. The present contribution aims more specifically at describing and analyzing the contribution of African regional courts and tribunals in the development of international environmental law. Before focusing on the jurisprudence of the said courts and tribunals (Sect. 10.4), it is important to retrace the birth and evolution of international environmental law within the African continent (Sect. 10.2) and to describe the rich panorama of environmental rules and principles that have been formulated in different sub-regions of Africa (Sect. 10.3).

---

[1] ICJ, *Gabčíkovo-Nagymaros Project (Hungary v Slovakia)*, Judgment, 25 September 1997, ICJ Reports 1997, Separate Opinion of Vice-President Weeramantry, p. 98. On this opinion, see Mbengue 2020b.

[2] In reality, the Manden Charter was never adopted as a formal written text since African societies at that time were still using the oral tradition. The Manden Charter has been transcribed on the basis of the knowledge shared by traditional griots.

[3] UNESCO 2014, p. 39.

10.2 'Wisdom of Elders':[4] The Birth of International Environmental Law in the African Continent

Achieving the goal of preservation of the environment has long informed policies within the African continent. The beginning of the development of environmental law and policy in Africa can be traced to the colonial times, with the colonial powers considering measures to preserve to a certain extent the environment of the territories under their control.[5] These measures were largely directed towards sustaining the trade in forest products and wildlife.[6] However, they proceeded to form the foundation of the modern environmental law and policy of Africa.

The Convention Designed to Ensure Conservation of Various Species of Wild Animals in Africa Which are Useful to Man or Inoffensive (1900)[7] is a good example of a treaty regarding environmental protection in Africa during the colonial period, and is perhaps the first modern environmental treaty ever concluded. It aimed to ensure the conservation of diverse animal species and prevent their indiscriminate killing. The goal, however, was to ensure that there remained a steady supply of wildlife and products for traders of ivory, animal skins and hunters.[8] In other words, the Convention was of a purely utilitarian perspective. It privileged the protection of 'harmless species' (which held certain commercial value) and advocated for the 'reduction' of some 'harmful species' such as lions, poisonous snakes and pythons.[9] This reduction was permitted based only on the perceived dangerousness of the animal, and did not account for any cultural, nutritional or spiritual value attributed to them by the local population. The Convention did not contemplate the benefits of protecting the environment for the well-being of the local population, and made no reference to the protection of forests or any plant species.[10]

The 1900 Convention—which never entered into force—was succeeded by the Convention Relative to the Preservation of Fauna and Flora in Their Natural State (1933).[11] This treaty did come into effect, and was built on the same premise as its predecessor. However, there were some differences worth noting. The 1933 Convention abandoned the approach of the 'reduction' of some species and instead provided for the creation of 'protected areas' such as national parks and reserves. The acts

---

[4] Title inspired by the music album of Shabaka and the Ancestors, *Wisdom of Elders*, Brownswood Recordings, 2016.

[5] Ogundere 1972, pp. 258–260.

[6] Dzidzornu 2015, p. 149. See also Takang 2014, p. 167.

[7] The Convention Designed to Ensure Conservation of Various Species of Wild Animals in Africa Which are Useful to Man or Inoffensive, 19 May 1900, British Parliamentary Papers 1900, pp. 825–837.

[8] Maluwa 1989, pp. 650–655.

[9] Such species were listed in Schedule V of the Convention.

[10] Takang 2014, p. 168.

[11] Convention Relative to the Preservation of Fauna and Flora in Their Natural State, 8 November 1933, 172 LNTS 241, entered into force 14 January 1936.

of capturing and killing species within these spaces were prohibited, and this colonial model still informs the environmental law and policy today of several African nations.[12] Apart from addressing fauna, the 1933 Convention also covered flora. The 1933 Convention remained applicable until the 1960s, which coincided with the wave of independence in Africa.

The utilitarian perspectives of the 1900 and 1933 Conventions should not overshadow their importance in the slow but progressive development of the 'international law relating to the protection of the environment'.[13] Most environmental treaties of that era reflected that utilitarian dimension. For instance, the preamble of the 1946 International Convention for the Regulation of Whaling[14]—whose object and purpose in light of contemporary international environmental law has been a subject of a dispute before the ICJ[15]—indicates that the said Convention was concluded 'to provide for the proper conservation of whale stocks and thus *make possible the orderly development of the whaling industry*'.[16]

If colonization planted the seed of environmental protection in modern Africa, decolonization has allowed the inception of a truly African perspective in the development of international environmental law. The Organization of African Unity (OAU)[17] played an important role in such development. The OAU, which was established in 1963, aimed to secure the economic and social sustainability of African nations. Although the Charter of the OAU contained no direct references to the preservation of the environment, its Preamble emphasized the 'responsibility to harness the *natural* and human resources of our continent for the total advancement of our peoples in all spheres of human endeavor'. It was thus under the aegis of the OAU, and taking into account its implicit powers as derived from the Preamble of its constitutive charter, that 38 newly independent African States concluded the African Convention on the Conservation of Nature and Natural Resources at Algiers (1968),[18] commonly referred to as the Algiers Convention. The Convention entered into force in 1969 and marked a watershed moment in the history of environmental protection on a pan-African level but also in the genesis of international environmental law per se. Indeed, one could even consider that international environmental law was born in

[12] Maluwa 1989, pp. 650–655. See also Doumbé-Billé 2005, pp. 5–17.

[13] To borrow the expression of the International Court of Justice (ICJ) in *Gabčíkovo-Nagymaros Project (Hungary v Slovakia)*, above n 1, p. 41, para 53.

[14] International Convention for the Regulation of Whaling, 2 December 1946, 161 UNTS 72, entered into force 10 November 1948.

[15] ICJ, *Whaling in the Antarctic (Australia v Japan: New Zealand intervening)*, Judgment, 31 March 2014, ICJ Reports 2014, p. 226, para 43.

[16] Preamble, para 7. Emphasis added.

[17] Charter of the Organization of African Unity (OAU) Charter, 25 May 1963, 479 UNTS 39, entered into force 13 September 1963.

[18] African Convention on the Conservation of Nature and Natural Resources, 15 September 1968, 1001 UNTS 3, entered into force 16 June 1969.

Algiers as opposed to Stockholm as is quite often claimed, including in the case-law of international courts and tribunals.[19]

The Algiers Convention was essentially built upon the African Charter for the Protection and Conservation of Nature (1963) which was adopted in Dar es Salaam.[20] Though only a small number of African States were parties to the African Charter for the Protection and Conservation of Nature, the latter embodied several important provisions which would inform the Algiers Convention. For instance, its Article 5 required (already!) African States to conduct an evaluation of all major development projects to assess their impact on the environment.[21]

Prior to the Algiers Convention, conservation of the environment by the colonial powers had solely been for utilitarian purposes, i.e. to regulate and allocate specific natural resources for their use. The Algiers Convention thus marked a radical shift by acknowledging that there existed a common responsibility on African nations for managing the environment, guided by a sustainable and rational use of available natural resources.[22] However, the Convention did not provide for institutional structures that would help effectuate its implementation by the parties, nor did it create mechanisms to enforce or monitor compliance of the obligations contained therein. The objective of the treaty thus remained far from achieved.[23]

It is these shortfalls, together with significant developments in international environmental law, that triggered the revision of the Algiers Convention under the aegis of the African Union (AU), the successor to the OAU. The Algiers Convention was revised in 2003 to become the Maputo Convention. The latter adopted a fresh approach of integrating the concern of environmental conservation with the goal of socio-economic development, that is sustainable development. As pointed out by the *Iron Rhine* Tribunal: 'Today, […] international […] law require(s) the integration of appropriate environmental measures in the design and implementation of economic development activities'.[24] The Maputo Convention is reflective of these new developments in international environmental law. It also adopts a more general and comprehensive approach towards preservation of the environment than its predecessor.

At this continental or pan-African level, the African Commission on Human and Peoples' Rights (hereinafter, the Commission) and the African Court on Human and Peoples' Rights (hereinafter, the African Court) form two important dispute

---

[19] See, e.g., the *Iron Rhine* Tribunal which explicitly traced back the birth of international environmental law to the 1972 Stockholm Conference on the Human Environment: 'Since the Stockholm Conference on the Environment in 1972 there has been a marked development of international law relating to the protection of the environment'. See *Iron Rhine Arbitration (Belgium/Netherlands),* Decision, 24 May 2005, 23 RIAA 35, p. 66, para 59.

[20] African Charter for the Protection and Conservation of Nature, Commission for Technical Co-operation in Africa South of the Sahara, 18th Session, 4–9 February 1963 (CCTA-CSA Pub).

[21] Maluwa 1989, pp. 650–655.

[22] African Convention on the Conservation of Nature and Natural Resources, above n 18, Preamble.

[23] Takang 2014, p. 168.

[24] *Iron Rhine Arbitration (Belgium/Netherlands)*, above n 19, p. 66, para 59.

settlement mechanisms that adjudicate on matters related, inter alia, to environmental protection.[25] Their jurisdiction *ratione materiae* relates to claims in connection with the African Charter on Human and Peoples' Rights (1981).[26] The African Charter on Human and Peoples' Rights recognizes that 'all people shall have the right to a general satisfactory environment favourable to their development'.[27] In this respect, the African Charter on Human and Peoples' Rights (hereinafter, the African Charter) is the first human rights treaty to recognize the human right to a healthy environment.[28]

The Commission was established in 1987 by the OAU, as a quasi-judicial body to address violations of the human rights enumerated in the Charter. Established pursuant to Article 30 of the Charter, the decisions of the Commission are non-binding recommendations. However, they influence the interpretation of the Charter at the continental and sub-regional levels.[29] For many years the Commission worked without a court. This changed in 2004 with the establishment of the African Court. The relationship between the two bodies is complex but, in essence, the Court was established to complement the mandate of the Commission. The Commission has the power to bring cases to the African Court for its consideration.[30] The actual and potential role of both the Commission and the African Court in the implementation and interpretation of a right to a healthy environment shows that the OAU and the African Union did not limit themselves to developing a set of substantive provisions in relation to the environment. They have also developed, to a certain extent, procedural tools to ensure effective protection of the environment. Such a clear balance between substantive provisions and procedural provisions is necessary for enhancing the preservation of the environment in Africa.

The OAU and the AU have, thus, been fertile grounds for the development of international environmental law. It is not surprising then that regional economic organizations in Africa have followed the same path as the continental organization and developed a network of legal instruments, rules and principles to govern environmental protection in different sub-regions of Africa.

---

[25] Mackenzie et al. 2010, pp. 387–414.

[26] African Charter on Human and Peoples' Rights, 27 June 1981, 1520 UNTS 217, entered into force 21 October 1986.

[27] Ibid., Article 24.

[28] That right was first enunciated in the Stockholm Declaration: United Nations General Assembly 1972, Resolution on Development and Environment, UN Doc A/RES/2849 (XXVI) (Stockholm Declaration), Principle 1: 'Man has the fundamental right to freedom, equality and adequate conditions of life, in an environment of a quality that permits a life of dignity and well-being, and he bears a solemn responsibility to protect and improve the environment for present and future generations.'

[29] Ankumah 1996, p. 24 and p. 74.

[30] Harrington 2002, p. 307.

10.3 'We Are Sent Here by History':[31] Regionalizing International Environmental Law in Africa

Though the OAU was successful in pushing for the decolonization of the entire continent, it proved to be less effective in addressing concerns regarding poverty reduction and economic development. This, coupled with an increase in the influence of globalization, led several sub-regions of Africa to organize themselves into Regional Economic Communities (RECs).[32] All of the 54 Member States of the AU today are a part of at least one of the RECs. These sub-regional bodies were formed with the goal of promoting stronger coordination and integration among the Member States.[33] This section describes RECs and the judicial mechanisms that most of them have established. A panorama of environmental provisions within the constitutive instruments of RECs will then be highlighted.

10.3.1 Mapping African Regional Courts and Tribunals in the Context of RECs

RECs were established based on the Lagos Plan of Action for Development of Africa (1980)[34] and the Treaty Establishing the African Economic Community (1991).[35] These instruments considered the establishment of RECs as the building blocks of African integration, which would eventually lead to the integration of the continent as a whole.

There exist eight RECs at the moment, which are the Arab Maghreb Union (AMU),[36] the Common Market for Eastern and Southern Africa (COMESA),[37]

---

[31] Title inspired from the music album of Shabaka and the Ancestors, *We are sent here by history*, Impulse! Records, 2020.

[32] Thompson 1993, p. 744.

[33] Onwuka and Sesay 1985, p. 220.

[34] Lagos Plan of Action for Development of Africa (1980), available at: https://www.resakss.org/node/6653. Accessed 21 July 2020.

[35] Treaty Establishing the African Economic Community, 3 June 1991, entered into force 12 May 1994, available at: https://au.int/en/treaties/treaty-establishing-african-economic-community. Accessed 21 July 2020.

[36] Arab Maghreb Union (AMU) Treaty, 17 February 1989, 1546 UNTS 151, entered into force 1 July 1989.

[37] Treaty establishing the Common Market for Eastern and Southern Africa (COMESA), 5 November 1993, 2314 UNTS 265, entered into force 8 December 1994.

the Community of Sahel-Saharan States (CEN-SAD),[38] the East African Community (EAC),[39] the Economic Community for Central African States (ECCAS),[40] the Economic Community of West African States (ECOWAS),[41] the Intergovernmental Authority on Development (IGAD)[42] and the Southern African Development Community (SADC).[43]

Each of these RECs have their own constitutive treaties which, inter alia, lay down the objectives of the REC, the overarching policy framework to guide the Member States, areas of cooperation and certain obligations. A majority of the treaties, as will be described in the present contribution, integrate the preservation of the environment and the attainment of sustainable development as key objectives.

In addition, some of the constitutive instruments of RECs also establish courts or tribunals. Article 7 of the COMESA Treaty established the COMESA Court of Justice in 1994, which has been operational since 1998. The East African Court (EAC) Court of Justice was established in 1999 under Article 9 of the EAC Treaty and has been operational since 2001. The ECOWAS Community Court of Justice has been established since the 1975 ECOWAS Treaty. It was then reestablished under Articles 6 and 15 of the 1993 Revised ECOWAS Treaty.[44] The Court only became operational in December 2000.

The SADC Tribunal was established in 1992 pursuant to Article 16 of the SADC Treaty. A Protocol on the Tribunal was adopted in 2000,[45] but the SADC Tribunal only became operational in 2005. It was then suspended in 2012 during the SADC Summit following harsh criticism against the Tribunal.[46] Subsequently, a new Protocol amending the jurisdiction of the SADC Tribunal has been adopted but has yet to come into force.

Last but not least, the constitutive treaties of AMU, IGAD and CEN-SAD do not envisage such adjudicatory mechanisms, while the Court of Justice of the ECCAS, though established in 1992 by the ECCAS Treaty, is still not operational.

---

[38] Community of Sahel-Saharan States (CEN-SAD) Treaty, 3 February 1998, revised in 2013, available at: http://extwprlegs1.fao.org/docs/pdf/Mor178294.pdf. Accessed 21 July 2020.

[39] Treaty for the establishment of the East African Community (EAC), 30 November 1999, 2144 UNTS 255, entered into force 7 July 2000.

[40] Treaty establishing the Economic Community for Central African States (ECCAS), 18 October 1983, entered into force 18 December 1984, available at: https://www.wipo.int/edocs/lexdocs/treaties/en/eccas/trt_eccas.pdf. Accessed 21 July 2020.

[41] Economic Community of West African States (ECOWAS) Treaty, 28 May 1975, 1010 UNTS 17, provisionally entered into force 28 May 1975. Revised in 1993.

[42] Agreement establishing the Intergovernmental Authority on Development (IGAD), 21 March 1996, IGAD/SUM-96/AGRE-Doc.

[43] Declaration and Treaty of the Southern African Development Community (SADC), 17 August 1992, entered into force 5 October 1993.

[44] The details for the operation of the Court were established by the 1991 Protocol on the ECOWAS Community Court of Justice.

[45] Protocol on Tribunal in the Southern African Development Community, 7 August 2000, entered into force 14 August 2011, available at: https://www.sadc.int/files/1413/5292/8369/Protocol_on_the_Tribunal_and_Rules_thereof2000.pdf. Accessed 21 July 2020.

[46] Alter et al. 2016, pp. 293–328. See also Mbengue 2020a, Mbengue and Schacherer 2022.

The mandates of the various African regional courts and tribunals vary in practice. The SADC Tribunal, for example, was established with the duty to ensure adherence to and proper interpretation of the Treaty and its subsidiary instruments, and to adjudicate disputes referred to it (Article 16(1)). The Tribunal has jurisdiction over the interpretation and application of the Treaty, protocols and subsidiary instruments of SADC and on all matters arising from specific agreements between Member States, whether within the SADC Community or amongst themselves. In 2019, an Agreement Amending the Protocol on SADC Tribunal[47] withdrew from the jurisdiction of the Tribunal disputes initiated by natural or legal persons against SADC Member States. This means that no claims from individuals regarding the environment can be brought before the SADC Tribunal against a SADC Member State. Only disputes between natural or legal persons and the SADC (i.e. the Organization) are now under the jurisdiction of the SADC Tribunal (Article 18 of the Revised Protocol).

On its side, the jurisdiction of the EAC Court of Justice is not governed by a specific Protocol like the SADC Tribunal. The jurisdiction of the Court is addressed only in the EAC Treaty. Article 23 of the EAC Treaty provides that: 'The Court shall be a judicial body which shall ensure the adherence to law in the interpretation and application of and compliance with this Treaty.' Article 27, para 1 further provides that: 'The Court shall initially have jurisdiction over the interpretation and application of this Treaty: Provided that the Court's jurisdiction to interpret under this paragraph shall not include the application of any such interpretation to jurisdiction conferred by the Treaty on organs of Partner States [which is the designation used in the EAC to refer to the Member States].' Noteworthy is the fact that Article 27, para 2 specifies as follows: 'The Court shall have such [...] human rights and other jurisdiction as will be determined by the Council at a suitable subsequent date. To this end, the Partner States shall conclude a protocol to operationalise the extended jurisdiction.' An interpretation based on the ordinary meaning of the terms of Article 27, para 2 indicates that, in principle, the EAC cannot deal at the present time with disputes in relation to the right to a healthy environment.

The ECOWAS Court of Justice, like the SADC Tribunal, is governed by a specific Protocol.[48] Article 9 of the Protocol (after it was amended in 2005) provides that:

> The Court has competence to adjudicate on any dispute relating to the following:
>
> (a) The interpretation and application of the Treaty, Conventions and Protocols of the Community;
>
> (b) The interpretation and application of the regulations, directives, decisions and other subsidiary legal instruments adopted by ECOWAS;
>
> (c) The legality of regulations, directives, decisions and other legal instruments adopted by ECOWAS;

---

[47] SADC Agreement Amending the Protocol on Tribunal, 7 July 2019, available at: https://www.sadc.int/files/3515/6525/8317/Agreement_Amending_the_Protocol_on_the_Tribunal_-_2007_-_English.pdf. Accessed 21 July 2020.

[48] Protocol A7P.1/7/91 on the Community Court of Justice (1991), available at: http://prod.courtecowas.org/wp-content/uploads/2018/11/Protocol_AP1791_ENG.pdf. Accessed 21 July 2020.

(d) The failure by Member States to honor their obligations under the Treaty, Conventions and Protocols, regulations, directives, or decisions of ECOWAS;

(e) The provisions of the Treaty, Conventions and Protocols, regulations, directives or decisions of ECOWAS Member States;

[…]

4. The Court has jurisdiction to determine cases of violation of human rights that occur in any Member State.

The ECOWAS Court of Justice has perhaps the broadest jurisdiction among African regional courts and tribunals and, therefore, a higher propensity of having disputes in relation to environmental protection being submitted to it. The jurisdiction of the ECOWAS Court of Justice is in this respect even broader than the jurisdiction of the COMESA Court of Justice, which is larger than the jurisdictions of the SADC Tribunal and the EAC Court of Justice. The COMESA Treaty provides that the COMESA Court of Justice has, for instance, jurisdiction to deal with disputes in which 'a Member State considers that another Member State or the Council has failed to fulfil an obligation under the Treaty or has infringed the provisions of the Treaty' or in disputes that 'any person who is a resident in a Member State refers for determination by the Court the legality of any act, regulation, directive, or decision of the Council or Member State alleging that such act, directive, decision or regulation is unlawful or infringes any provision of the Treaty provided such person has first exhausted local remedies in the national courts or tribunals of the Member State.'

Therefore, even if only the Courts of Justice of the EAC and ECOWAS have for the time being delivered judgments concerning the protection of the environment, it appears that most existing African regional courts and tribunals have more or less broad jurisdiction that can encompass disputes relating to environmental protection. The spectrum of environmental provisions contained in the primary and derived law[49] of RECs confirm the elasticity of such jurisdiction with respect to the environment and sustainable development issues.

[49] The concept of 'primary law' refers to the constitutive instruments of the RECs. The concept of 'derived law' relates to specific conventional instruments adopted by the RECs after their establishment.

10.3.2 A Panorama of Environmental Provisions in the Constitutive Instruments of RECs

The constitutive instruments of SADC,[50] ECOWAS,[51] EAC,[52] CEN-SAD[53] and IGAD[54] recognize the achievement and continuation of sustainable development as a key objective. Nevertheless, the vast majority of them limit themselves to the connection between sustainable development and poverty eradication rather than environmental protection or the preservation of the rights of future generations. For instance, the SADC Treaty mentions the objective to 'promote sustainable and equitable economic growth and socio-economic development that will ensure poverty alleviation with the ultimate objective of its eradication, enhance the standard and quality of life of the people of Southern Africa and support the socially disadvantaged through regional integration'.

This perspective contrasts with that in the Agreement establishing the World Trade Organization (1994)[55]—to which many of the RECs are actually connected to via Article XXIV of the GATT (1947)[56]—which in its preamble connects more explicitly sustainable development and environmental protection,[57] or with the approach under Principle 3 of the Rio Declaration on Environment and Development (1992)[58] which gives an intergenerational equity dimension to sustainable development.[59] Noteworthy is the fact that none of these constitutive instruments elevates sustainable development to the level of a *principle*. At the same time, it reflects the rather dominant view of the Sustainable Development Goals within the international legal

---

[50] SADC Treaty, above n 43, Article 5(1)(a), (last amended in 2015).

[51] Revised ECOWAS Treaty, above n 41, Article 3(2)(k), (2010).

[52] EAC Treaty, above n 39, Preamble and Article 5(3)(a), (1999).

[53] Revised Treaty of the CEN-SAD, above n 38, Article 3, (2013).

[54] Agreement Establishing the IGAD, above n 42, Article 7(1)(e), (1996).

[55] Agreement establishing the World Trade Organization, 15 April 1994, 1867 UNTS 154, 1 January 1995.

[56] General Agreement on Tariffs and Trade, 30 October 1947, 55 UNTS 187, entered into force 1 January 1948.

[57] See Preamble of the Agreement establishing the WTO (1994) : 'Recognizing that their relations in the field of trade and economic endeavour should be conducted with a view to raising standards of living, ensuring full employment and a large and steadily growing volume of real income and effective demand, and expanding the production of and trade in goods and services, *while allowing for the optimal use of the world's resources in accordance with the objective of sustainable development, seeking both to protect and preserve the environment* (…)'. Emphasis added.

[58] Rio Declaration on Environment and Development (1992), Annex 1 of Report of the UN Conference on Environment and Development, Rio de Janeiro, 3–14 June 1992, UN Doc. A/CONF.151/26/Rev.l (Vol l) (Rio Declaration).

[59] See Principle 3 of the Rio Declaration: 'The right to development must be fulfilled so as to equitably meet developmental and environmental needs of present and future generations.'

order which sees '[p]overty eradication [as] the greatest global challenge facing the world today and an indispensable requirement for sustainable development'.[60]

In that respect, the IGAD Treaty is an exception as it specifies that one of its aims and objectives is to: 'Initiate and promote programmes and projects for sustainable development of natural resources and environment protection'.[61] Here the emphasis on the environmental pillar of sustainable development is amplified.

Besides the general reference to the objective of sustainable development, several constitutive instruments of RECs also mention more specifically environmental protection as one of their core objectives. In general terms, the SADC Treaty lists 'effective protection of the environment' as one of its key objectives.[62] Similarly, the ECOWAS Treaty mentions 'the harmonization and co-ordination of policies for the protection of the environment'[63] as one of the aims and objectives it is pursuing. The ECOWAS Treaty actually goes a step further than the SADC Treaty and incorporates a specific Chapter on 'Cooperation in Environment and Natural Resources' (Chapter VI). Under that Chapter, ECOWAS Member States are required, for instance, to 'undertake to protect, preserve and enhance the natural environment of the region and co-operate in the event of natural disasters' (Article 29), and to 'undertake, individually and collectively, to take every appropriate step to prohibit the importation, transiting, dumping and burying of hazardous and toxic wastes in their respective territories' (Article 30).

The constitutive treaty of COMESA also goes in the same direction—albeit in a more detailed manner—than the ECOWAS Treaty and provides for an obligation for Member States to cooperate in the management and development of the environment. Chapter XVI of the COMESA Treaty addresses cooperation specifically in the development of natural resources, environment and wildlife, and contains obligations such as the sustainable management of natural resources and preservation of the environment from degradation and pollution. It requires Member States to develop a common environmental policy aimed at preserving ecosystems, preventing and reversing the effects of pollution, and declining biodiversity. Interestingly, the COMESA Treaty refers to certain principles of international environmental law, such as the principle of prevention ('preventive action') and the polluter-pays principle (Article 112, para 6).

The EAC Treaty is perhaps the most sophisticated constitutive instrument of a REC in Africa when it comes to specific provisions regarding the protection of the environment. First and foremost, it defines the 'environment' in a rather broad manner as: 'the natural resources of air, water, soil, fauna and flora, ecosystems, land, the man-made physical features, cultural heritage, the characteristic aspects of the landscape

[60] Rio + 20, United Nations Conference on Sustainable Development (2012), UN Doc A/RES/66/288, para 2.

[61] Agreement Establishing the IGAD, above n 42, Article 7(e).

[62] SADC Treaty, above n 43, Article 5 (last amended in 2015).

[63] Revised ECOWAS Treaty, above n 41, Article 3(2)(a).

and the socio-economic interaction between the said factors and any living and non-living organisms'.[64] Then it provides that one of the objectives of the EAC Treaty is for the Community to ensure 'the promotion of sustainable utilisation of the natural resources of the Partner States and the taking of measures that would effectively protect the natural environment of the Partner States'. As such, the EAC Treaty lays down several detailed obligations on Member States to manage and protect the environment. Some of those obligations relate to the management of the environment (Article 112) while others are specifically dealing with the Prevention of Illegal Trade in and Movement of Toxic Chemicals, Substances and Hazardous Wastes or the management of natural resources (Article 114) or again wildlife management (Article 116).

Because of its unique character, Article 111 of the EAC Treaty deserves to be fully quoted here:

> Environmental Issues and Natural Resources
>
> 1. The Partner States recognise that development activities may have negative impacts on the environment leading to the degradation of the environment and depletion of natural resources and that a clean and healthy environment is a prerequisite for sustainable development. The Partner States therefore:
>
> (a) agree to take concerted measures to foster co-operation in the joint and efficient management and sustainable utilisation of natural resources within the Community;
>
> (b) undertake, through environmental management strategy, to co-operate and co-ordinate their policies and actions for the protection and conservation of the natural resources and environment against all forms of degradation and pollution arising from developmental activities;
>
> (c) undertake to co-operate and adopt common policies for control of trans-boundary movement of toxic and hazardous waste including nuclear materials and any other undesirable materials;
>
> (d) shall provide prior and timely notification and relevant information to each other on natural and human activities that may or are likely to have significant trans-boundary environmental impacts and shall consult with each other at an early stage; and
>
> (e) shall develop and promote capacity building programmes for sustainable management of natural resources.
>
> 2. Action by the Community relating to the environment shall have the following objectives:
>
> (a) to preserve, protect and enhance the quality of the environment;
>
> (b) to contribute towards the sustainability of the environment;
>
> (c) to ensure sustainable utilisation of natural resources like lakes, wetlands, forests and other aquatic and terrestrial ecosystems; and

---

64 This is a definition that goes beyond the one retained by certain international courts and tribunals. See for instance the *Iron Rhine* Tribunal's definition: 'the Tribunal notes that in all of these categories 'environment' is broadly referred to as including air, water, land, flora and fauna, natural ecosystems and sites, human health and safety, and climate'.

(d) to jointly develop and adopt water resources conservation and management policies that ensure sustenance and preservation of ecosystems.

It is on the basis of the objectives, rules and principles enshrined in the constitutive instruments of the RECs that many of them have developed what may be described as *derived law regarding environmental protection*. For instance, the EAC Protocol on Environment and Natural Resources Management (2006)[65] is an example of such derived environmental law within the framework of RECs. The Protocol governs cooperation among EAC Member States in managing the natural resources and the environment which lie in their jurisdiction, including any transboundary resources. The Protocol also contains a non-exhaustive list of activities it applies to, such as conservation of biodiversity, management of wildlife resources and mitigation of climate change. The parties have the duty to ensure sound environmental and natural resource management in accordance with certain principles such as the fundamental right of the people to live in a clean and healthy environment, sustainable development, the precautionary principle and intergenerational equity.

Besides the derived environmental law, RECs have also shaped and formulated a broad array of environmental provisions within what can be referred to as 'environment-related instruments', i.e. instruments that do not deal primarily with environmental protection. The best examples are environmental provisions contained in African investment treaties. As stressed in the Report of the UN Secretary-General on 'Gaps in International Environmental Law and Environment-Related Instruments': 'Newly concluded investment treaties now tend to include environmental clauses, with such evolution particularly evident in Africa'.[66]

Examples of such new trends in the making of international environmental law in Africa, can be found in the ECOWAS Supplementary Act (2008)[67] which imposes upon investors, obligations to conduct a pre-establishment environmental impact assessment,[68] and to disseminate the results of such an EIA to the public. The ECOWAS Common Investment Code (ECOWIC) (2018)[69] was recently formulated in line with the ECOWAS Supplementary Act. It takes stock of the evolution of international environmental law and recognizes some principles *in statu nascendi*, such as the principle of non-regression.[70] The ECOWIC also makes mention of Multilateral

---

[65] EAC Protocol on Environment and Natural Resources Management, 3 April 2006, available at: www.eac.int/documents/EAC_protocol_on_enviro_and_natural_res_mgt.pdf Accessed 21 July 2020.

[66] UN Doc A/73/419* (2018), para 72.

[67] ECOWAS Supplementary Act A/SA.3/12/08 adopting community rules on investment and the modalities for their implementation with ECOWAS (2008).

[68] Ibid., Article 12.

[69] The ECOWAS Common Investment Code (ECOWIC) (2018), available at: https://nipc.gov.ng/wp-content/uploads/2019/12/ecowiccode.pdf Accessed 21 July 2020.

[70] Ibid., Article 21, para 3: 'The Member States further recognise that it is unlawful under this Code to encourage investment by relaxing national health, safety, or environmental measures. Accordingly, no Member State shall waive or otherwise derogate from, or offer to waive or otherwise derogate from, such measures as an encouragement for the establishment, acquisition, expansion, or retention of an investment in its national territory.'

Environmental Agreements (MEAs),[71] and implements certain principles of international environmental law such as environmental democracy (public participation, access to information and access to environmental justice).[72]

The Revised Investment Agreement for the COMESA Common Investment Area (CCIA) (2017)[73] also offers an interesting example of such a trend of incorporating environmental provisions in investment agreements. For instance, Article 31 of the CCIA provides that investors must apply the 'precautionary principle to their environmental impact assessment and to decisions taken in relation to a proposed investment, including any necessary mitigating or alternative approaches to the investment, or precluding the investment if necessary. The application of the precautionary principle by investors and investments shall be described in the environmental impact assessment'.[74]

In sum, African RECs have developed a strong corpus of rules and principles in relation to the protection of the environment. Those said rules and principles can be in many cases subject to disputes before African regional courts and tribunals. They can also inform the interpretation of what may be considered as African community law. Even if the jurisprudence of African regional courts and tribunals remains scarce at the present time with respect to the breadth of environmental norms, existing practice shows that African regional courts and tribunals have great potential to develop international environmental law and to contribute to more effective protection of the environment in Africa.

10.4 'Lest We Forget What We Came Here to Do':[75] Environmental Activism in the Jurisprudence of African Regional Courts and Tribunals

The jurisprudence of African regional courts and tribunals in the field of environmental protection remains scarce to say the least. In that respect, it is hard to speak in terms of *jurisprudence constante* yet when it comes to assessing their contribution to the development and implementation of international environmental law. This

[71] Ibid., Article 23, para 1: 'The Member States recognise that multilateral environmental agreements to which they are a party play a strategic role, globally, regionally, and nationally, in protecting the natural environment, and that their respective implementation of these agreements is critical to achieving the environmental objectives of these agreements. Each Member State affirms its commitment to implement in its national territory the multilateral environmental agreements to which it is a party.'

[72] Ibid., Articles 24 and 25.

[73] Investment Agreement for the COMESA Common Investment Area (CCIA) (2017), available at: https://www.comesa.int/wp-content/uploads/2019/04/COMESA-Gazette-Volume-21-Final_upload_web.pdf. Accessed 21 July 2020.

[74] Ibid., Article 31, para 5.

[75] Title inspired by the music album of Sons of Kemet, *Lest We Forget What We Came Here to Do*, Naim Jazz, 2015.

being said, African regional courts and tribunals have the potential of strengthening such a contribution. The existing case-law to date shows that they actually have been activists in the promotion of sustainable development considerations and in giving *effet utile* to some of the most important principles of international environmental law. Such an observation can be made for both dispute settlement mechanisms established at the continental level—i.e. the Commission and the African Court—then for some of the courts and tribunals established at the level of RECs—namely the ECOWAS Court of Justice and the EAC Court of Justice. Let us look at their jurisprudence *seriatim.*

10.4.1 Integrating Human Rights and the Environment: The Practice of the African Commission and the African Court on Human and Peoples' Rights

The African Commission on Human and Peoples' Rights was the first to address the question of protection of the environment in relation to the rights enshrined in the African Charter, in particular the right to a healthy environment. As a quasi-judicial body, its decisions are not binding. However, they hold high persuasive value and largely influenced the judgments rendered by the African Court in the *African Commission on Human and Peoples' Rights v Republic of Kenya* case[76] and the ECOWAS Court of Justice in the *SERAP v Nigeria* case.[77]

The landmark case in which the Commission took the opportunity to clarify the contours and scope of the right to a healthy environment and, concomitantly, to contribute to better effective protection of the environment in Africa is the *Ogoni* case.[78]

This case was brought before the Commission in 2001 by two NGOs, i.e. SERAC and CESR. Both of them mainly complained that the government of Nigeria had been directly engaged in production of oil through the Nigerian National Petroleum Company (NNPC), the operations of which caused severe environmental degradation and consequently health problems to the Ogoni people. The Communication filed by SERAC and CESR also asserted that the government withheld crucial information regarding the dangers and consequences of the activities of the oil companies and that the Ogoni were not involved in decisions important for the development of Ogoniland. According to SERAC and CESR the acts of Nigeria constituted a violation, *inter alia*, of Articles 16 and 24 of the African Charter. While Article 24 enshrines the right to a clean or healthy environment, Article 16 of the African Charter relates to the right

[76] ACHR, *African Commission on Human and People's Rights v Republic of Kenya*, Judgment, 26 May 2017, App No 006/2012, para 277 (the Ogiek case).

[77] ECOWAS Court of Justice, *Socio-economic Rights and Accountability Project (SERAP) v Nigeria,* Ruling, December 2010, ECW/CCJ/APP/08/09, paras 75–79.

[78] ACHPR, *Social and Economic Rights Action Centre (SERAC) and the Centre for Economic and Social Rights (CESR) v Nigeria*, 27 October 2001, No 155/96, para 52 (the Ogoni case).

to health *per se* ('Every individual shall have the right to enjoy the best attainable state of physical and mental health').

In that respect, and from a substantive point of view, the *Ogoni* case has been an opportunity for the Commission to strengthen the link between health and the environment, a link which is not always sufficiently stressed in international environmental law.[79] Indeed, the Commission, in its decision, stated that: 'the importance of a clean and safe environment that is closely linked to economic and social rights in so far as the environment affects the quality of life and safety of the individual.'[80] Interestingly, the Commission preferred to refer to a 'subsidiary means of interpretation'—to borrow the language of Article 38, paragraph 1 d) of the Statute of the ICJ—to support its legal interpretation of the relationship between the right to heath and the right to a clean environment. Indeed, the Commission referred to doctrine, and in particular, to the work of the late Professor Alexander Kiss.[81] It did neither refer to international jurisprudence nor to instruments of international environmental law. The Commission could have, for instance, referred to the Judgment of the ICJ in the *Gabcikovo-Nagymaros* case where the Court explicitly acknowledged that the environment 'represents […] the quality of life and the very health of human beings, including generations unborn';[82] but the Commission chose not do so. It could have referred to soft law instruments such as the 1992 Rio Declaration on Environment and Development, and in particular to Principle 1 of the Rio Declaration which embodies the right to a healthy environment by stating: 'Human beings are at the center of concerns for sustainable development. They are entitled to a healthy and productive life in harmony with nature'; here also, the Commission chose not to do so.

The Commission in the *Ogoni* case found it unnecessary to dwell upon general international environmental law and/or the case-law of international courts and tribunals to substantiate its interpretations of the right to a clean environment and or the relationship between the said right and the right to health. In short, it did not find it compelling, as the WTO Appellate Body, to invoke the 'contemporary concerns of the community of nations about the protection and conservation of the environment'[83] in its interpretation of what may be qualified as the legal environmental components of the right to a healthy environment.

---

[79] On this point, see Mbengue and Waltmann 2018, pp. 222–223.

[80] ACHPR, *Social and Economic Rights Action Centre (SERAC) and the Centre for Economic and Social Rights (CESR) v Nigeria*, above n 78, para 51.

[81] According to Prof. Kiss: 'an environment degraded by pollution and defaced by the destruction of all beauty and variety is as contrary to satisfactory living conditions and the development as the breakdown of the fundamental ecologic equilibria is harmful to physical and moral health.' See ACHPR, *Social and Economic Rights Action Centre (SERAC) and the Centre for Economic and Social Rights (CESR) v Nigeria*, above n 78, para 51.

[82] ICJ, *Gabčíkovo-Nagymaros Project (Hungary v Slovakia)*, above n 1, p. 41, para 53.

[83] *WTO, United States—Import Prohibition of Certain Shrimp and Shrimp Products*, Appellate Body Report, 12 October 1998, WTO/DS58/AB/R, (*US—Shrimp (Appellate Body Report)*), para 129.

The same line of thought can be also found with respect to the procedural obligations that the Commission identified as deriving from the right to a healthy environment. The Commission ruled that in order to comply with the 'spirit' of Articles of 16 and 24 of the Charter, an African State must:

> at least permit [...] independent scientific monitoring of threatened environments, require[e] and publicis[e] environmental and social impact studies prior to any major industrial development, undertak[e] appropriate monitoring and provid[e] information to those communities exposed to hazardous materials and activities and provid[e] meaningful opportunities for individuals to be heard and to participate in the development decisions affecting their communities.[84]

The Commission held that Nigeria had failed to fulfil any of these procedural obligations. It accepted that the Nigerian government had the right to generate revenue through oil extraction, and to utilize that income for promoting the socio-economic development of Nigerians. However, the Commission considered that Nigeria also had a duty of securing and protecting the rights of the Ogoni, including their procedural environmental rights.

One of the legal consequences that the Commission drew from its reasoning was that Nigeria would have to '[e]nsur[e] that appropriate environmental and social impact assessments are prepared for any future oil development and that the safe operation of any further oil development is guaranteed through effective and independent oversight bodies for the petroleum industry'.[85] What is interesting is that the Commission determined such a duty for Nigeria without making any reference to customary international environmental law or at least to principles of international environmental law such as the principle of environmental democracy.[86] The Commission seems simply to deduce that such a duty to conduct an environmental impact assessment (EIA) is inherent in the right to a clean and healthy environment. The approach of the Commission is different from the one adopted, for instance, by the ICJ in the *Gabcikovo-Nagymaros* case—which invoked 'new norms (that) have to be taken into consideration, and [...] new standards [that have to be] given proper weight'[87] —or in the *Pulp Mills* case where the Court invoked 'a practice, which in

[84] ACHPR, *Social and Economic Rights Action Centre (SERAC) and the Centre for Economic and Social Rights (CESR) v Nigeria*, above n 78, para 53.

[85] Ibid., para 69.

[86] See Principle 10 of the 1992 Rio Declaration on Environment and Development: 'Environmental issues are best handled with the participation of all concerned citizens, at the relevant level. At the national level, each individual shall have appropriate access to information concerning the environment that is held by public authorities, including information on hazardous materials and activities in their communities, and the opportunity to participate in decision-making processes. States shall facilitate and encourage public awareness and participation by making information widely available. Effective access to judicial and administrative proceedings, including redress and remedy, shall be provided.'

[87] ICJ, *Gabčíkovo-Nagymaros Project (Hungary v Slovakia)*, above n 1, p. 41, para 140.

recent years has gained so much acceptance among States that it may now be considered a requirement under general international law to undertake an environmental impact assessment'.[88]

The Commission's 'self-contained' implementation and interpretation of the right to a healthy environment in the *Ogoni* case, at least with respect to its relationship with general international environmental law, should not overshadow the great contribution it made in strengthening the link between human rights and environmental protection. It was, therefore, not surprising that the Inter-American Court of Human Rights, in its pioneering Advisory Opinion on *The Environment and Human Rights*, took inspiration from the *Ogoni* case in the following terms:

> In this regard, the African Commission on Human and Peoples' Rights underscored that the right to a healthy environment imposed on States the obligation to take reasonable measures to prevent pollution and ecological degradation, to promote conservation, and to secure an ecologically sustainable development and use of natural resources, as well as to monitor projects that could affect the environment.[89]

In another case, the *Endorois* case,[90] the Commission was much more open to the idea of referring to general international law and to the case-law of other international courts and tribunals, and in particular the jurisprudence of the Inter-American Court of Human Rights in *Moiwana v Suriname* and *Saramaka v Suriname*. The *Endorois* case concerned the rights of the Endorois, an indigenous community which had been allegedly evicted from its ancestral land by the government of Kenya. The Endorois argued that this eviction violated, inter alia, their right to property, their right to freely dispose of their natural resources and their right to development—all of which were linked to possessing a satisfactory environment. The government argued that the eviction was for the preservation of wildlife and the environment, which it was achieving by converting the contested land into a game reserve.

In its decision, the Commission recognized the Endorois' right to culture, religious worship, to own land and to partake in their development. It rejected the government's argument, as it had failed to undertake an environmental and social impact assessment to substantiate its claims. It observed that the government had failed to facilitate any effective participation of the Endorois community in the decision of declaring their land a game reserve, nor had it shared any profit with the community. The failure to provide conditions for the Endorois people to develop amounted to a violation of their right to development. The destruction of the environment, and the pollution of their traditional ecosystems were considered as relevant while concluding that the right to development had been violated.

---

[88] ICJ, *Pulp Mills on the River Uruguay, (Argentinia v Uruguay)*, Judgment, 20 April 2010, ICJ Reports 2010, p. 14.

[89] *The Environment and Human Rights (State Obligations in Relation to the Environment in the Context of the Protection and Guarantee of the Rights to Life and to Personal Integrity—Interpretation and Scope of Articles 4(1) and 5(1) of the American Convention on Human Rights)*, Advisory Opinion OC-23/18, 15 November 2017, IACtHR Ser. A, No 23, para 61.

[90] ACHPR, *Centre for Minority Rights Development (Kenya) and Minority Rights Group International on behalf of Endorois Welfare Council v Kenya*, Decision, 4 February 2010, Comm No 276/2003, para 152. Hereinafter the Endorois case.

Noteworthy is the fact that the right to a healthy environment was not formally speaking at stake in the *Endorois* case. The Commission took into account environmental concerns in the determination of whether certain rights under the African Charter were violated by Kenya; but it did not proceed as such with an interpretation of the contours, content and scope of the right to a healthy environment. The different interpretative methodologies in the *Ogoni* case and in the *Endorois* case seem to indicate that the Commission is more comfortable at the present time to refer to general international law and the case-law of other international courts and tribunals—in particular human rights courts—when the claims do not directly relate to the right to a healthy environment but merely to some environmental concerns that arise in the context of other human rights protected under the African Charter. The Commission tends, therefore, to favour a more *informal* approach to the development of international environmental law than a *formal* approach that means referring to instruments of international environmental law, whether they be hard law instruments or soft law instruments. What explains such a posture is perhaps the legal uncertainty that quite often characterizes the status, scope or content of several principles of international environmental law. The UN Secretary General himself in his Report on Gaps in International Environmental Law and Environment-Related Instruments has pointed to the uncertainty that surrounds international environmental law generally.[91] The hesitation towards environmental principles was also manifest in the award rendered by the *Iron Rhine* Tribunal when it declared: 'There is considerable debate as to what, within the field of environmental law, constitutes 'rules' or 'principles'; what is 'soft law'; and which environmental treaty law or principles have contributed to the development of customary international law.'

Despite the undeniable activism of the Commission towards environmental protection, judicial caution seems to be a constant trend in the African system of human rights when it comes to *legal pronouncements* about international environmental law. Indeed, the African Court followed the same cautious approach of the Commission in the first case—and only case to date—in which it had to deal indirectly with claims regarding the protection of the environment. In the *Ogiek* case,[92] the African Court was asked to adjudge if the eviction of the Ogiek, an indigenous community from the Mau Forest situated in the Rift Valley (Kenya), violated the African Charter. The Ogiek argued that this eviction violated, inter alia, the right to land (Article 14), the right to life (Article 4), the right to culture (Article 17(2) and

[91] UN Doc A/73/419* (2018), para 102: 'There are important deficiencies with respect to principles of international environmental law, in particular with respect to their content and legal status. There are instances where there is no clarity as to the nature and content of a principle, or no judicial consensus as to its applicability, or no recognition in binding legal instruments, or all of the above. The degree of legal uncertainty surrounding many of these principles has a direct and indirect impact on the predictability and implementation of sectoral environmental regimes. Some principles, such as access to information, participation in decision-making and access to justice, have only regional application. Others, such as a right to a clean and healthy environment and the principles of non-regression and progression, have only recently, and only in a limited number of legal instruments, been recognized and have not yet been fully developed [...]'.

[92] ACHR, *African Commission on Human and People's Rights v Republic of Kenya*, above n 76, para 7.

(3)), the right to freely dispose of wealth and natural resources (Article 22) and the right to development (Article 21) under the African Charter. The eviction was ordered as the forest was a 'reserved water catchment zone'. The government characterized this eviction as a measure to protect and conserve the environment 'for the benefit of its entire citizenry under its national laws as well as under the African Convention on Conservation of Nature and Natural Resources'.[93]

In its 2017 judgment, the African Court ruled that the degradation of the environment taking place in the Mau forest was not a consequence of the presence of the Ogiek peoples. In fact, the government had produced no evidence to substantiate this claim. Rather, in the view of the African Court it was a result of 'encroachment upon the land by other groups and government excisions for settlements, ill-advised logging concessions.'[94] The Court thus located the cause of the degradation in the actions of the government, and not the practices of the Ogiek. Consequently, it held that the eviction of the Ogiek was neither a necessary nor a proportionate measure taken to preserve the ecosystems of the forest.

Here again, it is important to note that the case was not *per se* about the right to a healthy environment since no direct claim of violation of Article 24 of the African Charter was made by the Ogiek. Nevertheless, there was room for the African Court to at least consolidate or better clarify the relationship between international environmental law and human rights law in the African context. As mentioned above, Kenya did not limit itself to invoking its domestic law to justify the eviction of the Ogiek. Kenya also invoked the African Convention on Conservation of Nature and Natural Resources (Maputo Convention). The Court did not find it necessary to make pronouncements on the relevance of the Maputo Convention for the interpretation of rights under the African Charter, including the right to a healthy environment. Perhaps the Court did not have to do so for reasons of judicial economy. But it was definitely a missed opportunity to better integrate African environmental law and African human rights law. Both the Maputo Convention and the African Charter on Human and Peoples' Rights are part of the *acquis* of the African Union and as such systemic integration between the two regimes could only benefit the progressive development of international environmental law in Africa. African regional courts and tribunals seemed to have followed the approach of systemic integration.

[93] Ibid., para 220.

[94] Ibid., para 130.

10.4.2 Reinforcing Due Diligence to Protect the Environment: The Practice of the ECOWAS Court of Justice

The ECOWAS Court of Justice had an opportunity to engage with claims of environmental degradation in the *SERAP v Nigeria* case.[95] The case was initiated by an NGO called the Socio-Economic Rights and Accountability Project (SERAP), which filed a complaint with the ECOWAS Court of Justice against the Government of Nigeria and several oil companies (i.e. Nigerian National Petroleum Company, Shell Petroleum Development Company, ELF Petroleum Nigeria Ltd, AGIP Nigeria PLC, Chevron Oil Nigeria PLC, Total Nigeria PLC and Exxon Mobil). SERAP complained of alleged violations of the right to health, the right to an adequate standard of living and to economic and social development of the people of the Niger Delta, as well as the failure of the Defendants to enforce laws and regulations to protect the environment and prevent pollution. The Niger Delta, according to SERAP, had suffered from several oil spills over decades which had destroyed crops, damaged the productivity and fertility of the soil, and contaminated the water consumed by communities living in the forest.

More specifically, SERAP requested the ECOWAS Court of Justice to declare 'that everyone in the Niger Delta is entitled to the internationally recognised human right to an adequate standard of living, including adequate access to food, to healthcare, to clean water, to a clean and healthy environment; to social and economic development; and the right to life and human security and dignity'[96] and that 'the systematic denial of access to information to the people of the Niger Delta about how oil exploration and production will affect them, is unlawful as it violates the International Covenant on Economic, Social and Cultural rights, the International Covenant on Civil and Political Rights, and the African Charter on Human and Peoples' Rights.'[97]

The Government of Nigeria raised a series of preliminary objections, and in particular that SERAP as an NGO had no *locus standi* before the ECOWAS Court of Justice and that corporations and individuals could not be sued before the Court. Addressing the *locus standi* of SERAP in its decision on preliminary objections, the ECOWAS Court of Justice paved the way for an *actio popularis* in the field of environmental protection in West Africa. The Court developed a test consisting of a consideration that where serious violations of human rights concern '*entire communities*'[98] and relate to '*environmental devastation* without sufficient and protective intervention from public authorities',[99] then *locus standi* before the Court should be granted to any NGO duly constituted according to the national law of any ECOWAS Member

[95] ECOWAS Court of Justice, *Socio-economic Rights and Accountability Project (SERAP) v Nigeria,* above n 77, para 7.

[96] African Charter on Human and Peoples' Rights, above n 26, para 19(a).

[97] Ibid., para 19(d).

[98] ECOWAS Court of Justice, *Socio-economic Rights and Accountability Project (SERAP) v Nigeria,* above n 77, para 55.

[99] Ibid.

State, and enjoying observer status before an ECOWAS institution. It then observed that: 'There is a large consensus in International Law that when the issue at stake is the violation of rights of entire communities, as in the case of the damage to the environment, the access to justice should be facilitated.'[100]

Interestingly, and in order to base the so-called 'large consensus' on concrete roots, the ECOWAS Court of Justice invoked mainly Article 2(5) of the Convention on Access to Information, Public Participation in Decision-Making and Access to Justice in Environmental Matters (commonly referred to as the Aarhus Convention).[101] According to the Court, the said provision defines the 'public concerned' with environment protection as the 'public affected or likely to be affected by, or having an interest, in the environmental decision-making; for the purposes of this definition, nongovernmental organization promoting environmental protection and meeting any requirements under national law shall be deemed to have an interest'. Furthermore, the Court also invoked Article 9 of Aarhus Convention which grants access to justice to the 'public concerned' as defined in Article 2(5).[102] In the words of the Court:

> Although the (Aarhus) convention is not a binding instrument on African States, its importance, as a persuasive evidence of an international communis opinio juris in allowing NGOs to access the Courts for protection of Human Rights related to the environment, cannot be ignored or underestimated by this Court.[103]

The Aarhus Convention is, indeed, a conventional instrument that has been adopted in the context of the United Nations Economic Commission for Europe (UNECE) to implement the principle of environmental democracy that is enshrined in Principle 10 of the 1992 Rio Declaration on Environment and Development. Although the Aarhus Convention has been opened for universal participation, no African country has acceded to it yet. The porosity of the ECOWAS Court of Justice to international environmental law in the *SERAP* case is striking and reveals a sharp contrast with the approach of the Commission and the African Court of Human and Peoples' Rights. Its openness to a treaty that no African State has signed or ratified shows also a radically different perspective from that adopted by the ICJ in the *Pulp Mills* case. In this case, Argentina invoked another UNECE Convention, the 1991 Convention on Environmental Impact Assessment in a Transboundary Context,[104] to allege that Uruguay failed to conduct a proper EIA under international law and practice. The position of the Court was simply to judge the Espoo Convention as

---

[100] Ibid., para 56.

[101] Convention on Access to Information, Public Participation in Decision-Making and Access to Justice in Environmental Matters, 25 June 1998, 2161 UNTS 447, entered into force 30 October 2001 (Aarhus Convention).

[102] ECOWAS Court of Justice, *Socio-economic Rights and Accountability Project (SERAP) v Nigeria,* above n 77, para 57.

[103] Ibid., para 58.

[104] Convention on Environmental Impact Assessment in a Transboundary Context (UNECE), 25 February 1991, 1989 UNTS 309, entered into force 19 September 1997.

irrelevant to specify the scope and content of an EIA since Argentina and Uruguay were not parties to it.[105]

It is true that in the *SERAP* case, the ECOWAS Court was not asked to decide whether there had been a violation of the Aarhus Convention. However, the fact that it sees the Aarhus Convention 'as a persuasive evidence of an international communis opinio juris' demonstrates that it has given full legal effect to the Convention in the context of a dispute involving an African country. Yet, it remains a mystery which customary rule of interpretation the ECOWAS Court of Justice relied upon to reach such a conclusion. In the future, it might be useful for the Court to better substantiate its reasoning: is it on the basis of Article 31.3(c) of the 1969 Vienna Convention on the Law of Treaties? Or on the basis of a *renvoi* to international law in the ECOWAS Treaty?

The judicial activism of the ECOWAS Court has been tempered by its refusal to establish that it had jurisdiction over the oil extracting corporations, despite the Court insisting on the need to render multinationals accountable under international law.[106] It considered in the context and legal framework of ECOWAS that only Member States and Community Institutions can be sued before it for alleged violation of human rights,[107] including the right to a healthy environment.

Another level of judicial activism in favour of environmental protection can be denoted in the way the ECOWAS Court has objectivized the subject-matter of the dispute at the merits stage of the *SERAP* case. Albeit SERAP alleged several violations of human rights and invoked more than 20 legal provisions, the ECOWAS Court of Justice decided to circumscribe the dispute to the right to a clean and healthy environment. In the words of the ECOWAS Court of Justice: 'As such, the heart of the

---

[105] ICJ, *Pulp Mills on the River Uruguay, (Argentinia v Uruguay)*, above n 88, para 205.

[106] According to ECOWAS Court of Justice, *Socio-economic Rights and Accountability Project (SERAP) v Nigeria,* above n 77, para 73: 'the lack of jurisdiction of the Court on individuals sued for human rights violation applies entirely in the cases, as the instant, where the alleged perpetrators of the violation are other non-state actors like corporations. Neither individuals nor corporations are parties to the treaties that the international Tribunal with jurisdiction over human rights are empowered to enforce'. In more recent years, some international courts and tribunals have been more progressive with the international subjectivity of corporations and their accountability under international law, see for instance, *Urbaser S.A. and Consorcio de Aguas Bilbao Bizkaia, Bilbao Biskaia Ur Partzuergoa v The Argentine Republic*, Award, 8 December 2016, ICSID Case No ARB/07/26, para 1195: 'The Tribunal may mention in this respect that international law accepts corporate social responsibility as a standard of crucial importance for companies operating in the field of international commerce. This standard includes commitments to comply with human rights in the framework of those entities' operations conducted in countries other than the country of their seat or incorporation. In light of this more recent development, it can no longer be admitted that companies operating internationally are immune from becoming subjects of international law. On the other hand, even though several initiatives undertaken at the international scene are seriously targeting corporations human rights conduct, they are not, on their own, sufficient to oblige corporations to put their policies in line with human rights law. The focus must be, therefore, on contextualizing a corporation's specific activities as they relate to the human right at issue in order to determine whether any international law obligations attach to the non-State individual.'

[107] ECOWAS Court of Justice, *Socio-economic Rights and Accountability Project (SERAP) v Nigeria,* above n 77, para 71.

dispute is to determine whether, in the circumstances referred to, the attitude of the Federal Republic of Nigeria, as a party to the African Charter on Human and Peoples' Rights, is in conformity with the obligations subscribed to in the terms of Article 24 of the said instrument, which provides: 'All peoples shall have the right to a general satisfactory environment favourable to their development". This approach of '[isolating] the real issue in the case and [identifying] the object of the claim'[108] is in line with the practice of international courts and tribunals such as the ICJ and arbitral tribunals.[109]

In its judgment on the merits, the ECOWAS Court of Justice continued on the same path than in its decision on preliminary objections; it gave some more West African flavour, texture and colour to the obligation of due diligence in the field of environmental protection. Most importantly, and by contrast to the Commission and African Court, it fostered the interaction between human rights law and international environmental law. Indeed, the ECOWAS Court in a pioneering manner considered that the right to a clean and healthy environment under Article 24 of the African Charter requires due diligence from States with respect to the protection of the environment.

And, in doing so, it engaged in proactive cross-fertilization by mentioning the case-law of the ICJ and the work of the *Institut de droit international*:

> Thus, the duty assigned by Article 24 to each State Party to the Charter is both an obligation of attitude and an obligation of result. The environment, as emphasised by the International Court of Justice, 'is not an abstraction but represents the living space, the quality of life and the very health of human beings, including generations unborn' (Legality of the Threat or Use of Nuclear Arms, ICJ Advisory Opinion of 8 July 2006, paragraph 28). It must be considered as an indivisible whole, comprising the biotic and abiotic natural resources, notably air, water, land, fauna and flora and the interaction between these same factors (International Law Institute, Resolution of 4 September 1997, Article 1). The environment is essential to every human being. The quality of human life depends on the quality of the environment.[110]

Nevertheless, in cross-fertilizing with the ICJ, the ECOWAS Court of Justice went further than the Court, innovated and contributed to the development of general or customary international environmental law by strengthening the content of due diligence. In the opinion of the ECOWAS Court, due diligence is not only an obligation of conduct ('obligation of attitude') but also an obligation of result. The dominant position in international jurisprudence at the present time has been to qualify due diligence merely as an obligation of conduct. In the *Pulp Mills* case, the ICJ considered

---

[108] See ICJ, *Nuclear Tests (Australia v France)*, Judgment, ICJ Reports 1974, p. 253, para 29.

[109] See Permanent Court of Arbitration, *Dispute Concerning Coastal State Rights in the Black Sea, Sea of Azov, and Kerch Strait (Ukraine v the Russian Federation)*, Preliminary Objections, 21 February 2021, para 151: 'However, it is ultimately for the Arbitral Tribunal itself to determine on an objective basis the nature of the dispute dividing the Parties by '[isolating] the real issue in the case and [identifying] the object of the claim'.

[110] ECOWAS Court of Justice, *Socio-economic Rights and Accountability Project (SERAP) v Nigeria*, above n 77, para 100.

that '[a]n obligation to adopt regulatory or administrative measures either individually or jointly and to enforce them is an obligation of conduct.'[111] The same approach has been followed by the Seabed Disputes Chamber of the International Tribunal for the Law of the Sea when it stated that '[t]he notions of obligations 'of due diligence' and obligations 'of conduct' are connected'.[112]

The ECOWAS Court explained its reasoning in the following terms:

> Article 24 of the Charter thus requires every State to take every measure to maintain the quality of the environment understood as an integrated whole, such that the state of the environment may satisfy the human beings who live there, and enhance their sustainable development. It is by examining the state of the environment and entirely objective factors, that one judges, by the result, whether the State has fulfilled this obligation. If the State is taking all the appropriate legislative, administrative and other measures, it must ensure that *vigilance and diligence are being applied and observed towards attaining concrete results.*[113]

Effective environmental protection requires '*concrete results*'. This is particularly true in the African context where many countries have sophisticated environmental regulatory frameworks that are often not implemented and enforced. This is perhaps the reason why the ECOWAS Court of Justice opted to depart from the *jurisprudence constante* of many international courts and tribunals and ruled that due diligence is both an obligation of conduct and an obligation of result. Most of the reasoning of the ECOWAS Court in its judgment actually focuses on the 'results' that Nigeria should have achieved in terms of environmental protection. The ECOWAS Court, for instance, emphasized that:

> It is significant to note that despite all the laws it has adopted and all the agencies it has created, the Federal Republic of Nigeria was not able to point out in its pleadings a single action that has been taken in recent years to seriously and diligently hold accountable any of the perpetrators of the many acts of environmental degradation which occurred in the Niger Delta Region.[114]

Although the Nigerian government did present an exhaustive list of regulatory/legislative measures that it had enacted, the ECOWAS Court observed that the said measures did not suffice to prevent the continued environmental degradation of the region. It pointed out that 'adoption of legislation, no matter how advanced it may be…as well as the allocation of financial resources in equitable amounts…may still fall short of the compliance with *international obligations in matters of environmental protection...* if these measures…are not accompanied by additional and concrete measures aimed at preventing the occurrence of damage or ensuring accountability, with the effective reparation of the environmental damage

[111] ICJ, *Pulp Mills on the River Uruguay, (Argentina v Uruguay)*, above n 88, para 187.

[112] ITLOS, *Responsibilities and obligations of States with respect to activities in the Area*, Advisory Opinion, 1 February 2011, ITLOS Reports 2011, p. 10, para 111.

[113] ECOWAS Court of Justice, *Socio-economic Rights and Accountability Project (SERAP) v Nigeria*, above n 77, para 109 (emphasis added).

[114] Ibid., para 110.

suffered'.[115] The Court held that Nigeria had failed to effectively implement its legislation and regulations and was in fact, unable to demonstrate any action taken on its part. It appears, therefore, that the ECOWAS Court is more concerned with the 'effective enforcement' dimension of the duty of due diligence when it comes to environmental protection. And, it is for this reason that the Court rejected the argument of Nigeria according to which the oil companies, as license holders, had the duty to preserve the environment. The Court observed that the damage caused by the oil industries to the environment, which is a 'vital resource of such importance to all mankind'[116] could not be left to the discretion of oil companies or any agreements of compensation entered into between the companies and the victims. The Court, thus, concluded that Nigeria's *omission* to prevent environmental damage and punish those responsible for the environment's degradation violated the right to clean and healthy environment under Article 24 of the African Charter. The government had, with its inaction, violated its duty of 'vigilance and diligence' imposed by the said provision.[117]

The emphasis on the 'effective enforcement' dimension of due diligence prompted the Court to adopt an original approach to the remedies in this case. The Court went again a step further and ordered Nigeria as follows:

> Take all effective measures, within the shortest possible time, to ensure restoration of the environment of the Niger Delta;
>
> Take all measures that are necessary to prevent the occurrence of damage to the environment;
>
> Take all measures to hold the perpetrators of the environmental damage accountable.

The 'environmental remedies' ordered by the ECOWAS Court of Justice indicates some willingness to ensure effective environmental protection. Again, this judicial posture distinguishes the ECOWAS Court from other international courts and tribunals which have shied away from ordering extended and proactive remedies in the context of environmental disputes.[118]

There is no doubt that the ECOWAS Court's judgment in the *SERAP* case is a good benchmark for the development of international environmental law. In developing its reasoning and legal interpretations, the ECOWAS Court took into account the specificities of Africa in general and of West Africa in particular with respect to

---

[115] ECOWAS Court of Justice, *Socio-economic Rights and Accountability Project (SERAP) v Nigeria*, Judgment, December 2012, ECW/CCJ/JUD/18/12, para 105.

[116] Ibid., para 109.

[117] Ibid.

[118] See, for instance, the approach of the ICJ in *Certain Activities Carried Out by Nicaragua in the Border Area (Costa Rica v Nicaragua) and Construction of a Road in Costa Rica along the San Juan River (Nicaragua v Costa Rica), Judgment*, ICJ Reports 2015, p. 665, para 228: 'the Court notes that Costa Rica has begun mitigation works in order to reduce the adverse effects of the construction of the road on the environment. It expects that Costa Rica will continue to pursue these efforts in keeping with its due diligence obligation to monitor the effects of the project on the environment. It further reiterates the value of ongoing co-operation between the Parties in the performance of their respective obligations in connection with the San Juan River.'

environmental protection. But beyond the African context, the ECOWAS Court was also resolute in advancing international environmental law. Such a concern allows us perhaps to understand why the ECOWAS Court did not mention the *Ogoni* case at all in its Judgment, despite the fact that SERAP referred to that case in its arguments. Even if this is to be regretted—as a reference to the *Ogoni* case would have contributed to shaping an African jurisprudence on the protection of the environment—it is perfectly understandable. The ECOWAS Court of Justice engaged more with general international environmental law in its application and interpretation of Article 24 of the African Charter; it also wished to stress how environmental protection 'is both vital and important in the highest degree';[119] this was not the case of the Commission in the *Ogoni* case. Yet, it is to be hoped that in the future the ECOWAS Court of Justice will make more explicit reference to principles of international environmental law, such as the precautionary principle or the principle of prevention. The judgment in the *SERAP* case does not mention those principles in the context of due diligence. The ECOWAS Court could have seized the opportunity to highlight the importance of those principles even in the specific context of the right to a healthy environment. This is the approach followed by the Inter-American Court of Human Rights in its Advisory Opinion on *The Environment and Human Rights* where it stated that, in order to comply with the obligations to respect and ensure human rights, including the right to a healthy environment:

> States must fulfill a series of obligations with regard to both damage that has occurred within their territory and transboundary damage [...] (1) the obligation of prevention; (2) the precautionary principle; (3) the obligation of cooperation, and (4) the procedural obligations relating to environmental protection in order to establish and determine the State obligations derived from the systematic interpretation of these provisions together with the obligations to respect and to ensure (human) rights [...].[120]

This being said, one common denominator between the ECOWAS Court of Justice and the Commission as well as the African Court, is that they have looked at environmental protection through the lens of human rights. The experience of the EAC Court of Justice shows that it is also possible for African regional courts and tribunals to deal with the protection of the environment *per se* and independently from any human rights concerns.

[119] Expression borrowed from WTO case-law. See for instance *Brazil—Measures affecting Import of Retreated Tyres,* Panel Report, 12 June 2007, WT/DS332/R, para 7.210.

[120] Inter-American Court of Human Rights, above n 89, para 125.

10.4.3 Rethinking Remedies in Environmental Disputes: The Practice of the EAC Court of Justice

The East African Court of Justice dealt for the first time with the protection of the environment in the *ANAW v Tanzania* case.[121] The case addresses the obligation to protect the environment *per se*, without any link whatsoever to securing the right to a healthy environment of a given community.

The *ANAW* case is the African equivalent of the *Iron Rhine* arbitration. The dispute arose out of Tanzania's project to upgrade, tarmac, pave, realign, construct, create, commission or construct the 'Natta - Mugumu - Tabora B - Klein's Gate - Loliondo Road' (known as the 'North Road') across the Serengeti National Park, and subsequently open it for the use of the general public. ANAW, an NGO, alleged that such a project would breach the provisions of the EAC Treaty, and requested the Court to grant a permanent injunction to prevent this action. As a reminder, Article 30(1) of the EAC Treaty enables 'natural and legal persons to refer, for determination by this Court, the legality of any Act, regulation, directive, decision or action of a Partner State on the grounds that it is unlawful or is an infringement of the Treaty.'

Tanzania raised preliminary objections to the jurisdiction of the EAC Court to deal with the ANAW's application. In particular, Tanzania asserted that the EAC Court was barred from exercising jurisdiction under Article 30(3) of the EAC Treaty which provides that: 'The Court shall have no jurisdiction under this Article where an Act, regulation, directive, decision or action has been reserved under this Treaty to an institution of a Partner State'. The First Instance Division of the EAC Court, for its part, had no flicker of doubt that the action being complained of came within the ambit of actions envisaged under Article 30(3) of the Treaty.[122] It thus overruled Tanzania's objections.

Tanzania then appealed the decision of the First Instance Division of the EAC Court of Justice before the Appellate Division of that Court. The latter took the opportunity of this first case to expound on what it called its 'environmental jurisdiction'.[123] First, it pointed to the peculiarity of the EAC Treaty with respect to environmental protection. As mentioned earlier in this present contribution, the EAC Treaty sets forth the most sophisticated and comprehensive system of rules governing the protection of the environment in the constellation of African RECs. The Appellate Division of the EAC Court took judicial notice of this fact in the following terms:

> From this long catalogue of Treaty provisions, it is more than abundantly clear that the Partner States have bound themselves to observe a variety of express undertakings and obligations, concerning the promotion, preservation, conservation and protection of the environment. The scope and import of the environmental obligations voluntarily and freely undertaken

---

[121] EACJ, *Africa Network for Animal Welfare (ANAW) v The Attorney General of the United Republic of Tanzania*, Appeal Judgment No 3, 2012, p. 13.

[122] EACJ, *Africa Network for Animal Welfare (ANAW) v The Attorney General of the United Republic of Tanzania*, First Instance Judgment No 9, 20 June 2014, para 15.

[123] EACJ, *Africa Network for Animal Welfare (ANAW) v The Attorney General of the United Republic of Tanzania*, above n 121, p. 8.

> by the Partner States under the Treaty, is broad and all-encompassing. The purpose of these Treaty provisions cannot and must not be allowed to be undermined by a narrow or restrictive reading of those provisions. Rather the provisions must be given a purposive interpretation, construction, application and implementation. Such is the essence of the Vienna Convention on the Interpretation of Treaties.[124]

ANAW had alleged a violation of several provisions of the EAC Treaty.[125] These articles embody the environmental obligations to which Member States of the EAC are bound. For the Appellate Division, 'it is quite evident that all the (said) provisions impose on the Partner States of the EA Community one obligation or another; one duty or another; and one undertaking or another with regard to their mutual co-operation in the environmental field.'[126] In addition to its jurisdiction under Article 27(1) of the EAC Treaty (to *interpret and apply* the Treaty) and its mandate under Article 23(1) of the same Treaty (*to ensure compliance with the provisions of the Treaty*), the Appellate Division found it compelling for the EAC Court to exercise its jurisdiction in the *ANAW* case. Indeed, the Appellate Division indicated that because of the transboundary and *erga omnes* considerations surrounding the North Road project, the project would not only have implications in Tanzania but it could affect also the interests of Kenya, as a neighboring State of Tanzania (in particular the Masai Maara National Park in Kenya) and, most importantly, 'the interests of the entire international community' since the Serengeti National Park is classified as a UNESCO World Heritage site.[127]

The merits phase in the *ANAW* case (2014) is also interesting to assess the contribution of the EAC Court of Justice in the field of environmental protection. During that stage—which first took place before the First Instance Division of the EAC Court—ANAW fine-tuned some of its arguments regarding the relevant applicable law. In addition to the environmental provisions of the EAC Treaty as well as the UNESCO obligations, ANAW invoked other instruments of international environmental law. Indeed, it advanced that Tanzania's actions are unlawful and in conflict with its obligations under the 2003 African Convention on the Conservation of Nature and Natural Resources, the 1992 Rio Declaration on Environment and Development, the 1972 Stockholm Declaration on Human Environment and the 1992 United Nations Convention on Biodiversity.[128] In this respect, Tanzania raised again a preliminary

---

[124] Ibid., pp. 10–11.

[125] EAC Treaty, above n 39, Articles 5(2) and (3); 8(1) (c); 111(1) (d); 111(2); 112(1) and (2); and 114(1).

[126] EACJ, *Africa Network for Animal Welfare (ANAW) v The Attorney General of the United Republic of Tanzania*, above n 121.

[127] Ibid., p. 11.

[128] EACJ, *Africa Network for Animal Welfare (ANAW) v The Attorney General of the United Republic of Tanzania*, above n 122, para 15; Convention on Biological Diversity, 5 June 1992, 1760 UNTS 79, entered into force 29 December 1993.

objection arguing that reference before the EAC to 'the violation of articles of international conventions and declarations on environmental and natural resources is untenable for being placed and enforced before the wrong forum.'[129]

Therefore, the weight to be accorded to general international environmental law in a dispute primarily based on the constitutive instrument of a regional organization, was an important feature of the *ANAW* case. The EAC Court of Justice acknowledged that it did not have the power to 'operate outside the framework of the Treaty and usurp the powers of other organs created for the enforcement of obligations created by other instruments including the African Charter'.[130] However, the EAC Court recalled that the *renvoi* to international law under Article 130(1) of the EAC Treaty ('The Partner States shall honour their commitments in respect of other multinational and international organizations of which they are members') would allow it to render decisions to ensure compliance with other international commitments than those contained in the EAC Treaty.[131] *In casu*, it decided not to proceed considering 'that while the Applicant mentioned those instruments in its pleadings and submissions, it failed to show what parts of them were violated and in fact it was the Respondent who spent considerable time in his submissions in a bid to show that there were no violations of any of those International Instruments'.[132]

Instead of engaging in interpretative gymnastics under Article 31.3(c) of the 1969 Vienna Convention on the Law of Treaties to determine which rules or principles of international environmental law outside the EAC Treaty would be relevant in the context of the *ANAW* case, the EAC Court opted for another strategy. It simply replaced in a creative manner international environmental *law* with international environmental *facts*. Indeed, the EAC Court was more concerned with determining whether the Tanzanian project as initially planned would have negative implications on the Serengeti if it were implemented. It was not as such preoccupied with developing or clarifying the scope of the environmental obligations under the EAC Treaty. This is a major difference with the ECOWAS Court of Justice's approach in the *SERAP* case. In this latter case, the ECOWAS Court of Justice was keen in clarifying

---

[129] EACJ, *Africa Network for Animal Welfare (ANAW) v The Attorney General of the United Republic of Tanzania*, above n 122, para 30.

[130] Ibid., para 48.

[131] It is interesting to note that the Appellate Division of the EAC Court of Justice went a bit further in its judgment on the merits (after the judgment of the First Instance Division was appealed by Tanzania) and qualified certain principles contained in those conventions as reflecting general principles of law in the meaning of Article 38.1c) of the Statute of the ICJ: 'But even if the Trial Court had in fact considered aspects of these International Instruments (as otherwise alleged by the Appellant) we, for our part, would not have been unduly alarmed. By being signatories to these other International Conventions and Declarations, the EAC Partner States, do subscribe to the various standards, norms and values of those Conventions—which standards, norms and values are also gleaned from the general principles of law recognized by the comity of Nations (…)'; EACJ, *Africa Network for Animal Welfare (ANAW) v The Attorney General of the United Republic of Tanzania*, above n 122, para 48. On environmental principles as general principles of law, see Mbengue and McGarry 2019, pp. 408–441.

[132] EACJ, *Africa Network for Animal Welfare (ANAW) v The Attorney General of the United Republic of Tanzania*, above n 122, para 75.

and even expanding the legal content of the right to a healthy environment and the legal implications of the obligation of due diligence in that respect. In the *ANAW* case, the First Instance Division of the EAC Court of Justice sought mainly to make factual findings with respect to the environmental effects of the project in order to determine whether or not Tanzania had complied with its environmental obligations under the EAC Treaty.

In this context, the EAC Court gave weight to the expert evidence before it. And, when experts of the parties would differ, the Court would simply give weight to the expertise of UNESCO. The following passage of the 2014 Judgment is revealing:

> The experts called by the Parties have differed on the consequences of negative impacts but agree on all the negatives. Happily for us, UNESCO, a renowned world body and objective on the subject has given us the answer to the question […] it stated that: (i) The proposed alignment of the road could result in irreversible damage to the property's (Serengeti's) Universal value; (ii) It supports a Strategic Environmental and Social Assessment which would include a southern alignment which would avoid the Serengeti.[133]

Such an approach is somewhat reminiscent of the judgment of the ICJ in the *Whaling in Antarctica* case. In its judgment, the ICJ relied to a certain extent on the agreements among the experts of both parties to the dispute to make some of its findings.[134] The incursions of the EAC Court into UNESCO Reports are similar, to a lesser extent, to the references that the ICJ made to reports of the International Finance Corporation (IFC) in the *Pulp Mills* case. In the latter case, Argentina and Uruguay disagreed on the authority and reliability of the studies and reports by the experts of the IFC. Uruguay argued before the Court that 'expert statements and evaluations issued by a competent international organization, such as the IFC, or those issued by the consultants engaged by that organization should be regarded as independent and given 'special weight''.[135] Even if the Court did not take a clear position on the value or impartiality of IFC reports, it made several references to them throughout its judgment.

The judgment of the EAC Court of Justice in the *ANAW* case is, thus, confirming a trend before international courts and tribunals wherein they rely increasingly on science and on expert evidence for the settlement of environmental disputes. Throughout the judgment in the *ANAW* case, several references to UNESCO reports are made to substantiate the reasoning of the Court and it is on the basis of the UNESCO findings—not contradicted by the experts of Tanzania—that the Court came to the conclusion that the 'North Road' project, if implemented, would have an irreversible impact on the environment:

> Having anxiously considered the matter and as can be seen above, we have found that all evidence points to the fact that if the road project is implemented as originally intended, then following UNESCO's findings it could have an irreversible negative impact on the Serengeti environment and ecosystem. While this view is not expressly shared by the Respondent, we are persuaded by those findings. In fact, the Respondent seemed to have taken note of that

[133] Ibid., para 68.

[134] On this point, see Mbengue 2016a, 2016b, p. 545.

[135] ICJ, *Pulp Mills on the River Uruguay, (Argentina v Uruguay)*, above n 88, para 166.

> fact and has effectively suspended the project and that is an admission that it has realized the error in the initial decision. His own consultant also gave a long list of possible negative impacts and which tally with those given by the Applicant.[136]

The EAC Court of Justice, because of the unique circumstances of the *ANAW* case, decided to order a permanent injunction restraining Tanzania from operationalising its initial proposal or proposed action of constructing or maintaining a road of bitumen standard across the Serengeti National Park subject to its right to undertake such other programmes or initiate policies in the future which would not have a negative impact on the environment and ecosystem in the Serengeti National Park. The issuance of such an order denotes once again the environmental activism that characterizes the actual jurisprudence of African regional courts and tribunals. 'Preventative'[137] remedies are actually necessary in a field where irreversibility is the default rule and reversibility the exception. As the ICJ has recognized, 'in the field of environmental protection, vigilance and prevention are required on account of the often irreversible character of damage to the environment and of the limitations inherent in the very mechanism of reparation of this type of damage.'[138] Vigilance and prevention should also apply to remedies in the context of environmental disputes.[139] The protection of the environment requires anticipation; and traditional remedies before international courts and tribunals do not effectively allow this need for anticipation to be taken into account.[140]

The First Instance Division of the EAC Court opted for such 'preventative' orders and the reasoning behind such a remedy is found in the following passage of the judgment:

> The Reference (i.e. the application) raises issues that are today the subject of wide debate across the world, including; environmental protection, sustainable development, environmental rule of law and the role of the State in policy formulation in matters relating to the environment and natural resources. In addition, the role of the Court in balancing its interpretative jurisdiction against the needs of ensuring that Partner States are not unduly hindered in their developmental programs has come to the fore. All these issues must however

---

[136] EACJ, *Africa Network for Animal Welfare (ANAW) v The Attorney General of the United Republic of Tanzania*, above n 122, para 81.

[137] Ibid., para 78: 'Whatever orders we must make therefore must be preventative and geared towards restraining it from pursuing the bituminized road project and secure the Serengeti ecosystem and any roads in the Serengeti should generally be used by wildlife, tourists and Park administrators and not the general public because of the attendant risks associated with such use.'

[138] ICJ, *Gabčíkovo-Nagymaros Project (Hungary v Slovakia)*, above n 1, p. 41, para 140.

[139] See Rudall 2020, pp. 112–113.

[140] See for instance the rather timid approach of the ICJ in *Certain Activities Carried Out by Nicaragua in the Border Area (Costa Rica v Nicaragua) and Construction of a Road in Costa Rica along the San Juan River* (*Nicaragua v Costa Rica*), above n 118 : 'The Court further considers that Nicaragua's request to order Costa Rica not to undertake any future development in the border area without an appropriate environmental impact assessment must be rejected (…) Costa Rica's obligation to conduct an environmental impact assessment only applies to activities carrying a risk of significant transboundary harm, and there is no reason to suppose that Costa Rica will not comply with its obligations under international law, as outlined in this Judgment, as it conducts any future activities in the area, including further construction works on the road.'

> be looked at from the one common thread running through the Reference viz. the need to protect the Serengeti ecosystem for the sake of future generations and whether the road project has potential for inflicting irreparable damage to the environment. The damage will be irreversible and we have already ruled on that subject based on the evidence before us and no more. And we have also restrained ourselves from merely approving the decision of the United Republic of Tanzania because it may be a popular decision with its policy makers. Whatever orders we must make therefore should be preventative and for obvious reasons; the environment, once damaged is rarely ever repaired.[141]

This passage demonstrates that African regional courts and tribunals can develop international environmental law without focusing on its *modus operandi*—i.e. the principles upon which it is based—but rather on its *ratio legis*—that is the purpose behind it. The ultimate *raison d'être* of international environmental law is to prevent significant harm to the environment. The judgment in the *ANAW* case purports to reinforce prevention and, as such, is a great contribution to the development of international environmental law before international courts and tribunals.

10.5 Conclusion

In concluding its judgment on the appeal in the *ANAW* case, the Appellate Division of the EAC Court of Justice pinpointed that the case has been 'a long, complex and harrowing judicial odyssey to bring the Reference to closure.'[142] The exhaustion by Tanzania of all available remedies before the EAC Court—despite its failure at each stage—brings to light the complex political challenges that African regional courts and tribunals might face when dealing with environmental disputes. Most environmental disputes involve economic projects that could bring large socio-economic benefits to African nations. These nations are all developing countries or least-developed countries and are, as a consequence, very much attached to their right to development.

African regional courts and tribunals cannot ignore this political environment. Otherwise, judicial activism towards environmental protection can lead to backlash against those courts. Past experiences faced by the SADC Tribunal, the ECOWAS Court of Justice and the EAC Court of Justice after their decisions were subjected to harsh criticism by States show that African regional courts are between a rock and a hard place when it comes to the development of international environmental law and effective protection of the environment. Some of the courts might be tempted to follow the advice of the Tribunal in the *Kishenganga* arbitration according to which it is not appropriate for an adjudicatory mechanism to 'assume the role of policymaker in determining the balance between acceptable environmental change

[141] EACJ, *Africa Network for Animal Welfare (ANAW) v The Attorney General of the United Republic of Tanzania*, above n 122, para 85.

[142] EACJ, *Africa Network for Animal Welfare (ANAW) v The Attorney General of the United Republic of Tanzania*, above n 121, para 81.

and other priorities'.[143] Some others, such as the ECOWAS and the EAC Courts of Justice, might prefer to continue the odyssey for more effective environmental protection within Africa. They can and they should. However, in such a quest, they should pursue a sustainable development rhetoric. The legitimacy and effectiveness of their judgments would depend on how much African States will be convinced that their developmental needs and concerns have been fully taken on board by African courts and tribunals.

References

Alter KJ, Gathii JT, Helfer LR (2016) Backlash against International Courts in West, East and Southern Africa: Causes and Consequences. European Journal of International Law 27:293–328.
Ankumah EA (1996) The African Commission on Human and Peoples' Rights. Nijhoff, The Hague.
Doumbé Billé S (2005) La nouvelle Convention africaine de Maputo sur la conservation de la nature et des ressources naturelles. Revue juridique de l'environnement 5:17.
Dzidzornu D M (2015) Environment Protection in Africa: A Panorama of the Law and Practice. Journal of Energy and Natural Resources Law 22:148.
Harrington J (2002) The African Court on Human and Peoples' Rights. In: Evans M, Murray R (eds) The African Charter on Human Rights: The System in Practice 1986–2000. CUP, Cambridge.
Killander M (2018) Regional Co-operation and Organization: African States. Max Planck Encyclopedia of International Law, OUP, Oxford.
Mackenzie R, Romano CPR et al, (2010) The African Commission and Court on Human and Peoples' Rights. In: Mackenzie R, Romano CPR et al. (eds) The Manual on International Courts and Tribunals. OUP, Oxford.
Maluwa T (1989) Environment and Development in Africa: An Overview of Basic Problems of Environmental Law and Policy. African Journal of International and Comparative Law 1:650.
Mbengue MM (2015) Between law and science: A commentary on the Whaling in the Antarctic case. Questions of International Law, Zoom-in 14:3–12.
Mbengue MM (2016a) Scientific Fact-finding at the International Court of Justice: An Appraisal in the Aftermath of the Whaling Case. Leiden Journal of International Law 29:529–550.
Mbengue MM (2016b) Reparation in International Environmental Law. Proceedings of the Annual Meeting of the American Society of International Law, pp 293–297.
Mbengue MM (2020a) La portée globale d'une lutte locale (Mike Campbell c. Zimbabwe). In: Watt HM et al. (eds) Tournant Global en Droit international privé. Pedone, Paris.
Mbengue MM (2020b) On Sustainable Development: A Conversation with Judge Weeramantry. In: Mbengue MM, Forlati S, McGarry B (eds) The Gabcikovo-Nagymaros Judgment and its Contribution to the Development of International Law. Brill, Boston/The Hague.
Mbengue MM, McGarry B (2019) General Principles of International Environmental Law in the Case-Law of International Courts and Tribunals. In: Andenas M, Fitzmaurice M, Tanzi A, Wouters J (eds) General Principles and the Coherence of International Law. Brill, Boston/The Hague.
Mbengue MM, Schacherer S (2022) International Investment Law before African Courts. In: Ruiz Fabri H, Stoppioni E (eds) International Investment Law: An Analysis of Major Decisions. Hart Publishing, Oxford.
Mbengue MM, Waltmann S (2018) Health and the Environment. In: Burci G-L, Toebes B (eds) Research Handbook on Global Health Law. Elgar, USA.

[143] *Indus Waters Kishenganga Arbitration (Pakistan v India)*, Final Award, 20 December 2013, 31 RIAA 309, para 112.

Ogundere JD (1972) The Development of International Environmental Law and Policy in Africa. The Natural Resources Journal 12:255.
Onwuka RI, Sesay A (eds) (1985) The Future of Regionalism in Africa. Macmillan, London.
Rudall J (2020) Compensation for Environmental Damage Under International Law. Routledge, Abingdon.
Takang JM (2014) From Algiers to Maputo: The Role of the African Convention on the Conservation of Nature and Natural Resources in the Harmonization of Conservation Policy in Africa. Journal of International Wildlife Law & Policy 17:165.
Thompson B (1993) Economic Integration in Africa: A Milestone—The Abuja Treaty. African Journal of International and Comparative Law 5:743.
UNESCO (2014) Philosophy Manual: A South-South Perspective. Paris, p 39.

Makane Moïse Mbengue is Professor of International Law and Director of the Department of Public International Law and International Organization, Faculty of Law, University of Geneva; Affiliate Professor, Sciences Po Paris (School of Law), makane.mbengue@unige.ch. The author is thankful to Ms. Maitreyee Dixit for her excellent research and assistance throughout the preparation and drafting of this contribution.

Chapter 11
Environmental Protection in International Investment Arbitration: From Defences to Counterclaims

Diane A. Desierto

Contents

Abstract This chapter examines how environmental protection has been invoked as basis for host State defences against investor claims, host State counterclaims against investors, and as a separate ground for investor claims against host States—all with relative degrees of success before investor-State arbitration tribunals. When invoked in these ways as a key substantive ground for legal defences, claims, and counterclaims, environmental protection poses issues of interdisciplinary complexity for tribunals when it comes to evidentiary assessment, the standard of diligence and precaution required of States as well as non-State actors, and the concurrent interaction of States' environmental protection obligations with their investment treaty obligations. While investor-State arbitration may (and should probably) not be the court of first resort to achieve environmental protection, it should also not be seen as the court of last resort when it comes to producing sound, competent, and credible adjudication that is mindful of the role of scientific expertise, public regulatory concerns, and desired environmental outcomes. At the very least, the jurisprudential record examined in this chapter provides some qualitative evidence of the feasibility of investor-State arbitration as an adjudicative process, capable of accommodating various scientific, fact-finding, expert-driven, and interdisciplinary methodologies towards resolving questions raised by either host States or investors concerning environmental protection.

D. A. Desierto (✉)
Notre Dame Law School, University of Notre Dame, Notre Dame, IN, USA
e-mail: ddesiert@nd.edu

Keough School of Global Affairs, University of Notre Dame, Washington, DC, USA

E. Sobenes et al. (eds.), *The Environment Through the Lens of International Courts and Tribunals*, https://doi.org/10.1007/978-94-6265-507-2_11

Keywords Environmental protection · Environmental impacts · Expropriation · Fair and equitable treatment · Compensation quantum · Due diligence principle · Precautionary principle · Multidimensional environmental analysis

11.1 Introduction

Environmental protection has increasingly arisen as one of the key issues in disputes between investors and host States that are brought to international investment arbitration.[1] This is to be expected, since foreign investment projects have been shown to generate significant environmental impacts on host States and their respective populations.[2] When host States' environmental measures are challenged in international investment arbitration due to alleged injurious impacts, and investors rely on the protective cover of investment treaty provisions[3] or foreign investment contract clauses,[4] there are mixed outcomes for actual environmental protection.[5] Precisely because international investment arbitration has largely been a paradigm of redress for violation of investment treaty or contract protections,[6] it has not been the jurisdictional remit of arbitral tribunals to examine or put forward reparative measures (either against the host State, or applicable to both the claimant investor and the respondent host State) designed to achieve environmental protection.[7] At best, therefore, environmental protection has assumed a defensive posture in international investment arbitration proceedings thus far—as a basis to justify a host State's allegedly injurious measure towards investors.[8] It has not been the source of possible host State counterclaims[9] against investors alleged to have committed environmental degradation, although there are extant proposals to this effect still pending in reforms contemplated for international investment law.[10]

---

[1] See e.g. Boisson de Chazournes 2017; Asteriti 2015 and Beharry and Kuritzky 2015.

[2] See e.g. Anh et al. 2019; Borregaard and Dufey 2002; Demena and Afesorgbor 2020.

[3] See Marisi 2020; Gordon and Pohl 2011.

[4] See Tienhaara 2011.

[5] See Mistura 2019; Da Silva 2018.

[6] See Ho 2018, pp. 222–253.

[7] See in comparison Payne 2017.

[8] See e.g., *Mesa Power Group LLC v Government of Canada*, Award, 24 March 2016, PCA Case No 2012-17, para 672; *Methanex v United States of America*, Final Award on Jurisdiction and Merits, 3 August 2005, NAFTA/UNCITRAL (*Methanex Award*) (https://www.italaw.com/sites/default/files/case-documents/ita0529.pdf—accessed 23 April 2021).

[9] See Harrison 2016; *Burlington Resources Inc v Republic of Ecuador*, Decision on Ecuador's Counterclaims, 7 February 2017, ICSID Case No ARB/08/5, para 1075 (awarding compensation to Ecuador for environmental harm caused by the investor in breach of Ecuador's environmental laws); *Urbaser S.A. and Consorcio de Aguas Bilbao Bizkaia, Bilbao Biskaia Ur Partzuergoa v The Argentine Republic*, Award, 8 December 2016, ICSID Case No ARB/07/26, paras 1182–1192 (*Urbaser Award*) (recognizing that in general, investors could be bound by international human rights law, such as the right to water, but in the specific circumstances of the case, such rights had to be incorporated first in the investment contract).

[10] See De Luca 2020.

In this chapter, I categorise current international investment arbitral jurisprudence on environmental protection into three sections. In Sect. 11.2, I examine how host States have argued regulatory measures in the name of environmental protection that may impair investor expectations of returns and risks to foreign investment, and whether arbitral tribunals have been receptive—even deferential—to the claimed environmental protection as the objective of these measures.[11] Section 11.3 discusses the emerging frequency of host State counterclaims in international investment arbitration, which is expected to proliferate even more with States' climate change commitments.[12] Section 11.4 explores how foreign investor claims could themselves be anchored on their legal expectations of the host State's compliance with its own environmental protection commitments.[13] The *Conclusion* recognizes that the imperfect system of international investment arbitration contains structural and evidentiary challenges, which militate against arriving at investment arbitral awards that are most responsive to all needs of environmental protection.[14] I consider how investor-State arbitration could potentially be a feasible dispute settlement mechanism for environmental protection claims and counterclaims, especially if investment treaties recognise the host State's environmental protection obligations as part of the applicable law to any covered investment, as seen from some of the later generations of investment treaties.

11.2 Environmental Protection as Host State Defence

Host States have argued environmental protection as a substantive defence, either calling for an environmentally-sensitive interpretation of investment treaty standards of treatment (such as expropriation, fair and equitable treatment, among others), or for the application of exceptions. *Methanex v United States*[15] involved both types of host State defences. To recall, Methanex Corporation had challenged the ban and related regulatory measures imposed by California on the sale and use of the gasoline additive methyl tertiary-butyl ether (MBTE), alleging breaches of the North American Free Trade Agreement (NAFTA) provisions on national treatment (Article 1102), fair and equitable treatment (Article 1105), and expropriation (Article 1110).[16] Among its findings of fact, the *Methanex* tribunal[17] found that California's measures were 'motivated by the honest belief, held in good faith and on reasonable scientific grounds, that MTBE contaminated groundwater and was difficult and expensive to

[11] See e.g., Romson 2012.

[12] Sharma 2020; Gleason 2020.

[13] See Viñuales and Dupuy 2013.

[14] See e.g., ibid., pp. 281–292; Sweify 2015; Mahla and Duggal 2020.

[15] *Methanex Award*, above n 8.

[16] Ibid., paras 26–28.

[17] Composed of J. William F. Rowley, V. V. Veeder and W. M. Reisman.

clean up'.[18] The Tribunal rejected the alleged breach of the NAFTA Article 1102 national treatment standard, because 'the California MTBE ban did not differentiate between foreign and domestic MTBE producers; nor, if it is relevant, did it differentiate between foreign and domestic methanol producers'.[19] There being no discriminatory treatment established at all in any way by Methanex, the tribunal also rejected the alleged breach of fair and equitable treatment under NAFTA Article 1105.[20] The *Methanex* tribunal also rejected the alleged breach of NAFTA Article 1110 on expropriation, since 'a non-discriminatory regulation for a public purpose, which is enacted in accordance with due process and, which affects, inter alios, a foreign investor investment is not deemed expropriatory and compensable unless *specific commitments* had been given by the regulating government to the then putative foreign investor contemplating investment that the government would refrain from such regulation'.[21] The tribunal went on to discuss, on findings of fact, that:

> No such commitments were given to Methanex. Methanex entered a political economy in which it was widely known, if not notorious, that governmental environmental and health protection institutions at the federal and state level, operating under the vigilant eyes of the media, interested corporations, non-governmental organizations and a politically active electorate, continuously monitored the use and impact of chemical compounds and commonly prohibited or restricted the use of some of those compounds for environmental and/or health reasons. Indeed, the very market for MTBE in the United States was the result of precisely this regulatory process. Methanex appreciated that the process of regulation in the United States involved wide participation of industry groups, non-governmental organizations, academics and other individuals, many of these actors deploying lobbyists. Methanex itself deployed lobbyists...Methanex entered the United States market aware of and actively participating in this process. It did not enter the United States market because of special representations made to it....[22]

Methanex is a successful example of a host State effectively framing environmental protection measures well within the actual terms and substantive criteria in investment treaty standards, so as to negate the existence of alleged discrimination (in this case, the national treatment and fair and equitable treatment standards). At the same time, the *Methanex* tribunal introduced the concept of *specific commitments* when evaluating an alleged breach of the NAFTA expropriation provision in Article 1110. This raises the threshold of expected due diligence of investors, to be aware of the host State's environmental regulations as the default regulatory environment, implementation of which would not ordinarily be compensable (even if injury occurs to investment) unless the host State government provides specific commitments to protect the investment even amid the environmental protection regulations.

Similar reasoning upheld the host State's defences of environmental protection regulatory measures and environmental regulatory enforcement in the case of *David*

---

[18] *Methanex Award*, above n 8, para 102, item no. 2.

[19] Ibid., Part IV, Chapter B, p. 19, para 38.

[20] Ibid., Part IV, Chapter C, pp. 5–12, paras 9–27.

[21] Ibid., Part IV, Chapter D, p. 4, para 7. Italics added.

[22] Ibid., Part IV, Chapter D, p. 5, paras 9 and 10.

Aven and Others v The Republic of Costa Rica.[23] This case was brought under Chapter Ten of the Dominican Republic-Central America Free Trade Agreement (DR-CAFTA), which was unique for not only containing treatment clauses on investment, but also specific provisions that respected the environmental regulatory prerogatives of the host State of the investment. Claimants in this case developed tourism properties (the Las Olas Project) in Costa Rica that became the subject of environmental regulatory enforcement by the Costa Rican government, ultimately resulting in the shutdown of the development of the projects.[24] The claimants alleged breaches of the DR-CAFTA provisions on fair and equitable treatment, minimum standard of treatment, and expropriation,[25] in particular emphasising the frustration of their legitimate investment-backed expectations due to the alleged arbitrary and bad faith manner[26] by which Costa Rica conducted its environmental regulatory enforcement procedures which ultimately resulted in the stoppage of the development.[27] Costa Rica argued, among others, that environmental protection is explicitly prioritised under the DR-CAFTA, and as such 'the rights of investment protection granted to investors under the Treaty may be subordinated to the protection of the environment'.[28] Article 10.11 of DR-CAFTA provides that 'nothing shall be construed to prevent a Party from adopting, maintaining, or enforcing any measure otherwise consistent with this Chapter that it considers appropriate to ensure that investment activity in its territory is undertaken in a manner sensitive to environmental concerns'.[29] Ultimately, Costa Rica maintained that 'the actions of Costa Rica are non-discriminatory regulatory actions designed and applied to protect the environment, these actions have not permanently deprived Claimants of the value or control of their investment, [Costa Rica's] actions have not interfered with Claimants' reasonable expectations. And the actions taken are *bona fide* exercise of police powers'.[30] Environmental protection has constitutional importance in Costa Rica's constitution and related administrative law, as well as Costa Rica's international environmental treaty commitments.[31]

The *Aven* Tribunal scrutinized the right to regulate invoked by Costa Rica and found, on the facts, that 'despite the efforts and good faith actions of Claimants…it does not appear they sought and received proper advice to develop the Las Olas Project, and if they did, they chose to ignore it'.[32] The Tribunal also held that the

---

[23] *David Aven and Others v Republic of Costa Rica*, Final Award, 18 September 2018, DR-CAFTA/UNCITRAL, Case No UNCT/15/3 [Members of the Tribunal: Eduardo Siqueiros, Presiding Arbitrator, C. Mark Baker and Pedro Nikken, Co-Arbitrators) (*Aven Award*).

[24] Ibid., para 6.

[25] Ibid., paras 18–20, 360.

[26] Ibid., paras 370–374.

[27] Ibid., para 369.

[28] Ibid., para 7.

[29] Ibid., para 385.

[30] Ibid., para 384.

[31] Ibid., para 394.

[32] Ibid., para 449.

claimants had the duty and obligation to 'advise the competent authority in matters that affect any impact to the environment'[33] and to show that, at the time they filed their applications for permits, to provide 'evidence that no such adverse impact on the Las Olas Project site was to occur as a consequence of the development',[34] such as the possible presence of wetlands or protected forest reserves on the properties being developed. Because the claimants had 'failed to do so, they thus cannot now attempt to shield their omission on the alleged failure [of the government agency or regulator] to inspect the property to verify the existence of wetlands'.[35] Moreover, the Tribunal found that wetlands in the Las Olas Project were 'indeed impacted by works undertaken by Claimants, and that the reaction taken by [Costa Rica] as a consequence was merited under the laws of Costa Rica, which are not inconsistent with international law…the actions taken by [Costa Rica] are not arbitrary nor in breach of the obligations under DR-CAFTA'.[36] Thus, similar to the *Methanex* case, the *Aven* Tribunal recognised the distinct due diligence duties of the investors entering into a jurisdiction that had already clearly established environmental protection as part of the regulatory fabric governing investments, not just through the DR-CAFTA treaty terms but through the Costa Rican Constitution and related administrative and environmental laws. The *Aven* Tribunal thus dismissed all of the claims put forward by the claimant investors.[37]

Not all assertions of environmental protection by the host State, however, are successful defences to claims of investment treaty breaches.[38] Costa Rica was found liable to compensate the claimant in the amount of around USD 16 Million, in the case of *Compania Del Dessarollo De Santa Elena S.A. v The Republic of Costa Rica*.[39] In reaching this assessment of the quantum of compensation, the Tribunal deliberately did not take environmental protection purposes into consideration: 'While an expropriation or taking for environmental reasons may be classified as a taking for a public purpose, and thus may be legitimate, the fact that the Property was taken for this reason does not affect either the nature of the measure of the compensation to be paid for the taking…The international source of the obligation to protect the environment makes no difference'.[40] Again, the Tribunal stressed: '[e]xpropriatory environmental measures—no matter how laudable and beneficial to society as a whole—are, in this respect, similar to any other expropriatory measures that a State may take in order to implement its policies: where property is expropriated, even for environmental

[33] Ibid., para 552.

[34] Ibid., para 553.

[35] Ibid., para 558.

[36] Ibid., para 585.

[37] Ibid., Part XIV, *dispositif.*

[38] See Marisi 2020, pp. 19–28.

[39] *Compania Del Desarrollo De Santa Elena S.A. v The Republic of Costa Rica*, Final Award, 17 February 2000, ICSID Case No ARB/96/1 [Members of the Tribunal: Yves Fortier, President; Prof. Sir Elihu Lauterpacht, and Prof. Prosper Weil, Tribunal Members].

[40] Ibid., para 71.

purposes, whether domestic or international, the state's obligation to pay compensation remains'.[41] This blanket reasoning was surprising, since the Tribunal did not differentiate between situations where the environmental protection measure of expropriation also redounded to the benefit of the investor (who presumably also is among the subjects of environmental protection). This case also antedated *Methanex* by five years, and unlike the *Methanex* tribunal which carefully drew the line with respect to specific commitments made by a State, the *Santa Elena* tribunal categorically rejected any distinctions for non-compensability, considerations of mitigation of compensation, or modifications to the quantum of compensation where a State implements an environmental protection measure that ultimately results in a *de facto* or *de jure* expropriation.

In sum, when considering the role of environmental protection as a legal defence of the host State, attention has to be paid to the legal standard or investment treaty norm against which environmental protection is raised as a defence. Reinterpreting a broad treaty norm such as fair and equitable treatment to take into account the host State's simultaneous regulatory duties such as environmental protection may be possible in some cases where the treaty is linguistically elastic enough to admit such interpretation within the unitary system of treaty interpretation under Article 31 of the Vienna Convention on the Law of Treaties. Where, as in the *Aven* case, the investment treaty itself contains a provision that enables host States to maintain their environmental treaty or environmental law obligations alongside investment treaty obligations, the interpretation of the investment treaty standard of protection at issue will undoubtedly be influenced by the interaction with the host State's environmental treaty obligations.

11.3 Environmental Protection as Host State Counterclaim

Environmental protection has been admitted as a basis for host States' counterclaims, but it has not necessarily been successful. In *Paushok v Mongolia,* an investor claim arising out of the application of domestic laws such as tax laws, Mongolia as the host State asserted seven counterclaims, which included the counterclaim that 'Claimants violated their environmental obligations towards Mongolia'.[42] The Tribunal declined jurisdiction over all of Mongolia's, including the allegation of breach of environmental obligations, finding that this counterclaim 'cannot be seen as having a close connection with the primary claim to which (they are) a response…they are clearly matters which strictly concern [third party GEM] and they all relate to subjects being

[41] Ibid., para 72.

[42] *Sergei Paushok, CJSC Golden East Company, CJSC Vostokneftegaz Company v The Government of Mongolia,* Award on Jurisdiction and Liability, 28 April 2011, UNCITRAL, para 678(5) [Tribunal President Hon. Marc Lalonde, Tribunal Members: Dr. Horacio Grigera Naon, Professor Brigitte Stern].

the object of Mongolian legislation and regulation'.[43] This case emphasizes that the framing of the host State counterclaim must hew closely to the primary claim—if the primary claim has no reasonable nexus with the counterclaim based on environmental protection, the Tribunal will very likely decline to exercise jurisdiction, especially to avoid giving a prohibited extraterritorial legislative effect to the host State's environmental laws through the use of the host State counterclaim in the investor-State arbitration process itself.

Urbaser v The Argentine Republic[44] presents an interesting example of a Tribunal's wide acceptance of international law and human rights law relating to environmental matters (e.g., the right to water) as part of the applicable law. As described by the Claimants, the case involved a dispute relating to a water and sewage concession in the Province of Greater Buenos Aires, Argentina:

> ...it was granted in early 2000 to Aguas Del Gran Buenos Aires S.A. (AGBA), a Company established by foreign investors and shareholders, including Claimants in the present proceeding. Claimants assert that they faced numerous obstructions on the part of the Province's authorities, which rendered the efficient and profitable operation of the Concession extremely difficult. The Concession was running into deadlock when Argentina suffered its economic crisis beginning in mid-2001, culminating in the emergency measures taken in January 2002, including a conversion of 1:1 between USD and Argentine Peso at a time when the Peso had depreciated by more than two thirds of its value. AGBA's numerous requests for a new valuation of its tariffs and for a complete review of the Concession all failed in front of the Province's lack of any serious commitment to bring the required renegotiation process to a successful end. Political reasons related to the fate of other concessions finally caused the Province to declare AGBA's concession terminated in July 2006. This was just the final step of a long process of persistent neglect of AGBA shareholders' interests on the part of the Province, comprising several violations by the Argentine Republic of Articles III, IV, and V of the Spain-Argentine BIT.[45]

Argentina denied all claims and rejected:

> all of the Claimants' allegations in relation to purported violations of the Concession Contract on part of Argentine authorities, all of which are in any event not under the jurisdiction of the Tribunal. The difficulties the Concession was faced with were in large part grounded on AGBA and its shareholders' deficient management, most expressly demonstrated by their incapacity to proceed efficiently in collecting bills from the network's users. In addition, and even more importantly, the Concession was fundamentally undermined by the investors' failure to perform their obligations when it was confirmed that nothing efficient had been done to provide even minimal investment for the first years of operation, with resources either from third parties or from the shareholders themselves. After one and a half year of operation, AGBA was already compelled to declare its incapacity to fulfil its undertakings in view of the expansion of the network. This situation having never been remedied, even with the assistance of the Province during a renegotiation process conducted over more than a year, there remained no other solution than to declare the Concession Contract terminated.[46]

---

[43] Ibid., para 696.

[44] *Urbaser Award*, above n 9 [Tribunal President: Professor Andreas Bucher; Tribunal Members: Professor Pedro Martinez-Fraga, Professor Campbell McLachlan QC].

[45] Ibid., para 34.

[46] Ibid., para 36.

Argentina put forward a Counterclaim, 'based on Claimants' alleged failure to provide the necessary investment into the Concession, thus violating its commitments and its obligations under international law based on the human right to water'.[47] The Tribunal found that the Spain-Argentina BIT 'accepts a possibility for [Respondent Argentina] to raise a counterclaim'.[48] The Tribunal further observed that the factual link between the claim and counterclaim:

> …is manifest. Both the principal claim and the claim opposed to it are based on the same investment, or the alleged lack of sufficient investment, in relation to the same Concession. This would be sufficient to adopt jurisdiction over the Counterclaim as well. The legal connection is also established to the extent the Counterclaim is not alleged as a matter based on domestic law only. Respondent argues indeed that Claimants' failure to provide the necessary investments caused a violation of the fundamental right for access to water, which was the very purpose of the investment agreed upon in the Regulatory Framework and the Concession Contract and embodied in the protection scheme of the BIT. It would be wholly inconsistent to rule on Claimants' claim in relation to their investment in one sense and to have a separate proceeding where compliance with the commitment for funding may be ruled upon in a different way. Reasonable administration of justice cannot tolerate such a potential inconsistent outcome.[49]

Simply put, because Argentina had uniquely premised its counterclaim on the right to water under international human rights law, the *Urbaser* Tribunal differentiated itself from the situation articulated by the Tribunal in *Paushok* about the investor-State arbitration process being instrumentalized to provide the prohibited extraterritorial effect of domestic laws.

In evaluating the merits of Argentina's counterclaim, the *Urbaser* Tribunal significantly accepted a deep nexus between the Spain-Argentina BIT with international law and human rights. The Tribunal's reasoning on this point is highly significant, and is reproduced below:

> 1194. A principle may be invoked in this regard to which corporations are by nature not able to be subjects of international law and therefore not capable of holding obligations as if they would be participants in the State-to-State relations governed by international law. While such principle had its importance in the past, it has lost its impact and relevance in similar terms and conditions as this applies to individuals. A simple look at the MFN Clause of Article VII of the BIT shows that the Contracting States accepted at least one hypothesis where investors are entitled to invoke rights resulting from international law…If the BIT therefore is not based on a corporation's incapacity of holding rights under international law, it cannot be admitted that it would reject by necessity any idea that a foreign investor company could not be subject to international law obligations.
>
> 1195. The Tribunal may mention in this respect that international law accepts corporate social responsibility as a standard of crucial importance for companies operating in the field of international commerce. This standard includes commitments to comply with human rights in the framework of those entities' operations conducted in countries other than the country of their seat or incorporation. In light of this more recent development, it can no longer be admitted that companies operating internationally are immune from becoming

[47] Ibid., last sentence.

[48] Ibid., para 1150.

[49] Ibid., para 1151.

> subjects of international law. On the other hand, even though several initiatives undertaken at the international scene are seriously targeting corporations human rights conduct, they are not, on their own, sufficient to oblige corporations to put their policies in line with human rights law. The focus must be, therefore, on contextualizing a corporation's specific activities as they relate to the human right at issue in order to determine whether any international law obligations attach to the non-State individual.[50]

The Tribunal went on to identify various instruments of international human rights, where even multinational companies or private corporations cannot act in disregard of such rights, such as the 1948 Universal Declaration of Human Rights, the 1966 International Covenant on Economic, Social and Cultural Rights and its interpretations by the Committee on Economic, Social and Cultural Rights, the United Nations General Assembly Resolution 64/292 on the right to safe and clean drinking water and sanitation as a human right, and the International Labor Organization's 1977 Tripartite Declaration of Principles concerning Multilateral Enterprises and Social Policy.[51] However, notwithstanding these instruments, the *Urbaser* Tribunal was careful to delineate the question of whether Claimants, as investors:

> were bound by an obligation based on international law to provide the population living on the territory of the Concession with drinking water and sanitation services. Respondent does not, in fact, go so far. Even if this obligation could be imposed upon Claimants, Respondent does not state that such obligation is based on international law...while Respondent correctly introduces the principle of pacta sunt servanda as a principle of international law, it identifies the relevant pactum as Claimants' obligation to invest in expansion work, thus relying again on the Concession Contract and admitting that international law does not provide a cause of action for the Counterclaim.[52]

Thus, by latching on to what Argentina itself had argued as the basis of the obligations of the investors, e.g., the concession contract, the *Urbaser* Tribunal could readily conclude that

> none of the provisions of the BIT has the effect of extending or transferring to the Concessionaire an obligation to perform services complying with the residents' human right to access to water and sewage services...For such an obligation to exist and to become relevant in the framework of the BIT, it should either be part of another treaty (not applicable here) or it should represent a general principle of international law....The human right to water entails an obligation of compliance on the part of the State, but it does not contain an obligation for performance on part of any company providing the contractually required service. Such obligation would have to be distinct from the State's responsibility to serve its population with drinking water and sewage services.[53]

The *Urbaser* Tribunal emphasized even further that:

> the investor's obligation to ensure the population's access to water is not based on international law. This obligation is framed by the legal and regulatory environment under which the investor is admitted to operate on the basis of the BIT and the host State's laws...the

50 Ibid., paras 1194–1195.

51 Ibid., paras 1196–1198.

52 Ibid., para 1206.

53 Ibid., paras 1207 and 1208.

> enforcement of the human right to water represents an obligation to perform. Such obligation is imposed upon States. It cannot be imposed on any company knowledgeable in the field of provision of water and sanitation services. In order to have such an obligation to perform applicable to a particular investor, a contract or similar legal relationship of civil and commercial law is required. In such a case, the investor's obligation to perform has as its source domestic law; it does not find its legal ground in general international law.[54]

In the particular case of the Claimants, the *Urbaser* Tribunal narrowed the applicability of the human right to water more markedly to only that which could have been specifically built in the concession contract or the BIT:

> [n]o human rights obligation to provide access to water existed on the part of Claimants before they entered into the Concession. The acceptance of the Bid and the Concession Contract could not have as an effect that the obligations arising out of this Contract became, in addition or in parallel, obligations based on international law. The BIT does not contain any indication in such a direction, and its reference to general principles of international law in Article X(5) cannot let emerge an obligation that did not exist on charge of the investing companies before they entered into their investment in the Argentine Republic.[55]

On this reasoning, the *Urbaser* Tribunal had little problem rejecting Argentina's counterclaim premised on the investors' alleged violation of the human right to water. It made it clear that, for the counterclaim to have prospered, the onus was an Argentina to establish that respect for the human right to water under international law was actually and intentionally part of the domestic regulatory framework governing the concession long before the concession contract was awarded. As the Tribunal noted, Argentina:

> does not state any legal ground for any individual's right to claim damages as a consequence of an alleged violation of the human right to water. Respondent does not demonstrate either that the alleged violation of such human right entails a duty of reparation equally based on international law, with the effect that the individuals concerned by such an alleged harm obtain an appropriate compensation. Respondent failed to state such a claim. This would be a reason sufficient to dismiss Respondent's counterclaim. The Tribunal adds that such failure can also be explained by the lack of any legal ground based on international law that would entitle a group of individuals to raise a claim for performance for delivery of water and sewage services directed against a company or any other private party. Accordingly, there does not exist a claim for compensation in case of lack of such performance not based on an obligation under international law.[56]

Three main observations can be made with respect to the *Urbaser* Tribunal's rejection of the Argentine counterclaim premised on the violation of the human right to water. First, while it broadly accepted that international human rights treaties and instruments do recognize that private parties have a legal duty to respect the right to water and a counterpart legal duty not to act or otherwise engage in activity that would destroy the right, the *Urbaser* Tribunal required a further nexus between these legal duties of private parties and the concession contract binding the investors in this case. The Tribunal closely followed Argentina's own submissions, and instead

---

[54] Ibid., paras 1209 and 1210.

[55] Ibid., para 1212.

[56] Ibid., para 1220.

pinned Argentina to its own statements that narrowly characterized the legal obligations of the investors concerned to the concession contract that they signed with Argentina. The Tribunal was not prepared to admit the independent existence of international legal obligations that bound corporations to observe human rights in extraterritorial activities, notwithstanding the increasing proliferation of litigation against such corporations in their home States that recognized such a scope to international human rights law,[57] including for environmental protection-related rights such as the human right to water.

Second, *Urbaser* was also decided before the Committee on Economic, Social and Cultural Rights issued its General Comment No. 24 (2017) on State obligations under the International Covenant on Economic, Social and Cultural Rights in the context of business activities.[58] In this General Comment No. 24, the Committee had clarified that 'under international standards, business entities are expected to respect Covenant rights regardless of whether domestic laws exist or are fully enforced in practice'.[59] The Committee stressed that, in accordance with international law, States parties to the Covenant could be held 'directly responsible for the action or inaction of business entities: (1) if the entity concerned is in fact acting on that State party's instructions or is under its control or direction in carrying out the particular conduct at issue, as may be the case in the context of public contracts; (2) when a business entity is empowered under the State Party's legislation to exercise elements of governmental authority or if the circumstances call for such exercise of governmental functions in the absence or default of the official authorities; or (3) if and to the extent that the State party acknowledges and adopts the conduct as its own'.[60] It remains an open question if the *Urbaser* Tribunal would have altered its reasoning and permitted Argentina's counterclaim, had Argentina argued from General Comment No. 24 that the human rights violations of investing companies in this case potentially exposed Argentina to legal liability for reparations towards its own population that suffered the violation at the hands of the private sector concessionaire that Argentina authorized under the concession.

Finally, there is a fundamental paradox in the *Urbaser* Tribunal's position on the admissibility of a counterclaim, vis-à-vis its ability to succeed on the merits. To recall, *Urbaser* admitted Argentina's counterclaim because it was based on a source of law *outside* of domestic law, which did not trigger the *Paushok* Tribunal's concerns against giving a prohibited extraterritorial legislative effect to the host State's environmental laws through the use of the host State counterclaim in the investor-State arbitration process itself. However, upon admission of Argentina's counterclaim, the *Urbaser* Tribunal then turns the reasoning on its head, and requires,

[57] See Joseph 2004, pp. 8–15; Augenstein and Kinley 2013; Bernaz 2017, Chapter 10 (on business and human rights litigation).

[58] Committee on Economic, Social and Cultural Rights, General Comment No. 24 (2017) on State obligations under the International Covenant on Economic, Social and Cultural Rights in the Context of Business Activities, 10 August 2017, E/C.12/GC/24, full text at https://www.refworld.org/docid/5beaecba4.html (last accessed 23 April 2021).

[59] Ibid., para 5.

[60] Ibid., para 11.

for the counterclaim to succeed on the merits, that the international human rights obligations on the right to water to first be transformed into the domestic regulatory and contractual framework over the concession in order to be directly applicable to the investors in this case. This poses a contradiction. If Argentina had indeed incorporated the human right to water in the concession contract and the domestic regulations and laws that govern the concession, its counterclaim would not be admissible since the investor-State arbitral process cannot supposedly be used to give the prohibited extraterritorial effect to domestic law. If Argentina did not incorporate the human right to water in domestic law and the concession contract, then its counterclaim would be admissible but unsuccessful on the merits. The only way, it appears, for the *Urbaser* Tribunal to have accepted this counterclaim was for an extraordinary threshold to have been met: that first, Argentina would allege as the legal basis for its counterclaim the existence of independent legal obligations outside of Argentine domestic law, and second, those same independent legal obligations would have mirroring provisions in the concession contract granted to the investors in this case. But how realistic is this dual threshold of identical international and domestic legal requirements given the deep diversity of actual regulatory and statutory practices of privatized water concessions in developing countries?[61] *Urbaser* is intriguingly silent on this point.

While it may appear from the *Paushok* and *Urbaser* arbitrations that host State counterclaims premised on environmental protection are hard to win on the merits, *Perenco v Ecuador*[62] provides a significant and promising counterfactual. The investors in this case brought their claim alleging Ecuador's breach of treaty obligations in the France-Ecuador bilateral investment treaty as well as two participation contracts for the exploration of Blocks 7 and 21 in the Ecuadorian Amazonian region.[63] Ecuador brought counterclaims alleging Perenco's liability for environmental and infrastructural damage in said Blocks 7 and 21,[64] alleging that 'its experts had determined the existence of an environmental catastrophe in the two oil blocks situated in the country's Amazonian rainforest that had been worked by the consortium under Perenco's operatorship'.[65]

At the outset, the *Perenco* Tribunal agreed that 'if a legal relationship between an investor and the State permits the filing of a claim by the State for environmental damage caused by the investor's activities and such a claim is substantiated, the State is entitled to full reparation in accordance with the requirements of the applicable law…a State has wide latitude under international law to prescribe and adjust its environmental laws, standards and policies in response to changing views and a

---

[61] See e.g., Marques and Simoes 2020; Jensen 2017; Gerlach and Franceys 2010.

[62] *Perenco v Ecuador LTD. v The Republic of Ecuador and Empressa Estatal Petroleos de Ecuador (Pertoecuador)*, Interim Decision on Environmental Counterclaim, 11 August 2015, ICSID Case No ARB/08/6 [Tribunal President: Judge Peter Tomka; Tribunal Members: Mr. Neil Kaplan and Mr. J. Christopher Thomas].

[63] Ibid., para 4.

[64] Ibid., para 5.

[65] Ibid., para 34.

deeper understanding of the risks posed by various activities, including those of extractive industries such as oilfields'.[66] The Tribunal found that Perenco had 'agreed to comply with all laws and regulations in Ecuador applicable to the Participation Contracts…[and] agreed to preserve the existing ecological equilibrium in [Blocks 7 and 21] and would clean up the area to allow the potential return to environmental conditions similar to those encountered at the beginning of operations. But it would not be liable for pre-existing environmental conditions…'.[67] A key issue was in the nature of environmental liability under Ecuadorian law. The 2008 Ecuadorian Constitution provided for a strict liability regime that, in Ecuador's view, 'there was a presumption of causation and Perenco can only escape liability by establishing that the contamination [of the Blocks 7 and 21] was caused by force majeure, Ecuador, or a third party…as a result of the presumption of causation established by the 2008 Constitution, the entity responsible for operations in an adversely impacted area bears the burden of demonstrating that such an impact was not caused by its own operations'.[68] However, Ecuadorian law before the promulgation of the 2008 Constitution had provided for a fault-based regime.[69]

The *Perenco* Tribunal first approached two questions on the legal framework governing the dispute: 1) the relationship between the 2008 Ecuadorian Constitution's rules (e.g., on the objective of full restoration and the protection of nature itself as a subject of environmental rights, its rule on the imprescriptibility of environmental torts, its potential impact on the burden of proof and causation issues) alongside the environmental impact that oilfield operations are permitted to have under Ecuadorian domestic law; and 2) whether the Constitution's establishment of a strict liability regime can be applied to all of Perenco's activities, given that most of them (e.g., until 20 October 2008) took place when the 1998 Constitution was in effect.[70] The Tribunal declared that 'although the 2008 Constitution contains important provisions dealing with the protection of the environment and has effect as a set of foundational legal rules, it does not purport to prescribe the environmental regulatory regime governing hydrocarbon operations. Rather, the specific rules governing the environmental aspects of hydrocarbon exploitation are to be found within [Ecuadorian domestic statutes], all of which preceded the 2008 Constitution's making but which have continued to remain in force since its entry into force'.[71] The Tribunal decided that instead of retroactively applying the 2008 Ecuadorian Constitution to the environmental governance over Blocks 7 and 21, it would "look at the Ecuadorian technical standards as promulgated by the relevant bodies of the Ecuadorian State and as applied 'on the ground' both before and after the 2008 Constitution's promulgation'.[72] The Tribunal insisted that 'a distinction must be drawn between

[66] Ibid., paras 34 and 35.

[67] Ibid., paras 109–110.

[68] Ibid., para 355.

[69] Ibid., para 354.

[70] Ibid., para 320.

[71] Ibid., para 323.

[72] Ibid., para 352.

pre- and post- 2008 constitutional regimes'[73] for purposes of determining the nature of the environmental liability regime that applied to the environmental damage in Blocks 7 and 21:

> 357. The Tribunal considers that where a particular regime can give rise to damages claims has governed the conduct of a complex activity such as hydrocarbons exploitation, although the standards can be made more stringent with respect to activities engaged in after their entry into force, in respect of attempts to impose tortious liability after the fact, an operator can in general be held only to the legal standards that applied to its conduct at the time…as the Tribunal understands the law prior to 2008 Ecuadorian law created a strong presumption that the operator was responsible for the damage and this presumption could only be rebutted by demonstrating that some other party was responsible.[74]

The *Perenco* Tribunal thus bifurcated the applicable law according to the pre- and post- 2008 Constitution regimes: it applied the fault liability regime for damage that occurred before the promulgation of the 2008 Ecuador Constitution on 20 October 2008, and then the strict liability regime under said Constitution after 20 October 2008.[75] Under the fault-based regime, the Tribunal employed the following burden of proof as well as proof of causation:

> 371…the approach taken by the Ecuadorian courts prior to 2008 was to employ a relatively stringent burden of proof rule which presumed that the operator engaged in a hazardous activity and benefiting therefrom was responsible for any resulting damage. This, however, is a rebuttable presumption.
>
> 372. In considering the burden of proof, the Tribunal is mindful of the problems of proof when an oilfield is operated over a period of years by a single operator or, to make matters more complicated, by successive operators. The problem here is that the environmental claim is not based on a single event but rather on an accumulation of discrete events occurring at different sites at different times (and in circumstances where the operator is itself responsible for reporting any spills or other contamination). How, for example, does a tribunal differentiate between the acts of successive operators or even differentiate between the cumulative effect of the acts of the same operator on a particular platform? While it agrees with Perenco that it cannot presume that Perenco is the author of all the harm that has been detected, once a regulatory exceedance resulting from a potentially hazardous activity is shown, Perenco is prima facie responsible therefor…
>
> 374. Given the special difficulties attendant in proving the commission of an environmental tort, it appears to the Tribunal to be wrong in principle that an operator can simply plead that a spill occurred in the ordinary course of business and it is not liable therefor unless it is proved to have acted negligently. *The Tribunal is thus inclined to employ a strong rebuttable presumption that if there is a regulatory exceedance, that in itself is evidence of fault.* Any alternative approach would make it too onerous for a claimant because it would likely lack sufficient evidence to demonstrate that the operator failed in its duty of care in many if not most instances in which regulatory exceedances have occurred. The Tribunal considers that regulatory exceedances are indicative of operational failures and therefore should be taken as falling below the standard of care…

---

[73] Ibid., para 356.

[74] Ibid., paras 357–358.

[75] Ibid., para 359.

> 379. In sum, if a regulatory exceedance occurred, Perenco is to be taken to have fallen below the requisite duty of care and will be held liable unless it can prove on a preponderance of evidence: (i) an occurrence of a force majeure event; (ii) that it did not fall below the standard of care in respect of that specific instance of contamination; or (iii) that some other person caused harm.[76]

Upon its review of the evidence, the Tribunal found that 'Perenco's claims of strong environmental law compliance are not made out. While the Tribunal is not prepared to find that Perenco consistently sought to conceal instances of contamination, there is some evidence that it was less than forthcoming in some instances'.[77] Among the key decisions and findings of the Tribunal in its 2015 Interim Decision on the Environmental Counterclaim, several are noteworthy on the issue of the applicable law of environmental protection and liability as well as the role of independent environmental expertise: (1) for the period commencing 4 September 2002 (when Perenco first acquired its interests in Blocks 7 and 21) through to 19 October 2008, the 1998 Constitution's fault-based regime applies; (2) for any contamination in excess of regulatory standards shown to have occurred after 20 October 2008 up until the Consortium suspended operations on 16 July 2009, Perenco is strictly liable in accordance with the 2008 Constitution's strict liability regime for environmental damage; (3) with regard to any environmental harm occurring in Blocks 7 and 21 from 16 July 2009, when Petroamazonas took over the Blocks, Perenco bears no liability. Its remediation obligation extends only to regulatory exceedances that predate Petroamazonas' activities and which themselves have not been overtaken by Petroamazonas' new works; and (4) the Tribunal shall appoint an independent environmental expert to assist the Tribunal in ascertaining the environmental condition of the Blocks in accordance with the legal and factual findings made by the Tribunal.[78] After reviewing the evidence of the parties and the reports of the experts, especially the independent environmental expert, the *Perenco* Tribunal awarded Ecuador the amount of US$54,439,517 to be paid by Perenco.[79]

Burlington Resources Inc. v Republic of Ecuador also involved a similar counterclaim from Ecuador against a US corporation (Burlington Resources Inc.),[80] also involving oilfield operations in the Ecuadorian Amazon. The Tribunal granted Ecuador US$39,199,373 for its environmental counterclaims, and US$2,577,119.77 for its infrastructure counterclaims.[81] The *Burlington* Tribunal also dealt with similar issues concerning the strict liability regime under Ecuador's 2008 Constitution and the fault liability regime that existed prior to the 2008 Constitution.[82] However, it

[76] Ibid., paras 371, 372, 374 and 379 (emphasis added).

[77] Ibid., para 447.

[78] Ibid., para 611.

[79] Ibid., para 899.

[80] *Burlington Resources Inc. v Republic of Ecuador*, Decision on Counterclaims, 7 February 2017, ICSID Case No ARB/08/5 [Tribunal President: Professor Gabrielle Kaufmann-Kohler; Tribunal Members: Professor Brigitte Stern, Mr. Stephen Drymer].

[81] Ibid., para 1075.

[82] Ibid., paras 195–249.

differed slightly from the *Perenco* Tribunal by concluding that 'in Ecuadorian law strict liability governed instances of environmental harm at the latest since the Delfina Torres decision was handed down in 2002'.[83] Similar to the *Perenco* Tribunal, the *Burlington* Tribunal took the view that 'environmental harm is defined by reference to regulatory criteria. In the case of oilfield operations, these regulatory criteria are to be found primarily in [Ecuadorian domestic legislation]. In other words, an oilfield operator could not be considered to have caused environmental harm if permissible limits were observed, since precisely these permissible limits allow determining when a negative impact crosses the threshold of harm….any exceedance of applicable limits triggers extra-contractual civil liability and the ensuing obligation of full restoration back to these limits, independently from parallel administrative liability and possible sanctions'.[84] The *Burlington* Tribunal applied the regulatory criteria to the facts before it to ultimately reach its conclusions regarding the impermissible environmental damage caused by the actions of the claimant.

11.4 Environmental Protection in Investor Claims

The case of *Peter A. Allard v The Government of Barbados*[85] is an interesting example of an investor who alleged investment treaty breaches by a host State resulting from the host State's alleged failure to meet its own environmental laws. In this case, Claimant Mr. Allard undertook to acquire and develop land (otherwise known as 'Sanctuary') in Barbados to create an ecotourism attraction.[86] The Sanctuary comprised 34.25 acres of land ('Graeme Hall Swamp'), with a forest of red and white mangroves, a lake, and ponds connected to the ocean by a canal,[87] which opened to the public in 2004.[88] A year later, there was an emergency discharge of raw sewage into the Graeme Hall Swamp as a result of a failure at the South Coast Sewage Treatment Plant operated by the Barbados Water Authority.[89] Two years later, Mr. Allard started trying to sell the Sanctuary. In initiating his claim against Barbados, Mr. Allard argued that the 'actions and inactions of Barbados…-caused and/or failed to mitigate a significant degradation of the environment and the 'tourist experience' at the Sanctuary, to an extent obliging the Claimant to close the Sanctuary, and thereby depriving him of the entire benefit of his investment in

---

[83] Ibid., para 247.

[84] Ibid., paras 291–292.

[85] *Peter A. Allard v The Government of Barbados*, Award, 27 June 2016, PCA Case No 2012-06 [Members of the Tribunal: Dr. Gavan Griffith (President), Professor Andrew Newcombe, Professor W. Michael Reisman].

[86] Ibid., para 33.

[87] Ibid., para 34.

[88] Ibid., para 42.

[89] Ibid., para 43.

Barbados'.[90] Claimant Mr. Allard alleged that Barbados breached guarantees of fair and equitable treatment, full protection and security, and the rules on expropriation under the 1996 Canada-Barbados bilateral investment treaty (BIT).[91] Respondent Barbados argued that the Claimant had 'closed the Sanctuary for business reasons unrelated to the environmental conditions at the site. During the relevant period, the environmental conditions at the Sanctuary were not degraded, but either stayed the same or improved. Alternatively, any degradation as did occur, arose from external causes and the Claimant's own actions and inactions...Barbados took appropriate steps for the environmental protection of the Sanctuary...[and] complied with all of its obligations under the BIT'.[92]

After an extensive review of the environmental and scientific evidence, the *Allard v Barbados* Tribunal found that the Claimant failed to establish with evidence that his decision to cease Sanctuary operations as an ecotourism attraction indeed arose out of any relevant degradation of the environment at the Sanctuary (e.g., as to water salinity and other parameters of water quality, the health of the mangroves, the diversity and health of fish, the diversity and number of birds, and the number of crabs).[93] The Tribunal also concluded that, 'even if it had found that there was a degradation of the environment at the Sanctuary during the Relevant Period (which it did not), it would not have been persuaded that such degradation was caused by any actions or inactions of Barbados'.[94]

Most importantly, beyond the above factual conclusions that Claimant Mr. Allard had not proven loss and damage attributable to actions or inactions of Barbados, the Tribunal also clarified the nature of the treatment standards invoked by the claimant in the particular context of environmental protection. With respect to the fair and equitable treatment standard under the 1996 Canada-Barbados BIT, the Tribunal identified three factual cumulative conditions for examination: '(1) was there a specific representation?, (2) did the investor rely on it, i.e., was it critical to his making of the investment; and (iii) was the investor's reliance reasonable?'[95] The Tribunal found that 'none of the statements relied upon by the Claimant are amenable to characterization as a specific representation capable of creating a legitimate expectation on the part of Mr. Allard that Barbados would take any specific steps with regard to the environmental protection of the Sanctuary. The terms and context of these statements do not suffice to support the expression of an intention to create an obligation for the State. Nor is each reasonably amenable to be interpreted by an investor to create such an obligation'.[96] The Tribunal altogether sidestepped the impact of Barbados' international obligations from environmental treaties on the formation of

[90] Ibid., para 50.
[91] Ibid., para 51.
[92] Ibid., para 52.
[93] Ibid., para 139.
[94] Ibid., para 166.
[95] Ibid., para 194.
[96] Ibid., para 199.

the investor's legitimate expectations: 'Having found no direct and specific representation capable of giving rise to legitimate expectations on the part of Mr. Allard regarding the environmental protection of the Sanctuary generally, the Tribunal need not address the question of whether Barbados' international obligations arising from its environmental treaties confirmed or reinforced the legitimacy of the Claimant's expectations'.[97] Ultimately, the Tribunal found that Mr. Allard's investment was not made out of any reliance on any representations of Barbados as to its environmental policies.[98]

Claimant Mr. Allard again tried to inject Barbados' environmental treaty obligations into the interpretation of the full protection and security clause in Article II(2) of the 1996 Canada-Barbados BIT, arguing that Barbados' environmental treaty obligations heightened the due diligence required of the host State to protect investments against injury by private parties and required reasonable preventive measures.[99] The Tribunal found that Barbados was 'aware of the environmental sensitivities of the Sanctuary…[and] took reasonable steps to protect it'.[100] The Tribunal rejected the possible effect of environmental treaties on the full protection and security clause: 'The [due diligence] obligation is limited to reasonable action, and a host State is not required to take any specific steps that an investor asks of it. The fact that Barbados is a party to the Convention on Biological Diversity and the Ramsar Convention does not change the standard under the BIT, although consideration of a host State's international obligations may well be relevant in the application of the standard to particular circumstances'.[101]

Finally, Claimant Mr. Allard argued that Barbados committed indirect expropriation, when it designated the area as a 'wetland of international importance' under the Ramsar Convention and the Sanctuary as a 'natural heritage site', making the property unusable for anything other than as a conservation project.[102] The Tribunal declared that there was no deprivation amounting to an expropriation, since Mr. Allard 'remains the owner of the Sanctuary grounds, on which he continues to operate a café, and acknowledged…that there is some kind of business remaining there…the Claimant has not been deprived of his entire investment in Barbados'.[103] With all of the claims rejected, the Tribunal ordered the Claimant Mr. Allard to pay Barbados the amounts of USD 567,162 for the costs of arbitration, and USD 2,508,144 for its costs.

The *Allard v Barbados* arbitration is a unique instance of an investor seeking to internalize the host State's environmental treaty obligations, in a manner that would have imposed a higher standard of due diligence and preventive action on the host State. On the facts and the evidence before the Tribunal, the Claimant in this case

[97] Ibid., para 208.

[98] Ibid., paras 222–223.

[99] Ibid., para 229–230.

[100] Ibid., para 242.

[101] Ibid., para 244.

[102] Ibid., para 255.

[103] Ibid., para 264.

failed to establish any environmental damage that was attributable to the actions or inactions of the host State. The case is instructive in how it treats the burden of proof in allegations of environmental damage (which in this case rested entirely with the Claimant), and an arbitral tribunal's careful interpretation of BIT standards of treatment (fair and equitable treatment, full protection and security, expropriation) when the investor invokes the host State's environmental treaty obligations to justify reinterpreting BIT standards in his favour.

11.5 Conclusion: Multidimensional Environmental Protection in Investor-State Arbitration

The foregoing discussion of environmental protection featuring as legal defences of the host State, bases for counterclaims by the host State, or possible sources of investor claims against host States, is not meant to be exhaustive of all possible jurisprudence on environmental issues in investor-State arbitration. Other cases have dealt with alleged breaches of a host State of environmental law, such as, for example, the North American Free Trade Area (NAFTA) tribunal's award in *Bilcon v Canada*,[104] where the tribunal majority found that Canada had breached Canadian environmental law on environmental impact assessment, and concomitantly, the minimum standard of treatment under NAFTA.[105] Unlike the *Allard* Tribunal which dealt with the Claimant's failed attempt to impose a higher standard of environmental due diligence on, and substantive duties of preventive action by, the host State, the *Bilcon* Tribunal resolved the issue of the substantive and procedural fairness of the environmental assessment process and found against the respondent host State Canada. Claimants in *Bilcon* argued that 'the treatment they received at every stage of the [environmental assessment by Nova Scotia and the Canadian Federal Government] was unfair, politically biased and discriminatory',[106] and that their proposed operation of a quarry and mining terminal was 'consistent with environmental integrity and economic development'.[107] Canada, in turn, responded that its regulatory evaluations and environmental assessment process were undertaken in a lawful, normal, and consistent manner.[108] On its review of the evidence before it, the *Bilcon* Tribunal ultimately ruled that the environmental assessment process was

---

[104] *William Ralph Clayton, William Richard Clayton, Douglas Clayton, Daniel Clayton, and Bilcon of Delaware Inc. v Government of Canada*, Award on Jurisdiction and Liability, 17 March 2015, PCA Case No 2009-04 [Tribunal President: Judge Bruno Simma; Tribunal Members: Professor Donald McRae, Professor Bryan Schwartz].

[105] Ibid., paras 588–604. See para 602 ('The Tribunal at this stage simply holds that the applicant was not treated in a manner consistent with Canada's own laws, including the core evaluative standard under the [Canadian domestic environmental statute] and the standards of fair notice required by Canadian public administrative law').

[106] Ibid., para 5.

[107] Ibid., para 26.

[108] Ibid., paras 27–39.

apparently laden with 'arbitrariness'[109] and that 'there was a fundamental departure from the methodology required by Canadian and Nova Scotian law'.[110] In its Award on Damages, the *Bilcon* Tribunal awarded the Claimants the amount of US$7 Million in compensation for Canada's breaches of NAFTA Article 1105 (Minimum Standard of Treatment) and Article 1102 (National Treatment), and also awarded interest.[111]

Other cases have also dealt with environmental protection in its particular applications on climate change and renewable energy projects, marine environmental resources and specialized environmental protection regimes, such as those involving involve a host State's policies and regulatory incentives to shift away from fossil fuel-based energy sources towards more renewable energy sources, as seen in the many relatively recent arbitrations brought by investors against Spain concerning renewable energy projects.[112] More recently, inter-State disputes and mixed State and non-State actor disputes have been brought to the Permanent Court of Arbitration, especially relating to the United Nations Convention on the Law of the Sea, as well as under select international environmental treaties.[113]

The investor-State arbitral jurisprudence that were purposely featured in this chapter were selected in order to demonstrate how arbitral reasoning conceptualizes and visualizes environmental protection, whether from the perspective of the host State mustering a legal defence or submitting a counterclaim, or from the vantage point of an investor that seeks to vindicate claims against a host State that allegedly did not perform its international environmental obligations in a manner that supposedly prejudiced the investment. What is clear, at least from the arbitral awards surveyed, is that the arbitral tribunals surveyed here were conscious of the expertise required to adjudicate issues involving environmental protection, liberally resorting to expert scientific and multidisciplinary advice on all dimensions of environmental protection, as well as embracing a myriad of fact-finding methodologies to determine the outcome most consistent with the objective of environmental protection. What is equally clear from the investor-State arbitral jurisprudence surveyed here is that arbitral tribunals side with interpretations that favour the greatest possible environmental protection, and not simply environmental protection *de minimis*. Arbitral tribunals carefully parse the allocation of risk of environmental damage in investment activities between the due diligence of the host State and the counterpart due diligence of the investor. There is no *a priori* assumption that investors or host States bear the

---

[109] Ibid., para 591.

[110] Ibid., para 600.

[111] Ibid., para 742. See *William Ralph Clayton, William Richard Clayton, Douglas Clayton, Daniel Clayton, and Bilcon of Delaware Inc. v Government of Canada*, Award on Damages, 10 January 2019, UNCITRAL, PCA Case No 2009-04, para 400.

[112] See *Charanne B.V Construction Investments S.A.R.L. v The Kingdom of Spain*, Award, 21 January 2016, ICSID Case No 062/2012; *Eiser Infrastructure Limited and Energia Solar Luxembourg S.A.R.L. v The Kingdom of Spain*, Award, 4 May 2017, ICSID Case No ARB/13/36; *Isolux Netherlands B.V. v Kingdom of Spain*, Final Award, 17 July 2016, SCC Case No V2013/153; *Novenergia II—Energy & Environment (SCA) (Grand Duchy of Luxembourg), SICAR v The Kingdom of Spain*, Final Award, 15 February 2018, SCC Case No 2015/063.

[113] See Meshel 2016; Stephens 2009, pp. 21–60; Garimella 2016.

sole or exclusive burden when it comes to achieving the desired legal environmental protection in these cases, and instead, arbitral tribunals are cognizant of the necessary partnership entailed in foreign investment activities between the private sector and the host State to realize environmental protection for the wider population that is impacted by investment. These demonstrated careful, cautious, scientifically deferential, but also quite progressive tendencies of several investor-State arbitral tribunals to resolve environmental protection disputes that augur well for future investor-State arbitral cases where more complexity as to environmental protection issues would be expected, such as in climate change (and the necessary industry, economy, and societal transformations required to meet climate change targets),[114] as well as in global public health crises from epidemiological diseases related to environmental factors.[115]

Understandably, some academic and scholarly concerns focus on the appropriateness of international investment arbitration to realize environmental protection outcomes.[116] My argument in this chapter is more modest. This chapter does not argue that international investment arbitration ought to be the primary forum for achieving environmental protection outcomes, or that there is empirical evidence that this form of dispute settlement is the most efficient and effective in realizing any environmental protection outcome. This form of dispute settlement was not designed to be so, even if environmental protection measures often feature within investor-State disputes. For the task of robustly or rigorously evaluating defences, justifications, claims, as well as counterclaims based on environmental protection measures within the context of pending investor-State disputes, the qualitative evidence shown here demonstrates that certain arbitral tribunals are well-capable of designing the evidentiary fact-finding process in a manner that considers scientific, environmental, regulatory, community inputs and expertise. I do not hypothesize if this will be a uniform experience for all investor-State arbitrations, as it is the parties in concert with the arbitral tribunal that ultimately shape the contours of evidentiary fact-finding processes in investor-State arbitration. To the extent that the parties and arbitral tribunals in the cases analysed in this chapter were able to fully utilize the evidentiary processes and possibilities for resort to independent expertise, one could potentially remark on the fairness and openness of investor-State arbitration as a particular form of dispute resolution process for disputes that intricately weave environmental protection with foreign investment protection issues. One would have to do a closer empirical and analytical survey of *all* investor-State arbitrations that encompassed environmental protection measures, before we could attempt to reach hard conclusions about the ultimate suitability (or unsuitability) of international investment arbitration to help realize environmental protection objectives and outcomes. At best, one could observe from the qualitative analysis done in this chapter that, contrary to the many popular biases and criticisms against this form of dispute resolution process, investor-State arbitration may not be the court of first resort to achieve environmental protection,

[114] See Boute 2012.
[115] See O'Gorman et al. 2020.
[116] See e.g., Latifah et al. 2020; Di Benedetto 2013, pp. 3–82; Robert-Cuendet 2019.

but it is also not the court of last resort when it comes to producing sound, competent, and credible adjudication that is mindful of the role of scientific expertise, public regulatory concerns, and desired environmental outcomes. At the very least, the jurisprudential record examined in this chapter provides some qualitative evidence of the feasibility of investor-State arbitration as an adjudicative process, capable of accommodating various scientific, fact-finding, expert-driven, and interdisciplinary methodologies towards resolving questions raised by either host States or investors concerning environmental protection.

References

Anh Hoang To, Dao Thi-Thieu Ha, Ha Minh Nguyen, Duc Hong Vo (2019) The Impact of Foreign Direct Investment on Environment Degradation: Evidence from Emerging Markets in Asia. https://www.ncbi.nlm.nih.gov/pmc/articles/PMC6539116/. Accessed 23 April 2020.

Asteriti A (2015) Environmental Law in Investment Arbitration: Procedural Means of Incorporation. Journal of World Investment & Trade 16:248–273.

Augenstein D, Kinley D (2013) When Human Rights 'Responsibilities' Become 'Duties': The Extraterritorial Obligations of States that Bind Corporations. In: Deva S, Bilchitz D (eds) Human Rights Obligations of Business: Beyond the Corporate Responsibility to Respect? Cambridge University Press, Cambridge, pp 271–294.

Beharry C, Kuritzky M (2015) Going Green: Managing the Environment through International Investment Arbitration. American University International Law Review 30:383–430

Bernaz N (2017) Business and Human Rights History, Law and Policy. Routledge, London/New York.

Boisson de Chazournes L (2017) Environmental Protection and Investment Arbitration: Yin and Yang. Anuario Colombiano de Derecho Internacional 10:371–400.

Borregaard N, Dufey A (2002) Environmental Effects of Foreign Investment versus Domestic Investment in the Mining Sector in Latin America. https://www.oecd.org/env/1819617.pdf. Accessed 23 April 2021.

Boute A (2012) Combating Climate Change through Investment Arbitration. Fordham International Law Journal 35:614–664

Da Silva M (2018) Compensation Awards in International Environmental Law: Two Recent Developments. New York University Journal of International Law and Politics 50:1417–1430.

De Luca A (2020) UNCITRAL Working Group III: Counterclaims in ISDS—Challenges and Prospects in light of the UNCITRAL Reform Process. http://arbitrationblog.kluwerarbitration.com/2020/03/28/uncitral-working-group-iii-counterclaims-in-isds-challenges-and-prospects-in-light-of-the-uncitral-reform-process/. Accessed 23 April 2021.

Demena BA, Afesorgbor SK (2020) The Effect of FDI on Environmental Emissions: Evidence from a Meta-Analysis. https://www.sciencedirect.com/science/article/pii/S0301421519307773. Accessed 23 April 2021.

Di Benedetto S (2013) International Investment Law and the Environment. Edward Elgar Publishing, Cheltenham.

Garimella SR (2016) Environmental Dispute Resolution, ADR Methods, and the PCA Arbitration Rules. ILI Law Review Summer 2016:199–222.

Gerlach E, Franceys R (2010) Regulating Water Services for All in Developing Economies. World Development 38:1229–1240.

Gleason T (2020) Examining Host-State Counterclaims for Environmental Damage in Investor-State Dispute Settlement from Human Rights and Transnational Public Policy Perspectives. International Environmental Agreements: Politics, Law and Economics. https://doi.org/10.1007/s10784-020-09519-y. Accessed 23 April 2021.

Gordon K, Pohl J (2011) Environmental Concerns in International Investment Agreements: A Survey, OECD Working Papers on International Investment. https://www.oecd.org/investment/investment-policy/WP-2011_1.pdf. Accessed 23 April 2021.

Harrison J (2016) Environmental Counterclaims in Investor-State Arbitration. Journal of World Investment and Trade 17:479–488

Ho J (2018) State Responsibility for Breaches of Investment Contracts. Oxford University Press, Oxford.

Jensen J (2017) Public-Private Partnerships for Water in Asia: A Review of Two Decades of Experience. International Journal of Water Resources Development 33:4–30.

Joseph S (2004) Corporations and Transnational Human Rights Litigation. Hart Publishing, London.

Latifah E, Imanullah MN, Angelia IR (2020) When International Investment Law and Environmental Law Are in Crossroads: How to Protect Investors and Environment in Tobacco Control Cases. 423 IOP Conference Series: Earth and Environmental Science. https://www.researchgate.net/publication/338632173_When_the_international_investment_law_and_environmental_law_are_in_crossroads_how_to_protect_investors_and_environment_in_tobacco_control_case. Accessed 17 March 2022.

Mahla M, Duggal KAN (2020) When the Answer is Becoming the Question: The Impact of Arbitrations on the Environment. http://arbitrationblog.kluwerarbitration.com/2020/11/29/when-the-answer-is-becoming-the-question-impact-of-arbitrations-on-the-environment/. Accessed 23 April 2021.

Marisi F (2020) Environmental Interests in Investment Arbitration: Challenges and Directions. Kluwer Law International, Alphen aan den Rijn.

Marques RC, Simoes P (2020) Revisiting the Comparison of Public and Private Water Service Provision: An Empirical Study in Portugal. Water 12:1477–1498.

Meshel T (2016) The Permanent Court of Arbitration and the Peaceful Resolution of Transboundary Freshwater Disputes. https://esil-sedi.eu/wp-content/uploads/2016/04/ESIL-Reflection-Tamar-Meshel_0.pdf. Accessed 23 April 2021.

Mistura A (2019) Enhancing Environmental Protection in International Investment Law through the Integration of International Civil Liability Principles. https://www.iisd.org/itn/en/2019/04/23/enhancing-environmental-protection-in-international-investment-law-through-the-integration-of-international-civil-liability-principles-alessandra-mistura/. Accessed 23 April 2021.

O'Gorman K, Stothard P, Valasek M (2020) Investor-State Claims in the Era of the COVID-19 Pandemic. https://www.nortonrosefulbright.com/-/media/files/nrf/nrfweb/knowledge-pdfs/international-arbitration-report---issue-14.pdf?la=en&revision=6edf090e-2dae-4845-a812-c912f12016d0. Accessed 23 April 2021.

Payne CR (2017) Developments in the Law of Environmental Reparations: A Case Study of the United Nations Compensation Commission. In: Stahn C et al (eds) Environmental Protection and Transitions from Conflict to Peace: Clarifying Norms, Principles, and Practices. Oxford University Press, Oxford, pp 329–366.

Robert-Cuendet S (2019) Protection of the Environment and International Investment Law. In: Krajewski M, Hoffman RT (eds) Research Handbook on Foreign Direct Investment. Edward Elgar Publishing, Cheltenham/Northampton, pp 596–618.

Romson A (2012) Environmental Policy Space and International Investment Law. Acta Universitatis Stockholmiensis. http://su.diva-portal.org/smash/get/diva2:510323/FULLTEXT01.pdf. Accessed 23 April 2021.

Sharma G (2020) Environmental Claims by States in Investment Treaty Arbitration. http://arbitrationblog.practicallaw.com/environmental-claims-by-states-in-investment-treaty-arbitration/. Accessed 23 April 2021.

Stephens T (2009) International Courts and Environmental Protection. Cambridge University Press, Cambridge.

Sweify M (2015) Investment-Environment Disputes: Challenges and Proposals. DePaul Business and Commercial Law Journal 14:133–208.

Tienhaara K (2011) Foreign Investment Contracts in the Oil & Gas Sector: A Survey of Environmentally Relevant Clauses. Sustainable Development Law & Policy 11:15–40.

Viñuales JE, Dupuy P-M (eds) (2013) Harnessing Foreign Investment to Promote Environmental Protection: Incentives and Safeguards. Cambridge University Press, Cambridge.

Diane A. Desierto Professor of Law and Global Affairs, LLM Faculty Director, Notre Dame Law School and Keough School of Global Affairs, University of Notre Dame. She can be reached at ddesiert@nd.edu

Chapter 12
Commercial Arbitration

Kirsten Odynski and Héloïse Broc

Contents

Abstract Commercial arbitration is considered a confidential means of resolving contractual disputes of a commercial nature between private parties. Yet, environmental issues have and will continue to be raised before commercial tribunals. For example, the rapid development of environmental legislation, in particular in respect of climate change, will impact the nature of the claims and defences brought forward by States and companies operating in the construction, engineering, and energy sectors, all of whom are existing users of commercial arbitration. This chapter explores whether commercial arbitration is an appropriate forum for the resolution of environmental disputes. The authors first consider the features of commercial arbitration that make it well suited to the resolution of environmental disputes, including its neutrality, the enforceability of awards, and the flexible procedure that can be tailored to the needs of a particular dispute. The authors then consider the impact of the private nature of commercial arbitration and the resulting lack of accessibility to the third parties and the public as a whole on this forum's suitability for the resolution of environmental disputes.

K. Odynski · H. Broc (✉)
White & Case LLP, Paris, France
e-mail: heloise.broc@whitecase.com

K. Odynski
e-mail: kirsten.odynski@whitecase.com

E. Sobenes et al. (eds.), *The Environment Through the Lens of International Courts and Tribunals*, https://doi.org/10.1007/978-94-6265-507-2_12

Keywords Party autonomy · Enforcement · Technical expertise · Selection of arbitrators · Interim measures · Time-efficiency · Public interest · Transparency · Confidentiality · Third party participation

12.1 Introduction

Commercial arbitration[1] is a consensual means of resolving disputes between parties acting in their private capacity arising out of commercial transactions.[2] Commercial tribunals are *ad hoc* and their authority is derived from and circumscribed by the parties' consent, materialized in the arbitration agreement.

Unlike investment arbitration, which arises under the terms of an international treaty and involves a State or State entity acting in its sovereign capacity, commercial arbitration has not played a central role in discussions about the suitability of arbitration for resolving environmental disputes. This is likely because the contractual and consensual nature of commercial arbitration prevents it from being a forum for typical disputes concerning the environment. This includes public actions against States seeking to enforce national and international obligations, and private tort actions against significant carbon emitters (the so-called 'Carbon Majors') seeking compensation for damages to the environment.[3] Additionally, the confidential nature of commercial arbitration,[4] where proceedings are typically conducted in private and awards are rarely published, makes it difficult to study the number of tribunals addressing environmental issues or the nature of the issues addressed.

Yet, the authors consider that tribunals presiding over commercial arbitrations have and will increasingly be called upon to consider and decide on disputes relating to environmental issues—in particular, in respect of climate change. This is for a number of reasons.

Commercial arbitrations are not solely the domain of private parties. Over the past forty years, globalization has fundamentally transformed the relationship between States and economic actors,[5] leading to '[various] forms of cooperation between

[1] Most legal systems distinguish between international and domestic arbitration. The discussion in this chapter focuses on international commercial arbitration, i.e., a commercial arbitration involving a foreign element. For example, pursuant to Article 1(3) of the UNCITRAL Model Law: 'An arbitration is international if: (1) the parties to an arbitration agreement have, at the time of the conclusion of that agreement, their place of business in different States; *or* (2) one of the following places is situated outside the State in which the parties have their place of business: (1) the place of arbitration if determined in, or pursuant to, the arbitration agreement; (2) any place where a substantial part of the obligation of the commercial relationship is to be performed of the place with which the subject-matter of the dispute is most closely connected; *or* (3) the parties have expressly agreed that the subject matter of the arbitration agreement relates to more than one country.'

[2] See e.g., Allsop 2019, p. 9.

[3] Baker and Stebbing 2018.

[4] See Sect. 12.3.1 below.

[5] Max Planck Institute, Transnational Private-Public Arbitration as Global Regulatory Governance: Charting and Codifying the Lex Mercatoria Publica. https://www.mpil.de/en/pub/research/archive/erc-project.cfm. Accessed 24 April 2021.

the state and private actors, prompted by the privatization of public functions and increases in public-private-partnerships'.[6] States and State entities regularly enter into contracts with private companies including concession contracts, contracts for the provision of public services, etc.[7] This has led to an increase in commercial arbitration 'between a public entity and a private entity under a contract which implicates the public interest' or the so-called 'public-private arbitration'.[8] In 2018, approximately 15% of the caseload of the International Chamber of Commerce (ICC), a leading institution for the administration of commercial arbitrations, involved a State or a State-owned entity.[9] That same year, approximately 38% of the cases for which the Permanent Court of Arbitration (PCA) provided registry service arose under contracts involving a State, intergovernmental organization or other public entity.[10] Disputes involving States and their entities are increasingly likely to touch on or concern environmental issues given the now wide spread recognition that 'climate change represents an urgent and potentially irreversible threat to human societies'.[11]

Further, commercial transactions—either purely private or public-private—are evidently not detached from environmental considerations. On the contrary, 'daily commercial activities … in one way or another address issues that have a bearing upon sustainability objective'.[12] This is particularly so in the construction and energy sectors, where commercial arbitration is already a preferred method of dispute resolution.[13] In 2017, 42% of the 186 new cases filed with the ICC were in the construction, engineering, and energy sectors.[14] Disputes arising in these sectors, even if purely contractual, often have environmental repercussions. Consider, for example, the environmental impact of claims relating to construction defects, such as a claim for damages due to the existence of a radioactive coolant leak in a plant,[15] or claims relating to the reconstruction of a plant due to the existence of gas-leak.[16]

National and international laws concerning environmental issues, including in the rapidly developing area of climate change, will increasingly be reflected in commercial contracts. As fellow arbitration practitioners have explained: '[w]here new risks manifest, parties invariably seek to mitigate and allocate such risks between them

---

[6] Ibid.

[7] Brekoulakis 2017.

[8] Brekoulakis and Devany 2016, p. 30.

[9] ICC Dispute Resolution (2018) Statistics, p. 9. http://files-eu.clickdimensions.com/iccwboorg-avxnt/files/web_icc_disputeresolution2018statistics.pdf. Accessed 24 April 2021.

[10] PCA Annual Report (2018), p. 18. https://docs.pca-cpa.org/2020/03/7d4bf644-pca-annual-report-2018.pdf. Accessed 24 April 2021.

[11] International Law Association (ILA) (2014) Committee on Legal Principle Relating to Climate Change, Declaration of Legal Principles Relating to Climate Change, Preamble, p. 1. https://ila.vettoreweb.com/Storage/Download.aspx?DbStorageId=1253&StorageFileGuid=f93d2f56-5629-40aa-a940-34c7da6e8545. Accessed 24 April 2021.

[12] Magnusson 2018, p. 396, para 17.42.

[13] Bishop et al 2018, p. 1; Brekoulakis and Thomas 2019, p. 1.

[14] ICC 2019, p. 13.

[15] Evans 2019, p. 289.

[16] Sanderson 2019.

contractually. Unsurprisingly, many contracts now include obligations to comply with or warrant compliance with environmental, human rights or sustainability obligations, and commitments to put in place back-to-back arrangements with counterparties further down the line'.[17] Evidently, disputes may arise in respect of the interpretation and application of such contractual provisions. For example, in 2017, an Austrian oil and gas group filed a € 34 million claim in a commercial arbitration against Romania arguing that the latter failed to pay environmental clean-up costs as agreed in the contract.[18] Also in 2017, the press reported that, in an arbitration arising out of a contract concerning a mining project, the Greek Ministry of Environment and Energy claimed that the company's proposal to use 'flash smelting' technology—a process for smelting ore containing sulphates—was in breach of the contract and the environmental terms of the project.[19]

The development of environmental legislation will also impact the nature of claims and defences raised in commercial arbitration, regardless of whether those laws have been incorporated into the contract. An oft cited example is the treatment of *force majeure* or hardship clauses. Such clauses operate as an exception to the binding nature of contractual commitments in circumstances where an event materially affects a party's ability to perform its obligations. Disputes may arise as to whether government measures intended to protect the environment, including climate change related legislation, may fall within the scope of such clauses.[20]

Users of commercial arbitration may also raise claims for non-compliance with legislative obligations. For example, as reported in a 2017 press article, in an arbitration arising out of a production sharing agreement, Sonatrach alleged that Total failed to operate a gas field in accordance with applicable environmental laws by extracting more gas than allowed by the geological models agreed when the contract was signed, thereby endangering the preservation of the field.[21]

Finally, although typically reserved for contractual disputes, public and private parties may determine it advantageous to submit purely environmental disputes to commercial arbitration. The submission of a dispute to commercial arbitration is entirely dependent on the parties' will such that parties may agree to submit any dispute to arbitration, even after the dispute has arisen. For example, in the case known as *Anderson and all v PG&E*, which inspired the Erin Brockovich movie, the

---

[17] Baker and Stebbing 2018.

[18] Young 2017.

[19] GAR (2017) Greece to bring claim against Canadian mining investor. https://globalarbitrationreview.com/article/1145341/greece-to-bring-claim-against-canadian-mining-investor. Accessed 24 April 2021. The Tribunal eventually dismissed the claim. For a definition of 'flash smelting' see Collins Dictionary. https://www.collinsdictionary.com/dictionary/english/flash-smelting Accessed 24 April 2021.

[20] An analysis of scope of *force majeure* and hardship clauses is outside the scope of this chapter and will depend on the applicable law, the language of the relevant clause, and the factual circumstances at issue.

[21] GAR (2017) Total and Sonatrach to drop ICC claims. https://globalarbitrationreview.com/article/1141140/total-and-sonatrach-to-drop-icc-claims. Accessed 24 April 2021. The parties eventually settled.

residents of Hinkley started arbitration against Pacific Gas and Electric Company one year after bringing the dispute before State courts. The parties agreed to arbitrate their dispute about whether PG&E had been contaminating the groundwater in Hinkley for more than 40 years after the judge wrote to the plaintiffs explaining that it could take up to five years before the case was assigned a trial date.[22] Parties may willingly agree to submit environmental disputes to commercial arbitration after they have arisen because, as set out further below,[23] it offers a number of advantages and the cross-border nature of many environmental disputes could be a challenge for national courts.

This clear nexus between commercial arbitration and environmental issues has been confirmed in recent reports issued by the ICC and the Stockholm Chamber of Commerce (SCC) concluding that commercial arbitration has witnessed a 'steady increase in disputes that arguably involve, or might involve, climate change related issues'[24] and will likely continue to be used to resolve both direct and ancillary environmental issues.

With that background in mind, this chapter considers the suitability of commercial arbitration for resolving environmental disputes. The authors first describe the features of commercial arbitration that make the forum well suited to addressing environmental disputes, including the fact that it offers a neutral forum, easily enforceable decisions, and flexible procedures that can be tailored to the needs of the parties and the nature of the dispute. The authors then consider how arbitration's confidential nature and the resulting lack of accessibility negatively affects the forum's appropriateness for resolving environmental disputes.

As commercial arbitral awards are rarely published and when published are typically redacted to protect the anonymity of the parties, the discussion that follows relies on the authors' experience, general principles, and press reports.

12.2 Is Commercial Arbitration a Suitable Forum to Resolve Environmental Disputes?

12.2.1 Neutrality

Disputes involving environmental issues are likely to arise out of international transactions, thus involving nationals of several jurisdictions, performance in different countries, and so on. Given the potential involvement of many different countries, a

[22] Chao 2017.

[23] See Sect. 12.2 below.

[24] ICC 2019, paras 24 and 75; SCC (2019) Green Technology Disputes in Stockholm, pp. 5 and 25. https://sccinstitute.com/about-the-scc/news/2019/just-published-green-technology-disputes-in-stockholm/. Accessed 24 April 2021.

forum detached from the parties' respective jurisdictions may be preferred.[25] This concern is heightened when the dispute involves a State party, which is not an infrequent occurrence in commercial transactions touching on environmental issues.[26] Indeed, the non-State party may be reluctant to have its dispute against a State or State-owned entity resolved before the national courts of that State. Further, the project underlying the dispute and its potential or actual impact on the environment may give rise to national political or media pressures. Commercial arbitration allows parties to select a neutral dispute resolution forum as the place of arbitration as well as to select arbitrators with a nationality other than those involved in the dispute.

12.2.2 *Ease of Enforceability*

International arbitral awards, including those rendered in commercial arbitrations, benefit from broad recognition and enforcement under the Convention on the Recognition and Enforcement of Foreign Arbitral Awards, adopted in New York in 1958 (New York Convention). This Convention, which now has 169 State parties,[27] imposes a general obligation on State courts to recognize and enforce international arbitral awards:

> Each Contracting State shall recognize arbitral awards as binding and enforce them in accordance with the rules of procedure of the territory where the award is relied upon, under the conditions laid down in the following articles. There shall not be imposed substantially more onerous conditions or higher fees or charges on the recognition or enforcement of arbitral awards to which this Convention applies than are imposed on the recognition or enforcement of domestic arbitral awards.[28]

The New York Convention also sets out an exhaustive list of grounds under which a domestic court may refuse to recognize and enforce an arbitral award:

1. invalidity of the arbitration agreement;
2. lack of proper notice of the arbitration proceedings or inability to present the case;
3. the scope of the dispute is not covered by the arbitration agreement;
4. the composition of the tribunal or the procedure violates the parties' agreement or (absent any agreement) the law of the seat, the award is not yet binding or has been set aside at the seat;

[25] Queen Mary and White & Case 2018 International Arbitration Survey: The Evolution of International Arbitration, p. 7 (Queen Mary and White & Case Survey). http://www.arbitration.qmul.ac.uk/media/arbitration/docs/2018-International-Arbitration-Survey---The-Evolution-of-International-Arbitration-(2).PDF. Accessed 24 April 2021.

[26] See Sect. 12.1 above.

[27] The entire list is available at: http://www.newyorkconvention.org/countries. Accessed 24 January 2022.

[28] Convention on the Recognition and Enforcement of Foreign Arbitral Awards, opened for signature 16 June 1956, entered into force 7 June 1959, 333 UNTS 3.

5. the dispute is not capable of being resolved through arbitration; or
6. recognition or enforcement of the award would be contrary to public policy in the enforcing State.[29]

As is evident from this list, these grounds are primarily procedural in nature and do not require the domestic court considering the enforceability of the award to re-examine the merits of the case. In fact, some countries, including France, expressly prohibit national courts from reviewing the merits of the case when considering the recognition and enforcement of an arbitral award.[30]

The New York Convention is 'arguably one of the most successful United Nations treaties in the area of international trade law',[31] with the enforcement of arbitral awards being granted 'in almost 90 per cent of the cases'.[32] Users perceive the ease of enforcement under the New York Convention as 'arbitration's most valuable characteristic'.[33]

This is an important benefit in the case of environmental disputes where a final decision rendered by arbitrators with appropriate expertise based on extensive witness

---

[29] Ibid., Article 5 ('(1) Recognition and enforcement of the award may be refused, at the request of the party against whom it is invoked, only if that party furnishes to the competent authority where the recognition and enforcement is sought, proof that: (1) The parties to the agreement referred to in article II were, under the law applicable to them, under some incapacity, or the said agreement is not valid under the law to which the parties have subjected it or, failing any indication thereon, under the law of the country where the award was made; or (2) The party against whom the award is invoked was not given proper notice of the appointment of the arbitrator or of the arbitration proceedings or was otherwise unable to present his case; or (3) The award deals with a difference not contemplated by or not failing with the terms of the submission to arbitration, or it contains decisions on matters beyond the scope of the submission to arbitration, provided that, if the decisions on matters submitted to arbitration can be separated from those not so submitted, that part of the award which contains decisions on matters submitted to arbitration may be recognized and enforced; or (4) The composition of the arbitral authority or the arbitral procedure was not in accordance with the agreement of the parties, or, failing such agreement, was not in accordance with the law of the country where the arbitration took place; or (5) The award has not yet become binding on the parties, or has been set aside or suspended by a competent authority of the country in which or under the law of which that award was made. (2) Recognition and enforcement of the arbitral award may also be refused if the competent authority in the country where recognition and enforcement is sought finds that: (a) the subject matter of the difference is not capable of settlement by arbitration under the law of that country; or (b) The recognition or enforcement of the award would be contrary to the public policy of that country').

[30] See e.g., Cour de cassation, Judgement, 30 January 2019, No 14–23.822 ('Whereas, the annulment judge is the judge of the award, admitting or denying its insertion into the French legal regime, and not the judge of the case for which the parties have entered into an arbitration agreement; that under the pretext of unsubstantiated objections based on the violation of Article 1502.3 of the Code of Civil Procedure, the objection, which accuses the Court of Appeal of not having censured an error of law allegedly committed by the arbitrators, only seeks a review of the merits; that it cannot be upheld'—automated translation).

[31] Kirtland and Connoly 2018.

[32] New York Convention in Brief. http://www.newyorkconvention.org/in+brief. Accessed 24 April 2021.

[33] Queen Mary and White & Case Survey, above n 25, p. 2.

and expert evidence is likely to be set aside only where a serious procedural irregularity has occurred (such as the improper constitution of the Tribunal or breach of due process for example). The New York Convention thus operates to ensure that national courts may not set aside a decision made in accordance with the procedure agreed to by the parties for political reasons.

Given its terms serve to promote the enforcement of arbitral awards, one might wonder whether the New York Convention could operate to allow the enforcement of arbitral awards that violate environmental regulations and objectives. It is highly unlikely that such an award would be issued and, even if it was, the recognition and enforcement of such an award could be refused under the New York Convention on the ground of public policy. While the interpretation and application of this ground is controversial, it is likely that in the not so distant future, at least some environmental regulations will form part of a country's public policy. The Paris Court of Appeal, for example, considers that a principle falls within the scope of public policy where (i) it is enshrined in an international text, and (ii) there is an international consensus upon it:

> [The resolution of the United Nations adopted on 14 December 1962] expresses an international consensus on the right of States to subject the exploitation of natural resources located on their territory to prior authorization and to control foreign investment in this field; that the provisions by which, in accordance with international law, States express their sovereignty over their natural resources are therefore part of international public policy.[34]

Where environmental regulations have risen to the level of public policy, domestic courts could refuse to recognize and enforce awards that fail properly to take into such regulations on grounds of public policy.

12.2.3 Procedural Flexibility

There are as many types of commercial arbitration as there are disputes. Commercial arbitral tribunals are *ad hoc* bodies established to rule on a particular dispute in accordance with the specific set of procedural rules agreed to by the parties. A fundamental characteristic of commercial arbitration is the principle of party autonomy: the parties' freedom to agree upon any procedure subject to limited mandatory requirements found in local or international laws, and in the applicable arbitration rules if any. The parties may directly agree on the rules of procedure or, more frequently, agree to arbitrate in accordance with a particular set of procedural rules developed by an institution or organization. To date, more than 75 different sets of procedural

[34] Paris Court of Appeal, *MK Group v SARL Onix*, Judgement, 16 January 2018, Case No 15/21703. The Paris Court of Appeal adopted a similar approach with respect to corruption in the *Belokon v Kyrgyzstan*, Judgement, 21 February 2017, Case No 15/01650.

rules are in use.[35] The ICC Rules of Arbitration[36] are the most widely used rules for institutional arbitration and the United Nations Commission on International Trade Law (UNCITRAL) Rules for *ad hoc* arbitrations.[37]

Environmental disputes have a number of unique features. For example, such disputes, particularly those concerning climate change, are by nature technical and time-sensitive. They also tend to raise issues of public interest. To address these unique features, parties to commercial contracts can adopt more specialized procedural rules such as the Permanent Court of Arbitration (PCA) Optional Rules for Arbitration of Disputes Relating to the Environment and/or Natural Resources (PCA Environmental Rules).[38] These rules, drafted by a committee of arbitration and environmental law experts, adapt commonly used arbitration rules, where necessary, to the needs of environmental disputes.[39] Parties can also develop procedural rules specific to the needs of their dispute. The sections that follow outline procedural elements that may be attractive to parties to an environmental dispute.

12.2.3.1 Appropriate Expertise

In 2019, the ICC published a report on 'Resolving Climate Change Related Disputes through Arbitration and ADR' (ICC Report), which considered the past and potential future role of arbitration, including commercial arbitration, in the resolution of climate change disputes.[40] This report was prepared by a task force that the ICC created, composed of business representatives, lawyers, arbitrators, arbitral institutions, and in-house counsels, as well as representatives of NGOs, business, industry groups and academics. The ICC Report is among the first comprehensive studies considering the suitability of commercial arbitration for resolving climate change disputes.

The ICC Report provides that 'the single most important feature of arbitrating climate change related disputes is the ability to ensure that appropriate expertise is available to the parties and the tribunal'.[41] In commercial arbitration, the 'appropriate

---

[35] Roe B (2018) Summary of Arbitral Rules. https://globalarbitrationnews.com/summary-of-arbitral-rules/. Accessed 24 April 2021.

[36] ICC Rules of Arbitration (2021) https://iccwbo.org/dispute-resolution-services/arbitration/rules-of-arbitration/. Accessed 24 April 2021.

[37] An 'institutional arbitration' is one in which an arbitral institution administers the arbitration process, whereas in case of an 'ad hoc arbitration', no institution is involved.

[38] PCA, Optional Rules for Arbitration of Disputes Relating to the Environment and/or Natural Resources (2001) (PCA Environmental Rules). https://docs.pca-cpa.org/2016/01/Optional-Rules-for-Arbitration-of-Disputes-Relating-to-the-Environment-and_or-Natural-Resources.pdf. Accessed 24 April 2021.

[39] See PCA, Environmental Dispute Resolution. https://pca-cpa.org/en/services/arbitration-services/environmental-dispute-resolution/. Accessed 24 April 2021.

[40] ICC 2019.

[41] Ibid., p. 19, para 5.7.

expertise' may be found in the arbitrators themselves (i.) or by the appointment of independent experts (ii.).

The Selection of Arbitrators

One of—if not the most—important features of commercial arbitration is the parties' ability to select their own decision-makers.[42] In addition to selecting individual arbitrators, parties may agree, either in the contract or after the dispute has arisen, on criteria that the arbitrator(s) must meet, such as, for example, having certain scientific or technical expertise. Failure to abide by the parties' agreement as to the necessary criteria may result in the annulment of the award.[43]

The parties' entitlement to select the arbitrators is enshrined in virtually all arbitration rules. In the case of a three-member tribunal (the most common scenario), under most arbitration rules, each party will nominate a co-arbitrator. The co-arbitrators, either with or without the involvement of the parties and their counsel, will then agree on a third arbitrator who will act as president of the tribunal. Article 7 of the PCA Environmental Rules, which is typical of most arbitration rules, provides for example:

> 1. If three arbitrators are to be appointed, each party shall appoint one arbitrator. The two arbitrators thus appointed shall choose the third arbitrator who will act as the presiding arbitrator of the tribunal. …
>
> 3. If within sixty days after the appointment of the second arbitrator the two arbitrators have not agreed on the choice of the remaining arbitrators and/or presiding arbitrator, the remaining arbitrators and/or presiding arbitrator shall be appointed by the appointing authority in the same way as a sole arbitrator would be appointed under article 6.[44]

Similarly, Article 9 of the UNCITRAL Rules provides:

> If three arbitrators are to be appointed, each party shall appoint one arbitrator. The two arbitrators thus appointed shall choose the third arbitrator who will act as the presiding arbitrator of the arbitral tribunal.[45]

In practice, the parties or the co-arbitrators agree on the president of the tribunal more often than not. For example, a review of the cases administered by the ICC in 2004 shows that the parties and co-arbitrators agreed upon the president in more than half of the cases presided over by a three-member tribunal.[46] In the absence of an agreement by the parties, the appointing authority within the institution or

---

[42] This feature of arbitration is often quoted as the parties' favourite. See e.g., ICEA 2015, p. 8; Queen Mary and White & Case Survey, above n 25, p. 7.

[43] Article V(1)(d) of the New York Convention (above n 28) provides that recognition and enforcement may be refused if '[t]he composition of the arbitral authority or the arbitral procedure was not in accordance with the agreement of the parties'.

[44] PCA Environmental Rules, above n 38, Article 7; see also, e.g., ICC Rules of Arbitration, above n 36, Articles 12(4) and 12(5).

[45] UNCITRAL Arbitration Rules (2013), Article 9. https://uncitral.un.org/sites/uncitral.un.org/files/media-documents/uncitral/en/uncitral-arbitration-rules-2013-e.pdf. Accessed 24 April 2021.

[46] Derains and Schwartz 2005, pp. 153–154

a State court judge in case of an *ad hoc* arbitration will intervene to select the arbitrator. When appointing an arbitrator, the relevant authority takes into account the candidate's '[e]xpertise, experience and qualifications with respect to the subject matter of the dispute'[47] and any criteria identified by the parties.

The appointment procedure is similar where the parties have agreed that a sole arbitrator will preside over the matter. In such cases, the parties have the opportunity to agree directly upon the sole arbitrator. Where, as is likely in the context of an ongoing dispute, cooperation is not possible,[48] the appointing authority in the case of institutional arbitration or the supporting authority in the case of an *ad hoc* arbitration will nominate the arbitrator.[49]

In practice, the arbitrators' selection is among the first critical issues considered in a commercial arbitration. It can be a time-consuming process, often involving extensive research into the background of potential candidates as well as his/her knowledge and experience in the industry. Word of mouth is an important source of information about arbitrators.[50] In environmental disputes, where counsel may be less familiar with experienced practitioners, lists of arbitrators may be useful. The PCA has, for example, published a 'specialized list of arbitrators considered to have expertise' in environmental disputes composed of academics, lawyers, former judges, and senior government officials.[51] At the time of writing, the PCA's list includes 12 candidates from 9 different countries.

Because environmental disputes are likely to entail complex technical and scientific questions, the opportunity of having a tribunal composed of 'both law-trained judges and science-technical decision makers (scientists, engineers, economist, planners, academics)' is particularly valuable.[52] Indeed, it 'brings two essential skill-sets into the adjudication process—law competence and scientific-technical competence'.[53] Nevertheless, practice has shown that parties may be reluctant to appoint arbitrators with scientific and/or technical expertise. Indeed, where the other party appoints an arbitrator with a background in law, there is a risk that the arbitrator appointed by the opposing party will have more sway in deciding the legal part of the case. However, there is evidence that this practice may be changing. According to a recent survey of the construction sector, 38% of respondents had experience of technical experts being appointed as arbitrators.[54]

---

[47] Fry et al 2012, p. 156, para 3.502.

[48] For example, in 2015, agreements between parties to a joint nomination of a sole arbitrator occurred in only 16% of ICC cases. See Bühler and Heitzmann 2017, pp. 138–139.

[49] See e.g., PCA Environmental Rules, above n 38, Article 6; ICC Rules of Arbitration, above n 36, Article 12(3); UNCITRAL Arbitration Rules, above n 45.

[50] In this regard, the 2018 White & Case and Queen Mary survey found that 77% of the Respondents use word of mouth as a source of information about arbitrators (above n 25, p. 20).

[51] List available at: https://pca-cpa.org/en/about/panels/panels-of-arbitrators-and-experts-for-environmental-disputes/. Accessed 24 January 2022.

[52] Pring and Pring 2016, p. 46.

[53] Ibid.

[54] See Queen Mary (2019) International Arbitration Survey: International Construction Disputes, p. 5. http://www.arbitration.qmul.ac.uk/research/2019/. Accessed 24 April 2021.

The Appointment of Independent Experts

Where it lacks the scientific or technical expertise necessary to resolve the dispute on its own, the tribunal may rely on independent experts.[55] The role of an expert is to 'assist, educate and advise the tribunal, in a fair and impartial manner, in specific fields in which the arbitrators do not themselves have the relevant expertise'.[56] In practice, experts have become "essential and indispensable" to commercial arbitration.[57] As scholars have explained, 'expert witnesses testimony is the predominant means of evidence when it comes to technical matters'.[58] Indeed, some authors consider that not retaining an expert in certain cases could be 'negligent'.[59]

Reflecting the traditions in both common and civil law systems, the use of both party- and tribunal-appointed experts is reflected in most arbitration rules. It is also found in the International Bar Association (IBA) Rules on the Taking of Evidence, which reflect the 'procedure in use in many different legal systems',[60] and the Guidelines on Party-appointed and Tribunal-appointed Experts adopted by the Chartered Institute of Arbitrators (CIArb) to 'set[] out the current best practice in international commercial arbitration on the appointment and use of party-appointed and tribunal-appointed experts'.[61] In practice, party-appointed experts are frequently appointed, with tribunal-appointed experts being used only rarely.[62]

Any expert, whether appointed by the parties or by the tribunal, must be independent from the parties, their counsel and the tribunal.[63] In addition, the more objective the expert appears, the more credible he/she is and the more weight the tribunal will give to his/her findings.[64] In recent years, party-appointed experts have been criticized for advocating for the party who appoints them. As explained by the tribunal in *Perenco v Ecuador*, an investment treaty case:

> However, with regard to many of the [experts'] differences, the Tribunal does not feel able to prefer one above the other. It seems to the Tribunal that each was attempting to achieve the

---

[55] See e.g., *Pulp Mills on the River Uruguay, (Argentina v Uruguay)*, Judgement, 20 April 2010, ICJ Reports 2010, Joint Dissenting Opinion of Judges Al-Khasawneh and Simma, p. 110, para 4 ('The Court on its own is not in a position adequately to assess and weigh complex scientific evidence of the type presented by the Parties. To refer to only a few instances pertinent for our case, a court of justice cannot assess, without the assistance of experts, claims as to whether two or three-dimensional modelling is the best or even appropriate practice in evaluating the hydrodynamics of a river, or what role an Acoustic Doppler Current Profiler can play in such an evaluation').

[56] Sachs and Schmidt-Ahrendts 2011, p. 147.

[57] Ibid.

[58] Voser and Bell 2019, p. 226.

[59] Ehle 2012, p. 76.

[60] IBA, Rules on the Taking of Evidence in International Arbitration (2010), Foreword, p. 11.

[61] CIArb, Guidelines on Party-appointed and Tribunal-appointed Experts, 2015, Introduction, p. 1. See also CIArb, Protocol for the Use of Party-Appointed Expert Witnesses in International Arbitration included as Appendix I.

[62] Sachs and Schmidt-Ahrendts 2011, p. 136.

[63] IBA Rules on the Taking of Evidence, above n 60, Articles 5(2)(c) and 6(2); CIArb Protocol for the Use of Party-Appointed Expert Witnesses in International Arbitration, above n 61, Article 4.

[64] Voser and Bell 2019, p. 230.

> best result for the party by whom they were instructed, and that they crossed the boundary between professional objective analysis and party representation.[65]

These criticisms combined with the high technicity of the case led the tribunal to appoint their own expert. A similar trend could materialize in cases where commercial tribunals are tasked with resolving environmental disputes involving highly technical issues.

In practice, an expert presents his or her direct testimony in the form of written reports,[66] and is then 'examined' during an oral hearing.[67] In general, each expert is questioned by the counsel of 'his/her' party (examination), and then cross-examined by the opposing party, with the possibility for the tribunal to ask questions directly. Expert witness conferencing, also known as 'hot-tubbing', has become increasingly popular as a means of saving time and costs and narrowing down the issues in dispute.[68] In that case, experts give evidence concurrently (as opposed to sequentially) with the tribunal leading the debate.

As with the selection of arbitrators, the selection of experts is a crucial decision for the parties to an international arbitration to make. As with arbitrators, parties with little prior familiarity in environmental disputes can consult lists of experts, including the one prepared by the PCA for environmental disputes.[69] Parties can also ask the ICC for assistance in identifying and appointing an expert with appropriate knowledge.[70]

The parties' and the tribunals' freedom to seek the assistance of a qualified independent expert, where appropriate is an important advantage of using commercial arbitration to resolve environmental disputes. This ensures that both the parties and the tribunal benefit from the expertise necessary to resolve the complex scientific and technical issues that such disputes often raise.

12.2.3.2 Availability of Urgent Relief

The ICC Report also states that '[u]rgency, timeliness and avoidance of delay is often critical for meaningful resolution of climate change related disputes'.[71] Commercial disputes involving these and other environmental issues are no exception to this

---

[65] *Perenco v Ecuador LTD. v The Republic of Ecuador and Empressa Estatal Petroleos de Ecuador (Pertoecuador)*, Interim Decision on Environmental Counterclaim, 11 August 2015, ICSID Case No ARB/08/6, para 581.

[66] See e.g., IBA Rules on the Taking of Evidence, above n 60, Articles 5(2) and 6(4).

[67] See e.g., Ibid., Articles 5(5) and 6(6).

[68] See e.g., Ibid., Articles 8(3)(f).

[69] The list is available at: https://pca-cpa.org/wp-content/uploads/sites/6/2016/07/Current-List-Annex-3-SP-SciEXP-update-20190930-184038-v6_.pdf. Accessed 24 April 2021.

[70] ICC Expert Rules. https://iccwbo.org/publication/icc-expert-rules-english-version/. Accessed 24 April 2021.

[71] ICC 2019, p. 26, para 5.34.

rule. For example, as reported in the press, the parties to a joint operating agreement relating to a Nigerian offshore oilfield disputed the appropriateness of drilling an additional well. The minority shareholder initiated an arbitration in an attempt to block the additional well arguing that drilling was premature and could cause damages to the environment resulting in potential liability.[72] In this case, both the parties' commercial interests (i.e., not having to pay a penalty), and their environmental interests (i.e., not causing environmental damage), commanded an urgent resolution of the dispute.

Efficiency is a guiding principle adopted by several arbitral institutions and parties can agree to implement an expedited procedure (1). In addition, the broad availability of interim relief counterbalances sometimes-lengthy commercial arbitration proceedings (2).

Efficiency and Expedited Procedures

As arbitration is '*la chose des parties*', the length of the procedure depends in large part on the complexity of the dispute and the will of the parties. On average, as illustrated in the figure below (see Fig. 12.1), it takes about two years between the request for arbitration and the issuance of the award.[73]

The parties can seek to reduce the length of the procedure by agreeing on strict time limits, either in the arbitration agreement or once the dispute has arisen. For example, parties can provide in their arbitration agreements that the award shall be issued within six months from the date of the request for arbitration. Parties may agree to different deadlines for different types of disputes. For example, in a decommissioning project in the oil and gas sector, the parties may agree that purely contractual issues that do not require in-depth factual or technical analysis, such as which party shall bear the clean-up costs, must be resolved within six months or less. Any agreed time limits are binding on the tribunal and the parties.

Some institutional arbitration rules require the parties and the tribunal to take steps to ensure the efficient resolution of the dispute.[74] For example, parties can bifurcate the proceedings to obtain more quickly a decision on a key or threshold issue, e.g., the tribunal's jurisdiction or a matter of contractual interpretation. Parties and the tribunal can also regularly hold case management conferences for the purpose of determining the most efficient way to resolve the dispute.

---

[72] Roddy L (2017) Contempt of Court Ruling Upheld in Nigerian Oilfield Dispute. https://globalarbitrationreview.com/article/1149125/contempt-of-court-ruling-upheld-in-nigerian-oilfield-dispute. Accessed 24 April 2021.

[73] Figure created by the authors on the basis of publicly available information.

[74] See e.g., ICC Rules of Arbitration, above n 36, Article 22 ('The arbitral tribunal and the parties shall make every effort to conduct the arbitration in an expeditious and cost-effective manner, having regard to the complexity and value of the dispute') and UNCITRAL Arbitration Rules, above n 45, Article 17 (the tribunal shall 'conduct the proceedings so as to avoid unnecessary delays and expenses and to provide a fair and efficient process for resolving the parties' disputes').

Several arbitral institutions have also adopted specific rules for fast track arbitration.[75] These rules are typically mandatory for small value claims and the parties can agree to apply such rules to disputes of any magnitude. Rules for fast track arbitration typically provide for short deadlines as well as a simplified procedure (e.g., sole arbitrator, limited document production, limited use of expert evidence, no oral hearing, and so on). In practice, fast track arbitrations are unlikely to be suitable for environmental disputes. Indeed, environmental disputes—and particularly those that arise in the construction or energy sectors—are likely to be highly technical in nature. Therefore, extensive evidence, including expert reports, may be necessary for the tribunal to address properly the issues in question.

Interim Relief

Given that a commercial arbitration may last for two years or more and the 'often irreversible nature of environmental harm',[76] interim measures are of particular importance in environmental disputes.

Interim relief is available before and after the constitution of the tribunal. Where the tribunal has not yet been constituted, parties may have recourse to State courts for interim relief without this constituting a waiver of the arbitration clause.[77] Additionally, parties may avail themselves of the 'emergency arbitrator' procedures offered by several arbitral institutions.[78] That is the parties can commence a separate arbitration to address the issue(s) requiring emergency relief. Emergency arbitrators are typically required to render a decision within one month of having received the file and are entitled to grant the interim measures described below.

Parties may seek interim relief from the tribunal itself following its constitution. Most arbitration rules expressly empower tribunals to grant interim measures. For example, Article 26 of the PCA Environmental Rules provides:

> Unless the parties otherwise agree the arbitral tribunal may, at the request of any party and having obtained the views of all the parties, take any interim measures including provisional orders with respect to the subject-matter of the disputes it deems necessary to preserve the

[75] See e.g., the ICC Rules of Arbitration, above n 36, or the SCC Arbitration Rules (2017). https://sccinstitute.com/our-services/rules/. Accessed 24 April 2021.

[76] Harrisson 2014, p. 519.

[77] See e.g., PCA Environmental Rules, above n 38, Article 26(3) ('A request for interim measures addressed by any party to a judicial authority shall not be deemed incompatible with the agreement to arbitrate, or as a waiver of that agreement'). See also ICC Rules of Arbitration, above n 36, Article 28(2) ('Before the file is transmitted to the arbitral tribunal, and in appropriate circumstances even thereafter, the parties may apply to any competent judicial authority for interim or conservatory measures. The application of a party to a judicial authority for such measures or for the implementation of any such measures ordered by an arbitral tribunal shall not be deemed to be an infringement or a waiver of the arbitration agreement and shall not affect the relevant powers reserved to the arbitral tribunal').

[78] See e.g., ICC Rules of Arbitration, above n 36, Article 29 and Appendix V; LCIA Arbitration Rules (2020), Article 9B. https://www.lcia.org/Dispute_Resolution_Services/lcia-arbitration-rules-2020.aspx. Accessed 24 April 2021.

> rights of any party or to prevent serious harm to the environmental failing within the subject matter of the dispute.[79]

Similarly, with respect to *ad hoc* arbitration, Article 26(1) of the UNCITRAL Rules provides: 'The arbitral tribunal may, at the request of a party, grant interim measures.'

Should the arbitration rules be silent, the tribunal may derive its power from the *lex arbitri* (i.e., the law of the seat or place of arbitration) or its inherent powers to do so.[80] This was confirmed by the tribunal in ICC Case No 10681 (2011):

> [I]nternational commercial arbitration practice shows that arbitration tribunals have inherent power to issue such orders as may be necessary to conserve the respective rights of the parties and to ensure that the tribunal jurisdiction and authority are made fully effective.[81]

Most arbitration rules leave the criteria to be considered when determining whether interim relief is warranted to the discretion of the tribunal.[82] While the criteria vary in practice depending on the legal background of the arbitrators and the circumstances of the case, the following three criteria are now widely accepted:

1. Urgency, which is the '*raison d'être*' of interim relief: the measure cannot await the final resolution of the dispute;
2. the threat of irreparable or substantial harm that cannot be compensated by damages; and
3. no pre-judgment of the merits of the case.[83]

Tribunals also have broad discretion as to the measure ordered. The ICC Rules provide that the tribunal may order 'any interim or conservatory measure it deems appropriate'.[84] The PCA Environmental Rules also permit 'any interim measures ... with respect to the subject-matter of the dispute [the tribunal] deems necessary' while recognizing the unique nature of environmental harm.[85] Broadly speaking, six types of interim measures are regularly awarded by arbitral tribunals: (1) preserving the *status quo*, (2) preserving evidence, (3) preserving property, (4) security for costs,

[79] See also ICC Rules of Arbitration, above n 36, Article 28(1) ('Unless the parties have otherwise agreed, as soon as the file has been transmitted to it, the arbitral tribunal may, at the request of a party, order any interim or conservatory measure it deems appropriate').

[80] The parties' agreement may also empower the tribunal to do so but it is rare in practice.

[81] ICC Bull., Special Supplement 2011: Interim, Conservatory and Emergency Measures in ICC Arbitration, Partial Award in ICC Case No 10681, p. 34.

[82] See e.g., ICC Rules of Arbitration, above n 36, UNCITRAL Arbitration Rules, above n 45; PCA Environmental Rules, above n 38.

[83] Lew 2000, paras 29–32.

[84] ICC Rules of Arbitration, above n 36, Article 28(1).

[85] PCA Environmental Rules, above n 38, Article 26(1) ('Unless the parties otherwise agree the arbitral tribunal may, at the request of any party and having obtained the views of all the parties, take any interim measures including provisional orders with respect to the subject-matter of the dispute it deems necessary to preserve the rights of any party or to prevent serious harm to the environment falling within the subject-matter of the dispute').

(5) securing the enforcement of the award by preserving assets, and (6) orders for interim payments.

However, the tribunal's power to award interim measures is not without limit. Due to the inherently consensual nature of arbitration, a tribunal cannot order an interim measure against a third party.

Finally, and importantly, arbitral tribunals lack the power to enforce the interim measures that they grant. It is unclear whether a decision granting an interim measure constitutes an 'award' under the New York Convention and can therefore benefit from its enforcement regime. Leading scholars have argued that the 'better view is that provisional measures should be and are enforceable as arbitral awards',[86] but the issue remains unsettled. In any event, tribunals have coercive tools to encourage the parties' compliance such as costs awards, peremptory orders, or accompanying the measure with monetary relief (*astreinte*).[87] And, in practice, most parties are inclined to comply with the decisions rendered by the tribunal hearing the merits of the case as they typically want to maintain their credibility and refrain from angering the tribunal at the outset of the proceedings.

In sum, the neutrality, ease of enforceability, and procedural flexibility characteristic of commercial arbitration make it well suited for the effective resolution of environmental disputes. Notably, the ICC Report reaches a similar conclusion finding that many of the same procedural features of commercial arbitration make it suitable for the resolution of climate change disputes.[88] These advantages together with the fact that commercial arbitration is already a preferred method of dispute resolution in sectors impacted by developments in environmental law means that commercial tribunals will be called on with increasing frequency to decide environmental disputes and issues. However, as the authors turn to next, the increased use of commercial arbitration to resolve environmental disputes is not without its challenges. These challenges stem from the private nature of commercial arbitration.

12.3 Is There a Need for Greater Accessibility When Commercial Arbitration Is Used to Resolve Environmental Disputes?

When considering the accessibility of commercial arbitration, one must keep in mind the fact that the tribunal's jurisdiction is circumscribed by the parties' consent. Yet, as parties often consent to arbitrate any dispute arising out of or in connection with the subject matter of the contract, this limitation on jurisdiction does not prevent

[86] Born 2014, p. 2514.

[87] Yesilirmak 2000, p. 33.

[88] ICC 2019, p. 19, para 5.5 ('This report assesses and confirms the capability of ICC to immediately offer adequate solutions in climate change related disputes through its several dispute resolution services, be it under the aegis of the ICC Court or ICC Centre or ADR').

commercial tribunals from hearing environmental disputes arising incidentally to commercial disputes.

The use of commercial arbitration to resolve environmental disputes, which are by nature disputes of public interest, creates a tension between the features of commercial arbitration intended to ensure the private resolution of disputes and the imperatives of transparency, which usually involve 'the disclosure of documents or other materials, open hearings, the participation of third parties in the arbitration process, and public access'.[89] The private nature of this dispute resolution mechanism risks a 'public perception that "secret courts" are rendering decisions with public interest implications, with no accountability'.[90] In addition, the often-confidential nature of commercial arbitration and the lack of a doctrine of precedent risk conflicting decisions and thus may negatively impact the development of environmental law.

12.3.1 The Tension Between Transparency and Confidentiality

For a long time, the confidential nature of commercial arbitration 'was accepted as a self-evident principle'.[91] Keeping information about the existence or substance of the dispute confidential[92] was thought to encourage an 'efficient, dispassionate dispute resolution, rather than an emotive "trial by press release" or efforts to gain extraneous leverage; reducing the risks of damaging disclosure of commercially-sensitive information to competitors, customers and others; and facilitating settlement by minimizing the role of public posturing'.[93]

Today, there is no uniform approach to confidentiality, as evidenced by the different treatment among different arbitration rules. The London Court of International Arbitration (LCIA) Rules, for example, contain a detailed confidentiality undertaking:

> The parties undertake as a general principle to keep confidential all awards in the arbitration, together with all materials in the arbitration created for the purpose of the arbitration and all other documents produced by another party in the proceedings not otherwise in the public domain, save and to the extent that disclosure may be required of a party by legal duty, to

---

[89] Poorooye and Feehily 2017, p. 282.

[90] Hay 2018, p. 216.

[91] Shore and Dimitrov 2009, p. 165.

[92] Such information may include the 'existence of the arbitral proceedings, documents created for the purpose of the arbitration such as the parties' submissions, documents produced during an arbitration in the course of document disclosure, the tribunal's procedural orders, hearing transcripts, the tribunal's deliberations, or any awards by the tribunal'. Hay 2018, p. 211.

[93] Born 2014, pp. 2780–2781.

protect or pursue a legal right, or to enforce or challenge an award in legal proceedings before a state court or other legal authority.[94]

By contrast, the ICC Rules do not specifically prevent parties from disclosing information about the arbitration. Rather, the ICC Rules empower tribunals to 'make orders concerning the confidentiality of the arbitration proceedings or of any other matters in connection with the arbitration'.[95] For their part, the PCA Environmental Rules and the UNCITRAL Rules provide that any awards issued in connection with the arbitration are confidential absent a contrary agreement of the parties.[96] In the case of the UNCITRAL Rules, it is worth recalling that in 2014, UNCITRAL adopted Rules on Transparency in Treaty-Based Investor-State Arbitration (UNCITRAL Transparency Rules).[97] These Rules provide for the publicity of the parties' pleadings, written submissions by *amicus curiae*, transcripts of hearings and any decisions from the tribunal.[98] Further, the Hague Rules on Business and Human Rights Arbitration (Hague Rules), launched on 12 December 2019, provide a framework to resolve business and human rights disputes, which encompass environmental disputes, and can apply to contractual disputes if the parties so decide.[99] These rules include six articles on transparency that reflect the principles in the UNCITRAL Transparency Rules.[100]

In practice, regardless of the rules applied, parties often agree to the confidentiality of the proceedings. Depending on the nature of the parties' agreement, the public may be unaware of the existence of the arbitration, the allegations of wrongdoing, the identity of the arbitrators, the legal issues at stake, or the content of the final award.[101]

This secrecy goes against 'the prevailing trend in environmental law to open decision-making processes to public scrutiny and participation'.[102] Indeed, with environmental disputes, which by nature are of interest to the public, the tension

[94] SCC Arbitration Rules, above n 75, Article 3 ('Unless otherwise agreed by the parties, the SCC, the Arbitral Tribunal and any administrative secretary of the Arbitral Tribunal shall maintain the confidentiality of the arbitration and the award').

[95] ICC Rules of Arbitration, above n 36, Article 22(3).

[96] PCA Environmental Rules, above n 38, Article 32(6) ('The award may be made public only with the consent of all the parties'); UNCITRAL Arbitration Rules, above n 45, Article 32(5) ('The award may be made public only with the consent of both parties').

[97] UNCITRAL Rules on Transparency in Treaty-based Investor-State Arbitration (2013). https://uncitral.un.org/sites/uncitral.un.org/files/media-documents/uncitral/en/rules-on-transparency-e.pdf. Accessed 24 April 2021.

[98] Ibid., Article 3.

[99] CILC, The Hague Rules on Business and Human Rights Arbitration (2019). https://www.cilc.nl/project/the-hague-rules-on-business-and-human-rights-arbitration/. Accessed 24 April 2021.

[100] Ibid., Articles 38 to 42.

[101] Magraw and Amerasinghe 2009, pp. 342–343. It should however be mentioned that the recognition and enforcement of the awards before national courts usually involve the submission of the award and hence some form of publicity.

[102] Meshel 2016, para 10.

between the parties' interest in preserving the confidentiality of the proceedings and the general public interest is 'heightened'.[103]

Mindful of this tension, several institutions have taken steps to enhance the 'legal transparency' of commercial arbitration through the publication of arbitral awards. The ICC for example, has long published redacted excerpts or summaries of arbitral awards rendered under its aegis in its quarterly *ICC Dispute Resolution Bulletin.* Other institutions, such as the International Centre for Dispute Resolution (ICDR) or the Vienna International Arbitration Centre (VIAC), have adopted a similar approach by publishing compilations of arbitral awards, albeit on a less regular basis.[104] In addition, some books regularly publish excerpts of arbitral awards under various rules, as for example the annual *Yearbook Commercial Arbitration.*

Further, since January 2016, the ICC has published on its website the names of the arbitrators, their nationality, their role within a tribunal, the method of their appointment, whether the arbitration is pending or closed, and, since 1 July 2019, the sector of industry involved as well as counsel representing the parties in the case.[105] Other institutions, such as the LCIA[106] and the SCC,[107] also publish reports containing details of past disputes, including the size, length, or cost.

Some States have also taken steps to increase the transparency of international arbitration. For example, Brazil enacted a new arbitration law on 26 May 2015 providing that 'public private arbitration' is subject to 'the principle of publicity' and all other laws governing transparency in public affairs.[108]

Finally, it is not uncommon for a party to disclose information about an ongoing arbitration, particularly in the case of an environmental dispute where 'publicity is often a significant win, even if the case is lost on legal merits'.[109]

In spite of these steps taken to enhance transparency, many, if not the majority, of commercial arbitrations, still take place in private without even the existence of the dispute being known to the public. The confidential nature of commercial arbitration thus detracts from its attractiveness for the routine resolution of environmental disputes. The lack of transparency of investment arbitration was one of the reasons for recent and very public opposition to this type of dispute resolution. This backlash against investment arbitration caused a number of countries and institutions to agree to use alternative dispute resolution methods. While the adoption of the UNCITRAL Transparency Rules, the Hague Rules and other similar measures have served to make the public more comfortable with investment arbitration, users of commercial arbitration may be reluctant to adopt and apply these rules.

---

[103] Poorooye and Feehily 2017, p. 298.

[104] The ICDR published the *ICDR Awards and Commentaries* which currently has two volumes. The VIAC published in 2015 a compilation of arbitral award (*VIAC, Selected Arbitral Awards*). There is only one volume at the time of writing.

[105] ICC 2019, paras 34–36.

[106] Available at: https://www.lcia.org/lcia/reports.aspx. Accessed 24 April 2021.

[107] Available at: https://sccinstitute.com/statistics/. Accessed 24 April 2021.

[108] Brazil, Law No 13.129, 26 May 2015, Articles 1(1) and 2(3).

[109] Baker and Stebbing 2018.

Indeed, the majority of users are private individuals valuing confidentiality such that the imposition of a general rule on transparency would constitute a drawback making commercial arbitration a less attractive forum for the resolution of their disputes. The adoption of the Brazilian-style exception described above, although appealing, could raise additional issues: the criteria applicable to qualify a 'public-private arbitration', the authority competent to determine that these criteria are met, etc.

Interestingly, the ICC Report notes that 'there is nothing in the ICC Arbitration Rules that would prevent the parties from agreeing to disclose information on pending arbitral proceedings to the public',[110] but does not go on to recommend that the existing ICC Rules be amended to require greater transparency. The authors agree with this approach: the burden of finding the right balance between transparency and confidentiality should lie with users of commercial arbitration. It is for the parties, and, more importantly, tribunals, to be mindful of the importance of public interest of the case and to adopt specific procedural features in this respect. The flexibility afforded to users of commercial arbitration lends itself to creative solutions. For example, instead of increasing the transparency of the arbitration proceedings themselves, parties could invite NGOs and other interested third parties to participate in the pre-arbitral stages of the dispute, i.e., in negotiations or, in the case of multi-tiered dispute resolution clauses, before dispute boards.

12.3.2 The Tension Between Transparency and Privacy

Given the contractual and consensual nature of commercial arbitration, absent a contrary agreement, only the parties to the arbitration agreement may participate (or observe) the proceedings. The private nature of commercial arbitration is enshrined in the vast majority of arbitration rules. Article 25(4) of the PCA Environmental Rules provides: 'Hearings shall be held in camera unless the parties agree otherwise'.[111] By contrast, the Hague Rules provide that 'hearings for the presentation of evidence or for oral argument shall be public'.[112] The Hague Rules are the only Rules to have adopted such a position at this time.

With respect to environmental disputes, this effective ban on the participation of non-parties to the arbitration conflicts with the call for greater participation of

[110] ICC 2019, para 5.77.

[111] PCA Environmental Rules, above n 38, Article 25(4). See also ICC Rules of Arbitration, above n 36, Article 26(3) of the ('The arbitral tribunal shall be in full charge of the hearings, at which all the parties shall be entitled to be present. Save with the approval of the arbitral tribunal and the parties, persons not involved in the proceedings shall not be admitted'); UNCITRAL Arbitration Rules, above n 45, Article 28(3) ('Hearings shall be held in camera unless the parties agree otherwise').

[112] CILC Hague Rules, above n 99, Article 41(1).

civil society and NGOs[113]. Traditionally, NGOs and other parties interested in the outcome of environmental disputes have sought to participate in two different ways: as parties or as *amicus curiae* (friends of the tribunal).[114]

12.3.2.1 Third Party Participation Is Unlikely

The participation of NGOs and other civil society members in environmental disputes is premised on the idea that such entities or the individuals that they represent could be directly affected by the outcome of the dispute. As sensible as this idea may be, it has oft been rejected in international fora[115] and is likely to be rejected in commercial arbitration.

Two procedural mechanisms operate to permit entities that are not parties to the arbitration agreement to participate: intervention and joinder. The difference between these mechanisms lies in the applicant: in case of joinder, an existing party to the arbitration requests the participation of a third party, and, in case of intervention, it is the third-party itself that requests to participate.

Most arbitral rules permit joinder only where the third party in question is bound by an arbitration agreement. The ICC Rules, for example, provide that a third party may be joined to the proceedings subject to the existence of 'an arbitration agreement under the Rules that binds' it.[116] Similarly, under the UNCITRAL Rules, the joinder of a third party is possible 'provided such person is a party to the arbitration agreement'.[117] Such provisions are obviously intended to address multi-party disputes, not public participation.

Other arbitration rules, including the LCIA,[118] Singapore International Arbitration Centre (SIAC),[119] and Hong Kong International Arbitration Centre (HKIAC)[120]

---

[113] In addition to NGOs, a variety of stakeholders may have an interest in participating in the proceedings (sub-contractors, suppliers, etc.). These 'contractual' third parties will not be addressed here.

[114] Osorio 2005.

[115] Ibid.

[116] ICC Rules of Arbitration, above n 36, Articles 6 and 7.

[117] UNCITRAL Arbitration Rules, above n 45, Article 17(5).

[118] LCIA Arbitration Rules, above n 78, Article 22.1(viii) ('The Arbitral Tribunal shall have the power, upon the application of any party … (viii) to allow one or more third persons to be joined in the arbitration as a party provided any such third person and the applicant party have consented to such joinder in writing following the Commencement Date or (if earlier) in the Arbitration Agreement').

[119] SIAC Arbitration Rules (2016), Rule 7.8 ('After the constitution of the Tribunal, a party or non-party to the arbitration may apply to the Tribunal for one or more additional parties to be joined in an arbitration pending under these Rules as a Claimant or a Respondent, provided that … all parties, including the additional party to be joined, have consented to the joinder of the additional party'). https://www.siac.org.sg/our-rules/rules/siac-rules-2016. Accessed 24 April 2021.

[120] HKIAC Administered Arbitration Rules (2018), Article 27(1) ('The arbitral tribunal … shall have the power to allow an additional party to be joined to the arbitration provided that … all parties,

Rules, empower tribunals to allow third parties that are not parties to the arbitration agreement to participate subject to the consent of all parties (including the third party). The Swiss Rules of International Arbitration, for their part, provide that the tribunal must only 'consult' with all the parties, including the third party,[121] although it is unlikely in practice that a tribunal will decide to join a third party in the face of a party's refusal.

Provisions like these may encourage tribunals and parties to permit the joinder of third parties. Nevertheless, in practice, third parties are unlikely to be able to participate absent the parties' agreement. Further, it is doubtful that a party facing claims that it caused environmental harm will permit the participation of NGOs and other interested third parties, given among other things that this has the potential to bias the tribunal and unnecessarily increase the cost of the proceedings. Where the participation is refused, NGOs and other groups can participate as a party's witness or expert. For example, in the *Arctic Sunrise Arbitration* case, an inter-State arbitration, Greenpeace's request to file an *amicus curiae* submission was denied by the tribunal.[122] Nevertheless, Greenpeace was then called as a witness by the Netherlands and submitted a statement of facts.[123] The same approach could be adopted by parties to commercial arbitrations.

The likely unavailability of joinder and intervention does not in and of itself preclude third party public participation as there is still the possibility of admitting *amicus curiae*.

12.3.2.2 *Amicus Curiae* Participation Is Possible

An *amicus curiae* is an entity (e.g., NGO, academic institution, not-for-profit organization, governmental agency, indigenous group, or business association) that has an interest in the outcome of the dispute and expertise in at least one aspect of the dispute's subject matter.[124] An *amicus curiae* is not a party to the proceedings so that, in principle, it will not have access to party's exhibits and will be prevented from participating in the hearings.

---

including the additional party, expressly agree'). https://www.hkiac.org/arbitration/rules-practice-notes/hkiac-administered-2018. Accessed 24 April 2021.

[121] SCAI Rules of International Arbitration (2012), Article 4(2) ('Where one or more third persons request to participate in arbitral proceedings already pending under these Rules or where a party to pending arbitral proceedings under these Rules requests that one or more third persons participate in the arbitration, the arbitral tribunal shall decide on such request, after consulting with all of the parties, including the person or persons to be joined, taking into account all relevant circumstances'). https://www.swissarbitration.org/Arbitration/Arbitration-Rules-and-Laws. Accessed 24 April 2021.

[122] *The Arctic Sunrise Arbitration (Netherlands v Russia)*, Procedural Order No 3 (Greenpeace International's Request to File an Amicus Curiae Submission), 8 October 2014, PCA Case No 2014-02. See also Chap. 15.

[123] *The Arctic Sunrise Arbitration (Netherlands v Russia)*, Award, 14 August 2015, PCA Case No 2014-02, paras 43 and 58.

[124] See e.g., Waincymer 2012, pp. 602–603.

Parties to commercial arbitration can agree on the participation of *amicus curiae*, either in their arbitration agreement or at any time during the course of the proceedings, and on the scope of this participation (i.e., whether the *amici* will have access to the documents and/or hearings).

Where parties fail to reach such an agreement, as may often occur in the case of private commercial contracts, arbitration rules expressly contemplating the intervention of third parties could serve as a basis for admitting *amicus curiae*. In particular, Article 4(2) of the Swiss Rules of International Arbitration provides:

> Where one or more third persons request to participate in arbitral proceedings already pending under these Rules or where a party to pending arbitral proceedings under these Rules requests that one or more third persons participate in the arbitration, the arbitral tribunal shall decide on such request, after consulting with all the parties, including the person or persons to be joined, taking into account all relevant circumstances.[125]

Similarly, the Hague Rules expressly provide that:

> After consultation with the parties, the arbitral tribunal may invite or allow a person or entity that is not a party ('third person(s)') to file a written submission with the arbitral tribunal regarding a matter within the scope of the dispute.[126]

Unexpectedly, although probably due to the relatively recent emergence of *amicus curiae* issue, the PCA Environmental Rules are silent on this subject.[127]

Where the parties have not expressly agreed on the filing of *amicus curiae* briefs and the applicable arbitration rules are silent, the issue is left to the discretion of the tribunal. Under most arbitration rules, the tribunal has broad discretion as to the conduct of the proceedings.[128] The ICC Rules provide that, in establishing the facts of the case, the tribunal 'may decide to hear … any other person'.[129] As the ICC has indicated, this general power provides the tribunal with the authority to allow *amicus curiae*.[130] The investment tribunal in *Methanex v United States* also relied on this general power to permit *amicus curiae*:

> The Tribunal considers that allowing a third person to make an amicus submission could fall within its procedural powers over the conduct of the arbitration, within the general scope of Article 15(1) of the UNCITRAL Arbitration Rules.[131]

---

[125] SCAI Rules of International Arbitration, above n 121, Article 4(2).

[126] CILC Hague Rules, above n 99, Article 28(1).

[127] Although not related to environmental disputes, it is worth noting that the Code of Sports-related Arbitration expressly allows for the submission of amicus curiae (see R41.4: 'After consideration of submissions by all parties concerned, the Panel may allow the filing of amicus curiae briefs, on such terms and conditions as it may fix').

[128] See e.g., ICC Rules of Arbitration, above n 36, Article 22; UNCITRAL Arbitration Rules, above n 45, Article 17.

[129] ICC Rules of Arbitration, above n 36, Article 25(3).

[130] ICC 2019, para 143.

[131] *Methanex v United States of America*, Decision on Petition from Third Persons to Intervene as Amicus Curiae UNCITRAL, 15 January 2001, NAFTA/UNCITRAL, para 31.

Similarly, an ICC tribunal held that it had the power to authorize *amicus curiae* despite the ICC Rules being silent on this subject:

> Upon further consideration the Tribunal now rules that the amicus curiae brief is admitted. While unknown not only to the regulations of the ICC and many other institutions but also to the traditional procedural laws of most legal systems in Europe, they are regularly submitted in proceedings before the European Court of Human Rights and other international courts and have recently been admitted by international tribunals, in particular in investment disputes. They frequently enhance a tribunal's knowledge by providing useful factual and legal information. Although a document of this kind does not enjoy any specific legal status (as it does in the civil procedure of certain jurisdictions or under the rules of procedure of certain international courts) it is—in any event in the case at hand—a welcome source of information and, in principle, capable of assisting the Arbitral Tribunal.[132]

Nevertheless, even if procedurally admitted, *amicus curiae* would still face a challenge: the confidentiality of the proceedings may prevent NGOs and others from learning of the existence of the proceedings, making participation impossible.

12.3.3 The Tension Between the Lack of a Doctrine of Precedent and the Protection of the Environment

To set straight any misconception, arbitral tribunals are required to apply the law except where the parties have expressly allowed the tribunal to decide as *amiable compositeur*, i.e., authorized by the parties to rule in equity by seeking the most appropriate solution.

All arbitration rules require the tribunal to apply the law chosen by the parties. Article 33 of the PCA Environmental Rules provides for example:

> In resolving the dispute, the arbitral tribunal shall apply the law or rules of law designated by the parties as applicable to the substance of the dispute.[133]

The parties' freedom to determine the law applicable to the dispute is not without limit. In particular, the parties may not be permitted to choose a whimsical law, unrelated to the dispute, with the sole purpose of evading environmental norms. Indeed, it is widely admitted that an arbitral tribunal can apply the mandatory law of a country other than the one whose rules the parties have agreed upon. In particular, the mandatory laws applicable at the seat of the arbitration or in one of the countries where the contract would be performed or the award enforced are relevant.[134]

---

[132] ICC Case No 16369, Final Award, 1 January 2011, 39 Yearbook Commercial Arbitration, 2014, 39:169.

[133] See e.g. PCA Environmental Rules, above n 38, Article 33(1). See also ICC Rules of Arbitration, above n 36, Article 21(1) ('The parties shall be free to agree upon the rules of law to be applied by the arbitral tribunal to the merits of the dispute'); UNCITRAL Arbitration Rules, above n 45, Article 35(1) ('The arbitral tribunal shall apply the rules of law designated by the parties as applicable to the substance of the dispute').

[134] See e.g., Brekoulakis 2009, paras 2–36.

Absent an agreement, the determination of the law applicable to the dispute is a complicated issue that is beyond the scope of the present chapter. For present purposes, it is sufficient to say that the tribunal will apply the law it considers appropriate.[135]

When applying the law governing the dispute, the tribunal must take into account the provisions of the contract, which may include environmental commitments (in the preamble or elsewhere), and, where appropriate, relevant trade usages.[136]

In addition, a tribunal may rely on transnational public policy when there is an international consensus on a specific public policy principle and when it is clear that it was violated.[137] As noted by a French Professor:

> Arbitrators have a social responsibility, as common judges of international trade law, in the construction of transnational public order, so as not to make arbitration a purely utilitarian justice but, on the contrary, a justice that conveys 'non-merchant' or humanist values.[138]

Although there is no consensus on whether environmental norms are part of transnational public policy, some scholars support the idea.[139]

It follows from the above that tribunals deciding commercial arbitrations may make determinations in respect of national and international environmental laws. Nevertheless, commercial arbitration is unlikely to have a significant impact of the development of international environmental law for two main reasons. First, as mentioned above, arbitral awards are binding only as between the parties to the dispute and are often confidential. Yet, as '[p]recedent cannot develop in a vacuum',[140] it is difficult to draw legal principles of general application from arbitral awards. Further, while arbitral awards may have a persuasive effect on subsequent tribunals, they have no binding effect. Therefore, it is entirely possible that two tribunals ruling on the same issue, such as for example the interpretation of a specific mitigation requirement under the Paris Agreement—and even under the same applicable law—could reach a completely different solution.

---

[135] See e.g., PCA Environmental Rules, above n 38, Article 33(1) ('Failing such designation by the parties, the arbitral tribunal shall apply the national and/or international law and rules of law it determines appropriate'); ICC Rules of Arbitration, above n 36, Article 21(1) ('In the absence of any such agreement, the arbitral tribunal shall apply the rules of law which it determines to be appropriate'); UNCITRAL Arbitration Rules, above n 45, Article 35 ('Failing such designation by the parties, the arbitral tribunal shall apply the law which it determines to be appropriate').

[136] See e.g., ICC Rules of Arbitration, above n 36, Article 21(2) ('The arbitral tribunal shall take account of the provisions of the contract, if any, between the parties and of any relevant trade usages'); UNCITRAL Arbitration Rules, above n 45, Article 35(3) ('In all cases, the arbitral tribunal shall decide in accordance with the terms of the contract, if any, and shall take into account any usage of trade applicable to the transaction').

[137] Mayer 2006, paras 2–35.

[138] Racine 2005, para 27.

[139] See e.g. Kessedjian 2007, p. 869 contending that transnational public policy should include prohibitions obligations such as 'the sustainable protection of the environment, human dignity, health, cultural objects and social justice'.

[140] Ramirez and Tagtachian 2017, p. 45.

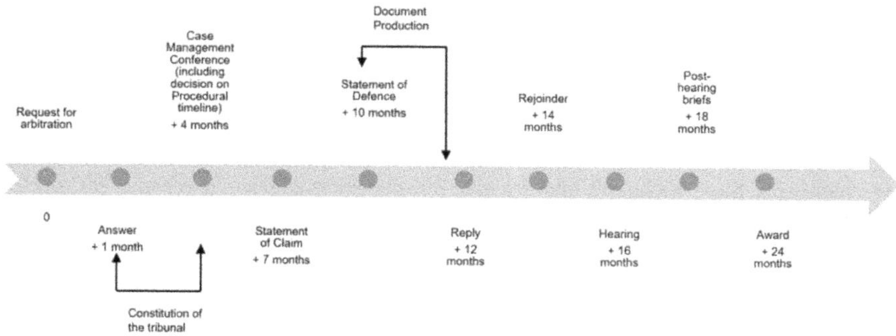

Fig. 12.1 Time between request for arbitration and issuance of an award. *Source* The authors

12.4 Conclusion

While commercial arbitration offers a procedure that is well suited to the resolution of environmental disputes, there is a tension between the private nature of the forum and the public nature of the issue. As environmental issues are likely to quickly become a fixture, users of commercial arbitration—including institutions and arbitrators—should continue to consider how best to modify procedures to ensure greater transparency and accessibility. Given its inherently flexible nature, users have a variety of options to consider when tailoring commercial arbitration procedure to suit the needs of environmental disputes.

References

Allsop J (2019) Commercial and Investor-State Arbitration: The Importance of Recognizing Their Differences. In: Kalicki J, Raouf M (eds) Evolution and Adaptation: The Future of International Arbitration. Kluwer Law International, Alphen aan den Rijn, pp 3–21.

Baker M, Stebbing H (2018) Acclimatising to Climate Change. https://globalarbitrationreview.com/article/1177029/acclimatising-to-climate-change. Accessed 24 April 2021.

Bishop D, Quintanilla Roché E, McBreaty S (2018) The Breadth and Complexity of the International Energy Industry. In: Rowley JWC et al (eds) Global Arbitration Review, The Guide to Energy Arbitrations. Law Business Research Ltd, London, pp 1–13.

Born G (2014) International Commercial Arbitration. Kluwer Law International, Alphen aan den Rijn.

Brekoulakis S (2009) Part I Fundamental Observations and Applicable Law, Chapter 2—On Arbitrability: Persisting Misconceptions and New Areas of Concern. In: Mistelis A, Brekoulakis S (eds) Arbitrability: International and Comparative Perspective. Kluwer Law International, Alphen aan den Rijn, pp 19–46.

Brekoulakis S (2017) The Protection of the Public Interest in Public Private Arbitrations. http://arbitrationblog.kluwerarbitration.com/2017/05/08/the-protection-of-the-public-interest-in-public-private-arbitrations/. Accessed 24 April 2021.

Brekoulakis S, Devany M (2016) Public-Private Arbitration and the Public Interest Under English Law. Modern Law Review 80:22–56.

Brekoulakis S, Thomas DB QC (2019) Introduction. In: Brekoulakis S, Thomas DB QC (eds) Global Arbitration Review, The Guide to Construction Arbitrations. Law Business Research Ltd, London pp 1–4.
Bühler M, Heitzmann P (2017) The 2017 ICC Expedited Rules: From Softball to Hardball? Journal of International Arbitration 34:121–148.
Chao D (2017) Environmental Justice Litigation in California: How Effective is Litigation in Addressing Slow Violence? https://scholarship.claremont.edu/cgi/viewcontent.cgi?article=2572&context=cmc_theses. Accessed 24 April 2021.
Derains Y, Schwartz E (2005) Guide to the ICC Rules of Arbitration. Kluwer Law International, The Hague.
Ehle B (2012) Practical aspects of using expert evidence in international arbitration. In: Roth M, Geistlinger M (eds) Yearbook on International Arbitration Volume II. Intersentia N.V., Antwerp, pp 75–84.
Evans J (2019) Construction Arbitrations in the Nuclear Sector. In: Brekoulakis S, Thomas DB QC (eds) Global Arbitration Review, The Guide to Construction Arbitrations. Law Business Research Ltd, London pp 288–300.
Fry J, Greenberg S, Mazza F (2012) The Secretariat's Guide to ICC Arbitration. International Chamber of Commerce, Paris.
Harrisson J (2014) Significant International Environmental Law Cases: 2012–14. Journal of Environmental Law 26:519–540.
Hay E (2018) Winds of Change? Confidentiality and in International Commercial Arbitration. In: González-Bueno C (ed) 40 under 40: International Arbitration. Dykinson, S.L., Madrid, pp 211–230.
ICC (2019) Resolving Climate Change Related Disputes through Arbitration and ADR. https://iccwbo.org/publication/icc-arbitration-and-adr-commission-report-on-resolving-climate-change-related-disputes-through-arbitration-and-adr/. Accessed 24 April 2021.
ICEA (2015) Dispute Resolution in the Energy Sector, Initial Report. https://www.scottisharbitrationcentre.org/wp-content/uploads/2015/05/ICEA-Dispute-Resolution-in-the-Energy-Sector-Initial-Report-Square-Booklet-Web-version.pdf. Accessed 24 April 2021.
Kessedjian C (2007) Transnational Public Policy. In: Van den Berg A (ed) International Arbitration 2006: Back to Basics? Kluwer Law International, ICCA, Alphen aan den Rijn, pp 857–870.
Kirtland M, Connoly K (2018) A comparison of the enforcement regimes under the New York and Washington Conventions—A tale of two cities. https://www.nortonrosefulbright.com/en/knowledge/publications/04f14b2a/a-comparison-of-the-enforcement-regimes-under-the-new-york-and-washington-conventions-mdashbra-tale-of-two-cities. Accessed 24 April 2021.
Lew J (2000) Commentary on Interim and Conservatory Measures in ICC Arbitration Cases. ICC Bull. 11:23–30.
Magnusson A (2018) Climate Disputes and Sustainable Development in the Energy Sector Bridging the Enforceability Gap. In: Sherer M (ed) International Arbitration in the Energy Sector. Oxford University Press, Oxford, pp 384–401
Magraw D, Amerasinghe N (2009) Transparency and Public Participation in Investor-State Arbitration. ILSA Journal of International & Comparative Law, 15:337–360.
Mayer P (2006) Effect of International Public Policy in International Arbitration. In: Mistelis L, Lew J (eds) Pervasive Problems in International Arbitration. Kluwer Law International, Alphen aan den Rijn, pp 61–69.
Meshel T (2016) Optional Rules for Arbitration of Disputes Relating to Natural Resources and/or the Environment: Permanent Court of Arbitration. Max Planck Encyclopedia of International Procedural Law.
Osorio (2005) International Arbitration & NGOs. https://www.transnational-dispute-management.com/article.asp?key=396#citation. Accessed 24 April 2021.
Poorooye A, Feehily R (2017) Confidentiality and Transparency in International Commercial Arbitration: Finding the Right Balance. Harvard Negotiation Law Review 2:275–324.

Pring G, Pring C (2016) UNEP, Environmental Courts & Tribunals A Guide for Policy Makers. https://wedocs.unep.org/bitstream/handle/20.500.11822/10001/environmental-courts-tribunals.pdf?sequence=1&isAllowed=y. Accessed 24 April 2021.

Racine JB (2005) Réflexions sur l'autonomie de l'arbitrage commercial international. Revue de l'arbitrage 2:305–360.

Ramirez EM, Tagtachian D (2017) The Precedential Effect of Increasing Transparency. ICC Bull. 2:41–47

Sachs K, Schmidt-Ahrendts N (2011) Protocol on Expert Teaming: A New Approach to Expert Evidence. In: Van den Berg AJ (ed) Arbitration Advocacy in Changing Times. Kluwer Law International/ICCA, Alphen aan den Rijn, pp 135–148

Sanderson C (2019) Multibillion Korean-Qatari ICC Case Settles. https://globalarbitrationreview.com/article/1193686/multibillion-korean-qatari-icc-case-settles. Accessed 24 April 2021.

Shore L, Dimitrov D (2009) Chapter II: The Arbitrator and the Arbitration Procedure—The Public Interest in Private Dispute Resolution. In: Klausegger C et al (eds) Austrian Arbitration Yearbook. Stämpfli Verlag AG, Bern, pp 163–174.

Voser N, Bell K (2019) Expert Evidence in Construction Disputes: Arbitrator Perspective. In: Brekoulakis S, Thomas DB QC (eds) Global Arbitration Review, The Guide to Construction Arbitrations. Law Business Research Ltd, London, pp 226–235.

Waincymer JM (2012) Procedure and Evidence in International Arbitration. Kluwer Law International, Alphen aan den Rijn

Yesilirmak A (2000) Interim and Conservatory Measures in ICC Arbitral Awards. ICC Bull. 11:31–36.

Young L (2017), Romania Faces Environmental Claim at ICC. https://globalarbitrationreview.com/article/1139979/romania-faces-environmental-claim-at-icc. Accessed 24 April 2021.

Kirsten Odynski (kirsten.odynski@whitecase.com) is a partner at White & Case LLP (Paris). The views reflected in this chapter are those of the authors and are not in any way intended to be legal advice.

Héloïse Broc (heloise.broc@whitecase.com) is an associate at White & Case LLP (Paris). The views reflected in this chapter are those of the authors and are not in any way intended to be legal advice.

Part II
Key Issues in International Environmental Proceedings

Chapter 13
Jurisdiction and Applicable Law (*Jurisdiction Ratione Materiae*)

Jessica Joly Hébert

Contents

Abstract This chapter will address questions of jurisdiction and applicable law, and how international courts and tribunals have considered these issues in disputes concerning the environment. First, it will establish the distinction between the jurisdiction of a court or tribunal to deal with a particular dispute and the applicable law it may use in doing so. The chapter then delves into the jurisdiction granted to different fora, more specifically arbitral tribunals, the ICJ, ITLOS and the dispute settlement body of the WTO. It does so by taking into account different methods for granting jurisdiction to a court or tribunal as well as the jurisdiction clauses found in various constitutive instruments. It further considers the law that each judicial body may apply, and has chosen to apply, in settling disputes of environmental law presented to it. Finally, issues related to forum shopping and to the selection of the most appropriate body to deal with particular claims related to the protection of the environment are discussed.

Keywords Jurisdiction · Applicable Law · Rules of Interpretation · ICJ · ITLOS · Arbitral Tribunals · WTO · Forum Shopping

J. Joly Hébert (✉)
CEDIN, Université Paris Nanterre, Paris, France

E. Sobenes et al. (eds.), *The Environment Through the Lens of International Courts and Tribunals*, https://doi.org/10.1007/978-94-6265-507-2_13

13.1 Introduction

Issues relating to jurisdiction and applicable law commonly arise in all types of disputes in international law, and ones concerning environmental matters are no exception. A few preliminary points are worth noting at the outset. There exists no specialized court or tribunal that deals exclusively with disputes concerning the environment, even though discussions have been ongoing for a few decades about the practicability of establishing such an institution.[1] As was demonstrated in Part I of this book, all courts or tribunals present their own peculiarities, including with regard to jurisdictional limitations found in their constitutive instruments and indications regarding the law they may apply in resolving the various types of disputes presented to them. It should also be noted that defining a dispute as an environmental one may not be always feasible.[2] Environmental disputes often form part of a wider dispute.[3] In fact, on most occasions, a case may raise issues concerning the protection of the environment but may not be qualified, in its entirety, as an environmental case *per se*, in light of the variety of issues in international law it presents. Environmental law also encompasses many sub-areas, for instance related to fisheries, air pollution, toxic waste and climate change. But as the field rapidly evolves, so too does the list of topics it comprises. These considerations are of particular relevance for the determination of the applicable law pertinent to specific disputes.

The present chapter aims to elucidate questions of jurisdiction and applicable law that different courts and tribunals may address when deciding disputes concerning environmental matters.[4] It will be divided as follows. First, the concepts of jurisdiction and applicable law will be distinguished on a theoretical level. Secondly, some jurisdictional considerations pertaining to specific courts and tribunals that deal with disputes concerning the environment will be analysed, followed thirdly by the applicable law that such institutions may apply once (and if) their jurisdiction has been confirmed. With regard to applicable law, clauses delimiting the law that those same courts or tribunals may apply will be analysed. Fourthly, concerns relating to forum shopping in cases of disputes with an environmental component will be addressed.

---

[1] See e.g. Sands and Peel 2018, p. 180.

[2] See the discussion, on a deeper level, by Boyle and Harrison 2013, pp. 247–250.

[3] See e.g. Okowa 1998, pp. 160–164; Stephens 2009, pp. 39–40; and Klein 2021, p. 1041.

[4] This chapter will focus particularly on inter-State disputes. Some other fora, such as the International Criminal Court or the European Court of Human Rights may also address matters that have an environmental protection component, but considering their specialty mandates, analysis of their particular jurisdiction and of the law they may apply has been left out. Nonetheless, for an interesting discussion with regard to inter-State disputes that can be presented in front of the European Court of Human Rights, see Pedersen 2018.

13.2 Distinguishing Jurisdiction from Applicable Law

First and foremost, the distinction between jurisdiction and applicable law must be clearly established at the conceptual level. Whether one is faced with a dispute concerning environmental matters or with any other dispute in international law, the foundational distinction applies. It is useful to refer to norms related to jurisdiction as 'norms of jurisdiction', and to norms that a particular tribunal may apply as 'norms of applicable law'.[5] In a nutshell, rules pertaining to jurisdiction 'are the only ones which could be judicially enforced (i.e. their violation could be sanctioned by the tribunal)' while rules of applicable law 'are only used to incidental ends (essentially to interpret the rules on which the tribunal has jurisdiction)'.[6] In more detail, this means that on the one hand, norms of jurisdiction are to be regarded as those with which compliance is required by the parties in a particular dispute. Jurisdiction is to be established in relation to those rules. On the other hand, norms of applicable law are all the rules that may be used by the court or tribunal to determine if the first set of rules has been complied with and incidentally, to resolve the dispute. For instance, they may be referred to in interpreting the first set of norms of jurisdiction.[7] What we are looking at are the interactions between norms 'derived from within [a] given regime'—norms of jurisdiction—and norms 'extraneous to the regime'—which may eventually be considered as norms of applicable law.[8]

In this regard, 'it is possible to have a court of limited *jurisdiction* in the sense of the disputes which it is to resolve, and yet not limit the *law applicable* by that court in resolving these disputes'.[9] For example, for a particular dispute, norms found in a treaty on the basis of which the jurisdiction of a court or tribunal would be established are considered as norms of jurisdiction. Those obviously may be applied, but other norms, such as norms of customary international law, can also form part of the body of applicable law.[10] As will be seen later,[11] the statutes of most courts and tribunals generally impose restrictions with regard to the types of norms that may be considered as part of the body of applicable law. The main distinction to retain at the moment is that a tribunal dealing with a particular dispute may only determine if the rules pursuant to which it has jurisdiction have been complied with, and not whether other rules on which it may rely to resolve the dispute, for example in an interpretation exercise—norms of applicable law—were violated.[12]

---

[5] Forteau 2011, pp. 151–152.

[6] Forteau 2013, p. 439. See also Oxman 2015, p. 414, where the author similarly explains the distinction, in this case in the context of disputes under UNCLOS.

[7] For a discussion under similar terms, see Parlett 2017, pp. 285–286; and Vranes 2005, p. 269.

[8] Gourgourinis 2011, p. 37.

[9] Bartels 2001, p. 502.

[10] On customary international law as applicable law in maritime delimitation cases, see McRae 2018, p. 92.

[11] See Sect. 13.4.

[12] One necessary point of precision: if a court or tribunal has based its jurisdiction not on the compromissory clause of a treaty, but on another mode of acceptance of its jurisdiction—such as

The distinction seems clear in theory. But when faced with a specific dispute in front of a court or tribunal, the notions can become blurred and have been confused by certain international courts and tribunals.[13] One example is the *Guyana v Suriname* case, which was heard by a tribunal constituted under Annex VII of the United Nations Convention on the Law of the Sea (hereinafter 'UNCLOS'). In that case, the Tribunal was asked to delimit the maritime boundary between the parties, but it was also asked to rule on the cross-boundary incidents at sea invoked by Guyana. The Tribunal first recalled that it was competent to apply Article 293,[14] para 1, of UNCLOS, which is the clause on applicable law. Referring to the *M/V 'SAIGA' (No. 2)* case previously heard by the International Tribunal for the Law of the Sea (hereinafter 'ITLOS'), the Tribunal interpreted this provision 'as giving it competence to apply not only the Convention, but also the norms of customary international law (including, of course, those relating to the use of force)'.[15] This is where the Tribunal confused its jurisdiction with the applicable law. As an Annex VII tribunal constituted under UNCLOS, the Tribunal had jurisdiction under Article 287 of UNCLOS.[16] Based on this title of jurisdiction, it may find that a party to the dispute has violated its obligations under UNCLOS and in doing so, it may need to refer to other rules of international law, such as the rules on the prohibition of the use of force. However, it is not competent to find breaches of any rules not contained in UNCLOS itself—the Tribunal had jurisdiction under that convention only and may therefore only find violations of norms found in the instrument on which its competence is based. Some provisions found in UNCLOS do refer to the use of force, such as Article 301 which concerns the peaceful uses of the sea, but considering that the Tribunal concluded that the actions of Suriname 'constituted a threat of the use of force in contravention of the Convention, the UN Charter and general international law',[17] it can be said that

---

an optional clause declaration at the ICJ—then violations of customary international law may be found, if they fall within the scope of the jurisdiction of the court. As noted by Boyle and Harrison, such cases 'may be able to take a more comprehensive approach to the dispute' (2013, p. 253).

[13] See Tzeng 2016, p. 243, invoking the following three cases: *M/V 'SAIGA'* (*No. 2*) (*Saint Vincent and the Grenadines v Guinea*); *Guyana v Suriname*; and *M/V 'Virginia G'* (*Panama/Guinea-Bissau*). See also Boyle and Harrison 2013, pp. 254–255; Crawford 2012, p. 477, in reference to the ICJ case *Military and Paramilitary Activities in und against Nicaragua* (*Nicaragua v United States of America*), Merits, Judgment, 27 June 1986, ICJ Reports 1986, p. 14; and Crawford 2019.

[14] The full text of this provision is reproduced under Sect. 13.4.1.2.

[15] *Guyana v Suriname*, Award, 17 September 2007, PCA Case No 2004-04, para 405, citing ITLOS, *M/V 'SAIGA'* (*No. 2*) (*Saint Vincent and the Grenadines v Guinea*), Judgment, 1 July 1999, ITLOS Reports 1999, p. 61, para 155.

[16] Article 287 UNCLOS reads as such: '[…] a State shall be free to choose […] one or more of the following means for the settlement of disputes concerning the interpretation or application of this Convention: (a) the International Tribunal for the Law of the Sea established in accordance with Annex VI; (b) the International Court of Justice; (c) an arbitral tribunal constituted in accordance with Annex VII; (d) a special arbitral tribunal constituted in accordance with Annex VIII for one or more of the categories of disputes specified therein.'

[17] *Guyana v Suriname*, above n 15, para 445.

the Tribunal exceeded its own jurisdiction as it concluded that there were violations of norms not contained in the instrument founding its competence.[18]

While this example does not concern environmental matters specifically, it is emblematic of the confusion between jurisdiction and applicable law that sometimes arises for adjudicative bodies that may be called upon to rule on disputes that include an environmental aspect. In contrast, in its Order no. 3 concerning the suspension of proceedings and provisional measures, the *MOX Plant* Annex VII of UNCLOS tribunal appears to have captured the necessary distinction between jurisdiction and applicable law. In this Order, it confirmed, first, 'that there is a cardinal distinction between the scope of its jurisdiction under Article 288, para 1, of the Convention, on the one hand, and the law to be applied by the Tribunal under Article 293 of the Convention, on the other hand'.[19] It further specified that 'to the extent that any aspects of Ireland's claims arise directly under legal instruments other than the Convention, such claims may be inadmissible.'[20] Likewise, in *Arctic Sunrise*, which case also partially concerned environmental matters,[21] the Tribunal held that 'Article 293(1) [of UNCLOS] does not extend the jurisdiction of a tribunal'.[22] Pursuant to this provision, the Tribunal concluded that in resolving the dispute presented to it, it could have regard 'to the extent necessary to rules of customary international law … not incompatible with the Convention, in order to assist in the interpretation and application of the Convention's provisions', but could not apply directly provisions found in other human rights treaties.[23] These findings support the distinction elaborated above between norms related to jurisdiction and norms of applicable law.[24]

Throughout this chapter, cases where courts and tribunals adequately distinguished between their jurisdiction to deal with a particular dispute and the law they may apply to interpret their constitutive instrument, and more generally to resolve that dispute, will be analysed.

13.3 Jurisdiction

Jurisdiction may be granted to courts and tribunals in a number of different ways. Many environmental law instruments include compromissory clauses that plan for the settlement of disputes in front of different judicial bodies, which may initially

---

[18] Tzeng 2016, pp. 248–251. See also Boyle and Harrison 2013, p. 255 for a wider criticism of the effect those decisions can have on a system of law based on consent.

[19] *The MOX Plant Case (Ireland v United Kingdom)*, Order N° 3, Suspension of Proceedings on Jurisdiction and Merits, and Request for Further Provisional Measures, 24 June 2003, para 19.

[20] Ibid. See also McLachlan 2005, pp. 301–302.

[21] *The Arctic Sunrise Arbitration* (*The Kingdom of the Netherlands v The Russian Federation*), Award on the Merits, 14 August 2015, PCA Case No 2014-02, paras 307–313.

[22] Ibid., para 188.

[23] Ibid., para 198; see also *The Duzgit Integrity Arbitration* (*The Republic of Malta v The Democratic Republic of São Tomé and Príncipe*), Award, 5 September 2016, PCA Case No 2014-07, para 207.

[24] For a general comment on relevant cases, see Parlett 2017.

direct States toward one forum over another if their dispute falls within the ambit of the subject-matter covered by a specific treaty. In the absence of such clauses, other forms of access to courts or tribunals may also be available to State parties to a dispute, depending on the forum they wish to seize.

13.3.1 Compromissory Clauses Found in Environmental Treaties

Many environmental treaties—if not most—contain compromissory clauses referring to certain dispute settlement bodies to which parties may bring their dispute and that are competent to issue binding decisions.[25] There is a broad variety in the wording of compromissory clauses found in environmental agreements. Some conventions provide for a fairly straightforward referral to arbitration or adjudication in case of an unresolved dispute.[26] Some other conventions add an additional step for binding settlement procedures to be activated. For example, the Convention on Biological Diversity first sets out, in Article 27, the requirement for parties to negotiate or to seek mediation, and then indicates that a State, upon acceptance, approval or accession to the Convention, may agree in writing for a dispute to be settled by arbitration, pursuant to the procedure set out in Annex II, Part 1, of the Convention, or by the International Court of Justice (hereinafter 'ICJ').[27]

Generally, a certain preference for recourse to arbitration, the ICJ or ITLOS is observed in international treaties, but regional agreements concerning the protection of the environment may also refer to institutions tied to the region. For example, Article XXX of the Revised African Convention on the Conservation of Nature and Natural Resources stipulates that parties must first attempt to settle their dispute through 'direct agreement' or through 'the good offices of a third party' and if those

---

[25] Stephens 2009, p. 23.

[26] See e.g. Convention for the Protection of the Marine Environment of the North-East Atlantic, 22 September 1992, 2354 UNTS 67, entered into force 25 March 1998 (OSPAR Convention), Art 32; 1996 Protocol to the Convention on the Prevention of Marine Pollution by Dumping of Wastes and Other Matter, 29 December 1972, 1046 UNTS 120, entered into force 30 August 1975, Article 16; Convention for the Protection of the Marine Environment and the Coastal Region of the Mediterranean, 16 February 1976, 1102 UNTS 27, entered into force 12 February 1978, Article 28.

[27] Clauses that are similarly worded have been included in the United Nations Framework Convention on Climate Change, 1 July 1992, 1771 UNTS 107, entered into force 21 March 1994 (Article 14) and in the Rotterdam Convention on the Prior Informed Consent Procedure for Certain Hazardous Chemicals and Pesticides in International Trade, 10 September 1998, 2244 UNTSS 337, entered into force 24 February 2004 (Article 20). See also, for an interesting discussion on the relation between the dispute settlement mechanism in UNCLOS and the one of the Convention on Biological Diversity, in the matter of the *South China Sea Arbitration* (*The Republic of the Philippines v The People's Republic of China*), Award on Jurisdiction and Admissibility, 29 October 2015, PCA Case No 2013-19, paras 281–289.

efforts prove unsuccessful, they may refer their issue to the Court of Justice of the African Union.[28]

In addition to the multilateral agreements they choose to adhere to, States have also concluded multiple bilateral agreements on questions concerning the protection of the environment. For example, Canada has entered into 28 bilateral agreements with States other than the United States aimed, in part or in whole, at the protection of the environment.[29] For this type of agreement, dispute settlement clauses appear to plan primarily for mediation or conciliation procedures, leaving aside resort to binding forms of dispute settlement such as arbitration or court procedures. However, some bilateral agreements do provide for the settlement of disputes leading to the issuing of a binding decision by an international court or tribunal. For instance, the bilateral treaty concluded between Uruguay and Argentina in 1975 on the Statute of the River Uruguay aims for the 'optimum and rational utilization of the River' and concerns, at least with regard to some of the provisions it contains, the protection of the environment.[30] In its Article 60, it provides for recourse to the ICJ in case of a dispute concerning the interpretation or application of the treaty.[31]

13.3.2 Aspects of the Jurisdiction of Certain Courts and Tribunals

Different courts and tribunals will have to deal with similar issues in addressing their jurisdiction. Each of them will have to interpret its own constitutive instrument

---

[28] Another example of a regional treaty is the Convention on the Conservation of European Wildlife and Natural Habitats, 19 September 1979, ETS No 104, entered into force 1 June 1982. Article 18, para 2 indicates that arbitration is the favoured mode of dispute settlement but reserves a role to the President of the European Court of Human Rights for the designation, in certain cases, of an arbitrator. Article 18, para 3, also makes provision for the participation of the European Union (referred to as the European Economic Community in the provision) as a party to the dispute, either by itself or jointly with the State concerned.

[29] See online: https://www.canada.ca/en/environment-climate-change/corporate/international-affairs/partnerships-organizations/participation-international-environmental-agreements.html. Another example is the Netherlands, which has concluded 12 bilateral agreements that have entered into force on the topic of the environment, such as the bilateral agreement between the Netherlands and Venezuela concerning the oil spill contingency plan to protect the coastal and marine environment, or more locally, the bilateral agreement between the Netherlands and the state of North Rhine-Westphalia in Germany to monitor the Rhine. See online: https://treatydatabase.overheid.nl/en/Verdrag/ZoekUitgebreidResultaat?topic=Environment&type=Bilateraal&isNLDepositary=False&isNLCurrent=True&pagina=1. Accessed 30 September 2020.

[30] See, i.e., Chapter VII on the use of water, Chapter VIII on the resources of the bed and subsoil, Chapter IX on the conservation, utilization and development of other natural resources, and Chapter X on pollution. Online: https://www.internationalwaterlaw.org/documents/regionaldocs/Uruguay_River_Statute_1975.pdf. Accessed 30 September 2020.

[31] See further, under Sect. 13.4.1.1, an analysis of the case *Pulp Mills on the River Uruguay (Argentina v Uruguay)* which was brought at the ICJ on the basis of that compromissory clause.

to determine what kinds of disputes it can settle in different instances. Due to the particularities of each of those instruments, in relation to which judicial bodies must affirm their jurisdiction, generalities may not be easily drawn. It is therefore worth looking in detail at some aspects of the jurisdiction of a few key courts and tribunals; they are key in that their jurisdiction is likely to be triggered to address disputes between States concerning the protection of the environment.

13.3.2.1 The ICJ

Taking first the ICJ, Article 36, para 1, of the Statute of the Court indicates that '[t]he jurisdiction of the Court comprises all cases which the parties refer to it and all matters specially provided for in the Charter of the United Nations or in treaties and conventions in force.' This means that State parties may conclude a special agreement to bring their dispute concerning environmental questions to the Court (or any dispute on a question of law for that matter).

Additionally, and as specified in Article 36, para 2, State parties can file an optional clause declaration recognizing the jurisdiction of the Court and use such declarations to bring a particular dispute to the attention of the Court. For example, the Court was able to hear the case *Certain Phosphate Lands in Nauru (Nauru v Australia)*, founding its jurisdiction on the declaration filed by Australia recognizing the Court's jurisdiction. In this case, issues relating to the responsibility of Australia for alleged environmental degradation could well have arisen, if the case had not been discontinued due to a settlement reached by the parties outside of Court. Indeed, Nauru claimed that Australia's mining activities on the island rendered the land 'completely useless for habitation, agriculture, or any other purpose unless and until rehabilitation was carried out'.[32]

In formulating their optional clause declarations, States may restrict the jurisdiction of the Court through the use of reservations or by wording a declaration in a restrictive manner. This way of proceeding is of particular relevance here because several States have, in their declarations, limited the jurisdiction of the Court in respect of environmental questions. Those declarations deserve scrutiny.

A number of States, such as Barbados, Japan, New Zealand and the Philippines, have carved out the jurisdiction of the Court with regard to cases concerning the 'exploration, exploitation, conservation or management' of 'living resources'[33] that may be found in certain specific marine areas appertaining to the State in question. Furthermore, three States—Poland, Slovakia and Romania—have adopted an even more explicit approach and have excluded from the Court's jurisdiction altogether 'disputes with regard to environmental protection'.[34] From an environmental

[32] ICJ, *Certain Phosphate Lands in Nauru* (*Nauru v Australia*), Application instituting proceedings, 19 May 1989, p 14, para 15.

[33] The declaration of the Philippines of 18 January 1972 refers more broadly to 'natural resources, including living organisms'.

[34] This is the language found in Poland's declaration of 25 March 1996. Similarly, Slovakia, in its declaration of 28 May 2004, excludes disputes 'with regard to the protection of environment'

perspective, this exclusion is troubling, especially given that it was not done in a concerted effort to deal with environmental issues in a more regionalized way.[35] For disputes involving one of those States, the Court would not be competent to deal with such matters on the basis of Article 36, para 2. Indeed, based on the principle of reciprocity of declarations, a Respondent State may refer to the declaration formulated by an Applicant State to refute the jurisdiction of the ICJ, even though it may not have itself limited the jurisdiction of the Court in any way.[36]

Some States have formulated other types of reservations in their declarations, the impact of which may not be so clear at first glance. Their effect however may be to restrict the Court's jurisdiction in the context of environmental cases. For example, Canada indicates in its declaration that the ICJ is not competent to deal with 'disputes arising out of or concerning conservation and management measures taken by Canada with respect to vessels fishing in the NAFO Regulatory Area'.[37] This formulation may exclude a wide variety of claims that affect the marine environment, but that are not clearly defined in the clause. Similarly, Pakistan has excluded any dispute concerning the exploitation of its maritime zones. Another example is the declaration of Malta in which it excludes from the ambit of the ICJ's jurisdiction disputes concerning 'the prevention or control of pollution or contamination of the marine environment in marine areas adjacent to [its] coast'.[38]

In addition, certain reservations excluding the jurisdiction of the Court on questions of reparation also have the effect of limiting the effective ability of the Court to fully resolve disputes concerning the environment. Declarations that exclude the Court's competence when it comes to 'the nature or extent of the reparation to be made for the breach of an international obligation'[39] make no distinction with regard to the subject-matter of the claims presented. However, considering that the full resolution of environmental disputes often requires a form of reparation, they may have an even more detrimental effect on disputes concerning the environment.[40]

States could also attempt to invoke broadly formulated reservations found in declarations to exclude environmental questions from the scope of jurisdiction of

---

and Romania, in its declaration of 23 June 2015, 'any dispute regarding to the protection of the environment'.

[35] One agreement concerning cooperation in the field of environmental protection between Germany, Poland and Slovakia of 1989 has been found, but none that concerns the three States at stake.

[36] ICJ, *Case of Certain Norwegian Loans*, Judgment, 6 July 1957, ICJ Reports 1957, p. 23. See also Fitzmaurice 2011, Section D.

[37] Declaration of Canada of 10 May 1994, point (2)(d).

[38] Declaration of Malta of 2 September 1983, point (2)(d).

[39] See, for example, the declaration of Bulgaria of 27 November 2015, of the Democratic Republic of the Congo of 8 February 1989, of Djibouti of 2 September 2005, of Sudan of 2 January 1958 and of Togo of 25 October 1979.

[40] Okowa 1998, p. 159; and Klein 2010, p. 387. See, for instance, the reparation phase in the case concerning *Certain Activities Carried Out by Nicaragua in the Border Area (Costa Rica v Nicaragua)*, Compensation, Judgment, ICJ Reports 2018, p. 15. In that case, the Court found that the total sum to be paid by Nicaragua to Costa Rica in compensation for the environmental damage caused and with respect to the restoration costs was of US$378,890.59. This is a considerable settlement (p. 58, para 156).

the Court. For instance, a number of States have formulated reservations excluding the Court's competence in 'disputes relating to matters which, by international law, are essentially within the[ir] domestic jurisdiction' or in 'disputes with regard to questions which by international law fall exclusively within the jurisdiction of' a particular State.[41] However, in the face of a claim that would concern the breach of an international obligation of environmental law, it seems unlikely that such reservations would be applicable. The Court already had the occasion to affirm, in its Advisory Opinion on the *Legality of the Threat or Use of Nuclear Weapons*, that 'the general obligation of States to ensure that activities within their jurisdiction and control respect the environment of other States or of areas beyond national control is now part of the corpus of international law relating to the environment.'[42] This affirmation, dating back to 1996, remains true and is especially relevant nowadays, in light of the current movement toward a better acknowledgment by States of their environmental obligations and of the emerging recognition, by many, of the *erga omnes* character of certain environmental obligations.[43]

13.3.2.2 ITLOS

Moving on from the ICJ, ITLOS may well be, or become, an institution of choice for a number of disputes concerning the environment that would arise under UNCLOS.[44] Under Article 287 of UNCLOS, parties to the Convention may choose to submit their dispute to ITLOS, among other courts or tribunals available. Under Article 288, para 1, it is specified that '[a] court or tribunal referred to in Article 287 shall have jurisdiction over any dispute concerning the interpretation or application of this Convention which is submitted to it in accordance with this Part.'

ITLOS is open to all 168 State parties to UNCLOS and in certain cases to other entities, such as international organisations.[45] Article 21 of its Statute, found in Annex VI of UNCLOS, indicates that '[t]he jurisdiction of the Tribunal comprises all disputes and all applications submitted to it in accordance with this Convention and all matters specifically provided for in any other agreement which confers jurisdiction on

[41] See, for instance, the declaration of Botswana of 16 March 1970, of Liberia of 20 March 1952, of Malawi of 12 December 1966, of Cambodia of 19 September 1957, of Canada of 10 May 1994, of the Gambia of 22 June 1966, of Kenya of 19 April 1965 and of Madagascar of 2 July 1992.

[42] ICJ, *Legality of the Threat of Nuclear Weapons,* Advisory Opinion, 8 July 1996, ICJ Reports 1996, p. 242, para 29.

[43] See for instance Robinson 2018; Dupuy and Viñuales 2018, p. 53; and Villalpando 2010. The ICJ also addressed the interaction between national laws and international environmental norms, thereby emphasizing the importance of environmental protection norms. In the case concerning *Certain Activities Carried out by Nicaragua in the Border Area* (*Costa Rica v Nicaragua*) *and Construction of a Road in Costa Rica along the San Juan River (Nicaragua v Costa Rica)*, the Court indicated that 'the fact that there may be an emergency exemption under Costa Rican law does not affect Costa Rica's obligation under international law to carry out an environmental impact assessment' (Judgment, ICJ Reports 2015, pp. 721–722, para 157).

[44] For a general discussion of the competence of ITLOS, see Popattanachai 2016, pp. 61–73.

[45] See Articles 291 and 305 of UNCLOS.

the Tribunal.' States can however limit, exclude or give precedence to the Tribunal's jurisdiction by filing a declaration concerning the choice of procedure under Article 287 of UNCLOS.[46] Through such declarations, some States have explicitly granted ITLOS priority to settle disputes based on the Convention. For example, Argentina sets out in its declaration, 'in order of preference', the jurisdiction of ITLOS first, then followed by the constitution of a special Annex VIII tribunal if the questions in dispute concern 'fisheries, protection and preservation of the marine environment, [or] marine scientific research and navigation'. Other States, such as Ecuador, list ITLOS, the ICJ and an arbitral tribunal constituted under Annex VII, but do not establish any order of preference.[47] There is a wide variety of declarations; some States specifically reject, or confirm, the jurisdiction of only one body—either the ICJ, ITLOS or an arbitral tribunal—for disputes arising under UNCLOS.[48] It is interesting to note that when an order of preference is in fact established, ITLOS always comes first, which may serve as an implicit recognition of the tribunal's special competence for all things UNCLOS. ITLOS has been subject to some criticism for not attracting a sufficient caseload,[49] in comparison with the ICJ which has received a constant stream of maritime delimitation cases in its recent past.[50] Nonetheless, the declarations under Article 287 of UNCLOS testify to the degree of confidence that States have put in this fairly new institution with regard to their UNCLOS disputes.

---

[46] To consult the declarations made pursuant to this provision, which vary widely in language and nature, see online: https://www.itlos.org/jurisdiction/declarations-of-states-parties/declarations-made-by-states-parties-under-article-287/. This procedure is different from that for the ICJ. Under Article 287 of UNCLOS, States can file declarations to determine which judicial body or bodies they wish to prioritise or exclude for the judicial settlement of UNCLOS related disputes. The ICJ declarations are specific to the World Court and rather focus on the subject-matter of disputes to be brought before the Court.

[47] When no order of preference is established in a specific declaration, the Applicant State can determine its choice of forum, but the Respondent State must also have accepted the jurisdiction of that particular forum. If States have not accepted the same jurisdiction, their dispute can be submitted only to arbitration under Annex VII of the Convention (see Article 287(3), (4) and (5)).

[48] See, for instance, the declarations filed by Guinea-Bissau which explicitly rejects the competence of the ICJ, while remaining silent with regard to its express choice of jurisdiction: '[Guinea-Bissau] does not accept the jurisdiction of the International Court of Justice'. Algeria, for its part, indicates that before a dispute may be submitted to the ICJ, the prior agreement of all parties concerned is required. Tanzania explicitly selects ITLOS and only this tribunal. Nicaragua, Norway and Spain, conversely, only accept the jurisdiction of the World Court. The Russian Federation, for its part, prioritizes the jurisdiction of arbitral tribunals, while recognizing ITLOS only for issues related to the prompt release of detained vessels and crews.

[49] Telesetsky 2018, p. 174 and ff. and more specifically p. 180. See also Seymour 2006 and, for a more positive assessment, Rothwell 2004. ITLOS also has asked more broadly as to whether there exists 'a new trend' moving 'away from binding judicial settlement of disputes and towards non-adversarial compliance mechanisms' (Golitsyn 2018, p. 9).

[50] See Sepúlveda Amor 2012; Telesetsky 2018, pp. 174 and 180.

13.3.2.3 The WTO

The World Trade Organization (hereinafter 'WTO') Appellate Body and panels have been seized in a number of cases that touch directly on environmental protection, even though those cases were mainly focused on trade restrictions.[51] In comparison to the other judicial bodies analysed above, the jurisdiction of the WTO judicial organs is quite restricted, 'to matters arising from the 'covered agreements', all of which are concerned exclusively with trade issues'.[52] Indeed, 'a WTO panel has jurisdiction only to decide whether or not an obligation *in the WTO treaty* has been violated'.[53] Because of this limited jurisdiction, environmental matters may be addressed incidentally, but the core of the subject-matter of a particular dispute in front of the WTO will always concern trade-related issues. For the present chapter, the interest of the WTO body of jurisprudence lies more specifically in its interpretation of the laws it may apply or refer to while deciding on the trade disputes it is competent to settle. Indeed, and as addressed below,[54] the WTO has allowed consideration for environmental norms in trade-oriented disputes, despite its specialization as a forum focused on trade issues.[55]

13.3.2.4 Arbitral Tribunals

Finally, one must not forget arbitral tribunals, which are in fact largely responsible for the settlement of numerous disputes relating to the environment. When negotiations or other non-binding methods of dispute settlement have failed, arbitration has been widely chosen by States as a preferred mode of settlement for such disputes, namely because of the flexibility it allows.[56] This same flexibility makes it difficult, however, to draw general conclusions regarding jurisdiction (or applicable law) unless a systemic and comprehensive analysis of those tribunals' jurisprudence were to be performed.

As it is the case for all courts and tribunals, rules governing the constitution and proper functioning of *ad hoc* arbitral tribunals, as well as the delimitation of the scope of their jurisdiction, depend on what has been agreed in the treaty which is constitutive of a specific arbitral tribunal. Differently though, those rules will vary for each newly formed arbitral tribunal. For example, Article 32, paras 3–10, of the OSPAR Convention, lays out the specific procedure for the constitution

[51] Sands and Peel 2018, p. 186.

[52] Stephens 2009, p. 48 and Annex 2 of the WTO Agreement—'Understanding on rules and procedures governing the settlement of disputes', Article 1.1.

[53] Pauwelyn et al 2004, p. 135.

[54] See further the discussion under Sect. 13.4.1.3.

[55] Klein 2021, p. 1043. See also Boyle and Harrison 2013, p. 249, where the authors point out that the WTO treaty regime's objective remains 'to further economic liberalization' despite the environmental issues that have been considered in a number of cases.

[56] Sands and Peel 2018, pp. 178–179; Stephens 2009, p. 28; and French 2006, p. 3.

and administration of an *ad hoc* tribunal. With regard to the jurisdiction of such a tribunal though, a large measure of discretion generally appears to be preferred. For example, Article 32, para 3(a), simply indicates that '[t]he request for arbitration shall state the subject matter of the application including in particular the Articles of the Convention, the interpretation or application of which is in dispute'. With regard to the law it may apply, Article 32, para 6 (a), specifies that '[t]he arbitral tribunal shall decide according to the rules of international law and, in particular, those of the Convention'. The distinction seen above between the jurisdiction and applicable law remains relevant.

If referral is made, rather, to an Annex VII tribunal under UNCLOS, the articles found in this specific section of the Convention are to be followed in order to appropriately constitute and operate the arbitral tribunal.[57] The same may be said for tribunals constituted under Annex VIII of UNCLOS which follow the rules laid out in that section of the Convention. A party to the dispute may nonetheless contest the jurisdiction of a tribunal constituted under those annexes, as the agreement of both parties is not required for proceedings to be instituted.[58]

13.3.3 Concluding Remarks on Jurisdiction

When faced with a particular dispute, and after having ascertained its jurisdiction, a judicial body will proceed to resolve the dispute for which it has competence (whether it is a dispute partly or fully concerned with the environment). As demonstrated above, different courts and tribunals will have jurisdiction to deal with disputes concerning the environment. Their jurisdiction may have been granted through a compromissory clause found in a treaty concerning the protection of the environment, through a special agreement between the parties concerned, by effect of a declaration recognising the competence of a judicial body, or by effect of the *forum prorogatum* doctrine. In any event, all courts and tribunals will face constraints with regard to their jurisdiction, which is circumscribed by their constitutive instrument.[59] On another note, notwithstanding the jurisdiction a court or tribunal may have to deal with a dispute, a body may still be ill-equipped or unwilling to tackle some of the environmental issues such a dispute presents; in practice, it may also reveal some prejudices in addressing the issues at hand.[60] As Shany puts it, 'regime courts' have their own biases and may be expected to act in a way that 'contribute[s] to the goals

[57] For instance, see Article 5 of Annex VII of UNCLOS: 'Unless the parties to the dispute otherwise agree, the arbitral tribunal shall determine its own procedure [...]'.

[58] Article 1 of Annex VII of UNCLOS and Article 1 of Annex VIII of UNCLOS.

[59] McLachlan 2005, p. 288.

[60] This criticism has been formulated, for example, with regard to the WTO. It has been argued that when faced with environmental cases, the WTO has 'ignored scientific evidence in favour of economic considerations' (Fox 2002, p. 330). See also Ahn 1999, pp. 821–822.

of the overarching regimes in which they operate',[61] which may not be necessarily aligned with the intention of the parties or the greater aim of norms related to the protection of the environment. While performing their activities, courts and tribunals have encountered difficulties in determining the norms they may apply, or refer to, in order to properly resolve a dispute in accordance with their mandate and principles of good administration of justice. These difficulties will now be addressed.

13.4 Applicable Law

As explained above, courts and tribunals have at times confused the law a violation of which it may validly pronounce (jurisdiction) with the law it may use to resolve a particular dispute (applicable law).[62] With regard to most of the courts and tribunals examined so far, a provision in their constitutive instrument informs what is the applicable law those bodies may refer to in order to settle the disputes presented to them. This is why, once again, it is worth looking separately at those different courts and tribunals, this time from the applicable law angle. Depending on the wording of those applicable law clauses—whether such provisions adopt a broader or more restrictive approach—and the particular practice of a judicial body in interpreting its applicable law provision, it will be shown that the determination of the law that may be applied in each given case may not be so simple.[63]

13.4.1 Applicable Law in the Context of Certain Courts and Tribunals

13.4.1.1 Applicable Law at the ICJ—Article 38 of the Statute

The applicable law clause found in Article 38 of the Statute of the Court is emblematic. While it defines the law that may be applied by the ICJ when settling disputes presented to it, it is also widely referred to as listing the sources of international law.[64] It reads as follows:

---

[61] Shany 2012, p. 246. 'Regime courts' are 'international courts [that] operate within the framework of specific regimes', such as the WTO, the European Union or the Council of Europe, to name only a few.

[62] See discussion above under Sect. 13.2.

[63] For this section, the applicable law that may be referred by *ad hoc* arbitral tribunals has been left out, because of the specificity and variety of it. Each convention planning for the constitution of an arbitral tribunal presents particularities, also with regard to the law it may apply. See also French 2006, p. 6.

[64] See, however, Pellet and Müller 2019, para 176: 'Article 38 gets its fame from the enumeration and concise definitions of the sources of international law contained in para 1—even though [….]

1. The Court, whose function is to decide in accordance with international law such disputes as are submitted to it, shall apply:
   a. international conventions, whether general or particular, establishing rules expressly recognized by the contesting states;
   b. international custom, as evidence of a general practice accepted as law;
   c. the general principles of law recognized by civilized nations;
   d. subject to the provisions of Article 59, judicial decisions and the teachings of the most highly qualified publicists of the various nations, as subsidiary means for the determination of rules of law.
2. This provision shall not prejudice the power of the Court to decide a case ex aequo et bono, if the parties agree thereto.

Undoubtedly, Article 38 is phrased in very broad terms and allows the Court to apply a wide variety of norms and rules while exercising its functions. It has, however, been criticized for being too formalistic[65] and for leaving out other valid manifestations of the law which could be understood as forming part of the applicable law body available to the Court, such as unilateral acts or decisions issued by international organizations.[66] Nonetheless, the Court has referred to sources not specifically mentioned in Article 38 on multiple occasions to resolve disputes. In the *Nuclear Test* cases, which concerned the testing of nuclear weapons and notably the environmental effects ensuing from those tests, the Court indicated that '[i]t is well recognized that declarations made by way of unilateral acts, concerning legal or factual situations, may have the effect of creating legal obligations'.[67] The unilateral statements pronounced publicly by France, outside of the context of Court proceedings, were relied upon by the Court to determine the Respondent State's obligations.[68] More recently, in its judgment on the merits in the case concerning the *Obligation to Negotiate Access to the Pacific Ocean (Bolivia v Chile)*, the Court reiterated its jurisprudence on unilateral acts and analysed Chile's declarations pronounced throughout the years that marked the dispute between the parties. Even though the Court ultimately found that the wording of the specific declarations relied upon '[did] not suggest that Chile has undertaken a legal obligation to negotiate Bolivia's sovereign access to the Pacific Ocean',[69] it did not dismiss the unilateral acts because of their mere nature, but because they were not demonstrative of Chile's intention

neither the jurisprudence nor, certainly, the doctrine, mentioned in para 1 (d) can be defined as a 'source', properly speaking.'

[65] Ibid., para 81.

[66] Ibid., para 87 and ff.: 'Other Sources of International Law—The *Lacunae* of Article 38'. Unilateral acts have been considered here as an additional source of international law, but in some cases, they could also be understood as being part of a customary rule of international law or of a general principle of law, and therefore be covered by Article 38 of the Statute.

[67] ICJ, *Nuclear Tests Case* (*Australia v France*), Judgment, 20 December 1974, ICJ Reports 1974, p. 253, p. 267, para 43 and ICJ, *Nuclear Tests Case* (*New Zealand v France*), Judgment, 20 December 1974, ICJ Reports 1974, p. 472, para 46.

[68] Ibid., p. 269, para 50 and ibid., p. 474, para 52.

[69] ICJ, *Obligation to Negotiate Access to the Pacific Ocean v*(*Bolivia v Chile*), Judgment, ICJ Reports 2018, p. 507, p. 555, para 147.

in this particular case. These cases provide an illustration of the law the Court is able and willing to apply when resolving disputes, irrespective of whether a particular source of law may be specifically mentioned in Article 38. In resolving future disputes concerning the protection of the environment, this level of openness toward a more varied set of norms will be welcome.

While the present chapter does not aim to demystify the ramifications of Article 38, needless to say that the ICJ benefits from the flexibility found in this provision in the law it chooses to apply in disputes with an environmental component. In recent judgments, the Court has been clearer in its delimitation of what is the applicable law in a given case, by dedicating a section of its judgments to it.[70] However, identifying the applicable law in a particular case is a task that the Court has always completed—if not explicitly, then implicitly. In each of the following cases that will be analysed, the Court, after having ascertained its jurisdiction, identified the law it would apply to resolve the dispute.

The Court has only had a few occasions to specifically deal with issues of environmental law, which more often than not constituted part of a wider dispute between the parties. This was true, for example, in the *Gabčíkovo-Nagymaros Project (Hungary/Slovakia)* case. This case concerned the construction and operation of a barrage system on the Danube river. Even though the questions touching upon the environment in this case have been qualified as 'incidental',[71] the Court made pronouncements on the environmental impact of the parties' actions, in accordance with the jurisdiction granted to it by special agreement. Indeed, it affirmed that 'the Project's impact upon, and its implications for, the environment are of necessity a key issue'.[72] The Court concluded that Articles 15 and 19 of the 1977 Treaty between the parties imposed on them an obligation 'to maintain the quality of the water of the Danube and to protect nature'.[73] The Court then proceeded to indicate that in the field of international environmental law and the law of international watercourses, 'new norms and standards have been developed' in the recent past and are 'set forth in a great number of instruments',[74] and that those new norms should be considered. This finding is in and of itself of systemic importance. The Court was able to identify as applicable law both norms found in the treaty at hand and norms of general international law. However, the Court remained evasive as to what norms and instruments it was specifically referring to. It was thus left to the parties to negotiate an agreed solution which would be cognisant of this vaguely identified applicable law.[75] More than fifteen years after the introduction of this case to the Court, it remains pending at

---

[70] See, i.e. the case concerning the *Frontier Dispute* (*Burkina Faso/Niger*), Judgment, 16 April 2013, ICJ Reports 2013, pp. 73–76, paras 60–69 and *Maritime Delimitation in the Black Sea* (*Romania v Ukraine*), Judgment, 3 February 2009, ICJ Reports 2009, pp. 74–78, paras 31–42.

[71] Okowa 1998, p. 162.

[72] ICJ, *Gabčíkovo-Nagymaros Project (Hungary v Slovakia)*, Judgement, 25 September 1997, ICJ Reports 1997, p. 77, para 140.

[73] Ibid., p. 78, para 140.

[74] Ibid.

[75] Ibid., p. 78, para 141. See also, Klein 2010, p. 394, citing Fitzmaurice 2001, p. 385.

the reparations phase. The Court's decision to leave it to the parties to negotiate may have been a satisfactory outcome for them at the time. However, the lack of specificity in the Court's pronouncements and overall vagueness as to the applicable law relating to the environmental aspect of the dispute on which the parties could have further relied in their negotiations may have contributed to the delayed settlement of the case.[76]

The Court also had to determine in its 1996 Advisory Opinion in the case concerning the *Legality of the Threat or Use of Nuclear Weapons* whether obligations of an environmental nature could be considered to resolve the main question it was asked, which concerned the legality of the use of force through nuclear weapons. It concluded that even though environmental treaties 'could [not be] intended to deprive a State of the exercise of its right of self-defence under international law because of its obligations to protect the environment', 'States must [nonetheless] take environmental considerations into account when assessing what is necessary and proportionate in the pursuit of legitimate military objectives'.[77] In that Opinion, the Court was more specific in its identification of the instruments to be considered as constituting the body of applicable law in this case, such as the Rio Declaration on Environment and Development of 1992 and General Assembly Resolution 47/37 of 25 November 1992 on the 'Protection of the Environment in Times of Armed Conflict'.[78] While these pronouncements are indeed instructive, it must be noted that they were made in the context of a non-binding advisory opinion, and so outside the context of a bilateral dispute.[79]

The following case is significant in light of the Court's pronouncement concerning the general international law applicable to an environmental dispute. The *Pulp Mills on the River Uruguay (Argentina v Uruguay)* case[80] concerned alleged breaches by Uruguay of its obligations under the Statute of the River Uruguay of 1975, a treaty in force between the parties and on which the jurisdiction of the Court was found.[81] More specifically, the Court was called upon to consider the effects of the pulp mills on the quality of the water of the river.[82] The Court determined that the parties, to comply with the obligations laid out in the treaty, were under an obligation to conduct an environmental impact assessment. To reach this conclusion, the Court analysed State practice and affirmed that 'the obligation to protect and preserve [...] has gained

---

[76] See also Yee 2016, p. 476, where the author acknowledges that the determination of the law applicable in a particular case may not always be straightforward.

[77] ICJ, *Legality of the Threat of Nuclear Weapons,* above n 42, p. 242, para 30. See also p. 243, para 33.

[78] See mentions in ibid., p. 242, para 30 and 32.

[79] See also IACHR, *The Environment and Human Rights—Requested by the Republic of Colombia,* Advisory Opinion, 15 November 2017, OC 23/17, which offers another example of the impact advisory opinions can have on the development of environmental law.

[80] See, for a general comment on the decision, Zhu and He 2012.

[81] ICJ, *Pulp Mills on the River Uruguay,* (*Argentina v Uruguay*), Judgment, 20 April 2010, ICJ Reports 2010, p. 40, para 48.

[82] ICJ, *Pulp Mills on the River Uruguay,* (*Argentina v Uruguay*), Application Instituting Proceedings of 4 May 2006, p. 5, para 2.

so much acceptance among States that it may now be considered a requirement under general international law to undertake an environmental impact assessment where there is a risk that the proposed industrial activity may have a significant adverse impact in a transboundary context'.[83] Even though the Court ultimately did not pronounce on any violation of substantial obligations found in the relevant treaty,[84] it stated that Argentina and Uruguay still had an obligation to cooperate and ensure the equitable use of the river and its protection.[85] These findings are noteworthy in that they illustrate the distinction between jurisdiction and applicable law, and identify the type of norms lying outside an instrument granting jurisdiction to a court or tribunal that such a body can use to resolve an environmental dispute. In that case, the Court affirmed its jurisdiction on the basis of the compromissory clause found in the 1975 treaty in force between the parties,[86] but referred to environmental principles of general international law in order to define the obligations of the parties under that instrument.

More recently, in the case concerning *Certain Activities Carried Out by Nicaragua in the Border Area (Costa Rica v Nicaragua),* the Court found that Nicaragua had violated its obligations under international environmental law and, for the first time, had the occasion to decide on the quantum to be awarded for reparation in a case concerning the protection of the environment.[87] In its judgment on the merits, the Court found that by its acts of excavation of two *caños*, Nicaragua had breached its obligations and that it had to compensate Costa Rica for the material damage it had caused.[88] The Court noted that the parties agreed on the existence of an obligation in general international law 'to conduct an environmental impact assessment concerning activities carried out within a State's jurisdiction that risk causing significant harm to other States, particularly in areas or regions of shared environmental conditions'.[89] The Court further based its reasoning on the customary law principle of prevention which has its origin in the due diligence that must be exercised by a State on its own territory[90] and on the principle that a State must avoid activities that would

[83] ICJ, *Pulp Mills on the River Uruguay, (Argentina v Uruguay),* above n 81, p. 83, para 204. See also Boyle and Harrison 2013, pp. 251–252, where the authors point out how the Court referred to norms of customary international law relating to the environment and applicable in the case at hand.

[84] Ibid., p. 106, para 282.

[85] Ibid., p. 101, para 266. For additional comments on the judgment, see the blog posts by Boyle 2010 and Payne 2010.

[86] Ibid., p. 40, para 48.

[87] ICJ, *Certain Activities Carried Out by Nicaragua in the Border Area (Costa Rica v Nicaragua),* above n 40, p. 15. See also Klein 2021, pp. 1053–1054.

[88] ICJ, *Certain Activities Carried out by Nicaragua in the Border Area (Costa Rica v Nicaragua) and Construction of a Road in Costa Rica along the San Juan River (Nicaragua v Costa Rica),* Judgment, 16 December 2015, ICJ Reports 2015, pp. 740–741, para 229.

[89] Ibid., p. 705, para 101 and p. 706, para 104.

[90] Ibid., p. 706, para 104, citing ICJ, *Pulp Mills on the River Uruguay, (Argentina v Uruguay),* above n 81, pp. 55–56, para 101.

cause significant damage to the environment of another State.[91] Moreover, the Court referred to Article 5 of the Ramsar Convention in order to inform its understanding as to whether Nicaragua had an obligation to consult with Costa Rica.[92] This case demonstrates that a court or tribunal does not need to distinguish between the sources of the environmental norms it refers to as part of the body of applicable law available to it. Here, norms found in customary international law and conventional norms were referenced by the Court, without any distinction being made regarding the different source of such norms.

13.4.1.2 Applicable Law for UNCLOS Bodies—Article 287 of UNCLOS

A few words may be added on the applicable law clause found in UNCLOS. Any court or tribunal listed in Article 287 which has jurisdiction to determine a particular dispute under the Convention (Article 288) must abide by Article 293 on applicable law. This clause is particular in that it applies to all judicial bodies mentioned in Article 287 that are competent to settle a dispute under Article 288 of the Convention, namely ITLOS, the ICJ and Annex VII and VIII tribunals. Article 293 reads as follows:

1. A court or tribunal having jurisdiction under this section shall apply this Convention and other rules of international law not incompatible with this Convention.
2. Paragraph 1 does not prejudice the power of the court or tribunal having jurisdiction under this section to decide a case *ex aequo et bono*, if the parties so agree.

As seen earlier, the interplay between Article 288 of UNCLOS regarding the jurisdiction of a particular court of tribunal, and Article 293 of the Convention which concerns the law that may be applied when jurisdiction has been affirmed with regard to a particular dispute, is of the utmost relevance.[93] Some cases have provided clarification as to what Article 293 means and to which 'other rules of international law' a judicial body may refer. In the *Arctic Sunrise Arbitration* analysed earlier, the Annex VII tribunal offered clarification with regard to the types of norms that may be considered to resolve a dispute brought under UNCLOS. It first specified that 'Article 293(1) does not extend the jurisdiction of a tribunal [but] ensures that [...] a tribunal can give full effect to the provisions of the Convention.'[94] It also indicated that rules of international law are incorporated in the Convention, but remained vague as to which provisions did so and which rules of international law were incorporated by them.[95] Going into more detail with regard to applicable law, the decision stated that it may be necessary for a tribunal faced with a dispute under the

[91] Ibid., pp. 711–712, para 118, citing ICJ, *Pulp Mills on the River Uruguay, (Argentina v Uruguay)*, above n 81, p. 56, para 101.

[92] Ibid., p. 709, para 110.

[93] See the discussion under Sect. 13.2. above.

[94] *The Arctic Sunrise Arbitration (The Kingdom of the Netherlands v The Russian Federation)*, above n 21, para 188. See also Parlett 2017, pp. 288–289 and generally on that case, Harrison 2016.

[95] *The Arctic Sunrise Arbitration (The Kingdom of the Netherlands v The Russian Federation)*, above n 21, para 188 and footnote 180 more precisely.

Convention 'to resort to foundational or secondary rules of general international law such as the law of treaties or the rules of State responsibility' or to 'primary rules of international law'.[96] It specified that rules of customary international law, including international human rights standards, may also be taken into account.[97] Accentuating the distinction between jurisdiction and applicable law, it made clear that 'Article 293 is not, however, a means to obtain a determination that some treaty other than the Convention has been violated, unless that treaty is otherwise a source of jurisdiction, or unless the treaty otherwise directly applies pursuant to the Convention.'[98]

In the arbitration between Barbados and Trinidad and Tobago, the Annex VII tribunal went further into what could be included as applicable law under Article 293 of UNCLOS. Indeed, it affirmed that this provision allowed 'for a broad consideration of the legal rules embodied in treaties and customary law as pertinent to the delimitation between the parties' as well as the 'general principles of international law and the contributions that the decisions of international courts and tribunals and learned writers have made to the understanding and interpretation of this body of legal rules'.[99] Both of these cases provide clarity in understanding what types of norms are usually expected to constitute the body of applicable law in any given case under UNCLOS.

Another case of relevance, which illustrates the distinction between the jurisdiction of a tribunal and the law it may apply to resolve a dispute presented to it, is the arbitration in the *South China Sea* case. In that case, the tribunal did not address in theory the distinction between Articles 288 and 293 of UNCLOS, but its pronouncements demonstrate it well.[100] It showed that a tribunal, while interpreting the norms found in the instrument granting it jurisdiction, may refer and be informed by other external norms to the Convention. In this arbitration, an Annex VII tribunal was constituted and its jurisdiction under Article 288 of UNCLOS to deal with the particular claims raised was confirmed.[101] At the merits stage, the tribunal was called upon to determine the law applicable to a number of claims. When addressing the issue of supervision of fishing vessels, the tribunal proceeded to an interpretation of certain provisions of UNCLOS. In its interpretative exercise, it referred to the Award of 2015 given by the Annex VII tribunal constituted in the *Chagos* case and to the Advisory Opinion of ITLOS in the *Fisheries* case.[102] When addressing

96 Ibid., para 190.

97 Ibid., para 197.

98 Ibid., para 192.

99 *Arbitration between Barbados and the Republic of Trinidad and Tobago, relating to the delimitation of the exclusive economic zone and the continental shelf between them*, Award, 11 April 2006, PCA Case No 2004-02, Volume XXVII, 27 RIAA 147, para 222.

100 See for instance the discussion in the *South China Sea Arbitration* (*The Republic of the Philippines v The People's Republic of China*), Award, 12 July 2016, PCA Case N°2013-19, para 956 and ff.

101 *South China Sea Arbitration* (*The Republic of the Philippines v The People's Republic of China*), above n 27, para 130 and ff.

102 *South China Sea Arbitration* (*The Republic of the Philippines v The People's Republic of China*), above n 100, para 735–744.

issues of traditional fishing, the tribunal referred to the arbitration in the case *Eritrea v Yemen*, where the notion was widely debated.[103] Moreover, the Philippines had claimed that China had engaged in wrongful conduct in the course of the ongoing proceedings and the tribunal had to address the law applicable when such allegations are made. It considered international jurisprudence and concluded that a principle existed according to which parties engaged in a dispute settlement procedure must refrain from aggravating or extending their dispute pending final settlement.[104] It further referred to the language found in other multilateral and bilateral conventions to confirm its interpretation of the obligation imposed on the parties.[105] The Court concluded that the principle of non-aggravation was implicit in different articles of UNCLOS, but that it nonetheless constituted an 'other rul[e] of international not incompatible with this Convention' pursuant to Article 293.[106] Throughout the case, while interpreting the provisions of UNCLOS, which instrument granted it jurisdiction, the tribunal considered other rules of international law found in conventions and addressed by the case-law, in conformity with Article 293 of UNCLOS.

13.4.1.3 Applicable Law in the WTO

The WTO deserves special attention when it comes to applicable law issues. Indeed, contrary to other judicial bodies analysed above, there is no specific clause concerning applicable law in the WTO Agreement.[107] Because of that, the WTO dispute settlement body has developed a particular practice relating to the law it may apply when settling disputes. Its approach raises difficult questions of interaction between the norms that can be applied *per se*, and the norms that may be referred to for interpretation purposes.

Article 3.2 of Annex 2 of the WTO Agreement—'Understanding on rules and procedures governing the settlement of disputes'—comes as close as possible to a clause on applicable law.[108] It indicates that the dispute settlement system of the organisation 'serves to preserve the rights and obligations of Members under the covered agreements, and to clarify the existing provisions of those agreements in accordance with customary rules of interpretation of public international law'. One must turn to the case law of the WTO to understand exactly what that means and what law can be referred to by the WTO dispute settlement organs.

---

[103] Ibid., para 795–796.

[104] Ibid., para 1169.

[105] Ibid., para 1170.

[106] Ibid., para 1173.

[107] See more specifically Annex 2 of the WTO Agreement: Understanding on rules and procedures governing the settlement of disputes.

[108] See Stephens 2009, pp. 48–49. This provision is also to be read alongside Article 7 of the Understanding on rules and procedures governing the settlement of disputes.

In its landmark pronouncement of *US—Gasoline*, the WTO affirmed, while referring to the customary rule of interpretation found in Article 31 of the Vienna Convention on the Law of Treaties (hereinafter 'VCLT' or 'Vienna Convention'), that its General Agreement is 'not to be read in clinical isolation from public international law'.[109] This pronouncement marked an explicit engagement by the WTO with regard to its approach to applicable law; its law is found in its own instruments, but may be interpreted in compliance with interpretation principles of the Vienna Convention.[110]

Other cases followed, referring once again to the VCLT rules of interpretation in order to properly settle trade disputes presented to the WTO. Of more interest for this chapter are the cases that comprised an element related to the protection of the environment. One of the most relevant cases remains the *US—Shrimp* case, which showed a 'greater willingness' on the part of the WTO to interpret its instruments 'in support of specific environmental efforts and multilateral environmental agreements more generally'.[111] In that case, the Appellate Body performed a detailed analysis of the term 'natural resources' found in Article XX(g) of the WTO Agreement. In doing so, it discussed the jurisprudence of the ICJ and concluded that the definition of such a term was not static, but in fact evolutionary. It also referred to UNCLOS as another convention which defines natural resources as both 'living and non-living resources'. It continued its analysis by discussing numerous other conventions, such as the Convention on Biological Diversity and the Convention on the Conservation of Migratory Species of Wild Animals.[112] All in all, principles found in decisions of other international courts and in international agreements were considered. It must be noted that the United States was not party to some of the treaties mentioned, but the Appellate Body did not see that as a bar to referring to them. In light of the applicable law it considered, the Appellate Body was able to conclude that the term 'natural resources' included living and non-living resources.[113]

A more recent case of importance is the *EC—Biotech* case, in that it raised issues related to the relevance of other rules of international law for the interpretation of the WTO Agreement in the context of Article 31(3)(c) of the VCLT.[114] This provision specifies that an interpreter shall take into account 'together with the context: any

---

[109] WTO, *United States—Standards for Reformulated and Conventional Gasoline,* Appellate Body Report, 29 April 1996, WT/DS2/AB/R, p. 17. By stating so, the WTO 'did not mean [however] that general international law is fully integrated into WTO dispute settlement' (Pauwelyn et al. 2004, p. 139). See further Bacchus 2015 and Pauwelyn 2001.

[110] For a further analysis, see Musto and Redgwell 2017, pp. 505–506.

[111] Klein 2010, p. 393.

[112] WTO, *United States—Import Prohibition of Certain Shrimp and Shrimp Products*, Appellate Body Report, 12 October 1998, WTO/DS58/AB/R, para 130. See also the analysis by McLachlan 2005, pp. 302–304.

[113] Ibid., para 131. See also the commentary by Gomula 2010, p. 409.

[114] WTO, *European Communities—Measures Affecting the Approval and Marketing of Biotech Products*, Panel Report, 29 September 2006, WT/DS291/R (*EC—Approval and Marketing of Biotech Products*). See, in general, section 7 of the report entitled 'Relevance of other rules of international law to the interpretation of the WTO agreements at issue in this dispute', p. 328 and ff.

relevant rules of international law applicable between the parties'.[115] In that case, the panel asked whether it could take into account principles found in the Convention on Biological Diversity and the Biosafety Protocol to interpret its own agreement.[116] It started its analysis by noting that Article 31(3)(c) of the Vienna Convention 'seems sufficiently broad to encompass all generally accepted sources of public international law' such as treaties, customary international law and general principles of law.[117] Further, it proceeded to analyse the exact meaning of the term 'applicable between the parties' found in Article 31(3)(c). The panel first noted that this provision does not refer specifically to the parties *in dispute*. Considering that the term 'party' signifies under Article 2(1)(g) of the VCLT 'a State which has consented to be bound by the treaty and for which the treaty is in force', it concluded that the rules applicable in the context of WTO disputes 'are the rules of international law applicable in the relations between the States which have consented to be bound by the treaty which is being interpreted, and for which that treaty is in force'.[118] Therefore, to be considered, rules of international law must be applicable to all WTO Members.[119] While this conclusion is logical and serves to preserve the interests of all WTO Members, it appears in stark contrast with the previous approach taken in *US—Shrimp* and may be overly restrictive.[120] The WTO comprises 164 Members.[121] To require that all of them be parties to a specific convention for it to be considered for interpretation purposes in a bilateral dispute is arguably excessive.[122]

Despite the findings of the Panel in the *EC—Biotech* case, some uncertainties remain as to the exact position of the WTO on the scope of Article 31(3)(c) of the VCLT and whether, in the future, a wider range of instruments could be used for interpretation of provisions under WTO agreements even if not all WTO Members are parties to them.[123]

There is also a debate in the literature which does not concern *per se* the WTO's interpretation of the VCLT, but questions whether the WTO is exceeding its authority

---

[115] See generally on this provision and the principle of systemic integration, McLachlan 2005 and Merkouris 2015. To see how the principle of systemic integration is used in front of Africa's international courts in the context of environmental disputes, see Gathii 2020, pp. 10–11.

[116] Gomula 2010, pp. 415–416.

[117] *EC—Approval and Marketing of Biotech Products*, above n 114, para 7.67.

[118] Ibid., para 7.68.

[119] Ibid., paras 7.68 and 7.70. See also WTO, *China—Measures Related to the Exportation of Various Raw Materials*, Panel Reports, 5 July 2011, WT/DS394/R, WT/DS395/R and WT/DS398/R para 7.377; Pauwelyn et al. 2004, p. 137.

[120] See McGrady 2008, more specifically at pp. 591–592.

[121] Since 29 July 2016, online: https://www.wto.org/english/thewto_e/whatis_e/tif_e/org6_e.htm.

[122] As McLachlan argues, if all parties to the WTO agreements must also be parties to other instruments for them to become 'applicable in the relations between the parties', 'it would have the ironic effect that the more membership of a particular multilateral treaty such as the WTO Covered Agreements expanded, the more those treaties would be cut off from the rest of international law' (2005, p. 314). See also Marceau 2002, p. 781.

[123] Musto and Redgwell 2017, p. 506.

in considering non-WTO law while settling disputes.[124] This debate may originate in the confusion that subsists between jurisdiction and applicable law. It may also originate from the fact that on a theoretical level, the distinction (if there is one) between rules referred to for interpretation purposes, and rules that are applied *per se* as part of the body of applicable law, has been debated.[125] Indeed, as authors note, 'the distinction between application and interpretation is not concrete and it may in some cases be difficult to determine whether a WTO tribunal is applying international law or simply using international law to interpret a WTO provision'.[126] Notwithstanding, in light of the distinction between jurisdiction and applicable law laid out earlier,[127] it is clear that the dispute settlement body of the WTO only has jurisdiction to entertain claims that are based on its agreements and could only sanction violations of obligations originating from these agreements. That being said, it is not prevented from considering other norms in solving the disputes validly presented to it, whether those are being considered as applied or only referred to in the process of an interpretation exercise.[128]

From the point of view of institutional policy, some authors also have argued that there is no need for the WTO to look for answers in law other than its own, even though international law may impact the dispute settlement system of the WTO by virtue of interpretation.[129] This may stem from the regime of speciality the WTO has attributed itself, despite its apparent willingness to consider issues of environmental law, outside of its specialty in the field of trade.[130] However, little reasoning can be offered in support of such a restrictive approach to the role of the WTO.

13.4.2 Concluding Remarks on Applicable Law

Despite differences in wording of applicable law clauses, or the lack thereof in the case of the WTO, it appears that courts and tribunals have found ways to rely on the applicable law they deem useful to resolve the disputes they are presented with. This is true for all types of disputes; environmental disputes are not special in that regard. Some may say that judicial bodies are in fact circumventing the clauses found in their constitutive instrument by allowing for consideration of norms that do not find their basis in the instrument granting jurisdiction to a specific body. However, that again confuses both concepts of jurisdiction and applicable law. The better view is

[124] See, emblematically, Pauwelyn et al. 2004, p. 142.

[125] For a wider discussion on this topic, see Gourgourinis 2011, p. 39.

[126] Mitchell and Heaton 2010, p. 570.

[127] See the discussion under Sect. 13.2. above.

[128] Pauwelyn et al. 2004, pp. 144–145 and Mitchell and Heaton 2010, p. 570 and ff.

[129] Pauwelyn et al. 2004, pp. 139 and 141.

[130] McLachlan pointed out that, in a number of cases, the Appellate Body of the WTO found that 'express obligations assumed by the parties under the Covered Agreements of the WTO overrode the principles of international environmental law whose application was sought' (2005, p. 304).

that in most cases, courts and tribunals, when considering other norms of international law, are appropriately exercising their jurisdiction. They are not sanctioning potential violations of those other norms referred to, but only using them to properly resolve the disputes they face, with appropriate consideration for the development of international environmental law which finds its expression in various conventions, custom and general principles of law external to their constitutive instrument.

As Forteau argues, '[v]ariations of applicable law depen[d] exclusively on the nature of the parties and of their bilateral obligations, not on the nature of the tribunal to which they decided to resort to'.[131] This may be true; in most instances, the entire body of international law is, in fact, potentially applicable.[132] A possible exception may be the WTO, which still appears reluctant to consider law that is not its own, and which may be, as its jurisprudence keeps on evolving, bound to refer to law that is only binding on all WTO Members.

Nonetheless, the norms that will end up being applied or considered for interpretation purposes will vary depending on the particular court or tribunal, which is limited by its constitutive instrument, but also by its institutional practice. Subject to a tribunal's self-understanding of its role and how it wishes to exercise its functions, the applicable law that will be considered in a given case will differ. The law related to the protection of the environment consists of a wide range of norms and is diverse in nature. Treaties have been concluded and customary international law has emerged, but this body of law is also largely influenced by recommendations, protocols, resolutions and other non-binding instruments, which can be considered as 'soft law'.[133] If one applies a certain hierarchy to the sources of international law, some of the most relevant norms of environmental law to resolve a particular dispute may not come high on that list. Depending on the level of formalism a judicial body wishes to exercise, or on its legal tradition or that of its members, such norms may end up being either put aside or brought into light. This reality exemplifies the particularities of each judicial body and is closely linked to the issue of forum shopping, i.e. the selection of the most appropriate forum for a particular dispute.

13.5 Forum Shopping

Forum shopping has been a divisive topic among scholars for many years.[134] When a State has opted to bring its dispute to a court or tribunal and is facing the options of multiple fora available, it is confronted with a choice, and its decision, which may be based on interests other than the mere settlement in justice, has been either frowned upon or celebrated. Celebrated, certainly, by States, which prefer to retain a level of

[131] Forteau 2013, p. 418.

[132] Forteau 2011, p. 143 and ff.

[133] Stephens 2009, pp. 92 and 275.

[134] See generally Mondré 2015.

discretion in their choice of forum.[135] Many factors can inform a State's selection of a forum over another.

States may more broadly consider 'the most favourable jurisdictional basis for their case',[136] meaning one which allows the court or tribunal to deal with the most issues. The 'significant divergence between forums as to what weight and what priority should be given to environmental issues'[137] has been noted as a reason to select a forum over another. As discussed earlier, in certain cases, courts and tribunals present a tendency to prioritise issues pertaining to their main area of expertise in the resolution of the disputes presented to them that comprise an element relating to environmental protection.[138] This reality may influence the choice of forum by a State. In the absence of an environmental court, States will undeniably have to ponder their interests.

It also has been set out above that the applicable law available to an institution is often similar notwithstanding the judicial body. Nonetheless, the court or tribunal's willingness or capacity to consider a wider scope of different types of norms, which is linked to a certain formalism or lack thereof within an institution, may impact a State's choice of forum. The 'degree of *openness*'[139] of a body with regard to the applicable law it can apply in a specific case at hand—meaning the degree to which a court or tribunal is willing to resolve a dispute or construe an instrument with consideration for norms of environmental law found in different conventions, in custom, in domestic law or in treaties not necessarily specifically referred to by the parties—may inform the decision of an Applicant party.

These considerations are linked to the specific expertise of a body with regard to a particular type of disputes.[140] Moreover, some tribunals or courts will be seen as better equipped to address complex issues regarding the evidence of environmental issues presented to them.[141] For example, Annex VIII of UNCLOS tribunals may be constituted to deal with disputes concerning the interpretation or application of some articles of the Convention which concern specific topics, such as fisheries or the protection and preservation of the marine environment. A list of experts for each field listed in Article 1 of Annex VIII is constituted and kept up to date (Article 2). In light of this procedure, a State may want to have recourse to such tribunals if its dispute is one concerning the listed fields of expertise. As a further example, ITLOS may be seized for its expertise in the law of the sea, for instance through its Seabed Disputes Chamber which has specific competence to deal with environmental issues arising

[135] Liénard 2009, p. 250.

[136] Boyle and Harrison 2013, p. 254.

[137] French 2006, p. 31.

[138] See Sect. 13.3.3 and Shany 2012, p. 246.

[139] Forteau 2013, p. 439.

[140] Stephens 2009, p. 277.

[141] Klein 2010, pp. 387–389; Bilder 1975, p. 225.

from the exploration and exploitation of marine resources.[142] Besides such inherent expertise, the ability of a court or tribunal to conduct fact-finding missions or to order experts to produce detailed reports may also be attractive to States, even though resort to such procedures would remain at the discretion of the judicial body.[143]

Conversely, States may wish to resort to a court or tribunal, not because of its specific expertise, but rather because of its more general competence. As mentioned above, most cases concerning the environment form part of a wider dispute which also touches upon questions of general international law. This reality explains why States may be more comfortable relying on a Court that can more aptly deal with all aspects of the dispute presented to it—environmental and non-environmental. The most obvious example of a court of general competence is the ICJ, which deals with varied and wide-ranging issues of international law.[144] States may choose recourse to the ICJ for its ability to 'provide a means to articulate the content or contours of particular substantive norms of international environmental law'.[145] Of value here is its particular knowledge and relatively consistent application of traditional concepts of public international law, such as treaty interpretation, State responsibility and principles related to reparation. The publicity of proceedings at the ICJ when compared to the relative secrecy of arbitration may also be appealing for States who wish not merely to settle their bilateral dispute, but also to contribute to the development of certain norms of environmental law of interest for the international community as a whole. However, this affirmation may be tainted by a certain level of wishful thinking and be too optimistic with regard to States' intentions.[146] The likelihood of compliance by parties with the Court's judgments may also make that institution attractive for States.[147]

The ICJ did attempt, in the past, to become even more attractive for States with regard to disputes concerning the environment. The Court, in 1993, created a chamber specialised in environmental law '[i]n view of the developments in the field of environmental law and protection which have taken place in the last few years'.[148] This may have been a decision taken in reaction to the creation of ITLOS[149]

---

[142] See the request for advisory opinion submitted to the Seabed Disputes Chamber of ITLOS, *Responsibilities and obligations of States with respect to activities in the Area*, Advisory Opinion, 1 February 2011, ITLOS Reports 2011, p. 10.

[143] See, for example, in the context of the ICJ, Article 50 of the Statute and Article 67 of the Rules of Court, and in the context of ITLOS, Article 15 of the Rules of the Tribunal (ITLOS/8).

[144] Jennings 1992, p. 242; Okowa 1998, p. 160.

[145] Klein 2010, p. 387.

[146] Stephens 2009, pp. 35–36, and 277. For instance, in Koskenniemi's view, it is only in rare circumstances that States would choose to resort to a settlement body to resolve their environmental disputes, and if they do so, they are seeking an acceptable outcome for themselves (Koskenniemi 1991, p. 82).

[147] Jennings 1992, p. 243.

[148] ICJ Press Release No 93/20 of 19 July 1993, p. 2, online: https://www.icj-cij.org/files/press-releases/7/10307.pdf. Accessed 30 September 2020. See also Okowa 1998, pp. 168–169.

[149] See Chartier 2018, para 8. UNCLOS entered into force in 1994 and ITLOS was inaugurated in 1996.

or to the pending cases the Court was hearing at the time, namely the *Certain Phosphate Lands in Nauru (Nauru v Australia)* and *Gabčíkovo-Nagymaros Project (Hungary/Slovakia)* cases, both of which comprised questions related to the environment.[150] The Chamber was reconstituted every year until 2006, but no State ever demanded that a case be heard by it, which ultimately caused its dismantlement.[151] It is true that there was no opportunity to demonstrate the expertise of such a chamber and the members composing it,[152] but it may also be that State parties did not see a need for such expertise.[153] As suggested by Raymond Ranjeva, a former ICJ judge, a court of general competence in public international law never encountered any particular difficulty in settling disputes in environmental law and in identifying the different principles of customary international law that apply,[154] which may explain the lack of demand for such a chamber. Moreover, the difficulty in defining disputes as completely environmental may also have been a factor.[155] All in all, it may be that an overly expert Court is not more attractive to parties than one which presents a more general and balanced approach toward international law.

All this being said, it remains rare that a particular dispute can be heard in front of multiple courts and tribunals. As we have seen in the above sections, the jurisdiction of courts and tribunals is often circumscribed, whether it is by the terms of a compromissory clause, or because States have limited a court or tribunal's competence by filing a declaration to that effect. More often than not, no choice is available. Overall, when looking at why States select one forum over another to settle their dispute concerning the environment, it is difficult to categorise forum shopping as either all negative or all positive. In an ever-developing field, the mere availability of a judicial court or tribunal to settle a dispute is welcome.

[150] While we can only speculate as to the exact reasons related to the creation of this chamber, specific mention of these two cases was made in the Communiqué announcing its creation (ICJ Press Release No 93/20 of 19 July 1993, p. 1, online: https://www.icj-cij.org/files/press-releases/7/10307.pdf). See also Chartier 2018, paras 8 and 20; and Palchetti 2019, para 22. In the latter author's view, 'the proliferation of international tribunals and a growing feeling that 'special fields' of international law exist' seem to have influenced the Court in the creation of its chamber.

[151] I.C.J. Yearbook 2006–2007, p. 29. For a parallel, see also the Permanent Court of Arbitration Optional Rules for Arbitration of Disputes relating to Natural Resources and/or the Environment, online: https://pca-cpa.org/wp-content/uploads/sites/6/2016/01/Optional-Rules-for-Arbitration-of-Disputes-Relating-to-the-Environment-and_or-Natural-Resources.pdf. Those were adopted in 2001 after years of consultation with leading experts to 'fill the gaps identified in existing environmental dispute resolution procedures' (Ratliff 2001, pp. 888 and 895; and Stephens 2009, pp. 31–34).

[152] Okowa 1998, p. 168.

[153] This is supported by the speech of the ICJ President, H.E. Rosalyn Higgins, to the General Assembly on 26 October 2006, where she said, justifying the decision not to renew the constitution of the environmental chamber, that '[a] survey of State practice suggests that States prefer environmental law not to be compartmentalized, but to find its place within international law as a whole' (p. 6, online: https://www.icj-cij.org/files/press-releases/9/13149.pdf). See also Chartier 2018, para 24.

[154] Ranjeva 1994, p. 438.

[155] Stephens 2009, pp. 39–40.

It would be tempting to conclude that one forum is necessarily preferable over another. However, that would overlook the number of considerations illustrated above that may come into play when a State chooses to bring its dispute in front of a judicial body over another. States, as sovereign entities, are free to prioritise their own interests in the way they see fit and make decisions accordingly at any given point in time.[156] All the courts or tribunals analysed throughout this piece and in the first part of this volume have their own strengths and weaknesses, specific expertise and shortcomings. In that light, forum shopping appears inevitable.

13.6 Conclusion

Issues relating to jurisdiction and applicable law are relevant for all types of disputes, environmental or otherwise. As demonstrated above, some fora may be in a better position to deal with certain issues concerning the protection of the environment than others, depending on the specific environmental question addressed and the will of the parties as they seek a peaceful resolution of their dispute. However, only the particulars of each case can dictate the most appropriate forum for each situation. Fundamental questions will continue to trouble all courts and tribunals having to address their jurisdiction and determine the law they can apply, aside from the substantive aspects of the environmental disputes presented to them. Despite these uncertainties, more frequent recourse to dispute settlement bodies able to issue binding decisions can only be celebrated in a field that is rapidly evolving.

References

Ahn D (1999) Environmental disputes in the GATT/WTO: before and after US – Shrimp case. Michigan Journal of International Law 20:819–870

Bacchus J (2015) Not in clinical isolation. In: Marceau G (ed) A history of law and lawyers in the GATT/WTO: the development of the rule of law in the multilateral trading system. Cambridge University Press, Cambridge, pp 507–516

Bartels L (2001) Applicable law in the WTO dispute settlement proceedings. Journal of World Trade 35:499–519

Bilder R B (1975) The settlement of disputes in the field of the international law of the environment. Collected Courses of the Hague Academy of International Law 144:139–240

Boyle A (2010) Pulp Mills case: a commentary. https://www.biicl.org/files/5167_pulp_mills_case.pdf Accessed 13 April 2020

Boyle A, Harrison J (2013) Judicial settlement of international environmental disputes: current problems. Journal of International Dispute Settlement 4:245–276

Chartier B (2018) Chamber for environmental matters: International Court of Justice (ICJ). Max Planck Encyclopedia of Public International Law

Crawford J R (2012) Jurisdiction and applicable law. Leiden Journal of International Law 25:471–479

[156] See generally Liénard 2009, pp. 214–215.

Crawford J R (2019) Military and Paramilitary Activities in and against Nicaragua case (Nicaragua v United States of America). Max Planck Encyclopaedia of Public International Law
Dupuy P-M, Viñuales J E (2018) International environmental law. Cambridge University Press, Cambridge
Fitzmaurice M A (2001) International protection of the environment. Collected Courses of the Hague Academy of International Law 293:9–488
Fitzmaurice M A (2011) International Court of Justice. Optional Clause. Max Planck Encyclopedia of Public International Law
Forteau M (2011) Forum shopping et fragmentation du droit applicable aux relations internationales – le regard de l'internationaliste publiciste. In: Berge J-S et al (eds) La fragmentation du droit applicable aux relations internationales – regards croisés d'internationalistes privatistes et publicistes – actes de la journée d'études du 16 avril 2010. Pedone, Paris, pp 143–163
Forteau M (2013) The diversity of applicable law before international tribunals as a source of forum shopping and fragmentation of international law: an assessment. In: Wolfrum R, Gätzschmann I (eds) International dispute settlement: room for innovations? Springer, Heidelberg, pp 417–441
Fox G (2002) Evaluating environmental trade disputes in the post-Seattle world. In: Brouwer F, Ervin D E (eds) Public concerns, environmental standards and agricultural trade. CABI Publishing, Wallingford, pp 325–347
French D (2006) Environmental dispute settlement: the first (hesitant) signs of spring? Hague Yearbook of International Law 19:3–32
Gaja G (2019) Relationship of the ICJ with other international courts and tribunals. In: Zimmermann A et al (eds) The Statute of the International Court of Justice: a commentary. Oxford University Press, Oxford, pp 647–660
Gathii J T (2020) The promise of international law: a third world view. Grotius Lecture, 2020 virtual meeting of the American Society of International Law
Golitsyn V V (2018) The potential role of the Tribunal in light of its experience after 20 years' judicial activity. ITLOS at 20: Looking into the future, symposium of 18 March 2017
Gomula J (2010) Environmental disputes in the WTO. In: Fitzmaurice M et al (eds) Research handbook on international environmental law. Edward Elgar, Cheltenham, Northampton, pp 401–425
Gourgourinis A (2011) The distinction between interpretation and application of norms in international adjudication. Journal of International Dispute Settlement 2:31–57
Harrison J (2016) The Arctic Sunrise Arbitration (Netherlands *v* Russia). The International Journal of Marine and Coastal Law 31:145–159
Jennings R (1992) The role of the International Court of Justice in the development of international environment protection law. Review of European, Comparative and International Environmental Law 1:240–244
Klein N (2010) Settlement of international environmental law disputes. In: Fitzmaurice M et al (eds) Research handbook on international environmental law. Edward Elgar, Cheltenham/Northampton, pp 379–400
Klein N (2021) International environmental law disputes before international courts and tribunals. In: Rajamani L, Peel J (eds) Oxford Handbook of International Environmental Law. Oxford University Press, Oxford, pp 1040–1055
Koskenniemi M (1991) Peaceful settlement of environmental disputes. Nordic Journal of International Law 60:73–92
Liénard Q (2009) La concurrence des procédures de règlement des différends internationaux environnementaux. II – Le choix du for pour le règlement des différends environnementaux : solutions conventionnelles et applications jurisprudentielles. In: Kerbrat Y (ed) Forum shopping et concurrence des procédures contentieuses internationales. Bruylant, Brussels, pp 211–250
Marceau G (2002) WTO dispute settlement and human rights. European Journal of International Law 13:753–814

McGrady B (2008) Fragmentation of international law or 'systemic integration' of treaty regimes: *EC – Biotech Products* and the proper interpretation of article 31(3)(c) of the Vienna Convention on the Law of Treaties. Journal of World Trade 42:589–618

McLachlan C (2005) The principle of systemic integration and article 31(3)(c) of the Vienna Convention. The International and Comparative Law Quarterly 54:279–319

McRae D (2018) The applicable law – the Geneva Convention on the Continental Shelf, the LOSC, and customary international law. In: Elferink A G O et al (eds) Maritime boundary delimitation: the case law – is it consistent and predictable? Cambridge University Press, Cambridge, pp 92–116

Merkouris P (2015) Article 31(3)(c) VCLT and the principle of systemic integration: normative shadows in Plato's cave. Brill Nijhoff, Leiden

Mitchell A D, Heaton D (2010) The inherent jurisdiction of WTO Tribunals: the select application of public international law required by the judicial function. Michigan Journal of International Law 31:559–620

Mondré A (2015) Forum shopping in international disputes. Palgrave Macmillan, Hampshire, New York

Musto C, Redgwell C (2017) US – Import Prohibition of Certain Shrimp and Shrimp Products (1998). In: Bjorge E, Miles C (eds) Landmark cases in public international law. Hart, Oxford/Portland, OR, pp 489–508

Okowa P N (1998) Environmental dispute settlement: some reflections on recent developments. In: Evans M D (ed) Remedies in international law: the institutional dilemma. Hart, Oxford, pp 157–172

Oxman B H (2015) Courts and tribunals: the ICJ, ITLOS, and arbitral tribunals. In: Rothwell DR et al (eds) The Oxford handbook of the law of the sea. Oxford University Press, Oxford, pp 394–415

Palchetti P (2019) Article 26. In: Zimmermann A et al (eds) The Statute of the International Court of Justice: a commentary. Oxford University Press, Oxford, pp 547–574

Parlett K (2017) Beyond the four corners of the convention: expanding the scope of jurisdiction of law of the sea tribunals. Ocean Development & International Law 48:284–299

Pauwelyn J (2001) The role of public international law in the WTO: how far can we go? The American Journal of International Law 95:535–578

Pauwelyn J, Trachtman J P, Steger D P (2004) The jurisdiction of the World Trade Organization. Proceedings of the Annual Meeting (American Society of International Law) 98:135–146

Payne C R (2010) Pulp Mills on the River Uruguay: the International Court of Justice recognizes environmental impact assessment as a duty under international law. https://www.asil.org/insights/volume/14/issue/9/pulp-mills-river-uruguay-international-court-justice-recognizes Accessed 13 April 2020

Pedersen O W (2018) The European Court of Human Rights and international environmental law. In: Knox J H, Pejan R (eds) The human right to a healthy environment. Cambridge University Press, Cambridge, New York, pp 86–96

Pellet A, Müller D (2019) Article 38. In: Zimmermann A et al (eds) The Statute of the International Court of Justice: a commentary, 3rd edn. Oxford University Press, Oxford, pp 819–962

Popattanachai N (2016) Environmental disputes from regional sea programmes before ITLOS: its potential role, contribution, and the challenges it would face in a land-based pollution case. New Zealand Yearbook of International Law 14:58–93

Ranjeva R (1994) L'environnement, la Cour internationale de Justice et la Chambre spéciale pour les questions de l'environnement. Annuaire français de droit international 40:433–441

Ratliff D P (2001) The PCA Optional Rules for Arbitration of Disputes Relating to Natural Resources and/or the Environment. Leiden Journal of International Law 14: 887–896

Robinson N A (2018) Environmental law: is an obligation *erga omnes* emerging? Panel Discussion at the United Nations, 4 June 2018

Rothwell DR (2004) Building on the strengths and addressing the challenges: the role of law of the sea institutions. Ocean Development and International Law 35:131–156

Sands Ph, Peel J (with Fabra A, Mackenzie R) (2018) Principles of international environmental law. Cambridge University Press, Cambridge

Sepúlveda Amor B (2012) The International Court of Justice and the law of the sea. Anuario Mexicano de Derecho Internacional, Décimo Aniversario 3–26

Seymour J (2006) The International Tribunal for the Law of the Sea: a great mistake? Indiana Journal of Global Legal Studies 13:1–35

Shany Y (2012) Assessing the effectiveness of international courts: a goal-based approach. American Journal of International Law 106:225–270

Stephens T (2009) International courts and environmental protection. Cambridge University Press, Cambridge

Telesetsky A (2018) The International Tribunal for the Law of the Sea: seeking the legitimacy of state consent. In: Grossman N et al (eds) Legitimacy and international courts. Cambridge University Press, Cambridge, pp 174–215

Tzeng P (2016) Jurisdiction and applicable law under UNCLOS. The Yale Law Journal 126:242–260

Villalpando S (2010) The legal dimension of the international community: how community interests are protected in international law. The European Journal of International Law 21:387–419

Vranes E (2005) Jurisdiction and applicable law in WTO dispute settlement. German Yearbook of International Law 48:265–290

Yee S (2016) Article 38 of the ICJ Statute and applicable law: selected issues in recent cases. Journal of International Dispute Settlement 7:472–498

Zhu X, He J (2012) International Court of Justice's impact on international environmental law: focusing on the *Pulp Mills* case. Yearbook of International Environmental Law 23:106–130

Jessica Joly Hébert Ph.D. candidate, CEDIN, Université Paris Nanterre. Former Associate Legal Officer at the International Court of Justice, jessica.joly.hebert@gmail.com. I would like to thank the editors for their useful comments on earlier versions of this chapter, as well as Judge Giorgio Gaja, Miles Jackson and Massimo Lando. All views expressed are entirely my own.

Chapter 14
Access to and Participation in Proceedings Before International Courts and Tribunals

Vladyslav Lanovoy

Contents

Abstract This chapter examines questions concerning access to and participation in proceedings before international courts and tribunals, with an emphasis on disputes that raise issues relevant to the environment. It compares the relevant legal framework and practice of international courts and tribunals which deal exclusively with inter-State disputes to those that primarily examine disputes between private parties and States. It argues that there are significant differences in the approach taken by these two categories of international courts and tribunals. While inter-State mechanisms can be said to have generally resisted broader access and participation of non-parties (with the limited exception of the WTO), regional human rights mechanisms and investor-State tribunals have adopted a more liberal approach. Although there may be benefits to a system which is open to non-party participation, there may also be significant risks from the standpoint of the administration of justice and the need to avoid any unnecessary burden on both the parties and the court or tribunal itself. This chapter seeks to distil and analyse why inter-State mechanisms on the one hand, and mechanisms involving private parties on the other hand, have adopted different approaches to the access to and participation in proceedings by non-parties.

Keywords Access · participation · non-parties · *amicus curiae* · international courts and tribunals

---

V. Lanovoy (✉)
Université Laval, Québec, Canada
e-mail: vladyslavlanovoy@graduateinstitute.ch

E. Sobenes et al. (eds.), *The Environment Through the Lens of International Courts and Tribunals*, https://doi.org/10.1007/978-94-6265-507-2_14

14.1 Introduction

This chapter examines questions relevant to access and participation in the proceedings before international courts and tribunals, with a particular focus on disputes that raise issues relevant to the environment. These questions have been often decried as a significant weakness of the international dispute resolution system insofar as disputes having an environmental aspect are concerned and have served as an argument in favour of establishing some form of permanent environmental court. As used in this chapter, the term 'access' on the one hand encompasses both standing and jurisdiction *ratione personae* in this context. The term 'participation' covers all forms of involvement in the proceedings, excluding requests by third States to formally intervene in the proceedings.[1] Thus, participation includes third States not seeking formal intervention, intergovernmental organizations, and non-governmental organizations who wish to make submissions in the context of contentious or advisory proceedings. These various entities will be referred to as non-parties.

First, this chapter compares the approach taken by various international courts and tribunals to access and participation with an emphasis, where possible, on disputes relating to the environment. It does so by examining, first, inter-State dispute settlement mechanisms, namely inter-State arbitration, the International Court of Justice (ICJ), the International Tribunal for the Law of the Sea (ITLOS), and the World Trade Organization Dispute Settlement Mechanism (WTO DSM). It then turns to those mechanisms that deal with disputes arising between private parties and States, including investor-State dispute settlement system (ISDS) and the three regional human rights mechanisms, namely the European Court of Human Rights (ECtHR), the Inter-American Commission on Human Rights (IACHR) and the Inter-American Court on Human Rights (IACtHR), as well as the African Commission on Human and Peoples' Rights (ACHPR) and the African Court on Human and Peoples' Rights (ACtHPR). While the focus of the chapter is intended to be on disputes with an environmental aspect, these are, of course, only a subset of the cases that serve to illustrate the framework for access and participation by non-parties.[2] That said, disputes with an environmental aspect have an important public law dimension that can be said to more readily justify participation by non-governmental organizations (NGOs) and civil society than disputes involving other subject matter.[3] In the broader sense, these disputes frequently have a direct and more tangible effect on the well-being of persons, their relationship with their government, or society at large. This holds true regardless of whether the case relates to the environment in a broader sense

[1] See e.g. Statute of the International Court of Justice, opened for signature 26 June 1945, entry into force 24 October 1945, Articles 62 and 63. See also Miron and Chinkin 2019a; Miron and Chinkin 2019b.

[2] For various aspects of these questions in the existing doctrine see, e.g., Chinkin 1993; Shelton 1994; Couvreur 1999; Bartholomeusz 2005; Leroux 2006; Vierucci 2008; Francioni 2009; Ishikawa 2010; Ronen 2012; Crema 2013; Gautier 2014; Wiik 2018; Born and Forrest 2019; Baltag 2020.

[3] For literature specifically focusing on the role of NGOs in the context of settlement of disputes having an environmental law component see, e.g., Beyerlin 2001; Lindblom 2005; Zengerling 2013; Lin 2017.

of community interests, be that universal (e.g., relating to climate change), regional or local (e.g., the risk of transboundary harm resulting from the use of common natural resources along the border). Environmental disputes also have an important public law dimension in a narrower sense owing to the impact they could have on smaller and underrepresented communities which may be affected, if not disappear, because of negative effects of, for instance, the exploration or exploitation of natural resources. As such, cases involving environmental law issues often lead to a difficult balancing of competing economic, human and social considerations.

In light of this public law dimension of environmental disputes, the facilitation of participation by non-parties who may have a genuine and substantial interest in the outcome of the dispute, would foster a more inclusive access to justice for victims of environmental harm. Moreover, the insights provided by non-parties may also be valuable, if not necessary, to judges to fully understand the relevant issues in dispute in the exercise of their contentious jurisdiction or to adequately respond to the legal questions posed to them in the context of advisory proceedings. At the same time, one should not lose sight of the need to ensure the efficient and sound administration of justice and the fact that the involvement of non-parties could delay the conduct of the proceedings and increase costs.

Second, this chapter aims to show that the two categories of dispute settlement mechanisms mentioned above, i.e., inter-State mechanisms and those addressing primarily disputes between private parties and States, have taken different approaches in respect of participation of non-parties, also widely referred to as *amicus curiae*.[4] In particular, it argues that inter-State dispute settlement mechanisms, perhaps with the exception of the WTO, have been less open to expanding the participation of NGOs and civil society, even when deciding on cases that have an important public dimension or raise issues of concern relating to common goods of the international community as whole, such as the environment or human rights.[5] By contrast, mechanisms dealing with disputes brought by private parties against the States have been much more accommodating of non-party participation, including from civil society and other interested stakeholders. It will be shown that there are important institutional, pragmatic, and strategic reasons that may explain this difference in approach.

The chapter proceeds as follows. Section 14.2 examines the legal framework that applies to questions of access to and participation in proceedings before international courts and tribunals. Section 14.3 highlights some of the reasons why inter-State dispute settlement mechanisms, on the one hand, and ISDS and regional human rights mechanisms, on the other hand, have taken different approaches to the access or participation of non-parties in the proceedings. Section 14.4 provides conclusions.

---

[4] The origins of the participation of *amicus curiae* are disputed among scholars, namely as to whether they are the creation of the Roman Law or of common law systems. See, e.g., Krislov 1963, p 694; *cf*. Covey Jr 1960, pp. 33–35. For the historical origin and the rationale beyond *amicus curiae*, see Bürli 2017, pp. 19–22.

[5] See generally Wojcikiewicz Almeida 2019 (arguing that the ICJ should 'assume expanded procedural powers' to reinforce the respect for certain community interests).

14.2 The Legal Framework Governing Access to and Participation in the Proceedings

This section examines the relevant legal framework and the practice of the two sets of dispute settlement mechanisms in respect of the question of access to and participation of non-parties in the proceedings. It starts with the key inter-State dispute settlement mechanisms, examining how their respective practice is similar and how it may diverge. It then turns to dispute settlement mechanisms under which a private party may directly espouse its claims against the State, namely ISDS and regional human rights mechanisms.

14.2.1 Inter-State Dispute Settlement Mechanisms

14.2.1.1 Inter-State Arbitration

The roots of the modern conception of dispute settlement can be traced to the 1899 and 1907 Hague Conventions for the Pacific Settlement of International Disputes.[6] Although these recognize a variety of peaceful means of settlement of inter-State disputes, the two Conventions sought to institutionalize international arbitration as a preferred means of settlement. To that end, States Parties established the Permanent Court of Arbitration (PCA), an intergovernmental organization which would facilitate the conduct and administration of arbitrations. International arbitration was foreseen as a chosen means for 'the settlement of differences between States by judges of their own choice, and on the basis of respect for law'.[7] After a series of arbitrations conducted in the pre-World War I period, the PCA entered a long period of dormancy, which coincided with the establishment of a first truly permanent dispute settlement mechanism, namely the Permanent Court of International Justice (PCIJ) in 1920 and its successor the International Court of Justice (ICJ) in 1945.

The renaissance of the PCA in the 1990s was possible due to two important legal developments, namely the proliferation of bilateral investment treaties providing for arbitration based on UNCITRAL Rules,[8] and the fact that the PCA was endowed with certain default functions under those rules, as well as the entry into force of the UN Convention on the Law of the Sea (UNCLOS).[9] Under Part XV of that

[6] Convention for the Pacific Settlement of International Disputes, opened for signature 29 July 1899, 1 Bevans 230, entered into force 5 September 1900 (1899 Convention); Convention for the Pacific Settlement of International Disputes, opened for signature 18 October 1907, 1 Bevans 577, entered into force 26 January 1910 (1907 Convention).

[7] 1899 Convention, above n 6, Article 15; 1907 Convention, above n 6, Article 37.

[8] 'Arbitration Rules of the United Nations Commission on International Trade Law', UN Doc. A/31/98, 15 December 1976 (1976 UNCITRAL Arbitration Rules).

[9] United Nations Convention on the Law of the Sea, opened for signature 10 December 1982, 1833 UNTS 3, entered into force 16 November 1994 (UNCLOS).

Convention, States Parties have a choice among various mechanisms to settle their disputes concerning the interpretation or application of UNCLOS, with an Annex VII arbitration operating by default in the absence of any forum choice made by the Parties or whenever their forum choices do not coincide.[10]

Over time, UNCLOS Annex VII arbitral tribunals have dealt with a number of important issues relating to the protection of the marine environment, including from the standpoint of access and participation by non-parties in the proceedings.[11] As a starting point, it is worth recalling that the procedural rules applicable to Annex VII arbitrations must be 'read and applied in the context of the Convention as a whole, and in particular Part XV, which sets out the dispute settlement system of the Convention'.[12] Article 5 of UNCLOS Annex VII provides that: 'unless the parties to the dispute otherwise agree, the arbitral tribunal shall determine its own procedure, assuring to each party a full opportunity to be heard and to present its case'.[13] This broad power comprises decisions with respect to *amicus curiae* participation and the approach taken to date in this regard by Annex VII tribunals has been largely consistent with that of other dispute settlement mechanisms foreseen under Article 287 UNCLOS, including ITLOS, as will be discussed below.[14]

The *Arctic Sunrise* and *South China Sea* arbitrations are emblematic of this framework, though the decisions taken by the tribunals on the issues of access and participation were very case-specific. The *Arctic Sunrise* case concerned measures taken by the Russian Federation in relation to a vessel operated by Greenpeace International, which staged a protest at the Russian offshore oil platform in the Pechora Sea, and thus had an obvious environmental component. Both ITLOS and an Annex VII tribunal were seized at two different stages of the dispute, namely the request for provisional measures, and the remainder of the procedure, respectively. Both mechanisms were faced with a request (with a submission attached) by Greenpeace International to participate in the proceedings; although not a party, the basis for Greenpeace's interest in the proceedings is obvious. In the absence of any objection to Greenpeace's request by the Netherlands (Russia was not participating), ITLOS 'decided that the request by Greenpeace International should not be accepted and

[10] Ibid., Articles 287(3) and (5). To date, the PCA has administered fourteen Annex VII arbitrations. See https://pca-cpa.org/en/services/arbitration-services/unclos/. Accessed 23 April 2021.

[11] See, e.g., *MOX Plant Case (Ireland v United Kingdom)*, Procedural Order No 3, 24 June 2003, PCA Case No 2002-01; *Dispute Concerning Access to Information Under Article 9 of the OSPAR Convention (Ireland v United Kingdom)*, Decision, 2 July 2003, PCA Case No 2001-03, 23 RIAA 59; *Chagos Marine Protected Area Arbitration (Mauritius v United Kingdom)*, Award, 18 March 2015, PCA Case No 2011-03, 21 RIAA 359; *The Arctic Sunrise Arbitration (Netherlands v Russia)*, Award on the Merits, 14 August 2015, PCA Case No 2014-02, 32 RIAA 205; *South China Sea Arbitration (Philippines v China)*, Award, 12 July 2016, PCA Case No 2013-19, 33 RIAA 153. See also Chap. 4.

[12] Wood and Sthoeger 2020, p. 72.

[13] UNCLOS, above n 9, Annex VII, Article 5.

[14] See Wood and Sthoeger 2020, p. 72 (arguing that this provision 'confers a broad power upon the Tribunal to determine its own procedure', with the tribunal being 'empowered to take any and all procedural steps that it considers necessary for the good administration of justice').

that its submissions would not be included in the case file'.[15] Once the tribunal was constituted under Annex VII, Greenpeace International again applied to participate (again attaching a submission).[16] Although the Netherlands again had no objection to Greenpeace's request and Russia maintained a position of non-appearance, the Annex VII tribunal held that there was 'no sufficient reason to grant Greenpeace International's application' with no further reasons provided.[17] In rejecting an unsolicited *amicus curiae* submission by a non-party (albeit one with an obvious interest in the proceedings), the tribunal adopted an approach, as will be discussed below, that was in line with that of ITLOS and the ICJ, which are the two other dispute settlement mechanisms listed in Part XV of UNCLOS. This is, perhaps, unsurprising since arbitral tribunals set up under Annex VII operate under the same conventional framework as ITLOS and the ICJ regarding the disputes relating to the interpretation or application of UNCLOS. Thus, the benefits of arbitration as a more flexible mechanism of settlement of disputes, which could be more open to non-party participation, are not as pronounced in this setting as they are for instance in the investment treaty arbitration context.[18]

In the *South China Sea* arbitration, a dispute which concerned *inter alia* alleged breaches of obligations under UNCLOS relating to the protection of the marine environment, the tribunal sought to accommodate third States who wished to participate in the proceedings, even though they did not make a formal request to intervene. This was indeed the case with Vietnam, which addressed a Note Verbale to the tribunal on the basis, *inter alia*, that 'its rights and interests of a legal nature in the South China Sea…may be affected'.[19] Vietnam requested that the tribunal 'give due regard to the position of Vietnam' on several issues including, as relevant to the present discussion, its support of 'the Tribunal's competence to interpret and apply' certain environmental obligations in UNCLOS, namely Articles 194(5) and 206.[20] At Vietnam's request, it was granted access to the pleadings and permitted to attend the otherwise closed hearings as an observer.[21] Vietnam also reserved 'the right to seek to intervene'.[22] The tribunal, for its part, stated that it would only address the permissibility of intervention in the event that Vietnam made a formal application to intervene, which it did not ultimately do.[23] Of note, Vietnam was not the only

---

[15] ITLOS, *The 'Arctic Sunrise' Case* (*Netherlands v Russia*), Provisional Measures, Order, 22 November 2013, ITLOS Reports 2013, p. 230, para 15.

[16] *The Artic Sunrise Arbitration* (*Netherlands v Russia*), Procedural Order No. 3, 8 October 2014, PCA Case No 2014-2, p. 2.

[17] Ibid.

[18] See Sect. 14.2.2.1 below.

[19] Socialist Republic of Vietnam, 'Statement of the Ministry of Foreign Affairs of the Socialist Republic of Vietnam Transmitted to the Arbitral Tribunal in the Proceedings between the Republic of the Philippines and the People's Republic of China' (14 December 2014), reproduced in Supplemental Written Submission of the Philippines, vol. VIII, Annex. 468.

[20] *South China Sea Arbitration* (*Philippines v China*), above n 11, pp. 192–193, para 36.

[21] Ibid., p. 188, para 15.

[22] Ibid., p. 193, para 36.

[23] Ibid., p. 195, para 43.

non-party expressing interest in the proceedings. Similar requests and accommodations were made by the tribunal for the informal participation of Malaysia, Japan, Indonesia, Thailand, and Brunei.[24] This informal participation of multiple third States in the proceedings arguably stands at odds with the approach adopted by both ITLOS and Annex VII Tribunal in the *Arctic Sunrise* arbitration in respect of Greenpeace's request to make submissions. There were of course broader and more sensitive issues of the exercise of sovereign rights in the *South China Sea* arbitration, which were certainly of a different nature than those regarding Greenpeace's request in the *Arctic Sunrise*.

Finally, it is noteworthy that various multilateral environmental agreements refer to arbitration as a potential means of dispute settlement.[25] Over its history and in particular in recent years, the PCA has developed substantial experience in administering inter-State arbitrations, including those involving an environmental aspect.[26] Significantly, in 2001, the PCA also adopted a set of Optional Rules for Arbitration of Disputes Relating to the Environment and/or Natural Resources (the 'PCA Environmental Rules') that may be used in settling any dispute concerning the environment, irrespective of whether the parties are States or non-State entities.[27] The PCA Environmental Rules have been used in six instances to date and the disputes in question have mainly involved carbon emissions projects and contracts between entities which buy and sell carbon credits.[28] Because these proceedings have not been made public, it is not known whether arbitral tribunals operating under the Environmental Rules have been asked to or have allowed participation by NGOs or civil society, though this is unlikely, precisely because the proceedings are not public.

---

[24] Ibid., p. 196, para 50.

[25] See, e.g., Convention on International Trade in Endangered Species of Wild Fauna and Flora, opened for signature 3 March 1973, 993 UNTS 243, entered into force 1 July 1975; Convention on the Conservation of Antarctic Marine Living Resources, opened for signature 20 May 1980, 1329 UNTS 47 entered into force 7 April 1982; Protocol to the Antarctic Treaty on Environmental Protection, opened for signature 4 October 1991, 2941 UNTS 9, entered into force 14 January 1998; Convention for the Conservation of Southern Bluefin Tuna, opened for signature 10 May 1993, 1819 UNTS 360, entered into force 20 May 1994; Protocol on Water and Health to the Convention on the Protection and Use of Transboundary Watercourses and International Lakes, opened for signature 17 June 1999, 2331 UNTS 202, entered into force 4 August 2005; Convention on the Transboundary Effects of Industrial Accidents, opened for signature 17 March 1992, 2105 UNTS 457, entered into force 19 April 2000.

[26] See, e.g., *Iron Rhine Arbitration* (*Belgium/Netherlands*), Decision, 24 May 2005, PCA Case No 2003-02, 23 RIAA 35; *Indus Waters Kishenganga Arbitration* (*Pakistan v India*), Final Award, 20 December 2013, PCA Case No 2011-03, 31 RIAA 309.

[27] PCA, 'Optional Rules for Arbitration of Disputes Relating to Natural Resources and/or the Environment', available at https://docs.pca-cpa.org/2016/01/Optional-Rules-for-Arbitration-of-Disputes-Relating-to-the-Environment-and_or-Natural-Resources.pdf (last accessed 15 February 2021). See also Ratliff 2001; Meshel 2016, para 11 (acknowledging the advantage of the Environmental Rules in ensuring 'greater accessibility to the process' in disputes related to climate change).

[28] Meshel 2016, para 14.

14.2.1.2 ICJ

Unlike arbitration, the ICJ is a permanent judicial body, which has certain inherent advantages in terms of continuity of its settled jurisprudence and thus predictability to States, but also important institutional and functional limitations. As a principal judicial organ of the United Nations (UN), its Statute forms an integral part of the UN Charter and thus the possibility of amendments is rather remote given the qualified majority that is required.[29] Thus, the ICJ's basic rules governing access and participation, which can be found in Articles 34, 65 and 66 of the Statute, in addition to Articles 62-63 concerning the formal intervention of third States, should be considered effectively permanent.

Pursuant to Article 34(1) of the Statute, only States may be parties in cases before the Court. However, this 'strict monopoly'[30] does not detract from the fact that the Court may request, pursuant to Article 34(2), information from 'public international organizations' if it deems it to be relevant to the case in the exercise of its contentious jurisdiction. Article 34(2), in turn, cross-refers to the Rules of Court, which unlike the Statute may be amended by the Court itself. In that context, Article 69 of the Rules of Court details the procedural framework in which 'public international organizations' can be requested to or may furnish information on their own initiative. Importantly, Article 69(4) of the Rules of Court limits the term 'public international organization' to international organizations of States. As a result of this narrow application of the Statute by the Court, only a limited set of entities may be allowed to take part in the proceedings. This includes third States who may apply to intervene on the basis of Articles 62 or 63 of the Statute, if a number of conditions are satisfied, or inter-governmental organizations which may be requested by the Court or furnish information on their own initiative in accordance with Article 34(2) of the Statute.

The wording of Article 66 of the Statute, however, which is applicable to advisory proceedings appears to be more inclusive, when it refers to 'any…international organization'. This has prompted considerable debate as to whether submissions by NGOs and members of civil society could fall within its scope of application. In its practice concerning advisory proceedings, however, the Court has consistently sought to align its interpretation of the term 'international organization' in Article 66(2) of the Statute with that of 'public international organization' under Article 34(2) of its Statute and 69(4) of the Rules of Court. On only one occasion, in its early history, had the Court taken the view that an organization which was not strictly speaking intergovernmental could submit its views in the advisory proceedings. This was in respect of the request originating from the International League for the Rights of Man in the context of the *International Status of South West Africa*, which the Court considered 'likely to assist [it] in its examination of legal questions put to it'.[31] The submission never actually materialized.

---

[29] Statute of the ICJ, above n 1, Article 69.

[30] Dupuy and Hoss 2019, para 1.

[31] *International Status of South West Africa*, Advisory Opinion, 11 July 1950, ICJ Reports 1950, Correspondence, Letter No 18, p. 327.

The subsequent practice of the Court has, however, held the line of limiting any such submissions to those made by intergovernmental organizations[32] and efforts to capitalize on the precedent of *International Status of South West Africa* have been unsuccessful.[33] In response to one such attempt by Professor Reisman to participate as an *amicus curiae* in the *Namibia* advisory opinion proceedings, the Registrar explained that the Court's willingness to receive a written statement from the International League for the Rights of Man was premised on the fact that it was 'an international organisation which could be considered by the Court as likely to be able to furnish information on the question' within the meaning of Article 66(2) of the Statute and was not to be interpreted as a precedent for the participation of private parties in advisory proceedings before the Court.[34] On that occasion, the Registrar of the Court informed Professor Reisman that he 'believe[d] that the Court would be unwilling to open the floodgate to what might be a vast amount of proffered assistance' and that in his opinion 'a negative answer must be given to [the question whether the Court would accept and consider a document, in the form of a memorial, from an individual or group], whatever justification for describing the volunteer as an *amicus curiae* may exist'.[35]

The *Legality of the Threat or Use of Nuclear Weapons* is one of the few advisory opinions in the Court's history which touches directly on questions regarding the environment. Because the Court stopped publishing correspondence (like the Registrar's communication above) in 1994, there is little public information on the various attempts of NGOs and civil society seeking to make submissions in those proceedings. However, the information which is available in the public domain suggests that a number of NGOs and other entities sought to participate in the proceedings.[36] For example, in his dissenting opinion in the *Legality of the Threat or Use of Nuclear Weapons*, Judge Weeramantry noted that '[a] multitude of organizations, including several NGOs, have also sent communications to the Court and submitted materials to it'.[37] He also noted that '[t]hough these organizations and individuals have not made formal submissions to the Court, they evidence a groundswell of global public opinion which is not without legal relevance'.[38] The Registrar of the Court at the time confirmed that the submissions from NGOs and individuals were placed at the

---

[32] See, e.g., *Legal Consequences for States of the Continued Presence of South Africa in Namibia (South West Africa) notwithstanding Security Council Resolution 276 (1970)*, Advisory Opinion, ICJ Reports 1971, Correspondence, Letters No 18, 21, 23, 29, 34, 35, 41, 42, 89, 94, 97, 98.

[33] See Lindblom 2005, pp. 303–310.

[34] *Legal Consequences for States of the Continued Presence of South Africa in Namibia (South West Africa) notwithstanding Security Council Resolution 276 (1970)*, Advisory Opinion, 21 June 1971, ICJ Reports 1971, Letter No 21, pp. 638–639.

[35] Ibid.

[36] Wiik 2018, p. 98.

[37] *Legality of the Threat or Use of Nuclear Weapons*, Advisory Opinion, 8 July 1996, ICJ Reports 1996, p. 226, Dissenting Opinion of Judge Weeramantry, p. 438.

[38] Ibid.

ICJ library for consultation by Members of the Court without forming part of the case file.[39]

In 2004, the Court adopted its Practice Direction XII, by which it clarified any ambiguity that may have been left in the Statute and the Court's practice in respect of submissions from NGOs and civil society in the context of advisory proceedings. Pursuant to that Practice Direction, such submissions will not form part of the case file but 'shall be treated as publications readily available and may accordingly be referred to by States and intergovernmental organizations presenting written and oral statements in the case in the same manner as publications in the public domain'.[40] Two points relating to the scope of application of this Practice Direction are well settled. First, the material scope of this Practice Direction is limited to advisory proceedings and does not apply in respect of the Court's contentious jurisdiction. Second, the Practice Direction only speaks of 'international non-governmental organizations', which would then exclude domestic NGOs or other private parties wishing to make submissions. Commentators have taken slightly different angles on the practical impact of this practice direction. Wiik, for instance, has argued that it 'constitutes a *de minimis* acknowledgement of the existence of submissions by entities other than those mentioned in Article 66(2) ICJ Statute' and while it 'solidifies the legal *status quo*…it can be seen as an assurance to parties that the Court will not rely on an inherent power to admit *amici curiae* against their express wishes'.[41] According to Watts, on the other hand, '[t]he Court has developed and put on a more formal footing its previous informal practice, reflecting a neat compromise between on the one hand treating non-governmental organizations in exactly the same way as governmental organizations and, on the other hand, banishing them from all participation in Advisory Opinion cases'.[42] Others have considered the Practice Direction XII to be a 'hesitant' acknowledgement of the growing importance of the work of NGOs and the reaction to their submissions in *Legality of the Threat or Use of Nuclear Weapons*.[43]

The absence of a formal mechanism for participation of non-parties before the Court has not prevented NGOs and civil society from making unsolicited submissions in the context of advisory proceedings or lobbying States to bring contentious cases before the Court. For instance, Dupuy and Hoss refer to the example of the *Obligation to Prosecute or Extradite* (*Belgium v Senegal*), a case in which the Human Rights Watch played an instrumental role in Belgium's decision to bring a case before the ICJ on the basis of the Convention against Torture.[44] In the *Arrest Warrant* (*DRC*

[39] Valencia-Ospina 2005, p. 231.

[40] ICJ, Practice Direction XII. https://www.icj-cij.org/en/practice-directions. Accessed 23 April 2021.

[41] Wiik 2018, pp. 99, 185–186.

[42] Watts 2004, pp. 392–393.

[43] Paulus 2019, pp. 1828–1829, para 26; Rosenne 2006, para 107.

[44] Dupuy and Hoss 2019, p. 666, para 4.

v Belgium) case, Belgium in its counter-memorial submitted and relied on a 750-page memorandum on universal jurisdiction prepared by the NGO Amnesty International.[45] Although the Court's judgment did not mention this memorandum, Judge *ad hoc* Van den Wyngaert referred to it on multiple occasions in her dissenting opinion.[46] NGOs' reports and statements have often figured prominently in the written pleadings of the parties in the context of disputes raising issues relevant to the environment.[47] Of course, the indirect participation of NGOs in the proceedings, whether through informal lobbying practices next to States or the use of their materials in the parties' pleadings, is fundamentally different from having formal standing to make submissions.

Finally, certain commentators have posited that NGOs and other members of civil society could be involved in ICJ proceedings through the framework set out for expert evidence, namely Article 50 of the Court's Statute, which refers to the Court's power to appoint as an expert 'any individual, body, bureau, commission or other organization'.[48] In general, the Court's practice of appointing its own experts remains relatively scant to date.[49] In a number of the environmental and scientifically complex cases decided in recent decades, the Court has refrained from appointing its own experts.[50] The Parties to disputes themselves, on the other hand, have presented expert evidence, including expert reports commissioned by NGOs. In *Certain Activities* (*Compensation*), for instance, an expert report commissioned by Costa Rica from a

[45] *Arrest Warrant of 11 April 2000* (*DRC v Belgium*), Counter-Memorial of the Kingdom of Belgium, 28 September 2001, pp. 80 and 104. See also Wiik 2018, pp. 436–437.

[46] *Arrest Warrant of 11 April 2000* (*DRC v Belgium*), Judgment, 14 February 2002, ICJ Reports 2002, Dissenting Opinion of Judge *ad hoc* Van den Wyngaert, pp. 154 and 165.

[47] See, e.g., *Gabčikovo-Nagymaros Project* (*Hungary v Slovakia*), Memorial of 2 May 1994, Vol. 5, Part 2, Annex 20, p. 841; ICJ, *Pulp Mills on the River Uruguay* (*Argentina v Uruguay*), Counter-Memorial of Uruguay, 20 July 2007, paras 3.16, 5.41 and 7.29; ICJ, *Aerial Herbicide Spraying* (*Ecuador v Colombia*), Memorial of Ecuador, 28 April 2009, para 6.14 and Vol. 4, Annex 162.

[48] Shelton 1994, p. 628; Lindblom 2005, pp. 309–310.

[49] See *Corfu Channel* (*Albania v United Kingdom*), Merits, Judgment, 9 April 1949, ICJ Reports 1949, pp. 20–22; *Corfu Channel* (*Albania v United Kingdom*), Compensation, Judgment, 15 December 1949, ICJ Reports 1949, p. 244; *Delimitation of the Maritime Boundary in the Gulf of Maine Area* (*Canada/United States*), Appointment of Expert, Order, 30 March 1984, ICJ Reports 1984, p 166; *Maritime Delimitation in the Caribbean Sea and the Pacific Ocean* (*Costa Rica v Nicaragua*), Decision to obtain an expert opinion, Order, 31 May 2016, ICJ Reports 2016, p 235 and Appointment of experts, Order of 16 June 2016, ICJ Reports 2016, p 240; *Armed Activities on the Territory of the Congo (DRC v Uganda)*, Appointment of experts, Order, 12 October 2020, available at https://www.icj-cij.org/public/files/case-related/116/116-20201012-ORD-01-00-EN.pdf (last accessed 23 April 2021).

[50] See, e.g., *Whaling in the Antarctic* (*Australia v Japan: New Zealand intervening*), Judgment, 31 March 2014, ICJ Reports 2014, p. 226; *Pulp Mills on the River Uruguay* (*Argentina v Uruguay*), Judgment, 20 April 2010, ICJ Reports 2010, p. 14, see in particular Joint Dissenting Opinion of Judges Al-Khasawneh and Simma, pp. 116–117, para 17; *Certain Activities Carried Out by Nicaragua in the Border Area* (*Costa Rica v Nicaragua*), Compensation, Judgment, 2 February 2018, ICJ Reports 2018, p. 15. For an excellent recent study on the environmental law dispute settlement in the Court's jurisprudence, see Sulyok 2021.

Costa Rican NGO, Fundación Neotrópica, provided the methodology that Costa Rica relied upon for its valuation of the environmental damages it alleged were caused by Nicaragua.[51]

14.2.1.3 ITLOS

ITLOS's legal framework and practice in relation to questions of access to and participation in the proceedings is very similar to that of the ICJ. Indeed, the latter's statute and rules served as a model for the former. There are, however, subtle but important differences between the two.

First, ITLOS is open to 'States Parties' to UNCLOS,[52] which includes entities other than States such 'international organizations in accordance with Annex IX'.[53] According to Article 1 of Annex IX UNCLOS, '"international organization" means an intergovernmental organization constituted by States to which its member States have transferred competence over matters governed by this Convention, including competence to enter into treaties in respect of those matters'.[54] In practice, the only international organization currently party to UNCLOS is the European Union (EU).

Second, ITLOS 'shall be open to entities other than States Parties only as specifically provided for in this Convention'. [55] This is a reference to 'States or international organisations that are not parties to the Convention', but which may still have access to ITLOS.[56] In this respect, under Article 20(2) of the Statute of ITLOS, access to ITLOS extends also to 'any case submitted pursuant to any other agreement conferring jurisdiction on the Tribunal which is accepted by all the parties to that case',[57] which is in line with the general clause on jurisdiction of Part XV UNCLOS dispute settlement mechanisms.[58] Moreover, the reference to 'entities other than States Parties' also covers entities that may be party to proceedings before the ITLOS Seabed Disputes Chamber, the jurisdiction of which is limited to the 'activities in the Area' in accordance with Articles 187 and 188 of the Convention.[59] Access to the ITLOS Seabed Disputes Chamber is open to a wide range of entities, including States Parties, the International Seabed Authority (ISA), the Enterprise, State enterprises, and natural and juridical persons sponsored by the State to undertake the activities in the Area.[60]

---

[51] *Certain Activities Carried Out by Nicaragua in the Border Area* (*Costa Rica v Nicaragua*), above n 50, p. 29, para 45.

[52] UNCLOS, above n 9, Article 291(1) and Annex VI, Statute of ITLOS, Article 20(1).

[53] Ibid., Article 305.

[54] Ibid., Annex IX, Article 1.

[55] Ibid., Article 291(2).

[56] See also Lekkas and Staker 2017, p. 2373, para 7.

[57] UNCLOS, above n 9, Annex VI, Statute of ITLOS, Article 20(2).

[58] Ibid., Article 288.

[59] See Treves 2017, p. 1880, para 4.

[60] UNCLOS, above n 9, Article 187.

Third, contrary to the Statute of the ICJ, the Convention and the Statute of ITLOS are silent on its general competence to render advisory opinions. In fact, only the ITLOS Seabed Disputes Chamber has the explicit authority to give advisory opinions at the request of the Assembly or the Council of the International Seabed Authority (ISA) on legal questions arising within the scope of their activities.[61] However, in the *Request for Advisory Opinion submitted by the Sub-Regional Fisheries Commission (SFRC)* (hereinafter '*Fisheries* Advisory Opinion'), ITLOS found that it had general competence to give an advisory opinion on the basis of Article 21 of its Statute, which refers to the jurisdiction of the Tribunal over '*all matters* specifically provided for in any other agreement which confers jurisdiction on the Tribunal', read together with Article 33 of the MAC Convention, the regional legal instrument on the basis of which the request was submitted.[62] ITLOS further held that Article 138 of its Rules, which expressly recognizes the Tribunal's advisory competence, 'furnishes the prerequisites that need to be satisfied before the Tribunal can exercise its advisory jurisdiction'.[63] Admittedly, the reasoning of the Tribunal is not beyond reproach, as demonstrated elsewhere.[64] This example does, however, demonstrate how international courts and tribunals may sidestep apparent limitations found in their foundational instruments concerning questions of competence and access, though as noted above in relation to the ICJ, they are not always willing to do so.

Fourth, insofar as participation of non-parties in the proceedings before ITLOS is concerned, similar limitations to those discussed in the context of the ICJ apply *mutatis mutandis*, albeit there are some noticeable differences in practice. As in the case of the ICJ, there is no formal means to make *amicus curiae* submissions or otherwise allow meaningful participation by entities other than States Parties or intergovernmental organizations. In the context of its contentious jurisdiction, ITLOS may request an intergovernmental organization or receive from an intergovernmental organization at its own initiative information relevant to a case before ITLOS.[65] Article 84(4) of its Rules defines an 'intergovernmental organization' in this context as 'an intergovernmental organization other than any organization which is a party or intervenes in the case concerned'.[66] This provision, however, has not yet been used.[67] As noted earlier, the only attempt thus far in the context of a preliminary stage of a contentious case before ITLOS was that by Greenpeace in the *Artic Sunrise* case, which was denied.[68] It is unclear on what basis Greenpeace's request was being

[61] Ibid., Article 191.

[62] ITLOS, *Request for an Advisory Opinion Submitted by the Sub-Regional Fisheries Commission (SFRC)*, Advisory Opinion, 2 April 2015, ITLOS Reports 2015, p. 22, para 58. MAC Convention stands for the Convention on the definition of the minimum access conditions and exploitation of fisheries resources within the maritime zone under the jurisdiction of SFRC Member States.

[63] Ibid., p. 22, para 59.

[64] Lando 2016.

[65] ITLOS Rules, Article 84.

[66] Ibid., Article 84(4).

[67] Wiik 2018, p. 101.

[68] ITLOS, *The 'Arctic Sunrise' Case (Netherlands v Russian Federation)*, above n 15, p. 230, para 15.

formulated, but in any case, one may conclude that Article 84 of ITLOS Rules was and is likely to be interpreted narrowly, thus effectively excluding NGOs from contentious proceedings.

By contrast, an interesting practice has developed in the context of the advisory proceedings before ITLOS, both in terms of access to and participation in such proceedings by both intergovernmental and non-governmental organizations. As with contentious cases, there is no express provision in the Statute or the Rules in respect of *amicus curiae* participation by non-parties. Articles 133 and 138 of the Rules of ITLOS do, however, require the Registrar of ITLOS to give notice to intergovernmental organizations which are likely to be able to furnish information on the question being considered by the Chamber or the Tribunal, respectively. As such, intergovernmental organizations may be invited to make written and oral submissions. The Statute and the Rules are, however, silent insofar as submissions by NGOs are concerned, a point which is worth retaining when briefly examining the practice of ITLOS and its Seabed Chamber in two advisory opinions proceedings concluded thus far.

In the Advisory Opinion on the *Responsibilities and Obligations of States with respect to Activities in the Area*, the Seabed Disputes Chamber clarified important features of the legal regime governing exploration and exploitation of the mineral resources in the Area, including the measures expected from States sponsoring contracts for the deep seabed mining and the scope of their liability in the event damage to the marine environment occurs.[69] A number of intergovernmental organizations participated in the proceedings on the basis of Article 133 of the Rules of ITLOS.[70] For our purposes, the most interesting aspect was the participation in the proceedings by the International Union for Conservation of Nature and Natural Resources (IUCN), which submitted a detailed written statement to the ITLOS Seabed Chamber. While the IUCN was invited to participate, its legal status as an intergovernmental organization may be questionable given that it comprises both governmental and non-governmental members.[71] Thus, the invitation extended to the IUCN to participate in written and oral proceedings indicates that ITLOS will approach the term 'intergovernmental organization' in Article 133 of the Rules of ITLOS with some flexibility. In other words, an organization which is, at least partially, composed of sovereign States would be considered as an 'intergovernmental organization' within the meaning of that provision.

The approach of allowing full participation to the IUCN can be contrasted with the way in which the Seabed Chamber considered an unsolicited joint written statement from two prominent international NGOs, Greenpeace International and the World Wildlife Fund for Nature (WWF), which sought to participate in the advisory proceedings. Although there is no express provision on unsolicited submissions from

---

[69] ITLOS, *Responsibilities and Obligations of States sponsoring persons and entities with respect to Activities in the Area*, Advisory Opinion, 1 February 2011, ITLOS Reports 2011, p. 10.

[70] ITLOS, *Responsibilities and Obligations of States sponsoring persons and entities with respect to Activities in the Area*, Order, 18 May 2010, ITLOS Reports 2010, p. 39, at p. 41.

[71] Gautier 2014, p. 213.

NGOs in UNCLOS, the Statute, or the Rules of ITLOS, the Seabed Chamber followed the same approach as the ICJ. It decided not to allow Greenpeace International and WWF to participate in the proceedings as *amici curiae* and did not include their joint statement in the case file, as their submission did not comply with Article 133 of the Rules of ITLOS. Nonetheless, the Chamber transmitted their joint statement to the States Parties, the ISA, and intergovernmental organizations participating in the advisory proceedings. The Chamber also decided that the joint statement would be made publicly available on its website.

This is at odds with the practice of the ICJ, which is to make such unsolicited submissions publicly available, but only at the Peace Palace in The Hague. 'Publicly available' is thus not tantamount to readily available as interested parties would need physical access to those documents at the Peace Palace. Thus, by posting such submissions on its website, ITLOS has taken the practice of the ICJ a step further by making them both publicly *and* readily available to all interested parties.[72] According to the former Registrar of ITLOS, now the Registrar of the ICJ, the Seabed Chamber 'followed an approach similar to the ICJ's, while developing its own practice'.[73]

ITLOS, in its full composition, when requested by the Sub-Regional Fisheries Commission (SFRC) to give an advisory opinion, followed the practice of its Seabed Chamber. Thus, in its 2015 *Fisheries* advisory opinion, ITLOS recognized that it had the competence to give an advisory opinion on a legal question if an international agreement related to the purposes of the Convention specifically provides for the submission to the Tribunal of a request for such an opinion. Beyond the intergovernmental organizations, including IUCN which was again invited to make submissions under Article 133 of the Rules of ITLOS,[74] the Tribunal received an unsolicited submission from the WWF and treated it in the same way as the Seabed Chamber, i.e., by publishing it on the website.[75] Interestingly, in their submissions, States Parties and intergovernmental organizations which participated in the proceedings referred to the WWF submission on several occasions.[76] This shows some level of impact of the NGO's views in the context of the advisory proceedings which consider environmental issues. As noted by Wiik, '[c]ompared with the ICJ, this facilitation of access to the submissions signals a greater openness to *amicus curiae* and encourages states parties and intergovernmental organizations to take them into account in their submissions'.[77]

---

[72] Wiik 2018, p. 102.

[73] Gautier 2014, p. 215.

[74] ITLOS, *Request for Advisory Opinion submitted by the Sub-Regional Fisheries Commission*, Order, 24 May 2013, ITLOS Reports 2013, p. 202.

[75] ITLOS, *Request for Advisory Opinion submitted by the Sub-Regional Fisheries Commission*, Advisory Opinion, 2 April 2015, above n 62, p. 13, para 23.

[76] Gautier 2014, p. 215.

[77] Wiik 2018, p. 102.

14.2.1.4 WTO

A final mechanism to be considered is that of World Trade Organization (WTO). The WTO Dispute Settlement Understanding (DSU) reflects many of the limitations inherent to inter-State dispute settlement mechanisms, like the ICJ or ITLOS, in particular by restricting access and jurisdiction *ratione personae* to States Parties, i.e., Members of the WTO. Only Member States may formally intervene as third parties in any given dispute.[78] While only parties to the dispute may appeal a panel report, third parties with a substantial interest in the matter may seek to make written and/or oral submissions before the Appellate Body.[79] That said, unlike other inter-State dispute settlement mechanisms, the WTO has developed a more considerable practice of when it should allow entities other than States to make submissions as *amici curiae* at both levels of its procedure, namely before Panels and the Appellate Body.[80] As a starting point, not unlike the Statutes of the ICJ or ITLOS, the DSU contains no provision on non-parties or *amici curiae*.[81]

The practice of the WTO in allowing submissions from non-parties starts with the *United States—Shrimp* (*1998*) case, which was incidentally 'the first dispute adjudicated under the [WTO] dispute resolution system in which the complex relationship between international trade regulation and the protection of the environment was at issue'.[82] In that case, the Panel received two unsolicited *amicus curiae* briefs from NGOs, namely the WWF and a joint submission by the Center for Marine Conservation (CMC) and the Center for International Environmental Law (CIEL). In response to these submissions, the complainants in that case (India, Malaysia, Pakistan and Thailand) requested that the Panel should not consider the content of those submissions.[83] The respondent, the US, on the other hand, stressed that the Panel could seek information from any relevant source under Article 13 of the DSU and urged the Panel to avail itself of any relevant information contained in the two submissions.[84] The Panel declined to consider the *amicus curiae* submissions on the basis that they were incompatible with the DSU framework. Specifically, it found that as the submissions had not been solicited by the Panel itself, they should not be accepted as 'pursuant to Article 13 of the DSU, the initiative to seek information

---

[78] WTO, Dispute Settlement Rules: Understanding on Rules and Procedures Governing the Settlement of Disputes, Marrakesh Agreement Establishing the World Trade Organization, Annex 2, opened for signature 14 April 1994, 1869 UNTS 401, 33 ILM 1226, Articles 4(11) and 10(2).

[79] Ibid., Article 17(4).

[80] Ibid., Article 2 sets out the competencies of the Dispute Settlement Body (DSB), which has 'the authority to establish panels, adopt panel and Appellate Body reports, maintain surveillance of implementation of rulings and recommendations, and authorize suspension of concessions and other obligations under the covered agreements'.

[81] WTO Secretariat 2017, p. 163.

[82] Oesch 2014, para 1.

[83] WTO, *United States—Import Prohibition of Certain Shrimp and Shrimp Products*, Panel Report, 15 May 1998, WT/DS58/R, para 5.1 et seq., para 7.7.

[84] Ibid.

and to select the source of information rests with the Panel. In any other situations, only parties and third parties are allowed to submit information directly to the Panel'.[85] The Appellate Body, however, disagreed with the Panel, opting for a broader interpretation of Article 13 DSU, considering that 'authority to seek information is not properly equated with a prohibition on accepting information which has been submitted without having been requested by a panel'.[86] The WTO Appellate Body also clarified that nothing prevented the disputing parties from incorporating into their own written submissions excerpts or reports prepared by NGOs and civil society.[87]

In the subsequent practice of the WTO DSM, the Appellate Body confirmed that the same principles in respect of the Panel's capacity to accept and consider unsolicited *amicus curiae* submissions applied *mutatis mutandis* to the Appellate Body itself. In *United States—Lead and Bismuth II (2000)*, the Appellate Body recalled that it had 'no legal duty to accept or consider unsolicited *amicus curiae* briefs submitted by individuals or organizations, not Members of the WTO'.[88] However, it found that it 'has broad authority to adopt procedural rules which do not conflict with any rules and procedures in the DSU or the covered agreements' and held that it had 'the legal authority to decide whether or not to accept and consider any information' it believed to be pertinent and useful in an appeal.[89] Ultimately, however, it did not find it necessary 'to take the two *amicus curiae* filed into account in rendering [its] decision'.[90]

In *European Communities (EC)—Asbestos*, the Appellate Body went much further by setting up a detailed *ad hoc* procedure for *amicus curiae* participation on the WTO website, which contained a generic invitation to all interested parties to apply for leave to make submissions.[91] This decision prompted a backlash from the WTO Member States. The adoption and the publication of this *ad hoc* procedure led to an urgently convened General Council meeting on 22 November 2000, at which the vast majority of member States condemned *amicus curiae* participation and accused the Appellate Body of acting *ultra vires*.[92] It is perhaps unsurprising then that the Appellate Body rejected all 17 *amicus curiae* submissions in that case on the basis of alleged procedural irregularities.[93] This also set a new trend for subsequent practice

[85] Ibid., para 7.8.

[86] WTO, *United States—Import Prohibition of Certain Shrimp and Shrimp Products*, Appellate Body Report, 12 October 1998, WTO/DS58/AB/R, para 108.

[87] Ibid., para 89.

[88] WTO, *United States—Imposition of Countervailing Duties on Certain Hot-Rolled Lead and Bismuth Carbon Steel Products Originating in the United Kingdom*, Appellate Body Report, 10 May 2000, WT/DS138/AB/R, para 41.

[89] Ibid., paras 36 and 42.

[90] Ibid., para 42.

[91] WTO, *European Communities—Measures Affecting Asbestos and Asbestos-Containing Products*, Appellate Body Report, 12 March 2001, WT/DS135/AB/R, paras 50–52 (*EC—Asbestos*).

[92] WTO General Council, Minutes of the Meeting of 22 November 2000, WT/GC/M/60, 23 January 2001, in particular paras 11–21. See also Wiik 2018, p. 110.

[93] *EC—Asbestos*, above n 91, para 56.

of the Appellate Body on any such unsolicited non-party submissions.[94] In most cases after the *EC—Asbestos*, the Appellate Body 'has either rejected the briefs without explanation or found them not necessary to consider.'[95]

Panels, on the other hand, have showed greater engagement with unsolicited non-party submissions, but have still normally considered discrete issues within those submissions or those parts that have been integrated, often *verbatim*, into the parties' pleadings.[96] As noted in an empirical analysis conducted by Squatrito in 2018:

> [i]n total, 21 of 144 (15%) panel reports have involved disputes to which there were *amici* filed. Amici were submitted in 17 out of 70 (or 24%) of the disputes reviewed by the Appellate Body where reports were circulated through 2014. Of all disputes brought to the WTO DSM, only 30 had *amicus* submissions at either or both the panel and AB.[97]

The number of *amici curiae* in the WTO dispute settlement proceedings are impressive when compared to other inter-State dispute settlement mechanisms. However, despite the initial openness showed by the Appellate Body to *amicus curiae* submissions, the political backlash that followed within the organization and the subsequent practice show a trend of much greater restraint in admitting such submissions. What is more, the treatment of such submissions is in nearly all cases limited to two or three lines in the introductory section of the Panel or Appellate Body reports, unless as noted above they have been integrated into the parties' pleadings. Thus, it could be said that the relative openness of the WTO DSM has only been partly successful. Be that as it may, it shows how the absence of a clear prohibition in the constitutive elements of the organization has allowed its dispute settlement mechanism to rely on its inherent powers so as to allow greater participation by NGOs and civil society, including in fundamental matters such as the environment.

14.2.2 Other Dispute Settlement Mechanisms

By comparison to the inter-State dispute settlement mechanisms analysed above, this section will examine the two examples of dispute settlement mechanisms which

[94] See, e.g., WTO, *European Communities —Measures Prohibiting the Importation and Marketing of Seal Products*, Appellate Body Report, 22 May 2014, WT/DS400/AB/R and WT/DS401/AB/R, para 1.15; WTO, *United States—Measures concerning the Importation, Marketing and Sale of Tuna and Tuna Products*, Appellate Body Report, 16 May 2012, WT/DS381/AB/R, para 8; WTO, *Brazil—Measures Affecting Imports of Retreaded Tyres*, Appellate Body Report, 3 December 2007, WT/DS332/AB/R, para 7; WTO, *United States—Final Countervailing Duty Determination with Respect to Certain Softwood Lumber from Canada*, Appellate Body Report, 19 January 2004, WT/DS257/AB/R, para 9.

[95] Squatrito 2018, pp. 71–73.

[96] See, e.g., WTO, *European Communities —Measures Affecting Asbestos and Asbestos-Containing Products*, Panel Report, 18 September 2000, WT/DS135/R, para 8.12; WTO, *Brazil—Measures Affecting Imports of Retreaded Tyres,* Panel Report, 12 June 2007, WT/DS332/R, para 1.8; WTO, *European Communities—Measures Prohibiting the Importation and Marketing of Seal Products*, Panel Report, 25 November 2013, WT/DS400/R and WT/DS401/R, para 1.17.

[97] Squatrito 2018, p. 70.

deal predominantly with cases between private parties and States. While some of the same limitations that have been encountered in inter-State context continue to apply here, these mechanisms have been more proactive in opening up their respective systems to involving non-parties in their proceedings and thus fostering a perception of greater substantive engagement with their submissions.

14.2.2.1 Investor-State Arbitral Tribunals

Investor-State Dispute Settlement (ISDS) arbitration proceedings have a number of distinct features when compared to the inter-State mechanisms analysed above. For one, their jurisdiction is not limited to States and the vast majority of cases concerns claims by investors against States (albeit with very limited recent examples of counterclaims) on the basis of international investment agreements (IIAs). These cases are normally conducted pursuant to a handful of procedural rules with varying degrees of prescriptiveness, which may partly explain the greater flexibility of this form of dispute settlement concerning the participation of non-parties. Depending on whether the arbitration is to be conducted under the auspices of the International Centre for Settlement of Investment Disputes (ICSID), in accordance with the UN Commission on International Trade Law Arbitration Rules (UNCITRAL), or some other set of rules, additional jurisdictional requirements may have to be satisfied. For example, Article 25 of the ICSID Convention sets out certain additional limitations to the exercise of jurisdiction *ratione personae* within the auspices of the Convention, namely by qualifying that it concerns 'any legal dispute arising directly out of an investment' and by defining what constitutes a 'national of another Contracting State'.[98] In other cases, where the specific rules are silent on additional requirements concerning jurisdiction *ratione personae*, the IIAs govern the question exhaustively. Jurisdictional objections thus frequently concern whether there is a qualifying investor or investment, or whether the investor has indeed the nationality of the other Contracting State, or whether the investor has satisfied the specific requirements of the arbitration clause in the IIA. Although access to ISDS is thus limited to qualifying investors, the nature of contested measures which often result from the host States' exercise of their regulatory powers in areas such as the environment, has increasingly triggered the interest of non-parties to participate as *amicus curiae*.

One of the first ISDS decisions to consider *amicus curiae* submissions was the 2001 *Methanex v United States* case. This was a NAFTA case considered under the 1976 UNCITRAL Arbitration Rules and had an important environmental component relating to the State of California's ban on the sale and use of the gasoline additive known as 'MTBE' (methyl tertiary-butyl ether). The tribunal ruled that there was 'nothing in either the [1976] UNCITRAL Arbitration Rules or [NAFTA Chapter 11] that either expressly confers upon the Tribunal the power to accept amici submissions

[98] Convention on the Settlement of Investment Disputes between States and Nationals of other States, opened for signature 18 March 1965, 575 UNTS 159, entered into force 14 October 1966.

or expressly provides that the Tribunal shall have no such power'.[99] By relying on the practice of the WTO Appellate Body and of the Iran-US Claims Tribunal, the tribunal ruled that it had an implied authority to permit *amicus* participation having regard to its broad procedural powers under Article 15(1) of the 1976 UNCITRAL Arbitration Rules.[100] Following the *Methanex* case, the NAFTA Free Trade Commission issued a Statement on Non-Disputing Party Participation on 7 October 2003, codifying the rules with respect to *amicus curiae* participation in NAFTA Chapter 11 proceedings,[101] which subsequent tribunals were able to apply.[102] Various developments aiming at ensuring greater transparency and participation of non-parties have also taken place in the context of the UNCITRAL Rules.[103] Although the 1976 and the new 2010 UNCITRAL Arbitral Rules are silent on non-party participation, the 2013 UNCITRAL Rules on Transparency in Treaty-Based Investor-State Arbitration explicitly acknowledge the tribunals' power to allow written submissions from non-parties and set out a detailed procedure and guidance for the tribunals in deciding whether to do so.[104]

Early ICSID tribunals took different positions on whether they had the power to allow non-party submissions in the absence of any specific provision in the applicable law. For example, in the first case raising *amicus curiae* participation in ICSID proceedings, *Aguas del Tunari SA v Bolivia*, the tribunal held that 'there [was] not at present a need to call witnesses or seek supplementary non-party submission at the jurisdictional phase'.[105] The tribunal elaborated in its reply to petitioners seeking to make submissions that 'it is manifestly clear to the Tribunal that it does not, absent

---

[99] *Methanex Corporation v United States*, Decision of the Tribunal on Petitions from Third Persons to Intervene as 'Amici Curiae', 15 January 2001, NAFTA/UNCITRAL, para 24.

[100] Ibid., paras 31–33.

[101] See, e.g., Statement of the Free Trade Commission on Non-Disputing Party Participation, 7 October 2003, available at http://www.sice.oas.org/TPD/NAFTA/Commission/Nondispute_e.pdf. Accessed 23 April 2021.

[102] See, e.g., *Glamis Gold Ltd v United States*, Decision on Application and Submission by Quechan Indian Nation, 16 September 2005, NAFTA/UNCITRAL, para 8-13 and Award, 8 June 2009, para 286.

[103] UNCITRAL, 'Settlement of Commercial Disputes: Revision of the UNCITRAL Arbitration Rules', UN Doc. A/CN.9/WG.II/WP.143, 20 July 2006, para 69 (suggesting that Article 15(1) of the 1976 UNCITRAL Arbitration Rules 'could be interpreted as encompassing power of the arbitral tribunal to accept such interventions, for example in the form of *amicus curiae* briefs').

[104] UNCITRAL Rules on Transparency in Treaty-Based Investor-State Arbitration (UNCITRAL Transparency Rules), Article 4. https://www.uncitral.org/pdf/english/texts/arbitration/rules-on-transparency/Rules-on-Transparency-E.pdf. Accessed 23 April 2021. Of course, the major limitation of these rules is that they apply only to arbitrations conducted on the basis of an IIA concluded on or after 1 April 2014, unless the parties otherwise agree. The 2014 UN Convention on Transparency in Treaty-Based Investor-State Arbitration, opened for signature 10 December 2014, UNTS Registration No 54749, entered into force 18 October 2017 (Mauritius Convention), sought to address this loophole by allowing States parties to an IIA concluded before 1 April 2014 to apply the UNCITRAL Transparency Rules, regardless of whether the arbitration is conducted under the UNCITRAL Arbitration Rules.

[105] *Aguas del Tunari SA v Bolivia*, Decision on Respondent's Objections to Jurisdiction, 21 October 2005, ICSID Case No ARB/02/03, para 18.

the agreement of the Parties, have the power to join a non-party to the proceedings; to provide access to hearings to non-parties and, *a fortiori*, to the public generally; or to make the documents of the proceedings public'.[106] In contrast, the *Suez* tribunal considered Article 44 of the ICSID Convention to be 'a grant of residual power to the Tribunal to decide procedural questions not treated in the Convention itself or the rules applicable to a given dispute', including the admissibility of non-party submissions.[107]

Following this initial uncertainty, and as a result of a two-year period of public consultation, certain amendments to the ICSID Arbitration Rules came into force on 10 April 2006. These amendments included Rule 37(2), which explicitly allows *amicus curiae* participation by non-parties to the dispute and sets out a number of criteria that tribunals may look at in making their decision on whether to grant leave:

> the Tribunal shall consider, among other things, the extent to which:
>
> (a) the non-disputing party submission would assist the Tribunal in the determination of a factual or legal issue related to the proceeding by bringing a perspective, particular knowledge or insight that is different from that of the disputing parties;
>
> (b) the non-disputing party submission would address a matter within the scope of the dispute;
>
> (c) the non-disputing party has a significant interest in the proceeding. The Tribunal shall ensure that the non-disputing party submission does not disrupt the proceeding or unduly burden or unfairly prejudice either party, and that both parties are given an opportunity to present their observations on the non-disputing party submission.[108]

The effect of this amendment was to settle the issue of whether arbitral tribunals had the power to consider non-party submissions and, as set out above, provide a non-exhaustive list of criteria that tribunals may take into account when exercising that power. This 'test' has become a helpful guidance in the subsequent practice of ICSID tribunals and has, to some extent, institutionalized *amici curiae*, in contrast to the treatment of non-party submissions in inter-State dispute settlement.[109] In some cases, investor-State arbitral tribunals have even proactively sought to invite *amici* participation, rather than adopting a passive attitude of awaiting submissions.[110] Many of these *amicus curiae* submissions have directly focused on the need for an

---

106 Ibid., para 17.

107 *Suez, Sociedad General de Aguas de Barcelona, S.A. and Vivendi Universal, S.A. v Argentina*, Order in Response to a Petition for Transparency and Participation as Amicus Curiae, 19 May 2005, ICSID Case No ARB/03/19, para 9.

108 ICSID Arbitration Rules, Article 37(2).

109 See, e.g., *Biwater Gauff (Tanzania) Ltd. v Tanzania*, Procedural Order No 5, 2 February 2007, ICSID Case No ARB/05/22, para 49.

110 See, e.g., *Pac Rim Cayman LLC v El Salvador*, Procedural Order Regarding Amici Curiae, 2 February 2011, ICSID Case No ARB/09/12. The Tribunal has done so on the basis of Rule 37(2) of ICSID Arbitration Rules and Article 10.20.3 of the Free Trade Agreement between Central America, the Dominican Republic and the United States of America (signed 5 August 2004, entered into force 1 January 2009), which provides that: 'The tribunal shall have the authority to accept and consider *amicus curiae* submissions from a person or entity that is not a disputing party'. See also *Apotex Holdings Inc. and Apotex Inc. v United States*, Invitation to Amici Curiae, 31 January 2013, ICSID

effective protection of the environment in the context of regulatory measures adopted by host States, particularly in respect of investments in the mining sector.[111]

Several trends can be identified in respect of non-party submissions in the ISDS context, when compared to inter-State dispute settlement mechanisms. First, even a cursory overview of the relevant cases shows that the consideration given to the substance of *amicus curiae* submissions is much more detailed in the reasoning of ISDS tribunals than compared to that in the context of inter-state dispute settlement mechanisms.[112] Second, a formal amendment of the relevant procedural rules or an authoritative interpretation may be preferable to leaving the question of non-party participation to unlimited discretion of tribunals, i.e., the wider or narrower interpretation they may give to their inherent powers, as the difference in the approaches of the *Methanex* and *Aguas del Tunari* tribunals demonstrate. Third, the effect of expressly providing conditions for the participation of non-disputing parties has potentially limited the possibility of 'opening the floodgates', in particular considering that nearly all ISDS cases implicate the State's ability to regulate, such as in relation to the environment. The ICSID Arbitration Rules, for example, have done so by emphasizing that the applicants seeking to make submissions must have a 'significant interest' in the proceedings, which has been interpreted as 'more than a "general" interest in the proceedings', which would include demonstrating that the outcome of the arbitration may have a direct or indirect impact on the rights or principles the applicant represents or defends.[113] Thus, tribunals are invited to scrutinize whether non-disputing party submissions are actually likely to 'assist in the determination of a factual or legal issue related to the arbitration by bringing a perspective, particular knowledge or insight that is different from that of the disputing parties'.[114] There is indeed a growing trend of cases in which tribunals have 'considered and addressed, in a reasoned manner, the criteria for *amicus* participation prescribed in institutional rules or similar instruments'.[115] However, what is perhaps peculiar about cases in which serious environmental or human rights concerns are at stake, is that tribunals

---

Case No ARB (AF)/12/1; *Mesa Power Group LLC v Canada*, Notification to Non-Disputing Parties and Potential Amicus Curiae, 28 May 2014, UNCITRAL, PCA Case No 2012-17; *RFP v Canada*, Notification to Non-Disputing Parties and Potential Amici Curiae, 8 May 2017, UNCITRAL, PCA Case No 2016-13; *Alicia Grace and Others v Mexico*, Procedural Order No 2 on Amicus Curiae and Non-Disputing Party Participation, 5 April 2019, ICSID Case No UNCT/18/4.

[111] See, e.g., *Pac Rim Cayman LLC v El Salvador*, Submission of Amicus Curiae Brief by the Center for International Environmental Law, 25 July 2014, ICSID Case No ARB/09/12; *Infinito Gold Ltd v Costa Rica*, Decision on Jurisdiction, 4 December 2017, ICSID Case No ARB/14/5, paras 124 ff.

[112] See, e.g., *Infinito Gold Ltd v Costa Rica*, Decision on Jurisdiction, 4 December 2017, ICSID Case No ARB/14/5, paras 121–140.

[113] See, e.g., *Eco Oro Minerals Corp. v Colombia*, Procedural Order No 6, 18 February 2019, ICSID Case No ARB/16/41, para 34.

[114] See, e.g., *Bear Creek Mining Corporation v Peru*, Procedural Order No 6, 21 July 2016, ICSID Case No ARB/14/21, para 38 and Partial Dissenting Opinion of Professor Philippe Sands QC appended to the Award of 30 November 2017, para 36.

[115] Born and Forrest 2019, p. 646. See also El-Hosseny 2021, pp. 356–359.

have more readily accepted the purported existence of a 'public interest' and, thus, the justification for the applicants to be allowed to make their submissions.[116]

14.2.2.2 Regional Human Rights Courts

The three regional human rights mechanisms, namely the ECtHR, the IACHR and the IACtHR as well as the ACHPR and the ACtHPR, stand out when compared to the dispute settlement mechanisms discussed above, both in terms of access to their jurisdiction, and the scope of participation by non-parties.

Access to regional human rights mechanisms is broad and allows for individuals to seek protection and enforcement of their human rights under the relevant legal instruments.[117] While individuals are able to directly lodge their applications with the ECtHR, in the American and African systems such applications shall be lodged with the respective Commissions.[118] Access to and standing before such mechanisms is expressly or impliedly premised on the legal notion of a victim. This is essential to understanding whether only those private parties who are directly or indirectly affected by the conduct of the State Party can bring cases, or whether associations or groups also have standing to bring a case on behalf of actual victims. There are nuanced differences between the three mechanisms in this respect.

For example, the ACHPR has recognized access and standing to a broad pool of potential applicants, including NGOs, even where they themselves are not alleged to have been directly or indirectly affected by a violation of the African Charter on Human and Peoples' Rights (African Charter), but rather appeared on behalf of actual victims.[119] In this sense, it can be said that the African Charter enshrines the conception of litigation in the public interest (*actio popularis*).[120] In contrast, under the European Convention on Human Rights (ECHR), the notion of 'victim' requires applicants to show that they are directly or indirectly affected by the measure or

---

[116] See, e.g., *Gabriel Resources Ltd and Gabriel Resources (Jersey) v Romania*, Procedural Order No 19, 7 December 2018, ICSID Case No ARB/15/31, para 75.

[117] Convention for the Protection of Human Rights and Fundamental Freedoms, opened for signature 4 November 1950, 213 UNTS 221, entered into force 3 September 1953 (European Convention of Human Rights); American Convention on Human Rights, opened for signature 22 November 1969, 1144 UNTS 123, entered into force 18 July 1978 (American Convention); African Charter on Human and Peoples' Rights, opened for signature 27 June 1981, 1520 UNTS 217, entered into force 21 October 1986 (African Charter).

[118] Note that the Protocol to the African Charter establishing the ACtHPR recognizes its jurisdiction to receive and examine communications from individuals and NGOs, but States Parties must make special declarations accepting the competence of the ACtHPR to do so. See Protocol to the African Charter (opened for signature 10 June 1998, entered into force 25 January 2004), Articles 5(3) and 34(6). Out of 30 Contracting States to the Protocol, only 9 have made such declarations. See ACtHPR, 'Activity Report, 1 January-31 December 2019', EX.CL/1204(XXXVI), paras 5–6.

[119] ACHR, *Social and Economic Rights Action Center and the Centre for Economic and Social Rights (CESR) v Nigeria (the Ogoni case)*, Decision, 27 May 2002, Comm No 155/96.

[120] Hampson et al. 2018, pp. 180–181; van den Eynde 2013; Bürli 2017.

practice in question.[121] Accordingly, 'for professional associations and NGOs to be regarded as victims they must show that they themselves are in some way affected by the measure complained of'.[122] They cannot initiate proceedings in the public interest. Finally, the practice of the IACHR and the IACtHR lies somewhere in-between the African and the European systems. Although the focus is kept on the notion of 'victim', individuals have been allowed to bring cases on behalf of their community.[123] Under the Inter-American system, even 'potential' victims could have standing to lodge applications, i.e., individuals who are 'at imminent risk of being directly affected by a legislative provision'.[124] NGOs are also specifically allowed to lodge petitions with the IACHR.[125]

In terms of the participation of non-parties in the proceedings, significant practice has developed before regional human rights mechanisms, even if the applicable legal instruments under which they operate are silent on *amici curiae* submissions, just like the inter-State dispute settlement mechanisms.[126] For example, it was not until the revised rules in 1983 that the President of the ECtHR was permitted, in the 'interest of the proper administration of justice', to invite other States not parties to the dispute or 'any other person' to submit comments or take part in the hearings.[127] This is now reflected in Article 36 of the ECHR, following the entry into force of Protocol 11 to the ECHR in 1998.[128] Similarly, the original rules of procedure of the IACtHR only implicitly allowed for *amici curiae*, and that was only made explicit with a subsequent revision of its rules in 2009.[129] The ACHPR's Rules of Procedure, as amended in 2020, authorize the Commission to 'invite or grant leave to an *amicus curiae* to intervene in the case by making written or oral submissions in order to assist the Commission in determining a factual or legal issue'.[130] They also recognize the right of non-parties to seek such leave and set out a detailed procedure for *amicus*

---

[121] ECtHR, Practical Guide on Admissibility Criteria 2014, pp. 11–14, paras 20–33, available at http://www.echr.coe.int/Documents/Admissibility_guide_ENG.pdf Accessed 15 February 2021.

[122] ECHR, Article 34. See also Vajic 2005, p. 94.

[123] IACHR, *Indigenous Community Yakey Axa of the Enxet-Lengua People v Paraguay*, Admissibility, Report No 2/02, 27 February 2002, Case No 12313, para 31; IACHR, *Xaxmok Kásek Indigenous Community v Paraguay*, Admissibility, Report No 11/03, 20 February 2003, Case No 322/01, para 29. See also IACtHR, *Kichwa Indigenous People of Sarayaku v Ecuador*, Merits and Reparation, Judgment, 27 June 2012, IACtHR Ser. C, No 245, para 231 (recognizing the rights of indigenous communities 'as collective subjects of international law and not only as members of such communities or peoples').

[124] IACHR, *Maria Morales de Sierra v Guatemala*, Admissibility, Report No 28/98, 6 March 1998, Case No 11625, para 35.

[125] American Convention, above n 117, Article 44.

[126] Hampson et al. 2018, pp. 182–183.

[127] 1983 Rules of the ECtHR, Rule 37(2).

[128] ECHR, above n 117, Article 36. See also Rules of the ECtHR, Rule 44(2)(a). For a comprehensive and up-to-date analysis of the ECtHR practice on non-party participation, see Bürli 2017, pp. 17–129.

[129] 2009 Rules of the IACtHR, Article 44.

[130] 2020 Rules of the ACHPR, Rule 104(1).

curiae participation.[131] The ACtHPR may also, 'in the interest of justice, authorise any other person who has interest in a case to intervene'.[132]

Given the very object and purpose of these mechanisms as a means to ensure compliance with human rights as enshrined in respective regional conventions, it is understandable that these mechanisms may be more inclined to seek to give greater voice in the proceedings to NGOs and civil society, and have done so through the amendments to their procedural rules. In so doing, their approach in practice has been less demanding in allowing *amici curiae*, when compared to inter-State mechanisms, and even when compared to the ISDS. This has prompted some authors to speak of human rights jurisdictions' 'liberal' approach in respect of participation in the proceedings when compared to more restrictive standards applied by other dispute settlement mechanisms in international law.[133]

To date, regional human rights mechanisms have permitted a substantial number of civil society actors to intervene in their proceedings, and the environment has often been at the forefront of their briefs.[134] It is then perhaps not surprising that the jurisprudence of regional human rights mechanisms has made a significant contribution towards the protection of various procedural and substantive rights of individuals and communities threatened by environmental degradation and pollution.[135] To give just one recent example, in an Advisory Opinion of 15 November 2017, the IACtHR reaffirmed that human rights depend on the existence of a healthy environment and stressed that States must take measures to prevent significant environmental harm within and outside their territories.[136] In that Advisory Opinion, the IACtHR made landmark legal findings on the right to a healthy environment as an

[131] Ibid., Rule 104(2) and 105.

[132] Ibid., Rule 61(2).

[133] El-Hosseny 2018, p. 224.

[134] See, e.g., ECtHR, *Hatton and Others v the United Kingdom*, Judgment, 8 July 2003, App No 36022/97, para 9; ACHR, *Centre for Minority Rights Development (Kenya) and Minority Rights Group International on behalf of Endorois Welfare Council v Kenya*, Decision, 4 February 2010, Comm No 276/2003; *Social and Economic Rights Action Center and the Centre for Economic and Social Rights (CESR) v Nigeria (the Ogoni case)*, above n 119; IACtHR, *Mayagna (Sumo) Awas Tingni Community v Nicaragua*, Judgment, 31 August 2001, IACtHR Ser. C, No 79, paras 29–62.

[135] Zengerling 2013, pp. 103–125; Stephens 2009, pp. 310–321. In the ECtHR context, see, e.g., *Lopez Ostra v Spain*, Judgment, 9 December 1994, App No 16798/90; *Guerra and Others v Italy*, Judgment, 19 February 1998, App No 14967/89; *Taskin and Others v Turkey*, Judgment, 10 November 2004, App No 46117/99; *Öneryildiz v Turkey*, Judgment, 30 November 2004, App No 48939/99; *Fadeyeva v Russia*, Judgment, 9 June 2005, App No 55723/00; *Giacomelli v Italy*, Judgment, 2 November 2006, App No 59909/00; *Tatar v Romania*, Judgment, 27 January 2009, App No 67021/01. In the IACtHR context, see, e.g., *Mayagna (Sumo) Awas Tingni Community v Nicaragua*, Judgment, 31 August 2001, above n 134; *Yakye Axa Indigenous Community v Paraguay*, Judgment, 17 June 2005, IACtHR Ser. C, No 125; *Kawas-Fernández v Honduras*, Judgment, 3 April 2009, IACtHR Ser. C, No 196; *Kichwa Indigenous People of the Sarayaku v Ecuador*, Judgment, 27 June 2012, above n 123.

[136] IACtHR, *The Environment and Human Rights (State Obligations in Relation to the Environment in the Context of the Protection and Guarantee of the Rights to Life and to Personal Integrity—Interpretation and Scope of Articles 4(1) and 5(1) of the American Convention on Human Rights)*, Advisory Opinion, 15 November 2017, OC-23/17.

'autonomous' human right and the scope of legal responsibility of States Parties to the American Convention.[137] It also recognized the various specific duties incumbent on States parties in preventing transboundary harm and cooperating with the potentially affected States, as well as ensuring a set of procedural rights under their jurisdiction, such as access to information, public participation and access to justice, in connection with policies and decision-making that could affect the environment.[138] In doing so, the IACtHR expressly indicated that the observations made by various non-governmental organizations, academic establishments and members of civil society, which were able to participate in the proceedings 'provided it with insight on the different questions raised'.[139]

14.3 The Reasons for the Different Approaches to Access and Participation in the Proceedings

The above review readily demonstrates that there is a clear difference in the approach of inter-State mechanisms and those mechanisms that deal mainly with cases brought by private parties against States as far as questions of access to and participation in proceedings are concerned. In this author's view, there are three principal reasons that explain why ISDS arbitral tribunals and regional human rights mechanisms have been significantly more receptive to opening up their proceedings to interested third parties, as opposed to their inter-State counterparts.

First, there are institutional or foundational reasons that explain this difference of approach. For example, the wording of the relevant provisions of the Statute of the ICJ and the longstanding practice developed on the basis of those provisions have shaped the approach of the institution to questions of access and participation, which are by now effectively set in stone.[140] Any modification of the Statute of the ICJ, just like the governing legal instruments of other inter-State mechanisms, namely the Statute of ITLOS or the DSU of the WTO, would require significant voting majorities in favour of any such amendments, and States have no real incentive to do so. Inter-State arbitration, on the other hand, is much more flexible and could potentially provide for greater involvement of interested stakeholders other than States and intergovernmental organizations. However, even in the context of inter-State arbitration, and in particular UNCLOS Annex VII arbitration, the approach to *amicus curiae* submissions has been similar, if not identical, to that of ITLOS for the reasons discussed above.

[137] Ibid., paras 62–64 and 244.

[138] Ibid., paras 211–241.

[139] Ibid., paras 6, 9 and 11.

[140] This also reflects the way other courts and tribunals have perceived the ICJ practice and procedure in this respect as a model for other mechanisms of dispute settlement. See, e.g., *United Parcel Service Inc. v Canada*, Decision of the Tribunal on Petitions for Intervention and Participation as Amicus Curiae, 17 October 2001, NAFTA/UNCITRAL, para 64.

Second, there are some pragmatic reasons that may explain the difference of approach. Mechanisms that deal predominantly with disputes between private parties and States have been more open to non-party participation, including by amending their governing instruments and procedural rules. Examples include, as discussed above, the amendment of the procedural rules of the ECtHR and IACtHR, the adoption of Protocol 11 to the ECHR, the authoritative interpretation of the rules on non-party participation in the context of NAFTA Chapter 11 arbitrations, the amendment of the ICSID Arbitration Rules, or the adoption of the new UNCITRAL Transparency Rules, which expressly recognize the capacity of non-parties to apply for leave to make submissions. We have not witnessed the same kind of procedural reaction on the part of inter-State mechanisms to increasing attempts of civil society to take part in the proceedings, even if they are the masters of their own procedure. Moreover, even where efforts were made to promote greater participation, as was the case of the WTO Appellate Body in the post *US-Shrimp* era, there was a backlash from Member States, which resulted in a practice today that is more in line with the other inter-State mechanisms. The ICJ, for example, rather than adopting, as it could do, an expansive interpretation of the concept of an 'international organization', has deliberately limited its reading of this provision to intergovernmental organizations.

The above pragmatic reasons may be said to be more acute in the context of an inter-State mechanism. Greater openness to participation by NGOs and civil society could lead to a significant burden upon these institutions, such as through the volume of submissions that would need to be processed, which could in turn hamper the proper administration of justice as between the States concerned. The limited capacity in terms of manpower and budgets of most of these inter-State mechanisms is certainly an important practical consideration. At the same time, this is also true in respect of human rights bodies. Although these are valid concerns, there are certainly ways to mitigate them, namely by designing a list of strict admissibility criteria for any such submissions and factors that may assist a court or tribunal in assessing the relevance of those submissions to the case before it, perhaps using the ICSID Arbitration Rules as a model.

Third and finally, there are also some strategic reasons which may explain the difference in the approach taken by the two sets of dispute settlement mechanisms in respect of access and participation. The so-called backlash against the lack of transparency and legitimacy of mechanisms such as the ISDS may at least in part explain the proclivity of arbitral tribunals in ISDS cases to consider more actively calls from NGOs and other members of civil society, particularly where investment disputes increasingly relate to important questions of public interest, the environment being chief amongst them.[141] At the same time, it would seem that the positions taken by such non-parties, at least in ISDS cases involving environmental issues, have been aligned with the positions taken by respondent States.[142] This may explain the relative openness of States to the idea of non-party participation in ISDS. Be

[141] See Baltag 2020, pp. 29–32; Mourre 2006, p. 270.

[142] See Born and Forrest 2019, p. 631; Ishikawa 2018, para 4.

that as it may, in the absence of similar threats directed at the institutional framework of inter-State mechanisms, perhaps with the exception of the WTO (though its current crisis is rather different in character and causes when compared to the ISDS), inter-State mechanisms have had no incentive to modify their approach to non-party participation in the proceedings. Finally, the very design, *raison d'être* and objectives of the human rights and the investment protection systems make them more amenable to non-party participation. Considering the inherent balancing exercise between public and private interests that regional human rights mechanisms and ISDS tribunals have to perform, the participation of non-parties may indeed make an important contribution to mechanism's analysis of the issues in dispute. These concerns of balancing public and private interests are present but are certainly not as pronounced in the context of inter-State dispute settlement mechanisms, which primarily concern sovereign interests.

14.4 Concluding Remarks

This chapter has considered the differences in terms of access to and participation in the proceedings before international courts and tribunals. The inherent limitations built into most instruments governing access to and the jurisdiction of inter-State mechanisms, but also to some extent ISDS and human rights mechanisms, can be mitigated by the exercise of their inherent powers in allowing greater participation of non-parties in the proceedings. This is particularly important in terms of disputes that raise public interest concerns and which relate to global commons such as the environment. However, as this chapter has demonstrated, calls for greater participation of non-parties, including NGOs and civil society, in the proceedings before international courts and tribunals have been met with differing rates of success. Notwithstanding the fact that the legal instruments governing the existing international courts and tribunals were originally silent on the question of participation of non-parties, this chapter has shown that inter-State mechanisms and those mechanisms dealing primarily with disputes arising between private parties and States have followed different approaches.

Regional human rights mechanisms and the ISDS tribunals have sought to fill in the void in their statutes and rules and, as a result, have broadly allowed for non-party participation in their proceedings, including in disputes raising issues relevant to the environment. By contrast, inter-State dispute settlement mechanisms have refrained from allowing non-parties, other than third States and intergovernmental organizations, to take part in the proceedings, whether contentious or advisory. The furthest they have gone in accommodating calls from civil society has been to design an *ad hoc* procedure for the filing of *amici curiae*, as the WTO Appellate Body did in the *EC—Asbestos*, or to publish unsolicited NGO submissions on their website, which has been ITLOS' practice thus far. However, as we have also seen, the willingness of international courts and tribunals to use their inherent powers so as to increase transparency and open the proceedings to a more meaningful participation by interested members of civil society is more limited when these courts and tribunals were essentially designed by and for sovereign States. There are, indeed, good reasons for exercising those inherent powers cautiously, as the example of the WTO Appellate Body's early approach to *amicus curiae* and the immediate political backlash it generated demonstrate.

It would be interesting to empirically analyse whether greater non-party participation, where it has been allowed, has an impact on the decisions rendered by international courts and tribunals. While there may be exceptions, it would seem that most of the existing impact of non-party submissions is rather nominal or parsimonious, unless and until the submissions of non-parties align with the position of one of the disputing parties, including in the context of disputes with an environmental component.[143] As noted by Baltag in the context of ISDS practice, 'to date, no tribunal has addressed the extent to which a submission by an *amicus curiae* has had a specific impact on its decision—or none at all'.[144] The limited treatment of such submissions in the decisions of international courts and tribunals may also be explained by the decision-maker's unwillingness to explicitly state what influence a submission may have had. Thus, it is either questionable or at least unknown whether greater participation of non-parties actually results in their views being taken into account by the court or tribunal in its decision-making process. The limited space devoted to the analysis of *amicus curiae* submissions in the reasoning of international courts and tribunals is a good indicator that this admittedly untested hypothesis may not be far from reality. Even if the participation of *amici curiae* may only have a negligible impact on the reasoning of the decisions rendered by courts and tribunals, NGOs and members of civil society continue nonetheless to seek participation in proceedings before international courts and tribunals. One would hope that they will continue to have at least some influence on how public interest issues such as those concerning the environment are considered by judges and arbitrators. In the end, the effective protection of the environment, whether domestically or internationally, may depend not only on the sound application of the existing law, but also on the means that private parties dispose of to exert pressure on governments and other public and private authorities.[145]

References

Baltag C (2020) The Role of Amici Curiae in Light of Recent Developments in Investment Treaty Arbitration: Legitimizing the System? ICSID Review 35:1-32

---

[143] See Lin 2017, p. 300 (arguing on the basis of three case studies in the ISDS context that 'arbitral tribunals seemed willing to [implicitly] consider the amici submissions only to the extent that the respondent states have advanced similar arguments').

[144] Baltag 2020, p. 29.

[145] Iovane 2008, p. 469.

Bartholomeusz L (2005) The Amicus Curiae before International Courts and Tribunals. Non-State Actors and International Law 5:209-286
Beyerlin U (2001) The Role of NGOs in International Environmental Litigation. ZaöRV 61:357-378
Born G, Forrest S (2019) Amicus Curiae Participation in Investment Arbitration. ICSID Review 34:626-665
Bürli N (2017) Third-Party intervention before the European Court of Human Rights. Intersentia, Cambridge
Chinkin C (1993) Third Parties in International Law. Clarendon Press, Oxford
Couvreur P (1999) Développements récents concernant l'accès des organisations intergouvernementales à la procédure contentieuse devant la Cour internationale de justice. In: Yakpo E, Boumedra T (eds) Liber Amicorum - Mohammed Bedjaoui. Kluwer Law International, The Hague, pp 293-323
Covey Jr F (1960) Amicus Curiae: Friend of the Court. DePaul Law Review 9:30-37
Crema L (2013) Testing Amici Curiae in International Law: Rules and Practice. Italian Yearbook of International Law 22:91-132
Dupuy P-M, Hoss C (2019) Competence of the Court: Article 34. In: Zimmermann A, Tams C, Oellers-Frahm K, Tomuschat C (eds) The Statute of the International Court of Justice: A Commentary. Oxford University Press, Oxford, pp 661-683
El-Hosseny F (2018) Civil Society in Investment Treaty Arbitration: Status and Prospects. Brill Nijhoff, Leiden
El-Hosseny F (2021) Third Party Intervention at the Proposed Multilateral Investment Court. In: de Brabandere E, Gazzini T, Kent A (eds) Public Participation and Foreign Investment Law. Brill Nijhoff, Leiden, pp 332–360
Francioni F (2009) Access to Justice, Denial of Justice and International Investment Law. EJIL 20:729-747
Gautier P (2014) Standing of NGOs and Third-Party Intervention before the International Tribunal for the Law of the Sea. Revue belge de droit international 47:205-224
Hampson F, Martin C, Viljoen F (2018) Inaccessible Apexes: Comparing Access to Regional Human Rights Courts and Commissions in Europe, the Americas and Africa. ICON 16:161-186
Iovane M (2008) La participation de la société civile à l'élaboration et à l'application du droit international de l'environnement. Revue générale de droit international public 112:465-519
Ishikawa T (2010) Third Party Participation in Investment Treaty Arbitration. ICLQ 59:373-412
Ishikawa T (2018) Intervention: Investment Arbitration. In: Ruiz Fabri H (ed) Max Planck Encyclopaedia of International Procedural Law. Oxford University Press, Oxford
Krislov S (1963) The Amicus Curiae Brief: From Friendship to Advocacy. Yale Law Journal 72:694-721
Lando M (2016) The Advisory Jurisdiction of the International Tribunal for the Law of the Sea: Comments on the Request for an Advisory Opinion Submitted by the Sub-Regional Fisheries Commission. Leiden Journal of International Law 29:441-461
Lekkas S-I, Staker C (2017) Article 20 Annex VI. In: Proelss A (ed) The United Nations Convention on the Law of the Sea. Hart, Oxford, pp 2370-2373
Leroux N (2006) NGOs at the World Court. International Community Law Review 8:203-221
Lin W-C (2017) Safeguarding the Environment? The Effectiveness of Amicus Curiae Submissions in Investor-State Arbitration. International Community Law Review 19:270-301
Lindblom A-K (2005) Non-Governmental Organisations in International Law. Cambridge University Press, Cambridge
Meshel T (2016) Optional Rules for Arbitration of Disputes Relating to Natural Resources and/or the Environment: Permanent Court of Arbitration (PCA). In: Ruiz Fabri H (ed) Max Planck Encyclopedia of International Procedural Law. Oxford University Press, Oxford
Miron A, Chinkin C (2019a) Chapter III. Procedure: Article 62. In: Zimmermann A, Tams C, Oellers-Frahm K (eds) The Statute of the International Court of Justice: A Commentary. Oxford University Press, Oxford, pp 1686-1740

Miron A, Chinkin C (2019b) Chapter III. Procedure: Article 63. In: Zimmermann A, Tams C, Oellers-Frahm K, Tomuschat C (eds) The Statute of the International Court of Justice: A Commentary. Oxford University Press, Oxford, pp 1741-1774

Mourre A (2006) Are Amici Curiae the Proper Response to the Public's Concerns on Transparency in Investment Arbitration? Law and Practice of International Courts and Tribunals 5:257-271

Oesch M (2014) US-Shrimp Case. In: Wolfrum R (ed) Max Planck Encyclopedia of Public International Law. Oxford University Press, Oxford

Paulus A (2019) Chapter IV. Advisory Opinions: Article 66. In: Zimmermann A, Tams C (eds) The Statute of the International Court of Justice: A Commentary. Oxford University Press, Oxford, pp 1812-1834

Ratliff D (2001) The PCA Optional Rules for Arbitration of Disputes Relating to Natural Resources and/or the Environment. Leiden Journal of International Law 14:887-896

Romano C (2000) The Peaceful Settlement of International Environmental Disputes. Kluwer Law International, The Hague

Ronen Y (2012) Participation of Non-State Actors in ICJ Proceedings. Law and Practice of International Courts and Tribunals 11:77-110

Rosenne S (2006) International Court of Justice (ICJ). In: Wolfrum R (ed) Max Planck Encyclopedia of Public International Law. Oxford University Press, Oxford

Shelton D (1994) The Participation of Nongovernmental Organizations in International Judicial Proceedings. AJIL 88:611-642

Squatrito T (2018) Amicus Curiae Briefs in the WTO DSM: Good or Bad News for Non-State Actor Involvement? World Trade Review 17:65-89

Stephens T (2009) International Courts and Environmental Protection. Cambridge University Press, Cambridge

Sulyok K (2021) Science and Judicial Reasoning: The Legitimacy of International Environmental Adjudication. Cambridge University Press, Cambridge

Treves T (2017) Article 291. In: Proelss A (ed) The United Nations Convention on the Law of the Sea: A Commentary. Hart, Oxford

Vajic N (2005) Some Concluding Remarks on NGOs and the European Court of Human Rights. In: Treves T et al. (eds) Civil Society, International Courts and Compliance Bodies. T.M.C. Asser Press, The Hague, pp 93-104

Valencia-Ospina E (2005) Non-Governmental Organisations and the International Court of Justice. In: Treves T et al. (eds) Civil Society, International Courts and Compliance Bodies. T.M.C. Asser Press, The Hague, pp 227-232

van den Eynde L (2013) An Empirical Look at the Amicus Curiae Practice of Human Rights NGOs before the European Court of Human Rights. Netherlands Quarterly of Human Rights 31:271-313

Vierucci L (2008) NGOs before International Courts and Tribunals. In: Dupuy P-M, Vierucci L (eds) NGOs in International Law: Efficiency in Flexibility? Elgar, Cheltenham, pp 155-180

Watts A (2004) The ICJ's Practice Directions of 30 July 2004. Law and Practice of International Courts and Tribunals 3:385-394

Wiik A (2018) Amicus Curiae before International Courts and Tribunals. Nomos Hart, Baden-Baden

Wojcikiewicz Almeida P (2019) International Procedural Regulation in the Common Interest: The Role of Third-Party Intervention and Amicus Curiae before the ICJ. Law and Practice of International Courts and Tribunals 18:163-188

Wood M, Sthoeger E (2020) Third-Party Intervention and Involvement in Inter-State Arbitration. In: Ruiz Fabri H, Franckx E, Benatar M, Meshel T (eds) A Bridge over Troubled Waters. Brill Nijhoff, Leiden, pp 61–82

WTO Secretariat (2017) A Handbook on the WTO Dispute Settlement System. Cambridge University Press, Cambridge
Zengerling C (2013) Greening International Jurisprudence: Environmental NGOs before International Courts, Tribunals and Compliance Committees. Nijhoff, Leiden

Vladyslav Lanovoy Assistant Professor, Université Laval, Québec, Canada. The author would like to thank Roel Walravens for his terrific research assistance in the preparation of this chapter.

Chapter 15
Provisional Measures

Cicely O. Parseghian and Benjamin K. Guthrie

Contents

Abstract Provisional measures are critical for the capacity of international courts and tribunals to protect the natural environment. By constraining or mandating certain party behaviours in order to prevent environmental harm while often lengthy proceedings are pending, they help to ensure that international dispute resolution remains a

C. O. Parseghian (✉)
Independent Attorney, Tucson, AZ, USA
e-mail: cicelyparseghian@gmail.com

B. K. Guthrie
Herbert Smith Freehills New York LLP, New York, NY, USA
e-mail: benjamin.guthrie@hsf.com

E. Sobenes et al. (eds.), *The Environment Through the Lens of International Courts and Tribunals*, https://doi.org/10.1007/978-94-6265-507-2_15

viable option for disputes with environmental components. Nearly all international courts and tribunals have the authority to order provisional measures, but the precise scope of that authority varies. Of particular note is that some tribunals are authorized to issue provisional measures primarily, or even solely, for the protection of the environment, while others may only issue such measures to protect party rights that are at issue in the dispute. There is general agreement among international courts and tribunals regarding the fundamental prerequisites for the ordering of provisional measures: there must be a risk of prejudice (though the precise threshold varies); the measures must be urgent; they must be proportional; and, in most situations, there must be a link between the measures and the rights in dispute in the proceedings. Recent years have seen international courts and tribunals issue an increasing number of provisional measures for protection of the environment. This chapter explores the significance of those orders, and of the distinctions between the approaches of particular courts and tribunals, for future environmental disputes.

Keywords Provisional Measures · Prevention · Rights *Pendente Lite* · Serious Harm to the Marine Environment · *Erga Omnes* Obligations · *Prima Facie* Jurisdiction · Plausibility · Link Requirement · Irreparable Prejudice · Urgency · Assurances · Undertakings · Proportionality · Discretion · Unilateral Obligations · Collaboration · Independent Experts · Environmental Impact Assessment

15.1 Introduction

Provisional or interim measures—orders requiring a party to a dispute to act or refrain from acting in a particular fashion during the pendency of their case—are a common feature of international judicial proceedings.[1] They reflect the fact that such proceedings 'take time, sometimes a lot of time, during which the rights at stake may be negatively affected by acts of one of the parties potentially resulting in an ineffective judgment.'[2]

In environmental disputes, the passage of time while a case is pending may have particularly dramatic consequences. For example, an industrial project may go from the planning phase to operational, with effects on the surrounding environment. Or an activity already causing adverse environmental impacts at the beginning of the proceedings—which may be the reason the proceedings were initiated—may continue unabated for years, with accumulating impacts, before a final decision is reached.

Depending on its nature, any harm that occurs while proceedings are pending may be difficult, or even impossible, to undo. Some resources regenerate quickly or can be replaced with relatively little overall impact. Others may take much longer

[1] In national jurisdictions, provisional measures are known by other names. For instance, in the United States, interim measures are called preliminary injunctions, and they are frequently sought in environmental litigation.

[2] Oellers-Frahm 2011, p. 1279.

to recover or be unique in ways that make them difficult to replace. Some damage may be irreversible. This makes disputes with environmental components different from a typical commercial litigation or arbitration, in which an award of monetary damages with interest is often like-for-like compensation for the harm suffered.

In environmental disputes, therefore, there may often be a particular need to prevent harm from occurring while the proceedings are pending, because that harm cannot always be easily erased in the final award. Because provisional measures are, by their nature, awarded with some urgency,[3] and because international courts and tribunals are generally afforded substantial discretion to craft the measures they deem necessary to achieve a particular purpose,[4] they may provide some unique potential for the prevention of environmental harm.[5] However, whether and to what extent provisional measures are available for environmental protection will depend in large part on which court or tribunal has been seized of the case, as well as the nature and facts of the dispute between the parties.

International courts and tribunals 'are free to adopt their own approach to provisional measures,' but 'a definable *jurisprudence constante* has emerged whereby most international courts follow the same process when deciding whether interim relief should be ordered.'[6] This chapter discusses the various elements of this process, areas of similarity, and areas of distinction.

It focuses principally on the ICJ, ITLOS, and state-to-state arbitration as these are the international tribunals that have been among the most active in considering provisional measures for protection of the environment.[7] In environmental cases, these bodies have been asked to issue provisional measures requiring respondents to:

- Cease atmospheric nuclear tests (granted)[8]
- Discontinue an experimental fishing program (granted)[9]
- Halt authorization, construction, and commissioning of industrial plants (denied)[10]
- Prohibit international shipment of radioactive materials (denied)[11]

---

[3] See Sect. 15.4.5, *infra.*

[4] See Sect. 15.5, *infra.*

[5] See Bendel 2019, pp. 491–92.

[6] Crawford 2016.

[7] The practice of the ICJ is also notable as it often serves as a reference for other international courts and tribunals.

[8] *Nuclear Tests Case (Australia v France)*, Provisional Measures Order, 22 June 1973, ICJ Reports 1973, p. 99; *Nuclear Tests Case (New Zealand v France)*, Provisional Measures Order, 22 June 1973, ICJ Reports 1973, p. 135.

[9] ITLOS, *Southern Bluefin Tuna Cases (New Zealand and Australia v Japan)*, Provisional Measures, 27 August 1999, ITLOS Reports 1999, p. 268.

[10] ITLOS, *The MOX Plant Case (Ireland v United Kingdom)*, Provisional Measures, 3 December 2001, ITLOS Reports 2001, p. 95; ICJ, *Case Concerning Pulp Mills on the River Uruguay (Argentina v Uruguay)*, Provisional Measures, 13 July 2006, ICJ Reports 2006, p. 113.

[11] ITLOS, *The MOX Plant Case (Ireland v United Kingdom)*, Provisional Measures, above n 10.

- Suspend land reclamation, dredging, or road construction works (denied)[12]
- Refrain from canal excavation in wetland areas (denied, but later granted)[13]
- Undertake emergency road remediation measures (denied)[14]
- Refrain from oil exploration and drilling operations (partially granted)[15]
- Provide project information (granted)[16]
- Transmit environmental impact assessments (denied)[17]
- Disperse environmental activists blockading an international bridge (denied)[18]
- Release a detained vessel and environmental activists (granted)[19]

The decision to grant or deny the requested order has depended on the particular facts and circumstances of each case and is not dispositive of whether a court or tribunal would grant or deny a request for a similar measure in a different case with different circumstances.

The authority of other international tribunals to order provisional measures is also well established, and insofar as the disputes before them implicate natural resources and the environment, their practice may become increasingly relevant as well.

Many disputes arising under investment treaties bear a relationship to environmental issues, either because the investment relates to natural resources or because the host state seeks to regulate the environmental impacts of the investment. Protection of the environment has not been a significant focus of provisional measures issued by investment arbitration tribunals to date, but it may be only a matter of time. For example, recent years have seen increased attention on the possibility of states asserting counter-claims, which could conceivably be accompanied by a request for provisional measures to prevent the investor from taking action that would cause

---

12 ITLOS, *Case Concerning Land Reclamation by Singapore in and around the Straits of Johor (Malaysia v Singapore),* Provisional Measures, 8 October 2003, ITLOS Reports 2003, p. 10; ICJ, *Certain Activities Carried Out by Nicaragua in the Border Area (Costa Rica v Nicaragua),* Provisional Measures, 8 March 2011, ICJ Reports 2011, p. 6; ICJ, *Construction of a Road in Costa Rica Along the San Juan River (Nicaragua v Costa Rica),* Provisional Measures Order, 13 December 2013, ICJ Reports 2013, p. 398

13 ICJ, *Certain Activities Carried Out by Nicaragua in the Border Area (Costa Rica v Nicaragua),* above n 12; ICJ, *Certain Activities Carried Out by Nicaragua in the Border Area (Costa Rica v Nicaragua),* Provisional Measures, 22 November 2013, ICJ Reports 2013, p. 354.

14 *Construction of a Road in Costa Rica Along the San Juan River (Nicaragua v Costa Rica),* above n 12.

15 ITLOS, *Dispute Concerning Delimitations of the Maritime Boundary between Ghana and Côte D'Ivoire in the Atlantic Ocean (Ghana/Côte D'Ivoire),* Provisional Measures, 25 April 2015.

16 *Case Concerning Land Reclamation by Singapore in and around the Straits of Johor (Malaysia v Singapore),*above n 12, p. 10.

17 *Construction of a Road in Costa Rica Along the San Juan River (Nicaragua v Costa Rica),* above n 12.

18 ICJ, *Case Concerning Pulp Mills on the River Uruguay (Argentina v Uruguay),* Provisional Measures, 23 January 2007, ICJ Reports 2007, p. 3.

19 *The 'Arctic Sunrise' Case (Kingdom of the Netherlands v Russian Federation),* Provisional Measures, 22 November 2013, ITLOS Reports 2013, p. 230.

harm to the natural environment.[20] Conversely, claimants sometimes request that a tribunal issue provisional measures suspending domestic proceedings against them.[21] Such a request could in theory relate to proceedings the outcome of which determines whether a certain environmental impact will occur.

In the realm of commercial arbitration, the prevalence of provisional measures orders bearing on environmental harm is difficult to assess as most proceedings are confidential. However, the International Chamber of Commerce observed in a 2019 report that it averaged three new environmental protection cases per year, and that other arbitral institutions reported similar figures.[22] It also noted that the majority of its cases relate to industries such as energy, construction, and transportation that are closely linked to climate concerns, and thus may have environmental implications.[23] The Permanent Court of Arbitration reports that it has administered nine confidential arbitrations related to the Kyoto Protocol's Clean Development Mechanism and Joint Implementation projects.[24]

15.2 Purposes and Nature of Provisional Measures

Like their equivalents in domestic courts, the purpose of provisional measures in international law is primarily 'to preserve rights that are the subject of litigation between the parties until such time as the dispute can be resolved, or *pendente lite*.'[25] This purpose is sometimes articulated as a need to safeguard or reestablish the *status quo* between the parties, in order to ensure that an eventual judgment will not be rendered meaningless in whole or in part due to changes that have occurred during the litigation.[26] Provisional measures may also be aimed at preventing aggravation or extension of the dispute between the parties. In international disputes, these functions take on 'special importance due to the relatively slow pace of proceedings, in which years may elapse before disputes are finally adjudicated.'[27]

Generally, provisional measures may be requested and ordered at any time during the proceedings.[28] A delay in making a request once the need for it arises may

---

[20] In its 2018 Award in *Aven v Costa Rica*, for example, the tribunal accepted that a respondent state might assert a counter-claim in relation to environmental damage, while dismissing the counter-claim on procedural grounds. See *Aven v Costa Rica*, Award, 18 September 2018, Case No. UNCT/15/3.

[21] See BIICL 2019, p. 12.

[22] ICC 2019, para 3.8.

[23] ICC 2019, Annex, para 17.

[24] Levine 2017, p. 26.

[25] Miles 2017, pp. 64.

[26] This purpose serves not only the interests of the parties, but also to protect the legitimacy of the tribunal itself, which will be harmed if its final decisions have, during the pendency of its cases, been rendered 'nugatory or of no effect'. Mensah 2002, p. 43.

[27] Miles 2017, p. 64.

[28] E.g., ICJ Rules, Article 73(1); ITLOS Rules, Article 89(1); ICSID Arbitration Rule 39(1).

diminish the chances of the request being granted, but if the need for provisional measures does not arise until midway through the proceedings, or even later, the option to seek provisional measures will be available.

Provisional measures have a preventive quality, but they are not a panacea and are subject to limitations. They are 'incidental by nature',[29] meaning they must generally arise from and be limited by the case in which they are ordered. They cannot go beyond the case already before the tribunal and cannot transform that case into a different one with different parties. However, as will be discussed below, certain tribunals enjoy broader authority, either because their power to issue interim relief is not constrained by reference to the rights of the parties, or because they are expressly authorized to order provisional measures aimed at the protection of the environment.[30] In those particular contexts, the utility of provisional measures for the protection of the environment may be expanded.

Because provisional measures necessarily involve some intrusion on the rights of one or more of the parties (and on the exercise of state sovereignty if that party is a state), and because they are generally awarded before jurisdiction has been conclusively established[31] and without in-depth review of the case's merits,[32] they are understood to be an exceptional form of relief.[33]

Finally, because decisions on provisional measures are supposed to be without prejudice to any later decision on the merits, they must not be an interim judgment or pre-judgment of any part of the claim at issue in the case.[34] As such, parties must carefully craft provisional measures requests that do not duplicate their requests for specific relief on the merits and, conversely, avoid including in their requests for relief on the merits remedies that would serve them better at an earlier point in the proceedings.[35]

15.3 Authority to Order Provisional Measures

Most international courts and tribunals are empowered to order provisional measures.[36] This power is often recorded expressly in the court's constituting treaty

[29] Tomka and Hernández 2011, § C.I.

[30] See Sect. 15.3.1, *infra*.

[31] See Sect. 15.4.1, *infra*.

[32] See Sect. 15.4.2, *infra*.

[33] See Miles 2017, pp. 287–88; Guilfoyle and Miles 2014, p. 279.

[34] Merrills 1995, p. 104; Tomka and Hernández 2011, Sect. C.I; Guilfoyle and Miles 2014, p. 284.

[35] See, e.g., *Construction of a Road in Costa Rica Along the San Juan River (Nicaragua v Costa Rica)*, above n 12, para 21 (rejecting Nicaragua's request for provisional measure ordering Costa Rica to transmit EIA for road project because request was 'exactly the same as one of Nicaragua's claims on the merits contained at the end of its Application,' at para 51(b)).

[36] Use of the term 'order' might have been controversial in the past, when the binding nature of provisional measures was disputed. However, as discussed below in Sect. 15.6, it is now widely

or an arbitral tribunal's rules. For example, Article 41 of the ICJ Statute, which served as the model for many corresponding provisions in other instruments,[37] provides:

> The Court shall have the power to indicate, if it considers that circumstances so require, any provisional measures which ought to be taken to preserve the respective rights of either party.[38]

The statutes or rules of the other major international tribunals discussed in this chapter, including ITLOS and tribunals constituted under UNCLOS, contain similar grants of authority to order provisional measures.[39]

In addition to these express provisions, many commentators also consider that international courts and tribunals have implied authority to order provisional measures, which derives from their inherent authority to regulate their proceedings.[40] It is generally unnecessary for tribunals to invoke such an implied authority, however, because their authority is made express in their constitutive instrument or applicable rules.[41]

Consequently, the question is not whether international courts and tribunals may order provisional measures, but rather the scope of their authority to do so.

15.3.1 Express Authority to Order Provisional Measures for Protection of the Environment

Provisions authorizing international courts and tribunals to order provisional measures vary with respect to the purpose for which provisional measures may be ordered. Specifically, there is divergence in whether provisional measures may be ordered only to protect the rights of the parties to the dispute, or also for the separate

understood that provisional measures are legally binding on the party or parties to whom they are directed, whether the court or tribunal in question 'indicates', 'prescribes', or 'recommends' them.

[37] Oellers-Frahm 2011, pp. 1280–81.

[38] Statute of the International Court of Justice, 26 June 1945, entry into force 24 October 1945, Article 41(1).

[39] See United Nations Convention on the Law of the Sea, 10 December 1982, 1833 UNTS 3, entered into force 16 November 1994 (UNCLOS), Article 290; UNCITRAL Arbitration Rules, 2013, Article 26; PCA Optional Environmental Rules, 19 June 2001, Article 26; Convention on the Settlement of Investment Disputes between States and Nationals of other States, adopted 18 March 1965, 575 UNTS 159, entered into force 14 October 1966 (ICSID Convention), Article 47.

[40] See Miles 2017, pp. 65, 198 and 232–33; Oellers-Frahm 2011, pp. 1281–83.

[41] A further source of authority could be the treaty or instrument under which the claim is brought. For example, in the *Kishenganga* Arbitration, the Indus Waters Treaty 'contained a specific power to grant interim relief,' which Pakistan argued 'furnished a self-contained set of rules,' making certain criteria generally applied by international courts and tribunals irrelevant. The tribunal 'adopted a nuanced view, holding that the provision "functions as a kind of *lex specialis* prescribed by the framers of the provision that makes unnecessary the imposition of further requirements,"' but nevertheless taking note of and referring to the jurisprudence of other courts and tribunals, including the ICJ. Miles 2017, pp. 208–09.

purpose of preventing serious harm to the environment (even when this goes beyond protecting the rights of a party).

Reflecting the traditional purpose of provisional measures—to protect rights of the parties pending resolution of the dispute—international courts and tribunals have broad authority to order provisional measures for that purpose.

In some cases, this focus on the rights of the parties forms an express limitation on the measures that may be ordered. The ICJ Statute permits the Court to indicate provisional measures only to 'preserve the respective rights of either party'.[42] Similarly, the ICSID Convention grants tribunals authority to recommend any provisional measure they deem necessary to 'preserve the respective rights of either party'.[43] The clear implication is that the Court or tribunal may not indicate provisional measures for other purposes when exercising its authority under these provisions.

Provisional measures issued under these provisions are, of course, capable of extending to protection of the environment so long as there is a nexus between the rights of one of the parties and the environment. When one of the parties is a sovereign state, that nexus may be present in the vast majority of cases, as international law recognizes harm to a state's natural environment as harm to the state itself.

However, two notable provisions go further, granting tribunals express authority not only to order provisional measures to protect the rights of the parties, but to protect the natural environment.

The first is Article 290 of UNCLOS, which applies to all judicial bodies empowered under Article 287: ITLOS, the ICJ (when acting pursuant to this provision[44]), *ad hoc* arbitral tribunals, and special arbitral tribunals constituted under UNCLOS Annexes VII and VIII.[45] Article 290(1) authorizes those tribunals to 'prescribe any provisional measures which it considers appropriate under the circumstances to preserve the respective rights of the parties to the dispute *or to prevent serious harm to the marine environment*, pending the final decision.'[46]

By expressly granting authority to issue measures to protect the marine environment, as distinct from measures to protect the rights of the parties, Article 290 does away with the requirement of a nexus between the environment and the rights of the

[42] ICJ Statute, above n 38, Article 41(1).

[43] ICSID Convention, above n 39, Article 47. See also ICSID Arbitration Rule 39(1) (party may request measures 'for the preservation of its rights').

[44] A dispute under UNCLOS will only be referred to the ICJ if both parties have so designated or otherwise agree. See UNCLOS, above n 39, Articles 287(1), (3)–(5). This has yet to occur, and it may, in fact, never occur given 'a relatively low number of states selecting the ICJ under UNCLOS Art 287(1).' Miles 2017, p. 191 n 100. Regardless, Article 290 of UNCLOS appears to apply to any 'court or tribunal' to which a dispute under UNCLOS has been duly submitted, and its provisions would presumably function as the *lex specialis* of any UNCLOS dispute referred to the ICJ, prevailing against any conflicting provisions in the Court's Statute or Rules. See Tomka and Hernández 2011, n 74.

[45] Miles 2017, p. 160.

[46] UNCLOS, above n 39, Article 290(1) (emphasis added).

parties.[47] Consequently, 'interim relief may be ordered not in relation to rights under dispute, but "mainly or even solely" to prevent harm to the environment.'[48]

Article 290's grant of authority to issue provisional measures for the 'wholly distinct purpose' of protecting the marine environment flows from the fact that UNCLOS 'devotes its part XII entirely to the protection of the marine environment as an integral part of the then-new law of the sea'.[49] Commentators have argued that this not only 'adds a new element to their link with the interests of the parties but also "reflects a change of international law from a mechanism providing for the coordination of States activities to one which also recognises and preserves common values of the community of States."'[50]

The second provision that expressly empowers international tribunals to order provisional measures for protection of the environment is Article 26 of the PCA's Optional Rules for Arbitration of Disputes Relating to Natural Resources and/or the Environment ('Optional Environmental Rules'), which provides:

> Unless the parties otherwise agree the arbitral tribunal may, at the request of any party and having obtained the views of all the parties, take any interim measures including provisional orders with respect to the subject-matter of the dispute it deems necessary to preserve the rights of any party *or to prevent serious harm to the environment falling within the subject-matter of the dispute.*[51]

This provision is more limited than Article 290 of UNCLOS insofar as it limits the environmental harm that may be addressed by an order of provisional measures to that 'falling within the subject-matter of the dispute'. This limitation represents a compromise between a desire to grant tribunals the power to protect the natural environment, on one hand, and a concern about tribunals over-extending that authority to affect third parties not participating in the arbitration.[52]

A third category of provisions falls between the express limitation seen in the ICJ and ICSID context and the express grant of authority seen in UNCLOS and the PCA Optional Environmental Rules. For example, the UNCITRAL Arbitration Rules provide that an 'arbitral tribunal may, at the request of a party, grant interim measures,' without specifying the purposes for which it may order such measures.[53] The Rules also require that the party seeking interim measures show that '[h]arm not adequately reparable by an award of damages is likely to result if the measure is not ordered,' but do not expressly stipulate that such harm must be to the party.[54]

---

[47] See Mensah 2002, pp. 45–46.

[48] Miles 2017, p. 162 (quoting Mensah 2002, p. 45).

[49] Tomka and Hernández 2011, Sect. B.IV.

[50] Ibid., n 39 (quoting Prof. Wolfrum); see also Tanaka 2014, p. 365 ('By referring to marine environmental protection as a justification for provisional measures, this provision is thought to give explicit textual expression to the enforcement of a community interest concerning marine environmental protection.'); Miles 2017, p. 453.

[51] PCA Optional Environmental Rules, above n 39, Article 26(1) (emphasis added).

[52] Meshel 2017, para 12; Ratliff 2001, pp. 892–93.

[53] UNCITRAL Arbitration Rules, above n 39, Article 26(1).

[54] Ibid., Article 26(3)(a).

Similarly, the ICC Rules of Arbitration provide that 'the arbitral tribunal may, at the request of a party, order any interim or conservatory measure it deems appropriate' without setting any express limitation.[55]

The limiting principle applicable to tribunals constituted under these rules, therefore, is not any express language in the rules themselves, but rather the fundamental principle that arbitral tribunals possess only the jurisdiction granted to them by the parties. In this regard, the ICC has noted that parties may wish to include express language in their agreement to arbitrate or terms of reference similar to Article 26 of the PCA Optional Environmental Rules, expressly providing that the tribunal may order provisional measures to avoid serious harm to the environment falling within the subject-matter of the dispute.[56]

A wrinkle in some tribunals' authority to indicate provisional measures only to preserve the rights of one of the parties comes in the form of *erga omnes* obligations. The ICJ recently indicated provisional measures at the request of Gambia to protect members of the Rohingya ethnic group located in Myanmar. The Court's order was premised upon its holding that Gambia had *prima facie* standing on the basis that it, like all other parties to the Genocide Convention, has 'a common interest to ensure that acts of genocide are prevented'.[57] That common interest was sufficient for Gambia to seek, and the Court to grant, provisional measures for the protection of non-Gambian nationals applicable outside the territory of Gambia. In the event that an environmental obligation *erga omnes* is recognized in the future, it could conceivably form the basis of a similar request for provisional measures to protect a third-party state or its nationals.[58]

15.3.2 Authority to Order Provisional Measures Proprio Motu

Many international courts and tribunals are only expressly empowered to order provisional measures when requested by one of the parties to a dispute. For example, the UNCITRAL Arbitration Rules provide that '[t]he arbitral tribunal may, *at the request of a party*, grant interim measures'.[59] Even UNCLOS Article 290 and the PCA

---

[55] ICC Arbitration Rules (2017), Article 28(1).

[56] ICC 2019, para 5.57.

[57] ICJ, *Application of the Convention on the Prevention and Punishment of the Crime of Genocide (Gambia v Myanmar)*, Provisional Measures, 23 January 2020, para 41.

[58] See Robinson 2018 ('It is realistic—not optimistic—to project that we shall witness in coming years an obligation *erga omnes* to safeguard Earth's environment.'); see also Miles 2017, p. 141; Bendel 2019, p. 521 (whether measures like those granted to address serious human rights violations are also available for environmental violations poses 'a significant question').

[59] UNCITRAL Arbitration Rules, above n 39, Article 26(1) (emphasis added); see also ICC Arbitration Rules (2017), Article 28; LCIA Arbitration Rules, Article 25; ICDR International Arbitration Rules, Article 24.

Optional Environmental Rules, which expressly authorize provisional measures for protection of the environment, require that one of the parties request such measures.[60]

In contrast, some courts and tribunals—including the ICJ and ICSID tribunals—are expressly empowered to order provisional measures on their own initiative, in the absence of a request from any of the parties.[61]

A court or tribunal's authority to order provisional measures *proprio motu* is potentially significant to the protection of the environment. Where provisional measures proceedings must be initiated by a party, the tribunal's ability to issue orders for protection of the environment is limited by the parties' willingness to request provisional measures, and whether such a request is consistent with their litigation strategy. Where a tribunal is empowered to issue provisional measures on its own initiative, it has greater flexibility to issue orders for protection of the environment even in situations in which the parties are not incentivized to request them.

It should be noted, however, that the Court has rarely utilized its power to order provisional measures *proprio motu*. And, although UNCLOS tribunals enjoy no such power and may only order provisional measures in response to a party request, they have nevertheless made interesting use of their broad discretion to order relief that differs, even substantially, from that requested.[62]

15.3.3 Express Authority to Order Provisional Measures Pending Constitution or Convening of Tribunal

Normally a court or tribunal ordering provisional measures does so in the context of proceedings over which it will continue to preside. One unique feature of UNCLOS is its Article 290(5), which grants ITLOS authority to award interim relief pending the constitution of a different tribunal. Provisional measures ordered in this fashion will remain in effect only until the subsequently constituted tribunal rules on the question,[63] meaning they may be in place to provide protection for shorter time periods than those ordered by other courts or tribunals.

In addition, when ITLOS is not in session or there is no quorum, the Chamber of Summary Procedure is also authorized to indicate provisional measures, although any measures prescribed in this manner are subject to review and revision by the full

---

[60] UNCLOS, above n 39, Article 290(3); PCA Optional Environmental Rules, above n 39, Article 26(1).

[61] ICJ Rules, Article 75(1); ICSID Arbitration Rule 39(3).

[62] E.g., ITLOS, *The MOX Plant Case (Ireland v United Kingdom)*, above n 10, para 78–81, 89(1) (granting measures entirely different from those requested). See Sect. 15.5, *infra*.

[63] See Case *Concerning Land Reclamation by Singapore in and around the Straits of Johor (Malaysia v Singapore)*, above n 12, para 65–69; see also Miles 2017, p. 309.

Tribunal.[64] This possibility has been called 'a major innovation', especially when compared to the practice of the ICJ on provisional measures.[65]

These express authorizations for the issuance of interim relief pending the constitution or convening of another tribunal is one that is uncommon among public international law tribunals[66] and 'raises questions of legitimacy in its exercise'.[67] Regardless, ITLOS has repeatedly made use of Article 290(5)'s unique grant of authority, with many of the key UNCLOS decisions on provisional measures involving environmental protection having been issued in that context.[68] On the other hand, the innovative authorization of the Chamber of Summary Procedure to prescribe provisional measures has yet to be utilized in practice.[69]

15.4 Criteria and Considerations

Before an international court or tribunal may order provisional measures, it must satisfy itself that certain preconditions are met and that the circumstances require the issuance of such relief. Although 'a measure of uniformity may be detected as between international courts and tribunals when considering the preconditions for interim relief,'[70] there are a number of important distinctions.

15.4.1 Jurisdiction

A request for provisional measures will usually be considered before the court or tribunal faced with the request has formally or finally determined the question of its jurisdiction over the underlying case. But, because interim measures 'are intended to make [a party] act, or more usually refrain from acting, in certain ways for a period of months, or possibly years, until the case is finally disposed of,' the 'consent of the respondent, and hence the question of substantive jurisdiction, cannot be entirely ignored.'[71]

---

[64] UNCLOS, above n 39, Article 25(2); ITLOS Rules, Article 91.

[65] Tomka and Hernández 2011, § B.IV.

[66] In contrast, provisions authorizing the appointment of emergency arbitrators to hear requests for provisional measures pending constitution of a full tribunal are more common in international commercial arbitration.

[67] Guilfoyle and Miles 2014, p. 274.

[68] *Southern Bluefin Tuna Cases (New Zealand and Australia v Japan),* Provisional Measures, 27 August 1999, ITLOS Reports 1999, p. 268; ITLOS, *The MOX Plant Case (Ireland v United Kingdom),* above n 10; *Case Concerning Land Reclamation by Singapore in and around the Straits of Johor (Malaysia v Singapore)*, above n 12.

[69] Miles 2017, p. 165-66.

[70] Ibid., p. 205.

[71] Merrills 1995, pp. 91–92. Where the respondent concedes jurisdiction or fails to challenge it, the tribunal will have less need to address the issue in depth.

The issue of jurisdiction in provisional measures proceedings was historically the subject of significant debate before the ICJ.[72] However, it 'has now been universally accepted—not only within the Court, but before other international bodies—that an essential prerequisite of interim relief is the establishment of jurisdiction *vis-à-vis* the main dispute on a *prima facie* basis.'[73] Under this standard, the applicant is given a degree of benefit of the doubt, and the court or tribunal will ask whether there is a *prima facie* basis to conclude jurisdiction will later be found.[74]

15.4.2 Possibility of Success on the Merits

In domestic jurisdictions, the availability of interim relief often depends on the 'applicant's capacity to demonstrate at least some possibility of victory if the matter proceeds to final judgment'.[75] For instance, in the United States, a showing of 'likelihood of success on the merits' is a prerequisite for a preliminary injunction. This is *not* the case in the international context, where preliminary consideration of a case's merits is considered 'problematic, due primarily to the consensual character of jurisdiction'.[76]

However, particularly since the legally binding nature of provisional measures was definitively clarified (including in the ICJ's 2001 Judgment in *LaGrand*),[77] most international courts or tribunals have now demonstrated that they will not order provisional measures without satisfying themselves that the applicant has at least some chance of securing relief on the merits.[78]

The standard applied by most of courts and tribunals addressed in this chapter is whether the rights forming the basis of the applicant's case on the merits are 'plausible'.[79] This requires an assessment of whether 'there is at least a reasonable possibility that the right which [the applicant] claims exists as a matter of law and will be adjudged to apply to that party's case'.[80] This is not a review of the applicant's

---

[72] Miles 2017, p. 209; see also pp. 210–12 (discussing cases).

[73] Ibid., p. 234. 'There is no particular reason, as a matter of logic or principle, why *this* needs to be [the] precise threshold, but it is adopted nonetheless more or less automatically, the sheer weight of the *jurisprudence constante* being such that the contemplation of any alternative would require a very good reason indeed (i.e. a *lex specialis*).' Ibid.

[74] Tomka and Hernández 2011, § C.I; Merrills 1995, p. 100; Miles 2017, pp. 213–24.

[75] Miles 2017, p. 255.

[76] Ibid.

[77] See Sect. 15.6, *infra*.

[78] Miles 2017, p. 255.

[79] Some investor-state tribunals have applied a more searching *prima facie* test, which tends to involve consideration of the *prima facie* strength of the parties' respective claims, counter-claims, and defences. See Crawford 2016; Miles 2017, pp. 15, 255, 268–69.

[80] *Certain Activities Carried Out by Nicaragua in the Border Area (Costa Rica v Nicaragua)*, above n 12, Declaration of Judge Greenwood, para 4.

prospects of success on the merits; it does not consider whether such rights have been breached, much less whether any such breach might be excusable.[81]

The plausibility test is part of the 'settled practice' of the ICJ,[82] and has also been adopted by tribunals constituted under UNCLOS.[83] In past orders, a range of environmental rights have been recognized as plausible, including:

- Right of a country to protect the natural environment in areas over which it is sovereign[84]
- Right to be free from transboundary harm[85]
- Right to request suspension of works that threaten transboundary environmental harm[86]
- Right to receive an environmental impact assessment ('EIA')[87]

Notably, the determination that the right sought to be protected is 'plausible' is a necessary, but not sufficient, condition for provisional measures. The other criteria discussed below must also be satisfied, and applicants have often cleared this preliminary hurdle only to have their requests for interim relief rejected for other reasons.

There is an important potential exception to the plausibility requirement under UNCLOS. That requirement, which relates to the plausibility of the rights that are contested on the merits, is not relevant for a tribunal's determination of whether provisional measures are merited to prevent serious harm to the marine environment—an objective under Article 290 that is separate from the protection of contested party rights.[88] Thus, even if the rights claimed by the applicant are rejected as implausible (which does not appear to be a common occurrence, even before the Court), ITLOS or another tribunal constituted under UNCLOS may nonetheless see fit to order provisional measures—whether requested by the applicant or not—for prevention of serious harm to the marine environment.[89] There do not yet appear to be examples of this in practice, but the possibility is intriguing.

[81] Miles 2017, p. 258.

[82] Ibid., pp. 259 and 262–63.

[83] See ibid., p. 263.

[84] *Certain Activities Carried Out by Nicaragua in the Border Area (Costa Rica v Nicaragua)*, above n 12, para 55; *Certain Activities Carried Out by Nicaragua in the Border Area (Costa Rica v Nicaragua)*, above n 13, para 28. See also *Case Concerning Pulp Mills on the River Uruguay (Argentina v Uruguay)*, above n 10, para 72.

[85] *Construction of a Road in Costa Rica Along the San Juan River (Nicaragua v Costa Rica)*, above n 12, paras 17–19.

[86] *Certain Activities Carried Out by Nicaragua in the Border Area (Costa Rica v Nicaragua)*, above n 12, para 59.

[87] *Construction of a Road in Costa Rica Along the San Juan River (Nicaragua v Costa Rica)*, above n 12, paras 17–19.

[88] See Miles 2017, pp. 263–64.

[89] Miles 2017, pp. 263–64.

15.4.3 Link Requirement

International courts and tribunals also tend to require that a close relationship exist between the provisional measures requested and the rights that are subject to final adjudication on the merits.[90] This stems from the limited nature of provisional measures as incidental to underlying proceedings, as well as their fundamental purpose: safeguarding the rights of the parties that are in dispute until a final decision can be reached.[91] For these reasons, unless a provision exists to broaden the scope of a particular tribunal's authority to order interim relief,[92] provisional measures may not be used to address issues that are not the subject of the main dispute, and they must not reach beyond what is required to preserve the respective rights of the parties at issue in the case.[93] The power is not one to protect *all* the rights of the parties to the dispute, much less the rights of non-parties. And, absent some provision to the contrary (e.g., UNCLOS Article 290), it is not a power to prevent more general damage, including damage to 'the environment'.

Because the measures requested must relate closely to the main claim, the rights or interests in question tend to be defined by the assertions contained in the document or documents filed by the claimant to initiate the case.[94] However, it is notable that provisional measures may be requested by either party. When a respondent applies for interim relief and has not filed a counterclaim articulating certain rights, 'the rights to be protected are a negative image of the claimant's application, in that the respondent may assert a right to pursue a course of conduct over the objections of the claimant.'[95]

The best example of this may be Uruguay's request for provisional measures in *Pulp Mills* regarding the blockading of an international bridge by Argentine civilian protesters. Although conceding that the acts of which it complained fell outside the Court's jurisdiction, Uruguay contended that they were a fundamental interference with the rights Uruguay was attempting to defend: its ability to construct and commission the pulp mills.[96] The Court agreed, finding that Uruguay's rights were 'not dependent solely' upon the manner in which Argentina had framed its case.[97] This was not a conclusion that Uruguay could seek interim protection for *any* right, without regard to the substance of the case. Rather, it was a recognition that 'Uruguay

---

[90] Crawford 2016; Miles 2017, pp. 285, 536.

[91] Merrills 1995, p. 100.

[92] See Sect. 15.3.1, *supra*.

[93] Merrills 1995, p. 100. See also *Case Concerning Application of the Convention on the Prevention and Punishment of the Crime of Genocide (Bosnia and Herzegovina v Yugoslavia (Serbia and Montenegro))*, Provisional Measures, 8 April 1993, ICJ Reports 1993, para 35 (Court 'ought not to indicate measures for the protection of any disputed rights other than those which might ultimately form the basis of a judgment').

[94] Miles 2017, p. 239.

[95] Ibid., p. 241.

[96] Ibid., p. 240.

[97] *Case Concerning Pulp Mills on the River Uruguay (Argentina v Uruguay)*, above n 18, para 28.

was entitled to request the protection of rights that formed the negative image of Argentina's complaint on the merits'[98]—the right, implied in Uruguay's defence, to authorize the construction and commissioning of the mills without Argentina's interference.

In its 2011 Order on provisional measures in *Certain Activities*, the Court first 'elevated the link between the measures sought and rights *pendente lite* to a condition precedent for the award of relief,'[99] having consistently articulated the requirement since, including in its most recent provisional measures decision.[100] There are indications that UNCLOS tribunals may also be moving toward treating the link requirement as a prerequisite to interim relief.[101] This is notably a higher standard than is applied by other international tribunals, such as in the investor-state arbitration context, where it is only required that the rights to be protected 'relate' to those to be determined on the merits.[102]

However, a distinction must be made here, too, regarding measures to 'prevent serious harm to the marine environment', which are available under UNCLOS even if rights pertaining to the marine environment are not directly the subject of the litigation.[103] As an illustration, in *Southern Bluefin Tuna*, none of the parties raised the issue, and 'ITLOS considered this aspect of the case on its own initiative,' ordering preventive measures accordingly.[104] This was possible because, for the purposes of disputes under UNCLOS Part XV, 'the marine environment is always considered to [be] a *de facto* right *pendente lite*.'[105]

15.4.4 *Qualifying Risk*

In order for the exceptional relief of provisional measures to be justified, there must be some risk of prejudice. But what level of harm suffices?

---

98 Miles 2017, p. 521.

99 Ibid., p. 243; see also *Certain Activities Carried Out by Nicaragua in the Border Area (Costa Rica v Nicaragua)*, above n 12, para 60–62.

100 *Certain Activities Carried Out by Nicaragua in the Border Area (Costa Rica v Nicaragua)*, above n 12, para 25, 29–33; *Construction of a Road in Costa Rica Along the San Juan River (Nicaragua v Costa Rica)*, above n 12, para 16, 20–23; *Application of the Convention on the Prevention and Punishment of the Crime of Genocide (Gambia v Myanmar)*, above n 57, para 44, 57-63.

101 Miles 2017, p. 247 (citing *Dispute Concerning Delimitations of the Maritime Boundary between Ghana and Côte D'Ivoire in the Atlantic Ocean (Ghana/Côte D'Ivoire)*, above n 15, para 63).

102 See ibid., p. 250 (citing *Plama v Bulgaria*) & 253–54 (discussing UNCITRAL rules and practice).

103 Miles 2017, p. 65; also p. 449.

104 Mensah 2002, p. 53.

105 Miles 2017, p. 450.

15.4.4.1 Irreparable Prejudice

At the ICJ, the long-established formulation is that the Court only has the power to indicate provisional measures when 'irreparable prejudice could be caused to rights which are the subject of the judicial proceedings'.[106] Although less settled, recent practice under UNCLOS also indicates that a party's right must be facing 'irreparable prejudice' for provisional measures to be justified.[107]

Although its predecessor applied this test literally, requiring a risk of damage that could not be remedied through monetary compensation, the Court now applies a 'somewhat more forgiving definition of irreparability', focusing on whether the alleged prejudice would impair the possibility for a full execution of a final judgment 'irrespective of the capacity for subsequent remediation or compensation'.[108] Miles argues that UNCLOS tribunals have demonstrated a similar willingness to 'accept a lesser standard of prejudice' to party rights in provisional measures proceedings.[109] He contends 'the field remains in a state of mild confusion' due to the continued use of the word 'irreparable' to describe the harm required 'when in reality meaning something less rigourous.'[110]

Where a risk to human life or health is at issue, the ICJ has demonstrated a willingness to find the 'irreparability' requirement easily satisfied, indicating that it 'considers risks to human life or health to be *ipso facto* irreparable'.[111] But what else counts as 'irreparable' harm in the context of environmental disputes?

In *Pulp Mills*, Argentina asked the Court to order Uruguay to suspend the authorization and construction of two paper pulp mills on the River Uruguay, in part to protect Argentina's procedural rights to prior notification and consultation.[112] The Court seems to have rejected the idea that harm to those rights could qualify as 'irreparable', indicating that any such violations could be remedied at the merits

[106] *Activities Carried Out by Nicaragua in the Border Area (Costa Rica v Nicaragua),* above n 13, para 34.

[107] See Guilfoyle and Miles 2014, p. 275; Miles 2017, pp. 301–06; see also *Dispute Concerning Delimitations of the Maritime Boundary between Ghana and Côte D'Ivoire in the Atlantic Ocean (Ghana/Côte D'Ivoire),* above n 15, para 41–43, 74, 86–96; *The 'Enrica Lexie' Incident (Italy v India)*, Provisional Measures, 24 August 2015, ITLOS Reports 2015, p. 182, para 87.

[108] Miles 2017, pp. 133–34, 292, 304.

[109] Ibid., p. 304.

[110] Ibid., p. 334. Miles argues the 'perceived severity' of the irreparable prejudice standard 'has created a backlash of sorts within ICSID arbitration in particular, such that a break in jurisprudence is now clearly observable.' Ibid., p. 287. In particular, he contends recent ICSID tribunals have required instead a 'putatively lower threshold of "significant" prejudice.' Ibid., p. 207. But there is some question about how different the two standards really are, or whether they are effectively the same. See ibid. p. 333; see also Crawford 2016.

[111] Miles 2017, p. 291. See, e.g., *Nuclear Tests,* above n 8, para 29–30; *Application of the Convention on the Prevention and Punishment of the Crime of Genocide (Gambia v Myanmar),* above n 57, para 70-75; *Certain Activities Carried Out by Nicaragua in the Border Area (Costa Rica v Nicaragua),* above n 12, para 75.

[112] *Case Concerning Pulp Mills on the River Uruguay (Argentina v Uruguay),* above n 10, para 4–6, 20(a), 34, 63–64 and 66.

stage.[113] This outcome could have important implications in future environmental cases, insofar as one party seeks provisional relief based on an alleged damage to its rights to certain procedures or to be consulted in a particular way prior to the initiation of a project.[114]

It is also important to recall, in the context of environmental disputes, that the threshold at which an international EIA becomes mandatory under general international law is when a risk of 'significant adverse impact in a transboundary context' exists.[115] This is not the same as a risk of 'irreparable prejudice'. Thus, a risk that is sufficient to require the preparation of an EIA may nonetheless *not* be sufficient to justify the indication of provisional measures. This explains how the Court in the *Road* case was able to reject Nicaragua's request for provisional measures on the ground that a risk of *irreparable* prejudice to the San Juan River from Costa Rica's road had not been established,[116] while later concluding that a risk of sufficiently *significant* adverse impact had existed to require Costa Rica to prepare an EIA for the project.[117]

The Court has stressed 'the great significance it attaches to respect for the environment',[118] and it has, on occasion, been satisfied of the existence of a risk of sufficiently irreparable harm to the environment to order provisional measures. In particular, in *Certain Activities*, the Court found in 2011 that Nicaragua's works in a disputed wetland area—which involved the clearing of a small channel (or *caño*), felling of trees, clearing of vegetation, and removal of soil, and which Costa Rica alleged would cause flooding and other damage[119]—were sufficient to require that

---

[113] Ibid., para 70.

[114] But see ITLOS, *The MOX Plant Case (Ireland v United Kingdom)*, above n 10, Separate Opinion of Judge Treves, para 7–9 (arguing that, although Tribunal did not explicitly say so, it implicitly considered requirement of urgency satisfied only with regard to Ireland's 'rights of a procedural character relating to cooperation and information' and ordered provisional measures accordingly, even where urgency had not been established regarding Ireland's substantive right 'not to be polluted or exposed to a risk of pollution' or regarding a 'risk to the marine environment' more generally; questioning whether Tribunal's 'precautionary approach is appropriate as regards the preservation of procedural rights').

[115] ICJ, *Case Concerning Pulp Mills on the River Uruguay (Argentina v Uruguay)*, Judgment, 20 April 2010, ICJ Reports 2010, para 204; see also *Construction of a Road in Costa Rica Along the San Juan River (Nicaragua v Costa Rica)*, above n 12, para 19; *Certain Activities/Road*, Judgment (2015), para 101, 104 and 153.

[116] *Construction of a Road in Costa Rica Along the San Juan River (Nicaragua v Costa Rica)*, above n 12, para 34. The timing of Nicaragua's request, immediately before the hearings on Costa Rica's second request for provisional measures in *Certain Activities*, cannot have helped.

[117] *Certain Activities/Road*, Judgment (2015), para 155–156 (finding threshold requiring EIA met for 160-km-long road, much of it immediately adjacent to San Juan River, due to 'risk of significant transboundary harm' to Nicaragua, principally 'the possible large deposition of sediment from the road, with resulting risks to the ecology and water quality of the river, as well as morphological changes').

[118] E.g., *Case Concerning Pulp Mills on the River Uruguay (Argentina v Uruguay)*, above n 10, para 72.

[119] *Certain Activities Carried Out by Nicaragua in the Border Area (Costa Rica v Nicaragua)*, above n 12, para 68.

Costa Rica be permitted to dispatch civilian personnel charged with protection of the environment to the area as 'necessary to ensure that no [irreparable] prejudice be caused' to the Ramsar-protected wetland.[120] And, in 2013, the Court ordered additional measures, finding that cutting of two new *caños* in the disputed area posed 'a real risk' of alteration of the course of the San Juan River.[121]

However, the Court has often found that the applicant state has failed to establish a risk of irreparable harm, rejecting provisional measures accordingly. This occurred in *Pulp Mills* with regard to the alleged environmental impacts of the construction and operation of the mills[122] and in *Certain Activities*, both regarding Costa Rica's request for an order suspending Nicaragua's program to dredge the San Juan River[123] and Costa Rica's later request for modification of earlier orders based on the presence and activities of Nicaraguan youths in the disputed area.[124]

The Court also unanimously rejected Nicaragua's request for provisional measures in the *Road* case, where there was no question that portions of a road built along the bank of the San Juan River were deteriorating, with sediment and debris being transferred to the river as a result. The dispute was whether this was resulting in 'harm', and the Court ultimately found no qualifying risk of prejudice.[125] In particular, the Court concluded that Nicaragua had failed to prove that the road works had 'led to a substantial increase in the sediment load in the river.'[126] Does this result imply that a party seeking provisional measures in an environmental case may be required to prove some level of existing harm before the Court will be willing to find a *risk* of irreparable harm? The Court also concluded that Nicaragua had failed to provide evidence of 'any long-term effect on the river by aggradations of the river channel', and had not explained how road works could endanger wetland species or 'identified

[120] Ibid., para 80, 86(2).

[121] *Certain Activities Carried Out by Nicaragua in the Border Area (Costa Rica v Nicaragua),* above n 13, para 49.

[122] *Case Concerning Pulp Mills on the River Uruguay (Argentina v Uruguay),* above n 10, para 73–75.

[123] *Certain Activities Carried Out by Nicaragua in the Border Area (Costa Rica v Nicaragua),* above n 12, para 81–82.

[124] ICJ, *Certain Activities Carried Out by Nicaragua in the Border Area (Costa Rica v Nicaragua); Construction of a Road in Costa Rica Along the San Juan River (Nicaragua v Costa Rica),* Order on Requests for the Modification of the March 2011 Provisional Measures, 16 July 2013, ICJ Reports 2013, para 19–20, 35.

[125] The Court's rationales were similar to those later expressed on the merits for rejecting Nicaragua's claims of environmental harm, raising questions about whether the decision on provisional measures prejudged the core issue on the merits to a certain extent. Compare *Construction of a Road in Costa Rica Along the San Juan River (Nicaragua v Costa Rica),* above n 12, para 34 and *Certain Activities/Road*, Judgment (2015), para 194, 196, 211, 213.

[126] *Construction of a Road in Costa Rica Along the San Juan River (Nicaragua v Costa Rica),* above n 12, para 34.

with precision which species [were] likely to be affected.'[127] These conclusions are informative about the level of proof the Court expects at the provisional measures stage.[128]

15.4.4.2 Serious Harm to the Marine Environment

As discussed above, UNCLOS authorizes tribunals to prescribe provisional measures they deem necessary to 'prevent serious harm to the marine environment'. Importantly, such measures are available 'even if there is no evidence that any specific right or rights of the party making the request for provisional measures are at risk'.[129] Thus, even if the applicant has failed to demonstrate an urgent risk of irreparable prejudice to its rights, measures for the prevention of serious harm to the marine environment may nonetheless be available.[130] ITLOS has also demonstrated that it may consider the need for such measures on its own initiative once a party has requested other measures, as it did in *Southern Bluefin Tuna*.[131]

When a tribunal under UNCLOS is ascertaining whether provisional measures are necessary to 'prevent serious harm to the marine environment'—whether at the request of a party or on its own initiative within the context of provisional measures proceedings initiated by a party on another basis—the concept of 'irreparable' prejudice does not come into play. This is because, by its express terms, Article 290 establishes the qualifying threshold: the harm in question must only be of a 'serious' character.[132] But what qualifies?

First, 'harm to the marine environment' is interpreted broadly and includes not only pollution, but also impacts to ecosystems, biodiversity, endangered species, and more.[133] Existing jurisprudence indicates that depletion of particular marine species,[134] pollution through releases of oil,[135] and the possible impacts of land reclamation activities (including sedimentation, bed level changes, and coastal erosion)[136] may all be harms that are sufficiently 'serious' to merit provisional measures.

---

[127] Ibid.

[128] They also raise interesting questions in the context of a dispute like the *Road* case, where baseline data did not exist due at least in part to Costa Rica's failure to prepare an EIA, in breach of international law. See *Certain Activities/Road*, Judgment (2015), para 162, 229(6).

[129] Mensah 2002, p. 46.

[130] E.g., *ITLOS, The MOX Plant Case (Ireland v United Kingdom)*, above n 10.

[131] Mensah 2002, p. 53.

[132] Miles 2017, p. 305.

[133] See Boyle 2007, p. 373; Miles 2017, pp. 305–06.

[134] *Southern Bluefin Tuna Cases (New Zealand and Australia v Japan)*, above n 68.

[135] See *The 'Arctic Sunrise' Case (Kingdom of the Netherlands v Russian Federation)*, above n 19, para 87 (fuel oil releases); *Dispute Concerning Delimitations of the Maritime Boundary between Ghana and Côte D'Ivoire in the Atlantic Ocean (Ghana/Côte D'Ivoire)*, above n 15, para 65 (oil extraction activities).

[136] See *Case Concerning Land Reclamation by Singapore in and around the Straits of Johor (Malaysia v Singapore)*, above n 12, para 22(3)(c)(d).

The jurisprudence of ITLOS also indicates that UNCLOS is concerned with preventing harm to the marine environment generally, not the marine environments of particular parties.[137] This reflects the '[o]verall sensitivity of the marine ecosystem' and a recognition that UNCLOS Article 290 authorizes the indication of provisional measures aimed at 'protecting a collective interest wider than that immediately subject to litigation'.[138]

Importantly, '[w]hen considering measures for the prevention of serious harm to the marine environment, ITLOS has indicated that it is willing to accept a lesser degree of proof when assessing the risk that harm will occur'[139] than it or the ICJ requires when considering alleged prejudice to party rights. This is clear from the Tribunal's decisions on provisional measures in *Southern Bluefin Tuna*,[140] *MOX Plant*,[141] and *Land Reclamation*,[142] as well as the Special Chamber's provisional measures decision in *Ghana/Côte d'Ivoire*.[143] In each of those cases, the tribunal found the evidence of potential harm either inconclusive or unpersuasive, but—emphasizing the need for 'prudence and caution'—erred on the side of caution, ordering provisional measures to prevent even possible harm to the marine environment.

15.4.5 Urgency

One area of consistency in the practice of international courts and tribunals on provisional measures relates to urgency, both procedural and substantive.

Procedurally, provisional measures requests are treated as a matter of urgency. This is required under the procedural rules of the various courts and tribunals. For instance, the ICJ's Rules require requests for provisional measures to be addressed 'as a matter of urgency,' with 'priority over all other cases,' including requiring

137 See Miles 2017, p. 311.

138 Miles 2017, p. 317.

139 Ibid., p. 314; see also Mensah 2002, p. 45 (evidence that serious harm 'might occur' sufficient).

140 *Southern Bluefin Tuna Cases (New Zealand and Australia v Japan),* above n 68, para 77–80 (noting scientific uncertainty, party disagreement, and Tribunal's inability to 'conclusively assess the scientific evidence presented by the parties').

141 ITLOS, *The MOX Plant Case (Ireland v United Kingdom),* above n 10, para 84, Joint Declaration (noting 'almost total lack of agreement on the scientific evidence with respect to the possible consequences' of plant operation), and Separate Opinion of Judge Treves, para 8–9 (scientific evidence 'not substantial and focused enough' to conclusively establish causal relationship between plant and risk to marine environment).

142 *Case Concerning Land Reclamation by Singapore in and around the Straits of Johor (Malaysia v Singapore),* above n 12, para 96, 99 (adverse effects to marine environment 'cannot be excluded' and 'possible implication' of works on environment sufficient to justify measures).

143 *Dispute Concerning Delimitations of the Maritime Boundary between Ghana and Côte D'Ivoire in the Atlantic Ocean (Ghana/Côte D'Ivoire),* above n 15, para 67–69, 72, 108(1)(c)–(d) (ordering measures even where evidence insufficient to prove imminent risk of serious harm to marine environment).

the prompt convening of the Court if it is not sitting when the request is filed.[144] Provisional measures requests under UNCLOS also have priority over other cases, with the rules requiring that a hearing on the request be scheduled at 'the earliest possible date'.[145] The possibility under Article 290(5) for the prescription of provisional measures even before the constitution or convening of a tribunal[146] means that requests for provisional measures—including those related to urgent environmental concerns—may be addressed even more quickly. ICSID tribunals are also required to give requests for provisional measures priority, and the Secretary General is empowered to schedule hearings on provisional measures immediately upon constitution of the tribunal.[147]

In practice, requests for provisional measures are indeed addressed promptly (relatively speaking), with hearings often occurring within a month or two after the submission of the request, and orders issuing shortly thereafter. This speed is one reason that provisional measures may be particularly useful for the purposes of environmental protection. However, the rapidity of the process may affect a party's ability to collect sufficient data or prepare adequate expert support to successfully prove or disprove a qualifying risk of harm.

The procedural urgency with which requests for provisional measures are addressed reflects the fact that they are understood to relate to issues presenting questions of substantive urgency: concerns that cannot wait for a final adjudication on the merits (or, in the case of ITLOS, even the constitution or convening of a tribunal). Thus, if the situation prompting the request is not actually urgent—if there is no risk that the rights or interests one party (or the court, if authorized to act *proprio motu*) seeks to protect will be harmed during the pendency of the case—then provisional measures are not justified and should not be ordered.

International courts and tribunals are consistent in their treatment of urgency as an essential precondition for the issuance of provisional measures, so long as some *lex specialis* does not create a different requirement.[148] It need not be proved with absolute certainty that the prejudice in question will necessarily materialize, but mere hypotheticals are insufficient. A 'real and imminent risk' of such prejudice must exist, 'the precise threshold of which is to be assessed on a case-by-case basis by reference to the ongoing factual matrix'.[149] Changes that occur after filing of application may be relevant for creating or eliminating urgency.[150]

In the context of provisional measures requested of ITLOS under Article 290(5), a higher degree of urgency must be demonstrated. It is not sufficient that the harm in question may materialize before a final adjudication on the merits; rather, such

[144] ICJ Rules, Article 74(1)–(2).

[145] ITLOS Rules, Article 90(1)-(2).

[146] See Sect. 15.3.3, *supra*.

[147] ICSID Arbitration Rule 39(2), (5).

[148] See Miles 2017, pp. 288, 306–10; see also Tomka and Hernández 2011, § C.II; Merrills 1995, p. 110.

[149] Miles 2017, p. 295.

[150] See ibid.

harm must be 'likely to occur'[151] before the Annex VII tribunal to be constituted is able to rule on the question, 'a period of time which in the ordinary course of events may be far shorter than the time until the giving of final judgment.'[152] Although this window may be quite short, ITLOS has found urgency justifying the prescription of provisional measures prior to the constitution of an arbitral tribunal on multiple occasions.[153]

15.4.6 Party Behaviour

The statements and conduct of the parties can bear significantly on whether the court or tribunal seized of their dispute will find a risk of prejudice that is both sufficiently significant and sufficiently urgent to justify the ordering of provisional measures. Most obviously, if a party's behaviour can be interpreted as confirming the existence of a qualifying risk or of the urgency of the situation, that behaviour is likely to be useful to the applicant.[154]

Declarations and assurances made by the parties have long been relied upon as bases for addressing whether provisional measures are necessary. Thus, there are many examples of respondents taking 'active steps to prevent the grant of provisional measures, usually by giving an undertaking or representation to the Court that it will not take certain actions or otherwise prejudice the *status quo*,'[155] often by laying out a timeline that undercuts a claim of urgency.[156]

---

[151] Mensah 2002, p. 47.

[152] Miles 2017, p. 308. It was formerly understood that the relevant time frame was constitution of the tribunal, but in *Land Reclamation*, ITLOS found urgency and ordered relief 'noting that the question to be asked was not when the Annex VII [tribunal] would be constituted, but rather when it would be in a position—having met, heard the arguments of the parties and allowed due time for deliberation—to 'modify, revoke or affirm those provisional measures,'' which may not be possible until well after the constitution of the tribunal. Ibid., p. 309.

[153] *Southern Bluefin Tuna Cases (New Zealand and Australia v Japan),* above n 68; ITLOS, *The MOX Plant Case (Ireland v United Kingdom),* above n 10; *Case Concerning Land Reclamation by Singapore in and around the Straits of Johor (Malaysia v Singapore)*, above n 12,; *The 'Arctic Sunrise' Case (Kingdom of the Netherlands v Russian Federation)*, above n 19.

[154] E.g., *Nuclear Tests,* above n 8, para 25–26 (France's official pronouncements); *Certain Activities Carried Out by Nicaragua in the Border Area (Costa Rica v Nicaragua)*, above n 12, para 72, 75 (Nicaragua's statements as indicating intent); *Artic Sunrise* and nonappearance of Russia, as discussed in Guilfoyle and Miles 2014, pp. 276–77.

[155] Miles 2017, p. 296.

[156] ITLOS, *The MOX Plant Case (Ireland v United Kingdom),* above n 10, para 79–80 (UK's assurance that no transport of fuel would occur until October 2002); *Case Concerning Pulp Mills on the River Uruguay (Argentina v Uruguay),* above n 10, para 46, 75 (finding persuasive Uruguay's assurance that mills 'would not be operational before August and June 2008 respectively, and that a number of further conditions would have to be met before that stage was reached,' including issuance of environmental permits); *Construction of a Road in Costa Rica Along the San Juan River (Nicaragua v Costa Rica)*, above n 12, para 33 (Costa Rica's assurances works would not resume until 'late 2014 or early 2015').

When the court or tribunal is willing to take the respondent at its word, such assurances may prove sufficient to allow the conclusion that a qualifying risk does not exist, or that there is no urgency.[157] In the UNCLOS context, ITLOS and Annex VII tribunals have likewise found the undertakings and representations of the respondent, as well as the public pronouncements of a party, sufficient to either eliminate the need for provisional measures entirely or to require the modification of the kind of relief deemed appropriate in the circumstances.[158]

When a court or tribunal formally places a party's assurance on the record in denying a request for certain provisional measures, this effectively binds the party to their promise even if no provisional measures are ordered. In *Land Reclamation*, ITLOS relied on Singapore's assurances 'that it would notify, consult and negotiate with Malaysia before proceeding with further works, while giving it the opportunity to comment and produce new evidence.'[159] This allowed Malaysia to secure at the provisional measures stage 'commitments that in substance addressed all of its rights to co-operation under [UNCLOS] and general international law.'[160] Professor Boyle calls this 'a very remarkable outcome for a provisional measures case—and one which effectively resolved the dispute without further proceedings on the merits.'[161] Even where the result is not so favourable, a court or tribunal's having formally placed one party's assurances on the record when denying provisional measures may ease the applicant's burden if it seeks provisional measures later due to a failure of the respondent to live up to its prior commitments.

However, the assurances of the party will not always be credited or sufficient to carry the day.[162] Such a result may be likely where a party's conduct is seen as particularly flagrant or brazen, or where the party has made public statements but refused to appear to respond to the request for provisional measures.

15.4.7 Proportionality

Although provisional measures are often sought by only one of the parties to a dispute, international courts and tribunals are generally authorized to order such

---

157 E.g., *Certain Activities Carried Out by Nicaragua in the Border Area (Costa Rica v Nicaragua)*, above n 12, para 71–74 (rejecting request based on Nicaragua's assurances); *Construction of a Road in Costa Rica Along the San Juan River (Nicaragua v Costa Rica)*, above n 12, para 37 (noting Costa Rica's assurances).

158 Miles 2017, pp. 310–11; see also ITLOS, *The MOX Plant Case (Ireland v United Kingdom)*, above n 10, para 78–81, 89(1); *The M/V 'Louisa" Case (Saint Vincent and the Grenadines v Spain)*, Provisional Measures, 23 December 2010, ITLOS Reports 2008–2010, para 74–75, 78 (crediting Spanish assurances regarding environmental monitoring).

159 Boyle 2007, p. 379.

160 Ibid., pp. 379–80.

161 Ibid., p. 380.

162 E.g., *Certain Activities Carried Out by Nicaragua in the Border Area (Costa Rica v Nicaragua)*, above n 13, para 40, 50; see also Miles 2017, pp. 311–12, 474 (discussing *Arctic Sunrise*).

relief to preserve the rights of *both* parties, not just those of the applicant. 'This means that there should be a measure of equity and justice to all the parties in the dispute, both in the nature of the measures ordered and in the effect of their application on the claims of the parties.'[163] The need for proportionality is also reflected in the procedural requirements of the tribunals in question, which uniformly require that both parties be provided the opportunity to be heard on the question of provisional measures before such relief is ordered,[164] even in those situations where the tribunal is acting *proprio motu*.

It is often not possible for provisional measures to affect both sides equally, particularly if the measures being ordered require only one party to cease or undertake certain actions. But 'care should be taken to ensure that, in seeking to preserve the rights of one party to the dispute, serious and unavoidable prejudice is not done to the rights or interests of the other party.'[165] This requires a balancing: sufficient relief to protect the right in question while interfering as little as possible with opposing rights.[166] Such proportionality works not only to reinforce the legitimacy of the particular court or tribunal in question, but also to increase the likelihood of compliance with the provisional measures it orders.[167] Conversely, unnecessary burdens on one party and any impression of bias undermine both the efficacy of the measures issued and the reputation of the institution issuing them.

15.5 Types of Measures Ordered

Once it has concluded that the circumstances require indication of provisional measures, a court or tribunal has broad discretion to decide what those measures should be. Indeed, the procedural rules of most tribunals establish that the tribunal may order measures that vary in whole or in part from those requested by the applicant, including measures directing the applicant (as well as the respondent) to act or refrain from acting.[168] This discretion—and the space it creates for the court or tribunal to determine creatively how best to preserve the rights of the parties and ensure the effectiveness of the final judgment (or, in the ITLOS context, to prevent

---

[163] Mensah 2002, p. 44.

[164] ICJ Rules, Article 74(3); UNCLOS, above n 39, Article 290(3); ICSID Arbitration Rule 39(4). Whether or not a party makes use of this opportunity is a separate question.

[165] Mensah 2002, p. 44.

[166] Miles 2017, p. 366. See, e.g., *Case Concerning Pulp Mills on the River Uruguay (Argentina v Uruguay),* above n 10, para 48 (considering likely impacts to Uruguayan economy of measures requested) & 80 (balancing); *Dispute Concerning Delimitations of the Maritime Boundary between Ghana and Côte D'Ivoire in the Atlantic Ocean (Ghana/Côte D'Ivoire),* above n 15, para 99–102 (considering financial costs to Ghana and environmental implications of measures requested).

[167] Miles 2017, p. 366.

[168] E.g., ICJ Rules, Article 75(2); ITLOS Rules, Article 89(5); ICSID Arbitration Rule 39(3).

serious harm to the marine environment)—is a key 'particularity' of interim protection.[169] The tribunal is left to consider the particular circumstances requiring the indication of provisional measures, the posture of the case and the parties, and to craft relief accordingly, constrained only by the fundamental limitations described above.

The courts and tribunals under review here have made frequent use of this discretion, ordering a range of measures. In cases with environmental dimensions, these measures have taken a variety of forms, relating to the need for environmental impact assessment or environmental monitoring, the suspension of certain works or projects, the remediation of environmental damage, and more.

Bendel contends the types of provisional measures ordered by international tribunals can be broken down into three categories: (1) 'orders that assign a unilateral obligation' on one party; (2) 'orders that demand collaboration between the parties'; and (3) 'orders that involve a third party in the execution of the order, as a mediator or guarantor of the order.'[170] This seems correct, broadly speaking, although measures falling into various categories are often ordered simultaneously.

15.5.1 Orders Assigning a Unilateral Obligation

Often, the unilateral obligation is express, requiring one party to either take or refrain from certain actions. Thus, for instance:

- France was ordered to 'avoid nuclear tests causing the deposit of radio-active fall-out' on the territories of Australia and New Zealand.[171]
- Singapore was ordered 'not to conduct its land reclamation in ways that might cause irreparable prejudice to the rights of Malaysia or serious harm to the marine environment'[172] (although the Tribunal generally permitted Singapore to continue its activities).
- Nicaragua was ordered to suspend *caño*-cutting activities in the disputed area and to fill a trench, providing proof of completion to the Court.[173]
- Ghana was ordered to monitor all existing activities in the disputed area to prevent environmental harm and to ensure no new drilling.[174]

---

[169] Oellers-Frahm 2011, p. 1281.

[170] Bendel 2019, p. 493.

[171] *Nuclear Tests,* above n 8, *dispositif.*

[172] *Case Concerning Land Reclamation by Singapore in and around the Straits of Johor (Malaysia v Singapore),* above n 12, para 106(2).

[173] *Certain Activities Carried Out by Nicaragua in the Border Area (Costa Rica v Nicaragua),* above n 12, para 53.

[174] *Dispute Concerning Delimitations of the Maritime Boundary between Ghana and Côte D'Ivoire in the Atlantic Ocean (Ghana/Côte D'Ivoire),* above n 15, para 108(1)(a), (c).

- Russia was ordered to release a Dutch vessel and Greenpeace activists upon payment of a bond.[175]

However, some tribunals issue measures appearing by their terms to order all parties to do or refrain from doing something, when the context actually makes clear that the order is directed at one party in particular.[176]

15.5.2 Orders Demanding Collaboration Between the Parties

ITLOS, in particular, has demonstrated a willingness to order parties involved in environmental disputes to cooperate and consult substantively in order to assess environmental impacts, ensure adequate environmental monitoring, and prevent or remediate environmental damage. In *Southern Bluefin Tuna*, ITLOS emphasized the need for the parties to cooperate to ensure conservation and promote optimum utilization, ordering them to 'resume negotiations without delay with a view to reaching agreement on measures for the conservation and management of southern bluefin tuna.'[177]

The Tribunal has also shown a willingness to issue orders of this sort even in cases where it has not seen fit to order the suspension of the challenged works. In both *MOX Plant* and *Land Reclamation*, 'notwithstanding findings that the evidence did not show that irreparable harm was either imminent or likely,' ITLOS ordered the parties to improve their cooperation, consult, exchange information regarding possible environmental consequences, monitor or assess the risks and effects of their activities, and devise measures to prevent pollution of the marine environment.[178] Although Singapore and Malaysia had agreed to such measures during the course of the *Land Reclamation* proceedings, in *MOX Plant* the Tribunal unanimously ordered them without either party having requested them,[179] and the Annex VII tribunal later affirmed.[180]

---

[175] *The 'Arctic Sunrise' Case (Kingdom of the Netherlands v Russian Federation)*, above n 19, para 105(1).

[176] E.g., *Southern Bluefin Tuna Cases (New Zealand and Australia v Japan)*, above n 68, para 90(1)(c)–(d) (ordering all parties to cease exceeding catch allocations and experimental fishing programs, when only Japan was engaged in one, prompting New Zealand and Australia to initiate the case).

[177] *Southern Bluefin Tuna Cases (New Zealand and Australia v Japan)*, above n 68, para 90(1)(e); see also Boyle 2007, p. 378.

[178] Boyle 2007, p. 378.

[179] ITLOS, *The MOX Plant Case (Ireland v United Kingdom)*, above n 10, para 27–30, 89(1) and Joint Declaration; see also Mensah 2002, p. 53; Tanaka 2014, p. 365.

[180] *The MOX Plant case (Ireland v United Kingdom)*, Order No 3: Suspension of Proceedings on Jurisdiction and Merits, and Request for Further Provisional Measures, 24 June 2003, *dispositif*, para 2.

These measures have been described as 'bold' and 'innovative'.[181] There are, as of yet, no examples of the ICJ ordering such substantive collaboration between the parties.[182] There may never be, insofar as the possibility for such orders in the UNCLOS context stems from the unique authority conferred by Article 290 to grant interim relief to 'prevent serious harm to the marine environment' or from a 'duty to cooperate' to prevent such harm that is in some way unique to the UNCLOS regime.[183]

Professor Boyle has argued that 'provisional measures applications may afford a useful method for tackling failure to do an EIA.'[184] However, to date, this has only proven to be true in the UNCLOS context;[185] the Court has yet to indicate any provisional measures addressing an alleged failure to conduct appropriate environmental assessments, even where the Court later concluded that such an assessment had been required under international law. The explanation may be that the unique grant of authority under UNCLOS to prescribe provisional measures for the protection of the marine environment permits ITLOS and other Annex VII tribunals to issue orders requiring party cooperation in the assessment of risks—even when those risks have been 'uncertain and the potential harm not necessarily irreparable'.[186] Whatever the reason for this different track record on EIA-related provisional measures, the fact that international law leaves the particulars of EIA to be specified at the domestic level[187] means that any provisional measures mandating cooperation between the parties in furtherance of EIA-related goals are unlikely to mandate specifics.

15.5.3 Orders to Involve Third Parties

In *Land Reclamation*, ITLOS not only ordered the parties to cooperate and consult with one another as it had done in *MOX Plant*, but to work together to 'promptly'

---

[181] Miles 2017, pp. 19 and 450.

[182] In *Certain Activities*, the Court did order Costa Rica to 'use its best endeavours to find common solutions with Nicaragua' for prevention of irreparable harm to the wetland, but this was an order without much substance. Order (2011), para 80 and 86(2). See also *Certain Activities Carried Out by Nicaragua in the Border Area (Costa Rica v Nicaragua); Construction of a Road in Costa Rica Along the San Juan River (Nicaragua v Costa Rica),* above n 124, para 14, 21 and 25–29 (rejecting Nicaragua's request that earlier measure be modified to allow for collaborative protection of wetland by environmental personnel of both parties).

[183] ITLOS, *The MOX Plant Case (Ireland v United Kingdom)*, above n 10, para 82; see also *Case Concerning Land Reclamation by Singapore in and around the Straits of Johor (Malaysia v Singapore),* above n 12, para 92.

[184] Boyle 2007, p. 378; see also Tanaka 2014, p. 366.

[185] E.g., *Case Concerning Land Reclamation by Singapore in and around the Straits of Johor (Malaysia v Singapore)*, above n 12, para 95, 106(1) (ordering EIA-type measures where Singapore had not undertaken assessment of impact of its works on Malaysian waters).

[186] Boyle 2007, p. 378.

[187] See *Case Concerning Pulp Mills on the River Uruguay (Argentina v Uruguay)*, above n 115, para 205.

establish a group of independent experts to study the effects of Singapore's works and propose measures to deal with any adverse effects. The Tribunal also expressly ordered the parties to utilize the findings and conclusions of the independent experts to guide their consultations and decision-making.[188] To the extent these measures were intended to facilitate resolution of the dispute, they have been dubbed 'a rousing success': Malaysia and Singapore resumed negotiations as ordered 'and the matter ended with an award on agreed terms by the Annex VII tribunal endorsing a complete settlement'.[189]

The ICJ has also 'demonstrated a willingness to co-opt third parties already peripherally involved into the dispute settlement process'.[190] In *Certain Activities*, the Court twice ordered Costa Rica to consult with the Ramsar Secretariat in its efforts to prevent irreparable damage to the wetland, providing notice to Nicaragua.[191] This approach was not without some criticism. In 2011, multiple judges dissented from the measure, questioning whether leaving Ramsar consultations and access to the disputed territory to only one party pre-judged the sovereignty question, failed to account for the interconnected nature of the wetlands in question, or set the stage for further aggravation of the dispute.[192]

If, as has been suggested, the goals in involving third-party institutions include enhancing collaboration between the parties and accounting for the multilateral nature of the rights at issue,[193] measures of the sort ordered by ITLOS requiring both parties to work together to interface with independent experts may be more effective than the sort ordered by the Court in *Certain Activities*, in which the role of interfacing with the third-party organization was left to only one party. Granted, the parties in *Land Reclamation* may have demonstrated a unique receptiveness to such measures during the hearings,[194] which may sometimes not exist. But the differing approaches, and their results, are instructive.

---

[188] *Case Concerning Land Reclamation by Singapore in and around the Straits of Johor (Malaysia v Singapore)*, above n 162, para 106(1)-(2).

[189] Miles 2017, p. 452.

[190] Ibid., p. 458.

[191] *Certain Activities Carried Out by Nicaragua in the Border Area (Costa Rica v Nicaragua)*, above n 12, para 86(2); *Certain Activities Carried Out by Nicaragua in the Border Area (Costa Rica v Nicaragua)*, above n 13, para 54, 59(E).

[192] See *Certain Activities Carried Out by Nicaragua in the Border Area (Costa Rica v Nicaragua)*, above n 12: Declaration of Judge Skotnikov, para 4–13; Declaration of Judge Xue; Separate Opinion of Judge Sepúlveda-Amor, para 4, 29–34; and Declaration of Judge *ad hoc* Guillaume, para 17–21. In 2013, only Guillaume voiced concern, declaring his continued preference for a more collaborative approach.

[193] See Bendel 2019, pp. 521–22; see also Miles 2017, pp. 455–58 (arguing purpose may be stabilizing force or enhancing likelihood of compliance).

[194] See *Case Concerning Land Reclamation by Singapore in and around the Straits of Johor (Malaysia v Singapore)*, above n 12, para 86.

15.5.4 Complementary Measures

It is common for courts and tribunals to direct the parties to refrain from taking any actions that will aggravate or extend the dispute. Miles contends that, although such measures can be seen as related to the need to protect the rights subject to litigation and the efficacy of the judicial process, they actually have 'a separate legal and historical basis.'[195] Nevertheless, since *LaGrand* and in what Miles argues is a departure from prior practice, the Court has made clear that it will only order these as measures as supplementary to and complimenting those that are ordered to protect rights *pendente lite.*[196] Whether or not this 'subordination of measures for non-aggravation'[197] is desirable, it is the current state of affairs.

A further category of complementary measures contains those requiring one or both of the parties to report back to the issuing court or tribunal regarding their compliance with the other measured issued. In the ITLOS context, such reporting requirements are mandatory under the Rules, which obligate the parties to provide a report to the issuing tribunal 'as soon as possible', including explaining 'the steps [the party] has taken or proposes to take in order to ensure prompt compliance with the measures prescribed'.[198] In the orders discussed in this chapter, ITLOS required the first report on compliance to be submitted by the parties very shortly after the issuance of the order, raising questions about how much can be achieved in such a short span of time.

Such reporting is not mandatory under the ICJ's Rules, which only provide that the Court 'may request information from the parties on any matter connected with the implementation of any provisional measures it has indicated.'[199] The practice may have been 'rare' in the past,[200] but it was utilized by the Court in *Certain Activities*. It is debatable whether this 'judicial supervision' helped to ensure the implementation of the measures ordered by the Court[201] or whether the reports instead served as a mechanism for the extension and aggravation of the dispute, as may often result, particularly where the parties interpret the meanings and requirements of the measures differently.[202]

---

[195] Miles 2017, p. 65; see also p. 274.

[196] See ibid., pp. 274–85.

[197] Miles 2017, p. 286.

[198] ITLOS Rules, Article 95(1).

[199] ICJ Rules, Article 78.

[200] Tomka and Hernández 2011, n. 24.

[201] Tanaka 2014, pp. 366–367.

[202] See ibid., p. 367.

15.5.5 *Modification or Revocation of Provisional Measures Previously Ordered*

Just as tribunals are authorized to award interim relief, so too are they generally authorized to revoke or modify provisional measures previously issued. As with the original issuance of such measures, there is some divergence as to whether the tribunal must act at the request of a party (ITLOS[203]) or may revoke or modify measures either at the request of a party or *proprio motu* (ICJ[204]). Either way, such a decision requires the tribunal to conclude that 'some change in the situation justifies such revocation or modification'.[205]

Although multiple parties to disputes before the ICJ have sought revocation or modification of earlier provisional measures, the Court has never seen fit to oblige.[206] The Court's response to the dueling requests from Costa Rica and Nicaragua in the joined cases regarding the San Juan River is the 'only instance in which the ICJ has engaged in substantive reflection on what is required for modification and revocation to be justified'.[207] Ultimately, the Court refused both requests, finding that Nicaragua had not identified a qualifying change and that, although Costa Rica had, irreparable harm and urgency had not been demonstrated.[208]

15.6 Legal and Practical Effect of Provisional Measures

If a litigant satisfies all of the criteria discussed above and successfully petitions an international court or tribunal for an order of provisional measures, what then?

'For nearly eight decades, the most significant controversy concerning provisional measures was the question of their binding effect.'[209] However, this dispute has now been definitively resolved in the affirmative—not only for tribunals constituted under

---

203 UNCLOS, above n 39, Article 290(3).

204 ICJ Rules, Article 76(1).

205 Ibid.; see also UNCLOS, above n 39, Article 290(2).

206 Miles 2017, p. 154.

207 Ibid., p. 500.

208 *Certain Activities Carried Out by Nicaragua in the Border Area (Costa Rica v Nicaragua); Construction of a Road in Costa Rica Along the San Juan River (Nicaragua v Costa Rica)*, above n 124.

209 Miles 2017, p. 336; see also Merrills 1995, p. 116; Oellers-Frahm 2011, pp. 1284–85.

UNCLOS, which explicitly provides for the binding effect of provisional measures 'prescribed' thereunder[210]—but also by the ICJ,[211] ICSID tribunals,[212] and others.

But the fact that the binding nature of provisional measures has now been established does not, unfortunately, guarantee their effectiveness. Most international courts and tribunals have limited power to enforce their orders beyond awarding costs or making adverse inferences, raising the perennial question of whether parties will comply.[213]

The record of compliance with provisional measures orders varies depending on the forum. Before the ICJ, that record is quite poor. A frequent criticism is that the Court's provisional measures orders 'are rarely complied with in full and often not at all,' with states often showing 'open defiance in whole or in part.'[214] Before other tribunals, the record is better. Litigants have largely, although not perfectly, complied with provisional measures ordered under UNCLOS Article 290 and in investor-state arbitrations.[215]

Litigants may be incentivized to comply with provisional measures by a desire not to lose credibility or create a bad impression with the tribunal that will later decide the merits of their case, or to avoid further measures by the tribunal. They may also comply so as not to damage their reputation or undermine their position to demand that other parties comply with their international obligations in other cases.[216]

Compliance may be more difficult in highly politicized cases, particularly where a state faces domestic pressure to maintain a certain position notwithstanding the order of an international tribunal. Ironically, it is in these cases where the need for judicially-ordered provisional measures may be greatest, as the likelihood of cooperation between the parties is correspondingly low.[217] States may attempt to find a middle ground by complying with the substance of an order under the guise of independent action, as Russia did in the *Artic Sunrise* case despite never recognizing the validity of the order.[218]

Because the provisional measures ordered by international courts and tribunals are binding on the parties, noncompliance gives rise to legal responsibility on the part of the breaching party.[219] The practical consequences of this, however, may vary.

[210] UNCLOS, above n 39, Article 290(6); see also Tomka and Hernández 2011, § B.I; Miles 2017, p. 347.

[211] ICJ, *LaGrand Case (Germany v United States of America)*, Judgment, 27 June 2001, ICJ Reports 2001, para 109. In its subsequent orders, 'the Court has invariably cited *LaGrand* as standing for the proposition that interim relief ordered pursuant to Article 41 is binding on the parties to a dispute.' Miles 2017, p. 357.

[212] Miles 2017, p. 357 (citing *Emilio Agustín Mafezzini v Spain*, Decision on Request for Provisional Measures, 28 October 1999, ICSID Case No. ARB/97/7).

[213] See Tanaka 2014, p. 365.

[214] Miles 2017, p. 506.

[215] Ibid., p. 506.

[216] Oellers-Frahm 2011, p. 1294; Miles 2017, p. 516.

[217] Merrills 1995, pp. 138–39.

[218] Miles 2017, pp. 374-75.

[219] Oellers-Frahm 2011, p. 1293.

In the practice of the ICJ, noncompliance with provisional measures has generally led only to a simple declaration that the party has breached its obligations.[220] The affected party may also be entitled to compensation for any damage caused by the wrongful act, but the Court has not historically granted other sanctions to penalize the breach of its order *per se*.[221]

This dynamic is illustrated by the Court's approach in *Certain Activities*. In its judgment on the merits, the Court held that Nicaragua had breached its obligations under the 2011 order indicating provisional measures.[222] While recognizing Costa Rica's right to compensation for environmental damage caused by that breach and the hypothetical possibility of the imposition of litigation costs,[223] the majority nonetheless rejected Costa Rica's request that Nicaragua pay the costs it incurred in obtaining the 2013 order in response to Nicaragua's breach.[224]

The imperfect record of compliance with provisional measures orders raises serious questions about their efficacy as a tool for preventing harm to the environment. However, it has been argued that even an order that is not complied with may have some value in altering the political calculus of the dispute, such as by encouraging the breaching party to settle rather than openly flout the order, or bringing increased public attention to the issue and granting a stamp of legitimacy to the requesting party's claim.[225]

15.7 Concluding Remarks

Provisional measures are a valuable tool for protection of the environment. Part of this value lies in their flexibility: international courts and tribunals across the board have broad discretion to shape the measures ordered, even when these are different in whole or in part from the measures requested.[226]

---

220 Miles 2017, p. 390.

221 Oellers-Frahm 2011, p. 1293.

222 ICJ, *Certain Activities Carried Out by Nicaragua in the Border Area (Costa Rica v Nicaragua); Construction of a Road in Costa Rica Along the San Juan River (Nicaragua v Costa Rica)*, Judgment, 16 December 2015, ICJ Reports 2015, p 665, para 129.

223 See ICJ Statute, above n 38, Article 64; ICJ Rules, Article 97.

224 ICJ, *Certain Activities Carried Out by Nicaragua in the Border Area (Costa Rica v Nicaragua); Construction of a Road in Costa Rica Along the San Juan River (Nicaragua v Costa Rica)*, above n 222, para 49(3)(c), (f), 143–44, 229(5). Four judges voted to award Costa Rica costs, 'the first occasion on which members of the Court reached such a conclusion.' Miles 2017, pp. 396–97; see Joint Declaration ('exceptional circumstances' warranting Court's first exercise of Article 64 power).

225 Miles 2017, pp. 516–17; Merrills 1995, pp. 139–40.

226 See Sect. 15.5, *supra*.

It has been said that international courts and tribunals are 'becoming bolder in their approach to provisional measures, directly impacting their relevance for environmental disputes.'[227] This evolution, however, is more marked in some courts and tribunals than others.

The ICJ embodies a comparatively 'restrictive' approach.[228] The scope of the provisional measures it may order are limited to those necessary to protect a right of one of the parties to the dispute,[229] and the Court requires a link to the subject matter of the case.[230] While the Court has authority to indicate provisional measures *proprio motu*, it has been reluctant to use that authority.[231] The Court also appears to be more likely to reject requests outright. That said, the Court has played a significant role in the development of the law regarding provisional measures, for protection of the environment and otherwise, and its orders create a foundation for orders in future cases.

ITLOS and tribunals constituted under UNCLOS have broader authority to order provisional measures for the protection of the environment.[232] They have demonstrated a 'strong willingness'[233] to do so in practice, even where evidence of harm is inconclusive or environmental harm is not the central focus of the underlying dispute.[234] They have also demonstrated a willingness to tailor relief beyond what the parties have requested for the prevention of possible environmental harm, including to enforce EIA and joint monitoring obligations and to promote conservation and pollution prevention.[235] Thus, as Professor Boyle concludes, ITLOS's provisional measures cases 'have established the utility of the Article 290 procedure as a means of protecting not only the rights of other States but also the marine environment in general.'[236]

---

[227] Bendel 2019, p. 493.

[228] Ibid., p. 520.

[229] See Sect. 15.3.1, *supra*.

[230] See Sect. 15.4.3, *supra*.

[231] See Sect. 15.3.2, *supra*.

[232] See Sect. 15.3.1, *supra*. See also Mensah 2002, p. 54 (noting 'different objectives' and 'different requirements' for provisional measures under UNCLOS for prevention of serious harm to marine environment).

[233] Tanaka 2014, p. 365.

[234] See Sect. 15.4.4, *supra*. It has been argued that provisional measures under UNCLOS to prevent serious harm to the marine environment 'possess a *sui generis* character within the wider regime of provisional measures in international law. They do not need to comply with the link test, the contemplated harm must be merely 'serious' and not 'irreparable,' and ITLOS has implied a willingness to consider the precautionary principle as relevant to the assessment of urgency.' Miles 2017, pp. 452–53.

[235] See Sect. 15.5.

[236] Boyle 2007, p. 380. It is interesting, however, that all three of the cases Professor Boyle references in this regard involved orders issued by ITLOS under Article 290(5), pending the constitution of another tribunal. Is ITLOS more willing to grant broader measures in part because such measures may remain in place for a shorter period of time?

Some have argued for greater use of provisional measures by other international courts and tribunals in order to achieve environmental protection. Bendel, in particular, contends that a reframing of provisional measures would allow 'interests other than the interests of the parties themselves [to] be protected.'[237] However, this is possible only if the tribunal possesses the authority to issue such measures to begin with—e.g., through an express provision in its foundational instrument, such as UNCLOS Article 290.[238] It is unlikely that the ICJ Statute will be amended to grant the Court such authority. However, it is an idea worth consideration for inclusion in future international environmental agreements, whether they contain consent to the jurisdiction of the ICJ or any other tribunal. Such agreements may seek to replicate (and perhaps expand) the relative success of provisional measures under UNCLOS, which is likewise a treaty in which protection of the environment plays a prominent role, an emphasis that has likely contributed to tribunals' willingness to issue provisional measures for protection of the environment.

References

Bendel J (2019) The Provisional Measures Orders in International Environmental Disputes: A Case for International Courts and Tribunals. Nordic Journal of International Law. 88:489-524

Boyle A (2007) The Environmental Jurisprudence of the International Tribunal for the Law of the Sea. Int'l J. of Marine & Coastal L. 22:369–381

British Institute of International and Comparative Law (BIICL) (2019) Empirical study: Provisional measures in investor-state arbitration. https://www.biicl.org/publications/2019-empirical-study-provisional-measures-in-investorstate-arbitration Accessed 30 May 2020

Crawford J (2016) Foreword. In: Miles C (ed) Provisional Measures before International Courts and Tribunals. Cambridge University Press, Cambridge

Guilfoyle D, Miles C (2014) Provisional Measures and the MV Arctic Sunrise. Am. J. Int'l L. 108:271-287

ICC (2019) Commission Report: Resolving Climate Change Related Disputes through Arbitration and ADR. https://iccwbo.org/content/uploads/sites/3/2019/11/icc-arbitration-adr-commission-report-on-resolving-climate-change-related-disputes-english-version.pdf Accessed 30 May 2020

---

[237] Bendel 2019, p. 492.

[238] With respect, Bendel's effort to locate such 'space for the operalisation of provisional measures that go beyond the protection of the rights of the parties' in phrases such as 'protection of the object of the dispute', 'maintenance of the *status quo*', and 'ensuring the situation is not aggravated' stretches the intended meaning of these phrases as used in legal instruments and jurisprudence, where they are understood as relating to the dispute and relationship between the parties, not to broader considerations. See Bendel 2019, pp. 496–97, 523. We cannot agree that 'the prevention of serious harm to the marine environment'—a basis for provisional measures that is understood to be unique to UNLOS, stemming from the treaty's express provisions in Part XII regarding the protection of the marine environment, see Tomka and Hernández 2011, § B.IV—somehow 'falls into the ICJ's interpretation of the avoidance of any aggravation or extension of the dispute'. Ibid., p. 498. See Miles 2017, pp. 450–53.

Levine J (2017) Adopting and Adapting Arbitration for Climate Change Related Disputes: The Experience of the Permanent Court of Arbitration. In: Dispute Resolution and Climate Change (ICC 2017). https://www.peacepalacelibrary.nl/ebooks/files/Adopting%20and%20Adapting%20Arbitration%20for%20Climate%20ChangeRelated%20Disputes.pdf Accessed 30 May 2020

Mensah T (2002) Provisional Measures in the International Tribunal for the Law of the Sea (ITLOS). ZaöRV 62:43-54

Merrills J (1995) Interim Measures of Protection in the Recent Jurisprudence of the International Court of Justice. Int'l & Comp. L. Q. 44:90-146

Meshel T (2017) Optional Rules for Arbitration of Disputes Relating to Natural Resources and/or the Environment. MPILux Working Paper 1

Miles C (2017) Provisional Measures before International Courts and Tribunals. Cambridge University Press, Cambridge

Oellers-Frahm K (2011) Expanding the Competence to Issue Provisional Measures—Strengthening the International Judicial Function. German L.J. 12:1279–1294

Ratliff D (2001) The PCA Optional Rules for Arbitration of Disputes Relating to Natural Resources and/or the Environment, Leiden J. Int'l L. 14:887-896

Robinson N (2018) Environmental Law: Is an Obligation Erga Omnes Emerging? United Nations Panel Discussion (4 June 2018). https://www.iucn.org/sites/dev/files/content/documents/2018/environmental_law_is_an_obligation_erga_omnes_emerging_interamcthradvisoryopinionjune2018.pdf Accessed 29 May 2020

Tanaka Y (2014) Provisional Measures Prescribed by ITLOS and Marine Environmental Protection. Proceedings of the Annual Meeting (ASIL), 108:365-367

Tomka P, Hernández G (2011) Provisional Measures in the International Tribunal for the Law of the Sea. In: Coexistence, cooperation and solidarity: Liber Amicorum Rüdiger Wolfrum. Brill, Leiden, pp 1763–1787

Cicely Parseghian (cicelyparseghian@gmail.com) is an US-trained attorney currently working for the courts of the state of Arizona. She spent ten years as an attorney at Foley Hoag LLP, where she served as counsel for various sovereign states in their disputes before the ICJ and ICSID tribunals, including many environmental disputes. Of particular relevance for the present chapter, she served as counsel to Uruguay in Pulp Mills (although after the provisional measures decisions discussed here) and to Nicaragua in the Certain Activities and Road cases.

Benjamin Guthrie (benjamin.guthrie@hsf.com, 917-542-7851) is an associate at Herbert Smith Freehills New York LLP. His practice focuses on focuses on international arbitration and dispute resolution. He has participated in cases before the ICJ, ICSID tribunals, and a range of international commercial arbitral tribunals.

Chapter 16
Proving Environmental Harm Before International Courts and Tribunals

Yuri Parkhomenko, Nour Nicolas and Benjamin Salas Kantor

Contents

Abstract This chapter analyses the decisions of international courts and tribunals dealing with claims concerning environmental harm and discusses practical aspects related to the burden of proof, standard of proof, and methods of proof, which could be relevant in preparing for international litigation involving proving environmental harm.

Keywords Burden of proof · Standard of proof · Methods of proof · Precautionary principle · Scientific evidence · Expert

Y. Parkhomenko (✉)
Foley Hoag LLP, Washington, DC, USA
e-mail: yparkhomenko@foleyhoag.com

N. Nicolas
Foley Hoag LLP, New York City, USA
e-mail: nnicolas@foleyhoag.com

B. Salas Kantor
Columbia Law School, New York, NY, USA
e-mail: bsalaskantor@foleyhoag.com

E. Sobenes et al. (eds.), *The Environment Through the Lens of International Courts and Tribunals*, https://doi.org/10.1007/978-94-6265-507-2_16

16.1 Introduction

One of the most striking trends before international courts and tribunals over the past decade has been the increase in the number of cases involving claims relating to prevention or infliction of environmental harm. Such cases require international courts and tribunals to address inherently fact-intensive issues. One of them frequently includes proving the existence and extent of environmental harm. This topic is vast and encompasses many issues. Addressing all of them is beyond the scope of this chapter. Instead, it will focus on those aspects relating to proving environmental harm that could be of practical relevance for preparing for possible litigation before an international court or tribunal. These aspects are addressed in four successive sections which analyse the practice of international courts and tribunals with respect to the burden of proof, standard of proof, and methods of proof in cases involving proving environmental harm.

16.2 Burden of Proof

It is a fundamental principle of international procedural law—one that international courts and tribunals have repeatedly endorsed—that the party claiming certain facts bears the burden of establishing them through sufficient evidence. In *Temple of Preah Vihear*, the International Court of Justice (ICJ) stated that the 'burden of proof in respect of [facts and contentions which are asserted or put forward by one Party or the other] will of course lie on the Party asserting or putting them forward'.[1] In the *Pulp Mills on the River Uruguay*, the Court reiterated that 'in accordance with the well-established principle of *onus probandi incumbit actori*, it is the duty of the party which asserts certain facts to establish the existence of such facts'.[2] This

---

[1] ICJ, *Case concerning the Temple of Preah Vihear (Cambodia v Thailand)*, Merits, Judgment, 15 June 1962, ICJ Reports 1962, p. 16.

[2] ICJ, *Pulp Mills on the River Uruguay (Argentina v Uruguay)*, Judgment, 20 April 2010, ICJ Reports 2010, para 162 (*Pulp Mills* (Judgment)). See also ICJ, *Case Concerning Military and Paramilitary Activities in and Against Nicaragua (Nicaragua v United States of America)* Merits, Judgment, 27 June 1986, ICJ Reports 1986, para 101 (*Military and Paramilitary Activities in and Against Nicaragua (Nicaragua v United States of America)* (Merits)) ('[I]t is the litigant seeking to establish a fact who bears the burden of proving it'); *Application of the Convention on the Prevention and Punishment of the Crime of Genocide (Bosnia and Herzegovina v Serbia and Montenegro)*, Merits, Judgment, 26 February 2007, ICJ Reports 2007, para 204 ('On the burden or onus of proof, it is well established in general that the applicant must establish its case and that a party asserting a fact must establish it'); *Sovereignty over Pedra Branca/Pulau Batu Puteh, Middle Rocks and South Ledge (Malaysia/Singapore)*, Judgment, 23 May 2008, ICJ Reports 2008, para 45 ('It is a general principle of law, confirmed by the jurisprudence of this Court, that a party which advances a point of fact in support of its claim must establish that fact'); *Maritime Delimitation in the Black Sea (Romania v Ukraine)*, Judgment, 3 February 2009, ICJ Reports 2009, para 68 ('As the Court has said on a number of occasions, the party asserting a fact as a basis of its claim must establish it'); *Ahmadou Sadio Diallo (Republic of Guinea v Democratic Republic of the Congo)*, Compensation, Judgment,

allocation of the burden of proof extends to proving the existence of environmental harm, the causal link between a wrongful act and alleged environmental harm, and the valuation of sustained environmental harm.[3] Each of these aspects are discussed in turn.

16.2.1 Existence of Environmental Harm

A claimant alleging environmental harm has the burden to prove that such harm is actual and significant, but this burden could reverse depending on the applicable law, as discussed in the subsections below.

16.2.1.1 Burden to Show that Environmental Harm Is Actual and Significant

International courts and tribunal dismissed claims of environmental harm where claimants failed to show actual harm. Two cases illustrate this. In *Certain Activities*, the Court had to address Nicaragua's claim that the increased sediment concentrations in the San Juan River as a result of Costa Rica's construction of the road caused significant harm to fish species, many of which belong to families that are vulnerable to elevated levels of sediments, to macro-invertebrates and to algal communities in the river.[4] The Court observed that Nicaragua did not present 'any evidence of actual harm to fish in the San Juan River,' nor did it identify 'with precision which species of fish have allegedly been harmed by the construction of the road'.[5] In the Court's view, the environmental diagnostic assessment relied upon by Nicaragua only showed that the construction of the road had a localized impact on macro-invertebrate communities and water quality in small Costa Rican streams draining into the San Juan River. However, the Court was not persuaded that the results of the

---

19 June 2012, ICJ Reports 2012, para 15 (*Diallo* (Compensation)) ('As a general rule, it is for the party which alleges a fact in support of its claims to prove the existence of that fact'); *Application of the Interim Accord of 13 September 1995 (the former Yugoslav Republic of Macedonia v Greece)*, Judgment, 5 December 2011, ICJ Reports 2011, para 72 ('[I]n general, it is the duty of the party that asserts certain facts to establish the existence of such facts').

[3] The ICJ explained in the *Diallo* case: 'As to each head of damage, the Court will consider whether an injury is established. It will then "ascertain whether, and to what extent, the injury asserted by the Applicant is the consequence of wrongful conduct by the Respondent", taking into account "whether there is a sufficiently direct and certain causal nexus between the wrongful act … and the injury suffered by the Applicant." … If the existence of injury and causation is established, the Court will then determine the valuation' (*Diallo* (Compensation), above n 2, para 14).

[4] ICJ, *Certain Activities Carried Out by Nicaragua in the Border Area (Costa Rica v Nicaragua) and Construction of a Road in Costa Rica along the San Juan River (Nicaragua v Costa Rica)*, Merits, Judgment, 15 December 2015, ICJ Reports 2015, para 208 (*Certain Activities; Construction of a Road* (Merits)).

[5] Ibid., para 211.

environmental diagnostic assessment and the follow-up study could be transposed to the San Juan River, which has an average width of nearly 300 m.[6] As regards the expert report submitted by Nicaragua, the Court found it difficult to attribute any differences in macro-invertebrate richness and abundance between the north and the south banks of the river to the construction of the road alone, as opposed to other factors such as the size of the catchment area and the nutrient levels therein.[7] On those grounds, the Court concluded that the construction of the road did not cause harm to the river's ecosystem.[8]

Another example comes from the Eritrea-Ethiopia Claims Commission, which rejected for want of proof the claims of Eritrea and Ethiopia against each with respect to environmental harm allegedly caused during an armed conflict. Eritrea claimed that Ethiopia released pesticides and chemicals, which allegedly killed thousands of livestock and sickened humans.[9] The Commission declined that claim for lack of sufficient evidence, given that it was 'supported solely by a report prepared by Eritrea's advocates, who are neither neutral nor environmental experts'.[10] The Commission made the same decision with respect to Ethiopia's claim against Eritrea for the alleged loss of trees.[11] The Commission observed that Ethiopia's claim 'was summarily presented in less than two pages', and 'the supporting evidence consisted of a claims form' prepared by an Ethiopian regional agricultural and natural resources development bureau, which 'did not identify the location of the lost plants, or the circumstances of their destruction'.[12] Nor did Ethiopia 'address the possibility that Ethiopian forces or civilians may have played some role in environmental degradation during the war'.[13] Taking account of 'the huge amount claimed, the lack of supporting evidence, the unanswered questions regarding the trees' location, and the manifold errors in calculating the claimed damages,' the Commission rejected Ethiopia's claim for environmental damage.[14]

Not any environmental harm is actionable under international law. In addition to showing actual harm, a claimant must still show that environmental harm meets or

---

[6] Ibid., para 212.

[7] Ibid., para 212.

[8] Ibid., para 213.

[9] Eritrea-Ethiopia Claims Commission, Final Award on Eritrea's Damages Claims, 17 August 2009, para 152.

[10] Ibid., para 155.

[11] Ibid., para 422.

[12] Ibid., para 423.

[13] Ibid., para 423.

[14] Ibid., para 425.

exceeds the threshold of significant harm.[15] *De minimis* effects are not enough.[16] The ILC's 2001 Articles on the Prevention of Transboundary Harm clarify that harm is 'significant' if it is 'more than "detectable"', but it need not be 'serious' or 'substantial'; what is significant depends on the circumstances of each case, and may vary over time.[17] It must lead to 'a real detrimental effect on matters such as, for example, human health, industry, property, environment or agriculture in other States,' and 'such detrimental effects must be susceptible of being measured by factual and objective standards'.[18]

For example, in the *MOX Plant Case* the ITLOS refused to grant provisional measures because the claimant had failed to prove the seriousness of the harm.[19] In so doing, the Tribunal heavily relied on the claimant's admission that the harm would not be of 'significant magnitude'.[20]

The ICJ authoritatively addressed this issue in *Certain Activities*, where Nicaragua claimed that Costa Rica's construction of the road resulted in the dumping of large quantities of sediment into the San Juan River, and an increase in sediment concentrations in the river, in and of itself, produced harm to the river, as sediment is a pollutant that had caused a number of adverse effects.[21] The 'core question' before

---

[15] See e.g., Article 290, para 1 of the United Nations Convention on the Law of the Sea (UNCLOS). See also *MOX Plant Arbitration (Ireland v United Kingdom)*, Suspension Of Proceedings On Jurisdiction And Merits, And Request For Further Provisional Measures, Procedural Order No 3, 24 June 2003, para 55 (*MOX Plant Arbitration* (Procedural Order No 3)) ('any harm caused, or likely to be caused, to the marine environment must be "serious" before the Tribunal's power to prescribe provisional measures on that basis arises'); *Pulp Mills* (Judgment), above n 2, para 101 (stating that a State is 'obliged to use all the means at its disposal in order to avoid activities which take place in its territory, or in any area under its jurisdiction, causing *significant damage* to the environment of another State').

[16] UNEP Governing Council decision 6/14 of 19 May 1978, UNEP, Environmental Law: Guidelines and Principles, No 2, Shared Natural Resources (Nairobi, 1978).

[17] International Law Commission, *Draft articles on Prevention of Transboundary Harm from Hazardous Activities, with commentaries* (2001), comment (4) to Article 2. Yearbook of the International Law Commission, 2001, vol. II, Part Two.

[18] Ibid.

[19] *MOX Plant Arbitration* (Procedural Order No 3), above n 15, para 54 ('As the Tribunal has already noted, the liquid wastes discharged from the MOX plant into the Irish Sea contain small quantities of radionuclides, some of which (e.g. Cs-137 and Pu-241) have an extremely long half-life. The wastes in question arise not as a direct by-product of reprocessing of spent nuclear fuels, but from ancillary activities such as the cleaning of the plant and sanitary operations') and para 55 ('the Tribunal does not consider that Ireland has established that any harm which may be caused to the marine environment by virtue of the operation of the MOX plant, pending the determination of this case on the merits, meets this threshold test').

[20] Ibid., para 54 ('The Attorney-General for Ireland, in opening the case, accepted that "…the level of discharges from the MOX plant…is not of a significant magnitude…").

[21] *Certain Activities; Construction of a Road* (Merits), above n 4, paras 174, 177, 178 ('First, it brought about changes in the river morphology, as large quantities of the sediment eroded from the road accumulated on the bed of the Lower San Juan, thereby exacerbating the problems for navigation in this stretch of the river and rendering additional dredging necessary to restore the navigability of the channel. Moreover, sediment eroded from the road created large deltas along the Costa Rican bank of the river that obstruct navigation. Secondly, Nicaragua argues that sediment

the Court was 'whether the construction of the road by Costa Rica has caused significant harm'.[22] The Court declined as unfounded the submission that 'any detrimental impact on the river that is susceptible of being measured constitutes significant harm'.[23] The Court reasoned based on presented evidence that sediment was naturally present in the river in large quantities, and Nicaragua did not show that the river's sediment levels were such that additional sediment eroded from the road passed 'a sort of critical level in terms of its detrimental effects'.[24] Moreover, the Court found that, contrary to Nicaragua's submissions, the present case did not concern a situation where sediment contributed by the road exceeded maximum allowable limits, which had not been determined for the San Juan River.[25] Thus, the Court was not convinced by the argument that the absolute quantity of sediment in the river due to the construction of the road caused significant harm *per se*.[26] The Court therefore proceeded to consider the relative impact of the road-derived sediment on the current overall sediment load of the San Juan River. In this regard, the Court noted that the total sediment load of the San Juan River had not been established and direct measurements of sediment levels in the river were not provided.[27] Based on the evidence before it, and taking into account the estimates provided by the experts of the amount of sediment in the river due to the construction of the road and of the total sediment load of the San Juan River, the Court observed that the road construction was contributing 'at most 2% of the river's total load,' and that 'significant harm cannot be inferred therefrom, particularly taking into account the high natural variability in the river's sediment loads'.[28]

That said, in other cases the relevant threshold of environmental harm could be determined by reference to standards specifically set out in the applicable law. For example, in the *Pulp Mills Case* Argentina alleged that a pulp mill was not compliant in terms of the discharges of effluent for each tonne of pulp produced.[29] To determine whether the concentrations of pollutants discharged by the pulp mill were within the

---

eroded from the road caused harm to the river's water quality and ecosystem. Thirdly, Nicaragua alleges that the construction of the road has had an adverse impact on tourism and the health of the river's riparian communities. In addition, Nicaragua maintains that Costa Rica's continuing failure to comply with road construction standards exposes Nicaragua to future harm, and that Costa Rica has failed to take appropriate remediation measures. Nicaragua further contends that additional risks derive from the possibility of spills of toxic materials into the river, the further development of the Costa Rican bank of the river and the likelihood of natural disasters caused by adverse events such as hurricanes, tropical storms and earthquakes').

[22] Ibid., para 187.

[23] Ibid., para 192.

[24] Ibid.

[25] Ibid.

[26] Ibid.

[27] Ibid., para 193. Costa Rica, based on its main expert's report, estimated the river's total sediment load to be approximately 12,678,000 tonnes per year using measurements from the Colorado River. Nicaragua has not provided a comparable figure, although its expert stated that the current total sediment load of the San Juan River is roughly 13,700,000 tonnes per year.

[28] Ibid., para 194.

[29] *Pulp Mills* (Judgment), above n 2, para 225.

regulatory limits, the Court had to assess them against the effluent discharge limits—both in terms of the concentration of effluents in each litre of wastewater discharged and the absolute amount of effluents that can be discharged in a day—prescribed by the applicable regulatory standards of the parties and the permits issued for the plant by the Uruguayan authorities, since the Digest of the Administrative Commission of the River Uruguay adopted by Argentina and Uruguay only set general limits on 'hydrocarbons', 'sedimentable solids', and 'oils and greases', but did not establish specific ones for the substances in contention between the parties.[30] Taking into account the data collected after the start-up of the mill as contained in the reports by Uruguay's National Directorate for the Environment of the Uruguayan Government and EcoMetrix, a consultancy specializing in environmental and industrial matters that was engaged by the International Financial Corporation to carry out environmental monitoring on the IFC's behalf, the Court found that the discharges from the pulp mill did no exceeded the limits set by the effluent standards prescribed by the relevant Uruguayan regulation.[31]

Similarly, in *Burlington v Ecuador* and *Perenco v Ecuador*, investment tribunals had to rely on Ecuadorian law, as will be discussed below, to determine whether contamination resulting from oil spills exceeded criteria prescribed by respondent in its regulations.[32]

In sum, a claimant bears a burden of showing actual environmental harm that has reached a requisite threshold determined by the applicable law.

16.2.1.2 The Allocation of the Burden of Proof May Depend on the Applicable Law

Although the principle of *onus probandi incumbit actori* is settled, in some circumstances, the burden of proof could be governed by an international treaty or domestic law, which may differently allocate the burden of proof based on the precautionary principle or specific liability regimes.

---

[30] Ibid., para 227. *See* also ibid., paras 242–243 ('The Court notes that CARU has not adopted a water quality standard relating to levels of total phosphorus and phosphates in the river. Similarly, Argentina has no water quality standards for total phosphorus. The Court will therefore have to use the water quality and effluent limits for total phosphorus enacted by Uruguay under its domestic legislation…to assess whether the concentration levels of total phosphorus have exceeded the limits laid down in the regulations of the Parties adopted in accordance with Article 41 (a) of the 1975 Statute').

[31] Ibid., para 228. For the sake of completion, the Court did find a few instances in which the concentrations exceeded the prescribed limits. However, 'in the absence of convincing evidence that this is not an isolated episode but rather a more enduring problem, the Court is not in a position to conclude that Uruguay has breached the provisions of the 1975 Statute.' Ibid., para 228.

[32] *Burlington Resources Inc. v Republic of Ecuador*, ICSID Case No ARB/08/5, Decision on Counterclaims, 7 February 2017 (*Burlington v Ecuador* (Counterclaims)); *Perenco Ecuador Limited v Republic of Ecuador*, ICSID Case No ARB/08/6, Interim Decision on the Environmental Counterclaim, 11 August 2015 (*Perenco v Ecuador* (Interim Decision on the Environmental Counterclaim)).

The Precautionary Principle and Burden of Proof

Does the precautionary principle reverse the burden of proof such that a party proposing to undertake activities potentially harmful to environment must show that such activities would not cause significant damage to environment? An answer may depend on the applicable law. Instructive in this regard is the ICJ's decision in the *Pulp Mills Case,* where Argentina argued that the precautionary principle reverses the burden of proof. Argentina instituted proceedings against Uruguay concerning alleged breaches by Uruguay of obligations incumbent upon it under the Statute of the River Uruguay, a treaty signed by the two States on 26 February 1975 ('the 1975 Statute') for the purpose of establishing the joint machinery necessary for the optimum and rational utilization of that part of the river which constitutes their joint boundary. Argentina alleged that Uruguay unilaterally authorized the construction of two pulp mills on the River Uruguay without complying with the obligatory prior notification and consultation procedures under the 1975 Statute. Argentina also claimed that those mills posed a threat to the river and its environment and were likely to impair the quality of the river's waters and to cause significant transboundary damage to Argentina.

Argentina contended that the 1975 Statute adopts an approach in terms of precaution whereby the burden of proof should be placed on Uruguay for it to establish that the pulp mill would not cause significant damage to the environment. It also argued that the burden of proof should not be placed on Argentina alone as the applicant, because, in its view, the 1975 Statute imposes an equal onus to persuade—for the one that the plant is innocuous and for the other that it is harmful. Uruguay, on the other hand, argued that the burden of proof is on Argentina, as the applicant, in accordance with the principle of *onus probandi incumbit actori*. Uruguay also strongly contested Argentina's argument that the precautionary approach of the 1975 Statute would imply a reversal of the burden of proof, in the absence of an explicit treaty provision prescribing it as well as Argentina's proposition that the Statute places the burden of proof equally on both Parties.

Regarding the arguments put forward by Argentina on the reversal of the burden of proof and on the existence, vis-à-vis each Party, of an equal onus to prove under the 1975 Statute, the Court considered that 'while a precautionary approach may be relevant in the interpretation and application of the provisions of the Statute, it does not follow that it operates as a reversal of the burden of proof'.[33] The Court also pointed out that 'there is nothing in the 1975 Statute itself to indicate that it places the burden of proof equally on both Parties'.[34] The Court thus reiterated that under 'the well-established principle of *onus probandi incumbit actori*, it is the duty of the party which asserts certain facts to establish the existence of such facts'.[35] It is therefore 'to be expected that the Applicant should, in the first instance, submit the

---

[33] *Pulp Mills* (Judgment), above n 2, para 164.

[34] Ibid., para 164.

[35] Ibid., para 162.

relevant evidence to substantiate its claims'.[36] The Court continued, that this does not, however, mean that 'the Respondent should not co-operate in the provision of such evidence as may be in its possession that could assist the Court in resolving the dispute submitted to it'.[37]

The same approach was adopted in the *Beef Hormones Case*, where the WTO Appellate Body examined the applicable treaty for language that might reverse the burden of proof.[38] Having found nothing in the text of the treaty that could justify the conclusion that the burden of proof has been shifted to the party proposing to undertake potentially harmful activities, the Appellate Body rejected the argument that the precautionary principle could reverse the burden of proof.[39]

By contrast, in *Aven v Costa Rica*, the investment arbitration tribunal reversed the burden of proof based on the precautionary principle embodied in the applicable Costa Rican law.[40] The respondent alleged that claimants did not identify the presence of wetlands and forests, conduct a biological survey to identify species that lived in those ecosystems, and propose measures to protect those species from the impacts of the proposed development. According to the respondent, this omission was an undeniable failure on the part of claimants, on whom the responsibility rested in accordance with Costa Rican law to disclose information that had been gathered during the process of carrying out the studies that would be attached to a development application.[41] This issue has a direct impact on whether or not there was a burden of proof imposed under Costa Rican law on the party that wishes to develop a real estate project and a duty to disclose any sensitive environmental area or potential damage to environment.[42] If the answer is in the affirmative, then the question was whether or not this was complied with by Claimants. This, in turn, included the question whether there is a duty to disclose in a development application situations or facts known to applicant that, in carrying out the development these could affect the environment, and whether there is a burden of proof on the applicant to evidence that there will be no adverse environmental impact.[43]

---

[36] Ibid., para 163.

[37] Ibid., para 163. In his separate opinion, Judge Greenwood confirmed that the 'nature of the case and of the obligations under the Statute does not alter the fundamental principle that, in proceedings before the Court, the burden of proving any given fact rests on the party asserting that fact.' *See* Separate Opinion of Judge Greenwood, para 24.

[38] WTO, *European Communities—Measures Concerning Meat and Meat Products (Hormones)*, Appellate Body Report, 16 January 1998, WT/DS26/AB/R; WT/DS48/AB/R, paras 97–109 (*EC—Hormones* (Appellate Body Report)).

[39] Ibid., paras 124–125.

[40] *David R. Aven, Samuel D. Aven, Carolyn J. Park, Eric A. Park, Jeffrey S. Shioleno, Giacomo A. Buscemi, David A. Janney and Roger Raguso v The Republic of Costa Rica*, Final Award, 18 September 2018, ICSID Case No UNCT/15/3, para 553 (*Aven v Costa Rica* (Final Award)).

[41] Ibid., para 525.

[42] Ibid., para 526.

[43] Ibid., para 527.

Costa Rica argued that the burden of proof fell on the applicant by reason of the precautionary principle.[44] According to Costa Rica, one of the main consequences of the application of the precautionary principle was that it should reverse the burden of proof on the party allegedly causing a risk of harm: the relevant person must show that it is not going to hurt the environment with the actions it intends to take rather than a burden on the government to prove the existence of harm. Costa Rica also referred to the precautionary principle recognized in Article 109 of the Costa Rican Biodiversity Law, which provides: 'The burden of proof, of the absence of non-permitted contamination, degradation or damage, shall correspond to whom requests the approval, the permit, or the access to biodiversity, or whom is accused of having caused the environmental harm'.[45] Relying on this legislation, the tribunal sided with the respondent and found a duty on claimants 'to advise the competent authority in matters that affect any impact to the environment'.[46] This duty transferred the burden of proof to claimants, and the burden was 'to evidence the absence of non-permitted pollution, degradation or affectation' from the proposed development.[47] This duty cannot be relieved 'by shifting the burden to Respondent's agencies to verify the accuracy of the information disclosed by Claimants' in their development application.[48]

It follows from these decisions that in the absence of express language to the contrary,[49] the precautionary principle does not reverse the burden of proof with respect to claims regarding environmental harm.

The Applicable Domestic Law and Burden of Proof

In some circumstances, the burden of proof may be governed by the applicable domestic law, which may allocate the burden of proof differently than the principle

---

[44] Ibid., para 444.

[45] Ibid., para 444.

[46] Ibid., para 552.

[47] Ibid., para 553.

[48] Ibid., para 554.

[49] For example, the Agreement on the Conservation and Management of Straddling Fish Stocks and Highly Migratory Fish Stocks (8 September 1995, 2167 UNTS 3, entered into force 11 December 2001) and the Stockholm Convention on Persistent Organic Pollutants (22 May 2001, 2256 UNTS 119, entered into force 17 May 2004) do not reverse the burden of proof, notwithstanding that both treaties are expressly based on the precautionary approach set out in Principle 15 of the Rio Declaration. By contrast, some treaties do reverse the burden of proof. See e.g., The Protocol to the Convention on the Prevention of Marine Pollution by Dumping of Wastes and Other Matter, 1972 (London Protocol) (7 November 1996, entered into force 24 March 2006); the Convention for the Protection of the Marine Environment of the North-East Atlantic (the 'OSPAR Convention') (22 September 1992, 2354 UNTS 67, entered into force 25 March 1998); Communication from the Commission of the European Communities on the Precautionary Principle (2000), IP/00/96 ('*Assigning responsibility for producing scientific evidence* is already a common consequence of these measures. Countries that impose a prior approval (marketing authorisation) requirement on products that they deem dangerous *a priori* reverse the burden of proving injury, by treating them as dangerous unless and until businesses do the scientific work necessary to demonstrate that they are safe') https://ec.europa.eu/commission/presscorner/detail/en/IP_00_96. Accessed 10 September 2021.

of *onus probandi incumbit actori*. For example, in *Burlington v Ecuador* and *Perenco v Ecuador*, Ecuador brought counterclaims against the investor for causing environmental harm, which were based on a violation of Ecuadorian environmental law. To decide on the allocation of the burden of proof both tribunals had to analyse whether the Ecuadorian law imposed a strict or fault-based liability regime. In *Burlington,* the claimant argued that fault-based and not strict liability governed Ecuador's environmental claim, with the result that Ecuador must prove the existence of environmental harm and that the harm was caused by the lack of diligence. In other words, for the claimant, Ecuador had to prove harm, fault and causation. For its part, Ecuador argued that the claimant's activities were subject to strict liability and therefore the claimant can only be exonerated if it establishes that the harm was caused by force majeure, a third party or the victim. A showing of diligence, or lack of fault, would not suffice. The *Burlington* tribunal agreed that in Ecuadorian law strict liability governed instances of environmental harm,[50] and the following elements characterized the strict liability regime for environmental harm under Ecuadorian law as established by jurisprudence: (i) the plaintiff must prove harm connected to the defendant's activities; (ii) fault is not required; and (iii) causation is presumed, the defendant being exonerated if he or she proves that the harm was caused by force majeure, the victim or a third party.[51] The environmental harm had to be proved by showing contamination exceedances above regulatory criteria.

A different conclusion was reached by the *Perenco* Tribunal. In the tribunal's view, although during the relevant period the Ecuadorian case law employed a relatively stringent burden of proof rule, which presumed that the operator engaged in a hazardous activity and benefiting therefrom was responsible for any resulting damage, it was a rebuttable presumption.[52] In considering the burden of proof, the Tribunal was mindful of the problems of proof when an oilfield is operated over a period of years by a single operator or by successive operators. The problem in that case was that the environmental claim was not based on a single event but rather on an accumulation of discrete events occurring at different sites at different times, and in circumstances where the operator was itself responsible for reporting any spills or other contamination. How could one differentiate between the acts of successive operators or even differentiate between the cumulative effect of the acts of the same operator on a particular platform? Although the tribunal agreed with the claimant that it cannot presume that the claimant was the author of all harm that has been detected, it concluded that 'once a regulatory exceedance resulting from a potentially hazardous activity is shown, the claimants is prima facie responsible therefor'.[53]

In sum, the standard allocation of the burden of proof, which requires a party asserting a fact to prove that fact, may be reversed in some circumstances where an applicable international treaty provides so based on the precautionary principle, or where the applicable provides for specific liability regimes.

---

[50] *Burlington v Ecuador* (Counterclaims), above n 32, para 247.

[51] Ibid., para 238.

[52] *Perenco v Ecuador* (Interim Decision on the Environmental Counterclaim), above n 32, para 371.

[53] Ibid., para 372.

16.2.2 Causation

Proving the existence of harm is not enough. A claimant must also show that there is 'a sufficiently *direct and certain causal nexus* between the wrongful act… and the injury suffered'.[54] Only if such causal nexus is established can the claimed injury be legally deemed the 'consequence',[55] or result, of the wrongful conduct. Indeed, some authors consider the causation requirement to inhere in the very notion of 'injury' in international law because, even if real, an injury is not claimable unless it can be considered the consequence of the wrongful act.[56] In international practice, the requirement of a 'sufficiently direct and certain causal nexus' is often expressed by stating that the wrongful act must be the 'proximate cause' of the injury. The proximate cause requirement can be found in the case law of many international courts and tribunals, and it excludes from the obligation to make reparation any injury that is indirect,[57] consequential or too remote from the wrongful act.[58] Likewise, if the damage is not 'foreseeable'[59] in the normal course of events, it is deemed to be too remote from the wrongful act and therefore not caused by it.

Establishing proximate cause in the context of environmental claims may be difficult, especially where harm could result from multiple sources. In *Certain Activities*, the ICJ acknowledged that 'in cases of environmental damage, particular issues may arise with respect to the existence of damage and causation'.[60] The damage may be due 'to several concurrent causes, or the state of science regarding the causal link between the wrongful act and the damage may be uncertain'.[61] In that case, the ICJ considered that it was for the Court to decide, in light of the facts of the case at hand and the evidence presented to it, whether there is a sufficient causal nexus between the wrongful act and the injury suffered.[62] Based on available evidence in that case, the Court concluded that Nicaragua had not established that the fact that sediment concentrations in the river increased as a result of the construction of the road '*in and of itself* caused significant transboundary harm'.[63]

---

[54] *Diallo* (Compensation), above n 2, para 14. *See also Certain Activities Carried Out by Nicaragua in the Border Area (Costa Rica v Nicaragua)* , Compensation, Judgment, 2 February 2018, ICJ Reports 2018, para 32 (*Certain Activities* (Compensation)).

[55] *Diallo* (Compensation), above n 2, para 14.

[56] Combacau and Sur 1995, p. 539.

[57] 'The Geneva Arbitration', in Moore 1898, p. 641.

[58] See *Yearbook of the International Law Commission*, 2001, Vol. II, Part 2, p. 93.

[59] *Responsabilité de l'Allemagne a Raison des Dommages Causés dans les Colonies Portugaises du Sud de l'Afrique*, Award, 31 July 1928, 2 RIAA 1011, p. 1031.

[60] *Certain Activities* (Compensation), above n 54, para 34.

[61] Ibid.

[62] Ibid., para 34.

[63] Ibid., para 196.

16.2.3 Valuation

Once the requisite causal link between the wrongful act and harm caused to environment is demonstrated, a claimant must still prove the valuation of the alleged harm to recover damages. It is consistent with the principles of international law governing the consequences of internationally wrongful acts, including the principle of full reparation, that 'compensation is due for damage caused to the environment, *in and of itself*, in addition to expenses incurred by an injured State as a consequence of such damage'.[64] Damage to the environment, and the consequent impairment or loss of the ability of the environment to provide goods and services, are compensable under international law.[65] Such compensation may include indemnification for the impairment or loss of environmental goods and services in the period prior to recovery and payment for the restoration of the damaged environment.[66]

Evaluating environmental harm could have unique difficulties, which are beyond the scope of this chapter. However, two points are important to highlight. First, as the ICJ explained in *Certain Activities,* 'international law does not prescribe any specific method of valuation for the purposes of compensation for environmental damage'.[67] International courts and tribunals would thus consider different valuation methods, 'tak[ing] into account the specific circumstances and characteristics of each case'.[68] For example, in *Certain Activities,* the Court considered that the most appropriate way to evaluate environmental damage in that case was from the perspective of the ecosystem as a whole, by adopting an overall assessment of the impairment or loss of environmental goods and services prior to recovery, instead of attributing values to specific categories of environmental goods and services and estimating recovery periods for each of them. Such an overall valuation, the Court reasoned, would allow it to take into account the capacity of the damaged area for natural regeneration.[69] The Court thus first proceeded to identify the most significant damage inflicted upon the area (i.e., the removal of trees during the excavation of the caños) and then assessed more ancillary harms (i.e., the raw materials, gas regulation and air quality services, and biodiversity in terms of habitat and nursery).[70]

Second, the absence of certainty as to the extent of damage does not necessarily preclude a court or tribunal from awarding an amount that it considers approximately to reflect the value of the impairment or loss of environmental goods and services. As the ICJ held in *Certain Activities,* 'the absence of adequate evidence as to the extent of material damage will not, in all situations, preclude an award of compensation for that damage'.[71] Quoting with approval the decision in the *Trail Smelter Case*, the

---

[64] Ibid., para 41.

[65] Ibid., para 42.

[66] Ibid.

[67] Ibid., para 52.

[68] Ibid.

[69] Ibid., para 81.

[70] Ibid., para 79.

[71] Ibid., para 35.

Court concluded that '[w]here the tort itself is of such a nature as to preclude the ascertainment of the amount of damages with certainty, it would be a perversion of fundamental principles of justice to deny all relief to the injured person, and thereby relieve the wrongdoer from making any amend for his acts'.[72] In such case, 'while the damages may not be determined by mere speculation or guess, it will be enough if the evidence show the extent of the damages as a matter of just and reasonable inference, although the result be only approximate'.[73]

16.3 Standard of Proof

The standard of proof concerns how a party in discharging its burden of proof, must convince a court or tribunal of its claims to the required standard.[74] As it has been already observed, there is clear standard of proof in international proceedings.[75] Rather, international jurisprudence 'has recognized the power of the courts to weigh the evidence freely' and 'has avoided a rigid rule regarding the amount of proof necessary to support the judgment'.[76] Just like with respect to other claims, precisely how much and precisely what kind of evidence will be required to convince a court of tribunal with respect to claims related to environmental harm will vary from case to case. Depending on the facts and circumstances of each case, a litigant should expect an international court or tribunal to apply different tests. In the context of litigating environmental claims, the following standards were applied most frequently: whether the evidence was 'sufficient' or 'convincing' to a court; whether the evidence shows a *prima facie* case; whether the preponderance of evidence shows that the claim of one party prevails over the claim of another party.

In the *Pulp Mills Case*, for example, the ICJ concluded that it was not '*convinced*' by Argentina's argument that an assessment of possible sites was not carried out prior to the determination of the final site,[77] or that the production of synthetic chemical compounds did not meet technological requirements.[78] Likewise, it concluded that Argentina had not 'convincingly' demonstrated that Uruguay had 'refused to engage in such co-ordination as envisaged by Article 36, in breach of that provision'.[79] However, in the same decision, the Court also observed that it had not been established

[72] Ibid., para 35 (citing to *Trail Smelter Arbitration*, Award, 11 March 1941, 3 RIAA, p. 1920).

[73] Ibid.

[74] Amerasinghe 2005; Kazazi 1996; Brown 2006.

[75] Brown 2006, p. 98 (the commentator identifies at pp. 98–101 five standards of proof that have been applied in international judicial proceedings).

[76] IACtHR, *Velásquez-Rodríguez v Honduras*, Judgement, Merits, 29 July 1988, 95 ILR 258, p. 285, referring to the ICJ Judgments in *Corfu Channel (Albania v United Kingdom)*, Merits, Judgment, 9 April 1949, ICJ Reports 1949, p. 4 and *Military and Paramilitary Activities in und against Nicaragua (Nicaragua v United States of America)*, Merits, Judgment, 27 June 1986, ICJ Reports 1986, p. 14.

[77] *Pulp Mills* (Judgment), above n 2, para 210.

[78] Ibid., paras 221–228.

[79] Ibid., para 189.

'to the satisfaction of the Court' that the algal bloom episode of 4 February 2009 was caused by the nutrient discharges from the pulp mill.[80] It also found the evidence on the record 'insufficient' to attribute an alleged increase in the level of concentrations of phenolic substances in the river to the operations of the pulp mill,[81] and that there was 'no clear evidence' to link the increase in the presence of harmful substances in the river to the operation of the pulp mill.[82] At the end, the Court found no 'conclusive evidence' in the record to show that Uruguay had not acted with the requisite degree of due diligence or that the discharges of effluent from the pulp mill had had deleterious effects or caused harm to living resources or to the quality of the water or the ecological balance of the river since it had started its operations.[83] Similarly, in *Certain Activities*, the Court considered that Costa Rica has not provided any 'convincing evidence' that sediments dredged from the river were deposited on its right bank, and that as such, 'a causal link between [the significant reduction in flow of the Colorado River] and Nicaragua's dredging programme has not been established'.[84] It also interchangeably referred to the 'sufficiency' of evidence.[85]

In the WTO context, the establishment of a *prima facie* case has been considered sufficient basis for a decision in favour a claimant. As the Appellate Body observed in the *EC-Hormones Case*, a 'prima facie case is one which, in the absence of effective refutation by the defending party, requires a panel, as a matter of law, to rule in favour of the complaining party presenting the prima facie case'.[86] However, 'precisely how much and precisely what kind of evidence will be required to establish such a presumption will necessarily vary from measure to measure, provision to provision, and case to case'.[87] In the *US-Shrimp Case*, the Appellate Body took the view that it has 'to assess the evidence before [it] in the light of the particular circumstances of this case,' which 'implie[d] that [it] may consider any type of evidence, and also that [it] may reach [its] conclusions regarding a particular claim on the basis of the level of evidence that [it considers] sufficient'.[88] In some cases, the WTO Panel has applied the balance of probabilities test to determine whether a *prima facie* case was made. In the *Asbestos Case*, the Panel applied the balance of probabilities test to verify the defending State's assertion that there existed a health risk justifying State

80 Ibid., para 250.

81 Ibid., para 254.

82 Ibid., para 259.

83 Ibid., para 265.

84 *Certain Activities* (Compensation), above n 54, para 119; see also para 192 ('Thus, the Court is not convinced by Nicaragua's argument that the absolute quantity of sediment in the river due to the construction of the road caused significant harm per se').

85 Ibid., para 206 ('Nicaragua has not presented sufficient evidence to prove that these deltas, which only occupy the edge of the river's channel on the Costa Rican bank, have had a significant adverse impact on the channel's morphology or on navigation').

86 *EC—Hormones* (Appellate Body Report), above n 38, para 104.

87 WTO, *United States—Measure Affecting Imports of Woven Wool Shirts and Blouses from India*, Appellate Body Report, 25 April 1997, WT/DS33/5, p. 14.

88 WTO, *United States—Import Prohibition of Certain Shrimp and Shrimp Products*, Appellate Body Report, 12 October 1998, WTO/DS58/AB/R, paras 7.14, 7.30.

intervention. It held that 'the evidence before [the Panel] *tends to show* that handling chrysotile-cement products constitutes a risk to health rather than the opposite'[89] and therefore concluded that 'EC has made a prima facie case for the existence of a health risk in connection with the use of chrysotile'.[90]

In conclusion, no generally applicable observation as to the applicable standard of proof can be articulated other than different tests may apply depending on the circumstances of each case, and litigants should therefore carefully examine jurisprudence of a court or tribunal before which it they intend to litigate their environmental claims.

16.4 Methods of Proof

Methods of proof refer to different types of evidence that a disputing party may consider relying on to prove its claims in environmental disputes. Collecting, submitting and analysing evidence have become increasingly relevant in the context of international environmental litigation, especially because courts and tribunals have to deal with scientific issues relating to environmental harm.

There are no highly formalized rules of procedure governing the admissibility and assessment of evidence.[91] A court or tribunal will consider all the evidence presented to it, assess its credibility, determine its weight and ensure that its factual findings have a proper basis in that evidence. Within these parameters, it is generally within the discretion of a court or tribunal to decide which evidence it chooses to utilize in making findings, and there is no requirement to accord to factual evidence of the parties the same meaning and weight as do the parties. All evidence once admitted is thus subject to an evaluation of its relevance, credibility and weight. As the ICJ stressed in two cases involving claims of environmental harm:

> It is the duty of the Court, after having given careful consideration to all the evidence in the record, to assess its probative value, to determine which facts must be considered relevant, and to draw conclusions from them as appropriate. In keeping with this practice, the Court will make its own determination of the facts, on the basis of the totality of the evidence presented to it, and it will then apply the relevant rules of international law to those facts which it has found to be established.[92]

---

[89] WTO, *European Communities—Measures Affecting Asbestos and Asbestos-Containing Products*, Appellate Body Report, 12 March 2001, WT/DS135/AB/R, para 8.193 (*EC—Asbestos* (Appellate Body Report)).

[90] Ibid., para 8.194.

[91] See e.g. Wolfrum and Moldner 2013. See also Tomka and Proulx 2016; *Pulp Mills* (Judgment), above n 2, para 14.

[92] *Certain Activities; Construction of a Road* (Merits), above n 4, para 176. See also IACtHR, *Kaliña and Lokono Peoples v Suriname*, Judgment, 25 November 2015, Ser. C, No 309, para 24 ('Based on its consistent case law concerning evidence and its assessment, the Court will examine and assess the documentary probative elements submitted by the parties and the Commission, the statements, testimony and expert opinions, and also the helpful evidence requested and incorporated by this Court, when establishing the facts of the case and ruling on the merits. To this end, it will abide by the principles of sound judicial discretion, within the corresponding legal framework, taking into

It is also clear from this statement that not all evidence presented to courts and tribunals are of equal probative weight. Some types of evidence may be considered stronger than others. Understanding an international court or tribunal's general approach to the assessment of evidence can help devise evidence collection strategies to focus on the types of evidence likely to be considered as having the greatest probative value. In proving environmental harm, three categories of evidence are normally presented before international courts and tribunals: documentary evidence, expert evidence, and testimonial evidence. The sections below discuss some of the practical aspects related to each of these categories of evidence in establishing environmental harm.

16.4.1 Documentary Evidence

Documentary evidence is by far the most common and important type of evidence in establishing environmental harm before international court and tribunals. It is a necessary corollary of the very nature of environmental claims because they involve highly technical issues that can be established convincingly through documentary materials.

In the context of environmental claims documentary evidence may take many forms and can fall in into the following categories: documents from international organization, official records, instruments, judicial decisions, and statements by governmental authorities of a State, press reports, affidavits, cartographic, photo, video and audio-visual materials. The probative value of such evidence would depend on the circumstances of each case. That said, some general propositions may be discerned from the practice of international courts and tribunals.

First, documentary evidence that could be given a particular weight includes admissions against interest. In *Perenco v Ecuador,* the investment arbitration tribunal considered as having a high probative value some internal documents of the claimant, an oil company, admitting the contamination of soil.[93] For example, Perenco's audits for relevant years 'showed an increase in non-conformities' and 'the increase in incidence of contamination'.[94] The audit reports served the basis for the Tribunal's conclusion that 'the number of non-conformities, including major non-conformities, [was] striking'.[95] The Tribunal also found 'very troubling' the Perenco's memorandum concerning the contamination of one area, admitting that 'the State will

account the body of evidence, and the arguments that have been submitted') (*Kaliña and Lokono Peoples v Suriname* (Judgment)).

93 *Perenco v Ecuador* (Interim Decision on the Environmental Counterclaim), above n 32, paras 410, 447.

94 Ibid., para 410.

95 Ibid.

probably assume that [Perenco] are hiding many more [environmental] damages and will scrutinize the operations area in search for more damages and it will probably find them'.[96]

Second, contemporaneous official records, instruments, judicial decisions, and statements by governmental authorities of a State may have a high probative value if they acknowledge facts unfavourable to the State,[97] not specially prepared for international litigation, or include findings obtained by examination of persons directly involved and subsequently cross-examined by judges skilled in examination and experienced in assessing large amounts of information. In *Philippines v China,* the Tribunal relied *inter alia* on contemporaneous reports of naval, coastguard and fisheries authorities of the Philippines and diplomatic exchanges between the Philippines and China to conclude that Chinese fishing vessels were involved in harvesting of threatened or endangered species and were engaged in the use of dynamite or cyanide in the disputed areas of the South China Sea.[98] However, the Tribunal did not take into account those incidents where the provenance of the vessels was uncertain due to the lack of contemporaneous reports, inventories, and photographs.[99]

Prior determinations of State authorities on regulatory exceedances were of a 'significant probative value' in *Perenco v Ecuador*.[100] The same was true with respect to the findings of state authorities, as affirmed in domestic judicial proceedings,

[96] Ibid., para 447.

[97] In *Lhaka v Argentina,* the IACtHR was confronted with a claim that indigenous communities' human rights were violated because Argentina failed to recognize and protect their lands from practices that caused environmental harm. The specific instances of environmental harm were demonstrated by testimonial evidence. Claimants also submitted to the Court the contemporaneous official documents indicating that Argentina was aware of the practices causing environmental harm but took no actions (*Case of Indigenous Communities of the Lhaka Honhat Association (Our Land) v Argentina,* Judgment, 6 February 2020, Series C, No 400 (Spanish only), paras 258 ('In more specific terms, it has been affirmed by the State that the Creole settlers raise "larger cattle" in the open field. The Honorary Advisory Commission created by Decree 18/93 of 1993 for the regularization of settlements in fiscal lot 55, pointed out that "livestock without grazing control has led to the destruction of resources, with the disappearance of around fifty herbaceous species and bushes in short time". He also highlighted that, as a result of uncontrolled grazing, there was "a general loss of biodiversity, due to the selectivity of livestock in their diet, while a transformation of the landscape occurs due to the elimination of areas of open grasslands') and para 262 ('Another aspect pointed out by the representatives is that of illegal logging. According to the representatives' observations, the "illegal" nature of the logging activity is supported by different provisions that, as of 1991, restricted forest exploitation (infra, para 269). State documentation has indicated as one of the causes of the "bio-socio-economic degradation of D[e]p[artamen] to […] Rivadavia" the "forestry activity" that is "carried out without the application of minimum standards of rationality nor of precautions that tend to assure the future of the wooded masses, and even less to make compatible with the livestock uses and the requirements of the fauna. The [vast] environmental legislation in force does not have any positive effect, […] clandestine forestry activity is almost a habitual thing').

[98] *South China Sea Arbitration (Philippines v China),* Award, 12 July 2016, PCA Case No 2013-19, paras 950, 968 (*South China Sea Arbitration* (Merits)).

[99] Ibid., para 969.

[100] *Perenco v Ecuador* (Interim Decision on the Environmental Counterclaim), above n 32, paras 838–839.

which were brought as evidence in *Jugheli and Others v Georgia.* In that case, the ECtHR had to deal with the dispute that concerned a thermal power plant in Tbilisi, which, according to claimants did not follow the pertinent regulations and was emitting toxic substances into the air that affected their health and well-being.[101] In the domestic judicial proceedings, the Georgian Regional Court had ordered the Ministry of Justice, the Ministry of Labour, Health and Social Affairs and the Ministry of the Environment to produce several expert reports to determine the environmental pollution and how it had affected human health.[102] The ECtHR decided to primarily rely on the findings of the domestic courts and the environmental studies commissioned by the authorities. The Court held that the expert opinions commissioned by the domestic courts and prepared by the competent State entities confirmed *inter alia* that the plant was emitting substances with toxicity twice the permitted level. However, the Court also stressed that it 'cannot rely blindly on the decisions of the domestic authorities, especially if they are obviously inconsistent or contradict each other.' In such situations, 'it has to assess the evidence in its entirety'.[103]

Third, international court and tribunals also tend to give great weight to reports by UN or other international organizations that are seen as being neutral and impartial. This is especially true when such organizations produce reports that are the product of independent and detailed fact-finding missions. In the *Pulp Mills Case,* the ICJ considered as helpful in refuting alleged environmental harm the technical and environmental impact assessment reports that the International Finance Corporation (IFC) commissioned before deciding to contribute to the financing of the planned pulp mills.[104] In *Certain Activities*, the ICJ took account of the Report of Ramsar Advisory Mission No. 69 of 17 December 2010, which was provided by Costa Rica and contained general information about the physical characteristics of the *Humedal Caribe Noreste.* In *Jugheli and Other v Georgia,* the ECtHR relied on Report by the

[101] ECHR, *Jugheli and Others v Georgia,* Judgment, 13 July 2017, No 38342/05, para 50 (*Jugheli and Others v Georgia* (Judgment)).

[102] Ibid., para 18. Among these were the following: (1) an expert examination of 28 October 2002 undertaken by the Expertise and Special Research Centre at the Ministry of Justice, which had concluded that the plant did not have a buffer zone around it and that it lacked a required filter system (ibid., 19); a report of the Institute of Environmental Protection at the Ministry of Environment, which had revealed that the plant's technical compliance document was defective because it had indicated the wrong height of the plant's chimneys, and its data on pollution could be 'misleadingly decreased' (ibid., para 20).

[103] Ibid., paras 63 and 67. In *Fadeyeva v Russia,* the ECtHR relied on official reports that illustrated a rise in pollution levels that exceeded the domestic norms, which demonstrated the existence of harm (*Fadeyeva v Russia,* Judgment, 30 November 2005, No 55723/00, para 83). In *Taskin v Turkey* the Court had to decide whether Turkey had breached the ECHR by permitting a gold mine to operate in Ovacik. The permits were issued by the local authorities in 1992, including a permit to use cyanide leaching in the mining process. The applicants challenged the permits and in 1997 the Supreme Administrative Court found in their favour. The ECtHR relied on the findings of the Turkish Supreme Administrative Court as well as the conclusions of the relevant environmental impact studies, to find that a risk to the environment and human health existed and Turkey was in breach of Article 8 of the Convention (*Taşkın and Others v Turkey,* Judgment, 10 November 2004, No 46117/99, paras 119, 121).

[104] *Pulp Mills* (Judgment), above n 2, paras 210, 226–228.

Institute of Scientific Research in Sanitation and Hygiene at the Ministry of Labour, Health and Social Affairs, which provided upon the request of Georgian courts independent and well-founded reports about the effect of environmental pollution on human health.[105]

Fourth, maps, photographs, satellite images and other visual materials can play an important role in establishing environmental harm if they come from independent sources and reflect a contemporaneous position on the ground and compare it with the position at the time of litigation. In *Certain Activities,* Nicaragua introduced photographs indicating sediment deltas on the Costa Rican bank of the San Juan River and sought to use them as evidence to prove that Costa Rica's construction of the road contributed sediment that caused significant harm to the river's morphology. The ICJ compared those photographs with the satellite images of the river, which demonstrated that at least two of those deltas pre-dated the road.[106] The satellite images corroborated other evidence that those deltas did not cause a significant adverse impact on the channel's morphology.[107]

Aerial photographs and satellite images were also dispositive evidence of environmental harm in the context of investment arbitration.[108] In *Aven v Costa Rica,* the respondent alleged that the claimants' development of a tourism project caused environmental harm to wetlands and forests. Although Costa Rica identified through the expert witness reports of KECE, an environmental consulting firm, that a total of eight wetlands on the site of the project were found, the claimants originally rejected the existence of any wetlands on the site during the arbitration proceedings. However, in their post-hearing brief, the claimants did not dispute the existence of wetlands in the studies and reports carried out in 2016 but argued that there was no proof that those conditions existed during the relevant time (2007–2011), when the claimants conducted their development. It was beyond dispute that one of the elements that define a wetland is the existence of hydric soils. The KECE report contained aerial photographs that showed the wetland area in 2005, the area of activity and construction work carried out in 2009 and 2010 by the claimants, and the situation of such area in 2016. Further, the KECE report identified within that wetland area the location of the bore holes made in a hydric analysis, and it was precisely in those locations that the experts found the existence of wetlands that had been drained and filled by the claimants.[109] The aerial photographs were 'clear evidence to the fact that the location of the wetland' was 'precisely' in the area where the claimants conducted the

[105] *Jugheli and Others v Georgia* (Judgment), above n 101, paras 68–69.

[106] *Certain Activities; Construction of a Road* (Merits), above n 4, paras 202, 206.

[107] Ibid., para 206.

[108] See e.g., *Burlington v Ecuador* (Counterclaims), above n 32, paras 459, 533, 630, 648, 706 (The Tribunal relied on satellite imagery and aerial photographs of the sites adjacent to oil platforms to assess the actual use of land surrounding the platform in order to decide what sensitivity analysis to apply in establishing environmental harm (ibid., para 343). Where the record contained no images or photographs from the relevant period, the Tribunal decided on the basis of the best available evidence (ibid., para 342).

[109] *Aven v Costa Rica* (Final Award), above n 40, para 584.

development works.[110] On that basis, the Tribunal determined that the wetland 'was indeed impacted by works undertaken' by the claimants.[111] The aerial photographs 'comparing the forest canopy in 2005, 2010, 2011 and 2016' were also dispositive for the Tribunal's conclusion that 'forests were also impacted' as a result of the claimants' cutting of trees.[112]

Fourth, press reports are generally not treated as evidence proving particular facts but may serve as useful context to corroborate facts established by other evidence. In *Philippines v China,* the reports of BBC and New York Times about the destruction of coral reefs, with schematic illustrations and video footage, corroborated other documentary evidence in the form of contemporaneous reports, photographs and satellite images showing the nature and scale of destruction of coral reefs by Chinese vessels.[113]

Because international courts and tribunals do not analyse each piece of evidence in isolation, it is important to collect different types of available documentary evidence that would comprehensively and convincingly show a fact that has to be proved.

16.4.2 Expert Evidence

Environmental issues invariably raise competing scientific claims. A court will often be called upon to adjudicate on two sharply differing views, in which mountains of scientific arguments may be presented in an equally compelling manner. Unlike many national systems that provide for environmental or scientific assessors to join panels and assist in deciphering technical information, the international judge likely will often find herself in a difficult position when seeking to decide on the relative merits of a scientific claim. Experts with specialized knowledge have proved particularly important in helping courts establish facts or evaluate the facts already elucidated.

Normally, experts are appointed by the disputing parties seeking assistance on complex scientific matters, which can be provided behind the scenes when preparing pleadings or in the form of expert opinions annexed to written pleadings and oral expert testimony. Some courts and tribunal also have authority to appoint experts and have exercised it as deemed necessary.[114]

---

[110] Ibid., para 582.

[111] Ibid., para 585.

[112] Ibid., para 586.

[113] *South China Sea Arbitration* (Merits), above n 98, paras 848, 968.

[114] Articles 48 and 50 of the Statute of the International Court of Justice and Article 67 of its Rules on the appointment of experts by the ICJ. One of the experts had to assess damages resulting from alleged illegal exploitation of natural resources. The Court relied on those provisions to appoint by Order of 12 October 2020 three experts in *Case Concerning Armed Activity on the Territory of the Congo (Democratic Republic of the Congo v Uganda).* In the WTO context, article 11.2 of the SPS Agreement and Article 13 of the DSU enable panels to seek information and advice as they deem appropriate in a particular case. These rules, however, 'leave to the sound discretion of a panel the determination of whether the establishment of an expert review group is necessary or appropriate'.

If experts are appointed by the disputing parties, it is important at the outset to clearly delineate the role of an expert to avoid such individuals acting both as an advocate and expert. In the *Pulp Mills Case,* some of these experts also appeared before the Court as counsel for one or the other of the parties to provide evidence.[115] The Court criticized both parties, noting that:

> Regarding those experts who appeared before it as counsel at the hearings, the Court would have found it more useful had they been presented by the Parties as expert witnesses under Articles 57 and 64 of the Rules of Court, instead of being included as counsel in their respective delegations. The Court indeed considers that those persons who provide evidence before the Court based on their scientific or technical knowledge and on their personal experience should testify before the Court as experts, witnesses or in some cases in both capacities, rather than counsel, so that they may be submitted to questioning by the other party as well as by the Court.[116]

Judge Greenwood observed in strong terms that for those persons to address the Court as counsel, rather than giving evidence as witnesses or experts, was 'both unhelpful to the Court and unfair to the other Party'.[117] He elaborated that 'the distinction between the evidence of a witness or expert and the advocacy of counsel is fundamental to the proper conduct of litigation before the Court (as it is before other courts and tribunals). A witness or expert owes a duty to the Court which is reflected in the declaration required by Article 64 of the Rules of Court. The duties of someone appearing as counsel are quite different'.[118] The problem is 'particularly acute where, as in the present case, some of those who addressed the Court as counsel had been actively and closely involved in the preparation of scientific reports which were part of the evidence before the Court'.[119]

As for the relative merits, reliability and authority of the documents and studies prepared by experts, they would depend both on the independence of the author, who must have no personal interest in the outcome of the dispute and must not be an employee of the Government, and the characteristics of the report itself, in particular the care with which its analysis was conducted, its completeness, the accuracy of the data used, and the clarity and coherence of the conclusions drawn from such data. This proposition is illustrated by decision of various courts.

In the *Pulp Mills Case*, both Argentina and Uruguay placed before the ICJ a vast amount of factual and scientific material in support of their respective claims. They

---

Hence, panels may seek information and advice as they deem appropriate in a particular case. This includes consulting with individual experts. In *Hormones* the Panel appointed experts—in their individual capacity—and sought their opinion on certain scientific and other technical matters raised by the parties to the dispute (*EC—Hormones* (Appellate Body Report), above n 38, paras 146–156. Similarly, in *Asbestos*, the panel based its conclusions with respect to the existence of a public health risk on the scientific evidence put forward by the parties and the comments of the experts consulted within the context of the present case (*EC—Asbestos* (Appellate Body Report), above n 89, paras 8.182, 8.188 and 8.19).

[115] *Pulp Mills* (Judgment), above n 2, para 165.

[116] Ibid., para 167.

[117] Ibid., Separate Opinion of Judge Greenwood, para 27.

[118] Ibid.

[119] Ibid.

also submitted reports and studies prepared by the experts and consultants commissioned by each of them, as well as others commissioned by the International Finance Corporation in its quality as lender to the project. Because some of the experts also appeared as counsel and thus could not have been cross-examined and questioned, it rendered their expert opinions not helpful, which prompted the Court to observe that 'it is the responsibility of the Court, after having given careful consideration to all the evidence placed before it by the Parties, to determine which facts must be considered relevant, to assess their probative value, and to draw conclusions from them as appropriate'.[120] The Court found helpful extensive data regarding the monitoring of effluent from the pulp mill, as contained in the various reports by EcoMetrix, a consultancy specializing in environmental and industrial matters that was engaged by the International Financial Corporation to carry out environmental monitoring on the IFC's behalf, in establishing the lack of significant environmental harm.[121] This supports the conclusion that expert statements and evaluations issued by a competent international organization, or those issued by the consultants engaged by that organization would be regarded as independent and given 'special weight.'

Similarly, the East African Court of Justice in *ANAW v Tanzania* relied on the expert opinion of UNESCO to decide whether the implementation of a road project would have an irreversible negative impact on the Serengeti Park, which is also listed on the UNESCO World Heritage List.[122] As the Court observed, '[h]appily for us, UNESCO, a renowned world body and objective on the subject has given us the answer to the question [and] stated that: (i) The proposed alignment of the road could result in irreversible damage to the property's (Serengeti's) Universal value; (ii) It supports a Strategic Environmental and Social Assessment which would include a southern alignment which would avoid the Serengeti'.[123] Based on the UNESCO expert report, which was not contradicted by the experts of a respondent, the Court concluded that the road project, if implemented, would have an irreversible impact on the environment.[124]

In *Aven v Costa Rica*, the Tribunal was presented with an expert report addressing a question whether the site where the investor developed a project contained wetlands before and after the development. The expert was questioned during the oral hearings

---

[120] *Pulp Mills* (Judgment), above n 2, para 168.

[121] Ibid., paras 226–228.

[122] EACJ, *Africa Network for Animal Welfare (ANAW) v The Attorney General of the United Republic of Tanzania*, Appeal Judgment No 3, 15 March 2012, p. 13.

[123] EACJ, *Africa Network for Animal Welfare (ANAW) v The Attorney General of the United Republic of Tanzania*, First Instance Division Judgment No 9, 20 June 2014, para 68.

[124] Ibid., para 81 ('Having anxiously considered the matter and as can be seen above, we have found that all evidence points to the fact that if the road project is implemented as originally intended, then following UNESCO's findings it could have an irreversible negative impact on the Serengeti environment and ecosystem. While this view is not expressly shared by the Respondent, we are persuaded by those findings. In fact, the Respondent seemed to have taken note of that fact and has effectively suspended the project and that is an admission that it has realized the error in the initial decision. His own consultant also gave a long list of possible negative impacts and which tally with those given by the Applicant').

as to whether his firm had carried out a soils survey, which was necessary because it was a component to determine the existence of hydric soils, which is one of the three elements of a wetland. The expert 'acknowledged that they did not carry out such survey, because that is something they do not do, but rely on the soils study undertaken by a third party'.[125] This meant in the view of the Tribunal that 'their conclusion as to the existence of wetlands was flawed from the outset, since without such soils study they could not reach the determination of the existence of wetlands'.[126] It was acknowledged by the expert during examination.[127] By contrast, the *Aven* Tribunal found convincing an expert opinion that was rigorously prepared in accordance with all applicable requirements and corroborated by another expert opinion.[128]

In some situations, the parties and their experts can be so deeply divided on a scientific matter that it could raise a significant problem for a tribunal. Tribunals have addressed it in significantly different ways. Some tribunals sought to supplement diverging expert opinions by a site visit. For example, in *Burlington v Ecuador* the Tribunal relied upon evidence presented by the experts of the disputing parties as augmented by the Tribunal's site visit to the oil blocks to determine the extent of contamination.[129]

Other tribunals appointed an independent expert, like in *Perenco v Ecuador*. There, the parties and their experts disagreed on the applicable regulatory criteria and proper

[125] *Aven v Costa Rica* (Final Award), above n 40, para 499.

[126] Ibid.

[127] Ibid. See also ibid., para 498 where the *Aven* Tribunal discounted another expert opinion for its incompleteness ('During the examination of environmental expert witnesses (wetlands and soils) during the December Hearing the discussion centred at one point on whether the soils in the wetlands alleged by Respondent to exist actually had hydric soils. Dr. Baillie argued in his report that he had not found such conditions, but when examined as to whether he shared the findings of Green Roots, Dr. Baillie indicated that he had not drilled to the depth of 105 cms, which is the depth of drills used by Green Roots, which they deemed necessary because in some of the areas there had been work undertaken. In other words, had the ground be untouched, the drills could be closer to the ground, but when it was clear that works had been performed, that it was indispensable to go deeper. And these works were precisely over the wetland referred to by Dr. Baillie as "Bajo 1" which is the same as that referred to in the KECE Report as Wetland # 1. Dr. Baillie indicated that he did not feel it was appropriate to drill that location as there had been development works there, and article 5(b) of the Executive Decree No 35803-MINAE contemplates a definition of hydric soils under natural conditions').

[128] Ibid., para 496 ('The First and Second Expert Reports from KECE conclude the existence of at least seven (7) wetlands on the Las Olas Project site, of which one was impacted. In addition, KECE was able to identify the location of another wetland outside of the project site but within what he referred to as the "Las Olas Ecosystem", based on the existence of the elements which the RAMSAR Convention and Costa Rica's law establish: (i) the dominance of hydrophytic vegetation; (ii) the presence of hydrological indicators, and (iii) the presence of hydric soils. These sites were referred to in a numerical order, starting from the southwestern end of the property, and then in a clockwise order along the property. Thus, Wetlands # 1 and 2 are located in the area of Easements, while the rest are located in the Condo Section. Wetland # 4 is located adjacent to the northwestern portion of the property. It is worthwhile to note that the site of defined Wetlands in the KECE Report matches those under the Baillie Reports; for example, KECE # 5 would correspond to "Bajo B2"; KECE 3 would correspond to "Bajo B4"; and KECE 2, would correspond to "Bajo B6"').

[129] *Burlington v Ecuador* (Counterclaims), above n 32.

testing methods to determine groundwater contamination caused by oil spills.[130] Summarizing the role of the parties appointed experts, the Tribunal observed: 'It seems…that each [expert] was attempting to achieve the best result for the party by whom they were instructed, and that they crossed the boundary between professional objective analysis and party representation. It is clear to the Tribunal that the experts were effectively shooting at different targets and this has made the work of this Tribunal most difficult'.[131] Accordingly, the Tribunal concluded that 'it must require an additional phase of fact-finding in order to arrive at a proper and just conclusion'[132] and decided to 'shall appoint an independent environmental expert to assist the Tribunal in ascertaining the environmental condition of the Blocks in accordance with the legal and factual findings made by the Tribunal in this Decision'.[133]

As regards the quality of the Independent Expert Report, the Tribunal stressed that the expert with his company conducted 'the sampling exercise transparently and considered suggestions made by the Parties' experts and representatives'.[134] The parties were given an opportunity to make written submissions and insert comments into the report.[135] They were also given the opportunity to cross-examine the expert, and the Tribunal found him to be 'a careful, credible, knowledgeable and objective

[130] *Perenco v Ecuador* (Interim Decision on the Environmental Counterclaim), above n 32, para 527.

[131] Ibid., para 581.

[132] Ibid., para 586.

[133] Ibid., para 618. In appointing an independent expert, the *Perenco* Tribunal took all necessary precautions to ensure the impartial and objective work of the expert, as reflected in paras 611(8), (11), (19) and (20): '611(8) The Tribunal will consult the Parties with regard to the appointment of the Tribunal's expert and will take their views into account but the decision as to the identity of and scope of work of the expert will be that of the Tribunal alone. … (11) The expert will be required to perform its work in accordance with the directions set out in this Decision and as set out in any protocol that might be issued by the Tribunal after consultation with the Parties. … (19) The Parties shall be entitled to send a representative to witness the expert's sampling activities. … (20) The Parties shall be given an opportunity to comment on the expert's report prior to the Tribunal's rendering a decision or award on this phase of the proceeding').

[134] *Perenco Ecuador Limited v Republic of Ecuador*, ICSID Case No ARB/08/6, Award, 27 September 2019, para 743. The Consolidated Independent Expert Report noted in this regard: 'It is important to note that the Parties have had the opportunity to pose questions and comment on my work throughout this engagement, including before and during the performance of the field campaign. In addition, representatives of the Parties were present during all onsite activities, including the initial exploratory visit to the Blocks as well as during the performance of sample mark-outs and collection of samples from all investigated media. The field program was implemented over a four-month period and issues raised by the Parties during that time were always considered; in certain cases, my approach was adjusted to incorporate expanded information or to address concerns (when these were reasonable and technically valid). It was not always possible to reach full agreement with both Parties, as their commitments to their clients and strategic approaches differed from my own. However, in all cases, a respectful dialogue was established with both Parties, and to my knowledge neither expressed concerns regarding bias for or against either Party in this matter. Relevant correspondence, emails, and other documentation of this dialogue between the Parties and myself or field personnel is included in Appendix B').

[135] Ibid., para 745.

expert witness'.[136] The Tribunal further noted that, although both parties had criticisms of the report, neither party challenged the results of the laboratory testing.[137] The Tribunal also stressed that 'the handling of the samples, from extracting them at site through to transporting them to [a laboratory], and their further…was conducted in accordance with best practices and therefore rendered the technical evaluation of the samples valid, accurate and reliable'.[138] All those hallmarks of quality in the expert testimony, prompted the Tribunal to observe that 'that is why [the expert] was appointed in the first place: to provide, in an objective and neutral fashion, the expertise and judgement which the Tribunal considered the Parties' experts had failed to provide'.[139]

Because expert evidence could be helpful in address the challenges posed by environmental disputes, which always involve complex scientific and technical issues, identifying an appropriate expert is very important—and it can be a very involved endeavour. In doing so, the following considerations might be kept in mind. *First*, counsel is well-served by immersing him or herself in the relevant scientific literature to gain as deep a familiarity with the relevant issues as possible. As part of this process, counsel should seek to identify those experts who might be able to opine on the issues at hand with the greatest authority and credibility. *Second*, in selecting the experts with whom to work, it is wise for counsel to bear in mind the need for skilled educators, not least because experts serve the critical function of helping to educate counsel about the strengths and limitations of claims and defences that may be under consideration. *Third*, it is important for an expert to be able to convey complex information in as straightforward a manner as possible, making it comprehensible to a non-expert audience. At the same time, experts must maintain the highest level of academic rigor because his or her views may be tested by the other side during cross-examination by opposing counsel and by a court or tribunal.

16.4.3 Testimonial Evidence

Testimonial evidence may come in two forms. One is direct oral testimony by a witness before a court. Another is an affidavit, which is testimonial evidence in written form, whereby parties seek to describe otherwise undocumented facts.[140] In international environmental disputes, testimonial evidence normally complements documentary evidence and expert testimony. However, it plays more prominent role in cases where proving environmental is an integral element of showing a violation of human rights.

---

[136] Ibid.

[137] Ibid., para 746.

[138] Ibid.

[139] Ibid., para 748.

[140] A deponent may be called to give oral testimony as a witness in proceedings and thus may also be subject to cross-examination and questioning.

This is illustrated by two decisions of the IACtHR. In *Lhaka v Argentina,* where the Court analysed the human right to a healthy environment, Argentina was held responsible for violating indigenous communities' human rights through its failure to recognize and protect their lands from practices that caused environmental harm. The Court relied *inter alia* on statements by indigenous communities that the environmental degradation of the territory had begun at the dawn of the twentieth century, simultaneously with the arrival of Creoles who introduced cattle and started felling the forests for their use in the lumber and charcoal industry and in the enclosures and fences.[141] This evidence was corroborated by live oral testimonies of two prominent chiefs from indigenous communities, who gave specific examples how logging and raising cattle on indigenous lands caused significant environmental harm and consequently altered the indigenous way of life and their cultural identity.[142] The Court thus held that Argentina failed to guarantee the indigenous communities' rights to a healthy environment, cultural identity, food, and water.[143]

In *Kaliña and Lokono Peoples v Suriname,* the IACtHR had to examine whether the respondent failed to comply with the safeguards of the right to collective property of indigenous people in relation to bauxite exploitation in a natural reserve that was established in order to protect and conserve nine unique ecosystems in part of the territory claimed as traditional by the Kaliña and Lokono peoples.[144] Evidence provided to the Court included affidavits and oral testimony of witnesses, including alleged victims. The Court found it 'pertinent to admit the testimony provided during the public hearing and by affidavit'.[145] However, the Court stressed that 'the statements made by the alleged victims cannot be assessed in isolation, but rather within the body of evidence in the proceedings, insofar as such statements may provide further information on the presumed violations and their consequences'.[146] The Court did just that. It carefully assesses affidavits and oral testimonies of victims, experts and witnesses of a bauxite extraction company, all of which corroborated that 'extraction operations had a widespread impact', because 'the noise of the construction work and the frequent dynamite explosions caused the animals and birds to leave

[141] *Lhaka Honhat Association (Our Land) v Argentina* (Judgment), above n 97, para 263.

[142] Ibid., para 265 ('Chief Rogelio Segundo, in the public hearing before this Court, explained that logging is something that "greatly harms the territory" because "the forest is degraded", "there is no flower or fruit", there are animals that leave and fewer hives to collect honey. He added that, despite the complaints made to the State, they have not been able to stop this activity, and that as a result of it, floods have been generated. Chief Francisco Pérez, for his part, pointed out that "the State does not control, the Creoles are the first to cut and we chieftains say 'we are going to denounce', and nothing, denounce, denounce and nothing, there is no answer." After consulting at the public hearing about how they get their medicines due to the scarcity of typical tree species, Mr. Pérez pointed out that his system of medicine depends on the forests and that "when [there is] rain the plants grow but the problem is that when the plant grows, sweetheart, the animals come and eat the plant, that's why there aren't any. We think that if [from] once the animals are removed, in two years we can have a beautiful forest"').

[143] Ibid., paras 286–289.

[144] *Kaliña and Lokono Peoples v Suriname* (Judgment), above n 92, para 199.

[145] Ibid., para 23.

[146] Ibid., para 25.

the area; the streams were contaminated, thus harming the fishing; the cutting down of trees and the noise of the operations drove away different types of wildlife..., and the soil was affected so that many of the traditional plants stopped growing'.[147] Those negative impacts on the environment and the indigenous natural resources were also acknowledged in an environmental sensitivity analysis prepared for the bauxite mining company, by admitting that some portions of the natural reserve 'had suffered considerable environmental damage as a result of the open-cast mining of bauxite'.[148] And although the mining company claimed that its remediation policies were rehabilitating the affected area, the claim was contradicted by the photographs showing the devastated area and witness testimony.[149] During its on-site procedure, the Court also verified that the area had clearly been damaged and 'the landscape altered radically'.[150]

In determining the probative value of testimonial evidence, international courts have considered several factors, which are equally relevant in the context of proving environmental harm. First, the weight given to direct oral testimony would depend on the perceived truthfulness of a witness, which would depend on various factors. For example, the *Perenco* Tribunal treated with caution the testimony by a witness in alleging that an environmental management company, a former employer of the witness, deliberately falsified various findings in its soil and groundwater sampling campaigns to establish environmental harm resulting from oil spills. The Tribunal found him 'to be a non-responsive witness who clearly bears a strong animus towards his former employer' and presented facts that were contradicted by contemporaneous evidence.[151] Another important element affecting the apparent reliability of a witness is whether he or she can be considered disinterested or independent, 'one who is not a party the proceedings and stands to gain or lose nothing from its outcome'.[152] As the ICJ has observed, for example, 'a member of the government of a State engaged in litigation' will '"probably tend to identify himself with the interests of his country."'

---

[147] Ibid., para 217. See also ibid., para 92 ('Regarding the adverse impact of the mining operations in the nature reserve, the hunting and fishing activities, which were traditional in the area, have declined considerably. In this regard, the noise and vibrations caused by the trucks and the dynamite explosions, the contamination of land and streams, and the destruction of fruit-bearing trees caused the wildlife to flee that the indigenous peoples hunted and fished to feed the members of the local communities. Also, access to the area of the mining concessions was prohibited to the indigenous peoples and to any other unauthorized person').

[148] Ibid., para 218.

[149] Ibid., para 219.

[150] Ibid., para 220.

[151] According to the Tribunal: '[The witness] provided details as to the number of times that he met with counsel and the amount he estimated that he was paid by Perenco to appear as a witness only when pressed by the Tribunal's President and even then he was vague. These aspects of the witness' demeanour, his seeking out Perenco's counsel to provide evidence against his former employer soon after arriving at a settlement with it, and the animus between him and [his former employer] leads the Tribunal to treat his evidence with caution' (*Perenco v Ecuador* (Interim Decision on the Environmental Counterclaim), above n 32, paras 550–553).

[152] *Military and Paramilitary Activities in and Against Nicaragua (Nicaragua v United States of America)* (Merits), above n 2, para 69.

Consequently, '"while in no way impugning the honour or veracity" of such a person, the Court should "treat such evidence with great reserve"'.[153] The same holds true with respect to affidavits. In assessing their probative value, the ICJ stressed as one of the factors 'whether they were made by State officials or by private persons not interested in the outcome of the proceedings'.[154]

Second, the probative value of direct oral testimony and an affidavit would depend on whether it attests to the existence of facts or represents only an opinion as regards certain events. In this regard, the ICJ repeatedly stated: 'The Court has not treated as evidence any part of the testimony given which was not a statement of fact, but a mere expression of opinion as to the probability or otherwise of the existence of such facts, not directly known to the witness. Testimony of this kind, which may be highly subjective, cannot take the place of evidence. An opinion expressed by a witness is a mere personal and subjective evaluation of a possibility, which has yet to be shown to correspond to a fact; it may, in conjunction with other material, assist the Court in determining a question of fact, but is not proof in itself. Nor is testimony of matters not within the direct knowledge of the witness, but known to him only from hearsay, of much weight'.[155]

Third, in some cases evidence which is contemporaneous with the period concerned may be of special value. Affidavits sworn later by a State official for purposes of litigation as to earlier facts will carry less weight than affidavits sworn at the time when the relevant facts occurred.[156] However, in other circumstances, where there would have been no reason for private persons to offer testimony earlier, affidavits prepared even for the purposes of litigation will be scrutinized by a court both to see whether what has been testified to has been influenced by those taking the deposition and for the utility of what is said.[157] Thus, courts will not find it inappropriate as such to receive affidavits produced for the purposes of a litigation if they attest to personal knowledge of facts by a particular individual.

Finally, the process of cross-examination enables the veracity of the witness testimony to be tested, and if it remains uncontradicted, it will be afforded greater weight than it may otherwise have been.[158]

---

[153] *Armed Activity on the Territory of the Congo (Democratic Republic of the Congo v Uganda)*, Judgment, 19 December 5005, ICJ Reports 2005, p. 36, para 65 (quoting *Military and Paramilitary Activities in and Against Nicaragua (Nicaragua v United States of America)* (Merits), above n 2, para 70).

[154] *Territorial and Maritime Dispute between Nicaragua and Honduras in the Caribbean Sea (Nicaragua v Honduras)*, Judgment, 8 October 2007, ICJ Reports 2007, p. 659, para 244.

[155] Ibid., para 244 (quoting *Military and Paramilitary Activities in and Against Nicaragua (Nicaragua v United States of America)* (Merits), above n 2, para 68).

[156] Ibid.

[157] Ibid.

[158] *Military and Paramilitary Activities in and Against Nicaragua (Nicaragua v United States of America)* (Merits), above n 2, para 67.

16.5 Conclusion

Courts do not adjudicate issues in the abstract. They are called upon to resolve actual disputes, and what makes a dispute concrete are the facts upon which it is based. Success, or failure, in proving environmental harm often hinges on whether claims are supported by evidence. As shown in this chapter, international courts and tribunals have their nuanced approaches with respect to evidential issues related to the burden of proof, standard of proof and methods of proof. That said, their decisions support some broad propositions. First, a claimant normally bears a burden of showing actual environmental harm that has reached a requisite threshold determined by the applicable law. However, the standard allocation of the burden of proof, which requires a party asserting a fact to prove that fact, may be reversed in some circumstances where an applicable international treaty provides so based on the precautionary principle, or where the applicable provides for specific liability regimes. Second, there is no clear rule on the standard of proof. However, international courts appear frequently to require the production of sufficient evidence. Third, there is no conclusive method of proof of environmental harm. No kind of evidence is sufficient by itself. Courts and tribunals consider all the evidence submitted by the parties in their totality and then determine which facts must be considered relevant, assess their probative value, and draw conclusions from them as appropriate. It is therefore imperative to collect and present, as corroborating each other, all kinds of authoritative and credible evidence ranging from documentary evidence to expert testimony, to witness testimony.

References

Amerasinghe CF (2005) Evidence in International Litigation. Nijhoff, Leiden

Boyle A, Harrison J (2013) Judicial Settlement of International Environmental Disputes: Current Problems. Journal of International Dispute Settlement 4:245–276

Brown Ch (2006) A Common Law of International Adjudication. Oxford University Press, Oxford

Combacau J, Sur S (1995) Droit International Public. Montchrestien, Paris

Del Mar K (2011) Weight of Evidence Generated through Intra-Institutional Fact-Finding before the ICJ. Journal of International Dispute Settlement 2:393–415

Foster C (2010) Science and the Precautionary Principle in International Courts: Expert Evidence, Burden of Proof and Finality. Cambridge University Press, Cambridge

Jennings R (1996) International Lawyers and the Progressive Development of International Law. In: Makarczyk J (ed) Theory of International Law at the Threshold of the 21st Century: Essays in Honour of Krzystof Skubiszewski. Kluwer Law International, The Hague, pp 413–424

Kazazi M (1996) Burden of Proof and Related Issues: A Study on Evidence before International Tribunals. Kluwer Law International, The Hague

Moore J (1898) History and Digest of The International Arbitrations to Which the United States Has Been a Party. Government Printing Office, Washington, DC

Tomka P, Proulx V-J (2016) The Evidentiary Practice of the World Court. In: Sainz-Borgo JC (ed) Liber Amicorum Gudmundur Eiriksson. University for Peace Press, San Jose, pp 361–382

Watts A (2001) Enhancing the Effectiveness of Procedures of International Dispute Settlement. In: Frowein J A, Wolfrum R (eds) Max Planck Yearbook of United Nations Law, Vol. 5

Wolfrum R, Moldner M (2013) International Courts and Tribunals, Evidence. In: Max Planck Encyclopaedia of Public International Law. Oxford University Press, Oxford, pp 1–25

Yuri Parkhomenko Partner at Foley Hoag LLP.

Nour Nicolas Associate at Foley Hoag LLP.

Benjamin Salas Kantor LLM candidate at Columbia Law School.

Chapter 17
State Responsibility and Liability

Malgosia Fitzmaurice

Contents

Abstract This chapter deals with the complex question of reparations for environmental damage. Section 17.2 is devoted to the brief presentation of responsibility for environmental damage and the content of the primary obligation to protect the environment. It is limited to State responsibility within the remit of public international law thus, and only refers briefly to civil liability regimes with particular focus on those which are connected to or derived from Multilateral Environmental Agreements. The question is considered whether a classical legal regime of reparations, as set out in the *Chorzow Factory* case, is suitable for environmental damage as it may be suggested that international environmental law has set new frontiers and challenges to classical rules of State responsibility. In the context of reparations for environmental damage, the work of the International Law Commission is analysed, as well as the case law of the international courts and tribunals, such as the International Court of Justice and the International Tribunal for the Law of the Sea. It is suggested that the existing classical framework of State responsibility and reparations for environmental harm is not entirely equipped to deal with the particularities of the environment.

Keywords State responsibility · Reparations · *Chorzow Factory* case · International Court of Justice · International Tribunal for the Law of the Sea ·

M. Fitzmaurice (✉)
Department of Law, Queen Mary University of London, London E1 4NS, England, UK
e-mail: m.fitzmaurice@qmul.ac.uk

E. Sobenes et al. (eds.), *The Environment Through the Lens of International Courts and Tribunals*, https://doi.org/10.1007/978-94-6265-507-2_17

International Law Commission · Environmental damage · Multilateral Environmental Agreements · Civil liability regimes

17.1 Introduction

This chapter deals with the complex and vexing question of State responsibility for environmental damage. The chapter is limited to State responsibility within the remit of public international law, thus only briefly analysing civil liability regimes, with particular focus on those which are connected to or derived from Multilateral Environmental Agreements (MEAs) .

Section 17.2 of this chapter indicates the differences between State responsibility and liability for environmental damage. In Sect. 17.3, consideration is given to whether the legal regime of State responsibility is suitable for environmental damage; it is suggested that international environmental law has set new frontiers and challenges to classical rules of State responsibility.[1] There are multiple fora dealing with environmental harm. This chapter does not purport to analyse practice of all of them but focuses on the International Court of Justice (ICJ), and investment arbitration on the basis of selected case law to evidence the similarities and differences in their approach to responsibility for environmental harm and the question of reparations.

Section 17.4 of this chapter is devoted to the question of reparations, and in particular whether the classical formula adopted by the Permanent Court of International Justice (PCIJ) in the *Chorzow Factory* case, is also reflective of reparations in international environmental law.[2] It was observed that '[t]he problems of defining and valuing "environmental damage" in international law are discrete but not fundamentally separate from those affecting reparation for material damage in general international law'.[3] This chapter examines whether principles of international law concerning reparations indeed retain their usefulness for international environmental law and to what extent international environmental law has developed its own principles in the context of reparations.

In this connection, it is important to recall the ICJ's statement in the 1997 *Gabcikovo-Nagymaros* case, in which it stated that it was:

> …mindful that, in the field of environmental protection, vigilance and prevention are required on account of the often irreversible character of damage to the environment and of the limitations inherent in the very mechanism of reparation of this type of damage.[4]

---

[1] On responsibility for environmental damage, e.g. Sands and Peel 2018, pp. 735–807; Mbengue 2016, pp. 293–297. See in general: Boyle 2002, pp. 17–26.

[2] 'Reparation must, as far as possible, wipe out all the consequences of the illegal act and re-establish the situation which would, in all probability, have existed if that act had not been committed', *Factory at Chorzow (Germany v Poland),* Merits, 1928 PCIJ (ser. A) No. 17, 47 (Sept. 13).

[3] Boyle 2002.

[4] ICJ, *Gabčíkovo-Nagymaros Project (Hungary v Slovakia),* Judgement, 25 September 1997, ICJ Reports 1997, para 140.

In the same vein, the Seabed Disputes Chamber of the International Tribunal for the Law of the Sea (ITLOS) in its 2011 Advisory Opinion has doubted the 'technical feasibility of restoring the situation to the status *quo ante*' in the case of potential damages to the deep seabed area.[5]

17.2 Distinguishing State Responsibility and Liability for Environmental Damage

This section deals with both State responsibility and liability for environmental damage. State responsibility, it may be said, entails more complex issues than State liability and is of more importance for environmental damage. Therefore, the greater part of this chapter analyses various aspects of State responsibility. The focus of this section therefore is to indicate the differences between these two concepts, rather than analyse State liability in-depth.

The law of State responsibility is based on the distinction between two types of rules: primary rules, which establish obligations of States, and secondary rules, which relate to breaches of primary rules and define consequences of such breaches. There are, however, cases of environmental damage which arise from lawful activities; these are covered by the rules of State liability. This distinction is based on a difference between liability *ex delicto* (based on a wrongful act) and *sine delicto* (deleterious acts resulting from lawful activities). The International Law Commission (ILC) struggled with this difference, in particular in relation to liability emanating from hazardous activities, such as nuclear power plants. These considerations prompted the ILC to begin with the 1978 Articles on Liability for Injurious Consequences of Acts Not Prohibited by International Law. This approach was, however, almost uniformly criticized as fundamentally misconceived. The key complaint of the critics was that in the law of State responsibility the issue is not whether the relevant activity as such is unlawful but whether the home State fulfils its due diligence duty to avoid causing the transboundary harm.[6]

---

[5] ITLOS, *Responsibilities and Obligations of States with Respect to Activities in the Area,* Advisory Opinion, 1 February 2011, ITLOS Reports p. 10, para 197.

[6] Following the criticism of the project, the ILC decided to divide the liability topic into two parts: one on prevention of harm arising out of transboundary activities and another on liability. The first part of the project resulted in the 2001 Articles on Prevention of Transboundary Harm from Hazardous Activities and the second part resulted in 2006 Principles of Allocation of Loss in the Case of Transboundary Harm Arising out of Hazardous Activities, see the text adopted by the International Law Commission at its fifty-third session, in 2001, and submitted to the General Assembly (A/56/10).

17.2.1 State Responsibility

The Draft Articles on State Responsibility (ASR) adopted by the ILC serve a 'triple function' in respect of an internationally wrongful act. Firstly, a preventive function, i.e. persuasion directed at States not to engage in conduct which could lead to an internationally wrongful act. Secondly, a corrective function, i.e. enforcement of primary international obligations. And thirdly, a compensatory or reparative function, i.e. restoring the status *quo ante* or compensation for damage caused by an internationally wrongful act.

The ASR adopted in Article 2 a definition of a wrongful act under international law: that is an act or omission, which is attributable to a State under international law, and constitutes a breach of an international obligation. Such a wrongful act engages the responsibility of the State (Article 1). Part One of Chapter 5 identifies circumstances precluding wrongfulness. These circumstances include the following: *force majeure*, distress, necessity, compliance with peremptory norms, self-defence, consent of a State against which an otherwise wrongful act has been committed, and the fact that the wrongful act constituted a countermeasure in response to a prior breach of international law (Articles 20–27). Part Two deals with the 'content of the international responsibility of States', which broadly refers to the issue of remedies. These remedies are defined in general terms as reparation for the injury, which can be accomplished in a number of ways, including restitution, compensation, and satisfaction. The final Part Three deals with implementation of the international responsibility of States, which includes rules on the 'invocation' of responsibility (Articles 42 and 48). Under the regime of Article 42 an 'injured' State may always invoke the responsibility of another State for a breach of international law. Article 48 provides for circumstances when responsibility may be invoked by States other than the injured State. Further, this Part fleshes out the concept of countermeasures—by which are meant measures taken by one State to induce another State which has committed a wrongful act to comply with its international obligations (Article 49).

The key question of importance in the area of State responsibility in relation to environmental harm is the threshold of harm and causation. Suffice to say that not all harm can constitute a wrongful act. There is a threshold accepted in the theory and practice of international law, which is so-called significant harm. This was defined during the codification of rules by the ILC on non-navigational uses of international watercourses,[7] where significant harm is defined as not minor or trivial but less than substantial or serious.[8] The question of causation is more problematic. A full analysis of causality exceeds the scope of this chapter.[9] However, it is observed that ASR left many unresolved questions. As Plakokefalos explains, international courts and tribunals employ causal analysis in determining the breach and the extent of the reparation. He notes that '[c]ausation is a necessary element of the breach when the primary obligation in question either directly or indirectly requires the existence of

[7] ILC Report, A/49/10, 1994, chap. III(B), para 219, *ILC Yearbook*, 1994, vol. II(2).

[8] McCaffrey 2019, p. 496.

[9] See on this Plakokefalos 2015. See also Chap. 16.

such a link'.[10] The same author has made several interesting comments on causation in relation to the prevention of transboundary harm. If it is an obligation of conduct, there may not be a wrongful act on the part of a State even if transboundary environmental harm occurs. He persuasively explains that 'causation might become part of the assessment of the breach of an obligation of conduct if the obligation itself demands that there must be damage for it to be breached [...] It will be considered an additional element of the breach if it stems not from the secondary rules of responsibility but, rather, from the primary rule in question'.[11] He has further opined that 'in the case of obligations of conduct things might be somewhat more complicated—for instance, when the breach of the obligation of conduct in questions related to the issue of reparation'.[12]

17.2.2 State Liability

As indicated above, the main feature distinguishing responsibility from liability is that the latter is not based on the commission of an internationally wrongful act. Such an approach has been seen as a possible alternative to the due diligence-based approach arising from the combination of the general rules on State responsibility and the duty of prevention of environmental harm. An approach based on strict and absolute liability (strict liability is understood as providing a greater range of exculpatory factors than absolute) is not free from misconceptions. Moreover, in practice, this approach has almost never been followed. The main illustration of a strict liability regime imposed on States is the 1972 Convention on International Liability for Damage Caused by Space Objects, and it only gave rise to one claim by Canada following the crash of a Soviet satellite with a nuclear reactor (Cosmo 954 claim) on Canadian territory. However, the claim was settled by an *ex gratia* payment of 3 million dollars by the USSR to Canada, without admitting liability.[13] Therefore, this case has no precedential value. The 1993 Council of Europe Lugano Convention for Damage Resulting from Activities Dangerous to the Environment is yet another failed attempt to impose an inter-State strict liability regime within an environmental context. It harmonizes laws on environmental damage; but due to several factors, such as incorporation of unlimited liability and the existence of sectoral liability regimes, it will probably never enter into force.

---

[10] Plakokefalos 2015, p. 481.

[11] Plakokefalos 2015, p. 482. He gives the following example: '... this is the case in the deep seabed, where the provisions on the obligations of the states sponsoring an exploration or exploitation activity in the area, carried out by a contractor, are obligations of conduct. Nonetheless, LOSC demands that in order for these obligations to be breached not only must the sponsoring state fail to abide by them but also that this failure must be causally connected to damage occurring in the deep seabed.'

[12] Plakokefalos 2015, p. 482.

[13] *Canada Claim against the Union of Soviet Republics for Damage Caused by Soviet Cosmos 954* 18 (4) (1979) *ILM*.

The Draft Articles on Prevention of Transboundary Harm Activities (2001 Articles) apply 'to activities not prohibited by international law which involve a risk of causing significant transboundary harm through their physical consequences'.[14] According to the principle of prevention '[t]he State of origin shall take all appropriate measures to prevent significant transboundary harm or at any event to minimize the risk thereof'.[15] Related to the 2001 Articles are the 2006 Draft Principles on Allocation of Loss in Case of Transboundary Harm Arising out of Hazardous Activities.[16] The 2006 Draft Principles 'apply to transboundary damage caused by hazardous activities not prohibited by international law'.[17] Damage 'means significant damage caused to persons, property or the environment; and includes: (i) loss of life or personal injury; (ii) loss of, or damage to, property, including property which forms part of the cultural heritage; (iii) loss or damage by impairment of the environment; (iv) the costs of reasonable measures of reinstatement of the property, or environment, including natural resources; (v) the costs of reasonable response measures'.[18] These 2006 Draft Principles regulate civil liability of an operator defined as 'any person in command or control of the activity at the time the incident causing transboundary damage occurs'.[19] States should 'take all necessary measures' 'to ensure that prompt and adequate compensation is available for victims of transboundary damage caused by hazardous activities located within its territory or otherwise under its jurisdiction or control'.[20] These measures should include the following:

> ...the imposition of liability on the operator or, where appropriate, other person or entity. Such liability should not require proof of fault [...] These measures should also include the requirement on the operator or, where appropriate, other person or entity, to establish and maintain financial security such as insurance, bonds or other financial guarantees to cover claims of compensation. In appropriate cases, these measures should include the requirement for the establishment of industry-wide funds at the national level. In the event that the measures under the preceding paragraphs are insufficient to provide adequate compensation, the State of origin should also ensure that additional financial resources are made available.[21]

The 2006 Draft Principles are based on the civil liability of an operator, not State responsibility; the State is obliged to make sure that the civil liability of an operator is implemented. Such obligations relate to the area of response measures, such as obtaining from the operator necessary information and the prompt notification to all States that are affected or likely to be affected (Principle 5(a)). The State of origin of the damage (with the appropriate involvement of the operator) has the duty to ensure that the appropriate response measures are adopted, and it should rely on the

---

[14] Article 1, above n 6.

[15] Article 3, above n 6.

[16] Text adopted by the International Law Commission at its fifty-eighth session, in 2006, and submitted to the General Assembly session (A/61/10). 899.

[17] Ibid., Principle 1.

[18] Ibid., Principle 2.

[19] Ibid.

[20] Ibid., Principle 4(1).

[21] Ibid., Principle 4.

best available technology (Principle 5(b)). The State of origin, as appropriate, should also consult with and seek the cooperation of States affected or likely to be affected to mitigate the effects of transboundary damage and, if possible, eliminate them (Principle 5(c)). States affected or likely to be affected by transboundary damage shall take all possible measures to mitigate and, if possible, eliminate effects of such damage (Principle 5(d)). According to Principle 5(e), the States concerned should, where appropriate, seek the assistance of competent international organizations or other States on mutually acceptable terms. In addition, the Draft Principles also encourage States to make all efforts to conclude specific international agreements relating to particular categories of hazardous activities, with provisions on compensation, response measures, and international and domestic remedies (Principle 7). As the ILC stated, these Draft Principles are significant as they intend 'to contribute to the process of development of international law both by providing appropriate guidance for States in respect of hazardous activities not covered by specific agreements, and by indicating the matters which should be dealt with in such agreements'.[22]

17.3 State Responsibility and International Environmental Law

17.3.1 Community Interests in International Environmental Law

The regime of State responsibility has not been entirely suitable for the redress of environmental damage, as a result of the inherently bilateral system of international law and the classical rule which links a claim for reparation to direct injury. Some of the concepts such as common concern of humankind, when related to climate change and biodiversity, presuppose an interest of the whole community of States that is in effect coterminous with obligations *erga omnes* and *erga omnes partes*. The legal character of such obligations are not entirely clear, though it is clear that they are non-reciprocal and not bilateralizable.[23] It also may be said that international law gives little guidance in terms of the identification of obligations *erga omnes*, apart from those that are already identified as such by the ICJ in its case law.[24] It is argued that the lack of clarity regarding the content and legal effects of obligations

---

[22] Draft principles on the allocation of loss in the case of transboundary harm arising out of hazardous activities, with commentaries, Yearbook of the International Law Commission, 2006, Vol. II, Part Two, available at https://legal.un.org/ilc/texts/instruments/english/commentaries/9_10_2006.pdf, p. 59.

[23] See in general on *erga omnes* obligations: Tams 2005; ICJ, *Barcelona Traction, Light and Power Co Ltd (Belgium v Spain)*, Judgement, 5 February 1970, ICJ Reports 1970, p. 3; Brunnée 2018.

[24] Duvic-Paoli 2018, p. 321.

erga omnes limits the willingness of States and scholars to go beyond this recognised category and there is no uniform approach to possible new entrants in this category.[25]

Duvic-Paoli has identified two major views regarding categories of *erga omnes* obligations in international environmental law scholarship. The first view argues that specific environmental law obligations (i.e. the prevention of pollution of the high seas), which are generally treaty based, are *erga omnes* as they cannot function on the basis of reciprocity. The second view adopts a wider approach by treating all environmental duties as *erga omnes*. On this view, all norms of international environmental law could arguably be obligations *erga omnes* in light of their objectives.[26] In view of the present author, Duvic-Paoli is correct to identify shortcomings of both approaches. The first one is too limiting due to its reliance primarily on treaty provisions without the reference to custom; the second, in contrast, is too inclusive as not all environmental obligations would qualify as *erga omnes* obligations. She further explains that to some extent, environmental obligations depend on the elements of 'importance', as adopted in the *Barcelona Traction* case.[27] However, the criterion of 'importance' is difficult to define. Finally, not all environmental obligations represent moral absolutes.[28]

A second category of obligations, which can be said to also represent community interests, is the obligations *erga omnes partes*, included in Article 48 of the ASR. They are based on the common interest of the parties to a multilateral treaty.

From a procedural point of view, Article 48 of the ASR recognises the *locus standi* of a State which is not directly injured but seeks to bring a claim on behalf of the whole community of States and in relation to the obligations *erga omnes* of any part to a treaty. When the Articles were adopted, this was considered to be a progressive development of international law. It may be said, however, that after the Judgments of the ICJ in *Belgium v. Senegal*,[29] *Whaling in the Antarctic*,[30] and the Advisory Opinion of the International Tribunal for Law of the Sea (ITLOS) on States Responsibilities and Obligations in the Area,[31] the redress of community interests has become more of a reality, albeit not without vexing questions, based on multilateral treaties.

In the *Whaling in Antarctic* case, Australia claimed to have brought the claim on behalf of the community of States, and was credited for having done so.[32] According to James Crawford, Australia invoked Japan's responsibility *erga omnes partes*

---

[25] Ibid., p. 321.

[26] Ibid., p. 322.

[27] *Barcelona Traction*, above n 23, para 3. 3.

[28] Duvic-Paoli 2018, p. 323.

[29] ICJ, *Questions Concerning the Obligation to Prosecute or Extradite (Belgium v Senegal)*, Judgment, 20 July 2012, ICJ Reports 2012, p. 422.

[30] ICJ, *Whaling in the Antarctic (Australia* v *Japan: New Zealand intervening)*, Judgment, 31 March 2014, ICJ Reports 2014, p. 226.

[31] ITLOS, *Responsibilities and obligations of States with respect to activities in the Area*, Advisory Opinion, 1 February 2011, ITLOS Reports 2011, p. 10.

[32] Fitzmaurice 2013, p. 377: '[b]ecause of the general and longstanding public interest in the protection of marine mammals, this case is likely to define the public perception of the Court as a protector of environmental concerns'.

under the International Convention for the Regulation of Whaling (ICRW).[33] During the proceedings, Australia claimed to act exclusively in defence of a general legal interest.[34] The ICJ's jurisprudence in this matter is so varied that is does not allow one to draw more general conclusions;[35] however, as Tams opines, perhaps the *Whaling* case could be seen as a logical follow-up to the 2011 Judgment in the *Belgium v Senegal* case. In that case, too, the Court surprised commentators by going out of its way to accept the applicant's standing to enforce a multilateral treaty protecting collective interests.[36] Interestingly, the Court has not mentioned at all the obligations *erga omnes partes* in its Judgment.

In relation to *Whaling in the Antarctic,* there were views expressed that the current ecosystem approach and the notion of *common heritage of humankind* may be considered by States as matters that give rise to obligations *erga omnes* and *erga omnes*

[33] Crawford 2013, p. 373.

[34] 'Australia does not claim to be an injured State because of the fact that some of the JARPA II take is from waters over which Australia claims sovereign rights and jurisdiction. ... Every party has the same interest in ensuring compliance by every other party with its obligations under the 1946 Convention. Australia is seeking to uphold its collective interest, an interest it shares with all other parties'.

[35] On the one hand we have ICJ, *South West Africa (Ethiopia and Liberia v South Africa)*, Judgment, 18 July 1966, ICJ Reports 1966, p. 6. (rejection of standing to enforce interests of the international community) and *East Timor (Portugal v Australia)*, Judgment, 30 June 1995, ICJ Reports 1995, p. 90. (jurisdictional limitations which prohibit public interest litigation), and on the other, *Barcelona Traction*, above n 23, (the *erga omnes* doctrine first mentioned) and the *Questions relating to the Obligation to Prosecute or Extradite*, above n 29, p. 422 in which the ICJ has recognised the standing of all treaty parties to enforce obligations *erga omnes partes*, see Tams 2016. Mention must be made of *The Gambia v Myanmar* case. On 11 November 2019, The Gambia filed an application at the International Court of Justice against Myanmar, alleging violation of obligations under the Genocide Convention. The Gambia contended that, since the obligations under the Genocide Convention are obligations *erga omnes partes*, any State party to the Genocide Convention is entitled to invoke the responsibility of another State party for the breach of its obligations, without having to prove a special interest. The Gambia argued during the provisional measures phase 'that the fact of being party to a treaty imposing obligations *erga omnes partes* suffices to establish its legal interest and legal standing before the Court.' See *Application of the Convention on the Prevention and Punishment of the Crime of Genocide (The Gambia v Myanmar),* Provisional Measures, Order, 23 January 2020, para 40. The Court agreed with The Gambia and considered that 'all the States parties to the Genocide Convention have a common interest to ensure that acts of genocide are prevented [...][and concluded that] not only a specially affected State, may invoke the responsibility of another State party with a view to ascertaining the alleged failure to comply with its obligations *erga omnes partes*, and to bring that failure to an end'.

[36] Tams 2016.

partes, and thus result in redress pursuant to Article 48 of ASR.[37] As Urs persuasively argues, this case illustrates that multilateral agreements such as the ICRW are not a simple sum of bilateral relationships.[38] Their multilateral effect is reflected by the interest of Australia and New Zealand in mutual compliance irrespective of their ability to make claims to specific injury arising out of Japan's violation. Therefore, 'as a result, irrespective of whether the ICRW was intended to prohibit commercial whaling as a conservationist effort, or simply to regulate states' access to a common resource, this emphasis by the Court reaffirms this trajectory in the development of international law'.[39]

Sakai expresses a different view from that adopted by the Court in the *Whaling* case on the question of standing (Article 48 of the ASR). He proposes that the Court's approach might be justified exclusively in the case of Conventions such as the Genocide Convention or the Convention against Torture. However, he considers that such obligations have no *raison d'être* in the case of the ICRW, even taking into account the allegedly 'special' character of whales.[40] Professor Sakai's approach to the applicability of the obligations *erga omnes* (*erga omnes partes*) in international litigation appears unduly restrictive. As explained above, some of the environmental obligations may qualify as *erga omnes* (*partes*), especially in light of the growing importance of preserving the environment (including its biodiversity) for future generations, which widens their scope beyond genocide.

The Seabed Disputes Chamber of ITLOS has referred to Article 48 of the ASR in finding that obligations to preserve the environment of the high seas and in 'the Area'[41] may be *erga omnes* or *erga omnes partes*. Accordingly, the ITLOS Chamber considered that the International Seabed Authority, acting on behalf of mankind and pursuant to the United Nations Law of the Sea Convention and Article 48 of ASR, could bring a claim in the case of environmental harm in the Area.[42]

---

[37] See also Giorgio Gaja 2011, pp. 171–80 who also expressed the view that the protection of natural resources can be within the realm of interests of the international community and the community interest can be also expressed through the imposition of certain restrictions on their exploitation. There is no doubt that the common heritage of mankind belongs to the category of concepts which engage general interest and that Article 48 of Articles on States Responsibility is to be relied on in case of breaches of obligations involving community interests. Shotaro Hamomoto also was of the view that multilateral environmental treaties are a source of collective interests therefore, arguing that Japan (even before the Judgment in the *Belgium v Senegal* case) would have been in a difficult position to claim inadmissibility of the claim by Australia on the basis of the lack of legal interest. According to Professor Hamamoto, the non-admissibility plea on the part of Japan, after *Belgium v Senegal*, the case against Australia, would be 'virtually hopeless', see Hamamoto 2014, p. 6.

[38] Urs Priya (2014) Are States Injured by Whaling in the Antarctic?, available at http://opiniojuris.org/2014/08/14/guest-post-states-injured-whaling-antarctic/, last accessed 8 October 2019.

[39] Ibid.

[40] Sakai 2016, pp. 10–11.

[41] 'The Area' is covered by Part 11 of the 1982 UNCLOS. The Area is covered by the concept of the Common Heritage of Humankind. It comprises the seabed and ocean floor and subsoil thereof, beyond the limits of national jurisdiction (Article 136 of the UNCLOS).

[42] See para 180 of the Advisory Opinion.

As previously noted, there is a host of vexing questions concerning the practical application of obligations *erga omnes* to environmental law within the paradigm of State responsibility. First of all, there are unresolved issues relating to the substantive and procedural division of obligations *erga omnes.* This was debated by the ILC during its work on the protection of the atmosphere. Special Rapporteur Murase[43] suggested that the general obligation to protect the atmosphere was an obligation *erga omnes,* a suggestion which was very divisive within the ILC. There was support for recognizing that the obligations pertaining to the protection of the atmosphere from transboundary atmospheric pollution of global significance and global atmospheric degradation are obligations *erga omnes.* Yet, a view expressed was that the legal consequences of such a recognition are not yet fully clear in the context of this topic.[44] Murase argued that a substantive obligation *erga omnes* could exist without a corresponding procedural obligation.[45] Although, standing in cases of obligations *erga omnes (partes)* can also be exercised by States that are not directly injured, a more complex question relates to the application of Article 48(1)(b). This provides for the possibility of invoking the responsibility of another State violating obligations of the international community as a whole.

As Duvic-Paoli states: '[w]hen it comes to prevention, courts and tribunals have traditionally been wary of accepting claims by parties that were acting as representatives of the international community but had not been directly affected by environmental harm'.[46] This can be exemplified by the United Nations Compensation Commission, Panel F4, which recognised the existence of common concern that entails the obligation towards both the international community and future generations. This statement of the Commission did not result in any direct legal consequences. It is argued that the Panel used the *erga omnes* character 'to examine the obligations of the claimants to prevent and mitigate environmental damage that occurred in neighbouring territories'[47]. The Commission did not extend, however, the scope of *locus standi* by such a qualification of the obligations.[48]

A very pertinent question is who are the beneficiaries? i.e. who benefits from environmental protection? As Duvic-Paoli explains the environment is the ultimate beneficiary but also the international community comprising States, individuals and communities benefit from harm avoidance.[49]

The other vexing problem is the kind of reparation that non-injured States can claim. It is assumed that the most beneficial kind would be restoration, but as it is often in practice, this may prove impossible.[50]

---

[43] Murase 2015.

[44] Report of the International Law Commission Sixty-eighth session (2 May–10 June and 4 July–12 August 2016), 287.

[45] Duvic-Paoli 2018, p. 341.

[46] Ibid.

[47] Duvic-Paoli 2018, p. 340.

[48] Ibid.

[49] Ibid.

[50] Ibid., pp. 342–43.

In view of the present author, the general judicial practice has definitely recognised the existence of *locus standi* in cases of substantive obligations *erga omnes* and *erga omnes partes,* as exemplified by recent case-law. However, as was highlighted in the *Whaling* case, the question of *locus standi* in relation to the environment is more complex and taxing because it is not quite certain whether all substitutive environmental obligations can be accorded the legal status of obligations *erga omnes* and *erga omnes partes.*

Finally, it may be said that the European Court of Human Rights, has applied the rules on *locus standi* more liberally. The Court's recent case law has indicated that it interprets the provisions of the European Convention on Human Rights in a less its rigid manner in order to give the widest possible effect to the protection of human rights. It has allowed claims brought by persons other than the actual victim, thus modifying the rigid direct victim requirement.[51]

17.3.2 Due Diligence and the Principle of Prevention

One of the most important—yet unresolved—issues, constituting a part of State responsibility, is the question of due diligence in relation to the obligation to prevent transboundary harm.[52] Such a duty has been recognised by the International Law Association (ILA)[53] and the ILC.[54] Due diligence is a general concept of international law. Although it has been widely analysed, what the concept requires of States (procedurally and substantively) is unclear. Apart from a straightforward definition, which is not controversial, there are many nuances, which make the practical application of due diligence problematic. The basic premise on which due diligence is based is that a responsible State has to comply with certain obligations and standards, which would vary depending on the circumstances of the case.[55] There are no uniform and general standards of due diligence fitting all situations.[56]

Regarding international environmental law, there are inherent—and we may even argue fundamental—problems with the concept of due diligence. There is no hard and fast division between substance and procedure which impacts on the due diligence concept (as exemplified by the case law of the ICJ, see below). Even more importantly, there is no agreement whether due diligence in international environmental law is an

---

[51] Ahmadov 2018, p. 169.

[52] Duvic-Paoli 2018, pp. 333–36; Plakokefalos 2012, pp. 32–36; Takano 2018, pp. 3–5. The ICJ indicated clearly that this an obligation of conduct, see *Case Concerning Application of the Convention on the Prevention and Punishment of the Crime of Genocide (Bosnia and Herzegovina v Yugoslavia (Serbia and Montenegro)),* Provisional Measures, 8 April 1993, ICJ Reports 1993. See Vinuales 2020.

[53] ILA 2016, p. 37.

[54] In general international law, see Draft Articles on State Responsibility with Commentaries adopted by the ILC on the first reading (1997) UN Doc.AS/CN.4528/Add.2.

[55] Koivurova 2010.

[56] Kulesza 2016; ILA Study Group on Due Diligence 2016, p. 2.

obligation of conduct (the majority view)[57] or the result of perhaps the mixture of both conduct and result.[58]

In international environmental law, due diligence is an element of the composite obligation to prevent transboundary harm.[59] Prevention comprises early notification; the obligation to conduct an Environment Impact Assessment (EIA); the obligation to exchange information; a duty to consult and a duty of cooperation in cases of environmental emergencies.[60] All of these components comprise separate obligations, which result in a complex legal framework regarding responsibility for environmental harm. The view is also expressed that the obligation of prevention constitutes one whole or in other words a continuum together with reparations, which further complicates the matter.[61]

In addition, and from a substantive point of view, the Seabed Chamber of ITLOS in its Advisory Opinion indicated that precaution[62] is also 'an integral part of the general obligation of due diligence'.[63] The other element of the substantive concept of due diligence is the principle of no-harm.

As Takano explains:

> With regard to whether the do-no-harm principle requires a duty to prevent all significant transboundary harm, as the *Advisory Opinion on the Legality of Nuclear Weapons* and the *Gabcikovo–Nagymaros* case indicate, states are only required to prevent harm caused as a result of an active disposition on or over their territory, which does not include the omission of protective measures.[64]

There are two landmark cases of the ICJ which shed some light on the procedural obligation of due diligence, though the findings of the ICJ have been subject to some criticism.[65] The ICJ in the *Pulp Mills* case stated that procedural obligations are an integrated and indivisible whole, and that procedural obligations exist separately from substantial obligations.[66] The analysis of both cases adjudged by the ICJ can

---

57 Duvic-Paoli 2018, p. 336; Dupuy 1999.

58 Duvic-Paoli 2018, p. 336.

59 Plakokefalos 2012.

60 Ibid.

61 Kosalapova 2013, p. 64.

62 The precautionary principle (Principle 15 of the Rio Declaration) is slowly gaining wider recognition in international environmental law as a norm of customary international law, a view supported by the 2011 Advisory Opinion of the Seabed Chamber of the ITLOS. This principle is also included in many environmental treaties. The reluctance to accord the precautionary principle a more defined status is linked, according to Sands and Peel, to 'doubts and differences as to what practical consequences of the precautionary principle or approach will be in particular field or in a specific case'. See Sands and Peel 2018, p. 240.

63 ITLOS, *Responsibilities and Obligations of States Sponsoring Persons and Entities with Respect to Activities in the Area*, Advisory Opinion, 1 February 2011, ITLOS Reports 2011, para 131.

64 Takano 2018, p. 3.

65 ICJ, *Case Concerning Pulp Mills on the River Uruguay (Argentina v Uruguay),* Judgment, 20 April 2010, ICJ Reports 2010, para 101; ICJ, *Certain Activities Carried out by Nicaragua in the Border Area (Costa Rica v Nicaragua) and Construction of a Road in Costa Rica along the San Juan River (Nicaragua v Costa Rica)*, Judgment, 16 December 2015, ICJ Reports 2015, p. 665.

66 McIntyre 2011, pp. 493–94.

lead to the conclusion that the Court has divided the principle of prevention into a substantive no-harm rule and procedural preventive obligations. The first obligation is breached only on evidence of a material breach; the second one when the required due diligence standards are not met.[67] Such a division has raised uncertainties. As Duvic-Paoli explains, if prevention is an obligation of due diligence, it can only be met when a number of other procedural obligations are fulfilled. It is difficult to understand how a breach of a procedural obligation does not automatically result in a breach of prevention. The two sides of prevention are organically linked. Therefore, a failure to fulfil a procedural obligation defeats the object and purpose of a treaty of harm prevention.[68]

There is an alternative route, focused on the breach of the obligation of due diligence to prevent environmental harm without a sharp distinction between due diligence and prevention. Thus, the prevention is the primary norm breached, notwithstanding the lack of material damage. Due diligence is then a standard of care, which breach leads to a violation of the obligation of prevention.[69] It may be said that these two approaches agree that due diligence will be breached without material damage, but they disagree whether the violated obligation is the obligation to prevent or the obligation of due diligence. The ICJ adopted the distinction of obligations whilst other tribunals have adopted the second alternative.[70] As an example, one can refer to the *South China Sea* arbitration,[71] where the Tribunal did not focus on whether the conduct of the State had breached its obligation of due diligence in the prevention of environmental harm. As Duvic-Paoli opines, 'the only difference from the existence of material damage is that it will have to be taken into account in the conduct of the assessment of the separations due to the affected State'.[72]

The other problematic issue is whether the violation of the procedural obligation of prevention, automatically results in the breach of a substantive obligation.[73] Theoretically such an approach is possible, but it brings a host of problems in practice, as both substantive and procedural obligations are inextricably connected. As Duvic-Paoli stated '[c]onsequently speaking, a failure to fulfil a procedural obligation defeats the objective and purpose of a treaty aiming at the prevention of harm'.[74]

Some of the problems with the applications of the rules of State responsibility to environmental claims are partly caused precisely because of the structure of the norm of prevention and its substantive and procedural elements, which are not clearly defined and uniformly applied, as for example the obligation to perform an EIA. The

---

[67] Duvic-Paoli 2018, p. 335.

[68] Duvic-Paoli 2018, 337.

[69] Ibid., p. 136.

[70] Ibid., p. 336.

[71] *South China Sea Arbitration (The Philippines v China),* Award, 12 July 2016, PCA Case No. 2013-19, para 941. Duvic-Paoli 2018, p. 335. See also Guo and Wang 2019, p. 235.

[72] Duvic-Paoli 2018, p. 336.

[73] As it is recalled, in both of the cases before the ICJ it was decided in the negative. See *supra* note 65.

[74] Duvic-Paoli 2018, p. 337.

pronouncement of the ICJ in the *Pulp Mills* case that the principle of EIA is already a norm of customary international law, was somewhat weakened by stating that its normative context is defined by States. The lack of clear content of principles such as the precautionary principle (approach) is also an obstacle in stating and quantifying environmental harm.

Therefore, it may be argued that '[...] tensions are visible in the position of the Court, which navigates rather uneasily between no-harm and prevention, between a traditional approach to damage and an awareness if the specificities of the environmental principle of prevention'[75] and that:

> [o]ne might say that the Court has taken two steps forward and one step back. The Court moved forward in concretizing the procedural aspects of the harm prevention framework, in particular the circumstances in which various procedural obligations are triggered. It appeared to move backward, however, in obscuring the relationship between procedure and substance, notably the due diligence duty of the harm prevention rule. We have to wait and see whether this turn to procedure proves to be mainly an effort to sidestep substance, or a pragmatic approach to enhancing the preventive power of customary international environmental law [...] For now, it seems that the price for greater clarity in preventive practice is confusion at a higher (read conceptual) level.[76]

17.4 State Responsibility and Reparations for Environmental Harm

According to the ILC: 'Every internationally wrongful act of a State entails the international responsibility of that State', and '[t]he State responsible for the internationally wrongful act is under an obligation: to cease that act, if it is continuing; and to offer appropriate assurances and guarantees of non-repetition, if circumstances so require.'[77]

The responsible State is under an obligation to make full reparation for the injury caused by the internationally wrongful act, including any damage, whether material or moral.[78] According to the *Chorzow Factory* case, reparation must 'wipe out all the consequences of the illegal act and re-establish the situation which would, in all probability, have existed if that act had not been committed'.[79]

Article 31 of ASR articulates a single system of reparation which applies to all breaches of international law, including environmental law.[80] The main principle is that: '(1) [t]he responsible State is under an obligation to make full reparation for the injury caused by the international wrongful act; (2) Injury includes any

[75] Ibid., p. 338.

[76] Brunnée 2016.

[77] 2001 ILC's Articles on the Responsibility of States for International Wrongful Acts (Article 30).

[78] Ibid., Article 31.

[79] PCIJ, *The Factory At Chorzow (Claim for Indemnity) (The Merits)*, Judgment, 13 September 1928, PCIJ Ser A No 17, p. 29.

[80] Crawford 2002, p. 295.

damage, whether material or moral, caused by the internationally wrongful act by a State'.[81] Article 35 on restitution describes it as the re-establishment of the situation that existed before the wrongful act was committed, unless restitution is materially impossible or involves a burden out of all proportion in order to benefit instead of compensation. Article 36 on compensation defines this obligation 'in so far as such damage is not made good by restitution'.[82] Compensation will cover any financially assessable damage, including loss of profits, insofar as it is established. Satisfaction is the form of reparation that is employed when restitution or compensation cannot be used. It may take the form of an acknowledgment of the breach, or expression of regret, or a formal apology.[83] Article 34 also stipulates that full reparation may only be achieved in particular cases by the combination of different forms of reparation.

In practice, a number of hurdles stand in the way of reparation for environmental harm. In addition, cases involving environmental harm often raise particularly complicated causation questions. In general, international law causation has a very important role and it also has many permutations.[84] In broad brushstrokes it is understood as one of the 'components that require a connection to be made between a conduct and an outcome'.[85]

In the law of State responsibility, causation has been linked with the question of the attribution of a wrongful act of an individual to a State. The ILC's pronouncements on this link are scant. Attribution as such is not included in ASR. The ILC has only stated that it is '[b]ased on criteria determined by international law and not on the mere recognition of a link of factual causality',[86] and that the link that must exist between the wrongful act and the injury in order for State responsibility to arise is a sufficient causal link, which is not too remote.[87] International courts and tribunals rely on causal analysis in determining the breach and in determining the extent of the reparation.[88]

However, an observation has been made that the application of causation by international courts and tribunals is capricious. It has been argued that cases before international courts and tribunals demonstrate very different causation standards.[89] Arbitral and judicial practice has developed five principal causation standards: (1)

---

[81] The forms of reparation envisaged by the law of State responsibility are the following: restitution, compensation and satisfaction, 'either singly or in combination' (Article 34).

[82] Compensation will cover any financially assessable damage, including loss of profits, insofar as it is established. Satisfaction is the form of reparation that is employed when restitution or compensation cannot be used. It may take the form of an acknowledgment of the breach, or expression of regret, or a formal apology (Article 37).

[83] Article 37, 2001 ILC's Articles on the Responsibility of States for International Wrongful Acts.

[84] See on this: Plakokefalos 2015, pp. 474–475.

[85] Plakokefalos 2015, p. 473. The subject –matter of causation has not attracted much attention in international law.

[86] 'State Responsibility, General Commentary' (ARSIWA Commentary), 2(2) *ILC Yearbook* (2001) 31, p. 81.

[87] Crawford 2002, p. 295.

[88] Plakokefalos 2015, p. 481.

[89] Tumonis 2012, p. 95.

direct versus indirect, (2) proximate versus remote, (3) foreseeable versus attenuated, (4) reasonable versus unreasonable, (5) certain versus speculative. In addition to the five principal standards, some writers add efficient and approximate causation standards.[90] It is argued that in some ICJ cases, the Court has applied a new standard.[91]

In international environmental law, causation is a complex question as the majority of environmental law obligations are those of conduct, such as the prevention of transboundary harm.[92] As has been explained: '[i]f a state takes the steps prescribed by the obligation (for example, conducts an environmental impact assessment, conducts negotiations and consultations and exchanges information with the possibly affected states), the state will have discharged its obligation even if transboundary environmental harm does occur'.[93]

At first blush, it may appear that such a type of obligation does not involve causation: i.e. that the assessment of the breach takes place at the normative level and is not connected to any particular result.[94] However, causation might become an element of the assessment of the breach within the context of the obligation of conduct if such an obligation includes damage for this obligation to be breached. Such an element of the breach is derived from the primary rules not secondary rules of State responsibility.[95]

The main forms of damage raise specific kinds of difficulties in the environmental context. Article 35 on restitution focuses on the restoration of the *status quo ante.*[96] In principle, the utility of restitution to remedy environmental harm should be obvious. It may avoid some controversies as it relates to restoration of a pre-existing factual situation, which does not involve the complex valuation questions associated with compensation. However, in many cases, environmental harms are irreversible, and hence restitution will be impossible (such as the extinction of species). As a result, restitution may not always be an option or may have to be complemented by compensation to ensure full reparation.

It is generally agreed that compensation is due only in the event of establishing 'financially assessable damage', including environmental harm. Indeed, the

---

[90] Ibid., p. 96.

[91] See e.g. ICJ, *Application of the Convention on the Prevention and Punishment of the Crime of Genocide (Bosnia and Herzegovina v Serbia and Montenegro),* Judgement, 26 February 2007, ICJ Reports 2007, para 462, where the Court applied the certain cause standard. See Tumonis 2012, p. 99, 100.

[92] Plakokefalos 2015, p. 481.

[93] Ibid., p. 481.

[94] Ibid., p. 482.

[95] Ibid. An example is given of the deep seabed, 'where the provisions on the obligations of the states sponsoring an exploration or exploitation activity in the area, carried out by a contractor, are obligations of conduct. Nonetheless, LOSC demands that in order for these obligations to be breached not only must the sponsoring state fail to abide by them but also that this failure must be causally connected to damage occurring in the deep seabed', p. 482.

[96] Crawford 2002, p. 213.

United Nations Compensation Commission assessed Iraq's liability for environmental damage and the depletion of natural resources.[97] The ILC certainly considered environmental harm to fall into a category of financially assessable damage, as the commentary to the ASR suggests by singling out pollution as one of the areas in which States may seek compensation for harm suffered. The ILC also observed in its commentary that, when compensation has been awarded, it is the general practice of States to make payments to reimburse the injured State for expenses reasonably incurred in preventing or remedying pollution or to compensate for the diminished value of polluted property. Therefore, as the law stands at present, compensation will include clean-up costs and property devaluation. The ILC acknowledged, however, that actual damage would often extend to such environmental values as biodiversity, amenity, or so-called 'non-use values', which are, 'as a matter of principle, no less real and compensable than damage to property, though [they] may be difficult to quantify'.[98] Similarly, it is unclear whether notional or non-market based value to depleted resources would be covered under the formulation of 'financially assessable damage', such as extinction of endangered wildlife.[99]

Finally, there are other forms of non-quantifiable, non-individual harm to the environment, which cannot be remedied based on available methods of reparation. The ILC Rapporteur pointed to the release of chlorofluorocarbons (CFCs) or other ozone wide-spread releases which can only be addressed by special treaty regimes that not only allocate risk but also introduce standards of conduct of the parties.[100]

The above considerations indicate that in some cases the general legal framework of the law of State responsibility is relevant for reparation of environmental harm, which can be evaluated on a traditional basis. However, other elements of environmental harm, such as the loss of biological diversity, wild fauna and flora, or ecosystems, escape that classical structure of reparation under the law of State responsibility. Therefore, when neither restitution nor compensation can be resorted to, satisfaction is the only remaining means of reparation for the injured State to rely on.

In light of the above, the value of the law of State responsibility in cases of transboundary harm is currently limited. There is no certainty as to the applicable standard of fault; and even if claims for compensation are limited to 'financially assessable damage', the interpretation of this phrase has yet to take full account of the particular demands of environmental evaluation. This does not suggest that we abandon the goal of compensating for environmental loss, but instead that we focus on methods of valuation and on overcoming the objection that something that is not

---

[97] UNCC, Governing Council Report and Recommendations Made by the Panel of Commissioners Concerning the Fifth Instalment of 'F4' Claims (30 June 2005) UN Doc. S/AC 26 /2005 /10 para 57.

[98] Crawford 2002, p. 123.

[99] Boyle 2007, p. 24.

[100] Crawford 2002, p. 118.

necessarily 'property' and that has no 'market value' has no 'financial or economic worth'.[101]

The complexity of reparation in environmental matters is illustrated by the recent Judgment of *Nicaragua v Costa Rica,* in which the Court determined the amount of compensation due to Costa Rica. The Judgment on compensation deals, *inter alia,* with the assessment of the sum due to Costa Rica for the impairment or loss of environmental goods and services and for the expenses incurred in monitoring or remedying the damaged environment by the unlawful activities of Nicaragua (so-called 'damage caused to the environment in and of itself'). It also included the excavation of some channels in an area in the northern part of Isla Portillos that the Court had recognized as under the sovereignty of Costa Rica as per the 2015 Judgment.[102]

The decision of the Court was described as a pioneering example of damage to the environment being litigated before an international tribunal.[103] Nonetheless, it has raised many questions—a full analysis of which exceeds the bounds of this chapter. The Court stated as follows:

> [I]n order to award compensation, the Court will ascertain whether, and to what extent, each of the various heads of damage claimed by the Applicant can be established and whether they are the consequence of wrongful conduct by the Respondent, by determining 'whether there is sufficiently direct and certain causal nexus between the wrongful act ... and the injury suffered by the Applicant[104]

The Court then observed that, in relation to environmental harm specifically, 'particular issues may arise with respect to the existence of damage and causation ... [and that] it is for the Court to decide whether there is a sufficient causal nexus between the wrongful act and the injury suffered'.[105] In confirming the general view on reparation for environmental damage it noted that 'damage to the environment, and the consequent impairment or loss of the ability of the environment to provide goods and services, is compensable under international law'.[106]

The Judgment was subject to a critique concerning the methodology used by the Court in arriving at compensation.[107] Both Costa Rica and Nicaragua, adopted a very different approach to what was compensable. Costa Rica relied on an 'ecosystem services approach' by reference to the goods and services that can be derived from

---

[101] Boyle 2002, pp. 25–6. The ICJ observed that the size of the area affected by Nicaragua's unlawful activities was 6.19 ha, ICJ, *Certain Activities Carried Out by Nicaragua in the Border Area (Costa Rica v Nicaragua),* Compensation, 2 February 2018, ICJ Reports 2018, para 54.

[102] ICJ, *Certain Activities Carried Out by Nicaragua in the Border Area (Costa Rica v Nicaragua),* Compensation, above n 101, p. 15; Fasoli 2019; Kindji and Faure 2019; Cittadino 2019; Rudall 2018.

[103] Rudall 2018, p. 288.

[104] *Certain Activities Carried Out by Nicaragua in the Border Area (Costa Rica v Nicaragua),* above n 101, para 32.

[105] Ibid., para 34.

[106] Ibid., para 42. See also ICJ, *Ahmadou Sadio Diallo (Guinea v Democratic Republic of Congo)* Compensation, 19 June 2012, ICJ Reports 2012, p. 324.

[107] Rudall 2018, p. 288.

the environment: some of them are tradeable on the market and have a 'direct use value while other goods and services are not tradeable on the market and have an "indirect use value"'. Based on this method Costa Rica claimed around USD$6.711 million in damages, with pre-judgment interest of around USD$0.5 million.[108]

Nicaragua adopted the 'replacement cost approach', which is the value to be used to calculate the compensation owed,[109] and arrived at an amount of damage estimated to be USD$188,504. In its further pleadings, Nicaragua applied the so-called 'corrected analysis', which is predicated upon the ecosystem services approach (as pleaded by Costa Rica) but with adjustments relating to the categories of environmental goods and services included and the values used.[110]

The Court has not relied on either of the approaches but introduced its own methodology, i.e. the method of overall valuation. The Court, in calculating the appropriate amount of compensation, considered Nicaragua's unlawful activities and the costs incurred by Costa Rica as a result (such as repairing the environmental damage). The Court's approach was dictated by:

> the specific characteristics of the affected area by the activities of Nicaragua, which is situated in the Northeast Caribbean Wetland, a wetland protected under the Ramsar Convention, where there are various environmental goods and services that are closely interlinked... such an overall valuation will allow the Court to take into account the capacity of the damaged area for natural regeneration[111]

The Court has allowed for a margin of uncertainty in evaluating environmental damage. In this respect, it relied on the *Trail Smelter* arbitration[112] and the case cited therein, introducing equitable considerations.[113]

In calculating the compensation owed, the Court appraised the existence and extent of the damage and established whether there existed a direct and certain causal link between the environmental harm and Nicaragua's wrongful acts. Where a link between the incurred cost and the wrongful act was lacking, the Court rejected compensation for the cost.[114] The Court thus awarded total compensation in the amount of USD$378,890.59, including pre-judgment interest.

There are several innovative and interesting features of this judgment. The Court has ascertained that damage to the environment itself is compensable under international law. It also clarified the questions regarding calculation of compensation.[115] However, and as mentioned above, there is serious criticism concerning the Court's judgment, starting with the methodology adopted by the ICJ which appears to be

---

[108] Ibid.

[109] Ibid., p. 289.

[110] Ibid.

[111] Ibid., paras 80–81.

[112] *Trail Smelter Arbitration*, Award, 11 March 1941, 3 RIAA 1905.

[113] US Supreme Court, *Story Parchment Co. v Paterson Parchment Paper Co.*, Judgement, 24 February 1931, 22 US 555.

[114] Rudall 2018, p. 291.

[115] Ibid.

unclear. First, the Court initially claimed to base its methodology on the equitable considerations for determining the amount of compensation in the event that the evidence is otherwise inconclusive. This methodology has not, however, been followed up in the final determination of the amount.[116] Second, although the Court awarded compensation to Costa Rica, it did so without spelling out clear legal criteria on which it based the quantification of damages. The Court had partially dismissed both methods proposed by the parties; at the same time, it decided to take into account those elements of each method which offered a reasonable basis for valuation.

There is no reasonable explanation in adopting such an approach.[117] The adoption of an 'overall assessment method' in order to offset the limitations of the methods proposed by the parties for the quantification of damages was justified on the basis of three reasons. First an overall assessment would allow the judges to take into account the consequences flowing from the most significant damage to the area, that is the removal of trees.[118] However, it is argued that the Court has not provided a reasonable justification for this approach.[119] Second, the Court used an 'overall assessment' method to quantify the damages of the ecosystem, such as wetlands (protected by the Ramsar Convention).[120] Yet, as Cittadino explains:

> In this case, both the significance of the wetlands and their importance as unitary ecosystems is supported by the existence of an international legal instrument protecting the wetland at stake to which Costa Rica and Nicaragua are parties. Therefore, the choice of using an 'overall assessment' method to quantify damages to ecosystems, such as wetlands, that are internationally protected for their inner interconnectedness, is justifiable purely in terms of legal reasoning.[121]

Third, such a system of evaluation 'will allow the Court to take into account the capacity of the damaged areas for natural regeneration'.[122] Nonetheless, the Court has not justified the period of regeneration with evidence.[123] It was observed that the Court adopted a restrictive approach to the issue of compensation because it appeared to be bound in many ways by its judgment of 16 December 2015, which established that Costa Rica was entitled to receive compensation for the material damage caused by Nicaragua's breaches. Therefore, the Court focused only on one form of repairing environmental harm and neglected all possible other options.

It was opined: '[a]lthough compensation may well be an appropriate way to repair environmental damage, it should not represent the option that had to prevail while

---

116 Cittadino 2019, p. 37.

117 Ibid., p. 38.

118 ICJ, *Certain Activities Carried Out by Nicaragua in the Border Area (Costa Rica v Nicaragua)*, Compensation, above n 101, para 79.

119 Cittadino 2019, p. 40.

120 ICJ, *Certain Activities Carried Out by Nicaragua in the Border Area (Costa Rica v Nicaragua)*, Compensation, above n 101, para 80.

121 Cittadino 2019, p. 40.

122 ICJ, *Certain Activities Carried Out by Nicaragua in the Border Area (Costa Rica v Nicaragua)*, Compensation, above n 101, para 81.

123 Cittadino 2019. See also Kindji and Faure 2019, p. 22.

seeking reparation',[124] when considering that State responsibility offers a wide range of means of reparation, which can also be applied in combination. Finally, it may be added that some Judges, such as Judge Dugard, have argued against compensation as a form of reparation for environmental harm as the environment may be impossible to repair. In case of environmental harm, long term effects of the illegal action should be considered and incentives for environmental protection provided.[125]

The 2018 *Costa Rica v Nicaragua* case may be contrasted in relation to the treatment of compensation with the ICSID investment arbitration case *Burlington Resources Inc. v Republic of Ecuador*[126] and *Perenco v Ecuador*.[127] In the *Burlington* case, the Arbitral Tribunal decided on an international investment dispute and the application of domestic environmental law to the conduct of foreign investors. Environmental concerns were raised in the counter-claim by Ecuador, in which it was argued that the investor was liable for causing damage to the environment.[128] In this case, the parties themselves consented to the tribunal having the jurisdiction over counter-claims. The case was based on private law and the 2018 Constitution of Ecuador, which establish strict liability for environmental damages. The Tribunal restricted the scope of the reparation on the grounds that the investor was one of multiple agents responsible for the damage.[129] Da Silva has identified differences between these two cases. In the *Costa Rica v Nicaragua* case, the ICJ relied on

---

[124] Kindji and Faure 2019, p. 24.

[125] ICJ, *Certain Activities Carried Out by Nicaragua in the Border Area (Costa Rica v Nicaragua)*, Compensation, above n 101, Separate Opinion of Judge *ad hoc* Dugard, para 47.

[126] *Burlington Resources Inc. v Republic of Ecuador,* Decision on Counterclaims, 7 February 2017, ICSID Case No. ARB/08/5; Da Silva 2018; Parlett and Ewad identify five ways upon which an investment tribunal might find that it has jurisdiction over a counterclaim by a State against an investor. First, the relevant treaty might explicitly provide for States to bring counterclaims. However, these are rare, and most treaties do not address the matter; Second, an investment tribunal might consider that it has jurisdiction over counterclaims even in the absence of a specific treaty provision. Other international courts and tribunals have recognised the possibility of counterclaims. The International Court of Justice, the International Tribunal for the Law of the Sea and the Iran-US Claims Tribunal have all adopted procedural rules to adjudicate counterclaims, even though they are not explicitly provided for in their constituent instruments. That might provide a basis for investment tribunals to conclude that their jurisdiction extends to counterclaims even in the absence of an express grant of jurisdiction in the underlying investment treaty. A third possibility is that the agreed arbitration rules permit counterclaims, and the parties' consent to those rules constitutes consent to a tribunal's jurisdiction over counterclaims. An example is Article 47 of the ICSID Convention might consider that it has jurisdiction over counterclaims even in the absence of a specific treaty provision; fourth possibility is that the parties themselves consent to the tribunal taking jurisdiction over counterclaims. A fifth possibility is that the dispute resolution clause in a BIT may permit claims to be brought by a State, see Parlett and Ewad 2017.

[127] *Perenco v Ecuador LTD. v The Republic of Ecuador and Empressa Estatal Petroleos de Ecuador (Pertoecuador),* Interim Decision on Environmental Counterclaim, 11 August 2015, ICSID Case No ARB/08/6; Rudall 2020, pp. 33–34; Da Silva 2018, p. 1418.

[128] Da Silva 2018, p. 1418. See also Rudall 2020, pp. 32–34. *Perenco v Ecuador LTD. v The Republic of Ecuador and Empressa Estatal Petroleos de Ecuador (Pertoecuador)*, above n 127.

[129] Da Silva 2018, p. 1418.

the sources of law listed in Article 38 of its Statute. The ICSID Tribunal's jurisdiction meanwhile was based on the law agreed between the parties or the law of the hosting state, and rules of general international law where applicable.[130] The strict liability regime resulted in the company only avoiding responsibility for environmental damage if it proved that the harm was caused by third parties or by the State itself.[131] In this case, the Tribunal decided 'that under Ecuadorian law, the company was not liable for the damage that occurred before or after its activities and did not have an obligation to fully restore the environment to pre-human conditions'.[132] The Tribunal, however, granted compensation for the harm, having concluded that the company had an obligation to remediate the harm caused only during the concession period; 'the Tribunal determined whether the compensation should be based on international or domestic prices and what the adequate technology for the recovery process would be'.[133] Burlington had argued that the 2008 Amendment to Ecuadorian environmental law (which introduced strict liability) did not apply retroactively, and that the relevant standard for liability should be negligence.[134] The Tribunal, however, stated that the 2008 Amendment was designed to bring Ecuadorian law in line with international norms and to ensure that Ecuador had satisfied its international obligations relating to hydrocarbon exploration.[135] Environmental harm, according to the Tribunal, 'is defined by reference to the regulatory criteria of the home state,' which upholds the home State's international obligations'.[136] Therefore, in this case, the Tribunal applied international law indirectly through its incorporation in the Constitution of Ecuador.

In the *Perenco v Ecuador* case, Ecuador brought a counter-claim amounting to USD$30 billion for pollution of parts of the Amazon rainforest from the same oil production facilities as in the previous case. Perenco's claim was governed by the France-Ecuador BIT and was decided by a different tribunal.[137] In its 2015 interim decision on counter-claims, the Tribunal acknowledged that 'a State has wide latitude under international law to prescribe and adjust its environmental laws, standards and policies in response to changing views and a deeper understanding of the risks posed by various activities'.[138] The Tribunal has stated that Ecuador has a treaty obligation to ensure the preservation of the Amazon and is entitled to modify its environmental

[130] Ibid., p. 1420.

[131] Ibid., p. 1423.

[132] Ibid.

[133] Ibid., p. 1428. See also Parlett and Ewad 2017. The Tribunal made onsite visits and relied on expert testimony and evidence collected in each concerned area. It may be mentioned, however, that the Arbitral Tribunal had to appoint their own experts due to the lack of agreement between party-appointed ones.

[134] *Burlington Resources Inc. v Republic of Ecuador*, above n 126, para 122; see also Sundararajan 2018, pp. 22–23.

[135] Ibid., para 81 and 159.

[136] Ibid., para 275, 291.

[137] Sundararajan 2018, p. 25.

[138] *Perenco v Ecuador LTD. v The Republic of Ecuador and Empressa Estatal Petroleos de Ecuador (Pertoecuador)*, above n 127, pp. 26–27.

regulation at any time to ensure compliance with this obligation. It is entitled to enforce this regulation against foreign investors operating in the regulated industry, regardless of when the initial investment was made or testate of domestic law at the time.[139] The Tribunal held that nothing in the France-Ecuador BIT can preclude Ecuador from enacting new regulations holding oilfield operators to more stringent environmental standards or prohibiting such activities altogether in areas which it considers to be particularly ecologically sensitive.[140]

However, the *Burlington* Tribunal and the *Perenco* Tribunal did not state that private companies were bound by the mandates of international environmental law.[141] The restriction on a State's exercise of its police powers here is the Ecuadorian Constitution and the State's other international legal obligations.[142] 'When choosing between certain disputed [but reasonable] interpretations of the Ecuadorian regulatory regime,' the Tribunal held, 'the interpretation which most favors the protection of the environment [should be] preferred'.[143] The Tribunal articulated a general responsibility imposed on States to provide its citizens with a pollution-free environment. This obligation is found both in international human rights law and in the Ecuadorian constitution, and the reason behind Ecuador's modifications to its regulatory regime.[144] As Sundararajan observed '[t]he Tribunal is therefore clear that it will respect Ecuador's right to impose environmental regulations on foreign investors to ensure compliance with international norms and will enforce those obligations against foreign investors, regardless of when the environmental regulation went into force'.[145] In 2019, the Tribunal in the realm of the *Perenco* case ordered the investor to compensate Ecuador USD$54 million.[146]

17.5 Conclusions on State Responsibility and Environmental Harm

As the above sections indicate, the application of the rules of State responsibility for internationally wrongful acts to the environment is not without problems. There are several reasons.

---

[139] Ibid., paras 34–35.

[140] Ibid., para 87.

[141] Sundararajan 2018, p. 26.

[142] Ibid., pp. 26–27, *Perenco v Ecuador LTD. v The Republic of Ecuador and Empressa Estatal Petroleos de Ecuador (Pertoecuador)*, above n 127, para 347.

[143] Sundararajan 2018, p. 27, *Perenco v Ecuador LTD. v The Republic of Ecuador and Empressa Estatal Petroleos de Ecuador (Pertoecuador)*, above n 127, para 322.

[144] *Perenco v Ecuador LTD. v The Republic of Ecuador and Empressa Estatal Petroleos de Ecuador (Pertoecuador)*, above n 127, para 37; Sundararajan 2018, p. 27.

[145] Sundararajan 2018, p. 27.

[146] *Perenco v Ecuador LTD. v The Republic of Ecuador and Empressa Estatal Petroleos de Ecuador (Pertoecuador)*, above n 127.

State responsibility plays a very modest role in the liability of private actors, who are largely responsible for environmental damage. Private civil liability regimes are few, and structured to fit a specific area. Some of them (the nuclear regime) have not proven to be very successful. Regimes attached to MEAs are usually contentious and their structures tend to be very complicated, reflecting tortuous negotiations. As such, the role of a State is limited to a vague obligation of general control over private actors by implementing relevant legislation.

As illustrated in the *Whaling in Antarctic* case, the extent to which States are responsible in relation to the environment towards the community of States generally (*erga omnes*) or towards a group of States based on a multilateral treaty regime (*erga omnes partes*) is unclear and the practical application is very limited. The fundamental principle on which environmental law rests, due diligence, is an ill-defined and variable concept, the implementation of which is very complex. The problem of woolliness and lack of precision of main principles of environmental law such as the precautionary principle exacerbates the difficulties of the application of State responsibility in respect of environmental disputes. The structure of the norm of prevention which comprises various elements, such as EIA, adds further complexity.

The ICSID Tribunal has engaged in an in-depth discussion about the extent of the liability of the investor, the required evidence to evaluate the damage, and the adequate method to recover the affected ecosystem.[147] Finally, the question of reparations for environmental harm, as evidenced by the *Costa Rica v Nicaragua* case presents a host of very important issues, starting with the method of calculation of damages and leading to a more general issue of experts. Although this judgment was criticised, the present author is of the view that this is a case of utmost importance, as it was the first time that the Court has engaged in the issue of compensation for environmental harm. In the future, it is hoped that a general rule of application for reparations in cases involving environmental damage will be formulated as the case-by-case approach is very limiting and not constructive. There are, however, certain concerns expressed as to the level of environmental knowledge of international courts and tribunals and the call for experts is made.[148] It is argued that an important aspect of the emerging practice on environmental compensation is that the assessment made by international courts and tribunals reflects the full picture of the environmental damage caused.[149] According to Rudall, one way to do it is to incorporate other values, such as the intrinsic value of the ecosystem or equitable considerations in the calculation of environmental compensation.

There is little doubt that the existing classical framework of State responsibility and reparations for environmental harm is not entirely equipped to deal with the particularities of the environment. However, there are significant developments towards considering environmental claims before international courts and tribunals, including by the ICJ, ITLOS, and investment arbitration.

---

[147] Da Silva 2018, p. 1429.

[148] Rudall 2020, p. 39.

[149] Ibid.

References

Ahmadov F (2018) The Rights of Actio Popularis before International Courts and Tribunals. Nijhoff/Brill, Leiden

Boyle A (2002) Reparation for Environmental Damage in International Law: Some Preliminary Problems. In: Bowman M, Boyle A (eds) Environmental Damage in International and Comparative Law: Problems of Definition and Valuation. Oxford University Press, Oxford

Boyle A (2007) Human Rights or Environmental Rights? A Reassessment. Fordham Environmental Law Review 18:3:471–511

Boyle A (2015) Human Rights and the Environment. What Next. In: Boer B (ed) Environmental Law Dimensions. Oxford University Press, Oxford, pp 201–239

Brunnée J (2016) Procedure and substance in international environmental law: Confused at a higher level? European Society of International Law 5:6

Brunnée J (2018) International Environmental law and Community Interests. In: Benvenisti E, Nolte G (eds) Community Interests Across International Law. Oxford University Press, Oxford, pp 151–175

Cittadino F (2019) Science novit curia? Damage evaluation methods and the role of experts in the Costa Rica v Nicaragua case. Question in International Law Zoom, pp 35–53

Crawford J (2002) The International Law Commission's Articles on State Responsibility: Introduction, Text and Commentaries. Cambridge University Press, Cambridge

Crawford J (2013) State Responsibility - The General Part: Breaches of Communitarian Norms. Cambridge University Press, Cambridge

Da Silva M (2018) Compensation Awards in International Environmental Law: Two Recent Developments. International Law and Politics 50:1417: pp 1418–1430

Dupuy PM (1999) Reviewing the difficulties of codification: on Ago's classification of obligations of means and obligations of result in relation to state responsibility. European Journal of International Law 2:10:375–81

Duvic-Paoli L-A (2018) The Prevention Principle in International Environmental Law. Cambridge University Press, Cambridge

Fasoli E (2019) The ICJ and the compensation for environmental damage in the Costa Rica/Nicaragua case: Does the application of equitable principles offset independent technical expertise? The Introduction. Question in International Law Zoom pp 1–4

Feria-Tinta M, Milnes SC (2016) The Rise of Environmental Law in International Dispute Resolution: The Inter-American Court of Human Rights Issues a Landmark Advisory Opinion on the Environment and Human Rights. Yearbook of International Environmental Law 27:1: pp 64–81

Fitzmaurice M (2013) The International Court of Justice and International Environmental Law. In: Tams C, Sloan J (eds) The Development of International Law by the International Court of Justice. Cambridge University Press, Cambridge, 353–374

Gaja G (2011) The Protection of General Interest in the International Community. General Course of Public International Law, RCADI 364: pp 171–180

Guo J, Wang P (2019) Due Diligence and Overlooked Evidence in the South China Sea Arbitration: A Note. Ocean Development & International Law, 50:2–3, 235–242, https://doi.org/10.1080/00908320.2019.1582631

Hamamoto (2014) Procedural Questions in the Whaling Judgment: Admissibility, Intervention and the Use of Experts, Japanese Society of International Law, The Honourable Shigeru Oda Commemorative Lectures, ICJ Judgment on Whaling in the Antarctic: Its Significance and Implications, http://www.jsil.jp/annual_documents/2014/2014manuscript_hamamoto.pdf

International Law Association (ILA) (2016) Study Group on Due Diligence in International Law, Second Report

Kindji K, Faure M (2019) Assessing reparation of environmental damage by the ICJ: A lost opportunity? Question in International Law Zoom, pp 5–33

Koivurova T (2010) Due Diligence. Max Planck Encyclopaedia of Public International Law

Kosolapova E (2013) Interstate liability for climate change related damage. Eleven International Publishing, The Hague

Kulesza J (2016) Due Diligence in International Law. Nijhoff/Brill, Leiden

Mbengue MM (2016) Critical Assessment of Reparations International Environmental Law. Proceedings of the ASIL Annual Meeting pp. 110, 293–297 doi:https://doi.org/10.1017/S027250370010326X

McCaffrey S (2019) The Law of International Watercourses. Oxford University Press

McIntyre O (2011) The world court's ongoing contribution to international water law: The Pulp Mills case between Argentina and Uruguay. Water Alternatives, Vol. 4:2: pp 124–144

Murase S (2015) ILC Second report of the Special Rapporteur Mr Shinya Murase on the Protection of the Atmosphere. UN Doc. A/CN 4/681, para 41

Parlett K, Ewad S (2017) http://arbitrationblog.kluwerarbitration.com/2017/08/22/protection-environment-investment-arbitration-double-edged-sword/

Plakokefalos I (2012) Prevention Obligation in International Environmental Law. Yearbook of International Environmental Law, Vol. 23:1: pp 3–43

Plakokefalos I (2015) Causation in the Law of State Responsibility and the Problem of Overdetermination: In Search of Clarity. The European Journal of International Law 26:2:471–492

Rudall J (2018) Certain Activities Carried Out by Nicaragua in the Border Area (Costa Rica v. Nicaragua) Compensation Owed by the Republic of Nicaragua to the Republic of Costa Rica, case-note. American Journal of International law, Vol. 112:2: pp 288–294

Rudall J (2020) Compensation for Environmental Damage under International Law. Routledge/Focus, Abingdon

Sakai H (2016) After the Whaling Case: Its Lessons from a Japanese Perspective. In: Fitzmaurice M, Tamada D (eds) Whaling in the Antarctic: The Judgment and its Implications. Brill/Nijhoff, Leiden, pp 308–345

Sands Ph, Peel J (2018) Principles of International Environmental Law. Cambridge University Press, Cambridge

Sundararajan A (2018) Environmental Counterclaims: Enforcing International Environmental Law Through Investor-State Arbitration, available at: https://www.salzburgglobal.org/fileadmin/user_upload/Documents/Anagha_Sundararajan__Environmental_Counterclaims.pdf Accessed 26 April 2021

Takano A (2018) Due Diligence Obligation and Transboundary Environmental Harm: Cybersecurity Applications. Laws 7:36:1–13

Tams C (2005) Enforcing Obligations Erga Omnes in International Law. Cambridge University Press, Cambridge

Tams C (2016) Roads Not Taken, Opportunities Missed: Procedural and Jurisdictional Questions Sidestepped in the Whaling Judgment. In: Fitzmaurice M, Tamada D (eds) Whaling in the Antarctic: The Judgment and its Implications. Brill/Nijhoff, Leiden, pp 193–217

Tumonis V (2012) The Complications of Conciliatory Judicial Reasoning: Causation Standards and Underlying Policies of State Responsibility. In: Mälksoo L, Ziemele I, Žalimas D (eds) Baltic Yearbook of International Law, Volume 11 (2011). Brill/Nijhoff, Leiden, The Netherlands

Vinuales JE (2020) Due Diligence in International Environmental Law–A Fine Grained Cartography. In: Krieger H, Peters A, Kreuzer L (eds) Due Diligence in International Legal Order. Oxford University Press, Oxford

Chapter 18
The Principles of International Environmental Law Through the Lens of International Courts and Tribunals

Edgardo Sobenes and John Devaney

Contents

Abstract Despite framing the language of discourse in international environmental law, the content and legal status of many of its core principles remains unsettled. The following principles, while frequently invoked, often defy precise understanding: Principle of Sovereignty and Responsibility; Principle of Good Neighborliness and International Cooperation; Principle of Preventive Action; Precautionary Principle; Principle of Sustainable Development; Polluter Pays Principle; and Principle of Common but Differentiated Responsibility. This chapter charts the treatment of these principles by International Courts and Tribunals (ICTs) in an effort to identify the development of both the content and legal status of each principle.

Keywords Principles of International Environmental Law · International Court of Justice · Customary International Law · Environmental Impact Assessment · International Courts and Tribunals

E. Sobenes (✉)
ESILA, The Hague, The Netherlands
e-mail: esobenes@gmail.com

J. Devaney
The Hague, The Netherlands
e-mail: jdevaney@law.gwu.edu

E. Sobenes et al. (eds.), *The Environment Through the Lens of International Courts and Tribunals*, https://doi.org/10.1007/978-94-6265-507-2_18

18.1 Introduction

During the last decades, while disputes concerning the substance and strength of the principles of international environmental law (IEL) have become more salient than ever, the legal status of some of the principles remain unsettled. This chapter addresses the interpretation and the scope of application of those principles that enjoy broad support and endorsement by International Courts and Tribunals (ICTs). In an effort to clarify the status of these principles, the authors chart their development by ICTs and examine how Courts and Tribunals have implemented the most relevant principles in international environmental proceedings or cases related to international environmental law. Specific attention is paid to the development of the principles through international litigation proceedings, and their acknowledgment as part of customary international law by ICTs, which reflects the importance of ICTs as means for the development and clarification of international law.

The principles in themselves are not new; the genesis of some date as far back as the dawn of the twentieth century. However, the voyage of each principle is unique; some have received scant attention from ICTs, while others have been extensively developed and recognised as part of the corpus of customary international law. In reading this chapter, it is important to bear in mind that, although each principle can stand alone, they are usually not independent from each other. Given the nature of IEL and the principles themselves, there is inevitable overlap in the elements of certain principles, which can exacerbate the challenges faced by ICTs in the adjudication of international disputes. Compounding these challenges, not all components and elements of each principle are settled, nor are all the principles part of customary international law despite their interconnection and parallel evolution.

Given the uneven development of these principles both across relevant ICTs and in relation to each other, chronological presentation is not always beneficial, especially in assessing the legal strength of a principle. Neither does the order in which the principles are presented reflect any hierarchy in their importance. For reasons that will become apparent in the reading, the structure chosen lends itself to the aims of this chapter. The principles addressed are: Principle of Sovereignty and Responsibility; Principle of Good Neighborliness and International Cooperation; Principle of Preventive Action; Precautionary Principle; Principle of Sustainable Development; Polluter Pays Principle; and Principle of Common but Differentiated Responsibility.

18.2 Principle of Sovereignty and Responsibility

The Principle of Sovereignty and Responsibility has been shaped by two fundamental concepts of IEL: the sovereignty of States over their natural resources, and the obligation of States not to cause damage to the environment.[1] The two underlying

[1] Sands et al. 2018, p. 201.

elements of this principle are set out in Principle 21 of the Stockholm Declaration[2] and Principle 2 of the Rio Declaration.[3] Both Declarations proclaim that a State's right to sovereignty over their natural resources and wealth is not absolute, but subject to a general responsibility not to cause damage to the environment of other States, or to areas beyond a State's national jurisdiction. These two elements, sovereignty and the responsibility not to cause damage, form a balance between the rights and obligations of States by establishing that the possession of rights involves the performance of corresponding obligations.[4] If the two were to be separated, the result would be a fundamental change in the principle's core and the balance would be lost.[5]

The elements of the principle have been the subject of a series of judgments and awards issued by ICTs, and can be traced back to the beginning of the twentieth century in the *Palmas* case,[6] long before the Stockholm and Rio Declarations were adopted. Not long after the Award in the *Palmas* case, the principle entered the corpus of international environmental law in the *Trail Smelter* case, where the Tribunal stated that under principles of international law, when the case is of serious consequence and the injury is established by clear and convincing evidence, 'no state has the right to use or permit the use of territory in such a manner as to cause injury by fumes in or to the territory of another or the properties or persons therein'.[7] The premise

[2] 'States have, in accordance with the Charter of the United Nations and the Principles of international law, the sovereign right to exploit their own resources pursuant to their own environmental policies, and the responsibility to ensure that activities within their jurisdiction or control do not cause damage to the environment of other States or of areas beyond the limits of national jurisdiction.' See the Stockholm Declaration on the Human Environment, in Report of the United Nations Conference on the Human Environment, UN Doc. A/CONF. 48/1 (Stockholm Declaration). There are several UNGA Resolutions that pre-dates the Stockholm Declaration, which refers to the Principle of Sovereignty of the States over their Natural Resources; See for example: UNGA Res. 626 (VII) (1952); UNGA Res. 1314 (XIII) (1958); and UNGA Res. 1515 (XV) (1960).

[3] Principle 2 of the Rio Declaration echoes Principle 21 and adds that States have the sovereign right to exploit their own resources pursuant to their own environmental and developmental policies. See the Rio Declaration on Environment and Development, UN Doc. A/CONF.151/26 (Vol I), 31 ILM 874 (1992) (Rio Declaration).

[4] See ICJ, *Legal Consequences for States of the Continued Presence of South Africa in Namibia (South West Africa) notwithstanding Security Council Resolution 276 (1970)*, Advisory Opinion, 21 June 1971, ICJ Reports 1971, p. 16.

[5] Sands et al. 2018, p. 201.

[6] In the *Palmas* case the Tribunal declared that all States were subject to an obligation to protect 'within their territories the right of other states, in particular their right to integrity and inviolability in peace and war'. *Island of Palmas Case, United States v Netherlands*, Award, 4 April 1928, PCA, 2 RIAA 829, ICGJ 392, p. 93. In the *Corfu Channel* case, the ICJ affirmed that 'every State's obligation not to allow knowingly its territory to be used for acts contrary to the rights of other States'. ICJ, *Corfu Channel (UK v Albania)*, Judgments, Merits, 9 April 1949, ICJ Reports 1949, p. 4.

[7] *Trail Smelter Arbitration*, Award, 11 March 1941, 3 RIAA 1905, p. 1965. See also the Dissenting opinion of Judge de Castro, in the case concerning *Nuclear Tests (Australia v France)*, Judgement, 20 December 1974, ICJ Reports 1974, p. 389.

underlying these holdings is the limitation on the sovereignty of a State emanating from the duty not to harm the interests of neighboring States.[8]

Similarly, in the *Lac Lanoux* Arbitration,[9] a dispute between France and Spain concerning the duty not to cause substantial damage to the environment of other States and the principles for the use of shared natural resources, specifically the water of Lac Lanoux, the Tribunal decided that France's diversion of waters was compliant with its treaty obligations towards Spain, with the caveat that the interests of Spain could not be ignored. The Tribunal held that Spain was entitled to demand that its 'rights be respected and that [its] interest be taken into consideration'.[10] A similar position was adopted by the Tribunal in the *Indus Waters* Arbitration between Pakistan and India, where the Tribunal rejected the notion of absolute sovereignty by concluding that India's right to divert the waters of the Kishenganga/Neelum was not absolute, and that Pakistan's existing uses of the waters had to be considered in the operation of India's plants.[11]

The principle was invoked again in the 1989 case brought by Nauru against Australia in respect to a 'dispute [...] over the rehabilitation of certain phosphate lands [in Nauru] worked out before Nauruan independence'.[12] In its Memorial, Nauru requested the Court to declare that Australia had breached its obligations concerning *inter alia* 'the principle of general international law that a State which is responsible for the administration of territory is under an obligation not to bring about changes in the condition of the territory which will cause irreparable damage to, or substantially prejudice, the existing legal interest of another State in respect of that territory'.[13] Later in the proceedings, the parties reached an out-of-court settlement, and the proceedings were discontinued. A bilateral settlement of a dispute should always be celebrated. However, as a result of the agreement, the Court missed an opportunity to further contribute to the development of the law on this fundamental principle.

Similarly, in 1995, New Zealand initiated proceedings against France on the basis of paragraph 63 of the 1974 *Nuclear Test* Judgment. New Zealand's case was based on the alleged environmental impact, in particular to the marine environment, of underground nuclear testing conducted by France.[14] In support of its claim, New Zealand referred to international treaties and general principles of international environmental law in advancing the position that Principle 21 of the Stockholm Declaration and Principle 2 of the Rio Declaration were 'well established proposition[s] of

[8] Oral 2013a, p. 409.

[9] *Affaire du Lac Lanoux (France v Spain),* Award, 16 November 1957, 12 RIAA 281.

[10] Ibid., p. 140.

[11] See *Indus Waters Kishenganga Arbitration, Pakistan v India,* Partial Award, 18 February 2013, PCA Case No 2011-01, para 436.

[12] See https://www.icj-cij.org/en/case/80 Accessed 26 February 2021.

[13] Memorial of Nauru, Submission VI, p. 250.

[14] New Zealand Application, 21 August 1995. See also Fitzmaurice 2013, p. 362.

customary international law'.[15] This was not challenged by France, and the recognition of the obligation of both States to respect and protect the natural environment was included by the Court in its Order without a clear expression of its own position on the matter, nor a direct reference to the principle as such.[16] In any case, in the preliminary phase of the proceedings, the Court found that it lacked jurisdiction to entertain New Zealand's Request and, thus, another chance to further develop and clarify the principle was missed.

It was not until the 1996 Advisory Opinion on *The Legality of the Threat or Use of Nuclear Weapon* that Principle 21 was considered to be part of customary international law by the ICJ. According to the Court, 'the existence of the general obligation of States to ensure that activities within their jurisdiction and control respect the environment of other States or of areas beyond national control is now part of the corpus of international law relating to the environment'.[17] This recognition was later reflected in the decision of the Court in the *Pulp Mills case,* where it restated that under customary international law, '[a] State is … obliged to use all the means at its disposal in order to avoid activities which take place in its territory, or in any area under its jurisdiction, causing significant damage to the environment of another State'.[18]

The recognition by the ICJ that this principle is now part of the *corpus* of customary international law provides a basis for bringing claims under customary law before ICTs,[19] yet ambiguity in its precise application demands caution.[20]

Among the difficulties encountered by judicial bodies is the determination of what actually constitutes environmental harm. This is because the principle cannot be applied in isolation from the specific circumstances of a case. The interaction between different factors requires certain clarification before determining whether the obligation has been met, including but not limited to, the determination of the environmental damage that would be prohibited under the principle.[21] The relevant question then becomes: what constitutes environmental harm? Or, perhaps more precisely, significant harm? The *Road* case between Nicaragua and Costa Rica is instructive in this regard. Nicaragua claimed that the construction of a road by Costa

[15] Ibid., para 98.

[16] ICJ, *Request for an Examination of the Situation in Accordance with Paragraph 63 of the Court's Judgment of 20 December 1974 in the Nuclear Tests (New Zealand v France) Case*, Preliminary Objection, Judgment, 22 September 1995, ICJ Reports 1995, p. 347.

[17] ICJ, *Legality of the Threat or Use of Nuclear Weapons*, Advisory Opinion, 8 July 1996, ICJ Reports 1996, pp. 241–2, para 29.

[18] ICJ, *Case Concerning Pulp Mills on the River Uruguay (Argentina v Uruguay),* Judgment, 20 April 2010, ICJ Reports 2010, p. 56, para 101 (*Pulp Mills case*). See also supra note 17.

[19] Sands et al. 2018, p. 211.

[20] For a detail discussion of the Principle as a rule of customary international law, see ibid., pp. 206–211.

[21] Sands et al. 2018, p. 206.

Rica along the San Juan River resulted in the dumping of large quantities of sediment into the river,[22] affecting the 'river morphology', 'the river's water quality and ecosystem' and the tourism and the health of the river's riparian communities.[23] Costa Rica denied Nicaragua's allegation, arguing that the construction of the road did not cause harm to Nicaragua.[24] The Court considered that '[t]he core question before [i]t [was] whether the construction of the road by Costa Rica has caused significant harm to Nicaragua'.[25] According to the Court:

> Nicaragua's submission that *any detrimental impact* on the river that is susceptible of being measured constitutes significant harm is unfounded. Sediment is naturally present in the river in large quantities, and Nicaragua has not shown that the river's sediment levels are such that additional sediment eroded from the road passes a sort of critical level in terms of its detrimental effects. Moreover, the Court finds that, contrary to Nicaragua's submissions, the present case does not concern a situation where sediment contributed by the road exceeds maximum allowable limits, which have not been determined for the San Juan River. Thus, the Court is not convinced by Nicaragua's argument that the *absolute quantity of sediment* in the river due to the construction of the road caused significant harm *per se*.[26]

The Court concluded that Nicaragua did not establish that the increase of sediment concentrations in the river from the construction of the road caused significant transboundary harm.[27] It was a matter of evidence concerning the threshold of damage. The evidence did not establish that the additional sediment passed any sort of critical level of detrimental effect. The Court clarified that, given the natural characteristic of the river, any detrimental impact did not necessarily equal significant harm, without clarifying what would have constituted significant harm or the contours of the maximum allowable limits. As a result, it concluded that Costa Rica did not breach its substantive obligations under customary international law concerning transboundary harm.[28]

As noted by Professor McCaffrey, the decision of the Court in the *Road* case underscores the difficulties faced by States in making out a case of transboundary environmental harm when the cause of the harm is incremental rather than sudden.[29] It also clarifies the importance of the baseline used by the parties to advance their arguments, as they must factor in the natural characteristics of the environmental feature that is the subject of the dispute.

---

[22] ICJ, *Certain Activities Carried Out by Nicaragua in the Border Area (Costa Rica v Nicaragua) and Construction of a Road in Costa Rica along the San Juan River (Nicaragua v Costa Rica)*, Judgment, 16 December 2015, ICJ Reports 2015, p. 726, para 177.

[23] Ibid., p. 727, para 178.

[24] Ibid., para 179.

[25] Ibid., p. 729, para 187.

[26] Ibid., pp. 730–1, para 192 (emphasis added).

[27] Ibid., pp. 731–1, para 196.

[28] Ibid., p. 737, para 217. See also Chap. 17.

[29] McCaffrey 2018, p. 366.

18.3 Principle of Good Neighborliness and International Cooperation

The Principle of 'Good-Neighbourliness' enunciated in Article 74 of the United Nations Charter in relation to social, economic and commercial matters has been translated into the development and application of rules promoting international environmental cooperation.[30] The Principle of International Cooperation places various obligations on States to minimise activities within their territory that are contrary to the rights of other States and which could harm other States or their inhabitants.[31] In that regard, it can be considered an application of the no harm principle and its maxim *sic utere tuo, et alienum non laedas* (you should use your property in such a way as not to cause injury to your neighbour's).[32] The engagement of ICTs with this principle charts its steady growth, both in its recognised subcomponents and its strength and standing in IEL.

The *Lac Lanoux* Arbitration contained an early statement of this principle in its most general form: 'France is entitled to exercise her rights; she cannot ignore the Spanish interests. Spain is entitled to demand that her rights be respected and that her interests be taken into consideration.'[33] The decision would go on to identify more specific obligations under the general duty to cooperate, including the obligations to provide information to and consult with the other State and to take the other State's interests into account. Ultimately, the Tribunal held that France had properly discharged its obligations, and recognised the principle as a potential limitation on territorial sovereignty in the following terms; '[t]erritorial sovereignty plays the part of a presumption. It must bend before all international obligations, whatever their source, but only for such obligations'.[34]

Subsequent jurisprudence has expanded upon and refined components of the principle of international cooperation and clarified its legal status. Though perhaps not an environmental case, the *Corfu Channel* case certainly has environmental implications as it involved the 'need to jointly manage shared natural resources'.[35] Its judgment concluded that Albania had a duty to warn and notify British sailors of a minefield in its waters.[36]

ICJ jurisprudence continues to identify additional components of the principle. In the *Gabcikovo-Nagymaros Project* case, Hungary attempted to distill the following

---

[30] Sands et al. 2018, p. 213.

[31] Valverde Soto 1996, p. 197.

[32] The maxim was invoked, for example, as a 'fundamental rule' by Hungary in its Original Application in the *Gabcikovo-Nagymaros Project* case, para 32 (citing in support of the maxim the *Corfu Channel* case (1949), the *Trail Smelter* case (1941), the Stockholm Declaration (1972), the World Charter for Nature (1982), the ILC Draft Articles on International Liability (1990) and the Rio Declaration (1992)).

[33] See supra note 9.

[34] Ibid.

[35] Craik 2020, p. 247.

[36] ICJ, *Corfu Channel (UK v Albania)*, above n 6, p. 22.

components from the principle, alleging Slovakia's failure: (1) to negotiate in good faith and in a spirit of co-operation; (2) to prevent disputes; (3) to provide timely notification of plans to carry out or permit activities which may entail a transboundary interference or a significant risk thereof; and (4) to engage in good faith consultations to arrive at an equitable resolution of the situation.[37] Ultimately, the Court would not engage on these proposed formulations, instead stressing the concepts of good faith and meaningfulness of negotiations. The Court recalled its statement on the principle in *North Sea Continental Shelf* cases: '[the Parties] are under an obligation so to conduct themselves that the negotiations are meaningful, which will not be the case when either of them insists upon its own position without contemplating any modification of it'.[38] It then invoked the principle of good faith, holding that the parties were obliged to apply their 1977 treaty 'in a reasonable way and in such a manner that its purpose can be realized'.[39]

The *Pulp Mills* case not only engaged in a more meaningful exposition of the procedural components of the principle but also established (somewhat perfunctorily) that the Principle expanded into the province of the substantive. Though the Court did hold that cooperation was a component of both procedural and substantive obligations, the bulk of its analysis in this regard would involve procedural obligations.[40] Regarding the latter, the Court concretely identified the procedural obligations of 'informing, notifying and negotiating' in the context of cooperation.[41] The Court then went on to explain how each obligation related to cooperation. The obligation to inform 'allows for the initiation of co-operation between the Parties which is necessary in order to fulfil the obligation'. The obligation to notify 'is intended to create the conditions for successful co-operation between the parties'.[42] The Court also invoked its jurisprudence in support of the proposition that negotiations must be meaningful.[43] Consequently, 'as long as the procedural mechanism for co-operation between the parties to prevent significant damage to one of them is taking its course, the State initiating the planned activity is obliged not to authorize such work and, a fortiori, not to carry it out.'[44] Therefore, Uruguay was in breach of its procedural obligations when it authorised the project before the procedural mechanisms contained in the 1975 Treaty were fulfilled.[45]

---

[37] Sands et al. 2018, p. 213. See also Hungary's Original Application, 22 October 1992, paras 27, 29 and 30.

[38] See original text in *North Sea Continental Shelf (Federal Republic of Germany/Denmark; Federal Republic of Germany/Netherlands)*, Judgment, 20 February 1969, ICJ Reports 1969, p. 47, para 85.

[39] See *Gabčíkovo-Nagymaros Project (Hungary v Slovakia)*, Judgement, 25 September 1997, ICJ Reports 1997, p. 79, para 142.

[40] *Pulp Mills on the River Uruguay (Argentina v Uruguay)*, above n 18, para 77.

[41] Ibid., p. 51, para 81.

[42] Ibid., p. 58, para 113.

[43] Ibid., p. 67, para 146, citing '*North Sea Continental Shelf (Federal Republic of Germany/Denmark; Federal Republic of Germany/Netherlands)*, above n 38, p. 47, para 85.

[44] Ibid., para 144.

[45] Ibid., paras 147–149.

Regarding the strength of the principle, it would not be until the *Road* case that the principle would be definitively recognised as customary international law. While one could argue that the principle had been recognised as customary law by the ICJ in *Gabcikovo-Nagymaros*[46] and the *Pulp Mills* case (at least in the context of EIAs),[47] never had it been stated so explicitly as in the *Road* case when the Court noted: 'the Parties concur on the existence in general international law of an obligation to notify, and consult with, the potentially affected State in respect of activities which carry a risk of significant transboundary harm'.[48] That this position was accepted by the Court without further assessment removes any doubt of the ICJ's position on the issue.

This assessment of the principle as part of customary international law has been echoed by ITLOS. In fact, the jurisprudence of ITLOS confirmed both the subcomponents and the customary status of the principle in more than one judgment. In the *Mox* case, in paragraph 82 of its Provisional Measures Order, ITLOS affirmed that: 'the duty to cooperate is a fundamental principle in the prevention of pollution of the marine environment under Part XII of the Convention and general international law and that rights arise there from which the Tribunal may consider appropriate to preserve under Article 290 of the UNCLOS'.[49]

In his separate opinion, Judge Wolfrum opined that 'the obligation to cooperate is the overriding principle of international environmental law, in particular when the interests of neighbouring States are at stake', and that the 'duty to cooperate denotes an important shift in the general orientation of the international legal order' as it 'balances the Principle of sovereignty of States'.[50] The final portion of that statement is, in fact, an echo of the Arbitral Tribunal in the *Lac Lanoux* Arbitration. Paragraph 82 has been invoked and quoted in subsequent ITLOS cases including the *Land Reclamation case (Malaysia v Singapore)*,[51] and the 2015 Advisory Opinion on a *Request submitted by the Sub-regional Fisheries Commission*.[52]

These ITLOS cases also identify many of the same components of the principle as the ICJ jurisprudence. The *Mox* Provisional Measures Order required consultations to exchange information, monitoring of risks, and devising, as appropriate, measures to prevent pollution. It recommended that the UK review with Ireland the whole system

---

[46] See *Gabčíkovo-Nagymaros Project (Hungary v Slovakia)*, above n 39, paras 140–141.

[47] *Pulp Mills on the River Uruguay (Argentina v Uruguay)*, above n 18, pp. 82–83, para 204.

[48] *Certain Activities Carried Out by Nicaragua in the Border Area (Costa Rica v Nicaragua) and Construction of a Road in Costa Rica along the San Juan River (Nicaragua v Costa Rica)*, above n 22, pp. 707–9, para 106. See also para 104.

[49] ITLOS, *Mox Plant case (UK v Ireland)*, Provisional Measures, 3 December 2001, ITLOS Reports 2001, p. 110, para 82.

[50] Ibid., Separate Opinion, Judge Rudiger Wolfrum, p. 135.

[51] See ITLOS, *Case Concerning Land Reclamation by Singapore in and around the Strait of Johor (Malaysia v Singapore)*, Provisional Measures, 8 October 2003, ITLOS Reports 2003, p. 25, para 92.

[52] See ITLOS, *Request for an Advisory Opinion submitted by the Sub-Regional Fisheries Commission*, Advisory Opinion, 2 April 2015, ITLOS Reports 2015, p. 43, para 140.

of intergovernmental notification and cooperation.[53] The ITLOS Order was affirmed by the Annex VII Tribunal by its Order of 24 June 2003, with a recommendation to establish further arrangements to address the Tribunals' concern that 'co-operation and consultation may not always have been as timely or effective as it could have been'.[54]

In the *Land Reclamation case (Malaysia v Singapore)*, ITLOS held that 'prudence and caution require that Malaysia and Singapore establish mechanisms for exchanging information on and assessing the risks or effects of land reclamation works'.[55] The Joint Declaration of *ad hoc* Judges Hossain and Oxman referred to 'the establishment of a common base of information' and consultation.[56] The 2015 Advisory Opinion on a *Request submitted by the Sub-regional Fisheries Commission* considered 'the rights and obligations of the coastal State in ensuring the sustainable management of shared stocks and stocks of common interest'.[57] ITLOS identified the obligation to 'seek to agree' and the obligation to cooperate as 'due diligence' obligations which require the States concerned to consult with one another, meaningfully, in good faith.[58]

The principle enjoys similar status and recognition in the environmental context of human rights law. The Inter-American Court of Human Rights has held that 'States have the obligation to cooperate, in good faith, to protect against environmental damage'.[59] In particular, 'States must notify other potentially affected States' and 'consult and negotiate in good faith with States potentially affected by significant transboundary harm', and have 'the obligation to ensure the right of access to information' concerning potential environmental impacts.[60]

Therefore, across a wide range of ICTs, the principle seems firmly established as customary international law.

[53] ITLOS, *Mox Plant case (UK v Ireland),* above n 49, p. 96.

[54] ITLOS, *Mox Plant case (UK v Ireland),* Order on Suspension of Proceedings on Jurisdiction and Merits, and Request for Further Provisional Measures, 24 June 2003, ITLOS Reports 2003, paras 66–7.

[55] See ITLOS, *Case Concerning Land Reclamation by Singapore in and around the Strait of Johor (Malaysia v Singapore),* above n 51, p. 26, para 99.

[56] Ibid., Joint Declaration, *ad-hoc* Judges Hossain and Oxman, p. 34.

[57] See *Request for an Advisory Opinion submitted by the Sub-Regional Fisheries Commission,* above n 52, para 175.

[58] Ibid., pp. 59–60, para 210.

[59] IACHR, *The Environment and Human Rights—Requested by the Republic of Colombia,* Advisory Opinion, 15 November 2017, OC 23/17, para 242 (d) (Original text: 'Los Estados tienen la obligación de cooperar, de buena fe, para la protección contra daños al medio ambiente […]').

[60] Ibid., para 242 (3).

18.4 Principle of Preventive Action

The Principle of Preventive Action is closely related to the previous principles.[61] It requires the prevention of transboundary harm and to 'reduce, limit or control activities that might cause or risk such damage'.[62] It also comprises the obligation of early notification, the obligation to conduct an Environment Impact Assessment (EIA); the obligation to exchange information; and a duty to consult and cooperate in accordance with international law.[63]

In the *Pulp Mills* case, the Court recognised the principle's status as a rule of customary international law, confirming that 'the Principle of prevention, as a customary rule, has its origins in the due diligence that is required of a State in its territory'.[64] The Court took a step forward and recognised that the obligation to carry out an EIA where there is a risk that the proposed activity may have a significant adverse impact in a transboundary context, is also 'a requirement under general international law'.[65]

Two points require emphasis. First, the Court recognised the origin of the principle and clarified that the principle constitutes a customary rule. Second, it recognised the obligation to carry out an EIA as a customary obligation,[66] which is central to the principle of prevention. Certainly, the preparation of an EIA provides substance to the obligation of due diligence to prevent significant harm.[67]

Regarding the activities that are covered by this principle, the Arbitral Tribunal in the *Iron Rhine case* clarified that the duty of prevention has become a principle of general international law that 'applies not only to autonomous activities but also to activities undertaken in implementation of specific treaties between the Parties'.[68] This approach was later reinforced and enlarged by the ICJ in the *Certain Activities* and the *Road* cases, where the Court, in referring to its previous Judgment in the *Pulp Mill* case, elucidated that the obligation to undertake an environmental impact assessment,[69] where there is a risk of a significant adverse impact in a transboundary

---

[61] As pointed out by Fitzmaurice in Chap. 17, the question of due diligence in relation to the obligation of prevention of transboundary harm is an unresolved issue. See also Duvic-Paoli 2018, pp. 333–36; Plakokefalos 2012, pp. 32–36; Takano 2018, pp. 3–5. The ICJ has indicated that this is an obligation of conduct, see *Application of the Convention on the Protection and Punishment of the Crime of Genocide (Bosnia v Serbia)*, Judgment, 26 February 2007, ICJ Reports 2007, para 430.

[62] Sands et al. 2018, p. 211.

[63] Plakokefalos 2012.

[64] *Pulp Mills on the River Uruguay (Argentina v Uruguay)*, above n 18, pp. 55–56, para 101.

[65] Ibid., para 204.

[66] Ibid.

[67] Tignino and Bréthaut 2020, p. 641.

[68] *Iron Rhine Arbitration, Belgium and Netherlands*, Award, 24 May 2005, PCA Case 2003-02, paras 59.

[69] In the *Gabčikovo-Nagymaros* case the Court noted that 'both Parties agree[d] on the need to take environmental concerns seriously and to take the required precautionary measures, but they fundamentally disagree[d] on the consequences this has for the joint Project', *Gabčíkovo-Nagymaros*

context, applies to all the activities which may have such significant adverse impact, and not only to industrial activities.[70]

Understanding the application of the principle by ICTs requires attention to at least two general comments. First, it bears emphasis that the principle of preventive action does not necessarily avoid environmental damage. Compliance with this obligation does not guarantee that the harm would not occur. As the *Iron Rhine* case recognises, the duty requires prevention or adoption and implementation of mitigation measures. This understanding is reflected across the case law of different ICTs. As explained by the Court in the *Certain Activities* case, if an environmental impact assessment confirms that there is a risk of significant transboundary harm, the State planning to undertake the activity is required, 'in conformity with its due diligence obligation, to notify and consult in good faith with the potentially affected State, where that is necessary to determine the appropriate measures to prevent or mitigate that risk'.[71]

The same approach was adopted by the ITLOS Chamber in its *Advisory Opinion in the Activities in the Area.* According to the Chamber '[w]here the sponsoring State has met its obligations [of due diligence], damage caused by the sponsored contractor does not give rise to the sponsoring State's liability',[72] and where the sponsoring States has not fulfilled its obligation of due diligence, but 'no damage has occurred, the consequences of such wrongful act are [to be] determined by customary international law'.[73]

Second, the principle, as a customary rule, has its origins in the due diligence that is required of a State in its territory. However, the precise scope of what is required from States under due diligence is unclear. Apart from the relatively straightforward definition, there are many nuances, which make the general practical application of due diligence problematic. The basic premise of due diligence is that a responsible State has to comply with certain obligations and standards, which would vary depending on the circumstances of the case.[74] For this reason, it is difficult to adopt general standards of due diligence that would fit all situations.[75] Some of the difficult aspects of the general application of due diligence are reflected in the *Advisory Opinion on Responsibility and Obligations in the Area.* In its Opinion, the Chamber stressed that the content of due diligence obligations may:

> not easily be described in precise terms. Among the factors that make such a description difficult is the fact that 'due diligence' is a variable concept. It may change over time as

Project (Hungary v Slovakia), above n 39, para 113. The Court did not affirm the obligation to carry out an environmental impact assessment before potentially damaging activities were to be authorized, nor did it refer to the content and scope of the EIA. *See* Juste-Ruiz 2013, p. 391.

[70] *Certain Activities Carried Out by Nicaragua in the Border Area (Costa Rica v Nicaragua) and Construction of a Road in Costa Rica along the San Juan River (Nicaragua v Costa Rica)*, above n 22, p. 706, para 104.

[71] Ibid.

[72] ITLOS, *Responsibilities and obligations of States with respect to activities in the Area*, Advisory Opinion, 1 February 2011, ITLOS Reports 2011, pp. 76–77.

[73] Ibid., p. 77. See also Chap. 17 by Fitzmaurice.

[74] Koivurova 2010.

[75] Kulesza 2016; see also ILA Study Group on Due Diligence 2016, p. 2.

> measures considered sufficiently diligent at a certain moment may become not diligent enough in light, for instance, of new scientific or technological knowledge. It may also change in relation to the risks involved in the activity. [..]. The standard of due diligence has to be more severe for the riskier activities.[76]

Despite the *Advisory Opinion* signalling some of the problems regarding the general application of the concept, the Chamber contributed significantly to its development by stating that the obligation constitutes an obligation of means, and not an obligation of result,[77] which accentuates the difference between a breach of the procedural obligation and a potential breach of the substantive obligation. The jurisprudence of the different ICTs in contentious cases has not meaningfully contributed to the clarification of the latter, nor has it provided the tools for an efficient and clear division between substance and procedure, which frustrates a comprehensive understanding of the concept of due diligence.

Regarding the *locus* reach of the obligation, the ICJ stated in the *Pulp Mills* case that the obligation to act with due diligence encompasses 'all activities which take place under the jurisdiction and control of' a State.[78] It also confirmed that the obligation: 'entails not only the adoption of appropriate rules and measures, but also a certain level of vigilance in their enforcement and the exercise of administrative control applicable to public and private operators such as the monitoring of activities undertaken by such operators'.[79]

The findings of the Court establish that the due diligence obligation is a standing obligation throughout the duration of the activities that could have an environmental harm on another State, and that it is not just required as an *a priori* step to the initiation of an activity. As reiterated by the Court in the *Certain Activities* case, these obligations are continuous and shall be taken throughout the life of the project.[80]

Regarding the EIA, the ICJ acknowledged in the *Pulp Mills* case that general international law does not specify the scope and content of an environmental impact assessment.[81] It emphasised that it is for each State to determine in its domestic legislation, or in the authorisation process for a project, the specific content of the environmental impact assessment required in each circumstance.[82] Without entering into detail on content, the Court highlighted that a State has to take due account of the

---

[76] *Responsibilities and obligations of States with respect to activities in the Area,* above n 72, p. 43, para 117.

[77] Ibid., p. 41, para 110.

[78] *Pulp Mills on the River Uruguay (Argentina v Uruguay),* above n 18, p. 79, para 197.

[79] Ibid.

[80] *Certain Activities Carried Out by Nicaragua in the Border Area (Costa Rica v Nicaragua) and Construction of a Road in Costa Rica along the San Juan River (Nicaragua v Costa Rica),* above n 22, p. 722, para 161. See also *Pulp Mills on the River Uruguay (Argentina v Uruguay),* above n 18, p. 83, para 205.

[81] *Pulp Mills on the River Uruguay (Argentina v Uruguay),* above n 18, para 205. Some Regional Conventions contain a comprehensive regulation of EIA, e.g. the Convention on Environmental Impact Assessment in a Transboundary Context, Espoo, 25 February 1991, and the Protocol on Strategic Environmental Assessment, Kiev, 21 May 2003.

[82] *Pulp Mills on the River Uruguay (Argentina v Uruguay),* above n 18, p. 83, para 205.

nature and magnitude of the potential adverse impact of the proposed development on the environment, as well as 'the need to exercise due diligence in conducting such an assessment'.[83] Moreover, the Court concluded that the obligations of due diligence 'would not be considered to have been exercised, if a party planning works liable to affect the regime of the river or the quality of its waters did not undertake an environmental impact assessment on the potential effects of such works'.[84]

Procedurally, the ICJ adopted a two-step process in the *Certain Activities* case. First, a State has to ascertain whether the proposed activity entails a risk of significant harm through a 'screening' process. If the screening process detects such a risk, the obligation to prepare an EIA is triggered.[85] However, if the screening process suggests that there is no such a risk, no further action is required by the State planning the activities.[86] Second, if the EIA confirms the risk of significant transboundary harm, the State 'planning to undertake the activity is required, in conformity with its due diligence obligation, to notify and consult in good faith with the potentially affected State, where that is necessary to determine the appropriate measures to prevent or mitigate that risk'.[87] These procedural obligations of consultation and notification will arise only if the State planning the activities decides to proceed with the contemplated activities, and where the EIA reveals a risk of significant harm.[88]

The ICJ provided further clarification on the international obligation to carry out an EIA in the *Road* case between Nicaragua and Costa Rica. The Judgment in this case is particularly relevant in two senses. First, it addresses potential exemption to the obligation due to an emergency under national law. Second, it explores the obligation to assess the environmental impact of the activities prior to its commencement.

In connection to the first point, Costa Rica denied that there was a risk of significant transboundary harm on Nicaragua's territory as a result of the construction of

[83] Ibid.

[84] Ibid., pp. 82–83, para 204. The Seabed Dispute Chamber of ITLOS took a step forward and, in contrast to the judgment of the ICJ in the *Pulp Mills case*, provided some guidelines on the scope and content of the obligation of EIA for deep seabed mining operations and its implementation. In the specific context of activities in the Area, the Chamber was able to clarify the content of the duty to conduct EIA under the specific Rules and Regulations concerning the activities in the Area. These Rules and Regulations, however, contain criteria that are applicable in a very limited context with specific actors, and thus may not readily be extended to other instances in which the duty also arises. According to Pineschi there are at least three specific issues that can be found in the Chamber's Opinion; (1) the scope of the obligation of prior EIA *ratione materiae*; (2) the scope of the obligation of prior EIA *ratione personae;* and (3) the functional relationship of the EIA obligation with the duty of cooperation with potentially affected States. The analysis of each of these specific issues falls beyond the scope of this chapter, for more see Pineschi 2013, pp. 427–35.

[85] McCaffrey 2018, p. 355.

[86] Ibid., p. 356.

[87] *Certain Activities Carried Out by Nicaragua in the Border Area (Costa Rica v Nicaragua) and Construction of a Road in Costa Rica along the San Juan River (Nicaragua v Costa Rica),* above n 22, p. 706, para 104.

[88] The Court acknowledged that the Parties concurred on 'the existence in general international law of an obligation to notify, and consult with, the potentially affected State in respect of activities which carry a risk of significant transboundary harm', see ibid. pp. 707–708, para 106.

a road alongside the San Juan Nicaraguan river, and that even if there was a risk, it 'was exempted from the requirement to prepare an environmental impact assessment because of the state of emergency created by Nicaragua's occupation of Isla Portillos'.[89] As mentioned above, ICTs have recognised that it is for each State to determine in its domestic legislation or in the authorisation process for a project, 'the specific content of the environmental impact assessment required in each case',[90] and it was on this basis that Costa Rica argued that its emergency decree exempts it from the requirement to conduct an EIA, 'either because international law contains a *renvoi* to domestic law on this point, or because it includes an exemption for emergency situations'.[91]

The Court, however, disagreed with Costa Rica. Referencing its finding in the *Pulp Mills* case,[92] the Court reiterated that domestic 'law does not relate to the question of whether an environmental impact assessment should be undertaken',[93] but to its content. It also emphasised that an emergency exemption under Costa Rican law 'does not affect Costa Rica's obligation under international law to carry out an environmental impact assessment'.[94] Ultimately, the Court concluded that Costa Rica did not demonstrate the existence of an emergency justifying constructing the road without undertaking an EIA, and decided that 'in the circumstances of this case, there was no emergency justifying the immediate construction of the road'.[95] Because of the lack of an emergency meriting justification, the Court concluded that there was no need to decide whether there is an emergency exemption from the obligation in cases where there is a risk of significant transboundary harm,[96] leaving unsettled the question of whether there is actually an emergency exemption under international law.

Regarding the second point, Costa Rica argued that even if international law required conducting an environmental impact assessment, it fulfilled this obligation by carrying out a number of environmental impact studies *a posteriori*,[97] which assessed the 'adverse effects that had already been caused by the construction of

---

[89] *Certain Activities Carried Out by Nicaragua in the Border Area (Costa Rica v Nicaragua) and Construction of a Road in Costa Rica along the San Juan River (Nicaragua v Costa Rica)*, above n 22, p. 719, para 148. See also paras 63–4.

[90] *Pulp Mills on the River Uruguay (Argentina v Uruguay)*, above n 18, p. 83, para 205.

[91] Above n 89.

[92] *Pulp Mills on the River Uruguay (Argentina v Uruguay)*, above n 18, p. 83, para 205.

[93] *Certain Activities Carried Out by Nicaragua in the Border Area (Costa Rica v Nicaragua) and Construction of a Road in Costa Rica along the San Juan River (Nicaragua v Costa Rica)*, above n 22, pp. 721–2, para 157.

[94] Ibid. This decision underlies that Article 27 of the Vienna Convention on the Law of Treaties is applicable to situations of declared emergency under domestic law.

[95] *Certain Activities Carried Out by Nicaragua in the Border Area (Costa Rica v Nicaragua) and Construction of a Road in Costa Rica along the San Juan River (Nicaragua v Costa Rica)*, above n 22, p. 722, para 159.

[96] Ibid.

[97] Ibid., p. 719, para 149.

the road on the environment and suggested steps to prevent or reduce them'.[98] This argument was dismissed by the Court. These studies were *post hoc* assessments of the environmental impact of the stretches of the road that had already been built, which the Court concluded violates the Principle of Prevention. According to the Court, the obligation of the States to exercise due diligence in preventing significant transboundary harm constitutes an obligation that requires an *ex ante* evaluation of the risk of significant transboundary harm, precisely with the aim of ensuring that the design and execution of any project would minimise the risk of significant transboundary harm.[99] As such, the obligation requires ascertaining whether there is a risk of significant transboundary harm *prior* to the undertaking of an activity having the potential to adversely affect or harm the environment of another State.[100] Only by carrying out this obligation *a priori* can States truly determine whether there is the subsequent obligation to conduct an environmental impact assessment.[101]

In determining the obligations of Costa Rica, the Court took into account the magnitude and nature of the project, the context in which it was carried out,[102] the location of the road along the San Juan River, and the geographic conditions of the river basin where the road was to be situated.[103] In light of these factors and the circumstances of the case, the Court concluded that the threshold for triggering the obligation to evaluate the environmental impact was met, and decided that Costa Rica had not complied with its obligation under general international law.[104] McCaffrey aptly summed up the relevant elements that can be gleaned from the Judgment concerning the EIA requirement for a particular project as including whether it is substantial in character, its proximity to the territory of another State, and the sensitivity of the receiving environment.[105] In addition, all of these elements are subject to, and controlled by, the overarching obligation of due diligence.[106]

Finally, the Court divided the Principle of Prevention into a substantive no–harm rule and procedural preventive obligations. In the *Road* case, the former obligation was not breached by Costa Rica,[107] but the latter was.[108] This case establishes that the ICJ is in a position to hold States to their procedural environmental obligations under international law, and also that it will require convincing evidence of significant harm

[98] Ibid., p. 722, para 160.

[99] Ibid., pp. 722–723, para 161.

[100] Ibid., p. 720, para 153.

[101] Above n 99.

[102] Ibid., pp. 720–1, para 155.

[103] Ibid. In regard to the wetland, the Court indicated that '[t]he presence of Ramsar protected sites heightens the risk of significant damage because it denotes that the receiving environment is particularly sensitive'.

[104] Ibid., p. 723, para 162. See also McCaffrey 2018, p. 358.

[105] Ibid.

[106] McCaffrey 2018, p. 359.

[107] See the operative clause of the Judgment, paras 6–7. See also para 217.

[108] Duvic-Paoli 2018, p. 335.

before finding a breach of the obligations to prevent transboundary environmental harm.

This analysis of the principle demonstrates its complexity, which necessitates careful attention to its interconnected components. However, whatever the exact content of the principle, the jurisprudence of ICTs has confirmed that it has become part of the *corpus* of customary international law, and as such, provides a basis for bringing claims under customary law before ICTs.

18.5 Precautionary Principle

Compared with many other principles, the Precautionary Principle is a relatively recent development. It did not appear in international legal instruments and treaties until the mid-1980s.[109] In contrast to the Principle of Prevention, which requires the obligation of due diligence to prevent environmental harm, the Precautionary Principle aims to provide guidance where there is scientific uncertainty.[110] Principle 15 of the Rio Declaration contains the main elements of the principle:

> In order to protect the environment, the precautionary approach shall be widely applied by States according to their capabilities. Where there are threats of serious or irreversible damage, lack of full scientific certainty shall not be used as a reason for postponing cost-effective measures to prevent environmental degradation.

As reflected in Principle 15, the lack of full scientific certainty shall not excuse failure to take the necessary measures to prevent environmental harm. This approach is echoed in Article 3(3) of the 1992 Climate Change Convention, which reads:

> The Parties should take precautionary measures to anticipate, prevent or minimize the causes of climate change and mitigate its adverse effects. Where there are threats of serious or irreversible damage, lack of full scientific certainty should not be used as a reason for postponing such measures, taking into account that policies and measures to deal with climate change should be cost-effective so as to ensure global benefits at the lowest possible cost. To achieve this, such policies and measures should take into account different socio-economic contexts, be comprehensive, cover all relevant sources, sinks and reservoirs of greenhouse gases and adaptation, and comprise all economic sectors. Efforts to address climate change may be carried out cooperatively by interested Parties.

The 1992 Convention conditions the application of the principle on a threat of serious or irreversible damage,[111] which has been the interpretation adopted by ICTs and in other multilateral treaties, such as the 1997 UN Watercourses Convention. Article 7 of the 1997 Convention provides that in utilising an international watercourse, States have an obligation to 'prevent the causing of significant harm' to other

---

[109] Sands et al. 2018, p. 230.

[110] Ibid.

[111] See also (e.g.) 1992 Baltic Convention, Article 3 (2); 1994 Danube Convention, Article 2(4-5); 1995 Fish Stock Agreement, Articles 5 and 6; 1996 Protocol to the 1972 London Convention, Article 3; 1999 Rhine Convention, Article 4.

states sharing the watercourse. McCaffrey opines that the inclusion of this provision in the section of the Convention entitled 'General Principles', implies that it is one of the fundamental obligations in the field.[112]

The position of the ICTs on the status of this principle is not unified. On the one hand, the Seabed Dispute Chamber (SDC) of ITLOS has recognised that there is an evident trend towards making the precautionary approach part of customary international law,[113] while on the other, the ICJ and a WTO panel have declined to acknowledge the customary international legal status of the principle. Among the elements that remain unclear are the level of scientific uncertainty that would trigger the obligation, and the burden of proof. Concerning the former, the Court missed a unique opportunity to further elaborate on the elements that would trigger the obligation in the *Gabčikovo-Nagymaros* case. Some commentators believe that this lack of consideration of the precautionary principle invoked by Hungary has affected the willingness of other ICTs to further develop the principle.[114]

One such example may be the *Southern Bluefin Tuna* case, where New Zealand and Australia requested the Tribunal to order 'that the parties act consistently with the precautionary principle in fishing for [southern bluefin tuna] pending a final settlement of the dispute'.[115] Stressing certain elements of the principle, such as scientific uncertainty, the Tribunal concluded that, although the evidence advanced by the parties was not conclusive enough to allow the Tribunal to assess the scientific evidence, 'measures should be taken as a matter of urgency to preserve the rights of the parties and to avert further deterioration of the southern bluefin tuna stock'.[116] This came without a determination on the customary status of the precautionary principle.[117]

---

[112] McCaffrey 2018, p. 467. See also *Pulp Mills on the River Uruguay (Argentina v Uruguay),* above n 18, pp. 55–6, para 101; and *Legality of the Threat or Use of Nuclear Weapons*, above n 17, p. 242, para 29.

[113] *Responsibilities and obligations of States with respect to activities in the Area,* above n 72, p. 47, para 135.

[114] Howley 2009, p. 12.

[115] Request for Provisional Measures, New Zealand, p. 6, 8 (3), Australia, p. 74–8 (3). See *Southern Bluefin Tuna (New Zealand and Australia v Japan),* Provisional Measures, Order, 27 August 1999, ITLOS Reports 1999.

[116] *Southern Bluefin Tuna (New Zealand and Australia v Japan),* Provisional Measures, Order, 27 August 1999, ITLOS Reports 1999, para 80, p. 296.

[117] Ibid., Separate Opinion Judge Laing, para 16. In the *Mox Plant case*, the Tribunal referred to the precautionary principle by stating that 'prudence and caution require that Ireland and the United Kingdom cooperate in exchanging information concerning risks or effects of the operation of the MOX plant and in devising ways to deal with them, as appropriate'. ITLOS, *Mox Plant case (UK v Ireland),* above n 49, p. 110, para 84. The same implicit recognition is reflected in the Order for Provisional Measures of the Tribunal in the *Land Reclamation case*, where the Tribunal stated that '[...]given the possible implications of land reclamation on the marine environment, prudence and caution require that Malaysia and Singapore establish mechanisms for exchanging information and assessing the risks or effects of land reclamation works and devising ways to deal with them in the areas concerned'. *Case Concerning Land Reclamation by Singapore in and around the Strait of Johor (Malaysia v Singapore),* above n 51, p. 26, para 99.

In the *Advisory Opinion on Responsibility and Obligations in the Area*, the SDC of ITLOS noted that direct obligations of sponsoring States are not limited to the obligation of due diligence, but also include 'the obligation to apply a precautionary approach'.[118] The Chamber recognised that there is a trend towards making the precautionary approach part of customary international law by referring to its incorporation into a growing number of international treaties and other instruments, many of which reflect the formulation of Principle 15 of the Rio Declaration.[119] The Chamber also referred to the criterion of feasibility, which requires States to apply the precautionary approach in accordance with their own capabilities.[120] In line with this criterion, States are expected to assess environmental risk consistently with their 'level of scientific knowledge and technical capability […] in the relevant scientific and technical fields'.[121] Although the Chamber declined to recognise the principle as part of the corpus of customary international law, the Opinion of the Chamber contributed to the development of the status and implementation of the Precautionary Principle as it relates to the protection of the marine environment under UNCLOS.[122] This contribution occurred primarily through an articulation of the elements of 'due diligence' under international law, which included, *inter alia*, the application of the precautionary approach, best environmental practices, and the use of environmental impact assessments.[123] As acknowledged by Lan Ngoc Nguyen in Chap. 3 of this book, even though the SDC did not explicitly state that the principle is a customary rule, its Opinion came closer to accepting the customary nature of the principle. Whether this formulation constitutes a first step towards a final confirmation of the principle as part of the *corpus* of customary international law, however, remains unsettled.[124]

The WTO panel in its case law has also declined to recognise that this principle forms part of customary international law,[125] and the ICJ, to date, has decided not to meaningfully engage with this question. The reluctance to accord the Precautionary Principle a more defined status is linked, according to Sands et al. to 'doubts and differences as to what practical consequences of precautionary principle or approach will be in a particular field or in a specific case'.[126] Such concerns are hardly unique to this particular principle, rendering their disproportionate effect upon it an interesting question. However, at least for the time being, it can be expected, as acknowledged

[118] *Responsibilities and obligations of States with respect to activities in the Area,* above n 72, p. 44, para 122.

[119] Ibid., p. 47, para 135.

[120] Ibid., p. 46, para 129.

[121] Ibid., p. 54, para 162.

[122] Oral 2013b, p. 419.

[123] Ibid.

[124] See WTO, *European Communities—Measures Affecting the Approval and Marketing of Biotech Products*, Panel Report, 29 September 2006, WT/DS291/R, para 7.89.

[125] Ibid.

[126] Sands et al. 2018, p. 240.

by ITLOS, that future decisions of ICTs will follow the trend towards making the precautionary approach part of customary international law.

Regarding the burden of proof, the key question becomes whether the burden of proof is on the State opposing the activities or with the State that is carrying out the activities? Contrary to what might be expected, ICTs' decisions are neither clear nor definitive on this point.

In the *Nuclear Test* case, New Zealand argued that the emergence of the Precautionary Principle has placed the burden of proof upon the party seeking to carry out the conduct that could give rise to environmental damage.[127] However, the Court declined to consider this argument and did not settle the matter. Judge Weeramantry reflected on this point in his Dissenting Opinion and expressed that:

> Where a party complains to the Court of possible environmental damage of an irreversible nature which another party is committing or threatening to commit, the proof or disproof of the matter alleged may present difficulty to the claimant as the necessary information may largely be in the hands of the party causing or threatening the damage.[128]

The Court neglected another opportunity to address this issue in the *Pulp Mills* case. In that case, Uruguay contested Argentina's argument that the precautionary approach placed the burden of proof on Uruguay, the Respondent in the case. However, the Court considered that while a precautionary approach may be relevant in the interpretation and application of the provisions of the Statute, it does not reverse the burden of proof, without elaborating any further.[129] In the *Whaling* case, Australia also sought an exception to the rule and to place the burden of proof on Japan under Article VIII.[130] Australia pointed out in its Memorial that '[t]he Contracting Governments to the ICRW have agreed to the adoption of a precautionary approach in a wide range of matters. As applied to Article VIII, this means that the uncertainty regarding the status of whale stocks requires Contracting Governments to act with prudence and caution by strictly limiting the grant of special permits under Article VIII'.[131] New Zealand, as an intervening party, also stressed that State parties to the ICRW do not have full discretion, in the form of a '*blank cheque*', to 'determine the number of whales to be killed under special permit under Article VIII',

---

[127] New Zealand Request, para 105. See above n 16.

[128] Dissenting Opinion of Judge Weeramantry, *Request for an Examination of the Situation in Accordance with Paragraph 63 of the Court's Judgment of 20 December 1974 in the Nuclear Tests (New Zealand v France) Case*, 22 September 1995, ICJ Reports 1995, p. 342.

[129] *Pulp Mills on the River Uruguay (Argentina v Uruguay),* above n 18, p. 71, para 164. In a precedent paragraph the Court reminded the well-established principle of *onus probandi incumbit actori* and underlined that 'it is the duty of the party which asserts certain facts to establish the existence of such facts [...]. This principle which has been consistently upheld by the Court applies to the assertions of fact both by the Applicant and the Respondent'. Ibid., p. 71, para 162.

[130] This Article states '[n]otwithstanding anything contained in this Convention...'. In general the use of the term 'notwithstanding' indicates an exception to a treaty, which could lead to the reversal of the burden of proof, as has been noted by the WTO Appellate body. See *European Communities—Conditions for the Granting of Tariff Preferences to Developing Countries*, Appellate Body Report, 20 April 2004, WT/DS246/AB/R, para 90.

[131] Memorial of Australia, pp. 173–176, paras 4.87–4.91.

and underlined that the number of whales to be killed ought to be 'necessary and proportionate to the objectives of the scientific research', pursuant to the precautionary approach, as related to 'the conservation and management of living marine resources'.[132] The Court did not decide on whether Article VIII was an exception to the rules concerning the burden of proof. However, the reasoning of the Court seems to suggest that it would have looked to Japan for an explanation on the history of the design of JARPA II, when stating that 'the Court will look to the authorizing state, which has granted special permits, to explain the objective basis for its determination'.[133] Due to the specific circumstances of the case, it seems that it was indeed Japan, and not Australia, who had the best access to all relevant evidentiary material.[134] Although not expressly stated by the Court, it appears that it did reverse the burden of proof to a certain extent, placing it on Japan. Judge Owada shared this point of view. In his Dissenting Opinion he expressed that the:

> Judgment appears to be applying the standard of objective reasonableness in such a way that it is the granting party that bears the burden of establishing that the scale and the size of the lethal take envisaged under the programme is reasonable in order for the programme to be qualified as a genuine programme 'for purposes of scientific research'.[135]

Indeed, several paragraphs of the reasoning of the Judgment hint that it was incumbent on Japan to provide the Court with the necessary evidence.[136] Nevertheless, the Court did not refer specifically to rules on burden of proof, nor did it indicate expressly that the burden swung to Japan.[137] If nothing else, this case seems to provide an instructive example on how, and in which situation, ICTs would consider reversal of the burden of proof.

To sum up, State practice and the consideration given by ICTs suggest that the principle is slowly gaining wider recognition in international environmental law as a norm of customary international law. If this trend continues, it may not take long for ICTs to recognise the principle as a customary rule, which could lead to clarification of the obligations of the States under the precautionary principle. Finally, it is important to highlight the inescapable paradox faced by ICTs: 'whereas environmental law is based on prevention, the Court's findings are based only on actual harm. This is clearly not in line with the precautionary measures that the Court itself considers to be required by current environmental law'.[138]

---

[132] *Whaling in the Antarctic (Australia v Japan: New Zealand intervening)*, Judgment, 31 March 2014, ICJ Reports 2014, Separate Opinion of Judge Trindade, paras 66–67.

[133] Ibid., p. 254, para 68. See also Foster 2016, p. 22.

[134] Foster 2011, pp. 206–208.

[135] *Whaling in the Antarctic (Australia v Japan: New Zealand intervening)*, above n 132, Dissenting Opinion of Judge Owada, para 43.

[136] See Foster 2016, p. 23, ft 55, referring to paras 137, 141, 144, 185, 193, 194, 206, 222, 226.

[137] Ibid., p. 23.

[138] Juste-Ruiz 2013, p. 399.

18.6 Principle of Sustainable Development

The ideas underlying the concept of sustainable development have a long history in international legal instruments, though the term itself only began to appear in treaties in the 1980s.[139] Earlier, the Stockholm Conference had culminated in the issuance of the Stockholm Declaration on Environment, with Principle 1 implicitly embodying the Principle of Sustainable Development:

> Man has the fundamental right to freedom, equality and adequate conditions of life, in an environment of a quality that permits a life of dignity and well-being, and he bears a solemn responsibility to protect and improve the environment for present and future generations.

The term itself is generally considered to have been officially coined by the 1987 Brundtland Report, which defined sustainable development as 'development that meets the needs of the present without compromising the ability of future generations to meet their own needs'.[140] The Principle of Sustainable Development consists of two core concepts: (1) the concept of 'needs', in particular the essential needs of developing nations, to which overriding priority should be given; and (2) the idea of limitations imposed, by the state of technology and social organisation, on the environment's ability to meet present and future needs.[141]

The most significant treatment of this principle comes from the ICJ in the *Gabcikovo-Nagymaros* case judgment of 1997. The case provides engagement on all the components, or subprinciples, commonly attributed to sustainable development: (1) the principle of intergenerational equity; (2) the principle of sustainable use; (3) the principle of equitable use; and (4) the principle of integration.[142] Engagement by the Court on these components is important, as in-depth analysis of these components by ICTs is limited, and usually quite general.

The dispute in *Gabcikovo-Nagymaros* concerned the development of a system of locks on the Danube River pursuant to a 1977 treaty between Hungary and Czechoslovakia for the purposes of producing hydroelectricity, improving navigation, and protecting against flooding. Hungary eventually decided to abandon the project, largely due to intense environmental criticism centring on threats to groundwater and wetlands. In response, Slovakia attempted to continue the project by unilaterally diverting the river to serve a power station on its territory.

The ICJ generally recognised the Principle of Sustainable Development as central to the future regime to be established by the parties, and gave arguably the most famous exposition on the principle by an ICT:

> Throughout the ages, mankind has, for economic and other reasons, constantly interfered with nature. In the past this was often done without consideration of the effects upon the

---

[139] Sands et al. 2018, pp. 217–218.

[140] *Gabčíkovo-Nagymaros Project (Hungary v Slovakia)*, above n 39, Separate Opinion of Judge Weeramantry, pp. 91–92; Valverde Soto 1996, p. 80; Report of the World Commission on Environment and Development.

[141] Sands et al. 2018, p. 218.

[142] Birnie et al. 2009; Sands et al. 2018, pp. 218–219.

> environment. Owing to new scientific insights and to a growing awareness of the risks for mankind – for present and future generations – of pursuit of such interventions at an unconsidered and unabated pace, new norms and standards have been developed [and], set forth in a great number of instruments during the last two decades. Such new norms have to be taken into consideration, and such new standards given proper weight, not only when States contemplate new activities, but also when continuing with activities begun in the past. This need to reconcile economic development with protection of the environment is aptly expressed in the concept of sustainable development.[143]

This analysis invokes all four of the subprinciples. The reference to preservation for 'future generations' is a hallmark of the principle of intergenerational equity.[144] The principle of sustainable use is embodied by the 'new norms and standards' juxtaposed with the old methods that were 'unconsidered' or 'without consideration' of effects on the environment.[145] The 'need to reconcile economic development with the protection of the environment' is a textbook formulation of the principle of integration.[146] The final subprinciple, equitable use, has been characterised as the recognition that 'use of one state must take account of the needs of other states'.[147] The Court recognises this subprinciple in both its formulation of the dispute as unilateral action by Slovakia,[148] and its solution to the dispute, invoking the *North Sea Continental Shelf cases*, in requiring the two States to conduct negotiations that are 'meaningful' and with each not merely 'insist[ing] upon its own position without contemplating any modification of it'.[149]

These subprinciples, at least in the context of sustainable development, are not further developed to any great extent in ICT jurisprudence. However, it is worth noting that an increasingly diverse range of tribunals are invoking these subprinciples, including regional and human rights courts.

The principle of intergenerational equity was only superficially invoked by the Arbitral Tribunal in the *Pacific Fur Seals* Arbitration in 1893,[150] and the ICJ in its 1996 *Nuclear Weapons* Advisory Opinion, recognising that 'the environment is not an abstraction but represents the living space, the quality of life and the very health of human beings, including generations unborn'.[151] This is a popular formulation of the subprinciple which has been invoked by a variety of ICTs including the Economic Community of West African States (ECOWAS) Court of Justice in the *SERAP v*

[143] *Gabčíkovo-Nagymaros Project (Hungary v Slovakia),* above n 39, pp. 77–8, para 140.

[144] Sands et al. 2018, p. 219.

[145] Ibid.

[146] Ibid.

[147] Ibid.

[148] *Gabčíkovo-Nagymaros Project (Hungary v Slovakia),* above n 39, paras 45, 58.

[149] *North Sea Continental Shelf (Germany/Netherlands),* above n 38, p. 47, para 85.

[150] *Award between the United States and the United Kingdom relating to the rights of jurisdiction of the United States in the Bering's sea and the preservation of fur seals,* Award, 15 August 1893, 18 RIAA 263.

[151] *Legality of the Threat or Use of Nuclear Weapons*, above n 17, pp. 241–2, para 29.

Nigeria case.[152] The East African Court of Justice recognised 'the need to protect the Serengeti ecosystem for the sake of future generations' as the 'one common thread' running through the reference, as 'the environment, once damaged, is rarely ever repaired'.[153]

Similarly, the principle of sustainable use received only limited development in the 2015 Advisory Opinion in response to a *Request by the Sub-Regional Fisheries Commission*, with ITLOS equating 'sustainable management' with 'conservation and development'.[154] In the *Shrimp/Turtle* case, the WTO Appellate Body, after acknowledging 'the objective of sustainable development'[155] concluded that sea turtles constitute an 'exhaustible natural resource'.[156]

The subprinciple of equitable use of natural resources was invoked by the ICJ in the *Pulp Mills* case, again in the context of State unilateral action, with the Court opining that utilisation of a river 'could not be considered to be equitable and reasonable' if 'the interests of the other riparian State in the shared resource and the environmental protection of the latter were not taken into account'.[157]

The subprinciple of integration of environment and development has enjoyed slightly more attention from ICTs. The Separate Opinion of Judge Weeramantry in *Gabcikovo-Nagymaros* noted that sustainable development seeks 'the resolution of tensions between two established rights' reaffirming 'in the arena of international law that there must be both development and environmental protection, and that neither of these rights can be neglected'.[158] The Arbitral Tribunal in the *Iron Rhine* case noted that 'emerging principles' now 'integrate environment protection into the development process', and 'stand not as alternatives but as mutually reinforcing, integral concepts', which create a duty to prevent, or at least mitigate significant harm to the environment caused by development.[159] The Arbitral Tribunal concluded that Belgium has such a duty of 'prevention and minimalisation of environmental harm' which must be 'integrated' with its transboundary 'economic development'.[160]

Human rights courts have also engaged with this issue in some depth. In the *Fredin* case,[161] the European Court of Human Rights found no violation of the applicant's

---

[152] *Socio-economic Rights and Accountability Project (SERAP) v Nigeria, ECW/CCJ/APP/08/09*, Ruling, ECOWAS, December 2010, para 111.

[153] *Africa Network for Animal Welfare (ANAW) v The Attorney General of the United Republic of Tanzania*, First Instance Division No 9, 2014, para 85.

[154] See *Request for an Advisory Opinion submitted by the Sub-Regional Fisheries Commission*, Advisory Opinion, 2 April 2015, ITLOS Reports 2015, p. 55, paras 190–1.

[155] WTO, *United States—Import Prohibition of Certain Shrimp and Shrimp Products*, Appellate Body Report, 12 October 1998, WTO/DS58/AB/R, (*US—Shrimp (Appellate Body Report)*), para 129, n. 107.

[156] Ibid., para 134.

[157] *Pulp Mills on the River Uruguay (Argentina v Uruguay)*, above n 18, pp. 74–5, para 177.

[158] *Gabčíkovo-Nagymaros Project (Hungary v Slovakia)*, above n 39, Separate Opinion of Judge Weeramantry, pp. 91–92.

[159] *Iron Rhine Arbitration, Belgium v Netherlands*, above n 68, pp. 27–28, para 59.

[160] Ibid., para 243.

[161] ECtHR, *Fredin v Sweden (No. 1)*, Judgment, 18 February 1991, App No 12033/86.

property rights where the Swedish government had struck a fair balance between the individual right (to extract gravel from a property) and the general interest in environmental protection. Similarly, in the *Posti and Rahko* case,[162] interference with two fishermen's property rights was justified, since it fulfilled the legitimate aim of preserving fish stocks. The Court formulated the issue, thus in *Hamer*:

> The environment is a cause whose defence arouses the constant and sustained interest of the public, and consequently the public authorities. Financial imperatives and even certain fundamental rights, such as ownership, should not be afforded priority over environmental protection considerations, in particular when the State has legislated in this regard.[163]

The African human rights bodies have similarly invoked this subprinciple in cases where the rights of indigenous peoples had to be weighed against economic development.[164] Such analysis recognises the importance of a clean and safe environment that is closely linked to economic and social rights in so far as the environment affects the quality of life and safety of the individual. The Commission would agree with Alexander Kiss when he states that '[i]ndeed an environment degraded by pollution and defaced by the destruction of all beauty and variety is as contrary to satisfactory living conditions and the development as the breakdown of the fundamental ecologic equilibria is harmful to physical and moral health'.[165]

The Inter-American Court of Human Rights and the Inter-American Commission on Human Rights have similarly dealt with the subprinciple in connection with indigenous peoples,[166] with the Court specifically acknowledging and building upon *Ogoni* in its Advisory Opinion on *The Environment and Human Rights*,

> In this regard, the African Commission on Human and Peoples' Rights underscored that the right to a healthy environment imposed on States the obligation to take reasonable measures to prevent pollution and ecological degradation, to promote conservation, and to secure an ecologically sustainable development and use of natural resources, as well as to monitor projects that could affect the environment.[167]

---

[162] ECtHR, *Posti and Rahko v Finland,* Judgment, 24 September 2002, App No 27824/95.

[163] ECtHR, *Hamer v Belgium,* Judgment, 27 November 2007, App No 21861/03, para 79.

[164] ACHR, *The Social and Economic Rights Action Center for Economic and Social Rights v Nigeria, African Commission on Human and Peoples' Rights,* Judgment, 27 October 2001, App No 155/96; ACHR, *Centre for Minority Rights Development (Kenya) and Minority Rights Group International on behalf of Endorois Welfare Council v Kenya,* Judgment, 4 February 2010, App No 276/2003, para 235; ACtHR, *African Commission on Human and People's Rights v Republic of Kenya,* Judgment, 26 May 2017, App No 006/2012, para 7.

[165] *The Social and Economic Rights Action Center for Economic and Social Rights v Nigeria,* above n 164, para 53.

[166] *Mayagna (Sumo) Awas Tingni Community v Nicaragua,* Judgment, 31 August 2001, IACtHR Ser. C No 79; *Yakye Axa Indigenous Community v Paraguay,* Judgment,17 June 2005, IACtHR Ser. C No 125; *Sawhoyamaxa Indigenous Community of the Enxet People,* Judgment, 29 March 2006, IACtHR Ser. C, No 146, paras 125–134; *Saramaka People v Suriname*, Judgment, 28 November 2007, IACtHR Ser. C, No 172; *The Human Rights Situation of the Indigenous People in the Americas,* Inter-Am. OEA/Ser.L/V/II.108, Doc 62 (2000).

[167] IACHR, *The Environment and Human Rights (State Obligations in relation to the Environment in the Context of the Protection and Guarantee of the Rights to Life and to Personal Integrity; Interpretation and Scope of articles 4(1) and 5(1) In Relation to Articles 1(1) and 2 of the American*

The lack of development of the Principle of Sustainable Development as a whole, both in and following *Gabcikovo-Nagymaros* has not gone unnoticed by scholars, many of whom considered the *Pulp Mills* case an opportunity for the ICJ to rectify the 'missed the opportunity' from *Gabcikovo-Nagymaros* to 'give further definition to the concept of sustainable development'.[168] *Pulp Mills* would, in fact, make at least two important developments regarding the principle. One relating to its substance and the other to its procedural component.

The applicability of the Principle of Sustainable Development was evident early on, with the Court stating at the provisional measures phase that 'account must be taken of the need to safeguard the continued conservation of the river environment and the rights of economic development of the riparian States'.[169] Relating to the procedural component, the ICJ considered that '[a]n obligation to adopt regulatory or administrative measures either individually or jointly and to enforce them is an obligation of conduct'.[170] It is worth noting that some subsequent ICT jurisprudence has sought to strengthen this procedural due diligence obligation from one of conduct to one of result, with the ECOWAS Court of Justice in the *SERAP v Nigeria* case holding that if 'the State is taking all the appropriate legislative, administrative and other measures, it must ensure that vigilance and diligence are being applied and observed towards attaining concrete results'.[171]

Turning again to the *Pulp Mills* case, in analysing Uruguay's compliance with substantive obligations, the ICJ highlights that 'the attainment of optimum and rational utilization requires a balance between the Parties' rights and needs to use the river for economic and commercial activities on the one hand, and the obligation to protect it from any damage to the environment that may be caused by such activities, on the other'.[172] It also highlights the 'interconnectedness between equitable and reasonable utilisation of a shared resource and the balance between economic development and environmental protection that is the essence of sustainable development'.[173] This has been characterised by scholars as a twofold balance that must be reached: 'on the one hand, a balance between the rights and needs of the parties and, on the other hand, a balance between the different uses of the river and the protection of the environment'.[174] This analysis suggests an alignment of the four subprinciples consisting of the principle of equitable use alone governing the former balance, with the integration of the other three subprinciples controlling the latter

Convention on Human Rights), Advisory Opinion OC 23/17, 15 November 2017, Requested by the Republic of Colombia, para 61.

168 Trevisan 2009, p. 40.

169 *Pulp Mills on the River Uruguay (Argentina v Uruguay)*, Order, Provisional Measures, 13 July 2006, ICJ Reports 2006, p. 133, para 80.

170 *Pulp Mills on the River Uruguay (Argentina v Uruguay)*, above n 18, p. 14, para 187.

171 *Socio-economic Rights and Accountability Project (SERAP) v Nigeria*, ECW/CCJ/APP/08/09, Ruling, ECOWAS, December 2010, para 109.

172 *Pulp Mills on the River Uruguay (Argentina v Uruguay)*, above n 18, p. 74, para 175.

173 Ibid., pp. 74–5, para 177.

174 Maljean-Dubois and Richard 2017, p. 316.

balance. The potential engagement of the subprinciples to form a balancing test is an intriguing concept. Unfortunately, the dearth of additional analysis in the case precludes further clarification on this twofold balance.

Just as the content of the principle remains somewhat undefined, so does its legal status. At best, there seems to be agreement on the fact that the principle has not reached the status of customary international law, as such. Scholars have opined that, though the ICJ in *Gabcikovo-Nagymaros* recommended the use of the principle in sovereign decision-making,[175] it 'stopped short of declaring or referring to sustainable development as a norm of customary international law'[176] or a core adjudicatory norm.[177] The Separate Opinion of Judge Weeramantry, who joined in the majority judgment and who some believe may have guided the drafting of paragraph 140 of the Judgment,[178] opined that the principle was 'a part of modern international law by reason not only of its inescapable logical necessity, but also by reason of its wide and general acceptance by the global community'.[179] The Arbitral Tribunal in the *Iron Rhine* case arguably went slightly further, invoking paragraph 140 in a discussion of sustainable development and concluding that, on the subprinciple of integration of environment and development, 'where development may cause significant harm to the environment there is a duty to prevent, or at least mitigate such harm' that 'in the opinion of the Tribunal, has now become a principle of general international law'.[180]

In the *Shrimp/Turtle* case, the WTO Appellate Body noted that the Preamble to the WTO Agreement explicitly acknowledges 'the objective of sustainable development', characterising it as a concept which 'has been generally accepted as integrating economic and social development and environmental protection'.[181]

In his Separate Opinion in the *Pulp Mills* case, Judge Cançado Trindade argued that '[t]here are strong reasons for recognizing sustainable development as a guiding general principle for the consideration of environmental and developmental issues'.[182] Judge Trindade further acknowledged the uncertain status of the principle by suggesting that the Court should have 'taken up, and further developed' its 'own *obiter dictum* in the *whole* (not only in part, as it did) of paragraph 140 of its Judgment in the *Gabcikovo-Nagymaros Project* case'.[183] Even as recently as the 2015 *Certain Activities* Judgment, in his Separate Opinion, Judge Bhandari only

---

[175] Gillroy 2006, p. 29.

[176] Taylor 1999, p. 110.

[177] Bosselmann 2008, p. 69.

[178] Sands et al. 2018, p. 220.

[179] *Gabčíkovo-Nagymaros Project (Hungary v Slovakia)*, above n 39, Separate Opinion of Judge Weeramantry, p. 92.

[180] *Iron Rhine Arbitration, Belgium v Netherlands*, above n 68, pp. 27–28, para 59.

[181] *US—Shrimp (Appellate Body Report)*, above n 155, para 129, n 107 and the accompanying text.

[182] *Pulp Mills on the River Uruguay (Argentina v Uruguay)*, above n 18, Separate Opinion of Judge Cançado Trindade, p. 137, para 139.

[183] Ibid., p. 190, fn 135.

goes so far as classifying the principle as 'an underlying concern in all negotiations and discussions of the international community relating to the environment'.[184]

Therefore, while the exact status of the principle in IEL may be up for debate, it seems that it is not customary international law in its entirety.

18.7 The Duty to Compensate for Harm (Polluter Pays Principle)

The Polluter Pays Principle is an environmental guideline which stipulates that the costs of pollution prevention, control and remediation should be borne by the polluter.[185] The principle has attracted broad support despite the fact that its exact meaning and its application to particular cases and situations remains open to interpretation, particularly in relation to the nature and extent of the costs included and the circumstances in which the principle will apply.[186] The Polluter Pays Principle has traditionally been characterised as a retrospective method of allocating loss after an incident resulting in transboundary harm has already occurred,[187] though this understanding may be evolving.[188] One ICJ Judge, citing Boyle, has opined that the principle could contribute to enhancing economic efficiency in the case of an incident that causes transboundary harm by judging the actions of polluters under a strict liability standard of care.[189]

ICTs have frequently applied the principle as a guideline, especially where it appears in treaties (see below), but there is consensus among the ICTs that the principle has not reached the status of customary international law.

Though it predated express formulation of the principle, the *Trail Smelter* case which held Canada liable for the environmental damage that it caused to the United States through air pollution and fixed the amount of compensation to be paid, is significant. The *Trail Smelter* case is frequently invoked by ICTs in the context of transboundary pollution.

The specific principle itself has its roots in the Organization for Economic Co-operation and Development (OECD), who introduced it in a 1972 recommendation as

[184] *Certain Activities Carried Out by Nicaragua in the Border Area (Costa Rica v Nicaragua) and Construction of a Road in Costa Rica along the San Juan River (Nicaragua v Costa Rica),* above n 22, Separate Opinion of Judge Bhandari, p. 793, para 13.

[185] Maguire 2012, p. 110.

[186] Sands et al. 2018, p. 240.

[187] *Supra* note 184, para 19. See also International Law Commission Draft Principles on the Allocation of loss in the case of transboundary harm arising out of hazardous activities, with commentaries (2006), p. 145–147, Session 58, UN doc. A/61/10; Rio Declaration, above n 3, Principles 13 and 16.

[188] See *Futura Immobiliare srl Hotel Futura and Others v Comune di Casoria,* 16 July 2009, Case C-254/08, ECR I-0000.

[189] Boyle 1991, pp. 363, 369.

one of the guiding principles concerning the international economic aspects of environmental policies.[190] The principle has also been established in EC law, appearing in several Environmental Action Programmes[191] and the Single European Act.[192] Additionally, the principle has been referred to or adopted in other environmental treaties, including the 1985 ASEAN Convention, the 1991 Alps Convention, the 1992 UNECE Transboundary Waters Convention, the 1992 OSPAR Convention, the 1992 Baltic Sea Convention, the 1994 Danube Convention, the 1994 Energy Charter Treaty, and the 2003 Carpathians Conventions.[193] Despite this widespread adoption, scholars have opined that it does not yet have the status of a principle of general international law,[194] and presently acts as merely a general guideline of public international law.[195]

ICTs' consideration of the issue is somewhat limited and does nothing to disturb this conclusion. However, with the doctrine being embedded in EC legislation, ECJ jurisprudence and the decisions of the European Commission have contributed to development of the principle. The European Commission has made rulings implicating the principle in relation to state aid. In Commission Decision 1999/272, the Commission held:

> it is clearly not compatible with the 'polluter pays' principle enshrined in Article 130r of the EC Treaty that a polluter should sell his contaminated land to one of his firms in order to avoid the clean-up costs, that the firm responsible for the contamination should file for bankruptcy and that the business activity should be carried on by the newly established firm.[196]

The Jurisprudence of the ECJ has engaged the principle in more depth. In *R v Secretary of State for the Environment and Ministry of Agriculture, Fisheries and Food, ex parte H.A. Standley and Others and D.G.D. Metson and Others*, the ECJ held that the Polluter-Pays Principle reflects a principle of proportionality, and does not mean that farmers must take on burdens for the elimination of pollution to which they have not contributed.[197] In the case of ERG and Others, the ECJ made an important ruling on burden of proof, allowing the presumption of a causal link between the alleged polluter and pollution where there is 'plausible evidence capable of justifying its presumption, such as the fact that the operator's installation is located close to the

---

[190] Ibid., OECD, Recommendation of the Council on Guiding Principles concerning International Economic Aspects of Environmental Policies, 26 May 1972, C (72)128.

[191] Official Journal of the European Communities (OJ C) 12, 20.12.1973, pp. 1–2, Title 2, sub 5, OJ C 46, 17.02.1983, pp. 1–16; OJ C 138, 17.05.1993, pp. 5–93.

[192] Single European Act, OJ L 169, 27.6.1987.

[193] Sands et al. 2018, p. 243.

[194] Declaration of the Human Environment, Report of the UN Conference on the Human Environment (Stockholm, 1972), UN doc. A/Conf.48/14/Rev1; Boyle 1991, pp. 363, 369; Crawford 2008, p. 359; Sands et al. 2003, p. 281.

[195] Cassese 2005, pp. 492–493.

[196] Commission Decision 1999/272, 1999 OJ L109.

[197] *The Queen v Secretary of State for the Environment and Ministry of Agriculture, Fisheries and Food, ex parte H.A. Standley and Others and D.G.D. Metson and Others,* 29 April 1999, Case C-293/97, ECR I-2603, paras 51–53.

pollution found and that there is a correlation between the pollutants identified and the substances used by the operator in connection with his activities'.[198] The ruling of the ECJ in the Immobilaire case expanded the scope of the principle even further, arguably beyond its commonly understood 'retrospective' role. The Immobilaire case upheld calculating an advance tax on potential polluters in the context of urban waste so long as it was not 'manifestly disproportionate to the volumes or nature of the waste that they are liable to produce'.[199] In the final analysis, though the ECJ jurisprudence helps to flesh out the content of the principle, it says little about the strength of the principle, specifically whether it constitutes customary international law.

In that regard, the GATT Dispute Settlement Panel has given consideration to the practice of the EC, and taken account of the potential role of the WTO in determining the impact of the polluter-pays principle on its subsidies rules,[200] but again, merely as a guideline. For example, the Dispute Settlement Panel considered an exception to the principle, concluding that rules on tax adjustment allow contracting parties to apply the Polluter-Pays Principle but do not require it.[201]

In the *Rhine Chlorides* cases, the Arbitral Tribunal has expressed the same conclusion, in particular emphasising the principle's importance in treaty law:

> The Tribunal observes that this principle features in several international instruments, bilateral as well as multilateral, and that it operates at various levels of effectiveness. Without denying its importance in treaty law, the Tribunal does not view this principle as being a part of general international law.[202]

Similarly, though the ICJ has yet to specifically address the principle in a majority judgment, reasoned review of its jurisprudence would lead to the same conclusion. Separate Opinions of Judges on the status of the principle have been mixed, and largely aspirational. In his dissenting opinion in the *Nuclear Weapons* case, Judge Weeramantry, opined that the 'polluter pays principle', along with a number of substantive principles of IEL, does 'not depend for [its] validity on treaty provisions' rather it is a 'part of customary international law', and 'part of the *sine qua* non for human survival'.[203] This reflects the views of Judge Weeramantry alone, who has often taken very progressive stances with respect to the environment.[204] On

---

198 *Raffinerie Mediterranee (ERG) SpA and Others v Ministero dello Sviluppo economico and Others,* 9 March 2010, Case C-378/08, ECR I-0000, paras 56–58.

199 *Futura Immobiliare srl Hotel Futura and Others v Comune di Casoria,* 16 July 2009, Case C-254/08, ECR I-0000, paras 52–58.

200 Sands et al. 2018, p. 244.

201 *United States—Taxes on Petroleum and Certain Imported Substances*, GATT Dispute Settlement Panel, 17 June 1987, L/6175—34S/136.

202 *Case Concerning the Auditing of Accounts between the Kingdom of the Netherlands and the French Republic Pursuant to the Additional Protocol of 25 September 1991 to the Convention on the Protection of the Rhine against Pollution by Chlorides of 3 December 1976*, Arbitral Award, 12 March 2014, PCA Case No 2000-02, p. 41, para 103.

203 See Dissenting Opinion of Judge Weeramantry to *Legality of the Threat or Use of Nuclear Weapons*, above n 17, pp. 502–04 (emphasis added).

204 Viñuales 2008, p. 247.

the other hand, in *Certain Activities*, the Separate Opinion of Judge Bhandari opined that:

> As the concept arose from the OECD and does not have the status of a principle of general international law, it presently acts as merely a general guideline of public international law.[205]

Judge Bhandari expanded upon these views in his separate opinion of 2018. He observed that, according to Indian courts, the 'polluter pays principle' is part of the concept of 'sustainable development', as well as of 'customary international law'.[206] He opined that the polluter pays principle should extend to punitive damages on the basis of the importance of deterrence of environmental destruction.[207]

Therefore, in the end, although the principle has an instinctive appeal and receives frequent use as a general principle of law, especially in treaty law, ICTs are virtually unanimous in their conclusions that it has not reached the status of customary international law.

18.8 Principle of Common but Differentiated Responsibility

The Principle of Common but Differentiated Responsibility (CBDR) developed from the application of equity in general international law, and the recognition that the special needs of developing countries must be considered in the development, application and interpretation of rules of international environmental law.[208]

As the name suggests, the principle contains two elements. The first is the common responsibility of States for the protection of the environment.[209] The second reflects the different circumstances of States, particularly between industrialised countries who have generally contributed more to global warming than underdeveloped countries, whose capacity to prevent damage may furthermore be less advanced.[210]

---

[205] See fn. 189 (internal citations omitted), citing Declaration of the Human Environment, Report of the UN Conference on the Human Environment (Stockholm, 1972), UN doc. A/Conf.48/14/Rev1; Boyle 1991, pp. 363, 369; Crawford 2008, p. 359.

[206] See above n 189.

[207] Ibid.

[208] Sands et al. 2018, p. 244.

[209] See Convention for the Establishment of an Inter-American Tropical Tuna Commission, 31 May 1949, 80 UNTS 72; Convention on Wetlands of International Importance Especially as Waterfowl Habitat, 21 December 1975, 996 UNTS 245; The Treaty on Principles Governing the Activities of States in the Exploration and Use of Outer Space, including the Moon and other Celestial Bodies, 27 January 1967, 610 UNTS 205.

[210] See Stockholm Declaration, above n 2, Principle 23; Rio Declaration, above n 3, Principle 11, 6; Convention for Cooperation in the Protection and Development of the Marine and Coastal Environment of the West and Central African Region (Abidjan), March 28, 1981, Article 4(1), 20 ILM 746; UN General Assembly, *United Nations Framework Convention on Climate Change: resolution / adopted by the General Assembly*, 20 January 1994, A/RES/48/189; Convention on the Law of the Sea, 10 December 1982, 1833 UNTS 397, Article 207.

The principle has been expressed in a number of international instruments, many relating to climate change, including at Principles 4 and 7 of the Rio Declaration, with Principle 7 formulating it thus:

> States shall cooperate in a spirit of global partnership to conserve, protect and restore the health and integrity of the Earth's ecosystem. In view of the different contributions to global environmental degradation, states have common but differentiated responsibilities. The developed countries acknowledge the responsibility that they bear in the international pursuit of sustainable development in view of the pressures their societies place on the global environment and of the technologies and financial resources they command.

The role of this principle in international litigation before ICTs is extremely limited. The principle has been recognized in various matters before the WTO, most notably the *US Shrimp* case.[211] The principle was invoked only implicitly by the appellate body, which stated that: 'discrimination results not only when countries in which the same conditions prevail are differently treated, but also when the application of the measure at issue does not allow for any inquiry into the appropriateness of the regulatory program for the conditions prevailing in those exporting countries'.[212]

However, the principle received explicit treatment from the WTO Panel in this case:

> The Panel urges Malaysia and the United States to cooperate fully in order to conclude as soon as possible an agreement which will permit the protection and conservation of sea turtles to the satisfaction of all interests involved and taking into account the Principle that States have common but differentiated responsibilities to conserve and protect the environment.[213]

The principle has long played a role in the arena of climate change. While the possibility of international climate litigation has been entertained by scholars, ultimately there are many challenges to be overcome for this to occur, which are beyond the scope of this chapter. However, the principle has been applied by domestic courts in cases of transboundary harm. In 2015, the Hague District Court rendered its decision in the case of *Urgenda v. Government of the Netherlands*. The Court ruled that, in order to meet its duty of care towards the plaintiffs, who represented current and future generations of Dutch citizens threatened by the risks of climate change, the Dutch government was required to reduce greenhouse gas emissions by at least 25% by 2020.[214] Scholars have heralded the case as ground-breaking in many regards, not the least of which being that it represented the first occasion on which a national court expressly used the international environmental law principle of CBDR to interpret the scope of a State's climate obligations.[215]

---

211 *US—Shrimp (Appellate Body Report)*, above n 155.

212 Ibid., para 165.

213 *US—Shrimp (Appellate Body Report)*, above n 155, para 7.2.

214 Netherlands Supreme Court, *State of the Netherlands (Ministry of Economic Affairs and Climate Policy) v Stichting Urgenda*, Judgment, 20 December 2019, ECLI:NL:HR:2019:2007 para 5.1.

215 Galvão Ferreira 2016, pp. 330–33.

Similarly, in 2020, a Norwegian Court of Appeal, when considering Norway's obligations under the Paris Agreement, concluded that current national contributions were insufficient to meet the mandated goal.[216] The Court referred to CBDR in concluding that the 'burdensharing principles in the Agreement are suited to strengthening Norway's responsibility'.[217] Though that decision was later reversed by the Supreme Court of Norway, the use of the principle by the Court of Appeal was not impugned.

Therefore, though this principle is strongly related to climate change, and has featured in environmental litigation at the national level- much of which has international, transboundary implications- it is virtually unaddressed in the jurisprudence of the ICTs.

References

Birnie P et al (eds) (2009) International Law and the Environment. Oxford University Press, Oxford

Bosselmann K (2008) The Principle of Sustainability: Transforming Law and Governance. Ashgate Publishing Ltd, Hampshire

Boyle A (1991) Making the Polluter Pay: Alternatives to State Responsibility in the Allocation of Transboundary Environmental Costs. In: Francioni F, Scovazzi T (eds) International Responsibility for Environmental Harm. Graham and Trotman, London, pp 363–379

Cassese A (2005) International Law. Oxford University Press, Oxford

Craik N (2020) The Duty to Cooperate in the Customary Law of Environmental Impact Assessment. International & Comparative Law Quarterly 69: 239–259

Crawford J (2008) Brownlie's Principles of International Law. Oxford University Press, Oxford

Duvic-Paoli L-A (2018) The Prevention Principle in International Environmental Law. Cambridge University Press, Cambridge

Fitzmaurice M (2013) The Development of International Law by the ICJ. In: Tams C, Sloan J (eds) The Development of International Law by the International Court of Justice. Oxford University Press, Oxford, pp 353–374

Foster C (2011) Science and the Precautionary Principle in International Courts and Tribunals; Expert, Evidence, Burden of Proof and Finality. Cambridge University Press, Cambridge

Foster CE (2016) Methodologies and Motivations: Was Japan's Whaling Programme for Purposes of Scientific Research? In: Fitzmaurice M, Tamada D (eds) Whaling on the Antarctic: The Significance and Implications of the ICJ Judgment. Brill Nijhoff, Netherlands, pp 9–37

Galvão Ferreira P (2016) Common But Differentiated Responsibilities' in the National Courts: Lessons from *Urgenda* v. *The Netherlands*. Transnational Environmental Law (52): 329–351

Gillroy J M (2006) Adjudication Norms Dispute Settlement Regimes and International Tribunals: The Status of 'Environmental Sustainability' in International Jurisprudence. Stanford Journal of International Law 42:1–52

Howley J (2009) The Gabčikovo-Nagymaros case: the influence of the International Court of Justice on the law of sustainable development. Queensland Law Student Review 2:1–19

[216] Shapovalova 2021, p. 11.

[217] Bogarting Court of Appeal, *Natur og Ungdom, Föreningen Greenpeace Norden, v the Government of Norway*, 23 January 2020, at 24 and 27. English translation available at https://www.domstol.no/globalassets/upload/hret/avgjorelser/2020/desember-2020/hr-2020-2472-p.pdf Accessed 10 April 2020.

International Law Association (ILA) (2016) Study Group on Due Diligence in International Law, Second Report
Juste-Ruiz J (2013) The International Court of Justice and International Environmental Law. In: Boschiero N et al (eds) International Courts and the Development of International Law - Essays in Honour of Tullio Treves. T.M.C. Asser Press, The Hague, pp 383–401
Koe A (1998) Damming the Danube: The International Court of Justice and the Gabcíkovo-Nagymaros Project (Hungary v Slovakia), Sydney Law Review 612. http://www6.austlii.edu.au/au/journals/SydLRev/1998/27.html Accessed 26 April 2021
Koivurova T (2010) Due Diligence. Max Planck Encyclopaedia of Public International Law
Kulesza J (2016) Due Diligence in International Law. Nijhoff/Brill, Leiden
Maguire R (2012) Incorporating International Environmental Legal Principles into Future Climate Change Instruments. Carbon & Climate Law Review 6:101–113
Maljean-Dubois S, Richard V (2017) The International Court of Justice's Judgement of 20 April 2010 in the Pulp Mills on the River Uruguay (Argentina v. Uruguay) case. In: Almeida P, Sorel J-M (eds) Latin America and the International Court of Justice. Routledge, Abingdon, pp 309–320
McCaffrey SC (2018) Environmental Law and Freshwater Ecosystems. In: Sobenes E, Samson B (eds) Nicaragua Before the International Court of Justice. Springer, Cham
Oral N (2013a) The International Court of Justice and International Environmental Law. In: Boschiero N et al (eds) International Courts and the Development of International Law - Essays in Honour of Tullio Treves. T.M.C. Asser Press, The Hague, pp 403–423
Oral N (2013b) Implementing Part XII of the 1982 UN Law of the Sea Convention and the Role of International Courts. In: Boschiero N et al (eds) International Courts and the Development of International Law, Essays in Honour of Tullio Treves. T.M.C. Asser Press, The Hague
Pineschi L (2013) The Duty of Environmental Impact Assessment in the First ITLOS Chamber's Advisory Opinion: Toward the Supremacy of the General Rule to Protect and Preserve the Marine Environment as a Common Value? In: Boschiero N et al (eds) International Courts and the Development of International Law - Essays in Honour of Tullio Treves. T.M.C. Asser Press, The Hague, pp 425–439
Plakokefalos I (2012) Prevention Obligation in International Environmental Law. Yearbook of International Environmental Law 23(1):3–43
Sands Ph et al (eds) (2003) Principles of International Environmental Law. Cambridge University Press, Cambridge
Sands Ph et al (eds) (2018) Principles of International Environmental Law. Cambridge University Press, Cambridge
Shapovalova D (2021) In Defense of the Principle of Common but Differentiated Responsibilities and Respective Capabilities. In: Mayer B, Zahar A (eds) Debating Climate Law. Cambridge University Press, Cambridge
Takano A (2018) Due Diligence Obligation and Transboundary Environmental Harm. Cybersecurity 833 Applications. Laws 7(36):1–13
Taylor P (1999) The Case concerning the Gabcikovo-Nagymaros Project: A Message from the Hague on Sustainable Development. New Zealand Journal of Environmental Law 3:109–126
Tignino M, Bréthaut C (2020) The Role of International case law in implementing the obligation no to cause significant harm. International Environmental Agreements: Politics, Law and Economics 20: 631–648
Trevisan L (2009) The International Court of Justice's Treatment of 'Sustainable Development' and Implications for Argentina v. Uruguay. Sustainable Development Law & Policy 10:40–85
Valverde Soto M (1996) General Principles of International Environmental Law. ILSA Journal of International & Comparative Law 3:193–209
Viñuales J E (2008) The Contribution of the International Court of Justice to the Development of International Environmental Law: A Contemporary Assessment. Fordham International Law Journal 232: 232–258

Edgardo Sobenes is an international lawyer and PIL Consultant with vast experience in the field of international law, settlement of international disputes, and diplomacy. He holds an Advanced LL.M in Public International Law and International Dispute Settlement from Leiden University, an International Master's in Law from the University of Barcelona and ISDE, and a LLB in Law and Economics from the Central-America University (UCA) (www.edgardosobenes.com).

John Devaney primarily practices international criminal law with a focus on cultural heritage crime. He has worked with various tribunals in The Hague and currently serves as an Associate Legal Officer. He began his career as a trial lawyer in the United States before earning an Advanced LL.M at Leiden University in Public International Law.

Part III
Future Opportunities and Developments

Chapter 19
Reflections on International Environmental Adjudication: International Adjudication Versus Compliance Mechanisms in Multilateral Environmental Agreements

Antonio Cardesa-Salzmann

Content

Abstract This chapter describes the general trend in Multilateral Environmental Agreements (MEA) towards the establishment of managerial compliance mechanisms, and discusses their main institutional and procedural features, before assessing their overall performance. This overview of compliance mechanisms in global MEA will in turn provide the backdrop for reflecting on some of the recent developments in the case law of the ICJ. It argues that *Whaling in the Antarctic* sheds light on some of the issues that may have kept States from bringing claims based on multilateral treaties before international courts—yet challenges remain for adjudicating international environmental disputes through international courts and tribunals. The chapter concludes with some reflections about the distinctive roles and potential complementarities between international environmental adjudication and regime-internal managerial compliance control in the broader picture of global environmental governance.

A. Cardesa-Salzmann (✉)
University of Strathclyde, Law School, Glasgow, Scotland
e-mail: antonio.cardesa-salzmann@strath.ac.uk

Strathclyde Centre for Environmental Law and Governance, Glasgow, Scotland

E. Sobenes et al. (eds.), *The Environment Through the Lens of International Courts and Tribunals*, https://doi.org/10.1007/978-94-6265-507-2_19

Keywords International environmental law · Multilateral environmental agreements · International courts and tribunals · Compliance mechanisms · Adjudicative dispute settlement · Managerialism · Inter-legality

19.1 Introduction: The Intrinsic Complexity of 'Environmental Disputes'

The emergence of international environmental law is intimately linked to international adjudication. Indeed, the origins of international environmental law, understood as the gradual adaptation of general principles of law and international customary law to regulate the legal consequences of environmental harms in transboundary contexts,[1] are a construct of jurisprudence. Standard textbooks on international environmental law will open with a historical reference to the landmark *Trail Smelter* Arbitral Award,[2] in which the arbiters relied on *sic utere tuo ut alienum non laedas* in order to formulate what has now become the bedrock principle of prevention of public international law relating to environmental protection.[3] After further consolidation in the case law of international courts and arbitral tribunals,[4] the principle of prevention was eventually enshrined in Principle 21 of the Stockholm Declaration[5] and Principle 2 of the Rio Declaration.[6] Moreover, international regimes that have grown out of key multilateral environmental treaties and have come to shape present-day 'global environmental law',[7] such as the UN Framework Convention on Climate Change,[8] the Convention on Biological Diversity,[9] or the UN Convention to Combat Desertification,[10] to name a few, rely in their construction on this principle.

---

[1] Boyle and Harrison 2013, p. 247.

[2] *Trail Smelter Arbitration*, Award, 11 March 1941, 3 RIAA 1905.

[3] Bodansky 2010.

[4] ICJ, *Corfu Channel (Albania v United Kingdom)*, Merits, Judgment, 9 April 1949, ICJ Reports 1949; *Lac Lanoux (France/Spain)*, Award, 16 November 1957, 12 RIAA 281.

[5] Declaration of the United Nations Conference on the Human Environment. In Report of the United Nations Conference on the Human Environment, Stockholm, 5–16 June 1972, UN Doc A/CONF.48/14/Rev.1, p. 3.

[6] Rio Declaration on Environment and Development. In Report of the United Nations Conference on Environment and Development, Rio de Janeiro, 3–14 June 1992, UN Doc A/CONF.151/26, Vol.I, Annex I.

[7] Yang and Percival 2009; Kulovesi et al. 2019.

[8] UN Framework Convention on Climate Change, 9 May 1992, 1771 UNTS 107, entered into force 21 March 1994. See Preamble, recital 8.

[9] Convention on Biological Diversity, 5 June 1992, 1760 UNTS 79, entered into force, 29 December 1993. See Article 3.

[10] UN Convention to Combat Desertification, 10 October 1994, 1954 UNTS 3, entered into force 26 December 1996. See Preamble, recital 15.

International courts and arbitral panels have thus been instrumental in adapting the existing general principles to emerging societal demands in international relations concerning the exploitation of common or shared natural resources. Over the past decades, however, growing scientific understanding about human impacts on global ecosystems has triggered a more profound change in public international law. In this process, international legal responses to transboundary environmental issues have been displaced gradually from the confined political and legal contexts of good neighbourliness, towards multilateral forums of cooperation. The pre-existing layer of general principles of law and reciprocal customary obligations between States has thus been complemented by an impressive amount of regional and universal multilateral treaties based on 'common concern' and 'common but differentiated responsibilities' in preserving ecosystems for present and future generations under the paradigm of 'sustainable development'.[11] While certainly not the only area of public international law to undergo such developments, international 'environmental' law is indeed one of the prominent examples of the trend that Bruno Simma famously coined as the evolution from bilateralism towards the protection of community interests in international law.[12]

Intuitively, considering the catalysing role of international courts and tribunals in the origins of international environmental law, one may expect this process of expansion of multilateral environmental treaty law to have led to a parallel increase in international (i.e., inter-state) environmental litigation. In the aftermath of the 1992 UN Conference on the Environment and Development, for instance, the International Court of Justice (ICJ) decided to set up a Chamber for Environmental Matters under Article 26(1) of its Statute. Yet, after more than a decade without a single referral of a dispute to the Chamber, the ICJ eventually decided to discontinue it in 2006. This latter example, however, should not convey the false impression that there has not been any increase. Contentious cases, such as the case concerning the *Gabčíkovo-Nagymaros Dam Project*,[13] the *Pulp Mills on the River Uruguay*,[14] the *Aerial Herbicide Sprayings* case,[15] *Whaling in the Antarctic*,[16] the case concerning *Certain Activities Carried Out by Nicaragua in the Border Area*,[17] or the *Dispute over the Status and Use of the Waters of the Silala*[18] stand for the handful of more

[11] See Chap. 1 in this volume.

[12] Simma 1994.

[13] ICJ, *Gabčíkovo-Nagymaros Project (Hungary v Slovakia)*, Judgment, 25 September 1997, ICJ Reports 1997, p. 7.

[14] ICJ, *Pulp Mills on the River Uruguay (Argentina v Uruguay)*, Judgment, 20 April 2010, ICJ Reports 2010, p. 14.

[15] ICJ, *Aerial Herbicide Spraying (Ecuador v Colombia)*, Removal from list, Order, 13 September 2013, ICJ Reports 2013, p. 278.

[16] ICJ, *Whaling in the Antarctic (Australia v Japan: New Zealand intervening)* Judgment, 31 March 2014, ICJ Reports 2014, p. 226.

[17] See, in particular, ICJ, *Certain Activities Carried Out by Nicaragua in the Border Area (Costa Rica v Nicaragua)*, Compensation, Judgment, 2 February 2018, ICJ Reports 2018, p. 15.

[18] See Application Instituting Proceedings filed in the Registry of the Court on 6 June 2016. *Dispute over the Status and Use of the Waters of the Silala (Chile v Bolivia)*.

or less clear-cut 'environmental' disputes dealt with by the ICJ alone. In addition to these contentious, inter-state cases, the ICJ also famously delved into public international law relating to environmental protection in the exercise of its advisory function in *Legality of the Threat or Use of Nuclear Weapons*.[19] Notwithstanding inter-state 'environmental' disputes brought before other international courts such as the International Tribunal of the Law of the Sea,[20] the WTO Dispute Settlement Body,[21] or arbitral tribunals,[22] what these latter cases brought before the ICJ suggest is that the adjudication of environmental disputes[23] has increased at a perhaps lower rate than expected some time ago, especially if compared with the general quantitative increase in international litigation. More importantly, however, it suggests some degree of uneasiness by States to engage in this type of litigation, as its complexity and unpredictable outcome makes it a high-risk endeavour.

To some extent, this complexity has to do with structural features derived from the somewhat blurry epistemological boundaries of 'environmental law' itself, which also apply to 'environmental disputes'. There is indeed some merit to the argument that there is no such thing as a clear-cut, distinct body of law that deals with environmental protection.[24] In this perspective, international environmental law cannot be reduced to the *sic utere* principle, the customary due diligence obligation not to cause significant transboundary harm, and a number of treaties that are generally recognised as multilateral environmental agreements (MEA), without incurring into over-simplification. For the same reasons, international environmental disputes cannot possibly be conceived as disputes that can or ought to be solved in accordance with international environmental law only. In the early 2000s, Cesare Romano provided a handy academic concept of 'international environmental dispute', by reliance on the classical concept of 'dispute' in the *Mavrommatis Palestine Concessions* case.[25] He defined them as 'conflict[s] of views or of interests between two or more States, taking the form of specific opposing claims and relating to an anthropogenic alteration of an ecosystem, having detrimental effect on human society and leading to environmental scarcity of natural resources'.[26] In real-world scenarios, however, environmental disputes are far from involving only States, but are much more complex and may involve other subjects of public international law, such as international organisations, as well as private persons, whether these are enterprises, or members of the public, non-governmental organisations (NGOs), or indigenous

---

[19] ICJ, *Legality of the Threat or Use of Nuclear Weapons*, Advisory Opinion, 8 July 1996, ICJ Reports 1996, p. 266.

[20] See Chap. 3 in this volume.

[21] See Chap. 5 in this volume.

[22] See Chaps. 11 and 12 in this volume.

[23] Stephens 2009; Romano 2000.

[24] Boyle and Harrison 2013, p. 247. See also *Case Concerning Aerial Herbicide Spraying (Ecuador v Colombia),* Memorial of Ecuador (Vol I), 29 April 2009.

[25] PCIJ, *Mavrommatis Palestine Concessions, Greece v United Kingdom,* Objection to the Jurisdiction of the Court, Judgment, 30 August 1924, PCIJ Ser. A, p. 11.

[26] Romano 2000.

peoples and local communities. Moreover, as already implied in the quoted definition, the environmental dimension to the claims of the parties in dispute is never the sole legal issue at stake. Rather, the centrality that environmental legal issues may take in a given dispute depends very much on the way in which parties decide to shape the dispute itself, a decision which in turn is more often than not inspired by complex political motivations that do not primarily relate to the preservation of ecosystems' integrity.[27]

When assessed in the context of inter-state disputes in which either part invokes 'environmental rules', different layers of general principles, customary rules and treaty regimes relating for example to the abatement of climate change, the conservation and sustainable management of biological diversity, sustainable land management and the prevention of desertification, or the international regulation of wildlife trade, will indeed be relevant to the case. However, these latter more or less clear-cut treaty-based 'environmental' rules often have to be balanced against other general principles, customary and/or treaty-based rules concerning (by way of mere example) the prevention of corruption and transnational organised crime, the fair and non-discriminatory conduct of international trade, the reciprocal furtherance of international investments, or the protection of human rights. In the *Aerial Herbicide Sprayings* case, for instance, Ecuador construed its claims not merely on the breach of territorial sovereignty and due diligence customary obligations arising out of the principle of prevention, but based aspects of its claims also on treaty-based international human rights obligations and the 1988 Narcotics Convention.[28] This is what Andreas Philippopoulos-Mihalopoulos refers to as the 'paradox of environmental law', an area of law which he qualifies as 'hazy yet urgent, undefinable yet omnipresent'.[29]

In elevating these reflections on the conceptualisation of 'environmental law' and that of 'environmental disputes' to another level altogether, it becomes clear that this slipperiness and omnipresence of legal rules relating in one way or another to environmental protection transcends the strict confines of public international law, hence reaching deep into the realm of transnational law,[30] or—to use a more provoking term – global law.[31] Legal disputes which have some kind of environmental dimension to it rarely rely on legal rules from only one legal system or jurisdiction, and require legal operators to engage in 'inter-legality', that is to say, seeking the solution to a dispute 'not by taking the one-jurisdiction-at-a-time perspective—the perspective of mutual alternative or exclusion—but by showing the relevance of—and the caring for—all the relevant normativities actually controlling the case'.[32] Emerging trends in public interest litigation to further locally global environmental

[27] See among many others Boyle and Harrison 2013, pp. 247–250.

[28] Ibid., p. 253.

[29] Philippopoulos-Mihalopoulos 2011, p. 19.

[30] Mai 2020.

[31] Cardesa-Salzmann and Cocciolo 2019. See also Chap. 22 in this volume.

[32] Klabbers and Palombella 2019, p. 3.

policy agendas, such as climate litigation,[33] enhance these calls for overcoming the fragmentation of rationalities and boundaries between international legal regimes, and between these and domestic legal systems, through convergence-promotion and divergence-accommodation even more compelling for (global) environmental law scholarship.[34]

Against the background of these introductory reflections on the intrinsic complexity of 'environmental disputes', this chapter will first describe the general move in MEA towards the establishment of managerial compliance mechanisms, which are bureaucratically led mechanisms aimed at supporting governments and facilitating the implementation of complex multilateral treaty regimes through bespoke assistance measures. I will argue that the structural legal features of international obligations arising out of MEA have furthered this shift towards managerialism, with the deliberate aim of 'avoiding disputes', as the international law of the treaties, the law governing state responsibility for internationally wrongful acts, and not least, international adjudication have shown only limited capacity to adapt to emerging regulatory trends in global environmental governance. I will then discuss the main institutional and procedural features of compliance mechanisms, before assessing their overall performance. This overview of compliance mechanisms in global MEA, will in turn provide the backdrop for reflecting on some of the recent developments in the case law of the ICJ, which especially after the *Whaling in the Antarctic* case, sheds light on some of the issues that may have kept States from bringing claims based on multilateral treaties before international courts. The chapter concludes with some reflections about the distinctive roles and potential complementarities between international environmental adjudication and regime-internal managerial compliance control in the broader picture of global environmental governance.

19.2 The Shift towards Managerialism: Compliance Mechanisms in MEA

One of the most repeated but still relevant citations within international legal scholarship is Louis Henkin's statement that 'almost all nations observe almost all principles of international law and almost all of their obligations almost all of the time.'[35] However, it is also well-known that environmental regulations suffer from structural implementation and compliance deficits, which are complex and multicausal in nature. Unfortunately, without fundamentally questioning the validity of Henkin's statement from a general perspective, international environmental law is not an exception to that structural deficit. It is well known that multilateral environmental treaties

[33] Sindico et al. 2021.

[34] Kulovesi et al. 2019.

[35] Henkin 1979, p. 47.

have developed over time a *sui generis* type of compliance mechanisms, specifically designed in order to address structural compliance issues within the confines of international treaty law relating to multilateral conventions from a managerial, non-confrontational and dispute-avoidance perspective. In this section I will discuss the scholarly debates, involving both academics and practitioners, which preceded and provided the intellectual breeding ground for the emergence and development of these characteristic mechanisms. I will then describe the main institutional and procedural features of these mechanisms, before appraising how they have performed, from a general perspective.

19.2.1 The Emergence of Endogenous Compliance Mechanisms in MEA

Academic literature interrogating the 'effectiveness' of multilateral regulatory treaties has been questioning for some time whether traditional approaches to international law enforcement under state responsibility, the international law of the treaties, and adjudicative dispute settlement suit the specific regulatory features and implementation needs of MEA.[36] Indeed, public international law analysts highlight the relevance of structural features of multilateral treaty obligations arising out of many MEA.[37] The collective, non-reciprocal nature of *erga omnes partes* obligations in some MEA, according to this strand of scholarly analysis, makes it hard to identify any injured or specially affected state as a consequence of their breach or non-compliance.[38] This latter feature of collective obligations begs the question about the purpose of traditional means of public international law to react to the breach of obligations arising out of multilateral treaties, such as the suspension or termination of the MEAs by any Party individually,[39] or the invocation of state responsibility.[40] Until the judgment rendered in 2012 in *Questions Relating to the Obligation to Prosecute or Extradite (Belgium v Senegal)*, [41] as we shall see, the adjudication of claims based on the breach of *erga omnes partes* obligations brought before international courts and tribunals by non-injured States, was also contested in the academic literature.[42]

---

[36] The most representative scholarly work is Chayes and Handler Chayes 1995; see also Ulfstein et al. 2007.

[37] Ehrmann 2000.

[38] Ibid.; Cardesa-Salzmann 2012.

[39] Article 60 (2) and (3) VCLT. See Fitzmaurice and Redgwell 2000, pp. 59–62; see also Koskenniemi 1992, p. 138.

[40] ILC Draft Articles on Responsibility of States for Internationally Wrongful Acts (2001), UN Doc A/56/10, Articles 42 and 48.

[41] ICJ, *Questions relating to the Obligation to Prosecute or Extradite (Belgium v Senegal)*, Judgment, 20 July 2012, ICJ Reports 2012, p. 422.

[42] Boyle and Harrison 2013, p. 256.

Given these difficulties of traditional enforcement mechanisms in public international law to cope with emerging structural features of environmental treaty regimes, scholars like Abram Chayes and Antonia Handler Chayes advocated for a pragmatic, pro-active approach to compliance with multilateral regulatory treaties.[43] Translating this strand of thought specifically to MEA, they argued that the complexity and dynamism of environmental problems addressed in environmental regimes, as well as their inter-woven nature, demanded a holistic, proactive approach in their 'management', rather than ex-post adjudication.[44] In so doing, advocates of managerialism distinguish themselves from narrower, economistic lines of thought, which regard States as 'rational utility maximisers' that will only comply with international treaty obligations if strong enforcement mechanisms provide for sanctions that outweigh the potential benefit of non-compliance.[45] According to managerialists, however, the parties to any MEA engage in complex, open-ended processes of cooperation based on the principle of common but differentiated responsibilities, in the context of which non-compliance cannot be reduced to economistic paradigms of rational utility maximisation without incurring into over-simplification. Rather, the accommodation of such heterogenous realities in MEA, especially in global MEA, signals a high degree of commitment by the ratifying parties, hence requiring a more subtle and nuanced approach to compliance-promotion through mutual consultation and deliberation for the sake of preserving the integrity of the treaty regime, rather than through hard enforcement.[46]

In particular, authors following this line of thought often emphasise structural complexities of adjudicative disputes settlement to cope with the multidimensionality or polycentricity of environmental disputes, given the eminently bilateralist structure of the adjudicative process.[47] On the other hand, they also emphasise how the complexity of international adjudication of environmental disputes is also conducive to fragmentation, as States engage in forum shopping, submitting the various aspects of the dispute to different available dispute settlement mechanisms that they deem most favourable to their claims. Most importantly, however, according to the standard managerialist discourse, adjudicative dispute settlement is by definition *ex-post* and too slow and cumbersome to deal appropriately with the issues at stake in environmental disputes.[48] Finally, as also implied in the Joint Dissenting Opinion of Judges Al-Khasawneh and Simma in the *Pulp Mills* case,[49] the reactive approach underlying adjudication in ascertaining breaches of or non-compliance with international environmental standards is also seen as a disadvantage, as environmental damage is

---

[43] Chayes and Handler Chayes 1995; for a critique of managerialism, however, see also Koskenniemi 2007.

[44] Chayes et al. 1998.

[45] See e.g. Downs et al. 2000; for a concise summary of this theoretical discussion, see Bodansky 2010, p. 236.

[46] Bodansky 2010, p. 236.

[47] Ohlhoff 2003, pp. 8–14; this assertion is critically discussed in Stephens 2009, pp. 95–102.

[48] Chayes et al. 1998, p. 54.

[49] ICJ, *Pulp Mills,* above n 14, p. 117.

frequently irreparable and remedial obligations arising out of state responsibility or liability regimes hardly provide for restitution or compensation.[50]

The previous paragraphs thus summarise the views of scholars and practitioners in favour of a managerialist approach to addressing the challenge of implementing the ever-growing number of MEA in the mid-1990s, towards making these treaties work effectively towards the achievement of their overarching objectives.[51] These views provided the intellectual breeding ground for creative approaches under already existing MEA, such as the 1973 Convention on International Trade in Endangered Species of Wild Fauna and Flora (CITES),[52] where the Secretariat of the Convention scrutinised the Parties' compliance with treaty obligations, allowing the Standing Committee and Conference of the Parties (COP) of the treaty to devise either facilitative strategies to support non-compliant parties to fully implement the treaty, or enforce it through the suspension of commercial trade in CITES species with non-compliant parties under Article XIV CITES.[53] Most importantly, however, the aforementioned debates also influenced the adoption of novel, endogenous mechanisms in newly adopted MEA, such as the non-compliance procedure contemplated in Article 8 of the 1987 Montreal Protocol on Ozone Depleting Substances.[54] As expressed by the leader of the US delegation in the negotiations of the Protocol, this provision was agreed upon in the closing stages of the *travaux préparatoires* given the broadly shared perception that monitoring and enforcement of the Protocol's commitments was absolutely essential, while lengthy negotiations over legalistic arguments regarding a dispute settlement clause, as had happened during the negotiations of Article 11 of the 1985 Vienna Convention on the Ozone Layer,[55] would only delay urgently required action.[56] After some initial learning curves,[57] the Montreal Protocol's non-compliance procedure was able to quickly gain institutional experience and build a successful track-record of eliciting compliance of the Parties that required some kind of technical and/or financial support to fully implement their commitments.

---

[50] Scovazzi 2001, p. 51; see also Brunnée 2004, p. 364.

[51] Ulfstein et al. 2007, pp. 9–11.

[52] Convention on International Trade in Endangered Species of Wild Fauna and Flora 3 March 1973, 993 UNTS 243, entered into force 1 July 1975.

[53] Sand 2013, pp. 251–252; Wettestad 2007; even if less successful than in CITES, managerial compliance-promoting strategies were also developed under the Ramsar Convention on Wetlands of International Importance especially as Waterfowl Habitat, 2 February 1971, 996 UNTS 245, entered into force 21 December 1975. See Ferrajolo 2011.

[54] Montreal Protocol on Substances that Deplete the Ozone Layer, 16 September 1987, 1522 UNTS 3, entered into force 1 January 1989. MOP Decision IV/5 and Annexes IV and V. UN Doc UNEP/OzL.Pro.4/15 (1992) (hereinafter, Montreal Protocol NCP). However, managerial approaches were already developed in the context of CITES. See Sand 2013; Wettestad 2007.

[55] Vienna Convention for the Protection of the Ozone Layer, 22 March 1985, 1513 UNTS 293, entered into force 22 September 1988.

[56] Benedick 1998, p. 270.

[57] Werksman 1996; see also Benedick 1998, pp. 276–286.

As I have argued elsewhere,[58] this much-praised success led to the replication of compliance mechanisms in most of the subsequently negotiated MEA. Indeed, since its inception, the Montreal Protocol's compliance mechanism has served as a model of inspiration for similar managerial procedures in other global and regional MEA. Global MEA featuring such mechanisms include:

- the Basel Convention on the Transboundary Movement of Hazardous Wastes and Their Disposal;[59]
- the Rotterdam Convention on the Prior Informed Consent Procedure for Certain Hazardous Chemicals and Pesticides in International Trade;[60]
- the Cartagena Protocol on Biosafety,[61] and the Nagoya Protocol on Access and Benefit-Sharing;[62]
- the Paris Agreement,[63] which is still in its very early stages and will come to substitute the one operating in the Kyoto Protocol;[64]
- the International Treaty on Plant Genetic Resources for Food and Agriculture;[65] and
- the Minamata Convention on Mercury.[66]

---

[58] Cardesa-Salzmann 2012.

[59] Basel Convention on the Control of Transboundary Movements of Hazardous Wastes and their Disposal, opened for signature 22 March 1989, 1673 UNTS 57, entered into force 5 May 1992. COP Decision VI/12, Appendix. UN Doc UNEP/CHW.6/40 (2003). Hereinafter, Basel Convention NCP

[60] Rotterdam Convention on the Prior Informed Consent Procedure for Certain Hazardous Chemicals and Pesticides in International Trade, 10 September 1998, 2244 UNTSS 337, entered into force 24 February 2004. COP Decision RC-9/7, Annex VII, UN Doc UNEP/FAO/RC/COP9/23 (2019), Hereinafter, Rotterdam Convention NCP.

[61] Cartagena Protocol on Biosafety to the Convention on Biological Diversity, 29 January 2001, 2226 UNTS 208, entered into force 11 September 2003. COP-MOP Decision BS-I/7, Annex. UN Doc UNEP/CBD/BS/COP-MOP/1/15 (2004). Hereinafter, Cartagena Protocol NCP.

[62] Nagoya Protocol on Access to Genetic Resources and the Fair and Equitable Sharing of Benefits arising from their Utilization to the Convention on Biological Diversity, 29 October 2010, 3008 UNTS, entered into force 12 October 2014. UN Doc UNEP/CBD/NP/COP-MOP/DEC/1/4 (2014) Annex (hereinafter, Nagoya Protocol NCP), para B.2.

Further managerial compliance mechanisms have also been established in other sectoral or issue specific biodiversity and nature protection regimes. See Cardesa-Salzmann 2017, sec. III.33.6 Annex.

[63] Decision 10/CMA.1. UN Doc FCCC/PA/CMA/2018/3/Add.2 (19 March 2019). Hereinafter, Paris Agreement NCP.

[64] Kyoto Protocol to the United Nations Framework Convention on Climate Change, 11 December 1997, 2303 UNTS 162, entered into force 16 February 2005. Decision 27/CMP1, Annex. UN Doc FCCC/KP/CMP/2005/8/Add.3. Hereinafter, Kyoto Protocol NCP.

[65] GB Resolution 2/2011, Annex. See <http://www.fao.org/3/be452e/be452e.pdf> Accessed 7 June 2021.

[66] Minamata Convention on Mercury, 10 October 2013, entered into force 16 August 2017, article 15. Decision MC-3/9, Annex, UN Doc UNEP/MC/COP3/Dec.9 (7 January 2020). Hereinafter, Minamata Convention NCP.

However, consensus to adopt such a mechanism remains elusive for some time now in the Stockholm Convention on Persistent Organic Pollutants.[67]

Regional MEA have also furthered the proliferation of compliance mechanisms, especially under the aegis of the UN Economic Commission for Europe (UNECE), where the compliance mechanism of the 1998 Aarhus Convention on the Rights of Access to Information, Public Participation in Decision-Making and Access to Justice in Environmental Matters,[68] has set unprecedented standards, allowing environmental civil society organisations to trigger proceedings against States Parties.[69] The 2018 Regional Agreement on Access to Information, Public Participation and Justice in Environmental Matters in Latin America and the Caribbean (Escazú Agreement) adopted under the aegis of the UN Economic Commission for Latin America and the Caribbean (ECLAC), also foresees an equivalent compliance mechanism, 'ensuring the significant participation of the public'.[70] The main focus of my discussions in this chapter, however, will focus on compliance mechanisms in global MEA.

19.2.2 Institutional and Procedural Features of Compliance Mechanisms in MEA

Compliance mechanisms in MEA typically rely on standing treaty bodies, which depending on the treaty are called either the Implementation Committee, or Compliance Committee, and are designed as small-sized, specialised subsidiary bodies to the MEA's plenary decision-making body, the Conference of the Parties (COP).[71] The concrete institutional design of these committees, as well as the procedural features of the mechanism, are carefully adapted and made bespoke to the specific regulatory features of the treaty regime in each MEA. Each compliance mechanism is therefore

---

[67] Stockholm Convention on Persistent Organic Pollutants, 22 May 2001, 2256 UNTS 119, entered into force 17 May 2004. Draft negotiation text in COP Decision SC-7/26, Annex. UN Doc UNEP/POPS/COP10/19 (2021). Hereinafter, Stockholm Convention Draft NCP.

[68] Convention on Access to Information, Public Participation in Decision Making and Access to justice in Environmental matters (Aarhus Convention), 25 June 1998, 2161 UNTS 447, entered into force 30 October 2001.

[69] Art 2(4) Aarhus Convention, and MOP Decision I/7, Annex, para 18. UN Doc ECE/MPPP/2/Add.8 (2004). Similar compliance mechanisms have been established in the following UNECE treaties: Protocol on Pollutant Release and Transfer Registers to the Convention on Access to Information, Public Participation in Decision-Making and Access to Justice in Environmental Matters, 21 May 2003, 2626 UNTS 119, entered into force 8 October 2009. Protocol on Water and Health to the Convention on the Protection and Use of Transboundary Watercourses and International Lakes, 17 June 1999, 2331 UNTS 202, entered into force 4 August 2005. Convention on Environmental Impact Assessment in a Transboundary Context (UNECE), 25 February 1991, 1989 UNTS 309, entered into force 19 September 1997.

[70] Regional Agreement on Access to Information, Public Participation and Justice in Environmental Matters in Latin America and the Caribbean, 4 March 2018, entered into force 22 April 2021 (Escazú Agreement), Article 18.

[71] Churchill and Ulfstein 2000, pp. 644–647.

unique, and generalisations should be taken with a grain of salt.[72] With this caveat in mind, however, this section will try to distil some general institutional and procedural features of compliance mechanisms in MEA with the aim of showcasing their distinct rationale vis-à-vis adjudicative dispute settlement of environmental disputes.

As anticipated above, taking the model of the Implementation Committee and the non-compliance procedure developed in the Montreal Protocol on Ozone Depleting Substances as a source of inspiration, the vast majority of MEA adopted over the past four decades have developed their own compliance mechanism. From a general perspective, these mechanisms follow a managerial approach and are conceived of as non-confrontational, non-adversarial procedures that do not aim to brand a Party as defaulting on its obligations or providing for remedies. Rather, their aim is to elicit Parties experiencing 'problems' back into compliance through bespoke assistance.[73] Thus designed to induce and promote compliance with the treaty obligations, their aim is to avoid the emergence of disputes and the resort to adjudicative settlement. As procedures that are collectively operated through the MEA's treaty bodies, they eschew the tricky question of the invocation of state responsibility.[74] This latter aspect is of particular relevance in the context of collective regimes, such as those of the Montreal Protocol, the Stockholm Convention, the Minamata Convention, the Nagoya Protocol, the Kyoto Protocol and, more recently, also the Paris Agreement, the central obligations of which are not owed vis-à-vis any specific Party, but *erga omnes partes*.

As opposed to international courts and tribunals, compliance mechanisms are praised for their flexibility and their capacity to address a broad range of issues of compliance, transcending the strict language of law.[75] In so doing, compliance mechanisms are instrumental to regime effectiveness, while preserving regime integrity. Accordingly, they are conceived and designed as bespoke procedures capable of 'managing' effectively compliance with and the implementation of dynamic environmental regimes, in which the basic legally binding treaty-based principles and standards are fleshed out through COP decisions, the legal nature of which is not always easily determined.[76] Endogenous, regime-specific compliance mechanisms are thus portrayed as better-suited to cope with underlying political tensions and delicate compromises among the Parties to an MEA, than international courts and tribunals. The latter focus primarily on the legal dimension of an environmental dispute between the contending parties only. As seen in *Whaling in the Antarctic*, moreover, the bilateralist approach of adjudicative dispute settlement, is perceived as a hindrance to accommodating the complex and delicate balance of interests in the adjudicative process that underlie global multilateral treaties, unless third-party intervention mechanisms are articulated. I shall return to this issue further below.

---

[72] Fodella 2009.

[73] Handl 1997, p. 34.

[74] Nègre 2010, p. 810.

[75] This, in turn, is encountered with strong objections in scholarship, See, e.g., Koskenniemi 2007, p. 13.

[76] Klabbers 2007, p. 1008; on the legal nature of COP decisions, see Brunnée 2002; Brunnée 2005.

Given this collective and managerial rationale of compliance mechanisms, the institutional design of Committees is fine-tuned to reflect not just an equitable geographical balance between the Parties to the MEA, but also other political compromises for the balancing of competing interests between them.[77] In specific MEA, for instance, such as the Kyoto Protocol[78] and the Paris Agreement,[79] the membership of the Committee must also feature representatives of small island developing States and the least developed countries. The Committee of the Nagoya Protocol, in turn, requires the representation of indigenous and local communities, either among the members of the Committee, or in any case with the appointment of observers entitled to participate in the deliberations, but not in the taking of decisions.[80] Accordingly, the size of Committees varies significantly. The Montreal Protocol and the Paris Agreement feature the smallest compositions, with ten and twelve members respectively, while the vast majority of Committees has fifteen members. The Kyoto Protocol's Compliance Committee can be singled out as featuring the so far most elaborate institutional design, with two branches—the Facilitative Branch and the Enforcement Branch – and twenty members. Decisions must be taken by consensus or, should this not be possible, by as a last resort by qualified majority.

A further significant distinctive feature of Compliance Committees comes with the mandate of its members. It is possible to distinguish between neatly political and managerial mechanisms, such as in the Montreal Protocol where Committee members are experts acting in a capacity of representatives of a Party,[81] from most of the other mechanisms, in which Committee members are mandated to act in their personal capacity as independent experts 'with recognised competence in relevant scientific, technical, socioeconomic or legal fields'.[82] This independent, expertise-based mandate, together with more elaborate procedural safeguards of due process and a mandate—not just to facilitate—but also to recommend enforcing measures, has led to qualify the compliance mechanisms under the Kyoto Protocol as quasi-judicial.[83] At the same time, the broad-based, interdisciplinary expertise built into the institutional design also allows these Committees to address compliance issues from a comprehensive perspective, capable of assessing complex factual and scientific-technical issues, rather than only from the legal perspective. This is a further institutional difference with respect to international courts and tribunals, especially the ICJ, where the conduct of evidence in complex environmental disputes has spurred internal debates, as epitomised in the Joint Dissenting Opinion of Judges Al-Khasawneh and Simma in *Pulp Mills*.

---

[77] Montreal Protocol NCP, para 5; Basel Convention NCP, paras 3–8; Rotterdam Convention NCP, paras 3–8; Cartagena Protocol NCP, para II.2; Minamata Convention, Article 15(3).

[78] Kyoto Protocol NCP, paras IV.1 and V.1.

[79] Paris Agreement NCP, para 5.

[80] Nagoya Protocol NCP, para B.2.

[81] Montreal Protocol NCP, para 5.

[82] Taken, by way of example, from the Paris Agreement NCP, para 5.

[83] Fodella 2009, pp. 359–362; see also Boisson de Chazournes and Mbengue 2007; Montini 2009.

In addition to outlining the institutional design of the Committee in charge of the compliance mechanism, the terms of reference also set out the procedures to carry out their mandate, as well as an indicative list of measures that can be forwarded to the COP for adoption in order to deal with situations of non-compliance by a Party. As with the institutional design, procedures and measures are tailored to the specific needs of each treaty regime. There are, however, some common features that are shared by the vast majority of compliance procedures. There are typically three different ways to trigger the mechanism and bring specific issues of non-compliance by a Party to the attention of the Committee.[84] In this sense, proceedings may be initiated on a Party-to-Party basis.[85] However, this way of triggering the procedure is only rarely used in practice, given the non-adversarial nature of the compliance mechanism. In the Paris Agreement, for instance, where the managerial and non-adversarial nature of the compliance mechanism was deliberately emphasised throughout the negotiation process, this way of initiating the compliance procedure was entirely left out of the terms of reference.[86]

Further, the terms of reference of all compliance mechanisms allow any Party that is not in compliance with its commitments, despite its best efforts to do, to refer itself to the Committee, especially where bespoke financial or technical assistance measures are required to comply with its commitments under the MEA.[87] In addition, the Secretariat (or other entitled treaty bodies) have the capacity to trigger the procedure when made aware of any compliance issues with respect to a Party.[88] It has to be said, however, that this latter trigger mechanism is only fully developed in the context of collective regimes based on *erga omnes partes* obligations.[89] However, the terms of reference of compliance mechanisms in MEA such as the Basel Convention and the Cartagena Protocol limit this triggering capacity of the Secretariat *ratione materiae* to general reporting obligations. In these treaties, the central treaty obligations concern the prior informed consent procedures to transboundary movements of controlled goods, which are of a bilateral nature.[90] Under the terms of reference

---

[84] Romanin Jacur 2009.

[85] See, e.g., Montreal Protocol NCP, para 1.

[86] Paris Agreement NCP, paras 20 and 22. Article 15 of the Minamata Convention on Mercury also omits this Party-to-Party mechanism.

[87] See for all, Montreal Protocol NCP, para 4.

[88] See, e.g., Montreal Protocol NCP, para 3. Under the Kyoto Protocol NCP, the triggering capacity is allocated to the expert review teams under article 8 of the Protocol (see Kyoto Protocol NCP, para VIII.3(a)), whereas in the Minamata Convention NCP, the Secretariat only plays a role channelling the information of national implementation reports, while the triggering function is left to the political discretion of the COP (see Article 15(4) (b) and (c)). This is also the case for the Nagoya Protocol NCP (see para D.1(c)).

[89] Montreal Protocol NCP, para 3; Kyoto Protocol NCP, para VI.1; Minamata Convention, Article 15(4); Paris Agreement NCP, para 20. In the Stockholm Convention Draft NCP, this issue is still controversial and subject to negotiation (see paras 17 and 17 (c) between brackets).

[90] Basel Convention NCP, para 9(c); For the Cartagena Protocol NCP, see COP-MOP Decision BS-V/1, para 1(b).

of the Rotterdam Convention, finally, the Secretariat or any other treaty body, lack any capacity to trigger the compliance procedure.[91]

Regional MEA, especially in the UNECE region, additionally allow for the initiation of compliance procedures by NGOs. As mentioned above, this relatively successful trend started with the Aarhus Convention under the aegis of the UNECE[92] has now been replicated in the Escazú Agreement in the region of Latin America and the Caribbean, where this innovation has still to be tested in practice. Global MEA, however, do not allow non-governmental organisations to trigger the compliance mechanism. The role of NGOs in compliance mechanisms is generally very limited in global MEA, in which some compliance mechanisms allow them to attend hearings that have been declared open to the public.[93] This is not to say, however, that NGOs are deprived of any kind of influence in compliance mechanisms. Even in mechanisms such as the one under the Montreal Protocol, in which the protection of the confidentiality of the technical information for the production of ozone depleting substances and its substitutes is emphasised, and where NGOs are formally excluded from the works of the Committee, the negotiators of the compliance mechanism already foresaw that civil society organisations would have indirect leverage through the Secretariat, for instance, by providing additional information relevant to the compliance record of a Party.[94] In MEA like the Nagoya Protocol, where the protection of the interests and rights of indigenous and local communities is at the very heart of the access and benefit-sharing regime, the Secretariat is explicitly mandated to channel relevant information to the Committee 'provided by a directly affected indigenous or local community, related to provisions of the Protocol',[95] hence allowing for an indirect triggering capacity.

19.2.3 Compliance Mechanisms as Compliance Promoters and Dispute Avoiders: An Appraisal

Once triggered, compliance procedures are conducive to the adoption of reactive measures seeking to gently elicit a non-compliant Party back into full or, at least, acceptable levels of compliance with its treaty obligations. Given the managerial, non-adversarial rationale that is common to these mechanisms, the measures devised by Committees are primarily of a facilitative nature. Only the compliance mechanisms of a few global MEA, such as the Montreal Protocol and the Kyoto Protocol, expressly foresee 'harder' enforcement measures. So, for instance, the

---

[91] Rotterdam Convention NCP, para 12.

[92] For a nuanced appraisal, see Samvel 2020.

[93] See, for instance, the Rules of Procedure of the Compliance Committee of the Kyoto Protocol, in Decision 4/CMP2, Annex, Rule 9. UN Doc FCCC/KP/CMP/2006/10/Add.1.

[94] Széll 1995, p. 100.

[95] Nagoya Protocol NCP, para 9.

indicative list of measures included in the terms of reference of the Montreal Protocol non-compliance procedure foresees:

A. Appropriate assistance, including assistance for the collection and reporting of data, technical assistance, technology transfer and financial assistance, information transfer and training.
B. Issuance of cautions.
C. Suspension, in accordance with the applicable rules of international law concerning the suspension of the operation of a treaty, of specific rights and privileges under the Protocol.[96]

The terms of reference under the Kyoto Protocol feature a much more detailed gradient of consequences that the Facilitative and the Enforcement Branches can adopt respectively. Facilitative measures may include the following measures:

(a) Provision of advice and facilitation of assistance to individual Parties regarding the implementation of the Protocol;
(b) Facilitation of financial and technical assistance to any Party concerned, including technology transfer and capacity building from sources other than those established under the Convention and the Protocol for the developing countries;
(c) Facilitation of financial and technical assistance, including technology transfer and capacity building [...]; and
(d) Formulation of recommendations to the Party concerned [...].[97]

Enforcement measures, in turn, may involve the suspension of the eligibility of a Party to participate in the emission trading schemes developed under Article 17 of the Protocol, as well as the joint implementation mechanism under Article 6 and the clean development mechanism under Article 12, if the Branch determines that a Party does not meet one or more of the eligibility requirements.[98] Most spectacularly, where the Enforcement Branch has determined that a Party has exceeded its assigned amount of anthropogenic greenhouse gas emissions under the Protocol, the enforcement measures that can be adopted also may involve the:

> deduction from the Party's assigned amount for the second commitment period of a number of tonnes equal to 1.3 times the amount in tonnes of excess emissions.[99]

With the exception of the prior two examples, however, the terms of reference of compliance mechanisms in other global MEA expressly limit the mandate of Committees to the adoption of facilitative measures only, and leave the adoption of harder enforcement measure to the political discretion of the COP.[100] In this sense,

---

[96] See MOP Decision IV/5, Annex V. UN Doc UNEP/OzL.Pro.4/15 (1992).
[97] See Kyoto Protocol NCP, para XIV.
[98] Ibid, para XV.4.
[99] Ibid, para XV.5.
[100] See e.g., Nagoya Protocol NCP, para F.3 (d).

the strong emphasis in the Paris Agreement's compliance mechanism on 'facilitating implementation and promoting compliance',[101] its deliberate avoidance of any enforcement language[102] and, in general, all the quasi-judicial features of its predecessor in the Kyoto Protocol, is quite remarkable. It is consistent, though, with the overall softer regulatory features of the Paris Agreement.[103]

The managerial and dispute-avoiding rationale of these mechanisms begs the question about their performance, in order to put them in context against adjudicative dispute settlement. In this context, it is important to remind that compliance mechanisms indeed seek 'securing an amicable solution of the matter on the basis of respect for the provisions' of the underlying MEA,[104] but apply themselves 'without prejudice to the operation of the settlement of disputes procedure' foreseen in the treaty.[105] Indeed, the operation and performance of these treaty-specific mechanisms varies greatly from one MEA to the other, given the bespoke nature of the procedures. A detailed account of their respective performance would exceed the scope of this chapter. In the remainder of this section, I will outline general patterns of performance of the above listed compliance mechanisms in global MEA. To that end, I will focus on those compliance mechanisms which have gathered the most significant institutional practice, like those under the Montreal Protocol, the Kyoto Protocol, the Basel Convention and the Cartagena Protocol, trying to illustrate general trends with specific examples from the operation of compliance mechanisms in other MEA. As highlighted by Klabbers, a general overview of this practice suggests that the majority of cases submitted to compliance mechanisms in global MEA concern issues of non-compliance by developing States.[106] Cases concerning countries with economies in transition to a market economy or developed countries have been less frequent, even though the practice of the Enforcement Branch of the Kyoto Protocol's Compliance Committee has precisely focused on this latter group of Parties.

In consistency with its managerial rationale, the average outcome of the non-compliance procedure in the Montreal Protocol is bespoke technical and financial assistance to the Parties under scrutiny. Whenever assistance measures are agreed, the Multilateral Fund of the Montreal Protocol and the executing agencies that are responsible for the implementation of *ex ante* technical and financial assistance to developing countries[107] (UNIDO, UNEP and UNDP) have to adapt their policies with respect to the non-compliant Party in accordance with the recommendations of the

[101] Paris Agreement NCP, para 30.

[102] Ibid, paras 28 and 30.

[103] Voigt 2016.

[104] Wording taken from the Montreal Protocol NCP, para 8.

[105] Wording taken by way of illustrative example from the preamble of the Montreal Protocol NCP For a discussion of the relationship between compliance mechanisms and dispute settlement, see Fitzmaurice and Redgwell 2000; Treves 2009.

[106] Klabbers 2007.

[107] In the jargon of the Montreal Protocol, these are the Parties operating under Article 5 of the Protocol.

Implementation Committee, as endorsed by the Meeting of the Parties (MOP).[108] The Committee and the MOP keep the evolution of non-compliant Parties under review until they are satisfied that no further action is required. Stronger measures, such as the issuance of cautions, are only applied if the situation extends in time and the Party under scrutiny fails to provide evidence of sufficient commitment in regaining compliance.

On the other hand, the Bureau of the Kyoto Protocol's Compliance Committee has never allocated any compliance issues raised by Expert Review Teams to its Facilitative Branch, nor have there been any self-referrals to this branch. Over the years, there has only been one instance Party-to-Party submission, effectuated in 2006 by South Africa (as chair of the G77 and China) with respect to 15 developed countries and countries with economies in transition. However, this submission did not substantiate, allegedly due to the lack of the required majority in the Branch in order to agree on its acceptance. These problems of infancy left aside, the Facilitative Branch has nevertheless been quite active, focussing its efforts on general functions of implementation review, providing parties with advice and support in the implementation of the protocol.[109] However, as I will develop in short, the main activity of the Kyoto Protocol's Compliance Committee has been undertaken by its Enforcement Branch.

Facilitative measures have now also been taken consistently by the compliance mechanisms of the Basel Convention and the Cartagena Protocol. The activity of the Committees in these latter MEA has been limited for some time to the general assessment of the respective MEA's implementation by all the Parties, but no specific cases of non-compliance had been submitted with respect to particular countries until relatively recently. Established in 2003, the Committee for Administering the Mechanism for Promoting Implementation and Compliance of the Basel Convention only received its first specific submissions by the Secretariat and self-referrals of Parties for their own non-compliance after 2009. These cases mainly concern structural difficulties of developing countries in complying with their reporting requirements.[110] As for the Compliance Committee of the Cartagena Protocol, an amendment of the terms of reference under COP-MOP's decision BS-V/1 has eventually allowed for referrals of issues of non-compliance with reporting obligations by the Secretariat, allowing the Committee to discharge its facilitative role in that regard. It is important to stress, however, that the specific cases of non-compliance submitted to the compliance mechanisms of these two MEA is materially limited to the fulfilment of periodical reporting obligations by the Parties. Accordingly, the financial and technical assistance agreed in these cases aims at developing national capacities in that regard.

Among the four compliance mechanisms selected for this performance overview, only those of the Montreal Protocol and the Kyoto Protocol are mandated for the

[108] Financial and technical assistance to countries with economies in transition has been provided mainly through the Global Environment Fund. See Boisson de Chazournes 2006, pp. 284–286.

[109] UN Doc CC/FB/20/2017/2, 1 August 2017.

[110] UN Doc UNEP/CHW/CC/8/25 (2011).

adoption of enforcement measures of a harder edge. An analysis of the of the practice regarding the adoption of 'sanctions' or enforcement measures in these two mechanisms reveals a mixed picture. The unique decisions adopted in the mid-1990s by the Montreal Protocol's MOP with respect to the non-compliance of certain countries with economies in transition, especially that concerning the Russian Federation in 1995,[111] were quite controversial, due to the severeness of the trade restrictions imposed.[112] In hindsight, such a strong and controversial reaction addressed what was perceived at the time as an existential challenge to the integrity of the ozone regime, but has also led to a process of regulatory and institutional development of the Montreal Protocol which has avoided so far resorting again to this type of measures.[113]

However, in accordance with the quasi-judicial features of the Kyoto Protocol's compliance mechanism, the suspension of rights and privileges has been a somewhat more frequent outcome of the decisions of the Compliance Committee's Enforcement Branch. It has so far transitorily suspended Greece,[114] Croatia,[115] Bulgaria,[116] Romania,[117] Lithuania,[118] Ukraine,[119] and currently also twice Kazakhstan,[120] from participation in the joint implementation mechanism, the clean development mechanism and the emission trading scheme under Articles 6, 12 and 17 of the Protocol, respectively.[121] While such hard enforcement measures are consistent with the legally binding quantified emission limitation or reduction commitments under the Kyoto Protocol, the completely revamped treaty regime under the Paris Agreement has made such an approach redundant.[122]

In conclusion, this overview of the rationale, the institutional and procedural features, and the operation of compliance mechanisms in practice does provide some insight into the reasons why States have found refuge in treaty-specific, non-adversarial procedures before carefully balanced international bureaucratic bodies in order to address the implementation and compliance deficit in global environmental governance, rather than allowing disputes to escalate and refer contending

---

[111] Montreal Protocol, MOP Decision VII/18, para 8. UN Doc UNEP/OzL.Pro.7/12 (1995).

[112] Fitzmaurice 2009, p. 473.

[113] Benedick 1998, pp. 276–286.

[114] UN Doc CC-2007-1-8/Greece/EB, 17 April 2008. Greece was reinstated in its eligibility to participate in the flexible mechanisms later that year (doc. CC-2007-1-13/Greece/EB, 13 November 2008).

[115] UN Doc CC-2009-1-8/Croatia/EB, 26 November 2009. Croatia has announced that it intends to appeal the final decision of the Enforcement Branch under §XI.1 Kyoto Protocol NCP (doc. CC-2009-1-9/Croatia/EB, 4 January 2010).

[116] UN Doc CC-2010-1-8/Bulgaria/EB, 28 June 2010.

[117] UN Doc CC-2011-1-8/Romania/EB, 27 August 2011.

[118] CC-2011-3-8/Lithuania/EB, 21 December 2011.

[119] UN Doc CC-2016-1-6/Ukraine/EB, 7 September 2016.

[120] CC-2019-1-6/Kazakhstan/EB, and Corr.1, 26 June 2019. See also CC-2020-1-4/Kazakhstan/EB, 13 January 2021.

[121] Less intense enforcement measures were also enacted vis-à-vis Slovakia and Monaco.

[122] Voigt 2016, p. 166.

parties to international courts. While the compliance mechanisms discussed in this appraisal show a varying degree of effectiveness, their underlying managerial approach promotes compliance with key treaty obligations and, in this way, does contribute to the avoidance of disputes. This begs the question whether there is a role for adjudicative dispute settlement of claims based on MEA, and whether international courts and tribunals should play a more prominent role in the principled development of the law, also in the context of global environmental governance.

19.3 Developments in the International Adjudication of Claims Based on *Erga Omnes Partes* Obligations

In this section, I will address the prior question by pointing to the structural issues that academic writing had identified as traditional shortcomings in international adjudicative dispute settlement for disputes of claims based on MEA. In so doing, I will highlight developments of the last decade in international adjudication, especially those regarding standing for collective claims, and third-party intervention (as of right), which remedy to some extent those traditional shortcomings. These considerations will pave the way for my final reflections about the distinctive roles and potential complementarities between international environmental adjudication and regime-internal managerial compliance control in the broader picture of global environmental governance.

When looking at the larger picture of international adjudicative dispute settlement in the last few decades, international environmental adjudication before the ICJ has been relatively scarce, even with the increase of 'environmental' cases seen after 2010. The environmental disputes that the ICJ has dealt (and is dealing) with are mostly bilateral, transboundary disputes concerning shared water resources. This is certainly so in the *Gabčíkovo-Nagymaros Dam* case,[123] the *Pulp Mills* case,[124] the *Silala* case,[125] and even the compensation of environmental harms in *Certain Activities Carried out by Nicaragua in the Border Area*[126] falls within this category. Equally, the *Aerial Herbicide Sprayings* case had a bilateral, transboundary environmental dispute at its core, albeit with much broader international legal implications.[127] While the parties' claims in the *Gabčíkovo-Nagymaros Dam* and the *Pulp Mills* cases were mainly (but not exclusively) based on bilateral treaties, the compensation claims by Costa Rica against Nicaragua in *Certain Activities*, as well as the respective 'environmental' claims of Ecuador and Colombia in *Aerial Herbicide Sprayings*, as well as chose of Chile and Bolivia in *Silala*, are based on customary rules of international law.

---

[123] ICJ, *Gabčíkovo-Nagymaros Project*, above n 13.

[124] ICJ, *Pulp Mills,* above n 14.

[125] ICJ, *Dispute over the Status and Use of the Waters of the Silala,* above n 18.

[126] ICJ, *Certain Activities Carried Out by Nicaragua in the Border Area*, above n 17.

[127] ICJ, *Case Concerning Aerial Herbicide Spraying*, above n 15.

As discussed in the previous sections, international cooperation aimed at addressing more comprehensively world-wide environmental problems is nowadays articulated through MEA. In the five decades after the UN Conference on the Human Environment, held in Stockholm in June 1972,[128] there has been an exponential increase in multilateral treaties relating to the environment. Until the *Whaling in the Antarctic* case, however, there was a striking absence of adjudication of claims articulated on the basis of multilateral treaties. This is what makes this latter case particularly interesting for our purposes. As anticipated in the prior section, before the judgment rendered by the ICJ in March 2014,[129] most of the academic writings would highlight a number of structural features that made the ICJ an elusive forum to adjudicate environmental disputes involving claims based on the interpretation or implementation of multilateral treaty obligations undertaken not merely on the basis of reciprocal interests, but in order to protect common interests.[130]

Jurisdiction of international courts and tribunals in order to adjudicate disputes between sovereign States is consent-based. Under Article 36 of the ICJ Statute, the Court's jurisdiction requires evidence of the acceptance of the States involved in the dispute, either on an ad hoc basis (a prior special agreement or a subsequent acceptance on the basis of *forum prorrogatum*) or a compromissory clause in a treaty, the interpretation or application of which gives rise to the dispute. Considering the blurry boundaries of international 'environmental' law vis-à-vis other branches of public international law, and consequently the inter-woven nature of 'environmental' legal issues with other concurring legal issues in international disputes, jurisdiction *ratione materiae* often proves tricky in international environmental adjudication.[131] The basic rules governing the jurisdiction of the ICJ in contentious cases mean that the adjudication of 'environmental' elements of an inter-state dispute against the backdrop of other relevant elements or dimensions of that same dispute are possible only when the contending States have either recognised the compulsory jurisdiction under Article 36(2) ICJ Statute, as was the case of Australia and Japan in *Whaling in the Antarctic* (and would have been in *Aerical Herbicide Sprayings*), or in the hypothetical case of a *compromis* (or through *forum prorrogatum*) attributing wider ranging jurisdiction *ratione materiae*. In the absence of such far reaching jurisdictional bases, which is the most common real-world scenario, jurisdiction over environmental disputes most commonly emanates from compromissory clauses in environmental treaties, whether these are bilateral or multilateral. However, as Boyle and Harrison have argued, another factor adding further complexity to the jurisdictional basis of international courts and tribunals in environmental disputes lies in the fact that, with the noticeable exception of the 'partly environmental'[132] UNCLOS,

[128] See above n 5.

[129] ICJ, *Whaling in the Antarctic,* above n 16.

[130] Ohlhoff 2003, pp. 204–209.

[131] On the ICJ's jurisdiction *ratione materiae*, see Chap. 13 in this volume.

[132] Boyle and Harrison 2013, p. 261.

which sets up compulsory dispute settlement by ITLOS or arbitral tribunals, the vast majority of MEA do not provide for compulsory adjudicative dispute settlement.[133]

One may conclude, therefore, that the jurisdictional basis of the ICJ and other international courts and tribunals for the adjudication of environmental disputes largely derives from compromissory clauses of scattered and overlapping MEA, which limit its material scope to the interpretation and application of underlying treaties only, giving rise to a 'picture of jurisdictional incoherence and complexity.'[134] As a result, cluster litigation and forum shopping are frequent phenomena associated to international environmental adjudication. This sees parties to a dispute bringing their respective claims to whichever international court or tribunal they deem most favourable to their interests, as paradigmatically exemplified by the *Swordfish* dispute between Chile and the European Union, which was brought simultaneously before ITLOS and the WTO Dispute Settlement Body. As a result, disputes are frequently apportioned into different 'clusters' of claims,[135] which are submitted to and litigated before different courts—like in the famous *MOX Plant* case between Ireland and the United Kingdom—with the subsequent risk of inconsistent outcome and fragmentation.

In addition to the consent-based nature of the ICJ's contentious jurisdiction and the relativity of the *res judicata* of its judgments, the traditional interpretation of provisions in the Statute of the ICJ governing the standing of parties to a multilateral treaty were seen as a hindrance to the construction of such cases before the ICJ.[136] As we shall see, this latter aspect has been addressed in the *Whaling in the Antarctic* case. In the remainder of this section, I will therefore explore the extent to which this latter case may have provided solutions to some of those hurdles, most notably the standing for claims based on *erga omnes partes* obligations, as well as third-party intervention under Article 63 ICJ Statute.

19.3.1 Standing for Claims Based on Multilateral Treaties

In the past, academic writings have extensively discussed the legal question of standing of a state party to a multilateral environmental treaty to institute proceedings against another state party for the breach of a treaty obligation which is not owed on a reciprocal basis, but *erga omnes partes*.[137] As discussed above, a wide range of treaty obligations undertaken in MEA addressing global environmental issues, such as climate change or the loss of biodiversity as a matter of common concern for humankind, often fall within this category.[138] In particular, two sorts of issues arise with respect to the litigation of claims based on *erga omnes partes* obligations

---

[133] Ibid., pp. 250–251.

[134] Ibid., p. 251.

[135] Harrison 2013, p. 505; Nollkaemper 2008.

[136] See below n 160.

[137] See above n 47.

[138] Cardesa-Salzmann 2012, pp. 108–111.

before international courts and tribunals: standing and the effect of *res judicata inter partes* for the integrity of multilateral treaty-regimes.

The question whether a single state can arrogate itself the legal interest for claiming the fulfilment of obligations, which are not owed to it on the basis of reciprocity, and from the breach of which it has not suffered significant harms, was very much at the heart of the work carried out by Rapporteur James Crawford.[139] It led to Article 48 of the 2001 Draft Articles on State Responsibility for Internationally Wrongful Acts.[140] In the commentary to Article 48, the recognition of the capacity to invoke state responsibility 'by a state other than an injured state' for the breach of an obligation established for the protection of a collective interest of a group of the international community as a whole, was expressly portrayed as a measure of progressive development of international law,[141] thus hinting at the controversial nature of this matter.

Translating this legal question from the domain of state responsibility to that of adjudicative dispute settlement, means asking whether—counter to what the ICJ established in 1966 in its judgment of the merits of the *South Western Africa* case[142]—public interest litigation[143] is possible under international law. Until the judgment rendered in 2012 *(Belgium v Senegal)*,[144] standing to institute proceedings before the ICJ on the basis of an alleged breach of *erga omnes partes* obligations was very much unclear. Academic writings would often highlight the ambiguities of paras 33 and 34 of the ICJ's 1970 judgment in the *Barcelona Traction* case and the ensuing interpretative discrepancies in scholarship as to their ultimate implications.[145] In addition, the problematic relationship of the legal interest of any State in the fulfilment of obligations *erga omnes* with the consent-based nature of the jurisdiction of international courts was also regarded as a significant hurdle to public interest litigation before the ICJ,[146] as seen in the dismissal of Portugal's claims against Australia in the *East Timor* case. This case was dismissed on the basis of the indispensable third party principle, which would have required the intervention of Indonesia, over which the ICJ however did not have jurisdiction.[147]

---

139 Third Report on State Responsibility by Mr. James Crawford, Special Rapporteur, UN Doc A/CN.4/507 2000.

140 ILC Draft Articles on Responsibility of States for Internationally Wrongful Acts, UN Doc A/56/10 (2001).

141 Ibid., p. 127.

142 ICJ, *South West Africa (Ethiopia and Liberia v South Africa)*, Judgment, 18 July 1966, ICJ Reports 1966, p. 6.

143 This terminology is used in Boyle and Harrison 2013, p. 256.

144 ICJ, *Questions relating to the Obligation to Prosecute or Extradite (Belgium v Senegal)*, Judgment, 20 July 2012, ICJ Reports 2012, p. 422.

145 Tams 2005, chapter 5.

146 Ibid., chapter 5; Ohlhoff 2003, pp. 167–176.

147 ICJ, *East Timor (Portugal v Australia)*, Judgment, 30 June 1995, ICJ Reports 1995, p. 90. The indispensable third party principle, however, was first established in Case of the Monetary Gold Removed from Rome in 1943 (Preliminary Question), Judgment of 15 June 1954: I.C.J. Reports 1954, p. 19.

While the indispensable third party rule indeed poses a jurisdictional limitation to public interest litigation before international courts and tribunals, the issue of standing before the ICJ for instituting proceedings on the basis of *erga omnes partes* obligations was explicitly recognised in *Belgium v Senegal*, when the Court established that:

> [t]he common interest in compliance with the relevant obligations under the Convention against Torture implies the entitlement of each State party to the Convention to make a claim concerning the cessation of an alleged breach by another State party. If a special interest were required for that purpose, in many cases no State would be in the position to make such a claim. It follows that any State Party to the Convention may invoke the responsibility of another State party with a view to ascertaining the alleged failure to comply with its obligations *erga omnes partes* [...] and to bring that failure to an end.[148]

Whaling in the Antarctic confirmed this trend, as Australia did not have to prove any special interest in Japan's compliance with its obligations under Article VIII of the 1946 International Convention for the Regulation of Whaling (ICRW),[149] other than being itself a party to the Convention. Being the first environmental dispute of claims based on *erga omnes partes* obligations adjudicated by the ICJ, this case clearly provides a precedent to draw from in future environmental public interest litigation before the Court. At the same time, for the purpose of contextualising the respective remits of international adjudication and compliance mechanisms in MEA, it is important to bear in mind that this landmark case would most certainly not have reached the ICJ, had there been a compliance mechanism in place in the ICRW.[150] Indeed, designed and negotiated as a fisheries treaty with for the time quite advanced language about 'safeguarding for future generations the great natural resources represented by the whale stocks' and the 'common interest to achieve the optimum level' of such stocks, the ICRW is nowadays seen as a multilateral treaty concerned with the conservation and sustainable exploitation of whales. Despite the objections lodged amongst others by Japan, the moratorium of all commercial whaling enacted in early 1980s and the establishment of the Indian Ocean Sanctuary and the Southern Ocean Sanctuary,[151] the vast majority of States Parties to the ICRW has shifted its focus towards conservation, rather than sustainable exploitation.

Given the original object and purpose of the ICRW and the historical context in which it was adopted, the institutional design of the International Whaling Commission (IWC)[152] and the decision-making procedures for the adoption of amendments the ICRW's schedule allows any State Party to opt out of proposed amendments through the issuance of objections.[153] However, these institutional and procedural

---

[148] ICJ, *Questions relating to the Obligation to Prosecute or Extradite*, above n 144, para 69.

[149] International Convention for the Regulation of Whaling, 2 December 1946, 161 UNTS 72, entered into force 10 November 1948 (hereinafter, ICRW).

[150] Boyle and Harrison 2013, p. 260.

[151] ICRW, Schedule, paras 6 and 7.

[152] ICRW, Article III.

[153] ICRW, Article V.

features are quite different from present day MEA, where for the sake of the preservation of regime integrity the leeway for regimes *à la carte* is avoided to the extent possible within the framework of international treaty law relating to multilateral conventions.[154] In this sense, present-day MEA typically feature clauses disallowing the formulation of reservations to the treaty. At the same time, procedures for the adoption of technical adjustments, amendments or additional protocols seek to ensure widest-possible adhesion and ratification by the Parties to the foundational treaty.[155] As opposed to current MEA, whose compliance mechanisms—as discussed above—are carefully designed for a proactive approach to support and encourage compliance by the parties, the IWC clearly lacks such a mandate. Enforcement is entirely left to national authorities and courts.[156]

These important institutional and regulatory differences between the ICRW and present-day MEA notwithstanding, *Whaling in the Antarctic* also addresses important legal questions about the relevance of *inter-partes* litigation regarding the interpretation and application of a multilateral treaty for other States Parties to the treaty. In this regard, scholarly writings focussing on the compliance with and effectiveness of multilateral environmental treaty-regimes have discussed the potential risk for regime integrity deriving from the *inter partes* effect of judgments of international courts and tribunals.[157] In this sense, as famously pointed out by Vice-President Weeramantry in his Separate Opinion to the judgment in the *Gabčíkovo-Nagymaros Dam* case,[158] the bilateralist approach underlying inter-state litigation is perceived as a hindrance to the adjudication of environmental disputes concerning common interests of humankind.

19.3.2 Third-Party Intervention on the Basis of Article 63 ICJ Statute

The discussions of the previous section show that compliance mechanisms allow for an institutionalised, cooperative approach towards compliance issues, the solution of which is agreed collectively through the Compliance Committee and the Conference of the Parties. Such a cooperative approach ensures the preservation of the often complex and sensitive balance of interests agreed upon in the negotiation of global MEA. On the other hand, the submission of such compliance issues to dispute settlement through adjudication can lead to an outcome which is legally binding for the contending Parties, given the *inter partes* effects of *res judicata.* Such an outcome, however, risks unravelling the wider, more complex balances enshrined in large multilateral treaties if the international court confronted with the dispute does

154 Churchill and Ulfstein 2000; Röben 2000; Brunnée 2002; Brunnée 2005; Wiersema 2009.

155 Röben 2000; Brunnée 2005.

156 ICRW, Article IX.

157 Stephens 2009, pp. 93–102.

158 ICJ, *Gabčíkovo-Nagymaros Project*, above n 13, p. 118.

not have the means to allow the other Parties in the treaty to make their respective representations in the proceedings.

The ICJ Statute does indeed foresee the possibility for third-party intervention as a way to accommodate claims and interest of other States which are not directly involved in the dispute. As highlighted by Judge Cançado-Trindade in his Separate Opinion to the Order granting intervention to New Zealand in the *Whaling in the Antarctic* case,[159] even if narrowly interpreted and little applied in the past, the ICJ Statute provides in Articles 62 and 63 avenues for intervention in the proceedings, not as a party in the dispute itself, but as third parties with an interest of a legal nature which may be affected by the decision in that case. Similar provisions exist with respect to arbitral tribunals and in the statute of ITLOS.[160] The 'discretionary intervention' of Article 62 and the 'intervention as of right' of Article 63, however, do differ quite significantly one from another.[161] Delving into the differences and respective remits of these two provisions of the ICJ Statute would outgrow the scope of this chapter, and have been discussed in some detail in the above-mentioned Separate Opinion of Judge Cançado-Trindade.[162]

However, given the structural significance of multilateral treaties present-day international environmental law, which give rise to fragmented, complex and polycentric patterns of governance[163] based on 'decentralized network of embedded, nested, clustered, and overlapping institutions',[164] third party intervention on the basis of Article 63 ICJ Statute indeed opens an avenue for accommodating collective interests and environmental regime integrity more effectively in *inter-partes* adjudicative dispute settlement. Of special interest for our purpose here, is Article 63(2) of the Statute. It confers the right of intervention in the proceedings to any party to a multilateral treaty other than those involved in the dispute, given their intrinsic interest not in the outcome of the case, but in the legal interpretation that the ICJ may adopt to that end. If a State decides to exercise this right of intervention under Article 63(2), however, the interpretation of the multilateral treaty rendered by the ICJ will be binding for it. It is also important to notice that this right of intervention is purely based on the common membership in the relevant treaty and does not require any other jurisdictional basis.[165]

As New Zealand's intervention in the dispute between Australia and Japan in *Whaling in the Antarctic* shows, Article 63 confers the other parties in a multilateral treaty, the provisions of which are at the core of the dispute, a suitable avenue to feed the views of the non-contending parties into the proceedings in the collective interest

---

[159] ICJ, *Whaling in the Antarctic*, Declaration of Intervention of New Zealand, Order of 6 February 2013, ICJ Reports 2013, p. 14.

[160] Statute of the International Tribunal for the Law of the Sea, 10 December 1982, 1833 UNTS 561, Article 32.

[161] See Chinkin 2012a; Chinkin 2012b, in particular pp. 1577–1578.

[162] Separate Opinion, above n 159, pp. 23–33.

[163] Kim 2019.

[164] Kim and Mackey 2013, p. 13.

[165] Chinkin 2012b, p. 1590.

of regime integrity. Obligations undertaken by States through multilateral treaties, especially those of an *erga omnes partes* nature, do not belong in exclusivity to the parties in dispute, but rather to the entirety of the parties. The intervention as of right of Article 63 thus provides a mechanism to protect the objective character of these obligations, as Judge Cançado-Trindade rightly pointed out, which are to be 'implemented collectively, singling out the predominance of considerations of general interest (or even *ordre public*), transcending the individual interest of States parties.'[166]

Of course, third party intervention on the basis of Article 63 has implications for procedural fairness in the proceedings before the Court, as the Japanese representation highlighted in the *Whaling in the Antarctic* case, who had to counter the arguments of the plaintiff and the intervening third party.[167] At the same time, as Judge Cançado-Trindade held, while there were valid elements to those concerns, these can be readily managed by the Court in order to ensure the procedural equality between the disputing parties on the basis or Article 86 of the Rules of Court.

To conclude with this set of reflections on the standing for claims based on multilateral treaties and third-party intervention, one may hope with Cançado-Trindade that the intervention granted to New Zealand in the *Whaling in the Antarctic* case on the basis of Article 63, together with prior interventions granted also on the basis of Article 62,[168] signifies a shift away from narrow and excessively formalistic interpretations of the past and towards a resurrection of third-party intervention for the future.[169] Going even further, one may even hope for a more liberal interpretation also of Article 34, paras (2) and (3) of the Statute, which seem to provide for similar avenues of third-party intervention also to relevant public international organisations, in order to accommodate the Statute to the more complex and polycentric reality of present-day public international law.[170] Whatever the attitude of the Court may be in the future, Cançado-Trindade rightly raises the argument that a more prominent space for third-party intervention before the ICJ will be critical not only for the effective litigation of disputes based on multilateral treaties, but also for the ICJ to overcome the sole dispute-settlement dimension of its functions and the fuller realisation of its mandate under Article 92 UN Charter as the main judicial organ of the United Nations.[171] In order to grasp the significance of the opportunities that the *Whaling in the Antarctic* case opens with respect to the use of Article 63 ICJ Statute for our purposes, however, one must also say that third-party intervention alone is unlikely to override the incentives provided by endogenous, treaty-specific compliance mechanisms to manage compliance issues through bespoke financial

---

[166] Separate Opinion, above n 159, p. 34.

[167] Boyle and Harrison 2013, p. 263.

[168] See, in particular, ICJ, *Jurisdictional Immunities of the State (Germany v Italy)*, Application for Permission to Intervene, Order of 4 July 2011, ICJ Reports 2011, p. 494.

[169] Separate Opinion, above n 159, p 33.

[170] Dupuy 2012, p. 604.

[171] Separate Opinion, above n 159, p. 37.

and technical assistance. However, it sets the required conditions for the adjudication of fundamental legal disputes arising out of MEAs, should the occasion arise. As the historical precedent of the challenges faced by the Montreal Protocol in the mid-1990s suggests, MEA and their institutional arrangements are resilient and adaptive bureaucracies.[172] However, they are not immune to crises, at which point third-party intervention under Article 63 ICJ Statute, as resuscitated in the *Whaling in the Antarctic* case, could make the resort to adjudicative dispute settlement before the ICJ seem like a viable option for States.

19.4 Concluding Reflections

The discussions engaged in in this chapter reveal a complex and patchworked scenario of multiple layers of general principles, customary rules of general international law and international treaties, most of which are multilateral, which provide the normative basis of what is generally known as international environmental law. However, whilst generally recognised as a distinct branch of public international law, its ontological and epistemological boundaries with respect to other branches of international law remain blurry. Structural features of international adjudication, such as in particular the atomised jurisdictional bases of international courts and tribunals for the adjudication of environmental disputes, or the accommodation of community interests through quintessentially bilateral adjudication (e.g. through extended standing and third-party intervention), remain bottlenecks for international environmental adjudication. As some authors have put it, '[w]hat is most remarkable in these circumstances is that there are any cases at all.'[173] In a largely parallel process to the progressive superseding of general principles and customary law with an ever-tighter web of MEA, endogenous, treaty-specific compliance mechanisms have come to provide an alternative, managerial approach to the promotion of implementation and compliance of international legal rules, which have come to coexist—and to some extent, displace—adjudicative dispute settlement of environmental disputes.

In turn, the scrutiny of the performance of compliance mechanisms across MEA also reveals a nuanced picture, according to which these managerial and non-adversarial approaches to the furtherance of implementation and compliance have proven particularly effective within treaty-regimes featuring *erga omnes partes* obligations. Their degree of success is perhaps more modest in treaty-regimes with a less intense protection of collective interests, in the context of which the catalysing role of treaty bodies in triggering compliance control and supportive measures is more limited.

[172] Werksman 1996.

[173] Boyle and Harrison 2013, p. 251.

The resulting scenario begs the question about the distinctive roles and potential complementarities between international environmental adjudication and regime-internal managerial compliance control in the broader picture of global environmental governance. In the past, I addressed this question by hypothesising the need for exploring and enhancing synergies between both types of mechanisms[174] in the interest of the international rule of law, and in order to allow the international legal order to come to terms with its own heterarchy and pluralism, by promoting systemic integrity and the respect for structural, transversal values.[175] A decade later, significant developments have taken place. On the one side, *Whaling in the Antarctic*[176] has provided a precedent of international environmental adjudication based on a multilateral treaty featuring obligations of an *erga omnes partes* character, consolidating the trend initiated in *Belgium v Senegal*[177] regarding standing in such cases, and opening a promising, more liberal approach towards third-party intervention on the basis of Article 63 ICJ Statute. After the criticism voiced against the practice of scientific fact-finding in environmental disputes in the *Pulp Mills* case, *Whaling in the Antarctic* also paved the way for fairer and methodologically more sound procedures for the uptake of complex and contingent scientific evidence. This said, and to put the significance of *Whaling in the Antarctic* in perspective, one must equally acknowledge that the substantiation of such a case before the ICJ was only possible due to the rather seldom coincidence of the two disputing parties' recognition of the Court's compulsory jurisdiction under Article 36(2) ICJ Statute. I also agree with Boyle's and Harrison's assessment that, even so, this case most probably would not have reached the ICJ, had the ICRW provided the basis for the IWC to develop managerialist approaches towards compliance.[178] While hypothetical, this latter remark is significant, as the managerialist approach advocates for constructive, non-punitive responses to non-compliance for the sake of regime integrity. Against this backdrop, the ironical twist in the story of this landmark case of international environmental adjudication was the withdrawal of Japan from the IWC as of 2019, resuming thereafter commercial whaling operations.

On the other side, the practice of managerial compliance control and assistance under MEA has silently continued over these years, allowing treaty bodies to accumulate valuable institutional knowledge, which has seen compliance mechanisms like those in the Basel Convention and the Cartagena Protocol finally becoming operative. The perhaps most remarkable development comes with the adoption and entry into force of the 2015 Paris Agreement, the compliance mechanism of which seemingly entails a shift away from the harder enforcement edge and quasi-judicial features of the compliance mechanism under the Kyoto Protocol,[179] towards decidedly more

---

174 Cardesa-Salzmann 2012.

175 Klabbers et al. 2009, pp. 43–44.

176 See above n 16.

177 See above n 41.

178 Boyle and Harrison 2013, p. 260.

179 Klabbers 2008.

facilitative and managerial patterns of operation.[180] As part of international bureaucratic governance structures,[181] moreover, compliance mechanisms in MEA provide technocratic forums for compliance monitoring and management which possibly harness the required technical expertise for scientific fact-finding more readily than international courts and tribunals. However, the technocratic nature of these mechanisms also confers a degree of opaqueness to these procedures, which compromises the deliberative quality of international environmental decision-making processes.[182] Participation of NGOs or of indigenous peoples and local communities in compliance mechanisms has only been addressed to some extent in the more liberal approaches taken by quasi-judicial compliance procedures like the one under the Kyoto Protocol, or the quite unique mechanism of the Nagoya Protocol[183] at global level, and those established under some regional MEA in the UNECE region.[184] From this perspective, some authors suggest that the increasing relevance of the best available science (BAS) standard for the discharge of international obligations undertaken in MEA, such as the Paris Agreement, and in UNCLOS, may well lead to litigation of the transparency and legitimacy of 'best' science, as well as gaps in the 'available' science, before international courts and tribunals.[185] While the compulsory dispute settlement system under UNCLOS makes this scenario more likely under that treaty system, the compliance mechanism in the Paris Agreement and the lack of provision for compulsory dispute settlement makes it less likely. However, time will tell.

These concluding reflections seem to confirm that compliance mechanisms of MEA and international courts and tribunals have continued to coexist in a largely autonomous manner. However, a more detailed scrutiny of the attitude of domestic and international courts vis-à-vis the actuations of compliance mechanisms may provide a more nuanced picture. As highlighted by Tabau and Maljean-Dubois some time ago, a closer look into the practice of the European Union with respect to the decisions of compliance mechanism in the Kyoto Protocol regarding its Member States, reveals a remarkable deferential approach by the European Commission and the Court of Justice of the European Union for the sake of consistency between the international and EU legal systems. [186] The spectacular rise in domestic climate change litigation across the globe also suggests that domestic courts are taking a much more demanding attitude towards national governments and legislatures in order to fully comply with the best available science standard under the Paris Agreement.[187] Of course, the willingness of courts, especially international courts, to seek the solution

[180] Voigt 2016.

[181] Biermann and Siebenhüner 2009.

[182] Dryzek and Stevenson 2011; Stevenson and Dryzek 2012; Stevenson and Dryzek 2014.

[183] Zheng 2021.

[184] Cardesa-Salzmann 2012, pp. 122–126.

[185] Cook 2018.

[186] Tabau and Maljean-Dubois 2010, p. 755; see also Cardesa-Salzmann 2012, p. 129.

[187] See e.g. the Judgment of the German Constitutional Court of 29 April 2021 in the *Neubauer* case, ECLI:DE:BVerfG:2021:rs20210324.1bvr265618. See also Chap. 20 in this volume.

to a dispute 'not by taking the one-jurisdiction-at-a-time perspective—the perspective of mutual alternative or exclusion—but by showing the relevance of—and the caring for—all the relevant normativities actually controlling the case,'[188] varies greatly and depends on the institutional and normative preferences or biases of the international legal framework from which it draws its mandate and jurisdiction.[189]

In this sense, I conclude by reiterating the desirability of enhancing synergies between compliance mechanisms in MEA and international courts and tribunals. While managerial compliance mechanisms have proven overall effective in supporting and facilitating the implementation and compliance of their respective MEA, they have equally performed well in avoiding disputes. At the same time, one may nevertheless agree with Stephens in that, in contrast to compliance procedures, international courts are 'more authoritative sites for independent decision-making, and therefore are potentially more useful for assisting in the principled development of the law'.[190] Put differently, other than endogenous, treaty-specific, managerial compliance mechanisms in MEAs, international courts and tribunals, and especially the ICJ, are in principle better placed to act as 'hubs of inter-legality.'[191] But I definitely also concur with Pineschi that the comity and mutual deference that judicial and non-judicial mechanisms ought to engage in for the sake of 'inter-legality', crucial as it indeed is, is unfortunately only a tiny part of the challenges we all face for the preservation of global ecosystems for future generations.[192]

References

Benedick RE (1998) Ozone Diplomacy. New Directions in Safeguarding the Planet, 2nd edn. Harvard University Press, Cambridge MA.

Bennouna M (2018) Experts before the International Court of Justice: What for? Journal of International Dispute Settlement 9:345–351. https://doi.org/10.1093/jnlids/idy009.

Biermann F, Siebenhüner B (2009) The Role and Relevance of International Bureaucracies: Setting the Stage. In: Biermann F, Siebenhüner B (eds) Managers of Global Change. The Influence of International Environmental Bureaucracies. MIT Press, Cambridge (MA), pp 1–14.

Bodansky D (2010) The Art and Craft of International Environmental Law. Harvard University Press, Cambridge MA.

Boisson de Chazournes L (2006) Technical and Financial Assistance and Compliance: The Interplay. In: Beyerlin U, Stoll PT, Wolfrum R (eds) Ensuring Compliance with Multilateral Environmental Agreements. A Dialogue Between Practitioners and Academia. Martinus Nijhoff, The Hague, p 273.

Boisson de Chazournes L, Mbengue MM (2007) À propos du caractère juridictionnel de la procédure de non-respect du Protocole de Kyoto. In: Maljean-Dubois S (ed) Changements climatiques, les enjeux du contrôle international. Documentation française, Paris, p 73.

[188] Klabbers and Palombella 2019, p. 3.

[189] Shany 2019, p. 328.

[190] Stephens 2009, p. 364.

[191] Shany 2019.

[192] Pineschi 2019.

Boyle A, Harrison J (2013) Judicial Settlement of International Environmental Disputes: Current Problems. Journal of International Dispute Settlement 4:245–276. https://doi.org/10.1093/jnlids/idt001.
Brunnée J (2002) COPing with Consent: Law-Making Under Multilateral Environmental Agreements. Leiden Journal of International Law 15:1–52. https://doi.org/10.1017/S0922156502000018.
Brunnée J (2004) Of Sense and Sensibility: Reflections on International Liability Regimes as Tools for Environmental Protection. International & Comparative Law Quarterly 53:351.
Brunnée J (2005) Reweaving the Fabric of International Law? Patterns of Consent in Environmental Framework Agreements. In: Wolfrum R, Röben V (eds) Developments of International Law in Treaty Making, Beiträge zum ausländischen öffentlichen Recht und Völkerrecht No 177. Springer, Heidelberg, p 101.
Cardesa-Salzmann A, Cocciolo E (2019) Global Governance, Sustainability and the Earth System: Critical Reflections on the Role of Global Law. Transnational Environmental Law 1–25.
Cardesa-Salzmann A (2012) Constitutionalising Secondary Rules in Global Environmental Regimes: Non-Compliance Procedures and the Enforcement of Multilateral Environmental Agreements. Journal of Environmental Law 24:103. https://doi.org/10.1093/jel/eqr022.
Cardesa-Salzmann A (2017) Monitoring and Compliance Mechanisms. In: Razzaque J, Morgera E (eds) Encyclopedia of Environmental Law: Biodiversity and Nature Protection Law. Edward Elgar, Cheltenham.
Chayes A, Handler Chayes A (1995) The New Sovereignty. Compliance with International Regulatory Agreements. Harvard University Press, Cambridge MA.
Chayes A, Handler Chayes A, Mitchell RB (1998) Managing Compliance: A Comparative Perspective. In: Brown Weiss E, Jacobson HK (eds) Engaging Countries. Strengthening Compliance with International Environmental Accords. MIT Press, Cambridge MA, p 39.
Chinkin C (2012a) Article 62. In: Zimmermann A, Tomuschat C, Oellers-Frahm K, Tams CJ (eds) The Statute of the International Court of Justice. A Commentary, 2nd edn. Oxford University Press, Oxford, pp 1529–1572.
Chinkin C (2012b) Article 63. In: Zimmermann A, Tomuschat C, Oellers-Frahm K, Tams CJ (eds) The Statute of the International Court of Justice. A Commentary, 2nd edn. Oxford University Press, Oxford, pp 1573–1597.
Churchill RR, Ulfstein G (2000) Autonomous Institutional Arrangements in Multilateral Environmental Agreements: A Little-Noticed Phenomenon. American Journal of International Law 94:623–659.
Cook K (2018) Judging 'Best Available Science': Emerging Issues and the Role of Experts. Journal of International Dispute Settlement 9:388–400. https://doi.org/10.1093/jnlids/idy012.
D'Aspremont J, Mbengue MM (2014) Strategies of Engagement with Scientific Fact-finding in International Adjudication. Journal of International Dispute Settlement 5:240–272. https://doi.org/10.1093/jnlids/idu004.
De Lucia V (2019) The 'Ecosystem Approach' in International Environmental Law. Genealogy and Biopolitics. Routledge, Abingdon.
Donoghue JE (2018) Expert Scientific Evidence in a Broader Context. Journal of International Dispute Settlement 9:379–387. https://doi.org/10.1093/jnlids/idy011.
Downs GW, Danish KW, Barsoom PN (2000) The Transformational Model of International Regime Design: Triumph of Hope or Experience? Columbia Journal of Transnational Law 38:465–514.
Dryzek JS, Stevenson H (2011) Global democracy and earth system governance. Ecological Economics 70:1865–1874. https://doi.org/10.1016/j.ecolecon.2011.01.021.
Dupuy P-M (2012) Article 34. In: Zimmermann A, Tomuschat C, Oellers-Frahm K, Tams CJ (eds) The Statute of the International Court of Justice. A Commentary, 2nd edn. Oxford University Press, Oxford, pp 585–605.
Ehrmann M (2000) Erfüllungskontrolle im Umweltvölkerrecht: Verfahren der Erfüllungskontrolle in der umweltvölkerrechtlichen Vertragspraxis. Nomos, Baden-Baden.

Ferrajolo O (2011) State Obligations and Non-Compliance in the Ramsar System. Journal of International Wildlife Law and Policy 14:243–260.
Fitzmaurice M (2009) Non-Compliance Procedures and the Law of the Treaties. In: Treves T, Pineschi L, Tanzi A et al. (eds) Non-Compliance Procedures and Mechanisms and the Effectiveness of International Environmental Agreements. T.M.C. Asser Press, The Hague, p 453.
Fitzmaurice M, Redgwell C (2000) Environmental Non-Compliance Procedures and International Law. Netherlands Yearbook of International Law 31:35–65.
Fodella A (2009) Structural and Institutional Aspects of Non-Compliance Mechanisms. In: Treves T, Tanzi A, Pineschi L, Pitea C, Ragni C, Romanin Jacur F (eds) Non-Compliance Procedures and Mechanisms and the Effectiveness of International Environmental Agreements. T.M.C. Asser Press, The Hague, pp 355–372.
Handl G (1997) Compliance Control Mechanisms and International Environmental Obligations. Tulane Journal of International and Comparative Law 5:29.
Harrison J (2013) Reflections on the Role of International Courts and Tribunals in the Settlement of Environmental Disputes and the Development of International Environmental Law. Journal of Environmental Law 25:501–514. https://doi.org/10.1093/jel/eqt018.
Henkin L (1979) How Nations Behave: Law and Foreign Policy, 2nd edn. Columbia University Press, New York.
Jasanoff S (2004) Heaven and Earth: The Politics of Environmental Images. In: Jasanoff S, Martello ML (eds) Earthly Politics: Local and Global Environmental Governance. MIT Press, Cambridge MA, pp 31–52.
Jasanoff S (2005) Law's Knowledge: Science for Justice in Legal Settings. American Journal of Public Health 95:49–58. https://doi.org/10.2105/ajph.2004.045732.
Kim RE, Mackey B (2013) International environmental law as a complex adaptive system. International Environmental Agreements: Politics, Law and Economics 14:5–24. https://doi.org/10.1007/s10784-013-9225-2.
Kim RE (2019) Is Global Governance Fragmented, Polycentric, or Complex? The State of the Art of the Network Approach. International Studies Review. https://doi.org/10.1093/isr/viz052.
Klabbers J, Palombella G (2019) Introduction: Situating Inter-Legality. In: Klabbers J, Palombella G (eds) The Challenge of Inter-Legality. Cambridge University Press, Cambridge, pp 1–21.
Klabbers J, Peters A, Ulfstein G (2009) The Constitutionalization of International Law. Oxford University Press, Oxford.
Klabbers J (2007) Compliance Procedures. In: Bodansky D, Brunnée J, Hey E (eds) The Oxford Handbook of International Environmental Law. Oxford University Press, Oxford, p 996.
Klabbers J (2008) The Commodification of International Law. In: Ruiz Fabri H, Jouannet E, Tomkiewicz V (eds) Select Proceedings of the European Society of International Law: Volume 1 2006. Hart Publishing, Oxford, p 341.
Koskenniemi M (1992) Breach of Treaty or Non-Compliance? Reflections on the Enforcement of the Montreal Protocol. Yearbook of International Environmental Law 3:123–162.
Koskenniemi M (2007) Constitutionalism as Mindset: Reflections on Kantian Themes About International Law and Globalization. Theoretical Inquiries in Law 8:9.
Kulovesi K, Mehling M, Morgera E (2019) Global Environmental Law: Context and Theory, Challenge and Promise. Transnational Environmental Law 8:405–435. https://doi.org/10.1017/S2047102519000347.
Lloyd EA, Oreskes N, Seneviratne SI, Larson EJ (2021) Climate Scientists Set the Bar of Proof Too High. Climatic Change 165:55. https://doi.org/10.1007/s10584-021-03061-9.
Mai L (2020) (Transnational) Law for the Anthropocene: Revisiting Jessup's Move from 'What?' to 'How?' Transnational Legal Theory 11:105–120.
Montini M (2009) Procedural Guarantees in Non-Compliance Procedures. In: Treves T, Tanzi A, Pineschi L, Pitea C, Ragni C, Romanin Jacur F (eds) Non-Compliance Procedures and the Effectiveness of International Environmental Agreements. T.M.C. Asser Press, The Hague, pp 389–405.

Morgera E (2017) The ecosystem approach and the precautionary principle. In: Biodiversity and Nature Protection Law. Edward Elgar Publishing, pp 70–80.
Morgera E (2019) Under the Radar: The Role of Fair and Equitable Benefit-Sharing in Protecting and Realising Human Rights Connected to Natural Resources. International Journal of Human Rights 23:1098–1139. https://doi.org/10.1080/13642987.2019.1592161.
Nègre C (2010) Responsibility and International Environmental Law. In: Crawford J, Pellet A, Olleson S (eds) The Law of International Responsibility. OUP, Oxford, p 803.
Nollkaemper A (2008) Cluster-litigation in Cases of Transboundary Environmental Harm. In: Faure M, Ying S (eds) China and International Environmental Liability. Legal Remedies for Transboundary Pollution. Edward Elgar, Cheltenham, p 11.
Ohlhoff S (2003) Methoden der Konfliktbewältigung bei grenzüberschreitenden Umweltproblemen im Wandel. Überwindung der Grenzen herkömmlicher Streitbeilegung durch systeminterne Flexibilität und systemexterne Innovation. Springer, Heidelberg.
Philippopoulos-Mihalopoulos A (2011) Towards a Critical Environmental Law. In: Philippopoulos-Mihalopoulos A (ed) Law and Ecology. New Environmental Foundations. Routledge, Abingdon, pp 18–38.
Pickering J, Persson Å (2019) Democratising planetary boundaries: experts, social values and deliberative risk evaluation in Earth system governance. Journal of Environmental Policy and Planning 1:13. https://doi.org/10.1080/1523908X.2019.1661233.
Pineschi L (2019) Inter-Legality and the Protection of Marine Ecosystems. In: Klabbers J, Palombella G (eds) The Challenge of Inter-Legality. Cambridge University Press, Cambridge, pp 188–205.
Popper KR (1963) Conjectures and Refutations: The Growth of Scientific Knowledge. Routledge, Abingdon.
Röben V (2000) Institutional Developments under Modern International Environmental Agreements. Max Planck Yearbook of United Nations Law 4:363–443.
Romanin Jacur F (2009) Triggering Non-Compliance Procedures. In: Treves T, Tanzi A, Pineschi L, Pitea C, Ragni C, Romanin Jacur F (eds) Non-Compliance Procedures and Mechanisms and the Effectiveness of International Environmental Agreements. T.M.C. Asser Press, The Hague, pp 373–387.
Romano C (2000) The Peaceful Settlement of International Environmental Disputes: A Pragmatic Approach. Kluwer Law International, The Hague.
Samvel G (2020) Non-Judicial, Advisory, Yet Impactful? The Aarhus Convention Compliance Committee as a Gateway to Environmental Justice. Transnational Environmental Law 9:211–238. https://doi.org/10.1017/S2047102519000426.
Sand PH (2013) Enforcing CITES: The Rise and Fall of Trade Sanctions. Review of European, Comparative and International Environmental Law 22:251–263. https://doi.org/10.1111/reel.12037.
Scovazzi T (2001) State Responsibility for Environmental Harm. Yearbook of International Environmental Law 12:43.
Shany Y (2019) International Courts as Inter-Legality Hubs. In: Klabbers J, Palombella G (eds) The Challenge of Inter-Legality. Cambridge University Press, Cambridge, pp 319–338.
Simma B (1994) From Bilateralism to Community Interest in International Law. In: Collected Courses of the Academy of International Law 250. pp 229–384.
Sindico F, Mbengue MM, McKenzie K (2021) Climate Change Litigation and the Individual: An Overview. In: Sindico F, Mbengue MM (eds) Comparative Climate Change Litigation: Beyond the Usual Suspects. Springer Nature, pp 1–33.
Stephens T (2009) International Courts and Environmental Protection. Cambridge University Press, Cambridge.
Stevenson H, Dryzek JS (2012) The discursive democratisation of global climate governance. Environmental Politics 21:189–210. https://doi.org/10.1080/09644016.2012.651898.
Stevenson H, Dryzek JS (2014) Democratizing Global Climate Governance. Cambridge University Press, Cambridge.

Széll P (1995) The Development of Multilateral Mechanisms for Monitoring Compliance. In: Lang W (ed) Sustainable Development and International Law. Graham & Trotman/Martinus Nijhoff, London/ Dordrecht/Boston MA, pp 97–109.
Tabau AS, Maljean-Dubois S (2010) Non-compliance Mechanisms: Interaction between the Kyoto Protocol System and the European Union. European Journal of International Law 21:749–763.
Tams CJ (2005) Enforcing Obligations Erga Omnes in International Law. Cambridge University Press, Cambridge.
Treves T (2009) The Settlement of Disputes and Non-Compliance Procedures. In: Treves T, Tanzi A, Pineschi L, Pitea C, Ragni C, Romanin Jacur F (eds) Non-Compliance Procedures and Mechanisms and the Effectiveness of International Environmental Agreements. T.M.C. Asser Press, The Hague, pp 499–520.
Trouwborst A (2009) The Precautionary Principle and the Ecosystem Approach in International Law: Differences, Similarities and Linkages. Review of European Community & International Environmental Law 18:26–37. https://doi.org/10.1111/j.1467-9388.2009.00622.x.
Ulfstein G, Marauhn T, Zimmermann A (2007) Making Treaties Work. Human Rights, Environment and Arms Control. Cambridge University Press, Cambridge.
Voigt C (2016) The Compliance and Implementation Mechanism of the Paris Agreement. Review of European, Comparative and International Environmental Law 26:161–173.
Werksman J (1996) Compliance and Transition: Russia's Non-Compliance Tests the Ozone Regime. Zeitschrift für ausländisches öffentliches R und Völkerr 56:750–773.
Wettestad J (2007) Monitoring and Verification. In: Bodansky D, Brunnée J, Hey E (eds) The Oxford Handbook of International Environmental Law. Oxford University Press, Oxford, pp 974–994.
Wiersema A (2009) The New International Law-Makers? Conferences of the Parties to Multilateral Environmental Agreements. Michigan Journal of International Law 31:231–287.
Yang T, Percival R V (2009) The Emergence of Global Environmental Law. Ecology Law Quarterly 36:615–664.
Zheng X (2021) Empowering Indigenous Peoples and Local Communities: A Human Rights-Based Appraisal of the Compliance Mechanism of the Nagoya Protocol. Review of European, Comparative and International Environmental Law 30:61–72. https://doi.org/10.1111/reel.12343.

Antonio Cardesa-Salzmann Lecturer, University of Strathclyde, Law School. Strathclyde Centre for Environmental Law and Governance, Glasgow (Scotland)

Chapter 20
Climate Change Litigation: National Courts as Agents of International Law Development

Sarah Mead and Lucy Maxwell

Contents

Abstract Climate change presents the single greatest threat to humans and the natural world. International climate negotiations have so far proven unable to effectively address the crisis. The Paris Agreement, adopted in 2015, set a long-term goal of keeping global temperature rise 'well below 2 °C above pre-industrial levels' while pursuing efforts to limit it to 1.5 °C. The world is not, however, on track to meet this goal. Against this backdrop is a rise in climate change litigation at the national, regional and international level. This chapter focuses on the role of *national* courts in developing international law and protecting human rights and the global environment. Through the lens of national climate change litigation, in particular the *Urgenda* litigation in the Netherlands and the *Thomson* case in New Zealand, the chapter highlights that international courts and tribunals are by no means the only site

Both authors contributed equally to the chapter, and the views expressed are their own.

S. Mead (✉) · L. Maxwell
Senior Legal Associate, Climate Litigation Network, Urgenda Foundation, Zaandam, The Netherlands
e-mail: sarah.mead@urgenda.nl

L. Maxwell
e-mail: lucy.maxwell@urgenda.nl

E. Sobenes et al. (eds.), *The Environment Through the Lens of International Courts and Tribunals*, https://doi.org/10.1007/978-94-6265-507-2_20

of international law activity and evolution: indeed, in respect of international climate change law, national courts could be said to be at the forefront of international legal development.

Keywords Climate change · litigation · international law · national courts · United Nations Framework Convention on Climate Change · Paris Agreement · *Urgenda* · *Thomson v Minister for Climate Change Issues*

20.1 Introduction

Climate change presents the single greatest threat to humans and the natural world. International climate negotiations have so far proven unable to effectively to address the crisis. The Paris Agreement, adopted in 2015, set a long-term goal of keeping global temperature rise 'well below 2 °C above pre-industrial levels' while pursuing efforts to limit it to 1.5 °C.[1] The world is not, however, on track to meet this goal. Global warming is already more than 1 °C,[2] and States are 'nowhere close' to taking the level of action needed to fight global warming.[3] Against this backdrop is a rise in climate change litigation at the national, regional and international levels. International law frequently plays an important role in these legal proceedings, but international law is also likely to be impacted by such proceedings.

This chapter departs from the focus in the preceding chapters in this book on international courts and tribunals and looks instead at the role of *national* courts in developing international law and protecting the global environment through the lens of national climate change litigation. It highlights that international courts and tribunals are by no means the only site of international law activity and evolution: indeed, in respect of international climate change law, national courts can fairly be described as a 'key agent' of international legal development.[4]

Section 20.2 of this chapter briefly sets out the role of national courts as enforcers and developers of international law. Section 20.3 introduces the international legal framework on climate change and the concept of climate change litigation, charting its steady increase over the last decade and the reasons for this. Bringing these two strands together, Sect. 20.4 narrows in on how courts are engaging with international law in national-level climate change litigation with a focus on the *Urgenda* litigation

[1] Paris Agreement, 12 December 2015, UN Doc. FCCC/CP/2015/L.9, Annex, entered into force 4 November 2016, Article 2(1)(a).

[2] IPCC 2018, p. 6.

[3] UN Secretary-General Antonio Guterres, UN Climate Press Release on the launch of Initial NDC Synthesis Report prepared by the UNFCCC, 26 February 2021, UNFCCC. Available at https://unfccc.int/news/greater-climate-ambition-urged-as-initial-ndc-synthesis-report-is-published.

[4] Tzanakopoulos 2016a.

in the Netherlands[5] and the *Thomson* case in New Zealand.[6] We have selected these cases because the judgments consider the respective mitigation claims on the merits, engage with the international climate change treaty regime in their reasoning, and are not currently on appeal.[7] The conclusion then considers what effect national climate change litigation may have on international law more generally and its ability to protect the global environment.

20.2 National Courts and International Law

The relationship between national courts and international law has been subject to intense academic scrutiny.[8] While initially treated as belonging to distinct systems of law, national courts are now widely accepted as key actors in the international legal system.

20.2.1 How National Courts Engage with International Law

The expansion of international law into areas traditionally governed by national law has expanded the scope for national courts to engage with international law and thereby to contribute to international law development. Traditionally, international law concerned inter-State relations with minimal interference in States' internal affairs: international law norms were generally 'outward-looking'.[9] As international law has increasingly sought to regulate affairs that take place *within* the domestic legal order, there has been a corresponding rise in 'inward-looking' international norms.[10] This is particularly notable in relation to international human rights law

---

[5] District Court of The Hague, *Urgenda Foundation v The State of The Netherlands*, Judgement, 24 June 2015, ECLI:NL:RBDHA:2015:7196 (English translation); The Hague Court of Appeal, *Netherlands v Urgenda Foundation*, Judgment, 9 October 2018, ECLI:NL:GHDHA:2018:2610 (English translation); Netherlands Supreme Court, *State of the Netherlands (Ministry of Economic Affairs and Climate Policy) v Stichting Urgenda*, Judgment, 20 December 2019, ECLI:NL:HR:2019:2007 (English translation).

[6] New Zealand High Court, *Thomson v Minister for Climate Change*, Judgment, 2 November 2017, [2017] NZHC 733.

[7] See further Sect. 20.4 below.

[8] For instance, see Falk 1963; Benvenisti 1993; Knop 1999; Bahdi 2002; Benvenisti and Downs 2009; Roberts 2011; Tzanakopoulos 2016a and 2016b.

[9] Benvenisti and Downs 2009, p. 62; Tzanakopoulos 2016a, p. 5.

[10] If the relevant rule refers exclusively to State-to-State relations on the international plane, then they are described as 'outward-looking'. If, conversely, the international rule prescribes, proscribes, or enables certain conduct on the domestic plane, i.e., within the State's domestic jurisdiction, then the relevant rules can be termed 'inward-looking'. Tzanakopoulos 2016b. See also: Tzanakopoulos and Tams 2013.

which imposes obligations on States with respect to individuals within their jurisdiction, but is also the case with respect to international environmental law. The result is a greater role for international law in domestic litigation.[11] A related yet distinct phenomenon is the effect of 'judicial globalisation', i.e. the 'global conversation' taking place between judges from different jurisdictions—which leads to a cross-fertilisation of judicial reasoning across different countries and regions.[12]

How national courts engage with international law depends on a myriad of country-specific features. A distinction is often made between domestic legal systems that treat international law as automatically incorporated (monist), and those that treat international law as requiring transformation by way of a domestic act (dualist). In reality, however, there are an '"infinite variety" of constitutional set-ups regulating the reception of international law within the domestic legal order of any given State'.[13] This is compounded by 'a subsequent infinite variety' of means by which domestic courts engage with these rules, often towards softening or moderating the effect of these rules.[14] For instance, to blunt the effect of a system of transformation, it is common for national courts to interpret domestic law consistently with international law[15]—an approach which will be touched on in more detail below. In the other direction, national courts might employ the doctrine of non-justiciability to blunt the effect of a system of incorporation. This 'paradoxical counter-move', an ILA Report on the subject notes, 'refers precisely to the seemingly paradoxical moderation of the opposing main positions of incorporation and transformation, so that irrespective of the local constitutional set-up, blunting or moderating may lead to similar outcomes in differently internationally inclined domestic legal orders.'[16] While this makes categorisation difficult, it also suggests that the differences between monist and dualist systems may be more apparent than real. This reflects what was observed in a study on national courts and international environmental law by Bodansky and Brunnée of over two decades ago. In relation to the study, they noted that: '[o]verall, the reports strongly suggest that the implementation of international environmental law by national courts is far less influenced by a country's civil law or common law tradition or its 'monist' or 'dualist' stance than by various other factors', including judicial attitudes.[17]

[11] Tzanakopoulos 2016a, para 15. Note, however, that this may be more the case in some States than in others. The Report notes: 'A recent study by a member of this Study Group demonstrates that citations to domestic case law in international law textbooks and in judgments of many international courts and tribunals come overwhelmingly from Western liberal democratic States in general and from a handful of those States in particular.'

[12] Constantinides 2012, p. 267.

[13] Tzanakopoulos 2016a, para 16.

[14] Ibid.

[15] D'Aspremont 2012, p. 143. D'Aspremont explains: 'If international law is not the 'law of the land' because it has not been incorporated, it may still yield effect in the domestic legal order if domestic judges interpret national law by drawing on international law.'

[16] Tzanakopoulos 2016a, para 29.

[17] Bodansky and Brunnée 1998, pp. 14.

20.2.2 How National Courts Impact on International Law

> International law not only percolates down from the international to the domestic sphere, but it also bubbles up.[18]

National courts play a dual role from the perspective of international law. National courts enforce international law—a fact long acknowledged given the limitations of their international counterparts in this respect. But national courts are also recognised as functioning as 'agents of development' of international law.[19] It is common ground that domestic jurisprudence may constitute 'subsequent practice' relevant to the interpretation of treaty law,[20] or play a subsidiary role in determining the rules of international law as 'judicial decisions'.[21] More generally, though, domestic jurisprudence has a role to play in the development of custom.

Formally, international law perceives domestic law and the decisions of national courts as mere facts. The PCIJ has opined: 'From the standpoint of International Law and of the Court which is its organ, municipal laws are merely facts which express the will and constitute the activities of States, in the same manner as do [domestic] legal decisions or administrative measures.'[22]

Facts are however highly relevant in the development and evolution of international law.[23] In terms of custom, domestic judgments can be evidence of State practice and/or *opinio juris* which may support or counter the existence of a customary law norm.[24] While the effect is limited given that national courts represent the practice of only one organ of one State,[25] the adjudicative function of courts—which invites them to interpret international norms—sets them apart. As argued by D'Aspremont, every act of interpretation and application of the law is an act constitutive of the law to some extent.[26] Tzanakopolous thus concludes that national courts 'engage in some limited form of lawmaking' which 'takes the form of consolidating and fine-tuning rules of international law, many times in less-than obvious ways, and in triggering acquiescence or reaction when going beyond well-established rules (or interpretations of rules)'.[27]

---

[18] Roberts 2011, p. 62.

[19] Tzanakopoulos 2016a and 2016b. See also: Roberts 2011.

[20] Article 31(3)(b). This provision provides that 'any subsequent practice in the application of the treaty which establishes the agreement of the parties regarding its interpretation'.

[21] Statute of the International Court of Justice, 26 June 1945, entry into force 24 October 1945, Article 38(1)(d).

[22] PCIJ, *Case concerning certain German interests in Polish Upper Silesia (The Merits)*, Judgement, 25 May 1926, Series A No 7 (emphasis added).

[23] Tzanakopoulos 2016b. In terms of the sources of international law, see Article 38 of the ICJ Statute.

[24] Roberts 2011; O'Keefe 2013.

[25] Alebeek 2013, p. 563.

[26] D'Aspremont 2012; Tzanakopoulos 2016b, p. 223.

[27] Tzanakopoulos 2016b, p. 239.

This chapter therefore proceeds on the understanding that domestic courts act as 'agents of legal development' in terms of international law.[28] This is not to suggest that the interpretation and application by domestic courts of international law norms is necessarily consistent or useful in terms of clarifying the law: the inconsistent application of international law norms by national courts can give rise to uncertainty and stall development. Nevertheless, whether the role of domestic courts is clarifying or complicating, they are undoubtedly a relevant actor in the development of international law norms. This function of national courts is explored in more detail with reference to climate change litigation in the following sections.

20.3 International Law and Climate Change Litigation

> Litigation has arguably never been a more important tool to push policymakers and market participants to develop and implement effective means of climate change mitigation and adaption than it is today.[29]

This section first introduces the concept of climate change litigation, before turning to introduce the international climate change treaty regime, and the role of national courts in interpreting and, in some cases, enforcing States' obligations pursuant to that regime. The aim is to highlight why national courts serve as a key site of international law development in the context of national-level climate change litigation.

20.3.1 Climate Change Litigation

Climate change litigation is a heterogenous, relatively young, and rapidly growing field of litigation. It includes proceedings against States and corporations initiated by individuals and communities, non-profit organisations, corporations, and local and regional governments,[30] at the sub-national and national, regional,[31] and international levels.[32] Given the complex and wide-ranging causes and effects of climate

---

[28] Tzanakopoulos and Tams 2013, p. 536. The word 'agent' is used in a broad sense, denoting a capacity to influence processes, in this case: processes of legal development.

[29] Burger and Gundlach 2017, p. 8.

[30] See Setzer and Byrnes 2020.

[31] See the proceedings initiated by ten families against the European Union in General Court, *Carvalho and Others v Parliament and Council*, Order, 8 May 2019, Case No T-330/18, ECLI:EU:T:2019:324 and the proceedings initiated by Portuguese children against 33 Member States of the Council of Europe in September 2020 <https://youth4climatejustice.org/>.

[32] See e.g. the communications initiated by individuals and groups against States before UN human rights treaty bodies. There has been one climate-related decision issued to date with respect to States' non-refoulement obligations: HRC, *Ioane Teitiota v New Zealand*, 7 January 2020,

change, identifying what qualifies as 'climate change litigation' can be complicated. As explained by Osofsky and Peel, '[w]hile most commentators would agree that lawsuits in courts with climate change as their central focus are climate change litigation, the outer boundaries are harder to establish'.[33] In general, the literature has tended to adopt a broad definition. A 2017 Report of the United Nations Environment Programme (UNEP), for instance, defines 'climate change litigation' as 'cases brought before administrative, judicial and other investigatory bodies that raise issues of law or fact regarding the science of climate change and climate change mitigation and adaptation efforts'.[34]

As at May 2020, climate change litigation had been brought in 36 countries.[35] There are certain discernible trends in the litigation. First, there has been a geographic expansion in recent years.[36] The vast majority of cases to date have been brought in high-income countries—in particular the United States, Australia and throughout Europe. Climate change litigation in the Global South is however increasing.[37] Secondly, the nature of the claims is evolving. International human rights law, for instance, is playing an increasingly important role in climate change litigation.[38] As regards the parties to climate change litigation, governments are the defendant in the vast majority of cases (75%), while plaintiffs range from individuals, corporations or non-governmental organisations.[39]

Within the broad field of climate change litigation, there is a small but growing number of national-level climate change cases in which claimants have invoked international law and, specifically, international treaties pertaining to climate change (outlined below), to substantiate States' obligations under domestic law. These cases are all 'pro-regulatory' in nature, insofar as the litigants seek to *increase* the ambition of States with respect to climate change action.[40] We have categorised these cases as follows:

CCPR/C/127/D/2728/2016. See also the pending communication filed with the UN Committee on the Rights of the Child on 23 September 2019 *Sacchi et al v Argentina et al* (Communication to the Committee on the Rights of the Child). A communication has also been filed by Torres Strait Islanders in 2019 with the Human Rights Committee against the Australian government for alleged infringements of their rights under the ICCPR. See <https://ourislandsourhome.com.au/#about>.

33 Osofsky and Peel 2013, p. 213.

34 Burger and Gundlach 2017, p. 10.

35 Setzer and Byrnes 2020, p. 4.

36 Setzer and Byrnes 2020. See also: Setzer and Vanhala 2019; Burger and Gundlach 2017, pp. 25–26.

37 Ibid., p. 4.

38 Ibid., p. 14.

39 Ibid., p. 9.

40 There are also a small number of 'pro-regulatory' proceedings initiated against large fossil fuel companies at the national level. See Setzer and Byrnes 2020, p. 18. See also: Ganguly et al. 2018.

- Proceedings initiated against national governments in relation to their overall efforts to mitigate dangerous climate change, as illustrated by their national GHG emissions reduction trajectories or targets ('systemic mitigation cases');[41]
- Proceedings initiated against national or sub-national governments in relation to sector or project-specific decisions that are alleged to have significant consequences for the State's overall GHG emissions. This includes: the approval of fossil-fuel intensive projects;[42] and approval of new fossil fuel exploration[43] and exploitation[44] ('sector or project-specific mitigation cases'); and
- Proceedings against national governments in relation to their obligations to effectively adapt to climate change ('adaptation cases').[45]

Each category offers opportunities to examine national courts' engagement with international law. In this chapter, we focus on two cases falling into the 'systemic mitigation' category. In the cases considered, the national courts interpret, and in some instances enforce, States' legal obligations and commitments regarding climate change mitigation under international law.[46] The judgments issued thus offer a particularly rich case-study of national courts' engagement with, and development of, international law.

20.3.1.1 The International Climate Change Treaty Regime

International climate change law is a 'vast and complex web of principles, rules, regulations and institutions'.[47] The UN climate change treaty regime sits at its core, but international climate change law is not a self-contained regime: rather '[i]t is anchored in the general rules, principles, and law-making practices of public international law and international environmental law, and intersects with other fields of

---

[41] These cases are defined in Sect. 20.4 below.

[42] For example, UK Supreme Court, *R (on the application of Friends of the Earth Ltd and others) (Respondents) v Heathrow Airport Ltd (Appellant)*, Judgment, 16 December 2020, [2020] UKSC 52.

[43] For example, Supreme Court of Norway, *Natur og Ungdom et al v The Government of Norway (Arctic Oil)*, Judgment, 22 December 2020, Case No HR-2020-846-J.

[44] For example, Land and Environment Court of New South Wales, *Gloucester Resources Limited v Minister for Planning (Rocky Hill)*, Judgement, 8 February 2019, 2019 NSWLEC 7.

[45] For example, Lahore High Court, *Ashgar Leghari v Federation of Pakistan*, Order,4 April 2015, Case No WP No 255012015. To date, there are very few cases regarding States' obligations with respect to climate change adaptation.

[46] In some proceedings, which are not considered here, litigants have invoked international law, but the case has been struck out at the initial stages without consideration of international law. For example, US Court of Appeal for the Ninth Circuit, *Juliana v United States*, 17 January 2020, No 18-36082 SC No 6:15-cv-01517-AA. Alternatively, the court has upheld the claim but has not referred to international law. For example, Supreme Court of Ireland, *Friends of the Irish Environment CLG v The Government of Ireland (Irish Climate Case)*, Judgment, 15 November 2020, Appeal No. 2015/19.

[47] Bodansky et al. 2017a, p. 10. See also Chapter 1.

international law, including most notably human rights, migration, and trade law.'[48] Canvasing the breadth of international climate change law is beyond the scope of this chapter. However, in order to understand why national courts play a particularly significant role in the development of this area of law, an introduction to the climate change treaty regime is necessary.

The main treaty instruments in the field of climate change are the UN Framework Convention on Climate Change (UNFCCC or the Convention),[49] the Kyoto Protocol,[50] and the Paris Agreement (together referred to as 'the climate change treaty regime'). Each treaty is a legally binding instrument, but provisions within these instruments 'vary in their legal force, ranging from those that merely provide context or narrative to those that establish legal obligations'.[51] Further, as will be shown, these treaties have distinctly 'inward-looking' provisions[52]—in particular the Paris Agreement, which make them ripe for national-level litigation.

The UNFCCC provides the framework for international cooperation to combat climate change. All States are party to the Convention.[53] The ultimate objective of the Convention 'is to achieve … [the] stabilization of [GHG] concentrations in the atmosphere at a level that would prevent dangerous anthropogenic interference with the climate system'.[54] The Convention provides a set of principles to guide the action of State Parties towards achieving this objective.[55] These include: that Parties should protect the climate system for future generations on the basis of equity and consistent with States' common but differentiated responsibilities and respective capabilities (CBDR-RC); the leading role of developed countries in combating climate change; and the need to adopt measures which are 'precautionary'.[56] The Convention sets a range of commitments for all State Parties towards achieving its objective.[57] In

[48] Bodansky et al. 2017a, p. 355.

[49] United Nations Framework Convention on Climate Change, 1 July 1992, 1771 UNTS 107, entered into force 21 March 1994 (UNFCCC).

[50] Kyoto Protocol to the United Nations Framework Convention on Climate Change, 12 March 1998, 2303 UNTS 162; entered into force 16 February 2005. The Kyoto Protocol set internationally binding targets for developed country parties for the period 1990–2012 to reduce GHG emissions. The Doha Amendment, which extended the Protocol, only passed into force on 31 December 2020.

[51] Bodansky et al. 2017a, pp. 17–19. The authors contend that 'legal bindingness' is a 'recurring theme' of the UN climate regime, reasoning that '[t]he potentially high costs of climate change action, combined with the deeply discordant political context in which the climate regime has evolved, have led to considerable innovation in developing legal instruments and provisions of varying degrees of normative force' (footnotes not included).

[52] See Sect. 20.2.1.

[53] As well as the State of Palestine, Niue, Cook Islands and the European Union (197 parties in total). See UNFCCC– Status of Ratification <https://treaties.un.org/Pages/ViewDetailsIII.aspx?src=IND&mtdsg_no=XXVII-7&chapter=27&Temp=mtdsg3&clang=_en> (accessed 1 November 2020).

[54] UNFCCC, above n 49, Article 2.

[55] Ibid., Article 3.

[56] Ibid.

[57] Ibid., Article 4. In particular, Article 4(2)(b) provides that developed countries will communicate policies and measures 'with the aim of returning individually or jointly to their 1990 levels

addition, each developed country Party is required to 'adopt national policies and take corresponding measures on the mitigation of climate change by limiting its anthropogenic emissions of [GHG] and protecting and enhancing [GHG] sinks and reservoirs'.[58]

Building on the Convention, the Kyoto Protocol created internationally binding mitigation targets.[59] The Protocol committed developed country Parties, as a group, to reduce GHG emissions by 'at least 5 per cent below 1990 levels in the commitment period 2008 to 2012'—with individual Parties agreeing to individualised binding targets.[60] In 2012, developed country Parties agreed to undertake new commitments under the Protocol for a second commitment period (2013–2020) by way of the Doha Amendment.[61] This Amendment however only received the requisite number of parties to pass into force in October 2020.[62]

The Paris Agreement, adopted in 2015, is the most recent instalment in the climate treaty regime. Its stated purpose is to enhance the implementation of the UNFCCC and to hold 'the increase in the global average temperature to well below 2 °C above pre-industrial levels and pursu[e] efforts to limit the temperature increase to 1.5 °C above pre-industrial levels'.[63] In order to achieve this long-term temperature goal, State Parties 'aim to reach global peaking of [GHG] emissions as soon as possible', and net zero emissions in the second half of the century 'on the basis of equity', among other principles.[64] The Paris Agreement expands upon a number of the key principles contained in the UNFCCC. The Agreement is 'guided by' the principle of equity and CBDR-RC 'in the light of different national circumstances',[65] and State Parties should 'respect, promote and consider their respective obligations on human rights' when taking action to address climate change.[66] Developed country Parties should also 'continue taking the lead by undertaking economy-wide absolute emission reduction targets' and by 'enhancing their mitigation efforts'.[67]

In terms of States' mitigation obligations, the Paris Agreement has been described as adopting a 'bottom-up' approach compared with the Kyoto Protocol's 'top-down'

---

these anthropogenic emissions of carbon dioxide and other greenhouse gases not controlled by the Montreal Protocol.'

[58] Ibid., Article 4(2)(a). 'Developed countries' refers to those countries listed in Annex 1 of the Convention—i.e. OECD countries and 'countries that are undergoing the process of transition to a market economy' (former Soviet and Socialist countries).

[59] Kyoto Protocol, above n 50, Article 3.

[60] Ibid., Article 3(1).

[61] *Doha Amendment to the Kyoto Protocol,* adopted 8 December 2012, CN.718.2012. TREATIES-XXVII.7.c.

[62] See https://unfccc.int/process/the-kyoto-protocol/the-doha-amendment Accessed 1 November 2020.

[63] Paris Agreement, above n 1, Article 2(1).

[64] Ibid., Article 4(1).

[65] Ibid., Preamble.

[66] Ibid.

[67] Ibid., Article 4(4).

approach of mandated emissions reduction targets for developed country Parties.[68] Under the Agreement, State Parties commit to adopt measures at the national level to achieve the stated 'purpose' of the Agreement, as defined in Article 2.[69] Most notably, all Parties are required to undertake and communicate nationally determined contributions (NDCs) reflecting their 'highest possible ambition' towards achieving the Agreement's objectives, to be updated in a progressive fashion every five years.[70] All Parties are also to 'pursue domestic mitigation measures' with the aim of achieving their NDCs.[71] Coupled with a comprehensive information sharing and transparency scheme and various review mechanisms, the Paris Agreement is designed to *guide* State Parties to set GHG emission reduction targets and other measures that will collectively achieve the long-term temperature goal. The Agreement does not, however, specify individual or collective GHG emissions reduction targets.

A key feature of the Paris Agreement is the existence of a 'dynamic mix' of treaty obligations with variations in legal bindingness.[72] There are provisions that can be characterised as *hard*:[73] i.e. those that are framed in mandatory terms ('shall') for individual parties with clear wording and no qualifiers, thereby creating rights and obligations that can be assessed for non-compliance (such as the obligation to set an NDC and to pursue domestic mitigation measures (Article 4(2)). Conversely, there are provisions which can be characterised as *soft*: i.e. norms which set standards, but are couched in discretionary or advisory wording ('should' or 'encourage'), or signal an expectation rather than an obligation ('will') (such as the obligation for developed countries to 'take the lead' (Article 4(4)). There is no clear line between these categories:each provision 'contains a unique blend of elements, and thus occupies its own place in the spectrum of legal character'.[74]

The precise legal status of Parties' obligations and commitments under the international climate change treaty regime has been the subject of extensive academic, political and diplomatic debate and consideration.[75] To date, this focus has not necessarily been mirrored in national courts' engagement with the treaty regime in systemic mitigation cases, as discussed in Sect. 20.4.

[68] Bodansky et al. 2017b, p. 213.

[69] Paris Agreement, above n 1, Article 3.

[70] Ibid., Article 4(2), (3) and (9).

[71] Ibid., Article 4(2).

[72] Bodansky et al. 2017b, p. 17; Rajamani 2017, p. 2.

[73] Bodansky et al. 2017b, p. 213.

[74] Ibid., pp. 213–214.

[75] Ibid., p. 17. The authors note one of the recurring themes in international climate change law is the legal bindingness, or otherwise, of its obligations.

20.3.2 *Role of National Courts in Interpreting, and Enforcing, the International Climate Change Treaty Regime*

National courts have assumed a particularly prominent role in interpreting the international climate change treaty regime. This is primarily due to 'nature of the beast'—climate change is inherently global and extremely urgent. Several features of the international climate change treaty regime, and international law in general, further contribute to this enhanced role for national courts.

First, the nature of climate change as an urgent global problem and one that raises novel questions of legal responsibility renders international law and practice a logical source of guidance and potential solutions for both litigants and national courts.[76] In this context, litigants and courts tend to look to international and comparative foreign jurisprudence for guidance in climate change cases; to seek inspiration as to how to approach a problem they have usually not been confronted with before.

Secondly, the 'bottom up' structure of States' mitigation obligations under the Paris Agreement (whereby contributions are 'nationally determined') also offers a distinct opportunity for national courts to interpret, and enforce, such obligations. In this respect, Wegener refers to the 'discernible domestic turn within the current international framework of climate change law and governance'.[77] He explains:

> Although the Paris Agreement does not contain substantive provisions comparable with the mitigation provisions of the Kyoto Protocol, it *nonetheless sets up a normative architecture of internationally agreed standards and expectations*. These are in need of translation into domestic governance and, finally, domestic action. While this may be primarily a task for legislatures, domestic courts can contribute by 'holding their governments to account, and … ensuring that … commitments are given practical and enforceable effect'. Rather abstract provisions, such as the collective temperature goal, which are not directly justiciable, are given practical effect when invoked in domestic courts. … Moreover, by referring to the non-binding standards set by the Paris Agreement and NDCs, national courts help to strengthen the legitimacy of those standards.[78]

Thirdly, litigants are also encouraged to turn to national courts owing to well-documented legal and political barriers to the effective utilisation of dispute resolution mechanisms at the international level. Chief among these are the State-based and consent-based nature of international law, with corresponding restrictions on the

[76] As noted in the *Urgenda* decision of the Supreme Court: '*Partly in view of the serious consequences of dangerous climate change* mentioned above in 4.2, it is not possible to accept the defence that a state does not have to take responsibility because other countries do not comply with their partial responsibility… If, on the other hand, this defence is excluded, then each country can be effectively held accountable for its share of emissions and all countries are most likely to make an effective contribution, in accordance with the principles set out in the Preamble of the UN Climate Convention cited above,' para 5.7.1 (emphasis added). See also paras 5.8 and 8.3.4.

[77] Wegener 2020, p. 18.

[78] Wegener 2020, p. 35 (emphasis added).

jurisdiction of international courts and tribunals.[79] This situation can be contrasted with the situation at the national level, where the consent of the parties is for the most part immaterial in determining whether the court has jurisdiction to hear the case. In addition, in proceedings seeking to enforce a State's obligations under international or regional human rights treaties, there is the general rule that requires claimants to exhaust local remedies before pursuing international remedies, which usually means having recourse to national courts first.[80]

Finally, there are also distinct benefits to interpreting and enforcing States' treaty obligations at the national level. The bindingness of national determinations and the relative expeditiousness of such proceedings in many jurisdictions is beneficial, especially given the urgency of the climate crisis. The almost universal ratification of the UNFCCC and the Paris Agreement also offers litigants, and judges, at the national level, the ability to engage in a 'global conversation' across jurisdictions regarding the interpretation of States' obligations under the climate change treaty regime.

20.4 National Courts and Climate Change Litigation: Engagement and Development

To assess how national courts are engaging with international law, this section turns to analysing the judgments in two 'systemic mitigation' cases in the Netherlands and New Zealand.

Identifying trends in national courts' approach to international law in any field is a complex undertaking given the multitude of country-specific features that influence a court's approach. In the case of climate change litigation, this exercise is rendered more complex owing to the nascent development of such jurisprudence, the small number of decided cases and the sheer diversity of national-level climate change cases. With this in mind, we analyse judgments issued in the *Urgenda* case in the Netherlands, focusing on the decision of the Dutch Supreme Court in late 2019, and the *Thomson* case in New Zealand issued by a court of first instance in 2017. We have selected these cases because the judgments consider the 'systemic mitigation'

---

[79] For an account of the barriers that face litigants—whether individuals, communities or States—in utilising international dispute resolution mechanisms to pursue responsibility in the context of climate change, see Bodansky et al. 2017a, pp. 288–289. The authors note at p. 289: '[g]iven the weaknesses of international dispute settlement procedures – in particular, the lack in most cases of compulsory jurisdiction or enforcement authority – international adjudication is unlikely to provide effective relief, either in reducing emissions or compensating victims.' See also: Verheyen and Zengerling 2016, p. 429: 'The main constraints for climate change litigation before the ICJ are the narrow access provisions—only States may be parties in contentious proceedings—and the limited willingness of States to accept the ICJ's jurisdiction or bring cases before the ICJ on a case- by-case basis'.

[80] There are exceptions. For example, see the argument made by the claimants in the recent communication filed with the UN Committee on the Rights of the Child against five State Parties to the UN Convention on the Rights of the Child (p. 91 of the CRC Complaint *Sacchi et al v Argentina et al*).

claim on the merits, engage with the international climate change treaty regime in their reasoning (to a greater or lesser extent), and are not currently on appeal.[81] Since the Dutch Supreme Court decision in *Urgenda* in late 2019, there has been a number of significant national judgments in other 'systemic mitigation' cases, but the courts' treatment of international law in the *Urgenda* and *Thomson* case remains instructive for the reasons identified.

In both cases, the claimants alleged that the State's efforts to mitigate dangerous climate change were unlawful on the basis (among others) that the country's projected GHG emissions were *not* in line with the emissions reductions required of developed countries to prevent dangerous climate change, which was defined as a global temperature increase of more than 2 °C. In each case, the claimants relied upon the State's commitments and obligations under the UNFCCC and, in *Thomson* (due to the timing of the filing of the case), the Paris Agreement. To demonstrate that the State's efforts to mitigate climate change were inadequate to prevent dangerous climate change, the claimants drew upon findings from the IPCC's Fourth Assessment Report (AR4) (2007) and decisions of the Conference of the Parties (COP) to the UNFCCC.

There are, however, some important differences in the legal architecture of the two claims. The Netherlands is a civil law jurisdiction, with an approach to international law that tends towards monism, while New Zealand is a common-law jurisdiction with a dualist approach. The legal bases of the claims are also distinct: the *Urgenda* case concerned alleged violations of rights protected in the European Convention on Human Rights (ECHR), and a breach of the State's duty of care in tort law. This can be contrasted with the *Thomson* case, which was a judicial review claim based on traditional public law grounds. These differences reflect the diversity of ongoing national-level climate change litigation, which are advanced on a range of legal bases in jurisdictions around the world.[82]

---

[81] As at June 2021, national courts have issued final judgments in several 'systemic mitigation' cases, ranging from courts of first instance to apex courts. They include: German Federal Constitutional Court (apex court), *Neubauer and Others v Germany*, Order of the First Senate of 24 March 2021, 1 BvR 96/20, 1 BvR 78/20, 1 BvR 288/20, 1 BvR 96/20, 1 BvR 78/20; Council of State (apex court), *Commune de Grande-Synthe v France*, Judgment, 19 November 2020, Case No 427301; Administrative Court of Paris, *Notre Affaire à Tous and Others v France*, Judgment, 3 February 2021, N°1904967, 1904968, 1904972, 1904976/4-1; Court of First Instance of Brussels, *VZW Klimaatzaak v Kingdom of Belgium & Others,* Judgment, 17 June 2021; Supreme Court of Ireland (apex court), *Friends of the Irish Environment CLG v The Government of Ireland (Irish Climate Case)*, above n 46; Colombian Supreme Court (apex court), *Future Generations v Ministry of the Environment and Others "Demanda Generaciones Futuras v Minambiente"*, Judgment, 4 April 2018, Case No 11001 22 03 000 2018 00319 00. For a full list, see Maxwell et al. 2022 (forthcoming).

[82] For an overview of systemic mitigation cases at the national-level, see: https://www.urgenda.nl/en/themas/climate-case/global-climate-litigation/.

20.4.1 The Urgenda Decisions (2015–2019) (The Netherlands)

The decisions of the Dutch courts in *Urgenda* represent, to date, the unequivocal 'high point' of national courts' engagement with, and development of, international climate change law. In three successive judgments, the Dutch courts determined that the State is required to reduce the country's GHG emissions by at least 25% by 2020 against 1990 levels. It was the first case globally in which a court ordered a State to reduce its GHG emissions by an absolute minimum amount based on its domestic legal obligations. While the basis of the District Court's decision differed from that of the higher courts, each court drew on international law (including soft law) and climate science to inform the content of the State's obligations under Dutch tort law and its positive obligations to protect the rights to life, and to private and family life, under Articles 2 and 8 of the ECHR, a regional human rights treaty.

The *Urgenda* case was initiated in 2013 by the Urgenda Foundation, a Dutch sustainability NGO and 886 Dutch citizens. The claimants alleged that the State's failure to take greater steps to reduce the country's GHG emissions by 2020 was unlawful. The claimants sought declaratory relief and a mandatory order that the State reduce its GHG emissions by 40%, or in the alternative by at least 25%, by 2020 against 1990 levels.

In 2015, the District Court of the Hague ruled in favour of Urgenda. It found that the Government had a legal duty to protect its citizens from dangerous levels of climate change pursuant to its duty of care under the tort of hazardous negligence, and ordered the Government to reduce Dutch emissions by 25% compared to 1990 levels by 2020. The District Court rejected the claimants' reliance on the ECHR on the basis that Urgenda, as an NGO, did not meet the 'victim' status requirement for standing under Article 34 of the ECHR.

In reaching its decision regarding the State's tortious duty of care to prevent dangerous climate change, the District Court engaged closely with the State's obligations and commitments under international climate change law, including principles of international environmental law contained therein and decisions taken by the COP to the UNFCCC. Specifically, the District Court drew on such materials pursuant to what it termed the 'reflex effect' of international law in domestic law.[83] This is a well-established principle of Dutch law—and common to other jurisdictions—by which courts *must* interpret the State's duties under national law in a manner, so far as is possible, that is consistent with its international law obligations.[84]

The District Court determined that while it was not possible, under Dutch constitutional law,[85] to *directly* enforce the State's obligations under the UNFCCC or the

---

[83] District Court of The Hague, *Urgenda Foundation v The State of The Netherlands*, above n 5, para 4.43.

[84] Ibid.

[85] The Court indicated that, under Dutch constitutional law, treaties and principles of international law are *not* directly enforceable against the State by individuals unless the instrument is 'binding on all persons' and that this test was not satisfied in the case of the UNFCCC at para 4.42. See

'no harm' principle of international law, it was appropriate to have regard to such sources in determining the existence and scope of the State's duty of care in tort pursuant to the 'reflex effect'. The Court reasoned that the duty of care in tort is an 'open-textured' norm that encompasses the concept of 'reasonableness', and the State's duties must be interpreted in a manner, so far as is possible, that is consistent with its 'international-law obligations'.[86] The District Court interpreted the concept of 'international-law obligations' broadly, encompassing non-binding obligations and principles of international environmental law contained in the UNFCCC. It held that the 'objectives and principles' contained in Articles 2 and 3 UNFCCC 'determine to a great extent the framework for and the manner in which the State exercises its powers'[87] and 'limi[t]' the State's 'discretion' with respect to its approach to climate change mitigation.[88] The Court referred to the State's 'responsibility'[89] and 'commitment'[90] under the UNFCCC, and referred extensively to the principles of CBDR-RC,[91] intergenerational equity[92] and the precautionary principle[93] in determining the scope of the State's duty to mitigate climate change under tort law.

The State appealed the decision, and Urgenda filed a cross-appeal with respect to the ECHR claim. In late 2018, the Court of Appeal upheld the decision of the District Court, while also allowing Urgenda's cross-appeal.[94] Importantly, the Court of Appeal accepted that Urgenda was permitted to rely upon the ECHR, and premised the State's obligation to reduce GHG emissions squarely on its positive obligations to protect the rights to life, and to private and family life, under Articles 2 and 8 respectively, of the ECHR.

The State appealed again. In September 2019, the Supreme Court's independent legal advisers (the Advocate-General and deputy Procurator-General) issued a lengthy Advisory Opinion recommending that the Supreme Court uphold the Court

---

Constitution of the Kingdom of the Netherlands, Article 93: "Provisions of treaties and of resolutions by international institutions which may be binding on all persons by virtue of their contents shall become binding after they have been published."

86 District Court of The Hague, *Urgenda Foundation v The State of The Netherlands*, above n 5, para 4.43.

87 Ibid., para 4.63.

88 Ibid., para 4.76.

89 See e.g. ibid., para 4.66: 'when it became a signatory to the UN Climate Change Convention and the Kyoto Protocol, the State expressly accepted *its responsibility* for the national emission level and in this context accepted the obligation to reduce this emission level as much as needed to prevent dangerous climate change' (emphasis added);

90 See e.g. ibid., para 4.79: 'in view of a fair distribution the Netherlands, like the other Annex I countries, has taken the lead in taking mitigation measures and has therefore *committed to* a more than proportionate [sic] contribution to reduction.'

91 See e.g. ibid., para 4.79.

92 See e.g. ibid., para 4.57.

93 See e.g. ibid., para 4.58. The precautionary principle was particularly significant in the Court's determination that the State has a duty of care to reduce GHG emissions in the short-term in order to mitigate climate change (see paras 4.64, 4.65).

94 The Court of Appeal did not, however, overrule the District Court's ruling with respect to the duty of care in tort.

of Appeal's ruling.[95] In December 2019, the Supreme Court of the Netherlands once again affirmed the order of the District Court, along with the Court of Appeal's reasoning with respect to the State's obligations under the ECHR. In so doing, the Supreme Court expanded upon the lower courts' engagement with international law: whereas the District Court interpreted the State's tortious duty of care in light of its 'international-law obligations' pursuant to the 'reflex effect', the Supreme Court, like the Court of Appeal, drew upon international law based on an articulated approach to the interpretation of the ECHR as a treaty, by reference to existing jurisprudence of the European Court of Human Rights (ECtHR).[96]

The Supreme Court determined, consistent with ECtHR jurisprudence, that it was required to interpret the ECHR so as to render its provisions 'practical and effective',[97] in light of its object and purpose as a treaty to protect individual human beings.[98] The Supreme Court determined that it 'must … take into account … relevant rules of international law', pursuant to Articles 31(1) and 31(3)(c) of the Vienna Convention on the Law of Treaties (VCLT).[99] The Court's approach to the interpretation of the ECHR thus included consideration of the State's non-binding commitments under the UNFCCC and soft law sources such as COP decisions. This was consistent with the view expressed in the Advisory Opinion prepared for the Supreme Court that, although soft law instruments are 'not legally binding in themselves, significance is increasingly attributed to them in the implementation of generally formulated obligations under international law and, by extension, in the implementation of open standards in national law'.[100]

Related to this is the 'common ground' method of interpretation to the ECHR, which has been developed by the ECtHR.[101] Referring to ECtHR jurisprudence, the Supreme Court determined that it was *required* to take into account instruments of

---

[95] Supreme Court of the Netherlands, Press Release (online, 13 September 2019) https://www.rechtspraak.nl/Organisatie-en-contact/Organisatie/Hoge-Raad-der-Nederlanden/Nieuws/Paginas/Advice-to-the-Supreme-Court-Court-of-Appeal-judgement-in-the-climate-case-Urgenda-can-be-upheld.aspx".

[96] See Netherlands Supreme Court, *State of the Netherlands (Ministry of Economic Affairs and Climate Policy) v Stichting Urgenda*, above n 5, paras 5.4.1–5.5.3.

[97] Ibid., para 5.4.1.

[98] See Footnote 97.

[99] Ibid., para 5.4.2. Citing ECtHR, *Nada v Switzerland*, Judgement, 12 September 2012 App No 10593/08.

[100] Netherlands Supreme Court, *State of the Netherlands (Ministry of Economic Affairs and Climate Policy) v Stichting Urgenda*, above n 5, 'Advisory Opinion on Cassation Appeal of the Procurator General in the Matter between the Netherlands v Urgenda' (Hoge Raad 2019) ECLI:NL:PHR:2019:1026, No. 19/00135, see para 2.31-2.33 regarding the role of soft law. Climate change is cited as an area of law in which soft law has often developed into hard law over the years in what is described as process of 'crystallization' of enforceable obligations, para 2.32.

[101] See Netherlands Supreme Court, *State of the Netherlands (Ministry of Economic Affairs and Climate Policy) v Stichting Urgenda*, above n 5, paras 5.4.1–5.4.3 and 6.3. Regarding the requirement to employ the common ground method, see paras. 5.4.2 and 5.8. For application of the method to the facts, see paras 7.2.1–7.2.11, in particular para 7.2.11.

international law other than the ECHR and State practice thereby,[102] as well as 'scientific insights and generally accepted standards'.[103] The 'common ground' method of interpretation was particularly important to the Supreme Court's determination of the State's 'minimum fair share' of emissions reductions, as outlined below.[104] As explained in the Advisory Opinion:

> The common ground method is somewhat comparable to the reflex effect that national courts, in implementing open standards into national law, can attribute to treaty provisions and 'soft law' that have no direct effect. This explains why the Court of Appeal in its contested judgment reached the same conclusion on the basis of Articles 2 and 8 ECHR as the District Court did on the basis of Article 6:162 [Dutch Civil Code]: for the concrete implementation of the reduction obligation, the District Court and the Court of Appeal sought to draw on the same climatological insights, objectives of international climate policy and principles of international law.[105]

The difference in approach (reflex effect versus common ground) reflects the different bases for the courts' judgments: while the District Court was concerned with interpreting domestic law standards and thus applied the reflex effect, the Supreme Court was tasked with interpreting the ECHR—a regional treaty, hence applying the 'common ground' approach.[106]

The Supreme Court drew upon international law in a number of stages in its judgment. The Supreme Court applied the precautionary principle in determining that the threshold test for the State's positive obligations under the ECHR was satisfied. The Court affirmed the Court of Appeal's determination that climate change poses a sufficiently 'real' and foreseeable risk of harm under Articles 2 and 8 ECHR, which triggers the State's obligations to take reasonable and adequate measures. The Court determined that this test was satisfied notwithstanding the existence of some uncertainty regarding the timing, nature and extent of the harm that climate change will cause in the Netherlands:[107]

> The fact that this risk will only be able to materialise a few decades from now and that it will not impact specific persons or a specific group of persons but large parts of the population does not mean—contrary to the State's assertions—that Articles 2 and 8 ECHR offer no protection from this threat [...]. *This is consistent with the precautionary principle* .... The

[102] Ibid., para 5.4.2.

[103] Ibid., ECtHR, *Demir and Baykara/Turkey*, Judgement, 12 November 2008, App No 34503/97, which referred to: 'The consensus emerging from specialized international instruments and from the practice of contracting States may constitute a relevant consideration for the Court when it interprets the provisions of the Convention in specific cases.'

[104] See Netherlands Supreme Court, *State of the Netherlands (Ministry of Economic Affairs and Climate Policy) v Stichting Urgenda*, above n 5, para 7.2.11.

[105] 'Advisory Opinion on Cassation Appeal of the Procurator General in the Matter between the Netherlands v Urgenda' (Hoge Raad 2019) ECLI:NL:PHR:2019:1026, No. 19/00135 para 2.72. Regarding the reflex effect, see para 2.30.

[106] The Supreme Court judgment makes no reference to the reflex effect, but rather applies the common ground approach as developed in ECtHR jurisprudence.

[107] Netherlands Supreme Court, *State of the Netherlands (Ministry of Economic Affairs and Climate Policy) v Stichting Urgenda*, above n 5, para 5.3.2.

> mere existence of a sufficiently genuine possibility that this risk will materialise means that suitable measures must be taken.[108]

The Court also invoked the principle of due diligence—which arises in both human rights law and in international environmental law—as part of inquiring into 'whether the measures taken by a State are reasonable and appropriate', 'consistent' and undertaken 'in a timely manner'.[109]

Having satisfied the threshold test, the Supreme Court indicated that the State was required to 'take appropriate measures against the threat of dangerous climate change' under Articles 2 and 8 ECHR.[110] To determine what constituted 'appropriate measures' to prevent climate change, the Supreme Court drew upon various principles in international law. First, the Court derived the State's *individual* responsibility to mitigate climate change from its binding obligations and non-binding commitments under the UNFCCC, the 'no harm' principle contained therein, and principles of proportionate liability under international and national law. Secondly, the Court drew upon the provisions of the UNFCCC and the Paris Agreement to formulate the State's duty to contribute its *'fair share'* of global emissions reductions.[111]

The Supreme Court articulated the individual responsibility of the Netherlands as obliging it 'to do "its part" in order to prevent dangerous climate change, even if it is a global problem.'[112] The Court indicated that this conclusion was 'based on' a number of grounds,[113] including principally the UNFCCC, which it described as follows:

> The UNFCCC is based on the idea that climate change is a global problem that needs to be solved globally. Where emissions of greenhouse gases take place from the territories of all countries and all countries are affected, measures will have to be taken by all countries. Therefore, all countries will have to do the necessary.[114]

The Supreme Court referred to the State's binding obligation under Article 4 of the UNFCCC, as well as the principles of CBDR-RC, intergenerational equity and the precautionary principle in Article 3, and determined that '[i]t follows from these provisions that each State has *an obligation* to take the necessary measures in accordance with its specific responsibilities and possibilities'.[115]

The Court indicated that this individual obligation to mitigate climate change 'corresponds to' the 'no harm' principle, as contained in both the preamble to the UNFCCC and under general international law:

> This understanding corresponds to what is commonly referred to as the 'no harm principle', a generally accepted principle of international law which entails that countries must not cause

[108] Ibid., para 5.6.2 (emphasis added).

[109] See ibid., para 5.3.3. See also para 6.5.

[110] Ibid., para 5.9.1.

[111] See ibid., paras 6.3 and 6.5 on the 'fair share'.

[112] Ibid., para 5.7.1.

[113] See Footnote 112.

[114] Ibid., para 5.7.2.

[115] Ibid., para 5.7.3 (emphasis added).

> each other harm. This is also referred to in the preamble to the UNFCCC … . Countries can be called to account for the duty arising from this principle. Applied to greenhouse gas emissions, this means that they can be called upon to make their contribution to reducing greenhouse gas emissions. This approach justifies partial responsibility: each country is responsible for its part and can therefore be called to account in that respect.[116]

The Court also introduced the notion that a State's individual contribution to climate change mitigation informs its 'partial responsibility' for the problem. The Court elaborated on this by referring to bodies of law on proportionate liability, including the International Law Commission's Draft Articles on Responsibility of States for Internationally Wrongful Acts (ARSIWA).[117] The Court indicated explicitly that a State's 'past emissions' are relevant to its current obligations to mitigate climate change:

> It is true that Article 3(1) UNFCCC [the principle of CBDR-RC]… entails that the distribution of the measures to be taken against climate change must not be based solely on the basis of responsibility for past emissions by a country, and that consideration must also be given to the possibilities for countries to reduce their emissions. But that does not detract from the fact that the underlying principle of these widely accepted rules is always that, in short, 'partial fault' also justifies partial responsibility.[118]

On the basis of the State's individual responsibility to mitigate climate change, and 'in view of the serious consequences of dangerous climate change',[119] the Court rejected the State's arguments that its contribution to global emissions was negligible, emphasising the detrimental impact on global efforts to combat climate change if such a defence were accepted and the need to provide an effective remedy pursuant to Article 13 of the ECHR (right to an effective remedy).[120]

The Court's next significant engagement with, and contribution to, international law was in its 'concretisation' of the State's positive obligations under Articles 2 and 8 ECHR regarding the action required to prevent dangerous climate change.[121] The Court articulated its task as being to determine 'whether the measures taken by the State are too little in view of what is clearly the lower limit of its share in the measures to be taken worldwide against dangerous climate change'.[122] To determine what constitutes the 'lower limit' of State action to reduce GHG emissions, the Court considered whether there existed 'agreements and/or consensus', as evidenced by 'the widely supported view of states and international organisations' and 'based on the insights of climate science'.[123]

---

116 Ibid., para 5.7.5.

117 Ibid., para 5.7.6: The Court explains that under the ARSIWA, 'the responsibility of each participating State is determined individually, on the basis of its own conduct and by reference to its own international obligations.'

118 Ibid., para 5.7.6.

119 Ibid., para 5.7.7.

120 Ibid., paras 5.7.7–5.7.9.

121 See Ferreira 2016.

122 Netherlands Supreme Court, *State of the Netherlands (Ministry of Economic Affairs and Climate Policy) v Stichting Urgenda*, above n 5, para 6.3.

123 Ibid., para 6.3.

In addressing this question, the Court considered whether there exists '*sufficient objective grounds from which a concrete standard can be derived*' regarding the action required of the State.[124] Relevant in this regard was evidence from IPCC reports regarding the impacts of warming at 1.5 °C and 2 °C, and the IPCC's finding that developed countries need to reduce their emissions by between 25 and 40% by 2020 in order to have a likely chance of holding temperature increase to below 2 °C (the 25–40% target).[125] It also took into account the fact that the 25–40% target had been referred to and endorsed in numerous decisions of the COP,[126] as well as by the European Union. The Court noted that the goal of holding temperature rise to 1.5 °C under the Paris Agreement 'necessitates a greater reduction in [GHG] emissions than is necessary for a target of no more than 2 °C'.[127] Finally, the Court referred to the risk of tipping points resulting in irreversible change,[128] and the lack of available technology to remove CO_2 from the atmosphere.[129] Citing the precautionary principle, the Court insisted that the State must not take 'irresponsible risks', such as reliance upon as yet undeveloped technology to remove CO_2 from the atmosphere,[130] nor seek to delay emissions reductions to the future:

> [I]t must be taken into account … that the maximum targets of 1.5 °C or 2 °C and the related concentrations of a maximum of 430 or 450 ppm are based on estimates. It is therefore possible that dangerous climate change will occur even with less global warming and a lower concentration of greenhouse gases, for example because a tipping point is reached or because ice melts at a higher rate … The *precautionary principle therefore means that more far-reaching measures should be taken* to reduce greenhouse gas emissions, rather than less far-reaching measures.[131]

On this basis, the Court concluded that an emissions reduction of at least 25% by 2020 was indeed 'to be regarded as an absolute minimum' for the State to discharge its positive obligations under Articles 2 and 8 of the ECHR.[132] In the authors' view, this concretisation of the State's positive obligations under Articles 2 and 8 ECHR—informed as it was by both international law and science—represents a significant contribution to the development of international climate change law.

Having identified the 'lower limit' of State action, the Court reiterated that, consistent with its duty of 'due diligence', the State was required to *substantiate* that its emissions reduction measures were 'responsible'.[133] The onus was therefore on the

---

[124] Ibid., para 6.4 (emphasis added).

[125] Ibid., para 7.2.1.

[126] Ibid., para 7.2.6.

[127] Ibid., para 7.2.8.

[128] Ibid., para 7.2.10.

[129] Ibid., para 7.2.5.

[130] Ibid., para 7.2.5. The Court determined that the State's actions must be 'responsible' (as well as 'fair') given the risks of harm posed by climate change. See references to 'responsible' and 'irresponsible' conduct in paras 7.2.5, 7.2.7, 7.2.11, 7.4.6, 7.5.1.

[131] Ibid., para 7.2.10 (emphasis added).

[132] Ibid., para 7.5.1.

[133] Ibid., para 7.2.1.

State to 'justify' that its policy met the minimum requirement.[134] In the circumstances, the Supreme Court found that 'the State has not been able to provide a proper substantiation of its claim that deviating from that target is nevertheless *responsible*'.[135] Further, the Court affirmed that the order would *not* constitute an 'impossible or disproportionate burden', as the State had 'not sufficiently substantiated' such effects,[136] particularly given that other EU countries pursued 'much stricter climate policies', and the State had been on notice of the order since the first court decision in 2015.[137] It, thus, affirmed that the State was required to reduce its emissions reduction by at least 25% by 2020 against 1990 levels.[138]

We now turn to the decision of the High Court of New Zealand in the *Thomson* case which illustrates a different approach to the use of international law in determining a State's obligations to mitigate climate change, before concluding with some reflections on the two approaches.

20.4.2 The Thomson Decision (2017) (New Zealand)

In 2017, the High Court of New Zealand, a court of first instance, dismissed an application for judicial review challenging the State's GHG emission reduction targets for 2030 and 2050.[139] The claim related to decisions taken by the relevant Minister pursuant to the Climate Change Response Act—an explicit purpose of which was to 'enable New Zealand to meet its obligations under the Convention, the Kyoto Protocol and any binding amendments to them (Purpose one)'.[140] The claim challenged both procedural and substantive aspects of the State's emission reduction targets, and drew upon the State's obligations under the UNFCCC and the Paris Agreement, as well as the District Court's decision in *Urgenda* as persuasive authority (the case being filed prior to the Court of Appeal's decision).[141]

The claim was brought by Ms Thomson, a law student, and comprised two elements: a challenge to the State's legislative 2050 emissions reduction target on procedural grounds; and a challenge to the State's 2030 emissions reduction target (which was tabled as its NDC under the Paris Agreement) on the basis that it constituted an inadequate level of GHG reduction. The challenge to the 2030 NDC included

[134] Ibid., para 5.3.3. Citing ECtHR, *Jugheli et al./Georgia*, Judgement, 13 July 2017, App No 38342/05 and No 2017/190, para 66.

[135] Netherlands Supreme Court, *State of the Netherlands (Ministry of Economic Affairs and Climate Policy) v Stichting Urgenda*, above n 5, para 7.5.1 (emphasis added).

[136] Ibid., para 7.5.3.

[137] See Footnote 136.

[138] Ibid., para 7.5.1.

[139] New Zealand High Court, *Thomson v Minister for Climate Change,* above n 6. Regarding the judgment, see: Palmer 2018; Winkelmann et al. 2019.

[140] Ibid., para 43.

[141] The claim did not, however, draw upon New Zealand's domestic human rights legal framework.

claims that the Minister had failed to take into account relevant considerations and that the target was irrational. While the latter ground entails a very high threshold for claimants, it does permit the court a degree of consideration of the substance or merits of the decision.

Turning first to the procedural challenge to the 2050 statutory target. The 2050 target had been set under legislation in 2011 and comprised a 50% reduction against 1990 levels. Under the Act (Section 224), the Minister had the power to set, amend or revoke a target at any time. The nub of the claimant's contention was that the Minister was required under the legislation to consider whether a review of the target was necessary, following the release of the IPCC's AR5 report in 2014 and in light of international climate change law, despite the absence of an express statutory requirement to do so.

The Court accepted the claimant's position that the Minister *was* required to consider a review, and determined that this was an implied mandatory consideration under the legislation, in order to 'give effect to the Act, and what New Zealand ha[d] accepted, recognised and committed to under the international instruments'.[142] The Court explained:

> [t]he Paris Agreement has been entered into in "pursuit of" the Convention's objective and guided by its principles. As a matter of statutory interpretation, s 224(2) can and therefore must be interpreted consistently with New Zealand's international obligations under these instruments. I consider s 224(2) is also to be interpreted consistently with matters that New Zealand has *recognised and accepted* in these instruments, as these aid in interpreting our obligations.[143]

The latter point indicates the Court's acceptance that it should consider, in addition to binding obligations, non-binding and hortatory provisions that the State has 'recognised and accepted' in international agreements in domestic statutory interpretation. Indeed, while the Court indicated that there was no binding obligation under international law for the State to review its NDC following the release of a new IPCC report,[144] several provisions of the UNFCCC and the Paris Agreement indicated that such review was necessary. The Court referred to the preamble of the UNFCCC and the Paris Agreement, the inclusion of the precautionary principle as a 'guiding principle' in the UNFCCC, and specific references to acting on the 'best available scientific knowledge', as well as the binding treaty obligations with respect to updating and reviewing measures to mitigate climate change.[145] It described the position as follows:

> These provisions [of the UNFCCC and the Paris Agreement] do not expressly require that New Zealand review any target it has set under its domestic legislation when an IPCC report is published. However collectively they do underline the pressing need for global action, that global action requires all Parties individually to take appropriate steps to meet the necessary

[142] New Zealand High Court, *Thomson v Minister for Climate Change,* above n 6, para 94.

[143] Ibid., para 88 (emphasis added).

[144] Ibid., para 91.

[145] Ibid., para 88–94.

> collective action, and that Parties should do so in light of relevant scientific information and update their individual measures in light of such information.[146]

The implied obligation that the Court derived from international climate change law was highly procedural in nature: it requires the Minister to *consider* the necessity of a *review* of the GHG mitigation target in light of a new IPCC report, and such review may or may not lead to a change in the target.[147] Nevertheless, the Court established an additional obligation on the part of the State to consider scientific developments in formulating its climate mitigation efforts, and one that might form the basis of subsequent climate change litigation. The Court concluded:

> In my view, what is express under s 225(3)(a), is implicit in s 224(2). The IPCC reports provide the most up to date scientific consensus on climate change. New Zealand accepts this. To give effect to the Act *and what New Zealand has accepted, recognised and committed to under the international instruments, and in light of the threat that climate change presents to humankind and the environment*, I consider the publishing of a new IPCC report requires the Minister to consider whether a target set under s 224 should be reviewed. That is, it is a mandatory relevant consideration in whether an existing target should be reviewed under s 224(2).[148]

The Court adopted a narrower approach to the relevance of international climate change law in its examination of the claimant's substantive challenge to the State's 2030 NDC target. The Court derived few boundaries from international climate change law with respect to the content of the State's emission reduction targets, and insisted that the State had a high degree of 'flexibility' in determining its NDC.[149]

The challenge to the State's 2030 NDC comprised several alleged grounds of unlawfulness. The State's target was a 30% reduction against 2005 levels or 11% against 1990 levels.[150] To recall, this is a significantly *lower* level of emissions reductions on a much longer timeframe than that enforced by the Dutch courts in *Urgenda*, based on IPCC's AR4 (25–40% by 2020).[151] The claimant alleged, inter alia, that the decision to set the target failed to take into account relevant considerations and was 'irrational'.

At the outset, the Court made an important determination as to the justiciability of the NDC, but ultimately dismissed all of the claims. The Court found that the NDC target was *prima facie* justiciable, contrary to the State's submissions.[152] It reviewed

---

[146] Ibid., para 91.

[147] Ibid., para 94.

[148] Ibid., para 94 (emphasis added). In the present case, the Court did not go on to enforce the procedural obligation, namely to order the relevant Minister to consider whether a review of the 2050 target was required in light of the IPCC's AR5 report. This was primarily because, following the hearing but prior to the judgment, a new national government was elected which committed to replace the target with a new zero by 2050 target.

[149] Ibid., para 38.

[150] Ibid., para 65.

[151] And as recognised by the IPCC in AR4 as necessary to be adopted by developed countries to have a likely chance of holding global temperature increase to 2 °C (let alone to achieve the 'well below 2°C' goal of the Paris Agreement), namely 25–40% by 2020 against 1990 levels.

[152] New Zealand High Court, *Thomson v Minister for Climate Change,* above n 6, paras 133–134.

other national-level climate change cases, including the District Court's decision in *Urgenda*, and concluded that there must be 'some scrutiny of the public power in addition to accountability through Parliament and the General Elections'.[153] The 'IPCC reports', in the Court's view, 'provide a factual basis on which decisions can be made', and remedies can be 'fashioned to ensure appropriate action is taken while leaving the policy choices about the content of that action to the appropriate state body'.[154] The Court noted, however, that there are 'constitutional limits' to the role of the judiciary,[155] and that, if a ground of review 'requires the Court to weigh public policies that are more appropriately weighed by those elected by the community', it may be necessary for the Court to 'defer to the elected officials'.[156]

The plaintiff challenged the Minister's decision to set the 2030 NDC on several public law grounds. First, Ms Thomson submitted that the Minister had unlawfully failed to take into account the cost of dealing with dangerous climate change in the economic modelling that underpinned the 2030 target. This consideration was necessary, the plaintiff submitted, owing to developed countries' obligation to take the lead in climate action and to put forward a 'fair and ambitious' contribution to addressing climate change.[157] In rejecting this claim, the Court noted that:[158]

> [N]either the Convention nor the Paris Agreement stipulate any specific criteria or process for how a country is to set its INDC and NDC, nor how it is to assess the costs of the measures it intends to take. The Paris Agreement seeks a contribution from a country that represents its "highest possible ambition" and developing countries should continue "taking the lead by undertaking economy-wide absolute emission targets" but it leaves these matters to be nationally determined.

Secondly, the claimant alleged that the Minister had unlawfully failed to consider 'the scientific consensus that the parties' combined INDCs fell short of the extent and speed of reductions needed to stabilize greenhouse gas concentrations in the atmosphere at a level that would prevent dangerous anthropogenic interference with the climate system'.[159] The contention was that the Minister failed to consider this between communicating New Zealand's INDC and confirming it as its NDC. In rejecting also this argument, the Court took the view that:

> There was no requirement [under the Paris Agreement] for countries to adopt a target that if adopted by all would achieve warming well below 2 °C, nor to alter its NDC because the combined INDCs were insufficient to meet the target. This stage of the process is about individual decision making (towards the common goal). The Paris process envisages a 2018 facilitative dialogue intended to assess the collective progress towards the long term temperature goal.[160]

---

[153] Ibid., para 134.

[154] Ibid., para 133.

[155] Ibid., paras 133–134.

[156] See Footnote 153.

[157] Ibid., para 137.

[158] Ibid., para 139.

[159] Ibid., para 158.

[160] Ibid., para 159.

The claimant also alleged that the decision to set the NDC was 'irrational' (in the public law sense) for several reasons, including: that the 2030 target was based on a 2 °C target, rather than the commitment to hold temperature increase to 'well below 2 °C' and to pursue efforts to limit the temperature increase to 1.5 °C under the Paris Agreement[161] (the temperature goal argument); that it did not reflect the State's obligations under the UNFCCC and the Paris Agreement as a developed country, including that it should 'take the lead' in emissions reduction (the equity argument); and that it did not represent a precautionary approach to emissions reduction as it relied heavily on negative emissions technology and failed to consider the risks and costs of delaying emissions reduction (the precautionary argument).[162]

The Court dismissed the temperature goal argument, in short order, on the basis of the State's evidence that it had indeed considered the temperature goals in the Paris Agreement.[163] It dismissed the equity argument without detailed examination of the concept of the State's CBDR-RC, in contrast to the approach of the Dutch courts. Controversially, the Court accepted the State's submissions that the practice of other developed countries offered an objective benchmark of 'equity' (or what contributes a 'fair' contribution to the global effort of emissions reduction) with respect to its NDC. The Court referred to a table submitted by the State's expert that provides a comparison of New Zealand's 2030 target against other developed countries' and concluded that '[t]he evidence shows that our target is fair when considered on this basis'.[164] This stands in contrast to the approach of the Dutch courts who referred primarily to the findings of the IPCC in AR4 to determine what constitutes 'equitable' or 'fair' emissions reductions of a developed country.

Finally, the Court dismissed the precautionary argument, in contrast to the position adopted by the Dutch Supreme Court, primarily on the basis that the State has flexibility to revise and update its NDC under the Paris Agreement process. The Court accepted evidence from the claimant's expert that a low emissions reduction target for 2030 will 'require substantially higher rates of emissions reductions from 2030 to 2050' and that 'technology required for large scale CO_2 removal does not presently exist'. The Court went on, however, to conclude that, '[t]his may all be so, but New Zealand's NDC does not remain set in stone until 2030. Reviews are envisaged. It is for the new Minister to consider any appropriate review'.[165]

The Court took a markedly different approach to that of the Dutch court in *Urgenda* with respect to the IPCC's findings regarding necessary emissions reductions to hold global temperature increase to below 2 °C. The Court correctly indicated that international agreements do not specify the emissions reductions required by States in their NDCs. However, the Court appeared to endorse the submissions of the State's experts that national emissions trajectories are 'not a question for science—but involves

[161] Ibid., para 162.
[162] Ibid., para 161.
[163] Ibid., para 164.
[164] Ibid., para 166.
[165] Ibid., para 169.

social, economic and political judgments about relative risks of over and under mitigation'.[166] The Court thus concluded that the Minister had not made 'any reviewable error for which the Court may intervene' and found that, '[t]he international framework has been followed' and '[i]t has not been demonstrated the NDC decision was outside the Minister's power under this framework'.[167]

20.4.3 *Reflections on the* Urgenda *and* Thomson *Decisions*

The judgments issued by the courts in the Netherlands and New Zealand in the *Urgenda* and *Thomson* cases highlight how national courts are engaging with international law as it applies to climate change—in some instances extensively, and illustrate the important role of national courts in the enforcement and interpretation of States' obligations under the international climate treaty regime. Though the judgments differ in terms of their outcome, each of the courts looked to international law to substantiate the State's obligations under domestic law. The judgments also exemplify the different legal bases in national law pursuant to which courts (and claimants) are currently engaging with States' obligations under the international climate change treaty regime, including tort law, human rights law and public law.

The approach adopted by the Dutch courts highlights the role of international law in substantiating open standards—in this case, the State's tortious duty of care and its positive obligations to protect human rights under a regional human rights treaty. The District Court clearly stipulated that Urgenda could not rely *directly* on the no-harm principle nor the UNFCCC or the Kyoto Protocol (the Paris Agreement not having been agreed yet) in its claim, but nevertheless acknowledged the 'reflex effect', such that 'when applying and interpreting national-law open standards and concepts … the court takes account of such international law obligations.'[168] It considered this to be 'a generally acknowledged rule in the legal system'.[169] This reflects the approach adopted by the High Court in *Thomson*. The Supreme Court in *Urgenda* meanwhile applied (as it considered it was required to do) the 'common ground' method to similar effect in determining the content of the State's positive obligations under Articles 2 and 8 of the ECHR by reference to international climate change law, soft law and scientific evidence.

Since the *Urgenda* case, national courts have adopted a similar approach to that of the Dutch courts. This includes the decisions of the Council of State in France (apex court) in *Grande-Synthe*,[170] and the first instance court in Belgium

---

[166] Ibid., para 171.

[167] Ibid., para 179.

[168] District Court of The Hague, *Urgenda Foundation v The State of The Netherlands*, above n 5, para 4.43.

[169] Ibid., para 4.43.

[170] See Council of State, *Commune de Grande-Synthe v France*, Judgment, 19 November 2020, Case No 427301, para 12.

in *Klimaatzaak*[171]—both of which are 'systemic mitigation' cases. In the *Grande-Synthe* case, for instance, the Council of State noted that, while the provisions of the UNFCCC and the Paris Agreement 'do not have any direct effect, they must nevertheless be taken into consideration in interpreting the provisions of national law'.[172] Also notable is the decision of the Dutch District Court in the case brought against Royal Dutch Shell regarding its contribution to climate change (the *Shell* case).[173] In this case, the Court acknowledged that while certain provisions of the Paris Agreement were not binding under international law, they nevertheless 'represent a universally endorsed and accepted standard that protects the common interest of preventing dangerous climate change', which is relevant to the interpretation of the unwritten standard of care.[174]

The judgment of the High Court in *Thomson* also illustrates an apparent willingness on the part of the Court to adopt a more expansive approach to the relevance of international climate change law when interpreting the *procedural* aspects of a State's efforts to mitigate climate change, but a disinclination to derive clear boundaries from international climate change law regarding the *substantive* content of a State's emission reduction targets. In this respect, unlike the Dutch courts in *Urgenda*, the Court did not seek to concretise the principle of CBDR-RC or equity, or the commitment of developed country Parties to 'take the lead' in combatting climate change. Nor did the New Zealand High Court find that the precautionary principle operated to preclude the State's reliance on uncertain technologies to remove CO_2 from the atmosphere, nor its ability to delay significant emissions reductions in the short-term. Rather, the judgment emphasised the 'flexibility' inherent in the Paris Agreement with respect to emissions reductions.[175]

Case-specific factors no doubt played a role in the High Court's approach in *Thomson*: New Zealand courts, like courts in many common law countries, are generally reluctant to be drawn into what might be perceived to be 'merits based review' in an action for judicial review.[176] Against this backdrop, it is notable that the High Court indicated a willingness to look to international law to determine the lawfulness of the Minister's actions. This interpretive approach has been flagged by

---

[171] See Court of First Instance of Brussels, *VZW Klimaatzaak v Kingdom of Belgium & Others,* Judgment, 17 June 2021 (unofficial translation), p. 59.

[172] Council of State, *Commune de Grande-Synthe v France*, Judgment, 19 November 2020, Case No 427301, para 12.

[173] District Court of the Hague, *Milieudefensie v Royal Dutch Shell,* Judgment, 26 May 2021, ECLR:NL:RBDHA:2021:5339 (official translation).

[174] Ibid., para 4.4.27.

[175] See e.g. New Zealand High Court, *Thomson v Minister for Climate Change,* above n 6, para 38.

[176] As noted by Palmer QC, 'Expansion [of the doctrine of judicial review] is slow because the judges are concerned not to overstep what is considered in New Zealand as the appropriate judicial role. What is sometimes labelled judicial activism in this field has not been evident in New Zealand and is not likely to be. Ministers have unlimited access to the legislative machinery to change the law should they feel threatened by judicial review of their actions. It is a sensitive line the judges tread. And not all judges feel familiar enough with the institutions and processes of government to have the confidence to intervene.' Palmer 2018, p. 203.

the Chief Justice of New Zealand and two of her fellow Supreme Court Justices as of potential significant for future climate change litigation:

> New Zealand courts apply a presumption to the interpretation of statutes that Parliament did not intend to legislate contrary to New Zealand's international obligations. We anticipate that international treaties in the climate change area will increasingly be used in this way in litigation and it may be that courts will, as they respond to the magnitude of the issue, seek to strengthen the presumption. Less clear is the status that courts will accord to New Zealand's undertakings outside of treaties, such as in the Paris Agreement.[177]

20.5 Conclusion

While national-level climate change litigation, especially 'systemic mitigation' cases, is presently at a nascent stage of development, these judgments suggest that national courts will play a significant role in influencing norms of international law relevant to climate change. This chapter has canvassed various reasons for an enhanced role for national courts as agents of international law development in the context of climate litigation. On the basis of the case analyses above, three further points can be added.

First, because national courts are usually referring to international law in order to substantiate the content of the State's obligations under national law (i.e. indirectly), the strict bindingness of the relevant provisions under international law is of less concern. This leaves more flexibility for national courts when invoking such provisions. While this is particularly notable in the Supreme Court judgment in *Urgenda,* it is also evident in *Thomson*, where the Court looked to matters that New Zealand had 'recognised and accepted'[178]—strict bindingness aside.

Secondly, related to this is a willingness on the part of national courts to draw on norms beyond the international climate change treaty regime, drawing on international human rights law and international environmental law. This process has led one academic to suggest that 'an international normative common ground' in climate litigation is emerging, which if confirmed by future litigation, 'would consolidate the … convergence of human rights, environmental protection, and climate governance'.[179]

Thirdly, contributing to these factors, is a rich 'global conversation' between litigants, scientific experts, courts, tribunals and other institutions that has come to characterise climate litigation. For example, the norms established in the *Urgenda* judgments regarding States' human rights obligations to mitigate climate change have been cited, and, in some cases, directly relied upon, by courts around the world including in Germany, Belgium, Norway, Ireland and Australia. Further, communities and lawyers have drawn upon these norms in their legal submissions in numerous pending climate cases globally. Other institutions are also taking note of judicial developments at the national level: the *Urgenda* judgment has been welcomed by the

---

177 Winkelmann et al. 2019, para 99.

178 New Zealand High Court, *Thomson v Minister for Climate Change,* above n 6, para 88.

179 Rodríguez-Garavito 2021.

President of the ECtHR,[180] the UN High Commissioner for Human Rights,[181] and the UN Special Rapporteur on Human Rights and the Environment,[182] reflecting the global nature of the dialogue.

Taken together, these dynamics create fertile ground for national courts to act as agents of international law development in this field, and as key actors in the protection of the environment and the global commons.

References

Alebeek RV (2013) Domestic Courts as Agents of Development of International Immunity Rules. Leiden Journal of International Law 26:559–578.

Bahdi R (2002) Globalization of Judgment: Transjudicialism and the Five Faces of International Law in Domestic Courts. George Washington International Law Review 555–604.

Benvenisti E, Downs GW (2009) National Courts, Domestic Democracy, and the Evolution of International Law. Eur J Int Law 20:59–72.

Benvenisti E (1993) Judicial Misgivings Regarding the Application of International Law: An Analysis of Attitudes of National Courts. European Journal of International Law 159–183.

Bodansky D, Brunnée J (1998) The Role of National Courts in the Field of International Environmental Law. Review of European Community and International Environmental Law 7:11–20.

Bodansky D, Brunnée J, Rajamani L (2017a) International Climate Change Law. Oxford University Press, Oxford, New York.

Bodansky D, Brunnée J, Rajamani L (2017b) Oxford Public International Law. Oxford University Press, online.

Burger M, Gundlach J (2017) The Status of Climate Change Litigation: A Global Review. UN Environment, Nairobi.

Constantinides A (2012) Transjudicial dialogue and consistency in human rights jurisprudence: a case study on diplomatic assurances against torture. In: Fauchald O K, Nollkaemper A (eds) The practice of international and national courts and the (de-)fragmentation of international law. Hart Publishing, Oxford.

---

[180] Speech of the President of the ECtHR on the occasion of the opening of the judicial year, 31 January 2020, p. 4: 'By relying directly on the Convention, the Dutch judges highlighted the fact that the European Convention of Human Rights really has become our shared language and that this instrument can provide genuine responses to the problems of our time.'

[181] UN High Commissioner for Human Rights Michelle Bachelet, 'Bachelet welcomes top court's landmark decision to protect human rights from climate change' (Press Release, 20 December 2019) https://www.ohchr.org/EN/NewsEvents/Pages/DisplayNews.aspx?NewsID=25450&LangID=E. Accessed 15 January 2021. The UN High Commissioner indicated that, 'the decision confirms that the Government of the Netherlands and, by implication, other governments have binding legal obligations, based on international human rights law, to undertake strong reductions in emissions of greenhouse gases.'

[182] UN Special Rapporteur on Human Rights and the Environment, David Boyd, referred to the *Urgenda* decision as 'the most important climate change court decision in the world so far, confirming that human rights are jeopardised by the climate emergency and that wealthy nations are legally obligated to achieve rapid and substantial emission reductions.' See Kaminski I, Dutch supreme court upholds landmark ruling demanding climate action (The Guardian, 20 December 2019) https://www.theguardian.com/world/2019/dec/20/dutch-supreme-court-upholds-landmark-ruling-demanding-climate-action Accessed 15 January 2021.

D'Aspremont J (2012) The Systemic Integration of International Law by Domestic Courts: Domestic Judges as Architects of the Consistency of the International Legal Order. In: Fauchald O K, Nollkaemper A (eds) The Practice of International and National Courts and the (De-)Fragmentation of International Law. Hart Publishing, Oxford.
Falk R A (1963) The Role of Domestic Courts in the International Legal Order Symposium on Procedural Aspects of International Law. Indiana Law Journal 429–445.
Ferreira P G (2016) 'Common But Differentiated Responsibilities' in the National Courts: Lessons from Urgenda v. The Netherlands. Transnational Environmental Law 5:329–351.
Ganguly G, Setzer J, Heyvaert V (2018) If at First You Don't Succeed: Suing Corporations for Climate Change. Oxford Journal of Legal Studies 38:841–868.
IPCC (2018) Special Report: Global Warming of 1.5°C. Summary for Policymakers.
Knop K (1999) Here and There: International Law in Domestic Courts Millennium Issue: Shaping the Parameters of International Law in the New Millennium. New York University Journal of International Law and Politics 501–536.
Maxwell L, Mead S, van Berkel D (2022) Standards for adjudicating the next generation of *Urgenda*-style climate cases. Journal of Human Rights and the Environment (forthcoming).
O'Keefe R (2013) Domestic Courts as Agents of Development of the International Law of Jurisdiction. Leiden Journal of International Law 26:541–558.
Osofsky H, Peel J (2013) Litigation's Regulatory Pathways and the Administrative State: Lessons from U.S. and Australian Climate Change Governance. Geo Intl Envtl Rev.
Palmer QC SG (2018) Can Judges Make a Difference? The Scope for Judicial Decisions on Climate Change in New Zealand Domestic Law. Victoria University of Wellington Law Review 49:191–210.
Rajamani L (2017) Elaborating the Paris Agreement: Implementation and Compliance. https://www.c2es.org/site/assets/uploads/2017/11/elaborating-the-paris-agreement-implementation-and-compliance-11-17.pdf Accessed 17 April 2021.
Roberts A (2011) Comparative International Law? The Role of National Courts in Creating and Enforcing International Law. International and Comparative Law Quarterly 60:57–92.
Rodríguez-Garavito C (2021) Litigating the Climate Emergency: The Global Rise and Impact of the 'Rights Turn' in Climate Litigation. In: Rodríguez-Garavito C (ed) Litigating the Climate Emergency: How Human Rights, Courts, and Legal Mobilization Can Bolster Climate Action. Cambridge University Press, UK.
Setzer J, Byrnes R (2019) Global Trends in Climate Change Litigation: 2019 Snapshot. Grantham Research Institute on Climate Change and the Environment and Centre for Climate Change Economics and Policy. London School of Economics and Political Science.
Setzer J, Byrnes R (2020) Global trends in climate change litigation: 2020 snapshot. Grantham Research Institute on Climate Change and the Environment and Centre for Climate Change Economics and Policy. London School of Economics and Political Science, London.
Setzer J, Vanhala LC (2019) Climate change litigation: A review of research on courts and litigants in climate governance. Wiley Interdisciplinary Review of Climate Change 10:e580.
Tzanakopoulos A, Tams CJ (2013) Introduction: Domestic Courts as Agents of Development of International Law. Leiden Journal of International Law 26:531–540.
Tzanakopoulos A (2016a) (Study group on) principles on the engagement of domestic courts with international law. Final Report: Mapping the Engagement of Domestic Courts with International Law. International Law Association (Johannesburg Conference).
Tzanakopoulos A (2016b) Domestic judicial lawmaking. In: Brolmann C, Radi Y (eds) Research Handbook on the Theory and Practice of International Lawmaking. Edward Elgar, Louvain.
United Nations Environment Programme (2019) The Emissions Gap Report 2019.
Verheyen R, Zengerling C (2016) International Dispute Settlement. In: Carlarne C P, Gray K R, Tarasofsky R G (eds) The Oxford Handbook of International Climate Change Law, Oxford University Press, Oxford.
Wegener L (2020) Can the Paris Agreement Help Climate Change Litigation and Vice Versa? Transnational Environmental Law 9:17–36.

Winkelmann H (C J), Glazebrook S, France E (2019) Climate Change and the Law. https://www.courtsofnz.govt.nz/assets/speechpapers/ccw.pdf Accessed 17 April 2021.

Sarah Mead LL.M (Leiden University), Senior Legal Associate at the Climate Litigation Network, a project of the Urgenda Foundation.

Lucy Maxwell LL.M (London School of Economics and Political Science), Senior Legal Associate at the Climate Litigation Network, a project of the Urgenda Foundation.

Chapter 21
A Growing Role for the UN Security Council?

Paul M. Romita and Eran Sthoeger

Contents

Abstract In the post-Cold War era, the Security Council has delved into a variety of environmental issues as they relate to international peace and security, including climate change, preventive diplomacy and trans-boundary waters, the impact on the environment of the exploitation of natural resources in armed conflict, and the

P. M. Romita (✉)
Security Council Report, 711 Third Avenue, 15th Floor, New York, NY 10017, USA
e-mail: p.romita@securitycouncilreport.org

E. Sthoeger
Independent Litigator and Consultant in International Law, New York City, USA
e-mail: Eran.Sthoeger@protonmail.com

Seton Hall Law School, Newark, NJ, USA

Brooklyn Law School, Brooklyn, NY, USA

E. Sobenes et al. (eds.), *The Environment Through the Lens of International Courts and Tribunals*, https://doi.org/10.1007/978-94-6265-507-2_21

protection of the environment in armed conflict. Such issues have been addressed in the context of a broadening understanding of the organ's mandate to maintain international peace and security, although the Council's engagement on them remains controversial among some of its members. In spite of these political difficulties, there has been significant activity in the Council in recent years on these matters, especially the relationship between climate change and security. The Security Council's role is not to protect the environment or to settle environmental disputes as a court or tribunal may. But the UN Charter and the Security Council's practice provide a framework that allows the Council to play a role—and, possibly, to play an even bigger role in the future—in addressing environmental disputes and in engaging more generally in environmental challenges, when it perceives that they are pertinent to the maintenance of international peace and security.

Keywords Security Council · Climate change · Sea level rise · International peace and security · Peaceful settlement of disputes · Conflict prevention · Collective security

21.1 Introduction

The United Nations (UN) Security Council is a political body tasked with primary responsibility for the maintenance of international peace and security. The understanding of what may endanger international peace security—and therefore falls within the scope of the Security Council's mandate—has expanded over the years. The founders of the UN may not have envisioned the scope of this expansion. In this regard, though not without controversy, environmental issues, such as climate change and water scarcity, have been discussed in the Security Council in recent years in various contexts, including as a conflict 'threat multiplier' that may be relevant for the Security Council's attempts to prevent or mitigate conflict. All the same, it is not always clear what concrete action the Security Council can take on such matters.

Though not a court or tribunal, the Security Council is granted the power in the Charter to make recommendations to states on how to peacefully settle their disputes that may endanger international peace and security.[1] If necessary, the Council also has the authority to pursue coercive, legally-binding measures to settle disputes.[2] To date, the Council's formal decisions on or related to environmental matters have generally (though not entirely) been of a softer, non-coercive nature.[3]

This chapter will assess the actual and possible role of the Security Council in addressing environmental issues that may endanger international peace and security—including as an aspect of its conflict prevention and mitigation work—and the

[1] Charter of the United Nations, opened for signature 26 June 1945, entered into force 24 October 1945 (UN Charter), Chap. VI.

[2] UN Charter, Article 41. See also Krisch 2012b, MN 30-33.

[3] See Sect. 21.3.

potential corollary impact of that role on the protection of the environment and the settlement of environmental disputes.

The chapter consists of five sections. After this brief introduction, Sect. 21.2 lays out the legal framework governing the powers of the Security Council. Section 21.3 then provides an overview of the Security Council's consideration of environmental issues thus far, followed by Sect. 21.4, which considers whether environmental issues are, in fact, relevant to the Security Council's work and why. Finally, Sect. 21.5 considers several avenues through which the Security Council has and may address environmental issues in the future.

21.2 The Legal Framework

21.2.1 The Mandate and Authority of the Security Council

Of the six principal organs of the UN,[4] the Security Council is the one tasked by Member States under Article 24 of the Charter with the 'primary responsibility for the maintenance of international peace and security' on their behalf.[5] Combined with Article 25, in which the Member States 'agree to accept and carry out the decisions of the Security Council',[6] the UN Charter grants the 15 members of the Security Council extensive authority to speak on behalf of—and bind—the wider membership by decisions taken without their input and over which they have no effective control.[7] The Charter makes clear that the functions of the Security Council do not preclude other UN organs, such as the General Assembly, from considering matters of international peace and security.[8] However, in the name of efficiency and expediency, the 'primary responsibility'—meaning that it is the principle organ on such matters while others play a secondary role—is vested with the 15 members of the Security Council.[9]

In order to maintain international peace and security, the Security Council was given the extraordinary and broad powers under Chapter VII of the Charter to not only make recommendations, but to impose binding enforcement measures on member states, from diplomatic and economic measures[10] to collective security measures and the authorization of the use of force.[11] These extraordinary measures are at the

[4] The other five are the General Assembly, the Trusteeship Council, the Economic and Social Council, the Secretariat and the International Court of Justice.

[5] UN Charter, Article 24(1).

[6] UN Charter, Article 25.

[7] Goodrich and Hambro 1946, p. 155; S/PV.91, Statement of the Secretary-General, 91st Meeting of the Security Council, 10 January 1947; Wood 1998, p. 77 and De Wet 2009, para 1.

[8] See, for example, UN Charter, Articles 10-14 and Wood 2007, para 21.

[9] Peters 2012, Article 24, MN 20; Goodrich and Hambro 1946, p. 155.

[10] UN Charter, Article 41.

[11] UN Charter, Article 42; Wood 1998, p. 77 and Wood 2007, para 18.

disposal of the Security Council where it has identified that a situation constitutes a 'threat to the peace, breach of the peace, or act of aggression'.[12] In making such a determination, the Council enjoys wide, though not necessarily unlimited, discretion.[13] Of the three, by far the most often used term in the practice of the Security Council is 'threat to the peace'.[14] Over time, the evolving practice of the Security Council, particularly since the end of the Cold War, has expanded the scope of what can be considered a threat to the peace and, more broadly, what may be considered relevant for the Council's mandate as a body concerned with international peace and security.[15]

Beyond the classic interstate warfare which was in the minds of the drafters of the Charter,[16] international peace and security has come to include situations internal to one territory or state,[17] terrorism as a global phenomenon,[18] proliferation of weapons of mass destruction,[19] violations of human rights law,[20] protection of civilians and violations of international humanitarian law,[21] piracy,[22] organized crime,[23] protection of democratic principles[24] and health crises (such as HIV/AIDS,[25] Ebola,[26] and COVID-19[27]). Indeed, soon after the Cold War ended, during a meeting held at the level of Heads of State and Government on 31 January 1992, the Security Council

[12] UN Charter, Article 39; de Wet and Wood 2013, para 9.

[13] ICTY Appeals Chamber, *Prosecutor v Duško Tadić*, 2 October 1995, Case No IT-94-1; Krisch 2012a, MN 4-6 and Wood 2007, para 26. See also discussion in De Wet 2009, para 16–20.

[14] Krisch 2012a, MN 12; De Wet 2009, para 6.

[15] See generally De Wet 2009; Matheson 2006, pp. 6–7.

[16] Krisch 2012a, MN 13.

[17] E.g., S/RES/918 of 17 May 1994; S/RES/713 of 25 September 1991; S/RES/1132 of 8 October 1997.

[18] E.g., S/RES/1368 of 12 September 2001; S/RES/1373 of 28 September 2001; S/RES/2178 of 24 September 2014 and S/RES/2462 of 28 March 2019.

[19] E.g., S/23500 of 21 January 1992; S/RES/1441 of 8 November 2002; S/RES/1540 of 28 April 2004 and S/RES/2105 of 5 June 2013.

[20] E.g., S/RES/688 of 5 April 1991; S/RES./713 of 25 September 1991 and S/RES/1325 of 31 October 2000.

[21] E.g., S/RES/767 of 24 July 1992; S/RES/918 of 17 May 1994; S/RES/1208 of 19 November 1998; S/RES/1314 of 11 August 2000 and S/RES/2165 of 14 July 2014.

[22] E.g., S/RES/2500 of 4 December 2019.

[23] E.g., S/PRST/2018/9 of 8 May 2018 and S/RES/2482 of 19 July 2019.

[24] E.g., S/RES/841 of 16 June 1993; S/RES/1132 of 8 October 1997 and S/RES/2337 of 19 January 2017.

[25] E.g., S/RES/2177 of 18 September 2014; S/PRST/2014/24 of 21 November 2014 and also S/PV.4087 of 10 January 2000, which was an open debate on the impact of AIDS on peace and security in Africa; S/RES/1308 of 17 July 2000 encouraged voluntary HIV/AIDS testing and counselling for peacekeeping troops.

[26] E.g., S/RES/2177 of 18 September 2014; S/RES/2439 of 30 October 2018; and S/PRST/2019/6 of 2 August 2019. See also S/PV.7279 of 14 October 2014; S/PV.7318 of 21 November 2014 and S/PV.7502 of 13 August 2015.

[27] S/RES/2532 of 1 July 2020 considered 'that the unprecedented extent of the COVID-19 pandemic is likely to endanger the maintenance of international peace and security'. See also S/2020/663 of

adopted a presidential statement, noting that 'non-military sources of instability in the economic, social, humanitarian and ecological fields have become threats to peace and security'.[28]

Though the Council has expanded the scope of what can be considered a matter of international peace and security, to what extent various issues and situations fall under the mandate of the Council remains divisive. For example, in the first Council meeting on human rights as a stand-alone issue in April 2017, contrasting views were reflected on the degree to which this issue should be in the Council's purview. Some Council members took the view that 'systematic violation of human rights is inherent to conflicts, which, in turn, can threaten international peace and security'.[29] Russia, like some others, took the view that:

> Various aspects of the issue are indeed present in the work of the Council. They are periodically addressed during thematic or country discussions. However, the Security Council is not intended to fulfil the tasks of ensuring the observance of human rights and is not adapted to a substantive analysis of the situation in this sphere. It is an organ with unique powers to make decisions, including those providing for the use of force in situations that pose a threat to peace, a breach of peace or an act of aggression. Under this mandate, the Council cannot serve as a forum for discussions about human rights situations, wherever they may be… We cannot agree with the assertion made in the concept note prepared for the meeting, according to which violations of human rights should be considered as an issue related to the primary responsibility of the Security Council for maintaining international peace and security, in accordance with the Charter.[30]

This divergence of views is highly relevant when considering the Council's potential role with regard to environmental issues and disputes.

21.2.2 The Security Council as a Dispute Resolution Body

The Security Council is not a judicial body and, while international law can play a role in its decision-making, it is one among many considerations.[31] It is a dispute resolution body nevertheless,[32] and can act as such both with respect to conflicts that have already erupted, as well as to prevent potential conflicts that may endanger international peace and security.

---

8 July 2020 and S/2020/765 of 30 July 2020 for a compendium of briefings and statements made at virtual Security Council meetings related to COVID-19.

[28] S/23500 of 21 January 1992.

[29] S/PV.7926 of 18 April 2017, Statement of Uruguay, p. 9, also statements of the United States, p. 4, United Kingdom, p. 19, Senegal, p. 18.

[30] S/PV.7926 of 18 April 2017, p. 12; see also statement of Kazakhstan, p. 8, Egypt, p. 9 and Bolivia, pp. 22–23.

[31] UN Charter, Article 1(1); Wolfrum 2012, MN 21-22.

[32] UN Charter, Chap. VI; Krisch 2012a, MN 27-29 and Krisch 2012b, MN 30-33.

In scenarios where conflicts may threaten the peace, breach the peace or are an act of aggression, the Council's binding powers may be used to maintain or restore international peace and security, by settling a dispute between the parties.[33]

The Security Council acted in this way in the aftermath of the Gulf War in 1990–1991, after the establishment of the Commission by the Secretary-General to demarcate the land and maritime boundary between Iraq and Kuwait, in accordance with resolution 687.[34] Iraq refused to accept the conclusions of the Commission and, in response, the Security Council, acting under Chapter VII, affirmed that the decisions of the Commission are final,[35] demanded that both parties respect the boundary as demarcated by the Commission,[36] and stated its intention to ensure the inviolability of the boundary,[37] presumably by taking further enforcement action if needed. Also in resolution 687, as will be discussed in detail below,[38] the Security Council determined that Iraq was legally liable for damages, including environmental damages, caused by its invasion and occupation of Kuwait.[39] Thus, the Security Council's enforcement powers may be utilized for the purpose of dispute resolution.[40]

Since the UN Charter does not, however, require the Security Council to wait until conflict erupts, it can also address 'threats' that can deteriorate into conflict.[41] The dispute settlement function of the Security Council applies both to situations of conflict, naturally, and to situations that have yet to result in conflict. Chapter VI of the UN Charter (Pacific Settlement of Disputes) focuses on the Council's dispute settlement function, with the intention that the organ shall concern itself with a dispute well before it materializes into a situation that threatens peace and security.[42]

In acting to settle disputes before they deteriorate into situations that endanger international peace and security, the Security Council fulfils one of the Purposes of the UN Charter, '[t]o maintain international peace and security, and to that end: to take effective collective measures *for the prevention and removal of threats to the peace*'.[43] Having raised the issue of 'preventive diplomacy'[44] in several statements

---

[33] Krisch 2012a, MN 27-29.

[34] S/RES/687 of 3 April 1991, para 3.

[35] S/RES/833 of 27 May 1993, para 4.

[36] Ibid., para 5.

[37] Ibid., para 6. See also S/RES/1862 of 14 January 2009 and S/RES/1907 of 23 December 2009, in which the Security Council imposed sanctions on Eritrea in order to force Eritrea, inter alia, to settle its dispute with Djibouti regarding their boundary and missing Djiboutian combatants.

[38] See Sect. 21.5.3.

[39] S/RES/687 of 3 April 1991, para 16.

[40] For more on this, see Krisch 2012a, MN 27-29.

[41] UN Charter, Article 39; Krisch 2012a, MN 13.

[42] Goodrich and Hambro 1946, p. 146.

[43] UN Charter, Article 1(1)—emphasis added; Goodrich and Hambro 1946, p. 40; Security Council Report 2017, p. 2.

[44] In 'An Agenda for Peace: Preventive Diplomacy, Peacemaking and Peace-keeping' (S/24111 of 17 June 1992, para 20), the Secretary-General defines 'preventive diplomacy' as 'action to prevent disputes from arising between parties, to prevent existing disputes from escalating into conflicts

through the 1990s,[45] the Security Council acknowledged in July 2000 the important role of conflict prevention and its relevance to its mandate under the Charter in a presidential statement[46] and, in 2002, it established a new subsidiary body, the 'Ad Hoc Working Group on Conflict Prevention and Resolution in Africa'.[47] During the 2005 World Summit, the Security Council also adopted resolution 1625, which contained a 'declaration on strengthening the effectiveness of the Security Council's role in conflict prevention, particularly in Africa'.[48] The resolution reaffirmed 'the need to adopt a broad strategy of conflict prevention, which addresses the root causes of armed conflict and political and social crises in a comprehensive manner'.[49] The Security Council further stressed the 'the importance of establishing effective comprehensive strategies of conflict prevention, focused on averting negative developments in the security, economic, social and humanitarian sectors'[50] and vowed to take concrete steps to strengthen prevention capacities, such as assessing regularly the developments in regions at risk of armed conflict and encouraging the Secretary-General to provide information to the Council on such developments.[51]

Over the years, conflict prevention elements have been part and parcel of the Security Council's consideration of a variety of issues.[52] Nevertheless, the Report of the High-Level Independent Panel on Peace Operations in June 2015, mandated to review UN peace operations and emerging needs, notes:

---

and to limit the spread of the latter when they occur'; see also S/2011/552 of 26 August 2011, the Secretary-General's report, 'Preventive Diplomacy, Delivering Results'.

45 S/PRST/1999/34 of 30 November 1999; S/PRST/1998/28 of 16 September 1998 and S/PRST/1997/46 of 25 September 1997. See also Security Council Report 2017, p. 7.

46 S/PRST/2000/25 of 20 July 2005.

47 Security Council Report 2017, p. 7; S/PRST/2002/2 of 31 January 2002.

48 S/RES/1625 of 14 September 2005.

49 Ibid., preamble.

50 Ibid., para 4.

51 Ibid., para 2.

52 E.g., S/PV.8546 of 12 June 2019, a briefing on 'Conflict prevention and mediation'; S/PV.7857 of 10 January 2017, a ministerial-level open debate on conflict prevention and sustaining peace; S/PV.7561 of 17 November 2015, a ministerial-level open debate on 'Security, development and the root causes of conflict'; S/RES/2150 of 16 April 2014 calling on states to prevent and fight against genocide, and other serious crimes under international law, reaffirming the principle of responsibility to protect populations from genocide, war crimes, ethnic cleansing and crimes against humanity; S/PRST/2013/4 of 15 April 2013 on 'Prevention of conflicts in Africa: addressing the root causes'; S/PRST/2011/18 of 22 December 2011 on preventive diplomacy. Prevention has also been a theme in the Security Council's attention to terrorism, for example S/PV.7690 of 11 May 2016, an open debate focusing on countering the narratives and ideologies of terrorism. On youth and violent extremism: S/PRST/2019/15 of 12 December 2019 on the role African youth can play in the prevention and resolution of conflicts S/RES/2419 of 6 June 2018 reaffirming the important role that youth and youth-led civil society can play in peacebuilding and sustaining peace; S/PV.7432 of 23 May 2015, a high-level open debate on the role of youth in countering violent extremism and promoting peace. Prevention was also a theme in the Council's discussion on conflict in the Middle East, S/PV.8600 of 20 August 2019, for example in the Statement of the Chef de Cabinet of the Secretary-General Maria Luiza Ribeiro Viotti, p. 3, Peru, p. 15, Kuwait, p. 16 and Côte d'Ivoire, p. 23; see also Security Council Report 2017, pp. 8–9.

> Despite its authority under Article 34 of the UN Charter to become involved at an early stage of a dispute, the Security Council has infrequently engaged in emerging conflicts. Instead, the Security Council has focused on dealing with armed conflicts and emergencies after they occur, leaving UN efforts at preventive diplomacy to the Secretariat in coordination with others. The Panel believes that the Security Council should increase its monitoring of emerging issues and expand its dialogue with the Secretariat on how best to support prevention and mediation efforts. Earlier Security Council engagement including interactive dialogues in informal formats and visits to turbulent areas would be important in addressing emerging threats.[53]

As will be shown in the next section, the Council's focus on conflict prevention has resulted in more opportunities to consider environmental issues that relate to international peace and security.

21.3 The Security Council on Environmental Issues

There are several ways in which the Security Council has grappled with the security implications of environmental issues in recent years. The Council's approach to these matters has been tentative. One problem is that some members are ambivalent at best about having environmental issues on the Council's agenda. Nevertheless, there has been burgeoning interest in climate change and security matters, and it is safe to say that this has become somewhat of a 'growth industry' in the Council's work, due largely to the initiative of elected members.[54] In recent years, the Council has also addressed water, peace and security issues; the protection of the environment in armed conflict; and the linkages between the exploitation of natural resources and conflict.

21.3.1 Climate Change and the Security Council: A Cautious Approach

The Security Council first addressed climate change on 17 April 2007 in a ministerial-level open debate on the relationship between energy, security and climate during the UK's presidency.[55]

---

[53] S/2015/446 of 17 June 2015, Report of the High-Level Independent Panel on Peace Operations, para 71; Security Council Report 2017, p. 10.

[54] Kron 2019, p. 249.

[55] S/PV.5663 and Resumption 1 of 27 April 2007. It should be noted the presidency of the Council rotates monthly in an order based on the English language alphabet. Among other functions, Council presidents chair the organ's meetings during the month and help to organize the monthly program of work with the Security Council Affairs Division of the UN Secretariat. In this later role, they often decide to pursue discretionary events or products (i.e., resolutions or presidential statements) reflecting their interests. Meetings held on climate change or other environmental issues are often such discretionary events.

From this inaugural meeting to today, this issue has been contentious. Over time, however, the Council has made inroads in incorporating climate-related issues both in its deliberations and in its formal outcomes (that is, resolutions and presidential statements).

Prior to the 2007 open debate, the Group of 77+China and the Non-Aligned Movement (NAM) submitted letters to the Council signalling their reservations, stating that, by hosting the meeting, the organ would infringe on the work of the General Assembly and the Economic and Social Council (ECOSOC).[56] These tensions continued during the debate, with two camps expounding opposing views. Several Council members maintained that focusing on this issue was in keeping with the organ's conflict prevention work. Consistent with this view was that of the Slovakian representative, who said that the topic 'is well in line with Security Council resolution 1625 of 14 September 2005 on comprehensively addressing the root causes of armed conflict and political and social crises, as highly stressed societies tend to be more violent societies'.[57] Similarly, the UK representative said: 'an unstable climate will exacerbate some of the core drivers of conflict, such as migratory pressures and competition for resources'.[58] In contrast, the representatives of China, Russia, and South Africa maintained that it was not within the Council's mandate to address climate change, positing that this is fundamentally a development issue inconsistent with the Council's mandate to uphold international peace and security.[59]

The different views among Council members were largely mirrored by those of non-Council members in the open debate, as 38 member states made statements in addition to the 15 Council members. Much of the concern came from developing countries that believed that the Council should not encroach on the work of other UN entities,[60] as had been foreshadowed in the letters submitted by the Group of 77+China and the NAM.

It was more than four years before the Council again held a meeting dedicated to climate and security. On 20 July 2011, Germany hosted an open debate during its presidency of the Council focused on 'the impact of climate change'.[61] A total of 62 member states (including the 15 Council members) and the EU participated in the debate. There were once again contrasting views on whether the Council was the appropriate forum to discuss climate change.

Germany's efforts to pursue a presidential statement also faced considerable difficulties. Ultimately, the Council managed to adopt the statement at the end of the meeting, but its adoption remained an open question as the proceedings began, and agreement was only reached after Germany made concessions that diluted

[56] S/2007/211 of 16 April 2007 is the Group of 77+China letter; S/2007/203 of 12 April 2007 is the NAM letter.

[57] S/PV.5663 of 17 April 2007, statement by Slovakia, p. 4.

[58] Ibid., statement by the United Kingdom, p. 2.

[59] Ibid., statements by China, pp. 12–13, Russia p. 17, and South Africa, pp. 15–17.

[60] Ibid., statements by Pakistan, pp. 24–25 and Namibia, pp. 31–32 and S/PV.5663 Resumption I of 17 April 2007, statements by Egypt, pp. 4–5; Sudan, pp. 11–12 and Cuba, pp. 26–27.

[61] S/PV.6587 and Resumption 1 of 20 July 2011.

the final product. While stating that the main tool for addressing climate change is the UN Framework Convention on Climate Change (UNFCCC),[62] the Council 'expresse[d] its concern that possible adverse effects of climate change, may, in the long run, aggravate certain existing threats to international peace and security'. It further expressed concern that 'possible security implications of loss of territory of some States caused by sea-level-rise may arise, in particular small low-lying island States'. The statement requested that the Secretary-General provide 'contextual information' in his reporting to the Council on the 'possible security implications of climate change…when such issues are drivers of conflict, represent a challenge to the implementation of Council mandates or endanger the process of consolidation of peace'.[63]

This remains the Council's only thematic outcome specifically focused on climate change. However, it seems that the Secretariat may have lacked the capacity to provide such 'contextual information'—which, as of September 2020, it was only beginning to develop[64]—leading to the conclusion that the statement has been inconsistently implemented at best.[65] It may also have been the case that the Secretariat did not feel pressure to produce on this front, given the ambivalence about the issue among some of the Council's more powerful members, although this cannot be substantiated.

In the ensuing seven years, the Council did not hold a formal meeting exclusively on climate change. At least in part this had to do with the political sensitivity of addressing the issue in the Council, especially in the aftermath of the contentious open debate in July 2011. Portugal, which served with Germany as an elected member in 2011-2012, was supportive of enhanced Security Council engagement on climate change as a security issue ;[66] during its November 2011 presidency, it decided to convene a briefing broadly focused on 'New Challenges to international peace and security and conflict prevention' such as transnational organized crime, terrorism, drug-trafficking and pandemics—in addition to climate change.[67] The wide ranging discussion diluted the heightened division that a meeting solely on climate change would have aroused. While Council members such as China, Russia and India again reiterated their view that the Council is not the right place to discuss climate change, they nonetheless addressed other challenges within the scope of the briefing that they believed to be firmly within the Council's purview.[68]

---

[62] UN Framework Convention on Climate Change, opened for signature 9 May 1992, 1771 UNTS 107, entered into force, 21 March 1994.

[63] S/PRST/2011/15 of 20 July 2011.

[64] This is the authors' interpretation based on various discussions with UN officials and Security Council diplomats.

[65] Cousins 2013, pp. 208–209.

[66] S/PV.6587 of 20 July 2011, p. 20. Portugal stated that the German-led initiative to discuss climate change and security in the Council should be 'a step towards a consistent and regular consideration of the issue by the Security Council, based on reliable information on specific situations where climate-related phenomena are negatively affecting peace and security.'

[67] S/PV.6668 of 23 November 2011.

[68] Ibid., statements by China, pp. 24–35, Russia, pp. 17–18 and India, pp. 23–24.

Like Portugal's initiative in November 2011, several other Council meetings in the years following the July 2011 open debate also dealt with climate change in broader contexts. These included an open debate during New Zealand's July 2015 presidency of the Council on 'Peace and security challenges facing small island developing states',[69] which also addressed issues such as transnational organized crime, drug and human trafficking and piracy; an open debate on 'Water, peace and security' in November 2016, hosted by Council president Senegal, that explored issues such as the negative impact that conflict can have on accessing clean water and the management of cross-border waterways;[70] and an open debate during Japan's December 2017 Council presidency on 'Addressing complex contemporary challenges to international peace and security' during which famine, pandemics, transnational organized crime, and drug trafficking were among the topics discussed.[71]

Despite continued resistance from a number of permanent members, elected members have been especially active in persevering against the political headwinds to integrate climate-security matters into the Council's work. In July 2018, seven years after the last official Council meeting on climate change, Sweden hosted a debate on 'Understanding and addressing climate-related security risks'[72] and in January 2019, the Dominican Republic initiated an open debate on 'Addressing the impacts of climate-related disasters on international peace and security'.[73] It should also be noted that the promotion of this issue within the Council has been bolstered by growing interest among the wider UN membership on the security implications of climate change. Seventy-five member states—in addition to the AU, the EU, and the Observer Mission of the Holy See—participated in the open debate hosted by the Dominican Republic, more member states than had participated in the Council's open debates on climate and security matters in 2007(53) and 2011(62). While developing countries such as India, Iran and Algeria reiterated long-standing concerns about Security Council encroachment on the prerogatives of other UN organs,[74] varying levels of support for Council involvement on climate change as a security issue were expressed by member states from different regions. Particularly vocal in their advocacy for Council engagement were a number of Small Island Developing States (SIDS)—Fiji, Maldives, St. Vincent and the Grenadines, and the Dominican Republic; for many SIDS, rising sea levels represent an existential threat, a point that

[69] S/PV.7499 of 30 July 2015, for example, in the statements of UN Secretary-General Ban Ki-moon, p. 3, Samoa, p. 5, Seychelles, pp. 8–9, Chile, p. 15, Spain, p. 16, Malaysia, pp. 18–19, United Kingdom, pp. 21–22, Jordan, p. 22, United States, p. 26 and Lithuania, p. 27.

[70] S/PV.7818 of 22 November 2015, for example, in the statements of New Zealand, p. 24, France, p. 25, Spain, p. 28 and Kazakhstan, p. 29.

[71] S/PV.8144 of 20 December 2017, for example, in the statements by UN Secretary-General Ban Ki-moon, p. 2, Japan, pp. 3–4, Sweden, p. 78, United Kingdom, p. 10, France, pp. 11–12 and Italy, p. 21.

[72] S/PV.8307 of 11 July 2018.

[73] S/PV.8451 of 25 January 2019.

[74] Ibid., statements by India, pp. 42–43, Iran, p. 64 and Algeria, pp. 80–82.

has consistently been made by the Pacific Island SIDS since the Council first began addressing climate and security issues.[75]

Germany co-organized an open debate via videoconference on climate and security (held remotely due to concerns about the COVID-19 pandemic) on 24 July 2020, in collaboration with fellow Council members Belgium, the Dominican Republic, Estonia, France, Niger, St. Vincent and the Grenadines, Tunisia, the United Kingdom, and Viet Nam.[76] Although divisions on the appropriateness of the Council as a venue for climate and security were predictably reiterated, most Council members (and many other participating member states)[77] were forward looking in their statements, highlighting ways that the Council could more effectively grapple with this global challenge. Among the ideas put forth for potential action were the establishment of an informal Security Council expert group on climate and security to help integrate climate-security considerations more firmly into the Council's work, the provision of training to UN mission personnel on climate-security risks, and the establishment of a Special Representative of the Secretary-General on climate-security matters to help coordinate the UN's response to this threat.[78] Some of the ideas proposed in the debate—including, for example, the establishment of an informal expert group and a Special Representative position—were incorporated in a draft resolution that Germany and the nine other co-organizers of the debate had wanted to pursue in the lead up to the meeting. Resistance from some of the veto-wielding members, especially the United States, ultimately caused this effort to be abandoned.

The failure of the draft resolution to gain traction has not deterred those Security Council members supportive of the climate and security agenda from continuing to pursue this issue in the Council. Climate-security matters or related topics were the focus of meetings convened virtually (due to COVID-19) in the ensuing months. These included an open debate on the 'Humanitarian Effects of Environmental Degradation and Peace and Security' in September 2020, organised by Niger;[79] an open debate on 'Contemporary Drivers of Conflict and Insecurity' in November 2020, spearheaded by Saint Vincent and the Grenadines;[80] and an open debate on 'Climate and Security' in February 2021, at the UK's initiative.[81]

Arria-formula meetings[82]have been another vehicle Council members have used to discuss controversial topics such as climate change. Given that they are not formal

---

[75] Ibid., statements by Fiji pp. 31–32, Maldives, pp. 28–29, St. Vincent and the Grenadines, p. 58 and the Dominican Republic, pp. 23–25.

[76] S/2020/751 of 28 July 2020.

[77] Non-Council members submitted their statements in writing in keeping with working methods adopted by the Council during the COVID-19 pandemic.

[78] S/2020/830 of 24 August 2020. This was a summary of the meeting produced by Germany.

[79] S/2020/929 of 21 September 2020, See Sect. 21.3.3.

[80] S/2020/1090 of 5 November 2020.

[81] S/2021/198 of 25 February 2021.

[82] Arria-formula meetings are not official Council meetings. They can be either closed or open to the wider UN membership and civil society. Experts with specialized knowledge from within and outside the UN system can participate in these meetings; this is different from the most common closed meeting format, closed consultations, in which only UN officials and Council members can

meetings of the Council, they do not require widespread support (or even acquiescence) among its members to convene. Any Council member(s) can organize them—including in conjunction with non-Council member states. Five public Arria-formula meetings were held on the security implications of climate change or related topics between 2013 and 2018.[83] A sixth Arria-formula meeting on climate and security was held on 22 April 2020, and explored the question: 'What can the UN do to prevent climate-related conflicts and how can we climate-proof UN in-country activities?'; the meeting was held through the virtual platform Zoom, again due to the impact of COVID-19 on the Council's working methods. While many of these meetings have led to a useful exchange of information, the fact that they were held outside of the Council's formal mechanisms reflects the difficulty for some members of Council involvement on these matters.

The increased frequency of climate-related meetings in recent years only tells a small part of the story of the Council's involvement on this issue. There have been efforts of a more lasting nature to anchor climate-security matters firmly on the Security Council's agenda.

The visiting mission that the Council undertook to the Lake Chad basin region in early March 2017 was a watershed moment for the organ's engagement on climate-security matters, in this respect.[84] In the Terms of Reference for the mission, the Council expressed the desire to 'receive briefings from the Governments in the region and United Nations country teams on the impact of climate and ecological changes, including desertification, land degradation and drought, on the humanitarian and security situation and long-term stability and development projects in the region, and their role in exacerbating the traditional drivers of conflict'.[85] During the visit, several interlocutors, including President Mohamadou Issoufou of Niger, conveyed to the Council the need to address climate change's impact on Lake Chad.[86]

After the visit, Resolution 2349, adopted on 31 March 2017, focused on the nexus between security, development, humanitarian and human rights issues in the Lake Chad basin region. While broad in scope, the resolution recognized: 'the adverse effects of climate change and ecological changes among other factors on the stability

participate. Open Arria-formula meetings can be used to enhance awareness of issues of particular interest to the host(s) of the meeting.

[83] They included: a meeting on the 'Security dimensions of climate change' (co-hosted by the United Kingdom and Pakistan on 15 February 2013); 'Climate change as a threat multiplier for global security' (Spain and Malaysia on 30 June 2015); 'Security implications of climate change: sea level rise' (Ukraine in cooperation with Germany on 10 April 2017); 'Preparing for security implications of rising temperatures' (France, Germany, Italy, Japan, Maldives, Morocco, Sweden, the Netherlands, Peru and the United Kingdom on 15 December 2017) and 'water, peace and security' (Bolivia, Côte d'Ivoire, the Netherlands, Belgium, the Dominican Republic, Germany, Indonesia and Italy on 26 October 2018).

[84] S/2017/403 of 5 May 2017 was the UN's report on the visiting mission.

[85] S/2017/181, para 2r.

[86] S/2017/403 of 5 May 2017, para 91.

of the Region, including through water scarcity, drought, desertification, land degradation, and food insecurity'.[87] It also 'emphasise[d] the need for adequate risk assessment and risk management strategies by governments and the United Nations relating to these factors'.[88] Since then, similar (and at times, nearly identical) language has been incorporated into a wide variety of Council products on specific countries and sub-regions in Africa: West Africa and the Sahel,[89] Central Africa,[90] the Central African Republic,[91] Somalia,[92] Mali,[93] Darfur,[94] the Democratic Republic of the Congo,[95]and South Sudan.[96] However, other than emphasizing the need for risk assessments and risk management strategies to address the adverse effect of climate change, ecological changes, and in some cases natural disasters, among other factors, on specific countries and regions, the Council has yet to suggest or mandate concrete measures to be pursued, with the exception of requesting the Secretary-General to 'provide information of…[risk] assessments in mandated reporting as appropriate' on Somalia[97] and Darfur.[98]

In January 2021, for the first time, the Council noted the impact of climate change in a region outside of Africa. In a resolution renewing the mandate of the UN Peacekeeping Force in Cyprus (UNFICYP), the Council recognized that 'effective contact and communication between the sides [the Turkish and Greek Cypriots] … helps to address island-wide matters, including health, crime, environmental protection, and issues related to the adverse impacts of climate change'. It is likely that further efforts will be made to continue to expand language on climate change and security to Council outcomes pertaining to cases outside of Africa.

A notable attempt to ensure the Council incorporates climate-security matters into its agenda occurred on 27 August 2020, when Germany and the nine other co-organizers of the 24 July open debate submitted a letter to the UN Secretary-General informing him of their intention to create an informal expert group on climate and security. The creation of the group is not sanctioned by a formal Council document: the fact that it is an informal, rather than a formal, subsidiary body means that no such founding document is essential, although the ten like-minded members would have preferred it. According to their letter, the group's purpose is to 'provide a space

[87] S/RES/2349 of 31 March 2017, para 26.

[88] Ibid.

[89] S/PRST/2020/3 of 11 February 2020, p. 3; S/PRST/2019/7 of 7 August 2019, p. 4; S/PRST/2018/16, p. 4.

[90] S/PRST/2019/10 of 12 September 2019, pp. 1–2; S/PRST/2018/17 of 10 August 2018, p. 2.

[91] S/RES/2499 of 15 November 2019, preamble; S/RES/2448 of 13 December 2018, preamble.

[92] S/RES/2474 of 31 May 2019, preamble; S/RES/2461 of 27 March 2019, para 21; S/RES/2431 of 30 July 2018, preamble and S/RES/2408 of 27 March 2018, preamble.

[93] S/RES/2480 of 28 June 2019, preamble and S/RES/2423 of 28 June 2018, preamble and para 68.

[94] S/RES/2429 of 13 July 2018, preamble and para 47.

[95] S/RES/2502 of 19 December 2019, preamble.

[96] S/RES/2567 of 12 March 2021, preamble.

[97] S/RES/2461 of 27 March 2019, para 21.

[98] S/RES/2429 of 13 July 2018, para 47.

for transparent, regular and systematic consultations between country experts [in Council delegations] and United Nations entities on climate-related security risks in order to improve the understanding of the adverse effects of climate change on peace and security and help strengthen the Council's efforts to mainstream the climate and security agenda in its daily work'.[99] While most current Council members are likely to attend meetings of the group, it is unlikely that naysayers on the Council will engage substantively in the group's work.

Resistance from China, Russia, and the United States during the Trump administration prevented the Council from pursuing more concrete actions, such as authorizing the deployment of climate advisors in UN peace operations, or incorporating climate-security language more widely, particularly in cases outside of Africa. Nonetheless, the consistent calls for risk assessments and risk management strategies make it clear that many Council members view the organ's engagement on climate-security matters largely in terms of conflict prevention. Members repeatedly emphasize the link between climate-security issues and the Council's conflict prevention agenda in public statements. In the 24 July 2020 open debate, France made perhaps the most direct connection in this regard, when it stated that 'the repercussions of climate change and the collapse of biodiversity on international security must imperatively become a key element of the conflict prevention agenda'.[100] Others drew this connection as well.[101] Furthermore, if we understand prevention in a broad context that encompasses the avoidance of conflict relapse, it is useful to note that some Council members have underscored that addressing climate-security threats should support peacebuilding efforts in post-conflict situations.[102]

21.3.2 Preventive Diplomacy and Trans-boundary Waters

Another environmental issue that has garnered some attention in the Security Council is the management of trans-boundary waters. The matter is often raised during semi-annual consultations on the work of the UN Regional Centre for Preventive Diplomacy for Central Asia (UNRCCA). In their January 2018 press statement on the UNRCCA, Council members 'commended the ongoing efforts of UNRCCA to assist the Central Asian states in transboundary water management and encouraged all Central Asian States to play a full and active role in this process'.[103] They further called on 'the Centre to continue to promote regional dialogue and encouraged all

[99] S/2020/849 of 27 August 2020.

[100] S/2020/751 of 28 July 2020, p. 21.

[101] Ibid., statements by Belgium, p. 10, Germany, p. 13, Estonia, p. 14, the United Kingdom, p. 16 and the Dominican Republic, pp. 19–20.

[102] Ibid., statements by the United Kingdom, p. 16 and Indonesia, p. 23.

[103] SC/13179 of 25 January 2018.

States in the region to engage constructively in consultations to reach agreement on how to meet energy and water resource challenges across the region'.[104]

The management of trans-boundary waters was a key feature of the open debate that Senegal convened on 'Water, peace and security' during its November 2016 Council presidency.[105] One of the featured briefers at the meeting, Secretary-General António Guterres spoke about the 'hydro-diplomacy' conducted by the UNRCCA, observing that it 'uses its good offices, convening power, analytical capacity and partnerships with regional organizations to promote dialogue and build trust'.[106] Danilo Türk, the Chair of the Global High-Level Panel on Water and Peace, also addressed the Council, maintaining that: 'Cooperation in shared water basins is a historically proven factor of post-conflict stabilization and peacebuilding'.[107]

Seven months later, Bolivia initiated a high-level briefing on 'Preventive diplomacy and transboundary waters' during its Council presidency in June 2017.[108] Secretary-General Guterres, again briefing, maintained that tensions regarding water access were increasing in all regions, and that without 'effective management of our water resources, we risk intensified disputes between communities and sectors and even increased tensions among nations'.[109] In highlighting the importance of international cooperation on trans-boundary waters, he observed how widely water resources are shared: 'All told, there are more than 270 internationally shared river basins that serve as the primary source of fresh water for approximately 40 per cent of the world's population. That is why it is essential that nations cooperate to ensure that water is shared equitably and used sustainably'.[110] The meeting came a year after Chile initiated a case against Bolivia over the use of the Silala river, which is pending before the International Court of Justice at time of writing.[111]

Most Council members expressed their support for both the November 2016 and the June 2017 meetings. Egypt, for example, called for a Security Council outcome addressing trans-boundary water management in the meeting on preventive diplomacy and transboundary waters.[112] However, Russia was dismissive of a Council role, particularly during the June 2017 meeting.[113] As with climate change, it maintained that water-related issues more broadly are essentially sustainable development concerns that are better addressed in other UN entities with relevant expertise.

---

104 Ibid.

105 S/PV.7818 of 22 November 2016.

106 Ibid., Statement by Secretary-General António Guterres, p. 3.

107 Ibid., Statement by Danilo Türk, p. 6.

108 S/PV.7959 of 6 June 2017.

109 Ibid., Statement by Secretary-General António Guterres, p. 2.

110 Ibid.

111 ICJ, *Dispute over the Status and Use of the Waters of the Silala (Chile v Bolivia)*. For background on the case, see https://www.icj-cij.org/en/case/162. Accessed 30 April 2021.

112 S/PV.7959 of 6 June 2017, Statement by Egypt, p. 13.

113 Ibid., Statement by Russia, pp. 13–14.

Ethiopia similarly stated that: ‘the topic is best addressed by the General Assembly and the Economic and Social Council’.[114]

Disagreements involving Egypt, Ethiopia and Sudan with regard to the Grand Ethiopian Renaissance Dam have also been discussed in the Security Council. This issue has important implications for the countries’ access to the Nile river. In May 2020, Egypt and Ethiopia wrote letters to the Council stating their positions. Egypt argued that the envisioned ‘unilateral filling and operation’ of the Dam by Ethiopia, ‘could cause significant harm to downstream communities’, negatively impacting water and food security and ‘potentially pos[ing] a serious threat to peace and security throughout the region’.[115] Ethiopia responded that its good faith efforts to negotiate a mutually beneficial solution to the Dam’s operation had not been reciprocated by Egypt in the context of ongoing negotiations among the two countries and Sudan on this issue.[116] Expressing historical grievances in the letter, Ethiopia asserted that: ‘Egypt, through colonial-based treaties to which Ethiopia is not a party, saw to it that it received the lion’s share of Nile water…leaving nothing to the remaining nine riparian countries’.[117] In a letter of 2 June 2020 to the Council, Sudan described potential positive and negative impacts of the dam,[118] and said that the three parties could resolve their difference through ‘strong political will and commitment’.[119]

Council members met in an open videoconference session to discuss this issue on 29 June 2020.[120] During the meeting, Under-Secretary-General for Political and Peacebuilding Affairs Rosemary DiCarlo emphasized that ‘climate change, combined with projected demographic growth and socioeconomic changes, will increase water management challenges — not only for Blue Nile riparian countries but worldwide’.[121] DiCarlo and Council members urged the parties to negotiate a mutually acceptable resolution to their dispute. African members Niger and South Africa urged the Council to defer to regional efforts by the AU to mediate the dispute. In April 2021, Egypt and Sudan wrote separate letters to the Security Council declaring that AU mediation had failed to produce results.[122] Ethiopia also wrote to the Council, accusing Egypt and Sudan of not negotiating in good faith.[123] As of early May 2021, it did not appear that the Security Council had the appetite to reengage on the issue and deal with it in a substantive way. This may be out of concern from some Council members that giving the dispute significant attention could set

---

[114] Ibid., Statement by Ethiopia, p. 19.

[115] S/2020/355 of 1 May 2020, p. 2.

[116] S/2020/409 of 14 May 2020.

[117] Ibid., p. 2.

[118] S/2020/480 of 2 June 2020, pp. 2–3.

[119] Ibid, p. 3.

[120] S/2020/636 of 1 July 2020.

[121] Ibid., p. 3.

[122] S/2021/351 of 12 April 2021 is the letter from Sudan. S/2021/354 of 13 April 2021 is the letter from Egypt.

[123] S/2021/376 (16 April 2021).

a precedent whereby the Council would be expected to respond to the multitude of other international disputes over transboundary waters.[124]

21.3.3 Protection of the Environment in Armed Conflict

The Security Council has regularly considered the topic of the protection of civilians in armed conflict and humanitarian law since 1999.[125] In recent years, Council members have also discussed the environmental dimension of armed conflict. Arria-formula meetings on the 'Protection of the Environment in Armed Conflict' were convened on 7 November 2018 and 9 December 2019. The 2018 meeting was initiated by Kuwait and Germany,[126] and the 2019 session was hosted by Kuwait, Germany, Peru and Estonia.[127] In these informal meetings, a number of Council members recognized the importance of considering environmental matters in the organ's work before, during and after conflict. Some members emphasized the need to uphold international humanitarian law with respect to protecting the environment in armed conflict, including by respecting its civilian character and by refraining from reprisal attacks on the environment.[128]

Not all were supportive of a Security Council role on protecting the environment in armed conflict, however. Russia expressed again its scepticism in both meetings. In the 2019 meeting, while emphasizing the importance of protecting the environment in armed conflict in international humanitarian law, Russia nonetheless argued that the Security Council is not the appropriate forum to address this issue.[129] It posited that international platforms such as the UN Environment Program (UNEP) and the UN Environmental Assembly are better suited in this regard.[130] Likewise, Bolivia said in the 2018 meeting that Council engagement on this issue would encroach on the responsibilities of other UN entities and could duplicate their efforts.[131]

---

[124] Interview with former Security Council diplomat, 10 May 2021.

[125] S/PV.3977 of 12 February 1999.

[126] Arria-formula meeting on "Protection of the Environment in Armed Conflict", 7 November 2018. http://webtv.un.org/search/protection-of-the-environment-during-armed-conflict-security-council-arria-formula-meeting/5859032430001/?term=Arria-formula%20Protection%20of%20the%20Environment%20during%20Armed%20Conflict&sort=date. Accessed 30 April 2021.

[127] Arria-formula meeting on "Protection of the Environment in Armed Conflict", 9 December 2019. http://webtv.un.org/search/arria-formula-meeting-on-protection-of-the-environment-during-armed-conflict/6114430670001/?term=Arria-formula%20Protection%20of%20the%20Environment%20during%20Armed%20Conflict&sort=date. Accessed 30 April 2021.

[128] E.g., Statements by Kuwait and Belgium in 7 November 2018 meeting, above n 126.

[129] Arria-formula meeting on 'Protection of the Environment in Armed Conflict', 9 December 2019, above n 127.

[130] Ibid.

[131] Arria-formula meeting on 'Protection of the Environment in Armed Conflict', 7 November 2018, above n 126.

In addition to these two Arria-formula meetings, the Council has also occasionally explored the environmental impacts of conflict in more formal meetings. Briefings from the UN Office for the Coordination of Humanitarian Affairs on the humanitarian situation in Yemen often include updates on negotiations with the Houthi rebels to permit a technical mission led by the UN to assess the condition of the FSO Safer oil tanker near the Ras Isa oil terminal north of Hodeidah in territory controlled by the Houthis, which has not been maintained since 2015.[132] The UN has expressed concern that 'the lack of maintenance of the 44-year old vessel could cause a major leak or explosion that would release its more than 1.1 million barrels of oil into the sea, creating an environmental catastrophe'.[133] On 15 July 2020, Council members held a videoconference meeting specifically devoted to the environmental threat posed by the FSO Safer,[134] a matter of widespread concern in the Council. During this session, Executive Director of UNEP Inger Andersen told members that 'an oil spill or an explosion would have a massive impact on the livelihoods and the health of the people relying on the area's natural resources, including fisheries'.[135] She also said that such a harmful effect on livelihoods 'would…contribute to a deterioration of security in the region, as the resources upon which the population relies would become polluted, scarce and contested'.[136] As of May 2021, the UN had yet to gain access to the FSO Safer, despite a commitment by the Houthis to permit such access.

More recently, Niger organized an open debate in videoconference format on the 'Humanitarian Effects of Environmental Degradation and Peace and Security' during its September 2020 Council presidency.[137] The meeting featured briefings by Peter Maurer, President of the International Committee of the Red Cross; Ibrahim Thiaw, the Executive Secretary of the Convention to Combat Desertification (UNCCD); and Inna Modja, a UNCCD Earth Ambassador. The briefers—as well as several Council members—described the complex interactions between environmental degradation, climate change, and peace and security.[138]

21.3.4 Natural Resources and the Environment

Over the years, the Council has held several debates on the relationship between natural resources and conflict.[139] Environmental issues have been raised in these

---

[132] Security Council Report (2020), Yemen: Mandate Renewal on UNMHA and Council VTC on the FSO Safer oil tanker. https://www.whatsinblue.org/2020/07/yemen-mandate-renewal-of-unmha-and-council-vtc-on-the-fso-safer-oil-tanker.php. Accessed 30 April 2021.

[133] Ibid.

[134] S/2020/721 of 17 July 2020.

[135] Ibid., p. 2.

[136] Ibid.

[137] S/2020/929 of 17 September 2020.

[138] SC/14307 of 17 September 2020.

[139] S/PV.5705 of 25 June 2007; S/PV.6982 of 19 June 2013 and S/PV.8372 of 16 October 2018.

meetings in two main ways. First, Council members have emphasized the environmental degradation often caused by the exploitation and mismanagement of natural resources.[140] Second, they have argued that climate change is leading to resource (namely water) scarcity, that can heighten the threat of conflict.[141] In some instances, the Security Council has imposed sanctions on individuals for providing support to armed groups by illegally exploiting or trading in natural resources, including minerals and wildlife.[142]

21.4 Should the Security Council Address Environmental Issues?

There are a number of arguments made against Security Council involvement on environmental issues: that they are not matters relevant to the Council's peace and security role, that the Council encroaches on the prerogatives of other UN entities when it addresses such issues, and even at times, that its involvement on these matters is a pretext for heavy-handed intervention in the domestic affairs of sovereign member states. These will be addressed in this section.

21.4.1 The Climate-Security Connection

A key challenge for those who believe that environmental issues should be a focus of the Security Council's attention is to provide evidence of linkages between those factors and conflict. In this regard, there has been significant discussion among scholars and among UN member states about the evidence of connections between security and climate change, including with regard to the Security Council's work. Penney has written: 'there is little evidence that climate change has been directly responsible for violent conflict outbursts. In fact, the link between the two remains uncertain'.[143] Brown, Hammill and McLeman have similarly noted that it is an 'analytical challenge…to disaggregate the role of climate change from other environmental, economic, social and political factors, if it is at all possible to do so'.[144] In the January 2019 debate on the impact of climate-related disasters on international

---

[140] E.g., S/PV.5705 of 25 June 2007, statement by Ghana, p. 13; S/PV.6982 of 19 June 2013, statements by Togo, p. 15 and Guatemala, p. 19 and S/PV.8372 of 18 October 2018, statement by Poland, p. 15.

[141] E.g., S/PV.5705 of 25 June 2007, statement by Ghana, p. 14; S/PV.6982 of 19 June 2013, statement by Republic of Korea, p. 22 and S/PV.8372 of 16 October 2018, statements by France, p. 16, the United Kingdom, p. 18 and Kazakhstan, p. 19.

[142] E.g., S/RES/2293 of 23 June 2016, para 7(g), preamble and S/RES/2399 of 30 January 2018, para 21(e), preamble.

[143] Penney 2018, p. 31.

[144] Brown et al. 2007, p. 1147.

peace and security, Russia stated that 'a generalized linking of the topic of climate change with peace can lead to the false assumption that the problems of the environment are unavoidable and always lead to conflict', while India noted that 'research findings on the generalized linkages between climate disasters and security remain ambiguous'.[145]

For these reasons, those member states wary of climate change as a Security Council agenda item insist on compelling evidence connecting climate change to security problems in specific cases before they see any merit in Security Council engagement, especially when there are other factors that are more direct drivers of conflict.[146]

Another concern shared by these states is that addressing climate change in the Council risks the possibility that coercive measures may be employed, although this criticism is rarely publicly expressed.[147] One time when this concern was voiced was during the debate on climate-related disasters in January 2019, when India said: 'Thinking in security terms usually engenders overly militarized solutions to problems that inherently require non-military responses to resolve them... As the saying goes, if you have a hammer, everything looks like a nail'.[148]

This argument captures the fears of developing countries worried about big powers intruding on their domestic affairs under false pretences. The NATO operation in Libya in 2011 reinforced the concerns of some member states that a humanitarian rationale for intervention can be a pretext for a wider agenda, including regime change.[149]

While drawing direct connections between climate change and security can be difficult,[150] many UN member states, and regional organizations, have taken a contrasting view, underscoring that climate change acts as a 'threat multiplier' that can exacerbate tensions over resources and contribute to conflict in specific cases.[151] Member states that believe that climate change should be an important part of the Council's agenda emphasize the linkages between climate change and security, and maintain that enhanced analysis of these connections can help the Council to assess and respond more effectively to specific security challenges.[152]

---

[145] S/PV.8451 of 25 January 2019, statements by Russia, p. 16, and India, p. 43.

[146] E.g., S/PV.8451 of 25 January 2019, statements by Russia, p. 16 and India, p. 43.

[147] Interview with UN Security Council diplomat, 24 March 2020.

[148] S/PV.8451 of 25 January 2019.

[149] See e.g., General Assembly 66th session, statements by Zimbabwe, 22 September 2011 (gadebate.un.org/en/66/Zimbabwe—accessed 30 April 2021), Cuba, 26 September 2011 (gadebate.un.org/en/66/cuba—accessed 30 April 2021) and Venezuela, 27 September 2011 (gadebate.un.org/en/66/Venezuela-bolivarian-republic—accessed 30 April 2021).

[150] On this challenge, see Conca 2019, pp. 6–8.

[151] E.g., S/PV.8212 of 22 March 2018, statement by Sweden, p. 11; S.PV.8307 of 11 July 2018, statement by Kazakhstan, p. 12 and S/PV.8451 of 25 January 2019, statements by Estonia, p. 34, the European Union, p. 44, Portugal, p. 47, the African Union, p. 55 and Trinidad and Tobago, p. 62.

[152] E.g., S/PV.8451 of 25 January 2019, statements by Germany, p. 12, France, p. 19, the Dominican Republic, pp. 24–25 and Sweden, p. 53.

Those member states that espouse Security Council engagement on climate change frequently maintain that this is part of the Council's conflict prevention work.[153] Assuming that environmental factors act as threat-multipliers or even contribute to the outbreak of conflict, Chapter VI offers a variety of largely recommendatory and non-binding avenues for action, as noted above.[154]

There have been some institutional structures created in recent years to explore the linkages between climate and security that may be useful to the Security Council. Since 2018, a small Climate Security Mechanism that relies on voluntary contributions from member states has operated in UN headquarters in New York; it consists of staff from the UN Department of Political and Peacebuilding Affairs, the UN Development Programme, and UNEP. It recently developed a 'tool box' of guidance documents on climate-related security matters in order to help inform UN staff working on peace and security issues. It has also gathered information on the security-related impacts of climate change that has been incorporated into reports of the Secretary-General to the Security Council in certain cases.[155]

A Climate Security Expert Network—consisting of an international group of some 30 experts—has also been formed that, according to its website, synthesizes 'scientific knowledge and expertise, advising on entry points for building resilience to climate-security risks, and helping to strengthen a shared understanding of the challenges and opportunities of addressing climate-related security risks'.[156] Its work is meant to support that of the UN's Climate Security Mechanism and the UN Group of Friends of Climate and Security.[157] The Climate Security Expert Network has produced detailed 'climate-fragility risk assessments' on various countries and regions, including Afghanistan,[158] South Asia,[159] and North Africa and the Sahel,[160] among others.

---

[153] E.g., S/PV.8451 of 25 January 2019, statements by Belgium, p. 10, Peru, p. 18, France, p. 19, Spain, p. 44, Portugal, p. 47 and Sweden, p. 53.

[154] See Sect. 21.2.

[155] Private discussion with UN Secretariat official, 23 March 2020.

[156] Climate Security Expert Network website. https://www.climate-security-expert-network.org/start. Accessed 30 April 2021.

[157] Initiated by Germany and Nauru in August 2018 and currently consisting of 50 member states, the goal of the Group of Friends to collaborate in generating ideas for climate change and security policy, enhancing public awareness of the issue, and strengthening the UN's engagement on climate-security matters.

[158] Brown 2019a.

[159] Jayaram 2019.

[160] Brown 2019b.

21.4.2 The Peace, Security and Development Nexus

As seen above,[161] some Security Council members have argued that climate change and other environmental issues are essentially sustainable development matters that in their view, are not within the Council's purview. In recent decades, however, there has been recognition in the decisions of the Security Council and the General Assembly of the interconnectedness among peace, security and development. This is consistent with the view that there should be a comprehensive approach to international peace and security. It assumes that even if environmental matters are considered primarily issues of sustainable development, they can have security implications, and thus, should be relevant to the Council's work. The 2005 World Summit Outcome document is a prominent example of the view that security and development are linked. Endorsed by the world's heads of state and government, it 'recognize[d] that development, peace and security and human rights are interlinked and mutually reinforcing',[162] a perspective reiterated in several Security Council outcomes, including its most recent formal product on conflict prevention in early 2018.[163]

Many other Council outcomes over the years have also emphasized the importance of promoting sustainable development as a way to address the root causes of conflict. This can be seen, for example, in resolution 1625, one of the Council's seminal resolutions on conflict prevention as mentioned above,[164] and resolution 2282, also known as the 'sustaining peace' resolution.[165] Resolution 1625 calls for attention to be paid to 'activities to prevent conflicts arising from competition for economic resources and to monitor...tension arising from economic and social issues'.[166] Resolution 2282, identical to a resolution adopted by the General Assembly on the same day,[167] is perhaps the clearest pronouncement by the Council that a holistic approach is required to prevent conflict and maintain peace. It says that 'sustaining peace' includes 'activities aimed at preventing the outbreak, escalation, continuance and recurrence of conflict...and should flow through all three pillars of the UN's engagement [peace and security, human rights and sustainable development] at all stages of conflict'.[168] The possible implication of these Council outcomes is that even if one were to consider most environmental issues primarily under the rubric of 'sustainable development', they could logically be considered acceptable for Council engagement, given Council precedent for drawing connections between 'sustainable development' and peace and security. One caveat to this view is that resolution 2282 also recognises that 'an integrated and coherent approach among relevant political, security and developmental actors, within and outside of the

---

[161] See Sect. 21.3.

[162] A/60/L.1 f 20 September 2005, para 9.

[163] S/PRST/2018/1 of 18 January 2018, p. 1.

[164] S/RES/1625 of 14 September 2005. See also Sect. 21.2.

[165] S/RES/2282 of 27 April 2016.

[166] S/RES/1625 of 14 September 2005, para 4a.

[167] A/RES/70/262 of 27April, 2016.

[168] S/RES/2282 of 27 April 2016, preamble.

United Nations system, *consistent with their respective mandates*, and the Charter of the United Nations, is critical to sustaining peace'.[169] This could be perceived as an expression of concern about possible Security Council infringement on the prerogatives of other UN organs, an issue that we turn to in the next section.

21.4.3 Encroachment on Other UN Organs and Bodies?

Some states take the view that the Security Council is encroaching on the mandate of other UN organs by considering climate change and other environmental issues. The main thrust of this perspective is that other UN organs—mainly the UN General Assembly and the Economic and Social Council—and specialized UN funds and programs are better suited than the Security Council to address environmental issues, even if they may have security implications, because of their expertise, resources and experience. There is also a political dimension to the encroachment argument. Some member states believe that the Security Council should not step on the toes of other UN organs on issues that have wide-ranging global implications because its composition and procedures are undemocratic.[170] Concern has further been raised that the 'securitization' of climate change diverts resources from development work.[171] The encroachment argument has frequently been raised in relation to the Security Council's involvement with climate change, although others have made the same argument with environmental issues more broadly.

In contrast, those espousing Security Council engagement on climate-security risks and other environmental challenges tend to believe that this organ is one of many UN actors that should strive to collaborate in a synergistic way to tackle these risks. These member states see the Council as one piece of a large puzzle, rather than as an ill-equipped interloper. They aspire for a UN system that confronts actual and potential environmental linkages to armed conflict in a coherent way that effectively coordinates resources and expertise.

With regard to climate change in particular, even staunch supporters of Security Council engagement, both in the Council and among the wider UN membership, recognize that the UNFCCC[172] is the primary forum in the UN system on this issue.[173]

---

[169] Ibid, emphasis added.

[170] Conca 2019, pp. 9–10; see also Kron 2019, p. 84.

[171] E.g., S/2020/751 of 28 July 2020, statement by Brazil, p. 46.

[172] The UNFCCC secretariat (known as UN Climate Change), established by the General Assembly in 1992, consists of some 450 staff persons and supports international climate change efforts, including the negotiations that led to the 2015 Paris Agreement.

[173] S/PRST/2011/15 of 20 July 2011. See also, for example, S/PV.8307 of 11 July 2018, statements by France, p. 14 and the Maldives, on behalf of the Alliance of Small Island States, p. 26 and S/PV.6587 of 20 July 2011, statements by Nauru, on behalf of the Pacific Small Island Developing States, p. 23 and by Australia, pp. 24–25.

However, the UNFCCC is not tasked with addressing the peace and security implications of climate change, nor does it have the authority to do so or engage in dispute resolution. Its work is geared toward climate mitigation and adaptation.

As a result, the Security Council's role on climate change can be viewed as complementary to that of the UNFCCC and other UN entities that work to address the many challenges associated with global warming. In this respect, at the open debate hosted by the Dominican Republic in January 2019, Belgium espoused 'finding ways to bring together the available know-how, in accordance with a unique and integrated United Nations approach' to address climate-related security risks,[174] while Peru emphasized the importance of 'develop[ing] synergies among the Council, the General Assembly and the Economic and Social Council, as well as with those competent bodies and agencies of the United Nations system with a view to having early warning systems for climate-related risks and other multidimensional threats'.[175]

Security Council practice and the UN Charter support such perspectives. The Council has traditionally delved into areas related to socio-economic development when it believes that they have peace and security implications. Furthermore, while the UN Charter outlines the responsibilities and functions of different UN organs, it envisions considerable overlap among them. The relationship among the Security Council, the General Assembly and ECOSOC—organs that the Security Council is sometimes accused of infringing upon—is no exception in this respect. These organs do not operate in silos, and there is considerable interaction among them, as is stipulated in the Charter. According to article 11(3), the General Assembly 'may call the attention of the Security Council to situations which are likely to endanger international peace and security'. Under article 12(1), the General Assembly may make recommendations to the Council, except on issues the Council is currently considering.[176]

The UN Charter provides for ECOSOC-Security Council interaction on environmental (and other economic and social) issues that have a potential impact on international peace and security. According to Article 65 of the Charter, ECOSOC 'may furnish information to the Security Council and shall assist the Security Council *upon its request*'.[177] In 1992, Secretary-General Boutros Boutros-Ghali noted in his report 'An Agenda for Peace' the potential relevance of Article 65 as part of an early warning system (for potential conflict), recommending that the Security Council invite ECOSOC to provide reports on 'those economic and social developments that may, unless mitigated, threaten international peace and security'. In resolution 1625,

[174] S/PV.8451 of 25 January 2019, statement by Belgium, p. 10.

[175] Ibid., statement by Peru, p. 18.

[176] For example, though the Security Council is regularly seized of the situation in Syria, in December 2016, the UN General Assembly adopted a resolution establishing the 'Independent, Impartial, and Independent Mechanism to Assist in the in the Investigation and Prosecution of Persons Responsible for the Most Serious Crimes under International Law Committed in the Syrian Arab Republic since March 2011', A/RES/71/248 of 21 December 2016, para 4. See also Johnson 2014, pp. 106–115.

[177] Emphasis added.

the Council requested ECOSOC to provide it 'as necessary and appropriate information and assistance', also consistent with Article 65. In practice, since 2002, the ECOSOC president has briefed the Security Council on several instances on a variety of country-specific and thematic issues.

21.5 Possible Future Role for the Security Council in the Protection of the Environment and Settling Environmental Disputes

The Security Council's role is not to protect the environment or to settle environmental disputes as a court or tribunal may. Nor should the Security Council be seen as a venue to bypass other processes such as the UNFCCC. But the Council can play a role, and indeed, has done so in the past, when it perceives that it is pertinent to the maintenance of international peace and security. Of course, when considering potential Council action, it is important to bear in mind that the political dynamics of a given situation, not just the framework discussed in this chapter, will influence the decision making of the Council.

21.5.1 The Environment and Conflict Prevention

A wide array of non-coercive tools are available to the Security Council under Chapter VI of the UN Charter that could be used to address environmental challenges to international peace and security, consistent with the view that exploring issues such as climate change and water security are part and parcel of its conflict prevention responsibilities.[178] The Council has investigatory powers under Article 34 of the UN Charter. Its efforts to learn more about the impacts of climate and ecological changes on the stability and security of the Lake Chad Basin region during its visiting mission there in March 2017, may be seen as an example of these powers.[179]

In fact, the Council has worked assiduously to expand its understanding of the links between climate change and security over the past decade. The Council has requested the UN Secretary-General to report where these linkages exist.[180] With the establishment of the climate-security mechanism in 2018—and assuming that UN peace operations develop greater capacity and expertise to analyse climate-security risks—it is foreseeable that improved reporting on this issue will be provided to the Council in the coming years. There has already been limited progress in reporting

[178] E.g., S/PV.8451 of 25 January 2019, statements by Belgium, p. 10, Poland, p. 13, Peru, p. 18, France, p. 19 and the Dominican Republic, p. 24 on climate change and S/PV.7818 of 22 November 2016, statements by Ukraine, p. 14, New Zealand, p. 23 and Egypt, p. 25 on water scarcity.

[179] See Sect 21.3.1.

[180] S/PRST/2011/15 of 20 July 2011, see Sect 21.3.1.

to the Council on climate-security issues, as reflected in the Secretary-General's reporting on Central Africa[181] and West Africa and the Sahel[182] in recent years. The knowledge base of the Council is also being enhanced on the relationship between security and climate change through various thematic Security Council meetings that have been held on climate-security matters. More briefings on environmental security challenges by civil society experts on country-specific issues could be useful sources of information for Council members; one example of such a briefing was when the Director of the Stockholm International Peace Research Institute addressed the Council on 24 February 2020 on climate-security risks in Somalia and how the UN Assistance Mission in Somalia could address them.[183]

There is also room for more collaboration among the Council and other UN organs in addressing environmental security threats. The 13 November 2018 joint meeting between ECOSOC and the Peacebuilding Commission, a subsidiary body of both the Security Council and the General Assembly, 'on linkages between climate change and challenges to peacebuilding and sustaining peace in the Sahel' is an example of cross-pollination between different UN organs to address climate and security issues.[184] Such meetings might be a helpful way for different parts of the UN system to share information and consider coordinated strategies for addressing environmental security risks.

While greater awareness and knowledge can help to inform the Council's deliberations, what proactive measures can this organ take to influence the decision-making of actors on the ground? Chapter VI of the UN Charter offers some non-coercive tools in this regard. Under article 33, the Council can call upon parties to resolve disputes through 'peaceful means of their choice', and this would certainly be an option for the Council in the case of a dispute related to climate change or other ecological factors endangering international peace and security. While politically unlikely, as the Security Council has only done this once,[185] the Council could also recommend that parties refer such disputes to the International Court of Justice.[186]

Although politically untenable at present, a future option for the Council could be to authorize the deployment of climate advisors in various UN peace operations. In terms of precedent for these positions, Germany has provided voluntary funding for an 'environmental security adviser' to 'work [with UN entities in Somalia] on issues related to the impact of climate change, environmental degradation and conflicts

[181] S/2019/913 of 29 November 2019, para 21–22, 82; S/2019/430 of 24 May 2019, para 26–27 and S/2018/1065 of 29 November 2018, para 25–26.

[182] S/2019/1005 of 30 December 2019, paras 59, 95; S/2019/549 of 5 July 2019, paras 28, 51, 56, 71, 88–89 and S/2018/1175 of 28 December 2018, paras 19, 20, 55, 62, 94.

[183] S/PV.8731 of 24 February 2020, statement by Dan Smith, pp. 6–8.

[184] S/2019/73 of 28 January 2019.

[185] S/RES/22 of 9 April 1947.

[186] The ICJ has dealt with several environmental disputes, e.g., *Aerial Herbicide Spraying (Ecuador v Colombia)*; *Pulp Mills on the River Uruguay, (Argentina v Uruguay)*, Judgement, 20 April 2010, ICJ Reports 2010, p. 14; *Nuclear Tests Case (Australia v France)*, Judgement, 20 December 1974, ICJ Reports 1974, p. 253 and *Nuclear Tests Case (New Zealand v France)*, Judgement, 20 December 1974, ICJ Reports 1974, p. 457.

over natural resources'.[187] This individual, who was deployed in the fall of 2020, is tasked with 'provid[ing] analysis on how these issues may affect dynamics or politics, security and conflicts' and enhancing 'coordination of environment-related programmes and projects in Somalia'.[188]

Funding such a position with UN assessed funds—that is, requiring member states to pay for such posts through their contributions to UN peacekeeping operations—would most likely be objectionable to some of the larger contributors among member states that object to Council engagement on environmental issues. It appears that climate advisors were a desired element of the draft resolution on climate and security that was aborted in July 2020, mainly due to US resistance. However, the creation of such posts could eventually become acceptable in specific cases, where there is clear evidence of the existence of a link between environmental factors and security and where the tasks associated with the post are not viewed as overly intrusive by the host government.

Finally, under Article 29 of the UN Charter, '[t]he Security Council may establish such subsidiary organs as it deems necessary for the performance of its functions'. Formal working groups—such as the Council's Working Group on Children and Armed Conflict—have been established through Council products.[189] Establishing a formal subsidiary body to address environmental security concerns would be difficult, if not impossible, at present, given the current dynamics in the Council. However, as we have seen, 10 Council members recently established an informal expert group on climate and security without a formal Security Council decision.[190] This could be used as a platform for generating language on the security risks of climate change or other ecological factors in the mandates of peace operations, just as the Council's Informal Experts Group on the Protection of Civilians has been a mechanism to discuss protection language in such mandates. It may also be a way for Council members to receive quality information from specialists on how ecological factors are impacting security in country- and region-specific cases.

[187] Eklöw and Krampe 2019, p. 37.

[188] Ibid.

[189] S/PRST/2002/2 of 31 January 2002 in the case of the ad-hoc Working Group on Conflict Prevention and Resolution in Africa; S/PRST/2001/3 of 31 January 2001 in the case of the Working Group on Peacekeeping Operations; and S/RES/1612 of 26 July 2005 in the case of the Working Group on Children and Armed Conflict.

[190] While the Informal Experts Group on Women, Peace and Security was established through resolution 2242 of 13 October 2015, the Informal Experts Group on Protection of Civilians was formed in 2009 without an authorizing Council product.

21.5.2 Addressing Environmental Disasters or Events with Environmental Aspects that Endanger International Peace and Security

Some states have expressed scepticism that the unique and broad enforcement powers given to the Security Council in the UN Charter are useful when it comes to environmental issues.[191] Indeed, it does not seem to be contentious that other UN bodies such as UNEP are better equipped to consider such matters. Moreover, universal action on challenges like climate change requires universal participation such as in multilateral treaties, and it is thus ill-suited for consideration by a body of 15 member states focused on security issues. While the Council may not be the appropriate forum to coordinate or dictate strategies and actions to protect the environment, when disputes or conflicts arise, there may be environmental aspects that can or should be addressed by the Security Council. Below are a few examples.

The Security Council has many times condemned alleged violations of international humanitarian law.[192] One such violation, found in Additional Protocol I[193] and customary international law,[194] is the prohibition on methods of warfare intended or expected to cause widespread, long-term and severe damage to the natural environment.[195] Thus, where relevant, the Security Council may condemn cases of serious environmental damages in armed conflict as violations of international humanitarian law. Where the Security Council has imposed sanctions on individuals for violations of international humanitarian law generally, this covers such practices as well.[196] Moreover, if relevant in a particular situation, the Security Council may deem it beneficial to impose sanctions on individuals partaking in such methods explicitly, as a stand-alone designation criterion.

Similarly, the Security Council has promoted accountability for perpetrators of mass crimes, including war crimes.[197] One such war crime can be: 'launching an attack in the knowledge that such attack will cause... widespread, long-term and

[191] S/PV.8451 of 25 January 2019.

[192] E.g., S/PRST/2019/8 of 20 August 2019 on the 70th anniversary of the Geneva Conventions; S/RES/2409 of 27 March 2018, paras 11, 14, 19, preamble and S/RES/2459 of 15 March 2019, paras 26, 37, preamble.

[193] Protocol Additional to the Geneva Conventions of 12 August 1949, relating to the protection of victims of international armed conflicts (Protocol I), opened for signature 8 June 1977, 1125 UNTS 3, entered into force 7 December 1978, Articles 35(3) and 55(1).

[194] Henckaerts and Doswald-Beck 2005, Rule 45, p. 151.

[195] See also ibid. Rule 44, p. 147 on due regard to the protection and preservation of the natural environment during conflict, as well as the application of the precautionary principle to environmental damage.

[196] See, for example, S/RES/2399 of 30 January 2018, para 21(b), which imposed sanctions on individuals '[i]nvolved in planning, directing, or committing acts in the CAR that violate international human rights law or international humanitarian law'.

[197] E.g., S/PRST/2019/8 of 20 August 2019, where the Security Council recalled the 'the importance of ensuring compliance with international humanitarian law and international human rights law, ending impunity for violations and abuses, and ensuring accountability'; S/RES/2499 of 15

severe damage to the natural environment which would be clearly excessive in relation to the concrete and direct overall military advantage anticipated'.[198]

Here too, the Security Council can condemn this crime and call on states to hold those that have knowingly caused excessive environmental damage during armed conflict accountable.

A potential precedent for such action was taken by the Council in 2011 in the context of piracy off the shores of Somalia. Here, the Security Council recognized the importance of preventing illegal dumping of toxic substances, and stressed the need to investigate allegations of such incidents.[199] The Security Council then requested the Secretary-General to report to it on the protection of Somali natural resources and waters, and on alleged illegal fishing and illegal dumping, including of toxic substances.[200] Moreover, it urged states to consider investigating allegations of 'illegal dumping, including of toxic substances, with a view to prosecuting such offences when committed by persons under their jurisdiction'.[201]

The Security Council may also find it necessary to take action, including enforcement action, to address immediate threats to international peace and security caused by environment-related events, such as natural disasters. This may be unlikely at present due to the view of some Security Council members, although not inconceivable. In May 2008, France took the view that Myanmar was not responding adequately to the humanitarian crisis resulting from Cyclone Nargis.[202] In discussions with Security Council members, it invoked the 'responsibility to protect' to argue that aid should be delivered to Myanmar, even without its consent if need be, by using the Security Council's enforcement powers.[203]

France's view failed to gain currency among Security Council members and ultimately no action was taken.[204] However, it is possible that, in the future, the Council

---

November 2019, paras 15, 21 and 33 and S/RES/2405 of 8 March 2018, paras 23, 33, 38 and preamble.

[198] Rome Statute of the International Criminal Court, opened for signature 17 July 1998, 2187 UNTS 3, entered into force 1 July 2002, Article 4.2.(b)(iv). Of course, in future referrals by the Security Council to the ICC, it is possible the ICC Prosecutor could eventually indict perpetrators for committing such acts.

[199] S/RES/1976 of 11 April 2011, preamble.

[200] Ibid., para 7.

[201] Ibid., para 8. See also S/RES/2020 of 22 November 2011, para 24. After the Secretary-General reported on the issue a couple of times, noting the difficulties of collecting relevant data due to lack of Somali capacity a suggesting that international anti-piracy forces take up the issue, the Security Council did not follow up with any concrete action on the issue of illegal dumping. See S/2011/661, Report of the Secretary-General on the protection of Somali natural resources and waters, of 25 October 2011; S/2012/783 of 22 October 2012, Section VIII and S/2013/623 of 21 October 2013, Section IX.

[202] Security Council Report 2008, Update Report No. 4: Myanmar, https://www.securitycouncilreport.org/update-report/lookup_c_glkwlemtisg_b_4130257.php. Accessed 30 April 2021.

[203] Ibid.

[204] Ibid. Other Council members were sceptic that such an approach was warranted and the relevance of the responsibility to protect to natural disasters. For more on this, see Conca 2019, p. 13; A/CN.4/3057, Summary record of the 3057th meeting of the International Law Commission of

could consider it necessary to take decisive action in response to a rapidly developing environmental or natural disaster, where the disaster—or the lack of adequate response by the relevant state—may impact international peace and security. If sea level rise reaches the point where it becomes an immediate existential threat to small island states as their territory becomes uninhabitable or even vanishes in the not-so-distant future—thus jeopardizing their sovereignty and territorial integrity, raising issues of statelessness and migration among others[205]—and the international community has yet to find an agreed legal framework to address this unprecedented event, the Security Council may be required to give an ad-hoc solution to a situation that threatens the existence of UN member states.[206] This could encompass, for example, recognizing the status and rights of such a state and of 'climate refugees', addressing their relocation, and helping to address their humanitarian needs.[207] Potential Security Council attention to these issues may also serve as an incentive for states to address them promptly and adequately to avoid the Council's scrutiny.

21.5.3 *Chapter VII Enforcement Measures to Settle Environmental Disputes*

We have established that the Council functions as a dispute settlement body,[208] exercising its authority under Chapters VI and VII to assist states in settling their disputes and, at times, settling the disputes for them. In the same vein, the Security Council's Chapter VII enforcement powers have been used to settle environmental issues in dispute in the past.

This was done in the aftermath of Iraq's invasion of Kuwait, where the Council, acting under Chapter VII, determined that Iraq was 'liable under international law for any direct loss, damage—including environmental damage and the depletion of natural resources—or injury to foreign Governments, nationals and corporations as a result of its unlawful invasion and occupation of Kuwait'.[209]

To ensure that Iraq pay reparations to the injured parties, the Security Council established a fund and a Commission to administer it, the UN Compensation Commission (UNCC).[210] Funded by proceeds of Iraqi oil sales,[211] the Commission

4 June 2010; Junk 2015, p. 88. Nevertheless, this does not take away from the capacity of the Security Council to use enforcement measures in such situations if it deems it necessary.

[205] Cousins 2013, pp. 201 and 206.

[206] Conca 2019, p. 14.

[207] See ibid., p. 12, on "climate refugees" and "statelessness".

[208] See Sect. 21.2.2.

[209] S/RES/687 of 3 April 1991, para 16.

[210] Ibid., para 18.

[211] S/RES/1483, para 21; see also the UNCC website, https://uncc.ch/home. Accessed 30 April 2021.

has to date paid an aggregate of $49.2 billion (out of $52.4 billion awarded) to individuals and corporations for death, injury, loss of or damage to property, commercial claims and claims for environmental damage.[212] Among the heads of claims paid off by the UNCC were 'F4' claims 'for direct environmental damage and depletion of natural resources resulting from Iraq's invasion and occupation of Kuwait'.[213] The Commission approved $4.3 billion in environmental damages from setting on fire 700 oil wells, as well as from 'burning construction of oil trenches; the piping of oil into the waters of the Persian Gulf; the laying of ordnance; the military mobilization of the Allied Forces; the movement of refugees; and even the extinguishing of the oil fires itself'.[214]

The Panel of Commissioners also made recommendations to the four injured States receiving compensation on how to best utilize these funds for environmental restoration projects.[215] In agreement with these states and Iraq, the UNCC Governing Council established the Follow-up Programme for Environmental Awards, to monitor the technical and financial aspects of environmental restoration projects funded by the awards.[216]

The decision that Iraq is liable and will compensate injured parties for environmental damages; the establishment of the compensation fund for that and other heads of claims; the establishment of the UNCC; the sum of $4.3 billion in awards for environmental damages caused by Iraq; and the environmental restoration projects they have funded were all a result of the Security Council utilizing its enforcement powers under Article 41 of the UN Charter. To date, this is the most forceful action the Security Council has taken on environmental issues.

Thus, the Security Council has made use of its enforcement powers to resolve an environmental dispute (which was one aspect of a wider dispute) and award compensation for environmental damages. In certain circumstances, the Security Council may again find it relevant to settle disputes that have an environmental aspect or an environmental dispute as such, if it believes they threaten international peace and security or relate to a conflict being addressed by the Security Council.

21.6 Conclusion

The Security Council has dealt with environmental issues in various contexts. Nonetheless, it does not have a meaningful record of dealing with environmental disputes, and it has had a limited impact at best in addressing ecological challenges to peace and security more generally. While the tools at its disposal are flexible and adaptable, the Council was not designed to address such matters, nor is it well suited

[212] See https://uncc.ch/home. Accessed 30 April 2021.

[213] E.g., S/AC.26/2005/10 of 30 June 2005, para 1.

[214] See https://uncc.ch/follow-programme-environmental-awards-0. Accessed 30 April 2021.

[215] See ibid.

[216] S/AC.26/Dec.258 of 8 December 2005. For an assessment of the UNCC's work, see Payne 2016.

to do so. However, it is plausible to assume that absent the implementation of effective mitigation strategies, climate change will increasingly contribute to water and food scarcity, desertification, and drought, exacerbating tensions over arable land, water, and other resources—the so-called 'threat-multipliers' frequently referred to by Council members.

In this context, continued efforts will persist to develop useful ways in which the Council can engage on the security impacts of environmental issues. In recent years, notwithstanding ongoing push back from a minority of members, there has been rising interest and effort in the Council to deal with these concerns. There is reason to believe that this organ will continue to search for a useful role in this regard, as UN member states (including those on the Council) are increasingly confronted with the environmental impacts of a warming planet on their own security and the welfare of their people. The change in the US administration in January 2021 has also added a powerful voice to the Council's efforts to address the security implications of environmental matters.

Looking forward, one important factor will be how effectively and convincingly linkages can be drawn between environmental phenomena and security challenges. The more concrete evidence that can be mustered to draw these connections in specific countries and regions, the more likely the doubters are to be won over to the need for Council involvement. It should also be noted that while the Council may not be the ideal forum to address environmental issues, its peace and security mandate dictates its responsibility to address the security implications of such matters. In this regard, it must find a way to work as effectively as possible with other stakeholders—inside and outside the UN system, ranging from the local and national levels to the regional and international levels—to address the potential and actual security threats of environmental factors.[217]

Acknowledgment The authors would like to thank Ewout Stoefs, Karin Landgren and Sir Michael Wood for their valuable comments on this chapter.

References

Brown O (2019a) Climate-Fragility Risk Brief: Afghanistan. https://climate-security-expert-network.org/sites/climate-security-expert-network.com/files/documents/csen_climate_fragility_risk_brief_-_afghanistan_0.pdf. Accessed 30 April 2021

Brown O (2019b) Climate-Fragility Risk Brief: North Africa and the Sahel. https://climate-security-expert-network.org/sites/climate-security-expert-network.com/files/documents/csen_climate_fragility_risk_brief_-_north_africa_sahel_.pdf. Accessed 30 April 2021

Brown O, Hammill A, McLeman R (2007) Climate Change as the 'new' security threat: implications for Africa. International Affairs 83:1141–1154

[217] Scott and Ku 2018, p. 2. On climate change in particular, the authors note: 'There has been growing recognition of the need for far-reaching, complementary efforts requiring enhanced coordination on the part of all international institutions'.

Conca K (2019) Is There a Role for the UN Security Council on Climate Change? Environment: Science and Policy for Sustainable Development 61:4–15
Cousins S (2013) UN Security Council: playing a role in the international climate change regime? Global Change, Peace & Security 25:191–210
de Wet E (2009) Peace, Threat to. MPEPIL
de Wet E, Wood M (2013) Collective Security. MPEPIL
Eklöw K, Krampe F (2019) Climate-Related Security Risks and Peacebuilding in Somalia. SIPRI, Policy Paper 53. https://www.sipri.org/sites/default/files/2019-10/sipripp53_2.pdf. Accessed 30 April 2021
Goodrich L, Hambro E (1946) The Charter of the United Nations: Commentary and Documents. World Peace Foundation, Boston MA
Henckaerts JM, Doswald-Beck L (2005) Customary International Humanitarian Law Volume I: Rules. Cambridge University Press, Cambridge
Jayaram D (2019) Climate-Fragility Risk Brief: South Asia. https://climate-security-expert-network.org/sites/climate-security-expert-network.com/files/documents/csen_climate_fragility_risk_brief_-_south_asia_0.pdf. Accessed 30 April 2021
Johnson L (2014) 'Uniting for Peace': Does It Still Serve Any Useful Purpose? AJIL Unbound 108:106-115
Junk J (2015) Testing Boundaries: Cyclone Nargis in Myanmar and the Scope of R2P. Global Security 60:78-93
Krisch N (2012a) Article 39. In: Simma B, Khan DE, Nolte G, Paulus A (eds) The Charter of the United Nations: A Commentary, 3rd edn. Oxford University Press, UK, pp 1272–1296
Krisch N (2012b) Article 41. In: Simma B, Khan DE, Nolte G, Paulus A (eds) The Charter of the United Nations: A Commentary, 3rd edn. Oxford University Press, UK, pp 1305–1329
Kron A (2019) Environmental Peacebuilding and the UN Security Council. In: Schrijver N, Blokker N (eds) Elected Members of the Security Council: Lame Ducks or Key Players? Brill/Nijhoff, Leiden/Boston, pp 248–266
Matheson M (2006) Council Unbound: The Growth of UN Decision Making on Conflict and Post-conflict Issues after the Cold War. United States Institute of Peace, Washington D.C.
Payne C (2016) Legal Liability for Environmental Damage: The United Nations Compensation Commission and the 1990-1991 Gulf War. In: Bruch C, Muffett C, Nichols S (eds) Governance, Natural Resources, and Post-Conflict Peacebuilding. Earthscan, Abingdon/New York, pp 719–760
Penney CK (2018) Climate change as a 'threat to international peace and security'. In: Scott SV, Ku C (eds) Climate Change and the UN Security Council. Edward Elgar Publishing, Northampton, pp 25–46
Peters A (2012) Art. 24. In: Simma B, Khan DE, Nolte G, Paulus A (eds) The Charter of the United Nations: A Commentary, 3rd edn. Oxford University Press, Oxford, pp 761–786
Scott SV, Ku C (2018) The UN Security Council and global action on climate change. In: Scott SV, Ku C (eds) Climate Change and the UN Security Council. Edward Elgar Publishing, Northampton, pp. 1–24
Security Council Report (2017) Can the Security Council Prevent Conflict? https://www.securitycouncilreport.org/atf/cf/%7B65BFCF9B-6D27-4E9C-8CD3-CF6E4FF96FF9%7D/research_report_conflict_prevention_2017.pdf. Accessed 30 April 2021
Wolfrum R (2012) Article 1. In: Simma B, Khan DE, Nolte G, Paulus A (eds) The Charter of the United Nations: A Commentary, 3rd edn. Oxford University Press, Oxford, pp 107–120
Wood M (1998) The Interpretation of Security Council Resolutions. Max Planck Yearbook of United Nations Law 2:77
Wood M (2007) Security Council. MPEPIL

Paul M. Romita Managing Editor, Security Council Report, 711 Third Avenue, 15th Floor New York, NY 10017, p.romita@securitycouncilreport.org, 1-917-576-0674

Eran Sthoeger, Esq. Litigator and consultant in international law, Adjunct Professor of international law at Seton Hall Law School and Brooklyn Law School, 5-49 Borden Ave, 2M, Long Island City, NY 11101, Eran.Sthoeger@protonmail.com, 1-917-355-3586

Chapter 22
Application of World Law by International Courts and Tribunals to Protect the Environment

Otto Spijkers

Contents

Abstract If States fail to conclude the necessary international legal agreements specifically designed to protect our common environment, then how far can (judges of) international courts and tribunals go in deriving the necessary obligations to protect our common environment from already existing norms and (general) principles of international law? To answer that question, this chapter draws inspiration from the so-called *world law* tradition, as it was developed in the United Kingdom and the United States (*world law*), the Netherlands (*wereldrecht*), and Japan (*sekai-hō).* This tradition calls upon (judges of) international courts and tribunals to use their authority and influence to claim a degree of independence from the will of States when identifying, interpreting and applying fundamental norms and principles of international law, based on global values, accepted and recognized by the international community as a whole as of fundamental importance, the observance of which is regarded as a shared legal interest of that international community. It is not disputed that a healthy environment is such a shared legal interest.

O. Spijkers (✉)
China Institute of Boundary and Ocean Studies (CIBOS), Wuhan University, Wuhan, China
e-mail: ottospijkers@whu.edu.cn

Research Institute of Environmental Law (RIEL), Wuhan University, Wuhan, China

E. Sobenes et al. (eds.), *The Environment Through the Lens of International Courts and Tribunals*, https://doi.org/10.1007/978-94-6265-507-2_22

Keywords Global values · world law · *wereldrecht* · *sekai-hō* · environmental protection · judicial freedom · International Court of Justice · World Court

22.1 Introduction

For various reasons, States have great difficulty agreeing on measures drastic and radical enough to effectively halt—or at least mitigate the negative effects of—climate change, biodiversity loss, destruction of forests, transboundary river pollution, and other types of damage caused by humankind to our natural environment. This raises the question: if States fail to bind themselves to robust enough legal obligations specifically intended to protect our common environment, then how much freedom can judges of international courts and tribunals permit themselves to derive the necessary obligations from already existing norms and general principles of international law? How far can they go in serving as a catalyst for international legal developments that aim to better protect our common environment? When does a court's liberal and elastic attitude to international law reach breaking point? When is the court's authority lost? When do its 'clients' move away from an overly creative court, preferring to settle their disputes elsewhere? When do international courts and tribunals lose their relevance, and become mere actors in a play that nobody takes seriously anymore?

To answer these questions, this chapter draws inspiration from the so-called world law tradition, as it was developed in the United Kingdom (UK) and the United States (US) (*world law*), the Netherlands (*wereldrecht*), and Japan (*sekai-hō*). More specifically, the aim of this chapter is to demonstrate the potential of the world law tradition, in its application by (judges of) the International Court of Justice (ICJ)—also referred to hereafter as the World Court[1]—and other international courts and tribunals to ensure environmental protection.[2] The chapter is forward-looking: an attempt is made to draw some lessons from past ideas and experiences that might be useful for the future.

This chapter first describes how world law was understood in the past, with a focus on the British and American *world law* traditions, and the Dutch *wereldrecht* tradition (Sect. 22.2). This is followed by some reflections on how world law was used—and can potentially be used—by (judges of) the World Court and other international courts and tribunals to claim a degree of freedom and independence from the will of States. In this second part of the chapter, the emphasis is on the Japanese *sekai-hō* tradition, because its founding father was himself a judge at the World Court (Sect. 22.3). It then turns more specifically to the domain of environmental protection. In this section, some examples are provided of international courts and tribunals—the World Court in particular—applying international law in a creative way to advance environmental protection, examples that may serve as inspiration for other international courts and

---

[1] In the world law literature, the preferred name for the International Court of Justice (ICJ) is 'World Court'. This chapter follows that approach.

[2] Hagiwara 2019.

tribunals (Sect. 22.4). The concluding section contains a number of general reflections on the potential value of the world law tradition, as applied by judges of international courts and tribunals, in today's efforts to stop environmental degradation (Sect. 22.5).

22.2 World Law

What is world law, and what purpose was it meant to serve? There are different world law traditions, which have developed in different parts of the world. In this section, I will draw on the British/American *world law* and Dutch *wereldrecht* traditions, just to give the reader an intuitive sense of what world law is all about. When zooming in on the actual and potential role of (judges of) international courts and tribunals in using world law to claim more independence, I will turn to the Japanese *sekai-hō* tradition (Sect. 22.3, below).

22.2.1 World Law in the United Kingdom

Let us begin in the UK, where some prominent politicians openly advocated world law in the period immediately after the Second World War. They saw world law as an alternative to the more traditional approach to international law, which saw international law as essentially a collection of contracts concluded between sovereign and independent States, trying to co-exist peacefully and respect the privacy (internal affairs) of the other States.

The most famous example is the address by British Foreign Secretary Ernest Bevin to the UK House of Commons of November 1945. Bevin proposed to establish a world parliament, mandated to make world law, and replace the old international legal order:

> From the moment you accept that [we need a world parliament], one phrase goes, and that is "international law". That phrase presupposes conflict between nations. It would be replaced by "world law", with a moral world force behind it, rather than a law built upon case made law and on agreements. It would be a world law with a world judiciary to interpret it, with a world police to enforce it, with the decision of the people with their own votes resting in their own hands, irrespective of race or creed, as the great world sovereign elected authority which would hold in its care the destinies of the people of the world.[3]

In today's world, a Foreign Minister calling for a world assembly, world judiciary, and world police, would probably not be taken very seriously. But in the years immediately following the Second World War, many British politicians were enthusiastic. In the UK, world law was advocated primarily by the World Federalist Movement,

---

[3] United Kingdom (UK), House of Commons Debate, 23 November 1945, Vol 416, Columns 759-846. These records can be consulted online at https://hansard.parliament.uk/.

and a considerable number of politicians aligned themselves with this movement.[4] On the other hand, despite speeches such as Bevin's speech just quoted, the response from the UK Government was generally somewhat lacking in enthusiasm. When Lord Merthyr, himself a world federalist, suggested that the United Nations should be developed into a World Federation with the authority to make and enforce world law, he was told by the representative of the UK Government that a single day spent inside the UK Foreign Office would make the honourable lord realise that his World Federation was never going to materialize.[5]

22.2.2 World Law in the United States of America

What about the world law tradition in the US? World law was most often and most vociferously championed in the US at the height of the cold war. The most influential blueprint for a reformed United Nations, capable of creating and enforcing world law, was *World Peace through World Law*, published in 1958 by Grenville Clark and Louis Sohn.[6] This plan, which was recently rediscovered and dusted off,[7] can best be described as a unique mix of a call to action and academic theory. It contained lots of ambitious proposals to enhance the authority of the World Court. One suggestion was to require States to submit all legal aspects of their international peace-threatening disputes to the World Court—i.e. to give it compulsory jurisdiction over such legal questions—and to refer all nonlegal questions to a World Conciliation Board and/or World Equity Tribunal.[8] Legal questions were defined as those questions 'susceptible of decision upon accepted legal principles'.[9] In essence, this included all questions relating to the interpretation or application of sources of international law (treaties, custom, general principles).[10] Moreover, to ensure greater independence for the judges of the World Court, it was suggested that the judges should be elected for life.[11] These proposals were not adopted by the Member States of the UN, but they were discussed widely, in academic circles and beyond.

In conclusion, it can be noted that the British/American world law tradition called for an approach to international law that was less dependent on the will of the sovereign States and agreements (treaties) based thereupon, and more grounded in what Bevin called 'a moral world force'. Moreover, it called for a strengthening of international courts and tribunals, the World Court in particular.

[4] Usborne, an active contributor to the British World Federalist Movement, is an example. See UK, House of Commons Debate, 28 July 1950, Vol. 478, Columns 913-44.

[5] UK, House of Lords Debate, 7 May 1953, Vol 182, Columns 348-85.

[6] Clark and Sohn 1958.

[7] Johnstone 2020.

[8] Ibid., p. 91, pp. 95–106.

[9] Ibid., p. 100.

[10] Ibid., pp. 337–338.

[11] Ibid., p. 337.

22.2.3 Wereldrecht *in the Netherlands*

Let us now turn to the Netherlands, where a more subtle kind of world law was developed. In 2010,[12] a special issue on *wereldrecht* was published by the *Nederlands Juristenblad*, with Leiden University professors Nico Schrijver and Janneke Gerards as guest editors.[13] In short, *wereldrecht* was said to refer to a limited set of fundamental principles and norms of public international law, based on global values, accepted and recognized by the international community as a whole as of fundamental importance (*jus cogens*), the observance of which was regarded as a legal interest of that international community (*erga omnes*).[14]

Elsewhere, I have defined global values as 'enduring, globally shared beliefs that a specific state of the world, which is possible, is socially preferable, from the perspective of all human beings, to the opposite state of the world'.[15] Such global values manifest themselves most clearly when the world is experiencing a fundamental lack. For example, a common desire to eradicate war is felt most strongly in times of world war; and the actual oppression and exploitation of peoples leads to a strong belief in human dignity and the self-determination of all peoples.[16] And in current times, the environmental degradation we witness all around us, and the outbreak of the coronavirus, make the global values of a healthy environment and a healthy population obvious to us all.

This *wereldrecht*, based on these globally shared values and interests, was meant to operate within the already existing constitutional framework of the United Nations Charter[17] and the basic rules contained therein, i.e. the principle of sovereign equality and territorial integrity of all States, the prohibition of threats to or use force in international relations, the principle of non-interference in the internal affairs of other States, and a general aspiration for equality and mutual benefit, and peaceful coexistence.[18]

In conclusion, we may note that the Dutch *wereldrecht* tradition urged us to single out a set of value-based norms and principles of fundamental importance to the international community as a whole and elevate these norms to a higher world law-type status. A healthy environment certainly belongs to that category of global values.

---

[12] The term *wereldrecht* first appeared much earlier, in the late 19th century. See 'Beginselen van een Algemeen Wereldrecht', *Vlaardingsche Courant*, 19 September 1877.

[13] Gerards and Schrijver 2010. See also Schrijver 2011. The latter book was used as textbook for an elective course on *wereldrecht*, which was offered at Leiden University School of Law, and taught by Nico Schrijver and myself.

[14] Spijkers 2010.

[15] Spijkers 2011, Chapter 2.

[16] Spijkers 2011.

[17] United Nations, Charter of the United Nations, 24 October 1945, 1 UNTS XVI, available at: https://www.refworld.org/docid/3ae6b3930.html Accessed 25 April 2021.

[18] These principles were first proclaimed in an agreement between India and the People's Republic of China of 29 April 1954, United Nations, Treaty Series, Vol 299, pp. 57–82. They have since been embraced by the great majority of States in this world.

22.3 Application of World Law by International Courts and Tribunals[19]

International courts and tribunals, and its judges, enjoy considerable authority and power. This provides them with unique possibilities to further develop and strengthen the fundamental norms of world law identified in the section above (Sect. 22.2). This authority can be formally confirmed in a particular document—such as the ICJ Statute—but it really is based on a global consensus that these courts are important and need to be taken seriously. This globally shared belief is very fragile and may evaporate at any time.[20] Anne Marie Bos came up with the following thought-experiment to make this clear:

> Imagine yourself in a building in The Hague, Netherlands. The building is called "Peace Palace". Imagine that you are attending a session of the International Court of Justice in the Great Hall of Justice. Try to forget about all prior knowledge you have as an international lawyer, and approach what you see with an open mind. You see many men - and a few women - sitting in a long line behind a long table. They are dressed in long black robes, with a white bib under their chin. They look serious, and one of them speaks. What kind of people are they? What are they doing there? You could reply: "These are the judges of the International Court of Justice. The International Court of Justice delivers a judgment in an international proceeding." With this answer, you give a legal-normative interpretation of the reality you have observed. This in itself sounds pretty obvious. But [...] what is this interpretation based on? [...] You could reply: "It is based on the UN Charter, on the Statute of the International Court of Justice, and on many more international legal norms. On the basis of these norms, we attribute a legal significance to the behaviour of these ladies and gentlemen." But this is a *possible* interpretation, there is no *necessity* whatsoever to arrive at this normative interpretation of what one perceives. Only if one accepts this interpretation, can we conclude that, what these ladies and gentlemen, all dressed in their black and stately attire, are doing behind the table, is to exercise the power attributed to them to adjudicate international disputes.[21]

The significance of what these ladies and gentlemen in the Great Hall say and do is thus based on an established reputation, and not on particular facts, symbols, clothes, or legal documents. When this reputation is shaken or undermined, the Great Hall is nothing more than a theatre, where a play is being staged.

The judges of the World Court—and those of other international courts and tribunals—are very much aware of the importance of maintaining their reputation. That is why they understand so well their limitations, and within those limitations they seek to find subtle ways to contribute to the progressive development of international law.

The challenge for the judges of the World Court, and the same applies to all other international courts and tribunals, is to be creative within the limitations imposed

---

[19] Since I am not fluent in the Japanese language myself, I have gratefully benefitted from the assistance and suggestions provided to me by Machiko Kanetake, Hirofumi Oguri, Mari Takeuchi, and Shin Kawagishi.

[20] Statute of the International Court of Justice, 26 June 1945, entry into force 24 October 1945 (ICJ Statute).

[21] Bos 2012, p. 154 (translated from the Dutch original by myself).

on them. Here, the Japanese tradition of *sekai-hō* ('world law') can provide some assistance.

22.3.1 **Sekai-hō** *in Japan*

Between 1932 and 1934, Japanese lawyer Kōtarō Tanaka presented us with his theory of *sekai-hō*.[22] His theory was rooted in natural law (as a counterpart to legal positivism), and can be seen as a reaction to the nationalist and militaristic atmosphere in Japan at that time.[23] Tanaka's main ambition was to 'liberate' international law from the State and the ethnic nation. He argued that the emergence of a world society, especially in an economic sense, implied the existence of *sekai-hō*.[24] Its emergence was thus a necessary and inevitable development, not a choice. International law could be deduced directly from human society, it was not a product of the States. At the time, he also presented his ideas in Europe, for example in France,[25] where they clearly had their influence.[26] Digging up norms and principles of world law was an undertaking for lawyers from all over the world, but Tanaka particularly encouraged scholars from Japan to take part in the unearthing of *sekai-hō*:

> Achieving justice is something that concerns not only one nation, but all the nations of the world. It belongs, like religion, to the domain of civilization, in the pursuit of which all nations must and can work together. In the future, Japanese jurists, too, will have to participate in the establishment and progress of this global legal community.[27]

From 1961 to 1970, Tanaka himself served as judge of the World Court. In this capacity, he wrote separate and dissenting opinions, which he used as a vehicle to promote his *sekai-hō*.[28]

For example, in his dissenting opinion to the World Court's judgment of 18 July 1966 in the South West Africa cases between Ethiopia/Liberia and South Africa, Tanaka made the argument that the international legal basis of human rights ought to be found in the general principles of international law, which existed independently of State consent. In his view, human rights existed largely independently of treaties, which were mere expressions of fortuitous State consent, and thus part of the more traditional international law. He referred to these general principles of international law as 'constituting a part of the law of the world community which may be designated as World Law, Common Law of Mankind (Jenks), Transnational Law (Jessup),

[22] Tanaka 1932–1934.

[23] Yokota 1974; Doak 2017, pp. 4–12.

[24] Takeshita 2013, pp. 229–230; Doak 2019, pp. 41–62.

[25] Tanaka 1938.

[26] Tanaka 1954, with contributions from, among others, Hans Kelsen.

[27] Tanaka 1938, p. 315 (translated from the French original by myself).

[28] Doak 2019, pp. 101–105.

etc.'—thereby suggesting that the exact term was not the most essential issue.[29] He then summarized the essence of his *sekai-hō* approach:

> [Article 38(1)(c) ICJ Statute[30]] extends the concept of the source of international law beyond the limit of legal positivism according to which, the States being bound only by their own will, international law is nothing but the law of the consent and auto-limitation of the State. But this viewpoint, we believe, was clearly overruled by [Article 38(1)(c) ICJ Statute], by the fact that this provision does not require the consent of States as a condition of the recognition of the general principles. States which do not recognize this principle or even deny its validity are nevertheless subject to its rule. From this kind of source international law could have the foundation of its validity extended beyond the will of States, that is to say, into the sphere of natural law and assume an aspect of its supra-national and supra-positive character.[31]

In 1966, Tanaka thus saw in the general principles of international law the foundation of *sekai-hō*.

In his dissenting opinion to the World Court's judgment of 20 February 1969 in the North Sea Continental Shelf cases between the Federal Republic of Germany, Denmark and the Netherlands, he referred to custom as its foundation. Tanaka argued that:

> The attitude which one takes vis-à-vis customary international law has been influenced by one's view on international law or legal philosophy in general. Those who belong to the school of positivism and voluntarism wish to seek the explanation of the binding power of international law in the sovereign will of States, and consequently, their attitude in recognizing the evidence of customary law is rigid and formalistic. On the other hand, those who advocate the objective existence of law apart from the will of States, are inclined to take a more liberal and elastic attitude in recognizing the formation of a customary law attributing more importance to the evaluation of the content of law than to the process of its formation. I wish to share the latter view.[32]

In Tanaka's view, the World Court, 'by according the equidistance principle the status of a world law [could have made] a contribution to the progressive development of international law', but, much to Tanaka's regret, the Court had missed that opportunity.[33] This was in part because not all judges on the World Court shared his view that general principles and custom need not be based on State consent, and could instead be deduced directly from the facts of human society.

Shortly after he retired from the Court, Tanaka further developed his *sekai-hō* theory in his scholarly writings. He regarded the influence of general principles of

---

[29] ICJ, *South West Africa (Ethiopia and Liberia v South Africa)*, Judgement, Dissenting opinion of Judge Tanaka, 18 July 1966, ICJ Reports 1966, p. 296.

[30] Article 38 ICJ Statute reads, above n 20, where relevant that '[t]he [World] Court, whose function is to decide in accordance with international law such disputes as are submitted to it, shall apply [..] (a) international conventions, whether general or particular, establishing rules expressly recognized by the contesting states; (b) international custom, as evidence of a general practice accepted as law; [and] (c) the general principles of law recognized by civilized nations'.

[31] ICJ, *South West Africa*, above n 29, p. 298.

[32] ICJ, *North Sea Continental Shelf (Federal Republic of Germany/Denmark/Netherlands)*, Judgment, Dissenting opinion of Judge Tanaka, 20 February 1969, ICJ Reports 1969, p. 178.

[33] Ibid., p. 196.

law on the jurisprudence of the World Court as the most pronounced sign of *sekai-hō*. Unlike treaties, these principles were binding on States, regardless of whether they had consented to them or not:

> [U]nlike the first source of law (international conventions) and the second one (international custom), the third source of law binds States regardless of their will. The first source of law (international conventions), is not of transnational character in the sense that such agreements are limited by the contracting States themselves. The second source of law (international custom) is not recognized as transnational because custom is also created by States. These two categories of law do not exist objectively and independently of the wills of States. Only the third source of law, that is the "general principles of law" can obtain the objective status as a source of international law existing above and independent from national wills.[34]

As will be demonstrated in more detail below (Sect. 22.4), this insight is of heightened relevance in the field of international *environmental* law, which is dominated by unwritten law, i.e. by (1) general principles we find formulated mainly in non-legally binding resolutions, world conference outcome documents, and other types of soft law documents, and by (2) international customary law.[35]

In Tanaka's view, general principles of international law gave the judges of the world's international courts and tribunals a certain freedom of interpretation, a certain autonomy from the sovereign States:

> [Article 38(1)(c) ICJ Statute] assures a large sphere of activity for the judges of the International Court of Justice. The sphere of a judge's discretion is wider in international law than in national law, for the former is still at a primitive stage with poorer sources of positive law in comparison with the latter. International law is the field where free law (*Freirecht, libre recherche scientifique*) can play its greatest role. And here, in this field, free law creates World Law.[36]

This, concluded Tanaka, made the International Court of Justice a true World Court, applying world law:

> Consequently, it can be said that the inclusion of the general principles of law in the sources of law by Article 38, paragraph 1 of the [ICJ] Statute significantly enlarges the quality of the functions of the International Court while at the same time infusing the quality of the activities of this Court with a transnational and World Law character.[37]

In the 1970s, Tanaka had to admit that the world law character of the World Court was still in development. But Tanaka predicted a great future for the World Court as an institution where disputes are settled on the basis of world law:

> The World Law element of the International Court of Justice is still very thin and weak today, both in structure and in function. Yet, I feel certain that this element is the starting point and foundation upon which the court will be able to realize through the rule of law the primary objective of the United Nations Charter: the ideal of permanent world peace.[38]

---

[34] Tanaka 1971, p. 19. Note that his view on the link between custom and State consent is not entirely consistent with his dissenting opinion of 1969.

[35] For the most important such declarations, see Sect. 22.4, below.

[36] Ibid., p. 20.

[37] Ibid., p. 21.

[38] Ibid., p. 22.

Tanaka himself admitted that he never fully refined his *sekai-hō theory*. He saw this as a task for the next generation.[39]

The future generation of Japanese scholars took on this challenge. In 1984 Yasuhiko Saito published a paper, building on the work of Tanaka. Saito defined *sekai-hō* as 'the ensemble of laws of the world community, which covers not only traditional legal relations between States, but also embraces all the multifarious traffic across national frontiers of the millions of individuals who compose the populations of States'.[40] Like the Dutch *wereldrecht* tradition, Saito paid particular attention to concepts such as *jus cogens*, obligations *erga omnes*, and *actio popularis*, as elements of *sekai-hō*.

This raises the question whether there already exist such elevated world law-type norms and principles in international *environmental* law. This question is addressed in more detail below (Sect. 22.4), but it may already be noted that, in view of Louis Kotzé, 'no international court or tribunal has explicitly identified any norm that has, or that could in future gain, peremptory status in the environmental domain; nor has any international court or tribunal invoked Articles 53 and 64 VCLT in practice to settle an environment-related treaty dispute'.[41] This may have been true when Louis Kotzé jotted down these sobering remarks in 2016, but, as will be argued more in-depth below, that should not lead us to conclude that norms and principles of international environmental law have not been elevated to a special, world law type status. Labelling a norm or principle as peremptory, or *jus cogens*, or as legal basis for obligations *erga omnes*, is not the only way to do so. Already in the 1997 *Gabčíkovo-Nagymaros* case, the World Court noted that '[n]either of the parties contended that new peremptory norms of environmental law had emerged'.[42] In making this remark, the World Court did appear to suggest that such contention could very well have been made, and that the Court would have been willing to embrace it.[43] At the same time, the above-quoted sentence from the *Gabčíkovo-Nagymaros* judgment also shows how the Court struggled to find a balance between respecting its jurisdictional limitations—based on State consent—and its freedom to interpret and apply the law creatively and innovatively.

Like Tanaka, Saito argued for more freedom for judges of international courts and tribunals when identifying, interpreting and applying fundamental norms and principles of international law. Judges should prefer a free, elastic and teleological

---

[39] Oguri 2020. This paper is in Japanese, but Hirofumi Oguri kindly provided me with an English summary.

[40] Saito 1984.

[41] Kotzé 2016, p. 252. The quote includes a reference to Article 53—on treaties conflicting with a peremptory norm of general international law (*jus cogens*)—and Article 64—on the emergence of a new peremptory norm of general international law (*jus cogens*) of the Vienna Convention on the Law of Treaties, concluded in Vienna on 23 May 1969, entry into force on 27 January 1980, in United Nations, Treaty Series, Vol 1155, p. 331.

[42] ICJ, *Gabčíkovo-Nagymaros Project (Hungary v Slovakia)*, Judgement, 25 September 1997, ICJ Reports 1997, para 112.

[43] More on this case in Sect. 22.4, below.

approach over the rigid and formalistic method, proposed Saito, which stems from an exaggerated respect for the absolute sovereignty of States.[44]

22.3.2 *World Judge as Guardian of World Law*

What about the current status of the world's judges as guardians of world law? What about the role of the judges of international courts and tribunals other than the World Court? Does Tanaka and Saito's line of argumentation in defence of judicial freedoms apply there as well? This was the central question of the doctoral research done by Mia Swart.[45] She focused on the international criminal tribunals. Swart began by noting that '[s]ince the *ad hoc* Tribunals, similar to the ICJ, are legal organs of the United Nations what is true for the ICJ must be true *a fortiori* for the *ad hoc* Tribunals who face the additional obstacle of having to apply the underdeveloped system of international criminal law'.[46] She then provided an overview of the most important arguments in favour of and against judicial lawmaking by the international criminal tribunals. Many of these arguments are specific to international criminal law and need not concern us here. But the arguments that (1) international courts and tribunals are part of a relatively undeveloped legal system, and that (2) a finding of a *non liquet* in international law must be avoided,[47] and that (3) the possibility of using general principles as a basis for a decision was permitted exactly to avoid such a *non liquet*, all three encourage judicial freedom, creativity, and activism, and all three apply also to all other international courts and tribunals.[48]

At the same time, (judges of) international courts and tribunals must operate carefully. Indeed, if international courts and tribunals distance themselves too much from the will of their creators and clients (the States), and claim to be the sole authors and guardians of this set of fundamental, value-based norms of international law, observance of which is considered in the interest of the international community as a whole, then they might lose their clients on the way. States may turn a blind eye and deaf ear to the world's courts, or even worse: they might attempt to crush their own creations, as Victor Frankenstein tried to do to the monster he had himself once created.

A brief anecdote may illustrate why this is not a theoretical, but a very real danger. It is about the lacklustre response of the US Government to the increasing confidence of the American world law tradition. In the early 1960s, there was a dispute between the US and the Soviet Union over the future of Berlin. Inspired by the World Law

---

[44] Saito 1984, p. 246.

[45] Swart 2006.

[46] Ibid., p. 283.

[47] The term *non liquet* literally means 'it is not clear'. It refers to the situation in which a court cannot decide a case because there is no applicable international law to use as foundation for a decision. Bodansky 2006.

[48] Swart 2006, pp. 283–293.

plan of Clark and Sohn (see Sect. 22.2, above), Charles S. Rhyne, former president of the American Bar Association, suggested that the US could ask the World Court for its opinion on the legal aspects of this so-called Berlin controversy.[49] In response, Dean Acheson, at the time consultant to the US Government, gave the following advice:

> We should make no further proposals to submit our right to be in Berlin - and to stay there - to the World Court. This proposal does not make the same impression abroad as it does in the United States. Many Americans are in the grip of the illusion inherent in the American Bar Association slogan "World peace through world law". No one else is; and we really do not believe it, either. Vital issues are political issues and are not judiciable. As we shall see, there is no "law" on these subjects; and no nation will accept third party adjudication - in effect arbitration - on matters affecting their world position and/or their vital interests. Nehru would not arbitrate Kashmir; or Sukarno, West New Guinea; or Nasser or Eden, Suez; or de Gaulle or the FLN, Algerian independence or their claims to the Sahara; or Khrushchev, Berlin. For us to do so means to the world that if the [World] Court should take jurisdiction and decide that we had no rights in Berlin, we would be willing to accept the decision. This, in turn, means to others that we cannot care very much one way or the other.[50]

What is particularly fascinating, is this last remark. It appears to suggest that States should not voluntarily submit controversies relating to their vital interests to an international court or tribunal, inviting it to settle such controversies on the basis of international law. Only issues that are not politically sensitive apparently are considered suitable for international adjudication on the basis of international law.[51]

It could be argued that it is no longer the case—if it ever was—that international courts and tribunals only deal with disputes that are not too politically sensitive. If we look at the current docket of the World Court, one is struck by the many cases that *do* relate to vital interests, such as the dispute between the Democratic Republic of the Congo and Uganda relating to armed activities on the territory of the Congo; or the dispute between Ukraine and the Russian Federation relating to events which occurred in eastern Ukraine and in Crimea from the spring of 2014 onwards; or the dispute between Palestine and the US on the relocation of the US Embassy to Jerusalem; or the case between the Gambia and Myanmar relating to genocidal acts allegedly committed by or under the effective control of Myanmar against members of the Rohingya group. At the time of writing, the Netherlands is preparing to lodge proceedings before an international dispute settlement mechanism against the Syrian Arab Republic, alleging that, through the latter's failure to prevent and punish acts of torture by its public officials or other person acting in an official capacity, Syria has breached several obligations enshrined in the Convention against Torture owed to the Netherlands as a State Party to that Convention (*erga omnes partes*).[52] Nobody will say that these disputes relate to mere trivial issues, but they have all been presented

---

[49] United States (US), Congressional Records Senate, 16 September 1961, p. 1989.

[50] Acheson 1961.

[51] For a very early example, see Bruncken 1925, in which the same argument is made.

[52] Letter from the Netherlands Minister of Foreign Affairs to the President of the Netherlands House of Representatives of the States-general, 18 September 2020, parliamentary document 32 735, No. 301, available at www.tweedekamer.nl.

to the World Court, and States have requested the Court to settle these controversies on the basis of international law.

The same can be said of the docket of other international courts and tribunals. For example, the International Tribunal for the Law of the Sea (ITLOS) currently has before it a dispute concerning delimitation of the maritime boundary between Mauritius and Maldives in the Indian Ocean,[53] and a dispute between Switzerland and Nigeria relating to the M/T 'San Padre Pio', a motor tanker flying the flag of Switzerland, which was arrested by Nigerian authorities while it was allegedly engaged in ship-to-ship transfers of gasoil in Nigeria's exclusive economic zone.[54] Of the latter it could be argued that this relates to a 'mere' incident; but the former certainly relates to issues of long-term political relevance.

The European Court of Human Rights currently has to deal with various inter-state applications lodged by Georgia and Ukraine against the Russian Federation, relating, *inter alia*, to alleged violations of the European Convention on Human Rights by the Russian Federation in Eastern Ukraine.[55] The Netherlands has lodged an application, also against the Russian Federation, relating to the downing of Malaysia Airlines Flight 17 (MH17), a passenger flight from Amsterdam to Kuala Lumpur, that was shot down over the territory of Eastern Ukraine on 17 July 2014.[56] And on 28 September 2020, Armenia lodged a request for interim measures against Azerbaijan in view of the recognition of the conflict in and around the region of Nagorno-Karabakh.[57] Again, it is difficult to make the argument that these cases relate to mere trivial or politically uncontroversial issues. Of more immediate relevance to the present research—which is, after all, on environmental protection—is that on 2 September 2020, a group of Portuguese youngsters lodged a complaint against 33 countries, accusing all countries of acting in breach of the European Convention on Human Rights by failing to take sufficient action to combat—or mitigate the negative effects of—climate change.[58] This case is likely to raise lots of highly contentious issues. It will certainly challenge the balance between the international court and the sovereign will of State governments: the question is who ultimately decides what measures ought to be taken to combat climate change.

All these highly political cases will need to be decided on the basis of rather vague and open norms, giving the relevant international courts and tribunals significant freedom to make a decision and thereby further develop international law.

What to conclude from all this? At the moment, international courts and tribunals are perhaps more relevant, and more highly regarded, than ever before. They are

[53] ITLOS, *Dispute Concerning Delimitation of the Maritime Boundary Between Mauritius and Maldives in the Indian Ocean (Mauritius/Maldives)*, Case No. 28.

[54] ITLOS, *The M/T 'San Padre Pio' (No. 2) Case (Switzerland/Nigeria)*, Case No. 29.

[55] ECHR, *Ukraine v. Russian Federation*, 13 March 2014, App No 8019/16; ECHR, *Georgia v. Russian Federation (IV)*, 22 August 2018 App. No 39611/18.

[56] ECHR, *The Netherlands v. Russian Federation*, Application 28525/20, 10 July 2020.

[57] ECHR, *Armenia v. Azerbaïdjan*, 28 September 2020, App. No 42521/20.

[58] At the time of writing, the application was not yet available on the Court's website. It can be found here: https://youth4climatejustice.org/the-case/.

asked to decide on highly political and fundamental issues and need to base their decision on relatively open and vague norms and principles of international law. They may thus be tempted to see how far they are allowed to go in moving international law forward, following the approach advocated by Tanaka's theory of *sekai-hō*. At the same time, they may have to acknowledge that their popularity might be due to their rather conservative approach, and that their popularity can just as easily and quickly be lost as it was once won.

22.4 World Law, International Courts, and Environmental Protection

Let us now turn to the role of international courts and tribunals in using international law to urge States to do more to protect our common environment. Let us begin with the past, and then turn to the future.[59]

Have we seen examples of international courts and tribunals, claiming for themselves the type of independence and freedom advocated by Tanaka, to encourage States to do more to protect our common environment? Above, we already alluded briefly to some environment-related case law of the World Court and the European Court of Human Rights, and we concluded that so far, not all that much case law exists which explicitly endows norms and principles that aim to protect our common environment with a special, world law-type status. In this section, this search for world law norms on environmental protection is continued.

As a first step, we need to establish whether there actually already exist fundamental norms and principles of international law that urge States to secure to all a healthy environment. In the early stages, international legal norms and principles to protect the environment consisted of declarations codifying principles of international customary law. Early examples include the Declaration on the Human Environment of 1972,[60] the Charter of Economic Rights and Duties of States of 1974,[61] and the World Charter for Nature of 1982.[62] The most important declaration is without any doubt the Declaration on Environment and Development, concluded at the end of the United Nations Conference on Environment and Development, held in Rio de

[59] Stephens 2018; Fitzmaurice 2013; Viñuales 2008.

[60] Declaration of the United Nations Conference on the Human Environment, adopted 16 June 1972, published in the Report of the United Nations Conference on the Human Environment, held in Stockholm, between 5 and 16 June 1972, UNDoc. A/CONF.48/14/Rev.1.

[61] Charter of Economic Rights and Duties of States, General Assembly resolution 3281(XXIX), adopted 12 December 1974.

[62] World Charter for Nature, annexed to General Assembly resolution 37/7, adopted 28 October 1982.

Janeiro in 1992.[63] This was followed by the Johannesburg Declaration on Sustainable Development of 2002,[64] and the Sustainable Development Goals of 2015.[65] With differing success, these declarations all purported to codify general principles and norms of customary international law relating to environmental protection.

In recent times, multilateral treaties to protect our common environment have been added to this wealth of customary norms and declarations of general principles. These include the following:

- Convention for the Protection of the Ozone Layer, concluded in Vienna on 22 March 1985, entry into force 22 September 1988, with 198 parties;[66]
- United Nations Framework Convention on Climate Change, concluded in New York on 9 May 1992, entry into force 21 March 1994, with 197 parties;
- Convention on Biological Diversity, concluded in Rio de Janeiro on 5 June 1992, entry into force 29 December 1993, with 196 parties;
- Paris Agreement, concluded in Paris on 12 December 2015, entry into force 4 November 2016, with 189 parties.

In 1996, André de Hoogh still had to conclude, to his chagrin, that 'the international community has not, at present, recognized obligations for the protection of the environment as obligations essential for the protection of its fundamental interests'.[67] It is difficult to keep rigidly to such scepticism in present times.

Indeed, from 1996 onwards, international courts and tribunals have played a modest but constructive role in the growth of international law in the field of environmental protection, with the World Court taking the lead. Around the same time that André de Hoogh came to his sobering conclusion, some interesting developments occurred in the Peace Palace. In its Advisory Opinion of 8 July 1996 on the Legality of the Threat or Use of Nuclear Weapons, the World Court:

> recognize[d] that the environment is under daily threat and that the use of nuclear weapons could constitute a catastrophe for the environment. The [World] Court also recognize[d] that the environment is not an abstraction but represents the living space, the quality of life and the very health of human beings, including generations unborn. The existence of the general obligation of States to ensure that activities within their jurisdiction and control respect the environment of other States or of areas beyond national control is now part of the corpus of international law relating to the environment.[68]

---

[63] Rio Declaration on Environment and Development, published in the Report of the United Nations Conference on Environment and Development, held in Rio de Janeiro, between 3 and 14 June 1992, UNDoc. A/CONF.151/26/Rev.l (Vol. 1).

[64] Johannesburg Declaration on Sustainable Development, published in the Report of the World Summit on Sustainable Development, held in Johannesburg (South Africa), between 26 August and 4 September 2002, UNDoc. A/CONF.199/20.

[65] Transforming Our World: The 2030 Agenda for Sustainable Development, General Assembly resolution 70/1, adopted 25 September 2015.

[66] Note that not all parties are States.

[67] de Hoogh 1996, p. 63.

[68] ICJ, *Legality of the Threat of Nuclear Weapons,* Advisory Opinion, 8 July 1996, ICJ Reports 1996, para 29.

And in its judgment of 25 September 1997, in the case concerning the Gabčíkovo-Nagymaros project, between Hungary and Slovakia, the World Court:

> ha[d] no difficulty in acknowledging that the concerns expressed by Hungary for its natural environment in the region affected by the Gabčíkovo-Nagymaros Project related to an 'essential interest' of that State.[69]

Earlier (in 1980), the International Law Commission (ILC) had already come to the conclusion, after assessing the practice of States, that 'ensur[ing] the survival of the fauna or vegetation of certain areas on land or at sea, to maintain the normal use of those areas or, more generally, to ensure the ecological balance of a region' could be seen as an essential interest of the State. The ILC added that '[i]t is primarily in the last two decades that safeguarding the ecological balance has come to be considered an "essential interest" of all States'.[70] In its judgment of 1997, the World Court referred to the ILC's conclusion of 1980, and affirmed it. And in 2001, the ILC in turn referred to the World Court's judgment of 1997 in support of its conclusion that 'safeguarding the environment' constituted an essential interest of a State.[71] This is an interesting example of cross-fertilisation between two institutions, both formally independent of States, jointly seeking to establish a particularly important principle of world law.

Let us get back to the World Court's ruling of 1997. After referring to the ILC report of 1980, the Court went on to recall that 'it has recently had occasion to stress [...] the great significance that it attaches to respect for the environment, not only for States but also for the whole of mankind'. It then quoted the paragraph from its own Advisory Opinion on the legality of the threat or use of nuclear weapons, already referred to above.

It might be recalled that Tanaka used the possibility to append Separate and Dissenting Opinions to World Court judgments as a vehicle to further promote the development of world law. Tanaka himself left the World Court in 1970, and thus he was no longer there to promote world law by the time the above-mentioned Advisory Opinion and Judgment were issued. But he found a successor. In a Separate Opinion to the Judgment of 25 September 1997, in the case concerning the *Gabčíkovo-Nagymaros* project, Vice-President Christopher Gregory Weeramantry wrote that:

> We have entered an era of international law in which international law subserves not only the interests of individual States, but looks beyond them and their parochial concerns to the greater interests of humanity and planetary welfare. In addressing such problems, which transcend the individual rights and obligations of the litigating States, international law will need to look beyond procedural rules fashioned for purely *inter partes* litigation. When we

[69] ICJ, *Gabčíkovo-Nagymaros Project*, above n 42, para 53.

[70] Article 33, Draft Articles on State Responsibility, with commentaries thereto, adopted by the International Law Commission at its thirty second session, published in the Yearbook of the International Law Commission, 1980, Vol II, Part Two, p. 39.

[71] Article 25, Articles on State Responsibility, with commentaries thereto, adopted by the International Law Commission at its fifty-third session, published in the Yearbook of the International Law Commission, 2001, Vol II, Part Two, p. 83.

> enter the arena of obligations which operate *erga omnes* rather than *inter partes*, rules based on individual fairness and procedural compliance may be inadequate. The great ecological questions now surfacing will call for thought upon this matter. International environmental law will need to proceed beyond weighing the rights and obligations of parties within a closed compartment of individual State self-interest, unrelated to the global concerns of humanity as a whole. The present case offers an opportunity for such reflection.[72]

He thus used his opinion to provide such reflection. In an extraordinarily rich opinion, he referred to treaties, State practice, policy documents, scholarly works, but also to works of fiction, poetry, ancient texts and traditions, and much more, to demonstrate the existence of a general obligation to protect the environment.

Although he did not explicitly use the term world law, Judge Weeramantry did make the argument that the obligation to protect the environment was rooted in various civilisations and cultures (i.e. that it was based on values, and derivable from the facts of human society); that it was reflected in a wide range of treaties, State practice, etc. (i.e. that it was accepted and recognized by the international community as a whole); and he argued extensively for its *erga omnes* character (i.e. that its observance must be regarded as a legal interest of the international community as a whole). In short, without using the label literally, he did make the argument that it was a norm of world law. And it is safe to say that the opinion had the desired effect. Lacking a legally binding character, the opinion nonetheless had a considerable influence on international environmental law scholarship, and thereby also on the development of world law to protect the environment.[73]

22.5 Some Reflections on the Potential of World Law Used by International Courts and Tribunals to Protect the Environment

How much freedom can (judges of) international courts and tribunals permit themselves to derive the obligations, necessary to protect our common environment, from customary norms and general principles of international (environmental) law? The British/American *world law* tradition has demonstrated that there is room for an approach to international law that is less dependent on the will of the sovereign States and agreements (treaties) based thereupon, and more grounded in global morality. The Dutch *wereldrecht* tradition provided us with criteria to single out world law-type norms and principles, i.e. they are value-based, of fundamental importance to the international community as a whole, and upholding them is considered a globally shared legal interest. The *sekai-hō* tradition added to this that (judges of) international courts and tribunals should claim for themselves more freedom when identifying, interpreting and applying such fundamental norms and principles of international

[72] Ibid., p. 118.

[73] Anghie and Weeramantry 1998; Anghie 2001.

law. At the same time, they need to be careful not to overdo it, and thereby lose the trust and confidence of their 'clientele' (the States).

Indeed, one might criticize the way in which Tanaka and Weeramantry used their competence as judges of the World Court to write Separate Opinions that served as booster rockets for world law. Is that really what Separate Opinions are meant to do? It is apt and appropriate, I believe, to finish this chapter with some constructive criticism of this self-proclaimed power of the world judge as producer of world law. After all, a little bit of modesty, unpretentiousness, and humility might be the best way to ensure the enduring effect and lasting life of the world law tradition.

Article 57 ICJ Statute reads that '[i]f the judgment does not represent in whole or in part the unanimous opinion of the judges, any judge shall be entitled to deliver a separate opinion'.[74] And Article 95 ICJ Rules of Court adds to this that '[a]ny judge may, if he so desires, attach his individual opinion to the judgment, whether he dissents from the majority or not'.[75] Many other international courts and tribunals allow for separate and dissenting opinions, with more or less the same freedom provided to the judges and arbitrators. For example, Article 30 Statute of the International Tribunal for the Law of the Sea (ITLOS) provides that '[i]f the judgment does not represent in whole or in part the unanimous opinion of the members of the Tribunal, any member shall be entitled to deliver a separate opinion'.[76] Article 125 ITLOS Rules adds that '[a]ny judge may attach a separate or dissenting opinion to the judgment'.[77]

These provisions from the Statutes and Rules of the ICJ and ITLOS could be interpreted as suggesting that judges at these international courts and tribunals should only produce a separate or dissenting opinion to express disagreement with the judgment, not to advance the development of a particular field or tradition, such as world law. At the same time, these provisions do not explicitly forbid judges from using their unique powers to contribute to the growth of world law.[78]

Tanaka and Weeramantry seem to have found a successor at the ICJ in Judge Cançado Trindade.[79] In 2018, the World Court for the first time had an opportunity to adjudicate a claim relating to compensation for environmental damage.[80] Trindade used this opportunity to write a Separate Opinion reflecting in a general sense on this obligation, referring to its history, grounding it in various cultures and traditions, and

[74] Article 57, ICJ Statute, above n 20.

[75] Rules of Court, adopted on 14 April 1978, entry into force 1 July 1978, last amended 14 April 2005.

[76] Article 30, Statute of the International Tribunal for the Law of the Sea, Annex VI of the United Nations Convention on the Law of the Sea, 10 December 1982, 1833 UNTS 3, entered into force 16 November 1994.

[77] Article 125, Rules of the Tribunal (ITLOS/8), adopted on 28 October 1997 and last amended on 25 September 2018. See also Article 135.

[78] Sarmiento Lamus 2020.

[79] For the practice of writing separate and dissenting opinions at regional human rights courts, see White and Boussiakou 2009, and Resende 2019.

[80] ICJ, *Certain Activities Carried Out by Nicaragua in the Border Area (Costa Rica v. Nicaragua)*, Compensation, 2 February 2018, ICJ Reports 2018, paras 41–43.

so on.[81] Even though he did not use the term world law, his approach—and this is not the first such separate opinion he has produced[82]—does fit within the tradition.

One might object that it is up to States—and not up to the judges of international courts and tribunals—to conclude international legal agreements and thereby determine how best to protect our common environment. By imposing obligations on all States, international courts and tribunals could be accused of trespassing on States' lawmaking territory. Similar debates take place at the domestic level, in the relations between the legislative and judicial branch of government.[83] These debates often relate to obligations in the field of environmental protection, for the simple reason that this is one of the most urgent global challenges at the moment, and it is also the challenge States are most reluctant to address sufficiently. Indeed, in the blogosphere, many people compare the global response to the coronavirus outbreak with the global response to climate change. The former is fundamental, sweeping, drastic, and far-reaching, and the latter is not.[84] And thus, the (domestic) courts jump in, obliging policymakers to take action.[85] This leads to muttering, grumbling and murmuring against activist judges.[86] In these debates, the term 'dikastocracy' is sometimes used, which refers to a world ruled by judges.[87] One can, of course, point out that (inter)national courts and tribunals are merely applying already existing law, and not making new law. But many norms of world law are very open and vague, and their meaning evolves over time. And if we accept Tanaka's argument, i.e. that general principles of international law emerge beyond State control and allow judges of international courts and tribunals a considerable degree of freedom, then we understand the urgency of the debate.

What to conclude from this? It appears that, so long as the (judges of) international courts and tribunals do not stretch their judicial freedom to breaking point, and lose the support of their creators and clients (the States), and come to be seen as a group of actors staging a play which has no societal relevance, they can certainly use their position of authority and influence to further develop international law, including in the field of environmental protection. Alter has recently made the argument that the World Court has not yet made full use of its potential as a catalyst for the development of international law, and that it allows itself to be too much constrained by the State-based nature of its jurisdiction.[88] As can be concluded from the above, individual judges also have considerable freedom to give shape to their own Separate

[81] Ibid., separate opinion of Judge Cançado Trindade.

[82] The most important example in the context of environmental protection is the separate opinion of Judge Cançado Trindade to ICJ, *Whaling in the Antarctic (Australia v Japan: New Zealand intervening)*, Judgment, 31 March 2014, ICJ Reports 2014, p. 226.

[83] Spijkers 2018.

[84] Cullet 2020.

[85] Spijkers 2021.

[86] Spijkers 2019.

[87] On 9 March 2020, a roundtable discussion of the Standing Committee for Interior Affairs of the Netherlands House of Representatives took place on the topic of Dikastocracy. The position papers are available at www.tweedekamer.nl/.

[88] Alter 2020.

Opinions, and thus one might assume that an abuse of this privilege could cause reputational damage to the court concerned.[89] So far, the majority of judges serving on international courts and tribunals have been acting within their limits, and have thereby avoided causing reputational damage to 'their' court or tribunal.[90]

The scholarly community can then use these rulings of international courts and tribunals, and/or the separate opinions issued by the more daring judges, to rally round. If we look at the current docket of international courts and tribunals, we find plenty of cases that offer an opportunity to make some general remarks about world law principles aiming to protect and preserve the world's environment. For example, the dispute between Chile and Bolivia over the status and use of the waters of the Silala could be used by the World Court as an opportunity to confirm that there exists a general obligation for all States to jointly protect and preserve the ecosystems of international watercourses. Such ruling would undoubtedly keep scholars of international water law content and occupied for decades; they can use the presumably somewhat vague references in the World Court ruling as basis for entire world water law theories. The dispute relating to alleged violations of sovereign rights and maritime spaces in the Caribbean Sea, between Nicaragua and Colombia, might permit the World Court to confirm the general obligation of all States not to cause harm to the living and non-living resources in another State's exclusive economic zone and continental shelf, with the same catalytic effect on law of the sea scholarship and thinking. And scholars are already thinking of creative ways to bring climate change to the World Court's attention.[91]

The most promising international case currently before an international *human rights* court is undoubtedly the complaint lodged by the Portuguese children against 33 States in Europe, accusing all of them of acting in breach of their obligations under human rights law by not doing enough to prevent dangerous climate change.[92] More generally, it appears that the most promising course to take is the human rights course, and the most promising fora are the international human rights courts, tribunals and committees.[93] How exactly to frame the issue, and how to leap over all jurisdictional and procedural hurdles, that is a topic for another time.

---

[89] Oxman examined the impact of separate opinions of ITLOS judges but did not draw any definite conclusions from his analysis. He did warn that 'the greater the number of [separate] opinions, the more difficult it may be [for the international tribunal] to maximize the impact of a decision either on the behavior of the parties or on the development of the law, or indeed even to assess that impact'. Oxman 2013, p. 51.

[90] A notable exception might be Judge Cançado Trindade of the World Court, to whom we have referred already. His habit of attaching lengthy separate opinions to almost every judgment has made him a somewhat controversial figure. See Milanovic 2012.

[91] Hernández et al. 2020.

[92] See Sect. 22.3, above.

[93] Council of Europe 2012, le Moli 2020, and Tigre 2020.

References

Acheson D (1961) Untitled Report of July 1961. Foreign Relations of the United States, 1961–1963, Volume XIV, Berlin Crisis, 1961–1962

Alter K J (2013) The New Terrain of International Law: Courts, Politics, Rights. Princeton University Press, Princeton, USA

Alter K J (2020) The ICJ In Comparison: Understanding the ICJ's Limited Influence. iCourts Working Paper Series, No. 195

Alter K J, Helfer L R, Madsen M R (eds) (2018) International Court Authority. Oxford University Press, Oxford, UK

Anghie A (2001) C.G. Weeramantry at the International Court of Justice. Leiden Journal of International Law 14:4, pp 829–850

Anghie A, Weeramantry C G (eds) (1998) Legal Visions of the 21st Century: Essays in Honour of Judge Christopher Weeramantry. Kluwer Law International, The Hague, The Netherlands

Bodansky D (2006) Non Liquet. Max Planck Encyclopedia of Public International Law

Bos A M (2012) Wereldrecht, Hoe Bestaat Het! In: Drosterij G (ed) Behulpzaam bij het Creëren van Orde en Vrede (Niet Gerechtigheid): Opstellen voor Liesbeth Huppes-Cluysenaer Bos. Digital Printing Partners, Houten, The Netherlands, pp 153–164

Bruncken E (1925) World Law and World Court. Marquette Law Review, 10:1, pp 10–21

Clark G, Sohn L B (1958) World Peace Through World Law. Harvard University Press, Cambridge MA, USA

Council of Europe (2012) Manual on Human Rights and the Environment. Council of Europe Publishing

Cullet P (2020) Learning from Coronavirus to Tackle Climate Change: The Imperative of Solidarity and Equity, available at https://www.soas.ac.uk/blogs/study/coronavirus-solidarity-equity/

de Hoogh A (1996) Obligations Erga Omnes and International Crimes: A Theoretical Inquiry into the Implementation and Enforcement of the International Responsibility of States. Kluwer Law International, The Hague, Netherlands

Doak K M (2017) Tanaka Kōtarō, Korea, and the Natural Law. Sungkyun Journal of East Asian Studies 17:1

Doak K M (2019) Tanaka Kōtarō And World Law: Rethinking the Natural Law Outside the West. Palgrave Macmillan, Cham, Switzerland

Fabra-Zamora J L (ed) (2020) Jurisprudence in A Globalized World. Edward Elgar Publishing Limited, Cheltenham, UK

Fitzmaurice M (2013) The International Court of Justice and International Envirsonmental Law. In: Tams C J, Sloan J (eds) The Development of International Law by the International Court of Justice. Oxford University Press, Oxford, UK, pp 352–374

Gerards J, Schrijver N (2010) Tot Zover de Aarde Strekt: Een Inleiding bij 65 Jaar Wereldrecht. Nederlands Juristenblad 85, pp 02-07

Hagiwara K (2019) Sustainable Development before International Courts and Tribunals: Duty to Cooperate and States' Good Faith. In: Voigt C (ed) International Judicial Practice on the Environment: Questions of Legitimacy. Cambridge University Press, Cambridge, UK, pp 167–s187

Hernández G, Nedeski N, Sparks T (2020) Judging Climate Change Obligations: Can the World Court Rise to the Occasion? (Part I and II). Voelkerrechtsblog

Hunter D B (2019) The Paris Agreement and Global Climate Litigation after the Trump Withdrawal. Maryland Journal of International Law 34:7, pp 224–248

Johnstone I (2020) Louis Sohn's Legacy. European Journal of International Law 31:2, pp 583–600

Kotzé L J (2016) Constitutional Conversations in the Anthropocene: In Search of Environmental Jus Cogens Norms. Netherlands Yearbook of International Law 46, pp 241–271

Lawrence P, Kohler L (2017) Representation of Future Generations through International Climate Litigation: A Normative Framework. German Yearbook of International Law 60, pp 639–666

le Moli G (2020) The Human Rights Committee, Environmental Protection and the Right to Life. International and Comparative Law Quarterly 69:3, pp 735–752

Maljean-Dubois S (2018) Climate Change Litigation. Max Planck Encyclopedia of International Procedural Law

Meguro M (2020) Litigating Climate Change Through International Law: Obligations Strategy and Rights Strategy. Leiden Journal of International Law 33:4, pp 933–951

Milanovic M (2012) Judging Judges: A Statistical Exercise, available at https://www.ejiltalk.org/judging-judges-a-statistical-exercise/

Oguri H (2020) Conceptions of International Law in Tanaka Kōtarō's Theory of World Law: Their Natural Law Basis and the Roles of General Principles of Law. Yearbook of World Law 39

Oxman B H (2013) Separate and Dissenting Opinions and Their Absence: A Window on Decision-Making in the Tribunal. In: Scheiber H N, Paik J-H (eds) Regions, Institutions, and Law of the Sea: Studies in Ocean Governance. Martinus Nijhoff, Leiden, Netherlands, pp 47–56

Resende R L (2019) Deliberation and Decision-Making Process in the Inter-American Court of Human Rights: Do Individual Opinions Matter? Northwestern Journal of Human Rights 17, pp 25–50

Saito Y (1984) International Law as a Law of the World Community: World Law as Reality and Methodology. In: United Nations Institute for Training and Research (ed) The Spirit of Uppsala: Joint UNITAR-Uppsala University Seminar on International Law and Organization for A New World Order. De Gruyter, Berlin, Germany

Sarmiento Lamus A D (2020) The Proliferation of Dissenting Opinions in International Law: A Comparative Analysis of the Exercise of the Right to Dissent at the ICJ and IACtHR. Meijers Series, Leiden University, Leiden, The Netherlands

Schrijver N (2011) Internationaal Publiekrecht als Wereldrecht: Een Inleiding. Boom Juridische Uitgevers, The Hague, The Netherlands

Spijkers O (2010) De Notie van Wereldrecht Vóór, Tijdens en Na de Oprichting van de Verenigde Naties. Nederlandsch Juristenblad 85:1, pp 12–15

Spijkers O (2011) The United Nations and the Evolution of Global Values. Intersentia, Cambridge

Spijkers O (2018) The Urgenda Case: A Successful Example of Public Interest Litigation for the Protection of the Environment? In: Voigt C (ed) Courts and the Environment. Edward Elgar Publishing, Cheltenham, UK, 305–344

Spijkers O (2019) Urgenda Tegen De Staat Der Nederlanden: Aan Wiens Kant Staat De Nederlandse Burger Eigenlijk? Ars Aequi, 2019

Spijkers O (2021) The Case between Urgenda and the State of the Netherlands. Hungarian Yearbook of International Law and European Law 8 (forthcoming)

Stephens T (2018) Environmental Principles and the International Court of Justice. In: Krämer L, Orlando E (eds) Principles of Environmental Law: Elgar Encyclopedia of Environmental Law, Vol. VI. Edward Elgar Publishing, Cheltenham, UK, pp 557–567

Swart M (2006) Judges and Lawmaking at the International Criminal Tribunals for the Former Yugoslavia and Rwanda. Dissertation, Faculty of Law, Leiden University, Leiden, The Netherlands

Takeshita K (2013) Sadajiro Atobe And Kōtarō Tanaka: The Universal Private International Law School of Thought in Japan. Japanese Yearbook of International Law 56, pp 217–242

Tanaka K (1932–1934) Sekai-Hō No Riron, Vol. 1-3. Iwanami Shoten, Tokyo, Japan

Tanaka K (1938) Une Esquisse d'une Théorie du Droit Mondial. Annales de l'Institut de Droit Compare de l'Université de Paris 3, pp 303–315

Tanaka K (1954) Natural Law and World Law: Essays to Commemorate the Sixtieth Birthday of Kōtarō Tanaka. Yuhikaku, Tokyo, Japan

Tanaka K (1971) The Character of World Law in the International Court of Justice. Japanese Annual of International Law 15

Tigre M A (2020) Inter-American Court of Human Rights Recognizes the Right to a Healthy Environment. ASIL Insight 24:14

Viñuales J (2008) The Contribution of the International Court of Justice to the Development of International Environmental Law. Fordham International Law Journal 32, pp 232–258
White R C A, Boussiakou I (2009) Separate Opinions in the European Court of Human Rights. Human Rights Law Review 9:1, pp 37–60
Wolfrum R (2010) Concluding Remarks. In: Wolfrum R, Kojima C (eds) Solidarity: A Structural Principle of International Law. Springer, Heidelberg, Germany
Yokota K (1974) Regret at the Passing of Chief Justice Kōtarō Tanaka. Japanese Annual of International Law 18, pp 4–8

Otto Spijkers Professor of International Law at the China Institute of Boundary and Ocean Studies (CIBOS) and at the Research Institute of Environmental Law (RIEL) of Wuhan University, China, e-mail: ottospijkers@whu.edu.cn

Chapter 23
General Conclusions

Philippe Couvreur

Abstract In these conclusions, we shall endeavour, as is customary, to extract the most essential substance from the many rich contributions that make up the book, to articulate a logical synthesis of them and to add, where appropriate, a few data and personal comments, before attempting to briefly sketch out a few possible prospects for the future, in the modest hope of helping the reader to develop his or her own thoughts. In view of the complexity of the subject, we will proceed in a series of steps, in an open and constructive spirit, and with the necessary caution, taking care not to make comparisons that are not appropriate or to make any snap value judgement as to the way in which the main jurisdictions in question, which are very different by nature, contribute, in the context and with the instruments that are specific to them, to the protection of the common good that is our environment. The reader will not be surprised that these conclusions dwell somewhat more on the International Court of Justice. There is an objective reason for this: the Court remains after all the 'mother' of international courts and tribunals; and a subjective one: the author of these lines has devoted 40 years of his life to its service.

International Environmental Law (IEL) is a body of law that has emerged and developed fairly rapidly. It is quite exemplary in the reactive and flexible way it addresses the growing concerns of the international community for environmental and related matters. From this point of view, it cannot be denied that IEL has more than successfully fulfilled the social function conferred to any rule of law.

However, it was forged in a rather complex social fabric, still dominated by sovereign States being the first source of law creation. These major social and legal actors, though, as a whole, increasingly conscious of the dangers that the environment is facing as well as of the need to act collectively in order to preserve this 'global common' and avoid disastrous consequences for mankind, often diverge regarding how and when to act, e.g. the identification of priorities, the adoption of strategies,

P. Couvreur (✉)
The Hague, The Netherlands
e-mail: ph.couvreur@icj-cij.org

E. Sobenes et al. (eds.), *The Environment Through the Lens of International Courts and Tribunals*, https://doi.org/10.1007/978-94-6265-507-2_23

their timing, the procedures to be adopted, etc. Political will is frequently determined by immediate constraints and short time considerations and interests, and scientific uncertainties, real or supposed, which should otherwise induce a precautionary approach, are still too often used as a convenient pretext to delay action. International life is commonly marked by tensions between particular immediate interests, favouring individual action, and common goals, perceived as more distant, which require close cooperation. These tensions are especially visible and difficult to overcome when affecting the environment, because of its complex linkage with other imperatives, the seriousness of the challenges and the urgency to take preventive measures.

It is therefore not surprising that new, imaginative paths, had to be taken, beyond traditional techniques, to develop IEL in what is still, despite the progress made, a poorly integrated international community. Resort to 'soft law', 'framework conventions' and other 'additional protocols' in order to progressively create and consolidate that law in a flexible way has been remarkable.[1] One can regret the typical lack of binding character *per se* and/or the vagueness of many of these instruments. According to a very famous *obiter* of the *Iron Rhine* Arbitral Tribunal, there was, at the time of the pronouncement of the Award (2005), 'considerable debate as to what, within the field of environmental law, constitutes 'rules' or 'principles'; what is 'soft law'; and which environmental treaty law or principles have contributed to the development of customary international law'.[2] More recently, in 2018, the UN Secretary General was not really more optimistic when he noted inter alia:

> There are important deficiencies with respect to principles of international environmental law, in particular with respect to their content and legal status. There are instances where there is no clarity as to the nature and content of a principle, or no judicial consensus as to its applicability, or no recognition in binding legal instruments, or all of the above.[3]

Be it as it may, history has shown that those original instruments played a unique role in the formation and development of IEL. Indeed, it appears, in retrospect, that initial recourse to classic instruments of 'hard law' would, in many cases, not have led to such a spectacular expansion of that body of law, which does at least exist, and is gradually consolidating, whatever its defects.

The original way in which IEL has developed over last decennia has not been neutral with respect to its very content. 'Declarations' such as those of Stockholm or Rio, as well as Resolutions of the UN General Assembly adopted by consensus, are typically setting out 'Principles', which status under international law is not always clear. If the 'principle of prevention' has undoubtedly acquired a customary character nowadays, it might probably also qualify as a 'general principle of law' recognised in most legal systems of the world. On the other hand, the status of the 'precautionary principle', as derived from the former, but designed to ensure full respect

[1] See Chapter 1, Sect. 1.4

[2] *Iron Rhine Arbitration (Belgium/Netherlands)*, Decision, 24 May 2005, PCA Case No 2003-02, 23 RIAA 35, para 58.

[3] Report on Gaps in International Environmental Law and Environment-Related Instruments, A/73/419, 2018, para 102.

thereof when there is a risk of serious or irreversible damage to the environment and a lack of scientific certainty,[4] is still debated.[5] The said 'Principles' are, by definition, formulated in broad terms, which may also raise a number of questions as to their exact meaning and scope when taken as such.[6] At the same time, their very nature enables them to be conveniently incorporated into 'hard law' instruments with different objects, and to inform that law, taking, in each case, a particular signification and relevance. The fact that basic 'environmental principles' have been 'scattered' over so many different legal instruments (bilateral, multilateral, etc.) ensures a certain degree of overall consistency of IEL, while allowing for the diversity of objectives and situations to be taken into account. Thus, the 'precautionary principle' is nowadays an integral part of important conventional rules governing such different fields as climate change,[7] conservation of living resources of the sea,[8] seabed exploitation,[9] or biosafety.[10]

IEL is not only unique by its mode of creation and development, as well as the ensuing consequences on the expression of its content. More than many other bodies of law, it derives from 'global values'[11] that visibly permeate its constitutional principles. Such principles may be regarded as ultimately founded in natural law. Because environment, taken as a whole, is also part of the common heritage of mankind, its protection is of common concern in space and in time. All relevant actors, be they (traditional) subjects of international law or not, have a common interest in its preservation. Thus, the most fundamental international obligations towards the environment have progressively been considered as being '*erga omnes (partes)*'.

This, concretely, has the advantage of placing the responsibility to protect global environment, and seek redress of failure to comply with such obligations, potentially on all subjects concerned. True, there remain uncertainties as to which environmental obligations precisely are '*erga omnes*' (though it would probably be easier to determine which ones are '*erga omnes partes*' in the framework of a multilateral treaty) and what are the exact consequences thereof. Much will undoubtedly depend on the legal context. However, these uncertainties, while impractical, should not question

---

[4] Rio Declaration on Environment and Development, 14 June 1992, 31 ILM 874, Principle 15.

[5] See e.g. Chap. 18, Sect. 18.5.

[6] See e.g. Chap. 17, Sect. 17.3.2, concerning the rather unclear articulation between 'prevention principle' and 'due diligence'. Cf. Chap. 18, Sect. 18.4.

[7] United Nations Framework Convention on Climate Change, 1 July 1992, 1771 UNTS 107, entered into force 21 March 1994 (UNFCCC), Article 3.

[8] Agreement on the Conservation and Management of Straddling Fish Stocks and Highly Migratory Fish Stocks, 4 August 1995, 2167 UNTS 3, entered into force 11 December 2001, Article 6.

[9] Regulations on Prospecting and Exploration for Polymetallic Nodules in the Area, July 2013, ISBA/19/C/17, Regulation 31(2); Regulations on Prospecting and Exploration for Polymetallic Sulphides in the Area, May 2010, ISBA/16/C/L.5, Regulation 33(2).

[10] Cartagena Protocol on Biosafety to the Convention on Biological Diversity, 29 January 2001, 2226 UNTS 208, entered into force 11 September 2003, Article 1.

[11] See Chap. 22.

the very existence in principle of obligations of such a nature. Practice should hopefully contribute to remove uncertainties. Thus, the Seabed Disputes Chamber of the International Tribunal of the Law of the Sea (ITLOS) considered, in its Advisory Opinion of 1 February 2011 on *Responsibilities and Obligations of States sponsoring Persons and Entities with respect to Activities in the Area*, that the Seabed Authority, which shall act on behalf of mankind, under Article 137, para 2, of UNCLOS, could bring a claim to preserve the environment in the Area and that each State Party might 'also be entitled to claim compensation in light of the *erga omnes* character of the obligations relating to preservation of the environment of the high seas and in the Area'.[12] In support of this view, the Chamber referred to Article 48 of the International Law Commission (ILC) Articles on State Responsibility.

Furthermore, since IEL ultimately derives from 'global values', and aims at meeting the imperative need to preserve, protect and manage a fundamental and integrative 'global common', many of its rules rest on and incorporate the concepts of equity and solidarity. While States are, as such, equal in rights and before the law, their overall position with respect to the protection of the environment is, to say the least, heterogenous. Not all States have unfortunately reached the same level of development. Not all have the same responsibility in the degradation of the global environment. Not all have the same potential to address that situation. The need to allow younger and poorer States to overcome the pressing challenge of their economic development without jeopardizing the environment, has led to the emergence of key 'bridging' concepts, like that of 'sustainable development', as from the 1970s.[13] As the International Court of Justice (ICJ) has put it in its *Gabcikovo-Nagymaros Project* Judgment of 25 September 1997, '[the] need to reconcile economic development with protection of the environment is aptly expressed in the concept of 'sustainable development''.[14] Present in substance in the 1972 Stockholm Declaration, this famous linkage between development and environment was given both substantive and procedural content in the 1992 Rio Declaration, while the 2002 Declaration of Johannesburg on Sustainable Development, in the aftermath of the 1995 Copenhagen Declaration, added 'social development' to economic development and environmental protection as interdependent pillars of sustainable development. A major step forward was the adoption of a common global agenda on the three pillars by the UN General Assembly in 2015 (the well-known 'Agenda 2030 for Sustainable Development'), comprising 17 indivisible Goals, which integrate Human Rights.[15] In that way, the 'natural' relation between environment, development and human rights was consolidated. It is of common knowledge that, despite progress made, discussions are still going on at the global level as to whether there is,

---

[12] ITLOS, *Responsibilities and Obligations of States sponsoring persons and entities with respect to Activities in the Area*, Advisory Opinion, 1 February 2011, ITLOS Reports 2011, p. 59, para 180. See also Chap. 17, Sect. 17.3.1.

[13] See e.g. Chap. 18, Sect. 18.6.

[14] *Gabčíkovo-Nagymaros Project (Hungary/Slovakia)*, Judgement, 25 September 1997, ICJ Reports 1997, p. 78, para 140.

[15] See Chap. 1, Sect. 1.2.

in present international law, a subjective right to a healthy environment, qualifying as an autonomous human right. The existence of such a right should nevertheless seem, nowadays, hard to contest, given the fundamental importance of a healthy environment as a self-sufficient requirement in human life. According to the 2020 Report of the UN Special Rapporteur on human rights obligations relating to the enjoyment of a safe, clean, healthy and sustainable environment, more than 80% of UN Member States have recognised this right in law (through their national Constitution, their national legislation, court decisions and/or regional treaties to which they are parties, such as the African Charter,[16] the San Salvador Protocol,[17] the Aarhus Convention[18] and the Escazu Agreement[19]).[20] The right to a healthy environment includes 'procedural elements' (access to environmental information, public participation in decision-making and access to justice), as well as 'substantive elements' (clean air, safe climate, healthy and sustainably produced food, access to safe water and adequate sanitation, non-toxic environments in which to live, work and play, and healthy ecosystems and biodiversity).[21]

Equity and solidarity also directly inform basic principles of IEL such as the common but differentiated responsibility principle (based on the finding that States contribution to the degradation of the global environment is variable)[22] or the inter- and intra-generational equity principle (reflecting the obligation for each generation to preserve the condition of the environment it will pass to the next one, as well as the observation that, within the same generation, there are glaring inequalities which should be mitigated). The great differences in the means available to States to contribute to the preservation of the environment were recognised and the consequences were drawn: thus, even Principle 15 of the Rio Declaration specifies that 'in order to protect the environment, the precautionary approach will be widely applied by States *according to their capabilities*'.[23]

In order to fulfil its social function, it is not sufficient for IEL to establish a legal framework addressing the most relevant environmental issues faced by the international community and regulating as comprehensively as possible the related actions

---

[16] African Charter on Human and Peoples' Rights, opened for signature 27 June 1981, 1520 UNTS 217, entered into force 21 October 1986.

[17] Additional Protocol to the American Convention on Human Rights in the Area of Economic, Social and Cultural Rights (Protocol of San Salvador), opened for signature 17 November 1988, Ser No 69, entered into force 16 November 1999.

[18] Convention on Access to Information, Public Participation in Decision Making and Access to justice in Environmental matters, opened for signature 25 June 1998, 2161 UNTS 447, entered into force 30 October 2001.

[19] Regional Agreement on Access to Information, Public Participation and Justice in Environmental Matters in Latin America and the Caribbean, opened for signature 4 March 2018, entered into force 22 April 2021.

[20] A/75/161, para 32 and A/HRC/43/53, Annex II.

[21] See also Right to a healthy environment: good practices, wedocs.unep.org. Accessed 30 April 2021.

[22] See e.g. Chap. 18, Sect. 18.8.

[23] Emphasis added.

of States and other subjects or actors. It must also be effective. The effectivity of a rule of law typically depends on the way it is applied. Many factors intervene here, and they are as diverse as the overall social context, the intrinsic characteristics of the rule itself, the attitude of its addressees, the availability of proper procedures to assure sanction of breaches, etc. As has already been noted, the current international society lacks integration, despite significant progress; IEL is a highly complex body of law, the content of which remains very heterogeneous; the addressees of it are mainly States, but not exclusively; and the procedures of settlement of international environmental disputes are various. Where the choice is made to resort to international courts and tribunals, or comparable mechanisms, the traditional limitations flowing from jurisdictional requirements apply. However, there are other potential difficulties, specific to environmental controversies. One immediately thinks, for example, about some aspects of the applicable law, in particular the law of international responsibility. The well-established components of international responsibility, as codified by the ILC, are not as such always suitable in case of environmental harm. Indeed, damage to the environment may—as it most frequently does—result from actions of private actors, without a State having committed a wrongful act other than a remote breach of a rather vague obligation to ensure control of activities carried out on its territory or otherwise under its jurisdiction. Even when directly caused by a State, environmental harm does not *per se* presuppose or generate a wrongful act. The best-known example is trans-boundary harm, which may be caused by an activity not prohibited by international law and for which State responsibility will arise only if the harm is 'significant'.[24] It is worth recalling here that, although international courts and tribunals have generally been cautious to rule in a pragmatic way, without entering into unnecessary theoretical considerations, the ILC had to face the complexity of issues raised in this context (1978,[25] 2001–2006[26]). Discussions held in the literature also reveal the difficulty of dealing in international law with concepts borrowed from domestic law systems, which hardly match (e.g. '(strict) liability'/'responsabilité objective'/'pour dommage'/'pour risque'), as well as the risks, for the effectivity of IEL, of attempting at all cost to 'rationally' classify every single concept, especially if definite legal consequences are to be almost mechanically inferred from such classifications. Thus, if there is a general duty of 'vigilance

[24] See for example *Pulp Mills on the River Uruguay, (Argentina v Uruguay)*, Judgement, 20 April 2010, ICJ Reports 2010, p. 56, para 101 (*Pulp Mills* (Judgment)); *Certain Activities Carried out by Nicaragua in the Border Area (Costa Rica v Nicaragua) and Construction of a Road in Costa Rica along the San Juan River (Nicaragua v Costa Rica)*, Judgment, 16 December 2015, ICJ Reports 2015, p. 711, para 118 and p. 737, para 217 (*Certain Activities; Construction of a Road* (Merits)).

[25] See Report of the Working Group on International Liability for Injurious Consequences Arising Out of Acts not Prohibited by International Law (doc. A/CN.4/L.284 and Corr.1).

[26] See the Draft Articles on Prevention of Transboundary Harm from Hazardous Activities, *Yearbook of the ILC*, 2001, Vol II, Part Two, pp. 144–170 and the Draft principles on the allocation of loss in the case of transboundary harm arising out of hazardous activities, *Yearbook of the ILC*, 2006, Vol II, Part Two, pp. 56–90.

and prevention' under IEL,[27] it does not seem so important to determine whether it formally belongs to a 'procedural' or a 'substantive' category of obligations. In the same vein, if, as we just recalled, there is a specific obligation not to cause significant transboundary harm under that law, it is not a priori fundamental to decide whether the duty of prevention is an obligation of 'conduct' or of 'result'. And even if, in theory, it may be interesting to seek defining the exact relation between 'prevention' (substantive obligation of result?) and 'vigilance'/ 'due diligence' (procedural obligation of conduct to fulfil the former?), it may not be *per se* indispensable, nor even desirable, if such an attempt is to lead to contestations and further confusions.[28] Another problem when it comes to applying the law of international responsibility to environmental matters is that the causal link, both to attribute the (wrongful) act and to establish that the damage (directly) results from it, may be highly complex, and therefore fairly difficult, if not impossible, to identify. In addition, environmental harm is 'often irreversible' and there are 'limitations inherent in the very mechanism of reparation of this type of damage':[29] where *restitutio* is not possible, compensation may not only be improper, because incapable to 'wipe out the consequences of the illegal act',[30] but also extremely complicated to evaluate.

Many jurisdictional bodies, of diverse nature, have emerged at the 'international', 'regional', 'transnational', etc. levels in recent decades, as IEL has developed. They have been unevenly seized with cases involving environmental aspects and have pronounced, in a variety of contexts, on issues of IEL of variable importance. The creation of these courts and tribunals has responded to different needs in time and space; their functions are not identical, and the scope of the jurisdiction conferred upon them by their founding texts differs. The decisions rendered by one or the other may therefore diverge on certain points. However, this heterogeneous panorama also reveals, as expected, similarities. Thus, the texts governing the activity of many jurisdictional bodies are inspired, directly or indirectly, by the Statute and the Rules of the International Court of Justice and, whatever lex specialis may be applicable, the basic principles of IEL as well as the normative developments to which they have given rise, always constitute a permanent frame of reference for the judge or the arbitrator. This volume conveniently presents an updated summary of the case-law of the main international courts and tribunals in that field.

The International Court of Justice continues to be nowadays, as was the case with the Permanent Court of International Justice—the Statute of which was adopted already more than one century ago— the only judicial body of a truly universal character and with general jurisdiction. The ICJ is the oldest and highest existing international court. With its exceptional level of legal expertise in all fields of international law, as its unique body of jurisprudence shows, and the flexibility of its procedures, notably with regard to the establishment of facts and the administration

---

[27] *Gabčíkovo-Nagymaros Project (Hungary/Slovakia)*, Judgement, 25 September 1997, above n 14, para 140.

[28] See Chap. 17, Sect. 17.3.2.

[29] *Gabčíkovo-Nagymaros Project (Hungary/Slovakia)*, Judgement, 25 September 1997, above n 14.

[30] *Factory at Chorzow*, Judgement, 26 July 1927, PCIJ Ser. A, No 17, p. 47.

of proof, the ICJ is well suited to deal with environmental disputes. Historically, the Court was seized of an increasing number of important cases in the context of which it had the opportunity to clarify many aspects of an evolving law. It first had to deal, although rather summarily, with environmental matters in proceedings concerning nuclear weapons. As is well known, an end was put to the *Nuclear Tests* cases on grounds of mootness, after France had publicly undertaken not to conduct further atmospheric tests in the Pacific, so that the Court was not called upon to rule on the merits.[31] However, it did not hesitate to indicate provisional measures ordering France to 'avoid nuclear tests causing the deposit of radio-active fall-out' on the territories of the Applicants.[32] The rather intricate formula used to justify this decision,[33] while contrasting with the more straight-forward one commonly used nowadays, in fact boils down to the same requirement: that there be a real and imminent risk of an irreparable prejudice. In its advisory opinion on the *Legality of the Threat or Use of Nuclear Weapons*, the Court examined IEL rather briefly and in general terms,[34] since that body of law was not the main ground on which States questioning the lawfulness of the threat or use of nuclear weapons were relying. Nevertheless, as is usually the case in advisory opinions, where it is not limited to the *petitum* of parties, the Court made some pronouncements of great significance. After having found that IEL as then in force did not specifically prohibit the use of nuclear weapons, the Court indicated that important environmental factors had to be taken into account in the implementation of the right of self-defence (governed by the principles of necessity and proportionality) as well as of humanitarian law;[35] it then added the famous *obiter* of para 29, so frequently quoted, concerning the potentially catastrophic consequences of the use of nuclear weapons for the environment, linking it with the quality of life and the health of human beings, 'including generations unborn'.[36]

Shortly thereafter, the Court was called upon to address environmental issues related to the regime and quality of river water. In the *Gabcikovo-Nagymaros Project* case, the main questions raised concerned treaty-law and the law of state responsibility, as a consequence of the breach by both Parties of their obligations under the 1977 Treaty between Czechoslovakia and Hungary on the construction and operation of a system of locks on the Danube. However, Hungary had invoked an 'ecological state of necessity' in order to suspend and abandon, as from 1989, the part of the works it was committed to perform in accordance with the Treaty. That Treaty itself contained important provisions relating to the preservation of the quality of water in

[31] *Nuclear Tests Case (Australia v France)*, Judgement, 20 December 1974, ICJ Reports 1974, p. 271, para 56.

[32] *Nuclear Tests Case (Australia v France)*, Interim Protection, Order, 22 June 1973, ICJ Reports 1973, p. 99, pp. 106 and 142.

[33] Ibid., pp. 105 and 141.

[34] *Legality of the Threat of Nuclear Weapons*, Advisory Opinion, 8 July 1996, ICJ Reports 1996, pp. 241–242.

[35] Ibid., 241

[36] Ibid., pp. 241–242.

the Danube (Article 15) and the protection of nature (Article 19). In the second part of its Judgment (the 'normative' part), the Court considered that the factual situation as it had developed since 1989 should 'be placed within the context of the preserved and developing treaty relationship'.[37] It noted inter alia that the Project's impact upon the environment was 'of necessity a key issue' and that 'in order to evaluate the environmental risks, current standards must be taken into consideration'.[38] The Court then formulated, in addition to the classic passage on 'vigilance and prevention' and 'the limitations inherent in the very mechanism of reparation of ... (environmental) damage' already referred to,[39] the well-known following obiter:

> owing to the new scientific insights and to a growing awareness of the risks for mankind - for present and future generations - (of human unconsidered interference with nature), new norms and standards have been developed, set forth in a great number of instruments during the last two decades. Such norms have to be taken into consideration, and such new standards given proper weight, not only when States contemplate new activities but also when continuing with activities begun in the past.[40]

Drawing the consequences thereof for the case at hand, the Court concluded that 'the Parties together should look afresh at the effects on the environment of the operation of the Gabcikovo power plant'.[41]

So far the ICJ had thus been seized rather incidentally of IEL issues. The situation then changed with the *Pulp Mills (Argentina v Uruguay)* case, as well as the joint cases concerning *Certain Activities Carried Out by Nicaragua in the Border Area (Costa Rica v Nicaragua)* and the *Construction of a Road Along the San Juan River (Nicaragua v Costa-Rica)*, in which such issues were central. The *Pulp Mills* case, like the *Gabcikovo Project* case, concerned the interpretation and application of a bilateral treaty, related to a border river, namely the 1975 Statute of the River Uruguay. However, this treaty, which established the 'regime for the use of the river', had a much stronger environmental content. Argentina maintained that Uruguay had breached its obligations thereunder, and that the breach had arisen out of the authorisation, construction and future commissioning of (originally) two pulp mills on the river, with a particular reference to the effects thereof on the quality of the waters. The Court, in its Order of 13 July 2006, decided not to indicate the provisional measures requested by Argentina (e.g. the suspension by Uruguay of the authorisations to construct and of the construction itself of the pulp mills). It found no evidence of an imminent 'threat' of irreparable damage to the 'substantive' rights (relating to e.g. the aquatic environment as well as to the economic and social interests of the riparian inhabitants) or the 'procedural' rights of Argentina. It is interesting to note that the Court did not consider that the simple fact that a possible damage to the

[37] *Gabčíkovo-Nagymaros Project (Hungary/Slovakia)*, Judgement, 25 September 1997, above n 14, p. 76, para 133.

[38] Ibid., p. 77, para 140.

[39] See footnotes 27 and 29 above.

[40] *Gabčíkovo-Nagymaros Project (Hungary/Slovakia)*, Judgement, 25 September 1997, above n 14, pp. 77–78, para 140.

[41] Ibid.

environment was involved should lead it to accept a lower test to indicate measures, as it sometimes did when (other) fundamental human rights were at stake.[42] On the contrary, it seems that the requirement of a 'threat' could be regarded as somewhat more demanding than that of a mere 'risk'; moreover, in certain passages of its Order, the Court only referred to the absence of 'irreparable damage', without even mentioning the otherwise sufficient threshold of a 'threat' or a 'risk'.[43] Be that as it may, the Court nonetheless made it clear, as it had done some 15 years before in the *Great Belt* case,[44] that, in proceeding with the authorisation and construction of the pulp mills, Uruguay could not create a *fait accompli* and beard all risks relating to any finding to the contrary on the merits.[45] The Court, once again, insisted on the importance of sustainable development and underlined that the 1975 Statute required cooperation between the Parties for activities affecting the river environment.[46] In its Judgment on the merits of 20 April 2010, it decided, as is well known, that, while Uruguay had breached certain of its 'procedural' obligations (in particular to inform the CARU and notify Argentina of its projected activities), there was no evidence in the record that it had breached any of its 'substantive' obligations under the 1975 Statute.

This Judgment contains many interesting and innovative developments. For example, the Court explained that, even if there was a 'functional link' between 'procedural' and 'substantive' obligations under the 1975 Statute, that did not prevent States parties from being required to answer for these obligations separately. Moreover, the Court noted that, while it had no jurisdiction to deal with the respect by Uruguay of its obligations under the many IEL instruments invoked by Argentina, since they had not been incorporated into the 1975 Statute, it had to interpret the latter in the light of international law as applicable between the Parties, in accordance with customary rules on treaty interpretation: this eventually allowed the Court to deal with many aspects of IEL.[47] Since the Court's (negative) decision on the alleged breach by Uruguay of its 'substantive' obligations (in particular the obligation to coordinate measures to avoid changes in the ecological balance of the river and the obligation to prevent pollution and preserve the aquatic environment) was almost entirely founded on the lack of evidence produced by Argentina, it is important to recall what the Court had to say on *onus probandi* in environmental disputes. It confirmed the applicability of the general rule *onus probandi incumbit actori,* as well

---

[42] See for example *Application of the International Convention on the Elimination of All Forms of Racial Discrimination (Georgia v Russian Federation)*, Provisional Measures, Order, 15 October 2008, ICJ Reports 2008, p. 353; *Application of the International Convention on the Elimination of All Forms of Racial Discrimination (Qatar v United Arab Emirates)*, Provisional Measures, Order, 23 July 2018, ICJ Reports 2018, p. 406.

[43] *Pulp Mills on the River Uruguay (Argentina v Uruguay)*, Provisional Measures, Order, 13 July 2006, ICJ Reports 2006, p. 132, paras 74–75 (*Pulp Mills* (Provisional Measures)) .

[44] *Passage through the Great Belt (Finland v Denmark)*, Provisional Measures, Order, 29 July 1991, ICJ Reports 1991, p. 19, para 33.

[45] *Pulp Mills* (Provisional Measures) , above n 43, p. 133, para 78.

[46] Ibid., paras 80–81.

[47] *Pulp Mills* (Judgment), above n 24, pp. 40 ff, paras 48 ff.

as of the overall duty of the Parties to cooperate in the provision of such evidence as may be in their possession that could assist the Court.[48] It further rejected the arguments put forward by Argentina on the reversal of the burden of proof and the existence of an equal *onus* to prove under the 1975 Statute: the Court specified that 'while a precautionary approach may be relevant in the interpretation and application of the provisions of the Statute, it does not follow that it operates as a reversal of the burden of proof';[49] in the same vein, the Court did not find in the 1975 Statute an indication that it placed the burden of proof equally on both Parties.[50] As to expert evidence, the Court observed that the Parties disagreed on the authority and reliability of the many studies and reports submitted by their respective experts as well as of those of the International Finance Corporation. It explained that, in order to adjudicate the case, it was not necessary for it to enter into a general discussion thereon and recalled that it was its responsibility:

> after having given careful consideration to all the evidence placed before it by the Parties, to determine which facts must be considered relevant, to assess their probative value, and to draw conclusions from them as appropriate...[by] apply[ing] the relevant rules of international law to those facts which it has found to have existed.[51]

Much has been said concerning the 'regrets' expressed by the Court that the Parties had resorted to experts intervening as members of their delegations, rather than as 'independent experts' under Articles 57 and 64 of the Rules of Court, so as to 'be submitted to questioning by the other party as well as by the Court'.[52] The import of that obiter has, in our opinion, somewhat been exaggerated. Indeed, there is a need to guard against any excessive formalism. On the one hand, a mere declaration pursuant to Article 64 of the Rules of Court seems, in itself, hardly sufficient to transform a 'pro parte expert' into a genuinely 'independent' one, especially when the expert in question, before making such a declaration at the hearing, was commissioned by a party to assist in preparing its written pleadings; this rather trivial observation does not in any way seek to question the honesty of any of the persons concerned: it is simply obvious that it will generally be extremely difficult for any professional having begun to work on a technical issue from a certain perspective and following a certain logic, to suddenly extricate them from such a context, change their approach and express different views. On the other hand, procedures before the Court are strictly informed by the principle audi et alteram partem ('principe du contradictoire'): any opinion, be it legal, scientific or technical, expressed, in writing or orally, by or on behalf of a party, is invariably submitted to the scrutiny of the other party and discussed in depth; moreover, the Court itself, or its Members individually, may easily ask for explanations or pose questions, either in writing or orally, in accordance with the relevant provisions of Articles 61 and 62 of the Rules of Court. As experience has

---

[48] Ibid., p. 71, paras 162–163.

[49] Ibid., para 164.

[50] Ibid.

[51] Ibid., para 168.

[52] Ibid., para 167.

shown, the procedure provided for in Article 65 of the Rules, though certainly more spectacular, but also sometimes in practice—it has to be admitted—little artificial, does not, in reality, offer many additional means to the Court, the decisions of which only marginally rely on evidence obtained in that way. The literature has also been widely reflecting the concerns, expressed in a well-known joint dissenting opinion, as to the appropriateness of the 'traditional' methodology adopted by the Court to assess evidence in such an 'exceptionally fact-intensive case'.[53] The dissenting Judges were inter alia of the opinion that, in such a case, the assessment of the many scientific questions at stake by external experts was indispensable and the Court should have either requested the Parties, under Article 62 of the Rules, to produce more evidence and explanations, or appointed its own experts under Article 67 of the Rules.[54] It is worth recalling that the system of evidence taking before the ICJ is characterised by the great freedom both of the parties to produce evidence and of the Court to assess it, without predetermined rigid standards and with respect for the 'intimate conviction' of the Judge.[55] As President Lachs once noted with regard to the 'accusatorial' or 'adversarial' system (in which the parties play a preponderant role) and the 'inquisitorial' one (in which the court predominates): 'the Statute and the Rules of Court ... [have] taken ... the best from both systems';[56] the 'Court [always] aim[s] to hold a middle course between these two systems'.[57] Recently, the Court has resumed its early practice in the *Corfu Channel* case of appointing its own experts.[58] Beyond these procedural aspects, the *Pulp Mills* case was the first opportunity for the Court to pronounce on substantial aspects of IEL, notably in interpreting Article 41 of the 1975 Statute in the light of IEL on subjects as varied as the obligation to carry out an environmental impact assessment (EIA), the choice of the siting of the mill, the consultation of affected populations, production technologies, the impact of discharges on the quality of waters, the effects on biodiversity, etc.

In the joined cases concerning *Certain Activities (Costa Rica v Nicaragua)* and the *Construction of a Road (Nicaragua v Costa Rica)*, the Court adopted globally the same approach as in *Pulp Mills*, with the important difference that, the basis of jurisdiction being broader here (namely Article XXXI of the Pact of Bogota and the declarations made by the Parties under Article 36, paras 2 and 5, of the Statute of the Court), it was not limited, as to the applicable law stricto sensu, to one particular treaty. True, the Court indicated provisional measures in the first case, as a consequence of works undertaken by Nicaragua in what was at the time a 'disputed territory'. The issue was mainly one of territorial sovereignty, but environmental aspects were also

53 Ibid., pp. 108 ff., especially paras 3ff.

54 Ibid., Joint Dissenting Opinion of Judges Al-Khasawneh and Simma, ICJ Reports 2010, pp. 111–112, paras 7–9.

55 See for example Couvreur 2018, p. 15.

56 Lachs 1981, p. 114.

57 Lachs 1992, p. 265.

58 See *Maritime Delimitation in the Caribbean Sea and the Pacific Ocean (Costa Rica v Nicaragua)*, Decision to obtain an expert opinion, Order, 31 May 2016, ICJ Reports 2016, p. 235 and *Armed Activities on the Territory of the Congo (Democratic Republic of the Congo v Uganda)*, Appointment of experts, Order, 12 October 2020.

present (e.g. the felling of trees). In its Order of 8 March 2011, the Court applied the current standard combining the requirement of a 'risk of irreparable prejudice' with that of 'urgency' under the formula 'real and imminent risk of irreparable prejudice'.[59] Nicaragua having announced the end of the contested works, the Court did not indicate the measures requested by Costa Rica to protect the environment in the area against the consequences of such continuing works (i.e. those measures aimed at prohibiting the enlargement of the *caño*, the felling of trees and the removal of vegetation or soil, as well as the dumping of sediments).[60] However the Court noted that Costa Rica had designated as wetland of international importance, under the Ramsar Convention, the 'Humedal Caribe Noreste', which included the 'disputed territory'. Accordingly, although it directed the Parties not to send or maintain any personnel in that territory, the Court allowed Costa Rica to 'dispatch civilian personnel charged with the protection of the environment to the disputed territory, including the *caño*, but only in so far as it (was) necessary to avoid irreparable prejudice being caused to the wetland where that territory (was) situated', and it prompted Costa Rica to 'consult with the Secretariat of the Ramsar Convention in regard to these actions, give Nicaragua prior notice of them and use its best endeavours to find common solutions with Nicaragua in this respect'.[61] On the other hand, the Court found that there was no evidence that the dredging, by Nicaragua, of the San Juan River was creating a risk of irreparable prejudice to Costa Rica's environment and that, even if such a risk existed, it would not be imminent.[62] The Court was seized by Costa Rica, on 24 September 2013, of a new request for provisional measures, based on new facts, i.e. the construction by Nicaragua of 'two artificial *caños*' in the 'disputed territory', as well as of a trench beginning at the seaward end of the eastern *caño*, with only a narrow stretch of sand separating it from the sea. In its Order of 22 November 2013, the Court observed the presence of Nicaraguan personnel in the 'disputed territory' as well as of a military camp. It further considered that there was a real risk that the trench would reach the sea and that an alteration of the course of the San Juan could ensue, with serious consequences for the rights claimed by Costa Rica. The Court concluded that the situation in the 'disputed territory' revealed the existence of a real risk of irreparable prejudice to these rights; it moreover considered that there was urgency. The Court thus indicated measures ordering Nicaragua to refrain from any activities in the 'disputed territory' as well as to fill the trench within two weeks, and to remove any personnel from the said territory; at the same time, it allowed Costa Rica, 'following consultation with the Secretariat of the Ramsar Convention and after giving Nicaragua prior notice, to take appropriate measures related to the

[59] *Certain Activities Carried Out by Nicaragua in the Border Area (Costa Rica v Nicaragua)*, Provisional Measures, Order, 8 March 2011, ICJ Reports 2011, pp. 21–22, paras 63–64.

[60] Ibid., p. 24, para 74.

[61] Ibid., p. 27, para 86.

[62] Ibid., p. 26, para 82.

two new *caños* to the extent necessary to prevent irreparable prejudice to the environment'.[63] In the *Construction of a Road* case, Nicaragua had requested the Court, at the time of filing its Memorial, to 'decide *proprio motu*' whether the circumstances of the case required the indication of provisional measures. The Court decided that the circumstances were not such as to require the exercise of its power under Article 75 of the Rules; given that there had not been any formal request for the indication of provisional measures, this decision did not take the form of an order, but of a letter from the Registrar to the Parties.[64] Then, on 11 October 2013, Nicaragua filed a request for the indication of provisional measures, contending that, with the rainy season, greater quantities of sediment and run off would be delivered into the San Juan's waters and that Costa Rica had still not provided an EIA to Nicaragua nor had it taken the necessary actions to avoid or mitigate the irreparable damage which was being inflicted on the river and its surrounding environment. As in the *Pulp Mills* case, the Court considered that the Applicant had not adduced sufficient evidence that the ongoing works created a real and imminent risk of irreparable prejudice to the river (there appeared in particular to be no evidence of a substantial increase in the sediment load in the river, no evidence as to any long-term effect on the river of the additional sediment and no evidence as to the alleged effects on the ecosystem).[65] The Court also emphasised that Costa Rica had acknowledged, in the course of oral proceedings, that it had a duty not to cause any significant transboundary harm as a result of the construction of the road, that Costa Rica had recognised the necessity of remediation works and that it had announced the filing, with its Counter-Memorial, of an 'Environment Diagnostic' study.[66]

In its Judgment of 16 December 2015 on the merits, the Court decided, in the *Certain Activities* case, that the 'disputed territory' belonged to Costa Rica and that, as a consequence, the activities carried out by Nicaragua in that territory were in breach of Costa Rica's territorial sovereignty. It concluded that Nicaragua was responsible for these breaches and incurred the obligation to make reparation for the damage caused. The Court was of the opinion that the Parties should engage in negotiations to assess the material damage and the amount of compensation due, adding that, were they to fail to reach such an agreement within 12 months of the date of the Judgment, it would itself, at the request of either Party, determine that amount.[67] As to the dredging activities carried out by Nicaragua to improve the navigability of the Lower San Juan river, the Court confirmed the findings it had made in its Order of 8 March 2011: it considered that these activities did not give rise to a risk of significant transboundary harm, either with respect to the flow of the Colorado River

[63] *Certain Activities Carried Out by Nicaragua in the Border Area (Costa Rica v Nicaragua); Construction of a Road in Costa Rica along the San Juan River (Nicaragua v Costa Rica)*, Provisional Measures, Order, 22 November 2013, ICJ Reports 2013, p. 370, para 59 (*Certain Activities* (Provisional Measures 2013)).

[64] Letters dated 11 March 2013.

[65] *Certain Activities* (Provisional Measures 2013) , above n 63, p. 407, para 34.

[66] Ibid., p. 408, para 37.

[67] *Certain Activities; Construction of a Road* (Merits), above n 24, pp. 740–741, para 229.

or to Costa Rica's wetland. In distinguishing between 'procedural' and 'substantive' obligations as in the *Pulp Mills* case, the Court inferred from the absence of such a risk that Nicaragua had not breached any obligation to proceed with an EIA or to notify, and consult with, Costa Rica, either under customary international law of the environment or treaty law, including the Ramsar Convention; it further concluded that, in the absence of evidence that Nicaragua's dredging programme had caused any harm to Costa Rica's territory, Nicaragua had not breached its obligations under the 1858 Treaty or current customary international law.[68] In the part of the same Judgment relating to the *Construction of a Road* case, the Court had this time to deal with the alleged breaches, by Costa Rica, of its procedural and substantive obligations under customary international law and treaty law. Nicaragua indeed contended, inter alia, that such a construction along the river, under its sovereignty, posed a significant risk of transboundary harm, because of the length and the location of the road, and that Costa Rica should therefore have carried out an EIA before commencing the works. Nicaragua also maintained that sediment concentrations in the river had increased as a result of the construction of the road and that this, in and of itself, had caused significant transboundary harm; it further claimed that the increased sediment had had an adverse effect on the morphology of the river, navigation and Nicaragua's dredging programme; and it additionally alleged that the construction works had damaged the water quality as well as the aquatic ecosystem, and had had an adverse effect on the health of the communities along the river. Concerning the procedural obligations of Costa Rica, the Court found that, given the magnitude of the project and the specific context in which it had to be implemented (e.g. the presence of wetlands of international importance), 'the threshold for triggering the obligation to evaluate the environmental impact of the road project was met'.[69] The Court emphasised, with reference to the *Pulp Mills* case, that, while it is for the domestic legislation to determine the specific content of an EIA in each case, having regard to various factors,[70] domestic law cannot derogate international law to determine under which circumstances such an EIA would be required.[71] It also recalled that, although the obligation to carry out an EIA is a continuous one, such an assessment has to be conducted prior to the implementation of the project concerned, and that a *post hoc* evaluation cannot qualify as an EIA. On the other hand, the Court found that Costa Rica had not breached its procedural obligations under treaty law, including several IEL instruments. Likewise, the Court dismissed Nicaragua's claims that Costa Rica had breached its substantive obligations both under customary and treaty law. It did so, as in the *Pulp Mills* case, mostly on the basis of the lack of evidence produced by the Applicant.[72]

---

68 Ibid., pp. 705 ff., paras 100 ff.

69 Ibid., p. 721, para 156.

70 *Pulp Mills* (Judgment), above n 24, p. 83, para 205.

71 *Certain Activities; Construction of a Road* (Merits), above n 24, pp. 721–722, para 157.

72 Ibid., p. 737, para 217; pp. 737–738, para 220 and p. 738, para 223.

It is interesting to note that, contrary to what had happened in that last case, and in the aftermath of the Court's observations referred to above,[73] the Parties, in the joined cases, called as 'independent experts', under Articles 57 and 64 of the Rules, the very experts whose reports they had annexed to their respective written pleadings in support of their theses. They did so at the request of the Court itself, after Nicaragua had suggested that the Court appoint a 'neutral expert' on the basis of Articles 66 and 67 of the Rules (which Costa Rica had found 'unnecessary') and Costa Rica had raised the possibility of a site visit (which Nicaragua had accepted, while suggesting that the expert appointed by the Court be included in the latter's delegation). This led to many exchanges of correspondence and a rather heavy procedure, including the production of written statements by the experts prior to the opening of the oral procedure as well as their cross-examination and reexamination at the hearing, with questions posed by Judges both to the experts and to the Parties.[74] It is striking that, despite all of this, the Court made no reference at all to the evidence given by the experts in the part of its Judgment on the merits relating to the *Certain Activities* case. Such a reference does appear in the part relating to the *Construction of a Road* case, but the Court's reliance on that evidence appears to have finally been rather modest. The Court indeed only indicated, in passing, that the Parties had 'submitted numerous reports and studies prepared by experts and consultants commissioned by each of them' on different questions and that '(s)ome of these specialists ha(d) also appeared before the Court to give evidence in their capacity as (independent) experts pursuant to Articles 57 and 64 of the Rules of Court'.[75] It then reaffirmed its statement in the *Pulp Mills* case, according to which it was its duty, 'after having given careful consideration to all the evidence in the record, to assess its probative value, to determine which facts must be considered relevant, and to draw conclusions from them as appropriate'.[76] The Court only dealt in some more detail with the experts' estimates concerning the volume of sediment contributed by the road. But it immediately observed that there was 'considerable disagreement amongst the experts on key data such as the areas subject to erosion and the appropriate erosion rates, which led them to reach different conclusions as to the total amount of sediment contributed by the road'; and, as in the *Pulp Mills* case, it went on to state that it saw 'no need to go into a detailed examination of the scientific and technical validity of the different estimates put forward by the Parties' (*sic*) experts'.[77] At the end, the Court considered it sufficient to note that it was not contested by the Parties that the amount of sediment in the river due to the construction of the road represented at most 2% of the river's total load. As already indicated, the Court eventually based its conclusions mostly on the lack of evidence adduced by the Applicant to substantiate its claims, and common sense. Beyond formal appearances, the methodology followed by the Court and the

---

[73] See earlier in these General Conclusions.

[74] *Certain Activities; Construction of a Road* (Merits), above n 24, pp. 676 ff., paras 30 and 32 ff.

[75] Ibid., p. 726, para 175.

[76] Ibid., para 176.

[77] Ibid., p. 729, para 186.

grounds on which it founded its decision were thus essentially the same as in *Pulp Mills*.

A last observation concerning this important Judgment of 16 December 2015 has to be made: it relates to the terminology used by the Court to define the duties of States in terms of transboundary harm, and in particular the way the Court articulated the concepts of 'prevention' and 'due diligence'.[78] In the part of the Judgment relating to the *Certain Activities* case, the Court quoted the passage of the *Pulp Mills* Judgment according to which 'the principle of prevention, as a customary rule, has its origins in the due diligence that is required of a State in its territory. It is 'every State's obligation not to allow knowingly its territory to be used for acts contrary to the rights of other States'.[79] Here the Court seemed to consider that, historically, the obligation of 'due diligence'—presumably an obligation of conduct, broader in scope—had preceded that of 'prevention', which proceeded from it and appeared to constitute an obligation of result. However, the Court immediately added, in its 2015 Judgment, that '[a] State is thus obliged to use all means at its disposal in order to avoid activities which take place in its territory ... causing significant harm to the environment'.[80] This additional statement seemed rather to merge the two obligations into one of conduct. Later in the same paragraph, the Court nevertheless defined the obligation for the fulfilment of which the ascertainment, prior to embarking on an activity, of whether there is a risk of significant transboundary environmental harm, has to be made, as 'an obligation to exercise due diligence in preventing (such a) harm'.[81] In this last passage, the accent was put again on the obligation of conduct, leaving open the question whether the obligation to prevent is a distinct one and, in the affirmative, is of a different nature (obligation of result). The same formula was used by the Court in the part of its Judgment relating to the *Construction of a Road* case.[82] The problem of the precise articulation between 'due diligence' and 'prevention' was thus not really solved by this Judgment, and, as already alluded to above, the question remains open.[83]

The Judgment of the Court of 2 February 2018 in the case concerning *Certain Activities* is highly innovative and of great importance for the development of IEL. As has already been commented in some detail earlier in the volume,[84] a few words will suffice here. Though it was regrettable that the Parties could not agree on the question of reparations due by Nicaragua to Costa Rica as a result of the former's unlawful activities on the territory of the latter, this gave the Court the unique opportunity to adjudicate for the first time a claim for reparation of environmental harm. It held that compensation was due for damage caused to the environment in and of itself, in

---

[78] Cf. 'vigilance' in *Gabčíkovo-Nagymaros Project (Hungary/Slovakia)*, Judgement, 25 September 1997, above n 14, para 140 and *Pulp Mills* (Judgment), above n 24, e.g. paras 188 and 197.

[79] *Certain Activities; Construction of a Road* (Merits), above n 24, p. 706, para 104 and *Pulp Mills* (Judgment), above n 24, pp. 55–56, para 101.

[80] *Certain Activities; Construction of a Road* (Merits), above n 24, p. 706, para 104.

[81] Ibid.

[82] Ibid., p. 720, para 153.

[83] See earlier in these General Conclusions.

[84] See Chaps. 2 and 17.

addition to expenses incurred by the injured State as a consequence of such damage, a more traditional issue which it treated separately. As to environmental damage, the Court distinguished between, on the one hand, indemnification for the impairment or loss of the ability of the environment to provide goods and services in the period prior to recovery and, on the other hand, payment for the restoration of the damaged environment.[85] It assessed the value to be assigned to both. However, before doing so, the Court observed that international law does not prescribe any specific method of valuation for purposes of compensation for environmental damage and that it had to take into account the particular circumstances and characteristics of each case. The Court considered, in the case at hand, that it was appropriate:

> to approach the valuation of environmental damage from the perspective of the ecosystem as a whole, by adopting an overall assessment of the value of the impairment or loss of environmental goods and services prior to recovery rather than attributing values to specific categories of goods and services, and estimating recovery periods for each of them.[86]

It explained in particular that the most significant damage to the area had been the removal by Nicaragua of trees during the excavation of the *caños* and that an overall approach could account for the correlation between the removal of trees and the harm caused to other environmental goods and services; the overall approach was also dictated by the fact that the activities of Nicaragua had affected a wetland protected under the Ramsar Convention where various environmental goods and services were closely interlinked; moreover, such an approach would allow the Court to take into account the capacity of the damaged area as a whole for natural regeneration.[87] On this basis, the Court awarded Costa Rica a sum of 120,000 USD for the impairment or loss of environmental goods and services of the impacted area in the period prior to recovery.[88] Despite the great interest of this reasoning, it unfortunately goes only part way inasmuch as the Court did not give any details as to how it had reached that precise amount. On the contrary, in relation to restoration, the Court rejected Costa Rica's claims for replacement of the soil, since there was evidence that Nicaragua had refilled the *caños* and there had been substantial revegetation. As to compensation for restoration measures in respect of the wetland, the modest sum awarded to Costa Rica (2,708.39 USD) was the one claimed by it.[89]

Lastly, the *Whaling in the Antarctic* case *(Australia v Japan: New Zealand intervening)* essentially concerned the interpretation and application of Article VIII of the 1946 Convention for the Regulation of Whaling, which authorises the parties to grant to their nationals special permits to kill, take and treat whales 'for purposes of scientific research'. As is well known, the Court found in its Judgment of 31 March 2014 that the permits granted by Japan under its 'JARPA II' program were not 'for purposes of scientific research', inter alia because of the extensive use of

---

[85] *Certain Activities Carried Out by Nicaragua in the Border Area (Costa Rica v Nicaragua)*, Compensation, Judgement, 2 February 2018, ICJ Reports 2018, p. 28, para 42.

[86] Ibid., p. 37, para 78.

[87] Ibid., pp. 37–38, paras 79–82.

[88] Ibid., pp. 38–39, para 86.

[89] Ibid., p. 39, para 87.

lethal methods and the sample sizes.[90] But obviously, the backdrop of this case was the preservation of marine mammals and the marine environment. The same observations may globally, and mutatis mutandis, be made here as with respect to the joined *Certain Activities* and the *Construction of a Road* cases concerning the presentation by the Parties of 'independent' experts under Articles 57 and 64 of the Rules. The Court did not accept to confine itself to the definition given by experts of the terms 'scientific research'. Moreover, while the Court engaged—rightly or wrongly so—in some exercise of scientific assessment of the JARPA II program, which justified a somewhat more frequent reference to the evidence given by the experts than in other cases, it finally based the essence of its decisions, here again, on the (lack of) evidence produced by the Parties. One of the most discussed aspects of the *Whaling* Judgment was indeed the rather heavy burden of proof placed on the Respondent, in apparent contradiction with the rule stated by the Court in the *Pulp Mills* case.[91]

It is trite to observe that the International Tribunal of the Law of the Sea (ITLOS) shares various characteristics with the ICJ: it is a permanent judicial body; its Statute and Rules are inspired by the ICJ's corresponding instruments; it has a link with the United Nations through UNCLOS and, while it does not have a 'universal character' as such, its jurisdiction ratione personae is nevertheless potentially broad. At the same time, it is a treaty organ, not a(n) (principal) organ of an international organisation, fully integrated into it; moreover, its jurisdiction rationae materiae is clearly 'specialized', not general. As we know, UNCLOS contains many provisions relating to the protection of marine environment. The bodies mentioned in Article 287 thus are destined to deal with environmental matters when entertaining disputes concerning the 'interpretation and application' of the Convention. Furthermore, if their jurisdiction ratione materiae is limited to such disputes, this does not prevent them from taking into account other principles and rules of IEL, if only under Article 31(3) of the Vienna Convention on the law of Treaties.

ITLOS has a special place among those bodies. On the one hand, it has a broad power to indicate provisional measures, not only to preserve the rights of the parties in dispute, as is usual, but also, more generally, to 'prevent serious harm to the marine environment',[92] without specific individual rights being directly at stake (though, in practice, it appears never to have used that power independently of the protection of the particular rights in dispute), and even to indicate such measures pending the constitution of an Annex VII Arbitral Tribunal to deal with the merits of the case.[93] On the other hand, ITLOS has (not without criticism) extended its advisory jurisdiction to the full Tribunal in 2015,[94] while UNCLOS only recognises such a competence

90 *Whaling in the Antarctic (Australia v Japan: New Zealand intervening)*, Judgment, 31 March 2014, ICJ Reports 2014, pp. 292–293, paras 223–227.

91 Ibid., Dissenting Opinion of Judge Abraham, p. 328 and Chap. 2, Sect. 2.3.2.

92 UNCLOS, Article 290(1).

93 Ibid., Article 290(5).

94 ITLOS, *Request for Advisory Opinion submitted by the Sub-Regional Fisheries Commission*, Advisory Opinion, 2 April 2015, ITLOS Reports 2015, p. 4.

to the Seabed Dispute Chamber.[95] Indeed, it is only in the framework of the exercise of those two functions that ITLOS was called upon to make pronouncements on the protection of the marine environment and to participate to the development of the law relating to it as well as to the clarification of more general principles of environmental law. Interestingly enough, it was in one of its earliest decisions, namely its Order of 27 August 1999, whereby it indicated provisional measures in the cases concerning the *Southern Bluefin Tuna (New Zealand v Japan; Australia v Japan)*,[96] that ITLOS almost formally recognised the 'precautionary principle' as an applicable rule of (customary) international law. The Tribunal noted that the southern bluefin tuna was 'severely depleted' and stocks at their 'historically lowest levels', and stated that, in the circumstances, parties should 'act with prudence and caution' (French: 'prudence et *précaution*', emphasis added) to ensure that effective conservation measures are taken to prevent serious harm to the stock of southern bluefin tuna'.[97] The decision of the Tribunal to indicate measures 'to preserve the rights of the Parties and to avert further deterioration of the southern bluefin tuna stock'[98] was based, inter alia, on the observation that there was some 'scientific uncertainty'[99] and that the Tribunal could not 'conclusively assess the scientific evidence presented by the Parties'.[100] However, like the ICJ would do later in the *Pulp Mills* case, ITLOS apparently considered that such a 'precautionary approach' should not operate as a reversal of the burden of proof. The Tribunal was more discrete as to that approach in its Order of 3 December 2001 in the *Mox Plant* case *(Ireland v United Kingdom)*[101] and its Order of 8 October 2003 in the case concerning *Land Reclamation by Singapore in and around the Straits of Johor (Malaysia v Singapore)*,[102] despite the invocation of the principle by the Applicants.

Almost ten years later, in its Advisory Opinion concerning *Responsibilities and Obligations of States sponsoring Persons and Entities with respect to Activities in the Area*,[103] the Seabed Dispute Chamber, which dealt with the precautionary principle as stipulated in the Regulations on Prospecting and Exploration for Polymetallic Nodules in the Area as well as the Regulations on Prospecting and Exploration for Polymetallic Sulphides in the Area, only recognised that the incorporation of the precautionary approach in a growing number of treaties had 'initiated a trend

---

[95] UNCLOS, Article 191. See Chap. 3, Sect. 3.2.2.

[96] ITLOS, *Southern Bluefin Tuna Cases (New Zealand and Australia v Japan)*, Provisional Measures, Order, 27 August 1999, ITLOS Reports 1999, p. 280.

[97] Ibid., p. 295, para 71 and p. 296, para 77.

[98] Ibid., para 80.

[99] Ibid., para 79.

[100] Ibid., para 80.

[101] ITLOS, *The MOX Plant Case (Ireland v United Kingdom)*, Provisional Measures, Order, 3 December 2001, ITLOS Reports 2001, p. 95.

[102] ITLOS, *Case Concerning Land Reclamation by Singapore in and around the Straits of Johor (Malaysia v Singapore)*, Provisional Measures, 8 October 2003, ITLOS Reports 2003, pp. 10 ff.

[103] *Responsibilities and Obligations of States sponsoring persons and entities with respect to Activities in the Area*, Advisory Opinion, above n 12, pp. 10 ff.

towards making this approach part of customary international law'.[104] On the other hand, a certain lack of clarity remained as to the normative articulation between the precautionary principle and duties such as the 'duty of due diligence' or the 'duty to cooperate', which ITLOS found to be duties under customary international law, closely related to the precautionary approach.[105] Lastly, it has to be noted that, while the Tribunal confirmed, in the context of UNCLOS, the relationship more generally established by the ICJ in *Pulp Mills* between the obligation to proceed to an EIA and the obligation to consult and to notify, it did not further elaborate on the normative content of the duty to conduct an EIA under Article 206 of UNCLOS or under customary law.[106]

The International Criminal Court (ICC) is, like ITLOS, a permanent judicial body, and a treaty organ maintaining certain relations with the United Nations (this time through the Security Council acting under Chapter VII of the Charter), with a potentially broad jurisdiction ratione personae as well as a specialised jurisdiction rationae materiae. It would probably, given these characteristics, be the most suitable forum to deal with 'crimes against the environment'.[107] At present, only one provision of the Rome Statute refers in express terms to the environment when describing specific acts capable of constituting war crimes within the jurisdiction of ICC. Thus Article 8(2)(b)(iv) mentions 'intentionally launching an attack in the knowledge that such attack will cause ... long-term and severe damage to the natural environment which would be clearly excessive in relation to the concrete and direct overall military advantage anticipated'. As is aptly explained in Chap. 6 of this book, the threshold for an act against the natural environment to become a war crime under this provision is extremely high, which leaves it unlikely to be applied in practice.[108] Although politically difficult to achieve, the proposal made at the end of that chapter, that 'crimes against the environment' (i.e. acts deliberately targeting the environment as a strategy in armed conflicts) be made a new crime under the Rome Statute, is therefore to be viewed with most sympathy.[109]

Regional Courts are, like the ICJ, ITLOS or the ICC, permanent judicial bodies. However, they operate with a (geographically) more limited jurisdiction ratione personae, even if they may be more broadly open to entities of various kinds other than States. Moreover, they generally belong to a more integrated institutional architecture, which reflects deeper solidarities as well as a closer pooling of values, objectives and resources. Such courts mostly operate in the field of economic integration and human rights. They primarily have to apply the specific law governing the activities

---

[104] Ibid., p. 47, para 135.

[105] See e.g. ibid., para 131 (duty of due diligence) or *The MOX Plant Case (Ireland v United Kingdom)*, Provisional Measures, above n 101, paras 82 ff. (duty to cooperate). See also Chap. 3, Sect. 3.3.1.

[106] Ibid., Sect. 3.3.3.

[107] The creation of a specialized court to that end would most likely be rather problematic, and in any event take time.

[108] See in particular Chap. 6, Sect. 6.8.1.

[109] Ibid., Sect. 6.9.

of the organisation of which they are an organ, or the specific law contained in the convention the integrity of which their mission is to protect, as well as other founding texts (e.g. casu quo, their Statute and Rules). It was usefully pointed out[110] that IEL was somehow born on the African Continent with the adoption in Dar es Salaam, in 1963, of the African Charter for the Protection and Conservation of Nature and the conclusion in Algiers, in 1968, of the Convention on the Conservation of Nature and Natural Resources, which was revised and expanded by the Maputo Convention of 2003, fully integrating the concept of sustainable development. Noteworthy is also that it was the African Charter on Human and People's Rights which, in 1981, for the first time recognised, as a human right, 'the right (of all people) to a general satisfactory environment favourable to their development'.[111] This right, as well as the substantive and procedural obligations derived from it, were extensively examined by the African Commission on Human and People's Rights (ACHPR) in its famous decision of 2001 in the *Ogoni* case.[112] The eviction of indigenous communities from their lands, at stake in the *Endorois* case before the Commission[113] and the *Ogiek* case before the African Court on Human and People's Rights (ACtHPR),[114] did not for its part directly deal with Article 24, but with other provisions of the Charter, including Article 22 concerning the right to freely dispose of own natural resources. Most other African Courts hold a sufficiently broad jurisdiction to also encompass environmental matters. Certain constitutive instruments, like those of the Economic Community of West African States (ECOWAS)[115] or the East African Community (EAC),[116] expressly include the protection of the environment among the objectives of the Community; and derived law has been adopted to develop these provisions. The *SERAP v Nigeria* case before the ECOWAS Court of Justice[117] concerned oil spills in the Niger Delta and the damages inflicted on crops, fertility of soil and contamination of the water consumed. The decision of the Court is well known, in particular as to its innovative extensive approach of *locus standi* 'when the issue at stake is the violation of rights of entire communities, as in the case of damage to

[110] See Chap. 10, Sect. 10.2.

[111] African Charter on Human and Peoples' Rights, opened for signature 27 June 1981, 1520 UNTS 217, entered into force 21 October 1986, Arts. 3 and 24.

[112] ACHPR, *Social and Economic Rights Action Centre (SERAC) and the Centre for Economic and Social Rights (CESR) (the Ogoniland case) v Nigeria*, Decision, 27 May 2002, Comm. No 155/96, para 52.

[113] ACHPR, *Centre for Minority Rights Development (Kenya) and Minority Rights Group International on behalf of Endorois Welfare Council v Kenya*, Decision, 4 February 2010, Comm. 276/2003.

[114] ACtHPR, *African Commission on Human and People's Rights v Republic of Kenya*, Judgment, 26 May 2017, App No 006/2012.

[115] Economic Community of West African States (ECOWAS) Treaty, 28 May 1975, 1010 UNTS 17, provisionally entered into force 28 May 1975, Chapter VI, Arts. 29–30.

[116] Treaty for the establishment of the East African Community (EAC), 30 November 1999, 2144 UNTS 255, entered into force 7 July 2000, Article 111.

[117] ECOWAS Court of Justice, *Socio-economic Rights and Accountability Project (SERAP) v Nigeria*, Ruling, December 2010, ECW/CCJ/APP/08/09.

the environment';[118] the Court referred in that respect to the Aarhus Convention, to which Nigeria was not a party, but which the Judges saw 'as a persuasive evidence of an international *communis opinio juris*'.[119] Moreover, the ECOWAS Court had the opportunity to come back to Article 24 of the African Charter and found that the 'right to a clean and healthy environment' generated for States an obligation of due diligence, which, contrary to the then prevailing opinion, it considered to be both an obligation of conduct and of result. The Court decided, *in casu*, that Nigeria had breached that obligation, because of its omission to prevent the damage and punish those responsible. It did not hesitate to order Nigeria to promptly take 'effective measures' to ensure restoration of the environment in the Delta of the Niger as well as 'all measures ... necessary' to prevent the occurrence of the damage.[120] For its part, the *ANAW v Tanzania* case before the EAC Court of Justice concerned the construction of a transboundary road across the Serengeti National Park and its conformity with environmental obligations under the EAC Treaty. The Judgments of the Court both on jurisdiction and on the merits are of interest from several points of view. First, the Court (Appellate Division) considered that the scope of the environmental obligations under the Treaty was broad and that, accordingly, the corresponding provisions had to 'be given a purposive interpretation, construction, application and implementation';[121] the Court further referred to the transboundary and *erga omnes* effects of the project, since that project could affect the interests of Kenya and even of the entire international community—the Serengeti being classified as a UNESCO World Heritage site—and found that it should exercise its jurisdiction in the case. Secondly, the Court gave weight to the evidence provided by the experts presented by the Parties, in particular when they agreed, as well as by UNESCO reports, especially when not contradicted by the experts of the Respondent.[122] And thirdly, having found that the implementation of the initial project would have an irreversible impact on the environment, and was therefore unlawful under the Treaty, the Court addressed a *permanent* injunction to Tanzania to refrain from implementing that project.[123]

The European panorama is somewhat different. The European Convention on Human Rights (ECHR) does not recognise—and hence does not seek to protect—a 'right to a clean and healthy environment' as such. This does of course not mean that the ECHR would offer no basis for the protection of the rights affected in case of environmental damage. On the contrary, there is an extensive jurisprudence of the European Court of Human Rights (ECtHR) dealing with environmental issues. But logically, the Court can only act within the limits of the jurisdiction ratione materiae conferred upon it by the Convention, which only guarantees individual (mostly civil

---

[118] Ibid., para 56.

[119] See Chap. 10, Sect. 10.4.2.

[120] ECOWAS Court of Justice, *Socio-economic Rights and Accountability Project (SERAP) v Nigeria*, above n 117.

[121] EACJ, *Africa Network for Animal Welfare (ANAW) v The Attorney General of the United Republic of Tanzania*, Appeal Judgment No 3, 15 March 2012, pp. 10–11.

[122] Ibid., Appeal Judgment No 4, 29 July 2014, p. 27.

[123] Ibid., p. 32.

and political) rights of human beings. As a result, the ECtHR ruled on disputes involving environmental elements by focusing exclusively on the rights expressly guaranteed by the ECHR that could be affected, such as the right to life (Article 2), the right to a fair trial (Article 6), the right to private and family life (Article 8), the right to information (Article 10), the right to property (Article 1 of Protocol No. 1), etc. It applied the 'positive obligation' for States, not only to 'respect' but also to 'protect' these rights, to cases concerning the environment in which they were at stake. As is clearly explained in Chap. 7 of the present volume, this led the Court to acknowledge 'positive environmental obligations', in particular in cases involving the right to private and family life. In that context, it recognised such important principles as the precautionary approach, the 'polluter/payer principle' or the duty to effect an EIA, to which these obligations were linked. The ECtHR also considered that the right guaranteed in Article 8 of the ECHR had to be interpreted in the light of the Aarhus Convention (which in turn guarantees the right to information, participation and access to justice in decision-making), ratified by almost all the States parties to the ECHR, in environmental cases. The Court thus efficiently protects the actual individual rights set out in the ECHR when subject to threats related to the environment. So far, the ECtHR has never dealt with general environmental protection, protection of common interests of nature or rights of future generations. It requests a direct link between the individual actual victim and the individual harm, and does not accept actio popularis. Global phenomena like climate change accordingly seem at present to, as such, escape the jurisdiction of the Court (as opposed to particular effects thereof affecting individual rights protected under the ECHR, like *refoulement*). Whether this situation could and would change over time appears unclear.

Since the European Single Act (1986) and the Treaty of Maastricht (1992), the environment has been increasingly present in the activities of the European Communities and the European Union (EU), in a wide variety of ways and forms. Competence in environmental matters is shared between the Union and its Member States. These matters are accordingly subject to the principle of subsidiarity. The Union's legislative activity in this area has nevertheless been particularly intense in the past, representing some two hundred instruments of secondary legislation, including many Directives. In accordance with Article 19 of the Treaty on the European Union, the Court of Justice of the EU (CJEU) is entrusted with the interpretation and application of the Treaties as well as secondary legislation. It is therefore not surprising that the Court had to entertain hundreds of cases relating to environmental protection and delivered very important decisions with respect to environmental law and principles. Thus the CJEU for example recently found that 'while Article 191(2) TFEU provides that the policy on the environment is to be based, inter alia, on the precautionary principle, that principle is also applicable in the context of other EU policies'; and it linked the obligation for the EU legislature to comply with the precautionary principle with the need to ensure, 'in particular, in accordance with Article 35 of the Charter of Fundamental Rights of the European Union and Article 9 and Article

168(1) TFEU, a high level of protection of human life'.[124] Unfortunately, as is aptly shown in Chap. 8, the procedural system in place, though efficient, is not favourable to direct actions of individuals or NGOs before the Court. Infringement proceedings for failure of Member States to comply with their obligations under EU law can only be initiated by the Commission or Member States themselves. In practice, most of these proceedings are initiated by the Commission. True, individuals and NGOs can lodge a complaint with the Commission, but the latter has full discretion as to the effect to give to such a complaint. Infringement proceedings are otherwise a powerful and effective tool, since the applicant may ask the Court to indicate interim measures of protection, even, in cases of urgency, on a provisional basis, without the defendant having had the opportunity to present observations. On the other hand, while direct actions of individuals and NGOs against *EU Institutions* are legally possible, actions for failure to act (rare in environmental matters), as well as actions for annulment, are rather difficult for them to initiate unless they are the addressees of the act they intend to challenge. Indeed, where they are not the addressees of an act, or that act is of general application, they only have a locus standi if they can show that they are both directly and individually concerned by the said act, i.e. if it alters their legal assets and affects them by reason of certain attributes or circumstances that set them apart, making them distinguishable from all others, as if they were the addressees.[125] In environmental matters, the EU, in practice, mostly adopts measures of general application; their implementation is left to Member States. It is thus not usual, for the EU, to exercise direct administrative functions in these matters, which substantially reduces the possibilities for individual actors to seize the CJEU. Regulation 1367/2006 (the 'Aarhus Regulation'),[126] adopted after the ratification of the Aarhus Convention by the EU in 2005, established a procedure whereby NGOs, whose primary-stated objective is the promotion of environmental protection, may request the EU Institutions, Agencies and bodies concerned to review an 'administrative act' (or omission) related with environmental protection. An 'administrative act' is restrictively defined in the Regulation as 'any measure of individual scope ... having legally binding and external effects'.[127] In the event of rejection of the request or infringement of the review procedure, the applicant may, under the Regulation, bring the matter before the Court of Justice 'in accordance with the relevant provisions of the Treaty'.[128] Because of the obstacles to direct actions by individuals and NGOs in environmental matters, the well-known procedure of preliminary ruling is of special interest here. National measures implementing EU law may in principle

[124] Court of Justice, *Blaise and Others*, Judgement, 1 October 2019, Case No C-616/17, ECLI:EU:C:2019:800, paras 41–42.

[125] Court of Justice, *Plaumann v Commission*, Judgement, 15 July 1963, ECLI:EU:C:1963:17. See Chap. 8, Sect. 8.3.2.

[126] Regulation (EC) No 1367/2006 of the European Parliament and of the Council on the application of the provisions of the Aarhus Convention on Access to Information, Public Participation in Decision-Making, and Access to Justice in Environmental Matters to Community institutions and bodies, 6 September 2006, OJEU 2006 L264, p. 13.

[127] Ibid., Article 2(1)(g).

[128] Ibid., Article 12.

easily be challenged before national courts, which *may or must* (when deciding in last instance) refer difficulties of interpretation of EU law, and *must* refer serious doubts concerning the validity of EU secondary legislation, to the Court of Justice of the EU for preliminary ruling. Effective access to national courts is therefore fundamental in that context. In the field of environmental protection, the adhesion to the Aarhus Convention entailed the adoption of EU secondary legislation (Directives) aimed at guaranteeing such an effective access to domestic courts, in particular when the legality of national measures taken within the scope of that legislation is concerned. The CJEU has also contributed to enhance access to national courts by interpreting that secondary legislation in the light of the Convention. Chapter 9 of this book very opportunely raises the issue of the conformity of the EU scheme with the Aarhus Convention, notably with Articles 9(3) and 9(4) thereof, and reminds us of the negative conclusions of the Convention Compliance Committee in that regard.[129]

The Inter-American System of Human Rights (ISHR) has, from the perspective of its origins and development, similarities with both the European and the African systems in terms of environmental preservation and the protection of human rights. In its original version (1969), the American Convention on Human Rights ('Pacto de San Jose') did not include any provisions relating to environmental rights. It contained only one—rather discreet—provision on economic, social and cultural rights (Article 26), which provided that States Parties, according to their means, would adopt measures to 'make effective the economic, social and cultural rights derived from the norms contained in the Charter of the OAS'. But the provision in question did not further define these rights. It is known that this shortcoming was partially remedied by the adoption in 1988 of the Additional Protocol to the Convention on Human Rights in the area of Economic, Social and Cultural Rights, or 'Protocol of San Salvador', which entered into force in 1999. Article 11 of that Protocol, entitled 'Right to a Healthy Environment', states that '[e]veryone shall have the right to live in a healthy environment and to have access to basic public services' and that '[t]he States Parties shall promote the protection, preservation, and improvement of the environment'. Unfortunately, it appeared to follow a contrario from Article 19(6) of the said Protocol that this right to a healthy environment was not as such directly 'justiciable', in the sense that violations of this right attributable to a State Party could not be the subject of an individual petition to the Inter-American Commission on Human Rights (IACHR) nor, when applicable, of a later seizing of the Inter-American Court of Human Rights (IACtHR).[130] Respect for the right in question could thus in principle only be monitored through the submission of reports by the States Parties. In 2012 and 2014, the OAS General Assembly (OASGA) has developed a formal mechanism for monitoring the implementation of the Protocol. Since the early 2000s, the OASGA has also been generally very active in developing the interrelation between the environment and human rights, notably through the

---

[129] See Chap. 8, Sect. 8.5 and Findings and recommendations of the Aarhus Convention Compliance Committee with regard to communication ACC/C/2008/32 concerning compliance by the European Union, Part I, 14 April 2011 and Part II, 17 March 2017.

[130] See e.g. Cerqueira 2020, p. 5.

adoption of numerous resolutions of great significance. Thus, the Inter-American Democratic Charter, adopted on 11 September 2001, recognises, in its Preamble, that 'a safe environment is essential to the integral development of the human being, which contributes to democracy and political stability'; and, in the terms of Article 15 thereof, it is essential that States Parties protect the environment in order 'to achieve sustainable development for the benefit of future generations'. Since 2001, the OASGA further adopts, every year, a resolution on 'Human Rights and Environment'[131] and, since 2008, a resolution on 'Human Rights and Climate Change in the Americas'.[132] The 2012 Social Charter of the Americas reiterates for its part, 'that a safe environment is essential to integral development'[133] and that Member States have to 'promote sustainable development' by means of the 'conservation and sustainable use of natural resources'[134] as well as to 'continue working to ensure (non-discriminatory) access to safe drinking water and sanitation services for present and future generations'.[135] Also of interest is for example Article XIX of the American Declaration on the Rights of the Indigenous Peoples, of June 2016, according to which indigenous peoples inter alia 'have the right to live in harmony with nature and to a healthy, safe, and sustainable environment, essential conditions for the full enjoyment of the right to life and to their spirituality, cosmovision, and collective well-being'.[136] As in the European system, the IACHR and the IACtHR have for decades rendered decisions relating to the protection of the environment, but always in cases involving directly justiciable 'civil' rights, such as the right to life guaranteed by Article 4 of the Inter-American Convention (and interpreted broadly so as to encompass a positive obligation for States to ensure a 'life in dignity') or the right to a collective property of indigenous and tribal peoples protected by Article 21 of the Convention.[137] In addition to its decisions on the merits, the IACHR has repeatedly indicated precautionary measures 'requesting' States to suspend eviction orders and the concession of mega-infrastructure projects in indigenous territories, or to protect other rights, such as the right to life, personal integrity or health, threatened by environmental damage. It has also repeatedly addressed the right to a healthy environment in the context of other types of activities such as site visits, the presentation of its Annual Report to the OASGA, the organisation of open thematic 'hearings', the distribution of press releases or the production of thematic reports on various subjects of great relevance, such as 'Business and Human Rights: Inter-American Standards' (containing an important section on climate change, the precautionary principle, extra-territorial obligations of States of registration of companies and claims against both of them for climate damages).[138] Among the IACtHR's most frequently cited

---

[131] See e.g. AG/RES.1819 (XXXI-O/01).

[132] See e.g. AG/RES.2429 (XXXVIII-O/08).

[133] Social Charter of the Americas, 4 June 2012 (doc AG/doc.5242/12 rev. 2), Preamble.

[134] Ibid., Article 10.

[135] Ibid., Article 20.

[136] AG/RES.2888 (XLVI-O/16).

[137] See Chap. 9, Sect. 9.2.1 (IACHR) as well as 9.2.2.1 and 9.3.3 (IACtHR).

[138] See e.g. Cerqueira 2020, p. 16.

environmental decisions based on the right to collective property are its 19 September 2006 ruling in *Claude Reyes and Others v Chile*,[139] which recognised access to information as a human right under the Inter-American Convention, and its 25 November 2015 ruling in *Kaliña and Lokono Peoples v Surinam*,[140] in which the Court inter alia examined in detail the ins and outs of the obligation to carry out an environmental and social impact assessment (ESIA)—respecting the traditions and culture of indigenous peoples—prior to the implementation of projects (*in casu* mining activities) likely to affect the territory of these peoples, as well as of the obligations to ensure, in addition to their effective participation by means of a consultation process, shared benefits for them.[141] But perhaps most remarkable is the spectacular breakthrough that the right to a healthy environment, as an autonomous, directly justiciable human right under Article 26 of the Inter-American Convention, has made in the IACtHR's jurisprudence of recent years. It has been the case first of all in the famous Advisory Opinion of 15 November 2017 (23/17), where this right was defined as including both a 'collective dimension' ('universal value' owed to both present and future generations) and an 'individual dimension' (since violations of this right can have direct or indirect repercussions on individuals, given its connection with other rights, such as the right to health, personal integrity or life). The Court qualified the right to a healthy environment as a 'fundamental right for the existence of humankind' in view of the irreparable harm that environmental degradation can cause to human beings.[142] But it also stressed that this right protects the various components of the environment (forests, rivers, seas, etc.) 'as legal interests in themselves', even in the absence of a risk to individuals, given their importance for the other living organisms with which human beings share the planet, recalling the emerging trend to recognise a form of legal personality, and accordingly rights, to nature.[143] The opinion further contains important developments on extra-territorial duties and responsibility of States, not only with respect to significant transboundary harm caused by activities carried out on national territory (and potentially climate change), but also for certain acts of individuals or companies operating abroad and considered as falling under their jurisdiction;[144] on the duty of prevention and the precautionary principle, as binding legal obligations under the Inter-American Convention; as well as on the obligations of States to cooperate (by way of information-sharing, notification, consultation, etc.) against environmental damage and to guarantee procedural environmental rights such as access to information and justice. The principles stated in Advisory Opinion 23/17 were subsequently confirmed in the IACtHR's Judgment of 6 February 2020

[139] IACtHR, *Claude Reyes v Chile*, Order, 19 September 2006, Series C, No 151.

[140] IACtHR, *Kaliña and Lokono Peoples v Surinam*, Judgement, 25 November 2015, Ser. C, No 309.

[141] IACtHR, *The Environment and Human Rights – Requested by the Republic of Colombia,* Advisory Opinion OC 23/17, 15 November 2017, IACtHR Ser. A, No 23, paras 199–230. See also *The Saramaka People v Surinam*, Judgement, 28 November 2007, IACtHR Ser. C, No 172, para 129.

[142] IACHR, *The Environment and Human Rights – Requested by the Republic of Colombia*, above n 141, para 59.

[143] Ibid., para 62.

[144] See Chap. 9, Sect. 9.3.1.

in the *Lhaka Honhat* case concerning the right of collective ownership of indigenous communities in northern Argentina and, inter alia, the sanitation of their traditional territory. This decision reiterates in particular that the right to a healthy environment is included in the rights protected by Article 26 of the Inter-American Convention, and is directly justiciable, given its relationship with the integral development of peoples which the OAS Charter obliges States Parties to promote.[145] It also contains considerations of primary importance on the obligations of States to prevent the environmental degradation of indigenous territories as a consequence of acts of individuals as well as on reparations due to indigenous peoples for the violation of their rights in such a context.

In view of their essentially autonomous and ephemeral character, inter-state arbitral tribunals are a priori likely to be, as such, the source of particular interpretations of international law, especially in branches where the law is sometimes as 'unstable' and 'vague' as in international environmental law. However, the reality has proved to be rather different. Since the famous *Trail Smelter* arbitration, such tribunals have globally made a remarkable contribution to the progressive development of IEL and the principles that inform it (e.g. sic utere tuo ut alienum non laedas (*Trail Smelter, Lac Lanoux*); 'neighbourly relations' and good faith (*Lac Lanoux*); due diligence (*Trail Smelter, South China Sea* arbitration); 'evolutive interpretation' (*Iron Rhine, Kishenganga,* etc.) , in general harmony with the work of courts and tribunals gradually established on a more permanent basis within the framework of institutional structures of universal or regional scope. The 'great' inter-state arbitrations that count in this respect have typically been the work of highly qualified personalities, including Members of the International Court of Justice. Their knowledge of international law and their wisdom, expressed, for example, in their concern to ensure the overall coherence of that law, have not only kept them from any particularistic drift in its interpretation but have also encouraged them to contribute to its consistent consolidation and enrichment. It is worth noting that, in recent UNCLOS arbitrations (e.g. *Arctic Sunrise, Duzgit Integrity*[146]), the tribunals concerned have considered that, while not having jurisdiction to determine breaches of obligations not originating in the Convention, they might have regard to customary international law (including human rights standards) 'not incompatible' with the said Convention.[147] Also of interest is the fact that, just as States have commonly preferred to bring their (environmental) cases before the full ICJ rather than before a (specialized) chamber thereof, they also do not appear to have shown, in environmental cases

[145] IACHR, *Indigenous Communities Members of the Lhaka Honhat Association v Argentina*, Judgement, 6 February 2020, Ser. C, No 400, paras 202 ff.

[146] *The Arctic Sunrise Arbitration (Netherlands v Russia)*, Award, 14 August 2015, PCA Case No 2014-02, paras 197–198 and *The Duzgit Integrity Arbitration (Malta v São Tomé and Príncipe)*, Award, 5 September 2016, PCA Case No 2014-07, paras 207–210.

[147] Compare, e.g. *Pulp Mills* (Judgment), above n 24, pp. 46–47, para 66 (reference to customary law only for the purposes of an interpretation in accordance with Article 31(3) of the Vienna Convention on the Law of Treaties).

brought before an arbitral tribunal, any particular interest in the very specific procedural rules adopted by the PCA in 2001 (which include a list of possible arbitrators 'specialized' in environmental matters).[148]

Investment arbitration if of course commonly concerned with tensions between private interests of the investor and collective interests of the investment State. Measures of public order taken by States to comply with their environmental duties, both under national law and international law, may raise problems with regard to the lex specialis governing a particular investment. When this is the case, arbitral tribunals, notably in the ICSID system, will carefully weigh, in particular, the legitimacy (objective necessity, proportionality and non-discriminatory character) of such measures and make sure they do not affect in an unacceptable manner the rights and legal expectancies of investors. Obviously measures of this nature cannot be tantamount to a de facto expropriation without the necessary compensation. While it appears that investment tribunals might nowadays become progressively more receptive to environmental constraints imposed on States, and at least take them indirectly into consideration, their decisions do not seem to be overall consistent and tend to remain globally focused mainly on the interests of investors, whatever the environmental importance of the measures at stake. We are dealing here with a major challenge for the future, since investments will remain essential to economic life while effective protection of the environment will become increasingly imperative, environmental law thus being set to grow and quickly to evolve. Is a reasonable balance likely to be found between the legal security due to investors and environmental necessities?[149]

As to commercial arbitration, it is clearly not, as such, intended to deal with environmental disputes, which normally involve, to varying degrees, public interest and State actors. However, public actors nowadays frequently enter into contracts with private ones and, as a consequence, a growing number of commercial arbitrations between them has emerged. Moreover, environmental law has been developing both at the national and international level. That law will thus be increasingly reflected in commercial contracts. Some of them already include environmental obligations and, as very well explained in Chap. 12 of this volume, it is expected that claims and defences somehow related to the environment will be more often presented in commercial arbitrations in the future. On the other hand, this mode of settling disputes undoubtedly offers advantages. First, it is a priori perceived by foreign private actors as more neutral than the national courts of the State entity concerned. Secondly, given the high number of States parties to the New York Convention of 1958, arbitral awards are broadly recognised and enforced by domestic courts (with the exception of awards tainted by serious procedural irregularities or contrary to public policy (ordre public), to which environmental regulations may belong). Thirdly, commercial arbitration is procedurally flexible: the parties may agree on rules of their choice, including a pre-established set of procedural rules (International Chamber of Commerce (ICC), UNCITRAL, PCA, etc.). These rules normally

---

148 See Chap. 4, Sect. 4.3.

149 See Chap. 11. See also e.g. Riofrio Piché 2014.

allow for the appointment of experts by the parties as well as by the tribunal, the indication of provisional measures (even before the constitution of the tribunal, by State courts, or as a result of 'emergency arbitrator' procedures[150]), etc., all instruments of recognised usefulness when it comes to disputes involving environmental aspects and in particular climate change issues. Unexpectedly, private arbitral practice shows in that respect many similarities with the 'ICJ model'. Further, it is even contended that provisional measures indicated by arbitral tribunals would be as enforceable as arbitral awards.[151] In this sense, commercial arbitration may appear as suitable for the effective resolution of environmental disputes, including climate change ones.[152] True, commercial arbitration is basically intended to ensure the private resolution of disputes and has therefore an important confidentiality dimension, which can generate tensions with the imperatives of transparency dictated by the public interest of environmental disputes. However, despite this 'private character' of commercial arbitration, adjustments are possible, as can be seen from certain rules in force. Confidentiality of the decisions may of course constitute an obstacle to the consistent development of the law concerned.

From this brief overview of the detailed panorama offered in the book, it emerges that IEL, despite its volatility and imprecision, has so far played a significant role in environmental protection in combination with other international instruments, such as those concerning the law of the sea, economic integration or the protection of individual rights. The international courts and tribunals which have had to apply the various related texts within the limits of their jurisdictions have, overall, made a rather remarkable contribution to their respect and harmonious development.[153] The diversity of the bodies concerned, the heterogeneity of the functions exercised and the specificity of the legal framework governing their activities do not appear to have given rise to worrying phenomena of 'fragmentation',[154] as had often been feared. On the contrary, it may be globally observed that these courts and tribunals have gradually endeavoured to take cognisance of their respective decisions, to examine them in their proper context and sometimes even to refer expressly to them, thus initiating

---

[150] See Chap. 12, Sect. 12.2.3.2.

[151] Ibid.

[152] Ibid., and ref. to ICC (2019) Resolving Climate Change Related Disputes through Arbitration and ADR. https://iccwbo.org/publication/icc-arbitration-and-adr-commission-report-on-resolving-climate-change-related-disputes-through-arbitration-and-adr/. Accessed 30 April 2021.

[153] Also noteworthy in this connection has been the role of non-compliance mechanisms and of treaty bodies established to monitor their application (see e.g. Chap. 19). Nor can the role of national courts in this area be overlooked: while they have always, inevitably and out of necessity, been at the forefront in litigations regarding environmental matters, with the increasing penetration of international law into domestic legal orders, these courts have progressively become more actively involved in the interpretation and development of IEL, sometimes spectacularly, for example when seized of complex issues concerning climate change, its effects and related liabilities (see, e.g. the *Urgenda* decisions of the Dutch Courts and more generally Chap. 20).

[154] This term, which has been widely used and abused, does not in any case seem to be the most felicitous to qualify a situation such as the one envisaged here, since etymologically it presupposes the existence of an original whole from which pieces or 'fragments' (lat. *fragmentum*) would later have been detached.

an interesting and promising process of 'cross-fertilization'. The adoption of more uniform and effective substantive rules, also allowing for greater convergence of jurisprudence on key aspects of IEL, obviously does not depend on the jurisdictional bodies concerned. It is essentially a question of political will.

The variety of the procedural means made available to international courts and tribunals by their founding texts or otherwise is of a completely different order. It is even more closely linked to the specific characteristics and particular requirements governing the exercise of their functions and is certainly not, as such, problematic. Although these means are often marked at the outset by the ICJ matrix, they have logically been adapted to the needs of each jurisdiction. Two procedures of particular importance in the field of environmental protection have been broadly discussed in the present volume: provisional measures and participation of third parties. With regard to the first one, it appears rather encouraging that, beyond the constraints of Article 41 of the ICJ Statute, other courts and tribunals may indicate provisional measures (otherwise generally similar in nature),[155] in defence of the environment, further than for the strict preservation of the rights in dispute (even if this may raise the issue of the fate of such measures once the case has been disposed of),[156] or without waiting for the constitution of the tribunal called upon to hear the case on the

[155] In addition, the conditions to which the indication of such measures is subject (jurisdiction *prima facie*, plausibility of the rights invoked, link between the measures requested and these rights, real and imminent risk of an irreparable prejudice to the said rights before the final decision is issued) are also globally comparable, beyond the many necessary nuances. It is interesting to note, in this regard, that, while conceptually distinct, the 'plausibility of the rights invoked' and the 'possibility of success on the merits' may turn out to be rather similar tests in practice. Thus, the ICJ has had to examine the rights claimed 'in context' and sometimes make a somewhat detailed analysis of particular facts at the outset in order to assess the applicability of these rights to the case in question; on the other hand, the Court has generally been more reluctant to engage in such an 'intrusion' into the facts when it has been called upon, in establishing its jurisdiction *ratione materiae* (be it *prima facie* or not), to determine whether the claims 'fall within the provisions' of the convention relied upon to found its jurisdiction and the rights asserted on the merits. Certain closely connected questions may indeed, in practice, prove to be relevant to the search for plausibility of the rights asserted and to the verification of *ratione materiae* jurisdiction, two steps, in themselves, of a radically different nature (*Application of the International Convention for the Suppression of the Financing of Terrorism and of the International Convention on the Elimination of All Forms of Racial Discrimination (Ukraine v Russian Federation)*, Provisional Measures, Order, 19 April 2017, ICJ Reports 2017, p. 118, paras 30–31 and pp. 131–132, paras 74–75; *Application of the International Convention for the Suppression of the Financing of Terrorism and of the International Convention on the Elimination of All Forms of Racial Discrimination (Ukraine v Russian Federation)*, Preliminary Objections, Judgment, 8 November 2019, ICJ Reports 2019, pp. 584 ff., paras 56 ff., especially paras 58 and 63).

[156] The ICJ could clearly not do so. It is immaterial whether the parties have agreed otherwise, since neither the Court nor the parties can derogate from the Statute, which is not 'at their disposal', being an integral part of the UN Charter and in any event hierarchically superior to any subsequent bilateral or multilateral agreement. Both the CPJI (see *Free Zones of Upper Savoy and the District of Gex*, Order, 19 August 1929, PCIJ Ser. A, No 22, p. 12) and the ICJ (*Frontier Dispute (Burkina Faso/Niger)*, Judgment, 16 April 2013, ICJ Reports 2013, p. 70, para 46) have recalled this obvious fact. In order to indicate provisional measures to 'prevent serious harm to the marine environment' under Article 290(1) of UNCLOS, the Court should therefore be able to establish a link with the rights in dispute between the parties. There is room for some judicial creativity here, given that the

merits.[157] As to the second, in matters of such general interest as the environment, it may be useful for certain tribunals (often dealing with disputes involving both public and private actors) to have the power to allow third entities to have access to or take part, in one way or the other, in the proceedings, more easily than the ICJ, which is exclusively seized of disputes between sovereign States generally anxious to defend the integrity of 'their' proceedings and to protect themselves against interferences from outside, which, at that level, are rarely diplomatically and politically neutral.[158]

Just as political will is indispensable to rationalise, consolidate and usefully develop IEL, it is essential when it comes to setting up effective non-jurisdictional means of protecting the environment at international level, preventing related disputes and resolving them. The editors of this book thus did well to include an interesting section on the role of the United Nations Security Council in these matters. It can a priori hardly be denied that the environment is capable of being the source of tensions that can undermine international peace and security, in the broad sense it has acquired nowadays. One need only think, for example, of climate change and the fearsome consequences it can have on territorial integrity, migration, equitable access to the most essential resources such as water, development, etc. Moreover, during armed conflicts, the environment is likely to be threatened or even targeted. Despite the obvious, the usual cleavages within the Security Council did not fail to play out when the question of its role in environmental matters arose. The link between certain major environment-related issues with far-reaching consequences, and the maintenance of international peace and security, has been questioned, which, in turn, has inevitably cast doubt on whether the Security Council should deal with them. On the other hand, the respective competencies of the General Assembly and the Economic and Social Council in this area were also invoked to discourage the Security Council from acting. However, this rather restrictive interpretation of the Security Council's powers was not shared by all Council members. Indeed, some members have tried to engage the Council further on environmental issues, either formally or informally, with uneven results.[159] The general assessment of the Council's activity in this area is therefore as contrasted as it is mixed overall. Divisions of a similar nature have typically appeared at the level of other international bodies with important political responsibilities, or on occasion of international conferences, as at the national level. The difficulties of all kinds (ideological, economic, etc.) that give rise to such obstacles must be overcome with lucidity and reason, taking into account the imperfect but

---

recognition of the existence of certain *erga omnes* obligations in relation to the environment (and specifically marine environment) is growing.

[157] See e.g. Chap. 15.

[158] See e.g. Chap. 14. Where the parties do not object to an application for permission to intervene under Article 62 of the ICJ Statute, the Court will in principle grant such a permission, its decision even taking the form of a simple Order (see *Land and Maritime Boundary between Cameroon and Nigeria, Application to Intervene*, Order, 21 October 1999, ICJ Reports 1999, p. 1029; *Jurisdictional Immunities of the State (Germany v Italy), Application for Permission to intervene,* Order, 4 July 2011, ICJ Reports 2011, p. 494).

[159] See Chap. 21, especially Sect. 21.3.1 (climate change) and 21.3.2 (preventive diplomacy and transboundary waters).

still encouraging achievements that have been consolidated in recent decades. Global awareness of environmental issues has been awakened and evolved positively: this is an essential condition for determined and effective political action. But undoubtedly much remains to be done, without further delay.

References

Cerqueira D (2020) El derecho a un medio ambiente sano en el marco normativo y jurisprudencia del Sistema Interamericano de Derechos Humanos. Fundacion para el Debido Proceso. http://dplf.org/sites/default/files/el_derecho_a_un_medio_ambiente_sano.pdf. Accessed 30 April 2021

Couvreur Ph (2018) Evidence before the International Court of Justice. International and Comparative Law Research Centre, Moscow

Lachs M (1981) La preuve et la Cour internationale de Justice. In: Perelman Ch, Foriers P (eds) La preuve en droit. Bruylant, Brussels

Lachs M (1992) Evidence in the Procedure of the International Court of Justice: Role of the Court. In: Bello EG, Brownlie I (eds) Essays in Honour of Judge Taslim Olawale Elias. Nijhoff, Dordrecht

Riofrio Piché M (2014) Les considérations environnementales dans l'arbitrage d'investissement sous l'égide du CIRDI. Université de Montréal. https://papyrus.bib.umontreal.ca/xmlui/bitstream/handle/1866/12431/Riofrio_Melanie_2014_memoire.pdf?sequence=2&isAllowed=y. Accessed 30 April 2021

Philippe Couvreur Ad Hoc Judge and former Registrar of the International Court of Justice.

Index

E. Sobenes et al. (eds.), *The Environment Through the Lens of International Courts and Tribunals*, https://doi.org/10.1007/978-94-6265-507-2

J

K

GPSR Compliance
The European Union's (EU) General Product Safety Regulation (GPSR) is a set of rules that requires consumer products to be safe and our obligations to ensure this.

If you have any concerns about our products, you can contact us on

ProductSafety@springernature.com

In case Publisher is established outside the EU, the EU authorized representative is:

Springer Nature Customer Service Center GmbH
Europaplatz 3
69115 Heidelberg, Germany

www.ingramcontent.com/pod-product-compliance
Ingram Content Group UK Ltd.
Pitfield, Milton Keynes, MK11 3LW, UK
UKHW020223290926
15470UKWH00001B/355
* 9 7 8 9 4 6 2 6 5 5 0 6 5 *